"The whole purpose of education is to turn mirrors into windows."

— Sydney J. Harris

Common Core State Standards EDITION

MIRRORS & WINDOWS

Connecting with Literature

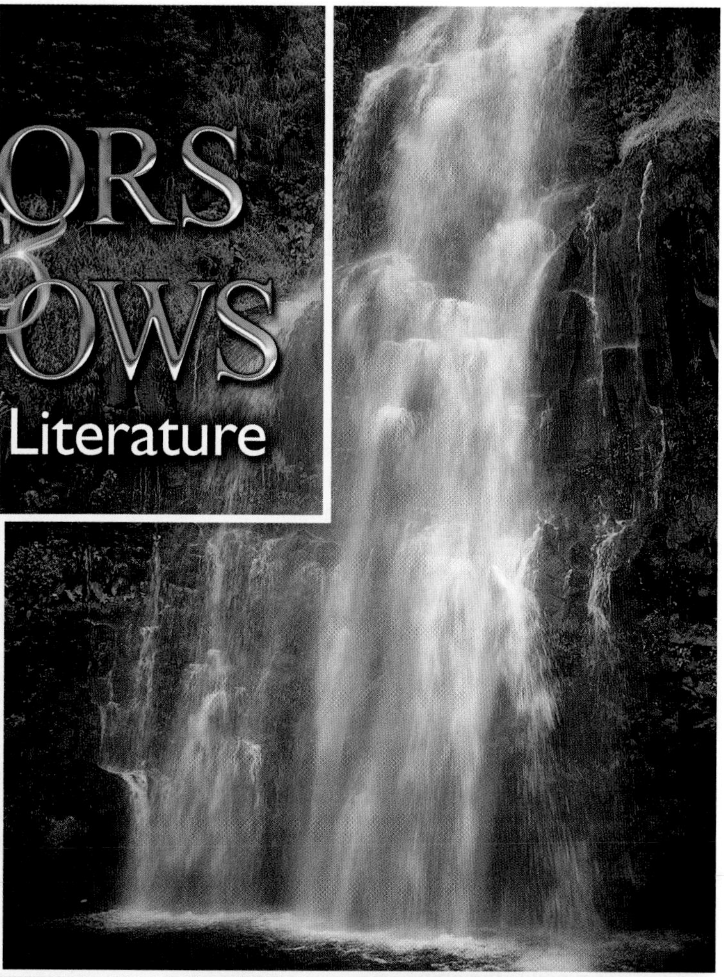

Level IV

EMC Publishing

ST. PAUL • INDIANAPOLIS

Staff Credits

Senior Editor: Brenda Owens
Associate Editors: Carley Bomstad, Keri Henkel Stifter, Stephanie Djock
Editorial Assistants: Erin Saladin, Lindsay Ryan
Writers: Carley Bomstad, Stephanie Djock, Sara Hyry Barry
Marketing Managers: Bruce Ayscue, Laurie Skiba
Permissions Coordinator: Valerie Murphy
Copy Editor: Nancy Papsin
Proofreaders: Kristen Melendez, Nancy Papsin, Carol Rogers
Indexer: Terry Casey
Photo Researchers: Brendan Curran, Paul Spencer
Production Editor: Courtney Kost
Cover Designer: Leslie Anderson
Text Design and Page Layout Lead: Matthias Frasch
Page Layout Designers: Matthias Frasch, Jack Ross, Lisa Beller, Jennifer Wreisner
Production Specialist: Petrina Nyhan

Literary Acknowledgments: Literary Acknowledgments appear following the Glossary of Vocabulary Words. We have made every effort to trace the ownership of all copyrighted material and to secure permission from copyright holders. In the event of any question arising as to the use of any material, we will be pleased to make the necessary corrections in future printings. Thanks are due to the authors, publishers, and agents for permission to use the materials indicated.

Art and Photo Credits: Art and Photo Credits appear following the Literary Acknowledgments.

ISBN 978-0-82196-035-6

875 Montreal Way
St. Paul, MN 55102
E-mail: educate@emcp.com
Web site: www.emcp.com

Printed in the United States of America

17 16 15 14 13 12 3 4 5 6 7 8 9 10

Consultants, Reviewers, and Focus Group Participants

Jean Martorana
Reading Specialist/English Teacher
Desert Vista High School
Phoenix, Arizona

Tracy Pulido
Language Arts Instructor
West Valley High School
Fairbanks, Alaska

Cindy Johnston
English Teacher
Argus High School
Ceres, California

Susan Stoehr
Language Arts Instructor
Aragon High School
San Mateo, California

John Owens
Reading Specialist
St. Vrain Valley Schools
Longmont, Colorado

Fred Smith
Language Arts Instructor
St. Bernard High School
Uncasville, Connecticut

Penny Austin-Richardson
English Department Chair
Seaford Senior High School
Seaford, Delaware

Cecilia Lewis
Language Arts Instructor
Mariner High School
Cape Coral, Florida

Jane Feber
Teacher
Mandarin Middle School
Jacksonville, Florida

Dorothy Fletcher
Language Arts Instructor
Wolfson Senior High School
Jacksonville, Florida

Tamara Doehring
English/Reading Teacher
Melbourne High School
Melbourne, Florida

Patti Magee
English Instructor
Timber Creek High School
Orlando, Florida

Margaret J. Graham
Language Arts/Reading Teacher
Elizabeth Cobb Middle School
Tallahassee, Florida

Elizabeth Steinman
English Instructor
Vero Beach High School
Vero Beach, Florida

Wanda Bagwell
Language Arts Department Chair
Commerce High School
Commerce, Georgia

Betty Deriso
Language Department Chairperson
Crisp County High School
Cordele, Georgia

Dr. Peggy Leland
English Instructor
Chestatee High School
Gainsville, Georgia

Matthew Boedy
Language Arts Instructor
Harlem High School
Harlem, Georgia

Patty Bradshaw
English Department Chair
Harlem High School
Harlem, Georgia

Dawn Faulkner
English Department Chair
Rome High School
Rome, Georgia

Carolyn C. Coleman
AKS Continuous Improvement Director
Gwinnett County Public Schools
Suwanee, Georgia

Elisabeth Blumer Thompson
Language Arts Instructor
Swainsboro High School
Swainsboro, Georgia

Toi Walker
English Instructor
Northeast Tifton County High School
Tifton, Georgia

Jeanette Rogers
English Instructor
Potlatch Jr.-Sr. High School
Potlatch, Idaho

Gail Taylor
Language Arts Instructor
Rigby High School
Rigby, Idaho

Carey Robin
Language Arts Instructor
St. Francis College Prep
Brookfield, Illinois

Patricia Meyer
English Department Chair
Glenbard East High School
Lombard, Illinois

Liz Rebmann
Language Arts Instructor
Morton High School
Morton, Illinois

Helen Gallagher
English Department Chair
Main East High School
Park Ridge, Illinois

Rosemary Ryan
Dean of Students
Schaumburg High School
Schaumburg, Illinois

Donna Cracraft
English Department Co-Chair/IB Coordinator
Pike High School
Indianapolis, Indiana

Consultants, Reviewers, and Focus Group Participants (cont.)

K. C. Salter
Language Arts Instructor
Knightstown High School
Knightstown, Indiana

Lisa Broxterman
Language Arts Instructor
Axtell High School
Axtell, Kansas

Shirley Wells
Language Arts Instructor
Derby High School
Derby, Kansas

Karen Ann Stous
Speech & Drama Teacher
Holton High School
Holton, Kansas

Martha-Jean Rockey
Language Arts Instructor
Troy High School
Troy, Kansas

Shelia Penick
Language Arts Instructor
Yates Center High School
Yates Center, Kansas

John Ermilio
English Teacher
St. Johns High School
Shrewsbury, Massachusetts

James York
English Teacher
Waverly High School
Lansing, Michigan

Mary Spychalla
Gifted Education Coordinator
Valley Middle School
Apple Valley, Minnesota

Shari K. Carlson
Advanced ILA Teacher
Coon Rapids Middle School
Coon Rapids, Minnesota

Rebecca Benz
English Instructor
St. Thomas Academy
Mendota Heights, Minnesota

Michael F. Graves
Professor Emeritus
University of Minnesota
330A Peik Hall
Minneapolis, Minnesota

Kathleen Nelson
English Instructor
New Ulm High School
New Ulm, Minnesota

Adonna Gaspar
Language Arts Teacher
Cooper High School
Robbinsdale, Minnesota

Sara L. Nystuen
English Department Chair; AP Instructor
Concordia Academy
Roseville, Minnesota

Tom Backen
English Teacher
Benilde-St. Margaret's School
St. Louis Park, Minnesota

Daniel Sylvester
Jr. High English & American Experience Teacher
Benilde-St. Margaret's School
St. Louis Park, Minnesota

Jean Borax
Literacy Coach
Harding High School
St. Paul, Minnesota

Erik Brandt
English Teacher
Harding High School
St. Paul, Minnesota

Kevin Brennan
High School English Teacher
Cretin-Derham Hall
St. Paul, Minnesota

Anna Newcombe
English Instructor
Harding High School
St. Paul, Minnesota

Rosemary Ruffenach
Language Arts Teacher, Consultant, and Writer
St. Paul, Minnesota

Nancy Papsin
English Teacher/Educational Consultant
White Bear Lake, Minnesota

Shannon Umfleet
Communication Arts Instructor
Northwest High School
Cedar Hill, Missouri

Ken Girard
Language Arts Instructor
Bishop LeBlond High School
St. Joseph, Missouri

Jessica Gall
Language Arts Instructor
Fremont High School
Fremont, Nebraska

Michael Davis
Language Arts Instructor
Millard West High School
Omaha, Nebraska

Lisa Larnerd
English Teacher
Basic High School
Henderson, Nevada

Jo Paulson
Title I Reading Teacher
Camino Real Middle School
Las Cruces, New Mexico

Stacy Biss
Language Arts Instructor
Hackensack High School
Hackensack, New Jersey

J. M. Winchock
Reading Specialist, Adult Literacy Instructor
Hillsborough High School
Hillsborough, New Jersey

Consultants, Reviewers, and Focus Group Participants (cont.)

Matthew Cahn
Department of English & Related Arts Supervisor
River Dell High School
Oradell, New Jersey

Jean Mullooly
Language Arts Instructor
Holy Angels High School
Trenton, New Jersey

Fenice Boyd
Assistant Professor, Learning and Instruction
State University of New York at Buffalo
Buffalo, New York

Michael Fedorchuk
Assistant Principal
Auburn High School
Auburn, New York

Robert Balch
English Instructor
Beacon High School
Beacon, New York

Rene A. Roberge
Secondary English/AP English Instructor
Hudson Falls High School
Hudson Falls, New York

Melissa Hedt
Literacy Coach
Asheville Middle School
Asheville, North Carolina

Jane Shoaf
Educational Consultant
Durham, North Carolina

Kimberly Tufts
Department Chair for ELA
Cranberry Middle School
Elk Park, North Carolina

Cheryl Gackle
English Instructor
Kulm High School
Kulm, North Dakota

Barbara Stroh
English Department Chair
Aurora High School
Aurora, Ohio

Mary Jo Bish
Language Arts Instructor
Lake Middle School
Millbury, Ohio

Judy Ellsesser-Painter
Language Arts Instructor
South Webster High School
South Webster, Ohio

Adele Dahlin
English Department Chair
Central Catholic High School
Toledo, Ohio

Joshua Singer
English Instructor
Central Catholic High School
Toledo, Ohio

Debbie Orendorf
Language Arts Instructor
Berlin Brothers Valley High School
Berlin, Pennsylvania

Dona Italiano
English Teacher/Language Arts Coordinator
Souderton Area High School
Souderton, Pennsylvania

Tina Parlier
Secondary English Instructor
Elizabethton High School
Elizabethton, Tennessee

Wayne Luellen
English Instructor
Houston High School
Germantown, Tennessee

Ed Farrell
Senior Consultant
Emeritus Professor of English Education
University of Texas at Austin
Austin, Texas

Terry Ross
Secondary Language Arts Supervisor
Austin Independent School District
Austin, Texas

Angelia Greiner
English Department Chair
Big Sandy High School
Big Sandy, Texas

Sharon Kremer
Educational Consultant
Denton, Texas

E. J. Brletich
Supervisor of English/Language Arts
Spotsylvania City School
Fredericksburg, Virginia

Jeffrey Golub
Educational Consultant
Bothell, Washington

Clifford Aziz
Language Arts Instructor
Washington High School
Tacoma, Washington

Becky Palmer
Reading Teacher
Madison Middle School
Appleton, Wisconsin

Mary Hoppe
English Teacher
Bonduel High School
Bonduel, Wisconsin

Lou Wappel
English, Humanities & Guidance Instructor
St. Lawrence Seminary High School
Mount Calvary, Wisconsin

Gregory R. Keir
Language Arts Instructor
East Elementary School
New Richmond, Wisconsin

CONTENTS IN BRIEF

Unit 1 Fiction 1

INDEPENDENT READING

Unit 3 Poetry 350

INDEPENDENT READING

Unit 4 Drama 484

Unit 5 Folk Literature 658

Unit 6 Independent Reading 824

LANGUAGE ARTS RESOURCES

LANGUAGE ARTS WORKSHOPS

Grammar & Style

Vocabulary & Spelling

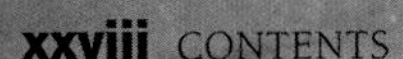

Speaking & Listening

Writing

Test Practice

INDEPENDENT READING

Fiction

Nonfiction

Poetry

Drama

Folk Literature

TO THE STUDENT

"The whole purpose of education is to turn mirrors into windows."

— Sydney J. Harris

Think about when you were young and about to start school for the first time. When you stood in front of the mirror, your view was focused on your own reflection and limited by your own experience. Then the windows of learning began to open your mind to new ideas and new experiences, broadening both your awareness and your curiosity.

As you discovered reading, you learned to connect with what you read and to examine your own ideas and experiences. And the more you read, the more you learned to connect with the ideas and experiences of other people from other times and other places. Great literature provides *mirrors* that help you reflect on your own world and *windows* that lead you into new worlds. This metaphor for the reading experience expresses the power of words to engage and transform you.

EMC's literature program, *Mirrors & Windows: Connecting with Literature,* provides opportunities for you to explore new worlds full of people, cultures, and perspectives different from your own. This book contains stories, essays, plays, and poems by outstanding authors from around the globe. Reading these selections will expand your appreciation of literature and your world view. Studying them will help you examine universal themes such as honesty, integrity, and justice and common emotions such as fear, pride, and belonging. You may already have thought about some of these ideas and feelings yourself.

As you read the selections in this book, try to see yourself in the characters, stories, and themes. Also try to see yourself as a citizen of the world—a world from which you have much to learn and to which you have much to offer.

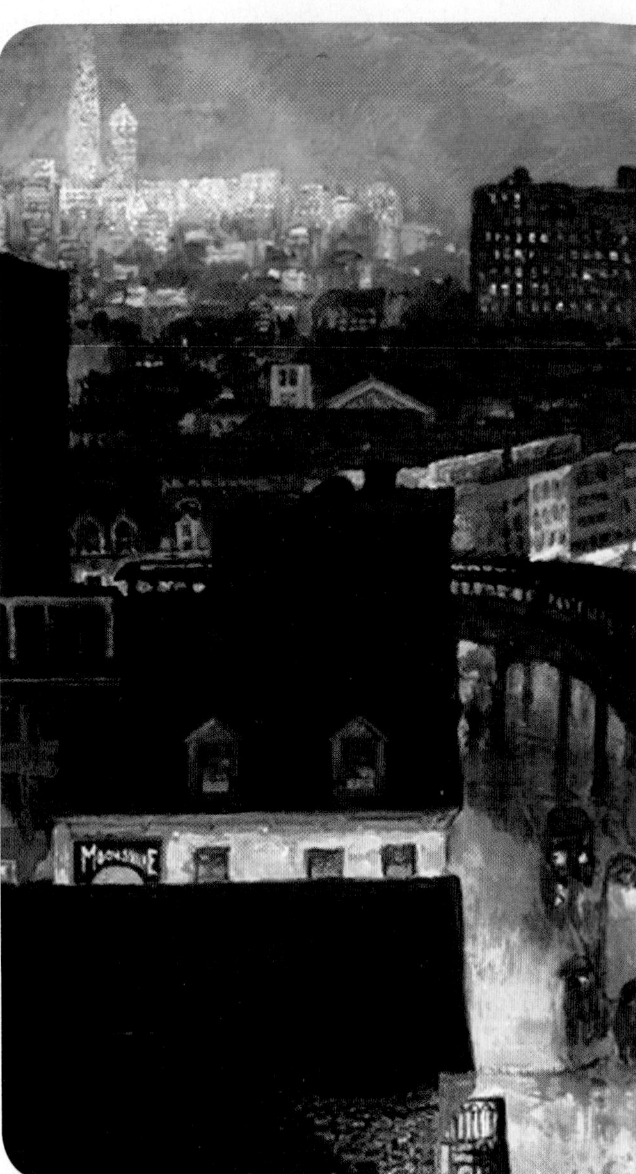

UNIT 1

Fiction

COFER

CONNELL

MAUPASSANT

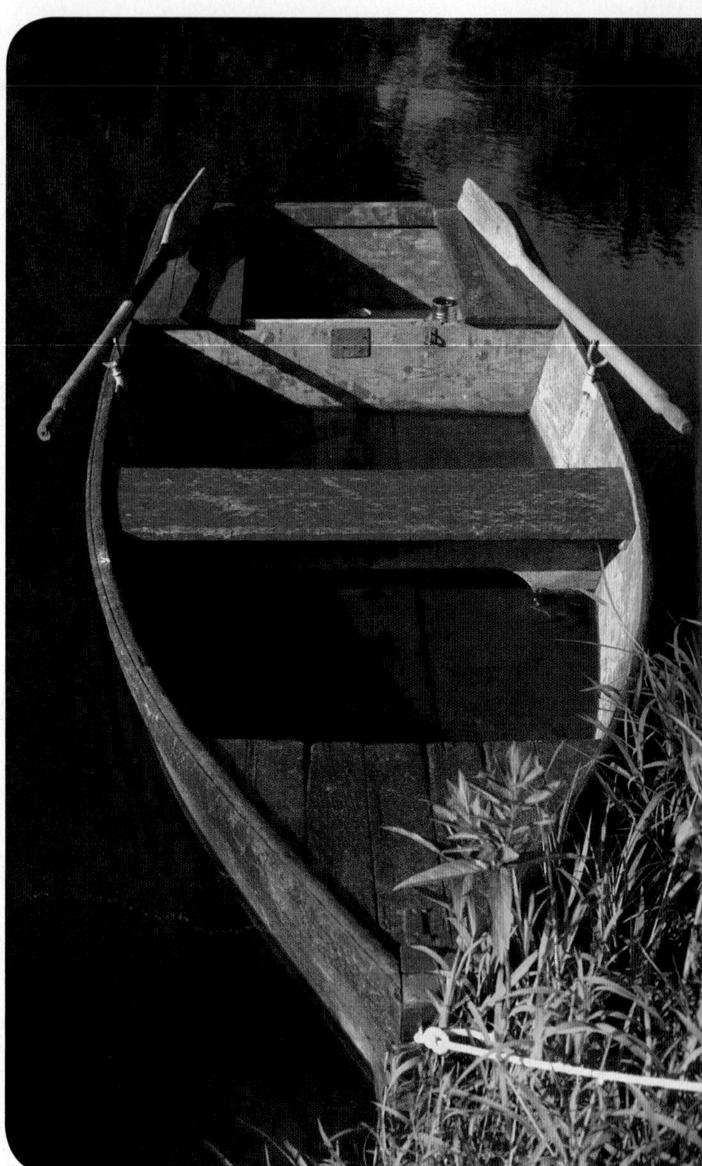

"Fiction is like a spider's web, attached ever so lightly perhaps, but still attached to life at all four corners. Often the attachment is scarcely perceptible."

—Virginia Woolf

Has anyone ever shown you a random act of kindness? Forgiven you or held a grudge against you? Think of the last time you sought revenge or the last time you were truly afraid. As you read the stories in this unit, compare your own experiences with those being expressed. You may find that, though invented, fiction mirrors everyday life.

POE

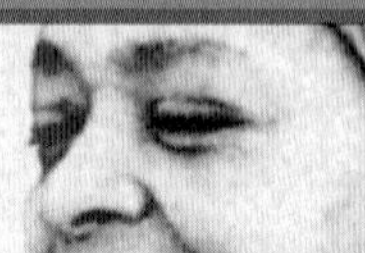

BAMBARA

HURST

INTRODUCTION TO FICTION

"You'll find this game worth playing," the general said enthusiastically. "Your brain against mine. Your wood-craft against mine. Your strength against mine."

—General Zaroff in "The Most Dangerous Game," by Richard Connell

Fiction is a popular choice for people who read mostly for entertainment. As with other forms of entertainment, the kind of fiction that might interest you depends on what kind of mood you may be in at the time. If you're feeling restless, you might enjoy a thriller or an adventure story like "The Most Dangerous Game, by Richard Connell (page 27). If you're feeling reflective, maybe you'll pick up a mystery or a romance like "The Gift of the Magi" by O. Henry (page 139).

THE GENRE OF FICTION

Genre is a type or category of literary composition, such as fiction, nonfiction, poetry, and drama. The genre known as **fiction** includes any work of prose that tells an invented or imaginary story. **Prose** is the broad term used to describe all writing that is not drama or poetry. It is more irregular in rhythm than poetry and more similar to the patterns of everyday speech.

The two main forms of fiction are the short story and the novel. A **short story** is a brief work of fiction that develops plot, conflict, characters, setting, mood, and theme all within a few pages. The majority of the selections in this unit are short stories. The **novel,** a close cousin of the short story, is a long work of fiction, which typically features an involved plot, many characters, and numerous settings.

Favorite Classic Novels

What makes a novel great? What elements make you want to read a book over and over again?

- *The Lord of the Rings* trilogy, by J. R. R. Tolkien
- *Gone With the Wind,* by Margaret Mitchell
- *To Kill a Mockingbird,* by Harper Lee
- *The Catcher in the Rye,* by J. D. Salinger
- *Adventures of Huckleberry Finn,* by Mark Twain

ELEMENTS OF FICTION

As you read, consider each of the elements discussed below. Notice how the author establishes a setting and mood, develops and advances the action, suggests one or more major themes, and breathes life into characters.

Plot

The **plot** is the series of events related to a central *conflict,* or struggle. Typically, the plot introduces a conflict, develops it, and eventually resolves it. The plot often falls into the same five parts: exposition, rising action, climax, falling action, and resolution. The **exposition,** or introduction, sets the tone or mood, introduces the characters and setting, and provides necessary background information. In the **rising action,** the conflict is developed and intensified. The **climax,** or turning point, is the high point of interest or suspense. The **falling action** consists of all the events that follow the climax. The **resolution,** or conclusion, is the point at which the central conflict is ended, or resolved. (See Understanding Plot, page 12.)

Point of View

Point of view is the vantage point or perspective from which the story is told. In **first-person point of view,** the story is told by someone who participates in or witnesses the action; this person, called the *narrator,* uses words such as *I* and *we* in telling the story. In **third-person point of view,** the narrator usually stands outside the action and observes, using words such as *she, he, it,* and *they.* There are two types of third-person point of view: limited and omniscient. In a *limited point of view,* the thoughts of only the narrator or a single character are revealed. In an *omniscient point of view,* the thoughts of all the characters are revealed. (See Understanding Point of View, page 46.)

Characters

The **characters** are the individuals that take part in the action of a story. The **protagonist** is the main character of a literary work; the **antagonist** is a character or force that is in conflict with the protagonist. In "The Most Dangerous Game" (page 27), Rainsford, the man who falls off a boat and swims ashore to a mysterious island, is the protagonist, and General Zaroff, the owner of the island, is the antagonist.

Characterization is the act of creating or describing a character. Writers create characters using three major techniques: showing what characters say, do, or think; revealing what other characters say or think about them; and describing what physical features, dress, and personalities the characters display. In "The Most Dangerous Game," you learn an essential fact about Rainsford when he declares, "The world is made up of two classes—the hunters and the hunted. Luckily, you and I are the hunters." (See Understanding Character, page 68.)

> ## Memorable Fictional Characters
>
> What makes a character memorable? Look over this list of fictional characters that have withstood the test of time. What is it about each character that makes him or her memorable or unique?
>
> - Sherlock Holmes
> - Oliver Twist
> - Tom Sawyer
> - Anne of Green Gables
> - Huckleberry Finn
> - Alice in Wonderland
> - Robin Hood
>
> 
>
> Alice.

Setting

The **setting** of a literary work is the time and place in which it occurs, together with all the details used to create a sense of a particular time period and location. Setting helps establish a context and a mood. **Mood,** or atmosphere, is the emotion created in the reader by part or all of a story. The setting of "The Sniper" (page 165) is Northern Ireland during a battle. The context of the story, a culture torn by internal war, helps to create a sinister, threatening mood. (See Understanding Setting, page 106.)

Theme

The **theme** is the central idea or perception about life that is revealed through a literary work. A *stated theme* is presented directly, whereas an *implied theme* must be inferred. Most works of fiction do not have a stated theme but rather several implied themes. An implied theme of "The Necklace" (page 143) is that acquiring money and wealth should not be the primary focus of life. As you read the story, you will probably find other themes, as well. (See Understanding Theme, page 136.)

FICTION READING MODEL

BEFORE READING

DURING READING | AFTER READING

BUILD BACKGROUND

- Determine the **context** of the story. Read the information in the **Build Background** section to find out where the story might be set or who the main characters are. Think about the context you bring to the selection based on your knowledge and experiences. What do you know about the topic? What do you want to know?

ANALYZE LITERATURE

- The **Analyze Literature** feature focuses on one or more literary techniques that are used in the selection. Make note of how the author uses these elements as you read.

SET PURPOSE

- Use the guidelines in the **Set Purpose** feature to preview the text. Skim the title and story to figure out what it's about and who the main characters are. What can you learn from the art or photos?

USE READING SKILLS

- Before reading, apply **reading skills** such as determining the author's purpose, analyzing text structure, and previewing new vocabulary.

BEFORE READING

DURING READING

AFTER READING

USE READING STRATEGIES

- **Ask questions** about things that seem unusual or interesting, such as why a character might have behaved in an unexpected way.
- **Visualize** by forming pictures in your mind to help you see the characters or actions.
- **Make predictions** about what's going to happen next. As you read, gather more clues that will either confirm or change your predictions.
- **Make inferences,** or educated guesses, about what is not stated directly. Things may be implied or hinted at, or they may be left out altogether.
- **Clarify** the story by taking notes about elements that seem important. After you finish reading, go back and reread sections that you didn't understand.

ANALYZE LITERATURE

- Determine what **literary elements** stand out as you read the story. Are the characters engaging and life-like? Is there a strong central conflict or theme?

MAKE CONNECTIONS

- Notice where there are **connections** between the story and your life or the world beyond the story. What feelings or thoughts do you have while reading the story?

BEFORE READING | DURING READING

AFTER READING

REFER TO TEXT

- Think about the facts. **Remember details** like characters' names, settings, and important actions in the story.
- **Determine the sequence of events** or the order in which things happened.
- **Reread** the story to pick up any details you may have missed the first time around.
- Try to **summarize** the story in a sentence or two based on the events.

REASON WITH TEXT

- **Analyze** the text by breaking down information into smaller pieces and figuring out how those pieces fit into the story as a whole.
- **Evaluate** the text. **Draw conclusions** by bringing together what you have read and using it to make a decision or form an opinion. Do you agree with the author's message?

ANALYZE LITERATURE

- **Apply** the ideas that you understand about the characters, plot, or theme to see if they help you answer any additional questions. **Review** how the author's use of literary elements increased your understanding.

EXTEND THE TEXT

- **Extend** your reading beyond the story by exploring ideas through writing or doing other creative projects.

Thank You, M'am

BEFORE READING **A Short Story by Langston Hughes**

BUILD BACKGROUND

Social Context "Thank You, M'am" tells the story of a boy who tries to steal and is surprised by the reaction of his victim. These two characters are typical of Hughes's literary characters. They portray the joys and miseries of ordinary African Americans living in Harlem, a section of New York City. Their dialect reflects the language of the common people.

Reader's Context Have you or someone you know been given a "second chance" to right a wrong? What lesson was learned from this experience?

ANALYZE LITERATURE: Character

A **character** is an individual that takes part in the action of a literary work. "When I get through with you, sir, you are going to remember Mrs. Luella Bates Washington Jones," declares one of the characters in "Thank You, M'am." Memorable characters give you clues to their personalities through what they say and do. You also learn more about a character through what the narrator or other characters say about them.

SET PURPOSE

As you read, pay attention not only to what you are told directly about the characters, but also what you can gather from other clues. Consider what the characters say and do, as well as what they perceive about one another.

MEET THE AUTHOR

Langston Hughes (1902–1967) was born in Joplin, Missouri, and grew up in Lawrence, Kentucky, and Cleveland, Ohio. He came from a family of abolitionists, people who fought for the end of slavery in the United States. Hughes started writing at an early age and published poetry and fiction in his high school magazine. After attending Columbia University for one year, he worked at a series of odd jobs while developing his skills as a writer. He then attended Lincoln University in Pennsylvania and graduated in 1929. By that time, he had published two books of poetry and had become known as a versatile and gifted poet. Hughes eventually settled in Harlem, New York, and wrote several poetry and short story collections as well as a novel and an autobiography.

USE READING SKILLS

Determine the Importance of Details Some details that appear in selections may be more important than others. These details provide the reader with a better understanding of a character, situation, and/or place. As you read the following selection, note any details that seem significant to the story and write them down or mark the page in some way. It might be helpful to note how the detail adds to the story.

PREVIEW VOCABULARY

Preview the vocabulary words from this selection as they are used in the sentences below. Try to unlock the meanings of the underlined words using the restatement clues provided in the sentences.

1. After being in a hospital bed for three months, Grandpa was too frail, or feeble, to walk to the car, so we decided to use a wheelchair.
2. The host was upset when he discovered that the hall was barren; in other words, no one had bothered to come to his party.
3. Our band teacher told us to look presentable for the concert; that is, good enough to be seen by an audience of family and friends.

Thank You, M'am

A Short Story by
Langston Hughes

Minnie, 1930.
William H. Johnson. Smithsonian
American Art Museum, Washington, DC.

"Shoes got by devilish ways will burn your feet."

> DURING READING
>
> **USE READING STRATEGIES**
>
> **Visualize** Picture the scene where the boy attempts to steal the purse. Where else in this story might it help to visualize?

She was a large woman with a large purse that had everything in it but hammer and nails. It had a long strap, and she carried it slung across her shoulder. It was about eleven o'clock at night, dark, and she was walking alone, when a boy ran up behind her and tried to snatch her purse. The strap broke with the single tug the boy gave it from behind. But the boy's weight and the weight of the purse combined caused him to lose his balance. Instead of taking off full blast as he had hoped, the boy fell on his back on the sidewalk and his legs flew up. The large woman simply turned around and kicked him right square in his blue-jeaned sitter. Then she reached down, picked the boy up by his shirt front, and shook him until his teeth rattled.

After that the woman said, "Pick up my pocketbook, boy, and give it here."

She still held him tightly. But she bent down enough to permit him to stoop and pick up her purse. Then she said, "Now ain't you ashamed of yourself?"

Firmly gripped by his shirt front, the boy said, "Yes'm."

The woman said, "What did you want to do it for?"

The boy said, "I didn't aim to."

She said, "You a lie!"

By that time two or three people passed, stopped, turned to look, and some stood watching.

"If I turn you loose, will you run?" asked the woman.

"Yes'm," said the boy.

"Then I won't turn you loose," said the woman. She did not release him.

"Lady, I'm sorry," whispered the boy.

"Um-hum! And your face is dirty. I got a great mind to wash your face for you. Ain't you got nobody home to tell you to wash your face?"

"No'm," said the boy.

"Then it will get washed this evening," said the large woman starting up the street, dragging the frightened boy behind her.

He looked as if he were fourteen or fifteen, frail and willow-wild,[1] in tennis shoes and blue jeans.

frail (frāl) *adj.*, weak; slight

The woman said, "You ought to be my son. I would teach you right from wrong. Least I can do right now is to wash your face. Are you hungry?"

"No'm," said the being-dragged boy. "I just want you to turn me loose."

"Was I bothering *you* when I turned that corner?" asked the woman.

"No'm."

"But you put yourself in contact with *me*," said the woman. "If you think that that contact is not going to last awhile, you got another thought coming. When I get through with you, sir, you are going to remember Mrs. Luella Bates Washington Jones."

DURING READING

ANALYZE LITERATURE

Character What kind of person is Luella Bates Washington Jones? Find the lines that suggest things about her character.

Sweat popped out on the boy's face and he began to struggle. Mrs. Jones stopped, jerked him around in front of her, put a half nelson[2] about his neck, and continued to drag him up the street. When she got to her door, she dragged the boy inside, down a hall, and into a large kitchenette-furnished room[3] at the rear of the house. She switched on the light and left the door open. The boy could hear other roomers

1. **willow-wild.** Thin, graceful, and flexible like a willow tree
2. **half nelson.** Wrestling hold in which one arm is pressed under the opponent's arm and one hand pressed to the back of the neck (as opposed to the full nelson in which both arms are pressed under the opponent's arms and both hands pressed to the back of the neck)
3. **kitchenette-furnished room.** A room with a small kitchen

Jim, 1930. William H. Johnson. Smithsonian American Art Museum, Washington, DC.

laughing and talking in the large house. Some of their doors were open, too, so he knew he and the woman were not alone. The woman still had him by the neck in the middle of her room.

She said, "What is your name?"

"Roger," answered the boy.

"Then, Roger, you go to that sink and wash your face," said the woman, whereupon she turned him loose—at last. Roger looked at the door—looked at the woman—looked at the door—*and went to the sink.*

"Let the water run until it gets warm," she said. "Here's a clean towel."

"You gonna take me to jail?" asked the boy, bending over the sink.

"Not with that face, I would not take you nowhere," said the woman. "Here I am trying to get home to cook me a bite to eat and you snatch my pocketbook! Maybe you ain't been to your supper either, late as it be. Have you?"

"There's nobody home at my house," said the boy.

"Then we'll eat," said the woman. "I believe you're hungry—or been hungry—to try to snatch my pocketbook!"

"I want a pair of blue suede shoes," said the boy.

"Well, you didn't have to snatch *my* pocketbook to get some suede shoes," said Mrs. Luella Bates Washington Jones. "You could of asked me."

"M'am?"

The water dripping from his face, the boy looked at her. There was a long pause. A very long pause. After he had dried his face and not knowing what else to do, dried it again, the boy turned around, wondering what next. The door was open. He could make a dash for it down the hall. He could run, run, run, *run!*

The woman was sitting on the daybed.[4] After a while she said, "I were young once and I wanted things I could not get." There was another long pause. The boy's mouth opened. Then he frowned, not knowing he frowned.

The woman said, "Um-hum! You thought I was going to say *but,* didn't you? You thought I was going to say, *but I didn't snatch people's*

DURING READING

USE READING STRATEGIES

Make Predictions What do you think Roger will do? Why?

4. **daybed.** Bed that can be a sofa during the day

pocketbooks. Well, I wasn't going to say that." Pause. Silence. "I have done things, too, which I would not tell you, son—neither tell God, if He didn't already know. Everybody's got something in common. So you set down while I fix us something to eat. You might run that comb through your hair so you will look presentable."

pre • sent • a • ble (pri zent' ə bəl) *adj.,* looking good enough to be shown to other people

In another corner of the room behind a screen was a gas plate and an icebox.[5] Mrs. Jones got up and went behind the screen. The woman did not watch the boy to see if he was going to run now, nor did she watch her purse, which she left behind her on the daybed. But the boy took care to sit on the far side of the room, away from the purse, where he thought she could easily see him out of the corner of her eye if she wanted to. He did not trust the woman *not* to trust him. And he did not want to be mistrusted now.

DURING READING

USE READING SKILLS

Determine the Importance of Details Why might the unattended purse be an important detail? What other actions within this paragraph seem significant?

"Do you need somebody to go to the store," asked the boy, "maybe to get some milk or something?"

"Don't believe I do," said the woman, "unless you just want sweet milk yourself. I was going to make cocoa out of this canned milk I got here."

"That will be fine," said the boy.

She heated some lima beans and ham she had in the icebox, made the cocoa, and set the table. The woman did not ask the boy anything about where he lived, or his folks, or anything else that would embarrass him. Instead, as they ate, she told him about her job in a hotel beauty shop that stayed open late, what the work was like, and how all kinds of women came in and out, blondes, redheads, and Spanish. Then she cut him a half of her ten-cent cake.

"Eat some more, son," she said.

When they were finished eating, she got up and said,

Elvis Presley.

The song "Blue Suede Shoes" topped the charts in 1956 and was covered by Elvis Presley. The song had been written and recorded by Presley's friend, Carl Perkins, in 1955. Perkins got the idea to write a song about blue suede shoes from fellow musician Johnny Cash.

5. **gas plate and an icebox.** gas plate—Small cooking surface fueled by gas; icebox—Cabinet containing ice for keeping food cold

"Now here, take this ten dollars and buy yourself some blue suede shoes. And next time, do not make the mistake of latching onto *my* pocketbook *nor nobody else's*—because shoes got by devilish ways will burn your feet. I got to get my rest now. But from here on in, son, I hope you will behave yourself."

She led him down the hall to the front door and opened it. "Good night! Behave yourself, boy!" she said, looking out into the street as he went down the steps.

The boy wanted to say something other than, "Thank you, m'am," to Mrs. Luella Bates Washington Jones, but although his lips moved, he couldn't even say that as he turned at the foot of the barren stoop and looked up at the large woman in the door. Then she shut the door. ❖

bar • ren (bar´ən) *adj.*, lacking interest or charm

Roger "did not trust the woman *not* to trust him. And he did not want to be mistrusted now." How do we learn to trust people? Are we more inclined to have faith in or to question the intentions of people we do not know well?

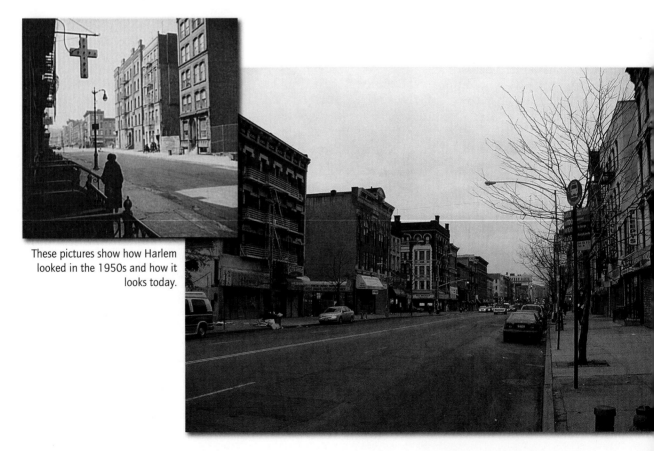

These pictures show how Harlem looked in the 1950s and how it looks today.

APPLY THE MODEL

AFTER READING

REFER TO TEXT	REASON WITH TEXT	
1a. What does Roger hope to steal from Mrs. Jones? What happens when he tries?	1b. Determine what Mrs. Jones's reaction to Roger says about her personality.	Understand **Find meaning**
2a. List the words in the story that are used to indicate the time period or when the story took place.	2b. Predict what would happen if a similar situation occurred today. How might the outcome be different?	Apply **Use information**
3a. Recall what Mrs. Jones tells Roger to do when they get back to her house. Does he obey her?	3b. Analyze why Roger might have made this choice when he had the opportunity to escape. What makes him trust Mrs. Jones?	Analyze **Take things apart**
4a. What personal information does Mrs. Jones share with Roger?	4b. Consider whether or not her past has any effect on her behavior toward Roger. Why or why not? Is the character of Mrs. Jones realistic? Explain.	Evaluate **Make judgments**
5a. State what Roger wants to say to Mrs. Jones as he leaves her house. Why isn't he able to say the words?	5b. Imagine Roger's life after his encounter with Mrs. Jones. What life lessons do you think he has learned?	Create **Bring ideas together**

ANALYZE LITERATURE: Character

Roger and Mrs. Jones are the characters who bring life to the story "Thank You, M'am." How are they different from each other? What do they have in common? Give examples of how the author makes these characters distinctive.

EXTEND THE TEXT

Writing Options

Creative Writing The way events are described can greatly influence a reader's perspective. In a detailed **narrative paragraph,** relate a series of events, true or fictional, by describing what happened. Consider how your description could influence a reader's perspective and what you would need to change within your description to alter that perspective.

Descriptive Writing Choose an unusual or intriguing person from your own neighborhood or family, and write a one- to two-paragraph **character description.** Include details about his or her physical appearance, personality, and interactions with others.

Collaborative Learning

Newspaper Article Pretend you are a reporter writing a newspaper story describing the "attempted robbery" of Mrs. Jones. With a classmate, create a newspaper article that answers the questions *who, what, when, where, why,* and *how.*

Critical Literacy

Author Presentation Langston Hughes wrote a number of poems and short stories. Read at least three poems and one other short story by Hughes to develop a sense of his writing style. What themes does he write about? How would you characterize his writing? Give a short presentation to your class about your discoveries.

Go to **www.mirrorsandwindows.com** for more.

Understanding Plot

PLOT

A **plot** is a series of related events that drive a story. Have you ever been so wrapped up in a book that you find yourself staying up until the early hours of the morning to finish it or flipping to the end of the book to see how it turns out? Books and stories that are hard to put down usually have an interesting or exciting plot.

ELEMENTS OF PLOT

A car is built around a frame, which gives it shape and stability. In the same way, the plot is the frame that gives a story its structure. In general, the main parts of a plot's framework are as follows:

Exposition: The characters are introduced; the setting is established; and necessary background information is provided.

Rising Action: The main character encounters and tries to solve a problem. This results in a conflict developing and growing in intensity.

Climax: At this crucial moment, the main character has to take action or make a decision. Sometimes, fate intervenes and forces the character's hand.

Falling Action: This part of a story explores the events that follow the climax, including the results of the main character's action or decision.

Resolution: This part of a story is sometimes called the *dénouement* (dā nü mä′). At this point, the conflict is resolved.

A **Plot Diagram** is a useful tool for keeping track of all the parts of a plot. To create a Plot Diagram, draw a pyramid shape and make notes on it about each part of the plot. Below is a Plot Diagram of the well-known story "Jack and the Beanstalk."

PLOT AND CONFLICT

A plot revolves around some type of **conflict,** or struggle. Usually, throughout the course of a story, a central conflict is introduced, developed, and resolved. In this unit, you'll read stories in which characters experience various kinds of conflict.

An *internal conflict*, such as the one Elena faces in "American History" (page 121), is a struggle that takes place within a character. In this case, Elena struggles with how she should feel about the things happening around her.

Plot Diagram for "Jack and the Beanstalk"

Exposition
Jack's mother sends him to market to sell their old cow. Instead, Jack trades it for some "magic beans." In anger at his foolishness, his mother throws them out the window. The beanstalk grows overnight, and Jack climbs it into the sky.

Rising Action
There, he is captured by a giant who wants to eat him. Jack steals some gold coins and escapes with the help of the giant's wife. After the money is gone, Jack climbs back up the beanstalk and steals from the giant a hen that lays golden eggs.

Climax
Still wanting more, Jack climbs back up and tries to steal a talking harp. The harp does not want to be stolen and calls out to the giant, who chases Jack down the beanstalk.

Falling Action
Jack cuts down the beanstalk before the giant reaches the ground. The giant falls to his death, pulling the beanstalk with him.

Resolution
Jack and his mother become rich with the harp and live happily ever after.

> That night, I lay in my bed trying to feel the right thing for our dead president. But the tears that came up from a deep source inside me were strictly for me.
>
> —from "American History"
> by Judith Ortiz Cofer

An *external conflict* is a struggle that takes place between a character and some outside force. One type of external conflict is between a character and nature. Another type of external conflict is between a character and society. In "The Necklace" (page 143), Matilda Loisel struggles against the social order as she tries to fit in with the rich and famous, even though she cannot afford the expensive dresses and jewels needed to transform herself into a woman of high society. The third type is between two main characters. This type is demonstrated in "The Cask of Amontillado" (page 59), as Montresor tries to manipulate Fortunato.

> The thousand injuries of Fortunato I had borne as I best could, but when he ventured upon insult, I vowed revenge. You, who so well know the nature of my soul, will not suppose, however, that I gave utterance to a threat. At length I would be avenged; this was a point definitely settled—but the very definitiveness with which it was resolved precluded the idea of risk. I must not only punish but punish with impunity.
>
> —from "The Cask of Amontillado"
> by Edgar Allan Poe

PLOT AND ORGANIZATION

A story has to have a beginning and an end. A story's plot, therefore, is often framed by time. Some stories focus on one hour in a person's life; others may span one hundred years. "The Most Dangerous Game" takes place over a period of around seventy-two hours. "The Cask of Amontillado" covers one afternoon. "The Necklace" spans more than ten years.

Most stories are told in **chronological order:** meaning that the writer unfolds events in the order in which they occur. Sometimes, writers play with time sequence. A **flashback** interrupts the chronological sequence of a literary work and presents an event that occurred earlier. A detective story might start with the central occurrence, such as a theft or murder, and then go back in time to trace the series of events that led up to the crime. This device can also be seen in "The Interlopers" (page 15), when Ulrich von Gradwitz thinks about past events that explain his feud with his neighbor.

> A famous lawsuit, in the days of his grandfather, had wrested it from the illegal possession of a neighboring family of petty landowners; the dispossessed party had never acquiesced in the judgment of the Courts, and a long series of poaching affrays and similar scandals had embittered the relationships between the families for three generations.
>
> —from "The Interlopers"
> by Saki

Writers use **foreshadowing** to present hints or clues to events that will occur later in a story. In "American History," Elena's mother warns her about getting her heart broken. This signals the reader that Elena will most likely suffer a romantic disappointment.

The Interlopers

BEFORE READING

A Short Story by Saki

GUIDED READING

BUILD BACKGROUND

Geographical Context **"The Interlopers"** is the story of two feuding families living in the Carpathian Mountains. Saki paints a vivid picture of that region, which extends from southern Poland to northeastern Romania. The Carpathians contain the vastest areas of montane (mountainous) forest in all of Europe. Over one-third of all European plant species, including some of the last remaining natural beech forests, are found there. Europe's largest populations of brown bears, wolves, and lynx also inhabit the Carpathians, where game hunting remains a common activity.

"The Interlopers" revolves around a feud between two men whose families have been fighting for three generations over the border between their lands. By the end of the story, however, each man realizes that he has a bigger problem than his neighbor's hatred.

Reader's Context Some people claim that hatred or grudges hurt those who hold them more than the people who are the object of their hostility. Do you agree or disagree? Why? How have you resolved a conflict or put an end to a grudge?

ANALYZE LITERATURE: Plot and Flashback

A **plot** is the series of events related to a central conflict, or struggle. A plot typically introduces a conflict, develops it, and eventually resolves it. A **flashback** interrupts the chronological sequence of a literary work and presents an event that occurred earlier. In "The Interlopers," Saki uses flashbacks to provide background information about the two main characters.

SET PURPOSE

Before you read, predict what will happen in the story. Make a prediction based on the Build Background section, pull quotes within the selection, and your own experience with grudges. Adjust your prediction as you learn more. Also, note how the author introduces the conflict and uses flashback to develop the conflict between the main characters.

MEET THE AUTHOR

When **Saki** (1870–1916), a British author, was killed in World War I at the age of forty-six, he left behind a literary legacy still appreciated today. Born Hector Hugh Munro in Burma, Saki wrote as a newspaper correspondent, but he is best known for his short stories. Many of Saki's works are satirical, poking fun at social conventions. In addition to short stories, Saki also wrote two novels, three plays, and one history.

USE READING SKILLS

Compare and Contrast

When you compare one thing to another, you describe their similarities. Contrasting describes their differences. As you read "The Interlopers" and "A Poison Tree" (page 22), take notes on the different subjects or characters presented. Afterward, determine how the main characters are different and how they are similar by creating a Venn Diagram as shown below. Write their similarities where the diagram overlaps. Write their differences in the outer parts of the circles.

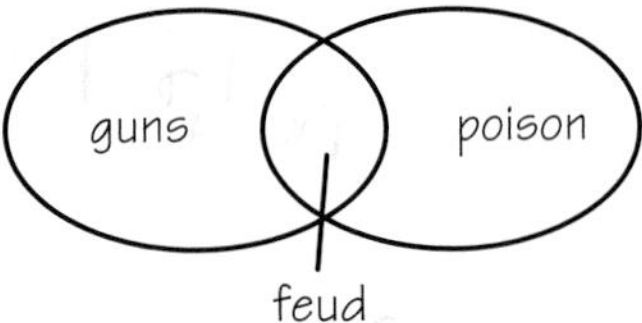

PREVIEW VOCABULARY

Use context clues to identify the meanings of the underlined words. Then identify a **synonym,** or word that has the same meaning, for each word.

1. The <u>precipitous</u> trail up the steep mountain was difficult even for the best climbers.
2. The <u>marauders</u> raided the villagers' stored crops and set their fields ablaze.
3. The <u>plight</u> of the heroine, cornered on the rooftop of a skyscraper, filled the audience with fear.
4. The speaker's dullness and the stifling room filled us with <u>languor</u>.
5. Jeff and Hallie put their long grudge aside and reached a <u>reconciliation</u>.

The Interlopers

A Short Story by **Saki**

Clearing in the Forest, 1825. Caspar David Friedrich. Neue Galerie, Linz, Austria.

The chance had come to give full play to the passions of a lifetime.

In a forest of mixed growth somewhere on the eastern spurs of the Carpathians, a man stood one winter night watching and listening, as though he waited for some beast of the woods to come within

The Carpathian Mountains.

the range of his vision, and, later, of his rifle. But the game for whose presence he kept so keen an outlook was none that figured in the sportsman's calendar as lawful and proper for the chase; Ulrich von Gradwitz patrolled the dark forest in quest of a human enemy.

The forest lands of Gradwitz were of wide extent and well stocked with game; the narrow strip of precipitous woodland that lay on its outskirt was not remarkable for the game it harbored or the shooting it afforded, but it was the most jealously guarded of all its owner's territorial possessions. A famous lawsuit, in the days of his grandfather, had wrested it from the illegal possession of a neighboring family of petty landowners;[1] the dispossessed party had never acquiesced in the judgment of the Courts, and a long series of poaching affrays[2] and similar scandals had embittered the relationships between the families for three generations. The neighbor feud had grown into a personal one since Ulrich had come to be head of his family; if there was a man in the world whom he detested and wished ill to it was Georg Znaeym, the inheritor of the quarrel and the tireless game-snatcher and raider of the disputed border-forest. The feud might, perhaps, have died down or been compromised if the personal ill-will of the two men had not stood in the way; as boys they had thirsted for one another's blood, as men each prayed that misfortune might fall on the other, and this wind-scourged winter night Ulrich had banded

ANALYZE LITERATURE

Flashback For how long has the feud between the two families been going on?

1. **petty landowners.** Owners of small pieces of land
2. **poaching affrays.** Attacks for the purpose of stealing game from someone else's property

pre • cip • i • tous (pri si´ pə təs) *adj.*, steep
em • bit • ter (im bi´tər) *v.*, make resentful
com • pro • mise (käm´prə mīz) *v.*, settle by having both sides make concessions

together his foresters to watch the dark forest, not in quest of four-footed quarry, but to keep a look-out for the prowling thieves whom he suspected of being afoot from across the land boundary. The roebuck,[3] which usually kept in the sheltered hollows during a storm-wind, were running like driven things tonight, and there was movement and unrest among the creatures that were wont to sleep through the dark hours. Assuredly there was a disturbing element in the forest, and Ulrich could guess the quarter from whence it came.

USE READING STRATEGIES

Make Predictions What do you think will happen if Ulrich discovers Georg Znaeym on his land?

He strayed away by himself from the watchers whom he had placed in ambush on the crest of the hill, and wandered far down the steep slopes amid the wild tangle of undergrowth, peering through the tree-trunks and listening through the whistling and skirling of the wind and the restless beating of the branches for sight or sound of the marauders. If only on this wild night, in this dark, lone spot, he might come across Georg Znaeym, man to man, with none to witness—that was the wish that was uppermost in his thoughts. And as he stepped round the trunk of a huge beech he came face to face with the man he sought.

The two enemies stood glaring at one another for a long silent moment. Each had a rifle in his hand, each had hate in his heart and murder uppermost in his mind. The chance had come to give full play to the passions of a lifetime. But a man who has been brought up under the code of a restraining civilization cannot easily nerve himself to shoot down his neighbor in cold blood and without word spoken, except for an offense against his hearth and honor.[4] And before the moment of hesitation had given way to action a deed of Nature's own violence overwhelmed them both. A fierce shriek of the storm had been answered by a splitting crash over their heads, and ere they could leap aside a mass of falling beech tree had thundered down on them. Ulrich von Gradwitz found himself stretched on the ground, one arm numb beneath him and the other held almost as helplessly in a tight tangle of forked branches, while both legs were pinned beneath the fallen mass. His heavy shooting-boots had saved his feet from being crushed to pieces, but if his fractures were not as serious as they might have been, at least it was evident that he could not move from his present position till someone came to release him. The descending twigs had slashed the skin of his face, and he had to wink away some drops of blood from his eyelashes before he could take in a general view of the disaster. At his side, so near that under ordinary circumstances he could almost have touched him, lay Georg Znaeym, alive and struggling, but obviously as helplessly pinioned down as himself. All round them lay a thick-strewn wreckage of splintered branches and broken twigs.

Relief at being alive and exasperation at his captive plight brought a strange medley of pious thank-offerings and sharp curses to Ulrich's lips. Georg, who was nearly blinded with the blood which trickled across his eyes, stopped his struggling for a moment to listen, and then gave a short, snarling laugh.

USE READING SKILLS

Compare and Contrast Examine this scene. Compare and contrast the situation of Georg and Ulrich. In what condition are the two men?

"So you're not killed, as you ought to be, but you're caught, anyway," he cried; "caught fast. Ho, what a jest, Ulrich von Gradwitz snared in his stolen forest. There's real justice

3. **roebuck.** Male of the roe deer
4. **hearth and honor.** Home and reputation

ma • raud • er (mə rôd´ ər) *n.,* person who raids and plunders
re • strain • ing (ri strān´ iŋ) *adj.,* controlling or disciplining
pin • ion (pin´ yən) *v.,* bind
plight (plīt) *n.,* dangerous situation

for you!" And he laughed again, mockingly and savagely.

"I'm caught in my own forest-land," retorted Ulrich. "When my men come to release us you will wish, perhaps, that you were in a better plight than caught poaching on a neighbor's land, shame on you."

Georg was silent for a moment; then he answered quietly:

"Are you sure that your men will find much to release? I have men, too, in the forest tonight, close behind me, and *they* will be here first and do the releasing. When they drag me out from under these damned branches it won't need much clumsiness on their part to roll this mass of trunk right over on the top of you. Your men will find you dead under a fallen beech tree. For form's sake I shall send my condolences to your family."

"It is a useful hint," said Ulrich fiercely. "My men had orders to follow in ten minutes' time, seven of which must have gone by already, and when they get me out—I will remember the hint. Only as you will have met your death poaching on my lands I don't think I can decently send any message of condolence to your family."

"Good," snarled Georg, "good. We fight this quarrel out to the death, you and I and our foresters, with no cursed interlopers[5] to come between us. Death and damnation to you, Ulrich von Gradwitz."

"The same to you, Georg Znaeym, forest-thief, game-snatcher."

Both men spoke with the bitterness of possible defeat before them, for each knew that it might be long before his men would seek him out or find him; it was a bare matter of chance which party would arrive first on the scene.

> "We have quarreled like devils all our lives over this stupid strip of forest..."

Both had now given up the useless struggle to free themselves from the mass of wood that held them down; Ulrich limited his endeavours to an effort to bring his one partially free arm near enough to his outer coat-pocket to draw out his wine-flask. Even when he had accomplished that operation it was long before he could manage the unscrewing of the stopper or get any of the liquid down his throat. But what a Heaven-sent draught it seemed! It was an open winter, and little snow had fallen as yet, hence the captives suffered less from the cold than might have been the case at that season of the year; nevertheless, the wine was warming and reviving to the wounded man, and he looked across with something like a throb of pity to where his enemy lay, just keeping the groans of pain and weariness from crossing his lips.

ANALYZE LITERATURE

Plot What other kind of conflict does the tree falling on the two men represent?

"Could you reach this flask if I threw it over to you?" asked Ulrich suddenly; "there is good wine in it, and one may as well be as comfortable as one can. Let us drink, even if tonight one of us dies."

USE READING STRATEGIES

Make Predictions What do you think Ulrich's statement might foreshadow?

"No, I can scarcely see anything; there is so much blood caked round my eyes," said Georg, "and in any case I don't drink wine with an enemy." Ulrich was silent for a few minutes, and lay listening to the weary screeching of the wind. An idea was slowly forming and growing in his brain, an idea that gained strength every time that he looked across at the man who was fighting so grimly against pain and exhaustion. In the pain and languor that Ulrich himself was feeling the old fierce hatred seemed to be dying down.

"Neighbor," he said presently, "do as you please if your men come first. It was a fair compact.[6] But as for me, I've changed my mind. If my men are the first to come you shall be the first to be helped, as though you were my guest. We have quarrelled like devils all our lives over this stupid strip of forest, where the trees can't even stand upright in a breath of wind. Lying

5. **interlopers.** People who meddle, or intrude, in other people's concerns

6. **compact.** Agreement

en • deav • our (in de´vər) *n.,* attempt; effort; British spelling of "endeavor"

lan • guor (laŋ´gər) *n.,* lack of interest; listlessness

here tonight, thinking, I've come to think we've been rather fools; there are better things in life than getting the better of a boundary dispute. Neighbor, if you will help me to bury the old quarrel I-I will ask you to be my friend."

Georg Znaeym was silent for so long that Ulrich thought, perhaps, he had fainted with the pain of his injuries. Then he spoke slowly and in jerks.

In all the countryside there are none that could hinder if we willed to make peace.

"How the whole region would stare and gabble[7] if we rode into the market-square together. No one living can remember seeing a Znaeym and a von Gradwitz talking to one another in friendship. And what peace there would be among the forester folk if we ended our feud tonight. And if we choose to make peace among our people there is none other to interfere, no interlopers from outside... You would come and keep the Sylvester night[8] beneath my roof, and I would come and feast on some high day at your castle....I would never fire a shot on your land, save when you invited me as a guest; and you should come and shoot with me down in the marshes where the wildfowl are. In all the countryside there are none that could hinder if we willed to make peace. I never thought to have wanted to do other than hate you all my life, but I think I have changed my mind about things too, this last half-hour. And you offered me your wine-flask....Ulrich von Gradwitz, I will be your friend."

USE READING STRATEGIES

Clarify Why might Georg's promise be especially significant to the hunters' developing friendship?

For a space both men were silent, turning over in their minds the wonderful changes that this dramatic reconciliation would bring about. In the cold, gloomy forest, with the wind tearing in fitful gusts through the naked branches and whistling round the tree-trunks, they lay and waited for the help that would now bring release and succor to both parties. And each prayed a private prayer that his men might be the first to arrive, so that he might be the first to show honorable attention to the enemy that had become a friend.

Presently, as the wind dropped for a moment, Ulrich broke silence.

"Let's shout for help," he said; "in this lull our voices may carry a little way."

"They won't carry far through the trees and undergrowth," said Georg, "but we can try. Together, then."

The two raised their voices in a prolonged hunting call.

"Together again," said Ulrich a few minutes later, after listening in vain for an answering halloo.

"I heard something that time, I think," said Ulrich.

"I heard nothing but the pestilential[9] wind," said Georg hoarsely.

There was silence again for some minutes, and then Ulrich gave a joyful cry.

"I can see figures coming through the wood. They are following in the way I came down the hillside."

7. **gabble.** Chatter; talk

8. **Sylvester night.** New Year's Eve, December 31; named after Saint Sylvester

9. **pestilential.** Of or related to a pestilence, regarded as dangerous or harmful

rec • on • cil • i • a • tion (re' kən si' lē ā´shən) *n.*, settling of problems or disputes

Both men raised their voices in as loud a shout as they could muster.

"They hear us! They've stopped. Now they see us. They're running down the hill towards us," cried Ulrich.

"How many of them are there?" asked Georg.

"I can't see distinctly," said Ulrich; "nine or ten."

"Then they are yours," said Georg; "I had only seven out with me."

"They are making all the speed they can, brave lads," said Ulrich gladly.

"Are they your men?" asked Georg. "Are they your men?" he repeated impatiently as Ulrich did not answer.

"No," said Ulrich with a laugh, the idiotic chattering laugh of a man unstrung with hideous fear.

"Who are they?" asked Georg quickly, straining his eyes to see what the other would gladly not have seen.

"Wolves." ❖

ANALYZE LITERATURE

Plot How is the event that follows the conflict resolution an example of irony?

Why do feuds often involve families? What is gained by feuding? What is lost? Could an interloper be the only answer to ending a feud?

REFER TO TEXT ▶▶▶▶	▶ REASON WITH TEXT	
1a. State the cause of the feud between Ulrich and Georg.	1b. Explain how the families of the main characters affect the feud.	**Understand** **Find meaning**
2a. Define what the men realize about their feud over the course of the story.	2b. Examine how the message of this selection might apply to the feuds of today. Explain your reasoning.	**Apply** **Use information**
3a. Identify who, other than Ulrich and Georg, is involved in the feud.	3b. Discuss how the reconciliation between Ulrich and Georg might affect those who live around them.	**Analyze** **Take things apart**
4a. How do the men react when they both decide to end the feud?	4b. Decide whether Ulrich and Georg's reconciliation was beneficial to anyone. Did the reconciliation make the final scene more or less tragic? Explain your answer.	**Evaluate** **Make judgments**
5a. Identify what Georg and Ulrich anticipate as a result of their reconciliation.	5b. Propose what will happen to the feud if both men die. How might their families respond? How might their hunting parties react when they discover the fallen leaders?	**Create** **Bring ideas together**

ANALYZE LITERATURE: Plot and Flashback

How does Saki's use of flashback help to develop the *exposition,* or background, for the plot? What is the central conflict in "The Interlopers"? Review the story to find an event that marks a major turning point in the plot. How is the conflict resolved? What other conflict arises? How does the last line in the story resolve that conflict?

Literature CONNECTION

William Blake (1757–1827) is one of England's finest artists and poets. Blake was an engraver's apprentice for seven years before attending the Royal Academy of Art's School of Design. Although he lived in relative obscurity and poverty, he established himself as an accomplished engraver, painter, and poet. In 1791, his poem **"A Poison Tree"** was published in *Songs of Innocence and Experience*, an illuminated book containing a collection of short lyric poems. Consider how "A Poison Tree" relates to the theme of "The Interlopers."

A Poison Tree

A Poem by **William Blake**

I was angry with my friend:
I told my wrath, my wrath did end.
I was angry with my foe:
I told it not, my wrath did grow.

And I water'd it in fears,
Night and morning with my tears;
And I sunnéd it with smiles,
And with soft deceitful wiles.

And it grew both day and night,
Till it bore an apple bright;
And my foe beheld it shine,
And he knew that it was mine,

And into my garden stole,
When the night had veil'd the pole:
In the morning glad I see
My foe outstretch'd beneath the tree. ❖

REFER TO TEXT ▶▶▶▶	▶ REASON WITH TEXT	
1a. Indicate whom the speaker is angry with in the first stanza.	1b. Infer why his anger ended when he told his friend.	**Understand** **Find meaning**
2a. Identify the ways in which the speaker tends to his wrath.	2b. Analyze what these images mean. Why would these actions cause his wrath to grow?	**Analyze** **Take things apart**
3a. Recall what the speaker sees in the morning. How does he feel about what he sees?	3b. Decide whether "A Poison Tree" is an appropriate title for this poem. What might the poison tree represent or symbolize?	**Evaluate** **Make judgments**

TEXT ◄TO► TEXT CONNECTION

Compare and contrast holding a grudge in "A Poison Tree" and "The Interlopers." How are the characters affected? What conclusions do the authors seem to make about holding a grudge?

AFTER READING

EXTEND THE TEXT

Writing Options

Creative Writing When people or characters are in extreme circumstances, they often act differently than they would otherwise. Imagine that Georg and Ulrich survive. Would they end their feud or would it begin again? Write a new **concluding paragraph** that shows what might happen if Georg and Ulrich survived. Compare your conclusion with those of your classmates.

Expository Writing Write a **conflict/resolution paragraph** about how to bring two opposing groups together to make peace or reach a settlement. You may choose any two groups you know about, whether it be two arguing friends or two political factions. Your audience depends on the groups you choose. Describe the conflict before making suggestions about how to settle the matter.

Lifelong Learning

Research a Family Feud The von Gradwitzes and the Znaeyms weren't the only mountain-dwelling families to get caught up in a famous feud. The legendary Hatfields and McCoys were real-life West Virginia clans who had a decades-long feud that allegedly began over the ownership of two pigs. The feud between the Capulets and the Montagues is the basis for the Shakespeare play *The Tragedy of Romeo and Juliet.* Use the library or the Internet to research a famous family feud. Write a brief essay comparing the feud in "The Interlopers" with your researched feud.

Critical Literacy

Create a Storyboard As a class, identify the following plot elements in the story: *exposition, rising action, climax, falling action,* and *resolution.* (See page 12 for more information on the elements of plot.) Divide into five groups; assign each group a part of the plot. Each group will illustrate the key event for their plot element. Illustrations may include captions or dialogue. Display the illustrations in the order the events occur in the story to create a storyboard.

Go to **www.mirrorsandwindows.com** for more.

READING ASSESSMENT

1. Read the following sentence: "Ulrich von Gradwitz patrolled the dark forest in quest of a human enemy." The author probably ended the first paragraph with this sentence to
   A. characterize Ulrich as a fine hunter.
   B. show that humans are generally uncivilized beings.
   C. introduce the conflict and create suspense.
   D. characterize Ulrich as cruel and inhumane.
   E. All of the above

2. Which is most likely the reason the author had the beech tree fall on the two men?
   A. to show that nature is stronger than humans
   B. to force the characters into a shared, difficult situation that would force them to communicate
   C. to show that people can hold grudges even under the most trying of circumstances
   D. to keep the characters from killing each other so the audience could see them interact
   E. to point out the men's shared hatred of the woods

3. As it is used on page 19, the word *languor* most nearly means
   A. sluggishness.
   B. compassion.
   C. dizziness.
   D. rage.
   E. bitterness.

4. Reread the last six lines from "A Poison Tree." If Ulrich had read these lines at the beginning of "The Interlopers," he would have
   A. thought it would be a fitting end for his foe, Georg.
   B. wondered how somebody could be so angry and hateful.
   C. thought that Georg was trying to poison him.
   D. wondered if anybody held such ill feelings toward him.
   E. wondered if the man was arrested for murder.

5. After the reconciliation, both men want to be first to "show honorable attention" to the other. Do you think they would have tried to outdo each other in being "honorable" and generous? If so, would this have been a case of people doing good things for the wrong reasons? Explain.

GRAMMAR & STYLE

UNDERSTAND THE CONCEPT APPLY THE SKILL

Subject and Verb Agreement

Subject and verb agreement is one of the ways in the English language to keep the meaning of a sentence clear. The **subject** of a sentence is who or what the sentence is about. In fact, the subject is the doer of the action of the sentence and is always a noun. The form of the verb needs to match the subject in terms of number; that is, if the subject is a singular noun, the verb must also be in singular form. If the subject is plural, the verb must be plural.

A **singular noun** stands for, or describes, one person, place, idea, or thing. A **plural noun** stands for, or describes, more than one person, place, idea, or thing.

EXAMPLES

singular nouns: cat, student, goose, apple, knife, boat, berry

plural nouns: cats, students, geese, apples, knives, boats, berries

In a sentence, a verb must be singular if its subject is singular. If a subject is plural, then its verb must be plural. This is called **agreement.**

EXAMPLES

singular subject and verb
The **cat smells** the fried fish.

plural subject and verb
The **cats smell** the fried fish.

singular subject and verb
The **student walks** back to the classroom.

plural subject and verb
The **students walk** back to the classroom.

singular subject and verb
The **knife spreads** the butter on the bread.

plural subject and verb
The **knives spread** the butter on the bread.

Usually, a verb directly follows the subject in a sentence. Sometimes, however, a prepositional phrase or an adjective clause separates the subject and verb. Even though the subject and verb may be separated, they must still agree in number.

EXAMPLES

A **tree** *in the forest* **falls** when it is struck by lightning. (singular subject and verb)
The **wolves** *who heard the men yelling* **wait** at the top of the clearing. (plural subject and verb)

What Great Writers Do

Find the subject and verb in each of the sentences from "The Interlopers" by Saki. Notice the distance between subject and verb.

> The roebuck, which usually kept in the sheltered hollows during a storm-wind, were running like driven things tonight, and there was movement and unrest among the creatures that were wont to sleep through the dark hours. Assuredly there was a disturbing element in the forest, and Ulrich could guess the quarter from whence it came.

REVIEW TERMS

- **subject:** the doer of the action
- **verb:** action word
- **singular noun:** stands for, or describes, one person, place, idea, or thing
- **plural noun:** stands for, or describes, more than one person, place, idea, or thing
- **phrase:** a group of words that functions as one part of speech
- **prepositional phrase:** a group of words that consists of a preposition, its object, and any modifiers of that object

UNDERSTAND THE CONCEPT

APPLY THE SKILL

Identify Subject-Verb Agreement

Identify each of the following sentences whose subjects and verbs do not agree. Using a separate sheet of paper, correct the subject-verb agreement of these sentences.

1. The forest lands of Gradwitz was of wide extent and well stocked with game.
2. But the game for whose presence he kept so keen an outlook was none that figured in the sportsman's calendar as lawful and proper for the chase.
3. The two enemies stand glaring at one another for a long silent moment.
4. A fierce shriek of the storm winds were answered by a splitting crash over their heads.
5. He have to wink away some drops of blood from his eyelashes before he could take in a general view of the disaster.
6. Each has a rifle in his hand, each has hate in his heart and murder uppermost in his mind.
7. When my men come to release us you will wish, perhaps, that you were in a better plight than caught poaching on a neighbor's land.
8. There is better things in life than getting the better of a boundary dispute.
9. In all the countryside there are none that could hinder if we willed to make peace.
10. There were silence again for some minutes, and then Ulrich gave a joyful cry.

Fix Subject-Verb Agreement

Fix the subject-verb agreement problems you find in the following paragraph about "The Interlopers."

> There are a lesson or two that you can learn from the story of "The Interlopers." The families of the main characters have a feud about hunting on a certain piece of land. When they meet one night, they plans to settle it first by killing one another. However, the wind that whips through the trees cause a branch to crash down upon them. Stuck under the branch, they decide to make peace. The two men each think they hears their group approaching, but neither are right. It is wolves.

EXTEND THE SKILL

Newspaper headlines often leave out auxiliary (or helping) verbs, such as *is, are, was, were,* in order to save space. Collect ten or more newspaper headlines that have been shortened in this way. On a separate sheet of paper, write out the headlines as complete sentences. You may need to add more than the auxiliary verbs.

The New York Times
METRO
PIONEER PRESS
SPORTS
WILD SPOTLIGHT KIM JOHNSSON
HEADY STUFF
Tackle tandem clearing the way

THE MOST DANGEROUS GAME

BEFORE READING

A Short Story by Richard Connell

BUILD BACKGROUND

Literary Context "The Most Dangerous Game" is a story of suspenseful drama. Richard Connell crafted a story around the central conflict of two characters. The **protagonist,** or main character, is Rainsford, a big-game hunter whose trip to Africa takes an unexpected turn when he meets General Zaroff, owner and inhabitant of a private island. Highly skilled and experienced hunters, the famous Rainsford and the cultured Zaroff share an enthusiasm for tracking big game. As the plot unfolds, the sport takes on new meaning, and Zaroff emerges as the **antagonist** in the story, or the character who is in conflict with the protagonist, Rainsford.

The "cat and mouse" plot that pits one hunter against the other has been adapted for several films, plays, and television shows. Connell helped write the screenplay for the 1932 film version of the story. In 1945, Orson Welles played Zaroff in a radio play adaptation of the story.

Reader's Context Do you or any of your friends or family enjoy the sport of hunting? Would you say that you relate more to the hunter or the hunted?

ANALYZE LITERATURE: Plot and Conflict

A story's **plot,** or series of events, centers around a conflict. A **conflict** is a struggle between two forces in a literary work. The central conflict may be *internal,* in which a character struggles against some element within himself or herself, or it may be *external,* in which a character struggles against nature, society or social norms, fate, or another character. A character may face more than one type of conflict, as does Rainsford in "The Most Dangerous Game."

SET PURPOSE

Think about the title of this selection. Read the opening quotation and look at other quotations and images within the story. To what kind of game do you think the title is referring? As you read, pay attention to the plot and identify the central conflict and other minor conflicts within the story.

MEET THE AUTHOR

Richard Connell (1893–1949) was born in Poughkeepsie, New York. At the age of ten, he covered baseball games for the local newspaper. Connell attended what is now Georgetown University and then graduated from Harvard University. After serving in World War I, he worked as an editor for various magazines and newspapers and continued to write. Connell created screenplays, numerous novels, and more than three hundred stories, many published in popular magazines such as the *Saturday Evening Post* and *Collier's.* "The Most Dangerous Game," published in 1924, is his most widely known story and won the O. Henry Memorial Award for short fiction.

USE READING SKILLS

Sequence of Events The order in which things happen is called **sequence.** When you read "The Most Dangerous Game," keep track of the sequence of events. You might do this by making a Sequence Map. Draw pictures that represent key events in the order they occur and include a caption under each image.

Rainsford sees the island

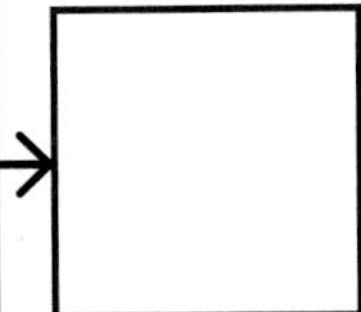

____

PREVIEW VOCABULARY

Use context clues to determine the meanings of the underlined words. Write each word in the context of a new sentence. Then confirm the meanings of the words by looking them up in the Glossary of Vocabulary Words in the back of your textbook.

1. Although I had no <u>tangible</u> evidence, I felt certain that someone had snooped through the contents of my locker.
2. The grumpy customer found the server's friendly personality <u>disarming</u>; he couldn't help smiling back and giving her a big tip.
3. Damon's <u>analytical</u> skills helped him score well on the math portions of his college entrance exams.
4. The practice of applying leeches to purify the blood seems <u>barbarous</u> to us now.
5. Concerned about the patient's welfare, the nurse <u>solicitously</u> asked questions about the older woman's injuries.

THE MOST DANGEROUS GAME

A Short Story by

Richard Connell

"THE WORLD IS MADE UP OF TWO CLASSES—
THE HUNTERS AND THE HUNTED."

"Off there to the right—somewhere—is a large island," said Whitney. "It's rather a mystery—"

"What island is it?" Rainsford asked.

"The old charts call it 'Ship-Trap Island,'" Whitney replied. "A suggestive name, isn't it? Sailors have a curious dread of the place. I don't know why. Some superstition—"

"Can't see it," remarked Rainsford, trying to peer through the dank tropical night that was palpable as it pressed its thick warm blackness in upon the yacht.

"You've good eyes," said Whitney, with a laugh, "and I've seen you pick off a moose moving in the brown fall bush at four hundred yards, but even you can't see four miles or so through a moonless Caribbean night."

"Nor four yards," admitted Rainsford. "Ugh! It's like moist black velvet."

"It will be light enough in Rio,"[1] promised Whitney. "We should make it in a few days. I hope the jaguar guns have come from Purdey's. We should have some good hunting up the Amazon. Great sport, hunting."

"The best sport in the world," agreed Rainsford.

"For the hunter," amended Whitney. "Not for the jaguar."

"Don't talk rot, Whitney," said Rainsford. "You're a big-game hunter, not a philosopher. Who cares how a jaguar feels?"

"Perhaps the jaguar does," observed Whitney.

"Bah! They've no understanding."

USE READING STRATEGIES

Make Inferences What does the name of the island suggest?

1. **Rio.** Rio de Janeiro, then the capital of Brazil

pal • pa • ble (pal´pə bəl) *adj.,* able to be touched or felt

"Even so, I rather think they understand one thing—fear. The fear of pain and the fear of death."

"Nonsense," laughed Rainsford. "This hot weather is making you soft, Whitney. Be a realist. The world is made up of two classes—the hunters and the hunted. Luckily, you and I are the hunters. Do you think we've passed that island yet?"

"I can't tell in the dark. I hope so."

"Why?" asked Rainsford.

"The place has a reputation—a bad one."

"Cannibals?" suggested Rainsford.

"Hardly. Even cannibals wouldn't live in such a God-forsaken place. But it's gotten into sailor lore, somehow. Didn't you notice that the crew's nerves seemed a bit jumpy today?"

"They were a bit strange, now you mention it. Even Captain Nielsen—"

"Yes, even that tough-minded old Swede, who'd go up to the devil himself and ask him for a light. Those fishy blue eyes held a look I never saw there before. All I could get out of him was: 'This place has an evil name among sea-faring men, sir.' Then he said to me, very gravely: 'Don't you feel anything?'—as if the air about us was actually poisonous. Now, you mustn't laugh when I tell you this—I did feel something like a sudden chill.

"There was no breeze. The sea was as flat as a plate-glass window. We were drawing near the island then. What I felt was a—a mental chill; a sort of sudden dread."

ANALYZE LITERATURE

Conflict Based on Whitney's comments, what type of conflict do you think Rainsford will encounter?

"Pure imagination," said Rainsford. "One superstitious sailor can taint the whole ship's company with his fear."

"Maybe. But sometimes I think sailors have an extra sense that tells them when they are in danger. Sometimes I think evil is a tangible thing—with wave lengths, just as sound and light have. An evil place can, so to speak, broadcast vibrations of evil. Anyhow, I'm glad we're getting out of this zone. Well, I think I'll turn in now, Rainsford."

"I'm not sleepy," said Rainsford. "I'm going to smoke another pipe on the afterdeck."[2]

"Good night, then, Rainsford. See you at breakfast."

"Right. Good night, Whitney."

There was no sound in the night as Rainsford sat there, but the muffled throb of the engine that drove the yacht swiftly through the darkness, and the swish and ripple of the wash of the propeller.

Rainsford, reclining in a steamer chair, indolently puffed on his favorite brier. The sensuous drowsiness of the night was on him. "It's so dark," he thought, "that I could sleep without closing my eyes; the night would be my eyelids—"

An abrupt sound startled him. Off to the right he heard it, and his ears, expert in such matters, could not be mistaken. Again he heard the sound, and again. Somewhere, off in the blackness, someone had fired a gun three times.

Rainsford sprang up and moved quickly to the rail, mystified. He strained his eyes in the direction from which the reports had come, but it was like trying to see through a blanket. He leaped upon the rail and balanced himself there, to get greater elevation; his pipe, striking a rope, was knocked from his mouth. He lunged for it; a short, hoarse cry came from his lips as he realized he had reached too far and had lost his balance. The cry was pinched off short as the blood-warm waters of the Caribbean Sea closed over his head.

He struggled up to the surface and tried to cry out, but the wash from the speeding yacht slapped him in the face and the salt water in

2. **afterdeck.** The rear half of a ship's deck

tan • gi • ble (tan´jə bəl) *adj.*, having substance or reality; capable of being touched his open mouth made him gag and strangle. Desperately he struck out with strong strokes after the receding lights of the yacht, but he stopped before he had swum fifty feet. A certain coolheadedness had come to him; it was not the first time he had been in a tight place. There was a chance that his cries could be heard by someone aboard the yacht, but that chance was slender, and grew more slender as the yacht raced on. He wrestled himself out of his clothes, and shouted with all his power. The lights of the yacht became faint and ever-vanishing fireflies; then they were blotted out entirely by the night.

Rainsford remembered the shots. They had come from the right, and doggedly he swam in that direction, swimming with slow, deliberate strokes, conserving his strength. For a seemingly endless time he fought the sea. He began to count his strokes; he could do possibly a hundred more and then—

Rainsford heard a sound. It came out of the darkness, a high screaming sound, the sound of an animal in an extremity of anguish and terror. He did not recognize the animal that made the sound; he did not try to; with fresh vitality he swam toward the sound. He heard it again; then it was cut short by another noise, crisp, staccato.

USE READING STRATEGIES

Clarify What is unusual about the sound that Rainsford hears?

"Pistol shot," muttered Rainsford, swimming on.

Ten minutes of determined effort brought another sound to his ears—the most welcome he had ever heard—the muttering and growling of the sea breaking on a rocky shore. He was almost on the rocks before he saw them; on a night less calm he would have been shattered against them. With his remaining strength he dragged himself from the swirling waters. Jagged crags appeared to jut into the opaqueness, he forced himself upward, hand over hand. Gasping, his hands raw, he reached a flat place at the top. Dense jungle came down to the very edge of the cliffs. What perils that tangle of trees and underbrush might hold for him did not concern Rainsford just then. All he knew was that he was safe from his enemy, the sea, and that utter weariness was on him. He flung himself down at the jungle edge and tumbled headlong into the deepest sleep of his life.

When he opened his eyes he knew from the position of the sun that it was late in the afternoon. Sleep had given him new vigor; a sharp hunger was picking at him. He looked about him, almost cheerfully.

"Where there are pistol shots, there are men. Where there are men, there is food," he thought. But what kind of men, he wondered, in so forbidding a place? An unbroken front of snarled and jagged jungle fringed the shore.

He saw no sign of a trail through the closely knit web of weeds and trees; it was easier to go along the shore, and Rainsford floundered along by the water. Not far from where he had landed, he stopped.

Some wounded thing, by the evidence a large animal, had thrashed about in the underbrush; the jungle weeds were crushed down and the moss was lacerated; one patch of weeds was stained crimson. A small, glittering object not far away caught Rainsford's eye and he picked it up. It was an empty cartridge.

"A twenty-two," he remarked. "That's odd. It must have been a fairly large animal too. The hunter had his nerve with him to tackle it with a light gun. It's clear that the brute put up a fight. I suppose the first three shots I heard was when the hunter flushed his quarry[3] and wounded it. The last shot was when he trailed it here and finished it."

He examined the ground closely and found what he had hoped to find—the print of hunting boots. They pointed along the cliff in the direction he had been going. Eagerly he hurried along, now slipping on a rotten log or a loose stone, but making headway; night was beginning to settle down on the island.

IN HIS HAND THE MAN HELD A LONG-BARRELED REVOLVER, AND HE WAS POINTING IT STRAIGHT AT RAINSFORD'S HEART.

Bleak darkness was blacking out the sea and jungle when Rainsford sighted the lights. He came upon them as he turned a crook in the coast line and his first thought was that he had come upon a village, for there were many lights. But as he forged along he saw to his great astonishment that all the lights were in one enormous building—a lofty structure with pointed towers plunging upward into the gloom. His eyes made out the shadowy outlines of a palatial château; it was set on a high bluff, and on three sides of it cliffs dived down to where the sea licked greedy lips in the shadows.

USE READING SKILLS

Sequence of Events
What has occurred up to this point in the story? Why might this last discovery be exciting?

"Mirage," thought Rainsford. But it was no mirage, he found, when he opened the tall spiked iron gate. The stone steps were real enough; the massive door with a leering gargoyle[4] for a knocker was real enough; yet about it all hung an air of unreality.

He lifted the knocker, and it creaked up stiffly, as if it had never before been used. He let it fall, and it startled him with its booming loudness. He thought he heard steps within; the door remained closed. Again Rainsford lifted the heavy knocker, and let it fall. The door opened then, opened as suddenly as if it were on a spring, and Rainsford stood blinking in the river of glaring gold light that poured out. The first thing Rainsford's eyes discerned was the largest man Rainsford had ever seen—a gigantic creature, solidly made and black-bearded to the waist. In his hand the man held a long-barreled revolver, and he was pointing it straight at Rainsford's heart.

Out of the snarl of beard two small eyes regarded Rainsford.

"Don't be alarmed," said Rainsford, with a smile which he hoped was disarming. "I'm no robber. I fell off a yacht. My name is Sanger Rainsford of New York City."

The menacing look in the eyes did not change. The revolver pointed as rigidly as if the giant were a statue. He gave no sign that he understood Rainsford's words, or that he had even heard them. He was dressed in uniform, a black uniform trimmed with gray astrakhan.[5]

"I'm Sanger Rainsford of New York," Rainsford began again. "I fell off a yacht. I am hungry."

The man's only answer was to raise with his thumb the hammer of his revolver. Then Rainsford saw the man's free hand go to his forehead in a military salute, and he saw him click his heels together and stand at attention. Another man was coming down the broad marble steps, an erect, slender man in evening clothes. He advanced to Rainsford and held out his hand.

3. **flushed his quarry.** Forced an animal out of its hiding place
4. **gargoyle.** Grotesquely carved figure of a human or an animal
5. **astrakhan.** Wool from a particular breed of Russian sheep

dis • arm • ing (dis ärm′iŋ) *adj.*, friendly or harmless

In a cultivated voice marked by a slight accent that gave it added precision and deliberateness, he said: "It is a very great pleasure and honor to welcome Mr. Sanger Rainsford, the celebrated hunter, to my home."

Automatically Rainsford shook the man's hand.

"I've read your book about hunting snow leopards in Tibet, you see," explained the man. "I am General Zaroff."

Rainsford's first impression was that the man was singularly handsome; his second was that there was an original, almost bizarre quality about the general's face. He was a tall man past middle age, for his hair was a vivid white; but his thick eyebrows and pointed military mustache were as black as the night from which Rainsford had come. His eyes, too, were black and very bright. He had high cheek bones, a sharp-cut nose, a spare, dark face, the face of a man used to giving orders, the face of an aristocrat. Turning to the giant in uniform, the general made a sign. The giant put away his pistol, saluted, withdrew.

"Ivan is an incredibly strong fellow," remarked the general, "but he has the misfortune to be deaf and dumb. A simple fellow, but I'm afraid, like all his race, a bit of a savage."

"Is he Russian?"

"He is a Cossack,"[6] said the general, and his smile showed red lips and pointed teeth. "So am I."

"Come," he said, "we shouldn't be chatting here. We can talk later. Now you want clothes, food, rest. You shall have them. This is a most restful spot."

Ivan had reappeared, and the general spoke to him with lips that moved but gave forth no sound.

"Follow Ivan, if you please, Mr. Rainsford," said the general. "I was about to have my dinner when you came. I'll wait for you. You'll find that my clothes will fit you, I think."

It was to a huge, beam-ceilinged bedroom with a canopied bed big enough for six men that Rainsford followed the silent giant. Ivan laid out an evening suit, and Rainsford, as he put it on, noticed that it came from a London tailor who ordinarily cut and sewed for none below the rank of duke.

The dining room to which Ivan conducted him was in many ways remarkable. There was a medieval magnificence about it; it suggested a baronial hall of feudal times[7] with its oaken panels, its high ceiling, its vast refectory table[8] where twoscore[9] men could sit down to eat. About the hall were the mounted heads of many animals—lions, tigers, elephants, moose, bears; larger or more perfect

USE READING STRATEGIES

Make Inferences
Based on his home and his response to Rainsford's arrival, what can be inferred about General Zaroff?

6. **Cossack.** Member of a group of people from southern Russia trained for difficult military combat
7. **baronial hall of feudal times.** Dining room in a medieval mansion
8. **refectory table.** Long table with heavy legs
9. **twoscore.** Forty

specimens Rainsford had never seen. At the great table the general was sitting, alone.

"You'll have a cocktail, Mr. Rainsford," he suggested. The cocktail was surpassingly good; and, Rainsford noted, the table appointments were of the finest—the linen, the crystal, the silver, the china.

> **"NO THRILL LEFT IN TIGERS, NO REAL DANGER. I LIVE FOR DANGER, MR. RAINSFORD."**

They were eating *borsch,* the rich, red soup with whipped cream so dear to Russian palates. Half apologetically General Zaroff said: "We do our best to preserve the amenities of civilization here. Please forgive any lapses. We are well off the beaten track, you know. Do you think the champagne has suffered from its long ocean trip?"

"Not in the least," declared Rainsford. He was finding the general a most thoughtful and affable host, a true cosmopolite.[10] But there was one small trait of the general's that made Rainsford uncomfortable. Whenever he looked up from his plate he found the general studying him, appraising him narrowly.

USE READING STRATEGIES

Make Inferences
Why is Rainsford uncomfortable when Zaroff studies him?

"Perhaps," said General Zaroff, "you were surprised that I recognized your name. You see, I read all books on hunting published in English, French, and Russian. I have but one passion in my life, Mr. Rainsford, and it is the hunt."

"You have some wonderful heads here," said Rainsford as he ate a particularly well cooked filet mignon. "That Cape buffalo is the largest I ever saw."

"Oh, that fellow. Yes, he was a monster."

"Did he charge you?"

"Hurled me against a tree," said the general. "Fractured my skull. But I got the brute."

"I've always thought," said Rainsford, "that the Cape buffalo is the most dangerous of all big game."

For a moment the general did not reply; he was smiling his curious red lipped smile. Then he said slowly: "No. You are wrong, sir. The Cape buffalo is not the most dangerous big game." He sipped his wine. "Here in my preserve on this island," he said in the same slow tone, "I hunt more dangerous game."

Rainsford expressed his surprise. "Is there big game on this island?"

The general nodded. "The biggest."

"Really?"

"Oh, it isn't here naturally, of course. I have to stock the island."

"What have you imported, General?" Rainsford asked. "Tigers?"

The general smiled. "No," he said. "Hunting tigers ceased to interest me some years ago. I exhausted their possibilities, you see. No thrill left in tigers, no real danger. I live for danger, Mr. Rainsford."

The general took from his pocket a gold cigarette case and offered his guest a long black cigarette with a silver tip; it was perfumed and gave off a smell like incense.

"We will have some capital hunting, you and I," said the general. "I shall be most glad to have your society."

"But what game—" began Rainsford.

"I'll tell you," said the general. "You will be amused, I know. I think I may say, in all modesty, that I have done a rare thing. I have invented a new sensation. May I pour you another glass of port, Mr. Rainsford?"

---

10. **cosmopolite.** Person who has a worldwide sophistication

a • men • i • ty (ə meˊ nə tē) *n.,* something that makes life easier or more pleasant

"Thank you, General."

The general filled both glasses and said: "God makes some men poets. Some He makes kings, some beggars. Me He made a hunter. My hand was made for the trigger, my father said. He was a very rich man with a quarter of a million acres in the Crimea,[11] and he was an ardent sportsman. When I was only five years old he gave me a little gun, specially made in Moscow for me, to shoot sparrows with. When I shot some of his prize turkeys with it, he did not punish me; he complimented me on my marksmanship. I killed my first bear in the Caucasus when I was ten. My whole life has been one prolonged hunt. I went into the army—it was expected of noblemen's sons—and for a time commanded a division of Cossack cavalry, but my real interest was always the hunt. I have hunted every kind of game in every land. It would be impossible for me to tell you how many animals I have killed."

Critical Viewing

Compare the illustration to General Zaroff's own hunting experiences. How are the depictions similar and how are they different?

ANALYZE LITERATURE

Conflict What do General Zaroff and Rainsford have in common?

The general puffed at his cigarette.

"After the debacle in Russia[12] I left the country, for it was imprudent for an officer of the Czar to stay there. Many noble Russians lost everything. I, luckily, had invested heavily in American securities, so I shall never have to open a tea room in Monte Carlo or drive a taxi in Paris. Naturally, I continued to hunt—grizzlies in your Rockies, crocodiles in the Ganges,[13] rhinoceroses in East Africa. It was in Africa that the Cape buffalo hit me and laid me up for six months. As soon as I recovered I started for the Amazon to hunt jaguars, for I had heard they were unusually cunning. They weren't." The Cossack sighed. "They were no match at all for a hunter with his wits about him and a high-powered rifle. I was bitterly disappointed. I was lying in my tent with a splitting headache one night when a terrible thought pushed its way into my mind. Hunting was beginning to bore me! And hunting, remember, had been my life. I have heard that in America businessmen often go to pieces when they give up the business that has been their life."

Relaxing After the Safari, 1922. Guy Arnoux, Stapleton Collection, London.

"Yes, that's so," said Rainsford.

The general smiled. "I had no wish to go to pieces," he said. "I must do something. Now, mine is an analytical mind, Mr. Rainsford. Doubtless that is why I enjoy the problems of the chase."

"No doubt, General Zaroff."

"So," continued the general, "I asked myself why the hunt no longer fascinated me. You are much younger than I am, Mr. Rainsford, and

11. **Crimea.** Peninsula on the Black Sea in southwestern Russia
12. **debacle in Russia.** Russian Revolution of 1917, during which the czar was overthrown and wealthy landowners lost their properties
13. **Ganges.** River in India

an • a • lyt • i • cal (a' nə li´ti kəl) *adj.*, skilled in breaking a whole into its parts and examining their relationships have not hunted as much, but you perhaps can guess the answer."

"What was it?"

"Simply this: hunting had ceased to be what you call 'a sporting proposition.' It had become too easy. I always got my quarry. Always. There is no greater bore than perfection."

The general lit a fresh cigarette.

> **USE READING STRATEGIES**
>
> **Clarify** What does General Zaroff enjoy most about hunting?

"No animal had a chance with me any more. That is no boast; it is a mathematical certainty. The animal had nothing but his legs and his instinct. Instinct is no match for reason. When I thought of this it was a tragic moment for me, I can tell you."

Rainsford leaned across the table, absorbed in what his host was saying.

"It came to me as an inspiration what I must do," the general went on.

"And that was?"

The general smiled the quiet smile of one who has faced an obstacle and surmounted it with success. "I had to invent a new animal to hunt," he said.

"A new animal? You're joking."

"Not at all," said the general. "I never joke about hunting. I needed a new animal. I found one. So I bought this island, built this house, and here I do my hunting. The island is perfect for my purposes—there are jungles with a maze of trails in them, hills, swamps—"

"But the animal, General Zaroff?"

"Oh," said the general, "it supplies me with the most exciting hunting in the world. No other hunting compares with it for an instant. Every day I hunt, and I never grow bored now, for I have a quarry with which I can match my wits."

Rainsford's bewilderment showed in his face.

"I wanted the ideal animal to hunt," explained the general. "So I said: 'What are the attributes of an ideal quarry?' And the answer was, of course: 'It must have courage, cunning, and, above all, it must be able to reason.'"

"But no animal can reason," objected Rainsford.

"My dear fellow," said the general, "there is one that can."

"But you can't mean—" gasped Rainsford.

"And why not?"

"I can't believe you are serious, General Zaroff. This is a grisly joke."

"Why should I not be serious? I am speaking of hunting."

> **ANALYZE LITERATURE**
>
> **Conflict** What conflict appears to be developing?

"Hunting? General Zaroff, what you speak of is murder."

The general laughed with entire good nature. He regarded Rainsford quizzically. "I refuse to believe that so modern and civilized a young man as you seem to be harbors romantic ideas about the value of human life. Surely your experiences in the war—"

"Did not make me condone coldblooded murder," finished Rainsford stiffly.

Laughter shook the general. "How extraordinarily droll you are!" he said. "One does not expect nowadays to find a young man of the educated class, even in America, with such a naive, and, if I may say so, mid-Victorian point of view.[14] It's like finding a snuff-box in a limousine. Ah, well, doubtless you had Puritan ancestors. So many Americans appear to have had. I'll wager you'll forget your notions when you go hunting with me. You've a genuine new thrill in store for you, Mr. Rainsford."

"Thank you, I'm a hunter, not a murderer."

"Dear me," said the general, quite unruffled, "again that unpleasant word. But I think I can show you that your scruples are quite ill founded."

14. **mid-Victorian point of view.** During Queen Victoria's reign, in the late nineteenth century, the English had a very strict code of moral behavior.

con • done (kən dōn´) *v.,* forgive or overlook an offense

"Yes?"

"Life is for the strong, to be lived by the strong, and, if need be, taken by the strong. The weak of the world were put here to give the strong pleasure. I am strong. Why should I not use my gift? If I wish to hunt, why should I not? I hunt the scum of the earth—a thoroughbred horse or hound is worth more than a score of them."

"But they are men," said Rainsford hotly.

"Precisely," said the general. "That is why I use them. It gives me pleasure. They can reason, after a fashion. So they are dangerous."

"But where do you get them?"

The general's left eyelid fluttered down in a wink. "This island is called Ship-Trap," he answered. "Sometimes an angry god of the high seas sends them to me. Sometimes, when Providence is not so kind, I help Providence a bit. Come to the window with me."

"LIFE IS FOR THE STRONG, TO BE LIVED BY THE STRONG, AND, IF NEED BE, TAKEN BY THE STRONG."

Rainsford went to the window and looked out toward the sea.

"Watch! Out there!" exclaimed the general, pointing into the night. Rainsford's eyes saw only blackness, and then, as the general pressed a button, far out to sea Rainsford saw the flash of lights.

The general chuckled. "They indicate a channel," he said, "where there's none; giant rocks with razor edges crouch like a sea monster with wide-open jaws. They can crush a ship as easily as I crush this nut." He dropped a walnut on the hardwood floor and brought his heel grinding down on it. "Oh, yes," he said casually, as if in answer to a question, "I have electricity. We try to be civilized here."

ANALYZE LITERATURE

Conflict What is the irony in General Zaroff's statement about being civilized?

"Civilized? And you shoot down men?" A trace of anger was in the general's black eyes; but it was there for but a second, and he said, in his most pleasant manner: "Dear me, what a righteous young man you are! I assure you I do not do the thing you suggest. That would be barbarous. I treat these visitors with every consideration. They get plenty of good food and exercise. They get into splendid physical condition. You shall see for yourself tomorrow."

"What do you mean?"

"We'll visit my training school," smiled the general. "It's in the cellar. I have about a dozen pupils down there now. They're from the Spanish bark San Lucar that had the bad luck to go on the rocks out there. A very inferior lot, I regret to say. Poor specimens and more accustomed to the deck than to the jungle."

He raised his hand, and Ivan, who served as waiter, brought thick Turkish coffee. Rainsford, with an effort, held his tongue in check.

"It's a game, you see," pursued the general blandly. "I suggest to one of them that we go hunting. I give him a supply of food and an excellent hunting knife. I give him three hours' start. I am to follow, armed only with a pistol of the smallest caliber and range. If my quarry eludes me for three whole days, he wins the game. If I find him"—the general smiled— "he loses."

"Suppose he refuses to be hunted?"

"Oh," said the general, "I give him his option, of course. He need not play the game if he doesn't wish to, I turn him over to Ivan. Ivan once had the honor of serving as official knouter to the Great White Czar,[15] and he has his own ideas of sport. Invariably, Mr. Rainsford, invariably they choose the hunt."

15. **Ivan...Czar.** During the reign of Alexander III (1881–1894) of Russia, Ivan was the official flogger, who whipped prisoners severely.

bar • ba • rous (bär´bə rəs) *adj.*, cruel; uncultured

"And if they win?"

The smile on the general's face widened. "To date I have not lost," he said.

Then he added, hastily: "I don't wish you to think me a braggart, Mr. Rainsford. Many of them afford only the most elementary sort of problem. Occasionally I strike a tartar.[16] One almost did win. I eventually had to use the dogs."

"The dogs?"

"This way, please. I'll show you."

The general steered Rainsford to a window. The lights from the windows sent a flickering illumination that made grotesque patterns on the courtyard below, and Rainsford could see moving about there a dozen or so huge black shapes; as they turned toward him, their eyes glittered greenly.

USE READING STRATEGIES

Make Inferences
What does the sound suggest?

"If anyone should try to get into my house—or out of it—something extremely regrettable would occur to him." He hummed a snatch of song from the Folies Bergère.

"And now," said the general, "I want to show you my new collection of heads. Will you come with me to the library?"

"I hope," said Rainsford, "that you will excuse me tonight, General Zaroff. I'm really not feeling at all well."

"Ah, indeed?" the general inquired solicitously. "Well, I suppose that's only natural, after your long swim. You need a good, restful night's sleep. Tomorrow you'll feel like a new man, I'll wager. Then we'll hunt, eh? I've one rather promising prospect—"

Rainsford was hurrying from the room.

"Sorry you can't go with me tonight," called the general. "I expect rather fair sport—a big, strong sailor. He looks resourceful—Well, good night, Mr. Rainsford; I hope you have a good night's rest."

The bed was good and the pajamas of the softest silk, and he was tired in every fiber of his being, but nevertheless Rainsford could not quiet his brain with the opiate of sleep. He lay, eyes wide open. Once he thought he heard stealthy steps in the corridor outside his room. He sought to throw open the door; it would not open. He went to the window and looked out. His room was high up in one of the towers. The lights of the château were out now, and it was dark and silent; but there was a fragment of sallow moon, and by its wan light he could see, dimly, the courtyard; there, weaving in and out in the pattern of shadow, were black, noiseless forms; the hounds heard him at the window and looked up, expectantly, with their green eyes. Rainsford went back to the bed and lay down. By many methods he tried to put himself to sleep. He had achieved a doze when, just as morning began to come, he heard, far off in the jungle, the faint report of a pistol.

General Zaroff did not appear until luncheon. He was dressed faultlessly in the tweeds of a country squire. He was solicitous about the state of Rainsford's health.

"As for me," sighed the general, "I do not feel so well. I am worried, Mr. Rainsford. Last night I detected traces of my old complaint."

To Rainsford's questioning glance the general said: "Ennui. Boredom."

Then, taking a second helping of crêpes suzette,[17] the general explained: "The hunting was not good last night. The fellow lost his head. He made a straight trail that offered no problems at all. That's the trouble with these sailors. They have dull brains to begin with, and they do not know how to get about in the woods. They do excessively stupid and obvious things. It's becoming most annoying. Will you have another glass of Chablis, Mr. Rainsford?"

"General," said Rainsford firmly, "I wish to leave this island at once."

The general raised his thickets of eyebrows; he seemed hurt. "But, my dear fellow," the

16. **strike a tartar.** Meet one who is difficult to control

17. **crêpes suzette.** Thin pancakes eaten as a dessert

so • lic • i • tous • ly (sə li´sə təs lē) *adv.,* showing concern general protested, "you've only just come. You've had no hunting—"

"I wish to go today," said Rainsford. He saw the dead black eyes of the general on him, studying him. General Zaroff's face suddenly brightened.

He filled Rainsford's glass with venerable Chablis from a dusty bottle.

"Tonight," said the general, "we will hunt— you and I."

Rainsford shook his head. "No, General," he said, "I will not hunt." The general shrugged his shoulders and delicately ate a hothouse grape. "As you wish, my friend," he said. "The choice rests entirely with you. But may I not venture to suggest that you will find my idea of sport more diverting than Ivan's?"

"OH, YOU CAN TRUST ME," SAID THE COSSACK. "I WILL GIVE YOU MY WORD AS A GENTLEMAN AND A SPORTSMAN."

He nodded toward the corner to where the giant stood, scowling, his thick arms crossed on his huge chest.

"You don't mean—" cried Rainsford.

"My dear fellow," said the general, "have I not told you I always mean what I say about hunting? This is really an inspiration. I drink to a foe worthy of me at last."

USE READING STRATEGIES

Make Predictions
What plans does General Zaroff have for Rainsford?

The general raised his glass, but Rainsford sat staring at him.

"You'll find this game worth playing," the general said enthusiastically. "Your brain against mine. Your woodcraft against mine. Your strength and stamina against mine. Outdoor chess! And the stake is not without value, eh?"

"And if I should win—" began Rainsford huskily.

"I'll cheerfully acknowledge myself defeated if I do not find you by midnight of the third day," said General Zaroff. "My sloop will place you on the mainland near a town." The general read what Rainsford was thinking.

"Oh, you can trust me," said the Cossack. "I will give you my word as a gentleman and a sportsman. Of course you, in turn, must agree to say nothing of your visit here."

"I'll agree to nothing of the kind," said Rainsford.

"Oh," said the general, "in that case—But why discuss that now? Three days hence we can discuss it over a bottle of Veuve Cliquot, unless—"

The general sipped his wine.

Then a businesslike air animated him. "Ivan," he said to Rainsford, "will supply you with hunting clothes, food, a knife. I suggest you wear moccasins; they leave a poorer trail. I suggest too that you avoid the big swamp in the southeast corner of the island. We call it Death Swamp. There's quicksand there. One foolish fellow tried it. The deplorable part of it was that Lazarus followed him. You can imagine my feelings, Mr. Rainsford. I loved Lazarus; he was the finest hound in my pack. Well, I must beg you to excuse me now. I always take a siesta after lunch. You'll hardly have time for a nap, I fear. You'll want to start, no doubt. I shall not follow till dusk. Hunting at night is so much more exciting than by day, don't you think? *Au revoir,*"[18] said the general, "Mr. Rainsford, *au revoir.*"

General Zaroff, with a deep, courtly bow, strolled from the room.

From another door came Ivan. Under one arm he carried khaki hunting clothes, a haversack of food, a leather sheath containing a long-bladed hunting knife; his right hand rested on a cocked revolver thrust in the crimson sash about his waist....

18. ***Au revoir.*** [French] Until we meet again

an • i • mate (a´ nə māt´) *v.*, to give life to; to move to action

Rainsford had fought his way through the bush for two hours. "I must keep my nerve. I must keep my nerve," he said through tight teeth.

He had not been entirely clearheaded when the château gates snapped shut behind him. His whole idea at first was to put distance between himself and General Zaroff, and, to this end, he had plunged along, spurred on by the sharp rowels of something very like panic. Now he had got a grip on himself, had stopped, and was taking stock of himself and the situation.

He saw that straight flight was futile; inevitably it would bring him face to face with the sea. He was in a picture with a frame of water, and his operations, clearly, must take place within that frame.

"I'll give him a trail to follow," muttered Rainsford, and he struck off from the rude paths he had been following into the trackless wilderness. He executed a series of intricate loops; he doubled on his trail again and again, recalling all the lore of the fox hunt, and all the dodges of the fox. Night found him leg-weary, with hands and face lashed by the branches, on a thickly wooded ridge. He knew it would be insane to blunder on through the dark, even if he had the strength. His need for rest was imperative and he thought: "I have played the fox, now I must play the cat of the fable."[19] A big tree with a thick trunk and outspread branches was nearby, and, taking care to leave not the slightest mark, he climbed up into the crotch, and stretching out on one of the broad limbs, after a fashion, rested. Rest brought him new confidence and almost a feeling of security. Even so zealous a hunter as General Zaroff could not trace him there, he told himself; only the devil himself could follow that complicated trail through the jungle after dark. But, perhaps, the general was a devil—

"I HAVE PLAYED THE FOX, NOW I MUST PLAY THE CAT OF THE FABLE."

An apprehensive night crawled slowly by like a wounded snake, and sleep did not visit Rainsford, although the silence of a dead world was on the jungle. Toward morning when a dingy gray was varnishing the sky, the cry of some startled bird focused Rainsford's attention in that direction. Something was coming through the bush, coming slowly, carefully, coming by the same winding way Rainsford had come. He flattened himself down on the limb, and through a screen of leaves almost as thick as tapestry, he watched. The thing that was approaching was a man.

It was General Zaroff. He made his way along with his eyes fixed in utmost concentration on the ground before him. He paused, almost beneath the tree, dropped to his knees and studied the ground. Rainsford's impulse was to hurl himself down like a panther, but he saw the general's right hand held something metallic—a small automatic pistol.

The hunter shook his head several times, as if he were puzzled. Then he straightened up and took from his case one of his black cigarettes; its pungent incense-like smoke floated up to Rainsford's nostrils.

Rainsford held his breath. The general's eyes had left the ground and were traveling inch by inch up the tree. Rainsford froze there, every muscle tensed for a spring. But the sharp eyes of the hunter stopped before they reached the limb where Rainsford lay; a smile spread over his brown face. Very deliberately he blew a smoke ring into the air; then he

USE READING STRATEGIES

Clarify How does this scene describe Rainsford? Is he described more as a man or an animal?

19. **I have played...fable.** He has used the trickery of the fox to escape his pursuer; now he must use the cunning of a cat to further escape.

fu • tile (fyü´ tl) *adj.*, having no result or effect

turned his back on the tree and walked carelessly away, back along the trail he had come. The swish of the underbrush against his hunting boots grew fainter and fainter.

The pent-up air burst hotly from Rainsford's lungs. His first thought made him feel sick and numb. The general could follow a trail through the woods at night; he could follow an extremely difficult trail; he must have uncanny powers; only by the merest chance had the Cossack failed to see his quarry.

Rainsford's second thought was even more terrible. It sent a shudder of cold horror through his whole being. Why had the general smiled? Why had he turned back?

Rainsford did not want to believe what his reason told him was true, but the truth was as evident as the sun that had by now pushed through the morning mists. The general was playing with him! The general was saving him for another day's sport! The Cossack was the cat; he was the mouse. Then it was that Rainsford knew the full meaning of terror.

"I will not lose my nerve. I will not."

He slid down from the tree, and struck off again into the woods. His face was set and he forced the machinery of his mind to function. Three hundred yards from his hiding place he stopped where a huge dead tree leaned precariously on a smaller, living one. Throwing off his sack of food, Rainsford took his knife from its sheath and began to work with all his energy.

ANALYZE LITERATURE

Plot What is Rainsford doing? How does this action change the plot of the story?

The job was finished at last, and he threw himself down behind a fallen log a hundred feet away. He did not have to wait long. The cat was coming again to play with the mouse.

Following the trail with the sureness of a bloodhound, came General Zaroff. Nothing escaped those searching black eyes, no crushed blade of grass, no bent twig, no mark, no matter how faint, in the moss. So intent was the Cossack on his stalking that he was upon the thing Rainsford had made before he saw it. His foot touched the protruding bough that was the trigger. Even as he touched it, the general sensed his danger and leaped back with the agility of an ape. But he was not quite quick enough; the dead tree, delicately adjusted to rest on the cut living one, crashed down and struck the general a glancing blow on the shoulder as it fell; but for his alertness, he must have been smashed beneath it. He staggered, but he did not fall; nor did he drop his revolver. He stood there, rubbing his injured shoulder, and Rainsford, with fear again gripping his heart, heard the general's mocking laugh ring through the jungle.

"Rainsford," called the general, "if you are within the sound of my voice, as I suppose you are, let me congratulate you. Not many men know how to make a Malay man-catcher. Luckily, for me, I too have hunted in Malacca.[20] You are proving interesting, Mr. Rainsford. I am going now to have my wound dressed; it's only a slight one. But I shall be back. I shall be back."

When the general, nursing his bruised shoulder, had gone, Rainsford took up his flight again. It was flight now, a desperate, hopeless flight, that carried him on for some hours. Dusk came, then darkness, and still he pressed on. The ground grew softer under his moccasins; the vegetation grew ranker, denser; insects bit him savagely. Then, as he stepped forward, his foot sank into the ooze. He tried to wrench it back, but the muck sucked viciously at his foot as if it were a giant leech. With a violent effort, he tore his foot loose. He knew where he was now. Death Swamp and its quicksand.

His hands were tight closed as if his nerve were something tangible that some one in the darkness was trying to tear from his grip. The softness of the earth had given him an idea. He stepped back from the quicksand a dozen feet

20. **Malacca.** Region in the southwestern Malay Peninsula in Asia

WORLD HISTORY CONNECTION

The Trenches of World War I
Rainsford's having "dug himself in in France" is a reference to World War I (1914–1918). The United States joined the war on the side of the Allies, which included Britain and France, in 1917. The setting for most of the fighting along the Western Front, or battle lines between Germany and France, was an elaborate system of trenches protected by barbed wire. The fortified trenches were an excellent system of defense, and the lines remained in nearly the same position throughout the war. However, life in the trenches was miserable and dangerous. A heavy rain could mean slopping around in standing water or deep mud for days, and the wet trenches provided a fertile breeding ground for various diseases. Compare Rainsford's situation to what he might have experienced in World War I.

or so, and, like some huge prehistoric beaver, he began to dig.

Rainsford had dug himself in in France, when a second's delay meant death. That had been a placid pastime compared to his digging now. The pit grew deeper; when it was above his shoulders, he climbed out and from some hard saplings cut stakes and sharpened them to a fine point. These stakes he planted in the bottom of the pit with the points sticking up. With flying fingers he wove a rough carpet of weeds and branches and with it he covered the mouth of the pit. Then, wet with sweat and aching with tiredness, he crouched behind the stump of a lightning-charred tree.

He knew his pursuer was coming; he heard the padding sound of feet on the soft earth, and the night breeze brought him the perfume of the general's cigarette. It seemed to Rainsford that the general was coming with unusual swiftness; he was not feeling his way along, foot by foot. Rainsford, crouching there, could not see the general, nor could he see the pit. He lived a year in a minute. Then he felt an impulse to cry aloud with joy, for he heard the sharp crackle of the breaking branches as the cover of the pit gave way; he heard the sharp scream of pain as the pointed stakes found their mark. He leaped up from his place of concealment. Then he cowered back. Three feet from the pit a man was standing, with an electric torch[21] in his hand.

"You've done well, Rainsford," the voice of the general called. "Your Burmese tiger pit[22] has claimed one of my best dogs. Again you score. I think, Mr. Rainsford, I'll see what you can do against my whole pack. I'm going home for a rest now. Thank you for a most amusing evening."

At daybreak Rainsford, lying near the swamp, was awakened by a sound that made him know that he had new things to learn about fear. It was a distant sound, faint and wavering, but he knew it. It was the baying of a pack of hounds.

Rainsford knew he could do one of two things. He could stay where he was and wait. That was suicide. He could flee. That was postponing the inevitable. For a moment he stood there, thinking. An idea that held a wild

21. **torch.** Flashlight (British)
22. **Burmese tiger pit.** Deep pit used to trap tigers in Burma, a country located in southeast Asia now known as Myanmar

chance came to him, and, tightening his belt, he headed away from the swamp.

The baying of the hounds drew nearer, then still nearer, nearer, ever nearer. On a ridge Rainsford climbed a tree. Down a watercourse, not a quarter of a mile away, he could see the bush moving. Straining his eyes, he saw the lean figure of General Zaroff; just ahead of him Rainsford made out another figure whose wide shoulders surged through the tall jungle weeds; it was the giant Ivan, and he seemed pulled forward by some unseen force; Rainsford knew that Ivan must be holding the pack in leash.

They would be on him any minute now. His mind worked frantically. He thought of a native trick he had learned in Uganda. He slid down the tree. He caught hold of a springy young sapling and to it he fastened his hunting knife, with the blade pointing down the trail; with a bit of wild grapevine he tied back the sapling.

Then he ran for his life. The hounds raised their voices as they hit the fresh scent. Rainsford knew now how an animal at bay feels.

He had to stop to get his breath. The baying of the hounds stopped abruptly, and Rainsford's heart stopped too. They must have reached the knife.

He shinned excitedly up a tree and looked back. His pursuers had stopped. But the hope that was in Rainsford's brain when he climbed died; for he saw in the shallow valley that General Zaroff was still on his feet. But Ivan was not. The knife, driven by the recoil of the springing tree, had not wholly failed.

Rainsford had hardly tumbled to the ground when the pack took up the cry again.

"Nerve, nerve, nerve!" he panted, as he dashed along. A blue gap showed between the trees dead ahead. Ever nearer drew the hounds. Rainsford forced himself on toward that gap. He reached it. It was the shore of the sea. Across a cove he could see the gloomy gray stone of the château. Twenty feet below him the sea rumbled and hissed. Rainsford hesitated. He heard the hounds. Then he leaped far out into the sea....

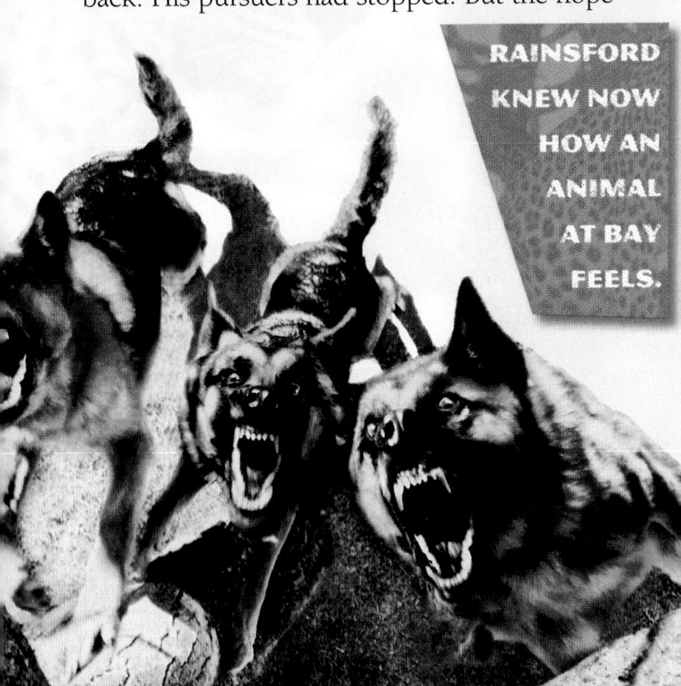
RAINSFORD
KNEW NOW
HOW AN
ANIMAL
AT BAY
FEELS.

When the general and his pack reached the place by the sea, the Cossack stopped. For some minutes he stood regarding the blue-green expanse of water. He shrugged his shoulders. Then he sat down, took a drink of brandy from a silver flask, lit a perfumed cigarette, and hummed a bit from *Madame Butterfly*.[23]

USE READING STRATEGIES

Visualize Visualize General Zaroff's actions as described in this passage. Do his actions seem out of place?

General Zaroff had an exceedingly good dinner in his great paneled dining hall that evening. With it he had a bottle of Pol Roger and half a bottle of Chambertin. Two slight annoyances kept him from perfect enjoyment. One was the thought that it would be difficult to replace Ivan; the other was that his quarry had escaped him; of course the American hadn't played the game—so thought the general as he tasted his after-dinner liqueur. In his library he read, to soothe himself, from the works of Marcus Aurelius.[24] At ten he went up to his bedroom. He was deliciously tired, he said to himself, as he

23. ***Madame Butterfly.*** Opera by Puccini
24. **Marcus Aurelius.** Roman emperor and philosopher who ruled from 160 to 180 CE

locked himself in. There was a little moonlight, so, before turning on his light, he went to the window and looked down at the courtyard. He could see the great hounds, and he called: "Better luck another time," to them. Then he switched on the light.

A man, who had been hiding in the curtains of the bed, was standing there.

"Rainsford!" screamed the general. "How in God's name did you get here?"

"Swam," said Rainsford. "I found it quicker than walking through the jungle."

The general sucked in his breath and smiled. "I congratulate you," he said. "You have won the game."

Rainsford did not smile. "I am still a beast at bay," he said, in a low, hoarse voice. "Get ready, General Zaroff."

The general made one of his deepest bows. "I see," he said. "Splendid! One of us is to furnish a repast for the hounds. The other will sleep in this very excellent bed. En garde, Rainsford..."

He had never slept in a better bed, Rainsford decided. ❖

"I am still a beast at bay." What does this statement mean for General Zaroff? What is the fate of General Zaroff and is it deserved?

AFTER READING

REFER TO TEXT	REASON WITH TEXT	
1a. Name the sport that Rainsford considers to be the best in the world.	1b. Paraphrase Rainsford's conversation with Whitney. Does he feel an allegiance to the hunters or the hunted? What does this conversation reveal?	**Understand** **Find meaning**
2a. Identify the type of big game that Rainsford believes is the most dangerous.	2b. According to General Zaroff, what is "the most dangerous game"? Discover the different meanings that the word *game* has within the story.	**Apply** **Use information**
3a. State why hunting had ceased to be "a sporting proposition" for General Zaroff.	3b. General Zaroff tells Rainsford, "No thrill left in tigers, no real danger. I live for danger, Mr. Rainsford." Analyze whether General Zaroff gets what he desires. Explain your reasoning.	**Analyze** **Take things apart**
4a. Recall what General Zaroff does after following Rainsford's trail to the base of the tree.	4b. Judge whether or not General Zaroff "plays fair." Give examples from the story to support your response.	**Evaluate** **Make judgments**
5a. Quote the statement that reveals that Rainsford has learned an important lesson during the course of the story.	5b. Propose how you think Rainsford will change after this experience. Explain your response.	**Create** **Bring ideas together**

ANALYZE LITERATURE: Conflict

What is the main conflict in this story? Does Rainsford struggle against an internal or external conflict? Who or what is Rainsford's adversary? Briefly summarize how the conflict is developed and resolved.

EXTEND THE TEXT

Writing Options

Creative Writing Create a new game and, in a few brief paragraphs, write a **set of rules** for the game. These directions should explain the purpose, basic setup, rules, and any strategies for playing.

Expository Writing For a writing magazine, write an **informative article** about techniques of characterization. Writers create characters using three major techniques: showing what characters say, do, or think; showing what other characters say or think about them; and describing what physical features, dress, and personality the characters display. In your article, explain the techniques of characterization and give examples of each type from "The Most Dangerous Game." In your article, analyze how well the characters are developed in this story.

Collaborative Learning

Debate the Practice of Hunting As a class, choose a proposition related to hunting. For example, "Congress should ban hunting of all animals in the United States" or "The hunting of deer should be legal in our region." Using library and Internet resources, research the topic. Then form teams to debate the issue. Each team should present a constructive speech stating its case for or against the proposition, and each team should be prepared to present a rebuttal speech to refute or attack its opponent's arguments while defending its own case. Once the debate is finished, ask the audience to consider the arguments that have been made and to vote for which side made the more persuasive case.

Critical Literacy

Participate in a Panel Discussion On several occasions,
Zaroff comments that he tries to be civilized on the island. Skim the story looking for references to being civilized. In small groups, conduct a panel discussion regarding what it means to be civilized. Group members should think of questions to ask the characters in the story and then choose characters to represent. The panel should ask the characters questions to clarify or elaborate and take notes to summarize the speaker's responses.

Go to **www.mirrorsandwindows.com** for more.

READING ASSESSMENT

1. General Zaroff explained that he had grown bored with hunting and was looking for a challenge. Why is Rainsford the perfect adversary for Zaroff?
   A. He has a stronger will to live than other men.
   B. He is smart, strong, and able to shoot a rifle.
   C. He was raised in the jungle.
   D. He is completely ruthless.
   E. He understands the art of hunting.

2. Which of the following events is an example of irony?
   A. Rainsford falls off the ship and lands on the island of a hunting enthusiast.
   B. General Zaroff wants Rainsford to hunt with him.
   C. The general sees no thrill left in hunting tigers.
   D. Rainsford, the world-renowned hunter, becomes General Zaroff's prey.
   E. Rainsford is impressed by the general's home and extensive collection of hunting trophies.

3. As it is used on page 34, the term *condone* most nearly means
   A. appreciate.
   B. hate.
   C. acknowledge.
   D. excuse.
   E. value.

4. Which of the following statements best foreshadows the end of the story?
   A. "Who cares how a jaguar feels?"
   B. "The place has a reputation—a bad one."
   C. "This place has an evil name among sea-faring men, sir."
   D. "You're a big game hunter, not a philosopher."
   E. "I drink to a foe worthy of me at last."

5. When the general stops beneath the tree Rainsford is hiding in, why does he blow a smoke ring before he turns and walks away?
   A. It is a signal for Ivan that he has found Rainsford.
   B. He is playing with Rainsford and wants him to know that he is saving him for another day.
   C. He is tired of the hunt and wants to turn in for the night.
   D. He has lost Rainsford's trail.
   E. All of the above

6. Earlier in the story, Rainsford accuses Zaroff of being a murderer, yet the implication at the end of the story is that Rainsford has fed Zaroff to the dogs. Is Rainsford, then, any better than Zaroff? Would there be any valid excuse for his actions? Explain.

UNDERSTAND THE CONCEPT | APPLY THE SKILL

Context Clues

Context clues are surrounding text or words that help readers understand the meaning of vocabulary. Context clues compare or contrast a word you do not know to other words you do know.

Comparison context clues provide familiar words or phrases that are similar to a word's meaning. Four common types of these clues are *restatement, apposition, cause and effect,* and *examples.* Words such as *like* and *as* may also help you identify comparison context clues.

- Using **restatement,** the author may tell you the meaning of the word you do not know by using different words to express the same idea in the same or another sentence. Some words that signal restatement are *that is, in other words,* and *or.*

EXAMPLES

Rainsford swam doggedly, that is, with determination, toward the island.

Rainsford's fear felt tangible, or like a *physical* part of himself that he hoped to cast off.

- **Apposition** renames something in different words. Look for a word or phrase that has been placed in the sentence to clarify the word you do not know.

EXAMPLES

They were eating borsch, the *rich, red soup with whipped cream* so dear to Russian palates.

Rainsford walked to the afterdeck, *the rear half of the ship's deck,* hoping to get some fresh air.

- **Cause and effect clues** require the reader to make an assumption based on what caused something to happen or result from its happening. Some words that signal cause and effect include *if...then, when...then, thus, therefore, because, so, due to, as a result of,* and *consequently.*

EXAMPLES

The city was completely surrounded; therefore, the king knew it was futile to keep fighting.

If the man had a disarming smile, then he'd appear harmless and we'd feel more comfortable letting him ride in our car.

- **Examples** used in a sentence can help illustrate a term you do not know. The writer may use the following expressions to introduce this type of clue: *for instance, for example, especially, particularly, including*, and *such as.*

EXAMPLES

Buffalo, lions, and deer are all types of big game.

Gargoyles are my favorite building feature, *particularly the type that are carved into the corners of old castles and look as though they are scowling at visitors.*

Contrast context clues can also unlock a word's meaning. These clues provide familiar words or phrases that are dissimilar or opposite to a word's meaning. In this case, you know what something means by what it is not. The word *but* frequently signals contrast context clues.

EXAMPLES

Rainsford might have expected a *rube* or *a country bumpkin* on the island, but he found a cosmopolite.

The general expected his latest opponent to be quite animated, but the sailor turned out to be *unexciting* and *lifeless.*

Context clues may appear in the same sentence as the word, or you may need to draw clues from the paragraph or passage in which you find the word.

UNDERSTAND THE CONCEPT

APPLY THE SKILL

Exercise A

Read the following lines from "The Most Dangerous Game." Define each underlined word and write a new sentence that will help the reader understand its meaning from the context.

1. He executed a series of intricate loops; he doubled on his trail again and again, recalling all the lore of the fox hunt.
2. Rainsford noted that the table appointments were of the finest—the linen, the crystal, the silver, the china.
3. "I started for the Amazon to hunt jaguars, for I had heard they were unusually cunning. They weren't." The Cossack sighed. "They were no match at all for a hunter with his wits about him and a high-powered rifle."
4. Laughter shook the general. "How extraordinarily droll you are!" he said.
5. To this end, he had plunged along, spurred on by the sharp rowels of something very like panic.

Exercise B

Find the following sentences within "The Most Dangerous Game." Using context clues in the sentences and surrounding text, estimate the meaning of the underlined vocabulary word. Write down both your estimated definition and note any surrounding context clues that assisted you.

1. "Can't see it," remarked Rainsford, trying to peer through the dank tropical night that was palpable as it pressed its thick warm blackness in upon the yacht.
2. "Don't be alarmed," said Rainsford, with a smile which he hoped was disarming.
3. "I had no wish to go to pieces," he said. "I must do something. Now, mine is an analytical mind, Mr. Rainsford. Doubtless that is why I enjoy the problems of the chase."
4. "Did not make me condone coldblooded murder," finished Rainsford stiffly.
5. He saw that straight flight was futile; inevitably it would bring him face to face with the sea.

Exercise C

Read the sentences below using context clues to figure out the meaning of each underlined word. Identify the type of context clues used and explain how they helped you figure out the meanings of the words.

1. She found their actions to be barbarous; that is, she thought what they had done was primitive and brutal.
2. The hotel's amenities, such as the complimentary valet and laundry service, made their stay even more enjoyable.
3. She knew he wasn't feeling well because his usual bright face had become sallow.
4. I found her scruples to be completely foreign; that is, her sense of right and wrong was so much different from my own.
5. Kyle didn't have a date, so Janelle solicitously asked him to dance; she didn't want anyone to feel left out.

SPELLING PRACTICE

Doubling the Final Consonant

When you add a suffix such as *-ed, -est, -ing* or certain other suffixes to a word that ends with consonant-vowel-consonant, you need to double the last consonant. For example, the word "sad" has the CVC pattern, so when we add *-er* or *-est*, we need to double the last letter to make "sadder" and "saddest." These words from "The Most Dangerous Game" are examples of words that have doubled the final consonant.

admitted	gripping	shrugged
beginning	hummed	sipped
biggest	jagged	sitting
blotted	lipped	slapped
charred	nodded	snapped
digging	occurred	splitting
doggedly	propeller	spurred
dragged	quizzically	stepped
dropped	regrettable	stopped
flattened	robber	swimming
forbidding	rotten	trimmed
getting	rubbing	whipped

Understanding Point of View

POINT OF VIEW

Point of view is the vantage point or perspective from which a story is told. The saying, "It all depends on how you look at it," suggests that the meaning of something can vary if you shift your perspective or point of view. In literature, it is much the same; so much depends on who is telling the story—whose point of view is interpreting the action.

TYPES OF NARRATION

The **first-person point of view,** or first-person narration, tells a story from the *I* or *we* perspective. "The Scarlet Ibis" (page 109) is told from the first-person point of view. The narrator is inside the story, even though he is recalling an event that happened long ago. Throughout much of the story, his perspective is limited by his direct involvement in the action. The first-person narration forces the reader to view the characters and events through the eyes of a single character.

First-person point of view can make a story seem more emotionally authentic, as in "The Scarlet Ibis." On the other hand, it may make you question the validity of what you are told, as in "The Cask of Amontillado" (page 59), which is told from the point of view of a seemingly unstable narrator, Montresor.

> "True," I replied; "the Amontillado."
> As I said these words I busied myself among the pile of bones of which I have before spoken. Throwing them aside, I soon uncovered a quantity of building stone and mortar. With these materials and with the aid of my trowel, I began vigorously to wall up the entrance of the niche.
>
> —from "The Cask of Amontillado"
> by Edgar Allan Poe

(Note that the *I* in first-person point of view appears in the text without quotation marks; you would not examine the dialogue in a story to determine the point of view, as any person speaking may say "I.")

Second-person point of view, or second-person narration, uses the word *you* and is relatively rare. It addresses the reader directly, positioning the reader within the story.

> You begin your journey on so high an elevation that your destination is already in sight—a city that you have visited many times and that, moreover, is indicated on a traveler's map you have carefully folded up to take along with you.
>
> —from "Journey"
> by Joyce Carol Oates (page 855)

She, He, and *it* are the pronouns marking **third-person point of view,** or third-person narration, the type most often encountered in fiction. The story "Thank You, M'am" (page 6) uses this type of narration, as does "The Most Dangerous Game" (page 27). The narrator is not a character in the story, but an observer and a recorder of the action. The third-person point of view has two variations: *limited point of view* and *omniscient point of view.*

- **Limited point of view** gives the reader an insight into the mind of only the narrator or of one other character. "The Most Dangerous Game," for instance, lets us know Rainsford's thoughts but not those of General Zaroff. "The Sniper" is another example of a story told from a limited third-person point of view. The narrator tells us only what the young man on the rooftop is thinking during the action.

> The pent-up air burst hotly from Rainsford's lungs. His first thought made him feel sick and numb. The general could follow a trail through the woods at night; he could follow an extremely difficult trail; he must have uncanny powers; only by the merest chance had the Cossack failed to see his quarry.
>
> —from "The Most Dangerous Game"
> by Richard Connell

- The **omniscient point of view** reveals to the reader the thoughts of all or most characters. In "The Good Deed" (page 83), for instance, the reader is shown the thoughts not just of Old Mrs. Pan, but of her son, Lili Yang, and of young Mr. Lim. "The Necklace" (page 143) is also an example of omniscient narration. The narrator knows everything about the characters and the unfolding plot.

> Mr. Pan was worried about his mother. He had been worried when she was in China, and now he was worried about her in New York, although he had thought that once he got her out of his ancestral village of Szechuen and safely away from the local bullies, who took over when the distant government fell, his anxieties would be ended....
>
> It soon became clear, however, that safety was not enough for old Mrs. Pan. She did not even appreciate the fact, which he repeated again and again, that had she remained in the village, she would now have been dead....
>
> —from "The Good Deed"
> by Pearl Buck

TYPES OF NARRATORS

Whether the story is in first- or third-person, the **narrator** is a character or speaker who tells a story. Sometimes, the narrator is a character in the story, as is the case with "Blues Ain't No Mockin Bird" (page 49) and "The Cask of Amontillado," but other times the narrator stands apart from the action.

Many narrators, whether in a first-person or third-person story, are reliable; you can trust their account of the events. Some, however, are *unreliable narrators*. For instance, Montresor in "The Cask of Amontillado" recounts events in great detail, but it is clear that he is mentally unstable or of a criminal temperament. Therefore, his contempt for Fortunato and his own feverish self-justification make him a doubtful recorder of experience.

Though the narrator of the third-person story "The Gift of the Magi" (page 139) is more reliable (and saner) than Montresor, the narration can still be questioned because the events of the story are not merely described; they are also commented upon. The narrator's remarks show a particular personality or opinion that may not be wholly objective. Notice how the narrator *editorializes* upon Della's actions:

> When Della reached home her intoxication gave way a little to prudence and reason. She got out her curling irons and lighted the gas and went to work repairing the ravages made by generosity added to love. Which is always a tremendous task, dear friends—a mammoth task.
>
> —from "The Gift of the Magi"
> by O. Henry

Determining Point of View

Ask yourself these questions to figure out the point of view of a story:

- ❑ Who is telling the story?
- ❑ Is the narrator a character in the story?
- ❑ From whose perspective is the story told? Is there more than one perspective?
- ❑ Does the narrator simply present the story, or offer commentary on the story?
- ❑ What biases, attitudes, or opinions do you think the narrator has? How might these assumptions color his or her view? Can I trust him or her to be truthful or objective?
- ❑ How might the story be different if told from another character's point of view?

Blues Ain't No Mockin Bird

BEFORE READING

A Short Story by Toni Cade Bambara

BUILD BACKGROUND

Cultural Context "Blues Ain't No Mockin Bird" is narrated by a young African-American girl who tells the story of what happens when two white filmmakers arrive at her grandmother's house. Granny Cain, described by her granddaughter as someone who "always got something to say" and who "teaches steady with no let-up," objects to the filmmakers filming the family and their home for the county's food stamp program. Granny Cain uses this opportunity as a teachable moment and, through her actions and storytelling, teaches her young granddaughter a lesson about human dignity, respect, and the right to privacy.

Reader's Context Do members of the news media take advantage of the plights of individuals in order to highlight problems in society? Who benefits from the news coverage? Explain.

ANALYZE LITERATURE: Point of View and Dialect

Point of view is the vantage point, or perspective, from which a story is told—in other words, who is telling the story. "Blues Ain't No Mockin Bird" is told from the perspective of Granny Cain's granddaughter, a minor character who plays a less significant role. A **dialect** is a version of a language spoken by the people of a particular place, time, or social group. The granddaughter and her family speak in a common dialect of their culture.

SET PURPOSE

In the Build Background section, how does the narrator's description of Granny Cain give you insight into her character? Look for the lessons Granny passes on through her storytelling. Also, consider how the point of view and the use of dialect affect the way you interpret the story.

MEET THE AUTHOR

Toni Cade Bambara (1939–1995) grew up in Harlem, New York, among other places, and described herself as "a writer since childhood." Born Miltona Mirkin Cade, she changed her first name to Toni, then took for her last name *Bambara*—the name of a West African tribe that she had found written on a sketchbook in her great-grandmother's trunk. Bambara devoted her life to writing and social activism. A natural storyteller with a sharp eye for human behavior and an ear for dialogue, Bambara said the short story was her favorite form of writing because it "makes a modest appeal for attention, slips up on your blind side and wrassles you to the mat before you know what's grabbed you." "Blues Ain't No Mockin Bird" appeared in Bambara's first collection of short stories, *Gorilla, My Love.*

USE READING SKILLS

Take Notes Record important details that you want to remember about characters in a story. As you read "Blues Ain't No Mockin Bird," use a Character Chart like the one below to keep track of Granny Cain's character traits and her responses to other characters.

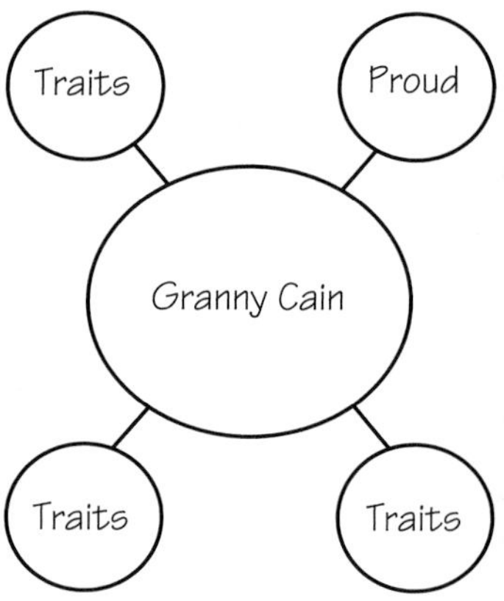

PREVIEW VOCABULARY

Use context clues to choose the best word from this list to complete the following sentences. Then write a new sentence using the vocabulary word in a new context.

original formality lasso

1. Shaking one another's hands was strictly a(n) ________, as neither of the two captains liked the rival team.
2. If she could ________ the target, then Emma would win the roping challenge.
3. "It's a(n) ________," the vendor told us. "You'll never find another quite like it."

Blues Ain't No Mockin Bird

"Get them persons out of my flower bed, Mister Cain...."

A Short Story by

Toni Cade Bambara

The puddle had frozen over, and me and Cathy went stompin in it. The twins from next door, Tyrone and Terry, were swingin so high out of sight we forgot we were waitin our turn on the tire. Cathy jumped up and came down hard on her heels and started tap-dancin. And the frozen patch splinterin every which way underneath kinda spooky. "Looks like a plastic spider web," she said. "A sort of weird spider, I guess, with many mental problems." But really it looked like the crystal paperweight Granny kept in the parlor. She was on the back porch, Granny was, making the cakes drunk. The old ladle dripping rum into the Christmas tins, like it used to drip maple syrup into the pails when we lived in the Judson's woods, like it poured cider into the vats when we were on the Cooper place, like it used to scoop buttermilk and soft cheese when we lived at the dairy.

"Go tell that man we ain't a bunch of trees."

"Ma'am?"

"I said to tell that man to get away from here with that camera." Me and Cathy look over toward the meadow where the men with the station wagon'd been roamin around all mornin. The tall man with a huge camera lassoed to his shoulder was buzzin our way.

"They're makin movie pictures," yelled Tyrone, stiff-enin his legs and twistin so the tire'd come down slow so they could see.

"They're makin movie pictures," sang out Terry.

"That boy don't never have anything original to say," say Cathy grown-up.

By the time the man with the camera had cut across our neighbor's yard, the twins were out of the trees swingin low and Granny was onto the steps, the screen door bammin soft and scratchy against her palms. "We thought we'd get a shot or two of the house and everything and then—"

"Good mornin," Granny cut him off. And smiled that smile.

"Good mornin," he said, head all down the way Bingo does when you yell at him about the bones on the kitchen floor. "Nice place you got here, aunty. We thought we'd take a—"

"Did you?" said Granny with her eyebrows. Cathy pulled up her socks and giggled.

"Nice things here," said the man, buzzin his camera over the yard. The pecan barrels, the sled, me and Cathy, the flowers, the printed stones along the driveway, the trees, the twins, the toolshed.

"I don't know about the thing, the it, and the stuff," said Granny, still talkin with her eyebrows. "Just people here is what I tend to consider."

Camera man stopped buzzin. Cathy giggled into her collar.

"Mornin, ladies," a new man said. He had come up behind us when we weren't lookin. "And gents," discoverin the twins givin him a nasty look. "We're filmin for the county," he said with a smile. "Mind if we shoot a bit around here?"

"I do indeed," said Granny with no smile. Smilin man was smiling up a storm. So was Cathy. But he didn't seem to have another word to say, so he and the camera man backed on out the yard, but you could hear the camera buzzin still.

"Suppose you just shut that machine off," said Granny real low through her teeth, and took a step down off the porch and then another.

"Now, aunty," Camera said, pointin the thing straight at her.

"Your mama and I are not related."

Smilin man got his notebook out and a chewed-up pencil. "Listen," he said movin back into our yard, "we'd like to have a statement from you...for the film. We're filmin for the county, see. Part of the food stamp campaign. You know about the food stamps?"[1]

Granny said nuthin.

"Maybe there's somethin you want to say for the film. I see you grow your own vegeta-bles," he smiled real nice. "If more folks did that, see, there'd be no need—"

1. **food stamps.** Coupons issued by the government and given to people with low incomes to be exchanged for food

las • so (la´ sō') *v.*, capture as if with rope
o • rig • i • nal (ə rij´ ə n'l) *adj.*, new; fresh and unusual; inventive

Granny wasn't sayin nuthin. So they backed on out, buzzin at our clothesline and the twins' bicycles, then back on down to the meadow. The twins were danglin in the tire, lookin at Granny. Me and Cathy were waitin, too, cause Granny always got somethin to say. She teaches steady with no let-up. "I was on this bridge one time," she started off. "Was a crowd cause this man was goin to jump, you understand. And a minister was there and the police and some other folks. His woman was there, too."

"What was they doin?" asked Tyrone.

"Tryin to talk him out of it was what they was doin. The minister talkin about how it was a mortal sin, suicide. His woman takin bites out of her own hand and not even knowin it, so nervous and cryin and talkin fast."

"So what happened?" asked Tyrone.

"So here comes…this person…with a camera, takin pictures of the man and the minister and the woman. Takin pictures of the man in his misery about to jump, cause life so bad and people been messin with him so bad. This person takin up the whole roll of film practically. But savin a few, of course."

"Of course," said Cathy, hatin the person. Me standin there wonderin how Cathy knew it was "of course" when I didn't and it was *my* grandmother.

After a while Tyrone say, "Did he jump?"

"Yeh, did he jump?" say Terry all eager. And Granny just stared at the twins till their faces swallow up the eager and they don't even care any more about the man jumpin. Then she goes back onto the porch and lets the screen door go for itself. I'm lookin to Cathy to finish the story cause she knows Granny's whole story before me even. Like she knew how come we move so much and Cathy ain't but a third cousin we picked up on the way last Thanksgivin visitin. But she knew it was on account of people drivin Granny crazy till she'd get up in the night and start packin. Mumblin and packin and wakin everybody up sayin, "Let's get on away from here before I kill me somebody." Like people

wouldn't pay her for things like they said they would. Or Mr. Judson bringin us boxes of old clothes and raggedy magazines. Or Mrs. Cooper comin in our kitchen and touchin everything and sayin how clean it all was. Granny goin crazy, and Granddaddy Cain pullin her off the people, sayin, "Now, now, Cora." But next day loadin up the truck, with rocks all in his jaw, madder than Granny in the first place.

"I read a story once," said Cathy soundin like Granny teacher. "About this lady Goldilocks who barged into a house that wasn't even hers. And not invited, you understand. Messed over the people's groceries and broke up the people's furniture. Had the nerve to sleep in the folks' bed."

"Then what happened?" asked Tyrone. "What they do, the folks, when they come in to all this mess?"

"Did they make her pay for it?" asked Terry, makin a fist. "I'd've made her pay me."

I didn't even ask. I could see Cathy actress was very likely to just walk away and leave us in mystery about this story which I heard was about some bears.

"Did they throw her out?" asked Tyrone, like his father sounds when he's bein extra nasty-plus to the washin-machine man.

"Woulda," said Terry. "I woulda gone upside her head with my fist and—"

"You woulda done whatcha always do—go cry to Mama, you big baby," said Tyrone. So naturally Terry starts hittin on Tyrone, and next thing you know they tumblin out the tire and rollin on the ground. But Granny didn't say a thing or send the twins home or step out on the steps to tell us about how we can't afford to be fightin amongst ourselves. She didn't say nuthin. So I get into the tire to take my turn. And I could see her leanin up against the pantry table, staring at the cakes she was puttin up for the Christmas sale, mumblin real low and grumpy and holdin her forehead like it wanted to fall off and mess up the rum cakes.

Behind me I hear before I can see Granddaddy Cain comin through the woods in his field boots. Then I twist around to see the shiny black oilskin cuttin through what little left there was of yellows, reds, and oranges. His great white head not quite round cause of this bloody thing high on his shoulder, like he was wearin a cap on sideways. He takes the shortcut through the pecan grove, and the sound of twigs snapping overhead and underfoot travels clear and cold all the way up to us. And here comes Smilin and Camera up behind him like they was goin to do somethin. Folks like to go for him sometimes. Cathy say it's because he's so tall and quiet and like a king. And people just can't stand it. But Smilin and Camera don't hit him in the head or nuthin. They just buzz on him as he stalks by with the chicken hawk slung over his shoulder, squawkin, drippin red down the back of the oilskin. He passes the porch and stops a second for Granny to see he's caught the hawk at last, but she's just starin and mumblin, and not at the hawk. So he nails the bird to the toolshed door, the hammerin crackin through the eardrums. And the bird flappin himself to death and droolin down the door to paint the gravel in the driveway red, then brown, then black. And the two men movin up on tiptoe like they was invisible or we were blind, one.

"Get them persons out of my flower bed, Mister Cain," say Granny moanin real low like at a funeral.

"How come your grandmother calls her husband 'Mister Cain' all the time?" Tyrone whispers all loud and noisy and from the city and don't know no better. Like his mama, Miss Myrtle, tell us never mind the formality as if we had no better breeding than to call her Myrtle, plain. And then this awful thing—a giant hawk—come wailin up over the meadow, flyin low and tilted and screamin, zigzaggin through the pecan grove, breakin branches and hollerin, snappin past the clothesline, flyin every which way, flyin into things reckless with crazy.

for • mal • i • ty (fôr ma´ lə tē) *n.*, behavior that follows accepted forms, rules, or customs

"He's come to claim his mate," say Cathy fast, and ducks down. We all fall quick and flat into the gravel driveway, stones scrapin my face. I squinch my eyes open again at the hawk on the door, tryin to fly up out of her death like it was just a sack flown into by mistake. Her body holdin her there on that nail, though. The mate beatin the air overhead and clutchin for hair, for heads, for landin space.

The camera man duckin and bendin and runnin and fallin, jigglin the camera and scared. And Smilin jumpin up and down swipin at the huge bird, tryin to bring the hawk down with just his raggedy ole cap. Granddaddy Cain straight up and silent, watchin the circles of the hawk, then aimin the hammer off his wrist. The giant bird fallin, silent and slow. Then here comes Camera and Smilin all big and bad now that the awful screechin thing is on its back and broken, here they come. And Granddaddy Cain looks up at them like it was the first time noticin, but not payin them too much mind cause he's listenin, we all listenin, to that low groanin music comin from the porch. And we figure any minute, somethin in my back tells me any minute now, Granny gonna bust through that screen with somethin in her hand and murder on her mind. So Granddaddy say above the buzzin, but quiet, "Good day, gentlemen." Just like that. Like he'd invited them in to play cards and they'd stayed too long and all the sandwiches were gone and Reverend Webb was droppin by and it was time to go.

They didn't know what to do. But like Cathy say, folks can't stand Granddaddy tall and silent and like a king. They can't neither. The smile the men smilin is pullin the mouth back and showin the teeth. Lookin like the wolf man, both of them. Then Granddaddy holds his hand out—this huge hand I used to sit in when I was a baby and he'd carry me through the house to my mother like I was a gift on a tray. Like he used to on the trains. They called the other men just waiters. But they spoke of Granddaddy separate and said, The Waiter. And said he had engines in his feet and motors in his hands and couldn't no train throw him off and couldn't nobody turn him round. They were big enough for motors, his hands were. He held that one hand out all still and it gettin to be not at all a hand but a person in itself.

"He wants you to hand him the camera," Smilin whispers to Camera, tiltin his head to talk secret like they was in the jungle or somethin and come upon a native that don't speak the language. The men start untyin the straps, and they put the camera into that great hand speckled with the hawk's blood all black and crackly now. And the hand don't even drop with the weight, just the fingers move, curl up around the machine. But Granddaddy lookin straight at the men. They lookin at each other and everywhere but at Granddaddy's face.

"We filmin for the county, see," say Smilin. "We puttin together a movie for the food stamp program...filmin all around these parts. Uhh, filmin for the county."

"Can I have my camera back?" say the tall man with no machine on his shoulder, but still keepin it high like the camera was still there or needed to be. "Please, sir."

Then Granddaddy's other hand flies up like a sudden and gentle bird, slaps down fast on top of the camera and lifts off half like it was a calabash[2] cut for sharing.

"Hey," Camera jumps forward. He gathers up the parts into his chest and everything unrollin and fallin all over. "Whatcha tryin to do? You'll ruin the film." He looks down into his chest of metal reels and things like he's protectin a kitten from the cold.

"You standin in the misses' flower bed," say Granddaddy. "This is our own place."

The two men look at him, then at each other, then back at the mess in the camera man's chest, and they just back off. One

2. **calabash.** Large, gourd-like fruit grown in the American tropics

sayin over and over all the way down to the meadow, "Watch it, Bruno. Keep ya fingers off the film." Then Granddaddy picks up the hammer and jams it into the oilskin pocket, scrapes his boots, and goes into the house. And you can hear the squish of his boots headin through the house. And you can see the funny shadow he throws from the parlor window onto the ground by the string-bean patch. The hammer draggin the pocket of the oilskin out so Granddaddy looked even wider. Granny was hummin now—high not low and grumbly. And she was doin the cakes again, you could smell the molasses from the rum.

"There's this story I'm goin to write one day," say Cathy dreamer. "About the proper use of the hammer."

"Can I be in it?" Tyrone say with his hand up like it was a matter of first come, first served.

"Perhaps," say Cathy, climbin onto the tire to pump us up. "If you there and ready." ❖

Where does pride come from? How can pride be both a positive and a negative character trait?

AFTER READING

REFER TO TEXT	REASON WITH TEXT	
1a. How do the men react to Granny asking them to stop filming?	1b. What do the men think of Granny Cain? Give examples from the text to support your answer.	Understand **Find meaning**
2a. List the things that the men notice as they film the yard.	2b. Examine why the men are excited about filming the Cain property. Why do you think this excitement bothers Granny Cain?	Apply **Use information**
3a. Recall how Granny Cain reacts to Granddaddy Cain when he first arrives.	3b. Find evidence in the story that the Cains are proud people.	Analyze **Take things apart**
4a. What does Granddaddy Cain do to Camera and Smilin's equipment?	4b. Decide if you think Granddaddy's treatment of Camera and Smilin is justified. Explain.	Evaluate **Make judgments**
5a. Point out how the children respond to the two men.	5b. Write how you would have reacted to the men if you were Granny Cain or Granddaddy Cain. Explain your response.	Create **Bring ideas together**

ANALYZE LITERATURE: Point of View and Dialect

Why did Bambara choose a minor character to narrate the story? How does the granddaughter's point of view affect the way the story is told and the way other characters are described? How might the story be different if it were narrated by Granny? by Smilin? How does the dialect contribute to the authenticity of the story?

EXTEND THE TEXT

Writing Options

Creative Writing In a few short paragraphs, write a **character description** that illustrates pride. Focus on the character's actions and interactions that show this character trait. It may be helpful to brainstorm how pride is demonstrated by organizing your thoughts in a graphic organizer similar to the one below.

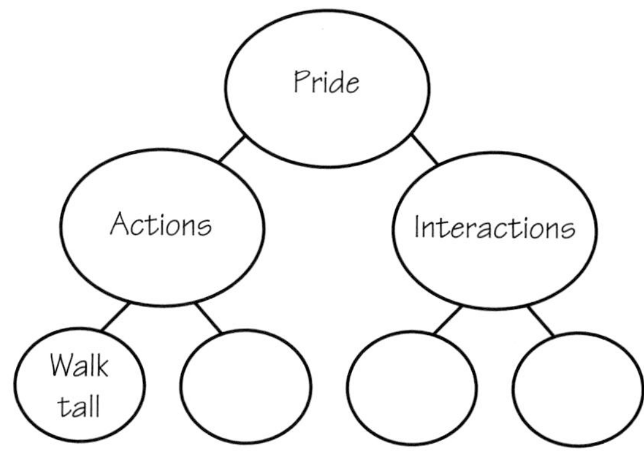

Expository Writing Give examples of dialect found within "Blues Ain't No Mockin Bird." In a **critical essay,** explain how dialect helps develop the characters and enhances the story's message.

Media Literacy

Write an editorial News broadcasts often cover personal tragedies or difficulties of people. Should reporters cover such stories or leave these stories and their subjects alone? Write an editorial for your local newspaper that argues one side of this issue. Give examples from news items you've seen on television or read about in the newspaper to support your position. Explain what you liked or didn't like about how the story was treated.

Lifelong Learning

Research the Blues What do you think the title of the story means? The mockingbird is well known for mimicking the sounds of other birds. What does that have to do with the musical style known as the blues? Use the Internet to research the history and characteristics of the blues. Use your research to draw conclusions about the meaning of the story's title, and write an essay in which you explain why the "blues ain't no mockin bird."

Go to **www.mirrorsandwindows.com** for more.

READING ASSESSMENT

1. Why does Granny want the men to leave?
   A. She values her privacy and does not like the way the men treat her.
   B. She's decided she doesn't want to be in the film for the county.
   C. She doesn't use food stamps.
   D. They are stepping on her flowers.
   E. They were making the children uncomfortable.

2. Which statement best describes the view of the cameraman and Smilin?
   A. They truly admire Granny and the pride she takes in her home.
   B. They are fascinated with a life that is not their own.
   C. They think what they see in Granny's yard will make a good movie.
   D. They are concerned about the welfare of Granny and her family.
   E. They don't want to intrude, but they have a job to do.

3. The term *formality,* found on page 52, most nearly means
   A. rudeness.
   B. gossip.
   C. stiffness.
   D. procedure.
   E. capture.

4. When Granny says of the cameraman "takin up the whole roll of film practically. But savin a few, of course," she implies that
   A. cameramen are wasteful.
   B. she would have gotten a good picture with only one or two shots.
   C. the cameraman should have been helping instead of shooting pictures.
   D. the cameraman was unfeeling and only interested in getting a good shot.
   E. None of the above

5. How does the story of "Goldilocks and the Three Bears" relate to the story of Granny and the filmmakers?

GRAMMAR & STYLE

UNDERSTAND THE CONCEPT

APPLY THE SKILL

Pronouns and Pronoun Agreement

A **pronoun** is a word used in place of a noun. Sometimes, a pronoun refers to a specific person or thing. There are different types of pronouns to stand for different kinds of nouns.

Types of Pronouns	Definition	Examples
personal pronoun	used in place of the name of a person or thing	I, me, we, us, it, he, she, him, her, you, they, them
indefinite pronoun	points out a person, place, thing, but not a specific or definite one	one, someone, anything, other, all, few, nobody
reflexive pronoun	refers back to a noun previously used	myself, herself, yourself, themselves, ourselves
interrogative pronoun	asks a question	who, whose, whom, what, which
demonstrative pronoun	points out a specific person, place, idea, or thing	this, these, that, those
possessive pronoun	shows ownership or possession	mine, yours, his, hers, ours, theirs

The word that a pronoun stands for is called its **antecedent.** The antecedent clarifies the meaning of the pronoun. The pronoun may appear in the same sentence as its antecedent or in a following sentence.

EXAMPLE

Where is *Tabitha? Vanya* thought *she* saw *her* in the garden.
(*Tabitha* is the antecedent of *her. Vanya* is the antecedent of *she.*)

When you use a pronoun, be sure that it refers clearly to its antecedent. A pronoun should agree in both number (singular or plural) and gender (masculine, feminine, or neutral) with its antecedent.

EXAMPLES

singular: The *puddle* had frozen over, and me and Cathy went stompin in *it.*
plural: And Granny just stared at the *twins* till *their* faces swallow up the eager and *they* don't even care anymore about the man jumpin.
feminine: "I read a story once," said Cathy soundin like Granny teacher. "About this lady *Goldilocks* who barged into a house that wasn't even *hers.*"
masculine: The tall *man* with a huge camera lassoed to *his* shoulder was buzzin our way.
neutral: Then Granddaddy picks up the *hammer* and jams *it* into the oilskin pocket.

REVIEW TERMS

- **pronoun:** a word used in place of a noun
- **antecedent:** the specific noun to which the pronoun refers
- **personal pronoun:** pronoun referring to a person or thing
- **indefinite pronoun:** pronoun referring to something/someone unspecific
- **reflexive pronoun:** pronoun referring back to a previously used noun
- **interrogative pronoun:** pronoun asking a question
- **demonstrative pronoun:** pronoun pointing out a specific noun
- **possessive pronoun:** pronoun showing ownership or possession
- **masculine:** referring to something/someone male
- **feminine:** referring to something/someone female
- **neutral:** referring to an object without gender

UNDERSTAND THE CONCEPT

APPLY THE SKILL

Identify Pronouns and Antecedents

Identify all of the pronouns and their antecedents in these sentences from "Blues Ain't No Mockin Bird." Note whether the pronouns are singular or plural and masculine, feminine, or neutral.

1. And the frozen patch splinterin every which way underneath kinda spooky. "Looks like a spider," Cathy said. But really it looked like the crystal paperweight Granny kept in the parlor.
2. She was on the porch, Granny was, making the cakes drunk.
3. The old ladle dripping rum into the Christmas tins, like it used to drip maple syrup into the pails when we lived in the Judson's woods.
4. Then Granddaddy holds his hand out—his huge hand I used to sit in when I was a baby.
5. "The men are makin movie pictures," yelled Tyrone, stiffenin his legs and twistin so the tire'd come down slow so they could see.
6. "Good morning," he said, head all down the way Bingo does when you yell at him about the bones on the kitchen floor.
7. "Did you?" said Granny with her eyebrows. Cathy pulled up her socks and giggled.
8. "Mornin, ladies," a new man said. He had come up behind us when we weren't lookin. "And gents," discoverin the twins givin him a nasty look.
9. "Takin pictures of the man in his misery about to jump, cause life so bad and people been messin with him so bad."
10. "Did they throw her out?" asked Tyrone, like his father sounds when he's bein extra nasty-plus to the washin-machine man.

Fix Pronoun Agreement

Fix the problems with pronoun agreement in the following paragraph about "Blues Ain't No Mockin Bird."

> The family in "Blues Ain't No Mockin Bird" is led by the strong characters of Granny and Granddaddy Cain. Her pride shows when they are approached by two camera men who are making a film about people on the food stamps program. He is turned away by Granny. They persist until Granddaddy Cain comes and takes his camera and breaks them with her own hands.

Use Pronouns Correctly in Your Writing

Hawks are birds of prey and mate for life. Examine the possible symbolism of the two hawks in "Blues Ain't No Mockin Bird" and write a brief paragraph explaining your own interpretation of the hawks, including who or what they might symbolize. After you have written the paragraph, look it over and make sure you have used pronouns correctly. Be certain that the pronouns are not too far removed from their antecedents. Correct any mistakes you may have made within your paragraph.

EXTEND THE SKILL

Close friends are often thought to be "on the same wavelength," meaning that they think similarly. Sometimes, this results in friends being able to have a conversation without the use of full sentences and other important words. The antecedents of the pronouns are understood, so the proper nouns are often left out. Create a humorous dialogue between two friends where a lot is communicated, but to the outside observer very little is understood. For example:

Friend 1: "So, how did it go?"
Friend 2: "You wouldn't believe it! Just what we thought!"
Friend 1: "No! I can't believe she would—"
Friend 2: "It was all over the table!"
Friend 1: "Did they take—?"
Friend 2: "All of it!"

Set the scene of your dialogue, such as in a school cafeteria, on a ball field, or at a store. Make sure you know what the conversation is about, but remove the parts that would be understood by both speakers. Substitute pronouns for specific nouns whenever possible.

The Cask of Amontillado

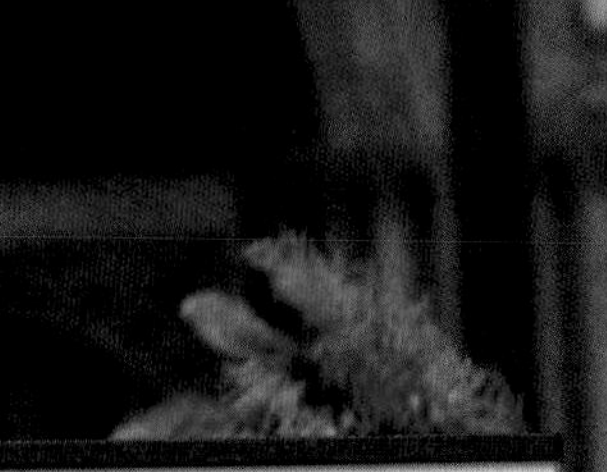

BEFORE READING

A Short Story by Edgar Allan Poe

DIRECTED READING

BUILD BACKGROUND

Literary Context Edgar Allan Poe defined the short story as a brief fictional work, the details of which are carefully chosen to create a "totality of effect." To create this effect in his fiction, Poe employed medieval settings, a dark atmosphere of horror and gloom, grotesque and violent incidents, and a first-person narrator whose internal thoughts often reveal the speaker's insanity or guilt. **"The Cask of Amontillado"** is no exception. First published in *Godey's Lady's Book* in 1846, the story, which is set in Italy, takes the characters deep into a murky vault.

Reader's Context Has anyone ever been cruel to you or someone you know? How did you or the person you know respond? Have you ever tried to get back at someone?

ANALYZE LITERATURE: Point of View and Narrator

Point of view is the vantage point from which a story is told. A **narrator** is a character or speaker who tells a story. This story is told from a first-person point of view by the narrator Montresor. Like many of Poe's narrators, Montresor is an *unreliable narrator,* or one that the reader cannot trust to be telling the truth.

SET PURPOSE

Poe carefully describes the setting using sensory details. As you read "The Cask of Amontillado," pay close attention to the descriptions of the catacombs and to the details that represent or imitate sound. Think about the mood that the setting helps create.

Note how the narrator, from the very beginning, refers to "you"—an implied listener to whom he is confessing a horrible deed. Look for details that indicate that Montresor may be unreliable as a narrator. What effect does the narrator have on the mood of the story?

MEET THE AUTHOR

Although **Edgar Allan Poe** (1809–1849) led a short and troubled life, few writers have had such enduring popularity and influence. After his father deserted the family and his mother died, Poe was informally adopted at age two by John Allan. Poe did well at the University of Virginia but was expelled from West Point because of poor attendance. In 1835 Poe married his cousin, Virginia Clemm, who died young. Briefly famous for his poem "The Raven," Poe nonetheless spent much of his life in poverty.

Regarded as the co-creator (with Nathaniel Hawthorne) of the American short story, Poe also invented detective fiction, wrote lyric poetry, and pioneered the psychological horror story.

USE READING SKILLS

Context Clues One type of context clue is cause and effect. This type of clue requires the reader to make an assumption based on the causes and results of behavior or events. Some words that signal cause and effect include *if...then, when...then, thus, therefore, because, so, due to, as a result of,* and *consequently.*

EXAMPLE

As a result of a low turnout during the first few days, the teacher considered terminating the remaining classes. (*Terminating* means ending or canceling.)

PREVIEW VOCABULARY

Use cause and effect clues to help define the vocabulary words within the following sentences. After discovering the meanings of the words, use them in new sentences.

1. Jake's car had been totaled in the accident, and he wanted retribution, so he took the other driver to court.
2. If he was a true masked avenger, then he never shared his identity with the world.
3. No one expected her to accost me in front of the teacher; consequently, everyone thought she was being immature and dramatic.
4. The problems came at us in succession; thus, we were never able to get ahead.
5. As a result of Simon's affliction, he wasn't able to attend the concert with his friends.

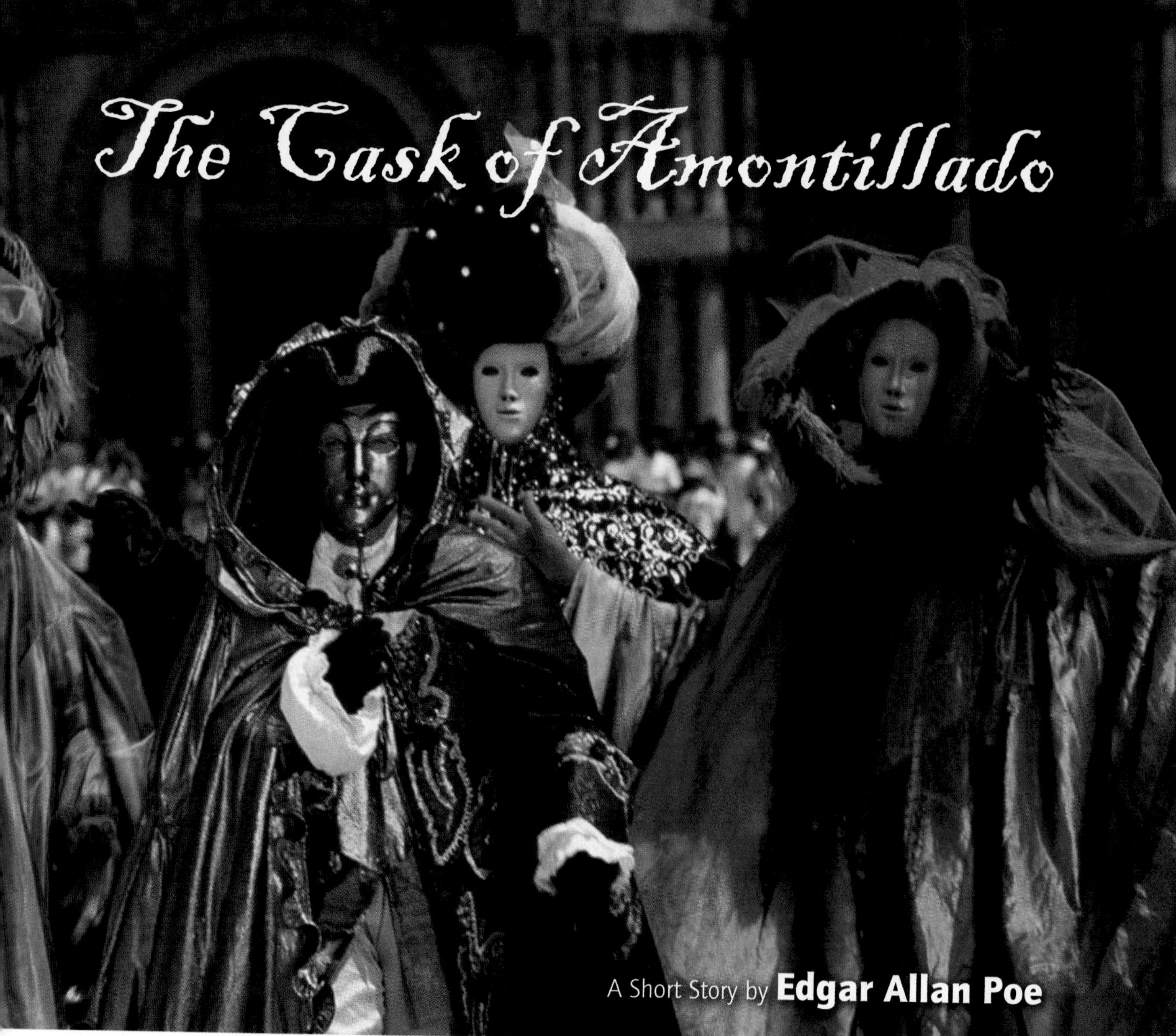

He did not perceive that my smile now was at the thought of his immolation.

The thousand injuries of Fortunato I had borne as best I could: but when he ventured upon insult, I vowed revenge. You, who so well know the nature of my soul, will not suppose, however, that I gave utterance to a threat. At length I would be avenged; this was a point definitely settled—but the very definitiveness with which it was resolved precluded the idea of risk. I must not only punish but punish with impunity.[1] A wrong is unredressed when retribution overtakes its redresser. It is equally unredressed when the avenger fails to make himself felt as such to him who has done the wrong.

1. **impunity.** Freedom from punishment or harm

pre • clude (pri klüd´) *v.*, prevent or make impossible beforehand
re • tri • bu • tion (re' trə byü´ shən) *n.*, punishment
a • veng • er (ə venj´ ər) *n.*, one who gets back at someone for a wrongdoing

CULTURAL CONNECTION

Carnival "The Cask of Amontillado" is set during the highly festive time of carnival, the last days before the Christian observance of Lent and its forty days of fasting and expressing sorrow for sins. During carnival, people indulge themselves with food and drink and celebrate with parades, elaborate costumes, and masked balls. The carnival tradition dates back to ancient Rome. Note the irony of the time in which Poe chose to place the events of this story.

It must be understood that neither by word nor deed had I given Fortunato cause to doubt my goodwill. I continued, as was my wont, to smile in his face, and he did not perceive that my smile *now* was at the thought of his immolation.[2]

He had a weak point—this Fortunato—although in other regards he was a man to be respected and even feared. He prided himself on his connoisseurship[3] in wine. Few Italians have the true virtuoso[4] spirit. For the most part their enthusiasm is adopted to suit the time and opportunity, to practice imposture upon the British and Austrian millionaires. In painting and gemmary, Fortunato, like his countrymen, was a quack—but in the matter of old wines he was sincere. In this respect I did not differ from him materially: I was skillful in the Italian vintages myself and bought largely whenever I could.

It was about dusk, one evening during the supreme madness of the carnival season, that I encountered my friend. He accosted me with excessive warmth, for he had been drinking much. The man wore motley.[5] He had on a tight-fitting parti-striped dress, and his head was surmounted by the conical cap and bells. I was so pleased to see him that I thought I should never have done wringing his hand.

I said to him, "My dear Fortunato, you are luckily met. How remarkably well you are looking today! But I have received a pipe[6] of what passes for amontillado,[7] and I have my doubts."

"How?" said he. "Amontillado? A pipe? Impossible! And in the middle of the carnival!"

"I have my doubts," I replied; "and I was silly enough to pay the full Amontillado price without consulting you in the matter. You were not to be found, and I was fearful of losing a bargain."

"Amontillado!"

"I have my doubts."

"Amontillado!"

"And I must satisfy them."

"Amontillado!"

"As you are engaged, I am on my way to Luchesi. If anyone has a critical turn it is he. He will tell me—"

"Luchesi cannot tell amontillado from sherry."

2. **immolation.** Death or destruction
3. **connoisseurship.** Expert judgment in matters involving taste and appreciation
4. **virtuoso.** One skilled in the fine arts
5. **motley.** Colorful jester's costume
6. **pipe.** Large cask used especially for wine or oil
7. **amontillado** (ə män´ tə läd´ ō). Pale, medium-dry sherry

ac • cost (ə kôst´) *v.*, approach in a challenging or an aggressive way

"And yet some fools will have it that his taste is a match for your own."

"Come, let us go."

"Whither?"

"To your vaults."

"My friend, no; I will not impose upon your good nature. I perceive you have an engagement. Luchesi—"

"I have no engagement; come."

"My friend, no. It is not the engagement, but the severe cold with which I perceive you are afflicted. The vaults are insufferably damp. They are encrusted with niter."[8]

"Let us go, nevertheless. The cold is merely nothing. Amontillado! You have been imposed upon. And as for Luchesi, he cannot distinguish sherry from amontillado."

Thus speaking, Fortunato possessed himself of my arm. Putting on a mask of black silk and drawing a *roquelaure*[9] closely about my person, I suffered him to hurry me to my *palazzo*.[10]

There were no attendants at home; they had absconded to make merry in honor of the time. I had told them that I should not return until the morning and had given them explicit orders not to stir from the house. These orders were sufficient, I well knew, to ensure their immediate disappearance, one and all, as soon as my back was turned.

I took from their sconces[11] two flambeaux, and giving one to Fortunato, bowed him through several suites of rooms to the archway that led into the vaults. I passed down a long and winding staircase, requesting him to be cautious as he followed. We came at length to the foot of the descent and stood together on the damp ground of the catacombs of the Montresors.

The gait of my friend was unsteady, and the bells upon his cap jingled as he strode.

"The pipe," said he.

"It is farther on," said I; "but observe the white web-work which gleams from these cavern walls."

He turned toward me, and looked into my eyes with two filmy orbs that distilled the rheum of intoxication.

"Niter?" he asked, at length.

"Niter," I replied. "How long have you had that cough?"

"Ugh! ugh! ugh!—ugh! ugh! ugh!—ugh! ugh! ugh!—ugh! ugh! ugh!—ugh! ugh! ugh!"

My poor friend found it impossible to reply for many minutes.

"It is nothing," he said, at last.

"Come," I said, with decision, "we will go back; your health is precious. You are rich, respected, admired, beloved; you are happy, as once I was. You are a man to be missed. For me it is no matter. We will go back; you will

8. **niter.** Potassium nitrate or sodium nitrate
9. ***roquelaure.*** [French] Knee-length cloak
10. ***palazzo.*** [Italian] Palace
11. **sconces.** Candlestick holders mounted on a wall

af • flict (ə flikt´) *v.*, distress or trouble so severely as to cause suffering

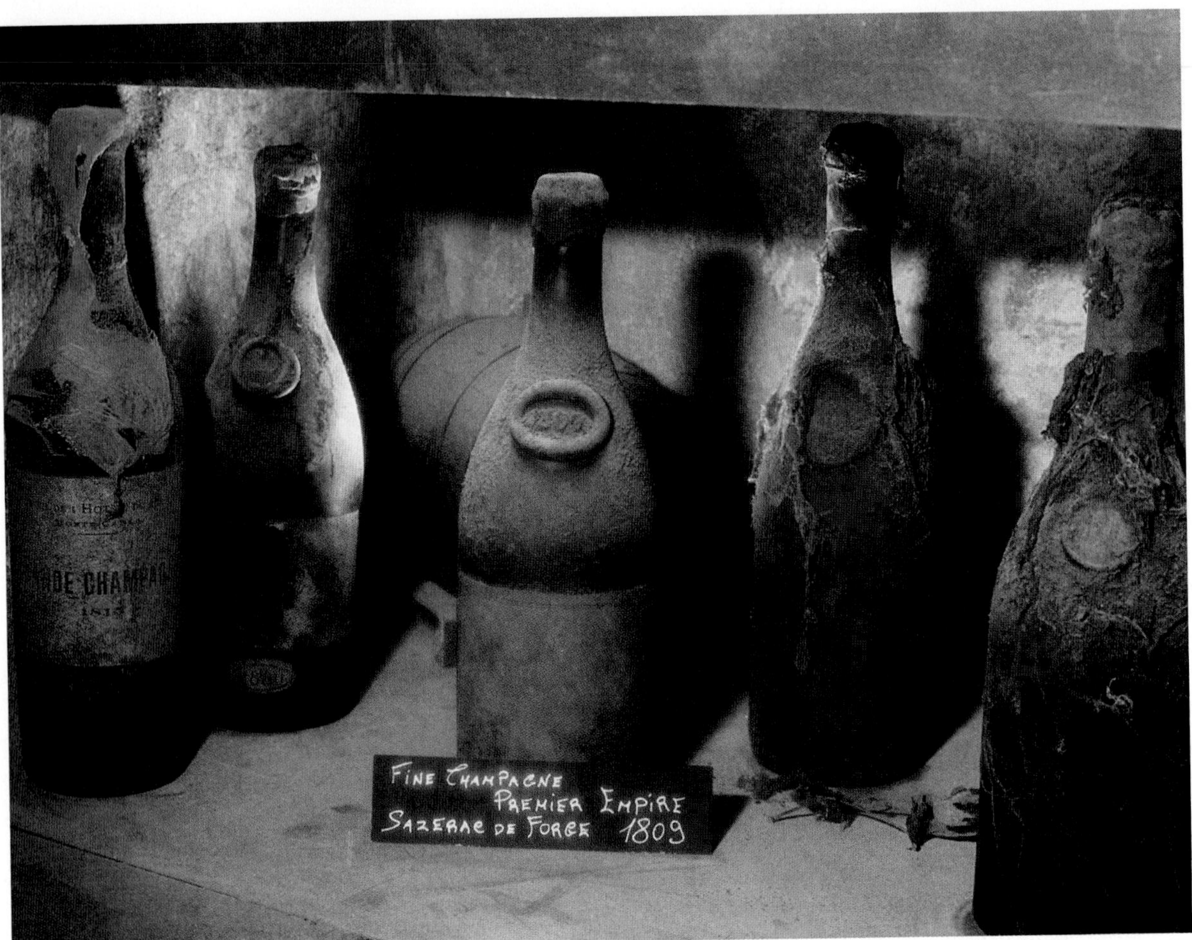

be ill, and I cannot be responsible. Besides, there is Luchesi—"

"Enough," he said; "the cough is a mere nothing; it will not kill me. I shall not die of a cough."

"True—true," I replied; "and, indeed, I had no intention of alarming you unnecessarily—but you should use all proper caution. A draft of this Medoc will defend us from the damps."

Here I knocked off the neck of a bottle which I drew from a long row of its fellows that lay upon the mold.

"Drink," I said, presenting him the wine.
He raised it to his lips with a leer. He paused and nodded to me familiarly, while his bells jingled.

"I drink," he said, "to the buried that repose around us."

"And I to your long life."

He again took my arm, and we proceeded.

"These vaults," he said, "are extensive."

"The Montresors," I replied, "were a great and numerous family."

"I forget your arms."

"A huge human foot d'or, in a field azure; the foot crushes a serpent rampant whose fangs are embedded in the heel."

"And the motto?"

"*Nemo me impune lacessit.*"[12]

"Good!" he said.

The wine sparkled in his eyes and the bells jingled. My own fancy grew warm with the Médoc. We had passed through walls of piled bones, with casks and puncheons[13] intermingling, into the inmost recesses of the catacombs. I paused again, and this time I

12. ***Nemo me impune lacessit.*** [Latin] No one attacks me with impunity.

13. **puncheons.** Large barrels

made bold to seize Fortunato by an arm above the elbow.

"The niter!" I said. "See, it increases. It hangs like moss upon the vaults. We are below the river's bed. The drops of moisture trickle among the bones. Come, we will go back ere it is too late. Your cough—"

"It is nothing," he said; "let us go on. But first, another draft of the Médoc."

I broke and reached him a flagon of de Grave. He emptied it at a breath. His eyes flashed with a fierce light. He laughed and threw the bottle upward with a gesticulation I did not understand.

I looked at him in surprise. He repeated the movement—a grotesque one.

"You do not comprehend?" he said.

"Not I," I replied.

"Then you are not of the brotherhood."

"How?"

"You are not of the masons."[14]

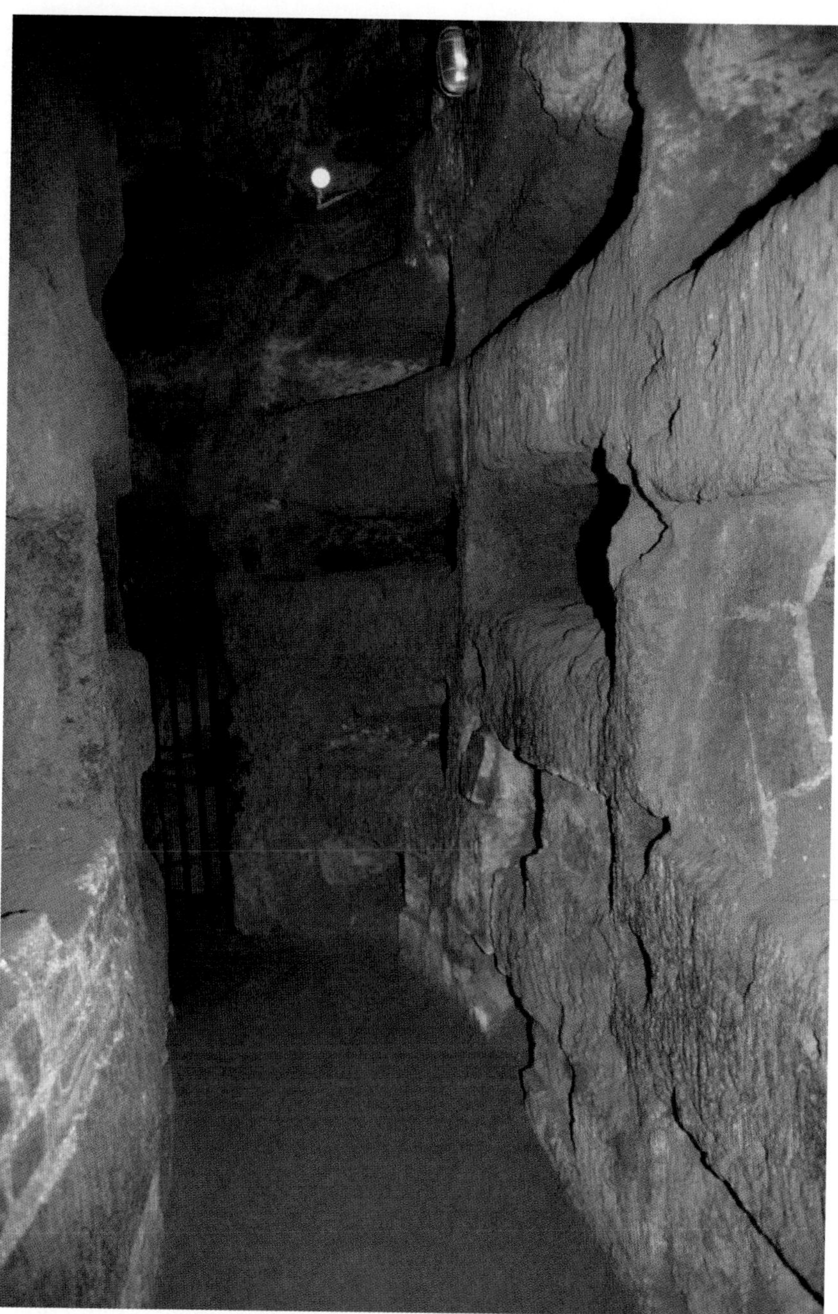

Ruins of Roman catacombs.

"Yes, yes," I said, "yes, yes."

"You? Impossible! A Mason?"

"A Mason," I replied.

"A sign," he said.

"It is this," I answered, producing a trowel from beneath the folds of my roquelaure.

"You jest," he exclaimed, recoiling a few paces. "But let us proceed to the amontillado."

"Be it so," I said, replacing the tool beneath the cloak and again offering him my arm. He leaned upon it heavily. We continued our route in search of the amontillado. We passed through a range of low arches, descended, passed on,

14. **masons.** Freemasons, members of an international secret society; also, skilled workers who build with stone, brick, or cement

gro • tesque (grō tesk´) *adj.*, bizarre; absurdly awkward and, descending again, arrived at a deep crypt in which the foulness of the air caused our flambeaux rather to glow than flame.

At the most remote end of the crypt there appeared another less spacious. Its walls had been lined with human remains, piled to the vault overhead, in the fashion of the great catacombs of Paris. Three sides of this interior crypt were still ornamented in this manner. From the fourth side the bones had been thrown down and lay promiscuously upon the earth, forming at one point a mound of some size. Within the wall thus exposed by the displacing of the bones, we perceived a still interior recess, in depth about four feet, in width three, in height six or seven. It seemed to have been constructed for no especial use within itself, but formed merely the interval between two of the colossal supports of the roof of the catacombs and was backed by one of their circumscribing walls of solid granite.

It was in vain that Fortunato, uplifting his dull torch, endeavored to pry into the depth of the recess.

It was in vain that Fortunato, uplifting his dull torch, endeavored to pry into the depth of the recess. Its termination the feeble light did not enable us to see.

"Proceed," I said; "herein is the amontillado. As for Luchesi—"

"He is an ignoramus," interrupted my friend, as he stepped unsteadily forward, while I followed immediately at his heels. In an instant he had reached the extremity of the niche, and finding his progress arrested by the rock, stood stupidly bewildered. A moment more and I had fettered him to the granite. In its surface were two iron staples, distant from each other about two feet horizontally. From one of these depended a short chain, from the other a padlock. Throwing the links about his waist, it was but the work of a few seconds to secure it. He was too much astounded to resist. Withdrawing the key, I stepped back from the recess.

"Pass your hand," I said, "over the wall; you cannot help feeling the niter. Indeed it is *very* damp. Once more let me *implore* you to return. No? Then I must positively leave you. But I must first render you all the little attentions in my power."

"The amontillado!" ejaculated my friend, not yet recovered from his astonishment.

"True," I replied; "the amontillado."

As I said these words, I busied myself among the pile of bones of which I have before spoken. Throwing them aside, I soon uncovered a quantity of building stone and mortar. With these materials and with the aid of my trowel, I began vigorously to wall up the entrance of the niche.

I had scarcely laid the first tier of the masonry when I discovered that the intoxication of Fortunato had in a great measure worn off. The earliest indication I had of this was a low moaning cry from the depth of the recess. It was *not* the cry of a drunken man. There was then a long and obstinate silence. I laid the second tier, and the third, and the fourth; and then I heard the furious vibrations of the chain. The noise lasted for several minutes, during which, that I might hearken to it with the more satisfaction, I ceased my labors and sat down upon the bones. When at last the clanking subsided, I resumed the trowel, and finished without interruption the fifth, the sixth, and the seventh tier. The wall was now nearly upon a

ter • min • a • tion (tʉr' mə nā´ shən) *n.*, ending; conclusion

Critical Viewing

How do the two figures in this illustration compare with your own impression of how Fortunato and Montresor appear?

An illustration of Fortunato and Montresor, by Arthur Rackham.

level with my breast. I again paused and, holding the flambeaux over the mason-work, threw a few feeble rays upon the figure within.

A succession of loud and shrill screams, bursting suddenly from the throat of the chained form, seemed to thrust me violently back. For a brief moment I hesitated—I trembled. Unsheathing my rapier, I began to grope with it about the recess; but the thought of an instant reassured me. I placed my hand upon the solid fabric of the catacombs and felt satisfied. I reapproached the wall; I replied to the yells of him who clamored. I reechoed—I aided—I surpassed them in volume and in strength. I did this, and the clamorer grew still.

It was now midnight, and my task was drawing to a close. I had completed the eighth, the ninth, and the tenth tier. I had finished a portion of the last and the eleventh; there remained but a single stone to be fitted and plastered in. I struggled with its weight; I placed it partially in its destined position. But now there came from out the niche a low laugh that erected the hairs upon my head. It was succeeded by a sad voice, which I had difficulty in recognizing as that of the noble Fortunato. The voice said—

"Ha! ha! ha!—he! he! he!—a very good joke indeed—an excellent jest. We will have many a rich laugh about it at the *palazzo*—he! he! he!—over our wine—he! he! he!"

"The amontillado!" I said.

"He! he! he!—he! he! he!—yes, the amontillado. But is it not getting late? Will not they be awaiting us at the *palazzo*—the Lady Fortunato and the rest? Let us be gone."

suc • ces • sion (sək se´ shən) *n.,* repeated following of one thing after another

"Yes," I said, "let us be gone."

"For the love of God, Montresor!"

"Yes," I said, "for the love of God!"

But to these words I hearkened in vain for a reply. I grew impatient. I called aloud—

"Fortunato!"

No answer. I called again—

"Fortunato!"

No answer still. I thrust a torch through the remaining <u>aperture</u> and let it fall within. There came forth in return only a jingling of the bells. My heart grew sick—on account of the dampness of the catacombs. I hastened to make an end of my labor. I forced the last stone into its position; I plastered it up. Against the new masonry I reerected the old rampart of bones. For the half of a century no mortal has disturbed them. *In pace requiescat!*[15] ❖

15. ***In pace requiescat!*** [Latin] May he rest in peace!

a • per • ture (ap´ ər chůr') *n.,* hole; gap; opening

Does a perceived insult result in a complete lack of judgment? Have you ever offended someone and not realized it at the time?

AFTER READING

REFER TO TEXT ▶▶▶▶	▶ REASON WITH TEXT	
1a. Record how Montresor reacts when he sees Fortunato on the street.	1b. Determine why Montresor would tell Fortunato about the Amontillado.	Understand **Find meaning**
2a. Name the image depicted on the Montresor coat of arms.	2b. Discuss the significance of Montresor's coat of arms and family motto.	Apply **Use information**
3a. Identify where Montresor leads Fortunato.	3b. What details indicate that Montresor's crime was premeditated?	Analyze **Take things apart**
4a. How does Montresor treat Fortunato as they make their way down the tunnels?	4b. A paradox is a self-contradictory statement that at first seems true. Assess whether Montresor's concern over the health of Fortunato, found on pages 61–63, is paradoxical. Explain your answer.	Evaluate **Make judgments**
5a. State how Montresor gets his revenge.	5b. Summarize the story of "The Cask of Amontillado."	Create **Bring ideas together**

ANALYZE LITERATURE: Point of View and Narrator

Poe frequently told stories from the point of view of unreliable narrators. Reread the first paragraph. Then skim the story, reviewing the dialogue between Montresor and Fortunato. Why do you think Poe chose such a narrator, and what effect does his choice have on the mood of the story?

EXTEND THE TEXT

Writing Options

Creative Writing Write an **introductory paragraph** to a horror story about revenge for a young-adult magazine. As Poe did in "The Cask of Amontillado," use precise details and vivid imagery to create a dramatic setting and mood. Your introduction should establish the setting, mood, narrator or main character(s), as well as the main conflict in the story.

Descriptive Writing Imagine you are a detective in charge of briefing the local police department on the events that took place in "The Cask of Amontillado." The police have asked you to analyze the victim's character. Based on Montresor's "confession," write a one-page **character analysis** of Fortunato. In your analysis, examine the aspects of Fortunato's character that enabled Montresor to entrap him. Use specific examples of his words or actions to support your analysis.

Collaborative Learning

Perform Reader's Theater Form a small group and choose one of Poe's horror stories to read aloud; possible choices include "The Cask of Amontillado," "The Masque of the Red Death," "The Fall of the House of Usher," and "The Pit and the Pendulum." As you prepare your reading, your group members should take specific character roles, such as Montresor and Fortunato in "The Cask of Amontillado." Use the tone and pitch of your voice as well as body language and gestures to convey the mood and dominant effect of each story and to heighten listeners' awareness of certain elements, such as sound effects and sound-imitating words.

Critical Literacy

Stage an Interview with Poe Work with a partner to research the life of Edgar Allan Poe. Find more information about his childhood, education, and adulthood by searching the Internet for websites dedicated to Poe, or by reading biographies you find in the library. When you are finished with your research, stage an interview with the author. Put together a list of questions you would want to ask Poe about the major events in his life and how they influenced his choice of themes in his short stories. One partner should play Poe, and the other the interviewer. Take notes to summarize the conversation.

Go to **www.mirrorsandwindows.com** for more.

READING ASSESSMENT

1. The narrator hates Fortunato because Fortunato
   A. stole some of the narrator's wine.
   B. has a better wine collection.
   C. insulted him.
   D. threatened his family.
   E. brags about his accomplishments.

2. The narrator most likely suggests he is going to ask Luchesi for help
   A. because he doesn't trust Fortunato.
   B. because Fortunato respects Luchesi's opinion.
   C. because he knows Fortunato hates Luchesi.
   D. to be considerate of Fortunato's prior engagements.
   E. to appeal to Fortunato's pride and make him jealous.

3. Why do you think Poe set the story during carnival?
   A. to contrast a mood of revelry with one of horror
   B. to create a likely situation for Montresor to carry off his murder unnoticed
   C. to increase the likelihood that Fortunato would be less suspicious of Montresor's generosity
   D. None of the above
   E. All of the above

4. As it is used on page 60, the term *accosted* most nearly means
   A. accused.
   B. belittled.
   C. confronted.
   D. handled.
   E. surprised.

5. What lines below, taken from the story, suggest a possible motive for Montresor's actions?
   A. "And yet some fools will have it that his taste is a match for your own."
   B. My heart grew sick—on account of the dampness of the catacombs.
   C. "Once more let me implore you to return. No? Then I must positively leave you."
   D. "You are rich, respected, admired, beloved; you are happy, as once I was."
   E. It must be understood that neither word nor deed had I given Fortunato cause to doubt my goodwill.

6. Identify the mood of the story and cite passages in which Poe uses carefully chosen sensory details to create this mood.

Understanding Character

CHARACTER

A **character** is an individual who takes part in the action of a literary work. A character is usually a person but may also be a personified plant, animal, object, or imaginary creature.

Have you heard of Sherlock Holmes? Most likely you would recognize him, even if you haven't read a single story by his creator, Sir Arthur Conan Doyle. Sherlock Holmes is a memorable literary character whom many people could describe: tall and thin; very intelligent and observant; smokes a pipe; wears a distinctive hat; lives in London; has a sharp, somewhat standoffish personality. Based on these traits, readers expect Holmes to act in certain ways.

TYPES OF CHARACTERS

Some characters you may like; others you may detest. However, all characters have some role to play in bringing a story to life. The characters around whom a story is centered are the **major characters.** In "The Good Deed" (page 83), for instance, Old Mrs. Pan is a major character. It is her actions, from deciding to cross the street one day to introducing two young friends to each other, that generate the story. Mr. Pan and his wife are **minor characters.** Minor characters play lesser roles in the story and may give the major characters points of interaction.

Major characters can also be classified as either *protagonists* or *antagonists.* The **protagonist** has the central role in a story; the **antagonist** works against the protagonist, and this friction creates conflict. Without Georg Znaeym in "The Interlopers" (page 15), Ulrich von Gradwitz would not have been patrolling the forest; the entire story is centered on their rivalry.

Have you ever noticed how some characters you remember long after reading and others you quickly forget? The difference could be attributed to whether the character is a *flat character* or a *round character.* Old Mrs. Pan in "The Good Deed" is a **round character;** she shows emotional complexity and development, at one time wasting away from homesickness, while at another being energized by the desire to help someone. Many characters that you encounter in fables and fairy tales, however, are **flat characters,** exhibiting only a single quality. Some flat characters play into common notions of how certain people think and behave. Such characters are considered *stereotypes.*

Another way to consider character is by noting *static characters* and *dynamic characters.* **Static characters** remain the same throughout the course of the story; the events in the plot do not alter them. **Dynamic characters,** on the other hand, are affected by plot events and therefore undergo change. The narrator in "The Scarlet Ibis" (page 109) is a dynamic character, as his attitude toward his brother changes; General Zaroff in "The Most Dangerous Game" (page 27) is a static character because he never changes his mind about his hunting practices.

The force or forces that drive a character to think, feel, or behave in a certain way is called **motivation.** Motivation can be relatively simple—the desire to shine in society, for example, or to exact revenge for an insult. It can also be complex, consisting of more than one need. The narrator of "The Scarlet Ibis" uncovers layers of motivation as he tells his sad tale: the humiliation of having an "odd" brother, the need to demonstrate his own normalcy and false pride in driving his brother to walk and to run, and finally, the overpowering necessity of trying to understand a tragic experience by retelling it in detail.

CHARACTERIZATION

The act of creating or describing a character is called **characterization.** There are three main techniques that an author uses to form a character:

- showing what characters say, do, or think
- showing what other characters say or think about them
- describing the physical features, dress, and personalities of the characters

The first two techniques are examples of *indirect characterization,* in which the writer shows what a character is like and allows the reader to judge that character. The third technique is considered *direct characterization,* in which the writer tells what the character is like. Consider the following examples:

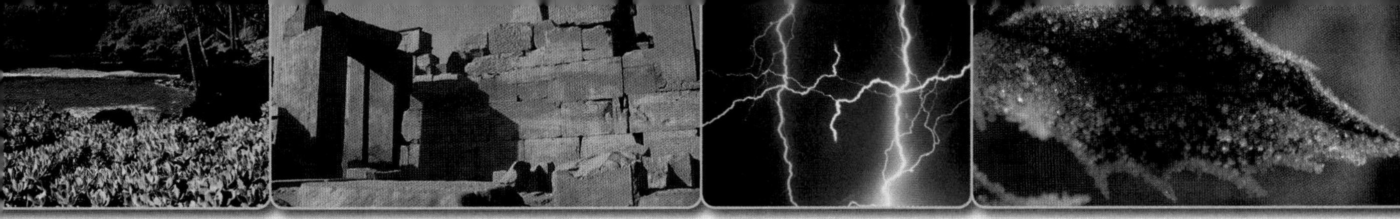

> He had a weak point—this Fortunato—although in other regards he was a man to be respected and even feared. He prided himself on his connoisseurship in wine…In painting and gemmary, Fortunato, like his countrymen, was a quack, but in the matter of old wines he was sincere.
>
> —from "The Cask of Amontillado"
> by Edgar Allan Poe (page 59)
>
> "I'll give him a trail to follow," muttered Rainsford, and he struck off from the rude paths he had been following into the trackless wilderness. He executed a series of intricate loops; he doubled on his trail again and again, recalling all the lore of the fox hunt, and all the dodges of the fox.
>
> —from "The Most Dangerous Game"
> by Richard Connell

In the first excerpt, Fortunato is depicted as snobbish and somehow powerful—"a man to be respected and even feared." In the second excerpt, Rainsford is characterized as cunning and experienced in the art of the dodge, recalling even in his desperate plight "all the lore of the fox hunt."

> He [Roger] looked as if he were fourteen or fifteen, frail and willow-wild, in tennis shoes and blue jeans.
>
> —from "Thank You, M'am"
> by Langston Hughes (page 6)
>
> Had the Queen of Sheba lived in the flat across the air shaft, Della would have let her hair hang out the window some day to dry just to depreciate Her Majesty's jewels and gifts.
>
> —from "The Gift of the Magi"
> by O. Henry (page 139)

Roger is characterized as a waif, whereas Della is characterized as innocently vain, capable of a childishly competitive action. With a few swift words, the authors of the two stories use direct characterization to capture something vital about each character.

The **dialogue,** or conversations between two or more characters, is also revealing. The content of the dialogue is a form of indirect characterization. A character may speak in a **dialect,** or a version of a language spoken by the people of a particular place, time, or social group. For example, when Mrs. Jones in "Thank You, M'am" says, "You a lie!" she is speaking in dialect, which makes her character more distinctive. We learn about her from what she says and how she says it:

> "I got a great mind to wash your face for you. Ain't you got nobody home to tell you to wash your face?"
>
> "No'm," said the boy.
>
> "Then it will get washed this evening," said the large woman starting up the street, dragging the frightened boy behind her.
>
> —from "Thank You, M'am"
> by Langston Hughes

As you read a story, use a Character Chart like the one below to characterize an important figure both directly and indirectly.

Characterization	Mrs. Jones	What Is Revealed
What she says	"I were young once and I wanted things I could not get."	Mrs. Jones grew up poor.
What she does	She gives ten dollars to Roger.	She is generous and compassionate.
What others say about her	"She was a large woman… hammer and nails."	She is strong and prepared for almost anything.

BEFORE READING **A Short Story by Louise Erdrich**

BUILD BACKGROUND

Social Context The story **"Destiny"** centers on an unusual young girl named Wallacette. Adored by her equally unusual grandmother and her grandmother's friend, the narrator, Wallacette is nonetheless a mystifying force to her parents and teachers. The story is set in Argus, North Dakota, a fictional town created by Erdrich as the setting for many of her stories, including her novel *The Beet Queen.*

Reader's Context How do you express strong feelings of like or dislike? Are you more likely to show your feelings openly, hide them, give subtle hints, or act in the opposite manner to what you're feeling?

ANALYZE LITERATURE: Character

A **character** is an individual that takes part in the action of a literary work. A *flat character* shows only one quality, or character trait. A *round character* shows the multiple character traits of a real person. A *static character* does not change during the course of the action. A *dynamic character* does change. Consider the role of the narrator in this story. Why do you think the author uses this character to tell the story of Celestine's family?

SET PURPOSE

Destiny is a supposedly predetermined or inevitable course of events that happens. Some define destiny as fate or what is meant to be. In this story, destiny comes into play during Wallacette's school pageant. What effect might destiny have on the characters in Erdrich's story? How do you think Wallacette, her parents, and Celestine regard the idea of destiny? Why?

MEET THE AUTHOR

Louise Erdrich (b. 1954) is, to date, the author of eleven novels, three books of poetry, and several publications of children's literature and nonfiction. She is the mother to six children (three of whom were originally adopted by her late husband Michael Dorris) and is the owner of a bookstore in Minneapolis, Minnesota. Like many of the characters in her books, she is of mixed Native American descent: Her mother is French Chippewa (Ojibwa), and her father is German-American. While Erdrich was growing up in North Dakota, her parents worked as teachers on a reservation. Today, she is a member of the Turtle Mountain Band of Chippewa. Erdrich has said, "To be of mixed blood is a great gift for a writer. I have one foot on tribal lands and one foot in middle-class life."

USE READING SKILLS

Draw Conclusions When you **draw conclusions,** you combine clues with your prior knowledge and make an educated guess, or inference, about what has happened, is happening, or will happen. Keep a Conclusions Chart to write down clues within the text that allow you to draw conclusions.

Conclusions Chart

Text: "I'm not going anywhere they put...radishes in Jell-O."
What I infer: Celestine is difficult to please.
Detail from text: "She has got a bug up her nose about the Swedes and their customs involving food."
Conclusions: The narrator views Celestine's attitude as immature and self-indulgent.

PREVIEW VOCABULARY

Choose the best word from the following list to complete each sentence.

earnest wield elude
premonition gloat

1. Mikhail had a(n) ______ that he would receive bad news.
2. The jewel thief continues to ______ the police despite their best efforts to catch him.
3. If you ______ every time you win, I won't play chess with you anymore.
4. The ______ expression on Kalisha's face convinced me that I could trust her.
5. You'll need to ______ a sword to complete the costume.

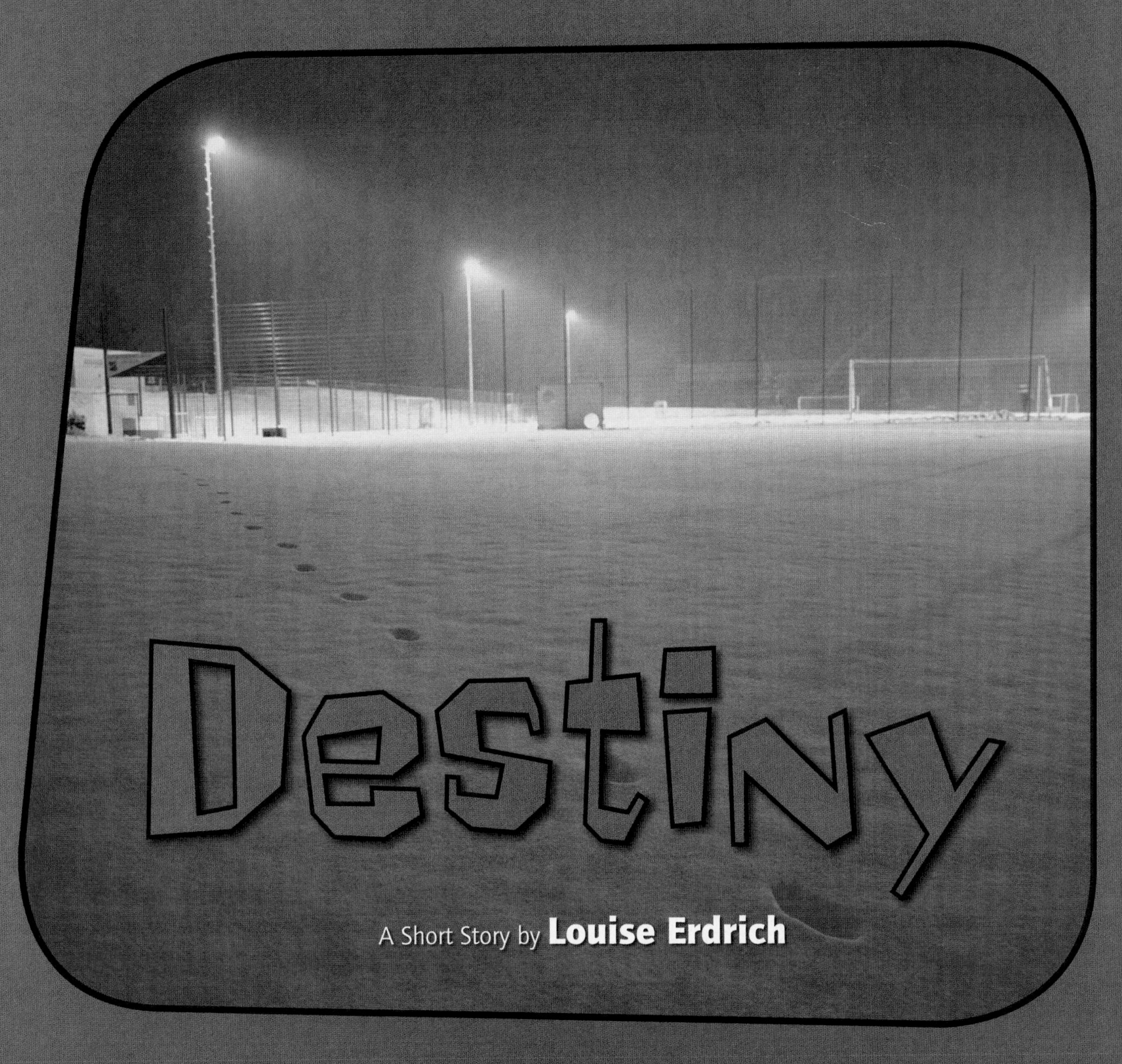

Tragedy, her favorite element, is in the air.

"I'm not going anywhere they put the radishes in Jell-O," says my friend and employee, Celestine Duval, when I mention visiting her son, Norris.

Yet that very night my shop catches fire, and she is out of a job until the insurance comes through. It is December. The nearest hydrant was frozen when they put a wrench to it, but I am lucky. Because I have a thick sliding door between the shop and the back room where I live, the only damage to my living quarters was stains from a few gray plumes of smoke blown up the walls.

"They lend an atmosphere," Celestine tells me.

She talks like a restaurant because Norris has opened a steakhouse in Argus, North Dakota, where he lives among the Swedes. This has led to Celestine's objections to the radishes. She has got a bug up her nose about the Swedes and their customs involving food. She went down to help Norris at the grand opening not so long ago, but she could not stand their habit of slicing odd things into the Jell-O.

Now, since the fire payment won't arrive for a week or so and the workmen won't start on the interior, we decide to close the shop and take a trip. We must get our minds off this disaster. We decide to go to Argus and visit Norris, his wife, Adele, and their daughter with the terrible name.

Like her mother, Wallacette is big and imposing, with a large-jawed grin full of teeth.

Wallacette is named after Adele's father, who died in the ninth month of Adele's pregnancy and left his daughter's mind unhinged with grief. Nothing that Norris said could persuade Adele to name their daughter something halfway normal. Wallacette she became.

Like her mother, Wallacette is big and imposing, with a large-jawed grin full of teeth. At eleven years old she towers above the rest of the children in her class, and she is mainly interested in fiercely pursuing love. To get boyfriends, she knocks boys down and grinds their faces in the snowy grit. To get girls, she ties the string waistbands of their dresses to her own dress strings, and drags them around the playground until they promise to write her a note.

The nuns don't know what to do with Wallacette, nor do her parents, for she is strong-willed and determined to get her way. These same traits, however, make her a favorite with Celestine and myself, for we think that she has got spunk, and we always look forward to what surprises each visit with her brings. But to visit Wallacette we must also contend with Norris and, worse, grim Adele, who insists that we help her out in their steakhouse. The Poopdeck[1] is the name of the place. I can't tell you why, except that this name was Adele's idea too.

The name does have to be an ocean-going kind of name, we admit. To save money on the renovations, Norris put in portholes rather than windows. Then he painted the outside white and blue, like a ship, and built a little captain's steering deck up top. He can't disguise the square shape of the building, though. It certainly doesn't look like it could sail anywhere.

After two hours of driving, we arrive in Argus. The Poopdeck's parking lot is jammed. Furry green plastic branches frame the portholes, decorations for the holidays. Within each porthole glows one red electric candle.

"Celestine," I say, "let's go somewhere else for lunch."

She is wearing a white turban on her head, and earrings that look like tiny red plungers. Christmas plungers. Her slanting eyes are sharp yellow, and the little purple spider veins in her cheeks have darkened like stitches.

"If we help out, they'll feed us afterward. All we can eat," she says.

But it's the helping I can do without.

1. **Poopdeck.** A partial deck above the ship's main afterdeck

It is Saturday, however, and we are pleased to see that Wallacette is behind the counter. Her job is to hand out paper boat flags and red and green Lifesavers to the children who eat at the Poopdeck. This she does with earnest enjoyment. Sometimes she forces the candy so eagerly on little children that they cry out in fear of her stony jaw and gleaming teeth.

She sees us. She ducks under the counter and hurls herself forward. I can hear the sharp *oof!* as the air is knocked out of Celestine's lungs. It is hard to think of Celestine as anyone's grandmother. But she seems right as Wallacette's. The girl's pale legs are brawny as a wrestler's. She wears dirty white anklets. A strange light shines in her face. Hunched in her black coat, under the turban with its blazing clip, Celestine looks strange too, and the same light glows within her eyes.

We join the cooks at the steam tables in the back. I am stationed at the deep-fryer, with wire baskets and bags of frozen products—fries, shrimp, onion rings, breaded fillets. The fish is always popular because of the boat theme, which is carried on in the menu.

"Old Tar Special," the waitress yells. "Clams Casanova! Fish Waikiki!"

Someone orders a Spinnaker Salad and a Lighthouse malt—a regular malt with a cherry "light."

I lower a basket of fantail shrimp into the popping grease. This is Wallacette's favorite item on the menu. I hear her voice through the cook's window, deep and loud.

"Sure you like candy. You do too. Take these."

A child's thin wail grows and is hushed. I peek out. The boy is hoisted into his mother's arms and carried out, staring over her shoulder, lip hanging. He doesn't know it, but his character has been strengthened by this encounter. Wallacette stands before another child. This time she is poking a striped paper flag through

ear • nest (ʉrn´ əst) *adj.,* sincere; serious

the child's buttonhole. The child stands stiffly, paralyzed, as if the slightest movement would cause the big girl to drive the tiny wooden pole into her heart.

"Don't be a sissy," she booms. "You like candy!"

When the noon rush is over, the three of us sit down in the end booth. The candles blaze in the little round portholes. Nets are draped across the walls. Wallacette has fried twenty-four fantail shrimp to place on a bed of coleslaw for herself. I am having the ham and pineapple rings. Celestine is having a steak and browned onions. She would normally accompany this with a salad, but not here. She won't go near the salad bar, because of Adele. In the cooler, Adele's creative Jell-O salads rest in brilliantly colored sheets. They are filled with walnuts, chopped celery, macaroni, onions, miniature pastel marshmallows, and, worst of all, sliced radishes.

"I'm sure glad you came back," Wallacette says to her grandmother. "Dad was worried that we'd have to come visit you."

The last time Celestine visited Norris and Adele, the nasty confrontation over the Jell-O took place. That is why, so far, Adele has avoided us.

"You're the one I came to see," Celestine tells her granddaughter. "Your mother and father can get along perfectly good without me."

"I guess they can," says Wallacette, who inherited Celestine's honesty. "But not me."

An expression that I've never seen forms on Celestine's face. She is watching Wallacette. It is as though her face is liable to break into pieces, as though the stitching spider veins barely manage to hold her face together. I am confused by this look, and then I realize what it is. Tenderness. The heart of Celestine is cold as clay, something even she'll admit. But she feels a true tenderness for Wallacette.

I am confused by this look, and then I realize what it is. Tenderness.

"You're in time!" Wallacette shouts suddenly. Light breaks over her broad pancake face. Her stony brow lifts. "You'll get to see our Christmas play!"

This is pleasing to both of us.

We enjoy Wallacette's successes and have already seen her in a piano recital, playing "Song of the Volga Boatmen" with tremendous expression. Celestine is chewing her steak eagerly, with pride and enthusiasm, for Wallacette has revealed to us that she will play a leading role.

"I am Joseph, father of the Christ child," she states. Then she grins, long and huge.

At first I think it's awful that they picked a little girl to play the father of Christ. Then I imagine Wallacette wearing a long grizzled beard and a coarse robe. I see the carpenter's maul[2] wielded in her fist. She will be convincing.

"*The Donkey of Destiny* is the name of this play," she tells us. Her face changes suddenly. "I hate the donkey."

The light goes out in the window. I distinctly hear Wallacette's teeth clench together and gnash. I've never heard the sound of gnashing teeth before, only read of it in books. Now I realize why this gnashing of teeth is mentioned so often. It is ominous and frightening to hear.

2. **maul.** A heavy wooden hammer used in carpentry

wield (wēld) *v.*, carry, as with a weapon

Adele and Norris have made their basement over into what they call a recreation center. A Hamm's beer lamp that shows a canoe on an endlessly revolving lake hangs off the side wall. This lamp makes Celestine raise her eyebrows and bend toward me.

"No comment," she whispers. We both dislike the lamp, with its foolish repetition, on sight. But we do not hurt any feelings. We smile and nod at Norris.

At one end of the room is a large cabinet television and a plush couch. In the middle of the room is a pool table that, as Norris now informs us, opens into a bed for guests. Norris seems anxious to demonstrate its double use, and so Celestine and I take our places against the wood-grain paneled walls while he struggles with the pool table. Norris is a small, washed-out, balding man. He is like a version of his mother, left too long in the water. But he is kinder than Celestine, and he wants very much to please us. Hinges creak and springs vibrate as he fiddles with the table. A loose ball rolls through the works. Norris slams his fist to dislodge a hidden latch, and the top springs up like the lid of a box. Then Norris bats a panel loose, and the bed folds into being. Sheets and pillows are secured, and we are ready for the night.

"I'll set the thermostat up for you," Norris says, wiping his brow, looking very much relieved. "Do you think you'll be all right down here?"

"As long as the table doesn't fold up on us," Celestine says. She is eyeing the bed suspiciously. I know that the ball is still loose inside of the pool-table bed, and that makes me a little hesitant. I've never heard this, but I can guess it is unlucky to sleep in a bed with what might be an eight ball folded up in its works. Still, we have no choice. Norris waves from the basement stairs. When he is gone, Celestine removes her shoes and turban and sits down carefully on her side of the bed.

"You want to hear the truth of the matter?" she says. "Wallacette loves the donkey."

"I don't understand this at first. I have forgotten about the donkey in the play. But Celestine goes on to explain.

"Wallacette tried to catch the boy who plays the donkey—the head, not the rear end, that is. So far he has outsmarted her. This makes her violent."

"We must tell her to go easy on the boy," I counsel.

Celestine seems to agree.

"Say it with flowers," she says abruptly, with a fierce nod.

I wonder, when she says this, if either of us knows enough to say what love is all about. Our husbands are long deceased. At one time we must have loved them. But for me love was not said with flowers, at least not until he died. Every spring now I change the artificial roses on his grave.

For the next several days of our visit Adele continues to elude us, while Norris is always late to get somewhere. We find evidence of Adele in fresh coffee, sweet buns, and little notes pinned or taped on various items in the house.

Only those two, Celestine and Adele, halfway enjoy their mortal combat.

"Don't touch the color tuner" is taped to the front of their television. "I'm saving the lemon bars for tonight" is taped on the refrigerator door. "Use the striped towels" is pinned to the correct towels in the bathroom.

Celestine laughs harshly every time she comes across another bold printed order from Adele.

"Out-and-out gall," she says, crumpling the bits of paper.

I get to wishing that the two of them would settle their account. It would make things much nicer for Norris, myself, and Wallacette. Only those two, Celestine and Adele, halfway enjoy their mortal combat.

When the morning of the play dawns, we are anxious and excited. Even Norris has heightened color. Wallacette's hair is curled with an electric iron, though it will be covered with a wig. She bundles up in a green pile coat and barges down the road. Norris and Adele drive off, leaving us alone in the house.

"There's a potluck dinner after the play," Celestine tells me. "I'm going to make a special secret dish."

Then she whisks herself off into the kitchen and hands me a cup of coffee and a bun through a crack in the door. I feel like a fifth wheel going downstairs to sit alone, first thing in the morning. I switch on the television, but the face of The Morning Hostess is pulsating blue, and I do not dare disobey Adele's note and adjust the dial.

The gymnasium that night is alive and noisy. The lights blaze in their steel-mesh covers. Folding chairs are lifted from a cart by dads with rolled-up sleeves and are added to the back rows. Mink-collared grandmothers are settled in firmly, ready to enjoy the pageant. The nuns are whispering together in their navy-blue veils. The run-down parish gym is also used as a dining hall and for bingo and budget meetings. The purple velveteen curtain is shabby, a castoff from the public school. Celestine insists that we sit far up front. In elbowing through the nuns we lose Adele and Norris.

"Accidentally on purpose," Celestine sniffs. We sit. She has already delivered her secret recipe, a long foil-covered pan, to the school kitchen. During the potluck dinner this dish will be unveiled. Celestine has taped Adele's name where it cannot be missed; she will be known as the author of the great work. For some reason I am uneasy that she has done this. Generosity is not her style.

The noise all around us mounts, and then suddenly it hushes. The lights go down. There is the sound of programs rustling. We have already found and admired the printed presence of Wallacette's name.

e • lude (ē lūd´) *v.*, avoid

When the curtains open, the spotlight shows a boy wearing a knit poncho and a huge sombrero, of the kind that people who have been to Mexico hang on their walls. This boy makes a long sad speech about his friend the donkey, whom he must sell to the glue factory in order to buy food. On a darkened set of bleachers behind him a vague chorus laments the donkey's fate.

The boy pulls the rope he has been twisting in his hands, and the donkey bumbles out of the wings. It is, of course, a makeshift donkey. It is wearing gray pants and tennis shoes. The body is barrel-shaped and lopsided, and the papier-mâché head lolls as if the donkey were drunk. The mouth, painted open in a grin, and the slanted, black-rimmed eyes give it a strange expression of cruelty.

Parents ooh and ahh, but some look startled. The donkey is an unpleasant creature. Its dyed burlap hide looks motheaten. One ear is long and one is short. Celestine must be the only person in the crowd who thinks the donkey is cute. "Oh, look at it prance," she whispers. Her long yellow Tartar[3] eyes gleam softly beneath the flashing buckle of her turban. Her gloves are in a tight ball, like socks. She smiles as the boy and his donkey start out on the long road to the glue factory. Tragedy, her favorite element, is in the air. Her eyes blaze when the chorus wails.

"*Amigos!*[4] We are *amigos!*" the boy shouts from beneath the sombrero. Then they slowly begin to walk across the stage. They are weeping. But before they reach the glue factory, Saint Joseph appears.

Saint Joseph has a long beard of spray-painted cotton, and an old piece of upholstery fabric is tied to her head. She wears a long brown terrycloth bathrobe that might belong to Norris. Her feet are bare. As in my vision of her, she is carrying a wooden maul. She looks grimmer than the mild church statues, and more powerful. I believe in her. The donkey sidles up

3. **Tartar.** Of Turkish or Central Asian descent
4. ***Amigos*** **(ä mē´ gōz).** [Spanish] Friends

to her with its evil, silly grin. She stands before it with her legs spread wide, balancing on the balls of her feet. All I can see of the boy whom, according to Celestine, she loves is a pair of gray corduroy knees and frayed black tennis shoes. Wallacette grabs the donkey around the neck and the gray legs twitch for a moment in the air. Then she sets the donkey down and says her lines to the donkey's *amigo*.

"Young man, where are you going with this donkey?"

"I must sell it to the glue factory, for my family is hungry," the boy says sadly.

"Perhaps I can help you out," Wallacette says. "My wife, Mary, myself, and our little boy, Baby Jesus, want to flee King Herod. My wife could ride this donkey if you would sell it."

"I will sell my donkey to help you," the boy shouts. "He will not be killed!"

"Of course not," Wallacette says. "We will only ride him across the desert to Egypt."

She takes some large coins made of crushed aluminum foil from her bathrobe pocket and gives them to the boy.

And so the transaction is accomplished. The Donkey of Destiny now belongs to Wallacette, who tries to pat its snarling papier-mâché muzzle. But then the episode occurs that we hope will not mar the mind of our favorite granddaughter for life. The donkey balks. Is this in the script? I glance at Celestine, wondering, but her look has narrowed to a flashlight focus of premonitions.

"Come along, little donkey," Saint Joseph says, through gritted teeth. She pulls, perhaps a bit roughly, at the rope on its neck. Suddenly a hand snakes from the front of the donkey's neck flap and rips the rope out of the grasp of a surprised Saint Joseph.

"Give it back!" she shouts in quick rage. "You're mine!"

The audience twitters; a few loud male guffaws are heard. Saint Joseph hears the audience—laughing at her! Fury tightens in her arms and she raises the maul high. I know what will happen. The audience gapes. Then she brings it down clean, like swift judgment, on the cardboard skull of the beast.

Fury tightens in her arms and she raises the maul high. I know what will happen.

The front of the donkey drops. The head flies off, smashed. The last of that scene that we see is Saint Joseph standing in criminal shock, maul gripped tight, over the motionless body of a towheaded[5] boy.

The curtain has closed and the audience is in a rumble of consternation. A fat, blonde, hysterical woman, the mother of the donkey's felled front end, flies down the aisle. Adele and Norris are nowhere to be seen.

"Come!" Celestine says, hoisting her handbag on her elbow. "Or the nuns will take it out of her hide!"

We leave the chairs, find the side stage door, and slip behind the curtains. Angels and shepherds are standing in dismayed clumps. The painted wood silhouettes of sheep and cattle look stupidly baffled. We see Adele, wide and flat-rumped in a red suit, and Norris, with his bald man's ring of hair, standing with the principal nun, gesturing and gabbling excit-

5. **towheaded.** Blond

pre • mo • ni • tion (prə mə ni´ shən) *n.*, vision of the future edly. The wounded boy is nowhere to be seen. Wallacette is gone too.

Adele sees us in the wings and strides over to Celestine.

"Mother," she says, "go home."

"Where's Wallacette?" Celestine asks, ignoring her daughter-in-law's order.

"She ran out the back door of the gym," Norris says bleakly, "and that's the last anyone has seen of her."

"Get out a search party, then!" Celestine says. "She's barefoot in the snow!"

But no search party forms at her words.

As it turns out, Wallacette was headed home. When we arrive there, she is sitting on the living room coffee table with her feet by the heat ducts.

"Young lady!" Adele cries out, marching toward her, but Norris gets there first.

"Wait," he said, "I think she's hurt."

Sure enough, the rare tear is in her eye. She sits in a lump, clutching her play beard, shaking with inner sobs. In Norris's bathrobe she looks, oddly, like an ordinary, middle-aged man. Her face is pale, streaked with misery, and her small blue eyes are dull and still. Adele and Norris look awed, watching her, and do not approach and hug her or pat her, as normal parents might. Perhaps they have never seen her cry before.

Celestine, however, kneels down next to her, and then suddenly, fiercely, she lunges and catches the girl full across the chest and neck with a stranglehold. I expect this to be the moment Wallacette breaks down. It will be good for the girl to shed real tears, I think sympathetically. But instead of melting and crying, Wallacette charges suddenly from the room like a bull, running right over her grandmother. Celestine goes tumbling in a black heap on the carpet, and a door down the hall slams. Adele follows, to pound on the door and reason with her daughter. Norris stays, bending apologetically over his mother, who looks perversely delighted with what has happened. She pushes Norris away and lifts herself up.

"Grandma's girl" is all she says, adjusting her turban.

That night, as we are lying side by side on the fold-out couch downstairs, I realize that something still bothers me, something that I wonder about. So I ask Celestine about the special secret dish that was to be placed among the others at the potluck dinner after the Christmas play.

"What was it?" I ask. "Was it your special chocolate bran cake?"

"It was not," Celestine says, waking quickly at my question. The sound of joy lights her voice. She crows.

"What?"

"The Jell-O. My special secret dish."

Of course I ask her what it was that made the Jell-O so special.

Bold as a weasel, she turns in the dark and fixes me with her proud, gleaming stare. She stares a long time, to let my anticipation sink in.

"Nuts and bolts," she finally says. "Washers of all types. I raided Norris's toolbox for the special ingredients."

Then she turns on her back to gloat up into the dark. I turn away from her, pretending to sleep.

But from my side of the bed I cannot escape the changing scenery of the beer lamp, still lit. I am forced to watch it revolve. So I watch, and after a while it isn't irritating anymore. In fact, it is almost as soothing as any real scenery you might find, and has the added advantage that you can relax and watch it in a dark room. Again and again I see the canoe leave the Minnesota lakeshore and venture through the water. The pines along the lake stand green-black and crisp. The water shimmers, lit within. The boat travels. I can almost see the fish rise, curious, beneath its shadow. ❖

gloat (glōt) *v.*, to consider in a victorious and boastful way

When Wallacette tries to catch the boy who plays the donkey, his outsmarting her makes her violent. How are feelings of love and hate similar? Why might a person act aggressively to someone they find attractive or whom they admire?

AFTER READING

REFER TO TEXT	REASON WITH TEXT	
1a. How does Wallacette interact with the other children at school?	1b. Discuss how the other children respond to Wallacette.	Understand **Find meaning**
2a. Indicate how Wallacette reacts when Celestine tries to comfort her.	2b. Based on what you know about Wallacette, why do you think she reacts the way she does? How is this related to her actions at the Christmas pageant?	Apply **Use information**
3a. Recall what Celestine creates for the school potluck.	3b. Analyze how Celestine might view her own actions. How might she perceive the relationship she has created with Adele? Explain.	Analyze **Take things apart**
4a. Identify what started the fight between Adele and Celestine.	4b. Do you think, as the narrator states, that Adele and Celestine actually enjoy arguing? Why or why not? How might their behavior affect Wallacette?	Evaluate **Make judgments**
5a. State the reasons why Wallacette might have attacked the "Donkey of Destiny."	5b. Why do you think the author titled her story "Destiny"? Summarize how each character has created his or her own "destiny" and derive ways that these destinies could be altered.	Create **Bring ideas together**

ANALYZE LITERATURE: Character

Compare the characters of Wallacette, Celestine, and Norris. Are these characters round characters or flat characters? Who is dynamic? Who is static? In what ways is there a family resemblance? How is each different? Which of these characters seems most realistic?

EXTEND THE TEXT

Writing Options

Creative Writing Write a **journal entry** for Wallacette that starts with the day her grandmother arrives for a visit and ends with the day after the pageant. Recall the main events of those days but tell them from Wallacette's point of view. How might she view other people's reactions to her? Conclude with ideas about how she will return to school and face the people who laughed at her.

Descriptive Writing Choose one of the characters in this story and write a two- to three-paragraph **character description.** Find text references to the character's physical appearance, as well as personality descriptions given by other characters, if applicable. Describe how the character acts in the story and offer suggestions to what his or her behavior indicates about the character.

Collaborative Learning

Create a Children's Book With a partner or small group, turn the story "Destiny" into a children's picture book. Decide which scenes in the story would work the best to have as illustrations and which parts of the text to use. Change the text to make it more suitable for younger audiences. You may also add a new ending to it. Decide who will draw and who will do the text. When you have your book compiled, read it to a group of younger children. On the title page, make sure to give credit to Louise Erdrich.

Critical Literacy

Deliver a Dramatic Monologue Choose one of the characters other than the narrator. Create a dramatic monologue, or long speech by one character, in which you pretend to be that character talking about the events in "Destiny." Try to stay true to the personality traits that the character exhibits in the story. Practice telling a shortened version of the story until you feel comfortable giving the monologue without notes or without having to look at your notes for most of it.

Go to **www.mirrorsandwindows.com** for more.

READING ASSESSMENT

1. Put these events in the correct sequence:
   ___ Wallacette smashes the skull of the donkey.
   ___ Adele and Celestine argue over the contents of Jell-O salad.
   ___ The narrator's shop burns down.
   ___ Celestine puts nuts and bolts in the Jell-O salad.
   ___ Wallacette "runs over" her grandmother to escape to her room.
   ___ Wallacette tries to hand out candy to young children.

2. Which of these words does *not* accurately describe Wallacette?
   A. brawny
   B. earnest
   C. ominous
   D. spunky
   E. determined

3. What does it mean that Norris is "like a version of his mother, left too long in the water"?
   A. She is flamboyant, but he is pale and mild.
   B. He has more wrinkles than she does.
   C. He is like her, only more concentrated.
   D. He seems cold, whereas she is warm.
   E. None of the above

4. Why does the narrator question whether either Celestine or she "knows enough to say what love is all about"?
   A. They have never been in love.
   B. They believe artificial flowers are a better gift than real ones.
   C. No one has treated them well, either.
   D. Their husbands have been dead a long time.
   E. They never wanted to be married.

5. As used on page 73, the word *earnest* most nearly means
   A. selfish.
   B. extreme.
   C. insincere.
   D. genuine.
   E. preoccupied.

6. Near the end of the story, the author writes, "Celestine, however, kneels down next to her, and then suddenly, fiercely, she lunges and catches the girl full across the chest and neck with a stranglehold." What does the language of the sentence suggest about Celestine and her feelings for Wallacette? How would you describe the relationships between the other characters? How are these relationships expressed?

The Good Deed

A Short Story by Pearl S. Buck

Tears of Autumn

A Short Story by Yoshiko Uchida

BEFORE READING

BUILD BACKGROUND

Cultural Context The selections, **"The Good Deed"** and **"Tears of Autumn,"** explore the experiences of coming to live in a new country, as well as traditional Chinese and Japanese marriage customs. "The Good Deed" tells the story of Mrs. Pan, an elderly immigrant from China, brought to the United States by her son. Mrs. Pan is surprised by many aspects of American life, especially that of young Americans choosing their own mates.

In "Tears of Autumn," Hana Omiya travels to America to marry a man she has never met. In the early 1900s, thousands of women came to the United States as "picture brides" for Japanese men who had come to the United States looking for new opportunities and who wanted Japanese wives.

Reader's Context Describe a good deed you have done or that somebody has done for you. How did it make you feel? Some people say that "one good turn deserves another." Do you believe that good deeds have a ripple effect? Explain your opinion.

USE READING SKILLS

Author's Purpose A writer's **purpose** is his or her aim or goal. An author may write with one or more purposes: to reflect, to entertain, to describe, to enrich, to tell a story, to inform, or to persuade. Use a chart like the one below to identify and summarize each author's purpose.

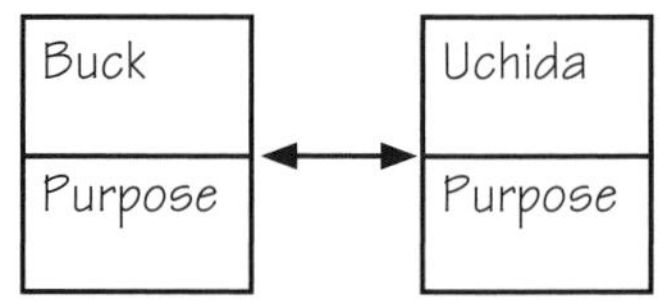

COMPARE LITERATURE: Motivation and Character

Motivation is a force that moves a **character,** or individual that takes part in a story's action, to think, feel, or behave in a certain way. Compare the characters of Mrs. Pan in "The Good Deed" and Hana Omiya in "Tears of Autumn." As you read, note their main traits or characteristics, and their motivations.

- Both Mrs. Pan and Hana have been removed from their countries. Consider how the degree of choice each had in that removal might have affected their opinions of America.
- Both characters make life-changing decisions: What motivates them to make these decisions? Consider the outside forces that affect their choices and determine the motivations of other characters who affect their choices.

MEET THE AUTHORS

BUCK

Pearl S. Buck (1892–1973) Born in West Virginia, Buck spent most of her childhood in China and spoke Chinese before she learned to speak English. After attending college in the United States, she returned to China, where she served as a translator and taught English. Buck received the Pulitzer Prize in 1932 for *The Good Earth.* In 1938, she was awarded the Nobel Prize in Literature, becoming the first American woman, and only the third American, to win that prize.

Yoshiko Uchida (1921–1992) was born in California to Japanese immigrants. She often recounted the experiences of Asian Americans in her writing, including stories about Japanese internment camps, which Uchida experienced firsthand during World War II. Uchida said, "Through my books I hope to give young Asian Americans a sense of their past and to reinforce their self-esteem and self-knowledge."

UCHIDA

THE GOOD DEED

丰功偉绩

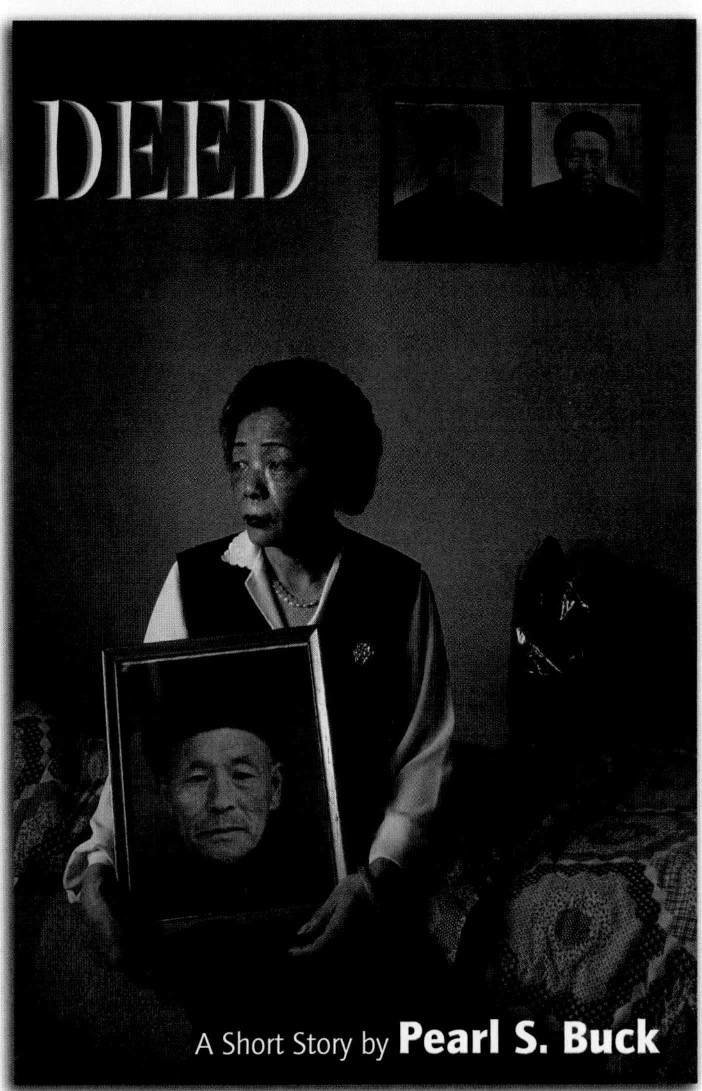

A good deed is a good deed whether one is in China or in America, for the same heaven stretches above all.

Mr. Pan was worried about his mother. He had been worried about her when she was in China, and now he was worried about her in New York, although he had thought that once he got her out of his ancestral village in the province of Szechuen and safely away from the local bullies, who took over when the distant government fell, his anxieties would be ended. To this end he had risked his own life and paid out large sums of sound American money, and he felt that day when he saw her on the wharf, a tiny, dazed little old woman, in a lavender silk coat and black skirt, that now they would live happily together, he and his wife, their four small children and his beloved mother, in the huge safety of the American city. It soon became clear, however, that safety was not enough for old Mrs. Pan. She did not even appreciate the fact, which he repeated again and again, that had she remained in the village, she would now have been dead, because she was the widow of the large land-owner who had been his father and therefore deserved death in the eyes of the rowdies in power.

Old Mrs. Pan listened to this without reply, but her eyes, looking very large in her small withered face, were haunted with homesickness.

"There are many things worse than death, especially at my age," she replied at last, when again her son reminded her of her good fortune in being where she was.

"How is it," she once asked her son, "that the children do not know how to obey?"

He became impassioned when she said this. He struck his breast with his clenched fists and he shouted, "Could I have forgiven myself if I had allowed you to die? Would the ghost of my father have given me rest?"

"I doubt his ghost would have traveled over such a wide sea," she replied. "That man was always afraid of the water."

Yet there was nothing that Mr. Pan and his wife did not try to do for his mother in order to make her happy. They prepared the food that she had once enjoyed, but she was now beyond the age of pleasure in food, and she had no appetite. She touched one dish and another with the ends of her ivory chopsticks,[1] brought with her from her home, and she thanked them prettily. "It is all good," she said, "but the water is not the same as our village water; it tastes of metal and not of earth, and so the flavor is not the same. Please allow the children to eat it."

She was afraid of the children. They went to an American school and they spoke English very well and Chinese very badly, and since she could speak no English, it distressed her to hear her own language maltreated by their careless tongues. For a time she tried to coax them to a few lessons, or she told them stories, to which they were too busy to listen. Instead they preferred to look at the moving pictures in the box that stood on a table in the living room. She gave them up finally and merely watched them contemplatively when they were in the same room with her and was glad when they were gone. She liked her son's wife. She did not understand how there could be a Chinese woman who had never been in China, but such her son's wife was. When her son was away, she could not say to her daughter-in-law, "Do you remember how the willows grew over the gate?" For her son's wife had no such memories. She had grown up here in the city and she did not even hear its noise. At the same time, though she was so foreign, she was very kind to the old lady, and she spoke to her always in a gentle voice, however she might shout at the children, who were often disobedient.

The disobedience of the children was another grief to old Mrs. Pan. She did not understand how it was that four children could all be disobedient, for this meant that they had never been taught to obey their parents and revere their elders, which are the first lessons a child should learn.

"How is it," she once asked her son, "that the children do not know how to obey?"

Mr. Pan had laughed, though uncomfortably. "Here in America the children are not taught as we were in China," he explained.

"But my grandchildren are Chinese nevertheless," old Mrs. Pan said in some astonishment.

"They are always with Americans," Mr. Pan explained. "It is very difficult to teach them."

Old Mrs. Pan did not understand, for Chinese and Americans are different beings, one on the west side of the sea and one on the east, and the sea is always between. Therefore, why should they not continue to live apart

1. **ivory chopsticks.** Thin pair of sticks used as eating utensils, made from elephant tusks

con • tem • pla • tive • ly (kən tem´plə tiv´lē) *adv.,* in a thoughtful or studious way
re • vere (re vir´) *v.,* regard with deep respect and love

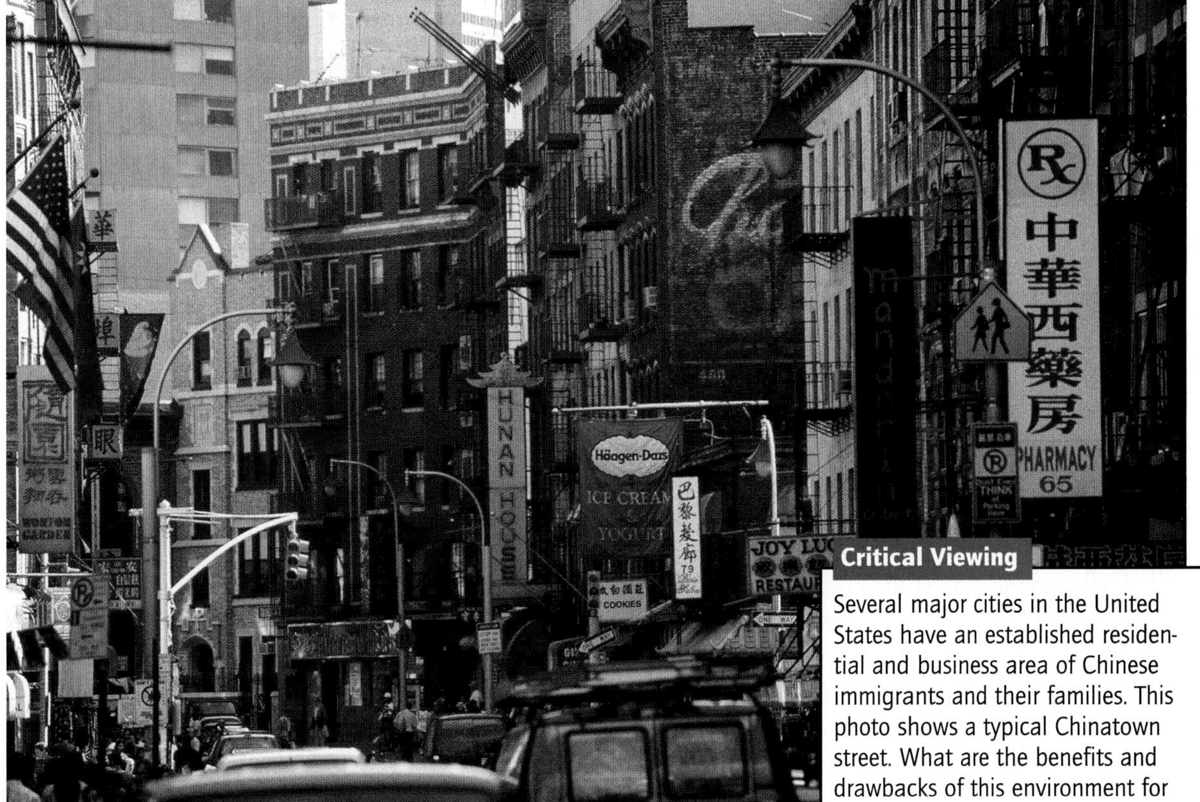

Chinatown, New York.

Critical Viewing

Several major cities in the United States have an established residential and business area of Chinese immigrants and their families. This photo shows a typical Chinatown street. What are the benefits and drawbacks of this environment for Chinese immigrants?

even in the same city? She felt in her heart that the children should be kept at home and taught those things which must be learned, but she said nothing. She felt lonely and there was no one who understood the things she felt and she was quite useless. That was the most difficult thing: She was of no use here. She could not even remember which spout the hot water came from and which brought the cold. Sometimes she turned on one and then the other, until her son's wife came in briskly and said, "Let me, Mother."

So she gave up and sat uselessly all day, not by the window, because the machines and the many people frightened her. She sat where she could not see out; she looked at a few books, and day by day she grew thinner and thinner until Mr. Pan was concerned beyond endurance.

One day he said to his wife, "Sophia, we must do something for my mother. There is no use in saving her from death in our village if she dies here in the city. Do you see how thin her hands are?"

"I have seen," his good young wife said. "But what can we do?"

"Is there no woman you know who can speak Chinese with her?" Mr. Pan asked. "She needs to have someone to whom she can talk about the village and all the things she knows. She cannot talk to you because you can only speak English, and I am too busy making our living to sit and listen to her."

Young Mrs. Pan considered. "I have a friend," she said at last, "a schoolmate whose family compelled her to speak Chinese. Now she is a social worker here in the city. She visits families in Chinatown and this is her work. I will call her up and ask her to spend some time here so that our old mother can be happy enough to eat again."

com • pel (kəm pel´) *v.*, force to do something

"Do so," Mr. Pan said.

That very morning, when Mr. Pan was gone, young Mrs. Pan made the call and found her friend, Lili Yang, and she explained everything to her.

"We are really in very much trouble," she said finally. "His mother is thinner every day, and she is so afraid she will die here. She has made us promise that we will not bury her in foreign soil but will send her coffin back to the ancestral village. We have promised, but can we keep this promise, Lili? Yet I am so afraid, because I think she will die, and Billy will think he must keep his promise and he will try to take the coffin back and then he will be killed. Please help us, Lili."

Lili Yang promised and within a few days she came to the apartment and young Mrs. Pan led her into the inner room, which was old Mrs. Pan's room and where she always sat, wrapped in her satin coat and holding a magazine at whose pictures she did not care to look. She took up that magazine when her daughter-in-law came in, because she did not want to hurt her feelings, but the pictures frightened her. The women looked bold and evil, their bosoms bare, and sometimes they wore only a little silk stuff over their legs and this shocked her. She wondered that her son's wife would put such a magazine into her hands, but she did not ask questions. There would have been no end to them had she once begun, and the ways of foreigners did not interest her. Most of the time she sat silent and still, her head sunk on her breast, dreaming of the village, the big house there where she and her husband had lived together with his parents and where their children were born. She knew that the village had fallen into the hands of their enemies and that strangers lived in the house, but she hoped even so that the land was tilled.[2] All that she remembered was the way it had been when she was a young woman and before the evil had come to pass.

She heard now her daughter-in-law's voice, "Mother, this is a friend. She is Miss Lili Yang. She has come to see you." Old Mrs. Pan remembered her manners. She tried to rise but Lili took her hands and begged her to keep seated.

"You must not rise to one so much younger," she exclaimed.

Old Mrs. Pan lifted her head. "You speak such good Chinese!"

"I was taught by my parents," Lili said. She sat down on a chair near the old lady.

Mrs. Pan leaned forward and put her hand on Lili's knee. "Have you been in our own country?" she asked eagerly.

Lili shook her head. "That is my sorrow. I have not and I want to know about it. I have come here to listen to you tell me."

"Excuse me," young Mrs. Pan said, "I must prepare the dinner for the family."

She slipped away so that the two could be alone and old Mrs. Pan looked after her sadly. "She never wishes to hear; she is always busy."

"You must remember in this country we have no servants," Lili reminded her gently.

"Yes," old Mrs. Pan said, "and why not? I have told my son it is not fitting to have my daughter-in-law cooking and washing in the kitchen. We should have at least three servants: one for me, one for the children and one to clean and cook. At home we had many more but here we have only a few rooms."

Lili did not try to explain. "Everything is different here and let us not talk about it," she said. "Let us talk about your home and the village. I want to know how it looks and what goes on there."

Old Mrs. Pan was delighted. She smoothed the gray satin of her coat as it lay on her knees and she began.

"You must know that our village lies in a wide valley from which the mountains rise as sharply as tiger's teeth."

"Is it so?" Lili said, making a voice of wonder.

2. **tilled.** Plowed and fertilized to be ready for planting

"It is, and the village is not a small one. On the contrary, the walls encircle more than one thousand souls, all of whom are relatives of our family."

"A large family," Lili said.

"It is," old Mrs. Pan said, "and my son's father was the head of it. We lived in a house with seventy rooms. It was in the midst of the village. We had gardens in the courtyards. My own garden contained also a pool wherein are aged goldfish, very fat. I fed them millet and they knew me."

"How amusing." Lili saw with pleasure that the old lady's cheeks were faintly pink and that her large beautiful eyes were beginning to shine and glow. "And how many years did you live there, Ancient One?"

"I went there as a bride. I was seventeen." She looked at Lili, questioning, "How old are you?"

Lili smiled, somewhat ashamed, "I am twenty-seven."

Mrs. Pan was shocked. "Twenty-seven? But my son's wife called you Miss."

"I am not married," Lili confessed.

Mrs. Pan was instantly concerned. "How is this?" she asked. "Are your parents dead?"

"They are dead," Lili said, "but it is not their fault that I am not married." Old Mrs. Pan would not agree to this. She shook her head with decision. "It is the duty of the parents to arrange the marriage of the children. When death approached, they should have attended to this for you. Now who is left to perform the task? Have you brothers?"

"No," Lili said, "I am an only child. But please don't worry yourself, Madame Pan. I am earning my own living and there are many young women like me in this country."

Old Mrs. Pan was dignified about this. "I cannot be responsible for what other persons do, but I must be responsible for my own kind," she declared. "Allow me to know the names of the suitable persons who can arrange your marriage. I will stand in the place of your mother. We are all in a foreign country now and we must keep together and the old must help the young in these important matters."

"It is the duty of the parents to arrange the marriage of the children."

Lili was kind and she knew that Mrs. Pan meant kindness. "Dear Madame Pan," she said. "Marriage in America is very different from marriage in China. Here the young people choose their own mates."

"Why do you not choose, then?" Mrs. Pan said with some spirit.

Lili Yang looked abashed. "Perhaps it would be better for me to say that only the young men choose. It is they who must ask the young women."

"What do the young women do?" Mrs. Pan inquired.

"They wait," Lili confessed.

"And if they are not asked?"

"They continue to wait," Lili said gently.

"How long?" Mrs. Pan demanded.

"As long as they live."

Old Mrs. Pan was profoundly shocked. "Do you tell me that there is no person who arranges such matters when it is necessary?"

"Such an arrangement is not thought of here," Lili told her.

"And they allow their women to remain unmarried?" Mrs. Pan exclaimed. "Are there also sons who do not marry?"

"Here men do not marry unless they wish to do so."

Mrs. Pan was even more shocked. "How can this be?" she asked. "Of course, men will not marry unless they are compelled to do so to provide grandchildren for the family. It is

a • bashed (ə bashd´) *adj.*, embarrassed; upset

CULTURAL CONNECTION

Arranged Marriages Arranged marriages, traditional in East Asian countries as well as in India, are created to join and strengthen two families and to ensure that the bride and groom are well matched. In China and Japan, careful consideration is given to a potential spouse's family history, health, and social status. While unions are usually initiated by the parents or heads of the household, the legwork is often done by a third party. These people, known as go-betweens or matchmakers, transmit correspondence between the two families, arrange meetings, and make sure the proposed couples are well-suited for one another. Part of the process includes an exchanging of letters and the reading of the bride's and groom's birthday by an astrologer. The astrologer makes certain that the union of the two individuals will not bring misfortune to either family. Also, because the bride traditionally leaves her own family to live with her husband's, the bride's parents scrutinize any potential spouse as well as his family. It is not only important that the groom can support and care for the bride, but that his family is able to as well. While not common in the past, today most young people involved in arranged marriages have a say in deciding their potential partners.

necessary to make laws and create customs so that a man who will not marry is denounced as an unfilial[3] son and one who does not fulfill his duty to his ancestors."

"Here the ancestors are forgotten and parents are not important," Lili said unwillingly.

"What a country is this," Mrs. Pan exclaimed. "How can such a country endure?"

Lili did not reply. Old Mrs. Pan had unknowingly touched upon a wound in her heart. No man had ever asked her to marry him. Yet above all else she would like to be married and to have children. She was a good social worker, and the head of the Children's Bureau sometimes told her that he would not know what to do without her and she must never leave them, for then there would be no one to serve the people in Chinatown. She did not wish to leave except to be married, but how could she find a husband? She looked down at her hands, clasped in her lap, and thought that if she had been in her own country, if her father had not come here as a young man and married here, she would have been in China and by now the mother of many children.

Instead what would become of her? She would grow older and older, and twenty-seven was already old, and at last hope must die. She knew several American girls quite well; they liked her, and she knew that they faced the same fate. They, too, were waiting. They tried very hard; they went in summer to hotels and in winter to ski lodges, where men gathered and were at leisure enough to think

3. **unfilial.** Not showing respect to one's parents

de • nounce (dē nouns´) *v.,* condemn strongly as evil or wrong about them, and in confidence they told one another of their efforts. They compared their experiences and they asked anxious questions. "Do you think men like talkative women or quiet ones?" "Do you think men like lipstick or none?" Such questions they asked of one another and who could answer them? If a girl succeeded in winning a proposal from a man, then all the other girls envied her and asked her special questions and immediately she became someone above them all, a successful woman. The job which had once been so valuable then became worthless and it was given away easily and gladly. But how could she explain this to old Mrs. Pan?

Old Mrs. Pan forgot herself for the first time since she had been hurried away from the village...

Meanwhile Mrs. Pan had been studying Lili's face carefully and with thought. This was not a pretty girl. Her face was too flat, and her mouth was large. She looked like a girl from Canton and not from Hangchow or Soochow. But she had nice skin, and her eyes, though small, were kind. She was the sort of girl, Mrs. Pan could see, who would make an excellent wife and a good mother, but certainly she was one for whom a marriage must be arranged. She was a decent, plain, good girl and, left to herself, Mrs. Pan could predict, nothing at all would happen. She would wither away like a dying flower.

Old Mrs. Pan forgot herself for the first time since she had been hurried away from the village without even being allowed to stop and see that the salted cabbage, drying on ropes across the big courtyard, was brought in for the winter. She had been compelled to leave it there and she had often thought of it with regret. She could have brought some with her had she known it was not to be had here. But there it was, and it was only one thing among others that she had left undone. Many people depended upon her and she had left them, because her son compelled her, and she was not used to this idleness that was killing her day by day.

Now as she looked at Lili's kind, ugly face it occurred to her that here there was something she could do. She could find a husband for this good girl, and it would be counted for merit when she went to heaven. A good deed is a good deed, whether one is in China or in America, for the same heaven stretches above all.

She patted Lili's clasped hands. "Do not grieve anymore," she said tenderly. "I will arrange everything."

"I am not grieving," Lili said.

"Of course, you are," Mrs. Pan retorted. "I see you are a true woman, and women grieve when they are not wed so that they can have children. You are grieving for your children."

Lili could not deny it. She would have been ashamed to confess to any other person except this old Chinese lady who might have been her grandmother. She bent her head and bit her lip; she let a tear or two fall upon her hands. Then she nodded. Yes, she grieved in the secret places of her heart, in the darkness of the lonely nights, when she thought of the empty future of her life.

"Do not grieve," old Mrs. Pan was saying, "I will arrange it; I will do it."

It was so comforting a murmur that Lili could not bear it. She said, "I came to comfort you, but it is you who comfort me." Then she got up and went out of the room quickly because she did not want to sob aloud. She was unseen, for young Mrs. Pan had gone to market and the children were at school, and Lili went away telling herself that it was all absurd, that an old woman from the middle of China who could not speak a word of English would not be able to change this American world, even for her.

Old Mrs. Pan could scarcely wait for her son to come home at noon. She declined to join the family at the table, saying that she must speak to her son first. When he came in, he saw at once that she was changed. She held up her head and she spoke to him sharply when he came into the room, as though it was her house and not his in which they now were.

...She had never before heard of a country where no marriages were arranged for the young, leaving to them the most important event of their lives and that at a time when their judgment was still unripe...

"Let the children eat first," she commanded, "I shall need time to talk with you and I am not hungry."

He repressed his inclination to tell her that he was hungry and that he must get back to the office. Something in her look made it impossible for him to be disobedient to her. He went away and gave the children direction and then returned.

"Yes, my mother," he said, seating himself on a small and uncomfortable chair.

Then she related to him with much detail and repetition what had happened that morning; she declared with indignation that she had never before heard of a country where no marriages were arranged for the young, leaving to them the most important event of their lives and that at a time when their judgment was still unripe, and a mistake could bring disaster upon the whole family.

"Your own marriage," she reminded him, "was arranged by your father with great care, our two families knowing each other well. Even though you and my daughter-in-law were distant in this country, yet we met her parents through a suitable go-between, and her uncle here stood in her father's place, and your father's friend in place of your father, and so it was all done according to custom though so far away."

Mr. Pan did not have the heart to tell his mother that he and his wife Sophia had fallen in love first, and then, out of kindness to their elders, had allowed the marriage to be arranged for them as though they were not in love, and as though, indeed, they did not know each other. They were both young people of heart, and although it would have been much easier to be married in the American fashion, they considered their elders.

"What has all this to do with us now, my mother?" he asked.

"This is what is to do," she replied with spirit. "A nice, ugly girl of our own people came here today to see me. She is twenty-seven years old and she is not married. What will become of her?"

"Do you mean Lili Yang?" her son asked.

"I do," she replied. "When I heard that she has no way of being married because, according to the custom of this country, she must wait for a man to ask her—" Old Mrs. Pan broke off and gazed at her son with horrified eyes.

"What now," he asked.

"Suppose the only man who asks is one who is not at all suitable?"

"It is quite possible that it often happens thus," her son said, trying not to laugh.

"Then she has no choice," old Mrs. Pan said indignantly. "She can only remain unmarried or accept one who is unsuitable."

in • dig • nant • ly (in dig´nənt lē) *adv.*, feeling anger as a reaction to ungratefulness

"Here she has no choice," Mr. Pan agreed, "unless she is very pretty, my mother, when several men may ask and then she has choice." It was on the tip of his tongue to tell how at least six young men had proposed to his Sophia, thereby distressing him continually until he was finally chosen, but he thought better of it. Would it not be very hard to explain so much to his old mother, and could she understand?

He doubted it. Nevertheless, he felt it necessary at least to make one point.

"Something must be said for the man also, my mother. Sometimes he asks a girl who will not have him, because she chooses another, and then his sufferings are intense. Unless he wishes to remain unmarried he must ask a second girl, who is not the first one. Here also is some injustice."

Old Mrs. Pan listened to this attentively and then declared, "It is all barbarous.[4] Certainly it is very embarrassing to be compelled to speak of these matters, man and woman, face to face. They should be spared; others should speak for them."

She considered for a few seconds and then she said with fresh indignation, "And what woman can change the appearance her ancestors have given her? Because she is not pretty is she less a woman? Are not her feelings like any woman's; is it not her right to have husband and home and children? It is well-known that men have no wisdom in such matters; they believe that a woman's face is all she has, forgetting that everything else is the same. They gather about the pretty woman, who is surfeited with them,[5] and leave alone the good woman. And I do not know why heaven has created ugly women always good but so it is, whether here or in our own country, but what man is wise enough to know that? Therefore his wife should be chosen for him, so that the family is not burdened with his follies."

Mr. Pan allowed all this to be said and then he inquired, "What is on your mind, my mother?" Old Mrs. Pan leaned toward him and lifted her forefinger. "This is what I command you to do for me, my son. I myself will find a husband for this good girl of our people. She is helpless and alone. But I know no one; I am a stranger and I must depend upon you. In your business there must be young men. Inquire of them and see who stands for them, so that we can arrange a meeting between them and me; I will stand for the girl's mother. I promised it."

Now Mr. Pan laughed heartily. "Oh, my mother!" he cried. "You are too kind but it cannot be done. They would laugh at me, and do you believe that Lili Yang herself would like such an arrangement? I think she would not. She has been in America too long."

Old Mrs. Pan would not yield, however, and in the end he was compelled to promise that he would see what he could do. Upon this promise she consented to eat her meal, and he led her out, her right hand resting upon his left wrist. The children were gone and they had a quiet meal together, and after it she said she felt that she would sleep. This was good news, for she had not slept well since she came, and young Mrs. Pan led her into the bedroom and helped her to lie down and placed a thin quilt over her.

When young Mrs. Pan went back to the small dining room where her husband waited to tell her what his mother had said, she listened thoughtfully.

"It is absurd," her husband said, "but what shall we do to satisfy my mother? She sees it as a good deed if she can find a husband for Lili Yang." Here his wife surprised him. "I can see some good in it myself," she declared. "I have often felt for Lili. It is a problem, and our mother is right to see it as such. It is not only Lili—it is a problem here for all young women, especially if they are not pretty." She looked <u>quizzically</u>

---

4. **barbarous.** Uncivilized
5. **is surfeited with them.** Has had enough of them

quiz • zi • cal • ly (kwiz´i kə lē) *adv.*, in a perplexed manner at her husband for a moment and then said, "I too used to worry when I was very young, lest I should not find a husband for myself. It is a great burden for a young woman. It would be nice to have someone else arrange the matter."

"Remember," he told her, "how often in the old country the wrong men are arranged for and how often the young men leave home because they do not like the wives their parents choose for them."

"Well, so do they here," she said pertly. "Divorce, divorce, divorce!"

"Come, come," he told her. "It is not so bad."

"It is very bad for women," she insisted. "When there is divorce here, then she is thrown out of the family. The ties are broken. But in the old country, it is the man who leaves home and the woman stays on, for she is still the daughter-in-law and her children will belong to the family, and however far away the man wants to go, she has her place and she is safe." Mr. Pan looked at his watch. "It is late and I must go to the office."

"Oh, your office," young Mrs. Pan said in an uppish[6] voice, "what would you do without it?"

They did not know it but their voices roused old Mrs. Pan in the bedroom, and she opened her eyes. She could not understand what they said for they spoke in English, but she understood that there was an argument. She sat up on the bed to listen, then she heard the door slam and she knew her son was gone. She was about to lie down again when it occurred to her that it would be interesting to look out of the window to the street and see what young men there were coming to and fro. One did not choose men from the street, of course, but still she could see what their looks were.

She got up and tidied her hair and tottered on her small feet over to the window and opening the curtains a little she gazed into the street really for the first time since she came. She was pleased to see many Chinese men, some of them young. It was still not late, and they loitered in the sunshine before going back to work, talking and laughing and looking happy. It was interesting to her to watch them, keeping in mind Lili Yang and thinking to herself that it might be this one or that one, although still one did not choose men from the street. She stood so long that at last she became tired and she pulled a small chair to the window and kept looking through the parted curtain.

Here her daughter-in-law saw her a little later, when she opened the door to see if her mother-in-law was awake, but she did not speak. She looked at the little satin-clad figure, and went away again, wondering why it was that the old lady found it pleasant today to look out of the window when every other day she had refused the same pleasure.

It became a pastime for old Mrs. Pan to look out of the window every day from then on. Gradually she came to know some of the young men, not by name but by their faces and by the way they walked by her window, never, of course looking up at her, until one day a certain young man did look up and smile. It was a warm day, and she had asked that the window be opened, which until now she had not allowed, for fear she might be assailed by the foreign winds and made ill. Today, however, was near to summer, she felt the room airless and she longed for freshness.

After this the young man habitually smiled when he passed or nodded his head. She was too old to have it mean anything but courtesy and so bit by bit she allowed herself to make a gesture of her hand in return. It was evident that he belonged in a china shop across the narrow street. She watched him go in and come out; she watched him stand at the door in his shirt sleeves on a fine day and talk and laugh, showing, as she observed, strong white teeth set off by two gold ones. Evidently he made money. She did not believe he was married, for she saw an old man who must be his father, who smoked a

6. **uppish.** Haughty or arrogant

as • sail (ə sāl´) *v.,* attack physically

Chinese wedding guestbook, invitation, and gift envelopes.

water pipe, and now and then an elderly woman, perhaps his mother, and a younger brother, but there was no young woman.

She began after some weeks of watching to fix upon this young man as a husband for Lili. But who could be the go-between except her own son?

She confided her plans one night to him, and, as always, he listened to her with courtesy and concealed amusement. "But the young man, my mother, is the son of Mr. Lim, who is the richest man on our street."

"That is nothing against him," she declared.

"No, but he will not submit to an arrangement, my mother. He is a college graduate. He is only spending the summer at home in the shop to help his father."

"Lili Yang has also been to school."

"I know, my mother, but, you see, the young man will want to choose his own wife, and it will not be someone who looks like Lili Yang. It will be someone who—"

He broke off and made a gesture which suggested curled hair, a fine figure and an air. Mrs. Pan watched him with disgust. "You are like all these other men, though you are my son," she said and dismissed him sternly.

Nevertheless, she thought over what he had said when she went back to the window. The young man was standing on the street picking his fine teeth and laughing at friends who passed, the sun shining on his glistening black hair. It was true he did not look at all obedient; it was perhaps true that he was no more wise than other men and so saw only what a girl's face was. She wished that she could speak to him, but that, of course, was impossible. Unless—

She drew in a long breath. Unless she went downstairs and out into that street and crossed it and entered the shop, pretending that she came to buy something! If she did this, she could speak to him. But what would she say, and who would help her cross the street? She did not want to tell her son or her son's wife, for they would suspect her and laugh. They teased her often even now about her purpose, and Lili was so embarrassed by their laughter that she did not want to come anymore.

Old Mrs. Pan reflected on the difficulty of her position as a lady in a barbarous and strange country. Then she thought of her eldest grandson, Johnnie. On Saturday, when her son was at his office and her son's wife was at the market, she would coax Johnnie to lead her across the street to the china shop; she would pay him some money, and in the shop she would say she was looking for two bowls to match some that had been broken. It would be an expedition, but she might speak to the young man and tell him—what should she tell him? That must first be planned.

This was only Thursday and she had only two days to prepare. She was very restless during those two days, and she could not eat. Mr. Pan spoke of a doctor whom she indignantly refused to see, because he was a man and also because she was not ill. But Saturday came at last and everything came about as she planned. Her son went away, and then her son's wife, and she crept downstairs with much effort to the sidewalk where her grandson was playing marbles and beckoned him to her. The child was terrified to see her there and came at once, and she pressed a coin into his palm and pointed across the street with her cane.

"Lead me there," she commanded and, shutting her eyes tightly, she put her hand on his shoulder and allowed him to lead her to the shop. Then to her dismay he left her and ran back to play and she stood wavering on the threshold, feeling dizzy, and the young man saw her and came hurrying toward her. To her joy he spoke good Chinese, and the words fell sweetly upon her old ears.

"Ancient One, Ancient One," he chided her kindly. "Come in and sit down. It is too much for you."

He led her inside the cool, dark shop and she sat down on a bamboo chair.

"I came to look for two bowls," she said faintly.

"Tell me the pattern and I will get them for you," he said. "Are they blue willow pattern or the thousand flowers?"

"Thousand flowers," she said in the same faint voice, "but I do not wish to disturb you."

"I am here to be disturbed," he replied with the utmost courtesy.

He brought out some bowls and set them on a small table before her and she fell to talking with him. He was very pleasant; his rather large face was shining with kindness and he laughed easily. Now that she saw him close, she was glad to notice that he was not too handsome; his nose and mouth were big, and he had big hands and feet.

"You look like a countryman," she said. "Where is your ancestral home?"

"It is in the province of Shantung," he replied, "and there are not many of us here."

"That explains why you are so tall," she said. "These people from Canton are small. We of Szechuen are also big and our language is yours. I cannot understand the people of Canton."

From this they fell to talking of their own country, which he had never seen, and she told him about the village and how her son's father had left it many years ago to do business here in this foreign country and how he had sent for their son and then how she had been compelled to flee because the country was in fragments and torn between many leaders. When she had told this much, she found herself telling him how difficult it was to live here and how strange the city was to her and how she would never have looked out of the window had it not been for the sake of Lili Yang.

"Who is Lili Yang?" he asked.

Old Mrs. Pan did not answer him directly.

That would not have been suitable. One does not speak of a reputable young woman to any man, not even one as good as this one. Instead she began a long speech about the virtues of young women who were not pretty, and how beauty in a woman made virtue unlikely, and how a woman not beautiful was always grateful to her husband and did not consider that she had done him a favor by the marriage, but rather that it was he who conferred the favor, so that she served him far better than she could have done were she beautiful.

To all this the young man listened, his small eyes twinkling with laughter.

"I take it that this Lili Yang is not beautiful," he said.

Old Mrs. Pan looked astonished. "I did not say so," she replied with spirit. "I will not say she is beautiful and I will not say she is ugly. What is beautiful to one is not so to another. Suppose you see her sometime for yourself, and then we will discuss it."

"Discuss what?" he demanded.

"Whether she is beautiful."

Suddenly she felt that she had come to a point and that she had better go home. It was enough for the first visit. She chose two bowls and paid for them and while he wrapped them up she waited in silence, for to say too much is worse than to say too little.

When the bowls were wrapped, the young man said courteously, "Let me lead you across the street, Ancient One." So, putting her right hand on his left wrist, she let him lead her across and this time she did not shut her eyes, and she came home again feeling that she had been a long way and had accomplished much.

One does not speak of a reputable young woman to any man, not even one as good as this one.

When her daughter-in-law came home she said quite easily, "I went across the street and bought these two bowls."

Young Mrs. Pan opened her eyes wide. "My mother, how could you go alone?"

"I did not go alone," old Mrs. Pan said tranquilly. "My grandson led me across and young Mr. Lim brought me back."

Each had spoken in her own language with helpful gestures.

Young Mrs. Pan was astonished and she said no more until her husband came home, when she told him. He laughed a great deal and said, "Do not interfere with our old one. She is enjoying herself. It is good for her."

But all the time he knew what his mother was doing and he joined in it without her knowledge. That is to say, he telephoned the same afternoon from his office to Miss Lili Yang, and when she answered, he said, "Please come and see my old mother again. She asks after you every day. Your visit did her much good." Lili Yang promised, not for today but for a week hence, and when Mr. Pan went home he told his mother carelessly, as though it were nothing, that Lili Yang had called him up to say she was coming again next week.

con • fer (kən fʉr´) *v.*, grant; bestow

Old Mrs. Pan heard this with secret excitement. She had not gone out again, but every day young Mr. Lim nodded to her and smiled, and once he sent her a small gift of fresh ginger root. She made up her mind slowly but she made it up well. When Lili Yang came again, she would ask her to take her to the china shop, pretending that she wanted to buy something, and she would introduce the two to each other; that much she would do. It was too much, but, after all, these were modern times, and this was a barbarous country, where it did not matter greatly whether the old customs were kept or not. The important thing was to find a husband for Lili, who was already twenty-seven years old.

So it all came about, and when Lili walked into her room the next week, while the fine weather still held, old Mrs. Pan greeted her with smiles. She seized Lili's small hand and noticed that the hand was very soft and pretty, as the hands of most plain-faced girls are, the gods being kind to such women and giving them pretty bodies when they see that ancestors have not bestowed pretty faces.

"Do not take off your foreign hat," she told Lili. "I wish to go across the street to that shop and buy some dishes as a gift for my son's wife. She is very kind to me."

Lili Yang was pleased to see the old lady so changed and cheerful and in all innocence she agreed and they went across the street and into the shop. Today there were customers, and old Mr. Lim was there too, as well as his son. He was a tall, withered man, and he wore a small beard under his chin. When he saw old Mrs. Pan he stopped what he was doing and brought her a chair to sit upon while she waited. As soon as his customer was gone, he introduced himself, saying that he knew her son.

"My son has told me of your honored visit last week," he said. "Please come inside and have some tea. I will have my son bring the dishes, and you can look at them in quiet. It is too noisy here." She accepted his courtesy, and in a few minutes young Mr. Lim came back to the inner room with the dishes while a servant brought tea.

Old Mrs. Pan did not introduce Lili Yang, for it was not well to embarrass a woman, but young Mr. Lim boldly introduced himself, in English.

"Are you Miss Lili Yang?" he asked. "I am James Lim."

"How did you know my name?" Lili asked, astonished.

"I have met you before, not face to face, but through Mrs. Pan," he said, his small eyes twinkling. "She has told me more about you than she knows."

Lili blushed. "Mrs. Pan is so old-fashioned," she murmured. "You must not believe her."

"I shall only believe what I see for myself," he said gallantly. He looked at her frankly and Lili kept blushing. Old Mrs. Pan had not done her justice, he thought. The young woman had a nice, round face, the sort of face he liked. She was shy, and he liked that also. It was something new.

Meanwhile old Mrs. Pan watched all this with amazement. So this was the way it was: The young man began speaking immediately, and the young woman blushed. She wished that she knew what they were saying but perhaps it was better that she did not know.

She turned to old Mr. Lim, who was sitting across the square table sipping tea. At least here she could do her duty. "I hear your son is not married," she said in a tentative way.

"Not yet," Mr. Lim said. "He wants first to finish learning how to be a Western doctor."

"How old is he?" Mrs. Pan inquired.

"He is twenty-eight. It is very old but he did not make up his mind for some years, and the learning is long."

The young woman had a nice, round face, the sort of face he liked.

"Miss Lili Yang is twenty-seven," Mrs. Pan said in the same tentative voice.

The young people were still talking in English and not listening to them. Lili was telling James Lim about her work and about old Mrs. Pan. She was not blushing anymore; she had forgotten, it seemed, that he was a young man and she a young woman. Suddenly she stopped and blushed again. A woman was supposed to let a man talk about himself, not about her.

"Tell me about your work," she said. "I wanted to be a doctor, too, but it cost too much."

"I can't tell you here," he said. "There are customers waiting in the shop and it will take a long time. Let me come to see you, may I? I could come on Sunday when the shop is closed. Or we could take a ride on one of the riverboats. Will you? The weather is so fine."

"I have never been on a riverboat," she said. "It would be delightful."

She forgot her work and remembered that he was a young man and that she was a young woman. She liked his big face and the way his black hair fell back from his forehead and she knew that a day on the river could be a day in heaven.

The customers were getting impatient. They began to call out and he got up. "Next

ten • ta • tive (ten´tə tiv) *adj.*, hesitant

Sunday," he said in a low voice. "Let's start early. I'll be at the wharf at nine o'clock."

"We do not know each other," she said, reluctant and yet eager. Would he think she was too eager?

He laughed. "You see my respectable father, and I know old Mrs. Pan very well. Let them guarantee us." He hurried away, and old Mrs. Pan said immediately to Lili, "I have chosen these four dishes. Please take them and have them wrapped. Then we will go home."

Lili obeyed, and when she was gone, old Mrs. Pan leaned toward old Mr. Lim.

"I wanted to get her out of the way," she said in a low and important voice. "Now, while she is gone, what do you say? Shall we arrange a match? We do not need a go-between. I stand as her mother, let us say, and you are his father. We must have their horoscopes[7] read, of course, but just between us, it looks as though it is suitable, does it not?" Mr. Lim wagged his head. "If you recommend her, Honorable Old Lady, why not?" Why not, indeed? After all, things were not so different here, after all.

"What day is convenient for you?" she asked.

"Shall we say Sunday?" old Mr. Lim suggested.

"Why not?" she replied. "All days are good, when one performs a good deed, and what is better than to arrange a marriage?"

"Nothing is better," old Mr. Lim agreed. "Of all good deeds under heaven, it is the best." They fell silent, both pleased with themselves, while they waited. ❖

7. **horoscopes.** Explanations about the effect on individuals of the positions of stars and planets at a particular point in time—in Chinese astrology, the most important time is conception—in this case, the time when Lili's or James's mother first began her pregnancy.

"That was the most difficult thing: She was of no use here." What does it mean to be a member of a community? Must people feel useful in order to feel accepted in a group?

REFER TO TEXT ▶▶▶▶▶	▶ REASON WITH TEXT	
1a. State the reason why Mr. Pan brought his mother to the United States.	1b. Give examples of why Mr. Pan would question his decision to remove his mother from danger.	**Understand** **Find meaning**
2a. How does Mrs. Pan react upon hearing that Lili is not married?	2b. Knowing what you do about Mrs. Pan, what is her main reason for helping Lili find a husband?	**Apply** **Use information**
3a. Recall how Lili reacts to James when they first meet. What does he already know about her?	3b. Analyze how the courtship between Lili and James is a blending of Chinese and American customs as described in the story.	**Analyze** **Take things apart**
4a. List the good deeds that are performed in the selection.	4b. Decide which deed you consider the most generous. Which do you consider the least generous? Explain your responses.	**Evaluate** **Make judgments**
5a. Identify what an acceptable marriage proposal requires, according to Mrs. Pan.	5b. What would Mrs. Pan think of personal ads? Internet match sites? speed dating? Explain your reasoning.	**Create** **Bring ideas together**

A Short Story by **Yoshiko Uchida**

Tomorrow, at last, the ship would dock in San Francisco and she would meet face to face the man she was soon to marry.

Hana Omiya stood at the railing of the small ship that shuddered toward America in a turbulent November sea. She shivered as she pulled the folds of her silk kimono close to her throat and tightened the wool shawl about her shoulders.

She was thin and small, her dark eyes shadowed in her pale face, her black hair piled high in a pompadour that seemed too heavy for so slight a woman. She clung to the moist rail and breathed the damp salt air deep into her lungs. Her body seemed leaden and lifeless, as though it were simply the vehicle transporting her soul to a strange new life, and she longed with child-like intensity to be home again in Oka Village.

She longed to see the bright persimmon dotting the barren trees beside the thatched roofs, to see the fields of golden rice stretching to the mountains where only last fall she had gathered plump white mushrooms, and to see once more the maple trees lacing their flaming colors through the green pine. If only she could see a familiar face, eat a meal without retching, walk on solid ground, and stretch out at night on a tatami[1] mat instead of in a hard narrow bunk. She thought now of seeking the warm shelter of her bunk but could not bear to face the relentless smell of fish that penetrated the lower decks.

Why did I ever leave Japan? she wondered bitterly. Why did I ever listen to my uncle? And yet she knew it was she herself who had begun the chain of events that placed her on this heaving ship. It was she who had first planted in her uncle the thought that she would make a good wife for Taro the lonely man who had gone to America to make his home in Oakland, California.

It all began one day when her uncle had come to visit her mother.

"I must find a nice young bride," he had said, startling Hana with this blunt talk of marriage in her presence. She blushed and was ready to leave the room when her uncle quickly added, "My good friend Takeda has a son in America. I must find someone willing to travel to that far land."

This last remark was intended to indicate to Hana and her mother that he didn't consider this a suitable prospect for Hana, who was the youngest daughter of what once had been a fine family. Her father, until his death fifteen years ago, had been the largest landholder of the village and one of its last samurai.[2] They had once had many servants and field hands, but now all that was changed. Their money was gone. Hana's three older sisters had made good marriages, and the eldest remained in their home with her husband to carry on the Omiya name and <u>perpetuate</u> the homestead. Her other sisters had married merchants in Osaka and Nagoya and were living comfortably.

Now that Hana was twenty-one, finding a proper husband for her had taken on an urgency that produced an embarrassing secretive air over the entire matter. Usually, her mother didn't speak of it until they were lying side by side on their quilts at night. Then, under the protective cover of darkness, she would suggest one name and then another, hoping that Hana would indicate an interest in one of them.

Her uncle spoke freely of Taro Takeda only because he was so sure Hana would never consider him. "He is a <u>conscientious</u>, hardworking man who has been in the United States for almost ten years. He is thirty-one, operates a small shop, and rents some rooms above the shop where he lives." Her uncle rubbed his chin thoughtfully. "He could provide well for a wife," he added.

"Ah," Hana's mother said softly.

"You say he is successful in this business?" Hana's sister inquired.

"His father tells me he sells many things in his shop—clothing, stockings, needles, thread, and buttons—such things as that. He also sells bean paste, pickled radish, bean cake, and soy sauce. A wife of his, would not go cold or hungry."

They all nodded, each of them picturing this merchant in varying degrees of success and <u>affluence</u>. There were many Japanese emigrating to America these days, and Hana had heard of the picture brides who went with nothing more than an exchange of photographs to bind them to a strange man.

"Taro San is lonely," her uncle continued. "I want to find for him a fine young woman who is strong and brave enough to cross the ocean alone."

"It would certainly be a different kind of life," Hana's sister ventured, and for a moment, Hana thought she glimpsed a longing ordinarily concealed behind her quiet, obedient face. In that same instant, Hana knew she wanted more for herself than her sisters had in their proper, arranged, and loveless marriages. She wanted to escape the smothering strictures of life in her

1. **tatami.** A floor mat made of reeds
2. **samurai.** A Japanese warrior-lord

per • pet • u • ate (pər pe´ chü āt) *v.*, to continue
con • sci • en • tious (kän' shē en´ shəs) *adj.*, careful; thoughtfully upright
af • flu • ence (a´ flü əns) *n.*, wealth

village. She certainly was not going to marry a farmer and spend her life working beside him planting, weeding, and harvesting in the rice paddies until her back became bent from too many years of stooping and her skin was turned to brown leather by the sun and wind. Neither did she particularly relish the idea of marrying a merchant in a big city as her two sisters had done. Since her mother objected to her going to Tokyo to seek employment as a teacher, perhaps she would consent to a flight to America for what seemed a proper and respectable marriage.

Almost before she realized what she was doing, she spoke to her uncle. "Oji San, perhaps I should go to America to make this lonely man a good wife."

"You, Hana Chan?" Her uncle observed her with startled curiosity. "You would go all alone to a foreign land so far away from your mother and family?"

"I would not allow it." Her mother spoke fiercely. Hana was her youngest and she had lavished upon her the attention and latitude that often befall the last child. How could she permit her to travel so far, even to marry the son of Takeda who was known to her brother?

But now, a notion that had seemed quite impossible a moment before was lodged in his receptive mind, and Hana's uncle grasped it with the pleasure that comes from an unexpected discovery.

"You know," he said looking at Hana, "it might be a very good life in America."

Hana felt a faint fluttering in her heart. Perhaps this lonely man in America was her means of escaping both the village and the encirclement of her family.

Her uncle spoke with increasing enthusiasm of sending Hana to become Taro's wife. And the husband of Hana's sister, who was head of their household, spoke with equal eagerness. Although he never said so, Hana guessed he would be pleased to be rid of her, the spirited younger sister who stirred up his placid life with what he considered radical ideas about

life and the role of women. He often claimed that Hana had too much schooling for a girl. She had graduated from Women's High School in Kyoto, which gave her five more years of schooling than her older sister.

"It has addled her brain—all that learning from those books," he said when he tired of arguing with Hana.

A man's word carried much weight for Hana's mother. Pressed by the two men, she consulted her other daughters and their husbands. She discussed the matter carefully with her brother and asked the village priest. Finally, she agreed to an exchange of family histories and an investigation was begun into Taro Takeda's family, his education, and his health, so they would be assured there was no insanity or tuberculosis or police records concealed in his family's past. Soon Hana's uncle was devoting his energies entirely

lat • i • tude (la´ tə tüd) *n.*, freedom of action and choice

to serving as go-between for Hana's mother and Taro Takeda's father.

When at last an agreement to the marriage was almost reached, Taro wrote his first letter to Hana. It was brief and proper and gave no more clue to his character than the stiff formal portrait taken at his graduation from middle school. Hana's uncle had given her the picture with apologies from his parents, because it was the only photo they had of him and it was not a flattering likeness.

Hana hid the letter and photograph in the sleeve of her kimono and took them to the outhouse to study in private. Squinting in the dim light and trying to ignore the foul odor, she read and reread Taro's letter, trying to find the real man somewhere in the sparse unbending prose.

By the time he sent her money for her steamship tickets, she had received ten more letters, but none revealed much more of the man than the first. In none did he disclose his loneliness or his need, but Hana understood this. In fact, she would have recoiled from a man who bared his intimate thoughts to her so soon. After all, they would have a lifetime together to get to know one another.

So it was that Hana had left her family and sailed alone to America with a small hope trembling inside of her. Tomorrow at last, the ship would dock in San Francisco and she would meet face to face the man she was soon to marry. Hana was overcome with excitement at the thought of being in America, and terrified of the meeting about to take place. What would she say to Taro Takeda when they first met, and for all the days and years after?

Hana wondered about the flat above the shop. Perhaps it would be luxuriously furnished with the finest of brocades and lacquers, and perhaps there would be a servant, although he had not mentioned it. She worried whether she would be able to manage on the meager English she had learned at Women's High School. The overwhelming anxiety for the day to come and the violent rolling of the ship were more than Hana could bear. Shuddering in the face of the wind, she leaned over the railing and became violently and wretchedly ill.

By five the next morning, Hana was up and dressed in her finest purple silk kimono and coat. She could not eat the bean soup and rice that appeared for breakfast and took only a few bites of the yellow pickled radish. Her bags, which had scarcely been touched since she boarded the ship, were easily packed, for all they contained were her kimonos and some of her favorite books. The large willow basket, tightly secured by a rope, remained under the bunk, untouched since her uncle had placed it there.

She had not befriended the other women in her cabin, for they had lain in their bunks for most of the voyage, too sick to be company to anyone. Each morning Hana had fled the closeness of the sleeping quarters and spent most of the day huddled in a corner of the deck, listening to the lonely songs of some Russians also traveling to an alien land.

As the ship approached land, Hana hurried up to the deck to look out at the gray expanse of ocean and sky, eager for a first glimpse of her new homeland.

"We won't be docking until almost noon," one of the deck-hands told her.

Hana nodded, "I can wait," she answered, but the last hours seemed the longest.

sparse (spärs) *adj.*, thin; meager

When she set foot on American soil at last, it was not in the city of San Francisco as she had expected, but on Angel Island, where all third-class passengers were taken. She spent two miserable days and nights waiting, as the immigrants were questioned by officials, examined for trachoma and tuberculosis, and tested for hookworm by a woman who collected their stools on tin pie plates. Hana was relieved she could produce her own, not having to borrow a little from someone else, as some of the women had to do. It was a bewildering, degrading beginning, and Hana was sick with anxiety, wondering if she would ever be released.

History Connection

Angel Island Known as the "Ellis Island of the West," Angel Island, off the coast of San Francisco, served from 1910 to 1940 as the first stop for immigrants who crossed the Pacific from Asia, Australia, and South America. During that time, immigration was restricted for citizens of certain countries, so Angel Island became the place where immigrants would wait for weeks, months, or even years while the Bureau of Immigration processed the applications. The processes were often humiliating and laborious: checking for parasites and a variety of diseases, and closely checking that the immigrant's story exactly matched that of his or her relatives or sponsors already in America. Failing an exam meant deportation. Conditions were harsh: The food was bad and the overcrowded buildings considered firetraps. Because of the Chinese Exclusion Act of 1882, Chinese citizens had an especially hard time gaining entry to the United States and, thus, often waited the longest.

On the third day, a Japanese messenger from San Francisco appeared with a letter for her from Taro. He had written it the day of her arrival, but it had not reached her for two days.

Taro welcomed her to America, and told her that the bearer of the letter would inform Taro when she was to be released so he could be at the pier to meet her.

The letter eased her anxiety for a while, but as soon as she was released and boarded the launch for San Francisco, new fears rose up to smother her with a feeling almost of dread.

The early morning mist had become a light chilling rain, and on the pier black umbrellas bobbed here and there, making the task of recognition even harder. Hana searched desperately for a face that resembled the photo she had studied so long and hard. Suppose he hadn't come. What would she do then?

Hana took a deep breath, lifted her head and walked slowly from the launch. The moment she was on the pier, a man in a black coat, wearing a derby and carrying an umbrella, came quickly to her side. He was of slight build, not much taller than she, and his face was sallow and pale. He bowed stiffly and murmured, "You have had a long trip, Miss Omiya. I hope you are well."

Hana caught her breath. "You are Takeda San?" she asked.

He removed his hat and Hana was further startled to see that he was already turning bald.

"You are Takeda San?" she asked again. He looked older than thirty-one.

"I am afraid I no longer resemble the early photo my parents gave you. I am sorry."

Hana had not meant to begin like this. It was not going well.

"No, no," she said quickly. "It is just that I...that is, I am terribly nervous..." Hana stopped abruptly, too flustered to go on.

"I understand," Taro said gently. "You will feel better when you meet my friends and have some tea. Mr. and Mrs. Toda are expecting you in Oakland. You will be staying

sal • low (sa´ lō) *adj.*, of a grayish yellow color

with them until..." He couldn't bring himself to mention the marriage just yet and Hana was grateful he hadn't.

He quickly made arrangements to have her baggage sent to Oakland then led her carefully along the rain-slick pier toward the streetcar that would take them to the ferry.

Hana shuddered at the sight of another boat, and as they climbed to its upper deck she felt a queasy tightening of her stomach.

"I hope it will not rock too much," she said anxiously. "Is it many hours to your city?"

Taro laughed for the first time since their meeting, revealing the gold fillings of his teeth. "Oakland is just across the bay," he explained. "We will be there in twenty minutes."

Raising a hand to cover her mouth, Hana laughed with him and suddenly felt better. I am in America now, she thought, and this is the man I came to marry. Then she sat down carefully beside Taro, so no part of their clothing touched. ❖

"Nothing ventured, nothing gained" is a common saying. How might people weigh risks and make choices when one option is relatively unknown? Is risk-taking a sign of bravery or recklessness?

REFER TO TEXT	REASON WITH TEXT	
1a. Identify the reason why Hana is traveling to America.	1b. Explain the ways that Hana feels she doesn't quite fit into her life at home.	**Understand** **Find meaning**
2a. What does Hana wonder about the flat above the shop?	2b. Predict how the reality of Takeda's life probably differs from what Hana and her family imagine.	**Apply** **Use information**
3a. State why Hana hasn't made friends on the ship.	3b. How does Hana feel about her trip? Point out details that reveal her feelings. How does the title reflect this?	**Analyze** **Take things apart**
4a. Describe how Hana envisions her life if she stays in Japan.	4b. Evaluate Hana's decision to come to America. Was her thinking rash or rational?	**Evaluate** **Make judgments**
5a. Name the area where Hana will be staying in Oakland.	5b. Predict how you think Hana will feel about her journey once she has been in America a few days. What might she find comforting in her new home? What might she find upsetting?	**Create** **Bring ideas together**

COMPARE LITERATURE: Motivation and Character

Do Mrs. Pan and Hana Omiya come to the United States for the same reason? Is what motivates Lili to accept Mrs. Pan's help in "The Good Deed" the same as Hana's motivation to volunteer for the marriage to Taro Takeda? How do you think each of the women view marriage? Explain.

AFTER READING

EXTEND THE TEXT

Writing Options

Creative Writing Lili and James plan to meet for a riverboat ride on Sunday. Hana and Taro will eventually have a marriage ceremony and move in together. Choose one of these events and write a one-page **narrative.** Choose a narrator, the actions that take place, and create descriptive details. Think about what you know about the couple's backgrounds and interests. Also consider the traits of each character. How would each react during the event?

Expository Writing You are creating a study guide about the pairing of "The Good Deed" and "Tears of Autumn" for other students. Write a one- to two-paragraph **plot analysis** of each story that identifies the main conflict and describes how it is introduced, developed, and resolved. Then explain what a reader can gain from reading the two stories together. What perspective does each cast on the other?

Lifelong Learning

Research Immigration With your classmates, create a display about the immigrant experience in America. Possible topics for research include the voyage over, quarantine and health inspections, picture brides, discrimination and prejudice, changing immigration laws, or immigration stations, such as Ellis Island and Angel Island. As a class, choose which topics you'll cover and how you will represent your findings. Some options include a time line, posters, illustrations, a video, maps, and replicas of artifacts.

Critical Literacy

Discuss Arranged Marriage Mrs. Pan believes in arranged marriages and is horrified by the idea of men and women approaching each other to find a potential spouse. Like Mrs. Pan, Hana Omiya sees the benefits of arranged marriages and agrees to marry a man she has never met. Marriages are still arranged today in some cultures. Consider the benefits and drawbacks of arranged and unarranged marriages. You may want to do some research on each custom. Then discuss in small groups the pros and cons and explain how you would prefer to find a spouse.

Go to **www.mirrorsandwindows.com** for more.

READING ASSESSMENT

1. What motivates Mrs. Pan to overcome her fear and leave the apartment building and cross the street?
   A. She wants to test her grandson and see if he will help her across.
   B. She is encouraged by the smiles and waves of the man from the china store and wants to speak with him.
   C. She has a strong desire to help Lili find a husband.
   D. She hopes that she will find replacements for the bowls she broke.
   E. It is a beautiful day, and she is tired of being inside the apartment all the time.

2. Why does Hana suggest herself as a match for Taro Takeda in "Tears of Autumn"?
   A. There was no one else in the village worth marrying.
   B. She wants to spite her sisters.
   C. She wants to improve her English.
   D. She likes the look of his photo.
   E. She wants to escape village life and family pressures.

3. Why does Uchida title her story "Tears of Autumn"?
   A. Hana has an uncomfortable voyage, misses her homeland, and is afraid of her future.
   B. The Omiya family misses Hana and wishes she hadn't left.
   C. Hana is very disappointed to see how her future husband looks.
   D. Hana is delighted that her life will start anew in America.
   E. Taro Takeda is overjoyed that someone will end his loneliness.

4. On page 92 of "The Good Deed," the term *assailed* most nearly means
   A. shielded.
   B. assaulted.
   C. abducted.
   D. approached.
   E. released.

5. According to the characters of both stories, what are the benefits of arranged marriage? Was Mrs. Pan's son justified in pretending his marriage had been arranged? Explain.

Understanding Setting

SETTING

Readers have the opportunity to experience the world through the pages of short stories. The stories in this unit take you from nineteenth-century Paris in "The Necklace" (page 143) to twentieth-century Northern Ireland in "The Sniper" (page 165). These selections derive their immediacy and color through the details of the settings.

The **setting** of a story is the time and place in which its action occurs. Setting can include the following: geographical location, time period, socio-economic conditions, and a specific room or building. In the story "American History" (page 121), the geographical location of the story is Paterson, New Jersey. The time period is very specific—November 22, 1963. The characters in the story are mostly working-class Puerto-Rican immigrants. The places described include Elena's tenement, her school, and her friend's house. The details create a lifelike impression that helps you envision Elena's circumstances.

> In August, Eugene and his family had moved into the only house on the block that had a yard and trees. I could see his place from my window in El Building. In fact, if I sat on the fire escape I was literally suspended above Eugene's backyard. It was my favorite spot to read my library books in the summer....
>
> ...By the time Eugene's family moved in, the yard was a tangled mass of weeds. The father had spent several days mowing, and when he finished, from where I sat, I didn't see the red, yellow, and purple clusters that meant flowers to me. I didn't see this family sit down at the kitchen table together. It was just the mother, a red-headed tall woman who wore a white uniform—a nurse's, I guessed it was; the father was gone before I got up in the morning and was never there at dinnertime.
>
> —from "American History"
> by Judith Ortiz Cofer

What Great Writers Do

Notice how Richard Connell uses details in the following excerpt to create a setting or backdrop for character and action:

> But as he forged along he saw to his great astonishment that all the lights were in one enormous building—a lofty structure with pointed towers plunging upward into the gloom. His eyes made out the shadowy outlines of a palatial château; it was set on a high bluff, and on three sides of it cliffs dived down to where the sea licked greedy lips in the shadows.
>
> —from "The Most Dangerous Game"
> by Richard Connell (page 27)

ELEMENTS OF SETTING

Sensory Details

Authors carefully select and arrange details to achieve a particular effect. The outdoor setting of "The Scarlet Ibis" (page 109) has an abundance of details that readers can hear, see, and smell. These are called **sensory details** because they appeal to several or all of the five senses (sight, sound, taste, smell, touch). One way to keep track of the details in a story is to use a Sensory Details Chart like the one on page 107.

> The flower garden was stained with rotting brown magnolia petals and ironweeds grew rank amid the purple phlox. The five o'clocks by the chimney still marked time, but the oriole nest in the elm was untenanted and rocked back and forth like an empty cradle. The last graveyard flowers were blooming, and their smell drifted across the cotton field and through every room of our house, speaking softly the names of our dead.
>
> —from "The Scarlet Ibis"
> by James Hurst

Sensory Details Chart for "The Scarlet Ibis"

Sight	Sound	Smell	Taste	Touch
gleaming white house green-draped parlor stained flower garden	graveyard flowers speaking the names of the dead	rotting magnolia petals smell of last grave-yard flowers	the taste of iced tea/bread from their dinner	cool feeling of the parlor

Setting and Mood

One reason why setting is important is that it provides background for the story. In "The Gift of the Magi" (page 139), readers are told that the mailbox of the apartment is too small and that the doorbell doesn't work. O. Henry's use of detail is sparse but telling; it indicates that the young couple of the story is poor. This is crucial information for understanding the story.

> In the vestibule below was a letter box into which no letter would go, and an electric button from which no mortal finger could coax a ring. Also appertaining thereunto was a card bearing the name "Mr. James Dillingham Young."
>
> —from "The Gift of the Magi" by O. Henry

Equally significant is the use of setting in creating a connection between the characters of a story and the context in which they are placed. This connection helps explain why characters speak or act in a certain way. That "American History" takes place on November 22, 1963, is significant because this was the day on which President John F. Kennedy was assassinated. The detail of the assassination is important to the way readers understand the thoughts and actions of Elena, the main character.

Setting also helps establish mood. **Mood,** or atmosphere, is the emotion created in the reader by part or all of a story. The mood of a story, for example, might be mysterious, happy, frightening, peaceful, serious, or tense. Details in the setting contribute to mood.

In "The Scarlet Ibis," the description of the setting frequently refers to the death of living things in autumn. If you feel apprehensive about looming death as you read this story, you are responding sensitively to the text. In "American History," the details used to describe the setting are devoid of color and light. This creates a dreary mood.

> Every Sunday we drove out to the suburbs of Paterson, Clifton and Passaic, out to where people mowed grass on Sundays in the summer, and where children made snowmen in the winter from pure white snow, not like the gray slush of Paterson, which seemed to fall from the sky in that hue.
>
> —from "American History" by Judith Ortiz Cofer

The Scarlet Ibis

BEFORE READING

A Short Story by James Hurst

BUILD BACKGROUND

Literary Context "The Scarlet Ibis" is a story about an older brother who struggles with his conflicted feelings for his younger brother, Doodle, who was born with physical disabilities. The **setting** for this story, that is, the time and place in which it occurs, is particularly important. According to the author, James Hurst, the setting becomes almost another character. Notice how Hurst describes colors, weather conditions, plants, and trees in great detail as he creates the world of the two main characters.

Reader's Context "If you believe it, you can do it." Do you agree with this statement? Are there times when it may not be true? Explain.

ANALYZE LITERATURE: Mood

Mood, or atmosphere, is the emotion created in the reader by a literary work. The description in the opening paragraph of "The Scarlet Ibis" establishes a haunting, lonely mood. Note the way the somber descriptions of nature in the first paragraph foreshadow, or hint at, the events to come. Watch for mood changes as the story unfolds.

SET PURPOSE

As you read, consider the author's claim that the setting of this story is almost another character. Hurst uses sensory details—words and phrases that describe how things look, sound, smell, taste, or feel—to make the story come alive. How do these details contribute to the mood of the story?

MEET THE AUTHOR

James Hurst (b. 1922) was raised on a farm in North Carolina. He studied chemical engineering at North Carolina State College and served in the U.S. Army during World War II. After the war, he pursued his dream of becoming an opera singer and took voice lessons at the Juilliard School, later traveling to Rome to continue his studies. Eventually, Hurst abandoned his musical aspirations and took a job in the international department of a bank in New York. He was employed at the bank for thirty-four years and spent his evenings writing. It was during this time that he wrote and published several short stories and a play. "The Scarlet Ibis" first appeared in *The Atlantic Monthly* in 1960 and was immediately recognized as a classic.

USE READING SKILLS

Cause and Effect As you read "The Scarlet Ibis," look for logical relationships between a cause or causes and one or more effects. Use a graphic organizer, like the one below, to recognize relationships between causes and effects. Transitional, or signal, words and phrases often indicate cause and effect (such as *one cause, another effect, as a result, therefore,* and *consequently)* and should be included in your organizer.

Cause	Effect	Summary Statement

PREVIEW VOCABULARY

Preview the sentences below and use context clues to infer the meanings of the underlined words.

1. His face went white with horror as we came careening around the corner of the house, unable to stop.
2. "It's not fair," he said sullenly. "I worked just as hard as they did, and I didn't get an award."
3. The end of the game was imminent, but Josh would not admit defeat.
4. The professor had believed his theory was infallible until his student pointed out the mistake that everyone else had overlooked.
5. The room was so loud that the speaker had to reiterate all of his arguments before the crowd understood his point.

The Scarlet Ibis

A Short Story by **James Hurst**

Doodle was just about the craziest brother a boy ever had.

It was in the clove of seasons,[1] summer was dead but autumn had not yet been born, that the ibis lit in the bleeding tree. The flower garden was stained with rotting brown magnolia petals and ironweeds grew rank amid the purple phlox. The five o'clocks by the chimney still marked time, but the oriole nest in the elm was untenanted and rocked back and forth like an empty cradle. The last graveyard flowers were blooming, and their smell drifted across the cotton field and through every room of our house, speaking softly the names of our dead.

It's strange that all this is still so clear to me, now that that summer has long since fled and time has had its way. A grindstone[2] stands where the bleeding tree stood, just outside the kitchen door, and now if an oriole sings in the elm, its song seems to die up in the leaves, a silvery dust. The flower garden is prim, the house a gleaming white, and the pale fence across the yard stands straight and spruce. But sometimes (like right now), as I sit in the cool, green-draped parlor, the grindstone begins to turn, and time with all its changes is ground away—and I remember Doodle.

Doodle was just about the craziest brother a boy ever had. Of course, he wasn't a crazy crazy like old Miss Leedie, who was in love with President Wilson[3] and wrote him a letter every day, but was a nice crazy, like someone you meet in your dreams. He was born when I was six and was, from the outset, a disappointment. He seemed all head, with a tiny body which was red and shriveled like an old man's. Everybody thought he was going to die—everybody except Aunt Nicey, who had

1. **clove of seasons.** Time between seasons
2. **grindstone.** Revolving stone disk for sharpening or polishing tools
3. **President Wilson.** Thomas Woodrow Wilson (1856–1924), twenty-eighth president of the United States

delivered him. She said he would live because he was born in a caul[4] and cauls were made from Jesus' nightgown. Daddy had Mr. Heath, the carpenter, build a little mahogany coffin for him. But he didn't die, and when he was three months old Mama and Daddy decided they might as well name him. They named him William Armstrong, which was like tying a big tail on a small kite. Such a name sounds good only on a tombstone.

I thought myself pretty smart at many things, like holding my breath, running, jumping, or climbing the vines in Old Woman Swamp, and I wanted more than anything else someone to race to Horsehead Landing, someone to box with, and someone to perch with in the top fork of the great pine behind the barn, where across the fields and swamps you could see the sea. I wanted a brother. But Mama, crying, told me that even if William Armstrong lived, he would never do these things with me. He might not, she sobbed, even be "all there." He might, as long as he lived, lie on the rubber sheet in the center of the bed in the front bedroom where the white marquisette curtains billowed out in the afternoon sea breeze, rustling like palmetto fronds.[5]

It was bad enough having an invalid brother, but having one who possibly was not all there was unbearable, so I began to make plans to kill him by smothering him with a pillow. However, one afternoon as I watched him, my head poked between the iron posts of the foot of the bed, he looked straight at me and grinned. I skipped through the rooms, down the echoing halls, shouting, "Mama, he smiled. He's all there! He's all there!" and he was.

When he was two, if you laid him on his stomach, he began to try to move himself, straining terribly. The doctor said that with his weak heart this strain would probably kill him, but it didn't. Trembling, he'd push himself up, turning first red, then a soft purple, and finally collapse back onto the bed like an old worn-out doll. I can still see Mama watching him, her hand pressed tight across her mouth, her eyes wide and unblinking. But he learned to crawl (it was his third winter), and we brought him out of the front bedroom, putting him on the rug before the fireplace. For the first time he became one of us.

As long as he lay all the time in bed, we called him William Armstrong, even though it was formal and sounded as if we were referring to one of our ancestors, but with his creeping around on the deerskin rug and beginning to talk, something had to be done about his name. It was I who renamed him. When he crawled, he crawled backwards, as if he were in reverse and couldn't change gears. If you called him, he'd turn around as if he were going in the other direction, then he'd back right up to you to be picked up. Crawling backward made him look like a doodlebug, so I began to call him Doodle, and in time even Mama and Daddy thought it was a better name than William Armstrong. Only Aunt Nicey disagreed. She said caul babies should be treated with special respect since they might turn out to be saints. Renaming my brother was perhaps the kindest thing I ever did for him, because nobody expects much from someone called Doodle.

Although Doodle learned to crawl, he showed no signs of walking, but he wasn't idle. He talked so much that we all quit listening to what he said. It was about this time that Daddy built him a go-cart and I had to pull him around. At first I just paraded him up and down the piazza,[6] but then he started crying to be taken out into the yard, and it ended up by my having to lug him wherever I went. If I so much as picked up my cap, he'd start crying to go with me and Mama would call from wherever she was, "Take Doodle with you."

He was a burden in many ways. The doctor had said that he mustn't get too

4. **caul.** Membrane enclosing a fetus or a baby at birth
5. **palmetto fronds.** Fan-shaped leaves of a palm tree
6. **piazza.** Large, covered porch

"It's so pretty," he said. "So pretty, pretty, pretty."

After that day Doodle and I often went down into Old Woman Swamp. I would gather wildflowers, wild violets, honeysuckle, yellow jasmine, snakeflowers, and water lilies, and with wire grass we'd weave them into necklaces and crowns. We'd bedeck ourselves with our handiwork and loll about thus beautified, beyond the touch of the everyday world. Then when the slanted rays of the sun burned orange in the tops of the pines, we'd drop our jewels into the stream and watch them float away toward the sea.

excited, too hot, too cold, or too tired and that he must always be treated gently. A long list of don'ts went with him, all of which I ignored once we got out of the house. To discourage his coming with me, I'd run with him across the ends of the cotton rows and careen him around corners on two wheels. Sometimes I accidentally turned him over, but he never told Mama. His skin was very sensitive, and he had to wear a big straw hat whenever he went out. When the going got rough and he had to cling to the sides of the go-cart, the hat slipped all the way down over his ears. He was a sight. Finally, I could see I was licked. Doodle was my brother and he was going to cling to me forever, no matter what I did, so I dragged him across the burning cotton field to share with him the only beauty I knew, Old Woman Swamp. I pulled the go-cart through the saw-tooth fern, down into the green dimness where the palmetto fronds whispered by the stream. I lifted him out and set him down in the soft rubber grass beside a tall pine. His eyes were round with wonder as he gazed about him, and his little hands began to stroke the rubber grass. Then he began to cry.

"For heaven's sake, what's the matter?" I asked, annoyed.

There is within me (and with sadness I have watched it in others) a knot of cruelty borne by the stream of love, much as our blood sometimes bears the seed of our destruction, and at times I was mean to Doodle. One day I took him up to the barn loft and showed him his casket, telling him how we all had believed he would die. It was covered with a film of Paris green[7] sprinkled to kill the rats, and screech owls had built a nest inside it.

Doodle studied the mahogany box for a long time, then said, "It's not mine."

"It is," I said. "And before I'll help you down from the loft, you're going to have to touch it."

"I won't touch it," he said sullenly.

"Then I'll leave you here by yourself," I threatened, and made as if I were going down.

7. **Paris green.** Green powdered insecticide

ca • reen (kə rēn´) *v.*, lurch from side to side, especially while moving rapidly
sul • len • ly (sul´ ən lē) *adv.*, gloomily

Critical Viewing

How does the image on this page reflect the mood of the story?

Doodle was frightened of being left. "Don't go leave me, Brother," he cried, and he leaned toward the coffin. His hand, trembling, reached out, and when he touched the casket he screamed. A screech owl flapped out of the box into our faces, scaring us and covering us with Paris green. Doodle was paralyzed, so I put him on my shoulder and carried him down the ladder, and even when we were outside in the bright sunshine, he clung to me, crying, "Don't leave me. Don't leave me."

When Doodle was five years old, I was embarrassed at having a brother of that age who couldn't walk, so I set out to teach him. We were down in Old Woman Swamp and it was spring and the sick-sweet smell of bay flowers hung everywhere like a mournful song. "I'm going to teach you to walk, Doodle," I said.

He was sitting comfortably on the soft grass, leaning back against the pine. "Why?" he asked.

I hadn't expected such an answer. "So I won't have to haul you around all the time."

"I can't walk, Brother," he said.

"Who says so?" I demanded.

"Mama, the doctor—everybody."

"Oh, you can walk," I said, and I took him by the arms and stood him up. He collapsed onto the grass like a half-empty flour sack. It was as if he had no bones in his little legs.

"Don't hurt me, Brother," he warned.

"Shut up. I'm not going to hurt you. I'm going to teach you to walk." I heaved him up again, and again he collapsed.

This time he did not lift his face up out of the rubber grass. "I just can't do it. Let's make honeysuckle wreaths."

"Oh yes you can, Doodle," I said. "All you got to do is try. Now come on," and I hauled him up once more.

It seemed so hopeless from the beginning that it's a miracle I didn't give up. But all of us must have something or someone to be proud of, and Doodle had become mine. I did not know then that pride is a wonderful, terrible thing, a seed that bears two vines, life and death. Every day that summer we went to the pine beside the stream of Old Woman Swamp, and I put him on his feet at least a hundred times each afternoon. Occasionally I too became discouraged because it didn't seem as if he was trying, and I would say, "Doodle, don't you *want* to learn to walk?"

He'd nod his head, and I'd say, "Well, if you don't keep trying, you'll never learn. Then I'd paint for him a picture of us as old men, white-haired, him with a long white beard and me still pulling him around in the go-cart. This never failed to make him try again.

Finally one day, after many weeks of practicing, he stood alone for a few seconds. When he fell, I grabbed him in my arms and hugged him, our laughter pealing through the swamp like a ringing bell. Now we knew it could be done. Hope no longer hid in the dark palmetto thicket but perched like a cardinal in the lacy toothbrush tree, brilliantly visible. "Yes, yes," I cried, and he cried it too, and the grass beneath us was soft and the smell of the swamp was sweet.

With success so imminent, we decided not to tell anyone until he could actually walk. Each day, barring rain, we sneaked into Old Woman Swamp, and by cotton-picking time Doodle was ready to show what he could do. He still wasn't able to walk far, but we could wait no longer. Keeping a nice secret is very hard to do, like holding your breath. We chose to reveal all on October eighth, Doodle's sixth birthday, and for weeks ahead we mooned around the house, promising everybody a most spectacular surprise. Aunt Nicey said that, after so much talk, if we produced anything less tremendous than the Resurrection,[8] she was going to be disappointed.

At breakfast on our chosen day, when Mama, Daddy, and Aunt Nicey were in the dining room, I brought Doodle to the door in the go-cart just as usual and had them turn their backs, making them cross their hearts and hope to die if they peeked. I helped Doodle up, and when he was standing alone I let them look. There wasn't a sound as Doodle walked slowly across the room and sat down at his place at the table. Then Mama began to cry and ran over to him, hugging him and kissing him. Daddy hugged him too, so I went to Aunt Nicey, who was thanks praying in the doorway, and began to waltz her around. We danced together quite well until she came down on my big toe with her brogans,[9] hurting me so badly I thought I was crippled for life.

Doodle told them it was I who had taught him to walk, so everyone wanted to hug me, and I began to cry.

"What are you crying for?" asked Daddy, but I couldn't answer. They did not know that I did it for myself; that pride, whose slave I was, spoke to me louder than all their voices, and that Doodle walked only because I was ashamed of having a crippled brother.

Within a few months Doodle had learned to walk well and his go-cart was put up in the barn loft (it's still there) beside his little mahogany coffin. Now, when we roamed off together, resting often, we never turned back until our destination had been reached, and to help pass the time, we took up lying. From the beginning Doodle was a terrible liar and he got me in the habit. Had anyone stopped to listen to us, we would have been sent off to Dix Hill.[10]

My lies were scary, involved, and usually pointless, but Doodle's were twice as crazy. People in his stories all had wings and flew wherever they wanted to go. His favorite lie was about a boy named Peter who had a pet peacock with a ten-foot tail. Peter wore a golden robe that glittered so brightly that when he walked through the sunflowers they turned away from the sun to face him. When Peter was ready to go to sleep, the peacock spread his magnificent tail, enfolding the boy gently like a closing go-to-sleep flower, burying him in the gloriously iridescent, rustling vortex. Yes, I must admit it. Doodle could beat me lying.

Doodle and I spent lots of time thinking about our future. We decided that when we were grown we'd live in Old Woman Swamp and pick dog-tongue for a living. Beside the

8. **Resurrection.** Jesus's return to life after the Crucifixion, according to Christian belief

9. **brogans.** Heavy work shoes

10. **Dix Hill.** The location of Dorothea Dix Hospital, a state institution for people with mental disabilities

im • mi • nent (im´ ə nənt) *adj.*, likely to happen soon
ir • i • des • cent (ir' i de´ sənt) *adj.*, having shifting changes in color
vor • tex (vôr´ teks) *n.*, whirlpool; eddy

stream, he planned, we'd build us a house of whispering leaves and the swamp birds would be our chickens. All day long (when we weren't gathering dog-tongue) we'd swing through the cypresses on the rope vines, and if it rained we'd huddle beneath an umbrella tree and play stickfrog. Mama and Daddy could come and live with us if they wanted to. He even came up with the idea that he could marry Mama and I could marry Daddy. Of course, I was old enough to know this wouldn't work out, but the picture he painted was so beautiful and serene that all I could do was whisper Yes, yes.

Once I had succeeded in teaching Doodle to walk, I began to believe in my own infallibility and I prepared a terrific development program for him, unknown to Mama and Daddy, of course. I would teach him to run, to swim, to climb trees, and to fight. He, too, now believed in my infallibility, so we set the deadline for these accomplishments less than a year away, when, it had been decided, Doodle could start to school.

That winter we didn't make much progress, for I was in school and Doodle suffered from one bad cold after another. But when spring came, rich and warm, we raised our sights again. Success lay at the end of summer like a pot of gold, and our campaign got off to a good start. On hot days, Doodle and I went down to Horsehead Landing, and I gave him swimming lessons or showed him how to row a boat. Sometimes we descended into the cool greenness of Old Woman Swamp and climbed the rope vines or boxed scientifically beneath the pine where he had learned to walk. Promise hung about us like the leaves, and wherever we looked, ferns unfurled and birds broke into song.

That summer, the summer of 1918, was blighted. In May and June there was no rain and the crops withered, curled up, then died under the thirsty sun. One morning in July a hurricane came out of the east, tipping over the oaks in the yard and splitting the limbs of the elm trees. That afternoon it roared back out of the west, blew the fallen oaks around, snapping their roots and tearing them out of the earth like a hawk at the entrails of a chicken. Cotton bolls were wrenched from the stalks and lay like green walnuts in the valleys between the rows, while the cornfield leaned over uniformly so that the tassels touched the ground. Doodle and I followed Daddy out into the cotton field, where he stood, shoulders sagging, surveying the ruin. When his chin sank down onto his chest, we were frightened, and Doodle slipped his hand into mine. Suddenly Daddy straightened his shoulders, raised a giant knuckly fist, and with a voice that seemed to rumble out of the earth itself began cursing heaven, the weather, hell, and the Republican Party. Doodle and I, prodding each other and giggling, went back to the house, knowing that everything would be all right.

And during that summer, strange names were heard through the house: Château-Thierry, Amiens, Soissons, and in her blessing at the supper table, Mama once said, "And bless the Pearsons, whose boy Joe was lost at Belleau Wood."[11]

So we came to that clove of seasons. School was only a few weeks away, and Doodle was far behind schedule. He could barely clear the ground when climbing up the rope vines and his swimming was certainly not passable. We decided to double our efforts, to make that last drive and reach our pot of gold. I made him swim until he turned blue and row until he couldn't lift an oar. Wherever we went, I purposely walked fast, and although he kept up, his face turned red and his eyes became glazed. Once, he could go no further, so he collapsed on the ground and began to cry.

"Aw, come on, Doodle," I urged. "You can do it. Do you want to be different from everybody else when you start school?"

"Does it make any difference?"

11. **Château-Thierry...Belleau Wood.** World War I battlefields in France

in • fal • li • bil • i • ty (in fal' ə bil' i tē) *n.,* correctness; incapacity for error

World History Connection

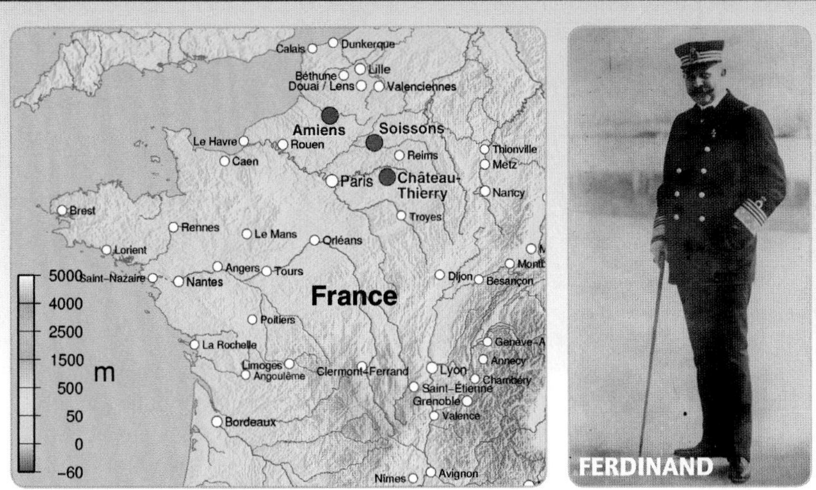

World War I The "strange names" mentioned on page 114 are sites of battles in France during World War I. The conflict began in 1914 when the Archduke Ferdinand, heir to the throne of the Austro-Hungarian empire, was assassinated by a Serbian terrorist in Sarajevo, Bosnia-Herzegovina. Most of Europe, the United States, Japan, and other nations around the world fought in this "war to end all wars" before a peace treaty was signed in 1918.

"It certainly does," I said. "Now, come on," and I helped him up.

As we slipped through dog days, Doodle began to look feverish, and Mama felt his forehead, asking him if he felt ill. At night he didn't sleep well, and sometimes he had nightmares, crying out until I touched him and said, "Wake up, Doodle. Wake up."

It was Saturday noon, just a few days before school was to start. I should have already admitted defeat, but my pride wouldn't let me. The excitement of our program had now been gone for weeks, but still we kept on with a tired doggedness. It was too late to turn back, for we had both wandered too far into a net of expectations and had left no crumbs behind.

Daddy, Mama, Doodle, and I were seated at the dining-room table having lunch. It was a hot day, with all the windows and doors open in case a breeze should come. In the kitchen Aunt Nicey was humming softly. After a long silence, Daddy spoke. "It's so calm, I wouldn't be surprised if we had a storm this afternoon."

"I haven't heard a rain frog," said Mama, who believed in signs, as she served the bread around the table.

"I did," declared Doodle. "Down in the swamp."

"He didn't," I said contrarily.

"You did, eh?" said Daddy, ignoring my denial.

"I certainly did," Doodle reiterated, scowling at me over the top of his iced-tea glass, and we were quiet again.

Suddenly, from out in the yard, came a strange croaking noise. Doodle stopped eating, with a piece of bread poised ready for his mouth, his eyes popped round like two blue buttons. "What's that?" he whispered.

I jumped up, knocking over my chair, and had reached the door when Mama called, "Pick up the chair, sit down again, and say excuse me."

By the time I had done this, Doodle had excused himself and had slipped out into the yard. He was looking up into the bleeding tree. "It's a great big red bird!" he called.

The bird croaked loudly again, and Mama and Daddy came out into the yard. We shaded our eyes with our hands against the hazy glare of the sun and peered up through the still leaves. On the topmost branch a bird the size of a chicken, with scarlet feathers and long legs, was perched precariously. Its wings hung down loosely, and as we watched, a feather

re • it • er • ate (rē it´ ə rāt') *v.*, repeat

dropped away and floated slowly down through the green leaves.

"It's not even frightened of us," Mama said.

"It looks tired," Daddy added. "Or maybe sick."

Doodle's hands were clasped at his throat, and I had never seen him stand still so long. "What is it?" he asked.

Daddy shook his head. "I don't know, maybe it's—"

At that moment the bird began to flutter, but the wings were uncoordinated, and amid much flapping and a spray of flying feathers, it tumbled down, bumping through the limbs of the bleeding tree and landing at our feet with a thud. Its long, graceful neck jerked twice into an S, then straightened out, and the bird was still. A white veil came over the eyes and the long white beak unhinged. Its legs were crossed and its clawlike feet were delicately curved at rest. Even death did not mar its grace, for it lay on the earth like a broken vase of red flowers, and we stood around it, awed by its exotic beauty.

"It's dead," Mama said.

"What is it?" Doodle repeated.

"Go bring me the bird book," said Daddy.

I ran into the house and brought back the bird book. As we watched, Daddy thumbed through its pages. "It's a scarlet ibis," he said, pointing to a picture. "It lives in the tropics—South America to Florida. A storm must have brought it here."

Sadly, we all looked back at the bird. A scarlet ibis! How many miles it had traveled to die like this, in *our* yard, beneath the bleeding tree.

"Let's finish lunch," Mama said, nudging us back toward the dining room.

"I'm not hungry," said Doodle, and he knelt down beside the ibis.

"We've got peach cobbler for dessert," Mama tempted from the doorway.

Doodle remained kneeling. "I'm going to bury him."

"Don't you dare touch him," Mama warned. "There's no telling what disease he might have had."

"All right," said Doodle. "I won't."

Daddy, Mama, and I went back to the dining-room table, but we watched Doodle through the open door. He took out a piece of string from his pocket and, without touching the ibis, looped one end around its neck. Slowly, while singing softly, "Shall We Gather at the River," he carried the bird around to the front yard and dug a hole in the flower garden, next to the petunia bed. Now we were watching him through the front window, but he didn't know it. His awkwardness at digging the hole with a shovel whose handle was twice as long as he was made us laugh, and we covered our mouths with our hands so he wouldn't hear.

CULTURAL CONNECTION

The Scarlet Ibis In ancient times, the **scarlet ibis** (ī´ bəs) was held sacred by the Egyptians, who believed it to be a reincarnation of Thoth, the god of knowledge. Mummified ibises have been found in the tombs of Pharaohs and in the ruins of temples. There are thirty-three species of ibises in the world; the bird featured in this story is the scarlet ibis, a native to coastal regions of tropical South America. This species is distinguished by its vivid red plumage. As you read, consider what the ibis symbolizes, or represents, in this story.

When Doodle came into the dining room, he found us seriously eating our cobbler. He was pale and lingered just inside the screen door. "Did you get the scarlet ibis buried?" asked Daddy.

Doodle didn't speak but nodded his head.

"Go wash your hands, and then you can have some peach cobbler," said Mama.

"I'm not hungry," he said.

"Dead birds is bad luck," said Aunt Nicey, poking her head from the kitchen door. "Specially *red* dead birds!"

As soon as I had finished eating, Doodle and I hurried off to Horsehead Landing. Time was short, and Doodle still had a long way to go if he was going to keep up with the other boys when he started school. The sun, gilded with the yellow cast of autumn, still burned fiercely, but the dark green woods through which we passed were shady and cool. When we reached the landing, Doodle said he was too tired to swim, so we got into a skiff[12] and floated down the creek with the tide. Far off in the marsh a rail was scolding, and over on the beach locusts were singing in the myrtle trees. Doodle did not speak and kept his head turned away, letting one hand trail limply in the water.

After we had drifted a long way, I put the oars in place and made Doodle row back against the tide. Black clouds began to gather in the southwest, and he kept watching them, trying to pull the oars a little faster. When we reached Horsehead Landing, lightning was playing across half the sky and thunder roared out, hiding even the sound of the sea. The sun disappeared and darkness descended, almost like night. Flocks of marsh crows flew by, heading inland to their roosting trees, and two egrets, squawking, arose from the oyster-rock shallows and careened away.

Doodle was both tired and frightened, and when he stepped from the skiff he collapsed onto the mud, sending an armada of fiddler crabs rustling off into the marsh grass. I helped him up, and as he wiped the mud off his trousers, he smiled at me ashamedly. He had failed and we both knew it, so we started back home, racing the storm. We never spoke (What are the words that can solder[13] cracked pride?), but I knew he was watching me, watching for a sign of mercy. The lightning was near now, and from fear he walked so close behind me he kept stepping on my heels. The faster I walked, the faster he walked, so I began to run. The rain was coming, roaring through the pines, and then like a bursting Roman candle, a gum tree ahead of us was shattered by a bolt of lightning. When the deafening peal of thunder had died, and in the moment before the rain arrived, I heard Doodle, who had fallen behind, cry out, "Brother, Brother, don't leave me! Don't leave me!"

The knowledge that Doodle's and my plans had come to naught was bitter, and that streak of cruelty within me awakened. I ran as fast as I could, leaving him far behind with a wall of rain dividing us. The drops stung my face like nettles, and the wind flared the wet glistening leaves of the bordering trees. Soon I could hear his voice no more.

I hadn't run too far before I became tired, and the flood of childish spite evanesced as well. I stopped and waited for Doodle. The sound of rain was everywhere, but the wind had died and it fell straight down in parallel paths like ropes hanging from the sky. As I waited, I peered through the downpour, but no one came. Finally I went back and found him huddled beneath a red nightshade bush beside the road. He was sitting on the ground, his face buried in his arms, which were resting on his drawn-up knees. "Let's go, Doodle," I said.

He didn't answer, so I placed my hand on his forehead and lifted his head. Limply, he fell backwards onto the earth. He had been bleeding from the mouth, and his neck and the front of his shirt were stained a brilliant red.

---

12. **skiff.** Small open boat
13. **solder.** Unite or make whole

ev • a • nesce (ev' ə nes´) *v.*, disappear

"Doodle! Doodle!" I cried, shaking him, but there was no answer but the ropy rain. He lay very awkwardly, with his head thrown far back, making his vermilion neck appear unusually long and slim. His little legs, bent sharply at the knees, had never before seemed so fragile, so thin.

I began to weep, and the tear-blurred vision in red before me looked very familiar. "Doodle!" I screamed above the pounding storm and threw my body to the earth above his. For a long time, it seemed forever, I lay there crying, sheltering my fallen scarlet ibis from the heresy of rain. ❖

her • e • sy (her´ i sē) *n.,* contradiction of what is generally believed to be true or right

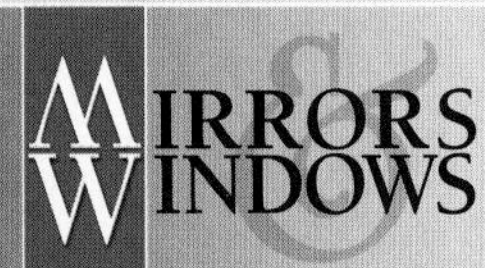

"They did not know that I did it for myself; that pride, whose slave I was, spoke to me louder than all their voices, and that Doodle walked only because I was ashamed of having a crippled brother." Does having the wrong motivation underscore or overpower the good that someone accomplishes?

AFTER READING

REFER TO TEXT	REASON WITH TEXT	
1a. Why did the narrator's family build a coffin for Doodle?	1b. Determine why the narrator would show Doodle the coffin in the barn loft.	Understand **Find meaning**
2a. Recall how the narrator motivates Doodle.	2b. Knowing what you do about the final outcome, would you use similar motivations for others? What rules would you follow if you were in charge of Doodle's success?	Apply **Use information**
3a. How does the narrator describe Doodle?	3b. Identify specific incidents in the story that tell the reader about the relationship between the two brothers.	Analyze **Take things apart**
4a. Identify what the brothers are trying to accomplish before Doodle goes to school.	4b. Judge whether or not the narrator is a good brother to Doodle. Is he responsible for what happens to Doodle at the end of the story? Explain.	Evaluate **Make judgments**
5a. What does Doodle do when the scarlet ibis dies?	5b. Explain why Doodle might appear so much more emotional than the rest of the family over the death of the scarlet ibis.	Create **Bring ideas together**

ANALYZE LITERATURE: Mood

What techniques does the author use to establish mood in various scenes of the story? What bits of dialogue and description especially affected you? How did they make you feel? Does the mood change during the story? If so, in what ways?

EXTEND THE TEXT

Writing Options

Creative Writing Assume that you have been asked to speak at Doodle's funeral. For the occasion, compose a **poem** about Doodle. Include details of his birth, life, death, personality, and the relationship with his brother. Also, include imagery from the story.

Descriptive Writing James Hurst creates a very vivid setting for "The Scarlet Ibis." Hurst does this by carefully using details that build a particular mood. Imagine that you are trying to describe the mood of this story to someone who hasn't read it. Write one or two **descriptive paragraphs** that examine the details of the setting you find most memorable, and how those details help develop the mood of the story. Include excerpts of particularly descriptive moments. Use a Sensory Details Chart like the one below to organize your details as you analyze the selection.

Sensory Details				
Sight	Sound	Smell	Taste	Touch
bleeding tree				

Collaborative Learning

Draw a Hurricane Map In "The Scarlet Ibis," the hurricane that destroys the family's cotton fields and cornfields also brings the unusual arrival of the tropical scarlet ibis to their North Carolina farm. With a partner or small group, use the Internet to research hurricane patterns and then create a hurricane map. Use a legend for the map to indicate the times of year when most hurricanes occur along the Atlantic coast.

Media Literacy

Create a Public Health Announcement In 1918, when "The Scarlet Ibis" takes place, a deadly disease known as Spanish influenza spread across the United States, killing more than 650,000. Imagine that you work for the health department. Research the Spanish influenza and create a public health announcement that describes its signs and symptoms and steps the public can take to stay healthy. Then compare the symptoms of the Spanish influenza with those Doodle experienced. Do you think Doodle was a victim of the epidemic? Support your answer with evidence from the story.

Go to **www.mirrorsandwindows.com** for more.

READING ASSESSMENT

1. Number these events in the correct sequence, with 1 being the first thing to happen in the story.
   ___ The narrator teaches Doodle to walk.
   ___ Doodle is shown his coffin.
   ___ Doodle dies.
   ___ A storm descends when the boys are outside.
   ___ Doodle buries the scarlet ibis.
   ___ The boys surprise their parents on Doodle's birthday.

2. The narrator in the story is motivated mainly by
   A. unselfishness.
   B. pride.
   C. high ideals.
   D. curiosity.
   E. irritation.

3. Which of the following does not foreshadow, or hint at, the end of the story?
   A. putting Doodle's go-cart away in the barn
   B. "the last graveyard flowers were blooming"
   C. the name William Armstrong "sounds good only on a tombstone"
   D. the arrival and death of the scarlet ibis
   E. the coming of the storm

4. Which of these descriptions sets a mood of gloom?
   A. "The flower garden is prim, the house a gleaming white, and the pale fence across the yard stands straight and spruce."
   B. "...the white marquisette curtains billowed out in the afternoon sea breeze, rustling like palmetto fronds."
   C. "I pulled the go-cart through the saw-tooth fern, down into the green dimness where the palmetto fronds whispered by the stream."
   D. "The flower garden was stained with rotting brown magnolia petals and ironweeds grew rank amid the purple phlox."
   E. "Then when the slanted rays of the sun burned orange in the tops of the pines, we'd drop our jewels into the stream and watch them float away toward the sea."

5. Why do you think Doodle tries so hard to learn the skills his brother wants to teach him? Why might he cling to his brother despite the fact that his brother can be cruel to him? Do you believe that Doodle behaves as most younger brothers behave? Why or why not?

AMERICAN HISTORY

BEFORE READING **A Short Story by Judith Ortiz Cofer**

DIRECTED READING

BUILD BACKGROUND

Historical Context "American History" takes place on November 22, 1963, the day President John F. Kennedy was assassinated. The narrator, a Puerto Rican girl named Elena, struggles "to feel the right thing" for the dead president, even while the national tragedy is overshadowed by a painful experience in her own life.

Sworn into office in 1961, John F. Kennedy was the thirty-fifth president of the United States and the youngest man and first Roman Catholic elected to be president. During his brief time in office, he called for civil rights legislation, fought for programs to fight poverty, and promoted leadership in space exploration. Even today, many Americans vividly remember where they were the moment they heard the tragic news of his assassination in Dallas, Texas.

Reader's Context Where were you on September 11, 2001? What effect did the events of that day have on you?

ANALYZE LITERATURE: Setting

The **setting** of a story is the time and place in which it occurs. Setting also includes the details used to create a sense of a particular time and place. In fiction, setting is most often revealed by means of description of such elements as landscape, scenery, buildings, furniture, clothing, the weather, and the season. It can also be revealed by how characters talk and behave. The description in the opening paragraph of "American History" establishes the story's setting.

SET PURPOSE

Think of how the title fits with the information in the Build Background section. Then preview the text, looking at any artwork and pull-out quotations. What other meaning could the title "American History" have? As you read, think about the role that setting plays in the story and how it affects what happens to the narrator and other characters. How does the setting provide a better understanding of the author's title choice?

MEET THE AUTHOR

Born in Puerto Rico, **Judith Ortiz Cofer** (b. 1952) immigrated to the United States with her family when she was young. She spent most of her childhood traveling back and forth between New Jersey and Puerto Rico. Cofer's family spoke only Spanish, but her American education was in English, and that became the language for her poetry, fiction, and nonfiction. She says, "It's important for the artist to retain some hold on her original self even if it is painful or unattractive.... How can you inject passion and purpose into your work if it has no roots?"

USE READING SKILLS

Main Idea The **main idea** within a piece of writing is the central point that the author develops with supporting details. It is a brief statement of what you believe the author wants you to know, think, or feel after reading the text.

As you read the selection, add details to a Main Idea Map like the one below. When you have finished reading the selection, use the details to draw conclusions and thus determine the selection's main idea.

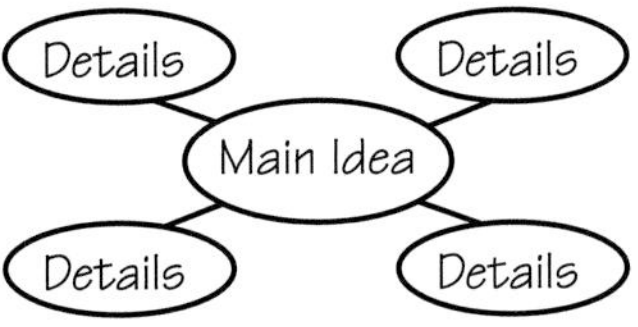

PREVIEW VOCABULARY

Try to unlock the meanings of the underlined vocabulary words using the context clues provided in the sentences below.

1. Martin Luther King Jr. became a martyr after he was assassinated for leading the Civil Rights movement.
2. My baby sister was enthralled with her new toy; she played with it for hours.
3. The athlete's elation upon winning a gold medal was clear from her smiling face.
4. The dilapidated iron factory stood in sharp contrast to its neighbor—a gleaming steel skyscraper.
5. When Felipe feels stressed, he seeks solace by listening to peaceful music in his darkened room.

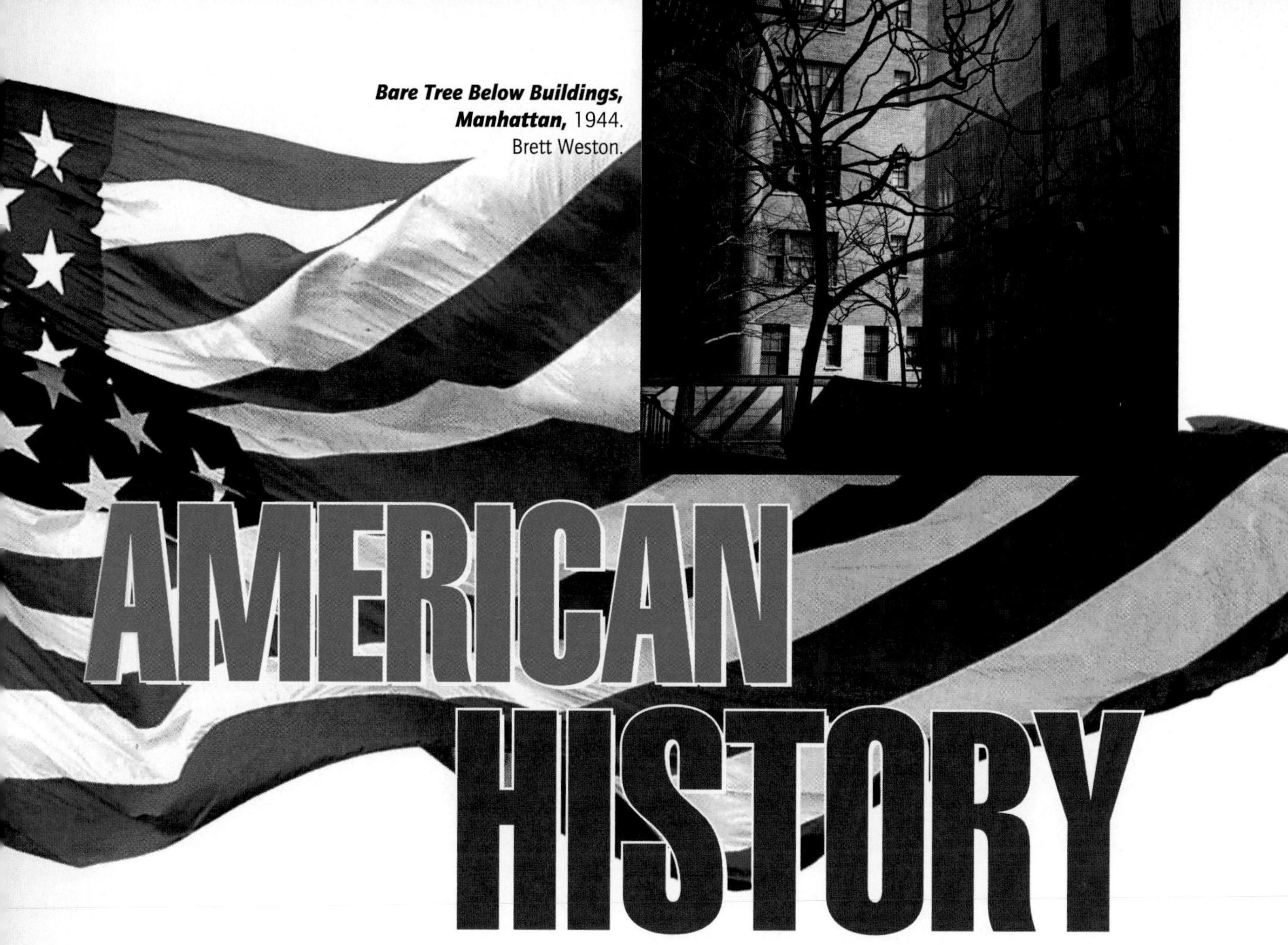

Bare Tree Below Buildings, Manhattan, 1944.
Brett Weston.

AMERICAN HISTORY

A Short Story by **Judith Ortiz Cofer**

"The President is dead, you idiots."

I once read in a "Ripley's Believe It or Not" column that Paterson, New Jersey, is the place where the Straight and Narrow (streets) intersect. The Puerto Rican tenement known as El Building was one block up from Straight. It was, in fact, *the* corner of Straight and Market; not "at" the corner, but the corner. At almost any hour of the day, El Building was like a monstrous jukebox, blasting out *salsas*[1] from open windows as the residents, mostly new immigrants just up from the island, tried to drown out whatever they were currently enduring with loud music. But the day President Kennedy was shot there was a profound silence in El Building; even the abusive tongues of *viragoes,*[2] the cursing of the unemployed, and the screeching of small children had been somehow muted. President Kennedy was a saint to these people. In fact, soon his photograph would be hung alongside the Sacred Heart and over the spiritist altars that many women kept in their apartments. He would become part of the hierarchy of martyrs

1. ***salsas*** (säl´ sas). [Spanish] Popular Latin American music
2. ***viragoes*** (vi rä' gōs). [Spanish] Loud, overbearing women

hi • er • ar • chy (hī´ ər är' kē) *n.*, group classified by grade or rank
mar • tyr (mär´ tər) *n.*, person who sacrifices his or her life for the sake of a principle or cause

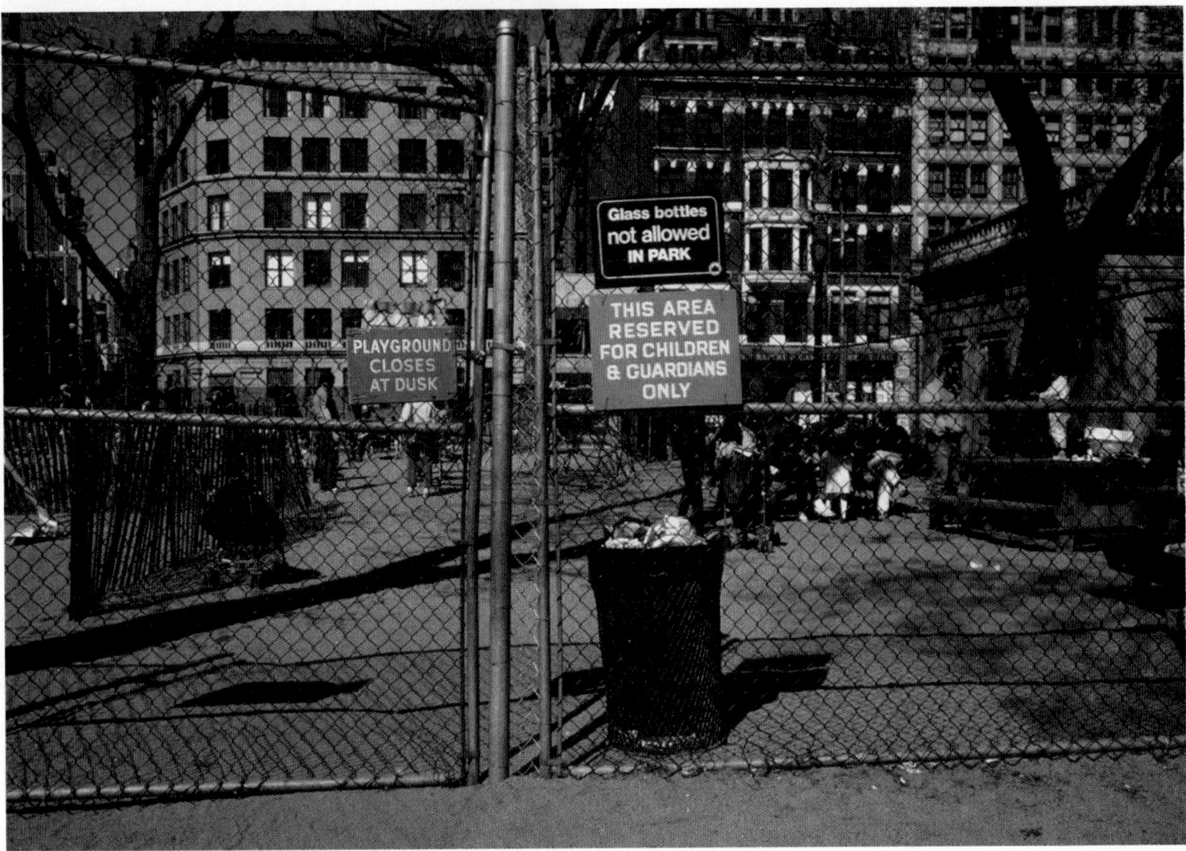

they prayed to for favors that only one who had died for a cause could understand.

On the day that President Kennedy was shot, my ninth grade class had been out in the fenced playground of Public School Number 13. We had been given "free" exercise time and had been ordered by our P.E. teacher, Mr. DePalma, to "keep moving." That meant that the girls should jump rope and the boys toss basketballs through a hoop at the far end of the yard. He in the meantime would "keep an eye" on us from just inside the building.

It was a cold gray day in Paterson. The kind that warns of early snow. I was miserable, since I had forgotten my gloves, and my knuckles were turning red and raw from the jump rope. I was also taking a lot of abuse from the black girls for not turning the rope hard and fast enough for them.

"Hey, Skinny Bones, pump it, girl. Ain't you got no energy today?" Gail, the biggest of the black girls had the other end of the rope, yelled, "Didn't you eat your rice and beans and pork chops for breakfast today?"

The other girls picked up the "pork chop" and made it into a refrain: "pork chop, pork chop, did you eat your pork chop?" They entered the double ropes in pairs and exited without tripping or missing a beat. I felt a burning on my cheeks and then my glasses fogged up so that I could not manage to coordinate the jump rope with Gail. The chill was doing to me what it always did; entering my bones, making me cry, humiliating me. I hated the city, especially in winter. I hated Public School Number 13. I hated my skinny flatchested body, and I envied the black girls who could jump rope so fast that their legs became a blur. They always seemed to be warm while I froze.

There was only one source of beauty and light for me that school year. The only thing I had anticipated at the start of the semester. That was seeing Eugene. In August, Eugene and his family had moved into the only house on the block that had a yard and trees. I could see his place from my window in El Building. In fact, if I sat on the fire escape I was literally suspended above Eugene's backyard. It was my favorite spot to read my library books in the summer. Until that August the house had been occupied by an old Jewish couple. Over the years I had become part of their family, without their knowing it, of course. I had a view of their kitchen and their backyard, and though I could not hear what they said, I knew when they were arguing, when one of them was sick, and many other things. I knew all this by watching them at mealtimes. I could see their kitchen table, the sink, and the stove. During good times, he sat at the table and read his newspapers while she fixed the meals. If they argued, he would leave and the old woman would sit and stare at nothing for a long time. When one of them was sick, the other would come and get things from the kitchen and carry them out on a tray. The old man had died in June. The last week of school I had not seen him at the table at all. Then one day I saw that there was a crowd in the kitchen. The old woman had finally emerged from the house on the arm of a stocky middle-aged woman, whom I had seen there a few times before, maybe her daughter. Then a man had carried out suitcases. The house had stood empty for weeks. I had had to resist the temptation to climb down into the yard and water the flowers the old lady had taken such good care of.

I was ready for rejection, snobbery, the worst.

By the time Eugene's family moved in, the yard was a tangled mass of weeds. The father had spent several days mowing, and when he finished, from where I sat, I didn't see the red, yellow, and purple clusters that meant flowers to me. I didn't see this family sit down at the kitchen table together. It was just the mother, a red-headed tall woman who wore a white uniform—a nurse's, I guessed it was; the father was gone before I got up in the morning and was never there at dinnertime. I only saw him on weekends when they sometimes sat on lawn chairs under the oak tree, each hidden behind a section of the newspaper; and there was Eugene. He was tall and blond, and he wore glasses. I liked him right away because he sat at the kitchen table and read books for hours. That summer, before we had even spoken one word to each other, I kept him company on my fire escape.

Once school started I looked for him in all my classes, but P.S. 13 was a huge, overpopulated place and it took me days and many discreet questions to discover that Eugene was in honors classes for all his subjects, classes that were not open to me because English was not my first language, though I was a straight A student. After much maneuvering I managed to "run into him" in the hallway where his locker was—on the other side of the building from mine—and in study hall at the library, where he first seemed to notice me, but did not speak; and finally, on the way home after school one day when I decided to approach him directly, though my stomach was doing somersaults.

I was ready for rejection, snobbery, the worst. But when I came up to him, practically panting in my nervousness, and blurted out: "You're Eugene. Right?" He smiled, pushed his glasses up on his nose, and nodded. I saw then that he was blushing deeply. Eugene liked me, but he was shy. I did most of the talking that day. He nodded and smiled a lot. In the weeks that followed, we walked home together. He would linger at the corner of El Building for a few minutes then walk down to his two-story house. It was not until Eugene moved into that house that I noticed that El Building blocked most of the sun, and that the only spot that got a little

dis • creet (di skrēt´) *adj.*, showing careful reserve in speech or action

SOCIAL STUDIES CONNECTION

Puerto Rico Puerto Rico, an island in the Caribbean, is a U.S. commonwealth acquired in 1898 as a result of the Spanish-American War. In 1917, Puerto Ricans became U.S. citizens and acquired most of the rights of U.S. citizenship. One exception is that Puerto Ricans cannot vote in presidential elections unless they are residents of the United States. This issue is currently under debate, as residents of Puerto Rico would like to vote in U.S. presidential elections. How does this information affect your understanding of the reaction of the Puerto Rican characters in the story to Kennedy's death?

sunlight during the day was the tiny square of earth the old woman had planted with flowers.

I did not tell Eugene that I could see inside his kitchen from my bedroom. I felt dishonest, but I liked my secret sharing of his evenings, especially now that I knew what he was reading since we chose our books together at the school library.

One day my mother came into my room as I was sitting on the windowsill staring out. In her abrupt way she said, "Elena, you are acting moony." *Enamorada* was what she really said, that is—like a girl stupidly infatuated. Since I had turned fourteen and started menstruating my mother had been more vigilant than ever. She acted as if I was going to go crazy or explode or something if she didn't watch me and nag me all the time about being a *señorita*[3] now. She kept talking about virtue, morality, and other subjects that did not interest me in the least. My mother was unhappy in Paterson, but my father had a good job at the bluejeans factory in Passaic and soon, he kept assuring us, we would be moving to our own house there. Every Sunday we drove out to the suburbs of Paterson, Clifton, and Passaic, out to where people mowed grass on Sundays in the summer, and where children made snowmen in the winter from pure white snow, not like the gray slush of Paterson, which seemed to fall from the sky in that hue. I had learned to listen to my parents' dreams, which were spoken in Spanish, as fairy tales, like the stories about life in the island paradise of Puerto Rico before I was born. I had been to the island once as a little girl, to grandmother's funeral, and all I remembered was wailing women in black, my mother becoming hysterical and being given a pill that made her sleep two days, and me feeling lost in a crowd of strangers all claiming to be my aunts, uncles, and cousins. I had actually been glad to return to the city. We had not been back there since then, though my parents talked constantly about buying a house on the beach someday, retiring on the island—that was a common topic among the residents of El Building. As for me, I was going to go to college and become a teacher.

But after meeting Eugene I began to think of the present more than of the future. What I wanted now was to enter that house I had watched for so many years. I wanted to see the other rooms where the old people had lived, and where the boy spent his time. Most of all, I wanted to sit at the kitchen table with Eugene like two adults, like the old man and his wife had done, maybe drink some coffee and talk about books. I had started reading *Gone With the Wind*.[4] I was enthralled by it,

3. ***señorita*** (sā' nyōr ē' ta). [Spanish] Young unmarried lady
4. ***Gone With the Wind.*** Famous novel by Margaret Mitchell set during the Civil War

hys • ter • i • cal (his ter' i kəl) *adj.*, displaying excessive emotion, often through uncontrollable laughter or tears
en • thralled (en thräld') *adj.*, being charmed or captivated

with the daring and passion of the beautiful girl living in a mansion, and with her devoted parents and the slaves who did everything for them. I didn't believe such a world had ever really existed, and I wanted to ask Eugene some questions since he and his parents, he had told me, had come up from Georgia, the same place where the novel was set. His father worked for a company that had transferred him to Paterson. His mother was very unhappy, Eugene said, in his beautiful voice that rose and fell over words in a strange, lilting way. The kids at school called him "the hick" and made fun of the way he talked. I knew I was his only friend so far, and I liked that, though I felt sad for him sometimes. "Skinny Bones" and the "Hick" was what they called us at school when we were seen together.

President John F. Kennedy.

The day Mr. DePalma came out into the cold and asked us to line up in front of him was the day that President Kennedy was shot. Mr. DePalma, a short, muscular man with slicked-down black hair, was the science teacher, P.E. coach, and disciplinarian at P.S. 13. He was the teacher to whose homeroom you got assigned if you were a troublemaker, and the man called out to break up playground fights, and to escort violently angry teenagers to the office. And Mr. DePalma was the man who called your parents in for a "conference."

That day, he stood in front of two rows of mostly black and Puerto Rican kids, brittle from their efforts to "keep moving" on a November day that was turning bitter cold. Mr. DePalma, to our complete shock, was crying. Not just silent adult tears, but really sobbing. There were a few titters from the back of the line where I stood shivering.

"Listen." Mr. DePalma raised his arms over his head as if he were about to conduct an orchestra. His voice broke, and he covered his face with his hands. His barrel chest was heaving. Someone giggled behind me.

"Listen," he repeated, "something awful has happened." A strange gurgling came from his throat, and he turned around and spat on the cement behind him.

"Gross," someone said, and there was a lot of laughter.

"The President is dead, you idiots. I should have known that wouldn't mean anything to a bunch of losers like you kids. Go home." He was shrieking now. No one moved for a minute or two, but then a big girl let out a "Yeah!" and ran to get her books piled up with the others against the brick wall of the school building. The others followed in a mad scramble to get to their things before somebody caught on. It was still an hour to the dismissal bell.

A little scared, I headed for El Building. There was an eerie feeling on the streets. I looked into Mario's drugstore, a favorite hangout for the high school crowd, but there were only a couple of old Jewish men at the soda-bar talking with the short order cook in tones that sounded almost angry, but they were keeping their voices low. Even the traffic on one of the busiest intersections in Paterson—Straight Street and Park Avenue—seemed to be moving slower. There were no horns blasting that day. At El Building, the usual little group of unemployed men were not hanging out on the front stoop making it difficult for women to enter the front door. No music spilled out from open doors in the hallway. When I walked into our apartment, I found my mother sitting in front of the grainy picture of the television set.

Though I wanted to feel the right thing about President Kennedy's death, I could not fight the feeling of elation that stirred in my chest.

She looked up at me with a tear-streaked face and just said, *"Dios mío,"*[5] turning back to the set as if it were pulling at her eyes. I went into my room.

Though I wanted to feel the right thing about President Kennedy's death, I could not fight the feeling of elation that stirred in my chest. Today was the day I was to visit Eugene in his house. He had asked me to come over after school to study for an American History test with him. We had also planned to walk to the public library together. I looked down into his yard. The oak tree was bare of leaves and the ground looked gray with ice. The light through the large kitchen window of his house told me that El Building blocked the sun to such an extent that they had to turn lights on in the middle of the day. I felt ashamed about it. But the white kitchen table with the lamp hanging just above it looked cozy and inviting. I would soon sit there, across from Eugene, and I would tell him about my perch just above his house. Maybe I should.

In the next thirty minutes I changed clothes, put on a little pink lipstick, and got my books together. Then I went in to tell my mother that I was going to a friend's house to study. I did not expect her reaction.

"You are going out *today?*" The way she said "today" sounded as if a storm warning had been issued. It was said in utter disbelief. Before I could answer, she came toward me and held my elbows as I clutched my books.

"*Hija,*[6] the President has been killed. We must show respect. He was a great man. Come to church with me tonight."

She tried to embrace me, but my books were in the way. My first impulse was to comfort her, she seemed so distraught, but I had to meet Eugene in fifteen minutes.

"I have a test to study for, Mama. I will be home by eight."

"You are forgetting who you are, *niña.*[7] I have seen you staring down at that boy's house. You are heading for humiliation and pain." My mother said this in Spanish and in a resigned tone that surprised me, as if she had no intention of stopping me from "heading for humiliation and pain." I started for the door. She sat in front of the TV holding a white handkerchief to her face.

I walked out to the street and around the chain-link fence, that separated El Building from Eugene's house. The yard was neatly edged around the little walk that led to the

5. ***Dios mío*** (dē´ ōs mē´ ō). [Spanish] My god
6. ***Hija*** (ē´ hä). [Spanish] Daughter
7. ***niña*** (nē´ nyä). [Spanish] Girl

ee • rie (ir' ē) *adj.*, frightening because of strangeness or mysteriousness
e • la • tion (i lā´ shən) *n.*, state of great joy and pride
dis • traught (di strôt´) *adj.*, upset by doubt or mental conflict

door. It always amazed me how Paterson, the inner core of the city, had no apparent logic to its architecture. Small, neat, single residences like this one could be found right next to huge, dilapidated apartment buildings like El Building. My guess was that the little houses had been there first, then the immigrants had come in droves, and the monstrosities had been raised for them—the Italians, the Irish, the Jews, and now us, the Puerto Ricans and the blacks. The door was painted a deep green: *verde,* the color of hope. I had heard my mother say it: *Verde—Esperanza.*

I knocked softly. A few suspenseful moments later, the door opened just a crack. The red, swollen face of a woman appeared. She had a halo of red hair floating over a delicate ivory face—the face of a doll—with freckles on the nose. Her smudged eye make-up made her look unreal to me, like a mannequin seen through a warped store window.

"What do you want?" Her voice was tiny and sweet sounding, like a little girl's, but her tone was not friendly.

"I'm Eugene's friend. He asked me over. To study." I thrust out my books, a silly gesture that embarrassed me almost immediately.

"You live there?" She pointed up to El Building, which looked particularly ugly, like a gray prison with its many dirty windows and rusty fire escapes. The woman had stepped halfway out and I could see that she wore a white nurse's uniform with St. Joseph's Hospital on the name tag.

"Yes. I do."

She looked intently at me for a couple of heartbeats, then said as if to herself, "I don't know how you people do it." Then directly to me: "Listen. Honey. Eugene doesn't want to study with you. He is a smart boy. Doesn't need help. You understand me. I am truly sorry if he told you you could come over. He cannot study with you. It's nothing personal. You understand? We won't be in this place much longer, no need for him to get close to people—it'll just make it harder for him later. Run back home now."

I couldn't move. I just stood there in shock at hearing these things said to me in such a honey-drenched voice. I had never heard an accent like hers, except for Eugene's softer version. It was as if she were singing me a little song.

"What's wrong? Didn't you hear what I said?" She seemed very angry, and I finally snapped out of my trance. I turned away from the green door, and heard her close it gently.

Our apartment was empty when I got home. My mother was in someone else's kitchen, seeking the solace she needed.

Father would come in from his late shift at midnight. I would hear them talking softly in the kitchen for hours that night. They would

di • lap • i • dat • ed (də la´ pə dā' təd) *adj.*, decayed; fallen into partial ruin through neglect
so • lace (sä´ ləs) *n.*, relief; consolation

not discuss their dreams for the future, or life in Puerto Rico, as they often did; that night they would talk sadly about the young widow and her two children, as if they were family. For the next few days, we would observe *luto*[8] in our apartment; that is, we would practice restraint and silence—no loud music or laughter. Some of the women of El Building would wear black for weeks.

That night, I lay in my bed trying to feel the right thing for our dead president. But the tears that came up from a deep source inside me were strictly for me. When my mother came to the door, I pretended to be sleeping. Sometime during the night, I saw from my bed the streetlight come on. It had a pink halo around it. I went to my window and pressed my face to the cool glass. Looking up at the light, I could see the white snow falling like a lace veil over its face. I did not look down to see it turning gray as it touched the ground below. ❖

8. ***luto*** (lü´ tō). [Spanish] Mourning

"I don't know how you people do it." What does Eugene's mother's comment tell you about her attitude toward the Puerto Rican community? Considering the events taking place within the story, why is that an ironic statement?

REFER TO TEXT ▶▶▶▶	▶ REASON WITH TEXT	
1a. How did Elena react to the news about President Kennedy's death?	1b. Describe how her reaction made her feel. Why doesn't Elena grieve for the dead president?	**Understand** **Find meaning**
2a. Identify how the atmosphere changes in El Building after the news of Kennedy's assassination.	2b. Examine why the death of Kennedy, in particular, would cause such great sorrow for the residents of El Building.	**Apply** **Use information**
3a. Indicate the source of beauty and light for Elena that school year.	3b. Compare and contrast El Building with the house next door. How does the neighbor's home life seem different from Elena's?	**Analyze** **Take things apart**
4a. Quote what Elena's mother tells her before she leaves for Eugene's house that night.	4b. Evaluate whether Elena was wrong to be more upset by the events in her personal life than with the death of President Kennedy.	**Evaluate** **Make judgments**
5a. What does Eugene's mother want to know about Elena when she knocks on their door?	5b. Why doesn't Eugene's mother want Eugene to spend time with Elena? Specify how Elena might persuade Eugene's mother to give her a chance to be friends with Eugene.	**Create** **Bring ideas together**

ANALYZE LITERATURE: Setting

What details does Judith Ortiz Cofer use to create a sense of a particular time? What details does she use to create a sense of particular places, such as El Building, Eugene's house, and the city of Paterson?

Informational Text CONNECTION

In 2003, forty years after the assassination of President Kennedy, many TV news broadcasts and documentaries featured the event and its impact on society. At the time of Kennedy's death, television was a relatively new medium, and this national tragedy was among the first covered by television news. **Joanne Ostrow,** a television and radio critic for the *Denver Post,* analyzes the effect of television in her article **"TV Coverage of JFK's Death Forged Medium's Role."** As you read, try to distinguish between the facts Ostrow presents and the opinions she expresses. (For more practice with distinguishing fact from opinion, see page 284.)

CRONKITE

DENVER POST Nov. 16, 2003

TV Coverage of JFK's Death Forged Medium's Role

by Joanne Ostrow

No amount of anniversaries and commemorations can erase the visceral impact of that November weekend in 1963.

But with the passage of 40 years, a number freighted with generational weight, we can view the media fallout from John F. Kennedy's assassination in the light cast by a more recent tragedy.

For Nov. 22, 1963, marked a shift in the media culture in a way that Sept. 11, 2001, marked a shift in America's awareness of its place in the global community.

The sense of connectedness via television was much the same in both instances. But in 1963, the feelings were new and the medium's growing pains in plain view.

Imagine, 90 percent of homes with TVs watched the JFK assassination coverage that weekend; A. C. Nielsen[1] said the average home tuned in for 31.6 hours.

Milton Berle, Lucille Ball and Ed Sullivan[2] had achieved mass TV moments, but television news never before had held a prolonged vigil. Suddenly, 'breaking news' took on a new definition. If this wasn't when television achieved legitimacy, it was at least when TV news became unavoidably dominant.

Vietnam was arguably a bigger milestone in the evolution of television news. By making it 'the living room war,' TV altered history, ending the killing sooner. For that matter, TV coverage of the 1962 Cuban missile crisis[3] offered a glimmer of how the events of a year later would rivet a nation.

But the JFK assassination coverage changed our expectations of the news and, by extension, the pace of our lives.

Strange how the most glamorous presidency

1. **A. C. Nielsen.** A television rating company, now called ACNielsen
2. **Milton Berle, Lucille Ball and Ed Sullivan.** Popular personalities on comedy and variety shows in the early days of television
3. **Cuban missile crisis.** Cold War confrontation that arose when the United States learned that the Soviet Union was building in Cuba sites for launching nuclear missiles within striking distance of the United States. The two powerful countries came dangerously close to nuclear war.

vis • cer • al (vi´ sə rəl) *adj.,* intensely emotional; felt as if in the internal organs
le • git • i • ma • cy (li ji´ tə mə sē) *n.,* authenticity

Mourners watching assassination and funeral coverage.

and the most controversial killing of the century are easily distilled into a discussion of media. It's true: 40 years later, the death of a young president pales next to the birth of a new media culture.

We learned that weekend that, in the media age, history amounts to iconic film moments. Shots of the limousine, the slumping figure and the pink suit are ingrained in memory. The images inspired many art works, none more surreal than the originals.

The pill-box hat[4] is part of our American vocabulary. And the sight of Walter Cronkite[5] removing his heavy black glasses and fighting tears became part of a pop-culture film loop endlessly replaying in our collective consciousness: 40 years of the same video art installation we call history.

As of Nov. 22, 1963, when the three existing networks broadcast 'wall-to-wall' news for the first time, newsprint yellowed before our eyes. The world of information changed. The lens opened and events and ideas came at us at the speed of light.

The shift from the primacy of print to the tyranny of TV—television as the first source of news—was cinched. ❖

4. **pill-box hat.** Small, round, brimless hat; Jacqueline Kennedy wore one on the day of her husband's assassination
5. **Walter Cronkite.** Television news announcer

i • con • ic (ī kä´ nik) *adj.*, having characteristics of an icon, an object of uncritical devotion
pri • ma • cy (prī´ mə sē) *n.*, state of being first in time, place, or rank
tyr • an • ny (tir´ ə nē) *n.*, oppressive power

REFER TO TEXT ▶▶▶▶	▶ REASON WITH TEXT	
1a. Recall what Ostrow says was responsible for changing "the pace of our lives."	1b. Summarize how the author supports this statement.	**Understand** **Find meaning**
2a. Ostrow states that with this event "the shift from the primacy of print to the tyranny of TV—television as the first source of news—was cinched." Indicate how the author's word choices reveal her attitude toward this change.	2b. Identify the degree in which this shift has been a positive development. What has perhaps been lost as a result?	**Analyze** **Take things apart**
3a. Forty years later, how does the death of a young president compare to the birth of a new media culture, according to Ostrow?	3b. Explain the main or controlling idea of this article. Do you agree or disagree with the author's message? State your reasons.	**Evaluate** **Make judgments**

TEXT ◀TO▶ TEXT CONNECTION

- Compare and contrast how the authors of "American History" and "TV Coverage of JFK's Death Forged Medium's Role" use Kennedy's assassination in their writing. What effect do you think each intended to have on the readers of her piece?
- Discuss the different purposes an author may have in writing about a real historical event from a fictional perspective.

AFTER READING

EXTEND THE TEXT

Writing Options

Creative Writing Write two **descriptive introductory paragraphs** for a short story. These paragraphs should establish setting in a way that is vivid and clear. In one paragraph, describe a place with which you are quite familiar in the present time. In the other paragraph, describe the same place but in a time set in the past or future. Try to use specific details of landscape, buildings, furniture, clothing, the weather, and the season in both paragraphs to make the setting as realistic as possible.

Persuasive Writing Assume that a friend says, "There was no hope of Elena and Eugene ever remaining friends." Do you agree or disagree? Share your opinion by writing a **persuasive character analysis** in which you examine each character's personality and background and collect details about them to support your opinion. Write the argument in a unified informative paragraph.

Collaborative Learning

Analyze Symbols In "American History," the door to Eugene's house is painted green, "the color of hope." The author uses other colors as symbols to stand for various ideas and feelings. Go back and skim the story, looking for other references to color, and jot these references in your notebook. Then meet with a small group to discuss the following questions: Where is color present in the story? What might the presence or absence of color mean in each situation?

Media Literacy

Participate in a Panel Discussion The mid-1960s was an important time for the U.S. Civil Rights movement. In a small group, research one of the following events from that time: the assassination of Medgar Evers; Martin Luther King Jr.'s "I Have a Dream" speech; the bombing of the Sixteenth Street Baptist Church in Birmingham, Alabama; or the passage of the Civil Rights Act of 1964. In a panel discussion, present your findings to the class. Discuss how the events of 1963 might have contributed to the passage of the Civil Rights Act the following year.

Go to **www.mirrorsandwindows.com** for more.

READING ASSESSMENT

1. Number these events from "American History" in the correct sequence, with 1 being the first thing to happen in the story.
   ____ Elena introduces herself to Eugene.
   ____ Elena tries to cry for the dead president.
   ____ President Kennedy is assassinated.
   ____ Eugene's mother answers the door.
   ____ Mr. DePalma yells at the students.
   ____ Elena watches the Jewish family from the fire escape.

2. Which of the following statements supports the author's assertion in "TV Coverage of JFK's Death..." that news coverage of the assassination led to TV becoming dominant in news reporting?
   A. "...Sept. 11, 2001, marked a shift in America's awareness of its place in the global community."
   B. "...A. C. Nielsen said the average home tuned in for 31.6 hours."
   C. "Vietnam was arguably a bigger milestone in the evolution of television news."
   D. "The sense of connectedness via television was much the same in both instances [that and Sept. 11, 2001]."
   E. "No amount of anniversaries and commemorations can erase the visceral impact of that November weekend in 1963."

3. "American History" might best be summarized by which statement?
   A. Personal disappointments can overshadow public tragedies.
   B. Prejudices are difficult to overcome.
   C. It is very difficult for people to escape their upbringing.
   D. Adults are constantly telling teenagers what to do and how to feel.
   E. It's important for people to do what is expected of them.

4. As it is used on page 124 of "American History," the word *enthralled* most nearly means
   A. overpowered.
   B. charmed.
   C. frustrated.
   D. confused.
   E. irritated.

5. Ostrow states that on Nov. 22, 1963, newsprint "yellowed before our eyes." What does that statement mean? Explain how Ostrow supports this statement. Do you think it is accurate? Why or why not?

VOCABULARY & SPELLING

UNDERSTAND THE CONCEPT

APPLY THE SKILL

Denotation and Connotation

The **denotation** of a word is its dictionary definition. The **connotation** of a word is an emotional association the word has in addition to its literal meaning.

Several types of connotation can influence the way you think about a word:

positive connotation: words that evoke a favorable response

negative connotation: words that provoke an unfavorable response

neutral connotation: words that cause no emotional response

For example, the words *cheap* and *thrifty* both denote "tending to spend less money," but *cheap* has a negative connotation similar to "stingy," whereas *thrifty* has a positive connotation that suggests being responsible with money. The best way of learning the connotation of a word is to pay attention to the context in which the word appears.

Different people may have different connotations for words. For example, the word *sunshine* has a positive connotation for many people. They may hear it and think warm and relaxing thoughts. However, if your skin is sensitive to the sun, the word *sunshine* may have a negative connotation for you.

Connotations also often express degree. For example, notice the slight differences in meaning among the following words:

wrathful
angry
frustrated
annoyed

Words also have *formal* and *informal* connotations. When you speak with or write to people who are in a position of authority, older people, or others you do not know well, you are most likely to use words with formal connotations. For example, you might address an elderly grandparent as *grandmother* instead of a less formal term like *granny*. Formal connotations tend to be either neutral or favorable. When you speak with or write to your friends, you are most likely to use words with informal connotations.

It is important to be aware of the connotations of words as well as their dictionary definitions. If you use a word with the wrong connotation, you might not convey the meaning you intended—or worse, you might offend your reader or listener. Politicians and salespeople are careful to use words with positive connotations. For example, most presidential speeches contain "feel-good" words such as *unite, freedom, equality,* and *progress.* Many sales pitches include words such as *modern, convenient,* and *value.*

Some dictionaries explain the differences in connotations between words with similar meanings. For example, if you look up the word *calm* in a dictionary, you may find a description of the differences between *calm, tranquil, serene, placid,* and *peaceful.*

Notice the slight differences in meaning between the following synonyms or near synonyms. They have very similar denotations, but differing connotations.

strong-willed / stubborn
flighty / unpredictable
solitude / loneliness
selective / picky
arrogant / self-confident

REVIEW TERMS

- **denotation:** the dictionary definition of a word
- **connotation:** the emotional association of a word in addition to its literal meaning
- **synonym:** a word that has the same basic meaning as another word
- **near synonym:** a word that has nearly the same meaning as another word but may have a different connotation

UNDERSTAND THE CONCEPT

APPLY THE SKILL

Exercise A

Use your prior knowledge, and a dictionary if needed, to identify the denotation of each of the following words from "The Scarlet Ibis" and "American History." Then tell whether the word for you has a positive, neutral, or negative connotation. Work with a partner to write sentences that use the words correctly. Make sure the context is appropriate for the connotation of the word.

1. martyr
2. discreet
3. hysterical
4. distraught
5. untenanted
6. stocky
7. snobbery
8. crazy
9. invalid
10. parade

Exercise B

In "The Scarlet Ibis," Doodle and his brother laugh with happiness when they know Doodle can learn to walk. With a partner, write down eight words expressing degrees of happiness, and rank them in order from least intense to most intense.

Exercise C

Working with your partner, brainstorm a list of words that have similar meanings, but different connotations. You may use a dictionary or thesaurus to help you. Then sort the words in a chart like the one below, showing which have negative connotations, which have positive connotations, and which are neutral.

Negative	Neutral	Positive
weird	unusual	unique
freakish	different	remarkable
bizarre	uncommon	extraordinary
abnormal	rare	unequaled

Exercise D

For each of the following words, think of a synonym with a more positive connotation. You may use a thesaurus to help you. Then write a sentence using each word.

1. fussy
2. stingy
3. nosy
4. fanatic
5. chatterbox
6. loner
7. skimpy
8. sickly
9. freak
10. selfish

SPELLING PRACTICE

Sounds of the Letter *C*

The letter *c* can pose problems for spelling because it can make a different sound depending on the letters that come after it. Generally, *c* before *e* or *i* sounds like the letter *s* as in the word "celery," though it can sometimes sound like *sh* as in "magician" or *k* as in some pronunciations of the word "Celtic." The digraph (set of two letters to make one sound) *ch* is usually pronounced as it is in the word "church," but it can also be pronounced like *k* in words like "mechanic." Read these words from "The Scarlet Ibis" and determine what sound the *c* makes in each word.

accidentally
accomplishments
ancestors
campaign
chimney
collapse
contrarily
descended
difference
discouraged
evanesced
fiercely
iridescent
magnificent
miracle
occasionally
precariously
scientifically
stomach
succeeded

GRAMMAR & STYLE

UNDERSTAND THE CONCEPT

APPLY THE SKILL

Sentence Variety

Too many simple sentences can make writing seem plodding and simplistic. Too many complex sentences may risk confusing the reader. A variety of sentence structures can give writing a rhythm and make it more interesting to read.

A **simple sentence** contains one independent clause and no subordinate clauses. A simple sentence is called an independent clause because it can stand by itself. It may have a compound subject, a compound predicate, and any number of phrases.

EXAMPLES

The two friends [subject] enjoyed similar activities [predicate].

Lynette and Jackee [compound subject] studied and spent time together [compound predicate].

A **compound sentence** consists of two sentences joined by a semicolon or by a comma followed by a coordinating conjunction. The most common coordinating conjunctions are *and, or, nor, for, but, so,* and *yet.* Each part of the compound sentence has its own subject and verb.

EXAMPLE

The two friends enjoyed similar activities [independent clause], and [coordinating conjunction] they often walked together to school [independent clause].

A **complex sentence** consists of one independent clause and one or more subordinate clauses.

EXAMPLE

Because they spent hours together during summer vacation [subordinate clause], the two friends became more like sisters [independent clause].

What Great Writers Do

Notice the sentence variety that Judith Ortiz Cofer uses in this paragraph from "American History" (page 121).

> It was a cold day in Paterson. The kind that warns of early snow. I was miserable, since I had forgotten my gloves, and my knuckles were turning red and raw from the jump rope. I was also taking a lot of abuse from the black girls for not turning the rope hard and fast enough for them.

Can you identify which sentence in this excerpt is actually a sentence *fragment* (a sentence that does not contain both a subject and a verb)? Professional writers sometimes use sentence fragments for effect, although you shouldn't do this in formal writing.

REVIEW TERMS

- **subject:** the doer of the action
- **predicate:** the part of the sentence that contains the verb phrase, including the objects, or recipients, of the action
- **clause:** a group of words that functions as one part of speech and that contains both a subject and a verb
- **phrase:** a group of words that functions as one part of speech but does not have both a subject and a verb
- **independent clause:** a complete sentence with a subject and a verb
- **subordinate clause:** a clause that contains a subject and a verb but cannot stand alone because it does not express a complete idea

UNDERSTAND THE CONCEPT

APPLY THE SKILL

Identify Sentence Structures

Identify each of the following sentences from "TV Coverage of JFK's Death Forged Medium's Role" as *simple, compound,* or *complex.*

1. The sense of connectedness via television was much the same in both instances.
2. If this wasn't when television achieved legitimacy, it was at least when TV news became unavoidably dominant.
3. The lens opened, and events and ideas came at us at the speed of light.
4. The pill-box hat is part of our American vocabulary.
5. As of Nov. 22, 1963, when the three existing networks broadcast "wall-to-wall" news for the first time, newsprint yellowed before our eyes.
6. In 1963, the feelings were new and the medium's growing pains were in plain view.
7. No amount of anniversaries and commemorations can erase the visceral impact of that November weekend in 1963.
8. At the time of Kennedy's death, television was a relatively new medium, and this national tragedy was among the first covered by television news.
9. Strange how the most glamorous presidency and the most controversial killing of the century are easily distilled into a discussion of media.

Improve Sentence Variety

Make the following paragraph about "The Scarlet Ibis" more interesting by revising some of the complex sentences to be simple or compound.

> Although the character of Doodle in "The Scarlet Ibis" was born with a disability, he is remarkably resilient. Despite not being able to walk at first, he pushes himself until he can walk, run, and even swim. Because his brother taunts him, Doodle tries harder. Even though Doodle is a small and weak boy, mentally he has a lot of strength.

Use Varied Sentence Structures in Your Writing

Write a short story about an unlikely friendship between two people or a brief essay about your own experience becoming friends with someone who seems to be very different from you. Choose your audience: a younger sibling who needs help making friends, or an adult who believes students of different backgrounds should be separated. After drafting your story, check for variety in your sentence structures. Which type of sentence structure did you use most often? Do you think that type is appropriate for the audience? Alter your sentence structures as needed for variety and audience appropriateness.

EXTEND THE SKILL

Examine the sentence structures in what you are currently reading, whether it be a textbook, novel, comic, or magazine. Note the number of simple versus complex or compound sentences. You may also wish to look at sentences in a children's book and compare them with the sentence structures in a novel for adults. For example, the first sentences from the following books show a wide range of sentence structures.

The Cat in the Hat, by Dr. Seuss (children's book)
Anne of Green Gables, by L. M. Montgomery (young adult)
The Diary of a Young Girl, by Anne Frank (young adult)
The Lion, the Witch, and the Wardrobe, by C. S. Lewis (young adult)
The Secret Garden, by Frances Hodgson Burnett (young adult)

Understanding Theme

THEME

Theme is a central idea in a literary work. You can also think of theme as the author's message. Some literary works have more than one theme, with one theme being more dominant than others. Do not confuse theme with plot. Plot outlines the events of a story; it answers the question, "What happens?" Theme, on the other hand, answers the question, "What is the point?"

In traditional literature, such as the fable or fairy tale, the theme is the moral of the story. The greedy dog of Aesop's fable snaps at his reflection in a river, and the bone he was enjoying falls from his jaws and is swept away by the current. The theme is obvious: The greedy lose what they have in trying to get more than their fair share. The moral of "Cinderella," featuring literature's most neglected stepdaughter, is also clear: Goodness triumphs over wickedness. Cinderella is beautiful and industrious, whereas her stepsisters are lazy and rather funny looking. The reader does not have to dig deep to find the theme.

Popular Themes in Literature

A common theme in literature is the search for personal identity. The following novels explore this theme:

Jane Eyre, by Charlotte Brontë
The House on Mango Street, by Sandra Cisneros
Great Expectations, by Charles Dickens
The Old Man and the Sea, by Ernest Hemingway
O Pioneers!, by Willa Cather

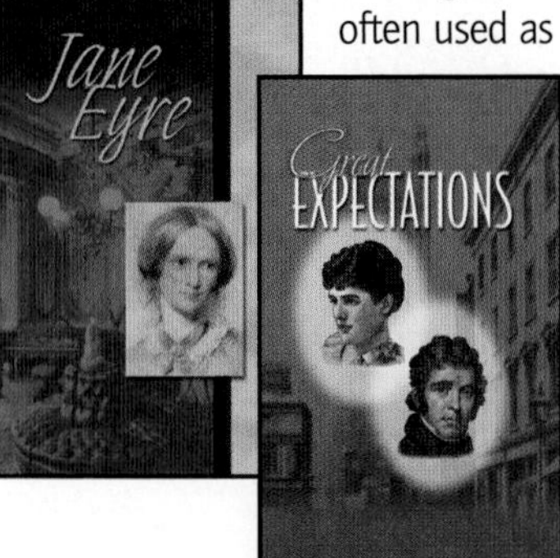

Other general topics that are often used as themes in literature include love, family, triumph over adversity, death and illness, greed and ambition, growing up, visions of the future, and courage and fear.

Modern literature, however, tends to be more sophisticated. That is partly because our worldview has shifted, and partly because the aim of the modern storyteller is somewhat different. There may be a moral in a modern tale, and in some stories, there are certainly clear consequences to human action. But most of today's authors would be embarrassed if a reader could so easily locate meaning that the story could be reduced to a one-sentence moral or theme.

ELEMENTS OF THEME

Symbols

Sometimes, the theme can be found in the symbolism of a work of literature. A **symbol** is anything that stands for or represents both itself and something else. This might be a *conventional* symbol, an object with which many people have associations, such as a flag, a star, or a particular color identified with a mood, as green is identified with envy. For instance, in "The Gift of the Magi" (page 139), the reader has no trouble associating a woman's long hair with the ideal of womanly beauty. The symbol may also be *personal* or *idiosyncratic,* one that assumes its secondary meaning because of the special use to which it is put by a writer. In that case, your job as the reader is to look for all the possible associations that could be attached to the symbolic object. In "The Scarlet Ibis" (page 109), the dying ibis is a personal symbol; the bird's fate is so central to the story, so tied to Doodle's fate, that you can predict the plot from the associations surrounding the symbol.

Character

When analyzing a theme in a work of fiction, it is also necessary to look at character. In "The Interlopers" (page 15), both von Gradwitz and Znaeym are angry and implacable men. As a wise philosopher remarked, "Character is fate." Because von Gradwitz and Znaeym are stubborn and vindictive, they are threatened with a terrible end. As you read the stories in this unit, notice how character and plot are intertwined, and how they work together to express the stories' themes.

Plot and Characterization

The theme of a fictional work, then, should be analyzed along with plot and characterization, and with the writer's attitude toward his or her material. As the plot unfolds, you may find a pattern to these events; in that case, the pattern may lead you to a significant theme. For example, "The Most Dangerous Game" (page 27), reveals a pattern in which a hunter hunts, is hunted, and, at last, hunts again. Rainford's position is relative to other events in the plot. What theme might the author be suggesting here? After you have read the story you should know whether the author's attitude is ironic, comic, or tragic. Until you understand the author's viewpoint, you cannot identify the prevailing theme or themes of the story. A work may have more than one possible theme or a theme that may be open to different interpretations by the reader. Now you can see why theme can be more subtle a concept than main idea.

TYPES OF THEMES

Most works of fiction do not directly state the theme. When the theme is presented directly, it is called a **stated theme.** For example, at the end of "The Gift of the Magi," O. Henry tells the reader what ideas he or she should take away from the reading. The story itself is centered on this single stated theme.

> But in a last word to the wise of these days let it be said that of all who give gifts these two were the wisest. Of all who give and receive gifts, such as they are wisest. Everywhere they are wisest. They are the magi.
>
> —from "The Gift of the Magi"
> by O. Henry

In contrast, Maupassant presents his story but leaves the reader to draw conclusions about the theme of "The Necklace" (page 143). This type of theme is called an **implied theme** and requires the reader to make inferences, or guesses, about the author's intent and perception of the events in the story.

Sometimes, a story character voices a theme. The narrator of "The Scarlet Ibis" suggests an important theme when he reflects on his conflicting feelings about his younger brother, which he aptly describes as the "knot of cruelty borne by the stream of love."

> There is within me (and with sadness I have watched it in others) a knot of cruelty borne by the stream of love, much as our blood sometimes bears the seed of our destruction, and at times I was mean to Doodle. One day I took him up to the barn loft and showed him his casket, telling him how we all had believed he would die.
>
> —from "The Scarlet Ibis"
> by James Hurst

DISCOVERING THEMES

To discover the theme or themes in a literary work, you can ask yourself the following questions about the work and make inferences based on your reading. These questions will help you explore the author's intentions in the story.

- What is the main idea?
- What does the author want me to think about?
- What seems to motivate the characters?
- What causes situations to change or events to happen?

After you find a general topic, consider what the author is saying about the topic to refine it into a more specific theme. For example, generosity is a dominant topic in "The Necklace." You could consider the general topic of "generosity" when comparing "The Necklace" to other selections with a similar topic. But, to analyze the theme of the individual piece, you will need to refine this broad topic into a specific theme. That is, you must figure out what the author is saying about generosity in this story. Is he saying that it is better to give than to receive, or that self-sacrifice is the greatest form of generosity?

The Gift of the Magi

A Short Story by O. Henry

The Necklace

A Short Story by Guy de Maupassant

COMPARING LITERATURE

BEFORE READING

BUILD BACKGROUND

Literary Context O. Henry's stories are famous for their distinctive surprise endings in which an ironic event occurs that violates expectations of the characters or the reader. **"The Gift of the Magi,"** published in 1906, contains one of the most famous surprise endings of all. Many of O. Henry's stories are set in the author's favorite locale, New York City, and are peopled with his favorite characters—lower middle-class workers, the unemployed, the homeless, and the forgotten.

"The Necklace" by Guy de Maupassant ironically depicts the fashionable life of Paris and the behavior of the middle class. His unemotional narration, meticulous detail, and accurate historical background are three of the techniques that mark his writing. As a *Naturalist* author, he sought to portray human beings and the society in which they live as accurately and truthfully as possible. For more on naturalism, see page 144.

Reader's Context What do you envy that others have? How might your life be different if you had what you wanted? What price would you pay to obtain it? To what lengths do you think somebody would be willing to go to get it for you?

USE READING SKILLS

Meaning of Words As you read, use context clues, find definitions in the dictionary, and decode words by recognizing common word parts. Create Word Maps, like the one below, to use as you read.

Word or Phrase	
Denotation	Connotation
Word Parts I Recognize	Synonyms
Word Origin	
Sentence Using Word or Phrase	Picture Illustrating Word or Phrase

COMPARE LITERATURE: Theme and Irony

A **theme** is a central idea or perception about life that is conveyed through a literary work. Wanting something you can't afford might be the topic of either story, but each has a distinct theme. **Irony** is the difference between appearance and reality. *Irony of situation* occurs when an event happens that violates the expectations of the characters, the reader, or the audience. How does each story use irony for effect?

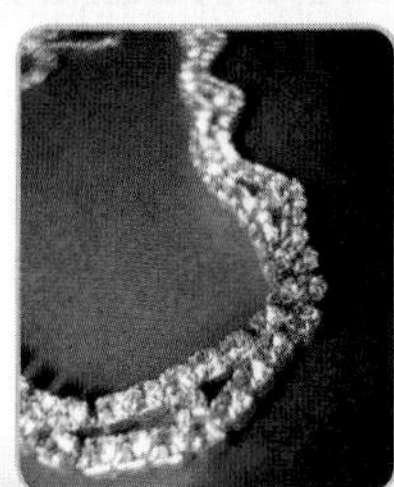

MEET THE AUTHORS

PORTER

William Sydney Porter (1862–1910) was raised in Greensboro, North Carolina, and was educated by his aunt who ran a private school. He adopted the pseudonym **O. Henry** while in jail. Porter was convicted of embezzling money and served more than three years in federal prison. After his release, he moved to New York City and began publishing a story a week.

Guy de Maupassant (1850–1893), one of the world's great short story writers, was born in Normandy, France. Through family connections, he met writer Gustave Flaubert, who mentored Maupassant and introduced him to other major writers of the day, including Emile Zola and Henry James. While Maupassant mainly wrote short stories, he also published six novels.

MAUPASSANT

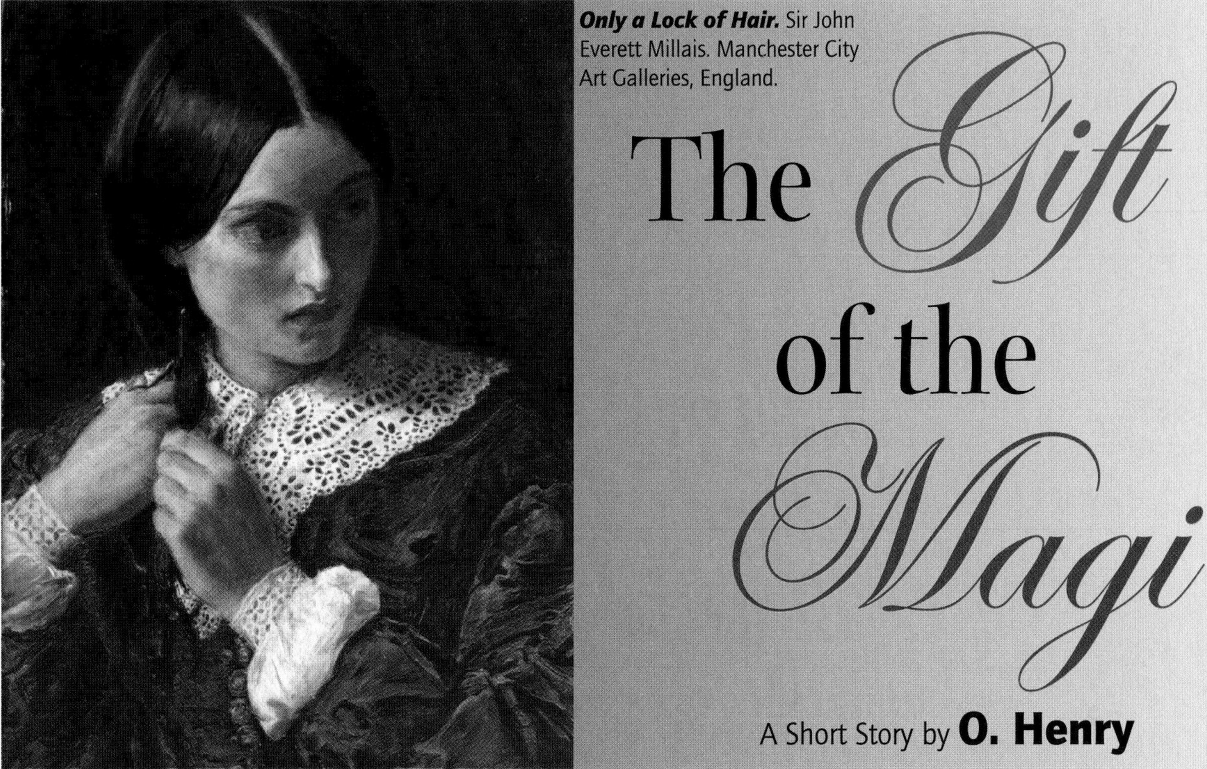

Only a Lock of Hair. Sir John Everett Millais. Manchester City Art Galleries, England.

The *Gift* of the *Magi*

A Short Story by **O. Henry**

Eight dollars a week or a million a year—what is the difference?

One dollar and eighty-seven cents. That was all. And sixty cents of it was in pennies. Pennies saved one and two at a time by bulldozing the grocer and the vegetable man and the butcher until one's cheeks burned with the silent imputation of parsimony that such close dealing implied. Three times Della counted it. One dollar and eighty-seven cents. And the next day would be Christmas.

There was clearly nothing to do but flop down on the shabby little couch and howl. So Della did it. Which instigates the moral reflection that life is made up of sobs, sniffles, and smiles, with sniffles predominating. While the mistress of the home is gradually subsiding from the first stage to the second, take a look at the home. A furnished flat at $8 per week. It did not exactly beggar description, but it certainly had that word on the lookout for the mendicancy[1] squad.

In the vestibule below was a letter box into which no letter would go, and an electric button from which no mortal finger could coax a ring. Also appertaining thereunto was a card bearing the name "Mr. James Dillingham Young."

The "Dillingham" had been flung to the breeze during a former period of prosperity when its possessor was being paid $30 per week. Now, when the income was shrunk to $20, the letters of "Dillingham" looked blurred, as though they were thinking seriously of contracting to a modest and unassuming D. But whenever Mr. James Dillingham Young came home and reached his flat above he was

1. **mendicancy.** Begging

im • pu • ta • tion (im' pyə tā´ shən) *n.,* accusation; insinuation
par • si • mo • ny (pär´ sə mō' nē) *n.,* stinginess; extreme thriftiness
pre • dom • i • nate (pri dä´ mə nāt') *v.,* holding advantage in numbers
ap • per • tain (a' pər tān´) *v.,* connecting to; being a part of

called "Jim" and greatly hugged by Mrs. James Dillingham Young, already introduced to you as Della. Which is all very good.

Della finished her cry and attended to her cheeks with the powder rag. She stood by the window and looked out dully at a gray cat walking a gray fence in a gray backyard. Tomorrow would be Christmas Day, and she had only $1.87 with which to buy Jim a present. She had been saving every penny she could for months, with this result. Twenty dollars a week doesn't go far. Expenses had been greater than she had calculated. They always are. Only $1.87 to buy a present for Jim. Her Jim. Many a happy hour she had spent planning for something nice for him. Something fine and rare and sterling—something just a little bit near to being worthy of the honor of being owned by Jim.

Della's beautiful hair fell about her rippling and shining like a cascade of brown waters.

There was a pier glass[2] between the windows of the room. Perhaps you have seen a pier glass in an $8 flat. A very thin and very agile person may, by observing his reflection in a rapid sequence of longitudinal strips, obtain a fairly accurate conception of his looks. Della, being slender, had mastered the art.

Suddenly she whirled from the window and stood before the glass. Her eyes were shining brilliantly, but her face had lost its color within twenty seconds. Rapidly she pulled down her hair and let it fall to its full length.

Now, there were two possessions of the James Dillingham Youngs in which they took a mighty pride. One was Jim's gold watch that had been his father's and his grandfather's. The other was Della's hair. Had the Queen of Sheba[3] lived in the flat across the air shaft, Della would have let her hair hang out the window some day to dry just to depreciate Her Majesty's jewels and gifts. Had King Solomon[4] been the janitor, with all his treasures piled up in the basement, Jim would have pulled out his watch every time he passed, just to see him pluck at his beard from envy. So now Della's beautiful hair fell about her rippling and shining like a cascade of brown waters. It reached below her knee and made itself almost a garment for her. And then she did it up again nervously and quickly. Once she faltered for a minute and stood still while a tear or two splashed on the worn red carpet.

On went her old brown jacket; on went her old brown hat. With a whirl of skirts and with the brilliant sparkle still in her eyes, she fluttered out the door and down the stairs to the street.

Where she stopped the sign read: "Mme. Sofronie. Hair Goods of All Kinds." One flight up Della ran, and collected herself, panting. Madame, large, too white, chilly, hardly looked the "Sofronie."

"Will you buy my hair?" asked Della.

"I buy hair," said Madame. "Take yer hat off and let's have a sight at the looks of it."

Down rippled the brown cascade.

"Twenty dollars," said Madame, lifting the mass with a practiced hand.

"Give it to me quick," said Della.

Oh, and the next two hours tripped by on rosy wings. Forget the hashed metaphor. She was ransacking the stores for Jim's present.

She found it at last. It surely had been made for Jim and no one else. There was no

---

2. **pier glass.** Narrow mirror set between two windows
3. **Queen of Sheba.** Biblical queen
4. **King Solomon.** Biblical king

de • pre • ci • ate (di prē´ shē āt') *v.*, lower in value other like it in any of the stores, and she had turned all of them inside out. It was a platinum fob chain[5] simple and chaste in design, properly proclaiming its value by substance alone and not by meretricious ornamentation—as all good things should do. It was even worthy of The Watch. As soon as she saw it she knew that it must be Jim's. It was like him. Quietness and value—the description applied to both. Twenty-one dollars they took from her for it, and she hurried home with the eighty-seven cents. With that chain on his watch Jim might be properly anxious about the time in any company. Grand as the watch was, he sometimes looked at it on the sly on account of the old leather strap that he used in place of a chain.

When Della reached home her intoxication gave way a little to prudence and reason. She got out her curling irons and lighted the gas and went to work repairing the ravages made by generosity added to love. Which is always a tremendous task, dear friends—a mammoth task. Within forty minutes her head was covered with tiny, close-lying curls that made her look wonderfully like a truant schoolboy. She looked at her reflection in the mirror long, carefully, and critically.

"If Jim doesn't kill me," she said to herself, "before he takes a second look at me, he'll say I look like a Coney Island[6] chorus girl. But what could I do—oh! what could I do with a dollar and eighty-seven cents?"

At seven o'clock the coffee was made and the frying pan was on the back of the stove hot and ready to cook the chops.

Jim was never late. Della doubled the fob chain in her hand and sat on the corner of the table near the door that he always entered. Then she heard his step on the stair away down on the first flight, and she turned white for just a moment. She had a habit of saying little silent prayers about the simplest everyday things, and now she whispered: "Please God, make him think I am still pretty."

The door opened and Jim stepped in and closed it. He looked thin and very serious. Poor fellow, he was only twenty-two—and to be burdened with a family! He needed a new overcoat and he was without gloves.

Jim stopped inside the door, as immovable as a setter at the scent of quail. His eyes were fixed upon Della, and there was an expression in them that she could not read, and it terrified her. It was not anger, nor surprise, nor disapproval, nor horror, nor any of the sentiments that she had been prepared for. He simply stared at her fixedly with that peculiar expression on his face.

Della wriggled off the table and went for him.

"Jim, darling," she cried, "don't look at me that way. I had my hair cut off and sold it because I couldn't have lived through Christmas without giving you a present. It'll grow out again—you won't mind, will you? I just had to do it. My hair grows awfully fast. Say 'Merry Christmas,' Jim, and let's be happy. You don't know what a nice—what a beautiful, nice gift I've got for you."

"You've cut off your hair?" asked Jim, laboriously, as if he had not arrived at that patent fact yet even after the hardest mental labor.

"Cut it off and sold it," said Della. "Don't you like me just as well, anyhow? I'm me without my hair, ain't I?"

Jim looked about the room curiously.

"You say your hair is gone?" he said, with an air almost of idiocy.

"You needn't look for it," said Della. "It's sold, I tell you—sold and gone, too. It's Christmas Eve, boy. Be good to me, for it went for you. Maybe the hairs of my head were numbered," she went on with a sudden serious

5. **fob chain.** Chain for a pocket watch
6. **Coney Island.** Section of Brooklyn, New York, known for its amusement park

mer • e • tri • cious (mer′ ə tri′ shəs) *adj.*, attractive in a false, showy way
pru • dence (prü′ d′n[t]s) *n.*, sound judgment

sweetness, "but nobody could ever count my love for you. Shall I put the chops on, Jim?"

Out of his trance Jim seemed quickly to wake. He enfolded his Della. For ten seconds let us regard with discreet scrutiny some inconsequential object in the other direction. Eight dollars a week or a million a year—what is the difference? A mathematician or a wit would give you the wrong answer. The magi[7] brought valuable gifts, but that was not among them. This dark assertion will be illuminated later on.

Jim drew a package from his overcoat pocket and threw it upon the table.

"Don't make any mistake, Dell," he said, "about me. I don't think there's anything in the way of a haircut or a shave or a shampoo that could make me like my girl any less. But if you'll unwrap that package you may see why you had me going awhile at first."

White fingers and nimble tore at the string and paper. And then an ecstatic scream of joy; and then, alas! a quick feminine change to hysterical tears and wails, necessitating the immediate employment of all the comforting powers of the lord of the flat.

For there lay The Combs—the set of combs, side and back, that Della had worshiped for long in a Broadway window. Beautiful combs, pure tortoise shell, with jeweled rims just the shade to wear in the beautiful vanished hair. They were expensive combs, she knew, and her heart had simply craved and yearned over them without the least hope of possession. And now, they were hers, but the tresses that should have adorned the coveted adornments were gone.

But she hugged them to her bosom, and at length she was able to look up with dim eyes and a smile and say: "My hair grows so fast, Jim!"

And then Della leaped up like a little singed cat and cried, "Oh, oh!"

Jim had not yet seen his beautiful present. She held it out to him eagerly upon her open palm. The dull precious metal seemed to flash with a reflection of her bright and ardent spirit.

"Isn't it a dandy, Jim? I hunted all over town to find it. You'll have to look at the time a hundred times a day now. Give me your watch. I want to see how it looks on it."

Instead of obeying, Jim tumbled down on the couch and put his hands under the back of his head and smiled.

"Dell," said he, "let's put our Christmas presents away and keep 'em awhile. They're too nice to use just at present. I sold the watch to get the money to buy your combs. And now suppose you put the chops on." The magi, as you know, were wise men—wonderfully wise men—who brought gifts to the Babe in the manger. They invented the art of giving Christmas presents. Being wise, their gifts were no doubt wise ones, possibly bearing the privilege of exchange in case of duplication. And here I have lamely related to you the uneventful chronicle of two foolish children in a flat who most unwisely sacrificed for each other the greatest treasures of their house. But in a last word to the wise of these days let it be said that of all who give gifts these two were the wisest. Of all who give and receive gifts, such as they are wisest. Everywhere they are wisest. They are the magi. ❖

7. **magi.** Wise men from the East who brought gifts to the infant Jesus

in • con • se • quen • tial (in['] kän[t]' sə kwen[t]´ shəl) *adj.*, unimportant
a • dorn • ment (ə dôrn´ mənt) *n.*, ornament; decoration
du • pli • ca • tion (dü' pli kā´ shən) *n.*, act or process of duplicating; a copy or double

How does the phrase "the best things in life are free" relate to this selection? What are some examples of things that money can't buy? Have you ever wanted to give a gift that you couldn't afford? What did you do?

REFER TO TEXT ▶▶▶▶	▶ REASON WITH TEXT	
1a. List the details which suggest that Della and Jim are relatively poor.	1b. Restate what Della's biggest concern is about not having much money.	**Understand** **Find meaning**
2a. Search the story and record the details that indicate a definite time period.	2b. Apply what you know and can guess about that era to determine why Della's haircut was such a big sacrifice.	**Apply** **Use information**
3a. What character traits of Della and of Jim prompt them to give the gifts they give?	3b. Identify what you think gives people the ability to put the needs of others before their own.	**Analyze** **Take things apart**
4a. Recognize how the narrator interacts with the reader in this story. Provide several examples that illustrate this interaction.	4b. Evaluate whether or not the narrator's commentary is helpful or intrusive. Give reasons to support your opinion.	**Evaluate** **Make judgments**
5a. Recall why the narrator states, "Of all who give and receive gifts, such as they are wisest." To whom is he referring?	5b. How does this passage relate to the title of the story? Propose what you believe to be the main idea or theme of the story.	**Create** **Bring ideas together**

The Necklace

A Short Story by **Guy de Maupassant**

How small a thing will ruin or save one!

She was one of those pretty, charming young ladies; born, as if through an error of destiny, into a family of clerks. She had no dowry,[1] no hopes, no means of becoming known, appreciated, loved, and married by a man either rich or distinguished; and she allowed herself to marry a petty clerk in the office of the Board of Education.

She was simple, not being able to adorn herself, but she was unhappy, as one out of her class; for women belong to no caste, no race, their grace, their beauty and their charm serving them in the place of birth and family. Their inborn finesse, their instinctive elegance, their suppleness of wit, are their only aristocracy, making some daughters of the people the equal of great ladies.

She suffered incessantly, feeling herself born for all delicacies and luxuries. She suffered from the poverty of her apartment, the shabby walls,

1. **dowry.** Wealth to be given by a bride to her husband when she marries

fi • nesse (fə nes´) *n.*, refinement; delicacy
sup • ple • ness (sʉ´ pəl nəs) *n.*, flexibility
in • ces • sant • ly (in' se´ sn´[t] lē) *adv.*, constantly; endlessly

LITERARY CONNECTION

ZOLA

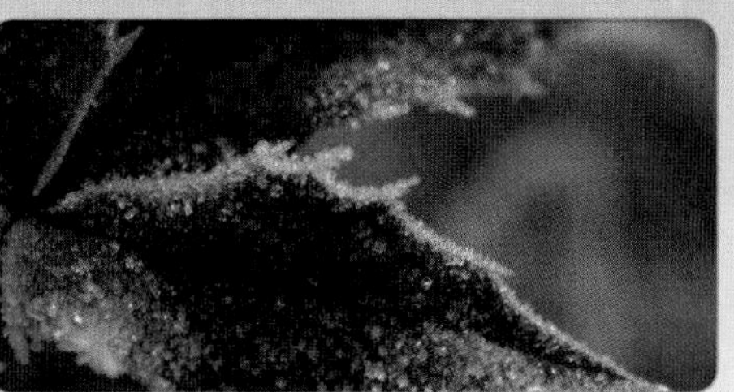

Naturalism "The Necklace" reflects the style and techniques of Naturalism, a literary movement of the late nineteenth and early twentieth centuries. It originated in France and was led by Emile Zola, whose essay "The Experimental Novel" came to represent the movement. Naturalist writers believed that human behaviors resulted from biological or environmental forces. Revolting against the Romantic school and its emphasis on subjectivity and imagination, Naturalist writers sought to portray human beings and the society in which they live as accurately and as truthfully as possible. As you read, notice how the author uses these techniques.

the worn chairs and the faded stuffs. All these things, which another woman of her station would not have noticed, tortured and angered her. The sight of the little Breton,[2] who made this humble home, awoke in her sad regrets and desperate dreams. She thought of quiet antechambers with their oriental hangings lighted by high bronze torches and of the two great footmen in short trousers who sleep in the large armchairs, made sleepy by the heavy air from the heating apparatus. She thought of large drawing rooms hung in old silks, of graceful pieces of furniture carrying bric-a-brac[3] of inestimable value and of the little perfumed coquettish apartments made for five o'clock chats with most intimate friends, men known and sought after, whose attention all women envied and desired.

When she seated herself for dinner before the round table, where the tablecloth had been used three days, opposite her husband who uncovered the tureen with a delighted air, saying: "Oh! the good potpie! I know nothing better than that," she would think of the elegant dinners, of the shining silver, of the tapestries[4] peopling the walls with ancient personages and rare birds in the midst of fairy forests; she thought of the exquisite food served on marvelous dishes, of the whispered gallantries, listened to with the smile of the Sphinx[5] while eating the rose-colored flesh of the trout or a chicken's wing.

She had neither frocks nor jewels, nothing. And she loved only those things. She felt that she was made for them. She had such a desire to please, to be sought after, to be clever and courted.

She had a rich friend, a schoolmate at the convent,[6] whom she did not like to visit. She suffered so much when she returned. And she wept for whole days from chagrin, from regret, from despair and disappointment.

◆ ◆ ◆

One evening her husband returned, elated, bearing in his hand a large envelope.

"Here, he said, "here is something for you."

2. **Breton.** Someone from Brittany, a rural province of France
3. **bric-a-brac.** Decorations
4. **tapestries.** Woven wall hangings
5. **Sphinx.** In Greek mythology, a creature with the body of a lion and the head of a woman that demanded that passersby in Thebes answer its riddles. A famous statue in Egypt features a mysterious smile.
6. **convent.** Residence of a religious order; sometimes also a school for girls

in • es • ti • ma • ble (i nes´ tə mə bəl) *adj.*, too valuable to be measured

cha • grin (shə grin´) *n.*, feeling of annoyance caused by failure or disappointment

Critical Viewing

How would you describe the different expressions on the faces of the two women depicted in this painting? Do these sentiments appear in the selection?

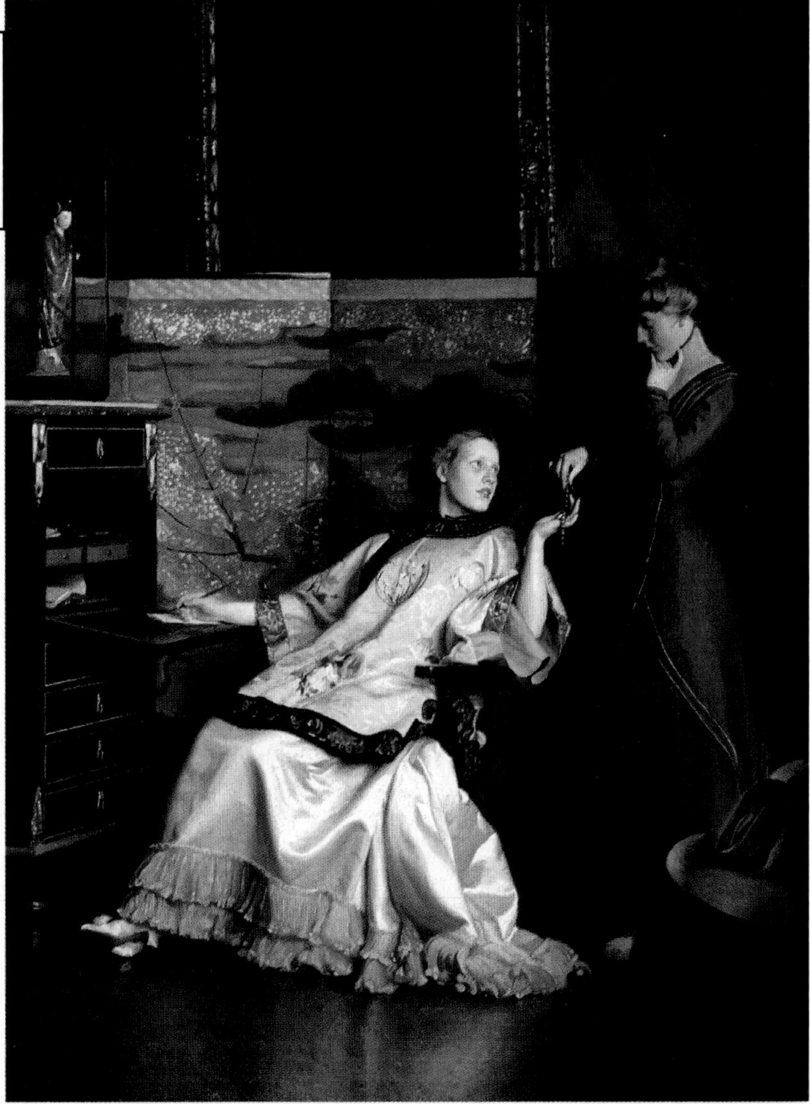

The New Necklace, 1910. William McGregor Paxton. Museum of Fine Arts, Boston.

She quickly tore open the wrapper and drew out a printed card on which were inscribed these words:

The Minister of Public Instruction and Madame George Ramponneau ask the honor of M. and Mme. Loisel's company Monday evening, January 18, at the Minister's residence.

Instead of being delighted, as her husband had hoped, she threw the invitation spitefully upon the table, murmuring:

"What do you suppose I want with that?"

"But, my dearie, I thought it would make you happy. You never go out, and this is an occasion, and a fine one! I had a great deal of trouble to get it. Everybody wishes one, and it is very select; not many are given to employees. You will see the whole official world there."

She looked at him with an irritated eye and declared impatiently: "What do you suppose I have to wear to such a thing as that?"

He had not thought of that; he stammered:

"Why, the dress you wear when we go to the theater. It seems very pretty to me."

He was silent, stupefied, in dismay, at the sight of his wife weeping. Two great tears fell slowly from the corners of her eyes toward the corners of her mouth; he stammered:

"What is the matter? What is the matter?"

By a violent effort she had controlled her vexation and responded in a calm voice, wiping her moist cheeks:

"Nothing. Only I have no dress and consequently I cannot go to this affair. Give your card to some colleague whose wife is better filled out than I."

He was grieved but answered:

"Let us see, Matilda. How much would a suitable costume cost, something that would serve for other occasions, something very simple?"

She reflected for some seconds, making estimates and thinking of a sum that she could ask for without bringing with it an immediate refusal and a frightened exclamation from the economical clerk.

Finally she said in a hesitating voice: "I cannot tell exactly, but it seems to me that four hundred francs[7] ought to cover it."

He turned a little pale, for he had saved just this sum to buy a gun that he might be able to join some hunting parties the next summer, on the plains at Nanterre,[8] with some friends who went to shoot larks up there on Sunday. Nevertheless, he answered:

"Very well. I will give you four hundred francs. But try to have a pretty dress."

◆◆◆

The day of the ball approached, and Mme. Loisel seemed sad, disturbed, anxious. Nevertheless, her dress was nearly ready. Her husband said to her one evening: "What is the matter with you? You have acted strangely for two or three days."

And she responded: "I am vexed not to have a jewel, not one stone, nothing to adorn myself with. I shall have such a poverty-laden look. I would prefer not to go to this party."

He replied: "You can wear some natural flowers. At this season they look very chic. For ten francs you can have two or three magnificent roses."

She was not convinced. "No," she replied, "there is nothing more humiliating than to have a shabby air in the midst of rich women."

Then her husband cried out: "How stupid we are! Go and find your friend Madame Forestier and ask her to lend you her jewels. You are well enough acquainted with her to do this."

She uttered a cry of joy. "It is true!" she said. "I had not thought of that."

The next day she took herself to her friend's house and related her story of distress. Mme. Forestier went to her closet with the glass doors, took out a large jewel case, brought it, opened it and said: "Choose, my dear."

She saw at first some bracelets, then a collar of pearls, then a Venetian cross of gold and jewels and of admirable workmanship. She tried the jewels before the glass, hesitated, but could neither decide to take them nor leave them. Then she asked:

"Have you nothing more?"

"Why, yes. Look for yourself. I do not know what will please you."

Suddenly she discovered in a black satin box a superb necklace of diamonds, and her heart beat fast with an immoderate desire. Her hands trembled as she took them up. She placed them about her throat, against her dress, and remained in ecstasy before them. Then she asked in a hesitating voice full of anxiety:

"Could you lend me this? Only this?"

"Why, yes, certainly."

She fell upon the neck of her friend, embraced her with passion, then went away with her treasure.

◆◆◆

The day of the ball arrived. Mme. Loisel was a great success. She was the prettiest of all, elegant, gracious, smiling and full of joy. All the men noticed her, asked her name and wanted to be presented. All the members of the Cabinet wished to waltz with her. The minister of education paid her some attention.

She danced with enthusiasm, with passion, intoxicated with pleasure, thinking of nothing, in the triumph of her beauty, in the glory of her success, in a kind of cloud of happiness that came of all this homage and all this admiration, of all these awakened desires and this victory so complete and sweet to the heart of woman.

She went home toward four o'clock in the morning. Her husband had been half asleep

7. **francs.** Former French currency
8. **Nanterre.** Suburb of Paris, France

im • mod • er • ate (i[m] mä´ d[ə] rət) *adj.*, excessive; unrestrained
hom • age (ä´ mij *or* hä´ mij) *n.*, respectful admiration

in one of the little salons[9] since midnight, with three other gentlemen whose wives were enjoying themselves very much.

He threw around her shoulders the wraps they had carried for the coming home, modest garments of everyday wear, whose poverty clashed with the elegance of the ball costume. She felt this and wished to hurry away in order not to be noticed by the other women who were wrapping themselves in rich furs.

Loisel detained her. "Wait," said he. "You will catch cold out there. I am going to call a cab."

But she would not listen and descended the steps rapidly. When they were in the street they found no carriage, and they began to seek for one, hailing the coachmen whom they saw at a distance. They walked along toward the Seine,[10] hopeless and shivering. Finally they found on the dock one of those old nocturnal coupés,[11] that one sees in Paris after nightfall, as if they were ashamed of their misery by day.

It took them as far as their door in Martyr Street,[12] and they went wearily up to their apartment. It was all over for her. And on his part he remembered that he would have to be at the office by ten o'clock.

She removed the wraps from her shoulders before the glass for a final view of herself in her glory. Suddenly she uttered a cry. Her necklace was not around her neck.

Her husband, already half undressed, asked: "What is the matter?"

She turned toward him excitedly:

"I have—I have—I no longer have Madame Forestier's necklace."

He arose in dismay: "What! How is that? It is not possible."

And they looked in the folds of the dress, in the folds of the mantle, in the pockets, everywhere. They could not find it.

He asked: "You are sure you still had it when we left the house?"

9. **little salons.** Small rooms or booths alongside a ballroom floor
10. **Seine.** River that runs through Paris
11. **nocturnal coupés.** Carriages that run at night
12. **Martyr Street.** Street named for religious martyrs, people who died under religious persecution

noc • tur • nal (näk tʉr´ n'l) *adj.,* active at night

"Yes, I felt it in the vestibule as we came out."

"But if you had lost it in the street we should have heard it fall. It must be in the cab."

"Yes. It is probable. Did you take the number?"

"No. And you, did you notice what it was?"

"No."

They looked at each other, utterly cast down. Finally Loisel dressed himself again.

"I am going," said he, "over the track where we went on foot, to see if I can find it."

Illustration depicting a jewelry store, circa 1854.

And he went. She remained in her evening gown, not having the force to go to bed, stretched upon a chair, without ambition or thoughts.

Toward seven o'clock her husband returned. He had found nothing.

He went to the police and to the cab offices and put an advertisement in the newspapers, offering a reward; he did everything that afforded them a suspicion of hope.

She waited all day in a state of bewilderment before this frightful disaster. Loisel returned at evening, with his face harrowed and pale, and had discovered nothing.

"It will be necessary," said he, "to write to your friend that you have broken the clasp of the necklace and that you will have it repaired. That will give us time to turn around."

She wrote as he dictated.

◆◆◆

At the end of a week they had lost all hope. And Loisel, older by five years, declared: "We must take measures to replace this jewel." The next day they took the box which had inclosed it to the jeweler whose name was on the inside. He consulted his books.

"It is not I, madame," said he, "who sold this necklace; I only furnished the casket."[13]

Then they went from jeweler to jeweler, seeking a necklace like the other one, consulting their memories, and ill, both of them, with chagrin and anxiety.

In a shop of the Palais-Royal they found a chaplet of diamonds which seemed to them exactly like the one they had lost. It was valued at forty thousand francs. They could get it for thirty-six thousand.

They begged the jeweler not to sell it for three days. And they made an arrangement by which they might return it for thirty-four thousand francs if they found the other one before the end of February.

Loisel possessed eighteen thousand francs which his father had left him. He borrowed the rest.

He borrowed it, asking for a thousand francs of one, five hundred of another, five louis of this one and three louis of that one. He gave notes, made ruinous promises, took money of <u>usurers</u> and the whole race of lenders. He compromised his whole existence, in fact, risked his signature without even

13. **casket.** Case

u • sur • er (yü´zhər ər *or* yüzh´ rər) *n.*, a person who lends money at an extremely high interest rate knowing whether he could make it good or not, and, harassed by anxiety for the future, by the black misery which surrounded him and by the prospect of all physical privations and moral torture, he went to get the new necklace, depositing on the merchant's counter thirty-six thousand francs.

When Mme. Loisel took back the jewels to Mme. Forestier the latter said to her in a frigid tone:

"You should have returned them to me sooner, for I might have needed them."

She did open the jewel box as her friend feared she would. If she should perceive the substitution what would she think? What should she say? Would she take her for a robber?

◆◆◆

Mme. Loisel now knew the horrible life of necessity. She did her part, however, completely, heroically. It was necessary to pay this frightful debt. She would pay it. They sent away the maid; they changed their lodgings; they rented some rooms under a mansard roof.[14]

She learned the heavy cares of a household, the odious work of a kitchen. She washed the dishes, using her rosy nails upon the greasy pots and the bottoms of the stewpans. She washed the soiled linen, the chemises and dishcloths, which she hung on the line to dry; she took down the refuse to the street each morning and brought up the water, stopping at each landing to breathe. And, clothed like a woman of the people, she went to the grocer's, the butcher's and the fruiterer's with her basket on her arm, shopping, haggling to the last sou her miserable money.

Every month it was necessary to renew some notes, thus obtaining time, and to pay others.

The husband worked evenings, putting the books of some merchants in order, and nights he often did copying at five sous a page.

And this life lasted for ten years.

At the end of ten years they had restored all, all, with interest of the usurer, and accumulated interest, besides.

Mme. Loisel seemed old now. She had become a strong, hard woman, the crude woman of the poor household. Her hair badly dressed, her skirts awry, her hands red, she spoke in a loud tone and washed the floors in large pails of water. But sometimes, when her husband was at the office, she would seat herself before the window and think of that evening party of former times, of that ball where she was so beautiful and so flattered.

How would it have been if she had not lost that necklace? Who knows? Who knows? How singular is life and how full of changes! How small a thing will ruin or save one!

One Sunday, as she was taking a walk in the Champs Elysées to rid herself of the cares of the week, she suddenly perceived a woman walking with a child. It was Mme. Forestier, still young, still pretty, still attractive. Mme. Loisel was affected. Should she speak to her? Yes, certainly. And now that she had paid, she would tell her all. Why not?

She approached her. "Good morning, Jeanne."

Her friend did not recognise her and was astonished to be so familiarly addressed by this common personage. She stammered:

"But, madame—I do not know—You must be mistaken."

"No, I am Matilda Loisel."

Her friend uttered a cry of astonishment: "Oh! my poor Matilda! How you have changed."

"Yes, I have had some hard days since I saw you, and some miserable ones—and all because of you."

14. **mansard roof.** Roof with two slopes all the way around, the lower slope being steeper than the upper

o • di • ous (ō´ dē əs) *adj.,* hateful and offensive

"Because of me? How is that?"

"You recall the diamond necklace that you loaned me to wear to the minister's ball?"

"Yes, very well."

"Well, I lost it."

"How is that, since you returned it to me?"

"I returned another to you exactly like it. And it has taken us ten years to pay for it. You can understand that it was not easy for us who have nothing. But it is finished, and I am decently content."

Mme. Forestier stopped short. She said:

"You say that you bought a diamond necklace to replace mine?"

"Yes. You did not perceive it then? They were just alike."

And she smiled with a proud and simple joy. Mme. Forestier was touched and took both her hands as she replied:

"Oh, my poor Matilda! Mine were false. They were not worth over five hundred francs!" ❖

"...there is nothing more humiliating than to have a shabby air in the midst of rich women." Mme. Loisel is very conscious of the social norms in her society. How important are social norms today? Do people place more importance on fitting in or being unique? What is important in your own culture?

REFER TO TEXT ▶▶▶▶	▶ REASON WITH TEXT	
1a. How does Mme. Loisel feel about her situation in life?	1b. Give examples of Mme. Loisel's thoughts that show she feels she should have had an aristocratic life.	**Understand** **Find meaning**
2a. Identify why Mme. Loisel is initially upset by the invitation.	2b. Applying what you know about Mme. Loisel, what motivates her to borrow the necklace from her friend?	**Apply** **Use information**
3a. What actions on the part of the husband show that he places his wife's happiness above his own?	3b. Analyze whether or not Mme. Loisel appreciates her husband. Give examples from the text to support your analysis.	**Analyze** **Take things apart**
4a. Recall why Mme. Loisel chooses not to tell Mme. Forestier the truth about losing the necklace right after it happens.	4b. Judge whether or not Mme. Loisel was justified in blaming Mme. Forestier for the hardships she had suffered. Why or why not?	**Evaluate** **Make judgments**
5a. State how long it takes Mme. Loisel to earn the money to pay for the diamond necklace.	5b. Generalize how Mme. Loisel's life is symbolized by the necklace. What sort of relationship between people and their social environment is described in this short story?	**Create** **Bring ideas together**

COMPARE LITERATURE: Theme and Irony

What do the themes of each story have in common? How are they different? What details in the stories help to express the themes? What is the ironic twist in each story? How does the use of irony affect the development of the themes?

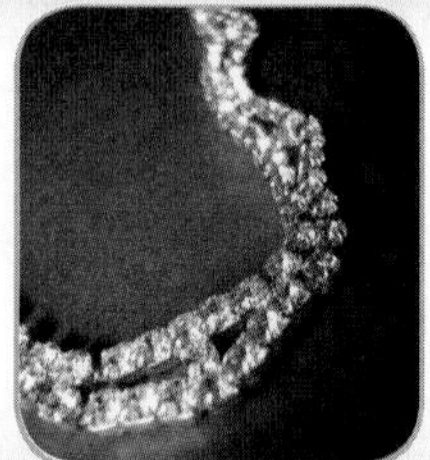

A **paradox** is a statement or situation that contradicts itself. Explain how the irony in each story presents a paradox for the characters.

EXTEND THE TEXT

Writing Options

Creative Writing Can material possessions make people happy? Write an **editorial** for the op-ed page (a reader-opinion page) of a local or national newspaper that answers this question. Use examples from your own life, from your observations, or from the stories to support your response. In your editorial, suggest a course toward happiness based on your opinion on the question.

Expository Writing Imagine you are going to present a paper at a convention of English teachers. The paper would compare "The Gift of the Magi" and "The Necklace." Write an **abstract** (a brief summary or an outline of the essay's main points) for the paper. In it, briefly summarize what you would cover in a comparative essay about the themes of the two stories. While you brainstorm, you may want to organize the information in a Cluster Chart similar to the one shown below.

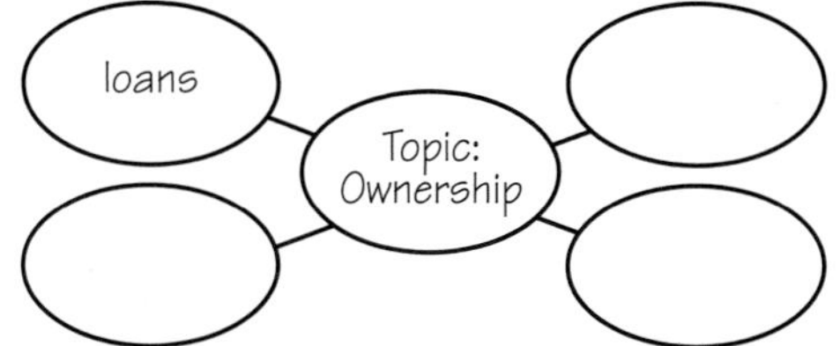

Media Literacy

Conduct Talk Show Interviews Use the story of Monsieur and Madame Loisel as the topic for a talk show. Divide into small groups of four, and choose roles: Madame Loisel, Monsieur Loisel, Madame Forestier, and the show host. Rehearse the interview: The host should ask questions about the characters' motivations and about how the incident with the necklace changed their lives and relationships; the characters should answer the questions. After rehearsing, each group should perform its interview for the class.

Collaborative Learning

Compose Alternate Endings How would Jim and Della have reacted if one person had gotten the other an expensive gift but the other only bought a gift within his/her means? What might have happened if Mme. Loisel had confessed the loss of the necklace immediately to her friend? With a partner, discuss how events may have turned out differently in each story. When you have come to an agreement about what might have happened, write a brief alternate ending to each story. How is the theme affected by the new endings?

Go to **www.mirrorsandwindows.com** for more.

READING ASSESSMENT

1. Which statement best describes Jim's reaction when he sees Della with short hair?
   A. He is horrified because Della looked ugly with short hair.
   B. He is sad that Della had to cut off her hair because he knows she loved it.
   C. He is surprised and didn't recognize her.
   D. He is upset because he had bought her hair combs that she now can't use.
   E. He is pleased she got a more modern hairstyle.

2. Which statement best describes Mme. Loisel's reaction when her husband gives her the invitation to the ball?
   A. She is overjoyed because she longs to mingle with society.
   B. She is amazed that her husband is able to get such an invitation.
   C. She is indifferent because she really doesn't like her husband's employers.
   D. She is irritated that her husband hadn't gotten an invitation earlier.
   E. She is upset because she has nothing appropriate to wear.

3. As used in "The Necklace" on page 144, the word *chagrin* most nearly means
   A. anger.
   B. embarrassment.
   C. excitement.
   D. sorrow.
   E. conceit.

4. What is ironic about Mme. Loisel being plunged into a "life of necessity"?
   A. Mme. Loisel yearned for a rich life, and her efforts to simulate one leads to her downfall.
   B. Mme. Loisel is forced to go to work for her rich friend to pay off her debt.
   C. Mme. Loisel always knew she was living in a station above herself.
   D. Mme. Loisel is surprised to learn that the jewels she had worked so hard to replace were fake.
   E. None of the above

5. Compare and contrast Della in "The Gift of the Magi" and Mme. Loisel in "The Necklace." Consider their desires, motivations, and experiences.

READING FICTION INDEPENDENTLY

Theme: Defining Moments

"A vision comes as a gift born of humility, of wisdom, and of patience. If from your vision quest you have learned nothing but this, then you have already learned much."

—Lame Deer,
from "The Vision Quest"

Who are you? The usual answer to that question is a name or sometimes a relationship, as in "I'm Julie's brother." But what characteristics make you who you are and how did you become that person? Defining moments are those times that call your beliefs, values, and personal strengths and weaknesses into question. Often a defining moment seems like arriving at a fork in the road; the path you choose to follow will determine who you become. Other times, the choice was made long ago, but recent events bring that decision into focus. As you read the selections in this section, decide what the defining moment is for the main characters and how they finally decide to define themselves.

USING READING SKILLS WITH FICTION

Identify the Main Idea

The **main idea** is a brief statement of what you think the author wants you to know, think, or feel after reading the text. In some cases, the main idea will actually be stated. Usually in fiction, the author will not tell you what the main idea is, and you will have to infer it.

In general, nonfiction texts have main ideas; literary texts, like the fictional stories in this unit, have **themes.** Sometimes, the term "main idea" is used to refer to the theme of a literary work. Both deal with the central idea in a written work.

A good way to find the main or overall idea of a whole selection (or part of a selection) is to gather important details of the story's actions into a Main Idea Map like the one below for "The Ravine." After reading the story, record the important details of the actions (plot) to find the purpose of those actions (the main idea or theme).

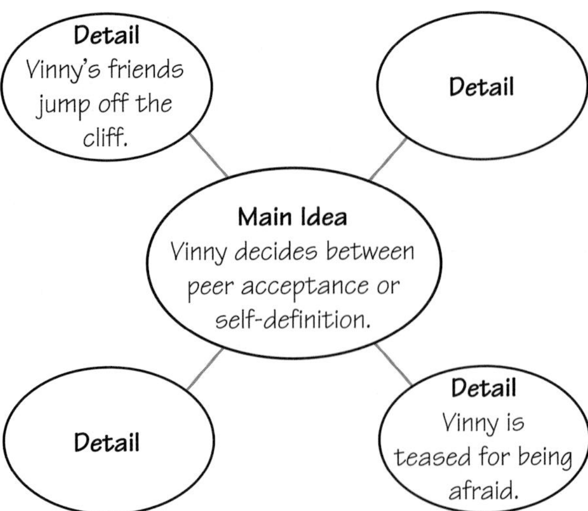
Detail
Vinny's friends jump off the cliff.
Detail
Main Idea
Vinny decides between peer acceptance or self-definition.
Detail
Detail
Vinny is teased for being afraid.

Understand Author's Purpose and Approach

The **author's purpose** is the reason the author wrote that story or what he or she hoped to achieve by doing so. Sometimes, there is a message or a point to the message; the author hopes you will think or feel a certain way about a subject after reading it. The purpose of other stories might be simply to entertain, whether to make you laugh or to scare you. If you can determine the author's purpose, you will be better able to critique or analyze the story for how effective the author was in achieving that purpose.

The literary elements, the terms and techniques used in literature, make up the **author's approach** to conveying his or her main idea or theme. Understanding the author's approach in fiction involves recognizing these literary elements:

- **Point of View** This is the vantage point, or perspective, from which a story or narrative is told. (See page 46 for more information on point of view.)
- **Characterization** This is the literary technique writers use to create characters and make them come alive. (See page 68 for more information on characterization.)
- **Mood** This is the atmosphere conveyed by a literary work. Writers create mood by using concrete details to describe the setting, characters, or events. Writers can evoke in the reader an emotional response—such as fear, discomfort, or longing—by working with descriptive language and sensory details. (See page 107 for more information on mood.)

Summarize Basic Events and Ideas

When you **summarize** a story, you recall the main events and points that outline the plot. A typical plot involves the introduction of a conflict, its development, and its eventual resolution. (See page 12 for more information on plot.) You do not need to restate every minor happening or detail, only the ones that answer the question, "What is this story about?" A basic summary explains who the main characters are, how they relate to one another, what the central conflict is, and what actions the characters take with regards to that conflict.

Framework for Fiction

When reading fiction, you need to be aware of the plot, the characters, and the setting. The following checklist of questions offers a framework for approaching fiction reading.

As you start to read...

- ☐ From which perspective is this story told?
- ☐ Who are the characters? What do I know about them?
- ☐ Where is the story set?

As you continue reading...

- ☐ What is the mood of the story?
- ☐ What do the characters or the setting look like?
- ☐ What do I predict will happen to the characters at the end?
- ☐ What is the central conflict?

After you've finished reading...

- ☐ What happens in the story?
- ☐ What message or point is the author trying to make?
- ☐ What am I supposed to understand after reading this?

What Good Readers Do

Use Fix-Up Ideas

If you experience difficulty in comprehending what you're reading, use one of the following Fix-Up Ideas:

- ☐ Reread
- ☐ Ask a question
- ☐ Read in shorter chunks
- ☐ Read aloud
- ☐ Retell
- ☐ Work with a partner
- ☐ Unlock difficult words
- ☐ Vary your reading rate
- ☐ Choose a new reading strategy

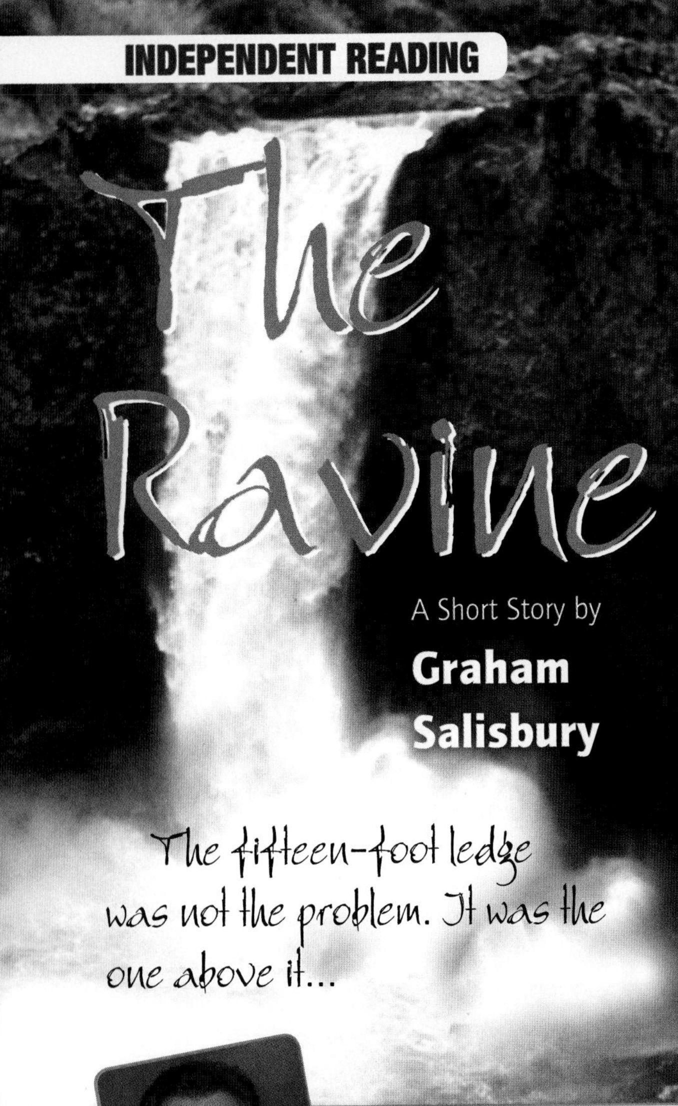

The Ravine

A Short Story by

Graham Salisbury

The fifteen-foot ledge was not the problem. It was the one above it...

Graham Salisbury grew up on the islands of Oahu and Hawaii. Born into a family that had a 100-year history of newspapermen working for the *Honolulu Advertiser,* Salisbury decided to "imagine rather than report." As Salisbury explains, "There are times when completely unexpected happenings take place as my fingertips walk the keyboard, things that make me laugh or get all choked up or even amaze me."

A *ravine* is a narrow, steep-sided valley that has been worn by running water. It is in a Hawaiian ravine that the four teenagers in **"The Ravine"** try to prove their bravery shortly after another boy died in the same spot. For one of the boys, the ravine tests not just his bravery but his definition of bravery, as well.

Have you ever been tempted to do something you felt uncomfortable about in order to be accepted by your peers?

When Vinny and three others dropped down into the ravine, they entered a jungle thick with tangled trees and rumors of what might have happened to the dead boy's body.

The muddy trail was slick and, in places where it had fallen away, flat-out dangerous. The cool breeze that swept the Hawaiian hill-side pastures above died early in the descent.

There were four of them—Vinny; his best friend, Joe-Boy; Mo, who was afraid of nothing; and Joe-Boy's haole[1] girlfriend, Starlene—all fifteen. It was a Tuesday in July, two weeks and a day after the boy had drowned. If, in fact, that's what had happened to him.

Vinny slipped, and dropped his towel in the mud. He picked it up and tried to brush it off, but instead smeared the mud spot around until the towel resembled something someone's dog had slept on. "Tst," he said.

Joe-Boy, hiking down just behind him, laughed. "Hey, Vinny, just think, that kid walked where you walking."

"Shuddup," Vinny said.

"You prob'ly stepping right where his foot was."

Vinny moved to the edge of the trail, where the ravine fell through a twisted jungle of gnarly trees and underbrush to the stream far below.

Joe-Boy laughed again. "You such a queen, Vinny. You know that?"

Vinny could see Starlene and Mo farther ahead, their heads bobbing as they walked, both almost down to the pond where the boy had died.

1. **haole.** Hawaiian term for foreigner or white person, not a local

"Hey," Joe-Boy went on, "maybe you going be the one to find his body."

"You don't cut it out, Joe-Boy, I going...I going..."

"What, cry?"

Vinny scowled. Sometimes Joe-Boy was a big fat babooze.

They slid down the trail. Mud oozed between Vinny's toes. He grabbed at roots and branches to keep from falling. Mo and Starlene were out of sight now, the trail ahead having cut back.

Joe-Boy said, "You going jump in the water and go down and your hand going touch his face, stuck under the rocks. Ha ha ha...a ha ha ha!"

Vinny winced. He didn't want to be here. It was too soon, way too soon. Two weeks and one day.

He saw a footprint in the mud and stepped around it.

The dead boy had jumped and had never come back up. Four search and rescue divers hunted for two days straight and never found him. Not a trace. Gave Vinny the creeps. It didn't make sense. The pond wasn't that big.

He wondered why it didn't seem to bother anyone else. Maybe it did and they just didn't want to say.

Butchie was the kid's name. Only fourteen.

Fourteen.

Two weeks and one day ago he was walking down this trail. Now nobody could find him.

The jungle crushed in, reaching over the trail, and Vinny brushed leafy branches aside. The roar of the waterfall got louder, louder.

Starlene said it was the goddess that took him, the one that lives in the stone down by the road. She did that every now and then, Starlene said, took somebody when she got lonely. Took him and kept him. Vinny had heard that legend before, but he'd never believed in it.

Now he didn't know what he believed.

The body had to be stuck down there. But still, four divers and they couldn't find it?

Vinny decided he'd better believe in the legend. If he didn't, the goddess might get mad and send him bad luck. Or maybe take *him,* too.

Stopstopstop! Don't think like that.

"Come on," Joe-Boy said, nudging Vinny from behind. "Hurry it up."

Just then Starlene whooped, her voice bouncing around the walls of the ravine.

"Let's *go,*" Joe-Boy said. "They there already."

Moments later, Vinny jumped up onto a large boulder at the edge of the pond. Starlene was swimming out in the brown water. It wasn't murky brown, but clean and clear to a depth of maybe three or four feet. Because of the waterfall you had to yell if you wanted to say something. The whole place smelled of mud and ginger and iron.

Starlene swam across to the waterfall on the far side of the pond and ducked under it, then climbed out and edged along the rock wall behind it, moving slowly, like a spider. Above, sun-sparkling stream water spilled over the lip of a one-hundred-foot drop.

Mo and Joe-Boy threw their towels onto the rocks and dove into the pond. Vinny watched, his muddy towel hooked around his neck. Reluctantly, he let it fall, then dove in after them.

The cold mountain water tasted tangy. Was it because the boy's body was down there decomposing? He spit it out.

He followed Joe-Boy and Mo to the waterfall and ducked under it. They climbed up onto the rock ledge, just as Starlene had done, then spidered their way over to where you could climb to a small ledge about fifteen feet up. They took their time because the hand and footholds were slimy with moss.

Starlene jumped first. Her shriek echoed off the rocky cliff, then died in the dense green jungle.

Mo jumped, then Joe-Boy, then Vinny.

The fifteen-foot ledge was not the problem.

It was the one above it, the one you had to work up to, the big one, where you had to take a deadly zigzag trail that climbed up and away from the waterfall, then cut back and forth to a foot-wide ledge something more like fifty feet up.

That was the problem.

That was where the boy had jumped from.

Joe-Boy and Starlene swam out to the middle of the pond. Mo swam back under the waterfall and climbed once again to the fifteen-foot ledge.

Vinny started to swim out toward Joe-Boy but stopped when he saw Starlene put her arms around him. She kissed him. They sank under for a long time, then came back up, still kissing.

Joe-Boy saw Vinny looking and winked. "You like that, Vinny? Watch, I show you how." He kissed Starlene again.

Vinny turned away and swam back over to the other side of the pond, where he'd first gotten in. His mother would kill him if she ever heard about where he'd come. After the boy drowned, or was taken by the goddess, or whatever happened to him, she said never to come to this pond again. Ever. It was off-limits. Permanently.

But not his dad. He said, "You fall off a horse, you get back on, right? Or else you going to be scared of it all your life."

His mother scoffed and waved him off. "Don't listen to him, Vinny, listen to me. Don't go there. That pond is haunted." Which had made his dad laugh.

But Vinny promised he'd stay away.

But then Starlene and Joe-Boy said, "Come with us anyway. You let your mommy run your life, or what?" And Vinny said, "But what if I get caught?" And Joe-Boy said, "So?"

Vinny mashed his lips. He was so weak. Couldn't even say no. But if he'd said, "I can't go, my mother won't like it," they would have laughed him right off the island. No, he had to go. No choice.

"Don't go there. That pond is haunted."

So he'd come along, and so far it was fine. He'd even gone in the water. Everyone was happy. All he had to do now was wait it out and go home and hope his mother never heard about it.

When he looked up, Starlene was gone.

He glanced around the pond until he spotted her starting up the zigzag trail to the fifty-foot ledge. She was moving slowly, hanging on to roots and branches on the upside of the cliff. He couldn't believe she was going there. He wanted to yell, Hey, Starlene, that's where he died!

But she already knew that.

Mo jumped from the lower ledge, yelling, "Banzaiiii!" An explosion of coffee-colored water erupted when he hit.

Joe-Boy swam over to where Starlene had gotten out. He waved to Vinny, grinning like a fool, then followed Starlene up the zigzag trail.

Now Starlene was twenty-five, thirty feet up. Vinny watched her for a while, then lost sight of her when she slipped behind a wall of jungle that blocked his view. A few minutes later she popped back out, now almost at the top, where the trail ended, where there was nothing but mud and a few plants to grab on to if you slipped, plants that would rip right out of the ground, plants that wouldn't stop you if you fell, nothing but your screams between you and the rocks below.

Vinny's stomach tingled just watching her. He couldn't imagine what it must feel like to

be up there, especially if you were afraid of heights, like he was. *She has no fear,* Vinny thought, no fear at all. Pleasepleaseplease Starlene. *I don't want to see you die.*

Starlene crept forward, making her way to the end of the trail, where the small ledge was.

Joe-Boy popped out of the jungle behind her. He stopped, waiting for her to jump before going on.

Vinny held his breath.

Starlene, in her cutoff jeans and soaked T-shirt, stood perfectly still, her arms at her sides. Vinny suddenly felt like hugging her. Why, he couldn't tell. *Starlene, please.*

She reached behind her and took a wide leaf from a plant, then eased down and scooped up a finger of mud. She made a brown cross on her forehead, then wiped her muddy fingers on her jeans.

She waited.

Was she thinking about the dead boy?

She stuck the stem end of the leaf in her mouth, leaving the rest of it to hang out.

When she jumped, the leaf would flap up and cover her nose and keep water from rushing into it. An old island trick.

She jumped.

Down, down.

Almost in slow motion, it seemed at first, then faster and faster. She fell feet first, arms flapping to keep balance so she wouldn't land on her back, or stomach, which would probably almost kill her.

Just before she hit, she crossed her arms over her chest and vanished within a small explosion of rusty water.

Vinny stood, not breathing at all, praying.

Ten seconds. Twenty, thirty…

She came back up, laughing.

She shouldn't make fun that way, Vinny thought. It was dangerous, disrespectful. It was asking for it.

Vinny looked up when he heard Joe-Boy shout, "Hey, Vinny, watch how a man does it! Look!"

Joe-Boy scooped up some mud and drew a stroke of lightning across his chest. When he jumped, he threw himself out, face and body parallel to the pond, his arms and legs spread out. *He's crazy,* Vinny thought, *absolutely insane.* At the last second Joe-Boy folded into a ball and hit. *Ca-roomp!* He came up whooping and yelling, "*Wooo! So good!* Come on, Vinny, it's hot!"

Vinny faked a laugh. He waved, shouting, "Naah, the water's too cold!"

Now Mo was heading up the zigzag trail—Mo, who hardly ever said a word and would do anything anyone ever challenged him to do. *Come on, Mo, not you, too.*

Vinny knew then that he would have to jump.

Jump, or never live it down.

Jump, or never live it down.

Mo jumped in the same way Joe-Boy had, man-style, splayed out in a suicide fall. He came up grinning.

Starlene and Joe-Boy turned toward Vinny.

Vinny got up and hiked around the edge of the pond, walking in the muddy shallows, looking at a school of small brown-backed fish near a ginger patch.

Maybe they'd forget about him.

Starlene torpedoed over, swimming underwater. Her body glittered in the small amount of sunlight that penetrated the trees around the rim of the ravine. When she came up, she broke the surface smoothly, gracefully, like a swan. Her blond hair sleeked back like river grass.

She smiled a sweet smile. "Joe-Boy says you're afraid to jump. I didn't believe him. He's wrong, right?"

Vinny said quickly, "Of course he's wrong. I just don't want to, that's all. The water's cold."

"Naah, it's nice."

Vinny looked away. On the other side of the pond Joe-Boy and Mo were on the cliff behind the waterfall.

"Joe-Boy says your mom told you not to come here. Is that true?"

Vinny nodded. "Yeah. Stupid, but she thinks it's haunted."

"She's right."

"What?"

"That boy didn't die, Vinny. The stone goddess took him. He's in a good place right now. He's her prince."

Vinny scowled. He couldn't tell if Starlene was teasing him or if she really believed that. He said, "Yeah, prob'ly."

"Are you going to jump, or is Joe-Boy right?"

"Joe-Boy's an idiot. Sure I'm going to jump."

Starlene grinned, staring at Vinny a little too long. "He is an idiot, isn't he? But I love him."

"Yeah, well…"

"Go to it, big boy. I'll be watching."

Starlene sank down and swam out into the pond.

Ca-ripes.

Vinny ripped a hank of white ginger from the ginger patch and smelled it, and prayed he'd still be alive after the sun went down.

He took his time climbing the zigzag trail. When he got to the part where the jungle hid him from view, he stopped and smelled the ginger again. So sweet and alive it made Vinny wish for all he was worth that he was climbing out of the ravine right now, heading home.

But of course, there was no way he could do that.

Not before jumping.

He tossed the ginger onto the muddy trail and continued on. He slipped once or twice, maybe three times. He didn't keep track. He was too numb now, too caught up in the insane thing he was about to do. He'd never been this far up the trail before. Once he'd tried to go all the way, but couldn't. It made him dizzy.

When he stepped out and the jungle opened into a huge bowl where he could look down, way, way down, he could see there three heads in the water, heads with arms moving slowly to keep them afloat, and a few bright rays of sunlight pouring down on them, and when he saw this, his stomach fluttered and rose. Something sour came up and he spit it out.

It made him wobble to look down. He closed his eyes. His whole body trembled. The trail was no wider than the length of his foot. And it was wet and muddy from little rivulets of water that bled from the side of the cliff.

The next few steps were the hardest he'd ever taken in his life. He tried not to look down, but he couldn't help it. His gaze was drawn there. He struggled to push back an urge to fly, just jump off and fly. He could almost see himself spiraling down like a glider, or a bird, or a leaf.

His hands shook as if he were freezing. He wondered, *Had the dead boy felt this way?* Or had he felt brave, like Starlene or Joe-Boy, or Mo, who seemed to feel nothing.

Somebody from below shouted, but Vinny couldn't make it out over the waterfall, roaring down just feet beyond the ledge where he would soon be standing, cascading past so close its mist dampened the air he breathed.

The dead boy had just come to the ravine to have fun, Vinny thought. Just a regular kid like himself, come to swim and be with his friends, then go home and eat macaroni and cheese and watch TV, maybe play with his dog or wander around after dark.

But he'd done none of that.

Where was he?

Inch by inch Vinny made it to the ledge. He stood, swaying slightly, the tips of his toes one small movement from the precipice.

Far below, Joe-Boy waved his arm back and forth. It was dreamy to see—back and forth, back and forth. He looked so small down there.

For a moment Vinny's mind went blank, as if he were in some trance, some dream where

Critical Viewing

What thoughts might you have if you were standing on a cliff similar to the one depicted in the image below?

he could so easily lean out and fall, and think or feel nothing.

A breeze picked up and moved the trees on the ridge-line, but not a breath of it reached the fifty-foot ledge.

Vinny thought he heard a voice, small and distant. Yes. Something inside him, a tiny voice pleading, *Don't do it. Walk away. Just turn and go and walk back down.*

"...I can't," Vinny whispered.

You can, you can, you can. Walk back down.

Vinny waited.

And waited.

Joe-Boy yelled, then Starlene, both of them waving.

Then something very strange happened.

Vinny felt at peace. Completely and totally calm and at peace. He had not made up his mind about jumping. But something else inside him had.

Thoughts and feelings swarmed, stinging him: *Jump! Jump! Jump! Jump!*

But deep inside, where the peace was, where his mind wasn't, he would not jump. He would walk back down.

No! No, no, no!

Vinny eased down and fingered up some mud and made a cross on his chest, big and bold. He grabbed a leaf, stuck it in his mouth. *Be calm, be calm. Don't look down.*

After a long pause he spit the leaf out and rubbed the cross to a blur.

They walked out of the ravine in silence, Starlene, Joe-Boy, and Mo far ahead of him. They hadn't said a word since he'd come down off the trail. He knew what they were thinking. He knew, he knew, he knew.

At the same time the peace was still there. He had no idea what it was. But he prayed it wouldn't leave him now, prayed it wouldn't go away, would never go away, because in there, in that place where the peace was, it didn't matter what they thought.

Vinny emerged from the ravine into a brilliance that surprised him. Joe-Boy, Starlene, and Mo were now almost down to the road.

Vinny breathed deeply, and looked up and out over the island. He saw, from there, a land that rolled away like honey, easing down a descent of rich Kikuyu grass pastureland, flowing from there over vast highlands of brown and green, then, finally, falling massively to the coast and flat blue sea.

He'd never seen anything like it.

Had it always been here? This view of the island?

He stared and stared, then sat, taking it in.

He'd never seen anything so beautiful in all his life. ❖

"But deep inside, where the peace was, where his mind wasn't, he would not jump. He would walk back down." When does it show more bravery to walk away than to follow the crowd? Have you ever been faced with a similar situation?

Refer and Reason

1. Distinguish the mood that the author creates by using details to describe the setting.
2. Compare and contrast Vinny with his friends. What type of characters are the friends? With which of the characters would you most likely be friends? Why?
3. Vinny's decision not to jump comes from "a place of peace." How do you think that might affect how his friends treat the incident? Discuss how things might have been different if he had jumped.

Writing Options

1. Create your own explanation for what happened to the boy who disappeared.
2. During the story, the teens draw symbols on themselves. In two or three paragraphs, evaluate their actions and their choices of symbols within the text.

 Go to **www.mirrorsandwindows.com** for more.

Genesis, 1993. Jaune Quick-to-See Smith. High Museum of Art, Atlanta.

The Vision Quest

Lame Deer, also known as John Fire, (1903–1976) was a Sioux born on the Rosebud Reservation in South Dakota. He tells in his autobiography, *Lame Deer, Seeker of Visions,* of his many jobs, including painter, shepherd, rodeo clown, rancher, and reservation police officer. In his book, he also describes Sioux rituals, such as the sun dance, healing rituals, and vision quest. **Richard Erdoes,** writer, illustrator, and photographer, was born in Europe. He moved to the United States in 1967, where he met Lame Deer and recorded his story.

Vision quests begin in the sweat lodge to purify the seeker. The seeker fasts and prays, hoping to hear the "voice of the Sacred." In **"The Vision Quest,"** Lame Deer describes a young man's vision quest.

What expectations do you have of yourself and your future?

A Short Story by **Lame Deer**

Recorded by **Richard Erdoes**

He spent the first night in the hole. . .trembling and crying out loudly.

A young man wanted to go on a Hanbleceya, or vision seeking, to try for a dream that would give him the power to be a great medicine man. Having a high opinion of himself, he felt sure that he had been created to become great among his people and that the only thing lacking was a vision.

The young man was daring and brave, eager to go up to the mountaintop. He had been brought up by good, honest people who were wise in the ancient ways and who prayed for him. All through the winter they were busy getting him ready, feeding him wasna,[1] corn, and plenty of good meat to make him strong. At every meal they set aside something for the spirits so that they would help him to get a great vision. His relatives thought he had the power even before he went up, but that was putting the cart before the horse, or rather the travois[2] before the horse, as this is an Indian legend.

"You're a brash young man, not yet ready or worthy to receive a vision."

When at last he started on his quest, it was a beautiful morning in late spring. The grass was up, the leaves were out, nature was at its best. Two medicine men accompanied him. They put up a sweat lodge to purify him in the hot, white breath of the sacred steam. They sanctified him with the incense of sweet grass, rubbing his body with sage, fanning it with an eagle's wing. They went to the hilltop with him to prepare the vision pit and make an offering of tobacco bundles. Then they told the young man to cry, to humble himself, to ask for holiness, to cry for power, for a sign from the Great Spirit, for a gift which would make him into a medicine man. After they had done all they could, they left him there.

He spent the first night in the hole the medicine men had dug for him, trembling and crying out loudly. Fear kept him awake, yet he was cocky, ready to wrestle with the spirits for the vision, the power he wanted. But no dreams came to ease his mind. Toward morning before the sun came up, he heard a voice in the swirling white mists of dawn. Speaking from no particular direction, as if it came from different places, it said: "See here, young man, there are other spots you could have picked; there are other hills around here. Why don't you go there to cry for a dream? You disturbed us all night, all us creatures and birds; you even kept the trees awake. We couldn't sleep. Why should you cry here? You're a brash young man, not yet ready or worthy to receive a vision."

But the young man clenched his teeth, determined to stick it out, resolved to force that vision to come. He spent another day in the pit, begging for enlightenment which would not come, and then another night of fear and cold and hunger.

When dawn arrived once more, he heard the voice again: "Stop disturbing us; go away!" The same thing happened the third morning. By this time he was faint with hunger, thirst, and anxiety. Even the air seemed to oppress him, to fight him. He was panting. His stomach felt shriveled up, shrunk tight against his backbone. But he was determined to endure one more night, the fourth and last. Surely the vision would come. But again he cried for it out of the dark and loneliness until he was hoarse, and still he had no dream.

Just before daybreak he heard the same voice again, very angry: "Why are you still here?" He knew then that he had suffered in vain; now he would have to go back to his people and confess that he had gained no knowledge and no power. The only thing he could tell them was that he got bawled out every morning. Sad and cross, he replied, "I can't help myself; this is my last day, and I'm crying my eyes out. I know you told me to go home, but who are you to give me orders? I don't know you. I'm going to stay until my uncles come to fetch me, whether you like it or not."

1. **wasna.** Food made of dried meat (often buffalo), dried berries, and fat or marrow that is high in energy

2. **travois.** Sled-like vehicle made by putting hide or netting between two poles that are pulled by a dog or horse

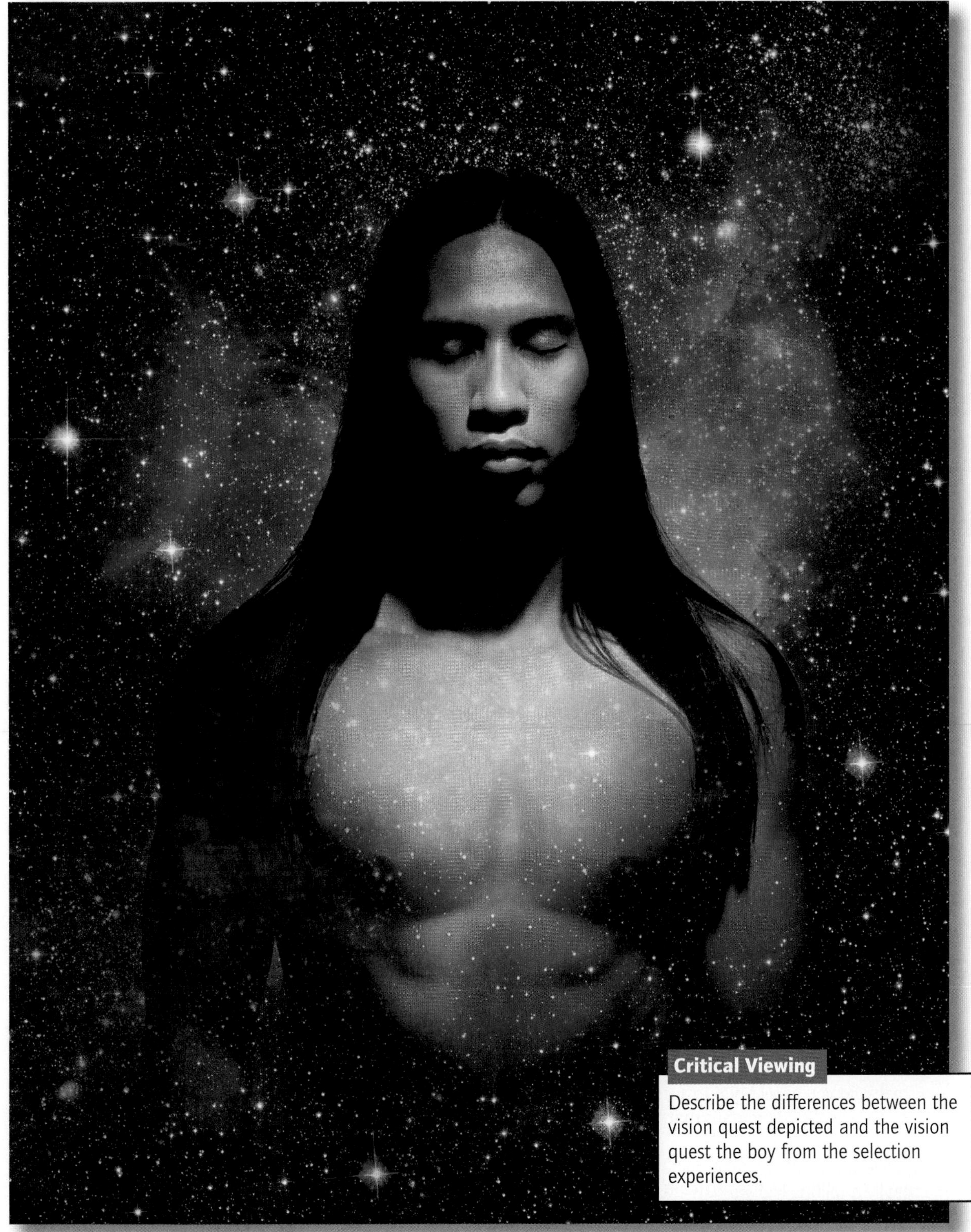

Critical Viewing

Describe the differences between the vision quest depicted and the vision quest the boy from the selection experiences.

All at once there was a rumble from a larger mountain that stood behind the hill. It became a mighty roar, and the whole hill trembled. The wind started to blow. The young man looked up and saw a boulder poised on the mountain's summit. He saw lightning hit it, saw it sway.

Slowly the boulder moved. Slowly at first, then faster and faster, it came tumbling down the mountainside, churning up earth, snapping huge trees as if they were little twigs. And the boulder was coming right down on him!

The young man cried out in terror. He was paralyzed with fear, unable to move. The boulder dwarfed everything in view; it towered over the vision pit. But just as it was an arm's length away and about to crush him, it stopped. Then, as the young man stared open-mouthed, his hair standing up, his eyes starting out of his head, the boulder *rolled up the mountain*, all the way to the top. He could hardly believe what he saw. He was still cowering motionless when he heard the roar and rumble again and saw that immense boulder coming down at him once more. This time he managed to jump out of his vision pit at the last moment. The boulder crushed it, obliterated it, grinding the young man's pipe and gourd rattle into dust.

Again the boulder rolled up the mountain, and again it came down. "I'm leaving, I'm leaving!" hollered the young man. Regaining his power of motion, he scrambled down the hill as fast as he could. This time the boulder actually leap-frogged over him, bouncing down the slope, crushing and pulverizing everything in its way. He ran unseeingly, stumbling, falling, getting up again. He did not even notice the boulder rolling up once more and coming down for the fourth time. On this last and most fearful descent, it flew through the air in a giant leap, landing right in front of him and embedding itself so deeply in the earth that only its top was visible. The ground shook itself like a wet dog coming out of a stream and flung the young man this way and that.

Gaunt, bruised, and shaken, he stumbled back to his village. To the medicine men he said: "I have received no vision and gained no knowledge. I have made the spirits angry. It was all for nothing."

"Well, you did find out one thing," said the older of the two, who was his uncle. "You went after your vision like a hunter after buffalo, or a warrior after scalps. You were fighting the spirits. You thought they owed you a vision. Suffering alone brings no vision nor does courage, nor does sheer will power. A vision comes as a gift born of humility, of wisdom, and of patience. If from your vision quest you have learned nothing but this, then you have already learned much. Think about it." ❖

What in life is owed to you? What part of your envisioned future do you have to fight for, and what part do you have to approach with wisdom and patience?

Refer and Reason

1. Based on the author's characterization of the young man, did you expect him to succeed in his vision quest? Identify the details that led to your expectation.
2. Judge whether the young man's vision quest is really a failure. Explain how the end of his vision quest is ironic.
3. Do you think the young man will try another vision quest? Why or why not? If he does, propose how he might change his approach.

Writing Options

1. Write an alternate ending to the story in which the young man experienced a vision that better satisfied his expectations of his quest. Describe what his vision revealed and how he would act when he returned to the village.
2. A moral is a lesson that relates to the principles of right and wrong and is intended to be drawn from a story. What moral does the selection provide? Write a two-paragraph theme analysis of this legend.

 Go to **www.mirrorsandwindows.com** for more.

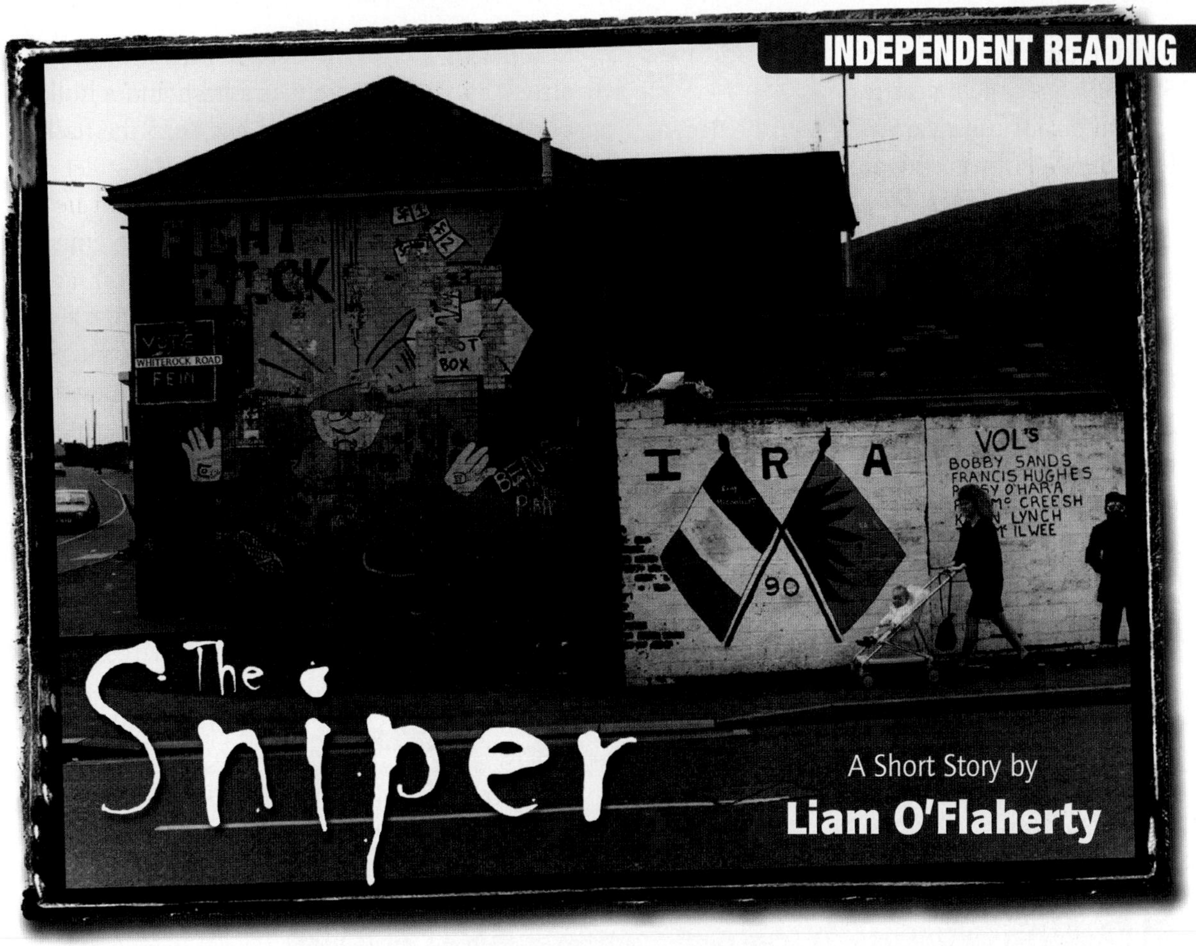

The Sniper

A Short Story by

Liam O'Flaherty

There was a flash and a bullet whizzed over his head.

Liam O'Flaherty (1896–1984) grew up off the west coast of Ireland on the Aran Islands. Many of his stories are set on these islands or in Dublin, Ireland. After a severe case of shell shock ended his brief stint with the Irish Guards, he joined in the Irish struggle for independence. O'Flaherty was well-traveled as well as politically active, and his writing reflects compassion for the common person.

Conflict between Ireland and England has existed for hundreds of years. During the late 1800s, pro-independent Irish formed a political party called the Irish Republican Brotherhood. In 1921, Southern Ireland became self-governed, but Northern Ireland stayed under British rule. In Liam O'Flaherty's **"The Sniper,"** the protagonist is a sniper for the Irish Republicans. O'Flaherty's story was published in 1923, two years after the British and the Irish agreed to establish self-government in Southern Ireland, or the Irish Free State.

What social or political issues are most important to you? How do you express your opinion in everyday life?

The long June twilight faded into night. Dublin lay enveloped in darkness but for the dim light of the moon that shone through fleecy clouds, casting a pale light as of approaching dawn over the streets and the dark waters of the Liffey. Around the beleaguered Four Courts the heavy guns roared. Here and there through the city, machine-guns and rifles broke the silence of the night, spasmodically, like dogs barking on lone farms. Republicans and Free Staters[1] were waging civil war.

On a roof-top near O'Connell Bridge, a Republican sniper lay watching. Beside him lay his rifle and over his shoulders were slung a pair of field glasses. His face was the face of a student, thin and ascetic, but his eyes had the cold gleam of the fanatic. They were deep and thoughtful, the eyes of a man who is used to looking at death.

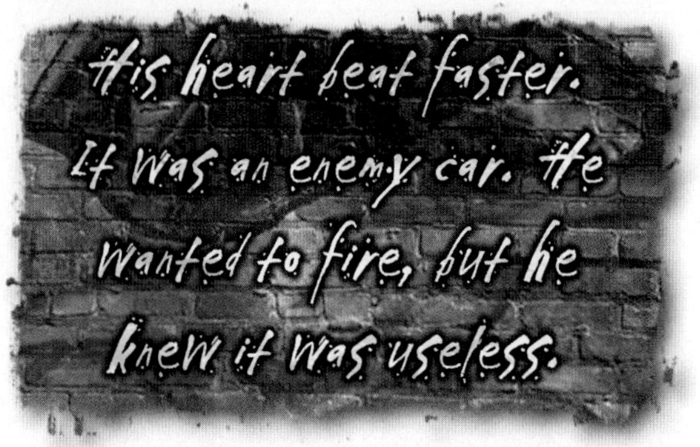
His heart beat faster.
It was an enemy car. He
wanted to fire, but he
knew it was useless.

He was eating a sandwich hungrily. He had eaten nothing since morning. He had been too excited to eat. He finished the sandwich, and, taking a flask from his pocket, he took a short draught.[2] Then he returned the flask to his pocket. He paused for a moment, considering whether he should risk a smoke. It was dangerous. The flash might be seen in the darkness and there were enemies watching. He decided to take the risk.

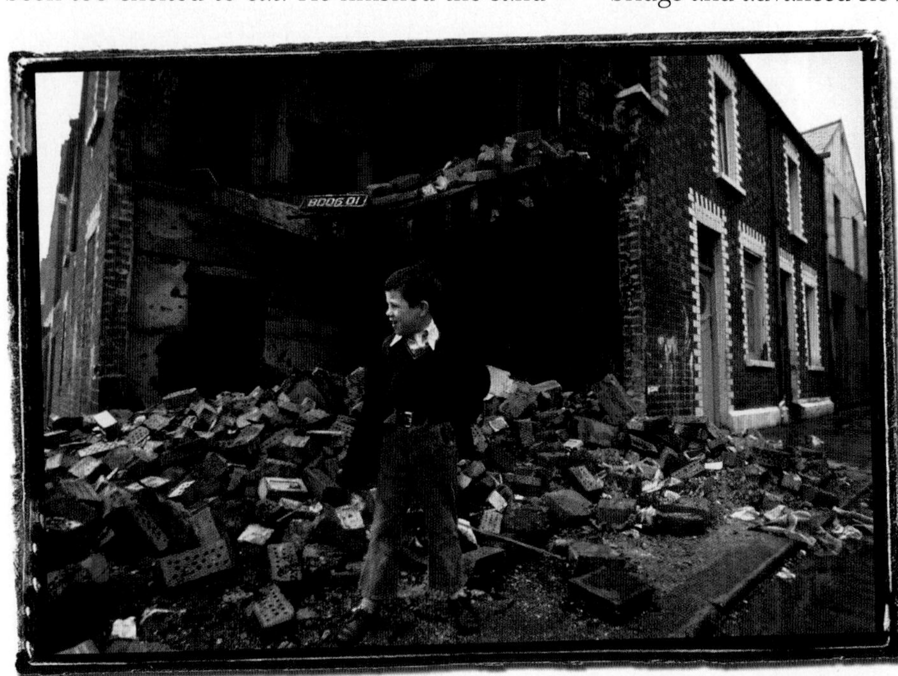

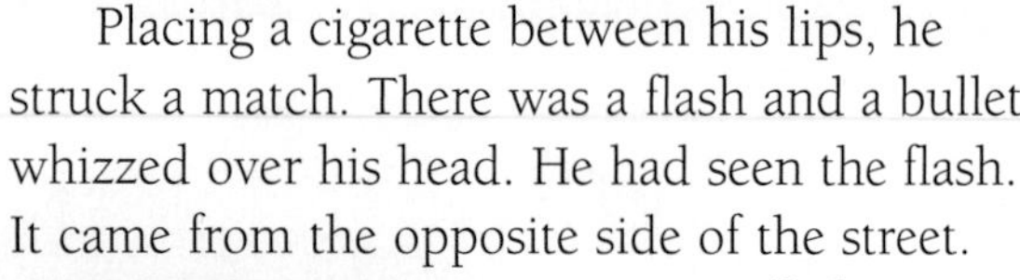

Placing a cigarette between his lips, he struck a match. There was a flash and a bullet whizzed over his head. He had seen the flash. It came from the opposite side of the street.

He rolled over the roof to a chimney stack in the rear, and slowly drew himself up behind it, until his eyes were level with the top of the parapet.[3] There was nothing to be seen—just the dim outline of the opposite housetop against the blue sky. His enemy was under cover.

Just then an armored car came across the bridge and advanced slowly up the street. It stopped on the opposite side of the street, fifty yards ahead. The sniper could hear the dull panting of the motor. His heart beat faster. It was an enemy car. He wanted to fire, but he knew it was useless. His bullets would never pierce the steel that covered the gray monster.

Then round the corner of a side street came an old woman, her head covered by a tattered shawl. She began to talk to the man in the turret[4] of the car.

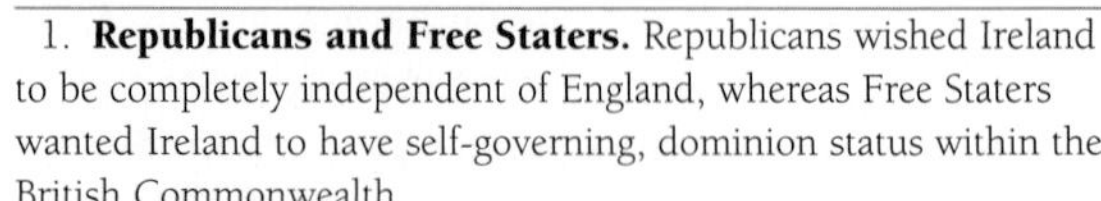

1. **Republicans and Free Staters.** Republicans wished Ireland to be completely independent of England, whereas Free Staters wanted Ireland to have self-governing, dominion status within the British Commonwealth.
2. **draught.** Drink
3. **parapet.** Low wall or railing, as along a balcony; wall used to screen troops from frontal fire
4. **turret.** Armored, usually revolving, structure on top of a tank or an armored car, used to hold a gun or guns

She was pointing to the roof where the sniper lay. An informer.

The turret opened. A man's head and shoulders appeared, looking toward the sniper. The sniper raised his rifle and fired. The head fell heavily on the turret wall. The woman darted toward the side street. The sniper fired again. The woman whirled round and fell with a shriek into the gutter.

Suddenly from the opposite roof a shot rang out and the sniper dropped his rifle with a curse. The rifle clattered to the roof. The sniper thought the noise would wake the dead. He stooped to pick the rifle up. He couldn't lift it. His forearm was dead.

"Blast!" he muttered, "I'm hit."

Dropping flat onto the roof, he crawled back to the parapet. With his left hand he felt the injured right forearm. There was no pain—just a deadened sensation, as if the arm had been cut off.

Quickly he drew his knife from his pocket, opened it on the breastwork of the parapet, and ripped open the sleeve. There was a small hole where the bullet had entered. On the other side there was no hole. The bullet had lodged in the bone. It must have fractured it. He bent the arm below the wound. The arm bent back easily. He ground his teeth to overcome the pain.

Then, taking out a field dressing, he ripped open the packet with his knife. He broke the neck of the iodine bottle and let the bitter fluid drip into the wound. A paroxysm of pain swept through him. He placed the cotton wadding over the wound and wrapped the dressing over it. He tied the ends with his teeth.

Then he lay against the parapet, and, closing his eyes, he made an effort of will to overcome the pain.

In the street beneath all was still. The armored car had retired speedily over the bridge, with the machinegunner's head hanging lifelessly over the turret. The woman's corpse lay still in the gutter.

The sniper lay still for a long time nursing his wounded arm and planning escape. Morning must not find him wounded on the roof. The enemy on the opposite roof covered his escape. He must kill that enemy and he could not use his rifle. He had only a revolver to do it. Then he thought of a plan.

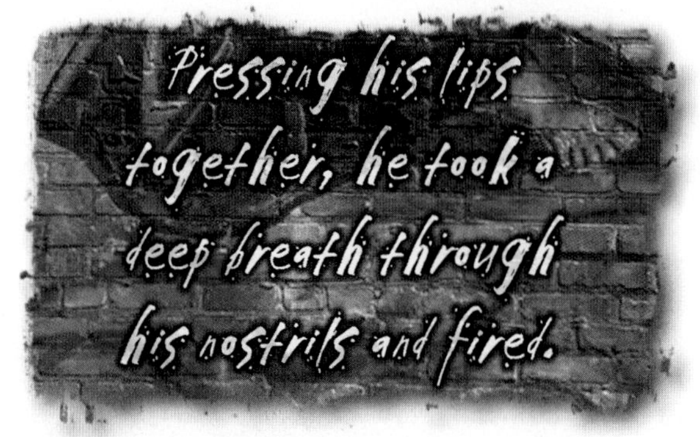
Pressing his lips
together, he took a
deep breath through
his nostrils and fired.

Taking off his cap, he placed it over the muzzle of his rifle. Then he pushed the rifle slowly over the parapet, until the cap was visible from the opposite side of the street. Almost immediately there was a report, and a bullet pierced the center of the cap. The sniper slanted the rifle forward. The cap slipped down into the street. Then, catching the rifle in the middle, the sniper dropped his left hand over the roof and let it hang, lifelessly. After a few moments he let the rifle drop to the street. Then he sank to the roof, dragging his hand with him.

Crawling quickly to the left, he peered up at the corner of the roof. His ruse had

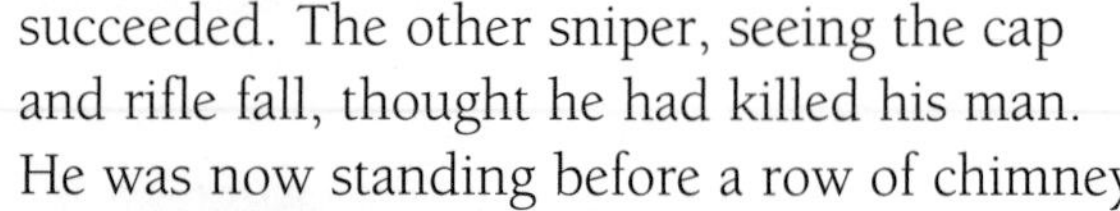

succeeded. The other sniper, seeing the cap and rifle fall, thought he had killed his man. He was now standing before a row of chimney pots, looking across, with his head clearly silhouetted against the western sky.

The Republican sniper smiled and lifted his revolver above the edge of the parapet. The distance was about fifty yards—a hard shot in the dim light, and his right arm was paining him like a thousand devils. He took a steady aim. His hand trembled with eagerness. Pressing his lips together, he took a deep breath through his nostrils and fired. He was almost deafened with the report and his arm shook with the recoil.[5]

Then when the smoke cleared, he peered across and uttered a cry of joy. His enemy had been hit. He was reeling over the parapet in his death agony. He struggled to keep his feet, but he was slowly falling forward, as if in a dream. The rifle fell from his grasp, hit the parapet, fell over, bounded off the pole of a barber's shop beneath, and then clattered on the pavement.

Then the dying man on the roof crumpled up and fell forward. The body turned over and over in space and hit the ground with a dull thud. Then it lay still.

5. **recoil.** Backward kick when a gun is fired

The sniper looked at his enemy falling, and he shuddered. The lust of battle died in him. He became bitten by remorse. The sweat stood out in beads on his forehead. Weakened by his wound and the long summer day of fasting and watching on the roof, he revolted from the sight of the shattered mass of his dead enemy. His teeth chattered, he began to gibber to himself, cursing the war, cursing himself, cursing everybody.

He began to gibber to himself, cursing the war, cursing himself, cursing everybody.

He looked at the smoking revolver in his hand, and with an oath he hurled it to the roof at his feet. The revolver went off with the concussion and the bullet whizzed past the sniper's head. He was frightened back to his senses by the shock. His nerves steadied. The cloud of fear scattered from his mind, and he laughed.

Taking the flask from his pocket, he emptied it at a draught. He felt reckless under the influence of the spirit. He decided to leave the roof now and look for his company commander, to report. Everywhere around was quiet. There was not much danger in going through the streets. He picked up his revolver and put it in his pocket. Then he crawled down through the skylight to the house underneath.

When the sniper reached the laneway on the street level, he felt a sudden curiosity as to the identity of the enemy sniper whom he had killed. He decided that he was a good shot, whoever he was. He wondered did he know him. Perhaps he had been in his own company before the split in the army. He decided to risk going over to have a look at him. He peered around the corner into O'Connell Street. In the upper part of the street there was heavy firing, but around here all was quiet.

The sniper darted across the street. A machine-gun tore up the ground around him with a hail of bullets, but he escaped. He threw himself face downward beside the corpse. The machine-gun stopped. Then the sniper turned over the dead body and looked into his brother's face. ❖

"He wondered did he know him. Perhaps he had been in his own company before the split in the army." What could turn a friend into an enemy? How difficult is it to understand an opposing viewpoint?

Refer and Reason

1. *Irony of situation* occurs when an event contradicts the expectations of the characters or the reader. What is ironic about the ending of the story? Why do you think the author uses an ironic ending?
2. What message does the story have about war? Evaluate whether or not the story is effective in teaching this lesson. Explain.
3. How do you imagine you would feel if you lived in a place where bombings and snipers were common? Do you think you would join the fighting? join a peace movement? just try to go about your life and stay safe? Explain your responses.

Writing Options

1. Imagine you are the sniper's brother. Describe your experiences that day on the rooftop.
2. Using examples from the selection, write a one-page persuasive essay on war.

Go to **www.mirrorsandwindows.com** for more.

Rules of the Game

The chessboard seemed to hold elaborate secrets waiting to be untangled.

A Short Story by

Amy Tan

Amy Tan (b. 1952) grew up in Oakland, California. Instead of becoming a doctor and a concert pianist as her mother wished, Tan studied English and linguistics and eventually pursued a writing career. In 1987, a trip to China with her mother inspired Tan to complete the book of stories that became *The Joy Luck Club.*

"Rules of the Game" is one of the stories that appears in *The Joy Luck Club.* The novel weaves together the stories of four women born and raised in China before 1949 and of their four American-born daughters. The events take place in San Francisco's Chinatown, where the immigrant women form the Joy Luck Club and begin meeting to play the Chinese game mah-jongg, invest in stocks, and tell their stories. Waverly, one of the daughters, is a chess prodigy. "Rules of the Game" explores her relationship with her mother.

How similar are your personality and interests to those of your parents or guardians? Do your differences cause problems within the family?

I was six when my mother taught me the art of invisible strength. It was a strategy for winning arguments, respect from others, and eventually, though neither of us knew it at the time, chess games.

"Bite back your tongue," scolded my mother when I cried loudly, yanking her hand toward the store that sold bags of salted plums. At home, she said, "Wise guy, he not go against wind. In Chinese we say, Come from

South, blow with wind—poom!—North will follow. Strongest wind cannot be seen."

The next week I bit back my tongue as we entered the store with the forbidden candies. When my mother finished her shopping, she quietly plucked a small bag of plums from the rack and put it on the counter with the rest of the items.

My mother imparted her daily truths so she could help my older brothers and me rise above our circumstances. We lived in San Francisco's Chinatown. Like most of the other Chinese children who played in the back alleys of restaurants and curio shops, I didn't think we were poor. My bowl was always full, three five-course meals every day, beginning with a soup full of mysterious things I didn't want to know the names of.

We lived on Waverly Place, in a warm, clean, two-bedroom flat that sat above a small Chinese bakery specializing in steamed pastries and dim sum.[1] In the early morning, when the alley was still quiet, I could smell fragrant red beans as they were cooked down to a pastry sweetness. By daybreak, our flat was heavy with the odor of fried sesame balls and sweet curried chicken crescents. From my bed, I would listen as my father got ready for work, then locked the door behind him, one-two-three clicks.

At the end of our two-block alley was a small sandlot playground with swings and slides well-shined down the middle with use. The play area was bordered by wood-slat benches where old-country people sat crackling roasted watermelon seeds with their golden teeth and scattering the husks to an impatient gathering of gurgling pigeons. The best playground, however, was the dark alley itself. It was crammed with daily mysteries and adventures. My brothers and I would peer into the medicinal herb shop, watching old Li dole out onto a stiff sheet of white paper the right amount of insect shells, saffron-colored seeds, and pungent leaves for his ailing customers. It was said that he once cured a woman dying of an ancestral curse that had eluded the best of American doctors. Next to the pharmacy was a printer who specialized in gold-embossed wedding invitations and festive red banners.

Farther down the street was Ping Yuen Fish Market. The front window displayed a tank crowded with doomed fish and turtles struggling to gain footing on the slimy green-tiled sides. A hand-written sign informed tourists, "Within this store, is all for food, not for pet." Inside, the butchers with their bloodstained white smocks deftly gutted the fish while customers cried out their orders and shouted, "Give me your freshest," to which the butchers always protested, "All are freshest." On less crowded market days, we would inspect the crates of live frogs and crabs which we were warned not to poke, boxes of dried cuttlefish, and row upon row of iced prawns, squid, and slippery fish. The sanddabs made me shiver each time; their eyes lay on one flattened side and reminded me of my mother's story of a careless girl who ran into a crowded street and was crushed by a cab. "Was smash flat," reported my mother.

At the corner of the alley was Hong Sing's, a four-table café with a recessed stairwell in front that led to a door marked "Tradesmen."

"Come from South, blow with wind—poom!—North will follow. Strongest wind cannot be seen."

1. **dim sum.** Traditional Chinese food consisting of a variety of items such as fried dumplings, chicken, or rice balls

My brothers and I believed the bad people emerged from this door at night. Tourists never went to Hong Sing's, since the menu was printed only in Chinese. A Caucasian man with a big camera once posed me and my playmates in front of the restaurant. He had us move to the side of the picture window so the photo would capture the roasted duck with its head dangling from a juice-covered rope. After he took the picture, I told him he should go into Hong Sing's and eat dinner. When he smiled and asked me what they served, I shouted, "Guts and duck's feet and octopus gizzards!" Then I ran off with my friends, shrieking with laughter as we scampered across the alley and hid in the entryway grotto[2] of the China Gem Company, my heart pounding with hope that he would chase us.

My mother named me after the street that we lived on: Waverly Place Jong, my official name for important American documents. But my family called me Meimei, "Little Sister." I was the youngest, the only daughter. Each morning before school, my mother would twist and yank on my thick black hair until she had formed two tightly wound pigtails. One day, as she struggled to weave a hard-toothed comb through my disobedient hair, I had a sly thought.

I asked her, "Ma, what is Chinese torture?" My mother shook her head. A bobby pin was wedged between her lips. She wetted her palms and smoothed the hair above my ear, then pushed the pin in so that it nicked sharply against my scalp.

"Who say this word?" she asked without a trace of knowing how wicked I was being. I shrugged my shoulders and said, "Some boy in my class said Chinese people do Chinese torture."

"Chinese people do many things," she said simply. "Chinese do business, do medicine, do painting. Not lazy like American people. We do torture. Best torture."

My older brother Vincent was the one who actually got the chess set. We had gone to the annual Christmas party held at the First Chinese Baptist Church at the end of the alley. The missionary ladies had put together a Santa bag of gifts donated by members of another church. None of the gifts had names on them. There were separate sacks for boys and girls of different ages.

One of the Chinese parishioners had donned a Santa Claus costume and a stiff paper beard with cotton balls glued to it. I think the only children who thought he was the real thing were too young to know that Santa Claus was not Chinese. When my turn came up, the Santa man asked me how old I was. I thought it was a trick question; I was seven according to the American formula and eight by the Chinese calendar. I said I was born on March 17, 1951. That seemed to satisfy him. He then solemnly asked if I had been a very, very good girl this year and did I believe in Jesus Christ and obey my parents. I knew the only answer to that. I nodded back with equal solemnity.

Having watched the other children opening their gifts, I already knew that the big gifts were not necessarily the nicest ones. One girl my age got a large coloring book of biblical characters, while a less greedy girl who selected a smaller box received a glass vial of lavender toilet water. The sounds of the box were also important. A ten-year-old boy had chosen a box that jangled when he shook it. It was a tin globe of the world with a slit for inserting money. He must have thought it was full of dimes and nickels, because when he saw that it had just ten pennies, his face fell with such undisguised disappointment that his mother slapped the side of his head and led him out of the church hall, apologizing to the crowd for

2. **grotto.** Cave or artificial recess or structure built to resemble a cave

her son who had such bad manners he couldn't appreciate such a fine gift.

As I peered into the sack, I quickly fingered the remaining presents, testing their weight, imagining what they contained. I chose a heavy, compact one that was wrapped in shiny silver foil and a red satin ribbon. It was a twelve-pack of Life Savers and I spent the rest of the party arranging and rearranging the candy tubes in the order of my favorites. My brother Winston chose wisely as well. His present turned out to be a box of intricate plastic parts; the instructions on the box proclaimed that when they were properly assembled he would have an authentic miniature replica of a World War II submarine.

The chessmen were more powerful than old Li's magic herbs that cured ancestral curses.

Vincent got the chess set, which would have been a very decent present to get at a church Christmas party, except it was obviously used and, as we discovered later, it was missing a black pawn and a white knight. My mother graciously thanked the unknown benefactor, saying, "Too good. Cost too much." At which point, an old lady with fine white, wispy hair nodded toward our family and said with a whistling whisper, "Merry, merry Christmas."

When we got home, my mother told Vincent to throw the chess set away. "She not want it. We not want it," she said, tossing her head stiffly to the side with a tight, proud smile. My brothers had deaf ears. They were already lining up the chess pieces and reading from the dog-eared instruction book.

I watched Vincent and Winston play during Christmas week. The chessboard seemed to hold elaborate secrets waiting to be untangled. The chessmen were more powerful than old Li's magic herbs that cured ancestral curses. And my brothers wore such serious faces that I was sure something was at stake that was greater than avoiding the tradesman's door to Hong Sing's.

"Let me! Let me!" I begged between games when one brother or the other would sit back with a deep sigh of relief and victory, the other annoyed, unable to let go of the outcome. Vincent at first refused to let me play, but when I offered my Life Savers as replacements for the buttons that filled in for the missing pieces, he relented. He chose the flavors: wild cherry for the black pawn and peppermint for the white knight. Winner could eat both.

As our mother sprinkled flour and rolled out small doughy circles for the steamed dumplings that would be our dinner that night, Vincent explained the rules, pointing to each piece. "You have sixteen pieces and so do I. One king and queen, two bishops, two knights, two castles, and eight pawns. The pawns can only move forward one step, except on the first move. Then they can move two. But they can only take men by moving crossways like this, except in the beginning, when you can move ahead and take another pawn."

"Why?" I asked as I moved my pawn. "Why can't they move more steps?"

"Because they're pawns," he said.

"But why do they go crossways to take other men? Why aren't there any women and children?"

"Why is the sky blue? Why must you always ask stupid questions?" asked Vincent. "This is a game. These are the rules. I didn't make them up. See. Here. In the book." He jabbed a page with a pawn in his hand. "Pawn. P-A-W-N. Pawn. Read it yourself."

My mother patted the flour off her hands. "Let me see book," she said quietly. She scanned the pages quickly, not reading the foreign English symbols, seeming to search deliberately for nothing in particular.

"This American rules," she concluded at last. "Every time people come out from foreign country, must know rules. You not know, judge say, Too bad, go back. They not telling you why so you can use their way go forward. They say, Don't know why, you find out yourself. But they knowing all the time. Better you take it, find out why yourself." She tossed her head back with a satisfied smile.

I found out about all the whys later. I read the rules and looked up all the big words in a dictionary. I borrowed books from the Chinatown library. I studied each chess piece, trying to absorb the power each contained.

I learned about opening moves and why it's important to control the center early on; the shortest distance between two points is straight down the middle. I learned about the middle game and why tactics between two adversaries are like clashing ideas; the one who plays better has the clearest plans for both attacking and getting out of traps. I learned why it is essential in the endgame to have foresight, a mathematical understanding of all the possible moves, and patience; all weaknesses and advantages become evident to a strong adversary and are obscured to a tiring opponent. I discovered that for the whole game one must gather invisible strengths and see the endgame before the game begins.

I also found out why I should never reveal "why" to others. A little knowledge withheld is a great advantage one should store for future use. That is the power of chess. It is a game of secrets in which one must show and never tell. I loved the secrets I found within the sixty-four black and white squares. I carefully drew a handmade chessboard and pinned it to the wall next to my bed, where at night I would stare for hours at imaginary battles. Soon I no longer lost my games or Life Savers, but I lost my adversaries. Winston and Vincent decided they were more interested in roaming the streets after school in their Hopalong Cassidy[3] cowboy hats.

I loved the secrets I found within the sixty-four black and white squares.

On a cold spring afternoon, while walking home from school, I detoured through the playground at the end of our alley. I saw a group of old men, two seated across a folding table playing a game of chess, others smoking pipes, eating peanuts, and watching. I ran home and grabbed Vincent's chess set, which was bound in a cardboard box with rubber bands. I also carefully selected two prized rolls of Life Savers. I came back to the park and approached a man who was observing the game.

"Want to play?" I asked him. His face widened with surprise and he grinned as he looked at the box under my arm.

"Little sister, been a long time since I play with dolls," he said, smiling benevolently. I quickly put the box down next to him on the bench and displayed my retort.

Lau Po, as he allowed me to call him, turned out to be a much better player than my brothers. I lost many games and many Life Savers. But over the weeks, with each diminishing roll of candies, I added new secrets. Lau Po gave me the names. The Double Attack from

3. **Hopalong Cassidy.** Fictitious cowboy character featured in Western movies

Dragon Character, 1986. Wu Zuoren. Collection of Robert A. Hefner III.

the East and West Shores. Throwing Stones on the Drowning Man. The Sudden Meeting of the Clan. The Surprise from the Sleeping Guard. The Humble Servant Who Kills the King. Sand in the Eyes of Advancing Forces. A Double Killing Without Blood. There were also the fine points of chess etiquette. Keep captured men in neat rows, as well-tended prisoners. Never announce "Check" with vanity, lest someone with an unseen sword slit your throat. Never hurl pieces into the sandbox after you have lost a game, because then you must find them again, by yourself, after apologizing to all around you. By the end of the summer, Lau Po had taught me all he knew, and I had become a better chess player.

A small weekend crowd of Chinese people and tourists would gather as I played and defeated my opponents one by one. My mother would join the crowds during these outdoor exhibition games. She sat proudly on the bench, telling my admirers with proper Chinese humility, "Is luck."

A man who watched me play in the park suggested that my mother allow me to play in local chess tournaments. My mother smiled graciously, an answer that meant nothing. I desperately wanted to go, but I bit back my tongue. I knew she would not let me play among strangers. So as we walked home I said in a small voice that I didn't want to play in the local tournament. They would have American rules. If I lost, I would bring shame on my family.

"Is shame you fall down nobody push you," said my mother.

During my first tournament, my mother sat with me in the front row as I waited for my turn. I frequently bounced my legs to unstick them from the cold metal seat of the folding chair. When my name was called, I leapt up. My mother unwrapped something in her lap. It was her chang, a small tablet of red jade which held the sun's fire. "Is luck," she whispered, and tucked it into my dress pocket. I turned to my opponent, a fifteen-year-old boy from Oakland. He looked at me, wrinkling his nose.

As I began to play, the boy disappeared, the color ran out of the room, and I saw only my white pieces and his black ones waiting on the other side. A light wind began blowing past my ears. It whispered secrets only I could hear.

"Blow from the South," it murmured. "The wind leaves no trail." I saw a clear path, the traps to avoid. The crowd rustled. "Shhh! Shhh!" said the corners of the room. The wind blew stronger. "Throw sand from the East to distract him." The knight came forward ready for the sacrifice. The wind hissed, louder and louder. "Blow, blow, blow. He cannot see. He is blind now. Make him lean away from the wind so he is easier to knock down."

"Check," I said, as the wind roared with laughter. The wind died down to little puffs, my own breath.

"Blow from the South," it murmured. "The wind leaves no trail."

My mother placed my first trophy next to a new plastic chess set that the neighborhood Tao[4] society had given to me. As she wiped each piece with a soft cloth, she said, "Next time win more, lose less."

"Ma, it's not how many pieces you lose," I said. "Sometimes you need to lose pieces to get ahead."

"Better to lose less, see if you really need." At the next tournament, I won again, but it was my mother who wore the triumphant grin.

"Lost eight piece this time. Last time was eleven. What I tell you? Better off lose less!" I was annoyed, but I couldn't say anything.

I attended more tournaments, each one further away from home. I won all games, in all divisions. The Chinese bakery downstairs from our flat displayed my growing collection of trophies in its window, amidst the dust-covered cakes that were never picked up. The day after I won an important regional tournament, the window encased a fresh sheet cake with whipped-cream frosting and red script saying, "Congratulations, Waverly Jong, Chinatown Chess Champion." Soon after that, a flower shop, headstone engraver, and funeral parlor offered to sponsor me in national tournaments. That's when my mother decided that I no longer had to do the dishes. Winston and Vincent had to do my chores.

4. **Tao (dou).** [Chinese] Chinese mystical philosophy founded in the 6th century BCE

"Why does she get to play and we do all the work," complained Vincent.

"Is new American rules," said my mother. "Meimei play, squeeze all her brains out for win chess. You play, worth squeeze towel."

By my ninth birthday, I was a national chess champion. I was still some 429 points away from grand master status, but I was touted as the Great American Hope, a child prodigy and a girl to boot. They ran a photo of me in *Life* magazine next to a quote in which Bobby Fischer said, "There will never be a woman grand master." "Your move, Bobby," said the caption.

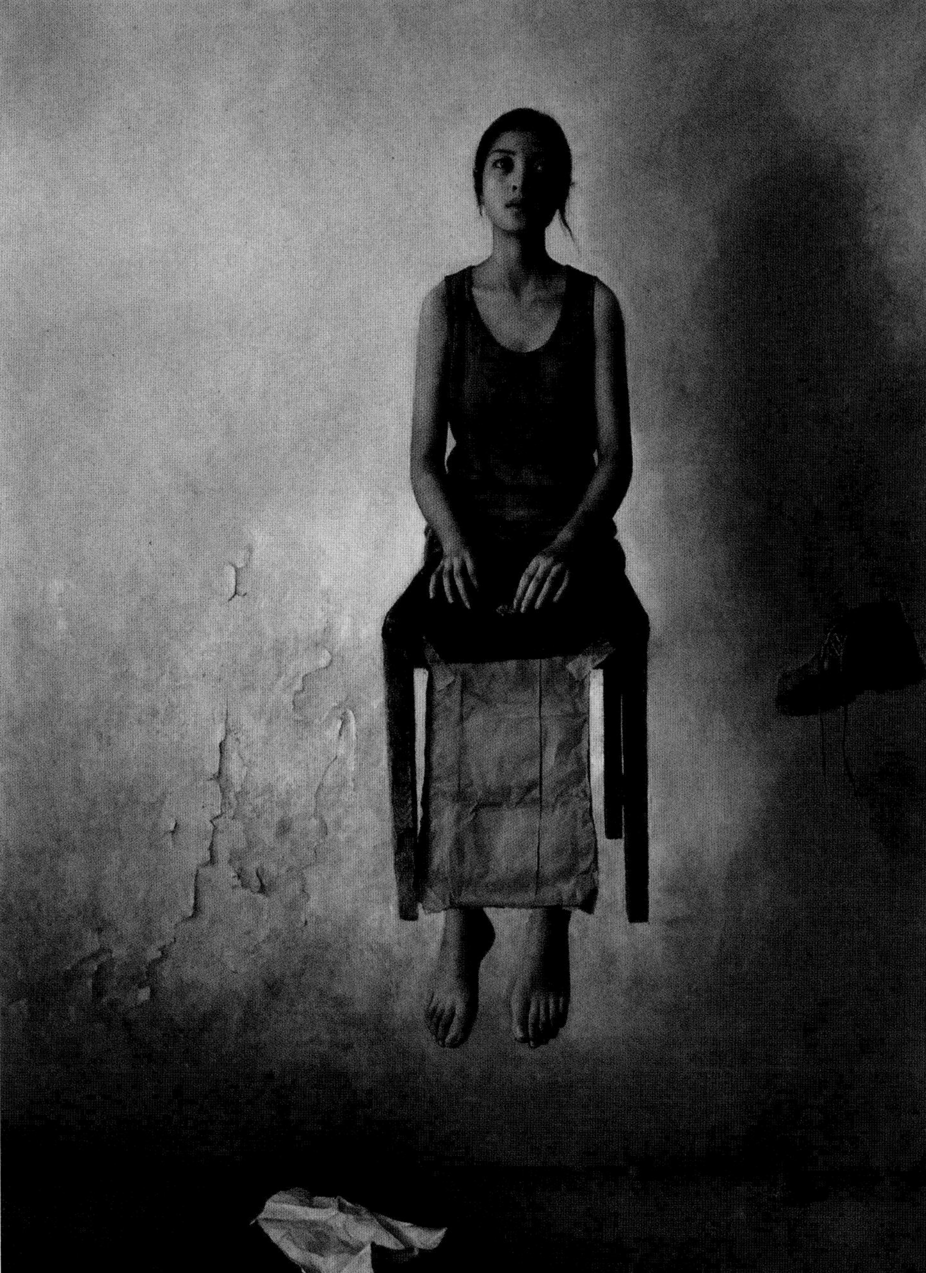

Dislocation, 1995. Kuang Jian.

Critical Viewing

What odd aspect of this painting suggests, or symbolizes, dislocation? In what way is the girl in Amy Tan's story becoming dislocated, or alienated, from her family and from her mother's traditional ideas?

The day they took the magazine picture I wore neatly plaited braids clipped with plastic barrettes trimmed with rhinestones. I was playing in a large high school auditorium that echoed with phlegmy coughs and the squeaky wooden floors. Seated across from me was an American man, about the same age as Lau Po, maybe fifty. I remember that his sweaty brow seemed to weep at my every move. He wore a dark, malodorous suit. One of his pockets was stuffed with a great white kerchief on which he wiped his palm before sweeping his hand over the chosen chess piece with great flourish.

In my crisp pink-and-white dress with scratchy lace at the neck, one of two my mother had sewn for these special occasions, I would clasp my hands under my chin, the delicate points of my elbows poised lightly on the table in the manner my mother had shown me for posing for the press. I would swing my patent leather shoes back and forth like an impatient child riding on a school bus. Then I would pause, suck in my lips, twirl my chosen piece in midair as if undecided, and then firmly plant it in its new threatening place, with a triumphant smile thrown back at my opponent for good measure.

I ran until it hurt and I realized I had nowhere to go, that I was not running from anything.

I no longer played in the alley of Waverly Place. I never visited the playground where the pigeons and old men gathered. I went to school, then directly home to learn new chess secrets, cleverly concealed advantages, more escape routes.

But I found it difficult to concentrate at home. My mother had a habit of standing over me while I plotted out my games. I think she thought of herself as my protective ally. Her lips would be sealed tight, and after each move I made, a soft "Hmmmmph" would escape from her nose.

"Ma, I can't practice when you stand there like that," I said one day. She retreated to the kitchen and made loud noises with the pots and pans. When the crashing stopped, I could see out of the corner of my eye that she was standing in the doorway. "Hmmmph!" Only this one came out of her tight throat.

My parents made many concessions to allow me to practice. One time I complained that the bedroom I shared was so noisy that I couldn't think. Thereafter, my brothers slept in a bed in the living room facing the street. I said I couldn't finish my rice; my head didn't work right when my stomach was too full. I left the table with half-finished bowls and nobody complained. But there was one duty I couldn't avoid. I had to accompany my mother on Saturday market days when I had no tournament to play. My mother would proudly walk with me, visiting many shops, buying very little. "This my daughter Wave-ly Jong," she said to whoever looked her way.

One day after we left a shop I said under my breath, "I wish you wouldn't do that, telling everybody I'm your daughter." My mother stopped walking. Crowds of people with heavy bags pushed past us on the sidewalk, bumping into first one shoulder, then another. "Aiii-ya. So shame be with mother?" She grasped my hand even tighter as she glared at me. I looked down. "It's not that, it's just so obvious. It's just so embarrassing." "Embarrass you be my daughter?" Her voice was cracking with anger. "That's not what I meant. That's not what I said." "What you say?" I knew it was a mistake to say anything more, but I heard my voice speaking, "Why do you have to use me to show off? If you want to show off, then why don't you learn to play chess?"

My mother's eyes turned into dangerous black slits. She had no words for me, just sharp silence.

I felt the wind rushing around my hot ears. I jerked my hand out of my mother's tight grasp and spun around, knocking into an old woman. Her bag of groceries spilled to the ground.

"Aii-ya! Stupid girl!" my mother and the woman cried. Oranges and tin cans careened down the sidewalk. As my mother stooped to help the old woman pick up the escaping food, I took off.

I raced down the street, dashing between people, not looking back as my mother screamed shrilly, "Meimei! Meimei!" I fled down an alley, past dark, curtained shops and merchants washing the grime off their windows. I sped into the sunlight, into a large street crowded with tourists examining trinkets and souvenirs. I ducked into another dark alley, down another street, up another alley. I ran until it hurt and I realized I had nowhere to go, that I was not running from anything. The alleys contained no escape routes.

My white pieces screamed as they scurried and fell off the board one by one.

My breath came out like angry smoke. It was cold. I sat down on an upturned plastic pail next to a stack of empty boxes, cupping my chin with my hands, thinking hard. I imagined my mother, first walking briskly down one street or another looking for me, then giving up and returning home to await my arrival. After two hours, I stood up on creaking legs and slowly walked home.

The alley was quiet and I could see the yellow lights shining from our flat like two tiger's eyes in the night. I climbed the sixteen steps to the door, advancing quietly up each so as not to make any warning sounds. I turned the knob; the door was locked. I heard a chair moving, quick steps, the locks turning-click! click! click!-and then the door opened.

"About time you got home," said Vincent. "Boy, are you in trouble."

He slid back to the dinner table. On a platter were the remains of a large fish, its fleshy head still connected to bones swimming upstream in vain escape. Standing there waiting for my punishment, I heard my mother speak in a dry voice.

"We're not concerning this girl. This girl not have concerning for us."

Nobody looked at me. Bone chopsticks clinked against the insides of bowls being emptied into hungry mouths.

I walked into my room, closed the door, and lay down on my bed. The room was dark, the ceiling filled with shadows from the dinnertime lights of neighboring flats.

In my head, I saw a chessboard with sixty-four black and white squares. Opposite me was my opponent, two angry black slits. She wore a triumphant smile. "Strongest wind cannot be seen," she said.

Her black men advanced across the plane, slowly marching to each successive level as a single unit. My white pieces screamed as they scurried and fell off the board one by one. As her men drew closer to my edge, I felt myself growing light. I rose up into the air and flew out the window. Higher and higher, above the alley, over the tops of tiled roofs, where I was gathered up by the wind and pushed up toward the night sky until everything below me disappeared and I was alone.

I closed my eyes and pondered my next move. ❖

Is it fair for parents, coaches, or teachers to take credit for the success of their children and students? What effect might this have on the sense of motivation and accomplishment the child experiences?

Informational Text CONNECTION

Chess is a game of strategy and skill that has been in existence since medieval times. The modern form of chess is thought to have been developed in the late 1400s in France, Italy, or Spain. Benjamin Franklin was among the earliest known U.S. chess players, but it wasn't until 1804 that chess began to gain popularity in the United States. Today, chess is played in local and national tournaments around the country, and even over the Internet.

How do you like to learn a new game or activity? What makes it easiest for you to understand?

The Rules of Chess

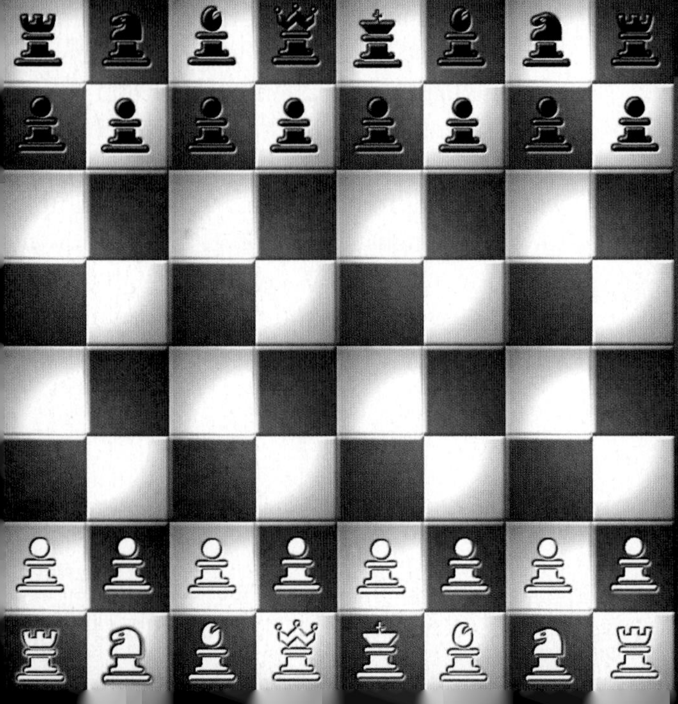

Chess is played by two players beginning in the position shown below. The player with the light-colored pieces (usually referred to as white) moves first. Then each player takes a single turn. The players must move in turn. A move cannot be skipped.

When setting up the pieces, keep in mind two things. The light colored square goes on the player's right, and Queens go on their color next to the Kings on the center files.

You may not move a piece to a square already occupied by one of your own pieces. You may capture an opposing piece by replacing that piece with one of your own pieces, if the piece can legally move there.

The King

The King is the most important piece. When it is trapped so it cannot move without being captured, then the game is lost. The trap is called checkmate.

The King can move one square in any direction. A King can never move into check or onto a square where it can be captured by an opponent's piece.

The Queen

The Queen is the most powerful piece. She can move to any square in any direction if her path is not blocked. Her range and ability to attack many pieces at once are the source of her power.

The Rook

The Rook is a very powerful piece because it can move to any square along its file or row as long as its path is not blocked. Its range is the source of its power.

The Bishop

The Bishop is a powerful piece because it can move to any square along its diagonals as long as it is not blocked. Its range is the source of its power.

The Knight

The Knight is nearly as powerful as the Bishop not because of its range but because it is the only piece that can hop over other pieces. It does so in an L-shaped path. This ability makes it particularly powerful in the early stages of a game when the board is crowded with pieces.

The Pawn

The Pawn is the least powerful piece because of its poor mobility. Ordinarily, it may move only one square forward. However, on its first move, it has the option of moving forward one or two squares. It may capture other pieces only by a diagonal move of one square. It may not capture forward. It may not move backward. The lowly Pawn usually does not last long, but if it is able to reach the eighth row or rank, then it can be promoted to any other piece except the King. A Pawn thus promoted is replaced by that piece. Therefore, it is possible to have more than one Queen or more than two Rooks, Bishops, or Knights on the board at one time.

The Objective in Chess

No one knows for certain where and when chess was invented, although a clue to its origins can be found in the word *checkmate*, a form of the Persian *shah-mat,* meaning, literally, "the king is dead." The objective in chess is to checkmate your opponent's King. When a King cannot avoid capture, then it is checkmated and the game is immediately over. If a King is threatened with capture but has a means to escape, then it is said to be in check. A King cannot move into check, and if in check must move out of check immediately. There are three ways to move out of check:

- By capturing the checking piece
- By blocking the line of attack by placing one's own piece between the checking piece and the King
- By moving the King out of check (away from its position)

If a King is not in check, and no other legal move is possible, then a stalemate, a draw or tie, occurs.

Over the years, various checkmate positions have acquired names given to them by players. The following illustration shows an example

of a checkmate position known as the "Fool's Mate." Only two moves into the game, the white player has foolishly left his or her King wide open. The black Queen slides down on a diagonal and traps the King to win the match.

Additional Information

If you decide that you want to learn to play chess, you need, in addition, to learn the rules governing moves, known as *castling* and *capturing en passant.* You can find the Official Rules of Chess of the United States Chess Federation at the Federation's site on the World Wide Web.

A good introduction to the game is Snyder, Robert M. *Chess for Juniors: A Complete Guide for the Beginner.* New York: McKay, 1991. ❖

Refer and Reason

1. Which chess piece is the most powerful and why? Analyze Waverly and her mother's relationship. What is the main conflict, and why might it be difficult to resolve?
2. Judge how effective Mrs. Jong's rules are in helping Waverly win at chess. How effective is her advice in other areas of Waverly's life?
3. Waverly becomes obsessed with playing chess. Imagine if her mother didn't support her talent. Summarize how the story would have developed if Mrs. Jong hadn't taken an interest in Waverly's abilities.

Writing Options

1. Write down the directions and rules for a game that you know or for a game of your own invention. Working in pairs, verbally explain the instructions to your partner and play a round of the game. Then switch roles and have your partner explain his or her game to you and try a round of that game.
2. The wind is used symbolically in this story. Write a two- to three-paragraph critical essay that explores the use of the wind in the story.

Go to **www.mirrorsandwindows.com** for more.

TEXT TO TEXT CONNECTION

- How do the rules of chess, as outlined here, compare to Mrs. Jong's rules in "Rules of the Game"? How might Mrs. Jong respond to these rules?
- How does strategy relate to "Rules of the Game"? Does either Mrs. Jong or this article teach strategy? Explain.

The Man to Send Rain Clouds

A Short Story by

Leslie Marmon Silko

"Did you find old Teofilo?" he asked loudly.

Leslie Marmon Silko (b. 1948), poet, novelist, and short story writer, grew up on the Laguna Pueblo Reservation in New Mexico and is of mixed Pueblo, Laguna, Mexican, and white heritage. After attending school on her reservation and at a Catholic school in Albuquerque, Silko studied law and then writing. Her stories reflect themes from her Native American heritage, including the relationship between humans and nature and the tensions of living within different cultures.

"The Man to Send Rain Clouds" explores the relationship between a Catholic priest and a Pueblo Indian community as they deal with the death of a member and the differences between their traditions. In the Pueblo tradition, Silko says, "Each adult works with every child, children belong to everybody and the way of teaching is to tell stories."

What types of traditions are practiced by your family or culture? What tradition is most important to you?

They found him under a big cottonwood tree. His Levi jacket and pants were faded light blue so that he had been easy to find. The big cottonwood tree stood apart from a small grove of winterbare cottonwoods which grew in the wide, sandy *arroyo*.[1] He had been dead for a day or more, and the sheep had wandered and scattered up and down the arroyo. Leon and his brother-in-law, Ken, gathered the sheep and left them in the pen at the sheep camp before they returned to the cottonwood tree. Leon waited under the tree while Ken drove the

1. ***arroyo*** **(ə rō´ yō).** [Spanish] Dry gully or channel carved by water

truck through the deep sand to the edge of the arroyo. He squinted up at the sun and unzipped his jacket—it sure was hot for this time of year. But high and northwest the blue mountains were still in snow. Ken came sliding down the low, crumbling bank about fifty yards down, and he was bringing the red blanket.

Before they wrapped the old man, Leon took a piece of string out of his pocket and tied a small gray feather in the old man's long white hair. Ken gave him the paint. Across the brown wrinkled forehead he drew a streak of white and along the high cheekbones he drew a strip of blue paint. He paused and watched Ken throw pinches of corn meal and pollen into the wind that fluttered the small gray feather. Then Leon painted with yellow under the old man's broad nose, and finally, when he had painted green across the chin, he smiled.

"Send us rain clouds, Grandfather." They laid the bundle in the back of the pickup and covered it with a heavy tarp before they started back to the *pueblo.*[2]

They turned off the highway onto the sandy pueblo road. Not long after they passed the store and post office they saw Father Paul's car coming toward them. When he recognized their faces he slowed his car and waved for them to stop. The young priest rolled down the car window.

"Did you find old Teofilo?" he asked loudly.

Leon stopped the truck. "Good morning, Father. We were just out to the sheep camp. Everything is O.K. now."

"Thank God for that. Teofilo is a very old man. You really shouldn't allow him to stay at the sheep camp alone."

"No, he won't do that any more now."

"Well, I'm glad you understand. I hope I'll be seeing you at Mass this week—we missed you last Sunday. See if you can get old Teofilo to come with you." The priest smiled and waved at them as they drove away.

Louise and Teresa were waiting. The table was set for lunch, and the coffee was boiling on the black iron stove. Leon looked at Louise and then at Teresa.

"We found him under a cottonwood tree in the big arroyo near sheep camp. I guess he sat down to rest in the shade and never got up again." Leon walked toward the old man's bed. The red plaid shawl had been shaken and spread carefully over the bed, and a new brown flannel shirt and pair of stiff new Levi's were arranged neatly beside the pillow. Louise held the screen door open while Leon and Ken carried in the red blanket. He looked small and shriveled, and after they dressed him in the new shirt and pants he seemed more shrunken.

It was noontime now because the church bells rang the Angelus.[3] They ate the beans with hot bread, and nobody said anything until after Teresa poured the coffee.

Ken stood up and put on his jacket. "I'll see about the gravediggers. Only the top layer of soil is frozen. I think it can be ready before dark."

Leon nodded his head and finished his coffee. After Ken had been gone for a while, the neighbors and clanspeople came quietly to embrace Teofilo's family and to leave food on the table because the gravediggers would come to eat when they were finished.

The sky in the west was full of pale yellow light. Louise stood outside with her hands in the pockets of Leon's green army jacket that was too big for her. The funeral was over, and the old men had taken their candles and medicine bags and were gone. She waited until the body was laid into the pickup before she said anything to Leon. She touched his arm, and he noticed that her hands were still dusty from the corn meal that she had sprinkled around the old man. When she spoke, Leon could not hear her.

"What did you say? I didn't hear you."

"I said that I had been thinking about something."

2. ***pueblo*** (pü äb´ lō). [Spanish] Village
3. **Angelus.** Prayer said at morning, noon, and evening to honor the birth of Jesus Christ

"About what?"

"About the priest sprinkling holy water for Grandpa. So he won't be thirsty."

Leon stared at the new moccasins that Teofilo had made for the ceremonial dances in the summer. They were nearly hidden by the red blanket. It was getting colder, and the wind pushed gray dust down the narrow pueblo road. The sun was approaching the long *mesa*[4] where it disappeared during the winter. Louise stood there shivering and watching his face. Then he zipped up his jacket and opened the truck door. "I'll see if he's there."

Ken stopped the pickup at the church, and Leon got out; and then Ken drove down the hill to the graveyard where people were waiting. Leon knocked at the old carved door with its symbols of the Lamb.[5] While he waited he looked up at the twin bells from the king of Spain[6] with the last sunlight pouring around them in their tower.

The priest opened the door and smiled when he saw who it was. "Come in! What brings you here this evening?"

The priest walked toward the kitchen, and Leon stood with his cap in his hand, playing with the earflaps and examining the living room—the brown sofa, the green armchair, and the brass lamp that hung down from the ceiling by links of chain. The priest dragged a chair out of the kitchen and offered it to Leon.

"No thank you, Father. I only came to ask you if you would bring your holy water to the graveyard."

The priest turned away from Leon and looked out the window at the patio full of

4. ***mesa*** **(mā´ sə).** [Spanish] A flat-topped hill or small plateau with steep sides

5. **Lamb.** Symbol of Jesus Christ

6. **twin bells...king of Spain.** Spain colonized the Americas in the fifteenth and sixteenth centuries; the Spanish monarchy sent priests and financed the building of churches.

Sunset Dance—Ceremony to the Evening Sun, 1924. Joseph Henry Sharp. Smithsonian American Art Museum, Washington, DC.

shadows and the dining-room windows of the nuns' cloister[7] across the patio. The curtains were heavy, and the light from within faintly penetrated; it was impossible to see the nuns inside eating supper. "Why didn't you tell me he was dead? I could have brought the Last Rites[8] anyway."

Leon smiled. "It wasn't necessary, Father."

The priest stared down at his scuffed brown loafers and the worn hem of his cassock. "For a Christian burial it was necessary."

His voice was distant, and Leon thought that his blue eyes looked tired.

"It's O.K. Father, we just want him to have plenty of water."

The priest sank down into the green chair and picked up a glossy missionary[9] magazine. He turned the colored pages full of lepers and pagans[10] without looking at them.

"You know I can't do that, Leon. There should have been the Last Rites and a funeral Mass at the very least."

7. **cloister.** Place of protection and seclusion for people who follow a religious vocation

8. **Last Rites.** Sacrament performed by a Catholic priest or deacon for someone who is dying

9. **missionary.** Person sent to convert others to a religion or to teach religious beliefs

10. **lepers and pagans.** *Lepers*—people afflicted with the disease known as leprosy; *pagans*—a word sometimes used to refer to people who are not Christians

Leon put on his green cap and pulled the flaps down over his ears. "It's getting late, Father. I've got to go."

When Leon opened the door Father Paul stood up and said, "Wait." He left the room and came back wearing a long brown overcoat. He followed Leon out the door and across the dim churchyard to the adobe[11] steps in front of the church. They both stooped to fit through the low adobe entrance. And when they started down the hill to the graveyard only half of the sun was visible above the mesa.

He sprinkled the grave and the water disappeared almost before it touched the dim, cold sand...

The priest approached the grave slowly, wondering how they had managed to dig into the frozen ground; and then he remembered that this was New Mexico, and saw the pile of cold loose sand beside the hole. The people stood close to each other with little clouds of steam puffing from their faces. The priest looked at them and saw a pile of jackets, gloves, and scarves in the yellow, dry tumbleweeds that grew in the graveyard. He looked at the red blanket, not sure that Teofilo was so small, wondering if it wasn't some perverse Indian trick—something they did in March to ensure a good harvest—wondering if maybe old Teofilo was actually at sheep camp corraling the sheep for the night. But there he was, facing into a cold dry wind and squinting at the last sunlight, ready to bury a red wool blanket while the faces of his parishioners[12] were in shadow with the last warmth of the sun on their backs.

His fingers were stiff, and it took him a long time to twist the lid off the holy water. Drops of water fell on the red blanket and soaked into dark icy spots. He sprinkled the grave and the water disappeared almost before it touched the dim, cold sand; it reminded him of something—he tried to remember what it was, because he thought if he could remember he might understand this. He sprinkled more water; he shook the container until it was empty, and the water fell through the light from sundown like August rain that fell while the sun was still shining, almost evaporating before it touched the wilted squash flowers.

The wind pulled at the priest's brown Franciscan robe and swirled away the corn meal and pollen that had been sprinkled on the blanket. They lowered the bundle into the ground, and they didn't bother to untie the stiff pieces of new rope that were tied around the ends of the blanket. The sun was gone, and over on the highway the eastbound lane was full of headlights. The priest walked away slowly. Leon watched him climb the hill, and when he had disappeared within the tall, thick walls, Leon turned to look up at the high blue mountains in the deep snow that reflected a faint red light from the west. He felt good because it was finished, and he was happy about the sprinkling of the holy water; now the old man could send them big thunderclouds for sure. ❖

11. **adobe** (ə dō´ bē). Brick made of sun-dried earth
12. **parishioners.** Members of a church district or parish

How important are cultural and religious traditions? When is it appropriate to modify your own practices to accommodate someone else's traditions or lifestyles? When does compassion win over traditional practices?

Literature CONNECTION

In **"Without Title,"** writer **Diane Glancy** (b. 1941) makes reference to an important Native American rite of passage—a rite the speaker's father never got to experience. The Missouri-born Glancy, whose own father was part Cherokee, calls her Native American ancestry a "heritage I feel every day." Consider whether or not the poem "Without Title" relates to the story "The Man to Send Rain Clouds." Explain your reasoning.

Without Title

A Poem by **Diane Glancy**

It's hard you know without the buffalo,
the shaman,[1] the arrow,
but my father went out each day to hunt
as though he had them.
He worked in the stockyards.[2]
All his life he brought us meat.
No one marked his first kill,
no one sang his buffalo song.[3]

1. **shaman.** Priest or healer
2. **stockyards.** Yards where cattle, sheep, pigs, or horses are kept before being slaughtered for market
3. **marked...buffalo song.** *Marked his first kill*—took notice of his first kill because it was important; *buffalo song*—song about the coming of age of a person who has just made his first kill

Without a vision he had migrated[4] to the city
and went to work in the packing house.[5]
When he brought home his horns and hides
my mother said
get rid of them.
I remember the animal tracks of his car
backing out the drive in snow and mud,
the aerial[6] on his old car waving
like a bow string.
I remember the silence of his lost power,
the red buffalo painted on his chest.
Oh, I couldn't see it
but it was there, and in the night I heard
his buffalo grunts like a snore. ❖

4. **migrated.** Moved from one country or place to another; moved from one climate to another in regular cycles

5. **packing house.** Plant or factory where meats are processed and packaged for sale

6. **aerial.** Antenna

Refer and Reason

1. Review the story, and identify the parts that reveal the priest's feelings about the community in which he lives. What kind of relationship exists between the people of this community and the priest? Why might this be?
2. Assess whether the priest's decision to sprinkle the holy water was appropriate. Why do you think the priest ultimately decides to sprinkle the holy water over Teofilo's body?
3. Tell how you think the father in "Without Title" feels about the absence of his people's traditions. What connections can be made between these feelings and what the priest experiences in "The Man to Send Rain Clouds"?

Writing Options

1. Imagine that you are the priest in the story. Write a letter to the bishop of your church explaining your decision to sprinkle holy water for an unorthodox purpose.
2. Write a three- to four-paragraph compare-and-contrast essay that describes how the father in "Without Title" could be compared with the priest from "The Man to Send Rain Clouds."

Go to **www.mirrorsandwindows.com** for more.

TEXT ⟷ TO ⟷ TEXT CONNECTION

In "Without Title" and "The Man to Send Rain Clouds," Native American characters are shown to have absorbed certain parts of the larger American culture but still preserved certain elements of their own. What do you think the narrator in the story and the speaker in the poem would consider the benefits of such a cultural blending? What might they consider to have been lost?

FINDING MIRACLES

by Julia Alvarez

Fifteen-year-old Milly Kaufman wants to fit in at her Vermont high school, so she hasn't mentioned that she's adopted. That all changes after Pablo, a refugee from a war-torn Latin American country, shows up at her school and suspects that she is also from his country.

DELTA WEDDING

by Eudora Welty

Riding on a train to her cousin's wedding in the Mississippi Delta in 1923, Laura McRaven is anxious—and with good reason. Although the cotton plantation world Laura enters seems timeless, the novel is about change; weddings, war, duels, death, and large historical events invade the family society.

JACK LONDON: FIVE GREAT SHORT STORIES

by Jack London

In this collection, lost sailors try to save their burning ship, a Mexican boy must deal with a mysterious source of gold coins, two men are marooned in a snowbound cabin, a sled dog musher is pinned under a fallen pine, and an Aleut islander searches for his lost bride.

GREAT EXPECTATIONS

by Charles Dickens

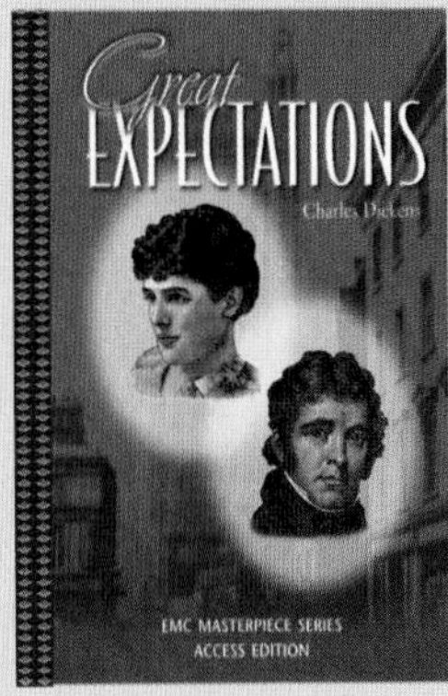

The poor orphan Pip expects little from life—until he meets three characters including the escaped convict Magwich, the bitter Miss Haversham, and her haughty niece, Estelle. Years later, he receives a gift from a mysterious benefactor. As Pip encounters cold hearts, revenge, but also love and gratitude, he learns what really counts in life.

ETHAN FROME

by Edith Wharton

A terrible accident has left Ethan Frome a disfigured, broken man. What tragic story lies behind Ethan's tortured face? The narrator leads you through one compelling vision of Ethan's story in Edith Wharton's vivid tale of life in the stark New England countryside.

THE ADVENTURES OF TOM SAWYER

by Mark Twain

For Tom Sawyer and his friends, every day is filled with adventure and mayhem. With murder mysteries to solve, pirate islands and robbers' dens to explore, and mischief to make, the quiet town of St. Petersburg doesn't remain sleepy for long!

Deliver a Narrative Presentation

Being a storyteller is about more that just having an interesting story to tell—it's knowing how to tell it. In this lesson, you will present a story, or narrative, to your classmates.

A **narrative** is a story with a beginning, middle, and an end. It can be fiction or nonfiction. The events of a narrative may be told in **chronological order**—that is, in the order they occurred.

1. Select a story

Select a simple story, such as a fairy tale, a ghost story, or an urban legend. Reread the story until you can retell it using your own words.

2. Map out the story line

Determine the beginning, the middle, and the end of the story. Find the climax, the point at which the conflict builds to the highest point, and the resolution, the point where the conflict is resolved. Decide on a good first and last line for the story, and commit these lines to memory. You don't have to memorize the entire story, however. The idea is to familiarize yourself with the main plot elements so that you can tell it in your own words. Each time you tell the story, you might embellish it or change details. Eventually, the story will become your own.

3. Visualize the story

What is the setting of the story? What sights, sounds, smells, tastes, and textures do you want your audience to have in mind while they listen? Plan how to add these sensory details to your story. You don't want to overload the story with description, but adding a few colorful lines will help create a vivid tale.

4. Think about mood, tone, and language

Is the story silly and humorous or dark and spooky? Is the message serious or lighthearted? What tone of voice should you use when telling the story? Consider your audience and topic—would formal or informal language be more appropriate?

5. Practice

Tell the story often—by yourself in front of a mirror or with a friend. Keep the following tips in mind:

- Choose your words and structure your sentences so that your audience can follow the story.
- Use appropriate intonation; that is, vary the pitch and tone of your voice, depending on the mood you want to set.
- Decide which parts of the story to stress, and find the best way of doing that—for example, by pausing or by raising your voice.
- Record your story and play it back. Are you speaking too fast? too softly? Is the story missing anything?

6. Present the narrative

Finally, present your narrative to the class, using facial expressions and gestures to bring the story to life. Try to tell the story without the aid of any notes. Remember, it's not the exact words of your story that matter—it's the way you tell it.

Speaking and Listening Rubric

Your presentation will be evaluated on these elements:

Content

- ☑ clear chronology—beginning, middle, and end
- ☑ strong opening and closing sentences
- ☑ vivid description
- ☑ simple vocabulary and sentence structure

Delivery and Presentation

- ☑ appropriate volume, pace, and enunciation
- ☑ effective tone, intonation, and stress
- ☑ effective nonverbal expression

Character Analysis

Assignment
Analyze a character from a short story
Purpose
To inform readers by giving insight into a character
Audience
Someone who has not read the story or someone who has read it and would like to discuss it

If you think about the short stories you read in this unit, you can probably recall certain characters that intrigued you. Perhaps they reminded you of yourself or of people you know. For instance, maybe you have felt rejected, like Elena in "American History," or have known someone who holds a grudge, like Georg and Ulrich in "The Interlopers." Other characters might have seemed to be people you would like to know, such as James and Della in "The Gift of the Magi," who will do anything to make one another happy.

Any of these characters would be a good topic for a **character analysis,** a type of expository (informational) writing that gives insight into a character from a literary work, such as a short story, novel, or play. In a character analysis, the writer states a main idea about the character and proves it using details from the work.

ASSIGNMENT

Choose a character from one of the short stories you read in this unit. Prewrite, draft, and revise a character analysis, stating a main idea about that character using details from the story to support it.

❶ PREWRITE

Select Your Topic

Brainstorm a list of memorable characters from the short stories in this unit. Choose the character that most interests you.

Gather Information

Reread the work in which your character appears, gathering information about appearance, actions, speech, and thoughts and feelings. Also, jot down comments the narrator or others make about the character. Use a chart like the one on the next page to record these details from the story. (See columns 1 and 2.)

Next, decide what these details reveal. Look for common threads running among the details—patterns that reveal something important about the character. Record your conclusions in column 3 of the chart.

Organize Your Ideas

Review the conclusions you entered in column 3 of the chart. As you do, ask yourself these questions: What are my character's main qualities? Is he or she generally a good or a bad person? Does the character change over the course of the story or stay the same throughout?

Circle the three conclusions from the chart that best describe the character. Number them in the order in which you would like to include them in your essay. Think about what order will be most effective in presenting your analysis of this character.

Writing Rubric

A successful character analysis

- ☑ has an **introduction** that identifies the title and author of the story, names the character being analyzed, and creates interest
- ☑ provides a clear **thesis statement** that expresses the main idea of the essay
- ☑ develops a **body** using evidence from the story—including both descriptions and quotations of details and dialogue—to support the main idea about the character
- ☑ ends with a **conclusion** that restates the main point and provides closure

Character Chart

Character: Montresor from "The Cask of Amontillado"		
Traits	**Details from the Story**	**What the Details Reveal**
Appearance	Wears a mask of black silk	He is secretive and sly.
Actions	Smiles at F. while plotting revenge Chains F. to wall and leaves him to die	He is calculating and insanely vengeful.
Speech	Speaks very flatteringly to F. Says he is concerned for F. even after chaining F. to the wall	He is manipulative and sarcastic.
Thoughts and Feelings	Claims he is "sick at heart" but then blames his condition on the dampness of the vaults	He is a cold person with no empathy.

Write Your Thesis Statement

Based on the conclusions you have drawn, write a one-sentence summary about your character. This is your **thesis statement.** Using the information from the Character Chart, one student, Adrienne, wrote this thesis statement about the character Montresor from Edgar Allan Poe's short story "The Cask of Amontillado":

> Montresor is a cold, calculating individual who is out for revenge.

❷ DRAFT

Write your essay by following this three-part framework: **introduction, body,** and **conclusion.**

Draft Your Introduction

In a character analysis, the **introduction** identifies the author and title of the story, gives a brief summary (one to two sentences) of the story's plot or theme, and names the characters being analyzed. The introduction also states the thesis, establishing the main idea or point of the analysis. Finally, a good introduction creates interest, drawing readers into the rest of the essay.

The introduction that Adrienne wrote during the Draft stage is shown in the first column of the chart on page 195. In the first two sentences, Adrienne states the author and title, gives a sense of what the story is about, and identifies Montresor. In the third sentence, she provides the thesis statement. She doesn't, however, do much to create interest. What could she add to the introduction to make readers want to continue?

What Great Writers Do

What can you tell about the character Montresor from the details given in the short story "The Cask of Amontillado," by Edgar Allan Poe?

- Montresor puts on "a mask of black silk," hiding his identity and taking on an evil appearance.
- Montresor smiles at Fortunato, his victim, saying that "he did not perceive that my smile *now* was at the thought of his immolation."
- Montresor rationalizes his behavior by saying, "My heart grew sick; it was the dampness of the catacombs that made it so."

- **Introduction**
  Identify the author, the title, and the character being analyzed. Briefly summarize the plot or theme. Include your thesis statement.
- **Body**
  Write one paragraph for each main point about the character. Support each point with evidence from the story.
- **Conclusion**
  Rephrase the thesis, and give your essay closure.

Draft Your Body

In the **body,** state each point you want to make about the character you are analyzing and then support or prove it with the details you listed in the Character Chart. Use the information that you already mapped out in the Prewrite stage.

Adrienne decided to start the body of her essay with details from the beginning of the story about Montresor's vengeful nature. Look at the draft of her first body paragraph in the left-hand column of the chart on the next page. Adrienne also drafted two more body paragraphs. She proved her thesis by offering specific details from the story, including several quotations.

Review the three statements you circled on your Character Chart and the order in which you decided to present them. Develop each statement into a paragraph by adding supporting details from the story. Every detail should relate clearly to the point you are making about this character, as stated in your thesis.

Draft Your Conclusion

Finally, write the **conclusion** of your character analysis. A good conclusion does two things: (1) It summarizes the main point made in the body of the essay, restating the thesis, and (2) it brings the discussion to a close, leaving readers with a sense of finality.

Does Adrienne do both these things in her conclusion? Look at the draft of her conclusion in the chart on the next page.

❸ REVISE

Evaluate Your Draft

You can evaluate your own writing or exchange papers with a classmate and evaluate each other's work. Either way, think carefully about what is done well and what can be improved.

What Great Writers Do

Improving word choices is one of the keys to effective revision. Mark Twain (1835–1910), author of *The Adventures of Huckleberry Finn,* made this point when he said,

"The difference between the right word and the almost right word is the difference between lightning and a lightning bug."

Start by looking at the content and organization. Make sure that the three parts of the essay—the introduction, body, and conclusion—work together to prove the thesis. Every paragraph should relate clearly back to that main idea. Use the Revision Checklist on page 196 to make this evaluation. Make notes directly on the essay about what changes need to be made.

Next, check the language for errors. Go back through your draft to make sure you have correctly applied the guidelines in the Grammar & Style workshops in this unit. Again, use the Revision Checklist to evaluate the writing. Think, too, about how the writing can be made more clear and interesting. One way to achieve this is to improve word choices, replacing general words with more specific words.

Revise for Content, Organization, and Style

Adrienne evaluated her draft and found a number of things to improve. Look at the chart on the next page (this time, the right-hand column) to see how she revised the three paragraphs we looked at earlier.

DRAFT STAGE		REVISE STAGE	
Introduction Edgar Allan Poe's short story "The Cask of Amontillado" is about one man luring another to his death as punishment for an insult. The story is narrated by Montresor, who is a distinguished man from a noble Italian family. Throughout the course of the story, readers find out that Montresor is a cold, calculating individual who is out for revenge.	Identifies author and title; gives sense of what story is about Identifies character to be analyzed States thesis	Edgar Allan Poe's short story "The Cask of Amontillado" is about one man casually luring another to his death as punishment for ~~an~~ some unknown insult. The story is narrated by its main character, Montresor, who is a distinguished man from a noble Italian family. Throughout the course of the story, readers find out that Montresor is a cold, calculating individual who is out for revenge. The name *Montresor* is only a few letters different from the word *monster,* and this may be no accident, as Montresor is monstrous and inhumane.	Adds details for clarity Adds sentence to create interest and draw readers into body
Body Paragraph Montresor shows how vengeful he is right from the beginning when he says that he wants to not only punish Fortunato but "punish [him] with impunity." This seems harsh, especially since we never learn exactly what Fortunato has done. He seems to be a harmless individual; in fact, he seems much more likable than Montresor.	Starts character analysis from beginning of story Uses quotation from story as proof	Montresor shows ~~how vengeful he is~~ that he is abnormally vengeful right from the beginning when he says that he wants ~~to not only~~ not only to punish Fortunato but to "punish [him] with impunity." This seems harsh, especially since we never learn exactly what Fortunato has done to Montresor—only that Fortunato has "insulted" him. ~~He seems to be a harmless individual; in fact, he seems much more likable than Montresor.~~	Rewords sentence to strengthen idea Fixes grammatical error: split infinitive Adds details for clarity Deletes details that are off topic
Conclusion At the end of the story, the reader understands that Montresor is truly evil. He is so cold and calculating that he feels no remorse for his crime.	Brings discussion to end of story Summarizes; restates thesis	At the end of the story, the reader ~~understands~~ has the chilling realization that Montresor is truly evil. He is so cold and calculating that he feels no remorse for his crime; rather, he takes delight in it. The reader has been drawn into the mind of a ruthless, inhumane killer—a true monster.	Uses more specific words for clarity and interest Adds detail; creates sentence variety Adds sentence to parallel introduction and provide closure

REVISION CHECKLIST

Content and Organization

- ❑ Is the title stated and author identified in the **introduction?** Does the introduction give a brief overview of the plot or theme?
- ❑ Does the **introduction** present a clear **thesis statement?** Does it accurately identify the main idea of the essay? Does it create interest?
- ❑ Does each **body** paragraph clearly relate back to the thesis?
- ❑ Does each **body** paragraph provide details from the story to support what's being said about the character? Are there enough supporting details? Are all the details relevant to the point being made?
- ❑ Does the **conclusion** summarize the essay and restate the thesis? Does it provide a sense of closure?

Grammar and Style

- ❑ Do **subjects and verbs agree?** (page 24)
- ❑ Do **pronouns agree?** (page 56)
- ❑ Are a **variety of sentence types** used? (page 134)

- **Introduction:** Adrienne added several details to clarify and thus strengthen her writing. She also added a sentence at the end to create interest.
- **Body:** Adrienne improved the language by correcting a grammatical error and using more specific words to state an idea more strongly. She improved the content and organization by adding an important detail and deleting one that didn't relate back to her thesis.
- **Conclusion:** By using more specific words and adding that Montresor takes delight in what he's doing, Adrienne adds interest, even drama. By adding the final sentence, she not only brings her analysis to a close, but she also returns to the idea she added to the introduction: Montresor is a monster.

Review the notes you or your partner made as you evaluated your draft. Respond to each comment and effectively revise your essay.

Proofread for Errors

The purpose of proofreading is to check for remaining errors. While you can look for errors as you evaluate your essay, you should focus on this purpose during proofreading. Use proofreader's symbols to mark any errors you find. (See the Language Arts Handbook 4.1 for a list of proofreader's symbols.) To complete the assignment, print out a final draft and read the entire essay once more before turning it in.

Take a look at Adrienne's final draft on the next page. Review how she worked through the three stages of the writing process: Prewrite, Draft, and Revise.

WRITING FOLLOW-UP

Publish and Present

- Find out whether your school has a magazine or journal that publishes students' writing. If it does, consider submitting your character analysis for publication. If it doesn't, look into other organizations and publications that accept students' literary interpretations.
- Draw a portrait of the character you chose. To create this image, use whatever details are provided in the text, along with your impressions from reading and writing.

Reflect

- Does the character you chose seem more or less interesting to you now that you have written this character analysis? Explain your answer.
- What did you learn about characterization as an element of fiction from doing this analysis? What can authors do to bring their characters to life for readers?

STUDENT MODEL

Montresor: A True Monster
by Adrienne Watt

Edgar Allan Poe's short story "The Cask of Amontillado" is about one man casually luring another to his death as punishment for some unknown insult. The story is narrated by its main character, Montresor, who is a distinguished man from a noble Italian family. Throughout the course of the story, readers find out that Montresor is a cold, calculating individual who is out for revenge. The name *Montresor* is only a few letters different from the word *monster,* and this may be no accident, as Montresor is monstrous and inhumane.

What is the writer's thesis statement?

Montresor shows that he is abnormally vengeful right from the beginning when he says that he wants not only to punish Fortunato but to "punish [him] with impunity." This seems harsh, especially since we never learn exactly what Fortunato has done to Montresor—only that Fortunato has "insulted" him.

What evidence does the writer provide that Montresor is vengeful?

Montresor is quite calculating in the way he carries out his crime. First, he chooses the carnival period, when the streets are full of activity and noise. Next, he tells his servants that he will not be home, knowing that they will leave the house, too. Montresor then lures his victim down to an isolated burial chamber far below ground, where no one will hear his screams. As the men walk, Montresor acts concerned for Fortunato, saying that they should turn back so he doesn't catch cold in the dampness. At the same time, Montresor flatters Fortunato by talking about his great taste in wines.

What evidence does the writer provide that Montresor is calculating?

Near the end of the story, it becomes clear how cold and cruel Montresor is when the reader realizes what he plans to do: He is going to chain up Fortunato and leave him to die in this underground chamber. Montresor actually seems to enjoy Fortunato's terror. When he chains up Fortunato, he says sarcastically, "Indeed, it is very damp. Once more let me implore you to return." Then as he bricks up the opening, he listens with "satisfaction" to the clanking of the chain as Fortunato tries to free himself. Montresor hesitates once when he hears Fortunato's screams but only because he is worried someone else might hear. After reassuring himself that the walls are too thick for the sound to get through, he continues. He claims that his heart grew sick, not because of the deed but because of the dampness!

What evidence does the writer provide that Montresor is cold and cruel?

How does the writer attach quotations about Montresor's cruelty to her own sentences?

At the end of the story, the reader has the chilling realization that Montresor is truly evil. He is so cold and calculating that he feels no remorse for his crime; rather, he takes delight in it. The reader has been drawn into the mind of a ruthless, inhumane killer—a true monster.

Where does the writer restate her thesis?

TEST PRACTICE WORKSHOP

Reading Skills

MAKE INFERENCES

You make inferences all the time. When you see a skinny cat with no collar and matted fur, you infer that it is a stray. If your friend storms into the room and slams down his books, you infer that he is angry about something. Making inferences means combining new clues with your prior knowledge in order to make an educated guess about what is happening.

Test-Taking Tips

- Read the passage carefully.
- Read and consider all of the answer choices before you choose the one that best responds to the question.
- Refer to the passage when answering the questions.

As you read, you gather clues from the text and use your prior knowledge to fill in the gaps. For example, read the following passage from "American History," by Judith Ortiz Cofer:

> There was only one source of beauty and light for me that school year. The only thing I had anticipated at the start of the semester. That was seeing Eugene.

From this passage, you might infer that the narrator has a crush on Eugene. You can test this inference by reading on and gathering more clues.

Answering Reading Comprehension Questions

Reading comprehension questions ask you to read a passage and answer questions about it. The following steps will help you answer the reading comprehension questions on standardized tests.

- Preview the passage and questions and predict what the text will be about.
- Use the reading strategies you have learned to read the passage. Mark the text and make notes in the margins.
- Reread the first question carefully. Make sure you know exactly what it is asking.
- Read the answers. If you are sure of the answer, select it and move on. If you are unsure of the answer, eliminate any answers that you know are incorrect and focus on the remaining choices. Then move on to the next step.
- Scan the passage to look for key words related to the question. When you find a key word, slow down and read carefully.
- Answer the question and go on to the next one. Answer each question in this way.

PRACTICE

Directions: Read the following story. The questions that come after it will ask you to make inferences using the clues in the passage.

Prose Fiction: The following passage is a short story titled "The One Sitting There" by Joanna H. Wo.

I threw away the meat. The dollar ninety-eight a pound ground beef, the boneless chicken, the spareribs, the hamsteak. I threw the soggy vegetables into the trashcan: the carrots, broccoli, peas, the Brussels sprouts. I poured the milk down the drain of the stainless steel sink. The cheddar cheese I ground up in the disposal. The ice cream, now liquid, followed. All the groceries in the refrigerator had to be thrown away. The voice on the radio hinted of germs thriving on the food after the hours without power. Throwing the food away was rational and reasonable.

In our house, growing up, you were never allowed to throw food away. There was a reason. My mother saved the peelings and spoiled things to put on the compost heap. That would go back into the garden to grow more vegetables. You could leave meat or potatoes to be used again in soup. But you were never allowed to throw food away.

I threw the bread away. The bread had gotten wet. I once saw my father pick up a piece of Wonder Bread he had dropped on the ground. He brushed his hand over the slice to remove the dirt and then kissed the bread. Even at six I knew why he did that. My sister was the reason. I was born after the war. She lived in a time before. I do not know much about her. There are no pictures. The only time my father talked about her was when he described how she clutched the bread so tightly in her baby fist that the bread squeezed out between her fingers. She sucked at the bread that way.

So I threw the bread away last. I threw the bread away for all the times that I sat crying over a bowl of cabbage soup my father said I had to eat. Because eating would not bring her back. Because I would still be the one sitting there. Now I had the bread. I had gotten it. I had bought it. I had put it in the refrigerator. I had earned it. It was mine to throw away.

So I threw the bread away for my sister. I threw the bread away and brought her back. She was twenty-one and had just come home from Christmas shopping. She had bought me a doll. She put the package on my dining room table and hung her coat smelling of perfume and the late fall air on the back of one of the chairs. I welcomed her as an honored guest. As if she were a Polish bride returning to her home, I greeted her with a plate of bread and salt. The bread, for prosperity, was wrapped in a white linen cloth. The salt, for tears, was in a small blue bowl. We sat down together and shared a piece of bread.

In a kitchen, where such an act was an ordinary thing, I threw away the bread. Because I could.

Multiple Choice

1. The narrator of this passage has just experienced
   A. a war.
   B. a power outage.
   C. a famine.
   D. a family conflict.

2. What seems to have happened to the narrator's sister?
   F. She died.
   G. She was taken away from the family.
   H. She ate a bad piece of bread.
   J. She left home and has just recently returned.

3. In line 50, the word *prosperity* means
   A. poverty.
   B. nutrition.
   C. happiness.
   D. success.

4. Which line indicates that what you read may not be what has actually happened?
   F. "The voice on the radio hinted of germs thriving on the food after the hours without power."
   G. "So I threw the bread away for my sister. I threw the bread away and brought her back."
   H. "I once saw my father pick up a piece of Wonder Bread he had dropped on the ground. He brushed his hand over the slice to remove the dirt and then kissed the bread."
   J. "As if she were a Polish bride returning to her home, I greeted her with a plate of bread and salt."

Constructed Response

5. In lines 11–12, the narrator says, "Throwing the food away was rational and reasonable." Does the narrator throw the food away for purely rational reasons? Why or why not? Use information from the passage to explain your answer.

Writing Skills

REFLECTIVE ESSAY

Many standardized tests include sections that ask you to demonstrate your writing ability by composing an essay in response to a *prompt.* Some prompts ask you to express your thoughts about a particular topic, often something that has happened to you.

You are asked to reflect on an issue, not give a straight report of the facts. Feel free to use "I" and give examples that are meaningful to you from your personal life or experiences. Take the time to explain your examples to fully develop your point of view. An essay with one or two thoughtful, well-developed reasons or examples is more likely to get a high score than an essay with several short, simplistic examples.

Support your ideas appropriately, and show that you can use language well. Remember that the reflective essay is an opportunity for you to say what you think about an important issue that's relevant to your life.

When you respond to a reflective prompt, keep these tips in mind:

- Narrow the topic to one specific aspect, experience, or event about which you have something to say.
- Don't just tell what happened; explain how it affected you, what you learned from it, or how it changed your thinking.
- Organize the information in your essay so that the reader can follow it.
- Include an introduction in which you identify your narrowed topic, a body in which you explain the topic and your insights about it, and a conclusion in which you sum up your reflections on the topic.
- Use a variety of sentence structures to make the writing interesting.
- Pay attention to grammar, usage, capitalization, spelling, and punctuation.

Writing Tips

- Practice writing in different formats and in real situations.
- Share your writing with others and get feedback.
- Strive for your writing to be well developed and well organized.
- Use precise, clear, and concise language.

PRACTICE

Timed Writing: 30 minutes

Think carefully about the issue presented in the following excerpt and the assignment below. Allow 30 minutes to write your response to the prompt.

Catastrophic national events such as the assassination of President John F. Kennedy on November 22, 1963, the terrorist attacks on September 11, 2001, and the damage and loss of life caused by Hurricane Katrina in August 2005 often change individuals' lives. The effects are personal and immediate for some individuals—for instance, those who lose friends or family in a disaster. The effects may be more subtle or indirect for other individuals, such as those who follow the disaster in the media or hear about it secondhand. Regardless, in both cases, individuals' lives are often changed forever by the disasters themselves and what happens in their aftermath.

Assignment: How have you been affected by a significant local or national disaster? Plan and write a reflective essay that explains your experience with a specific disaster. Use details such as examples, observations, and feelings to make your position clear.

Revising and Editing Skills

Some standardized tests ask you to read a draft of an essay and answer questions about how to improve it. As you read the draft, watch for errors like these:

- incorrect spellings
- disagreement between subject and verb; inconsistent verb tense; incorrect forms for irregular verbs; sentence fragments and run-ons; double negatives; and incorrect use of frequently confused words, such as *affect* and *effect*
- missing end marks, incorrect comma use, and lowercased proper nouns and proper adjectives
- unclear purpose, unclear main ideas, and lack of supporting details
- confusing order of ideas and missing transitions
- language that is inappropriate to the audience and purpose, and mood that is inappropriate for the purpose

After checking for errors, read each test question and decide which answer is best.

PRACTICE

Directions: In the passage that follows, certain words and phrases are numbered and underlined. In the questions below the passage, you will find alternatives for each underlined word or phrase. In each case, choose the alternative that best expresses the idea, that is worded most consistently with the style and tone of the rest of the passage, or that makes the text correct according to the conventions of standard written English. If you think the original version is best, choose alternative A or F, "MAKE NO CHANGE." To indicate your answer, circle the letter of the chosen alternative.

(1) <u>Like most of the people in our country,</u> I felt sorry for the people of New Orleans after Hurricane Katrina hit their city. (2) <u>But I have to admit the amount of damage and number of people killed didn't seem real to me.</u> (3) It was <u>way to much</u> to take in. (4) What finally made me understand was hearing about <u>how people had to leave there pets behind</u> when they escaped during the flooding.

1. A. MAKE NO CHANGE.
   B. Like most Americans,
   C. Like most of the people in the United States,
   D. Like most of us,

2. F. MAKE NO CHANGE.
   G. But I have to admit. The amount of damage and number of people killed didn't seem real to me.
   H. But I have to admit, the amount of damage and number of people killed didn't seem real to me.
   J. But I have to admit, the amount of damage, and number of people killed, didn't seem real to me.

3. A. MAKE NO CHANGE.
   B. way two much
   C. way too much
   D. too much

4. F. MAKE NO CHANGE.
   G. how people had to leave there pet's behind
   H. how people had to leave behind their pet's
   J. how people had to leave behind their pets

UNIT 2

Nonfiction

KING

NYE

ALEXIE

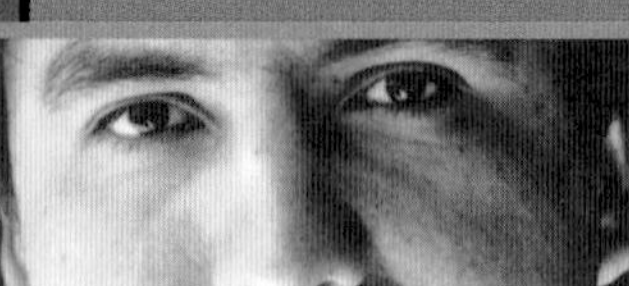

"Say not, 'I have found the truth,' but rather, 'I have found a truth.'"

—Kahlil Gibran

Learning about the experiences of others can be fascinating. It can reveal ideas and perceptions completely new to you and shape how you view the world. As you read the selections in the following unit, be conscious that while nonfiction is factual, it also contains the perceptions and opinions of the writers. It's possible that, as you read the upcoming nonfiction pieces, you will discover multiple "truths."

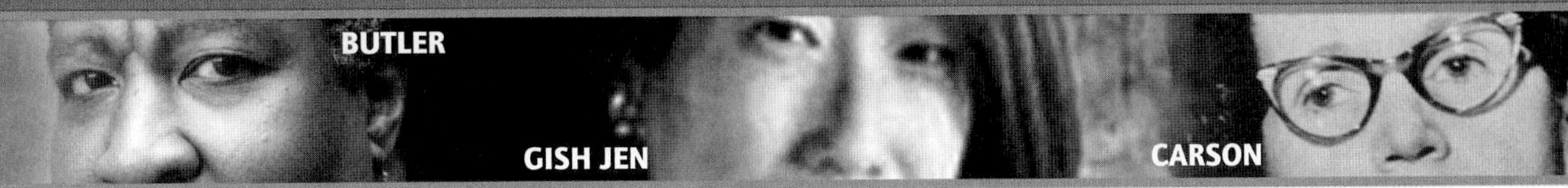

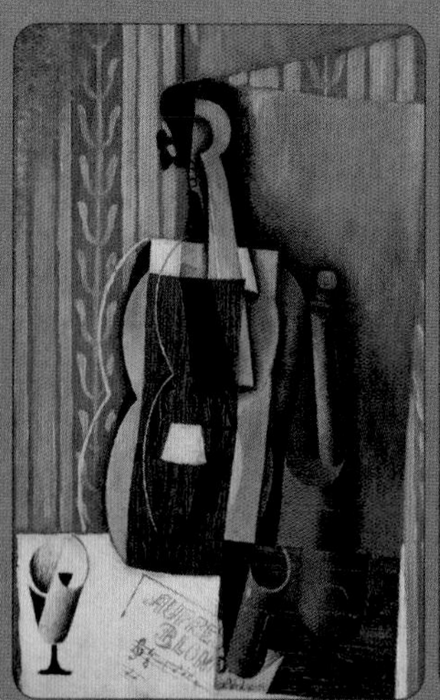

INTRODUCTION TO NONFICTION

"I felt a bit tearful to be parting from people whose lives had so intensely, if for a moment, touched mine."

—Julia Alvarez, from "Aha Moment"

"Truth is stranger than fiction." That is an old saying which suggests that real life is often more extraordinary than an imagined story. Whether or not you agree with this bit of folk wisdom, it is certain that well-crafted nonfiction can be just as interesting as a novel or short story. Nonfiction writing explores real people's lives, places, things, events, and ideas. The following selections include an autobiography about one woman's attempt to swim across a freezing sea, a biography of a young man who exceeded the world's expectations, and a speech that was given to unite a divided nation. If you have ever delved into the biography of a remarkable person or a news article about an exciting topic, you have already experienced the pleasure of reading good nonfiction.

THE GENRE OF NONFICTION

Nonfiction is prose writing about real events. Among popular forms of nonfiction are biographies, autobiographies, memoirs, essays, speeches, and inf ormational text. These forms often read like stories: They feature well-rounded characters, colorful settings, significant themes, and many other elements you will recognize from your reading of fiction.

Biography, Autobiography, and Memoir

A **biography** is the story of a person's life written by someone else. Lindsley Cameron's "Becoming a Composer" (page 233) is a biography of Hikari Oe, a man who was born with a severe brain defect, yet who possesses an extraordinary talent for music. Writers of biographies often rely on such sources as *letters, diaries, journals,* and *interviews,* which are also forms of nonfiction. The use of sources helps biographers find the most accurate and trustworthy information.

An **autobiography** is the story of a person's life written by that person. Like other types of personal narratives, the autobiography expresses the first-person point of view and uses the pronoun *I*. Lynne Cox wrote *Swimming to Antarctica* (page 223) as a record of her accomplishments as a famous cold-water swimmer.

A **memoir** is a type of autobiography that focuses on one incident or period in a person's life. Memoirs are often based on an individual's memories of, and reactions to, historical events. In his memoir "The Teacher Who Changed My Life" (page 215), Nicholas Gage tells the story of his immigrant experience and the teacher who had a profound impact on his later career as a writer. (See Understanding Biography, Autobiography, and Memoir, page 212.)

Essay

Another form of nonfiction, the **essay,** is a short work that presents a single main idea, or *thesis,* about a particular topic. There are several different kinds of essays, including *expository,* or *informative, essays,* which explore a topic with the goal of informing or enlightening the reader; *persuasive essays,* which aim to persuade the reader to accept a certain point of view; and *personal essays,* which explore a topic related to the life or interests of the writer. Unlike the formal essay, the personal essay is characterized by an intimate and informal style or tone. (See Understanding Essays, page 242.)

Speech

A **speech** is a public address that was originally delivered orally. Speeches may be formal or informal, depending on the situation or context in which they are presented and the audience. There are three main types of speeches:

- **Impromptu:** a speech given without advance preparation
- **Memorized:** a speech that has been written out and memorized word for word
- **Extemporaneous:** a speech in which the speaker refers to notes occasionally

As with writing, speeches usually have a specific purpose and message. A speech may be *informative,* used to share new and useful information, or *persuasive,* used to convince or persuade the audience to believe something, do something, or change their ways. Martin Luther King Jr.'s famous "I Have a Dream" speech (page 269) and Nelson Mandela's "Glory and Hope" speech (page 277) are examples of persuasive speeches. A *commemorative speech* honors an individual for outstanding accomplishments and exemplary character. (See Understanding Speeches, page 266.)

Informational Text

A form of nonfiction writing with which you are probably quite familiar is the **informational text.** Because of the Internet and easy access to most publications, people today have more information available at their fingertips than ever before. Included as informational texts are the following:

- An **article** is an informational piece of writing about a particular topic, issue, event, or series of events. Articles usually appear in newspapers, popular magazines, professional journals, or on websites. "Trapped New Orleans Pets Still Being Rescued" (page 287) is an example of a news article.
- An **editorial** is a magazine or newspaper article that represents the opinions of the editors or publishers. You will be able to identify the persuasive tone of the editorial, which distinguishes the form from a news article's objective tone and impersonal viewpoint.
- **How-to writing** is a type of informational writing that explains a procedure or strategy. The writer includes the steps in a particular process or provides a clear explanation of how to do something. Octavia Butler's "Furor Scribendi" (page 297) explains the procedure for writing effectively.
- Additional types of informational texts include **web pages, electronic media, visual media,** and **advertisements.** (See Understanding Informational Texts, page 284.)

PURPOSES AND METHODS OF WRITING IN NONFICTION

Author's Purpose

A writer's **purpose** is his or her aim, or goal. All writers, including those of nonfiction, write with some overall purpose in mind. The following chart lists some of the modes, or methods, and purposes of writing:

Mode of Writing	Purpose	Examples
expository	to inform	news article, research report
narrative	to express thoughts or ideas, or to tell a story	personal account, memoir
descriptive	to portray a person, place, object, or event	travel brochure, personal profile
persuasive	to convince people to accept a position and respond in some way	editorial, petition

NONFICTION READING MODEL

BEFORE READING | DURING READING | AFTER READING

BUILD BACKGROUND

- **Connect** your own knowledge and experiences to what you read. What do you already know about the topic? What questions do you still have about it?
- Based on the information in the **Build Background** and **Meet the Author** sections, what points or perspectives do you think the author will make in the selection?

ANALYZE LITERATURE

- The **Analyze Literature** feature focuses on one or more literary techniques that are used in the selection. Make note of how the author uses these elements as you read.

SET PURPOSE

- **Preview** the text to set a purpose for reading. Notice if there are any photographs, artworks, or charts accompanying the text. Your prior knowledge about the subject may also help you set a purpose.

USE READING SKILLS

- Before reading, apply **reading skills** such as determining the author's purpose, analyzing text structure, and previewing new vocabulary.

BEFORE READING | DURING READING | AFTER READING

USE READING STRATEGIES

- **Ask questions** about things that interest or confuse you. Consider the author's purpose. Does the information and the argument presented in the selection support this purpose?
- **Visualize** or form pictures in your head to help you mentally see the images that the author describes.
- **Make predictions** about what will happen next in narrative nonfiction selections. As you read, gather more clues that will either confirm or change your predictions.
- **Make inferences,** or educated guesses, about what is not stated directly. Some points may be implied or hinted at, or they may be left out altogether.
- **Clarify** your understanding of what you are reading by rereading or reading aloud portions of the text you didn't understand.

ANALYZE LITERATURE

- In nonfiction writing, pay attention to the **word choices** and **phrasing** to understand how the author feels about the subject. What do the author's words reveal about his or her attitude?

MAKE CONNECTIONS

- Notice where there are **connections** between your life and the selection.

BEFORE READING | DURING READING | AFTER READING

REFER TO TEXT

- Think about the **facts.** Remember **details,** such as descriptions of people, places, or situations. Who was involved? Where and when did it take place?
- Try to **summarize** the author's points or ideas in two or three sentences.
- With narrative nonfiction, recall the **sequence** of events or the order in which things happened.

REASON WITH TEXT

- **Apply** what you know about the subject from your prior knowledge or from one part of the text to answer any additional questions.
- **Analyze** the text by breaking down information into smaller units.
- **Evaluate** the text. Is the author effective in drawing you into his or her narrative nonfiction selection? Does it ring true? Has the author achieved his or her purpose?

ANALYZE LITERATURE

- Review the author's use of **literary techniques,** such as diction, or choice of language. What other techniques were used?

EXTEND THE TEXT

- Explore ideas beyond the nonfiction selection by writing or engaging in other creative projects.

AHA MOMENT

BEFORE READING

A Narrative by Julia Alvarez

BUILD BACKGROUND

Literary Context In **"Aha Moment,"** Julia Alvarez portrays one fateful flight taken while on a book tour. The impact on Alvarez's life from this event—her "aha moment"—remains long after the airplane lands. Her near-death experience teaches her valuable lessons about courage, camaraderie, and appreciation of life's blessings.

Reader's Context Think of a time when a machine or some technology let you down at a critical moment. How did you cope?

ANALYZE LITERATURE: Diction

Diction, when applied to writing, refers to word choice. Much of a writer's style is determined by the types of words that he or she chooses. Diction can be formal or informal, simple or complex, contemporary or old-fashioned, coarse or refined. For example, consider the difference between saying, "I had an aha moment" and "I had an epiphany." As you read, note the words Julia Alvarez has chosen to describe her eventful flight.

SET PURPOSE

When applied to literature, the term *epiphany* refers to a moment of sudden insight in which the essence, or nature, of a person, thing, or situation is revealed. Predict what kind of an epiphany the author might have had from a rough flight. Then, as you read, look for what Julia Alvarez describes as being "struck by lightning" or having an "aha moment."

MEET THE AUTHOR

Julia Alvarez (b. 1950) was born in New York but was raised in the Dominican Republic until age ten. At that time, her father joined an underground resistance movement against the dictatorship of Molina Trujillo, and the family was forced to flee and move back to the United States. A native speaker of Spanish, Alvarez explains that her love of language and writing came from having to pay so much close attention to the English in her classrooms in New York. Though she had won many awards for her poetry and essays, she did not publish her first novel, *How the García Girls Lost Their Accents,* until 1991.

USE READING SKILLS

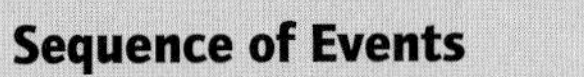

Sequence of Events
Sequence refers to the order in which things happen. When you read nonfiction, keep track of the sequence of events by making a Sequence Map like the one below.

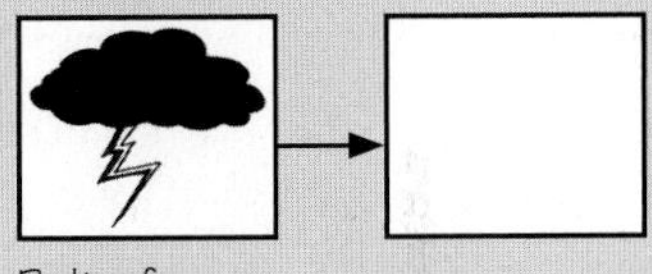

Bolt of lightning

PREVIEW VOCABULARY

Try to unlock the meanings of the underlined vocabulary words using the contrast clues provided in the sentences below.

1. The villagers were <u>stricken</u> by a mysterious sickness, but they tried to continue living a carefree existence.
2. Although her father has a Southern <u>drawl</u>, Bea has a chipper voice that bounces around the room.
3. The <u>indiscriminate</u> scolding angered the employees who were not guilty of stealing; however, the boss thought it was better than confronting the thief.
4. After the dentist tightened their braces, Marco was in <u>excruciating</u> pain, but his sister Jaclyn was only a little uncomfortable.
5. My father <u>lamented</u> the fact that he never took photos of the fish he caught; on the other hand, he enjoyed being able to exaggerate.

AHA MOMENT

A Narrative by **Julia Alvarez**

I heard vaguely through my fear,
"Engine number two...hit...emergency landing...."

DURING READING

ANALYZE LITERATURE

Diction What words does Alvarez use in the first paragraph to describe movement? How do those words provide insight into Alvarez's emotions at the time?

I was in the tiny bathroom in the back of the plane when I felt the slamming jolt, then the horrible swerve that threw me against the door. Oh, Lord, I thought, this is it! Somehow I managed to unbolt the door and scramble out. The flight attendants, already strapped in, waved wildly for me to sit down. As I lunged ahead toward my seat, passengers looked up at me with the stricken expression of creatures who know they are about to die.

strick • en (stri´ kən) *adj.,* plagued by fear, disease, or misfortune

"I think we got hit by lightning," the girl in the seat next to mine said. She was from a small town in east Texas, and this was only her second time on an airplane. She had won a trip to England by competing in a high school geography bee and was supposed to make a connecting flight when we landed in Newark.

In the next seat, at the window, sat a young businessman who had been confidently working. Now he looked worried—something that really worries me: when confident-looking businessmen look worried. The laptop was put away. "Something's not right," he said.

The pilot's voice came over the speaker. I heard vaguely through my fear, "Engine number two...hit...emergency landing...New Orleans." When he was done, the voice of a flight attendant came on, reminding us of the emergency procedures she had reviewed before takeoff. Of course I never paid attention to this drill, always figuring that if we ever got to the point where we needed to use life jackets, I would have already died of terror.

Now we began a roller-coaster ride through the thunderclouds. I was ready to faint, but when I saw the face of the girl next to me I pulled myself together. I reached for her hand and reassured her that we were going to make it. "What a story you're going to tell when you get home!" I said. "After this, London's going to seem like small potatoes."

DURING READING

USE READING SKILLS

Sequence of Events How might this scene be described? Why might this scene be significant?

"Yes, ma'am," she mumbled.

I wondered where I was getting my strength. Then I saw that my other hand was tightly held by a ringed hand. Someone was comforting *me*—a glamorous young woman across the aisle, the female equivalent of the confident businessman. She must have seen how scared I was and reached over.

"I tell you," she confided. "the problems I brought up on this plane with me sure don't seem real big right now." I loved her southern drawl, her indiscriminate use of perfume, her soulful squeezes. I was sure that even if I survived a plane crash, I'd have a couple of broken fingers from all the T.L.C.[1] "Are you okay?" she kept asking me.

drawl (drôl) *n.*, a slow manner of speech

in • dis • crim • i • nate (in' dis krim´ nət *or* in' dis kri´ mə nət) *adj.*, reckless; without concern for distinction

ex • cru • ci • at • ing (ik skrü´ shē ā tiŋ) *adj.*, very painful

Among the many feelings going through my head during those excruciating 20 minutes was pride—pride in how well everybody was behaving. No one panicked. No one screamed. As we jolted and screeched our way downward, I could hear small pockets of soothing conversation everywhere.

DURING READING

USE READING STRATEGIES

Ask Questions What is the gift of Alvarez's friend's dying father? Why would she think about that at a moment like this?

I thought of something I had heard a friend say about the wonderful gift his dying father had given the family. He had died peacefully, as if not to alarm any of them about an experience they would all have to go through someday.

And then—yes!—we landed safely. Outside on the ground, attendants and officials were waiting to transfer us to alternate flights. But we passengers clung together. We chatted about the lives we now felt blessed to be living, as difficult or rocky as they might be. The young businessman lamented that he had not had a chance to buy his two girls a present. An older woman offered him her box of expensive chocolates, still untouched, tied with a lovely bow. "I shouldn't be eating

la • ment (lə ment´) *v.*, express sadness or regret

1. **T.L.C.** Abbreviation for "tender loving care"

them anyhow," she said. My glamorous aisle mate took out her cell phone and passed it around to anyone who wanted to make a call, or to hear the reassuring voice of a loved one.

There was someone I wanted to call. Back in Vermont, my husband was anticipating my arrival late that night. He had been complaining that he wasn't getting to see very much of me because of my book tour. That's why I had decided to take this particular flight—oh, yes, those stories! I had planned to surprise him by getting in a few days early. Now I just wanted him to know I was okay and on my way. When my name was finally called to board my new flight, I felt a bit tearful to be parting from people whose lives had so intensely, if for a moment, touched mine.

DURING READING

ANALYZE LITERATURE

Diction What words and interjections are included in these last few paragraphs? How do these word choices contribute to the explanation of Alvarez's "aha moment"?

Now, back on terra firma,[2] walking down a Vermont road, I sometimes hear an airplane and look up at that small, glinting, piece of metal. I remember the passengers on that fateful, lucky flight and wish I could thank them for the many acts of kindness I witnessed and received. I am indebted to my fellow passengers and wish I could pay them back.

Just then, remembering my aisle mate's hand clutching mine while I clutched the hand of the high school student, I was struck by lightning all over again: The point is not to pay back kindness but to pass it on. ❖

2. **terra firma.** [Latin] "solid ground"

Have you ever been frightened but somehow found the strength to get through a difficult situation? What makes people pull together and support one another during a crisis?

APPLY THE MODEL

AFTER READING

REFER TO TEXT	REASON WITH TEXT	
1a. Recall what Alvarez sees when she steps out of the airplane bathroom.	1b. Why does Alvarez become more worried when she sees the businessman?	Understand **Find meaning**
2a. Review the first four paragraphs. List the thoughts that go through Alvarez's mind.	2b. Based on these paragraphs, make a generalization about how Alvarez handles frightening situations.	Apply **Use information**
3a. Note how the passengers conduct themselves during the flight.	3b. Identify why Alvarez is proud of the passengers on the plane.	Analyze **Take things apart**
4a. Quote what the author, in the final paragraphs, wishes she could do for her fellow passengers.	4b. Explain the author's main or controlling idea in this narrative. Assess the value of an experience like the one Alvarez writes about.	Evaluate **Make judgments**
5a. Identify Alvarez's epiphany, the "aha moment" of the title.	5b. Rewrite the ending to show the epiphany Alvarez might have had if the passengers had responded differently.	Create **Bring ideas together**

ANALYZE LITERATURE: Diction

Select a paragraph from the story that contains expressive vocabulary. Find the words that carry the most expression. Replace those words with your own that generally mean the same thing, such as replacing "scrambled" with "walked" or "hurried." How does the change in word choice affect the impact of the passage?

EXTEND THE TEXT

Writing Options

Creative Writing Pretend you are a news reporter assigned to cover the emergency landing in "Aha Moment." Write a **newspaper article** of approximately four paragraphs about the event. Imagine you interview Alvarez, the pilot, and several other passengers. Describe their accounts in your article. Make sure to include the five Ws of a news article: *who, what, where, when,* and *why.* Give your story a compelling headline.

Narrative Writing Think of a time when you learned a life lesson or when you experienced a revelation or an epiphany. Write a **narrative** about your "aha moment." Your essay should be about five paragraphs in length. The first paragraph should have a thesis statement and the next three paragraphs should support the thesis with details of your experience. Choose words and phrases that capture the mood of the experience. Finish with a strong concluding paragraph that relates to your thesis.

Collaborative Learning

Investigate an "Aha Moment" Sometimes, "aha moments" don't last. With a group of your classmates, identify a significant recent event that could become an "aha moment." Create a class presentation that explains the details of the event, and the things that could change positively as a result. Also consider why the "aha moment" may not last.

Critical Literacy

Research "Aha Moments" Life-changing moments certainly happen, but sometimes the evidence supporting the event is limited. Find an "aha moment" using Internet, library, or other media sources. Document your sources, including all website addresses. Write a brief one-page summary of the moment. Conclude your summary with your opinion of whether the "aha moment" event was real or imagined.

Go to **www.mirrorsandwindows.com** for more.

Understanding Biography, Autobiography, and Memoir

BIOGRAPHY, AUTOBIOGRAPHY, AND MEMOIR

A best-selling author reflects fondly on his favorite teacher. A young woman gives her harrowing account of nearly losing her life while swimming in frigid water. A boy with severe brain damage grows up to be an exceptional musician. Reading about other people's lives can be a fascinating experience. Perhaps this is why biography, autobiography, and memoir are such popular forms of writing.

Biography

A **biography** is the story of a person's life, told by someone other than that person. Most biographers write about people who are well-known, such as athletes, performers, writers, or political figures, but this isn't always the case. "Becoming a Composer" (page 233) is about Hikari Oe, the talented son of a famous Japanese author. Notice how the biographer selects the most telling details of Hikari's experience to convey what is remarkable about the young musician:

Hikari's physical handicaps precluded his developing much skill as a pianist. It was hard for him to see the notes and to see and control his fingers on the keys. But he clearly had interest in and aptitude for music. He mastered the contents of Japan's standard introductory piano textbook very quickly. He enjoyed the lessons with his mother, and he had perfect pitch—the ability to correctly identify any note heard instantly and to sing any tone accurately.

—from "Becoming a Composer" by Lindsley Cameron

Autobiography and Memoir

An **autobiography** is the story of a person's life, written by that person. Sometimes confused with autobiography is **memoir.** Though the two terms are often used interchangeably, the main difference between an autobiography and a memoir is that, generally, an autobiography includes all or most of the significant experiences of the subject's life, whereas a memoir typically focuses on one or more particular incidents or people who have been important to the writer. For example, the memoir "The Teacher Who Changed My Life" (page 215) is about specific events in Nicholas Gage's life, but the time and place in which the events occurred is also important to the memoir. Gage at the time of the events was a recent immigrant to the United States from a war-torn Greek village and had survived tragic and horrific circumstances that directly affected his life.

I kept writing, one line after another, telling how the Communist guerrillas occupied our village, took our home and food, how my mother started planning our escape when she learned that the children were to be sent to re-education camps behind the Iron Curtain and how, at the last moment, she couldn't escape with us because the guerrillas sent her with a group of women to thresh wheat in a distant village.

—from "The Teacher Who Saved My Life" by Nicholas Gage

Another difference between the two forms is the order in which events unfold. Autobiographies are often written in chronological order, with details arranged in the order in which they occur. Memoirs are usually less structured.

While autobiography and memoir clearly fall into the category of nonfiction, it is up to their authors to choose which details to include and which to leave out, as well as where to begin and end the retelling of events. This filtering of information allows writers to shape their stories to be understood by readers in a certain way.

HOW TO READ BIOGRAPHY, AUTOBIOGRAPHY, AND MEMOIR

When you are getting ready to read a biography, autobiography, or memoir, there are several approaches you can take. The approach you use, however, will depend on your purpose for reading. Below are some common purposes for reading a biography, autobiography, or memoir and the approach you might take reading with each purpose.

- **Read to find out about a person's life.** If you choose this purpose, you'll want to use a graphic organizer like a Sequence Map or Time Line (see below) to keep track of important events. The following graphic organizers record important events in the life of Nicholas Gage, author of "The Teacher Who Changed My Life." As you read, look for details about time and place.

Sequence Map

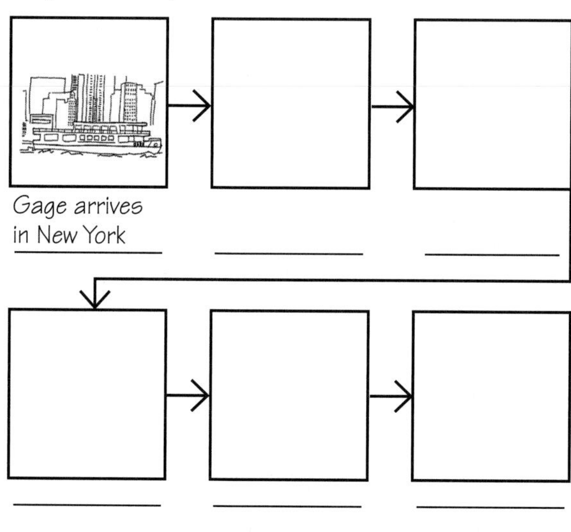

Time Line

Dates	1949	
Events	Gage arrives in New York	

- **Read to learn more about someone's character.** Imagine the biography of a public figure you've always admired has recently been published. You read it because you want to know what this person is really like in his or her everyday life. To read with this purpose, a Character Chart like the one on page 69 can be useful.

These two purposes will often overlap, and you may find a person's character is largely shaped by the events that have taken place in his or her life. You can use an Inference Chart like the one below to figure out how events have had an influence on a person's character.

Inference Chart

Text	What I Conclude
I clutched my Greek notebooks from the refugee camp, hoping that my few years of schooling would impress my teachers....	The speaker is concerned, but will work hard to earn his teacher's praise.

Additional Reading

If you enjoy reading about the lives of others, you may want to read the following titles:

- *Black Elk Speaks,* by Black Elk and John G. Neirhardt
- *California Palms,* by lê thi diem thúy
- *Hawk: Occupation Skateboarder,* by Tony Hawk
- *I Know Why the Caged Bird Sings,* by Maya Angelou
- *Mississippi Solo,* by Eddy L. Harris
- *There Comes a Time: The Struggle for Civil Rights,* by Milton Meltzer
- *Thinking Like a Mountain,* by Aldo Leopold

THE TEACHER WHO CHANGED MY LIFE

BEFORE READING

A Memoir by Nicholas Gage

GUIDED READING

BUILD BACKGROUND

Literary Context "The Teacher Who Changed My Life" is a memoir, or brief autobiography. In the memoir, Gage doesn't discuss everything that has happened to him so far. Instead, he focuses on a significant event in his life. The word *memoir* gives a clue to its meaning: Gage examines *memorable experiences* in his childhood and early adulthood and explains how these events helped shape his life. The title of the memoir indicates that Gage is describing a teacher who influenced him. What do the words "changed my life" suggest about the selection?

Reader's Context The author makes the statement, "For the first time I began to understand the power of the written word." What does the "power of the written word" mean to you? What do you think gives the written word its power?

ANALYZE LITERATURE: Memoir

A **memoir** is a type of autobiography that focuses on one incident or period in the writer's life. Memoirs are often based on writers' reactions to historical events. Read Meet the Author to begin to understand the historical events that influenced this memoir.

SET PURPOSE

As you read, think about the historical events that are the backdrop of Gage's memoir. As you read, think about the historical events that are the backdrop of Gage's memoir. Distinguish the most important from the less important details and events that the author included in his memoir. Consider these questions: How did these events change his life? How did Miss Hurd's instructions to write about what happened to his family in Greece change his life? Consider these questions: How did these events change his life? How did Miss Hurd's instructions to "write about what happened to your family in Greece" change his life?

MEET THE AUTHOR

Nicholas Gage (b. 1939), born Nikos Gatzoyiannis, lived in a small village in Greece. His mother, Eleni, was killed for sending him and his sisters to join their father in America. With the encouragement of his junior-high teacher, Miss Hurd, he received a scholarship to Boston University and later graduated from the Columbia University Graduate School of Journalism. Gage moved to Athens, Greece, to become a foreign correspondent for the *New York Times* but later quit and began searching for information about his mother. His experiences became the basis for his book *Eleni* (1983). Gage, the author of a number of other books, has received several awards for his works.

USE READING SKILLS

Summarize The ability to **summarize** a piece of writing, or recap its main ideas or events in your own words, is important to a successful reading experience. As you read the excerpt from "The Teacher Who Changed My Life," use a graphic organizer like the one below to summarize each part of the selection.

Topic: Finding your talents
Introduction: Nicholas Gage, a young Greek refugee, arrives in America with his sisters.
Body:
Conclusion:

PREVIEW VOCABULARY

Try to unlock the meanings of the underlined vocabulary words using the context clues in the sentences.

1. An <u>authoritarian</u> person gives orders and is unwilling to hear criticism.
2. Showing their disapproval, the unfriendly students looked <u>askance</u> at the newcomer.
3. By providing guidance and protection, a <u>mentor</u> takes you under his wing.
4. I'd expected my new boss to be <u>formidable</u>, but she was easygoing and supportive.
5. Although the attention <u>mortified</u> him at first, Jamel soon got over his embarrassment.

THE TEACHER WHO CHANGED MY LIFE

A Memoir by **Nicholas Gage**

"What are all you goof-offs doing here?" she bellowed...

Nicholas Gage and his teacher, Marjorie Hurd.

The person who set the course of my life in the new land I entered as a young war refugee—who, in fact, nearly dragged me onto the path that would bring all the blessings I've received in America—was a salty-tongued, no-nonsense schoolteacher named Marjorie Hurd. When I entered her classroom in 1953, I had been to six schools in five years, starting in the Greek village where I was born in 1939.

When I stepped off a ship in New York Harbor on a gray March day in 1949, I was an undersized 9-year-old in short pants who had lost his mother and was coming to live with the father he didn't know. My mother, Eleni Gatzoyiannis, had been imprisoned, tortured and shot by Communist guerrillas for sending me and three of my four sisters to freedom. She died so that her children could go to their father in the United States.

USE READING STRATEGIES

Ask Questions Why was it difficult for Nicholas and his family to leave Greece?

The portly, bald, well-dressed man who met me and my sisters seemed a foreign, authoritarian figure. I secretly resented him for not getting the whole family out of Greece early enough to save my mother. Ultimately, I would grow to love him and appreciate how he dealt with becoming a single parent at the age of 56, but at first our relationship was prickly, full of hostility.

As Father drove us to our new home—a tenement[1] in Worcester, Massachusetts—and pointed out the huge brick building that would be our first school in America, I clutched my Greek notebooks from the refugee camp, hoping that my few years of schooling would impress my teachers in this cold, crowded country. They didn't.

1. **tenement.** A house or an apartment, often one in poor condition

au • thor • i • tar • i • an (ə thär' ə ter´ ē ən) *adj.*, expecting or demanding strict obedience

When my father led me and my 11-year-old sister to Greendale Elementary School, the grim-faced Yankee principal put the two of us in a class for the mentally retarded. There was no facility in those days for non-English-speaking children.

> *Fixing me with a stern look, she added, "Nick, I want you to write about what happened to your family in Greece."*

By the time I met Marjorie Hurd four years later, I had learned English, been placed in a normal, graded class and had even been chosen for the college preparatory track in the Worcester public school system. I was 13 years old when our father moved us yet again, and I entered Chandler Junior High shortly after the beginning of seventh grade. I found myself surrounded by richer, smarter and better-dressed classmates, who looked askance at my strange clothes and heavy accent. Shortly after I arrived, we were told to select a hobby to pursue during "club hour" on Fridays. The idea of hobbies and clubs made no sense to my immigrant ears, but I decided to follow the prettiest girl in my class—the blue-eyed daughter of the local Lutheran minister. She led me through the door marked "Newspaper Club" and into the presence of Miss Hurd, the newspaper advisor and English teacher who would become my mentor and my muse.[2]

> **ANALYZE LITERATURE**
>
> **Memoir** Why would the idea of hobbies and clubs make no sense to the young Nicholas Gage?

A formidable, solidly built woman with salt-and-pepper hair, a steely eye and a flat Boston accent, Miss Hurd had no patience with layabouts. "What are all you goof-offs doing here?" she bellowed at the would-be journalists. "This is the Newspaper Club! We're going to put out a newspaper. So if there's anybody in this room who doesn't like work, I suggest you go across to the Glee Club now, because you're going to work your tails off here!"

I was soon under Miss Hurd's spell. She did indeed teach us to put out a newspaper, skills I honed during my next 25 years as a journalist. Soon I asked the principal to transfer me to her English class as well. There, she drilled us on grammar until I finally began to understand the logic and structure of the English language. She assigned stories for us to read and discuss; not tales of heroes, like the Greek myths I knew, but stories of underdogs—poor people, even immigrants, who seemed ordinary until a crisis drove them to do something extraordinary. She also introduced us to the literary wealth of Greece—giving me a new perspective on my war-ravaged, impoverished[3] homeland. I began to be proud of my origins.

One day, after discussing how writers should write about what they know, she assigned us to compose an essay from our own experience. Fixing me with a stern look, she added, "Nick, I want you to write about what happened to your family in Greece." I had been trying to put those painful memories behind me and left the assignment until the last moment. Then, on a warm spring afternoon, I sat in my room with a yellow pad and pencil and stared out the window at the buds on the trees. I wrote that the coming of spring always reminded me of the last time I said goodbye to my mother on a green and gold day in 1948.

I kept writing, one line after another, telling how the Communist guerrillas occupied

2. **muse.** A source of inspiration, especially for a writer
3. **impoverished.** Without money; poor

a • skance (ə skans´) *adv.*, with disapproval or scorn
men • tor (men´ tôr') *n.*, a trusted teacher; a role model
for • mi • da • ble (fôrm´ mə də bəl) *adj.*, causing fear or dread; inspiring awe

World History Connection

Civil War in Greece During World War II (1939–1945), the Germans brutally attacked Greece. After the conflict, Britain and the Soviet Union acted as overseers of the war-torn region. The two nations, along with the United States, had been allies during the war, but now hostility existed between the Soviet Union and the countries of Europe and North America. In Greece, a civil war broke out between the mostly wealthy conservatives and the struggling villagers. For their part, the Communist guerrillas—as Gage shows—were eager to gain a foothold in the region. Because the United States dreaded a Communist takeover of Athens, the American government supported the Greek army with money and supplies. Even so, the guerrillas were not defeated until the late 1940s.

USE READING SKILLS

Summarize Based on the connection box and Gage's own experience, summarize the conditions and events that led to his arrival in America.

our village, took our home and food, how my mother started planning our escape when she learned that the children were to be sent to re-education camps behind the Iron Curtain and how, at the last moment, she couldn't escape with us because the guerrillas sent her with a group of women to thresh wheat in a distant village. She promised she would try to get away on her own, she told me to be brave and hung a silver cross around my neck, and then she kissed me. I watched the line of women being led down into the ravine and up the other side, until they disappeared around the bend—my mother a tiny brown figure at the end who stopped for an instant to raise her hand in one last farewell.

I wrote about our nighttime escape down the mountain, across the minefields and into the lines of the Nationalist soldiers, who sent us to a refugee camp. It was there that we learned of our mother's execution. I felt very lucky to have come to America, I concluded, but every year, the coming of spring made me feel sad because it reminded me of the last time I saw my mother.

I handed in the essay, hoping never to see it again, but Miss Hurd had it published in the school paper. This mortified me at first, until I saw that my classmates reacted with sympathy and tact to my family's story. Without telling me, Miss Hurd also submitted the essay to a contest sponsored by the Freedoms Foundation at Valley Forge, Pennsylvania, and it won a medal. The Worcester paper wrote about the award and quoted my essay at length. My father, by then a "five-and-dime-store chef," as the paper described him, was ecstatic[4] with pride, and the Worcester Greek community celebrated the honor to one of its own.

For the first time I began to understand the power of the written word. A secret ambition took root in me. One day, I vowed, I would go back to Greece, find out the details of my mother's death and write about her life, so her grandchildren would know of her courage. Perhaps I would even track down the men who killed her and write of their crimes. Fulfilling that ambition would take me 30 years.

Meanwhile, I followed the literary path that Miss Hurd had so forcefully set me on. After junior high, I became the editor of my

4. **ecstatic.** Extremely happy; joyful

mor • ti • fy (môr´ tə fī) *v.*, embarrass deeply

school paper at Classical High School and got a part-time job at the Worcester Telegram and Gazette. Although my father could only give me $50 and encouragement toward a college education, I managed to finance four years at Boston University with scholarships and part-time jobs in journalism. During my last year of college, an article I wrote about a friend who had died in the Philippines—the first person to lose his life working for the Peace Corps—led to my winning the Hearst Award for College Journalism. And the plaque was given to me in the White House by President John F. Kennedy.

For a refugee who had never seen a motorized vehicle or indoor plumbing until he was nine, this was an unimaginable honor. When the Worcester paper ran a picture of me standing next to President Kennedy, my father rushed out to buy a new suit in order to be properly dressed to receive the congratulations of the Worcester Greeks. He clipped out the photograph, had it laminated in plastic and carried it in his breast pocket for the rest of his life to show everyone he met. I found the much-worn photo in his pocket on the day he died 20 years later. ❖

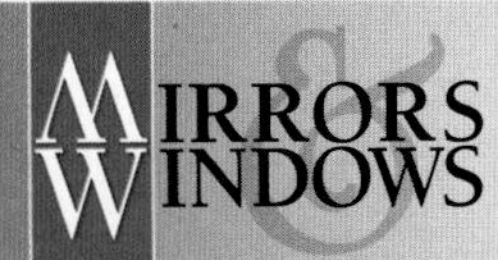

Who expects the most out of you? Is it your teachers, parents, friends, family, or yourself? Do people generally strive to accomplish what's expected of them?

AFTER READING

REFER TO TEXT	REASON WITH TEXT	
1a. Identify the writing topic Miss Hurd assigns Gage.	1b. Explain why Miss Hurd asks Gage to write on that particular topic.	Understand **Find meaning**
2a. Recall where Gage would have been sent if he had not escaped from Greece.	2b. The Iron Curtain was an area of Eastern Europe that was under Soviet control after WWII. Use this knowledge to explain why the Communists in Greece wanted to send children to re-education camps behind the Iron Curtain.	Apply **Use information**
3a. List the two types of stories that Miss Hurd assigns during English class.	3b. Compare and contrast the effects the two types of stories may have had on Gage.	Analyze **Take things apart**
4a. State how Gage uses his new writing skills in his adult life.	4b. Explain why you think it was important for Gage to find out what happened to his mother.	Evaluate **Make judgments**
5a. Point to the passage where Gage explains why he joined the Newspaper Club.	5b. Explain the controlling idea and the author's purpose in writing this memoir.	Create **Bring ideas together**

ANALYZE LITERATURE: Memoir

Memoirs may explore writers' feelings about themselves as individuals and also their relations with other people. In what way does the memoir "The Teacher Who Changed My Life" fit into both these categories? How does Gage show a clear connection between his individual experience and its historical context?

EXTEND THE TEXT

Writing Options

Creative Writing Imagine you are writing a fictional story of a family that escaped oppression and came to the United States. Create a one-page **outline** that summarizes your story including the names of the family members, where they are coming from and why, how they make the journey, and what they encounter when they arrive in America. Share the summary of your story with the class.

Narrative Writing Most people have had a mentor or role model in their lives. This person might not be as influential as Miss Hurd but is still someone you look up to and admire. Identify someone you would consider a mentor or role model. (It could be a family member, a person from your community, a teacher, or someone else.) Write a brief five-paragraph **narrative essay** describing your mentor and explaining the impact he or she has had on your life.

Collaborative Learning

Create an Advertising Campaign With a group of classmates, design a multimedia advertising campaign encouraging people to become teachers. Emphasize the importance of the profession to the community and to the nation, as well as the personal rewards of teaching. Create storyboards to illustrate commercials, website ads, newspaper and magazine ads, and any other creative media for your campaign. Work with your design team to build on the ideas of others and contribute relevant information. Develop a plan for consensus building and set ground rules for decision-making. Finally, assign representatives to present your campaign to the class.

Media Literacy

Research the Use of Propaganda Propaganda is colorful or emotional language meant to persuade others. Working individually or with a partner, research the use of propaganda and find one strong example of its use since 1950. Consider not only the details surrounding your example, but whether, in your judgment, the use of propaganda was effective. Write a brief five-paragraph paper summarizing your research. Be sure to list the sources of your information. For more information on propaganda, see page 285.

Go to **www.mirrorsandwindows.com** for more.

READING ASSESSMENT

1. Number these events in the correct sequence, with 1 being the first event to occur, and 6 being the last event.
   ___ Nicholas arrives in New York.
   ___ Nicholas's classmates respond with sympathy.
   ___ Nicholas's mother dies.
   ___ Nicholas writes about his mother's death.
   ___ Nicholas promises to look for his mother's killers.
   ___ Nicholas joins the Newspaper Club.

2. What does Nicholas admire most about Miss Hurd?
   A. She asks him to write about his experiences.
   B. She tells him to join the Glee Club.
   C. She introduces the students to Greek myths.
   D. She encourages her students to work hard.
   E. She was also forced to flee her native country.

3. As it is used on page 216, the term *askance* most nearly means
   A. with curiosity.
   B. with ridicule.
   C. with admiration.
   D. with uncertainty.
   E. with confusion.

4. Which of these statements suggests most clearly what is important to Nicholas?
   A. "I found myself surrounded by richer, smarter and better-dressed classmates, who looked askance at my strange clothes and heavy accent."
   B. "I found the much-worn photo in his pocket on the day he died 20 years later."
   C. "This mortified me at first, until I saw that my classmates reacted with sympathy and tact to my family's story."
   D. "For a refugee who had never seen a motorized vehicle or indoor plumbing until he was 9, this was an unimaginable honor."
   E. "The idea of hobbies and clubs made no sense to my immigrant ears, but I decided to follow the prettiest girl in my class—the blue-eyed daughter of the local Lutheran minister."

5. Why do you think Nicholas never wants to see the essay again after he hands it in? What lessons do you think he learned from Miss Hurd's attitude toward the assignment and the essay?

GRAMMAR & STYLE

UNDERSTAND THE CONCEPT

APPLY THE SKILL

Prepositional, Infinitive, and Participial Phrases

A **phrase** is a group of words used as a single part of speech. In your writing, be careful not to confuse a phrase with a sentence (a group of words that expresses a complete thought). Phrases contribute to sentences by helping you describe people, actions, settings, and so on. Remember, though, that phrases should always be a part of a sentence and shouldn't be written as if they were sentences, beginning with a capital letter and ending with a period or other end punctuation.

The three types of phrases you will probably use most often are prepositional phrases, infinitive phrases, and participial phrases.

A **prepositional phrase** contains a preposition, its object, and any modifiers of the object. A prepositional phrase modifies, or describes, another word or word group in the sentence. A prepositional phrase that modifies a noun is an adjective; a prepositional phrase that modifies an adjective, adverb, or verb is an adverb.

EXAMPLES

The boy clutched his notebooks *from the refugee camp*. [Here, *camp* is the object of the preposition *from*; the phrase *from the refugee camp* acts as an adjective modifying the noun *notebooks.*]

His friends reacted *with sympathy*. [The prepositional phrase acts as an adverb that modifies the verb. It describes how they reacted.]

Their response made him proud *of his work.* [The prepositional phrase also acts as an adverb. It modifies the adjective *proud.*]

Later *in the year,* he received an award. [The prepositional phrase acts as an adverb, too. It modifies the adverb *later.*]

An **infinitive phrase** contains an infinitive (the form of a verb with *to* in front of it) and any modifiers and complements (such as direct objects). Infinitive phrases can act as nouns, adjectives, or adverbs.

EXAMPLES

To become an American citizen, he thought, must be a dream. [The infinitive phrase is the subject of the verb *must be;* it is used as a noun.]

The plan *to cross the Atlantic during the winter* excited and terrified the family. [The infinitive phrase is used as an adjective, modifying the noun *plan*.]

The boy had learned *to speak English.* [The infinitive phrase is used as an adverb, modifying the verb *had learned.*]

A **participial phrase** contains a participle (the form of a verb usually ending in *–ing, –ed,* or *–d*) and any modifiers and complements (such as direct objects). Some participial phrases include prepositional phrases or infinitive phrases. Participial phrases are used as adjectives, to modify nouns or pronouns. When you use a participial phrase, be careful that the phrase modifies the noun or pronoun you want it to modify.

EXAMPLES

Standing on the deck of the boat, Nicholas saw the Statue of Liberty. [The participial phrase modifies the subject, *Nicholas.* The participial phrase includes two prepositional phrases.]

His mother, *forced by the guerrillas to work hard,* could not sail to the United States. [The participial phrase, which includes a prepositional phrase and an infinitive phrase, modifies the subject, *mother.*]

REVIEW TERMS

- **participial phrase:** contains a participle (the form of a verb ending in *–ing, –ed,* or *–d*) and any modifiers and complements
- **infinitive phrase:** contains an infinitive (the form of a verb with *to* in front of it) and any modifiers and complements
- **prepositional phrase:** contains a preposition, its object, and any modifiers of the object; modifies, or describes, another word or word group in the sentence

UNDERSTAND THE CONCEPT

APPLY THE SKILL

Identify Prepositional Phrases

Identify the prepositional phrase in each of the following sentences. Then indicate which word the phrase modifies.

1. The boy described the nighttime escape down the mountain.
2. In his senior year, he wrote his first newspaper article.
3. His father was ecstatic with pride when the boy received an award.

Use Prepositional Phrases Correctly

Answer each of the following questions by writing a sentence that contains a prepositional phrase.

EXAMPLE

Where did Miss Hurd think the lazy students should go?
She thought they should go *to the Glee Club.*

1. When and where did Nicholas's ship arrive?
2. Where does Nicholas say the camps were located?
3. Where did the blue-eyed girl lead Nicholas?

Identify Infinitive Phrases

Identify the infinitive phrase in each of the following sentences. Then indicate whether the phrase functions as a noun, an adjective, or an adverb.

1. They sent the women to thresh wheat in a faraway village.
2. The assignment to describe his youthful experiences was frightening to Nicholas.
3. To put out a newspaper each week seemed like an impossible task.

Use Infinitive Phrases Correctly

Answer each of the following questions by using an infinitive phrase correctly in a sentence.

EXAMPLE

What did the family want?
The family wanted *to come to the United States.*

1. How would Nicholas's feelings toward his father change over time?
2. Why did Nicholas's father go shopping after his son was photographed with the president?
3. What did the boy's mother learn about her children?

Identify Participial Phrases

Identify the participial phrase in each of the following sentences. Then indicate which noun the phrase modifies.

1. Deciding to follow the girl with blue eyes, Nicholas walked to the Newspaper Club.
2. His father, made a widower by historical events, met the children at the boat.
3. Drilled on grammar by Miss Hurd, the boy began to read and write English easily.

Use Participial Phrases Correctly

Combine the two sentences in each of the following items by turning one of the sentences into a participial phrase that modifies a noun in the other sentence.

EXAMPLES

Edith was assigned to write an essay. She delayed the work until the last minute.
Assigned to write an essay, Edith delayed the work until the last minute.

Can Carola teach French and Spanish? She knows both languages.
Can Carola, *knowing both languages,* teach French and Spanish?

1. She enrolled in the state university. It was located in her town.
2. She planned to major in Spanish. She took two courses in the language.
3. Will Miguel get a job this summer? He needs to earn money.

from *Swimming to Antarctica*

BEFORE READING

An Autobiography by Lynne Cox

GUIDED READING

BUILD BACKGROUND

Historical Context An excerpt from Lynne Cox's book *Swimming to Antarctica,* the following selection describes part of her childhood and her attempt to swim across the freezing Bering Sea. Cox was determined to make her way from Little Diomede Island, Alaska, to Big Diomede Island, in what was then the Soviet Union. What motivated her was the fact that, during the Cold War, people living on the two islands were forbidden to visit each other, even if they were related. She overcame the chilly waters to reach her goal and remarkably the presidents of the Cold War superpowers—Ronald Reagan of the United States and Mikhail Gorbachev of the Soviet Union—met together in Washington, DC, to congratulate her.

Reader's Context Have you ever done anything when no one believed you could? Have you ever wanted (or tried) to break a world record, or know of anyone who did?

ANALYZE LITERATURE: Autobiography

Swimming to Antarctica is an **autobiography,** or the author's own story of her life. In the selection, Cox describes what she does and the reasons for her actions. Pay attention to the parallels, or similarities, between the Cox you meet in the Bering Sea and the younger Cox, in the second part of the selection, at the swimming pool. Consider the personal qualities she reveals about herself in the two settings.

SET PURPOSE

As you read Cox's suspenseful account of her struggles with nature, think of the goals she has set for herself. What do these goals suggest about her as a person? Consider how the experiences of her childhood help explain how she came to swim in the Bering Sea.

MEET THE AUTHOR

Lynne Cox (b. 1957) began swimming in Manchester, New Hampshire, when she was nine years old. When she was just fifteen years old, Cox swam across the English Channel (perhaps the sport's greatest challenge) in record speed, a feat she repeated the following year. By this time, Cox had made a name for herself as a world-class swimmer and went on to swim in bodies of water never attempted. She is described as "the purist of marathon swimmers," as she does not wear a wet suit to protect herself from the cold, nor does she use a cage while swimming in shark-infested waters. She was inducted into the International Swimming Hall of Fame in 2000 and today is an author, a motivational lecturer, and a teacher of both indoor and open water swimming techniques.

USE READING SKILLS

Draw Conclusions When you **draw conclusions,** you are gathering pieces of information and then deciding what that information means. Use a chart like the one below to keep track of the information you find while you are reading as well as the conclusions you draw.

Drawing Conclusions Chart
Key Idea: Lynne Cox is taking a serious risk by attempting this swim.
Supporting Points: "Is my blood sugar dropping? ...Is my body temperature plunging? Am I hypothermic?"
Overall Conclusion: Swimming across the Bering Sea is a dangerous task.

PREVIEW VOCABULARY

Use context clues to help you choose the best word from the following list to complete the sentences below. You may need to change the form of the word.

ominous *deteriorating*
pervasively *pensively*
unbridled

1. The rumor was _____, leaving few families untouched.
2. After watching the horror movie, Albert's imagination was _____, and he kept imagining awful scenarios.
3. If our mother was pacing the floor _____, we knew something was wrong.
4. While Cassidy grew stronger, Gale's health was _____.
5. The good feelings Cerise had were ruined as she heard the bell strike _____ from the unseen clock.

from *Swimming to Antarctica*

An Autobiography by **Lynne Cox**

The Bering Sea. Mary Iverson.

I believe that this swim will create a thaw in the Cold War. I cannot fail.

Prologue

A Cold Day in August

It is August 7, 1987, and I am swimming across the Bering Sea. I am somewhere near—or across—the U.S.-Soviet border. The water stings. It's icy cold. My face feels as if it has been shot full of novocaine and it's separating from my skull. It's as if I'm swimming naked into a blizzard. My hands are numb, and they ache deep down through the bone. I can't tell if they are pulling any water. They feel as though they are becoming detached from my body. I look down at them through the ash-colored water: they are splotchy and bluish white; they are the hands of a dead person. I take a tight, nervous breath. Suddenly it occurs to me that my life is escaping through my hands.

This frigid and ominous sea is behaving like an enormous vampire

USE READING STRATEGIES

Ask Questions Why might the narrator be swimming in freezing cold water?

om • i • nous (ä´ mə nəs) *adj.,* suggesting that disaster is about to occur

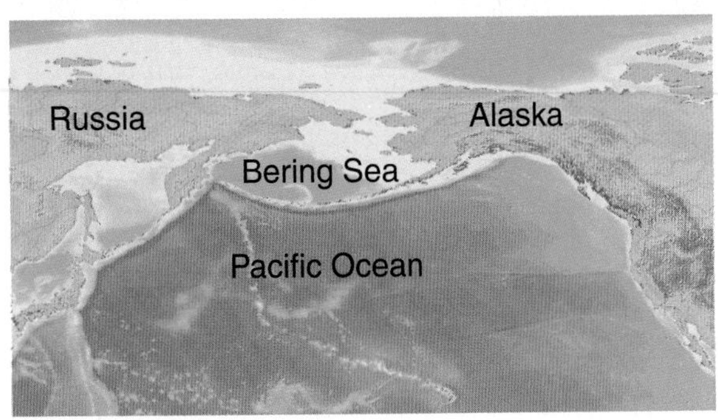

Map of the Bering Sea.

slowly sucking the warmth, the life from my body, and I think, *Oh my God, pick up your pace. Swim faster, faster. You've got to go as fast as you can. You've got to create more heat. Or you will die!*

I try to lift my arms over more rapidly. They are sore and sluggish. I am tired. I have been sprinting, swimming as fast as I can go, for more than an hour. But I sense that I am fading, becoming less of myself. *Is my blood sugar dropping? Is that why I feel so strange? Or is my body temperature plunging? Am I hypothermic?*[1] Systematically I check my body. *My lips feel pickled; my throat is parched and raw from the briny water. I want to stop to drink some fresh water and catch my breath. But the water is too cold to allow me to pause for even a moment. If I do, more heat will be drained from my body, heat that I will never regain.*

Through foggy goggles, I continue monitoring my body. I've never pushed myself this far. The coldest water I've ever swum in was thirty-eight degrees in Glacier Bay, Alaska, and that was only for twenty-eight minutes. This swim is five times longer. I am afraid of going beyond the point of no return. The problem is that my brain could cool down without my being aware of it, which would cause a dangerous loss of judgment. I glance at my shoulders and arms: they are as red as lobsters. This is a very good sign. My body is fighting to protect itself from the cold by employing a defense mechanism called vasoconstriction. It is diverting blood flow away from my hands and feet, arms and legs to the core of my body; it is keeping my brain and vital organs warm so they will continue to function normally.

I reach out and pull faster and, through muscle movement, try to create heat more quickly than I am losing it. My breaths are short and rapid, and my chest is heaving. My heart is pounding. I am afraid.

The fog is growing heavier; the air is saturated and raw. It feels as though I am trying to breathe through a wet blanket. With each breath, the chill rolls deeper into my lungs. Now I am cooling down from the inside out. I can't help myself; I think of David Yudovin.

David was a seasoned long-distance swimmer who, during an attempt to swim from Anacapa Island to the California mainland, technically died from hypothermia. His body tried to fight the cold by shunting the blood flow to his brain and vital organs. For a period of time, his core was protected. But at some critical point the blood vessels in his extremities[2] became paralyzed. Blood rushed from his core to his hands and feet, where it was cooled by the fifty-eight-degree water; when it flowed back into his torso, it caused his core temperature to drop. As a result, David became disoriented. His swimming speed dropped, and then his heart went into atrial fibrillation.[3] As he continued to cool down, his heart became less functional, until it suddenly stopped beating altogether.

There had been warning signs: his lips were purple, he was shivering, and his shoulders had turned blue. But his crew didn't recognize the severity of the situation. When they spoke to David, he said he was doing okay, and the decrease in his body temperature was so

USE READING STRATEGIES

Make Inferences Why might the author recall David Yudovin's experience?

1. **hypothermic.** Suffering from hypothermia, or dangerous loss of body heat
2. **extremities.** Hands and feet (the outermost parts of the body)
3. **atrial fibrillation.** Rapid, irregular contraction of muscles in the atrium, a chamber of the heart. This dangerous condition may be treated with a defibrillator.

World History Connection

GORBACHEV

The Cold War The decades-long conflict between Western Europe, North America, and Japan, on one side, and the Union of Soviet Socialist Republics (USSR) and several weaker nations of Eastern Europe, on the other side, motivated Cox to cross the icy waters of the Bering Sea. The military, political, and economic rivalry began in the mid-1940s, at the end of World War II, during which the Soviet Union and the West had joined forces to defeat Germany, Japan, and Italy. Conflict arose as the Soviet Union became more critical of the United States' capitalist society and the United States began to fear the spread of Communism. The term *Cold War* referred to the fact that no actual fighting occurred between the two sides. Even so, tensions were heightened by an arms race, in which both Washington, DC, and Moscow stockpiled nuclear weapons aimed at the other. Moreover, cooperation between the United States and the Soviet Union following World War II was hard to maintain, as the ban on visits between residents of Little Diomede, in Alaska, and Big Diomede, then in the USSR, suggests.

The Cold War ended as the 1990s began, when President Mikhail Gorbachev oversaw both the breakup of the Soviet Union into its various republics and the move from socialism to capitalism. Similar changes were made in the socialist economies of the smaller Eastern European nations.

gradual, they didn't notice his deteriorating condition. Neither did David. His brain had been cooled down so far that he wasn't able to recognize the warning signs. He had no idea he was dying.

At the hospital in Ventura doctors and nurses shot Adrenalin[4] directly into his heart and repeatedly shocked his heart with a defibrillator. They warmed his blood and had him breathe warmed oxygen. An hour and fifty minutes after his initial cardiac arrest, the medical team revived David. He had been lucky.

Will I be that lucky? The water here is twenty degrees colder. Will I be able to recognize if I've gone too far?

Yes. Yes. I will. I can do this. I've broken the world records for the English Channel, I've swum across the frigid waters of the Strait of Magellan, and I've done swims in icy waters where no one else has ever survived.

I can do it.

Thank God (or Ben & Jerry's) for my body fat; it's insulating me from the cold. Still, the cold is moving deep into the marrow of my bones. Chills are curling up my spine and spreading out across my shoulders. My teeth are clenched and my lips are quivering. My muscles are as tight as boards.

I am pushing myself to the limit. But I've got to do this. This swim is not about me. It's about all of us.

It's about doing something that's going to make a positive difference in the world. For eleven years, I have hoped when there was no reason to hope. I have believed when there was little to believe. For the last forty-two years we've been engaged in a Cold War with the Soviets. Somehow it has to be stopped. I believe

4. **Adrenalin.** A prescription medicine to increase the body's responses to threat. The medicine is chemically similar to a substance the body releases naturally.

de • te • ri • o • rat • ing (di tir´ ē ə rāt' ing *or* dē tir´ ē ə rāt' ing) *adj.,* worsening that this swim will create a thaw in the Cold War. I cannot fail. If I die doing this, the Soviets will regret giving me permission to make this swim. I can't let that happen. *Swim faster! Don't focus on the cold or the pain. Don't give any energy to it. Focus on the finish. Swim faster.*

> **USE READING SKILLS**
>
> **Draw Conclusions** Based on the information provided, why might the author's swim "create a thaw" in the Cold War?

I think of my parents, brother, and sisters, of friends and of the people who have gotten me this far. I conjure up their faces in my mind's eye. This gives me energy, and I imagine how wonderful it will feel to embrace the people who are waiting for us on Big Diomede Island and to hold their warm hands. This is inspiring. I replay a sentence in my head: *Hand to hand, heart to heart, we can change the world.* This is what I have grown to believe.

With every part of my being I am reaching forward, racing against time and the pervasively cold sea.

I lift my head and look up.

Something is very wrong.

Out in front of me, to the left and to the right, are the two thirty-foot-long walrus-skin boats that are supposed to be guiding and protecting me. On board the one to the right is a group of physicians who are monitoring me during the swim. To the left is a boatful of journalists huddled against the chill. Inuit guides—Eskimos who live on Little Diomede Island—are driving the walrus-skin boats. They are veering away from each other.

The dark fog has grown so thick that our visibility is down to twenty feet. We planned to meet the Soviets at the border so they could guide us to Big Diomede Island, to their shore. Our guides have never ventured across the border. They were afraid that the Soviets would pick them up and jail them in a Siberian prison. This had happened to relatives. They had been imprisoned for fifty-two days.

> **USE READING STRATEGIES**
>
> **Make Inferences** Why might the fact that the guides have never ventured over the border be significant?

Pat Omiak, the lead navigator from Little Diomede, asks Dr. Keatinge, one of the doctors, "Which direction do you think we should take?" Keatinge says, "I'm not sure."

Like Omiak, he has never ventured into these waters. But he recommends going straight ahead. I follow them. They are making abrupt turns to the right and left. I am frustrated. Each moment we spend off course diminishes our chances of making it across. It hits me that we are lost somewhere in the middle of the Bering Sea. But I keep swimming and I keep thinking, *Please, God, please let the Soviet boats find us.* I strain to see them through the fog, listen for high-pitched engine sounds in the water, feel for vibrations, and continue praying.

When I turn my head to breathe I notice that the boats are drifting away from me. I shout at the top of my lungs, "Move closer! Move closer!"

They have no idea how frightened I am. They don't know what's happened before. I don't know how long I can last.

1
Beginnings

"Please. Please. Please, Coach, let us out of the pool, we're freezing," pleaded three purple-lipped eight-year-olds in lane two.

Coach Muritt scowled at my teammates clinging to the swimming pool wall. Usually this was all he had to do to motivate them, and they'd continue swimming. But this day was different. Ominous black clouds were crouched on the horizon, and the wind was gusting from all different directions. Even though it was a mid-July morning in Manchester, New Hampshire, it felt like it would snow.

per • va • sive • ly (per vā´ siv lē) *adv.*, widespread; in a manner that affects many

Lynne Cox swimming in the Bering Sea.

Critical Viewing

How much encouragement would you need to swim in forty-two degree waters?

Cupping his large hands against his red face, and covering the wine-colored birthmark on his left cheek, Coach Muritt bellowed, "Get off the wall! Swim!"

"We're too cold," the boys protested.

Coach Muritt did not like to be challenged by anyone, let alone three eight-year-old boys. Irritated, he shouted again at the swimmers to get moving, and when they didn't respond, he jogged across the deck with his fist clenched, his thick shoulders hunched against the wind and his short-chopped brown hair standing on end. Anger flashed in his icy blue eyes, and I thought, *I'd better swim or I'll get in trouble too,* but I wanted to see what was going to happen to the boys.

Coach Muritt shook his head and shouted, "Swim and you'll get warm!"

But the boys weren't budging. They were shaking, their teeth chattering.

"Come on, swim. If you swim, you'll warm up," Coach Muritt coaxed them. He looked up at the sky, then checked his watch, as if trying to decide what to do. In other lanes, swimmers were doing the breaststroke underwater, trying to keep their arms warm. More teammates were stopping at the wall and complaining that they were cold. Laddie and Brooks McQuade, brothers who were always getting into trouble, were breaking rank, climbing out of the pool and doing cannonballs from the deck. Other young boys and girls were joining them.

USE READING STRATEGIES

Make Predictions
Predict how a man like Coach Muritt will handle the reluctant swimmers.

"Hey, stop it! Someone's going to get hurt—get your butts back in the water!" Coach Muritt yelled. He knew he was losing control, that he had pushed the team as far as we could go, so he waved us in. When all seventy-five of us reached the wall, he motioned for us to move toward a central lane and then he shouted, "Okay, listen up. Listen up. I'll make a deal with you. If I let you get out now, you will all change into something warm and we'll meet in the boys' locker room. Then we will do two hours of calisthenics."

Cheering wildly, my teammates leaped out of the pool, scurried across the deck, grabbed towels slung over the chain-link fence surrounding the pool, and squeezed against one another as they tried to be first through the locker room doors.

Getting out of the water was the last thing in the world I wanted to do. I hated doing calisthenics with the team. Usually we did them five days a week for an hour, after our two-hour swimming workout. A typical workout included five hundred sit-ups, two hundred push-ups, five hundred leg extensions, five hundred half sit-ups, two hundred leg lifts on our backs, and two hundred leg lifts on our stomachs. As we did the exercises, Coach Muritt counted and we had to keep pace with him. Between each set of fifty repetitions, he gave us a one-minute break, but if anyone fell off pace or did the exercises incorrectly, he made us start the set all over again. He wanted to make us tough, teach us discipline and team unity. And I didn't mind that. I liked to work hard, and I liked the challenge of staying on pace, but I detested having to start an exercise all over again because someone else was slacking off or fooling around. Brooks and Laddie McQuade were notorious for that. They were always trying to see how much they could get away with before they got caught. For them, it was a big game. Older boys on the team yelled at them and tossed kick-boards at them, but they didn't care; they liked the attention they were getting from the team and the coach. I didn't want to play their game, and I didn't want to do two long hours of calisthenics with them, so I shouted, "Coach Muritt, can I stay in the pool and swim?"

He was wiping his eyes and nose with a handkerchief, and asked incredulously, "Jeez, aren't you freezing?"

"If I keep swimming, I'm okay," I said, and smiled, trying my very best to convince him. I was a chubby nine-year-old, and I was a slow swimmer, so I rarely got a chance to stop and take a rest. But because I just kept going, I managed to constantly create body heat, and that way I stayed warm when all the other swimmers were freezing.

"Is there anyone else who wants to stay in the water?"

"We do," said three of his Harvard swimmers in lane one.

During the college season, Muritt coached the Harvard University Swim Team. He was considered to be one of the best coaches in all of New England; at least a dozen of his college swimmers had qualified for the U.S. Nationals. In the summer, most of his college swimmers worked out with our age groupers on the Manchester Swim Team, and they inspired us by their example. Somehow my parents knew from the start that to become your best, you needed to train with the best. And that's why I think they put my older brother, David, me, and my two younger sisters, Laura and Ruth, into Coach Muritt's swimming program.

Coach Muritt studied the sky, and we followed his gaze. "I still don't like the looks of those clouds," he said pensively.

"Coach, we'll get out immediately if it starts to thunder. I promise," I said, and held my breath, hoping he wouldn't make me do calisthenics.

He considered for a moment, but he was distracted by uproarious laughter, high-pitched hoots, and shouts coming from the locker room.

"Please, Coach Muritt, please can we stay in?" I said.

"Okay, but I'll have to take the pace clock or it's going to blow over—you'll have to swim at your own pace for the next couple of hours."

"Thank you, Coach," I said, and clapped my hands; I was doubly thrilled. I had escaped calisthenics and now I was going to be able to swim for three hours straight. I loved swimming and I loved swimming at my own pace, alone in my own lane, with no one kicking water in my face, and no one behind tapping my toes, telling me I had to swim faster. It was a feeling of buoyant freedom. But swimming into a storm was even better; waves were rushing around me, and lifting me, and tossing me from side to side. The wind was howling, slamming against the chain-link fence so strongly that it sounded like the clanging of a warning bell. I felt the vibrations rattle right through my body, and I wondered if the wind would tear the fence from its hinges. Turning on my side to breathe, I checked the sky. It looked like a tornado was approaching, only without the funnel cloud. I wondered for a second if I should climb out of the water. But I pushed that thought away; I didn't want to get out. I was immersed in unbridled energy and supernatural beauty, and I wanted to see what would happen next.

USE READING STRATEGIES

Visualize Visualize the author's surroundings as she swims in the pool. What do the author's choices reveal?

My world was reduced to the blur of my arms stroking as a cold, driving rain began. The raindrops that hit my lips tasted sweet and cold, and I enjoyed the sensations of every new moment. The pool was no longer a flat,

pen • sive • ly (pen´ siv lē) *adv.*, in a thoughtful or troubled manner

un • bri • dled (ən' brī´ d'ld) *adj.*, without restraint; left free boring rectangle of blue; it was now a place of constant change, a place that I had to continually adjust to as I swam or I'd get big gulps of water instead of air. That day, I realized that nature was strong, beautiful, dramatic, and wonderful, and being out in the water during that storm made me feel somehow a part of it, somehow connected to it.

When the hail began, the connection diminished considerably. I scrambled for the gutters while the college swimmers leaped out of the water and ran as fast as they could into the locker room. One looked back at me and shouted, "Aren't you getting out?"

"No, I don't want to," I said, crawling into the gutter by the stairs. The hail came down so fast and hard that all I heard was the rush and pinging of the stones as they hit the deck and pool. Thankful for the white bathing cap and goggles protecting my head and eyes, I covered my cheeks with my hands. Hailstones the size of frozen peas blasted my hands, neck, and shoulders, and I winced and cringed and tried to squeeze into a tighter ball, hoping that it would be over soon.

I realized that by putting myself in a situation different from everyone else's, I had experienced something different, beautiful, and amazing.

When the hail finally changed to a heavy rain, I crawled out of the gutter and started swimming again. As I pulled my arms through the water, I felt as if I were swimming through a giant bowl of icy tapioca. The hailstones floated to the water's surface and rolled around my body as I swam through them. I realized that by putting myself in a situation different from everyone else's, I had experienced something different, beautiful, and amazing.

In the parking lot outside, I saw Mrs. Milligan sitting in her car with her headlights aimed at me. Mrs. Milligan was Joyce's mother, and Joyce was the fastest and nicest girl on the team. Joyce had qualified for nationals a couple of times, and I wanted to be just like her. Once I'd asked her why she was so fast. She'd said that she did what Coach Muritt asked of her. It was such a simple statement, but one that was a revelation for me. If I did what Joyce did, then maybe I could also make it to nationals. I wondered how long Mrs. Milligan had been watching me. When I saw my teammates poking their heads out of the locker room, I knew the workout was over, so I climbed out of the pool.

Mrs. Milligan ran to me; her raincoat was plastered to her body and her short brown hair was standing on end. She was carrying a large towel, and when a gust hit it, the towel spread open like a sail. She wrapped it tightly around me and shouted, "How long have you been swimming in this storm?"

"The whole time," I said.

"Oh, my goodness. Coach Muritt let you swim in this?" she said, guiding me quickly into the girls' locker room and putting my hands between hers to warm them.

"He sure did, and I had a lot of fun." I grinned. It had been one of the most enjoyable workouts of my swimming career.

Rubbing the towel rapidly on my back, she bent over and said in my ear, with absolute certainty, "Someday, Lynne, you're going to swim across the English Channel."

It kind of took my breath away, but from the moment she said it, I believed that it could happen. After all, Mrs. Mulligan was Joyce's mother, and I knew how her encouragement had helped Joyce become a fast swimmer. Even though I was only nine years old at the time, I somehow knew that one day I would swim the English Channel.

ANALYZE LITERATURE

Autobiography What lessons did the young narrator learn on this day that she applies to her swim across the Bering Sea? What lesson might have been the most important?

When I stepped out of the locker room, Coach Muritt turned and looked at me with surprise and said, "Are you just getting out of the pool now?"

"Yes, thank you, Coach Muritt. I had so much fun. You know what? Mrs. Milligan said that someday I'm going to swim the English Channel."

He looked at me for a few moments and said, "Yes, I think you will."

I remember telling my mother, as she drove my siblings and me home from workout in her bright red Buick station wagon, "Mom, Mrs. Milligan said that someday I'm going to swim the English Channel."

Without giving it much consideration, she said, "Well, if you train hard, I'm sure someday you probably will."

I couldn't wait to get home. I ran upstairs, grabbed our National Geographic atlas, and flipped through it until I found the page that featured England and France. Then I began to wonder, How far across is the English Channel? Where do you start to swim? I studied the map and the idea began to take hold in my mind. Maybe someday I would swim the English Channel. ❖

"Someday, Lynne, you're going to swim across the English Channel." Some goals seem too impossible to consider. How does encouragement from someone you respect make dreams seem more attainable?

AFTER READING

REFER TO TEXT	▶ REASON WITH TEXT	
1a. Quote what Cox says when she notices that her arms and shoulders are bright red.	1b. Knowing what you do about Cox's and David Yudovin's swims, what is Cox's biggest concern physically?	**Understand** **Find meaning**
2a. State what international crisis was occurring during Cox's swim of 1987.	2b. Apply what you know about the conflict to decide whether Cox could "create a thaw." Explain your response.	**Apply** **Use information**
3a. List two reasons Cox wanted to stay in the pool even after everyone else went inside.	3b. Relate the feelings Cox describes in the swimming pool to her acceptance, as an adult, of serious challenges in the open seas.	**Analyze** **Take things apart**
4a. Who gives young Cox the idea to swim the English Channel? Indicate how others respond to the idea.	4b. Assess whether Cox's experience in the pool or the opinions of adults motivated her more in her decision to swim the Bering Sea. Explain.	**Evaluate** **Make judgments**
5a. Recall what Cox hopes to achieve by swimming across the Bering Sea.	5b. Tell other ways champion swimmers or other professional athletes might "make a positive difference in the world." If possible, document one or more examples of athletes making a difference.	**Create** **Bring ideas together**

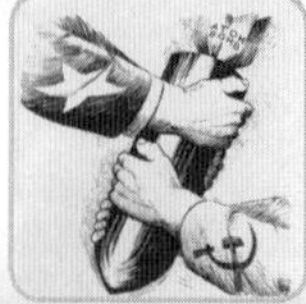

ANALYZE LITERATURE: Autobiography

Cox begins her autobiography with a swim she attempted as an adult but goes on to describe her early experiences as a swimmer. Why do you think she structured, or arranged, the opening of her book in this way? How might the effect of the narrative have changed if it occurred in chronological order, the order in which the events actually happened?

EXTEND THE TEXT

Writing Options

Creative Writing Imagine you are in one of the boats traveling alongside the author as she swims across the Bering Sea. In a **descriptive paragraph,** describe the conditions and surroundings you endure as well as your observations of Cox during her journey. You may want to organize your observations in a Sensory Details Chart such as the one below.

Sensory Details				
Sight	Sound	Touch	Taste	Smell
choppy sea				

Descriptive Writing The idea of swimming a long distance in a frigid sea is truly extraordinary. Do you know of other people who took remarkable risks, perhaps even endangering their own lives? In four or five paragraphs, write a **descriptive essay** describing an event where someone put his or her life at risk. Conclude your essay with a final paragraph reflecting on his or her motives.

Collaborative Learning

Prepare a Group Presentation Lynne Cox believed that if she could swim from the United States to the Soviet Union through the frigid Bering Sea it would have a positive impact on the entire world. Can a single event or a single person have such an effect? Working in groups, research a person who made a difference in the world. Prepare a class presentation on the individual and the surrounding events. Conclude the presentation with your group's opinion of the individual's long-term impact.

Media Literacy

Create a Cause-and-Effect Diagram The first part of the selection portrays a long-distance swimmer at great risk of hypothermia, or a dangerous loss of body heat. Individually or with a partner, research hypothermia and other dangers swimmers might face. To find a variety of facts and opinions on these dangers, check with a number of sources, such as medical websites and swimming clubs. Create a cause-and-effect diagram based on your research. Use your diagram in a flyer, on a poster, or on a web page devoted to swimming safety.

Go to **www.mirrorsandwindows.com** for more.

READING ASSESSMENT

1. Which passage does not express a sense of dread in the first part of the selection?
   - A. "With each breath, the chill rolls deeper into my lungs."
   - B. "They are making abrupt turns to the right and left."
   - C. "Will I be able to recognize if I've gone too far?"
   - D. "This gives me energy and I imagine how wonderful it will feel to embrace the people who are waiting for us..."
   - E. "I look down at them through the ash-colored water: they are splotchy and bluish white; they are the hands of a dead person."

2. Which emotion seems to motivate Cox the champion swimmer the most?
   - A. concern for peace
   - B. sense of freedom
   - C. ambition
   - D. competitiveness
   - E. pride

3. The most important idea in "Swimming to Antarctica" is summarized in which statement?
   - A. Competitive swimmers must learn to protect themselves from icy waters.
   - B. Swimming from one country to another can help solve international conflicts.
   - C. Dedication to one's sport and commitment to safety are vital to any athlete.
   - D. Athletes receive their greatest thrill when they are most in danger.
   - E. None of the above

4. As it is used on page 223, the term *ominous* most nearly means
   - A. unfeeling.
   - B. stinking.
   - C. heartless.
   - D. thick.
   - E. threatening.

5. What is the effect on the reader of the moment-by-moment details that Cox provides in the first part of the selection? Why do you think she leaves readers uncertain about what happened to her in the Bering Sea?

Becoming a Composer

BEFORE READING **A Biography by Lindsley Cameron**

DIRECTED READING

BUILD BACKGROUND

Literary Context "Becoming a Composer" is from Lindsley Cameron's book *The Music of Light* (1998), a nonfiction account of Hikari Oe, the son of the famous Japanese author Kenzaburo Oe and his wife Yukari. (The names are pronounced hee-KA-ree OH-eh, ken-ZAH-buh-roh, and yoo-KAH-ree.) Hikari, whose name means "light" in Japanese, was born with a serious brain disorder. The surgery that corrected the condition interfered with his ability to think. In addition, he was diagnosed with autism, a disorder which affects the development of social interaction and communication skills.

Despite his disabilities, Hikari showed an extraordinary talent for music. His parents encouraged this talent, and today Hikari is a world-famous composer. The first compact disc of his compositions was released to high praise when he was only twenty-nine.

Reader's Context Can you think of anyone who has a disability but is extraordinarily talented? Have you or someone you know ever exceeded the expectations of others?

ANALYZE LITERATURE: Biography

"Becoming a Composer" is part of a **biography,** the story of a person's life written by someone other than the subject of the work. Lindsley Cameron wrote this biography about Hikari Oe. This selection focuses on Hikari's love of music and how he learned to compose it.

SET PURPOSE

As you read the selection, identify the sources that the author, Lindsley Cameron, used to gather information on her subject, Hikari Oe. Consider what responsibilities a biographer has to his or her sources and to his or her subject.

MEET THE AUTHOR

Lindsley Cameron lived in Japan for eight years and later moved to New York, where she has written about Japanese and Chinese art and culture for the *New York Times* and *The New Yorker* magazine. In addition to *The Music of Light,* she has published a book of short stories, *The Prospect of Detachment* (1991).

Cameron first became aware of Kenzaburo Oe after reading his book *A Personal Matter,* a fictional account of his and his wife's decision to raise their son despite doctors' recommendations. Cameron later met Oe, when his first book was published in English. The many hours of interviews he granted Cameron led to her writing *The Music of Light.*

USE READING SKILLS

Comparison Clues A context clue that uses a comparison is the opposite of a contrast clue described in the first selection. For **comparison clues,** surrounding words are similar or comparable to the meaning of the unfamiliar word. Words and phrases that indicate this type of clue include *such as, like, also, similarly, just as,* and *in the same way.*

PREVIEW VOCABULARY

Read the following sentences and determine the definition of each underlined vocabulary word using the comparison clues provided.

1. The herbal tea helped <u>alleviate</u> my headache, as the ice pack helped my swollen ankle.
2. Lana <u>transcended</u> all of our expectations in the same way that the underdog team did when it won the state soccer tournament.
3. Like the other students who failed to buy a raffle ticket, Ian was <u>precluded</u> in the door prize contest.
4. Just as I was <u>reprimanded</u>, the other students were criticized in front of the entire class.
5. Lea needed to <u>transcribe</u> the conversation perfectly, like a machine that copied everything word for word.

Becoming a Composer

A Biography by **Lindsley Cameron**

Every day when he came home from school, all he wanted to do was listen to classical music.

Every day when he came home from school, all he wanted to do was listen to classical music.

Hikari has been hearing music all his life. During her pregnancy, his mother listened to lots of Mozart. "They say fetuses begin to hear during their fifth month in the womb," she says, "so maybe he started to like it then." And after he was born, to alleviate her depression, she played recordings of the works of her other favorite classical composers—Chopin and Beethoven, chiefly—over and over. "When he was a toddler, he loved Western classical music. He would listen to it for hours, perfectly absorbed. Whenever we wanted some peace, we'd just put a few symphonies on the record player, and we could be sure Pooh-chan[1] wouldn't bother us at all. At that time, I had no idea how unusual that was. It wasn't until I had my other children that I realized that most normal toddlers won't listen to *any* kind of music for hours in a row—and that Western classical music is something most of them get tired of very fast."

Not Hikari. In a memoir about him, she wrote of how, when he was an infant, she played her favorite Western classical[2] composers again and again until the records wore out. When a wornout record stuck and repeated a passage, Hikari wailed, as he did when a record stopped. She could quiet him only by playing another record. At first, she thought he enjoyed only Western classical music, but by the time he was a toddler she discovered that he liked children's songs and some other music, too. She also discovered

1. **Pooh-chan.** The family's nickname for Hikari, referring to Winnie the Pooh, a character in children's books by A. A. Milne
2. **Western classical.** Classical music from the West, that is, Europe and the Americas

al • le • vi • ate (ə lē´ vē āt') *v.,* relieve; make less severe that he could remember any tune he had ever heard. Entering a restaurant with his family, if classical music was being played, he could tell them at once what the piece was, even after hearing only a few notes.

When he was nine, Yukari began teaching him to read music and to play the piano, reasoning that even if he never got to be very good at it, the attempt might improve his coordination, and even if it didn't, he would probably enjoy it. Every day when he came home from school, all he wanted to do was listen to classical music. Many autistic[3] people limit their activities very narrowly; a tendency to have interests that are both highly restricted and very intense is listed in the diagnostic manual of the American Psychiatric Association as a symptom of autism. It can also be characteristic of genius, of course, but at this time no one suspected that Hikari's preoccupation would ultimately lead him to transcend the usual limits of his condition.

Hikari's physical handicaps precluded his developing much skill as a pianist. It was hard for him to see the notes and to see and control his fingers on the keys. But he clearly had interest in and aptitude for music. He mastered the contents of Japan's standard introductory piano textbook very quickly. He enjoyed the lessons with his mother, and he had perfect pitch—the ability to correctly identify any note heard instantly and to sing any tone accurately.

Inborn absolute pitch is rare. Musicians can be trained to develop relative pitch—that is, the ability to identify notes through recognizing intervals from given memorized pitches—and the earlier they begin musical training, the more likely they are to develop it. There is no definitive figure for the occurrence of inborn perfect pitch in the general population, since the phenomenon has chiefly been studied in musicians, but it is usually estimated as less than 4 percent. It is more common in people with disabilities like Hikari's, and it has recently been linked to a particular gene.

Hikari was extraordinarily sensitive to sounds of all kinds. He had (and to some extent still has) a horror of dogs, apparently because he disliked their barking and growling so. He had an excellent memory for the sounds of spoken language, too. He enjoyed exploiting the comic possibilities of language and was always making puns. And he was—and still is—a talented mimic; he could reproduce the routines of popular television entertainers. And he could remember nearly any piece of music he heard, even music he didn't like particularly. He could even remember that atonal[4] music he detested, if the piece wasn't too long or complicated. What he remembered best, though, was the eighteenth- and nineteenth-century Western classical music he preferred.

Although such talents made him easy to teach in some ways, Yukari, having three children to take care of, would probably not have been able to instruct him at all if Natsumiko had not proven extraordinarily helpful in taking care of Hikari. Even as a toddler, she understood that her brother needed her help and assumed responsibilities far beyond what might be expected at her age. When her mother went shopping with the children, Natsumiko would take care of the other two. By the time she was six—an age when most children need a parent to escort them when using a public bathroom—she was able to escort Hikari, who couldn't manage such things by himself. (In Japan at that time, most public toilets were unisex.) At home, she often took over the care of her brothers, freeing her mother to get on with her chores. Still, Yukari couldn't manage to give Hikari piano lessons—or even help with practicing—every

3. **autistic.** Suffering from autism, a mental disorder usually diagnosed in childhood and characterized by withdrawal, inability to interact socially, repetitive behavior, and a variety of ways of acting out

4. **atonal.** Refers to music not organized in one key or tonal center

tran • scend (tran[t] send′) *v.*, go beyond the limits of; overcome
pre • clude (pri klüd′) *v.*, rule out or make impossible in advance

day, and in any case she had only a beginner's skills herself, having taken lessons for a few years as a child.

Trouble began when Hikari, at age eleven, reached the point of trying to play with both hands simultaneously. He simply couldn't do it, and he stopped making progress. She reprimanded him for not trying hard enough; after all, he had been able to learn everything up to that time, however slowly and laboriously. As his parent, she wanted him to do well and became disappointed and frustrated when he couldn't. And he, of course, wanted to please her and earn her approval, so he, too, became disappointed and frustrated. The lessons weren't fun anymore; in fact, they had become something to be dreaded. Yukari thought it would be a terrible shame if he should come to hate playing the piano, when he seemed to love music more than anything else in the world.

A more knowledgeable teacher was the only solution. The Oes asked around among friends and acquaintances, trying to find someone willing and able to work with a pupil with special needs. Finally, Kumiko Tamura, an amateur classical singer, member of a chorus group, and the wife of a friend of Kenzaburo's, agreed to try, coming to the Oes' house for an hour once every two weeks.

She hadn't been informed in advance about Hikari's disabilities, and once his mother explained his condition, she concluded that she might best begin by teaching him to sing songs with her. She had never worked with a handicapped child before, but she and Hikari got along well from the start. When she found that he could already play the piano a little, she began teaching him to play chords, because his poor physical coordination ruled out the usual fingering exercises.

At first, communication was difficult, and Yukari had to serve as an interpreter at every lesson. But after a couple of months, as they grew used to each other, Ms. Tamura and Hikari were able to talk to each other without her aid, and the lessons became weekly. After the first year, Hikari and his teacher found a way to communicate fluently about musical concepts that were beyond Yukari's level of knowledge, and she couldn't understand what they were saying to each other at all. Ms. Tamura's willingness to accommodate her problematic pupil undoubtedly accelerated their achievements in communicating: in a memoir she wrote a few years ago, Yukari said, "What Hikari likes about his teacher is that she never forces him to practice. Hikari doesn't like to be told what to do and what not to do. He likes to do everything his own way. His teacher knows that and that's why Hikari gets along very well with her."

Among other things, Ms. Tamura taught him to improvise.[5] Sometimes she would play a melody and he would continue it; sometimes the two of them would work out a harmony together. "At such times it often happened that we would come up with a particularly attractive melody or harmony which it seemed a pity to lose, although…often…Hikari remembered such interesting passages and repeated them later," Ms. Tamura has written in the liner notes for his first CD. This was why she began

Kenzaburo and Hikari Oe look together at the liner notes of Hikari's second CD.

5. **improvise.** Compose, recite, sing, or play without preparation

rep • ri • mand (re´ prə mand') *v.,* scold harshly

teaching him how to write down the tunes he made up. He progressed rapidly; soon he could accurately write down anything she played for him. "I was especially eager for him to learn to transcribe music," Yukari remembers. "I had read about how Mozart would write down music as his father played it, and it seemed like the kind of thing Hikari would enjoy a lot."

It wasn't long before he had transcribed music from nearly every record the Oes owned. He enjoyed using his transcribing skills just for fun. He has always loved his maternal grandmother, who lived with the family off and on over the years, always treating him very affectionately.

"Once, when Hikari was still in elementary school, she was hospitalized briefly and we went to visit her. She told him she wanted to find a particular song. She didn't know who wrote it and couldn't remember anything about it but the melody. He took her request very seriously, and wrote the tune down for her on music paper as soon as he got home," Yukari said.

On another occasion, Kenzaburo had been watching a videotape when Hikari was in the room and told him afterward that he had liked the soundtrack, which had been composed by Toru Takemitsu, Japan's best-known composer. His highly original music had made him a celebrity in Japan at an early age, and in 1964, when he was thirty-four, the huge international success of the film *Woman in the Dunes,* with his haunting, otherworldly score, brought him fame all over the world. *November Steps,* a New York Philharmonic commission, a sensation when it was first performed in 1967 and still one of his best-loved pieces, solidified his reputation in the West. Takemitsu, one of Kenzaburo's oldest and closest friends, had been one of the first people he talked to about his son's condition, right after Hikari's birth. And Takemitsu got along in a friendly way with the grown-up Hikari. Kenzaburo especially liked the music for a particular scene in the tape he had been watching, about four minutes long, where a young woman was eating an apple. Hikari promptly transcribed it for him, then played it on the piano as well as he could. Later, Kenzaburo told Takemitsu about it. A journalist who was with them didn't believe that Hikari could have transcribed the music correctly from memory, but Kenzaburo happened to have the notebook Hikari had used and gave it to Takemitsu to check. The composer said it was exactly what he had written, with only a minor error or two.

Hikari had always enjoyed his lessons with Ms. Tamura, but now he could hardly wait for them. When entering a Japanese house, people normally exchange their shoes for slippers at the threshold. Hikari would greet Ms. Tamura at the door carrying not only slippers for her to put on but also an alarm clock set for the time the lesson was to begin; he apparently wanted to make certain that none of the time sacred to music was wasted on pleasantries.

He would show her what he had written in his music-manuscript notebook since the last time they met. At first, these were bits and pieces of music he had heard. But soon, by the time he was thirteen, he began writing down fragments he had composed himself, working entirely in his head, without a piano. At first, Ms. Tamura did not know what they were. His favorite compositional method at that time was filling up a manuscript page with broken chords or Alberti basses (a particular left-hand accompaniment of broken triads popular in the classical period), then thinking up a melody to go with them. He wrote mostly in an eighteenth-century idiom,[6] and she thought he must have heard something on the radio that she did not happen to recognize.

His mother thought so, too. "He was always listening to classical music, and he could remember whatever he heard. He knew many more pieces than I did, so I always assumed that he was writing down things I just didn't

6. **idiom.** A style or form of artistic expression

tran • scribe (tran skrīb´) *v.,* write down; make a written copy of happen to know." She said in a television interview that although Hikari would write "This Is My Song" on his music manuscripts, she told Ms. Tamura that he must just be transcribing things he'd heard.

But the day came when his teacher saw four measures she was absolutely certain were his and no one else's. As she put it, in the same television interview, "I yelled out, 'Mrs. Oe, Hikari's composing!' I'm embarrassed to say this, but it reminded me of Annie Sullivan and Helen Keller[7] and the water breakthrough. It was an emotional moment. I couldn't stop crying."

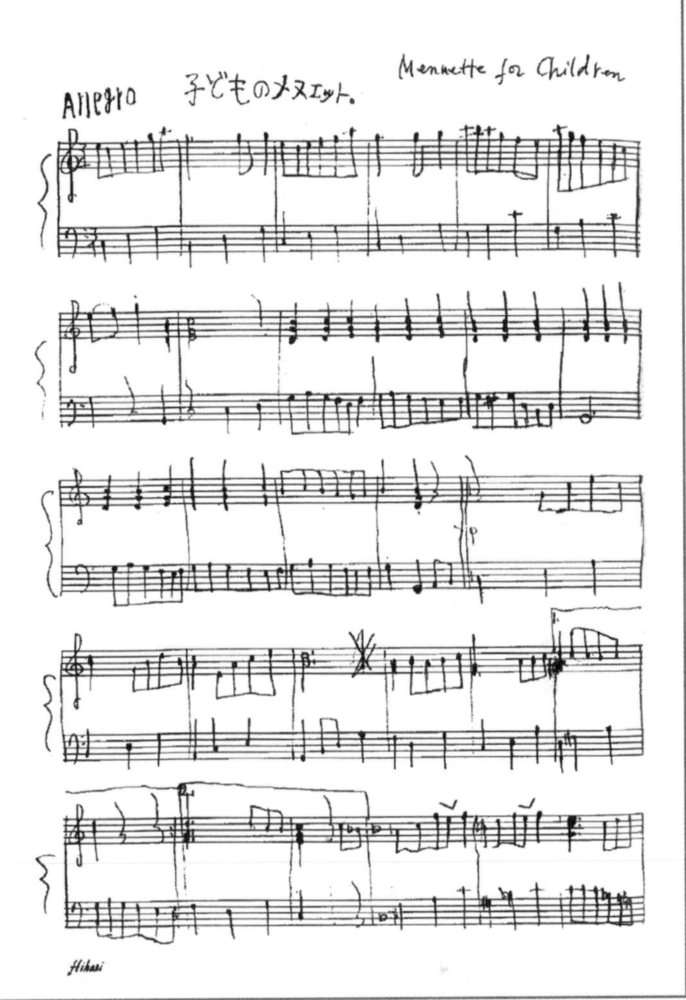

Hikari's handwritten musical notation of one of his compositions.

She told a Japanese magazine reporter some details about Hikari's progress: "While having fun with various keys, Hikari began to show very clear likes and dislikes about which keys were good for particular pieces. Hikari remembers everything that he plays on any given day because he has a good memory, and so we started listening practice, too, because he also has a good ear. Listening to the music, he writes it down on a score sheet and afterwards even goes so far as to write in the chords, having thought intently on it for a while. He also does the opposite, writing in the melody while listening to the harmony. He started to write a lot of melodies on notepads the way a small child draws pictures. A lot of these doodled score sheets started to pile up, but after a while I realized that there were pieces that I did not recognize mixed in. They appeared to be Hikari's own compositions. I really could not have been happier at the time! Still, I wondered at first if they might possibly be scores that I didn't know, because he knows everything when it comes to classical music, from symphonic to instrumental pieces."

Gradually, though, Ms. Tamura realized that all the works she couldn't identify were entirely Hikari's. And the day came when this was true of everything he wrote in the notebook.

It is not clear when Hikari himself realized that he was composing. He was thirteen when he presented his teacher with the finished score of a short piece by leaving it on the music rack of the piano encircled with a red ribbon tied in

7. **Annie Sullivan and Helen Keller.** Helen Keller became deaf, mute, and blind as a result of a childhood illness. Later on, she overcame her disabilities to become a famous author and lecturer. Annie Sullivan was the teacher who taught Helen to read and speak. The first word that Sullivan got the young girl to understand was *water.*

a bow; he seemed to know it was something he had made all by himself. "Birthday Waltz," written for his sister's birthday, was his first finished composition.

And when he graduated from elementary school, he wrote a setting for a poem his father had written called "Graduation." Kenzaburo, as always, took great pride and pleasure in his son's musical development. "Sitting nearby with a book, listening to his piano lessons," he wrote, "I can feel the best, most human things in his character finding lively and fluent expression." ❖

"I can feel the best, most human things in his character finding lively and fluent expression." In what different ways do people express themselves? What makes a person's talent truly remarkable?

AFTER READING

REFER TO TEXT	REASON WITH TEXT	
1a. Quote what Tamura says when she realizes Hikari is composing his own music.	1b. Explain why Tamura thinks of Annie Sullivan and Helen Keller when she discovers that Hikari is composing music.	**Understand** **Find meaning**
2a. Record the details that illustrate how Hikari feels about his lessons with Tamura.	2b. Generalize to create a list of personal qualities a parent or teacher must have to work with someone who has difficulty communicating and interacting with others. Cite passages where Tamura shows these qualities.	**Apply** **Use information**
3a. Identify the parts of music lessons that Hikari finds difficult.	3b. Classify Hikari's difficulties as primarily physical or as primarily emotional/mental. Explain how the two types of problems might affect each other.	**Analyze** **Take things apart**
4a. List details about Hikari's personality.	4b. Judge whether Cameron's narrative of Hikari avoids making the boy an object of pity or of disbelief. Defend your answer.	**Evaluate** **Make judgments**
5a. Cameron notes that a tendency toward restricted but intense interest is a symptom of autism and also a sign of genius. Recall what Cameron said people expected of Hikari.	5b. Consider these expectations of Hikari and what he went on to do. Create a slogan that generalizes and reflects on similar misunderstandings about people's abilities.	**Create** **Bring ideas together**

ANALYZE LITERATURE: Biography

How has Cameron interwoven the quotations from Hikari's mother, teacher, and father into the selection? How might the biography have been different if Cameron had known the Oe family when Hikari was born?

EXTEND THE TEXT

Writing Options

Creative Writing Suppose that Hikari's work has been nominated for a musical award. He is too shy to give an acceptance speech and has asked you to prepare and deliver the speech on his behalf in the event that he wins. Write a one- to two-paragraph **acceptance speech** to be delivered if Hikari wins the award.

Persuasive Writing If an author was preparing your biography, he or she would spend a great deal of time researching your life. The biographer would certainly interview people who interact with you or know you well enough to provide insight into your life. Write a brief **persuasive essay** of four or five paragraphs convincing your biographer who should be interviewed, why those people should be chosen, and what questions should be posed.

Critical Literacy

Research Autism Autism is a condition that is common throughout the United States, yet many people are unfamiliar with the disorder and how it can affect families. Working with a partner or small group, brainstorm a list of questions you have about autism. Find the answers to these questions and write a presentation that describes autism and answers your list of questions. If you know someone who is familiar with autism, consult with him or her for firsthand knowledge. Document your research sources, including any websites you visit.

Media Literacy

Be a Music Critic Imagine you are a music critic writing for a popular website. The website targets people ages 14 to 21 and reviews all types of music. Select a band, musical group, or live musical performance and write a brief review of three to five paragraphs. In your introduction, give the reader an outline of your overall opinion. Then give examples to support your opinion in the next paragraphs. Finally, conclude your review with a summary and restatement of your overall opinion. Remember, good critics provide precise language and clear supporting details so their readers clearly understand the critics' opinions.

MW Go to **www.mirrorsandwindows.com** for more.

READING ASSESSMENT

1. Number these events in the correct sequence, with 1 being the first event to happen in the selection, and 6 being the last event.
   ___ Tamura teaches Hikari to improvise.
   ___ Hikari has trouble using two hands simultaneously.
   ___ Hikari gives his teacher a composition wrapped in a red bow.
   ___ His mother listens to Mozart a great deal.
   ___ Hikari graduates from elementary school.
   ___ Yukari gives her son piano lessons.

2. Which of these statements probably represents Cameron's attitude toward the subject of her biography?
   A. She feels compassion for Hikari.
   B. She thinks his parents deserve to be recognized.
   C. She wants to publicize the misfortune of autism.
   D. She admires how much the boy had been able to accomplish with his parents' help.
   E. She feels that Hikari's parents have misrepresented him.

3. The author describes in detail the boy's ability to transcribe music after listening to the melody. She explains the topic at length because
   A. she doesn't believe that Hikari transcribed the music by himself.
   B. the topic is of particular interest to her.
   C. she doesn't have enough other information about Hikari.
   D. she wants to discuss Japan's best-known composer, Toru Takemitsu.
   E. she wants to provide believable evidence of Hikari's talent.

4. As used on page 234, the term *transcend* most nearly means
   A. accept.
   B. rise above.
   C. embrace.
   D. struggle.
   E. None of the above

5. Hikari's mother has written a memoir about her family (especially her son), and his father is the author of a novel based on his family. How might the experience of writing a true account differ from that of writing a fictional account of a family like the Oes?

UNDERSTAND THE CONCEPT | APPLY THE SKILL

Comma Usage

The punctuation mark that appears most often in most types of writing is the **comma,** the period with a tail that tells readers where to pause in a sentence. To use commas correctly, keep in mind a few guidelines for when commas are needed—and for when they are not needed.

1. Use a comma to separate items in a series. The items may be words, phrases, or clauses.

EXAMPLES

The musicians include *piano players*, *horn blowers*, and *drummers.* [nouns in a series]

The concert began after the conductor *bowed to the audience*, *greeted the orchestra*, and *raised her baton.* [phrases in a series]

Do you know *which composer wrote the music*, *who the soloist is*, and *how loud the music will be?* [clauses in a series]

2. Use a comma when you combine sentences with a conjunction, such as *and, but, or, nor, yet, so,* or *for.* In the combined sentence, place the comma before the conjunction.

EXAMPLE

Hai-ping has taken violin lessons**,** *but* she'd really like to play the trumpet.

3. Use a comma after an introductory word, phrase, or clause.

EXAMPLES

*Naturally***,** talented musicians should be encouraged to play instruments. [Without the comma, "Naturally" might be misread as modifying "talented musicians."]

*Made of shiny dark wood***,** the piano is a handsome musical instrument.

4. Use a comma to set off words, phrases, or clauses that interrupt a sentence. Use two commas if the interrupter appears in the middle of the sentence. Use one comma if the interrupter comes at the end of the sentence.

EXAMPLES

How might autism**,** *a serious brain disorder***,** be related to genius? [A word or phrase that identifies or renames another noun is called an *appositive.*]

These students could also take a class in the psychology of the brain**,** *of course.*

5. Use a comma between two or more adjectives that modify the same noun and that could be joined by *and.* (Note: If *and* is used, then you don't need the comma.)

EXAMPLE

The cello has a deep**,** haunting sound.

6. Use a comma to set off names in direct address.

EXAMPLES

We'll help you**,** *Miriam***,** to learn this solo.

Thanks for checking the information**,** *Candice.*

7. Use a comma to separate the parts of a date that include the month, day, and year. Do not use a comma if only the month and year are given.

EXAMPLES

Mozart was born on *January 27***,** *1756***,** in Austria. [A comma separates the date from the year and the year from any remaining part of the sentence.]

Beethoven was born in *December 1770* in Germany.

8. Use a comma to separate items in addresses. Do not use a comma between the state name (whether spelled in full or abbreviated) and the ZIP code.

EXAMPLE

Our music teacher lives at *36 West Piano Drive***,** *Delray Beach***,** *Florida 33483.*

9. Do not use unnecessary commas. Too many commas can make the sentence's meaning unclear and the style choppy.

EXAMPLE

The musician, would explain the difference, between the trombone, my favorite instrument, and the piano. [incorrect]

The musician would explain the difference between the trombone, my favorite instrument, and the piano. [correct: only the appositive phrase needs to be set off by commas.]

UNDERSTAND THE CONCEPT

APPLY THE SKILL

Use Commas Correctly

In the following sentences, add commas that are needed and remove commas that don't belong.

1. As you might expect the national language of Japan is Japanese.
2. Mount Fuji an active volcano is a well-known sight to the Japanese, and visitors to the island nation.
3. Without a doubt the most tragic dates in modern Japanese history are August 6 and 9 1945 the days the two atomic bombs were dropped on Hiroshima, and Nagasaki.
4. In August, 1945 the Japanese surrendered to the United States and World War II came to an end.
5. Do you know Anita that favorite foods in Japan include rice octopus and shrimp?
6. To do better in difficult demanding subjects some Japanese children go to school during the day, and in the evening.
7. Spending long hours in school every day of course has both advantages, and disadvantages.
8. The English language, contains a number of words from Japanese and you may know at least two: *kimono* a bathrobe and *sumo* a type of wrestling.
9. Sumo wrestlers in fact are famous for their huge size but they are skillful graceful athletes.
10. If you want to learn more about Japan write to *Tokyo Today,* 160 Island Avenue Santa Fe New Mexico 87501.
11. If you aren't busy Vladimir would like you to listen to him play.
12. Students interested in the topic of autism, the teacher suggested might read Kenzaburo Oe's book about his son.

The following excerpt from "Us and Them" by David Sedaris contains misplaced or missing commas. Read the excerpt and replace or delete the commas using the skills from the previous page.

> Word spread that Mr. Tomkey did not own a television and you began hearing that while this was all very well and good it was unfair for him to inflict his beliefs upon others, specifically his innocent, wife and children. It was speculated that just as the blind man develops a keener sense of hearing the family, must somehow compensate for their loss. "Maybe they read" my mother's friend said. "Maybe they listen to the radio, but you can bet your boots they're doing *something*."

EXTEND THE SKILL

Imagine that you are teaching an elementary school class about using commas correctly. Write a paragraph about the adventures of a character known as The Comma. Be as creative as you like in writing the paragraph, but be sure you have used all the commas correctly.

REVIEW TERMS

- **clause:** a group of words that functions as one part of speech and that contains both a subject and a verb
- **comma:** a punctuation mark that appears most often in most types of writing and that tells readers where to pause in a sentence
- **conjunction:** a word that joins words, phrases, clauses, and sentences together
- **phrase:** a group of words that functions as one part of speech but does not have both a subject and a verb

Understanding the Essay

THE ESSAY

You've heard it before—your teacher tells you to write an essay on a particular topic. Essays, however, are not only homework assignments. Many of the nonfiction selections you encounter are versions of the essay form.

An **essay** is a short nonfiction work that presents a main idea, or thesis, about a particular topic. The three most common types of essays are expository, persuasive, and personal. Some essays are a combination of these types.

TYPES OF ESSAYS

- An **expository essay** explores a topic with the goal of informing or enlightening the reader. In the excerpt "Becoming a Composer" from her biography *The Music of Light* (page 233), Lindsley Cameron writes to inform the readers about Hikari Oe's musical talents despite his disability.
- A **persuasive essay** aims to convince the reader to accept a certain point of view. "The Obligation to Endure" (page 253), from Rachel Carson's *Silent Spring,* is an example of a persuasive essay in which Carson tries to convince readers to advocate for safer pesticides. This selection is also an example of an expository essay, as Carson seeks to inform readers that chemical pesticides are a danger to the environment and to human beings.
- A **personal essay** explores a topic related to the life or interests of the writer. Personal essays are characterized by an intimate and informal style or tone. "Us and Them" (page 245) by David Sedaris is a personal essay, in which the author reflects on incidents and attitudes of his childhood and what they mean to him now.

THESIS STATEMENT

Perhaps the most important part of an essay is its thesis. The **thesis statement** is the essay's main idea. Most thesis statements identify a main idea the writer of the essay is trying to prove to his or her audience. For example, the thesis of Annie Dillard's "It's Not Talent; It's Just Work" (page 306) is "Doing something does not require discipline; it creates its own discipline...."

What Great Writers Do

In the paragraphs that follow the thesis, the writer, Annie Dillard, tries to prove with examples from her own life that doing something you love creates the diligence and discipline necessary to complete the task.

> Now, it happens that when I wrote my first book of prose, I worked an hour or two a day for a while, and then in the last two months, I got excited and worked very hard, for many hours a day. People can lift cars when they want to. People can recite the Koran, too, and run in marathons. These things aren't ways of life; they are merely possibilities for everyone on certain occasions of life. You don't lift cars around the clock or write books every year. But when you do, it's not so hard. It's not superhuman. It's very human. You do it for love. You do it for love and respect for your own life; you do it for love and respect for the world; and you do it for love and respect for the task itself.
>
> —from "It's Not Talent; It's Just Work"
> by Annie Dillard

If you're able to identify an essay's thesis, you will be able to better determine the writer's purpose and locate points in the essay that support the thesis. In most essays, the thesis is somewhere near the end of the introduction. An exception is the personal essay, where the thesis might be positioned near the end of the essay by way of pointing out a moral or offering a reflection on what has come before.

ORGANIZATION

There are several different ways to organize an essay. The most common methods of organization are listed on the following page.

Method	Characteristics	Example
Chronological Order	• Events are given in the order in which they occurred. • Events are connected by transition words such as *when, next, then, finally,* and *at last.* (Personal essays, because they tell a story, are often written in chronological order.)	When my family first moved to North Carolina, we lived in a rented house three blocks from the school where I would begin the third grade.... Within a year we would move again.... Our next house was less than a mile away.... —from "Us and Them" by David Sedaris (page 245)
Order of Importance	• Details are given in the order of importance or familiarity. • Details are connected by transition words such as *more important, less important, most important,* and *least important.*	First forget inspiration. Habit is more dependable....Forget talent. If you have it, fine. Use it. If you don't have it, it doesn't matter.... Finally, don't worry about imagination. You have all the imagination you need,.... —from "Furor Scribendi," by Octavia Butler (page 297)
Comparison and Contrast Order	• When comparing two things (or ideas), like apples and oranges, there are two methods of organization: 1) List all the characteristics of apples, usually in one paragraph, followed by all the characteristics of oranges; or 2) list one characteristic of apples and compare it with one characteristic of oranges. Follow this with another characteristic applied to both apples and oranges. • The things being compared are connected by transition words such as *likewise, similarly, in contrast, a different kind,* and *another difference.*	The more you fail in private, the less you will fail in public.... If you forget this—if you let down your guard, or lower your standards, or compromise too quickly, or leave in something that should be rejected—you'll have to deal with the other, more painful kind of failure, the public kind. —from "An 'A' in Failure" by Twyla Tharp (page 325)
Cause and Effect Order	• One or more causes are presented followed by one or more effects, or one or more effects are presented followed by one or more causes. • Transition words that indicate cause and effect include *one cause, another effect, as a result, consequently, because,* and *therefore.*	The whole process of spraying seems caught up in an endless spiral. Since DDT was released for civilian use, a process of escalation has been going on in which ever more toxic materials must be found. This has happened because insects, in a triumphant vindication of Darwin's principle of the survival of the fittest, have evolved super races immune to the particular insecticide used, hence a deadlier one has always to be developed—and then a deadlier one than that. —from "The Obligation to Endure" by Rachel Carson (page 253)

Us and Them

BEFORE READING

A Personal Essay by David Sedaris

BUILD BACKGROUND

Literary Context A **personal essay** is a type of writing that explores a topic related to the life or interests of the writer. Personal essays are characterized by an intimate and informal style or tone. **"Us and Them"** is a personal essay from David Sedaris's popular collection *Dress Your Family in Corduroy and Denim.* In this essay, Sedaris explains his boyhood fascination with neighbors who did not have a television set. The essay examines what it means to be an insider or an outsider as well as the role TV plays in our culture.

Reader's Context What behaviors, customs, or ideas did you find strange as a child that you now understand better? How did you react to these differences?

ANALYZE LITERATURE: Irony

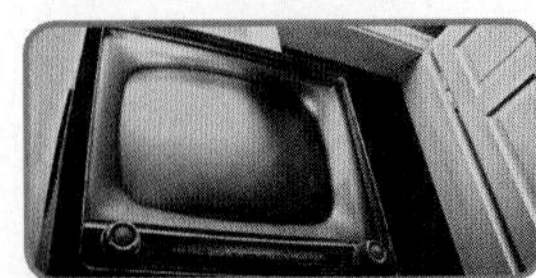

In "Us and Them," David Sedaris uses irony to add humor to his account. **Irony** is the difference between appearance and reality or expectations and reality. Much of what makes this essay funny has to do with the differences between what the young Sedaris thinks and what the adult Sedaris and the reader know.

SET PURPOSE

Read the Build Background section. Think about the Reader's Context questions. Use your responses to these questions to make one or two preliminary predictions about what Sedaris might say about differences in his essay. Then, as you read, notice the areas where the author uses irony to express these differences.

MEET THE AUTHOR

David Sedaris (b. 1956) began his working life as a housecleaner in Chicago. Though he has been writing since he was twenty, he didn't publish a book until he was thirty-seven. Sedaris's talent for humor was finally discovered by Ira Glass, a host on National Public Radio, at an open-mike performance. Sedaris often writes satire, a type of humorous writing or speech that points out falsehoods or failings, drawing upon his own experiences and poking fun at himself. Sedaris reads his humorous pieces on National Public Radio's *This American Life.* His published work includes several popular books, among them *Naked* (1997), *Me Talk Pretty One Day* (2000), and *Dress Your Family in Corduroy and Denim* (2004).

USE READING SKILLS

Evaluate Cause and Effect
As you read "Us and Them," look for logical relationships between a cause or causes and one or more effects. To track cause-and-effect connections, create a chart like the one below. As you read the story, fill in each cause and its effect.

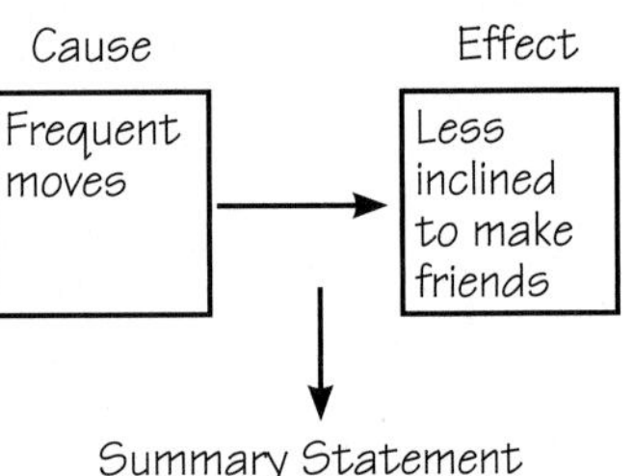
Cause
Effect
Frequent moves
Less inclined to make friends
Summary Statement
Since the narrator's family moves often, he is okay with not making friends

PREVIEW VOCABULARY

Preview vocabulary words from this selection as they are used in the sentences below. Try to unlock the meanings of the underlined words using the context clues in the sentences.

1. Because she hadn't studied for the test, Lindsay wrote down answers <u>indiscriminately</u> without even reading the questions.
2. Don't <u>inflict</u> your anger on others when you are mad at yourself.
3. Your performance would hardly <u>merit</u> applause, never mind a standing ovation.
4. If you <u>mutilate</u> the book, you must pay for a replacement.
5. <u>Synthetic</u> fabrics dry more quickly than natural ones like cotton.

Us and Them

A Personal Essay

by **David Sedaris**

"Maybe they listen to the radio, but you can bet your boots they're doing something."

When my family first moved to North Carolina, we lived in a rented house three blocks from the school where I would begin the third grade. My mother made friends with one of the neighbors, but one seemed enough for her. Within a year we would move again and, as she explained, there wasn't much point in getting too close to people we would have to say good-bye to. Our next house was less than a mile away, and the short journey would hardly merit tears or even good-byes, for that matter. It was more of a "see you later" situation, but still I adopted my mother's attitude, as it allowed me to pretend that not making friends was a conscious choice. I could if I wanted to. It just wasn't the right time.

Back in New York State, we had lived in the country, with no sidewalks or streetlights; you could leave the house and still be alone. But here, when you looked out the window, you saw other houses, and people inside those houses. I hoped that in walking around after dark I might witness a murder, but for the most part our neighbors just sat in their living rooms, watching TV. The only

mer • it (mer´ ət *or* me´ rət) *v.*, be worthy of

place that seemed truly different was owned by a man named Mr. Tomkey, who did not believe in television. This was told to us by our mother's friend, who dropped by one afternoon with a basketful of okra. The woman did not editorialize—rather, she just presented her information, leaving her listener to make of it what she might. Had my mother said, "That's the craziest thing I've ever heard in my life," I assume that the friend would have agreed, and had she said, "Three cheers for Mr. Tomkey," the friend likely would have agreed as well. It was a kind of test, as was the okra.

To say that you did not believe in television was different from saying that you did not care for it. Belief implied that television had a master plan and that you were against it. It also suggested that you thought too much. When my mother reported that Mr. Tomkey did not believe in television, my father said, "Well, good for him. I don't know that I believe in it, either."

Because they had no TV, the Tomkeys were forced to talk during dinner.

"That's exactly how I feel," my mother said, and then my parents watched the news, and whatever came on after the news.

Word spread that Mr. Tomkey did not own a television, and you began hearing that while this was all very well and good, it was unfair of him to <u>inflict</u> his beliefs upon others, specifically his innocent wife and children. It was speculated that just as the blind man develops a keener sense of hearing, the family must somehow compensate for their loss. "Maybe they read," my mother's friend said. "Maybe they listen to the radio, but you can bet your boots they're doing *something*."

I wanted to know what this something was, and so I began peering through the Tomkey's windows. During the day I'd stand across the street from their house, acting as though I were waiting for someone, and at night, when the view was better and I had less chance of being discovered, I would creep into their yard and hide in the bushes beside their fence.

Because they had no TV, the Tomkeys were forced to talk during dinner. They had no idea how puny their lives were, and so they were not ashamed that a camera would have found them uninteresting. They did not know what attractive was or what dinner was supposed to look like or even what time people were supposed to eat. Sometimes they wouldn't sit down until eight o'clock, long after everyone else had finished doing the dishes. During the meal, Mr. Tomkey would occasionally pound the table and point at his children with a fork, but the moment he finished, everyone would start laughing. I got the idea that he was imitating someone else, and wondered if he spied on us while we were eating.

When fall arrived and school began, I saw the Tomkey children marching up the hill with paper sacks in their hands. The son was one grade lower than me, and the daughter was one grade higher. We never spoke, but I'd pass them in the halls from time to time and attempt to view the world through their eyes. What must it be like to be so ignorant and alone? Could a normal person even imagine it? Staring at an Elmer Fudd lunch box, I tried to divorce myself from everything I already knew: Elmer's inability to pronounce the letter *r*, his constant pursuit of an intelligent and considerably more famous rabbit. I tried to think of him as just a drawing, but it was impossible to separate him from his celebrity.

One day in class a boy named William began to write the wrong answer on the blackboard, and our teacher flailed her arms, saying,

in • flict (in flikt´) *v.*, cause something unpleasant to be endured

"Warning, Will. Danger, danger." Her voice was synthetic and void of emotion, and we laughed, knowing that she was imitating the robot in a weekly show about a family who lived in outer space. The Tomkeys, though, would have thought she was having a heart attack. It occurred to me that they needed a guide, someone who could accompany them through the course of an average day and point out all the things they were unable to understand. I could have done it on weekends, but friendship would have taken away their mystery and interfered with the good feeling I got from pitying them. So I kept my distance.

In early October the Tomkeys bought a boat, and everyone seemed greatly relieved, especially my mother's friend, who noted that the motor was definitely secondhand. It was reported that Mr. Tomkey's father-in-law owned a house on the lake and had invited the family to use it whenever they liked. This explained why they were gone all weekend, but it did not make their absences any easier to bear. I felt as if my favorite show had been canceled.

Halloween fell on a Saturday that year, and by the time my mother took us to the store, all the good costumes were gone. My sisters dressed as witches and I went as a hobo. I'd looked forward to going in disguise to the Tomkeys' door, but they were off at the lake, and their house was dark. Before leaving, they had left a coffee can full of gumdrops on the front porch, alongside a sign reading DON'T BE GREEDY. In terms of Halloween candy, individual gumdrops were just about as low as you could get. This was evidenced by the large number of them floating in an adjacent dog bowl. It was disgusting to think that this was what a gumdrop might look like in your stomach, and it was insulting to be told not to take too much of something you didn't really want in the first place. "Who do these Tomkeys think they are?" my sister Lisa said.

The night after Halloween, we were sitting around watching TV when the doorbell rang. Visitors were infrequent at our house, so while my father stayed behind, my mother, sisters, and I ran downstairs in a group, opening the door to discover the entire Tomkey family on our front stoop. The parents looked as they always had, but the son and daughter were dressed in costumes—she as a ballerina and he as some kind of a rodent with terry-cloth ears and a tail made from what looked to be an extension cord. It seemed they had spent the previous evening isolated at the lake and had missed the opportunity to observe Halloween. "So, well, I guess we're trick-or-treating *now*, if that's okay," Mr. Tomkey said.

I attributed their behavior to the fact that they didn't have a TV, but television didn't teach you everything. Asking for candy on Halloween was called trick-or-treating, but asking for candy on November first was called begging, and it made people uncomfortable. This was one of the things you were supposed to learn simply by being alive, and it angered me that the Tomkeys did not understand it.

"Why of course it's not too late," my mother said. "Kids, why don't you…run and get…the candy."

"But the candy is gone," my sister Gretchen said. "You gave it away last night."

syn • the • tic (sin the´ tik) *adj.,* produced artificially

"Not *that* candy," my mother said. "The other candy. Why don't you run and go get it?"

"You mean *our* candy?" Lisa said. "The candy that we *earned?*"

This was exactly what our mother was talking about, but she didn't want to say this in front of the Tomkeys. In order to spare their feelings, she wanted them to believe that we always kept a bucket of candy lying around the house, just waiting for someone to knock on the door and ask for it. "Go on, now," she said. "Hurry up."

My room was situated right off the foyer,[1] and if the Tomkeys had looked in that direction, they could have seen my bed and the brown paper bag marked MY CANDY. KEEP OUT. I didn't want them to know how much I had, and so I went into my room and shut the door behind me. Then I closed the curtains and emptied my bag onto the bed, searching for whatever was the crummiest. All my life chocolate has made me ill. I don't know if I'm allergic or what, but even the smallest amount leaves me with a blinding headache. Eventually, I learned to stay away from it, but as a child I refused to be left out. The brownies were eaten, and when the pounding began I would blame the grape juice or my mother's cigarette smoke or the tightness of my glasses—anything but the chocolate. My candy bars were poison but they were brand-name, and so I put them in pile no. 1, which definitely would not go to the Tomkeys.

I tore off the wrappers and began cramming the candy bars into my mouth, desperately, like someone in a contest.

Out in the hallway I could hear my mother straining for something to talk about. "A boat!" she said. "That sounds marvelous. Can you just drive it right into the water?"

"Actually, we have a trailer," Mr. Tomkey said. "So what we do is back it into the lake."

"Oh, a trailer. What kind is it?"

"Well, it's a *boat* trailer," Mr. Tomkey said.

"Right, but is it wooden or, you know… I guess what I'm asking is what *style* trailer do you have?"

Behind my mother's words were two messages. The first and most obvious was "Yes, I am talking about boat trailers, but also I am dying." The second, meant only for my sisters and me, was "If you do not immediately step forward with that candy, you will never again experience freedom, happiness, or the possibility of my warm embrace."

I knew that it was just a matter of time before she came into my room and started collecting the candy herself, grabbing indiscriminately, with no regard to my rating system. Had I been thinking straight, I would have hidden the most valuable items in my dresser drawer, but instead, panicked by the thought of her hand on my doorknob, I tore off the wrappers and began cramming the candy bars into my mouth, desperately, like someone in a contest. Most were miniature, which made them easier to accommodate, but still there was only so much room, and it was hard to chew and fit more in at the same time. The headache began immediately, and I chalked it up to tension.

My mother told the Tomkeys she needed to check on something, and then she opened the door and stuck her head inside my room. "What the *devil* are you doing?" she whispered, but my mouth was too full to answer. "I'll just be a moment," she called, and as she closed the door behind her and moved toward my bed, I began breaking the wax lips and candy necklaces pulled from pile no. 2. These were the second-best things I had received, and while it

1. **foyer.** Entrance hallway

in • dis • crim • i • nate • ly (in' dis krim´ ən at lē *or* in' dis kri´ mən at lē) *adv.*, without picking and choosing

Critical Viewing

Would the narrator have approved of the family in this photograph? Is watching television still a family event? Consider whether television brings people together or drives them apart.

hurt to destroy them, it would have hurt even more to give them away. I had just started to mutilate a miniature box of Red Hots when my mother pried them from my hands, accidentally finishing the job for me. BB-size pellets clattered onto the floor, and as I followed them with my eyes, she snatched up a roll of Necco wafers.

"Not those," I pleaded, but rather than words, my mouth expelled chocolate, chewed chocolate, which fell onto the sleeve of her sweater. "Not those. Not those."

She shook her arm, and the mound of chocolate dropped like a horrible turd upon my bedspread. "You should look at yourself," she said. "I mean, *really* look at yourself."

Along with the Necco wafers she took several Tootsie Pops and half a dozen caramels wrapped in cellophane. I heard her apologize to the Tomkeys for her absence, and then I heard my candy hitting the bottom of their bags.

"What do you say?" Mrs. Tomkey asked.

And the children answered, "Thank you."

While I was in trouble for not bringing my candy sooner, my sisters were in more trouble for not bringing theirs at all. We spent the early part of the evening in our rooms, then one by one we eased our way back upstairs, and joined our parents in front of the TV. I was the last to arrive, and took a seat on the floor beside the sofa. The show was a Western, and even if my head had not been throbbing, I doubt I would have had the wherewithal[2] to follow it. A posse of outlaws crested a rocky hilltop, squinting at a flurry of dust advancing from the horizon, and I thought again of the Tomkeys and of how alone and out of place they had looked in their dopey costumes. "What was up with that kid's tail?" I asked.

"Shhhh," my family said.

For months I had protected and watched over these people, but now, with one stupid act, they had turned my pity into something hard and ugly. The shift wasn't gradual, but immediate, and it provoked an uncomfortable feeling of loss. We hadn't been friends, the Tomkeys and I, but still I had given them the gift of my curiosity. Wondering about the Tomkey family had made me feel generous, but now I would have to shift gears and find plea-

2. **wherewithal.** Ability

mu • ti • late (myü´ tə lāt') *v.,* cut or tear up; damage sure in hating them. The only alternative was to do as my mother had instructed and take a good look at myself. This was an old trick, designed to turn one's hatred inward, and while I was determined not to fall for it, it was hard to shake the mental picture snapped by her suggestion: here is a boy sitting on a bed, his mouth smeared with chocolate. He's a human being, but also he's a pig, surrounded by trash and gorging himself so that others may be denied. Were this the only image in the world, you'd be forced to give it your full attention, but fortunately there were others. This stagecoach, for instance, coming round the bend with a cargo of gold. This shiny new Mustang convertible. This teenage girl, her hair a beautiful mane, sipping Pepsi through a straw, one picture after another, on and on until the news, and whatever came on after the news. ❖

Why are we often uncomfortable with things that are unfamiliar to us? How can people find common ground with those whose backgrounds or behaviors are different from their own?

AFTER READING

REFER TO TEXT ▶▶▶▶	▶ REASON WITH TEXT	
1a. List things the narrator thought the Tomkeys did not know because they did not have television.	1b. Summarize the narrator's ideas about television.	**Understand** **Find meaning**
2a. What candy does the narrator's mother want her children to bring to her? What does the narrator do when he goes to retrieve his candy?	2b. Use what you know about the narrator to explain why he acted the way he did. Choose two words to describe his behavior.	**Apply** **Use information**
3a. Identify what the family does after the Tomkeys leave from trick-or-treating.	3b. Recognize how the narrator uses television. What is he avoiding and how does watching television assist him?	**Analyze** **Take things apart**
4a. Record how the Tomkeys are different according to the narrator.	4b. Consider whether it is beneficial or harmful to the narrator to classify the Tomkeys as different from his own family. Explain your response.	**Evaluate** **Make judgments**
5a. Recall why the Tomkeys didn't go trick-or-treating on October 31.	5b. A **paradox** is a statement or situation that contradicts itself. Explain how the narrator's feelings are paradoxical when the Tomkeys naively come trick-or-treating the day *after* Halloween and his mother makes him give them his own candy.	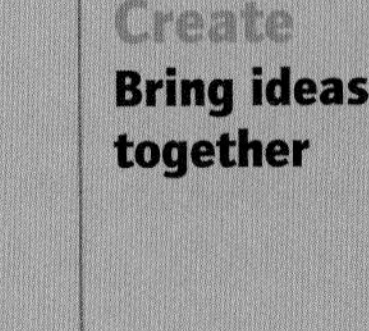 **Create** **Bring ideas together**

ANALYZE LITERATURE: Irony

How is irony used to compare the Sedaris and Tomkey families? What does this essay suggest about how and why people categorize others? What does it say about television? Are these two ideas related in any way?

EXTEND THE TEXT

Writing Options

Creative Writing Imagine if you didn't have access to television or the Internet. Would it affect your current lifestyle? How? What might you do instead? Create a **weekly calendar** that assumes television and Internet viewing is not available. Write down your other scheduled activities. Finally, write down things you'd schedule during your newly created free time.

Expository Writing Do people have to be similar to be real friends? Can friendship exist between people who seem to have nothing in common? Write a **position statement** of three or more paragraphs about how differences affect relationships. Use your own experiences to support and illustrate your opinion.

Collaborative Learning

Create a Theatrical Poster Imagine that you want to create a theatrical version of "Us and Them" and need a poster for advertising. The producer wants you to create a photo collage of images that best describes your vision of the essay. Working with a partner or small group, collect photographs from a variety of sources and create a movie poster that best illustrates the essay. You can use your own photos or collect images from magazines, newspapers, and advertisements.

Media Literacy

Evaluate the Impact of Media Media can be found everywhere in our society and will likely have a great impact in shaping our future. Consider whether this is an encouraging prospect or if there could be negative consequences. Choose a form of media (such as the Internet, magazines, or billboards) and analyze how messages in media are conveyed through visual and sound techniques. Write a persuasive essay that either supports or opposes the future growth of media. Find evidence that supports your position. Your essay should have a clear thesis explaining your position, followed by at least three supporting paragraphs. Your conclusion should restate your thesis and summarize your argument.

Go to **www.mirrorsandwindows.com** for more.

READING ASSESSMENT

1. What reason do the neighbors give for being concerned that the Tomkeys don't own a television?
   A. They are worried that the Tomkeys don't know things that watching television could teach them.
   B. They are concerned that the Tomkey family can't afford a television.
   C. They question if they should also not own a television.
   D. They are worried that Mr. Tomkey is forcing his views on his family.
   E. They are offended that the Tomkeys don't want to be like everyone else.

2. Why does the narrator pity the Tomkey family?
   A. The Tomkeys fight every night during dinner.
   B. He feels the Tomkeys don't have adequate knowledge of the world.
   C. The Tomkey children have no friends.
   D. The neighborhood goes out of its way to be rude to the family.
   E. The Tomkeys are not wealthy enough to afford a television.

3. As it is used on page 248, the term *indiscriminately* most nearly means
   A. deliberately.
   B. in disgust.
   C. haphazardly.
   D. immediately.
   E. angrily.

4. Why might the author have chosen to end the story with the family watching television?
   A. It illustrates how television can soothe a troubled mind.
   B. It shows how normal the Sedaris family is compared with the Tomkey family.
   C. It reinforces the narrator's reliance on television to distract himself from his own emotions.
   D. It shows how television can bring a family together.
   E. None of the above

5. Sedaris writes, "My candy bars were poison but they were brand-name, and so I put them in pile no. 1, which definitely would not go to the Tomkeys." What is the significance of this statement? Why do you think the writer included this detail, and how does it portray the narrator?

The Obligation to Endure *from Silent Spring*

BEFORE READING

A Persuasive Essay by Rachel Carson

DIRECTED READING

BUILD BACKGROUND

Literary Context A letter from a *Boston Globe* reporter in 1958 first interested Rachel Carson in the harmful effects of DDT. The insecticide (the word ending *–cide* means "killer of") was being used to eliminate mosquitoes in Boston, Massachusetts, and it was destroying birds as well. Carson began to question the use of insecticides and other dangerous chemicals.

Carson's book *Silent Spring* inspired the first pesticide-control laws in U.S. history. Since the publication of the work in 1962, people have become more aware of environmental hazards, and pesticides are now available that target particular species (so birds wouldn't suffer the same fate as mosquitoes) and that are, in general, less harmful.

Reader's Context If you were given the choice of knowing or not knowing the facts about environmental pollution, would you prefer to have the information or not? Explain your response.

ANALYZE LITERATURE: Persuasive Essay

A **persuasive essay,** like the excerpt from *Silent Spring,* tries to convince readers to agree with the writer's opinions, or **argument.** For their part, readers of a persuasive essay should evaluate the evidence the writer provides. They should consider the kinds of facts, examples, and other details the writer uses to support the argument.

SET PURPOSE

As you read the selection, think about Carson's purpose or goal. What kind of response does she hope to bring to mind in her readers? What facts, examples, and other details does she use to achieve her goal? What use does she make of experts in science? Evaluate her evidence and decide whether you agree with her argument.

MEET THE AUTHOR

Rachel Carson (1907–1964) grew up on a farm in rural Springdale, Pennsylvania. There, as a child, she developed a deep interest in both nature conservation and writing. After attending graduate school at the Marine Biological Laboratory, Carson wrote pamphlets and scripts for the Fish and Wildlife Service. Gifted with the ability to explain scientific issues to a wide audience, Carson wrote *The Sea Around Us,* which won the National Book Award in 1952. The volume sold so well that she could resign from her government job and become a full-time writer. Carson has said that "the discipline of the writer is to learn to be still and listen to what his subject has to tell him."

USE READING SKILLS

Distinguish Fact from Opinion As you read "The Obligation to Endure," keep notes on statements that appear to be opinions as well as statements that could be easily proved. Create a Fact or Opinion Chart, like the one below, by jotting down the facts and opinions you found within the selection. Support your reasoning by offering "proof" for each statement.

Fact or Opinion Chart	
Fact: Since the mid-1940s over 200 basic chemicals have been created for use in killing pests.	**Opinion:** Future historians may well be amazed by our distorted sense of proportion.

PREVIEW VOCABULARY

Read over the following vocabulary words used in Rachel Carson's "The Obligation to Endure": *barrage, advent, inevitable, detrimental,* and *prudent.* Select the best possible word choice for each incomplete sentence below.

1. I was being _____ when I asked for a list of references before I gave her the job.
2. The constant _____ of music was enough to make anyone's head hurt.
3. Omar has asked everyone to avoid anything that would be _____ to the team's success.
4. I suppose it's _____ that Shayna would get the lead in the school play; she is the luckiest girl in our class.
5. Jameson swore that he had been around during the _____ of television, but none of us believed him.

Environmental Study, 1999. Julie Delton.

The Obligation to Endure

A Persuasive Essay by **Rachel Carson**

> "...the chemical war is never won, and all life is caught in its violent crossfire."

The history of life on earth has been a history of interaction between living things and their surroundings. To a large extent, the physical form and the habits of the earth's vegetation and its animal life have been molded by the environment. Considering the whole span of earthly time, the opposite effect, in which life actually modifies its surroundings, has been relatively slight. Only within the moment of time represented by the present century[1] has one species—man—acquired significant power to alter the nature of his world.

During the past quarter century this power has not only increased to one of disturbing magnitude but it has changed in character. The most alarming of all man's assaults upon the environment is the contamination of air, earth, rivers, and sea with dangerous and even lethal materials. This pollution is for the most part irrecoverable; the chain of evil it initiates not only in the world that must support life but in living tissues is for the most part irreversible. In this now universal contamination of the environment, chemicals are the sinister and little-recognized partners of radiation in changing the very nature of the world—the very nature of its life. Strontium 90, released through nuclear explosions into the air, comes to earth in rain or drifts down as fallout, lodges in soil, enters into the grass or corn or wheat grown there, and in time takes up its abode in the bones of a human being, there to remain until his death. Similarly, chemicals sprayed on croplands or forests or gardens lie long in soil, entering into living organisms, passing from one to another in a chain of poisoning and death. Or they pass mysteriously by underground streams until they emerge and, through the alchemy[2] of air and sunlight, combine into new forms that kill vegetation, sicken cattle, and work unknown harm on those who drink from once pure wells. As Albert Schweitzer[3] has said, "Man can hardly even recognize the devils of his own creation."

It took hundreds of millions of years to produce the life that now inhabits the earth—eons of time in which that developing and evolving and diversifying life reached a state of adjustment and balance with its surroundings. The environment, rigorously shaping and directing the life it supported, contained elements that were hostile as well as supporting. Certain rocks gave out dangerous radiation; even within the light of the sun, from which all life draws its energy, there were short-wave radiations with power to injure. Given time—time not in years but in millennia— life adjusts, and a balance has been reached. For time is the essential ingredient; but in the modern world there is no time.

The rapidity of change and the speed with which new situations are created follow the impetuous[4] and heedless pace of man rather than the deliberate pace of nature. Radiation is no longer merely the background radiation of rocks, the bombardment of cosmic rays, the ultraviolet of the sun that have existed before there was any life on earth; radiation is now the unnatural creation of man's tampering with the atom. The chemicals to which life is asked to make its adjustment are no longer merely the calcium and silica and copper and all the rest of the minerals washed out of the rocks and carried in rivers to the sea; they are the synthetic creations of man's inventive mind, brewed in his laboratories, and having no counterparts in nature.

To adjust to these chemicals would require time on the scale that is nature's; it would require not merely the years of a man's life but the life of generations. And even this, were it by some miracle possible, would be futile, for the new chemicals come from our laboratories in an endless stream; almost five hundred annually find their way into actual use in the United States alone. The figure is staggering

1. **the present century.** *Silent Spring* was published in the twentieth century (1962)

2. **alchemy.** Scientific method of transmutation, changing a thing into something else

3. **Albert Schweitzer** (1875–1965). Medical missionary to Africa and noted humanitarian

4. **impetuous.** Behavior that is based on sudden action rather than on careful consideration

and its implications are not easily grasped—500 new chemicals to which the bodies of men and animals are required somehow to adapt each year, chemicals totally outside the limits of biologic experience.

Among them are many that are used in man's war against nature. Since the mid-1940s over 200 basic chemicals have been created for use in killing insects, weeds, rodents, and other organisms described in the modern vernacular[5] as "pests"; and they are sold under several thousand different brand names.

These sprays, dusts, and aerosols are now applied almost universally to farms, gardens, forests, and homes—nonselective chemicals[6]

that have the power to kill every insect, the "good" and the "bad," to still the song of birds and the leaping of fish in the streams, to coat the leaves with a deadly film, and to linger on in soil—all this though the intended target may be only a few weeds or insects. Can anyone believe it is possible to lay down such a barrage of poisons on the surface of the earth without making it unfit for all life? They should not be called "insecticides," but "biocides."

The whole process of spraying seems caught up in an endless spiral. Since DDT was released for civilian use, a process of escalation has been going on in which ever more toxic materials must be found. This has happened because insects, in a triumphant vindication of Darwin's principle of the survival of the fittest, have evolved super races immune to the particular insecticide used, hence a deadlier one has always to be developed—and then a deadlier one than that. It has happened also because, for reasons to be described later, destructive insects often undergo a "flareback," or resurgence, after spraying, in numbers greater than before. Thus the chemical war is never won, and all life is caught in its violent crossfire.

Along with the possibility of the extinction of mankind by nuclear war, the central problem of our age has therefore become the contamination of man's total environment with such substances of incredible potential for harm—substances that accumulate in the tissues of plants and animals and even penetrate the germ cells to shatter or alter the very material of heredity upon which the shape of the future depends.

Some would-be architects of our future look toward a time when it will be possible to alter the human germ plasm by design. But we may easily be doing so now by inadvertence,[7] for many chemicals, like radiation, bring about gene mutations. It is ironic to think that man might determine his own future by something so seemingly trivial as the choice of an insect spray.

All this has been risked—for what? Future historians may well be amazed by our distorted sense of proportion. How could intelligent beings seek to control a few unwanted species by a method that contaminated the entire environment and brought the threat of disease and death even to their own kind? Yet this is precisely what we have done. We have done it, moreover, for reasons that collapse the moment we examine them. We are told that

5. **vernacular.** Common, everyday language

6. **nonselective chemicals.** Substances that affect both their targets and other animals or plants

7. **inadvertence.** Accident; result of inattention

bar • rage (bə räzh´ *or* bə räj´) *n.,* rapid outpouring of many things at once

Biology Connection

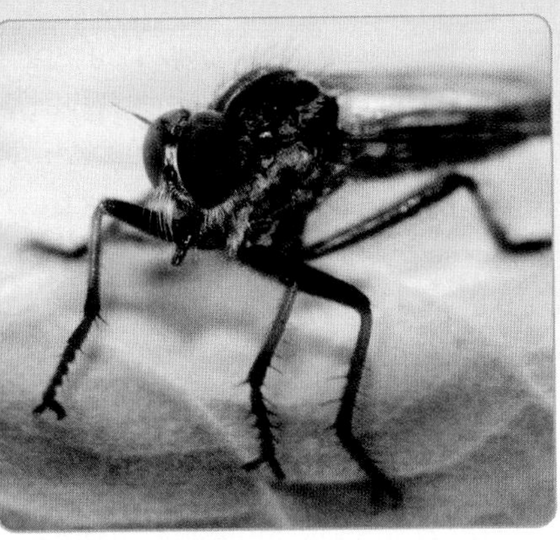

History of DDT In 1939, Paul Müller, a Swiss chemist, discovered that DDT, which seemed harmless to humans and other mammals, was extremely toxic, or poisonous, to insects. The chemical quickly gained a reputation as a miraculous agent for controlling insects such as mosquitoes and other pests that attack crops and forests. For his findings, he was awarded the Nobel Prize in Medicine in 1948. Later, the United States recognized the dangers of DDT and in 1972 banned its use as an insecticide.

the enormous and expanding use of pesticides is necessary to maintain farm production. Yet is our real problem not one of *overproduction?* Our farms, despite measures to remove acreages from production and to pay farmers *not* to produce, have yielded such a staggering excess of crops that the American taxpayer in 1962 is paying out more than one billion dollars a year as the total carrying cost of the surplus-food storage program. And is the situation helped when one branch of the Agriculture Department tries to reduce production while another states, as it did in 1958, "It is believed generally that reduction of crop acreages under provisions of the Soil Bank will stimulate interest in use of chemicals to obtain maximum production on the land retained in crops."

All this is not to say there is no insect problem and no need of control. I am saying, rather, that control must be geared to realities, not to mythical situations, and that the methods employed must be such that they do not destroy us along with the insects.

The problem whose attempted solution has brought such a train of disaster in its wake is an accompaniment of our modern way of life. Long before the age of man, insects inhabited the earth—a group of extraordinarily varied and adaptable beings. Over the course of time since man's advent, a small percentage of the more than half a million species of insects have come into conflict with human welfare in two principal ways: as competitors for the food supply and as carriers of human disease.

Disease-carrying insects become important where human beings are crowded together, especially under conditions where sanitation is poor, as in time of natural disaster or war or in situations of extreme poverty and deprivation. Then control of some sort becomes necessary. It is a sobering fact, however, as we shall presently see, that the method of massive chemical control has had only limited success, and also threatens to worsen the very conditions it is intended to curb.

Under primitive agricultural conditions the farmer had few insect problems. These arose with the intensification of agriculture—the devotion of immense acreages to a single crop. Such a system set the stage for explosive increases in specific insect populations. Single-crop farming does not take advantage

ad • vent (ad´ vent') *n.,* coming into being or use; arrival of the principles by which nature works; it is agriculture as an engineer might conceive it to be. Nature has introduced great variety into the landscape, but man has displayed a passion for simplifying it. Thus he undoes the built-in checks and balances[8] by which nature holds the species within bounds. One important natural check is a limit on the amount of suitable habitat for each species. Obviously then, an insect that lives on wheat can build up its population to much higher levels on a farm devoted to wheat than on one in which wheat is intermingled with other crops to which the insect is not adapted.

These invasions, both the naturally occurring and those dependent on human assistance, are likely to continue indefinitely.

The same thing happens in other situations. A generation or more ago, the towns of large areas of the United States lined their streets with the noble elm tree. Now the beauty they hopefully created is threatened with complete destruction as disease sweeps through the elms, carried by a beetle that would have only limited chance to build up large populations and to spread from tree to tree if the elms were only occasional trees in a richly diversified planting.

Another factor in the modern insect problem is one that must be viewed against a background of geologic and human history: the spreading of thousands of different kinds of organisms from their native homes to invade new territories. This worldwide migration has been studied and graphically described by the British ecologist Charles Elton in his recent[9] book *The Ecology of Invasions.* During the Cretaceous Period,[10] some hundred million years ago, flooding seas cut many land bridges between continents and living things found themselves confined in what Elton calls "colossal separate nature reserves." There, isolated from others of their kind, they developed many new species. When some of the land masses were joined again, about 15 million years ago, these species began to move out into new territories—a movement that is not only still in progress but is now receiving considerable assistance from man.

The importation of plants is the primary agent in the modern spread of species, for animals have almost invariably gone along with the plants, quarantine[11] being a comparatively recent and not completely effective innovation. The United States Office of Plant Introduction alone has introduced almost 200,000 species and varieties of plants from all over the world. Nearly half of the 180 or so major insect enemies of plants in the United States are accidental imports from abroad, and most of them have come as hitchhikers on plants.

In new territory, out of reach of the restraining hand of the natural enemies that kept down its numbers in its native land, an invading plant or animal is able to become enormously abundant. Thus it is no accident that our most troublesome insects are introduced species.

These invasions, both the naturally occurring and those dependent on human assistance, are likely to continue indefinitely. Quarantine and massive chemical campaigns are only extremely expensive ways of buying time. We are faced, according to Dr. Elton, "with a life-and-death need not just to find new technological means of suppressing this plant or

8. **checks and balances.** Methods of balancing one factor against another to keep their effects equal

9. **recent.** That is, relative to 1962

10. **Cretaceous Period.** The geologic period during which, most scientists believe, dinosaurs became extinct, and small mammals and plants began to develop on earth.

11. **quarantine.** Period in which plants and animals brought from overseas are kept in isolation to prevent the spread of disease or of pests

that animal"; instead we need the basic knowledge of animal populations and their relations to their surroundings that will "promote an even balance and damp down the explosive power of outbreaks and new invasions."

Much of the necessary knowledge is now available but we do not use it. We train ecologists in our universities and even employ them in our governmental agencies but we seldom take their advice. We allow the chemical death rain to fall as though there were no alternative, whereas in fact there are many, and our ingenuity could soon discover many more if given opportunity.

Have we fallen into a mesmerized state that makes us accept as inevitable that which is inferior or detrimental, as though having lost the will or the vision to demand that which is good? Such thinking, in the words of the ecologist Paul Shepard, "idealizes life with only its head out of water, inches above the limits of toleration of the corruption of its own environment.... Why should we tolerate a diet of weak poisons, a home in insipid[12] surroundings, a circle of acquaintances who are not quite our enemies, the noise of motors with just enough relief to prevent insanity? Who would want to live in a world which is just not quite fatal?"

Yet such a world is pressed upon us. The crusade to create a chemically sterile, insect-free world seems to have engendered[13] a fanatic zeal on the part of many specialists and most of the so-called control agencies. On every hand there is evidence that those engaged in spraying operations exercise a ruthless power. "The regulatory entomologists...function as prosecutor, judge and jury,[14] tax assessor and collector and sheriff to enforce their own orders," said Connecticut entomologist Neely Turner. The most flagrant[15] abuses go unchecked in both state and federal agencies.

It is not my contention that chemical insecticides must never be used. I do contend that we have put poisonous and biologically potent chemicals indiscriminately into the hands of persons largely or wholly ignorant of their potentials for harm. We have subjected enormous numbers of people to contact with these poisons, without their consent and often without their knowledge. If the Bill of Rights contains no guarantee that a citizen shall be secure against lethal poisons distributed either by private individuals or by public officials, it is surely only because our forefathers, despite their considerable

12. **insipid.** Dull; unstimulating
13. **engendered.** Created
14. **regulatory entomologists...jury.** The laws relating to insects are developed by the entomologists (experts on insects) who work in government agencies; therefore, even bad laws go unchallenged because the agencies won't criticize their staff members.
15. **flagrant.** Openly offensive

in • ev • i • ta • ble (i ne´ və tə bəl) *adj.,* unable to be avoided
det • ri • men • tal (de' trə men´ t'l) *adj.,* harmful

wisdom and foresight, could conceive of no such problem.

I contend, furthermore, that we have allowed these chemicals to be used with little or no advance investigation of their effect on soil, water, wildlife, and man himself. Future generations are unlikely to condone our lack of prudent concern for the integrity of the natural world that supports all life.

There is still very limited awareness of the nature of the threat. This is an era of specialists, each of whom sees his own problem and is unaware of or intolerant of the larger frame into which it fits. It is also an era dominated by industry, in which the right to make a dollar at whatever cost is seldom challenged. When the public protests, confronted with some obvious evidence of damaging results of pesticide applications, it is fed little tranquilizing pills of half truth. We urgently need an end to these false assurances, to the sugar coating of unpalatable facts. It is the public that is being asked to assume the risks that the insect controllers calculate. The public must decide whether it wishes to continue on the present road, and it can do so only when in full possession of the facts. In the words of Jean Rostand, "The obligation to endure gives us the right to know." ❖

pru • dent (prü´ d'nt) *adj.*, cautious; careful

Are people today obligated to save or protect the environment? If so, how? When is a problem *your own* problem? When does a problem become *everyone's* problem?

REFER TO TEXT ▶▶▶▶	▶ REASON WITH TEXT	
1a. Quote Carson to identify the "significant power" humankind has in this century.	1b. In your own words, give examples that emphasize the "disturbing magnitude" of this power.	**Understand** **Find meaning**
2a. Recall what human beings have been trying to destroy since the 1940s with "over 200 basic chemicals."	2b. Illustrate what effect our attempt to "control a few unwanted species" might have on humans and the world.	**Apply** **Use information**
3a. According to Carson, what happens when the public protests?	3b. Infer why the public is given "false assurances."	**Analyze** **Take things apart**
4a. Identify Carson's response to the idea that pesticides are needed to maintain production.	4b. Assess whether Carson makes reasonable demands on users of insecticides. Support your response.	**Evaluate** **Make judgments**
5a. Indicate how modern agriculture is more damaging to the environment than prehistoric farming was.	5b. Propose regulations on pesticides that you think Carson would endorse. Explain what effect you think these regulations would have on the world.	**Create** **Bring ideas together**

ANALYZE LITERATURE: Persuasive Essay

Summarize the main points about pollution that Carson makes. Then list the types of evidence she provides in support of her opinions. Finally, write a short critique of the essay, in which you take a stand or express your own opinion on the issue.

DEINLEIN

Informational Text CONNECTION

Mary Deinlein is an education specialist at the Smithsonian Migratory Bird Center. Part of the Smithsonian Institution in Washington, DC, the Center's goal is to promote a "greater understanding, appreciation, and protection of the grand phenomenon of bird migration." One way to reach this goal is to study the behavior, habitats (natural homes), migration patterns, and diseases of birds. **"When It Comes to Pesticides, Birds Are Sitting Ducks"** is a scientific article that examines the dangers of pesticides to the world's bird population.

The French philosopher Michel de Montaigne (1533–1592) wrote, "Let us permit nature to have her way. She understands her business better than we do." As you read the article, decide whether you agree or disagree with this quotation.

When It Comes to Pesticides, Birds Are Sitting Ducks

A Scientific Article by Mary Deinlein

The Legacy of Silent Spring

In 1962, Rachel Carson's eloquent and best-selling book, *Silent Spring,* drew international attention to the environmental contamination wrought[1] by pesticides, particularly the insecticide DDT. Carson cited declines in the number of songbirds due to poisoning as a key piece of evidence.

Six years later came documentation of a more insidious[2] effect of pesticide use. Accumulations of DDE, a compound produced when DDT degrades, were causing reproductive failure in several species of predatory birds, including peregrine falcons, brown pelicans, osprey, and bald eagles. Not only was DDE toxic to developing embryos, it also caused eggs to be laid with abnormally thin shells. So fragile were the shells that the eggs would easily break under the weight of the adult bird during incubation.[3]

DDT belongs to a class of insecticides known as organochlorines, which also includes dicofol, dieldrin, endrin, heptachlor, chlordane, lindane, and methoxychlor, among others. Some of these pesticide ingredients, such as dieldrin and heptachlor, are poisonous in very small amounts. However, the most dangerous traits of the organochlorines are their persistence—that is, their tendency to remain chemically active for a long time—and their solubility in fat, which means they become stored in fatty tissues within organisms and can accumulate over time. Because of these two traits, contaminant levels become more concentrated with each step up in a food chain—a process known as *biomagnification*. For example, when ospreys repeatedly feed on fish contaminated with DDT, increasing amounts of the pesticide are stored within their bodies.

1. **wrought.** Forced into existence
2. **insidious.** Harmful and happening in a manner barely noticed
3. **incubation.** The act of sitting on eggs to provide the proper environment (heat) for growth and hatching of young

OVER 5 BILLION POUNDS OF PESTICIDES ARE USED ANNUALLY. WHAT DOES THIS MEAN FOR THE HEALTH OF OUR ENVIRONMENT? BIRDS PROVIDE SOME OF THE ANSWERS.

Biomagnification accounts for why predatory birds, being at the top of the food chain, are most severely affected by organochlorine pesticides.

Thanks partly to the fervor[4] generated by Carson's book and partly to a study done by the National Institutes of Health which found DDT or its byproducts in 100% of the human tissues it examined, DDT and most other organochlorines were banned for use in the United States in the early 1970s. Since the ban, numbers of the more severely affected bird species have slowly recovered. However, the fate of some populations of peregrine falcons remains uncertain because DDT, its breakdown products, and other organochlorines are still prevalent in the environment.

If DDT was banned in the United States in the early 1970s, why is there still a problem today? One reason is that the United States continues to export DDT, along with other pesticides known to be hazardous to the environment and to human health. The countries of Latin America, the wintertime destination for many of the migratory birds that breed in the United States and Canada (including many peregrine falcons), are also the destination for many of these exported pesticides.

New Pesticides, New Problems

Because of the ban on DDT and the tight restrictions placed on other organochlorines, a new arsenal of pesticides predominates today. Organophosphates and carbamates are now two of the most common classes of active ingredients found in pesticide products. Although organophosphate and carbamate compounds are not as persistent as the organochlorines, they are much more acutely toxic, which means that even very small amounts can cause severe poisoning.

It is estimated that of the roughly 672 million birds exposed annually to pesticides on U.S. agricultural lands, 10%—or 67 million—are killed. This staggering number is a conservative estimate that takes into account only birds that inhabit farmlands, and only birds killed outright by ingestion of pesticides. The full extent of bird fatalities due to pesticides is extremely difficult to determine because most deaths go undetected.

Nevertheless, sobering numbers of dead birds have been documented. For example, in 1995, the pesticide monocrotophos, sprayed to kill grasshoppers, was responsible for the deaths of at least 20,000 Swainson's hawks in Argentina. Thanks to the efforts of the American Bird Conservancy and other organizations, Novartis (formerly Ciba-Geigy), a major manufacturer of monocrotophos, has recently agreed to phase out the production and sale of this pesticide.

Over 150 bird "die-offs," involving as many as 700 birds in a single incident, have been attributed to diazinon, an organophosphate insecticide commonly used for lawn care. In 1990, diazinon was classified as a restricted ingredient, and banned for use on golf courses and turf farms, marking the first time regulatory action has been taken specifically on behalf of birds. However, in most states diazinon is still available over the counter for use on home lawns and parks. So, despite the restricted-use status, as much as 10 million pounds of diazinon are still used yearly in the United States, primarily by home owners. Continued reports of bird fatalities, and additional evidence concerning the extreme toxicity of diazinon and its metabolites[5] to aquatic invertebrates and mammals have prompted the U.S. Fish and Wildlife Service and a consortium[6] of environmental organizations headed by the Rachel Carson Council to petition the Environmental Protection Agency to further restrict uses of diazinon....

4. **fervor.** Overwhelming emotion and passion
5. **metabolites.** Products of specific chemical breakdowns
6. **consortium.** Gathering of various groups to work toward achieving the same goal

Lessons from the Birds and the Bees

As evidence mounts regarding links between pesticide exposure and rates of sterility, cancers, hormonal disruption, and immune system disorders in humans, should we heed the warning signs provided by birds, or continue to pay the high environmental and social costs of rampant pesticide use? Here are a few thoughts and figures to consider. The benefits of pesticides are often cited in terms of their contribution to world food production, and yet it is estimated that crop losses to pests would increase only 10% if no pesticides were used. Between 1945 and 1989, pesticide use in the U.S. increased tenfold and yet crop losses doubled from 7–14%. Consider also that all of us, everywhere, are exposed to some pesticide residues in food, water, and the atmosphere. Residents of the United States eat an estimated 2 billion pounds of imported produce tainted with banned pesticides each year.

Scientist Paul Ehrlich has compared pesticides to heroin in that "they promise paradise and deliver addiction." Pesticide use leads to dependency by killing not only the targeted pests but also the natural predators and parasites of those pests and through the development of resistance in the pests. The destruction of natural enemies and increased resistence are countered by heavier and more frequent pesticide applications, thus maintaining the "pesticide habit" and increasing the costs of supporting it.

Honey bees and wild bees are among the victims of pesticide poisoning and their numbers are on the wane,[7] a fact that is gaining increasing attention because of their economic, ecological, and agricultural importance as pollinators.[8] With something as fundamental as the birds and the bees at stake, shouldn't we all be concerned?

If you want to help reduce global contamination and its costs, here are some things you can do:

*educate yourself and others about the effects of pesticides and alternative pest control methods,

* buy organically grown products, and support organizations working to reduce society's dependence on pesticides ❖

7. **wane.** Process of decreasing

8. **pollinators.** Organisms that pollinate, or spread pollen (the reproductive units of various plants)

REFER TO TEXT ▶▶▶▶	▶ REASON WITH TEXT	
1a. What does scientist Paul Ehrlich compare pesticides to?	1b. What is the significance of this comparison? How might it support Carson's assertion that "false assurances" need to end?	**Analyze** Take things apart
2a. Why, if it was banned in the early 1970s, does DDT still appear today?	2b. Is the exportation of banned pesticides irresponsible or acceptable? Explain.	**Evaluate** Make judgments
3a. What solutions or suggestions does Deinlein propose regarding pesticides?	3b. If you were allowed to add your own suggestions regarding the use of pesticides, what would your suggestions be?	**Create** Bring ideas together

TEXT ↔ TO TEXT CONNECTION

- Compare and contrast how Deinlein and Carson address their similar topics. Analyze how effective the language and tone used by each author is for their audience and purpose.
- Locate and read one or more current articles about DDT and compare and contrast them with these two selections. How do the viewpoints vary among the texts? Provide evidence from each text to support your findings.

AFTER READING

EXTEND THE TEXT

Writing Options

Creative Writing Write a **letter** to a fictional chemical company expressing concern over its production of pesticides. Cite the evidence found in "The Obligation to Endure" and the related article "When It Comes to Pesticides, Birds Are Sitting Ducks." Your letter should be polite yet forceful and should contain three clear elements: the reason you are writing, the evidence that supports your position, and the course of action you expect the company to take.

Expository Writing Research an endangered species and write a brief (four- or five-paragraph) **informational article** that might appear in a magazine. Be sure to include details a reader would find informative and interesting, including maps, drawings, and photos. In the course of your article, be sure to explain what needs to change for the animal to survive.

Collaborative Learning

Debate the Pesticide Issue DDT is now banned in all major countries. However, there is increasing debate about allowing pesticides to be used in developing nations struggling with malaria and West Nile virus. With a partner or in a small group, research how developing nations might benefit from the immediate effects of a pesticide. Be sure to document your sources. Develop an argument that either supports or opposes the use of DDT in these nations and debate a team with an opposing view.

Media Literacy

Create a Persuasive Brochure Imagine you work with the Smithsonian Migratory Bird Center and have been asked to create a brochure explaining the negative effects of pollution, DDT, and other chemicals on the bird population. Use the previous selections, newspaper and magazine articles, the Internet, and other sources as references to create a four-panel brochure (fold a sheet of paper in half to create the four panels). Adding illustrations, diagrams, maps, and photos will make your brochure more interesting. Be sure to include suggestions for those people who want to become more actively involved.

Go to **www.mirrorsandwindows.com** for more.

READING ASSESSMENT

1. Which of these statements is most important to Carson's argument?
   A. In nature, animal life is influenced by the environment.
   B. In nature, the environment is influenced by animal life.
   C. Human beings alter, or change, the environment.
   D. Human beings should be careful about altering the environment.
   E. All of the above

2. Which of these statements does *not* explain why insects have become a major environmental problem in the last century?
   A. The government is unable to control the use of pesticides.
   B. On many farms, there is not enough diversity, or variety, of crops planted.
   C. When plants and animals are brought to regions where they did not exist before, they may have no natural enemies.
   D. Pesticides often kill natural predators of the insects the pesticides were designed to control.
   E. None of the above

3. As it is used on page 259, the term *prudent* most nearly means
   A. sensible.
   B. reckless.
   C. anxious.
   D. rightful.
   E. unyielding.

4. Which of these considerations was probably the least significant for Carson as she wrote *Silent Spring?*
   A. She shouldn't overwhelm her readers with details and explanations.
   B. She should avoid offending the pesticide industry.
   C. Her suggestions for reform shouldn't go beyond the realistic.
   D. Her readers should be expected to do more than sigh at the state of the environment.
   E. She should give examples that her readers would relate to and understand.

5. What relationship between knowledge (and understanding) and preservation of the environment does Carson stress in "The Obligation to Endure"?

GRAMMAR & STYLE

UNDERSTAND THE CONCEPT

APPLY THE SKILL

Possessive Nouns and Pronouns

Nouns that show ownership or possession are called **possessive nouns.** A possessive noun indicates that an object or idea *belongs to* someone or something. Possessive nouns can be singular or plural. In writing possessive nouns correctly, you should keep in mind the following three guidelines.

1. To form the possessive of a singular noun, add an apostrophe and an *s* to the end of the word.
2. To form the possessive of a plural noun that ends in *s,* add an apostrophe after the *s.*
3. To form the possessive of a plural noun that does not end in *s,* add an apostrophe and an *s* to the correct plural form of the noun.

EXAMPLES

possessive form of a singular noun

The *earth's* plants and animals have been influenced by the environment. [singular noun *earth* + apostrophe + *s*]

The *boss's* assistant left the office. [Possessive singular nouns ending in *ss* are also followed by an apostrophe + *s.*]

We missed hearing *Fannie Jones's* speech. [Possessive proper nouns that end in *s,* including personal names like *Fannie Jones,* also take an apostrophe + *s.*]

possessive form of a plural noun ending in *s*

The *mosquitoes'* larvae were destroyed by the insecticide. [plural noun *mosquitoes* + apostrophe]

possessive form of a plural noun not ending in *s*

The *women's* environmental group formed a food network. [plural noun not ending in *s* + apostrophe + *s*]

A **possessive pronoun,** a word used in place of a noun, may also be used to show possession. A possessive pronoun may stand alone and function as a pronoun. It may also be used before a noun or gerund and function as an adjective.

EXAMPLES

possessive pronoun used as pronoun

The candy bars are *mine.*

Hers were not offered to the neighbors.

The bucket of gumdrops was *theirs.*

possessive pronoun as an adjective before a noun

You mean *our* candy?

All *my* life chocolate has made me ill.

It was unfair of him to inflict *his* beliefs upon others.

possessive pronoun as an adjective before a gerund

Her laughing is becoming tiresome.

Becoming friends would have interfered with *my* pitying them.

They were not ashamed of *their* talking during dinner.

Do not confuse possessive pronouns and **contractions,** which combine two words by joining them and adding an apostrophe. Some possessive pronouns and contractions sound alike, but they have different meanings and spellings. Possessive pronouns do not contain an apostrophe.

your / you're
their / they're
theirs / there's
its / it's

REVIEW TERMS

- **noun:** word that names a person, place, or thing
- **possessive noun:** noun that shows ownership or possession
- **pronoun:** word used in place of a noun
- **possessive pronoun:** pronoun that shows ownership or possession
- **adjective:** word that modifies a noun or pronoun
- **gerund:** a verb ending in *–ing* that acts like a noun
- **contraction:** combines two words by shortening them and joining them with an apostrophe

UNDERSTAND THE CONCEPT

APPLY THE SKILL

Identify Possessive Nouns

Indicate whether the underlined nouns in the following sentences are plural or possessive or both plural and possessive.

1. Do you know how many species of insects there are on the planet?
2. Scientists' studies have discovered nearly one million species.
3. An insect's body is made up of three parts: head, thorax, and abdomen.
4. The class listened to Mr. Williams's discussion of plants that trap insects.
5. The plants' leaves have a pitcher-like shape filled with a liquid that attracts insects.

Use Possessive Nouns Correctly

In the following sentences, write the correct possessive form of each underlined noun.

1. Among dangerous chemicals are the products used in humankinds war against insects.
2. The title of Charles Eltons book is *The Ecology of Invasions.*
3. Scientists have documented childrens sensitivity to these chemicals.
4. As could be expected, *Silent Spring* did not meet with industrys approval.
5. Nicholass family has planted a garden to attract butterflies.

Identify Possessive Pronouns

Identify the possessive pronouns in the following excerpt from "Us and Them" by David Sedaris. Then indicate if they are used as pronouns or adjectives.

> My room was situated right off the foyer, and if the Tomkeys had looked in that direction, they could have seen my bed and the brown paper bag marked MY CANDY, KEEP OUT. I didn't want them to know how much I had, and so I went into my room and shut the door behind me. Then I closed the curtains and emptied my bag onto the bed, searching for whatever was the crummiest. All my life chocolate has made me ill. I don't know if I'm allergic or what, but even the smallest amount leaves me with a blinding headache. Eventually, I learned to stay away from it, but as a child I refused to be left out.

Use Possessive Pronouns Correctly

In the following sentences, write the correct possessive form of each underlined pronoun.

1. For hers efforts in writing *Silent Spring,* Rachel Carson was attacked by the chemical industry.
2. Some believe that life modifies it's surroundings.
3. It's a miracle that their not harmed by the use of pesticides.
4. Spreading the word on the dangers of pesticides was mine intention.
5. I was cautious, because the plants were not my.
6. Ours science project was ruined because I had used too much insecticide.
7. Logan supports the use of pesticides, but I disagree with hims reasons.
8. Rachel Carson gave many examples of how pesticides affect humans and they're surrounding world.
9. It's important to note that ours essay on the environment received a good grade.
10. Angela tried to argue with our thesis, but hers supporting points were not as strong as ours.

EXTEND THE SKILL

With a partner, make a list of fifteen insect-related nouns, such as *antenna, grasshopper, thorax,* and *horsefly.* Then write the correct singular possessive and plural possessive forms of each noun on your list.

Understanding Speeches

SPEECHES

When you think about giving a speech, you might envision yourself standing in front of a group of people, trembling and sweating, your eyes darting back and forth, your hands nervously clenching your note cards. Speaking in front of a crowd is not always easy. Many people throughout history, however, have been in the same situation, and their speeches were so significant that they were reprinted to be read over and over again. You will read two such famous speeches in this unit.

A **speech** is a public address that was originally delivered orally. The nature of a speech, whether formal or informal, is usually determined by the situation or context in which it is presented. Formal speeches generally call for a greater degree of preparation. A *formal speech* situation might exist when presenting an assigned speech to classmates, or giving a presentation to a community group or ceremony. The more formal a speech is the more preparation it requires. *Informal speech* situations are more casual and might include telling a story among friends, giving a pep talk to your team at halftime, or presenting a toast at a dinner table. The three main types of speeches are impromptu, memorized, and extemporaneous speeches.

TYPES OF SPEECHES

Impromptu Speech

A speech that requires no advance preparation is called an **impromptu speech.** If you were to give this type of speech, you would simply get up and talk. For example, if you were surprised by a gift or an award, you might be called upon to give a brief speech that was not written or rehearsed. The famous line spoken by Neil Armstrong from the surface of the moon, "That's one small step for man, one giant leap for mankind," could be considered an impromptu speech.

Memorized Speech

A **memorized speech** requires more preparation in that the speaker writes and memorizes the speech word for word. This is difficult to do, and memorized speeches sometimes seem stiff and devoid of expression.

Extemporaneous Speech

Most speeches that have become famous are **extemporaneous speeches.** If you were to give this type of speech, you would prepare and refer to notes or outlines, and you would rehearse until you felt comfortable giving the speech. The speech delivered by John F. Kennedy from which came the line, "Ask not what your country can do for you...ask what you can do for your country," is an example of an extemporaneous speech.

What Great Speakers Do

Notice how in his "I Have a Dream" speech, Martin Luther King Jr. uses both parallelism and repetition:

But one hundred years later, the Negro still is not free; one hundred years later, the life of the Negro is still sadly crippled by the manacles of segregation and the chains of discrimination; one hundred years later, the Negro lives on a lonely island of poverty in the midst of a vast ocean of material prosperity; one hundred years later, the Negro is still languished in the corners of American society and finds himself in exile in his own land...

ELEMENTS OF SPEECHES

Most of the time, speeches are delivered orally to a public audience. When you are able to read a copy of a speech, however, you have more of a chance to absorb and reflect on its message. To understand and analyze a speech you are reading, it helps to consider its purpose or occasion, its main idea, and its use of rhetorical devices.

Purpose

When a person writes a piece for publication, he or she has a **purpose,** or goal. The same is true when a person gives a speech. The most common purposes for giving a speech are to either explain something

(informative) or to convince people to accept a position and respond in some way (persuasive). Historical speeches are also often connected to an occasion of some sort. Nelson Mandela delivered his speech "Glory and Hope" (page 277) on the occasion of taking the office of president of South Africa. The purpose of his speech was to urge listeners to look to the future and dedicate themselves to the well-being of their country.

Main Idea

The **main idea,** or central message, of a speech may be stated directly, usually in the introduction. More often than not, however, the main idea is implied, or not directly declared. In his speech "I Have a Dream" (page 269), Martin Luther King Jr.'s main idea, that he dreams of a world in which all people treat each other as brothers and sisters, is implied.

Good speakers understand the need to support their main ideas. Common types of support include facts and statistics, firsthand experiences or examples, opinions of experts, logical reasoning, comparisons and contrasts, causes and effects, research results, and appeals to emotion. Martin Luther King Jr. uses a variety of support. He points to historical events such as slavery and current events such as segregation, draws on his own experiences, and appeals to the emotions of Americans who desire freedom for all people.

Rhetorical Devices

Rhetorical devices are techniques used by speakers to achieve a particular effect, especially to persuade or influence. Three common types of rhetorical devices are listed below:

- **Parallelism** Using this rhetorical device, a writer emphasizes the equal value or weight of two or more ideas by expressing them in the same grammatical form.
- **Repetition** This is a writer's intentional reuse of a sound, word, phrase, or sentence. Writers often use repetition to emphasize ideas.
- **Rhetorical Question** This kind of question is asked for effect but is not meant to be answered. A rhetorical question will get the audience thinking about something. For example, a person giving a speech meant to persuade the residents of a community to adopt a curfew might say, "It's ten o'clock at night. Do you know where your children are?" This question is not meant to be answered but to draw attention to the purpose of the speech.

Famous Speeches

Many historical speeches are still well known and regarded today. Below is a short list of famous speeches. You can find the transcripts of these and other speeches online. A few good places to start are USinfo, AmericanRhetoric, and Digital History.

Patrick Henry's "Give Me Liberty, or Give Me Death..." (Mar. 23, 1775)
Abraham Lincoln's "Gettysburg Address" (Nov. 19, 1863)
Sojourner Truth's "Ain't I a Woman" (Dec. 1851)
Franklin Delano Roosevelt's "Pearl Harbor Address to the Nation" (Dec. 8, 1941)
John F. Kennedy's Inaugural Address (Jan. 20, 1961)
Martin Luther King Jr.'s "I Have a Dream" (Aug. 28, 1963)

Patrick Henry Speaking Against the Stamp Act, 1800s. American artist. The Granger Collection.

I Have a Dream

BEFORE READING

A Speech by Dr. Martin Luther King Jr.

DIRECTED READING

BUILD BACKGROUND

Literary Context On August 28, 1963, Martin Luther King Jr. delivered his speech **"I Have a Dream"** at the foot of the Lincoln Memorial to an interracial audience of more than two hundred thousand. King made skillful use of **rhetoric** (the art of speaking effectively), repeating words and phrases and using the rhythm of biblical language to describe his vision of a world in which people would be "not judged by the color of their skin, but the content of their character." Since that time, "I Have a Dream" has become one of the most widely recognized and quoted speeches ever delivered.

Reader's Context If you were given the power to change one law in the United States, what change would you make? Why? Whom might this change affect?

ANALYZE LITERATURE: Rhetorical Devices

The speech "I Have a Dream" contains many examples of **rhetorical devices**—techniques that a speaker or writer uses to achieve a particular effect on the audience. Rhetorical devices in this speech include the **repetition** of words, phrases, and passages, and **figurative language**—wording meant to be understood imaginatively, not literally. In particular, look for **metaphors,** in which one thing is spoken of as if it were something else (example: "a lonely island of poverty").

SET PURPOSE

During King's speech, reminders of the Civil War were inescapable. As King noted, the goals of equality and justice for which the nation had engaged in that bloody conflict had not been fulfilled. As you read, think about the historical setting of King's speech and note the references to America's past.

MEET THE AUTHOR

Martin Luther King Jr. (1929–1968), the son and grandson of Baptist ministers, was born in Atlanta, Georgia. A gifted student, King entered Morehouse College at the age of fifteen and decided to enter the ministry. At Crozer Theological Seminary, in Chester, Pennsylvania, King became influenced by two men who had stressed nonviolent resistance to injustice: American essayist Henry David Thoreau (1817–1862) and Indian leader, Mohandas Gandhi (1869–1947). After receiving his doctoral degree from Boston University in 1955, King founded the Southern Christian Leadership Conference and led protests throughout the South. In 1964, King was awarded the Nobel Peace Prize, and four years later, he was assassinated. In the decades following King's death, countless others, including his widow, Coretta Scott King (1927–2006), continued to speak out for a just society.

USE READING SKILLS

Text Organization
Understanding different methods of text organization can help you comprehend what you read. Look for an introduction that states the author's thesis, a body that provides details to support the argument, and a conclusion that reviews the points of the argument and makes a call for action or a final statement about the speaker's position. Use a chart like the one below to record the main ideas in each section of the speech.

Introduction:	Body	Conclusion
100 years ago Lincoln freed the slaves		

PREVIEW VOCABULARY

Preview the vocabulary words from this selection as they are used in the sentences below. Try to unlock the meanings of the underlined words using the context clues in the sentences.

1. The cook <u>seared</u> the steaks to brown the meat and seal in the juices.
2. Education and training usually provide <u>mobility</u> for job seekers.
3. After Jeremy's girlfriend had left him, he tried not to <u>wallow</u> in self-pity.
4. When an organization announces its <u>creed</u>, the public knows what the group's values and goals are.
5. The coach, who would not tolerate <u>discord</u> among the players, encouraged teammates to respect each other.

I Have a Dream

Martin Luther King Jr.

August 28, 1963

Lincoln Memorial, Washington, DC

I say to you today, my friends, so even though we face the difficulties of today and tomorrow, I still have a dream.

I'm happy to join with you today in what will go down in history as the greatest demonstration for freedom in the history of our nation.

Fivescore[1] years ago, a great American, in whose symbolic shadow we stand today, signed the Emancipation Proclamation.[2] This momentous decree came as a great beacon light of hope to millions of Negro slaves who had been seared in the flames of withering injustice.

1. **Fivescore.** One hundred; one score equals twenty
2. **Emancipation Proclamation.** Document signed by Abraham Lincoln in 1863 that legally set free all people held as slaves in the United States

sear (sir) *v.*, burn; destroy

American History Connection

Civil Rights Movement For years after the Supreme Court ruled, in 1954, that segregation in the schools is illegal, little changed in the United States. In 1963, when President John F. Kennedy asked Congress for a law requiring equal treatment regardless of race, southern representatives blocked the bill. Civil Rights leaders responded with a peaceful demonstration in Washington, DC. King's "I Have a Dream" speech, delivered at that demonstration, is considered the turning point for the Civil Rights movement. A year later, President Lyndon B. Johnson signed the first of several pieces of legislation giving African Americans equal rights. (Vice President Johnson had become president after Kennedy was assassinated in November 1963.)

It came as a joyous daybreak to end the long night of their captivity.

But one hundred years later, the Negro still is not free; one hundred years later, the life of the Negro is still sadly crippled by the manacles[3] of segregation[4] and the chains of discrimination; one hundred years later, the Negro lives on a lonely island of poverty in the midst of a vast ocean of material prosperity; one hundred years later, the Negro is still languished[5] in the corners of American society and finds himself in exile in his own land....

Nineteen sixty-three is not an end, but a beginning. And those who hope that the Negro needed to blow off steam and will now be content, will have a rude awakening if the nation returns to business as usual. There will be neither rest nor tranquility in America until the Negro is granted his citizenship rights. The whirlwinds of the revolt will continue to shake the foundations of our nation until the bright day of Justice emerges....

There are those who are asking the devotees of Civil Rights, "When will you be satisfied?" We can never be satisfied as long as the Negro is the victim of the unspeakable horrors of police brutality; we can never be satisfied as long as our bodies, heavy with the fatigue of travel, cannot gain lodging in the motels of the highways and the hotels of the cities; we cannot be satisfied as long as the Negro's basic mobility is from a smaller ghetto[6] to a larger one; we can never be satisfied as long as our children are stripped of their selfhood and robbed of their dignity by signs stating "For Whites Only"; we cannot be satisfied as long as the Negro in Mississippi cannot vote and a Negro in New York believes he has nothing for which to vote. No! No, we are not satisfied, and we will not be satisfied until "justice rolls down like waters and righteousness like a mighty stream."[7]

I am not unmindful that some of you have come here out of great trials and tribulations.[8] Some of you have come fresh from narrow

3. **manacles.** Handcuffs; shackles; restraints
4. **segregation.** Enforced separation of people according to group characteristics
5. **languished.** Suffering from lost vigor or strength
6. **ghetto.** Section of a city in which many members of a minority group live, either by choice or because of economic or social pressure
7. **"justice rolls down...stream."** Reference to the biblical passage Amos 5:24
8. **tribulations.** Misery or distress caused by oppression

mo • bil • i • ty (mō bi´ lə tē) *n.*, ability to move from place to place

Critical Viewing

How does this image illustrate the magnitude of Martin Luther King Jr.'s speech?

March on Washington at Lincoln Memorial, August 28, 1963.

Let freedom ring from Stone Mountain of Georgia; let freedom ring from Lookout Mountain of Tennessee; let freedom ring from every hill and molehill of Mississippi. From every mountainside, let freedom ring.

jail cells. Some of you have come from areas where your quest for freedom left you battered by the storms of persecution and staggered by the winds of police brutality. You have been the veterans of creative suffering. Continue to work with the faith that unearned suffering is redemptive.[9] Go back to Mississippi. Go back to Alabama. Go back to South Carolina. Go back to Georgia. Go back to Louisiana. Go back to the slums and ghettos of our northern cities, knowing that somehow the situation can and will be changed. Let us not wallow in the valley of despair.

I say to you today, my friends, so even though we face the difficulties of today and tomorrow, I still have a dream. It is a dream deeply rooted in the American meaning of its creed, "We hold these truths to be self-evident, that all men are created equal."[10] I have a dream that one day on the red hills of Georgia, sons of former slaves and the sons of former slave owners will be able to sit down together at the table of brotherhood. I have a dream that one day even the state of Mississippi, a state sweltering with the heat of injustice, sweltering with the heat of oppression, will be transformed into an oasis of freedom and justice. I have a dream that my four little children will one day live in a nation where they will not be judged by the color of their skin, but the content of their character.

I have a dream today!

I have a dream that one day down in Alabama—with its vicious racists, with its governor having his lips dripping with the words of interposition and nullification[11]—one day right there in Alabama, little black boys and black girls will be able to join hands with little white boys and white girls as sisters and brothers.

I have a dream today!

I have a dream that one day "every valley shall be exalted[12] and every hill and mountain shall be made low. The rough places will be made plain and the crooked places will be made straight, and the glory of the Lord shall be revealed, and all flesh shall see it together."[13]

This is our hope. This is the faith that I go back to the South with. With this faith we shall be able to transform the jangling discords of our nation into a beautiful symphony of brotherhood. With this faith we will be able to work together, to pray together, to struggle together, to go to jail together, to stand up for freedom together, knowing that we will be free one day.

And this will be the day. This will be the day when all of God's children will be able to sing with new meaning, "My country 'tis of thee, sweet land of liberty, of thee I sing. Land where my fathers died, land of the pilgrim's pride, from every mountainside, let freedom ring."[14] And if

9. **redemptive.** Freeing from the consequences of sin
10. **"We hold these truths to be self-evident, that all men are created equal."** First line of the second paragraph of the Declaration of Independence
11. **governor...interposition and nullification.** King is referring to the Alabama governor's refusal to obey a federal requirement to allow African-American children to attend public schools. *Interposition* is the disputed theory that a state can reject a federal order. *Nullification* refers to the refusal of a state to enforce any federal law.
12. **exalted.** Raised in status; elevated by praise
13. **"every valley shall be...see it together."** Reference to the biblical passage Isaiah 40:4–5
14. **"My country 'tis of thee...let freedom ring."** Lines from a well-known patriotic song

wal • low (wä´ lō) *v.*, allow oneself to accept a state of helplessness
creed (krēd) *n.*, set of fundamental beliefs
dis • cord (dis´ kôrd) *n.*, a combination of musical sounds that strikes the ear harshly

America is to be a great nation this must become true....

So let freedom ring from the prodigious hilltops of New Hampshire; let freedom ring from the mighty mountains of New York; let freedom ring from the heightening Alleghenies of Pennsylvania; let freedom ring from the snow-capped Rockies of Colorado; let freedom ring from the curvaceous slopes of California. But not only that. Let freedom ring from Stone Mountain of Georgia; let freedom ring from Lookout Mountain of Tennessee; let freedom ring from every hill and molehill of Mississippi. From every mountainside, let freedom ring.

And when this happens and when we allow freedom to ring, when we let it ring from every village and every hamlet, from every state and every city, we will be able to speed up that day when all God's children, black men and white men, Jews and gentiles, Protestants and Catholics, will be able to join hands and sing in the words of the old Negro spiritual: "Free at last. Free at last. Thank God Almighty, we are free at last." ❖

What is leadership and who today embodies your definition? What is heroism? How are leadership and heroism related? How are they unrelated?

REFER TO TEXT ▶▶▶▶	▶ REASON WITH TEXT	
1a. In encouraging his listeners to return to their homes, what did King predict would happen?	1b. Explain the purpose of King reiterating that the struggle was not over.	**Understand** **Find meaning**
2a. List phrases King repeats during his speech.	2b. Examine why King repeats "I have a dream."	**Apply** **Use information**
3a. Outline the specific injustices King refers to during his speech.	3b. Classify those in King's audience. To do so, consider which audiences he probably had in mind when he outlined these injustices.	**Analyze** **Take things apart**
4a. Recall who had gathered at the Lincoln Memorial to listen to King's speech.	4b. The success of a persuasive speech depends on its effect on its audience. Critique King's speech and identify features of the speech that may have been particularly effective.	**Evaluate** **Make judgments**
5a. Quote the beginning of the speech to show what King thought of the event.	5b. Prepare a list of questions you would ask if you were to interview someone who had listened to King's speech at the Lincoln Memorial.	**Create** **Bring ideas together**

ANALYZE LITERATURE: Rhetorical Devices

Identify examples of repetition within the speech. What group of words is repeated most often and how is it helpful? Point out metaphors in the speech. Try rewording the phrases in simpler, more literal language. How does the effect of the phrases change when you restate them in ordinary words? Identify examples of repetition within the speech. What group of words is repeated most often and how is it helpful? Point out metaphors in the speech. Try rewording the phrases in simpler, more literal language. How does the effect of the phrases change when you restate them in ordinary words? How does the organization of the text help to achieve the author's purpose?

Literature CONNECTION

King's work was an inspiration for many people. The following poem, **"Martin Luther King Jr.,"** is a tribute to the late Civil Rights leader. **Gwendolyn Brooks** (1917–2000) had published roughly seventy-five lyric, narrative, and dramatic poems by the age of sixteen. She wrote about life in the African-American community in South Chicago. In 1950 she became the first African-American recipient of the Pulitzer Prize. Themes in her later work included protests against poverty and racism.

Martin Luther King Jr.

A Poem by **Gwendolyn Brooks**

A man went forth with gifts.

He was a prose poem.
He was a tragic grace.
He was a warm music.

He tried to heal the vivid volcanoes.
His ashes are
  reading the world.

His Dream still wishes to anoint
  the barricades of faith and of control.

His word still burns the center of the sun,
  above the thousands and the
  hundred thousands.

The word was Justice. It was spoken.

So it shall be spoken.
So it shall be done. ❖

REFER TO TEXT ▶▶▶▶▶	REASON WITH TEXT	
1a. According to Brooks's poem, what did King do?	1b. What do you think Brooks means when she says that King "tried to heal the vivid volcanoes"?	**Analyze** **Take things apart**
2a. What metaphors does Brooks use to describe Martin Luther King Jr.?	2b. How does the author's description of King relate to what you know or imagine about him? Judge whether or not her descriptions are accurate and appropriate. Explain.	**Evaluate** **Make judgments**
3a. What does King leave behind after he is gone?	3b. What person in the news or in history would inspire a similar poem? Create a similar poem that exemplifies that person's attributes and contributions.	**Create** **Bring ideas together**

TEXT ◀TO▶ TEXT CONNECTION

- How do Martin Luther King Jr. and Gwendolyn Brooks describe or refer to racism and social injustice within these two selections?
- What descriptive words and phrases illustrate the social climate? How are these descriptions similar? In your opinion, which selection is most vivid? Why?

AFTER READING

EXTEND THE TEXT

Writing Options

Creative Writing What might it have been like to experience Martin Luther King Jr. deliver his "I Have a Dream" speech firsthand? Imagine that you were in the audience at the nation's capital listening to the speech. If possible, go online to HPOL (History and Politics Out Loud) and listen to the live recording. Write an imaginary **personal letter** to a friend or relative describing the experience. Highlight King's use of rhetorical devices as you explain the impact of the speech on the crowd and on you.

Expository Writing Write a five-paragraph **organization analysis** of the speech "I Have a Dream." Identify and describe the sections of the speech and the purpose of each section. Explain how the organization of the speech enhances its effectiveness and has a positive impact on the crowd. Suggest some rules a speechwriter should learn from "I Have a Dream."

Critical Literacy

Identify Allusions An allusion is a reference to a well-known person, event, object, or work from history or literature. In "I Have a Dream," Martin Luther King Jr. makes several allusions to famous historic documents and to speeches, biblical passages, songs, and other works. Reread the speech and identify the allusions you find. In small groups, discuss the images or emotions the allusions you identified might have called up in King's audience. How do the allusions help to support the important ideas in the speech?

Lifelong Learning

Deliver a Persuasive Speech Write a three- to five-minute speech that persuades an audience of your peers to participate in your vision for a better world. For example, you might try to persuade classmates to sponsor a child through a relief organization, send money to help refugees, feed homeless people, or help build a home for Habitat for Humanity. Organize your speech by clearly stating your position, providing your supporting evidence, and concluding with a convincing summary. Before delivering your speech, practice the techniques you can use to be persuasive, including varying your tone of voice and asking your listeners rhetorical questions.

Go to **www.mirrorsandwindows.com** for more.

READING ASSESSMENT

1. According to Dr. King, there will be "neither rest nor tranquility" in the United States until
   A. blacks and whites meet on the hills of Georgia.
   B. African Americans are given full rights as citizens.
   C. all American citizens support the Civil Rights movement.
   D. Dr. King's dream comes true.
   E. the nation returns to business as usual.

2. Why would Dr. King state, "Continue to work with the faith that unearned suffering is redemptive"?
   A. to encourage civil rights activists to continue fighting
   B. to assure his audience that their struggle would eventually be rewarded
   C. to assure his audience that, in the future, racists would suffer for the injustices they practiced today
   D. only A and B
   E. All of the above

3. As it is used on page 272, the term *wallow* most nearly means
   A. rejoice.
   B. bring yourself down.
   C. gather together.
   D. fight one another.
   E. hide.

4. Which of the following excerpts is not a metaphor?
   A. "the content of their character"
   B. "a beautiful symphony of brotherhood"
   C. "He was a warm music" (from Brooks's poem)
   D. "an oasis of freedom and justice"
   E. "a state sweltering with the heat of injustice"

5. In a movement for social justice, why must both the supporters and the opponents of the cause understand the goals of the struggle?

Glory and Hope

BEFORE READING **A Speech by Nelson Mandela**

DIRECTED READING

BUILD BACKGROUND

Historical Context Using the same nonviolent methods employed by Martin Luther King Jr., Nelson Mandela fought for the freedom of blacks in South Africa. Eventually, he came to believe that civil disobedience was the only way to obtain that freedom. After having been jailed for twenty-seven years, he was released and on May 10, 1994, he was installed as the first democratically elected president of South Africa. At his inauguration, he delivered the speech **"Glory and Hope,"** in which he asks all South Africans to work together to build a nation based on justice.

Reader's Context How do you feel after you have completed a long and difficult task? How do you behave after a victory? How do you address your competition?

ANALYZE LITERATURE: Persuasive Speech

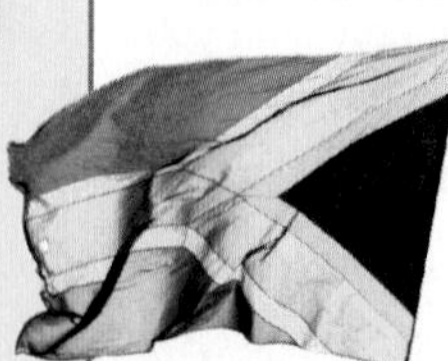

A **persuasive speech** is used to convince an audience to side with an opinion and adopt a plan. The speaker tries to persuade the audience to believe something, do something, or change their ways. A speaker will use facts and research to support and analyze his or her opinion and may also include emotionally charged words and imagery to sell his or her viewpoint to the audience.

SET PURPOSE

Remember that South African citizens, distinguished guests, and people around the world heard Mandela's speech. As you read, consider what persuasive elements Mandela used within his speech. What opinion or plan was he asking his listeners to adopt? Which of his opinions are substantiated with facts? What is the relevance of his statements in opposition to the past government of Africa?

MEET THE AUTHOR

Nelson Mandela (b. 1918) grew up in Transkei, South Africa. Expected to become a councillor for Thembuland's acting chief, like his father, Mandela became a lawyer instead. By the 1940s, Mandela had become a well-known leader in the fight against *apartheid.* Apartheid was South Africa's strict segregation and discrimination against black and mixed-race people. Mandela and many others became enemies of the government and were repeatedly harassed. In 1962, Mandela was convicted and jailed for illegally leaving South Africa and inciting a strike. He was later tried for sabotage and sentenced to life in prison. Pressured by an international boycott, the South African government released Mandela in 1990. Even after his many years in prison, Mandela remained a powerful symbol of the fight to defeat apartheid. In 1999, he retired from the presidency.

USE READING SKILLS

Paraphrase As you read, use footnotes and vocabulary words to paraphrase passages, or translate them into your own words. Pay special attention to passages that give insight into the country's history as well as Mandela's objectives. A Paraphrasing Chart like the one below might help you.

Original Passage	Paraphrased Version
...we saw it spurned... because it has become the universal base of pernicious ideology...and racial oppression.	...we were rejected by the world... because our country was filled with destructive beliefs...and discrimination.

PREVIEW VOCABULARY

Try to unlock the meanings of the underlined vocabulary words using the context clues in the sentences.

1. The <u>chasm</u> that exists in communication between adults and children is often referred to as the generation gap.
2. Because the U.S. Constitution guarantees the <u>inalienable</u> rights of life, liberty, and the pursuit of happiness, every citizen is guaranteed these rights.
3. The library declared a period of <u>amnesty</u> by allowing borrowers to return overdue books without paying late fees.

Glory and Hope

A Speech by **Nelson Mandela**

The moment to bridge the chasms that divide us has come.

Your majesties, your royal highnesses, distinguished guests, comrades and friends: Today, all of us do, by our presence here, and by our celebrations in other parts of our country and the world, confer[1] glory and hope to newborn liberty.

Out of the experience of an extraordinary human disaster that

1. **confer.** Give or award

WORLD HISTORY CONNECTION

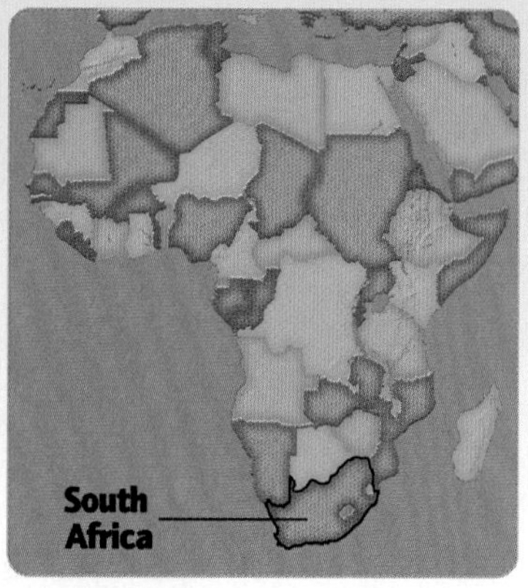

Apartheid *Apartheid,* the policy of racial segregation, was practiced officially by the South African government between 1948 and 1991. The policy established white minority rule—that is, the nation was governed by whites, even though blacks outnumbered them in population. Moreover, blacks faced severe restrictions in education, jobs, land ownership, and even mobility within the country. To push for an end to apartheid, nations around the world participated in international sanctions against South Africa, breaking off commercial, cultural, and diplomatic ties with that country. Even its athletes were not allowed to take part in the Olympics. Finally, South Africa agreed to eliminate apartheid, for two reasons: because South Africans strongly protested it, and because international sanctions were creating financial hardships and a sense of isolation. The transition to a democracy not based on race was completed with Mandela's election to the presidency.

lasted too long must be born a society of which all humanity will be proud.

Our daily deeds as ordinary South Africans must produce an actual South African reality that will reinforce humanity's belief in justice, strengthen its confidence in the nobility of the human soul and sustain all our hopes for a glorious life for all.

All this we owe both to ourselves and to the peoples of the world who are so well represented here today.

To my compatriots,[2] I have no hesitation in saying that each one of us is as intimately attached to the soil of this beautiful country as are the famous jacaranda trees of Pretoria[3] and the mimosa trees of the bushveld.[4]

Each time one of us touches the soil of this land, we feel a sense of personal renewal. The national mood changes as the seasons change.

We are moved by a sense of joy and exhilaration when the grass turns green and the flowers bloom.

That spiritual and physical oneness we all share with this common homeland explains the depth of the pain we all carried in our hearts as we saw our country tear itself apart in terrible conflict, and as we saw it spurned, outlawed and isolated by the peoples of the world, precisely because it has become the universal base of the pernicious[5] ideology[6] and practice of racism and racial oppression.

We, the people of South Africa, feel fulfilled that humanity has taken us back into its bosom, that we, who were outlaws not so long ago, have today been given the rare privilege to be host to the nations of the world on our own soil.

We thank all our distinguished international guests for having come to take possession with the people of our country of what is, after all, a common victory for justice, for peace, for human dignity.

We trust that you will continue to stand by us as we tackle the challenges of building peace, prosperity, nonsexism, nonracialism and democracy.

2. **compatriots.** People from one's own country; fellow citizens
3. **Pretoria.** Administrative capital of South Africa
4. **bushveld.** Grasslands in South Africa that are characterized by shrubbery and thorny vegetation
5. **pernicious.** Causing great harm; destructive
6. **ideology.** A set of beliefs shared by members of a group

spurn (spʉrn) *v.,* reject or refused with scorn

South African crowd cheering at the inauguration of Nelson Mandela.

We deeply appreciate the role that the masses of our people and their democratic, religious, women, youth, business, traditional and other leaders have played to bring about this conclusion. Not least among them is my Second Deputy President, the Honorable F. W. de Klerk.[7]

We would also like to pay tribute to our security forces, in all their ranks, for the distinguished role they have played in securing our first democratic elections and the transition to democracy, from bloodthirsty forces which still refuse to see the light.

The time for the healing of the wounds has come.

The moment to bridge the chasms that divide us has come.

The time to build is upon us.

We have, at last, achieved our political emancipation. We pledge ourselves to liberate all our people from the continuing bondage of poverty, deprivation, suffering, gender and other discrimination.

We succeeded to take our last steps to freedom in conditions of relative peace. We commit ourselves to the construction of a complete, just and lasting peace.

We have triumphed in the effort to implant hope in the breasts of the millions of our people. We enter into a covenant[8] that we shall build the society in which all South Africans, both black and white, will be able to walk tall, without any fear in their hearts, assured of their inalienable right to human dignity—a rainbow nation at peace with itself and the world.

As a token of its commitment to the renewal of our country, the new Interim Government of National Unity will, as a matter of urgency, address the issue of amnesty for various categories of our people who are currently serving terms of imprisonment.

We dedicate this day to all the heroes and heroines in this country and the rest of the world who sacrificed in many ways and surrendered their lives so that we could be free.

Their dreams have become reality. Freedom is their reward.

We are both humbled and elevated by the honor and privilege that you, the people of South Africa, have bestowed on us, as the first President of a united, democratic, nonracial and nonsexist South Africa, to lead our country out of the valley of darkness.

---

7. **F. W. de Klerk.** Member of the ruling white minority and president of South Africa before Mandela. His presence during Mandela's administration helped to unite the country.

8. **covenant.** Formal, binding agreement made by two or more people or groups

chasm (ka´ z'm) *n.,* marked division, separation, or difference
dep • ri • va • tion (de' prə vā´ shən) *n.,* state of having something taken away
in • a • li • en • able (i' nāl´ yə nə bəl *or* i' nā´ lē ə nə bəl) *adj.,* impossible to give up or take away
am • nes • ty (am´ nə stē) *n.,* pardon for past offenses

We understand it still that there is no easy road to freedom.

We know it well that none of us acting alone can achieve success.

We must therefore act together as a united people, for national reconciliation, for nation building, for the birth of a new world.

Let there be justice for all.

Let there be peace for all.

Let there be work, bread, water and salt for all.

Let each know that for each the body, the mind and the soul have been freed to fulfill themselves.

Never, never and never again shall it be that this beautiful land will again experience the oppression of one by another and suffer the indignity of being the skunk of the world.

The sun shall never set on so glorious a human achievement!

Let freedom reign. God bless Africa! ❖

"Forgive and forget" is a common phrase. What are the benefits of forgiving a wrong? Are there some things that should not be forgiven?

AFTER READING

REFER TO TEXT	REASON WITH TEXT	
1a. Quote what Mandela says to his compatriots about their connection to South Africa.	1b. What does Mandela mean when he says that South African compatriots experience a sense of "personal renewal" when they touch the soil?	Understand **Find meaning**
2a. Indicate what Mandela asks of the international community.	2b. Apply what you know about the international boycott to explain why Mandela makes this request.	Apply **Use information**
3a. Identify Mandela's audience.	3b. Consider South Africa's history and recognize why Mandela referred to the new South Africa as a "rainbow nation." Point out other symbolic reasons Mandela might have for using the term *rainbow.*	Analyze **Take things apart**
4a. List the goals of the new government.	4b. Select the goal you think will be hardest to fulfill. Why do you think this goal will be so hard to meet?	Evaluate **Make judgments**
5a. For which two groups, according to Mandela, does South Africa have the obligation to create a just society?	5b. Give examples of Mandela's opinions that are substantiated in the text and those that are unsubstantiated.	Create **Bring ideas together**

ANALYZE LITERATURE: Persuasive Speech

Most of Mandela's speech is written using formal language. Near the end, however, Mandela uses the phrase "skunk of the world" to describe South Africa's historical poison. What might have been the effect of this informal phrase on the listeners? How would this expression assist Mandela's persuasive speech?

EXTEND THE TEXT

Writing Options

Creative Writing Imagine you are a reporter covering the inauguration of Nelson Mandela for a worldwide news service. Your story will be read by many people who may be completely unaware of Mandela, South Africa, and the apartheid. Write a **news article** of two hundred words or less that informs your readers. Be sure to give your article an interesting headline.

Expository Writing Mandela and King shared a common vision, dedicated their lives to fundamental human rights, and inspired countless people worldwide to fight for their own rights. Locate and read a current speech on human rights. Then write a **compare-and-contrast essay** of about five paragraphs comparing these three speeches. Plan your essay by making a list of how these speeches are similar and how they are different. Use this list to develop your paragraphs and organize your essay. Provide evidence from each speech to support your statements. It may be helpful to examine the social and political atmosphere during the delivery of the speech and determine how these climates influenced each speaker.

Collaborative Learning

Create a Human Rights Presentation Working as part of a group, research a current human rights issue and develop an informative presentation for your class. Add interest to your presentation by including pictures, maps, charts, and illustrations. Find a phrase from the Mandela speech that could be the title of the report, such as "...there is no easy road to freedom" or "The moment to bridge the chasms that divide us has come."

Media Literacy

Analyze a Great Speech Write a five-paragraph essay analyzing a memorable speech. Use the Internet or library resources to find a speech that is reasonably well-known and that you find interesting. In your analysis, consider the time and place the speech was delivered, the speaker's use of rhetorical devices, the speech's impact or historical significance, and its personal appeal. Be sure to document your research. Include a reference location for the original speech.

Go to **www.mirrorsandwindows.com** for more.

READING ASSESSMENT

1. Who are the "bloodthirsty forces which still refuse to see the light"?
   A. international guests
   B. the security forces
   C. bordering nations
   D. people in prison
   E. the supporters of apartheid

2. As it is used in the selection, the term *amnesty* most closely means
   A. reprieve.
   B. reimbursement.
   C. acknowledgment.
   D. treatment.
   E. conviction.

3. Which of the following was one of Mandela's goals in giving the speech?
   A. to blame the whites of South Africa for years of trouble and mistreatment
   B. to assure the people of South Africa that the nation would have an easy time and that the most important task was to celebrate the creation of the new government
   C. to criticize the nations of the world for their boycott of South Africa
   D. to seek the people's help in moving beyond past injustices
   E. to show his enemies that he had finally prevailed

4. Which of the following is not an effect of repetition in the speech?
   A. It helps listeners follow what the speaker is saying.
   B. It suggests that some of the listeners had little education.
   C. It helps listeners to remember important points.
   D. It gives added emphasis to major ideas or themes within the speech.
   E. All of the above

5. The phrase "inalienable rights"appears in the U.S. Declaration of Independence, written in 1776. Why, do you think, has Mandela used the expression here? Under which circumstances might rights become "alienable"?

UNDERSTAND THE CONCEPT | APPLY THE SKILL

Use Figurative Language

To make their writing more colorful and memorable, authors use **figurative language**—words and phrases intended to be understood imaginatively and not literally.

EXAMPLE

> Each one of us is as intimately attached to the soil of this beautiful country as are the famous jacaranda trees of Pretoria and the mimosa trees of the bushveld.

Mandela did not expect his listeners to consider themselves as actually rooted to the earth. Rather, he assumed that they would, in their imaginations, view their emotional bonds to their country to be as strong as the roots of a jacaranda tree.

You can develop your vocabulary, especially in reading, by recognizing and interpreting figurative language. Here are some of the types of figurative language you'll encounter.

Simile: A **simile** is a comparison using the word *like* or *as* and usually suggests an imaginative similarity between two unlike things. Mandela's comparison of the South Africans' attachment to their country and the strongly rooted jacarandas is a simile.

Metaphor: Imaginative comparisons that do not use *like* or *as* are called **metaphors.**

EXAMPLE

> The moment to bridge the chasms that divide us has come.

Mandela was suggesting that the wide gaps separate us, but we can unite by means of an imaginary link (actually, hard work and dedication).

Some metaphors may appear as noun phrases—for example, "rainbow nation" could also be written as "the nation is a rainbow."

Knowing how to interpret similes and metaphors can help you understand the meanings of unfamiliar or odd-sounding phrases. The statement "The sun shall never set on so glorious a human achievement" may seem confusing, but in fact it's a metaphor, in which the setting sun suggests death as well as darkness.

And how does the sentence "We are moved by a sense of joy and exhilaration when the grass turns green and the flowers bloom" fit into the speech? The greening and blossoming of springtime is a frequently used metaphor for psychological or personal rebirth. Here, springtime renewal of the earth suggests the new South Africa.

An effective way to add figurative language to your writing is to start out using a Sensory Details Chart like the one below to write down sensory details that can be used to write a colorful description of your subject.

Sight	Sound	Touch	Taste	Smell
grass turns green; flowers blooming				

REVIEW TERMS

- **figurative language:** words and phrases intended to be understood imaginatively and not literally
- **simile:** a comparison using the word *like* or *as* that usually suggests an imaginative similarity between two unlike things
- **metaphor:** an imaginative comparison that does not use *like* or *as*

UNDERSTAND THE CONCEPT

APPLY THE SKILL

Identify Similes and Metaphors

Indicate whether each of the following statements is a simile or a metaphor. Then, in a sentence, explain the comparison.

EXAMPLE

Nicholas Gage's teacher had a Boston accent and salt-and-pepper hair.

Answer: "Salt-and-pepper hair" is a metaphor. The comparison means that her hair was both white and black.

EXAMPLE

The birds killed by the pesticides were scattered around the field like smashed apples that had fallen before harvest time.

Answer: "Like smashed apples that had fallen before harvest time" is a simile. It suggests that the dead birds had fallen from the sky, injured and neglected—much like apples falling to the ground.

1. This frigid and ominous sea is behaving like an enormous vampire slowly sucking the warmth, the life from my body. (from *Swimming to Antarctica*)
2. The state of Mississippi will be transformed into an oasis of freedom. (from "I Have a Dream")
3. I tore off the wrappers and began cramming the candy bars into my mouth, desperately, like someone in a contest. (from "Us and Them")
4. In most states, dangerous chemicals are as commonplace as old movies on late-night TV.
5. Just then, remembering my aisle mate's hand clutching mine while I clutched the hand of the high school student, I was struck by lightning all over again. (from "Aha Moment")
6. His ashes are reading the world. (from "Martin Luther King Jr.")
7. Mia said she was her brother Garrett's secret weapon.
8. As Albert Schweitzer has said, "Man can hardly even recognize the devils of his own creation." (from "The Obligation to Endure")
9. I felt as if I were swimming through a giant bowl of icy tapioca. (from *Swimming to Antarctica*)
10. Because of pollution, spring is as silent as a forest of dead birds.

Use Figurative Language Effectively

Read over the sentences below and rewrite the sentences using colorful and descriptive words while maintaining their original purpose.

1. The people gathered to watch Nelson Mandela speak.
2. Martin Luther King Jr., gave a speech during the March on Washington.
3. His neighbors were different.
4. The boy had trouble learning to play the musical instrument.
5. The water was cold.
6. The woman next to me looked afraid.
7. I was happy to have landed safely.
8. He worried about the environment.
9. It was unfair that I had to share with him.
10. The teacher told us to write a paper.

SPELLING PRACTICE

Commonly Misspelled Words

The following words from "Glory and Hope" present a challenge to spellers. Study the list and see if you can figure out a spelling rule to help you remember how to spell each word.

achievement	confidence	precisely
appreciate	democracy	privilege
beautiful	exhilaration	society
belief	friends	strengthen
building	government	succeeded
challenges	physical	
chasms	possession	

Understanding Informational Text

INFORMATIONAL TEXT

If you want to find out who won last night's football game, or how to bake a cake, where would you look? Whether you use websites on the Internet, a newspaper, or a cookbook to find out what you need to know, you are using informational texts. **Informational texts** are forms of nonfiction writing that aim to explain information.

TYPES OF INFORMATIONAL TEXT

Articles

An **article** is an informational piece of writing about a particular topic, issue, event, or series of events. Articles usually appear in newspapers, popular magazines, professional journals, or on websites. An **editorial** is a magazine or newspaper article that gives the opinions of the editors or publishers. A **review** is an article that is a critical evaluation of a work, such as a book, play, movie, or musical performance or recording.

How-to Writing

How-to writing does exactly that—tells you, in detail, how to do something. Some how-to documents use numbered lists to give instructions; others explain procedures with diagrams or in paragraph form. "Furor Scribendi" (page 297) is how-to writing that explains the procedure for writing for publication. It uses numbered steps followed by explanations.

> Writing for publication may be both the easiest and the hardest thing you'll ever do. Learning the rules—if they can be called rules—is the easy part. Following them, turning them into regular habits, is an ongoing struggle. Here are the rules....
> —from "Furor Scribendi" by Octavia Butler

Websites

A **website** is an electronic source of information that is available through the Internet. Anybody can create a website, and the information found there is very rarely monitored or censored. Websites that are created by credible organizations or experts usually contain trustworthy information that could serve as a valuable research source. However, many websites also contain misinformation. Make sure to evaluate the credibility of what you find by checking it against authorized sources.

Graphic Aids

Charts, graphs, maps, diagrams, spreadsheets, drawings, and illustrations are visual materials that present information in understandable ways. When you work with a graphic aid, look for elements such as its title, labels, column or row headings, a key aid or legend, a scale or unit of measurement, and its source.

CRITICAL READING

Just because an article is printed in a reputable newspaper or magazine doesn't mean all the information is reliable or presented objectively. When you read an article critically, you first look for the facts and then look beyond the facts at what the writer is trying to say. Ask yourself these questions:

- What is the writer's main idea? Is it clear?
- What evidence does the writer give to support his or her main idea? For example, does the article contain facts and statistics, quotations from experts, or statements from eyewitnesses?
- Does the evidence come from reliable sources?
- How much evidence is presented? Is it convincing?
- Is there another side of the story? What is a possible opposing viewpoint?

Recognize Bias

Something to look out for while you read critically is a writer's bias. **Bias** is a personal judgment about something, or a mental leaning in one direction or the other. You may think bias is a negative thing, but everyone is biased in some way.

Look for What's Missing

You should also direct a critical eye to the facts that a writer may have left out. Look for quotations from experts that seem to be out of context or seem inconsistent with other statements the experts have made.

Distinguish Fact from Opinion

A **fact** is a statement that could be proven by direct observation or supported by reliable resources. Every statement of fact is either true or false. An **opinion,** on the other hand, expresses an attitude or a desire, not a fact about the world. You can agree or disagree with an opinion, but not prove it to be true or false.

Opinions can take different forms: value statements, policy statements, or predictions. **Value statements** use judgment words, such as *good, bad, nice, cheap, ugly,* and *hopeless.* **Policy statements** express rules or ideas about how things should be. Words such as *should, should not, must,* or *must not* are often used. **Predictions** make statements about the future and are signaled by words such as *may, might,* and *could.* Because the future is largely unknowable, predictions are considered opinions.

Both facts and opinions require analysis on the part of the reader. When evaluating a fact, ask yourself whether it can be proven through observation or by checking a reliable, unbiased source. An opinion can also be evaluated by checking the facts that support it.

Use a Fact or Opinion Chart like the one below to record statements of fact and opinion and the proof or support that backs up the statement. An example has been provided for you, based on the newspaper article "Trapped New Orleans Pets Still Being Rescued" (page 287).

Fact or Opinion Chart	
Fact: Two thirds of households in the United States have pets. **Proof:** Survey by the American Veterinary Medical Association	**Opinion:** "They're shaggy-looking, they're suffering the same emotional loss that people are." **Support:** Quotation by a St. Bernard Parish councilman

Be Aware of Propaganda

The intentional use of false arguments to persuade others is called **propaganda.** Propaganda most often appears in nonfiction. There are many types of faulty arguments of which a discerning reader should be aware. Refer to the chart below.

Type of Argument	Definition	Example	Analysis
glittering generality	statement given to make something sound more appealing than it actually is an appeal to emotion and can be difficult to prove	This video game system is the best one ever made!	Nothing in this statement tells why the video game system is the best.
spin	a technique of creating misleading statements used to manipulate public perception of the news	The accident was a minor incident in that only twenty-five people were injured.	The fact is that twenty-five people were injured; this does not make the accident a minor incident.
stereotype	an overgeneralization about a group of people, one based on a lack of knowledge or experience	All teenagers want to do is find ways to get into trouble.	There is no proof for this statement, as some teenagers do get into trouble, but others do not.
circular reasoning	the error of trying to support an opinion by restating it in different words	That adventure film was exciting because it was full of action.	The "reason" given for the film being exciting is really just another way of saying it was exciting.
loaded words	words that stir up strong feelings, either positive or negative	The new coach is incredibly kind and a lot of fun.	This statement is not a reasonable evaluation of the coach's skills or abilities.
bandwagon appeal	statement that plays to a person's desire to be part of the crowd—to be like everyone else and do what everyone else is doing	Those who want to be cool wear Star jeans.	This statement suggests you aren't really part of the "in" crowd unless you wear this brand of jeans. It doesn't say anything about the quality of the clothing.

Trapped New Orleans Pets Still Being Rescued

BEFORE READING

A News Article by Laura Parker and Anita Manning

DIRECTED READING

BUILD BACKGROUND

Historical Context In late August 2005, Hurricane Katrina hit New Orleans, Louisiana, and other communities along the Gulf of Mexico. As a result of powerful winds and flooding, the region was nearly destroyed. Many homes were submerged in water up to the roof; the streets had turned into rivers; and residents were told to *evacuate,* or leave the area as quickly as possible. Not everyone could just pick up and go, however, especially families without cars or without friends or relatives in undamaged areas. Amid the chaos, one group of victims was especially at risk. As the *USA Today* news article **"Trapped New Orleans Pets Still Being Rescued"** describes, thousands of dogs, cats, and other pets had to be left behind by owners fleeing the flooded city.

Reader's Context Have you ever lost a pet or something very important to you? What were you able to do, or would have liked to try, to remedy the situation? What was the outcome?

ANALYZE LITERATURE: Thesis

A **thesis** is a main idea that is supported in a work of nonfiction. The best essays and articles support their main ideas effectively. Writers may use facts, statistics, examples, or other details to support their theses. As you read "Trapped New Orleans Pets Still Being Rescued," be aware of the writers' message.

SET PURPOSE

As you read, ask yourself whether the authors support their thesis effectively and whether you agree or disagree with their perspective. As you read, ask yourself whether the authors support their thesis effectively and whether you agree or disagree with their perspective. Distinguish the most important from the less important details that support the author's purpose. Use a Main Idea Chart like the one below to write down the main idea and the points the authors use to support their thesis. To help you decide, use a Main Idea Chart like the one below to write down the main idea and the points the authors use to support their thesis.

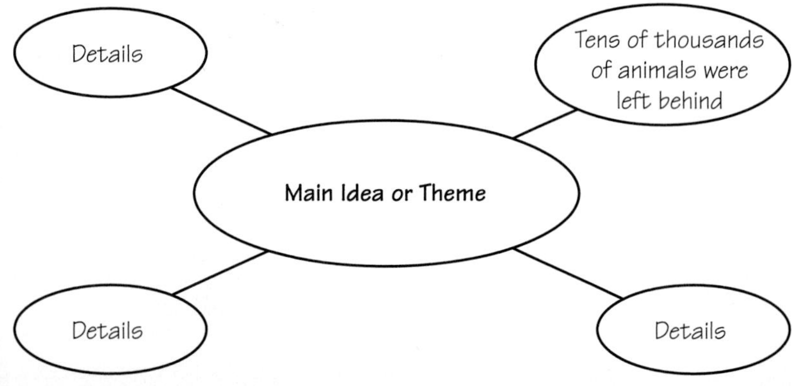

USE READING SKILLS

Identify the Author's Purpose As you read "Trapped New Orleans Pets Still Being Rescued," try to discern the purpose of the article. An **author's purpose** is his or her aim or goal. Being able to understand the intended purpose is an important reading skill. An author may write to inform, to express ideas or tell a story, to describe something, or to persuade. The purpose often corresponds to a specific mode, or type, of writing. Review the Modes of Writing Chart on page 205.

As you read, determine the form and mode this article utilizes. Once you have identified the authors' purpose, evaluate, or judge, how well the article achieved that purpose.

PREVIEW VOCABULARY

Using the selection vocabulary words listed, choose the best possible word to complete the sentences below. You may need to alter the word for it to work within the sentence.

emaciate
diaspora
euthanize

1. Karla didn't know how she felt about ______ unwanted pets; for her, the idea seemed barbaric.
2. The man rescued from the island was ______ and unable to walk by himself.
3. Many of the towns surrounding the evacuated areas felt the effects of the ______.

Trapped New Orleans Pets Still Being Rescued

In the first few days after Katrina hit, animals seemed to be everywhere in New Orleans.

A News Article by **Laura Parker** and **Anita Manning**

USA Today Oct. 6, 2005

NEW ORLEANS— For weeks after Hurricane Katrina struck, the only noise here in the empty neighborhoods of sodden houses was the barking of dogs. Then the barking stopped. Dogs are still here, but many are too hoarse and weak to make a sound. Many others have died. But hundreds of volunteer pet rescuers insist it's not too late.

"The animals we are finding now are emaciated and sick and lonely, but we are still finding them alive," says Wayne Pacelle, president of the Humane Society of the United States.

Across the New Orleans area, the largest pet rescue operation in U.S. history has been a backdrop to the human suffering and the questions of how and when communities can be rebuilt. But from the start, pets have been part of the story—from the tens of thousands of animals left behind by their owners because shelters and hotels wouldn't accept them, to the scattered residents who risked their lives

ema • ci • ate (i mā´ shē āt') *v.,* to waste away physically; to lose flesh so as to become very thin and refused to evacuate so they could stay with their pets.

Five weeks after the flooding began, animal rescue teams continue to fan across New Orleans and surrounding parishes[1] every day at dawn in a race against diminishing odds.[2] They gather up hundreds of desperate pets every day—more than 8,000 so far. And they leave behind fresh water and dry food for the dogs and cats roaming the streets that rescuers do not have enough staff to find or collect.

"We have left out tens of thousands of pounds of food and water to extend their lives," Pacelle says.

The Humane Society of the United States, the American Society for the Prevention of Cruelty to Animals (ASPCA) and other rescuers say they have no way of knowing precisely how many pets were left behind when the area was evacuated just before the storm hit Aug. 29. Surveys by the American Veterinary Medical Association indicate that two-thirds of U.S. households have at least one pet.

The number of rescued animals has so overwhelmed the temporary shelters set up by the Humane Society in nearby Gonzales, Louisiana, and Hattiesburg, Mississippi, that some pets are being flown to shelters in two dozen other states. The need for shelter space also has led the Humane Society to send more than 200 animals to temporary quarters on the grounds of two Louisiana prisons, where inmates are caring for rescued animals, Pacelle says.

It's become a small-scale version of the hurricane diaspora that displaced more than one million people in Louisiana, Mississippi and Texas. The rescue effort, which includes reconstruction of animal shelters in Louisiana and Mississippi, will cost more than $15 million, Pacelle says. The Humane Society has raised about $17 million in donations so far.

"They're shaggy-looking, they're suffering the same emotional loss that people are," Mark Madary, a St. Bernard Parish councilman, says of the homeless pets he has helped to round up in the communities south of New Orleans that were swamped by Katrina's 21-foot storm surge. "They're scared. They want food. They want somebody to take care of them.

"Most of the dogs got loose because the flood destroyed front doors," Madary says. "They're coming up to [rescuers'] vehicles. You'd think they'd go for water first, but they go for food. They're starving."

Madary spent the first week after Katrina helping to rescue more than 7,000 residents by boat. Last week, he helped other volunteers in St. Bernard collect 400 pets that were sent to the large shelter in Gonzales, set up in the horse stalls at the Lamar-Dixon Expo Center.

From there, many pets from St. Bernard were flown to shelters in California, where they will stay until they are reclaimed by their owners or adopted. Most rescued pets are kept at the large shelters in Mississippi and Louisiana for 48 hours before they are shipped out.

The animals are fed, watered, treated by veterinarians and petted. Every animal is photographed. The mug shots are posted on www.petfinder.com, a website set up by the consortium of animal groups overseeing the rescue, to help displaced pet owners locate their animals.

There are only about 50 reunions between owners and pets a day, Pacelle says.

Happy reunion

Francis Louis Jr., who lives north of downtown New Orleans, is one of the few local owners reunited with his dog. He left Roscoe, a

1. **parishes.** What counties are called in Louisiana
2. **diminishing odds.** The increasing likelihood of disappointment or failure

di • as • po • ra (dī as´ p(ə) rə) *n.,* the movement, migration, or scattering of a people away from an established or ancestral homeland

Critical Viewing

How well does this image portray the needs of pets that were left behind, and how well does the image support the article?

5-year-old shepherd mix, in his backyard with enough food and water to last a week. Then Louis fled.

"We figured we'd be back in a day or so, but then the worst came to pass," Louis says.

When he returned home three weeks later, he found a note saying that Roscoe had been rescued and taken to the shelter in Gonzales, about 50 miles northwest of New Orleans. When Louis was reunited with Roscoe, the dog was whining and crying. Louis was overjoyed.

Pets whose owners have been found are shipped home to them, wherever home is these days.

Most of the rescued animals have been cats or dogs, but the refugee population also includes exotic birds, snakes, fish, hamsters, rabbits, goats and a few pot-bellied pigs. At first, local animal shelters filled up so quickly that volunteers couldn't keep up with cleaning the cages. "We ship 300 out in a day and get 400 in," Pacelle says.

More than 1,000 veterinarians, animal control officers and activists from state chapters of the ASPCA are involved in rescue efforts here. About 80 animals were so aggressive or so close to death when they were rescued that they were euthanized, Pacelle says. But most rescued pets bounce back quickly once they receive food and water.

After Oct. 15, most of the pets that have not been claimed can be put up for adoption under applicable state laws, Pacelle says. However, he says that deadline could be extended because so many pets are still arriving at shelters. Animals that are not claimed will be kept at the shelters across the

eu • tha • nize (yü′ thə nīz′) *v.*, the practice of killing or permitting the death of hopelessly sick or injured animals in a relatively painless way for reasons of mercy

Hurricane Katrina aftermath.

country until they can be adopted, he says.

The images of residents on their roofs, stranded after staying behind with their pets, and packs of gaunt, frightened dogs roaming through debris after Katrina have led to changes in evacuation policies.

As Hurricane Rita approached last month, Texas suspended rules that barred pets from shelters there. The state's homeland security chief, Steve McCraw, urged evacuees to take their pets with them.

The Humane Society is urging Congress to pass a bill that would require state and local emergency management agencies that receive federal funding to allow pets to be included in evacuation plans.

Animals still in houses

In the first few days after Katrina hit, animals seemed to be everywhere in New Orleans.

"Where there was water, you would see packs of dogs swimming," says Cory Smith, 32, a former animal control officer in Washington, DC, who has been helping to rescue pets here.

About two weeks ago, when it became clear that the volunteers couldn't round up all the stray animals, they began to leave out food and water. Pacelle says it has made a noticeable difference in the health of the pets living on the streets.

The concern now is for animals still trapped in houses. More than 5,000 pet owners have called the Humane Society and asked volunteers to enter their houses and retrieve or feed animals. That has been a slow process: At many addresses, the volunteers have heard the sounds of pets trapped in nearby houses, so they've entered those homes as well.

Jane Garrison, a Humane Society staffer in Washington, DC, has divided the city into 35 sectors and dispatches search teams after dawn each day. The volunteers are armed with pet food, water, cages and a lot of ingenuity. Garrison says that when she entered one home, she went through the homeowners' old mail, found a cellphone bill and called the owner. "I said, 'I was just in your house, [and] forgive me for going through your mail, [but] I just rescued your two cats.' He was thrilled," she says.

Rescuers also have found heart-breaking scenes—dogs that drowned after being chained to porches, pets that starved to death in carriers. One dog, Garrison says, tried unsuccessfully to chew its way out of a carrier before it died.

National Guardsmen across the region have given rescuers lists of dogs they've seen while on patrol. A week ago, several Guardsmen pointed out a St. Bernard-mastiff still stuck on a roof, which Garrison helped rescue and reunite with its owner. "He was standing there, panting and drooling," Garrison says. "He drank three gallons of water before we left the house."

Even with that, the dog weighed 40 pounds—less than half what the veterinarians in Gonzales calculated he should have weighed.

On a recent mission, volunteer rescuers Smith and Drew Moore, of Corvallis, Oregon, searched door-to-door in the Mid City area, where the floodwaters had reached 12 inches or higher.

With spray paint, they scrawled coded messages on each searched house: "F/W SPCA 1 DOG," said one note, meaning they'd left food and water behind for a dog they had not seen. The work was tedious. It took a crowbar to get inside some houses, and Smith and Moore didn't find many pets. Some had been retrieved or set loose by neighbors.

At one house, Smith paused, sure she had heard the bark of a small dog. She disappeared inside, followed by Moore. But they found nothing, despite the "Beware of Dog" sign on the fence. "It was a little dog," she said as the pair moved down the street. "It's so scary. That bark was maybe his last."

By afternoon, they had retrieved three cats and a small collie. The collie ran away when they first approached him, but followed their truck to the next address. When Smith and Moore emerged from another house, the collie was waiting for them, ready to be rescued. ❖

Would you expect someone to risk his or her own safety to assist a family pet? How much responsibility should people have for their pets in the aftermath of a disaster?

REFER TO TEXT	REASON WITH TEXT	
1a. List the actions volunteers took when scouring the streets for pets.	1b. Summarize why it was difficult for volunteers to rescue abandoned and stray animals.	**Understand** **Find meaning**
2a. According to the article, how much money has been donated to assist in the recovery of New Orleans's pets?	2b. Generalize about the relationship between pets and people based on financial support and volunteer time donated to the rescue effort.	**Apply** **Use information**
3a. Identify the people mentioned in the article who attempted to rescue the animals of New Orleans.	3b. Analyze the Katrina emergency and explain why the rescue of animals was left to volunteer or nonprofit organizations rather than being handled by state or national emergency officials.	**Analyze** **Take things apart**
4a. Why were many pets left behind?	4b. Argue for or against people being allowed to bring pets to emergency shelters.	**Evaluate** **Make judgments**
5a. Recall where unclaimed pets were ending up.	5b. Imagine you were in charge of getting abandoned pets adopted. Design a plan for finding suitable new homes for the unclaimed animals.	**Create** **Bring ideas together**

ANALYZE LITERATURE: Thesis

An essay is a short nonfiction work that presents a single main idea, or thesis, about a particular topic. Summarize the main ideas of this essay and determine the thesis. Then write a short critique of the essay, in which you evaluate how effectively the authors have supported their thesis.

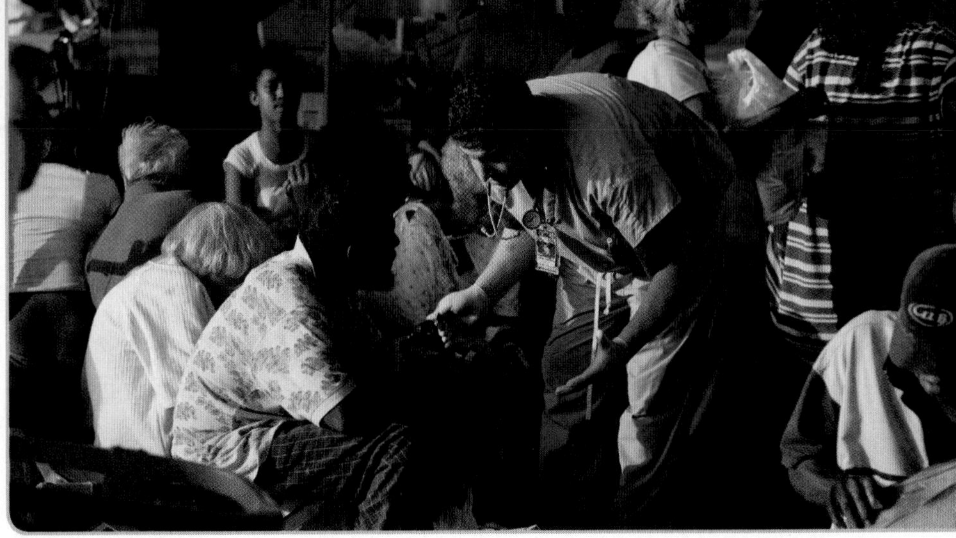

VERGHESE

Literature
CONNECTION

"Close Encounter of the Human Kind," which appeared in the *New York Times Magazine* on September 18, 2005, is a personal essay rather than a news article. The author, **Dr. Abraham Verghese,** describes his experiences giving medical treatment to Hurricane Katrina refugees. As you read, consider how Dr. Verghese responds to the medical and emotional needs of patients uprooted from their homes by the pitiless storm. How might the essay differ from an objective news account of the same event?

Close Encounter of the Human Kind

A Personal Essay by Abraham Verghese, M.D.
Published: September 18, 2005

With the first busloads of Katrina refugees about to arrive in San Antonio, the call went out for physician volunteers, and I signed up for the 2 AM to 8 AM shift. On the way, riding down dark, deserted streets, I thought of driving in for night shifts in the I.C.U.[1] as an intern many years ago, and how I would try to steel myself, as if putting on armor.

Within a massive structure at Kelly U.S.A. (formerly Kelly Air Force Base), a brightly lighted processing area led to office cubicles, where after registering, new arrivals with medical needs came to see us. My first patient sat before me, haggard, pointing to what ailed her, as if speech no longer served her. I peeled her shoes from swollen feet, trying not to remove skin in the process. Cuts from submerged objects and immersion in standing water had caused the swelling, as well as infection of both feet. An antibiotic, a pair of slip-ons from the roomful of donated clothing and a night with her feet elevated—that would help.

1. **I.C.U.** Abbreviation for intensive care unit, where the most seriously ill or injured patients are treated

The ailments common among the refugees included diarrhea, bronchitis, sore throat and voices hoarse or lost. And stress beyond belief. People didn't have their medications, and blood sugars and blood pressures were out of control.

I prayed, as I wrote prescriptions, that their memories of particular pills were accurate. For a man on methadone maintenance who was now cramping and sweating, I prescribed codeine to hold him. Another man, clutching a gym bag as if I might snatch it from him, admitted when I gently probed that he was hearing voices again. We sat together looking through the Physicians' Desk Reference. "That's it," he said, recognizing the pill he hadn't taken since the storm hit.

Hesitantly, I asked each patient, "Where did you spend the last five days?" I wanted to reconcile the person in front of me with the terrible locales on television.[2] But as the night wore on, I understood that they *needed* me to ask; to not ask was to not honor their ordeal. Hard men wiped at their eyes and became animated in the telling. The first woman, the one who seemed mute from stress, began a recitation in a courtroom voice, as if preparing for future testimony.

It reminded me of my previous work in field clinics in India and Ethiopia, where, with so few medical resources at hand, the careful listening, the thorough exam, the laying of hands *was* the therapy. And I felt the same helplessness, knowing that the illness here was inextricably[3] linked to the bigger problem of homelessness, disenfranchisement[4] and despair.

Near the end of my shift, a new group of patients arrived. A man in his 70's with gray hair and beard came in looking fit and vigorous. One eye was milky white and sightless, but the glint in his good eye was enough for two. His worldly belongings were in a garbage bag, but his manner was dignified.

He was out of medicine, and his blood sugar and blood pressure were high. He couldn't pay for his medication, so his doctor always gave him samples: "Whatever he have. Whatever he have." He had kept his shoes on for five days, he said, removing the battered, pickled but elegant pair, a cross between bowling shoes and dancing shoes. His toes were carved ebony,[5] the tendons on the back like cables, the joints gnarled but sturdy. All night I had seen many feet; in his bare feet I read resilience.

He told me that for two nights after the floods, he had perched on a ledge so narrow that his legs dangled in the water. At one point, he said, he saw Air Force One[6] fly over, and his hopes soared. "I waited, I waited," he said, but no

2. **I wanted to reconcile...television.** The author is referring to the round-the-clock TV coverage of the hurricane victims who were housed in large arenas in New Orleans, with inadequate medical care, sanitary conditions, and food and water.

3. **inextricably.** Permanently; without expectation of change

4. **disenfranchisement.** Removal of a legal right, especially the right to vote

5. **His toes were carved ebony.** This is a metaphor, or imaginative comparison.

6. **Air Force One.** Airplane in which the president of the United States flies; George W. Bush flew over but did not stop in New Orleans, on the trip from his home in Crawford, Texas, to Washington, DC

help came. Finally a boat got him to a packed bridge. There, again, he waited. He shook his head in disbelief, smiling though. "Doc, they treat refugees in other countries better than they treated us."

"I'm so sorry," I said. "So sorry."

He looked at me long and hard, cocking his head as if weighing my words, which sounded so weak, so inadequate. He rose, holding out his hand, his posture firm as he shouldered his garbage bag. "Thank you, Doc. I needed to hear that. All they got to say is sorry. All they got to say is sorry."[7]

I was still troubled by him when I left, even though he seemed the hardiest of all. This encounter between two Americans, between doctor and patient, had been carried to all the fullness that was permitted, and yet it was incomplete, as if he had, as a result of this experience, set in place some new barriers that neither I nor anyone else would ever cross.

Driving home, I remembered my own metaphor of strapping on armor for the night shift. The years have shown that there is no armor. There never was. The willingness to be wounded may be all we have to offer. ❖

---

7. **"All they got to say is sorry."** The patient wished that the government had apologized for not helping the storm victims sooner.

REFER TO TEXT ▶▶▶▶	▶ REASON WITH TEXT	
1a. As an intern, how did the author prepare himself for night shifts at the intensive care unit?	1b. Why might a doctor feel the need to prepare himself in this way? What does the imagery imply about his experiences and the patients he encountered?	**Understand** **Find meaning**
2a. According to the author, what did each refugee need him to do?	2b. Do you agree with the author that "the illness here was inextricably linked to the bigger problem of hopelessness, disenfranchisement and despair"?	**Analyze** **Take things apart**
3a. Which patient troubled Dr. Verghese the most?	3b. Evaluate the text organization of the essay. Infer how the conclusion of the essay ties back to the beginning. Which sentence best expresses the author's message or purpose?	**Evaluate** **Make judgments**

- Describe the **tone**—the writer's attitude toward the subject—of "Close Encounter of the Human Kind" and that of "Trapped New Orleans Pets Still Being Rescued." Contrast the tones of the two pieces and analyze how the difference in purpose might affect the difference in tone.
- Recall who or what the authors of the articles focus on in their opening paragraphs.
- Which of the works is a more personal account of the events narrated?

AFTER READING

EXTEND THE TEXT

Writing Options

Creative Writing Newspapers usually invite their readers to submit letters expressing personal opinions. The letters, which may be printed in a newspaper in a section titled "Letters to the Editor," provide a wide variety of opinions. Write an imaginary **letter to the editor** paying tribute to those who helped with the animal rescues in New Orleans. Use examples from "Trapped New Orleans Pets Still Being Rescued" to inform people of the efforts and risks of the rescuers.

Descriptive Writing There have been a number of hurricane-related disasters that have devastated the United States. Write a brief five-paragraph **comparative essay** that compares a different disaster with what happened in New Orleans. Plan your essay by listing the facts, and use these facts to develop good paragraphs.

Lifelong Learning

Research Volunteer Organizations Working as part of a group, identify two local volunteer organizations that provide charity, assistance, or community service. You might find groups that provide meals for the homeless, support environmental protection, provide shelter for animals, or mentor foster-care children. Research the organizations and discuss how you might become involved. Call their offices to obtain information or look up the organizations on the Internet. In a group presentation to your class, discuss two of the organizations and explain how people could become involved.

Media Literacy

Investigate Weather Forecasting Research a form of severe weather (such as hurricanes and tornadoes). Analyze how meteorologists predict or forecast these events as well as how these events are covered by the media. Look on the Internet for weather-related websites that provide maps, charts, and documents that explain visually the process of weather forecasting. Create either a poster-board display of your pictures accompanied by explanatory paragraphs or a visual illustration and present the process to your classmates.

Go to **www.mirrorsandwindows.com** for more.

READING ASSESSMENT

1. Because the purpose of this news article is primarily to inform the reader, the authors have
   A. not included any upsetting incidents.
   B. provided quotations from animal rescuers.
   C. narrated their account in chronological, or time, order.
   D. avoided expressing their feelings.
   E. attempted to persuade their readers to think a certain way.

2. The main idea of "Close Encounter of the Human Kind" may best be summarized by which statement?
   A. Medical treatment for the poor in the United States is often no better than in Third World countries.
   B. Until the American government and the American people treat all members of society with equality and respect, even the best medical treatment won't help much.
   C. People need to apologize to others when the government has failed them.
   D. Patients suffering from the effects of a natural disaster are most in need of medical attention.
   E. Knowing important medical information is crucial in the event of a natural disaster.

3. The majority of rescue workers described in "Trapped New Orleans Pets Still Being Rescued" would agree with which statement?
   A. Pets are important members of society.
   B. The care and safety of animals are important to plan in the event of a disaster.
   C. It is necessary to invade private property if an animal is in danger.
   D. Further planning is needed to prevent an incident similar to New Orleans from recurring.
   E. All of the above

4. As used on page 288 of "Trapped New Orleans Pets Still Being Rescued," the term *diaspora* most closely means
   A. outpouring of emotions.
   B. effects.
   C. damage of homes.
   D. warnings.
   E. various relocations of people.

5. What do you think is the effect of full-time television coverage of the refugees sheltered in arenas or other large public places? If you were the producer of the coverage, what might be your main concerns? What would you want to communicate to viewers? Why?

Furor Scribendi

A How-to Writing by Octavia Butler

How to Write a Letter

A How-to Writing by Garrison Keillor

COMPARING LITERATURE

BEFORE READING

BUILD BACKGROUND

Literary Context The how-to essay **"Furor Scribendi"** (Latin for "A Rage for Writing") appears in Octavia Butler's collection *Bloodchild and Other Stories* (1995). This story collection has received many honors, including being named as the *New York Times* Notable Book of the Year. The essay advises readers on the art of becoming a good writer.

Like Butler, Garrison Keillor refuses to believe that writing is something only a few people can or should do. In his essay **"How to Write a Letter,"** Keillor tells why it's important to keep letter writing alive as an art and as a skill. This selection is an excerpt from Keillor's book *We Are Still Married: Stories and Letters,* published in 1989.

Reader's Context Do you write for pleasure? How often do you write to someone via letter or e-mail? How might writing be a valued hobby to a person?

USE READING SKILLS

Analyze Authors' Approach Being able to recognize how an author approaches his or her subject and audience will assist you in understanding the selection. An author may be informative, humorous, persuasive, or forceful when presenting his or her work. As you read, determine how the authors of these selections approach their subjects and how they present them to readers. Consider how the choice of approach affects the selection.

COMPARE LITERATURE: How-to Writing

A **how-to writing** usually provides the steps to a process. Writers may use explanations, examples, and other details to make the process clearer. "Furor Scribendi" and "How to Write a Letter" both give how-to advice about writing. As you read the essays, think about what each author wants you to know, think, feel, or do. Compare Butler's purpose in "Furor Scribendi" to Keillor's purpose in "How to Write a Letter."

MEET THE AUTHORS

BUTLER

Octavia Butler (1947–2006) is best known as a science fiction writer. Starting in the late 1970s, she wrote a number of novels that were well-received by the public. Her best-known book, *Kindred,* was published in 1988. Butler has received numerous awards, including the Hugo Award from the World Science Fiction Society and the Nebula Award from the Science Fiction Writers of America. In 1995, Butler was awarded a "genius grant" from the MacArthur Foundation. In a note of self-mockery, Butler said that "nobody made me take an IQ test before I got [my grant]. I knew I'm no genius."

Garrison Keillor (b. 1942) is the host of the award-winning public radio show *A Prairie Home Companion,* a variety show loosely based on radio broadcasts of the pre-television era. The best-known portion of the show is "The News from Lake Wobegon," in which Keillor describes with humor and warmth the lives of average people in a fictitious Minnesota town. Keillor has been a contributor to *The New Yorker* and other magazines, has written several books, and has edited collections of poetry.

KEILLOR

Girl Writing, 1908. Pierre Bonnard.

Furor Scribendi

A How-to Writing by

Octavia Butler

You want to be the writer who keeps readers up late at night, not the one who drives them off to watch television.

Writing for publication may be both the easiest and the hardest thing you'll ever do. Learning the rules—if they can be called rules—is the easy part. Following them, turning them into regular habits, is an ongoing struggle. Here are the rules:

1. Read. Read about the art, the craft, and the business of writing. Read the kind of work you'd like to write. Read good literature and bad, fiction and fact. Read every day and learn from what you read. If you commute to work or if you spend part of your day doing relatively mindless work, listen to book tapes. If your library doesn't have a good supply of complete books on audio tape, companies like Recorded Books, Books on Tape, Brilliance Corporation, and the Literate Ear will rent or sell you a wide selection of such books for your pleasure and continuing education. These provide a painless way to ponder use of language, the sounds of words, conflict, characterization, plotting, and the multitudes of ideas you can find in history, biography, medicine, the sciences, etc.

2. Take classes and go to writers' workshops. Writing is communication. You need other people to let you know whether you're communicating what you think you are and whether you're doing it in ways that are not only accessible and entertaining, but as compelling as you can make them. In other words, you need to know that you're telling a good story. You want to be the writer who keeps readers up late at night, not the one who drives them off to watch television. Workshops and classes are rented readers—rented audiences—for your work. Learn from the comments, questions, and suggestions of both the teacher and the class. These relative strangers are more likely to tell you the truth about your work than are your friends and family who may not want to hurt or offend you. One tiresome truth they might tell you, for instance, is that you need to take a grammar class. If they say this, listen. Take the class. Vocabulary and grammar are your primary tools. They're most effectively used, even most effectively abused, by people who understand them. No computer program, no friend or employee can take the place of a sound knowledge of your tools.

3. Write. Write every day. Write whether you feel like writing or not. Choose a time of day. Perhaps you can get up an hour earlier, stay up an hour later, give up an hour of recreation, or even give up your lunch hour. If you can't think of anything in your chosen genre, keep a journal. You should be keeping one anyway. Journal writing helps you to be more observant

of your world, and a journal is a good place to store story ideas for later projects.

4. Revise your writing until it's as good as you can make it. All the reading, the writing, and the classes should help you do this. Check your writing, your research (never neglect your research), and the physical appearance of your manuscript. Let nothing substandard slip through. If you notice something that needs fixing, fix it, no excuses. There will be plenty that's wrong that you won't catch. Don't make the mistake of ignoring flaws that are obvious to you. The moment you find yourself saying, "This doesn't matter. It's good enough." Stop. Go back. Fix the flaw. Make a habit of doing your best.

5. Submit your work for publication. First research the markets that interest you. Seek out and study the books or magazines of publishers to whom you want to sell. Then submit your work. If the idea of doing this scares you, fine. Go ahead and be afraid. But send your work out anyway. If it's rejected, send it out again, and again. Rejections are painful, but inevitable. They're every writer's rite of passage. Don't give up on a piece of work that you can't sell. You may be able to sell it later to new publications or to new editors of old publications. At worst, you should be able to learn from your rejected work. You may even be able to use all or part of it in a new work. One way or another, writers can use, or at least learn from, everything.

6. Here are some potential impediments for you to forget about:

First forget *inspiration*. Habit is more dependable. Habit will sustain you whether you're inspired or not. Habit will help you finish and polish your stories. Inspiration won't. Habit is persistence in practice.

Forget *talent*. If you have it, fine. Use it. If you don't have it, it doesn't matter. As habit is more dependable than inspiration, continued learning is more dependable than talent. Never let pride or laziness prevent you from learning, improving your work, changing its direction when necessary. Persistence is essential to any writer—the persistence to finish your work, to keep writing in spite of rejection, to keep reading, studying, submitting work for sale. But stubbornness, the refusal to change unproductive behavior or to revise unsalable work can be lethal to your writing hopes.

Finally, don't worry about imagination. You have all the imagination you need, and all the reading, journal writing, and learning you will be doing will stimulate it. Play with your ideas. Have fun with them. Don't worry about being silly or outrageous or wrong. So much of writing is fun. It's first letting your interests and your imagination take you anywhere at all. Once you're able to do that, you'll have more ideas than you can use. Then the real work of fashioning them into a story begins. Stay with it.

Persist. ❖

in • e • vit • a • ble (in ev´ ə tə b'l) *adj.*, unavoidable
im • ped • i • ment (im ped´ ə mənt) *n.*, obstacle; roadblock; interference
le • thal (lē´ th'l) *adj.*, deadly

"Learning the rules—if they can be called rules—is the easy part. Following them, turning them into regular habits, is an ongoing struggle." Why is it sometimes difficult to be disciplined to follow rules that we know will benefit us? How can we turn following rules into good habits?

REFER TO TEXT	REASON WITH TEXT	
1a. List a writer's two "primary tools."	1b. Explain why it is important to use all of your writer's tools.	**Understand** Find meaning
2a. State what, according to Butler, is essential to any writer.	2b. Apply Butler's advice to another part of your life, such as a relationship, an activity, or schoolwork. How might her advice assist you?	**Apply** Use information
3a. Identify who might have difficulty being honest and open when responding to your writing.	3b. How would questions and criticism help during the writing process? Infer why strangers might offer better criticism than friends and family.	**Analyze** Take things apart
4a. Recall what Butler claims is more reliable than inspiration and talent.	4b. Critique the idea that writers should not rely on inspiration and talent. Explain your response.	**Evaluate** Make judgments
5a. Identify the intended audience of the selection.	5b. Modify Butler's essay so that it can serve as a guide for your classmates about the art of writing for classes. Choose advice that you can use from the selection, and identify advice you should alter or add.	**Create** Bring ideas together

How to Write a Letter

A How-to Writing by **Garrison Keillor**

We need to write, otherwise nobody will know who we are.

We shy persons need to write a letter now and then, or else we'll dry up and blow away. It's true. And I speak as one who loves to reach for the phone, dial the number, and say, "Big Bopper here—what's shakin', babes?" The telephone is to shyness what Hawaii is to February, it's a way out of the woods, *and yet:* a letter is better.

Such a sweet gift—a piece of handmade writing in an envelope that is not a bill, sitting in our friend's path when she trudges home from a long day spent among wahoos and savages, a day our words will help repair. They don't need to be immortal, just sincere. She can read them twice and again tomorrow: *You're*

someone I care about, Corinne, and think of often and every time I do you make me smile.

We need to write, otherwise nobody will know who we are. They will have only a vague impression of us as A Nice Person, because, frankly, we don't shine at conversation, we lack the confidence to thrust our faces forward and say, "Hi, I'm Heather Hooten: let me tell you about my week." Mostly we say "Uh-huh" and "Oh, really." People smile and look over our shoulder, looking for someone else to meet.

So a shy person sits down and writes a letter. To be known by another person—to meet and talk freely on the page—to be close despite distance. To escape from anonymity and be our own sweet selves and express the music of our souls.

Same thing that moves a giant rock star to sing his heart out in front of 123,000 people moves us to take ballpoint in hand and write a few lines to our dear Aunt Eleanor. *We want to be known.* We want her to know that we have fallen in love, that we quit our job, that we're moving to New York, and we want to say a few things that might not get said in casual conversation: *Thank you for what you've meant to me, I am very happy right now.*

The first step in writing letters is to get over the guilt of *not* writing. You don't "owe" anybody a letter. Letters are a gift. The burning shame you feel when you see unanswered mail makes it harder to pick up a pen and makes for a cheerless letter when you finally do. *I feel bad about not writing, but I've been so busy,* etc. Skip this. Few letters are obligatory, and they are *Thanks for the wonderful gift* and *I am terribly sorry to hear about George's death* and *Yes, you're welcome to stay with us next month,* and not many more than that. Write those promptly if you want to keep your friends. Don't worry about the others, except love letters, of course. When your true love writes, *Dear Light of My Life,*

an • o • nym • i • ty (an' ə nim´ ə tē) *n.,* quality or state of not being known
ob • lig • a • to • ry (ō blig´ ə tō rē) *adj.,* required

Joy of My Heart, O Lovely Pulsating Core of My Sensate[1] *Life,* some response is called for.

Some of the best letters are tossed off in a burst of inspiration, so keep your writing stuff in one place where you can sit down for a few minutes and *(Dear Roy, I am in the middle of a book entitled* We Are Still Married *but thought I'd drop you a line. Hi to your sweetie, too)* dash off a note to a pal. Envelopes, stamps, address book, everything in a drawer so you can write fast when the pen is hot.

A blank white eight-by-eleven sheet can look as big as Montana if the pen's not so hot—try a smaller page and write boldly. Or use a note card with a piece of fine art on the front; if your letter ain't good, at least they get the Matisse.[2] Get a pen that makes a sensuous line, get a comfortable typewriter, a friendly word processor—whichever feels easy to the hand.

Tell us what you're doing and tell it like you were talking to us.

Sit for a few minutes with the blank sheet in front of you, and meditate on the person you will write to, let your friend come to mind until you can almost see her or him in the room with you. Remember the last time you saw each other and how your friend looked and what you said and what perhaps was unsaid between you, and when your friend becomes real to you, start to write.

Write the salutation—*Dear You*—and take a deep breath and plunge in. A simple declarative sentence[3] will do, followed by another and another and another. Tell us what you're doing and tell it like you were talking to us. Don't think about grammar, don't think about lit'ry style; don't try to write dramatically, just give us your news. Where did you go, who did you see, what did they say, what do you think?

If you don't know where to begin, start with the present moment: *I'm sitting at the kitchen table on a rainy Saturday morning. Everyone is gone and the house is quiet.* Let your simple description of the present moment lead to something else, let the letter drift gently along.

The toughest letter to crank out is one that is meant to impress, as we all know from writing job applications; if it's hard work to slip off a letter to a friend, maybe you're trying too hard to be terrific. A letter is only a report to someone who already likes you for reasons other than your brilliance. Take it easy.

Don't worry about form. It's not a term paper. When you come to the end of one episode, just start a new paragraph. You can go from a few lines about the sad state of pro football to the fight with your mother to your fond memories of Mexico to your cat's urinary-tract infection to a few thoughts on personal indebtedness and on to the kitchen sink and what's in it. The more you write, the easier it gets, and when you have a True True Friend to write to, a *compadre,*[4] a soul sibling, then it's like driving a car down a country road, you just get behind the keyboard and press on the gas.

Don't tear up the page and start over when you write a bad line—try to write your way out of it. Make mistakes and plunge on. Let the letter cook along and let yourself be bold. Outrage, confusion, love—whatever is in your mind, let it find a way to the page.

Writing is a means of discovery, always, and when you come to the end and write *Yours ever* or *Hugs and kisses,* you'll know something you didn't when you wrote *Dear Pal.*

---

1. ***Sensate.*** Appealing to the senses
2. **Matisse.** (1869–1954) Henri Matisse, French painter
3. **declarative sentence.** Sentence that makes a direct statement and that is punctuated with a period
4. ***compadre*** **(kəm pä′ drā *or* kəm pä′ drē).** [Spanish] Close friend or pal

Probably your friend will put your letter away and it'll be read again a few years from now—and it will improve with age. And forty years from now, your friend's grandkids will dig it out of the attic and read it, a sweet and precious relic *of the ancient eighties* that gives them a sudden clear glimpse of you and her and the world we old-timers knew. You will then have created an object of art. Your simple lines about where you went, who you saw, what they said, will speak to those children and they will feel in their hearts the humanity of our times.

You can't pick up a phone and call the future and tell them about our times. You have to pick up a piece of paper. ❖

After reading this selection, has Keillor persuaded you to write letters to friends and family members? How is writing an e-mail similar and different?

REFER TO TEXT ▶▶▶▶	▶ REASON WITH TEXT	
1a. Recall what type of person Keillor says needs to write a letter. What does such a person gain by writing a letter?	1b. Keillor says, "The telephone is to shyness what Hawaii is to February…." In your own words, explain this comparison.	**Understand** **Find meaning**
2a. Identify the first step in writing letters.	2b. In what way does guilt prevent a person from getting started on a letter? Apply this idea to other situations: How might guilt or embarrassment prevent someone from taking certain actions?	**Apply** **Use information**
3a. Name the future recipient of your letter. What might the person think of it?	3b. Infer Keillor's meaning when he refers to the "humanity of our times."	**Analyze** **Take things apart**
4a. State why, according to Keillor, a letter is a "sweet gift."	4b. Evaluate whether Keillor's view of work, described in paragraph 2, is realistic. What is his purpose in describing a workday in this manner?	**Evaluate** **Make judgments**
5a. Quote what Keillor says moves a shy person to write and a rock star to perform.	5b. Using what Keillor has said about letters, deduce how he would likely respond to seeing letters in the Library of Congress by great authors such as George Washington and Abigail Adams.	**Create** **Bring ideas together**

COMPARE LITERATURE: How-to Writing

The essays by Octavia Butler and Garrison Keillor give advice to would-be writers. What similarities and differences did you find? To what degree do the differences in the advice they give result from their dissimilar tone and purpose? Do you think using humor adds to or takes away from the effectiveness of Keillor's essay?

AFTER READING

EXTEND THE TEXT

Writing Options

Creative Writing Write five **descriptive sentences** explaining how to be successful in an English class. Make sure the sentences are in the proper order and are clear enough for the reader to understand. Then repeat the exercise, only this time tell someone how to be unsuccessful!

Applied Writing Write a **how-to paper** entitled "How to Write an Essay." In your own words, write five or more paragraphs explaining to a reader the steps to composing an essay. Start by making a list of the correct steps to writing (in their proper order). Create an introductory paragraph that explains the purpose and overview of your essay, a paragraph explaining each writing step on your list, and a concluding paragraph summarizing your essay.

Collaborative Learning

Create Directions Identify locations or sites in your city or town (such as buildings, landmarks, or geographic features). Choose one and find out how to get to the location using your school as the starting point. Working in pairs, verbally give the directions slowly to your partner to write down, but don't reveal where your directions lead. See if your partner can use your step-by-step instructions to find out the final destination. Then reverse roles and have your partner give you directions to the location he or she selected.

Media Literacy

Research Historic Letters Working individually or with a partner, research important historic letters. Visit the library or explore websites such as the Library of Congress to help with your research. Remember to document all your sources. Choose a letter you feel provides the most meaningful insight into history. In a brief class presentation, explain the significance of your letter and why you chose it. Be sure to read excerpts of or the entire letter out loud as part of your presentation.

Go to **www.mirrorsandwindows.com** for more.

READING ASSESSMENT

1. Number the steps in Butler's writing process in "Furor Scribendi" in the correct sequence, with 1 being the first step and 6 being the last.
   ___ Write every day.
   ___ Avoid worrying about inspiration and talent.
   ___ Read as much as you can and learn from what you read.
   ___ Submit your work for publication.
   ___ Revise your writing until it's as good as you can make it.
   ___ Take writing classes and go to writers' workshops.

2. Which of the following ideas does Butler *not* express in "Furor Scribendi"?
   A. Persistence is good, but stubbornness is bad.
   B. If your work is rejected, you should probably find another activity.
   C. Don't overlook even minor errors.
   D. Strangers can be better critics than family and friends.
   E. Answers B and D

3. Which of the following statements best represents Butler's views in "Furor Scribendi"?
   A. Talent will get you nowhere.
   B. You can rely on the judgment of strangers.
   C. To become a good writer, you must work at your goal.
   D. Imagination is the key to good writing and is necessary for success.
   E. Don't conform or change your writing style.

4. Which of the following statements best represents Keillor's views in "How to Write a Letter"?
   A. A letter to a friend isn't necessarily something you have to write, but doing so can benefit you as much as the person who receives the letter.
   B. Writing letters to friends shouldn't be taken too seriously.
   C. Love letters are the most important ways of communicating.
   D. When you write to friends, you should follow certain guidelines.
   E. Letters are special and should be saved for occasions when you have something important to say.

5. Butler cautions writers against waiting for inspiration, whereas Keillor says it may sometimes come in a burst. With which writer do you agree? Explain.

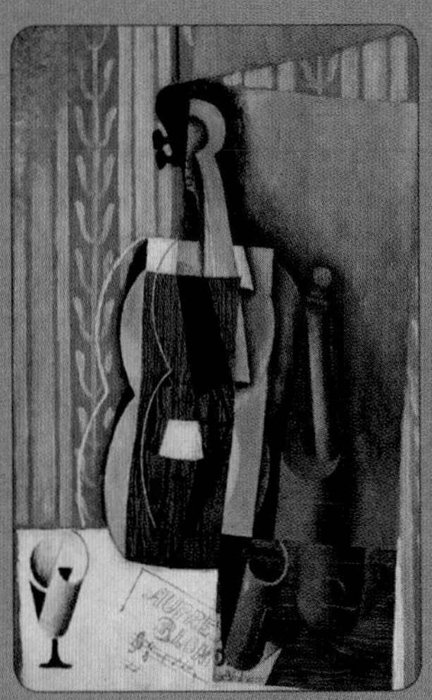

READING NONFICTION INDEPENDENTLY

Theme: Facing Challenges

"My favorite heroes in The Odyssey *are the older warriors who have been through many wars. They don't hide their scars, they wear them proudly as a kind of armor."*

–Twyla Tharp, from "An 'A' in Failure"

The road of life rarely runs smoothly; everybody faces challenges and obstacles from time to time. Sometimes, the challenges come from things outside you, larger in scope than any day-to-day trouble might be. War, racial discrimination, and poverty force people to find new ways to cope. Other challenges, however, are more exclusive to you alone. Whether it's grappling with shyness, disability, or fear, these personal challenges can also be a large force in shaping who you are. As you read the selections in this section, consider what challenges the central figures face.

USE READING SKILLS WITH NONFICTION

Identify Supporting Details

Supporting details are the facts and information that provide the evidence and structure that make up nonfiction writing. To identify supporting details, you need to do the following:

- **Locate basic facts,** such as names, dates, and events.
- **Determine the importance** of those facts to the understanding of the selection. Some facts or details will be more important than others. The main ideas are what the selection is about; the minor ideas and details provide support for the main ones.
- **Determine the mode of writing** the author is using. The possible modes and types of writing that employ those modes are listed on page 205.
- **Interpret subtly stated details.** These details can help clarify the author's stance or purpose, or they may give fuller meaning to the basic facts.
- **Understand the function** of a part of a passage. Is the author providing information, supporting a previously made point, presenting a conflicting argument, building suspense? Pay attention to how your understanding of a topic or your feelings toward it changes as you read.
- **Draw conclusions** about how the author uses the supporting details to achieve his or her desired result. Put together clues from the text with your prior knowledge to make inferences.

Distinguish Fact from Opinion

A **fact** is a statement that could be proven by direct observation. Every statement of fact is either true or false.

EXAMPLE

Many Greek myths deal with human emotion. (This statement is a fact that can be proven by examining the content of Greek myths.)

An **opinion** is a statement that expresses an attitude or a desire, not a fact about the world. One common type of opinion statement is a value statement. A *value statement* expresses an attitude toward something.

EXAMPLE

Ancient Greece produced some *beautiful* and *inspiring* myths. (The adjectives used to describe myths express an attitude or opinion toward something that cannot be proven.)

A *policy statement* is an opinion that tells not what is but what someone believes should be.

EXAMPLES

The president *should* be reelected.
You *must not* play your radio during study hall.

A *prediction* makes a statement about the future. Because the future is unpredictable, most predictions can be considered opinions.

EXAMPLES

People will live longer in the future.
Tomorrow will be partly cloudy.

When evaluating a fact, ask yourself whether it can be proven through direct observation or by checking a reliable source such as a reference book or an unbiased expert. An opinion is only as good as the facts that support it. When reading, be critical about the statements that you encounter.

Fact or Opinion Chart	
Fact: Two thirds of households in the United States have pets. **Proof:** Survey by the American Veterinary Medical Association	**Opinion:** "They're shaggy-looking, they're suffering the same emotional loss that people are." **Support:** Quotation by a St. Bernard Parish councilman

Framework for Nonfiction

When reading nonfiction, you need to be aware of what type of writing it is, how it uses supporting details, and what the author's intent is. The following checklist of questions offers a framework for approaching nonfiction reading.

As you start to read...

- ❑ What are the basic facts, such as names, dates, locations, and events?
- ❑ What is the mode or purpose of the writing? Narrative, informative, persuasive, descriptive, or personal?

As you continue reading...

- ❑ What seem to be the most important ideas in this selection?
- ❑ Are there more facts or opinions?
- ❑ How are the opinions supported?

After you've finished reading...

- ❑ How does the author use supporting details to convey his or her message?
- ❑ What can you infer by the author's choice of words and details about how the author regards the subject or wants the reader to regard the subject?

What Good Readers Do

Monitor Your Reading Progress

All readers encounter difficulty when they read, especially if the reading material is not self-selected. When you have to read something, note problems you are having, and make a plan to fix them.

- ❑ Because I do not understand this part, I will...
- ❑ Because I am having trouble staying interested in the selection, I will...
- ❑ Because the words are too hard, I will...
- ❑ Because the selection is very long, I will...
- ❑ Because I cannot remember what I have just read, I will...

It's Not Talent; It's Just Work

We want to believe that other people are natural wonders; it gets us off the hook.

An Essay by **Annie Dillard**

Annie Dillard won a Pulitzer Prize for *Pilgrim at Tinker Creek,* which was published in 1974. Although best known for that detailed account of the four seasons she spent living in the wilderness at Tinker Creek in Virginia, Dillard has also published poetry, fiction, memoirs, and creative nonfiction. Dillard said of writing, "What impels the writer is a deep love for and respect for language, for literary forms, for books.... You don't do it from willpower; you do it from an abiding passion for the field." She explores this idea in **"It's Not Talent; It's Just Work,"** first published in *Seventeen* magazine.

Many people debate whether talent is the result of "nature or nurture." In other words, are we born with talent, or does our environment allow us to develop talent? Dillard takes a unique approach, focusing on the love within us that allows us to achieve.

What prevents you from being the best at any given activity? How might someone disagree with your perspective?

It's hard work, doing something with your life. The very thought of hard work makes me queasy. I'd rather die in peace. Here we are, all equal and alike and none of us much to write home about—and some people choose to make themselves into physicists or thinkers or major-league pitchers, knowing perfectly well that it will be nothing but hard work. But I want to tell you that it's not as bad as it sounds. Doing something does not require discipline; it creates its own discipline—with a little help from caffeine.

People often ask me if I discipline myself to write, if I work a certain number of hours a day on a schedule. They ask this question with envy in their voices and awe on their faces and a sense of alienation all over them, as if they were addressing an armored tank or a talking giraffe or Niagara Falls. We want to believe that other people are natural wonders; it gets us off the hook.

Now, it happens that when I wrote my first book of prose

I worked an hour or two a day for a while, and then in the last two months, I got excited and worked very hard, for many hours a day. People can lift cars when they want to. People can recite the Koran,[1] too, and run in marathons. These things aren't ways of life; they are merely possibilities for everyone on certain occasions of life. You don't lift cars around the clock or write books every year. But when you do, it's not so hard. It's not superhuman. It's very human. You do it for love. You do it for love and respect for your own life; you do it for love and respect for the world; and you do it for love and respect for the task itself.

If I had a little baby, it would be hard for me to rise up and feed that little baby in the middle of the night. It would be hard but certainly wouldn't be a discipline. It wouldn't be a regimen I imposed on myself out of masochism, nor would it be the flowering of some extraordinary internal impulse. I would do it, grumbling, for love and because it has to be done.

Of course it has to be done. And something has to be done with your life too: something specific, something human. But don't wait around to be hit by love. Don't wait for anything. Learn something first. Then, when you are getting to know it, you will get to love it, and that love will direct you in what to do. So many times when I was in college, I used to say of a course like seventeenth-century poetry or European history, "I didn't like it at first, but now I like it." All of life is like that—a sort of dreary course which gradually gets interesting if you work at it.

I used to live in perpetual dread that I would one day read all the books that I would ever be interested in and have nothing more to read. I always figured that when that time came I would force myself to learn wildflowers, just to keep awake. I dreaded it, because I was not very interested in wildflowers but thought I should be. But things kept cropping up and one book has led to another and I haven't had to learn wildflowers yet. I don't think there's much danger of coming to the end of the line. The line is endless. I urge you to get in it, to get in line. It's a long line—but it's the only show in town. ❖

1. **Koran.** Holy book of the Islamic faith

"Doing something does not require discipline; it creates its own discipline...." If people love doing something, is it really work? What motivates people to do their best at something?

Refer and Reason

1. List commonly held beliefs about talent that Dillard identifies. Compare her ideas with these beliefs.
2. Quote Dillard's analogy about having a baby. Assess whether the analogy strengthens her argument.
3. Recall how Dillard feels about work. Thomas Edison once said that genius is one percent inspiration and ninety-nine percent perspiration. Compose the response you think Dillard would give if asked whether she agrees with Edison's statement.

Writing Options

1. Annie Dillard makes an analogy or comparison between life and a show. Write an analogy comparing success or perseverance to an object, such as a door, a window, or a light bulb. Include a description of the object and its function in your comparison.
2. Answer the following imaginary college application prompt in an essay that answers all parts: What do you want to do with your life? How and why will you work for it, and how will your college experience help you accomplish this goal?

Go to **www.mirrorsandwindows.com** for more.

INDEPENDENT READING

An Ethnic Trump

A Personal Essay by **Gish Jen**

Gish Jen (b. 1956) is the American-born daughter of immigrant Chinese parents, who wanted her to go to business school. Gish Jen had internalized that dream and said later, "Only after many years was I able to realize that I had to be a writer, or die." In her novels, short fiction, and nonfiction, she writes of themes related to immigration, assimilation, and occasional discord with other ethnicities.

"An Ethnic Trump" is a personal essay about Gish Jen's experiences as the mother of a biracial child. The author ponders what it means to be multiracial in American society and how important it really is to hold on to one's ethnic heritage.

Does your own ethnic heritage play a role in your daily life? Of what aspects in your own heritage are you particularly proud?

That my son, Luke, age four, goes to Chinese-culture school seems inevitable[1] to most people, even though his father is of Irish descent. For certain ethnicities[2] trump others; Chinese, for example, trumps Irish.

This has something to do with the relative distance of certain cultures from mainstream American culture, but it also has to do with race. For as we all know, it is not only certain

1. **inevitable.** Unavoidable
2. **ethnicities.** Cultural origins or backgrounds of individuals, including country or tribe of origin, religion, and language

For certain ethnicities trump others; Chinese, for example, trumps Irish.

ethnicities that trump[3] others but certain colors: black trumps white, for example, always and forever; a mulatto[4] is not a kind of white person, but a kind of black person.

And so it is, too, that my son is considered a kind of Asian person whose manifest destiny[5] is to embrace Asian things. The Chinese language. Chinese food. Chinese New Year. No one cares whether he speaks Gaelic[6] or wears green on Saint Patrick's Day. For though Luke's skin is fair, and his features mixed, people see his straight black hair and "know" who he is.

But is this how we should define ourselves, by other people's perceptions? My husband, Dave, and I had originally hoped for Luke to grow up embracing his whole complex ethnic heritage. We had hoped to pass on to him values and habits of mind that had actually survived in both of us.

Then one day, Luke combed his black hair and said he was turning it yellow. Another day, a fellow mother reported that her son had invited all blond-haired children like himself to his birthday party. And yet another day, Luke was happily scooting around the Cambridge Common playground when a pair of older boys, apparently brothers, blocked his way. "You're Chinese!" they shouted, leaning on the hood of Luke's scooter car. "You are! You're Chinese!" So brazen[7] were these kids that even when I, an adult, intervened, they continued to shout. Luke answered, "No, I'm not!"—to no avail; it was not clear if the boys even heard him. Then the boys' mother called to them from some distance away, outside the fence, and though her voice was no louder than Luke's, they left obediently.

Behind them opened a great, rippling quiet, like the wash of a battleship.

Luke and I immediately went over things he could say if anything like that ever happened again. I told him that he was 100 percent American, even though I knew from my own childhood in Yonkers that these words would be met only with derision.[8] It was a sorry chore. Since then, I have not asked him about the incident, hoping he has forgotten about it, and wishing that I could, too. For I wish I could forget the sight of those kids' fingers on the hood of Luke's little car. I wish I could forget their loud attack, but also Luke's soft defense: No, I'm not.

Chinese-culture school. After dozens of phone calls, I was elated to discover the Greater Boston Chinese Cultural Association nearby in West Newton. The school takes children at three, has a wonderful sense of community, and is housed in a center

3. **trump.** To override or outrank
4. **mulatto.** A person of mixed white and black ancestry
5. **manifest destiny.** A future event accepted as inescapable
6. **Gaelic.** The Irish language
7. **brazen.** Overly bold; disrespectful
8. **derision.** Ridicule; mockery; sarcasm

And if there were going to be incidents on the playground, we wanted him to know what Chinese meant.

paid for, in part, by great karaoke[9] fund-raising events. (Never mind what the Japanese meant to the Chinese in the old world. In this world, people donate at least two hundred dollars each for a chance at the mike, and the singing goes on all night.) There are even vendors who bring home-style Chinese food to sell after class—stuff you can't get in a restaurant. Dave and I couldn't wait for the second class, and a chance to buy more bao[10] for our freezer.

But in the car on the way to the second class, Luke announced that he didn't want to go to Chinese school anymore. He said that the teacher talked mostly about ducks and bears and that he wasn't interested in ducks and bears. And I knew this was true. I knew that Luke was interested only in whales and ships. And what's more, I knew we wouldn't push him to take swimming lessons if he didn't want to, or music. Chinese school was a wonderful thing, but there was a way in which we were accepting it as somehow nonoptional. Was that right? Hadn't we always said that we didn't want our son to see himself as more essentially Chinese than Irish?

Yet we didn't want him to deny his Chinese heritage, either. And if there were going to be incidents on the playground, we wanted him to know what Chinese meant. So when Luke said again that he didn't really want to go to Chinese school, I said, "Oh, really?" Later on, we could try to teach him to define himself irrespective[11] of race. For now, though, he was going to Chinese school. I exchanged glances with Dave. And then together, in a most carefully casual manner, we squinted at the road and kept going. ❖

9. **karaoke.** Device that plays musical accompaniment while the user sings along

10. **bao (baù).** [Chinese] Steamed bun, often filled with meat or vegetables

11. **irrespective.** Regardless

"But is this how we should define ourselves, by other people's perceptions?" Jen asks. Have you ever let what others may think about you affect your self-image? Do people tend to embrace one cultural heritage more than another?

Refer and Reason

1. List the evidence which shows that Luke is perceived as more Chinese than Irish. Analyze the reasons that some ethnicities trump others.
2. Recall why Luke did not want to go to Chinese-culture school anymore. Assess Luke's parents' decision that Luke should continue to go to Chinese-culture school.
3. Quote the taunt of the boys on the playground. Create a dialogue that you think reflects the feelings of Luke and his mother about this incident.

Writing Options

1. Write a letter to your parents requesting to either attend or not attend a school that focuses on your own ethnic and cultural background. Support your preference.
2. Write an expository essay in which you evaluate Gish Jen's approach in writing about ethnicity. Focus on the major question that she addresses in her essay, the types of supporting details she provides, and her response to the major question.

Go to **www.mirrorsandwindows.com** for more.

Literature CONNECTION

Like "An Ethnic Trump," **"Saying Yes"** deals with the issue of cultural blending. In the poem, award-winning writer and painter **Diana Chang** (b. 1934) addresses a personal conflict common among people who identify with two different cultures: Must they be one or the other, or can they be both?

Saying Yes

A Poem by **Diana Chang**

"Are you Chinese?"
"Yes."

"American?"
"Yes."

"*Really* Chinese?"
"No...not quite."

"*Really* American?"
"Well, actually, you see..."

But I would rather say
yes

Not neither-nor,
not maybe,
but both, and not only

The homes I've had,
the ways I am

I'd rather say it
twice,
yes ❖

TEXT ←TO→ TEXT CONNECTION

- Why do you think people, such as the ones encountered in "An Ethnic Trump" and "Saying Yes," feel the need to classify people into neat categories?
- What advantages and disadvantages do you think the two writers would say their biracial and bicultural identities have given them?

Literature CONNECTION

Sherman Alexie (b. 1966) spent his early years on the Spokane Indian Reservation, in Wellpinit, Washington. Although he attended reservation schools through junior high, he preferred to go to a public high school, where he was one of the few ethnic-minority students.

Alexie's short story, titled **"Indian Education,"** focuses not so much on learning as on the interactions between students and their non-Native American teachers. In his many books, mostly poetry and short stories, Alexie writes about the Native American tradition in which he was raised, as well as about the comedy and tragedy of life in Anglo society.

Indian Education

A Short Story by

Sherman Alexie

And I said, Yes, I am. I am Indian. Indian, I am....

FIRST GRADE

My hair was too short and my U.S. Government glasses were horn-rimmed, ugly, and all that first winter in school, the other Indian boys chased me from one corner of the playground to the other. They pushed me down, buried me in the snow until I couldn't breathe, thought I'd never breathe again.

They stole my glasses and threw them over my head, around my outstretched hands, just beyond my reach, until someone tripped me and sent me falling again, facedown in the snow.

I was always falling down; my Indian name was Junior Falls Down. Sometimes it was

Bloody Nose or Steal-His-Lunch. Once, it was Cries-Like-a-White-Boy, even though none of us had seen a white boy cry.

Then it was a Friday morning recess and Frenchy SiJohn threw snowballs at me while the rest of the Indian boys tortured some other *top-yogh-yaught* kid, another weakling. But Frenchy was confident enough to torment me all by himself, and most days I would have let him.

But the little warrior in me roared to life that day and knocked Frenchy to the ground, held his head against the snow, and punched him so hard that my knuckles and the snow made symmetrical bruises on his face. He almost looked like he was wearing war paint.

But he wasn't the warrior. I was. And I chanted *It's a good day to die, it's a good day to die*, all the way down to the principal's office.

SECOND GRADE

Betty Towle, missionary teacher, redheaded and so ugly that no one ever had a puppy

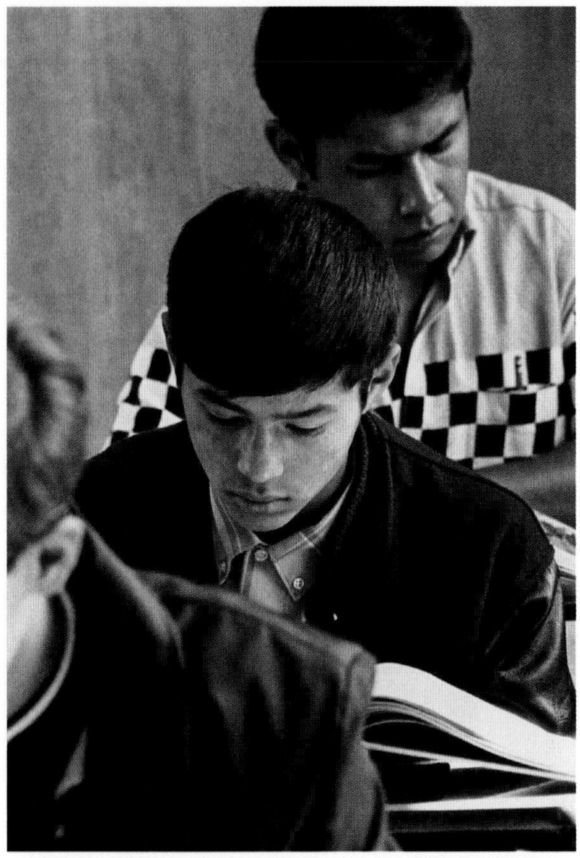

crush on her, made me stay in for recess fourteen days straight.

"Tell me you're sorry," she said.

"Sorry for what?" I asked.

"Everything," she said and made me stand straight for fifteen minutes, eagle-armed with books in each hand. One was a math book; the other was English. But all I learned was that gravity can be painful.

For Halloween I drew a picture of her riding a broom with a scrawny cat on the back. She said that her God would never forgive me for that.

Once, she gave the class a spelling test but set me aside gave me a test designed for junior high students. When I spelled all the words right, she crumpled up the paper and made me eat it.

"You'll learn respect," she said.

She sent a letter home with me that told my parents to either cut my braids or keep me home from class. My parents came in the next day and dragged their braids across Betty Towle's desk.

"Indians, indians, indians." She said it without capitalization. She called me "indian, indian, indian."

And I said, *Yes, I am. I am Indian. Indian, I am....*

FOURTH GRADE

"You should be a doctor when you grow up," Mr. Schluter told me, even though his wife, the third grade teacher, thought I was crazy beyond my years. My eyes always looked like I had just hit-and-run someone.

"Guilty" she said. "You always look guilty."

"Why should I be a doctor?" I asked Mr. Schluter.

"So you can come back and help the tribe. So you can heal people."

That was the year my father drank a gallon of vodka a day and the same year that my mother started two hundred different quilts but never finished any. They sat in separate, dark places in our HUD house and wept savagely.

I ran home after school, heard their Indian tears, and looked in the mirror. *Doctor Victor,* I called myself, invented an education, talked to my reflection. *Doctor Victor to the emergency room....*

SIXTH GRADE

Randy, the new Indian kid from the white town of Springdale, got into a fight an hour after he first walked into the reservation school.

Stevie Flett called him out, called him a squawman,...and called him a punk.

Randy and Stevie, and the rest of the Indian boys, walked out into the playground.

"Throw the first punch," Stevie said as they squared off.

"No," Randy said.

"Throw the first punch," Stevie said again.

'No," Randy said again.

"Throw the first punch!" Stevie said for the third time, and Randy reared back and pitched a knuckle fastball that broke Stevie's nose.

We all stood there in silence, in awe.

That was Randy, my soon-to-be first and best friend, who taught me the most valuable lesson about living in the white world: *Always throw the first punch....*

NINTH GRADE

At the farm town high school dance, after a basketball game in an overheated gym where I had scored twenty-seven points and pulled down thirteen rebounds, I passed out during a slow song.

As my white friends revived me and prepared to take me to the emergency room where doctors would later diagnose my diabetes, the Chicano teacher ran up to us.

"Hey," he said. "What's that boy been drinking? I know all about these Indian kids. They start drinking real young."

Sharing dark skin doesn't necessarily make two men brothers....

ELEVENTH GRADE

Last night I missed two free throws which would have won the game against the best team in the state. The farm town high school I play for is nicknamed the "Indians," and I'm probably the only actual Indian to ever play for a team with such a mascot.

This morning I pick up the sports page and read the headline: INDIANS LOSE AGAIN.

Go ahead and tell me none of this is supposed to hurt me very much.

TWELFTH GRADE

I walk down the aisle, valedictorian of this farm town high school, and my cap doesn't fit because I've grown my hair longer than it's ever been. Later, I stand as the school board chairman recites my awards, accomplishments, and scholarships.

I try to remain stoic for the photographers as I look toward the future.

Back home on the reservation, my former classmates graduate: a few can't read, one or two are just given attendance diplomas, most look forward to the parties. The bright students are shaken, frightened, because they don't know what comes next.

They smile for the photographer as they look back toward tradition. ❖

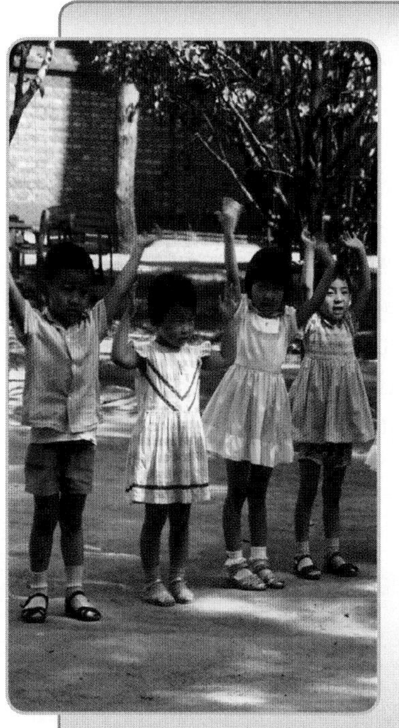

TEXT ◄TO► TEXT CONNECTION

- The narrator in Sherman Alexie's short story "Indian Education" responds to his teacher, *"Yes, I am. I am Indian. Indian, I am."* In the poem "Saying Yes" by Diana Chang, on page 311, the narrator says "yes" both to being Chinese and to being American. How does Gish Jen's son Luke in "An Ethnic Trump," on page 308, react when older boys on the playground call him Chinese? How important do these authors think it is to identify with their ethnic heritage?
- Stereotypes are the uncritically accepted, usually unfavorable ideas about an ethnic or other group of people. What stereotypes of Indian family life does the narrator in "Indian Education" experience? In "An Ethnic Trump" what stereotypes does Luke have to deal with on the playground? What stereotypes do you encounter in your own school? How might people eliminate stereotypes?

ONLY DAUGHTER

I WAS/AM THE ONLY DAUGHTER AND *ONLY* A DAUGHTER.

A Personal Essay by

Sandra Cisneros

Through her award-winning poems, novels, essays, and short stories, **Sandra Cisneros** (b. 1954) has helped bring the Chicana—an American woman or girl of Mexican descent—perspective into mainstream literature. Born into a large Mexican-American family, Cisneros defied male-dominated cultural expectations by earning college degrees and pursuing a writing career. Cisneros writes about conflicts directly related to her upbringing, including divided cultural loyalties and feelings of alienation. She has said, "We're amphibians and bridges to communities at war with each other, but it's our job in the new millennium to help bridge and translate."

In Cisneros's personal essay **"Only Daughter,"** the author shares her feelings about her father and about being the only daughter and "only the daughter" in a traditional Mexican family of seven children. The essay originally appeared in *Glamour* magazine in November 1990.

Of all the members of your family and your friends, whose opinion is the most important to you?

Once, several years ago, when I was just starting out my writing career, I was asked to write my own contributor's note for an anthology[1] I was part of. I wrote: "I am the only daughter in a family of six sons. *That* explains everything."

Well, I've thought about that ever since, and yes, it explains a lot to me, but for the reader's sake I should have written: "I am the only daughter in a *Mexican* family of six sons." Or even: "I am the only daughter of a Mexican farmer and a Mexican-American mother." Or: "I am the only daughter of a working-class family of nine." All of these had everything to do with who I am today.

I was/am the only daughter and *only* a daughter. Being an only daughter in a family of six sons forced me by circumstance to spend a lot of time by myself because my brothers felt it beneath them to play with a *girl* in public. But that aloneness, that loneliness, was good for a would-be writer—it allowed me time to think and think, to imagine, to read and prepare myself.

Being only a daughter for my father meant my destiny would lead me to become someone's wife. That's what he believed. But when I was in the fifth grade and shared my plans for college with him, I was sure he understood. I remember my father saying, "*Que bueno, mi'ja*,[2] that's good." That meant a lot to

1. **anthology.** A collection of selected literary pieces, works of art, or music

2. ***Que bueno, mi'ja*** **(ke bwe´ nō mē´ hä).** [Spanish] That is good, my daughter.

Critical Viewing

What feeling is portrayed in the image at right? How might this feeling present itself within the selection?

El Pan Nuestro, 1923–1928. Diego Rivera. Ministry of Education, Mexico City, Mexico.

me, especially since my brothers thought the idea hilarious. What I didn't realize was that my father thought college was good for girls—good for finding a husband. After four years in college and two more in graduate school and still no husband, my father shakes his head even now and says I wasted all that education.

In retrospect, I'm lucky my father believed daughters were meant for husbands. It meant it didn't matter if I majored in something silly like English. After all, I'd find a nice professional eventually, right? This allowed me the liberty to putter about embroidering my little poems and stories without my father interrupting with so much as a "What's that you're writing?"

But the truth is, I wanted him to interrupt. I wanted my father to understand what it was I was scribbling, to introduce me as "My only daughter, the writer." Not as "This is only my daughter. She teaches." *Es maestra*—teacher. Not even *profesora.*[3]

In a sense, everything I have ever written has been for him, to win his approval even though I know my father can't read English words, even though my father's only reading includes the brown-ink *Esto* sports magazines from Mexico City and the bloody *¡Alarma!* magazines that feature yet another sighting of *La Virgen de Guadalupe*[4] on a tortilla or a wife's revenge on her philandering[5] husband by bashing his skull in with a *molcajete* (a kitchen mortar[6] made of volcanic rock). Or the

3. ***profesora*** (prō fe sō´ rä). [Spanish] Professor
4. ***La Virgen de Guadalupe*** (lä vēr´ hen de gwä dä lü´ pe). [Spanish] The Virgin of Guadalupe, the virgin mother of Jesus, who, according to legend, appeared in Mexico in 1531
5. **philandering.** Having many love affairs
6. **mortar.** A bowl in which hard foods are ground

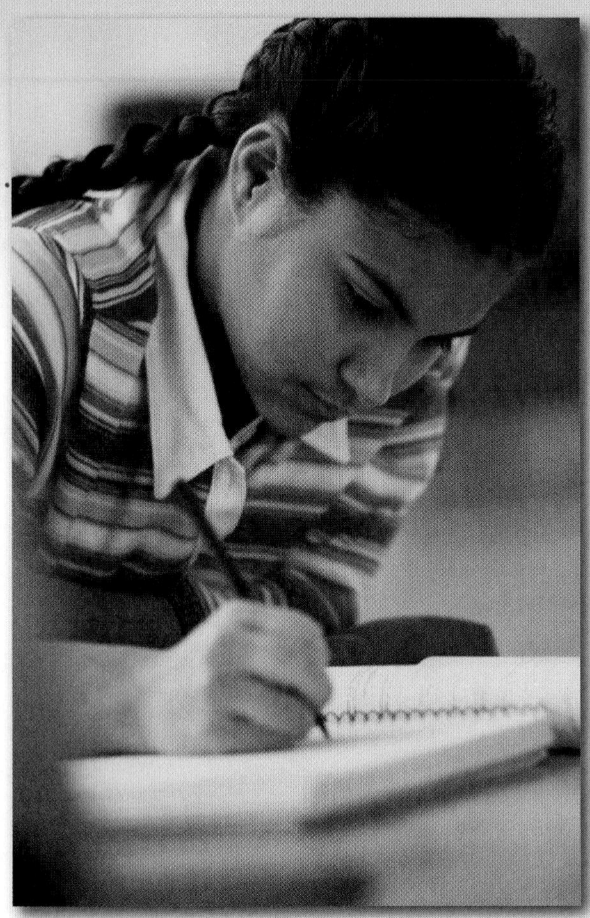

fotonovelas, the little picture paperbacks with tragedy and trauma erupting from the characters' mouths in bubbles.

My father represents, then, the public majority. A public who is disinterested in reading, and yet one whom I am writing about and for and privately trying to woo.

When we were growing up in Chicago, we moved a lot because of my father. He suffered bouts of nostalgia. Then we'd have to let go our flat, store the furniture with mother's relatives, load the station wagon with baggage and bologna sandwiches, and head south. To Mexico City.

We came back, of course. To yet another Chicago flat, another Chicago neighborhood, another Catholic school. Each time, my father would seek out the parish priest in order to get a tuition break and complain or boast: "I have seven sons."

He meant *siete hijos,* seven children, but he translated it as "sons." "I have seven sons." To anyone who would listen. The Sears Roebuck employee who sold us the washing machine. The short-order cook where my father ate his ham-and-eggs breakfasts. "I have seven sons." As if he deserved a medal from the state.

My papa. He didn't mean anything by that mistranslation, I'm sure. But somehow I could feel myself being erased. I'd tug my father's sleeve and whisper: "Not seven sons. Six! and *one daughter.*"

When my oldest brother graduated from medical school, he fulfilled my father's dream that we study hard and use this—our heads, instead of this—our hands. Even now my father's hands are thick and yellow, stubbed by a history of hammer and nails and twine and coils and springs. "Use this," my father said, tapping his head, "and not this," showing us those hands. He always looked tired when he said it.

Wasn't college an investment? And hadn't I spent all those years in college? And if I didn't marry, what was it all for? Why would anyone go to college and then choose to be poor? Especially someone who had always been poor.

Last year, after ten years of writing professionally, the financial rewards started to trickle in. My second National Endowment for the Arts Fellowship.[7] A guest professorship at the University of California, Berkeley. My book, which sold to a major New York publishing house.

At Christmas, I flew home to Chicago. The house was throbbing, same as always; hot *tamales*[8] and sweet *tamales* hissing in my mother's pressure cooker, and everybody—my mother, six brothers, wives, babies, aunts, cousins—talking too loud and at the same

7. **National Endowment for the Arts Fellowship.** Funding awarded by the government to people working in the arts

8. ***tamales*** (tä mä´ les). [Spanish] Ground meat rolled in cornmeal dough that is then wrapped in cornhusks and steamed

time, like in a Fellini[9] film, because that's just how we are.

I went upstairs to my father's room. One of my stories had just been translated into Spanish and published in an anthology of Chicano writing, and I wanted to show it to him. Ever since he recovered from a stroke two years ago, my father likes to spend his leisure hours horizontally. And that's how I found him, watching a Pedro Infante[10] movie on Galavisión[11] and eating rice pudding.

I SAT ON THE BED NEXT TO MY FATHER AND WAITED. HE READ IT VERY SLOWLY.

There was a glass filmed with milk on the bedside table. There were several vials of pills and balled Kleenex. And on the floor, one black sock and a plastic urinal that I didn't want to look at but looked at anyway. Pedro Infante was about to burst into song, and my father was laughing.

I'm not sure if it was because my story was translated into Spanish or because it was published in Mexico or perhaps because the story dealt with Tepeyac,[12] the *colonia* my father was raised in and the house he grew up in, but at any rate, my father punched the mute button on his remote control and read my story.

I sat on the bed next to my father and waited. He read it very slowly. As if he were reading each line over and over. He laughed at all the right places and read lines he liked out loud. He pointed and asked questions: "Is this So-and-so?"

"Yes," I said. He kept reading.

When he was finally finished, after what seemed like hours, my father looked up and asked: "Where can we get more copies of this for the relatives?"

Of all the wonderful things that happened to me last year, that was the most wonderful. ❖

9. **Fellini.** Federico Fellini (1920–1993), Italian film director
10. **Pedro Infante.** A popular Mexican film star
11. **Galavisión.** A Spanish cable television network
12. **Tepeyac.** A district of Mexico City

How much do you value your family's approval? Do people need approval from family or peers to feel proud of their accomplishments? Is it enough for people to know that they worked hard and achieved an important goal?

Refer and Reason

1. Review "Only Daughter." Point out parts of the essay in which the author reveals her feelings toward her father. Classify her feelings and point out any contradictions in them.
2. Recall what Cisneros's father expected her destiny to be. Why do you think he held the opinions about women that he did? Judge how he feels about his daughter at the end of the essay.
3. Rewrite the new ending to the essay to reflect how Cisneros might have felt if her father had refused to read her story or had read it but reacted unfavorably.

Writing Options

1. Imagine you are Cisneros's father and describe in a journal entry your feelings upon reading your daughter's story.
2. Write a narrative essay that reflects on an incident in your life that taught you something. To get started, ask yourself: Why did I identify this incident? What did it teach me about myself and about other people? What is the lasting value of the incident?

 Go to **www.mirrorsandwindows.com** for more.

This Is Not Who We Are

A Personal Essay by

Naomi Shihab Nye

I'm idling in the drive-through line at a fast-food franchise in Texas, the kind of place I usually avoid, because my hungry teenager *needs* a hamburger, when a curling strand of delicate violin rises from National Public Radio. I know immediately it's Simon Shaheen, the Arab-American virtuoso[1] violinist, an elegant man who wears starched white shirts and black suits and plays like an angel.

"It is our duty to be hopeful."

A calm washes over me that I haven't felt in days. The commentator says his name. I raise the volume; our car fills up with grace. I place my head on the steering wheel, tears clouding my eyes.

"Mom! Are you all right? You are *so weird!*"

No. I am simply an Arab-American in deep need of cultural uplift to balance the ugliness that has cast a deep shadow over our days.

Play Ali Jihad Racy, Um Kalthoum, Marcel Khalife, Hamza El Din, Matoub Lounes…any melodious Middle Eastern music to counteract the terrible sorrow of this time! With so many precious people and lands grieving and no way that we, simple citizens, can solve it or get our full minds around it, what shall we do with our souls?

I grew up in St. Louis in a tiny house full of large music—Mahalia Jackson and Marian Anderson singing majestically on the stereo, my German-American mother fingering *The Lost Chord* on the piano as golden light sank through trees, my Palestinian father trilling in

Naomi Shihab Nye (b. 1952) was born to a Palestinian father and a German-American mother. Poet, essayist, editor, and children's author, Nye writes of everyday events from a new perspective and says, "For me, the primary source of poetry has always been local life, random characters met on the streets, our own ancestry sifting down to us through small essential daily tasks."

In **"This Is Not Who We Are,"** Nye writes about the emotional burden of being Arab American, especially after the September 11 tragedy. The title of her essay is taken from words her grandmother spoke to her in a dream after September 11: "Say this is not who we are."

How have the events of September 11 affected you and your own family and friends?

1. **virtuoso.** A highly skilled musical performer

Arabic in the shower each dawn. He held single notes so long we thought he might faint.

The world rang rich counterpoint, mixed melodies, fragrances, textures: crushed mint and garlic in the kitchen, cardamom brewing in coffee, fabulously embroidered Palestinian pillows plumped on the couch. And always, a thrumming underchord, a hovering, hopeful note: Things had been bad, but they would get better. Our dad had lost his home, but he would make another one.[2] People suffered everywhere, but life would improve.

I refuse to let that hope go.

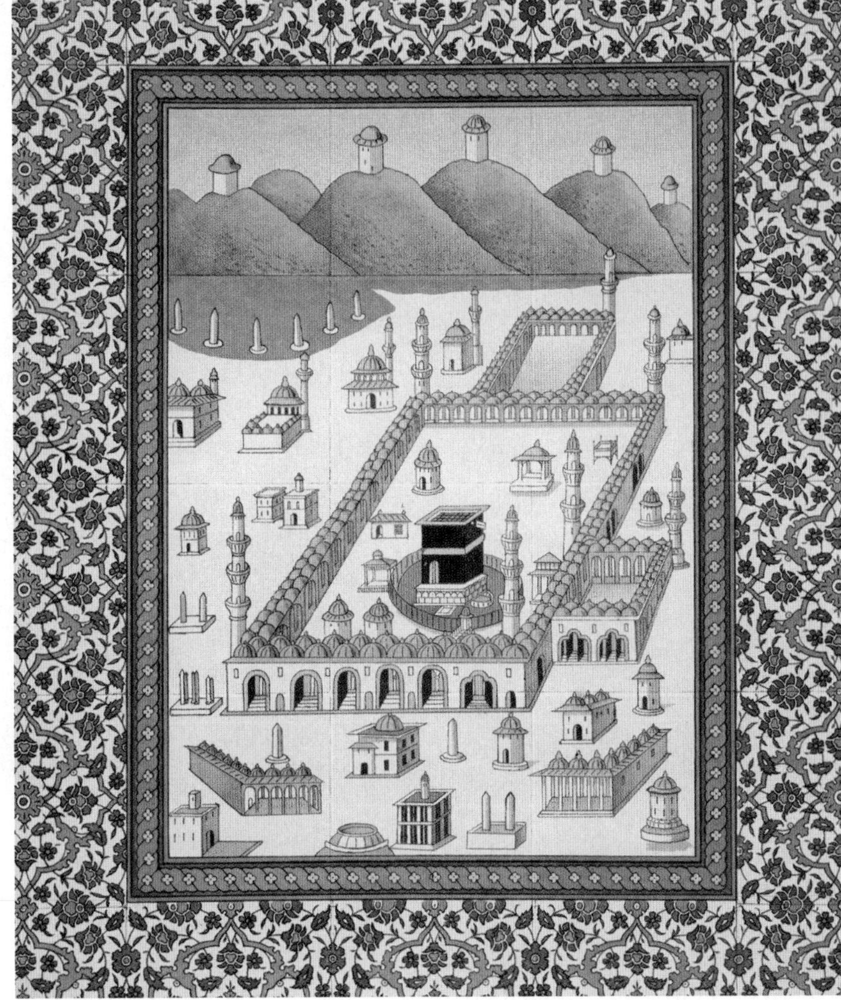

Lithograph of Mecca, 1800s.

Because men with hard faces do violent things, because fanaticism[3] seizes and shrinks minds, is no reason for the rest of us to abandon our songs.

Maybe we need to sing them louder.

I hold in my heart so many sorrowing individuals. All families and friends of innocent victims everywhere. All dedicated advocates of peace—keep speaking out wherever you can! All people related to the Middle East who despise bad behavior. All gentle immigrants—how much harder their lives may be now. All citizens who trust the great potential of humanity. All children who want to be happy. All mothers and sisters of violent men.

I wish for world symbols more than SUVs wearing American flags like hula skirts—aren't images that embrace all humanity, all nations and variations, the only thing that will save us now? My friend Milli makes me an exquisite peace bracelet with a miniature globe on it, alongside an ivory dove and beads from many countries. I wear it every day.

A friend I don't know sends an e-mail: "It is our duty to be hopeful." Her words flicker inside me, a small torch penetrating gloom.

The words of children console us, not the other way around. During a local poetry

2. **Our dad...would make another one.** When Israel won the war and gained independence, hundreds of thousands of Palestinians, including the author's father and grandmother, were forced from their homes.

3. **fanaticism.** Excessive enthusiasm or intense uncritical devotion

workshop with fourth-graders, a girl hands me a folded note: "Poetry is eating all my problems." My great-niece stomps her foot. "Adults are forgetting how to have fun!"

I keep thinking, we teach children to use language to solve their disputes. We teach them not to hit and fight and bite. Then look what adults do!

I read about the Seeds of Peace teenagers, Arabs and Israelis who come together in Maine and Jerusalem for deepened dialogue and greater understanding. Their gatherings are not easy. They cry and fear and worry. But they emerge from their sessions changed. Every weapon on earth betrays their efforts, but we need them desperately, to balance the cruel tides.

Condolence cards fan out on my table—kind women I haven't seen in years, writing "We care." Everyone advises me to stay balanced, practice yoga again, eat well, laugh out loud. They understand that an Arab-American might be feeling sicker than most people these difficult days. I grip these lovely messages as if they were prescriptions from the best doctor. My wonderful Japanese-American friend Margaret in Hawaii is particularly vigilant, writing "How are you? You are strongly in our thoughts" every single week.

Critical Viewing

Consider why the dove is a symbol of peace. What other images are symbols of peace?

I treasure the welcoming world of women…laughing, tending, nourishing, mending, wrapping language around one another like a warm cloak. I try to think of supportive women in my community whom I could surprise—friends who might be able to use a bunch of red ranunculuses, a plate of hot gingerbread when it is not even their birthday.

And I keep thinking of my Palestinian grandmother, who lived to be 106 years old and didn't read or write, though she always said she could "read the sky" and the tea leaves in the bottom of everyone's cups. She claimed she didn't want to die "until everyone she didn't like died first." We think she succeeded.

HISTORY CONNECTION

Israeli and Palestinian Conflict Israelis and Palestinians have an intensely conflicted relationship over territory that both consider their homeland. The Jews call this place Israel; the Arabs, Palestine. In 1948, the United Nations declared the creation of the state of Israel, sparking a war between the newly created state and Arabs whose ancestors had been living in Palestine, Egypt, Jordan, Syria, and Lebanon for centuries. Israel won the war and gained independence, but hundreds of thousands of Palestinians were forced from their homes.

The truth was, she was very popular. She liked everybody and they all loved her. The Israeli anthropologist who did an oral history project in her village found me years later to say, "Her warmth changed my life—I consider her my grandmother, too." Even though she had lost her home to Israel in 1948, she said, "I never lost my peace inside."

The only place she ever traveled beyond Palestine was to Mecca, by bus. She was proud to be called a hajji,[4] to wear layered white clothes afterward. In her West Bank village, she worked hard to get stains out of everyone's dresses—scrubbing them with a stone over a big tin tub in the courtyard, under her beloved lemon tree. If we told her, "You are very patient," she would joke, "What choice do I have?"

I think she would consider the recent tragedies a terrible stain on her religion. She would weep. She never fussed at my father for not praying five times a day in the traditional way. As she excused herself from our circle for her own prayers, he might say something like "I'm praying all the time, every minute," and she would grin.

She wanted people to worship in whatever ways they felt comfortable. To respect one another, enjoy one another's company, tell good stories, sit around the fire drinking tea and cracking almonds, and never forget to laugh no matter what terrible things they had been through. Laughter was the power.

What wisdom did she possess that other people can't figure out?

I thought I was done writing about her—for years she starred in my essays and poems. But after September 11, she started poking herself into my dreams again, kindly, sorrowfully: "Say this is not who we are."

Apparently the entire United States has taken to reading more poetry, which can only be a good sign. Journalists ask, "Why do you suppose people are finding strength in poetry now?" Those of us who have been reading poetry all our lives aren't a bit surprised. As a direct line to human feeling, empathic[5] experience, genuine

4. ***hajji*** **(ha´ jē).** [Arabic] One who has made a pilgrimage to Mecca, Saudi Arabia, a destination of pilgrims in the Islamic world

5. **empathic.** Understanding, being sensitive to, and vicariously experiencing the feelings, thoughts, and experiences of others

language and detail, poetry is everything that headline news is not. It takes us inside situations, helps us imagine life from more than one perspective, honors imagery and metaphor—those great tools of thought—and deepens our confidence in a meaningful world.

I feast on *The Poetry of Arab Women,* a contemporary collection published last year. Deema K. Shehabi wrote, "And where is that mountain / that will fold us inward slowly / …enemy of melancholy, ally of life / glistening darkly / in silence."

Nazik al-Malaika wrote, "How do we forget pain, / how do we forget pain? / Who will light for us / the night of its memory?"

From Fadwa Tuqan, the brave Palestinian who has lived all these difficult years in Nablus on the West Bank: "Give us love, so we may build the collapsed universe within us / anew…."

Then I read Coleman Barks's vibrant translations of Rumi, the 13th-century Sufi poet who has for the past few years been one of the best-selling poets in the United States. It's rumored he's also the poet most often read aloud on the radio in Afghanistan. Open *The Soul of Rumi* anywhere and find something helpful. On page 158: "Why am I part of this disaster, this / mud hole for donkeys?" Later in the same poem, "I ask / a flower, 'How is it you are so wise so / young?' "

Yes. I breathe deeply, closing my eyes. *And how are we educated human beings so old and so stupid?*

Now that I have tears in my eyes even while making baba ghanouj, our famous eggplant dip, so what? This is my cultural sorrow—not the first ever in the world. Admit it and move on. There is still so much good work to do.

When a gentle man I don't know approaches me in a crowd at a literary conference to say, "I am afraid for my daughter to admit she is half-Arab now. What should we do?" I am momentarily tongue-tied.

Later I wish I had told him, "Tell her never deny it. Maybe Arab-Americans must say we are twice as sad as other people. But we are still proud, of everything peaceful and beautiful that endures. Then speak beauty if we can—the beauty of culture, poetry, tradition, memory, family, daily life. Each day, live in honor of the ones who didn't have this luxury or time. We are not alone." ❖

In what ways do people show pride in their cultural or family background? How might that pride be tested or challenged?

Refer and Reason

1. List details about the author's grandmother. Identify several other people whose words or actions positively influenced the author. Recognize the admirable characteristics of these people.
2. State the fear of the man at the literary conference. Justify the man's concern.
3. Quote the comparison the author makes between poetry and headline news. Choose a headline from the newspaper. Compose a poem about the subject of the news story. Does your poem live up to the author's expectations of poetry?

Writing Options

1. Write a letter to an imaginary pen pal in another country, and describe yourself, your interests, and America. Include details about your local community and school.
2. Write a position statement and essay regarding the issues that appear in "This Is Not Who We Are" and imagine that it will be sent to the governor of your state.

 Go to **www.mirrorsandwindows.com** for more.

An "A" in Failure

A How-to Writing by **Twyla Tharp**

Every creative person has to learn to deal with failure, because failure, like death and taxes, is inescapable.

A math professor at Williams College bases ten percent of his students' grades on failure. Mathematics is all about trying out new ideas—new formulas, theorems, approaches—and knowing that the vast majority of them will be dead ends. To encourage his students not to be afraid of testing their quirkiest ideas in public, he rewards rather than punishes them for coming up with wrong answers.

Every creative person has to learn to deal with failure, because failure, like death and taxes, is inescapable. If Leonardo and Beethoven and Goethe failed on occasion, what makes you think you'll be the exception?

I don't mean to romanticize failure, to parrot the cliché "If you're not failing, you're not taking enough risks," especially if that view "liberates" you to fail too often. Believe me, success is preferable to failure. But there is a therapeutic power to failure. It cleanses. It helps you put aside who you aren't and reminds you who you are. Failure humbles.

The best failures are the private ones you commit in the confines of your room, alone, with no strangers watching. Private failures are great. I encourage you to fail as much as you want in private. It will cost you a little in terms of efficiency—the more you fail, the longer it takes to finish—but no one has to see this.

Twyla Tharp (b. 1941) is an innovative and award-winning dancer and choreographer who often infuses humor into her work. Tharp's dance compositions include a diverse mix of music, such as Mozart, Scott Joplin, Fats Waller, and the Beach Boys.

"An 'A' in Failure" is an excerpt from *The Creative Habit: Learn It and Use It for Life,* Tharp's guide to being creative published in 2003. She says, "Failure is going to happen, so you might as well make the most of it.... You always do your best work after your worst failures." Tharp believes everyone can be creative, saying, "The notion that the artist is given this divine gift is not only inaccurate, but destructive." The book offers exercises to help people develop their own creativity.

Have you ever failed miserably at something you wanted to succeed at? Did you learn anything from that failure?

Dancers, 1877. Edgar Degas.

Some of my favorite dancers at New York City Ballet were the ones who fell the most. I always loved watching Mimi Paul; she took big risks onstage and went down often. Her falls reminded you that the dancers were doing superhuman things onstage and when she fell, I would realize,...she's human." And hitting the ground seemed to transform Mimi: It was as though the stage absorbed the energy of her fall and injected it back into her with an extra dose of fearlessness. Mimi would bounce back up, ignore the fall, and right before my eyes would become superhuman again. I thought "Go Mimi!" She became greater because she had fallen. Failure enlarged her dancing.

That should be your model for dealing with failure.

When you fail in public, you are forcing yourself to learn a whole new set of skills, skills that have nothing to do with creating and everything to do with surviving.

Jerome Robbins[1] liked to say that you do your best work after your biggest disasters. For one thing, it's so painful it almost guarantees that you won't make those mistakes again. Also, you have nothing to lose; you've hit bottom, and the only place to go is up. A fiasco compels you to change dramatically. The golfer Bobby Jones said, "I never learned anything from a match I won." He respected defeat and he profited from it.

Failure creates an interesting tug of war between forgetting and remembering. It's vital to be able to forget the pain of failure while

Private failures are the first drafts that get tossed in the wastebasket, the sketches crumpled up on the floor, the manuscripts that stay in the drawer. They are the not-so-good ideas you reject en route to finding the one that clicks.

When I tape a three-hour improvisational session with a dancer and find only thirty seconds of useful material in the tape, I am earning straight A's in failure. Do the math: I have rejected 99.7 percent of my work that day. It would be like a writer knocking out a two-thousand-word chapter and upon re-reading deciding that only six words were worth keeping. Painful, yes, but for me absolutely necessary.

What's so wonderful about wasting that kind of time? It's simple: The more you fail in private, the less you will fail in public. In many ways, the creative act is editing. You're editing out all the lame ideas that won't resonate with the public. It's not pandering. It's exercising your judgment. It's setting the bar a little higher for yourself, and therefore your audience.

If you forget this—if you let down your guard, or lower your standards, or compromise too quickly, or leave in something that should be rejected—you'll have to deal with the other, more painful kind of failure, the public kind.

1. **Jerome Robbins.** American choreographer who choreographed and directed many Broadway plays including *West Side Story* and *Fiddler on the Roof*

retaining the lessons from it. I've always found it easier to put something that wasn't very successful behind me than to move on to something new after an effort that was acclaimed. After a certifiable success, I always think, "I could lose this," and so I cling to it. (For this reason, Duke University basketball coach Mike Krzyzewski banned his teams from calling themselves the "defending national champions," because he felt this made them think defensively. Also, he argued that you only defend something that can be taken away from you, and your past successes will always be yours no matter what.) A part of me hates to let go of success and move on. After a certifiable failure, however, I can't wait to move on. I'm thinking, "Get back to work. Fix it. Do it different and better the next time."

Failure creates an interesting tug of war between forgetting and remembering.

That's the tug of war. You have to forget the failure: to get it behind you, but at the same time you have to remember the reasons for it. People accommodate this duality in their own ways. I know one writer who frames all his rejection letters and hangs them up in the guest bathroom for every visitor to see. He scoffs at failure. I know an actress who does the same with her most vicious reviews, mocking those who mock her. That which to anyone else is a loss is to the artist a gain.

My heroes in *The Odyssey* are the older warriors who have been through many wars. They don't hide their scars, they wear them proudly as a kind of armor. When you fail—whether your short film induces yawns or your photographs inspire people to say "That's nice" (ouch!) or your novel is trashed in a journal of opinion that matters to you—the best thing to do is acknowledge your battle scars and gird yourself for the next round. Tell yourself, "This is a deep wound. But it's going to heal and I will remember this wound. When I go back into the fray it will serve me well." ❖

"If you're not failing, you're not taking enough risks." Do you agree with this statement? When can we learn from our mistakes and failures?

Refer and Reason

1. Give three examples of failure mentioned in the memoir. Identify the main points Tharp illustrates with her many examples.
2. State what every creative person has to learn to deal with. The selection is called "An 'A' in Failure." Judge whether the selection is really about failure or success. Explain your response.
3. Review the background material on page 325 and quote Tharp's beliefs about artists. Compare her ideas with Annie Dillard's ideas about talent in her essay on page 306. Compose a letter from Tharp to a person who has said "I'm not creative."

Writing Options

1. Write a parable, a brief story that teaches a lesson or moral, in which a character succeeds in the end by learning about failure. Choose one of these audiences for your parable: business people, creative artists, high school students.
2. Write a two- to three-paragraph response to "An 'A' in Failure" using examples and observations from your own life to support or challenge Tharp's thesis.

Go to **www.mirrorsandwindows.com** for more.

Mia Hamm.

The Burden of Expectations

A Biography by **Jere Longman**

THE GIRLS OF SUMMER
THE U.S. WOMEN'S SOCCER TEAM AND HOW IT CHANGED THE WORLD
JERE LONGMAN

Mia Hamm was the first player, male or female, to be named the U.S. soccer champion for three years in a row: 1994, 1995, and 1996. Her story is the subject of **"The Burden of Expectations,"** from Jere Longman's biographical book, *The Girls of Summer.* In the selection, the author examines Hamm not just as a talented player but as an individual, a member of an unusual family, and a team player.

Jere Longman has been on the sports beat for the *New York Times* for a number of years. Before his assignment with that big-city newspaper, he covered Eagles football games for the *Philadelphia Inquirer.* Besides the book *The Girls of Summer,* he's written *Among the Heroes,* a story about the passengers of Flight 93, one of the four airplanes hijacked on September 11, 2001.

Who is your favorite actor, author, or athlete? What about that person helps you appreciate his or her work?

A native of Selma, Alabama, Hamm lived a road-atlas childhood in Texas, California, Virginia and Italy, where her father, Bill, an Air Force colonel, was drawn weekly to the national spasm over soccer. Mia was born with a club foot, and treatment required her to sleep in corrective shoes connected by a steel bar. When she was very young, she wore a cast, and once a week, her mother would awaken at four in the morning, put her in the tub to dissolve the plaster support, then drive 50 miles to Montgomery, Alabama, so Air Force

"Ever since you're old enough to have someone make an impression on you, you're searching for an identity." 

doctors could stretch the tendons and ligaments in her foot and turn it outward. At 15 months, Hamm and her family moved to Florence, Italy, where her father rode his bike two miles to the stadium every other Sunday to watch Fiorentina play in the Italian professional league. Mia was about 18 months old when she showed her first interest in soccer. Her mother remembers the moment as if it were a photograph: Mia in a lavender dress, white lace tights, and white corrective shoes, coming down a slide in a park, seeing a man and his son kicking a soccer ball, and running toward them.

"It was like watching a movie," Stephanie Hamm said of her daughter. "She ran until she got to the ball and she booted it. She kept kicking the ball. She wouldn't let them play. Finally, the little boy gave up and Mia and the father played for the next 25 minutes. She was no taller than a minute."

At age six, living then in Wichita Falls, Texas, Hamm played her first organized soccer. She scored one goal in the fall league, her father said, and she was like any six-year-old during a soccer match, spending as much time looking at rocks and clouds in the sky as she did looking at the soccer ball. In the spring league, though, she scored 23 goals. "No longer did they insist that she stand in one place and wait for the ball," Bill Hamm said.

Mia reminded Stephanie Hamm of her own mother, determined, competitive, the same clenched jaw, a woman who regularly beat her husband at tennis and swam expertly and stood up on roller coasters. For a shy girl whose life was frequently uprooted by military life, sport provided reliable constancy for Mia. "Ever since you're old enough to have someone make an impression on you, you're searching for an identity," she said. "How do you fit into elementary school, junior high, college? Sports is how I fit in. That was my voice. It made me feel good about myself."

When Hamm was five, her parents adopted an eight-year-old Thai-American orphan named Garrett, whose legs and arms seemed wondrously suited to propelling a ball off a bat, through a hoop, into a net. Mia followed him from one neighborhood game to the next, football to baseball to soccer, and Garrett unfailingly chose his younger sister for his team.

"I was his secret weapon," Hamm said.

Her athleticism was such that, at age 10, she joined an 11-year-old boys' soccer team and led it in scoring. As a seventh-grader in Wichita Falls, Texas, she played end and quarterback and cornerback on a junior-high football team. "Even in pads she was fast," her father said. In a desperate moment of the 1995 World Cup, the Americans made her a goalkeeper and she did not let a shot elude her. At a practice at the Citrus Bowl in Orlando, Florida, before the 1999 World Cup, someone brought a football and Hamm repeatedly knocked in field goals from 35 yards. She was also the best golfer on the soccer team.

"Growing up, I played against boys and you never had to apologize for knocking someone over or going in hard for a tackle," Hamm said. "I think guys are taught that more than girls, to compete hard and not apologize for being successful."

Even in junior high, she exhibited two traits that would define her professional career and would sometimes fall into direct conflict: a fierce passion to play and succeed and a famous reluc-

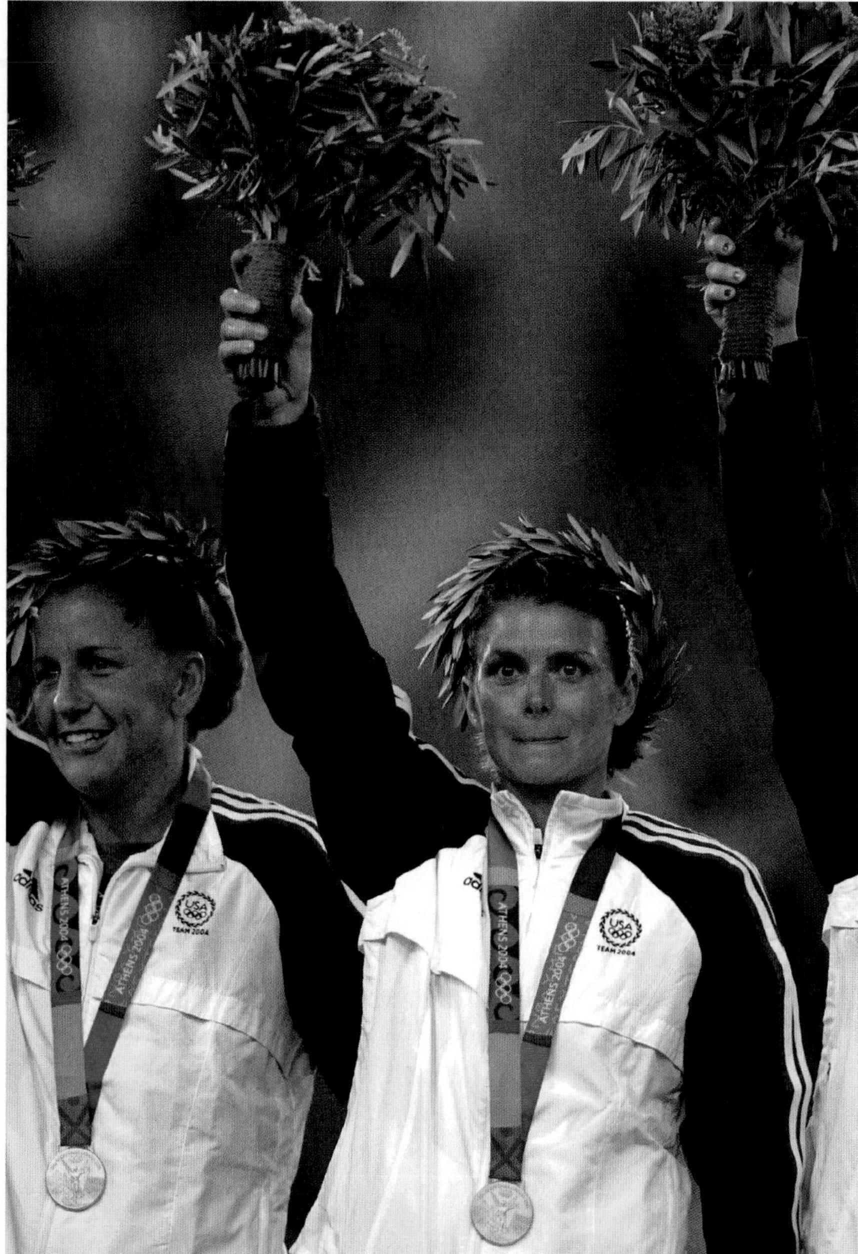
Mia Hamm at the Athens 2004 Olympic Games after the United States defeated Brazil 2–1 to win the gold medal.

tance to be in the spotlight. She declined to play football in the eighth grade, her mother said, because too much attention had been paid to the girl and not the team in the seventh grade.

As a young girl, Mia said, she became so frustrated over losing that she quit every game she played, neighborhood pickup games, family board games. When she wanted to play, her older sisters would ask, "Are you going to quit?" She was what she called a "screamer," a person who "reacted emotionally as opposed to thinking how a situation needed to be handled and then always going around and apologizing for things." Even after she had won an Olympic gold medal and two World Cups, losing would feel like heartburn. Following the 1999 World Cup, the Americans would lose four consecutive games to a world all-star team on an indoor victory tour. The games were only exhibitions, they meant nothing, but Hamm, spotting two reporters in an arena hallway after the fourth loss, would say in a loud voice, "I HATE LOSING!"

"The thing about emotion is, it's so unpredictable," Hamm said. "It can be my biggest strength or my biggest weakness. You never know how it's going to motivate you. I've worked on it. In college, I used to get really upset, down, every time I made a mistake. I'd take myself out of the game for five minutes. We worked on trying to turn it into positive energy by working hard defensively, or getting mad. You're going to take this player on again, and not let this big doubt come into your head that you're going to mess up."

"A champion is someone who is bent over, drenched in sweat, at the point of exhaustion when no one else is watching."

At 15, she became the youngest player, male or female, to join the national soccer team. Hamm wrote in her autobiography that Anson Dorrance, who was then the coach, pulled her aside and said, "You can become the best soccer player in the world." Taking night classes, Hamm graduated from high school in three years, and she followed Dorrance to North Carolina, where she won four national championships and met her husband, Christiaan Corry, a Marine pilot.

'While her husband was in attendance at the final, her brother Garrett was not. He suffered from a rare blood disorder, aplastic anemia, and although Mia raised $50,000 for his care through a benefit soccer game, he contracted a fungal infection after a bone-marrow transplant and died in April of 1997 at the age of 28. She started the Mia Hamm Foundation in his honor for research into bone marrow diseases and to develop sporting opportunities for young women.

"He embodied what I was always reaching for in sports," Hamm said. "He never gave up. And he never made me feel I couldn't participate because I was a girl."

Donna de Varona, the chairwoman of the World Cup organizing committee, said she wondered whether her brother's death affected Mia's own struggle for self-assurance on the field. "Maybe she feels guilty about her brother," de Varona said. "She was so close to him and profoundly affected by his death. Maybe it's simply that she's alive and he's not. She gets to play and he didn't make it."

She would become soccer's all-time leading scorer, a willing pioneer but a diffident celebrity. It would be one of a number of fundamental contradictions in her personality. She was a superstar who deferred constantly to[1] her teammates. A scorer who was a selfless passer. A forward who was as reserved with her words as she was explosive with her feet. A driven player who was impatient with failure but self-doubting about success.

"It's like these actors you see on the big screen, they put themselves up there to be criticized by everyone, but they're insecure," Chastain[2] said. "I don't see how those things parallel each other. They seem opposite poles to me.

Why the insecurity alongside unsurpassed[3] talent? "There's this kind of struggle inside herself to want to be the best and never believing she's gotten there," her mother said, "like 'I haven't done enough for my teammates, I haven't seen enough opportunities, I haven't made enough goals.' I'm sure there are games where she's not up to it physically, emotionally or psychologically, but she never wants to let down. There's never a reason not to work very hard."

As a teenager, she was out of house by 8 in the morning in the summer, practicing her shooting and dribbling and passing alone, before the sun turned from light to heat in Wichita Falls. Dorrance saw her running sprints alone one morning at North Carolina during the off-season and sent her a note: "A champion is someone who is bent over, drenched in sweat, at the point of exhaustion when no one else is watching."

1. **deferred...to.** Submitted to the wishes of; showed respect for
2. **Chastain.** Brandi Chastain, member of the 1999 U.S. Women's Soccer team
3. **unsurpassed.** Unequaled

Mia Hamm leaps into the arms of teammate Abby Wambach after the USA defeated Norway 1–0 in the Women's World Cup quarterfinal game in Foxboro, Massachusetts, October 1, 2003.

Having grown up in a military family with three sisters and two brothers, Hamm possessed a reserve, almost a sense of rank, as if she should aspire to succeed at a high level but that she should not stand out from the others or be treated differently. Even her handshake was noncommittal, as if it might reveal too much. She did not want her spotlight to keep her teammates permanently in the shadows, so she spoke of them constantly, a point guard handing off verbal assists. Most of her goals were layups, she said dismissively,[4] "harder to miss it than make it."

Before the World Cup, she turned down a photo shoot for a possible cover of *Newsweek* magazine, she declined to appear with David Letterman, she gave few one-on-one interviews, she declined to publicize her own autobiography and she insisted that her teammates be included in Nike's advertising campaign. "I don't like the spotlight being just about me," Hamm said. "I think they had the idea of getting everyone involved anyway. That was the motivation of the whole tournament, that there was more than one athlete on the team."

"Her work ethic was above everyone else's," said Lou Pearce, who coached Hamm for two years in high school in Wichita Falls and said she was the best player on a boy's varsity team. "While the boys were sleeping till 12, she was out at 8, on the side of the high school, working for an hour and a half—30 minutes of foot drills warming up, 30 minutes of shooting, 30 minutes of running. The goal didn't have a net. She'd kick the ball where she wanted, and then she'd go get it, never walking, always jogging."

Like her fellow North Carolina alum, Michael Jordan, Hamm understood the basic

4. **dismissively.** Without taking seriously

What she had to give she would give most of it to her team.

incongruity in what Americans wanted from their athletes, that they be educated and articulate but unwilling to offer contentious[5] opinion. Neither she nor Jordan spoke up against Nike's sweatshop labor practices in Asia. Some reporters found Hamm to be difficult, unforthcoming, a prima donna. She was available for interviews only certain days during the World Cup. Some of her teammates wanted her to be more visible in promoting the tournament. But she had set her priorities. What she had to give she would give most of it to her team. "I didn't want it to be Mia Hamm's World Cup from the media perspective," she said. "I put enough pressure on myself. It takes me a certain amount of time to get ready for games, to focus. I don't want to put any doubt in my own head that I'm not the player right now that I want to be." If her elusiveness was frustrating for reporters, in a way it was also refreshing and fascinating. How rare to find privacy in a society where celebrity honeymoons proceed right from the bedroom to the video store. In this confessional age of scandalous tell-all, she remained a rare mystery, as effortless and guarded as DiMaggio.[6]

"Some people love the attention," co-captain Julie Foudy said. "Mia says, 'I want to be able to have a life after soccer. I don't want to walk into a coffee shop and I'm with my husband and people are coming up for autographs.' I think that's why she stays out of the limelight as much as she can. Because she feels, 'I want a life. I don't want to have to change my life because everyone knows who I am.'" ❖

5. **contentious.** Argumentative

6. **DiMaggio.** Joe DiMaggio, a three-time MVP winner and thirteen-time All-Star for the N.Y. Yankees baseball team

What makes athletes and celebrities fascinating to the majority of society? What separates athletes from other types of celebrities?

Refer and Reason

1. Note the contradiction Longman identifies in Hamm, the driven player. Analyze how self-doubt can both motivate people to succeed and prevent success.
2. Recall how Hamm reacted to sweatshop labor practices. Argue whether star athletes should speak out against injustices or other social issues.
3. List some of the expectations people have of Mia Hamm because of her star athlete status. Compile a list of expectations people have of you. Categorize those expectations that are a burden and those you think you are able to meet.

Writing Options

1. Imagine that you are one of Mia's teammates. Write a letter to the companies endorsing Mia. Describe your feelings about having Mia as a teammate.
2. Assume you are a writer at a newspaper. Prepare an op-ed, or opinion essay, about the role of the individual player and of the team in a sport of your choice. Provide details, such as examples or statistics, to support your opinion.

 Go to **www.mirrorsandwindows.com** for more.

Climbing Mount Fuji

(Partway)
(In a Bus)
(At Least We Think
That Was Mount Fuji)

A Personal Narrative by **Dave Barry**

Dave Barry (b. 1947) wrote a humor column for twenty-five years and has written as many books. Material from two of his books was used for a television show called *Dave's World.* In 1988, Barry won a Pulitzer Prize for Commentary. When asked about his writing habits, Barry said, "Panicky despair is an underrated element of writing." He also noted, "Good writing is almost always hard, and what I think sometimes happens is that writers forget how hard it is, or don't want to do the work any more and they call this 'writer's block.'"

Dave Barry writes about the popular tourist attraction Mount Fuji in **"Climbing Mount Fuji,"** a chapter from his book *Dave Barry Does Japan.* Mount Fuji, Japan's highest mountain at about 12,380 feet, is a volcano that has been dormant, or inactive, since 1707. Mount Fuji is open for climbing in July and August. As many as a million people may try to climb the mountain in any given year, most of them scrambling to reach the top in time for sunrise.

If you could go to any destination or visit any tourist attraction, where would you go? What would you expect on your visit to this location?

...if we squinted really hard, we could see something that might have been Mount Fuji.

The last major tourism thing we did in Japan was make the traditional pilgrimage up picturesque Mount Fuji, a dormant volcano, which is defined, geologically as "a volcano that may not in fact exist." At least *we* never saw it. It was reputed to be quite large, but we never saw a trace of it the whole time we were in Japan, because it was always covered by a thick layer of picturesque clouds. So although we spent several hundred dollars for a Mount Fuji tour, during which we rode for ten hours in a tour bus that was allegedly driving around, and on, Mount Fuji, all we ever saw, through the dense fog, was the part of Mount Fuji directly below the bus window. It looked a lot like a road. I would say it was dormant.

From time to time, our guide would point out the window and say: "If you look over there, maybe you can just see top of mountain," and we'd all squint into the fog, and if we squinted really hard, we could see something that might have been Mount Fuji. Or it could have been window dirt, or one of those brown things that float around inside your eyeball. (Try not to think about them. They're probably harmless.)

We weren't the only people attempting to enjoy the picturesque beauty of Mount Fuji that day. It was the height of vacation season, and Mount Fuji is one of Japan's most popular destinations. As the guide put it when our bus set out: "Very traffic jam can be expected."

This turned out to be, if anything, a very understatement. As far as we could tell, the entire Japanese nation had been waiting for a day like this, featuring maximum cloud density, to make the Mount Fuji trip.

So we spent the first few hours grinding slowly along on a car-choked highway, passing the time by eating cookies from a package labeled "Varieties of Bland New Type." The other major entertainment medium on the bus was Brazilians. There was a group of Brazilian tourists on the bus, and they were sociable to the point of mass civil disorder. After three weeks among the Japanese, who tend to be, by American standards, quite reserved, I had come to think of us as quite outgoing and lively and demonstrative; but we are The Night of the Living Dead compared with Brazilians, at least the Brazilians on our bus. They communicated mainly by shouting—happy, vibrant shouts, interspersed with loud laughs and heartfelt emotional greetings, whenever two of them were reunited again after an absence caused by, for example, walking to the other end of the bus.

Their favorite thing to shout was "*Hai!*" This is the Japanese word for "yes," and it appeared to be the only Japanese word that the Brazilians knew. But they *loved* it, and they used it at every available opportunity. The guide, pointing at the fog, would say, "Now maybe you can just see top of mountain," and the Brazilians, not even looking out the window, would shout "*HAI!*" and then collapse with laughter.

Thus we whiled away the hours, inching our way through the traffic to Mount Fuji, then gradually up the slope until we reached the Fifth Station, which is the highest point you can drive to on Mount Fuji. There we found a very traffic jam indeed. I am quite sure that many of those cars are still up there.

We got out of the bus and wandered for a while in the fog along with thousands of other people. Many of them were hikers on their way to the top, which was a five-hour climb from where we were. It was so crowded that people were waiting in line to get onto the trail, which disappeared up the mountainside, into the gloom. A loudspeaker on a pole constantly blared instructions at the hikers, the noise echoing up and down the slope. I asked our guide what it was saying, and he said, "Mainly it says be careful not to fall down."

Being a bold adventurer who is always ready to take on a physical challenge, I myself set off briskly up the mountain, and I did not rest until about fifteen feet later, where there was a soft-drink vending machine. I would have continued all the way to the top, but our tour itinerary required us to be back on the bus in forty-five minutes, so we could resume sitting in traffic.

One lucky break for us was that there was a large and busy gift shop, which sold every conceivable kind of Mount Fuji souvenir. With an eye toward having something to do on the bus ride home, I bought a nice set of Mount Fuji toenail clippers (the box said "Family Size"). The clerk spent several minutes carefully wrapping the box, as though it were a gift. I hadn't asked him to do this, but by then I was used to it; the Japanese are big on packaging, and your purchases often get wrapped. (Once, in Tokyo, Robby and I and Tom Reid of the Washington *Post* had purchased desserts in a bakery. Our plan was to take the desserts outside, a distance of maybe ten feet, and eat them, but first the clerk put each dessert into a separate box, which he carefully fastened shut with tape. When we got outside and opened them, we discovered that we were short one plastic spoon, so Tom went back inside to get it. The clerk, who could see that we were eating right outside, nevertheless wrapped the plastic spoon in paper, which he put into a little bag, which he taped shut, before he gave it to Tom. Just doing his job.)

Not that I am complaining about Japanese packaging mania. It was kind of festive, opening my toenail clippers on the bus.

We left the Fifth Station and drove back down the mountain to the popular, by which I mean comically overcrowded, tourist destination of Hakone, where we went to a restaurant. Our group made quite an entrance. There were maybe fifty vacationing Japanese, eating and chatting quietly, and suddenly

HAI!

Fifty heads jerked around simultaneously to see who was shouting "YES!" at them. It was, of course, our Brazilians, whose mood seemed to improve the longer they sat on the bus...soon they were striding around inside the restaurant, doing little dance steps, hurling *hais* left and right and holding long-distance conversations with each other across the room, over the heads of stunned, staring Japanese, who would not make this kind of noise if they were undergoing surgery without anesthesia. It's probably no accident that Brazil and Japan are located so far apart.

It's probably no accident that Brazil and Japan are located so far apart.

While waiting for the traffic to build up for our return trip to Tokyo, we spent some time in the Hakone area, which is quite pretty and features a spectacular view of the clouds covering Mount Fuji. It also features snack bars where you can buy a popular dish made by frying tiny baby eels until they form a yellowish brown mass of what looks like melted-together spaghetti with zillions of little spots on it. The spots are what's left of the baby eels' eyes. As a bold culinary adventurer I certainly would have tried this dish, but I had to sit down with my head between my legs.

When the traffic was dense enough for our purposes we got back onto the bus and began inching back toward Tokyo. It had been a long day, and eventually even the Brazilians became dormant, as did the rest of us. As night began to fall, I drifted off to sleep listening to the monotonous, reassuring sound of our guide saying that if we looked *now*, maybe we could just see the top of... ❖

What do you do when events in your life don't measure up to your expectations or go according to your plan? What can people learn from these experiences?

Refer and Reason

1. Recall Barry's comparisons of Japanese, Americans, and Brazilians. Analyze Barry's cultural observations to make some generalizations about Japanese and Brazilian people. Are the generalizations fair?
2. Evaluate whether Barry's humorous and sometimes sarcastic tone is a positive or a negative addition to the selection. Explain.
3. List three facts about Mount Fuji. Using details from Barry's piece and the background information, write a brief description of Mount Fuji.

Writing Options

1. Choose a scene from the selection and write a paragraph describing it from the perspective of a Japanese citizen.
2. Write a brief analysis of hyperbole, which is the use of exaggeration for effect, in "Climbing Mount Fuji." Explain how it adds humor to the selection.

Go to **www.mirrorsandwindows.com** for more.

FOR YOUR READING LIST

SELECTIONS FROM THE JOURNALS

by Henry David Thoreau, edited by Walter Harding

For twenty-five years, Henry David Thoreau kept a journal, recording his observations on both the natural and the man-made worlds. In the book, miniature portraits of daily life are mixed with thoughtful meditations on their meaning. This slim volume of excerpts from his journal conveys the keen eye, humor, and poetry found in Thoreau's fourteen-volume larger work.

FAREWELL TO MANZANAR: A TRUE STORY OF JAPANESE AMERICAN EXPERIENCE DURING AND AFTER THE WORLD WAR II INTERNMENT

by Jeanne Wakatsuki Houston and James Huston

If FBI agents led your father away saying he was a Japanese saboteur and sent the rest of the family to a desert camp enclosed by barbed wire, what would you do? This is what happened to seven-year-old Jeanne Wakatsuki in 1942. This true account pre-sents a young person's view of a dark episode in American history.

HIGH EXPOSURE: AN ENDURING PASSION FOR EVEREST AND UNFORGIVING PLACES

by David Breashears

At age twelve, David Breashears became hooked on the sport of extreme climbing. Starting on the rock faces outside of Boulder, Colorado, he tackled more diffi-cult climbs until he was ready for Everest. Four times he reached its summit, including when he was one of the rescuers who tried to reach a party caught in a fatal blizzard.

GRAND MOTHERS: POEMS, REMINISCENCES, AND SHORT STORIES ABOUT THE KEEPERS OF OUR TRADITIONS

edited by Nikki Giovanni

This collection is a tribute to the women who tell stories, offer wisdom, and pass on family lega-cies to their grandchildren. The writers within this anthology write about grandmothers who are strong, silent, a little bit scary, indulgent—even those who can only be found on scraps of old paper. This anthology reminds readers of the basic human needs that grandmothers fulfill.

SILENT SPRING

by Rachel Carson

Released in 1962, Rachel Carson's widely acclaimed book brought the detrimental use of pesticides into the public aware-ness. The novel provides examples of mankind's misuse of poisons on farmland, cities, and neighbor-hoods and urges its readers to become advocates for ecological awareness.

SWIMMING TO ANTARCTICA

by Lynne Cox

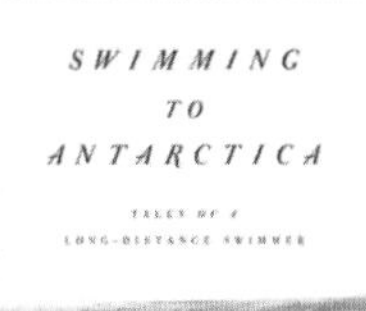

Beyond the icy waters of the Bering Strait, Cox's autobiography details her journeys across many bodies of water. Wearing only a bathing suit, cap, and goggles, Cox enters iceberg-filled waters and encounters dolphins and sharks. Her account describes not only her experiences but also her motivation and love of swimming.

Deliver a Persuasive Speech

An effective way to convince others to adopt your opinion is by delivering a persuasive speech. The goal of this type of speech is to change someone's mind or way of thinking about a topic. You must portray yourself as the authority figure, so you need to know your material well. In a persuasive speech, do not be afraid to show a little emotion—this is not a sterile or static speech. Your body and voice must match the tone of your words. Use the following guidelines to present your speech to your audience. Prepare by rehearsing your speech in pairs or small groups.

1. Be sincere and enthusiastic

Feel strongly about your topic. Apathy is infectious and will quickly spread to your audience. When you are trying to convince someone of something, you must first establish your credibility, or in other words, you must sell yourself before you sell your message. You must be committed to the ideals and goals of your speech and what you are saying. Do not use words such as "maybe" or "might"—use positive words such as "will" and "must."

2. Maintain good but relaxed posture

Don't slouch or lean. It's fine to move around a bit; doing so releases normal nervous tension. Keep your hands free to gesture naturally instead of clutching note cards, props, or the podium so often or hard that you "tie up" your hands.

3. Speak slowly

Oral communication is more difficult for audiences to process and understand than written language and visual images. Pause briefly before each major point and before any direct quotations, allowing important or complex information to sink in. Don't be afraid of silence. Focus on communicating with the audience. By looking for feedback from the audience, you will be able to pace yourself appropriately.

4. Maintain genuine eye contact

Treat the audience as individuals, not as a mass of people. Look at individual faces.

5. Speak in a genuine, relaxed, conversational tone

Don't act or stiffen up. Be yourself, but make sure to vary your pitch and volume. Avoid speaking in a monotone. Let your words speak for themselves; reflect your nature through your voice.

6. Communicate with the audience

Focus on conveying your message, not on "getting through" the speech. Concentrate on communicating with the audience, not speaking at or to them.

Speaking Tip

Remain confident and composed. Remember that listeners are generally supportive of speakers and usually don't detect any signs of nervousness. To help yourself overcome initial apprehension, take two or three deep breaths as you are stepping up to speak.

Listening Tip

As you listen to your classmates' persuasive speeches, evaluate the effectiveness of their arguments. Does the speaker offer relevant evidence to support his or her main idea?

Speaking and Listening Rubric

Your presentation will be evaluated on these elements:

Content

- ☑ clear chronology—beginning, middle, and end
- ☑ strong opening and closing sentences
- ☑ persuasive and well-supported thesis
- ☑ simple vocabulary and sentence structure

Delivery and Presentation

- ☑ appropriate volume, pace, and enunciation
- ☑ effective tone, intonation, and stress
- ☑ effective nonverbal expression and gestures

Persuasive Essay

Assignment
Write a persuasive essay

Purpose
To persuade readers to consider your point of view

Audience
Adults and peers affected by your topic who may or may not agree with your position

Persuasive words have power: Martin Luther King Jr.'s "I Have a Dream" speech, Nelson Mandela's "Glory and Hope" speech, and Rachel Carson's book *Silent Spring* all inspired important changes in society. Each author stated his or her opinion and provided convincing, reasonable evidence to support it. They felt passionately about the truth of their position. Their words have had a lasting effect.

Expressing an informed opinion is an attempt to win an audience, to convince people to agree with or understand your point of view. You encounter persuasive language every day. Advertisers persuade you to make a purchase; newspaper editorials persuade you to consider an opinion on an issue. Persuasion combines passion with logic and reasoning to influence the minds and sometimes change the lives of others.

For this assignment, choose a topic you believe in and care about. Prewrite, draft, and revise an informed **persuasive essay** that expresses your opinion of this important topic.

❶ PREWRITE

Select Your Topic

Brainstorm a list of topics that concern you. To find ideas, read through a newspaper or current events magazine. Choose a topic that you not only have a strong opinion about, but a topic that either you or a relative have had some experience with. It is important that you have both emotional and logical argumentation for your essay to be persuasive and effective.

Writing Rubric

A successful persuasive essay

- has an **introduction** identifying the topic and generating interest in it
- includes a **thesis statement** that clearly establishes the writer's position on the topic
- provides at least three informed reasons in the **body** and supporting evidence for each reason
- acknowledges opposing viewpoints and offers responses to those objections
- presents ideas in a reasonable, respectful, and sincere way
- issues a call-to-action or a recommendation for the reader in the **conclusion**

Gather Information

Read more articles on your topic. Talk with people about the issue you chose. Remember that there are two or more sides to every issue. Anticipating opposing viewpoints can help you make a strong case for your own argument. Take notes on the different ideas and perspectives you discover.

Next, pose a question about your topic and write it at the top of a chart like the one on page 341. Then list pro and con reasons to support both sides of the argument—for and against. Don't evaluate your ideas at this point.

Organize Your Ideas

Review the pro and con reasons you listed in your chart. Consider which points, or arguments, you feel most strongly about. If any seem particularly weak, cross them out.

You need at least three reasons to support your thesis statement. To gradually convince your readers, present your arguments in order of importance, ending with the strongest point. Number your reasons, one through three, in a logical progression.

Pro and Con Chart

Topic Question: Should separate math and/or science classes be offered for girls and boys?	
Pro	Con
• Reduces distraction • Allows for a teaching style that is more aligned to gender learning style • Balances attention and encouragement • Reduces the number of girls who are dropping out of math	• 2 Doesn't parallel real world • 3 Fosters notion that separate is good • 1 Offers a defeatist approach and encourages gender bias

Write Your Thesis Statement

Determine the general idea that the numbered points on your graphic organizer support. Write a **thesis statement** that answers, in your opinion, the question at the top of your graphic organizer. One student, Rhonda, wrote this thesis statement in response to her initial question, "Should separate math and/or science classes be offered for girls and boys?":

Girls should compete with boys in math and science classes.

❷ DRAFT

Write your essay by following the three-part framework described on page 342: **introduction, body,** and **conclusion.**

Draft Your Introduction

In a persuasive essay, the **introduction** grabs readers' attention, drawing them in. You might want to start out with a significant quotation, an anecdote or a story, or an important fact or statistic. The introduction should also identify and briefly explain the issue, both to inform readers and to alert them to the problem. Declare your opinion on the issue in your thesis statement.

Rhonda's introduction, shown in the first column of the chart on page 343, presents the issue and gets the readers' interest in the first sentence. Next, she provides the rationale for having separate math and science classes for boys and girls. At the end of the introduction, in her thesis statement, she opposes gender-segregated classrooms. Her tone, however, is too strong and informal. She risks offending her readers. How could she state her opinion in a more respectful tone?

Draft Your Body

In the **body,** you support your thesis statement. You provide reasons why you hold your opinion. You already have them—the numbered points in your chart.

What Great Writers Do

Great writers don't shy away from a highly debatable thesis statement. Notice how they also respectfully acknowledge possible opposition to their views:

- "I am not unmindful that some of you have come here out of great trials and tribulations." —Martin Luther King Jr.
- "We understand it still that there is no easy road to freedom." —Nelson Mandela
- "All this is not to say there is no insect problem and no need of control. I am saying, rather, that control must be geared to realities..." —Rachel Carson

- **Introduction** Identify your topic and include a thesis that states your opinion about it.
- **Body** Provide at least three logical reasons with supporting evidence to back up your opinion, and to inform and persuade your readers.
- **Conclusion** Rephrase your thesis, appeal to your readers with a call-to-action or recommendation, and give your essay closure.

Develop your ideas by providing additional supporting evidence for your reasons, such as facts, statistics, expert opinion, or personal experience. Remember to respond to possible opposition to your opinion.

Rhonda begins the draft of her body with her point that gender-separated classes might send the wrong message. She develops that idea, as you can see from the draft of her first body paragraph in the left-hand column of the chart on page 343. Later, she establishes other reasons why she believes segregated classrooms will not work.

Review the numbered pro and con reasons in your chart. Expand each reason into a fully developed paragraph. Organize your reasons logically; develop them in the order you decided to present them. Use your thesis statement to guide and focus your writing.

Draft Your Conclusion

In the **conclusion,** or last paragraph, of a persuasive essay, summarize the points you made in the body. Rephrase your thesis statement, use convincing language, and include a call-to-action or recommendation for the reader. Build on the introduction to provide closure and strengthen the argument. Show your conviction, and leave the reader with something to think about.

Examine the draft of Rhonda's essay, in the chart on page 343. Is she on her way to writing a strong, convincing conclusion?

❸ REVISE

Evaluate Your Draft

Evaluate your own writing or exchange essays with a classmate and evaluate each other's work. Read over the writing and think about how you can improve it.

Consider the essay's content, organization, and language. Make sure the introduction, body, and conclusion work well together. Make sure every paragraph supports the thesis statement. Use the Revision Checklist on page 344 to guide your evaluation, checking off each item as you complete it. Write notes on the essay about what's been done well and what can be improved.

Next, check the language for errors. Go through the draft, paying attention to the guidelines in the Grammar & Style workshops in this unit. Think about how the writing can be made more clear and interesting. Ways to achieve this are to strengthen transitions, improve word choices, and eliminate unnecessary wordiness.

What Great Writers Do

Part of your purpose in revision is to clarify your passionate ideas and beliefs about your topic. Harper Lee (b. 1926), author of *To Kill a Mockingbird,* said,

"Before I can live with other folks I've got to live with myself. The one thing that doesn't abide by majority rule is a person's conscience."

Revise for Content, Organization, and Style

When Rhonda evaluated her draft, she discovered ways to improve it. Look at the right-hand column of the chart on page 343 to see how she revised the three paragraphs we looked at earlier.

- **Introduction:** Rhonda more clearly and assertively introduced her topic to strengthen her introduction. She also replaced vague, informal writing with specific, respectful language.

DRAFT STAGE		REVISE STAGE	
Introduction Do female students do better in female-only classes, especially in math and science? I read one study that said separate classes allow females to get more attention and encouragement. While it might seem logical, this idea is actually pretty lame. Girls should compete with boys in math and science classes.	Identifies topic Provides context for the issue States opinion in thesis	A recent study found that female students do better in female-only classes, especially in math and science. ~~I read one study that said~~ Separate classes, the study said, allow females to get more attention and encouragement. While the logical conclusion seems to be that high schools should segregate math and science classes by gender, this idea is actually ~~pretty lame~~ flawed. The reality is, girls should compete with boys in the math and science classroom.	Introduces topic in the form of a sentence, not a question. Replaces vague idea with specific, more respectful language Adds a transitional phrase
Body Having separate classes sends the message that girls are bad at math and science. Studying with boys is not a distraction, as the study also suggests. Male and female classmates gain a lot by studying with each other.	Creates topic sentence from a reason that supports her thesis statement Responds to opposing views	Having separate classes sends the message that girls are not as good at math and science as boys are. My cousin, a college sophomore, is in a mixed-gender math study group. She says studying with men is not a distraction, as the study also suggested. Instead, both her male and female classmates gain a lot by studying with each other. With separate classes, there is a risk of lowered standards in the female classes.	Uses a paragraph transition; rewords sentence to strengthen idea Provides an example Use commas correctly Restates topic sentence for emphasis
Conclusion We can't just accept the attitude that female students cannot compete with males in the "hard classes" or that men are better than women. Anyone who believes that is living in the Dark Ages. Men and women benefit from studying and working together. Schools that try to help females by isolating them from males will do everyone a disservice.	Brings discussion to end of story Summarizes main points Restates thesis	~~We can't just~~ Ultimately, to accept the attitude that female students cannot compete with males in the "hard classes"~~or~~ is to accept the attitude that men are better than women. ~~Anyone who believes that is living in the dark ages.~~ Men and women benefit from studying and working together. Both male and female students should protest gender separation. Schools that try to help females by isolating them from males will do everyone a disservice.	Tightens language Deletes lines that might offend readers Includes a call-to-action for readers

REVISION CHECKLIST

Content and Organization

- ❑ Is your topic identified in your **introduction?** Does your introduction provide context for the issue and grab the readers' attention?
- ❑ Is the **thesis** clearly stated in the **introduction?** Does it respectfully state your opinion?
- ❑ Does each **body** paragraph develop ideas that support the thesis statement? Do you explain your reasoning and include supporting evidence?
- ❑ Are your **body** paragraphs organized in a logical order, building to the strongest argument?
- ❑ Does your **conclusion** restate your thesis? Does it issue a call-to-action or make a recommendation for readers? Does it provide closure and leave readers with something to think about?

Grammar and Style

- ❑ Do you use prepositional, infinitive, and participial phrases correctly? (page 220)
- ❑ Do commas appear in the appropriate locations? (page 240)
- ❑ Does your writing use possessive nouns and pronouns correctly? (page 264)

- **Body:** Rhonda strengthened sentences by rewording and adding transitions where needed. She also decided to include an example to support her paragraph's main idea. She added a final statement that reflects back to the topic sentence, giving the paragraph unity.
- **Conclusion:** To give her argument integrity and to respect her readers, Rhonda tightened her language and deleted a potentially offensive statement. She also included a call-to-action for readers.

Review the notes you or your partner made in working with your draft. Use the suggestions to effectively revise your essay.

Proofread for Errors

When you proofread, look specifically for mechanical errors in capitalization, spelling, punctuation, and grammar. You can certainly fix these errors as you revise your essay, but focusing on them intently during proofreading guarantees a clean, finished copy. Use proofreader's symbols to mark any errors you find. (See Language Arts Handbook 4.1 for a list of proofreader's symbols.) Print out your final draft and read through it once more before turning it in.

Read Rhonda's finished, polished essay on the next page. See how her final version reflects her work in the three stages of the writing process: Prewrite, Draft, and Revise.

WRITING FOLLOW-UP

Publish and Present

- Deliver your persuasive essay as a speech. (See the Speaking & Listening Workshop "Deliver a Speech" on page 339.) Prepare your speech by rehearsing it in pairs or small groups.
- Facilitate (that is, lead) a group discussion about your essay topic with a group of your classmates. As the facilitator, ask relevant questions about the topic, provide information, and listen carefully to your classmates' responses. As the facilitator, model the same respectful language when you speak that you used in writing your essay.

Reflect

- In the process of writing your essay, what did you learn about your topic? What helped you see your topic from another viewpoint? How did examining the pros and cons of the issue benefit you?
- Now that you have practiced the art of persuasion, where do you recognize persuasive language in advertising, news reporting, and politics? Collect examples of both effective and ineffective uses of persuasive language.

STUDENT MODEL

XX + XY is the Best Formula
by Rhonda Cobb

A recent study found that female students do better in female-only classes, especially in math and science. Separate classes, the study said, allow females to get more attention and encouragement. For some students, they also reduce the distraction created by the opposite sex. While the logical conclusion seems to be that high schools should segregate math and science classes by gender, this idea is actually flawed. The reality is, girls should compete with boys in math and science classes.

What is the writer's thesis statement?

One problem is that separate classes send the message that girls are not as good at math and science as boys are. The study said girls would get much-needed attention in a female-only classroom. However, we shouldn't have to resort to separate classes for girls to get the attention and encouragement they deserve. My cousin, a college sophomore, is in a mixed-gender math study group. She says studying with men is not a distraction, as the study also suggested. Instead, both her male and female classmates gain a lot by studying with each other. With separate classes, there is a risk of lowered standards in the female classes.

Where does she acknowledge opposing views?

Furthermore, separate classes in math and science for males and females simply doesn't match what is happening in the real world. Men and women are not segregated in the workplace. These days, you find as many women doctors and scientists as men. You also see women lawyers, business owners, police officers, and construction workers. Across the employment spectrum, women are doing jobs that used to be handled only by men. How did these women achieve their career goals? Not by sitting in a segregated classroom, but by learning to compete with men.

What evidence does the writer give to support her views?

In fact, separate classrooms may promote the dated notion that gender separation is good. Women have already struggled for more than a century in this country to be considered equal to men, to have equal rights and equal opportunities. By separating male and female students, schools will encourage our society to move backward, rather than forward.

Ultimately, to accept the attitude that female students cannot compete with males in the "hard classes" is to accept the attitude that men are better than women. If that attitude leaked into the working world, women might be denied the same jobs as men. Men and women both benefit from studying and working together. Both male and female students should protest gender separation. Schools that try to help females by isolating them from males will do everyone a disservice.

What call-to-action does the writer make in the conclusion?

Where does the writer restate the thesis?

TEST PRACTICE WORKSHOP

Reading Skills

IDENTIFY THE AUTHOR'S PURPOSE

A writer's **purpose** is his or her aim, or goal. Being able to figure out a writer's purpose, or purposes, is an important reading skill. An author may write with one or more of the following purposes: (1) to inform or explain; (2) to entertain, describe, enrich, or enlighten; (3) to tell a story or narrate a series of events; or (4) to persuade.

Test-Taking Tips
To identify the author's purpose, ask yourself these questions:

- Why did the author create this piece of writing?
- Is the author simply sharing information or trying to convince me of something?
- Is he or she writing to entertain or trying to make a point?

Once you identify what the author is trying to do, you can evaluate how well he or she has achieved that purpose. For example, you may judge that the author of a persuasive essay made a convincing argument. Or, you may decide that the author of a humorous true story failed to entertain you because the sequence of events was confusing. Read the following excerpt from Garrison Keillor's "How to Write a Letter." Try to determine whether Keillor's main purpose here is to reflect, entertain, inform, describe, enrich, tell a story, or persuade. Think about what leads you to this answer.

> Sit for a few minutes with the blank sheet in front of you, and meditate on the person you will write to, let your friend come to mind until you can almost see her or him in the room with you. Remember the last time you saw each other and how your friend looked and what you said and what perhaps was unsaid between you, and when your friend becomes real to you, start to write.

You can recognize that Keillor's purpose in this excerpt is to inform. In these two sentences, Keillor is *not* describing a letter, reflecting on his attitude toward letter writing, entertaining us with a funny story about someone writing a letter (although Keillor's writing is somewhat humorous), or trying to convince us to write a letter. His purpose is to explain to the reader one of the steps to take in writing a letter.

PRACTICE

Directions: The passage in this test is followed by several questions. After reading the passage, choose the best answer to each question.

Nonfiction: The passage that follows is Sojourner Truth's Speech to the Convention of the Equal Rights Association, New York City, 1867.

...I feel that if I have to answer for the deeds done in my body just as much as a man, I have a right to have just as much as a man. There is a great stir about colored men getting their rights, but not a word about the colored women; and if colored men get their rights, and not colored women theirs, you see the colored men will be masters over the women, and it will be just as bad as it was before. So I am for keeping the thing going while things are stirring; because if we wait till it is still, it will take a great while to get it going again. White women are a great deal smarter, and know more than colored women, while colored women do not know scarcely anything. They go out washing, which is about as high as a colored woman gets, and their men go about idle, strutting up and down; and when the women come home, they ask for their money and take it all, and then scold because there is no food. I want you to consider on that, chil'n. I call you chil'n; you are somebody's chil'n, and I am old enough to be mother of all that is here. I want women to have their rights. In the courts women have no rights, no voice; nobody speaks for them. I wish woman to have her voice there among the pettifoggers. If it is not a fit place for women, it is unfit for men to be there.

I am above eighty years old; it is about time for me to be going. I have been forty years a slave and forty years free, and would be here forty years more to have equal rights for all. I suppose I am kept here because something remains for me to do; I suppose I am yet to help to break the chain. I have done a great deal of work; as much as a man, but did not get so much pay. I used to work in the field and bind grain, keeping up with the cradler; but men doing no more, got twice as much pay.... We do as much, we eat as much, we want as much. I suppose I am about the only colored woman that goes about to speak for the rights of the colored women. I want to keep the thing stirring, now that the ice is cracked. What we want is a little money. You men know that you get as much again as women, when you write, or for what you do. When we get our rights, we shall not have to come to you for money, for then we shall have money enough in our own pockets; and maybe you will ask us for money. But help us now until we get it. It is a good consolation to know that when we have got this battle once fought we shall not be coming to you any more....

Multiple Choice

1. What is Sojourner Truth's main purpose?
   A. to reflect
   B. to narrate a series of events
   C. to inform
   D. to persuade
   E. to confuse

2. Which of the following sentences from the first paragraph of the excerpt seems to be contrary to the speaker's main purpose?
   A. "So I am for keeping the thing going while things are stirring; because if we wait till it is still, it will take a great while to get it going again."
   B. "White women are a great deal smarter, and know more than colored women, while colored women do not know scarcely anything."
   C. "I call you chil'n; you are somebody's chil'n, and I am old enough to be mother of all that is here."
   D. "If it is not a fit place for women, it is unfit for men to be there."
   E. None of the above

3. As used in line 49, the word *consolation* most nearly means
   A. joined together.
   B. source of comfort.
   C. contest for those who have lost earlier.
   D. accident.
   E. deception.

4. *Dialect* is a language spoken by the people of a particular place, time, or social group. Identify the sentence below that is *not* an example of dialect.
   A. "I want you to consider on that, chil'n."
   B. "In the courts women have no rights, no voice; nobody speaks for them."
   C. "I used to work in the field and bind grain, keeping up with the cradler..."
   D. "I wish woman to have her voice there among the pettifoggers."
   E. All of the above

Constructed Response

5. Name at least three techniques Sojourner Truth uses to achieve her purpose and provide a specific example to support each one.

Writing Skills

Test-Taking Tip
Plan your essay by spending a limited period of time on prewriting. In your writing test booklet, briefly jot down the following:

- the stance or side of the topic that you plan to discuss
- reasons that support your stance
- examples or evidence for support
- opposing arguments and your possible responses

Completing this prewriting step will help you organize your ideas in a logical order before you begin writing your essay.

PERSUASIVE WRITING

Many high-stakes tests, including college entrance exams and statewide tests, ask that you write a persuasive essay on a selected topic. Writing prompts on such tests typically introduce the topic, giving information about two different perspectives on it. You are then asked to choose a perspective or side and, using reasons and supporting evidence, write a persuasive essay. Essays must be completed within a specified period of time, often 30 minutes.

As with any writing assignment, make sure to apply the basic steps of the writing process: prewrite, draft, and revise. Organize your essay into the three-part framework: introduction, body, and conclusion.

- **Introduction** Identify your topic and include a thesis that states your opinion about it.
- **Body** Provide at least three logical reasons and supporting evidence to inform and persuade your readers.
- **Conclusion** Rephrase your thesis and give your essay closure.

Take a few minutes before the end of the testing session to read over your essay and correct any mistakes in grammar, usage, punctuation, and spelling. Scorers will take into account the limited time frame given to write your essay. They will evaluate your ability to:

- take a position on the topic
- focus on the topic throughout the essay
- support your ideas logically and thoroughly
- organize your ideas in a logical way
- use language clearly and effectively according to the conventions of standard written English

PRACTICE

Timed Writing: 30 minutes

Think carefully about the issue presented in the following excerpt and the assignment that follows. Allow 30 minutes to write your response.

Some parents feel that their teenage children are given too many material things and don't value property because they haven't had to work for it. Other parents want to give their teenage children advantages that they can afford and don't see any harmful effects in doing this. In your opinion, should parents buy everything for their teenage children without making them work to earn it?

Assignment:

Write an essay in which you take a position on this topic. You may choose to support one of the two points of view given, or you may write about a third perspective on the topic. Support your position with specific reasons and examples.

Revising and Editing Skills

Some standardized tests ask you to read a passage and answer multiple-choice questions about how to improve it. As you read the passage, keep the following tips in mind.

- Pay attention to the writing style used in each passage.
- Consider the elements of writing, such as tone or emphasis, that are included in the passage.
- Be aware that you may be asked questions about a section of the passage or about the passage as a whole.
- Examine each answer choice and determine how it differs from the others.
- Read and consider all of the answer choices and eliminate the answers that you know are incorrect.
- Reread the sentence using your selected answer to make sure it is correct.

PRACTICE

Directions: Read each question, and consider each answer to determine which one is best. If you think the original version is best, choose alternative A or F, "Make no change."

(1) Buying me my own computer would be a good idea. (2) First, it wouldn't cost my parents a hole lot of money, and it would be an investment in my future. (3) First off, I'd only need about $500 from my parents. (4) I would be willing to spend my savings that I worked real hard for to pay the rest of it. (5) I'd do lots of checking beforehand to get the very best deal on a computer that will last a long time. (6) I'd no longer have to be bothering them about using their laptop beings how I would have my own computer.

1. What change, if any, should you make to sentence 2?
   A. Make no change.
   B. Change *First* to *Firstly.*
   C. Change *hole* to *whole* or delete it entirely.
   D. Change the comma after *money* to a semi-colon.
   E. Change *future* to *past.*

2. Which unnecessary words could be deleted?
   A. First off (sentence 3)
   B. lots of (sentence 5)
   C. beforehand (sentence 5)
   D. very (sentence 5)
   E. All of the above

3. Which of the following would be the best way to revise sentence 4?
   A. I would be willing to spend my savings, for which I worked really hard, to pay the rest of the cost.
   B. I would be willing to spend my savings to pay the rest of it; I worked really hard for these savings.
   C. Even given how hard I worked for them, I would spend my savings to pay the rest.
   D. I worked hard for my savings but would be willing to spend them to pay the rest of it.
   E. I'd pay with my savings.

4. Which of the following would be the best way to revise sentence 6?
   A. Make no change.
   B. being I would have my own computer
   C. due to I would have my own computer
   D. since I would have my own computer
   E. being that I had one

UNIT 3

POETRY

SEXTON

DUNBAR

WALKER

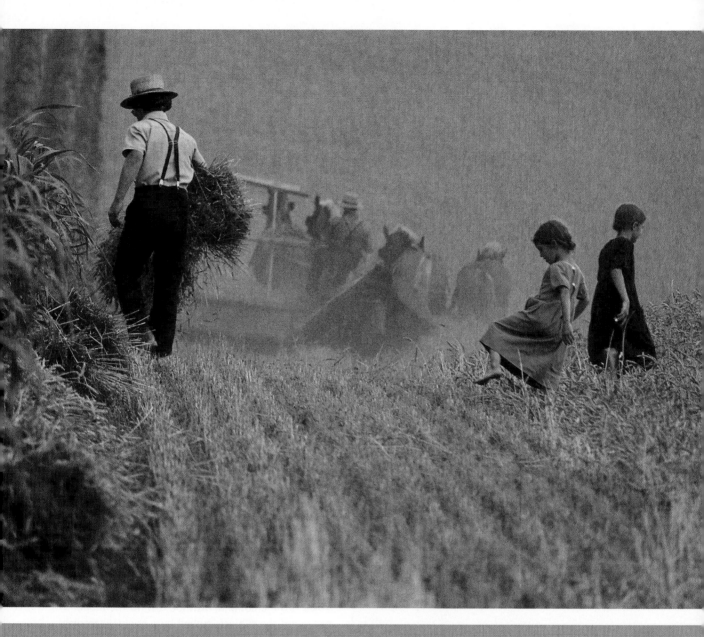

"Poetry is life distilled."

—Gwendolyn Brooks

Could you describe your world in just a paragraph? Try expressing your dreams, opinions, and emotions in a few sentences. Is this possible? As you read the following unit, observe how complex ideas are condensed into a modest selection of words. You may find that while it is usually shorter than prose, poetry speaks volumes.

Introduction to Poetry

Poetry is . . .

"language at its most distilled and most powerful."

—Rita Dove

"just the evidence of life. If your life is burning well, poetry is just the ash."

—Leonard Cohen

"when an emotion has found its thought and the thought has found words."

—Robert Frost

"a deal of joy and pain and wonder, with a dash of the dictionary."

—Kahlil Gibran

"the rhythmical creation of beauty in words."

—Edgar Allan Poe

"the art of creating imaginary gardens with real toads."

—Marianne Moore

Finding a good definition for poetry is difficult, especially because poems can take so many forms. How would you define poetry?

THE GENRE OF POETRY

The word "poem" comes from the Greek word *poíma,* which means "work," and is derived from *poieín,* "to make." **Poetry** uses imaginative and musical language to communicate experiences, thoughts, or emotions. Of all the literary forms, it packs the most meaning into the fewest words. Because poetry is often arranged in lines and stanzas as opposed to sentences and paragraphs, it has more freedom than prose in its ordering of words and use of punctuation.

ELEMENTS OF POETRY

Speaker and Tone

The **speaker** of a poem is the character who speaks in, or narrates, the poem—the voice assumed by the writer. The speaker and the writer of the poem are not necessarily the same person. Since the speaker is the voice of the poem, the voice sets the tone.

Tone is the emotional attitude toward the reader or toward the subject implied by a poem. Examples of different tones include familiar, ironic, playful, sarcastic, serious, and sincere. (See Understanding Speaker and Tone, page 360.)

Setting and Context

The **setting** of a literary work is the time and place in which it occurs, together with all the details used to create a sense of a particular time and place. Poets often create setting by using **sensory details,** or words and phrases that describe how things look, sound, smell, taste, or feel. In poetry, **context** refers to the conditions in which the poem occurs. Context is closely related to setting but focuses more on the environment of the time and place. Two common types of context include historical and cultural. (See Understanding Setting and Context, page 372.)

Figurative Language

Figurative language is writing or speech that is meant to be understood imaginatively instead of literally. Figurative language may be used in all types of writing but is especially common in poetry.

- A **metaphor** is a comparison in which one thing is written about as if it were another. An example of a metaphor is "My joy is the joy of sunlight," found in the poem "Gifts," by Shu Ting (page 363).
- A **simile** is a comparison that uses *like* or *as.* Judith Ortiz Cofer uses simile within her poem "Cold as Heaven" (page 367), with the lines "how wrapped like mummies in layers of wool / that almost immobilized us, we could only / take hesitant steps like toddlers / toward food, warmth, and shelter."
- **Personification** is a figure of speech in which an animal, a thing, a force of nature, or an idea is described as if it were human or is given human qualities. Ishmael Reed uses personification in the line, "the hunger of this poem is legendary / it has taken in many victims" from "BEWARE: Do Not Read This Poem," on page 357. (See Understanding Figurative Language, page 384.)

Sight and Sound

Imagery Poetry uses descriptive language, or **imagery,** to create a vivid picture in the mind of the reader and to appeal to the senses—primarily sight but also sound, touch, taste, and smell. For example, in "Courage" (page 471), Anne Sexton uses the image of "picking the scabs off your heart, / then wringing it out like a sock" to describe having courage when faced with despair and loss.

Rhythm The pattern of beats, or stresses, in a line of poetry is called **rhythm.** Rhythm can be regular or irregular. A regular rhythmic pattern is called a **meter.** Typically, stressed syllables are marked with a [/] and unstressed syllables with a [⌣]. Notice how Maya Angelou uses meter in "Caged Bird" (page 406).

⌣ / ⌣ / ⌣⌣ / ⌣ /
The free bird thinks of another breeze

⌣ ⌣ / ⌣ / ⌣ ⌣ / ⌣ /
and the trade winds soft through the sighing trees

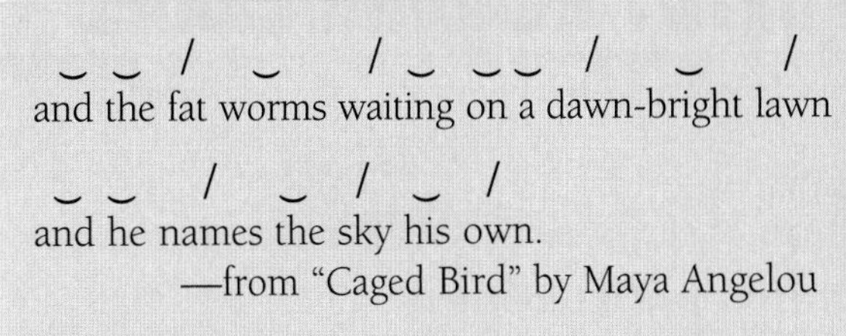
⌣ ⌣ / ⌣ / ⌣ ⌣⌣ / ⌣ /
and the fat worms waiting on a dawn-bright lawn

⌣ ⌣ / ⌣ / ⌣ /
and he names the sky his own.

—from "Caged Bird" by Maya Angelou

Rhyme Some forms of poetry use the repetition of sounds at the ends of words to create **rhyme,** as in *day* and *away.*

- **Internal rhyme** is rhyme that occurs within lines; **end rhyme** is rhyme that occurs at the ends of lines.
- **Slant rhyme,** or *near rhyme,* is the use of words that do not rhyme exactly but have a similar sound, as in *rave* and *rove* or *rot* and *rock.*
- **Rhyme scheme** is the pattern of end rhyme designated by assigning a different letter of the alphabet to each rhyme, for example, *abab.*

(See Understanding Sight and Sound, page 390.)

Structure and Form

Structure Whereas stories and essays are divided into paragraphs, poems can be divided into **stanzas,** or groups of lines. The type of stanza is determined by the number of lines. Two lines are a **couplet,** three a **tercet** or **triplet,** four a **quatrain,** five a **quintet** or **quintain,** six a **sestet,** seven a **septet,** and eight an **octave.** It is sometimes possible to determine the type of poem by the stanza type, if the poem is not in free verse.

Form A single poem may contain numerous recognizable elements. For instance, a poem may feature a set pattern of lines or syllables, end rhyme, strong rhythm, and specialized sound devices. Or it may be written in free verse, which avoids use of regular rhythm, rhyme, meter, or division into stanzas.

Types of Poetry

There are many different types of poetry. One thing that poems have in common, however, is precision of language; each word of a poem is carefully chosen to convey a tone, viewpoint, and perception of an object or an experience. (See Understanding Structure and Form, page 412.)

POETRY READING MODEL

BEFORE READING | DURING READING | AFTER READING

BUILD BACKGROUND

- Make **predictions** about what the poem will be about by reading the title and the **Build Background** feature and by looking over any footnotes.
- Read the **Meet the Author** feature to look for information about the author's writing style.

ANALYZE LITERATURE

- The **Analyze Literature** feature will focus on one or more literary techniques or elements that are used in the selection. In poetry, the author may use figurative language or stanza structure in a way that supports the meaning of the poem.

SET PURPOSE

- **Preview** the text to set a purpose for reading. A purpose for reading poetry might be to see how the poet creates moods, messages, or images in the reader's mind.

USE READING SKILLS

- Before reading, apply reading skills, such as analyzing text structure and previewing new vocabulary words. The **Use Reading Skills** feature will give you instructions on how to apply the skills while you read, such as using a graphic organizer.

BEFORE READING | **DURING READING** | AFTER READING

USE READING STRATEGIES

- **Read aloud** in order to hear and feel how the language is used, which is key both to understanding and appreciating poetry.
- **Visualize** by forming pictures in your mind to help you see any scenes or people described in the poem. Poetry often makes use of strong images.
- **Ask questions** about things that seem unusual or interesting or things you don't understand. For instance, you might ask why the author chose certain images to express his or her ideas.
- **Make inferences,** or educated guesses, about what is not stated directly. Things may be implied or hinted at, or they may be left out altogether.
- **Clarify** your understanding of the poem by rereading it. Often you will gain new insights into the language and meaning of the poem.

ANALYZE LITERATURE

Determine which **literary elements** stand out as you read the poem. What figurative language, sound devices, and imagery are used? What is the poem's form and structure?

MAKE CONNECTIONS

Notice where there are **connections** between the selection and your life or the world beyond the poem. How might the topic of the poem apply to you or to people you know?

BEFORE READING | DURING READING | **AFTER READING**

REFER TO TEXT

- **Remember details,** such as the key images.
- Try to **summarize** the meaning of the poem in a sentence or two. Ask yourself, what is this poem about?

REASON WITH TEXT

- **Interpret** the ideas and images in the poem to help you clarify meaning.
- **Analyze** the text by breaking down information into smaller pieces and discovering how those pieces fit into the poem as a whole.

ANALYZE LITERATURE

- **Review** how the author's use of literary elements increased your understanding or enjoyment of the poem.

EXTEND THE TEXT

- **Extend** your reading beyond the selection by exploring ideas through writing or engaging in other creative projects.

BEWARE: Do Not Read This Poem

BEFORE READING

A Lyric Poem by Ishmael Reed

BUILD BACKGROUND

Literary Context Studying your reflection in a mirror can be insightful. Are there times when the image you see may not be how you see yourself or what you want others to see? Ishmael Reed's poem **"BEWARE: Do Not Read This Poem"** explores how poetry is another way by which we can see our true selves. The poem was first published in 1972 in a volume of poetry titled *Conjure;* it was followed by *Chattanooga* (1973), *A Secretary of Spirits* (1978), and *New and Collected Poems* (1988).

Reader's Context Do you think a mirror reflects your true self? Where else can you look for reflections of who you really are?

ANALYZE LITERATURE: Metaphor

Like most poems, "BEWARE: Do Not Read This Poem" uses figurative language, notably metaphor. A **metaphor** is a figure of speech in which one thing is spoken of or written about as if it were another. The two "things" involved are the writer's actual subject, the *tenor* of the metaphor, and another thing to which the subject is likened, the *vehicle* of the metaphor.

SET PURPOSE

Examine the central metaphor in "BEWARE: Do Not Read This Poem." Consider also the word choices the author uses. Choosing words with the correct connotations, or implied meanings, is important as synonyms can evoke a variety of different feelings. How do the metaphor and word choices work together to create the mood of the poem?

MEET THE AUTHOR

Ishmael Reed (b. 1938) has written novels, poetry, essays, plays, and even operas. In all of these forms, Reed likes to defy convention by mixing radically different kinds of material. "No one says a novel has to be one thing," he notes. "It can be anything it wants to be, a vaudeville show, the six o'clock news, the mumblings of wild men saddled by demons." He adds, "In poetry one strives for pure originality." Satirical humor, used like a weapon, is one of Reed's most effective tools as a writer.

USE READING SKILLS

Author's Approach When applied to writing, **diction** refers to an author's word choice, an important aspect of a writer's style. For example, Reed uses an everyday vocabulary and casually abbreviates many words. What effect does that have on the tone of the poem? Why would the poet choose to write with this style? Below is a small list of Reed's diction choices as well as their meanings. Find other examples as you read the poem.

Diction Choice	Meaning
abt	about
w/	with
ol	old
back off	leave alone
woman/s	woman's

PREVIEW VOCABULARY

Examine the following words from the selection. Brainstorm a list of **synonyms** (different words that have the same meaning) for each word and write down your choices. When you are finished reading the selection, substitute your chosen synonyms and note how word choices can alter the tone of the selection.

swift
disappeared
tenant
legendary
resist

BEWARE: Do Not Read This Poem

A Lyric Poem by **Ishmael Reed**

tonite, *thriller* was
abt an ol woman, so vain she
surrounded her self w/
many mirrors

It got so bad that finally she
locked herself indoors & her
whole life became the
mirrors

one day the villagers broke
into her house, but she was too
swift for them. she disappeared
into a mirror
each tenant who bought the house
after that lost a loved one to
the ol woman in the mirror:
first a little girl
then a young woman
then the young woman/s husband

the hunger of this poem is legendary
it has taken in many victims
back off from this poem
it has drawn in yr feet
back off from this poem
it has drawn in yr legs
back off from this poem
it is a greedy mirror

DURING READING

USE READING STRATEGIES

Visualize After reading lines 1–12, close your eyes and visualize the scene. Sketch your visualization in your notebook.

swift (swift) *adj.*, fast

ten • ant (te´ nənt) *n.*, resident

leg • end • ar • y (le´ jən dār' ē) *adj.*, famous; mythical; of legend

DURING READING

ANALYZE LITERATURE

Metaphor How is the poem described? What idea is the poet trying to convey by using these images and ideas?

you are into this poem. from
    the waist down
nobody can hear you can they?

this poem has had you up to here
    belch
this poem aint got no manners
you cant call out frm this poem
relax now & go w/ this poem
move & roll on to this poem

    do not resist this poem
    this poem has yr eyes
    this poem has his head
    this poem has his arms
    this poem has his fingers
    this poem has his fingertips

this poem is the reader & the
    reader this poem

statistic: the us bureau of missing persons reports
    that in 1968 over 100,000 people disappeared
    leaving no solid clues
    nor trace   only
a space   in the lives of their friends ❖

DURING READING

USE READING SKILLS

Author's Approach Why might the author have chosen casual language and abbreviations while describing the act of being eaten by a poem?

DURING READING

USE READING STRATEGIES

Make Inferences What is the point of including the statistic at the end of the poem? What meaning does it shed on the rest of the poem?

"...you are into this poem. from / the waist down / nobody can hear you can they?" What do these lines describe? In what ways might someone be consumed? In what ways might an obsession be similar?

APPLY THE MODEL

AFTER READING

REFER TO TEXT ▶▶▶▶▶	REASON WITH TEXT	
1a. Recall why the old woman surrounds herself with mirrors.	1b. Conclude why the poet emphasizes images of mirrors.	**Understand** **Find meaning**
2a. State what happens to the tenants who move into the house after this incident.	2b. Apply the idea of being consumed by something to other aspects of life.	**Apply** **Use information**
3a. Write what is legendary about this poem. Identify how the poem shows its greediness in lines 19–29.	3b. Analyze how the speaker draws the reader into the poem.	**Analyze** **Take things apart**
4a. Identify the words or lines that you think best express the tone of the poem.	4b. Interpret the tone of the poem. Did you find this poem intimidating or approachable? Do you think the speaker has a friendly or reserved attitude toward the reader? Explain.	**Evaluate** **Make judgments**
5a. Indicate how the qualities of "this poem" change in lines 34–41.	5b. Write a summary that covers the main ideas in this poem.	**Create** **Bring ideas together**

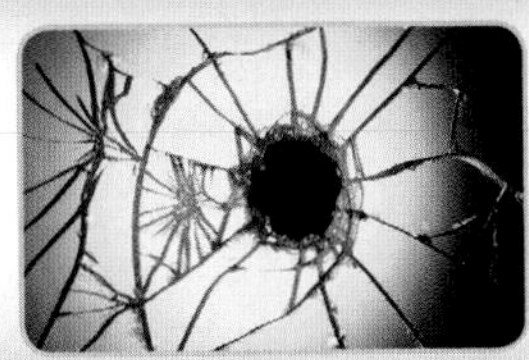

ANALYZE LITERATURE: Metaphor

In lines 25–26, the speaker in Reed's poem says "back off from this poem / it is a greedy mirror." How does the poet develop this metaphor throughout the poem? In what way is a poem like a mirror? Cite examples from the poem in your explanation.

EXTEND THE TEXT

Writing Options

Creative Writing Pretend that you are an advice columnist and someone has written to you expressing worry about being eaten by a poem. You will need to write the **letter** from the worried person, as well as the **response** of the columnist. Consider the metaphorical meaning of "being eaten by a poem" as you write this letter and response.

Expository Writing Write a one-page **poetry analysis,** focusing on what the speaker is trying to communicate about reading poetry. The title of the poem is a warning, and the poem concludes with a statistic about missing people. How do these things connect with the warnings given in the poem? How does the poet get his idea across?

Collaborative Learning

Research Mirrors People have long been fascinated with mirrors. With a partner or small group, research some aspect of this fascination: Explore how mirrors are made, how many different types of mirrors there are, or how people have used mirrors in science and the arts. You may want to start by doing an Internet search using "mirror" and "reflection" as key words.

Media Literacy

Present an Oral Interpretation Give a dramatic reading of "BEWARE: Do Not Read This Poem." To prepare, reread the poem several times to form a clear image of the speaker in your mind. Then, on a copy of the poem, make notes about where you will increase or decrease your pace and raise or lower your volume, as well as any gestures or facial expressions you will use to convey emotion. In a small group, take turns presenting the poem. Share your comments on the strong points of each oral interpretation.

Go to **www.mirrorsandwindows.com** for more.

Understanding Speaker and Tone

SPEAKER AND TONE

Poetry has survived the centuries because of its ability to convey emotions and images. One of the reasons so many poems are cherished is that they speak to the reader's heart, mind, or imagination. Yet, who really is speaking? Is it the author? a created character in the poem? The **speaker** of a poem is the character who speaks in, or narrates, the poem—the voice assumed by the writer. The speaker and the writer of the poem are not necessarily the same person.

Since the speaker is the voice of the poem, the voice sets the tone. **Tone** is the emotional attitude toward the reader or toward the subject implied by a poem. Examples of different tones include familiar, ironic, playful, sarcastic, serious, and sincere. Writers can establish tone by their use of voice, irony, and diction.

ELEMENTS OF SPEAKER AND TONE

Voice

Voice is the way a writer uses language to reflect his or her unique personality and attitude toward a topic, form, and audience. The speaker in Shu Ting's poem "Gifts" (page 363) conveys a sense of determination about achieving freedom and passing ideas on to future generations through such sentences and phrases as "I'll climb from the roots to the veins," "Igniting golden flames," and "Flying from hardship and failure." The images in the poem are simple and natural but show strength and growth. The attitude of the speaker suggests that the freedom to express one's ideas is also a natural element.

Irony

One aspect of voice to consider is irony. **Irony** is the difference between appearance and reality. Different types of irony include the following:

- **dramatic irony:** something is known by the reader or audience but unknown to the characters
- **verbal irony:** a character says one thing but means another
- **irony of situation:** an event occurs that violates the expectations of the characters, the reader, or the audience

What Great Writers Do

The speaker in "Patterns" by Amy Lowell (page 467) expresses frustration and anguish about the imposed patterns in which she finds herself. The reader sees events from her perspective, although it is suggested that those viewing her situation from the outside would not understand or necessarily appreciate her feelings. This intimate perspective allows the reader to appreciate the frustration of the speaker to express herself or be understood by those around her.

> What is Summer in a fine brocaded gown!
> I should like to see it lying in a heap upon
> the ground.
> All the pink and silver crumpled up on the
> ground.
>
> I would be the pink and silver as I ran
> along the paths,
> And he would stumble after,
> Bewildered by my laughter.
>
> —from "Patterns" by Amy Lowell

Verbal irony operates when a speaker says one thing but means something quite different. Irony can be subtle, suggesting that the speaker has in mind several different shades of meaning. An ironic statement may also be rather crude and obvious, as in the case of sarcasm. As you read, be aware of this gap between what is said and what is intended.

Diction

Diction, when applied to writing, refers to the author's or poet's choice of words and how those word choices express ideas or emotions. As you know, poets choose words very carefully, and every word is important. As you read, consider specific word choices and think about why a poet chooses certain words instead of others. Ishmael Reed's "BEWARE: Do Not Read This Poem" on page 357 contains unconventional diction that sets the tone for the poem.

ASSESSING SPEAKER AND TONE

Discovering the tone of a poem is more than knowing what the poem is about or what it is trying to accomplish. For example, in "Gentle Communion" by Pat Mora (page 368) and "Cold as Heaven" by Judith Ortiz Cofer (page 367), both of the speakers are granddaughters speaking about their grandmothers. In "Gentle Communion," the grandmother has died; in "Cold as Heaven," the grandmother is dying. The tone of the two poems is very similar. Both show respect and love for the grandmothers, though both also portray the grandmother as having an almost childlike quality.

> Even the long-dead are willing to move.
> Without a word, she came with me from
> the desert.
> Mornings she wanders through my rooms
> making beds, folding socks.
> —from "Gentle Communion" by Pat Mora
>
> Before there is a breeze again
> before the cooling days of Lent, she may
> be gone.
> My grandmother asks me to tell her
> again about the snow.
> —from "Cold as Heaven"
> by Judith Ortiz Cofer

To determine the tone of a poem, use the following methods:

- **Read Aloud** First, try reading it aloud. Sometimes, hearing the words will help reveal the tone or mood of the piece.
- **Notice Words That Stand Out** Pay attention to the words in a poem that seem to follow a certain pattern or invoke similar emotions. In "Cold as Heaven," for instance, the words *cooling, white, mummies, stone,* and *purifying* suggest the coldness of death and a certain respectful calmness.
- **Be Aware of Word Choice** Another thing to think about is the connotations of words. The **denotation** of a word is its dictionary meaning without any emotional associations. The **connotation** of a word is the set of ideas or emotional associations it suggests, in addition to its actual meaning. For example, the connotation of the word *warm* suggests comfort and security, whereas the connotation of the word *stuffy* suggests a feeling of being closed in and uncomfortable.
- **Consider the Speaker** It may also help to consider the speaker as a character instead of a neutral observer. What bias might the speaker show? What attitude do you think the speaker or poet expresses?
- **Compare and Contrast Similar Poems** Comparing poems with similar themes or subjects can help you to analyze the tone of each poem. "The Secret" (page 401) and "Poetry" (page 402) both deal with writing poetry. "Sympathy" (page 405) and "Caged Bird" (page 406) each express ideas of freedom versus oppression and captivity. The speaker's voice and perspective are different in each poem, so naturally, each will have its own particular tone.

Consider these adjectives as a starting point for how to describe tone:

hopeful	frustrated
sad	amused
wistful	scared
mournful	thrilled
determined	regretful
celebratory	impassioned
joyful	boastful
bitter	worried

GIFTS / To the Oak

Lyric Poems by Shu Ting
Translated by Donald Finkel and Carolyn Kizer

BEFORE READING

BUILD BACKGROUND

Literary Context Lyric poems express personal feelings. In **"Gifts,"** Shu Ting expresses her faith in the human spirit by alluding to China's troubled past. **"To the Oak"** is written as a love poem, expressing the poet's deep connection with nature.

Figurative language is writing or speech that is meant to be understood imaginatively instead of literally. Many writers, especially poets, use figurative language to help readers see things in new ways. These poems use a type of figurative language called metaphor to convey their ideas. A **metaphor** is a figure of speech in which one thing is spoken of or written about as if it were another.

Literary Context Studying your reflection in a mirror can be insightful. Are there times when the image you see may not be how you see yourself or what you want others to see?

ANALYZE LITERATURE: Tone

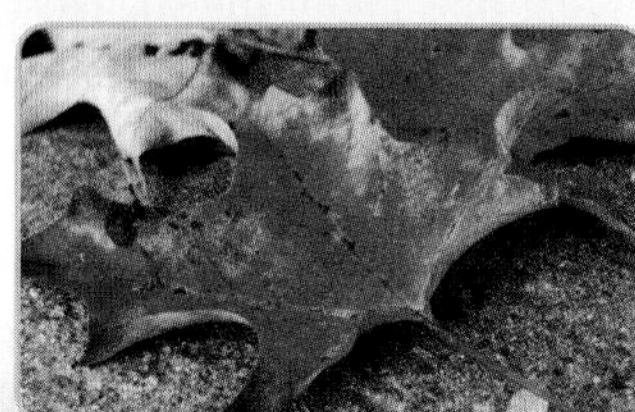

Tone is the emotional attitude toward the reader or toward the subject implied by a literary work. Think about the emotions the speaker conveys in "Gifts" and "To the Oak," and how metaphor is used to convey these emotions or attitudes.

SET PURPOSE

Read about the Misty Poets in the section below and determine whether the following two poems reflect the main themes of the Misty Poets. As you read the poems, determine the tone and how the tone is developed by the speakers.

MEET THE AUTHOR

Shu Ting (b. 1952) is the pen name of the poet Gong Peiyu. Shu Ting was considered the leading poet in China in the 1980s. She belongs to a group of Chinese writers known as the Misty Poets. These poets emerged in the 1970s after the death of China's longtime dictator Mao Tse-tung. Under Mao, poets and artists were not allowed to express their feelings or personal views. Instead, they were expected to celebrate the accomplishments of the Communist government, the Communist Party, and the people. The Misty Poets focused on three main themes: individualism, humans' relationship with the natural world, and the struggle against oppression. Through her poetry, Shu Ting has helped to nurture the struggle for democracy in China.

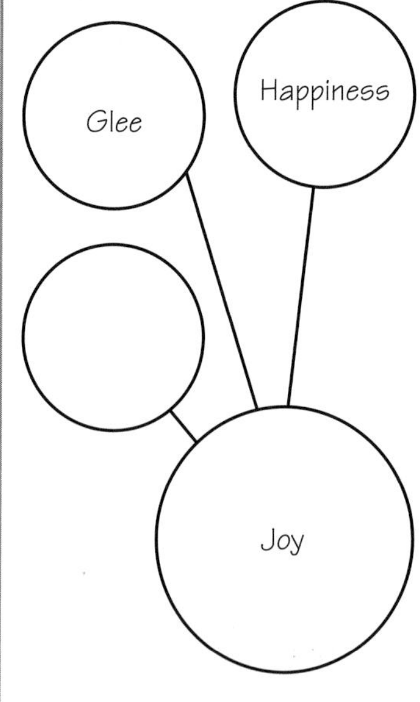

USE READING SKILLS

Meaning of Words Grouping words into categories can help you think about how they are both similar and different in meaning. With a partner, brainstorm ten words that relate to the word *joy.* For example, you could think of words that mean the same or almost the same thing as joy, such as *glee* and *happiness.* You could also think of words describing occasions on which people feel joy, such as *birthday* and *reunion.*

If you get stuck, consult a dictionary or a thesaurus. Include both familiar and new words in your list. Next, brainstorm ten words related to the word *grief.* Finally, for each of the words *joy* and *grief,* make a Cluster Chart like the one below. Group the words into appropriate categories. Add more circles as needed.

Cluster Chart

Glee
Happiness
Joy

GIFTS

A Lyric Poem by **Shu Ting**

Translated by Donald Finkel

> **USE READING STRATEGIES**
>
> **Visualize** The poet uses many images to convey her ideas. Picture these images in your mind.

> **USE READING STRATEGIES**
>
> **Clarify** Read the second stanza aloud. What initial consonant sound is repeated? What is the effect of that alliteration?

My dream is the dream of a pond
Not just to mirror the sky
But to let the willows and ferns
Suck me dry.
I'll climb from the roots to the veins,
And when leaves wither and fade
I will refuse to mourn
Because I was dying to live.

My joy is the joy of sunlight.
In a moment of creation
I will leave shining words
In the pupils of children's eyes
Igniting golden flames.
Whenever seedlings sprout
I shall sing a song of green.
I'm so simple I'm profound!

My grief is the grief of birds.
The Spring will understand:
Flying from hardship and failure
To a future of warmth and light.
There my blood-stained pinions[1]
Will scratch hieroglyphics[2]
On every human heart
For every year to come.

Because all that I am
Has been a gift from earth. ❖

1. **pinions.** The tips of a bird's wings
2. **hieroglyphics.** Pictures that represent words or ideas

How might the phrase "ashes to ashes and dust to dust" reflect the poem? Are humans indebted to the earth?

To the Oak

A Lyric Poem by **Shu Ting**

Translated by Carolyn Kizer

If I love you
I won't imitate the morning glory
Borrowing your high branches to display myself;
If I love you
I won't imitate those infatuated birds
Who repeat their monotonous flattery to the foliage,
Nor the fountain
With its solace of cool waters;
I won't even be those background vistas
That serve to make you more majestic.
Not even sunshine,
Not even spring rain,
No, none of these!

I would like to be a kapok tree
Standing beside you as an equal,
Our roots touching underground,
Our leaves touching in the clouds;
And with every gust of wind
We would bow to each other.

But no one else understands our language;
You have your branches
Like daggers or swords
While my big red flowers
Are heavy sighs.
Though it seems we are separated forever
We are eternally together.
This is great love,
This is fidelity.
Love—
Not only for your splendid trunk
But also for the earth you stand on. ❖

USE READING SKILLS

Meaning of Words
What other words might be grouped with the word *fidelity*?

How can one demonstrate his or her commitment to a relationship? Is it possible to be in a serious relationship and yet remain an individual?

AFTER READING

REFER TO TEXT ▶▶▶▶	▶ REASON WITH TEXT	
1a. Recall what the pond lets the willows and ferns do in "Gifts."	1b. In your own words, explain what sacrifice the speaker makes in dreaming as the pond.	**Understand** Find meaning
2a. State why the speaker in "Gifts" refuses to mourn when the leaves "wither and fade."	2b. Relate the idea of sacrifice to the idea of a struggle for freedom.	**Apply** Use information
3a. In "Gifts," what causes the pupils of children's eyes to ignite "golden flames"?	3b. Analyze the images the poet uses in stanza 2. How do they express the speaker's joy and hopefulness?	**Analyze** Take things apart
4a. List the images that the speaker in "To the Oak" compares him- or herself to.	4b. Rank the images in the poem based on the power they had on you, the reader. Explain what the most powerful image expresses to you.	**Evaluate** Make judgments
5a. For what two things does the speaker express his or her love in the last stanza of "To the Oak"?	5b. Summarize the feelings the speaker expresses in this poem. Explain whether any emotion overshadows others.	**Create** Bring ideas together

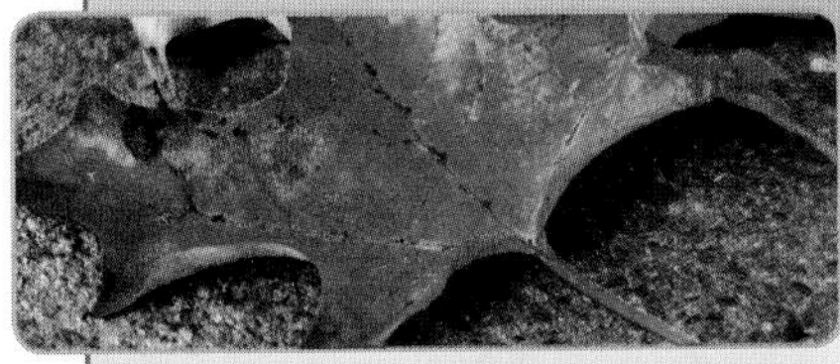

ANALYZE LITERATURE: Tone

Who are the speakers in each of the poems? Is it the poet or someone else? How do the poet's words suggest the speaker's tone?

EXTEND THE TEXT

Writing Options

Creative Writing Write a short **lyric poem** that uses metaphors to convey an idea or ideas to other young people. First, decide what tone you want to set: encouraging, questioning, frightening, or any other tone that fits your intention. Second, decide who the speaker will be; that is, decide on the perspective that's presenting the idea or ideas. Third, think about images that would convey the appropriate tone. (For more on metaphor, see page 384.) Finally, share your poem with the class.

Expository Writing Imagine that you are trying to explain the meaning of one of these poems to a classmate. In two paragraphs, write a **critical analysis** that explains what the poem is about. Explain who the intended audience for the poem is, and what ideas you believe the speaker is trying to convey. You will need to discuss the relevant information about the poem's cultural and historical context, as well as describe the imagery used in the poem.

Collaborative Learning

Artistically Express a Struggle Brainstorm to make a list of the struggles that you experience or know about. These struggles can be serious, such as an ongoing war or a problem in the community, or they can be humorous, such as the struggle to stay awake in a certain class or to get a date for a school dance. Using a form similar to that in "Gifts" where the speaker states "My grief is the grief of birds," create your own metaphors and images to convey this struggle. Break into small groups and decide how to express your collective metaphors and images: in posters with brief captions, in a song, in a poetic skit, in a slide show, or in a video. Share your work with the rest of the class.

Lifelong Learning

Research the Misty Poets Use the Internet and the library to identify other Misty Poets from China. Choose one poet and research his or her life and work. Imagine that person is coming to your school to do a reading. Create a poster advertising the event. Include on your poster key biographical details and accomplishments of the poet.

Go to **www.mirrorsandwindows.com** for more.

Cold as Heaven

A Lyric Poem by Judith Ortiz Cofer

Gentle Communion

A Lyric Poem by Pat Mora

BEFORE READING

BUILD BACKGROUND

Literary Context Judith Ortiz Cofer's poem **"Cold as Heaven"** was published in 1995 in *Reaching for the Mainland and Selected New Poems.* Cofer's poem recounts a conversation between a person and his or her dying grandmother, in which talking about the weather helps to take their minds off of elements beyond their control. Cofer has said that, "In a sense I have been connected through my imagination.... My poetry is my emotional and intellectual connection to my heritage."

Important themes within Pat Mora's work include family, Mexican-American culture, and the desert. Mora has said that many of her ideas come from the desert where she grew up, which included "open spaces, wide sky, all that sun and all those animals that scurry across the hot sand or fly over the mountains." Mora's poem **"Gentle Communion"** appeared in *Communion,* a collection of poems first published in 1991. In the poem, Mora writes about a person remembering his or her grandmother who has died and the relationship that they shared.

Reader's Context Think of one thing you would like your grandparent to know, and one thing you would like to know about his or her life.

COMPARE LITERATURE: Speaker and Tone

A **speaker** is the character who speaks in, or narrates, a poem. While you read, think about the speaker in each poem. Is the author writing as herself, or as someone else? Also consider the tone of each poem. **Tone** is the emotional attitude toward the reader or toward the subject implied by a literary work. What techniques does each author use to achieve the tone?

USE READING SKILLS

Important Details It is helpful to write down your own thoughts on ideas, issues, and themes within a poem. Consider what the poem describes, and what it reminds you of. Then select a topic that is presented in the poem. Write that topic in the main circle of a Cluster Chart. In the surrounding circles, jot down any details from your notes. Consider creating two diagrams or using a different color pen to easily compare and contrast two poems with similar topics. After reading, infer the themes of the poems.

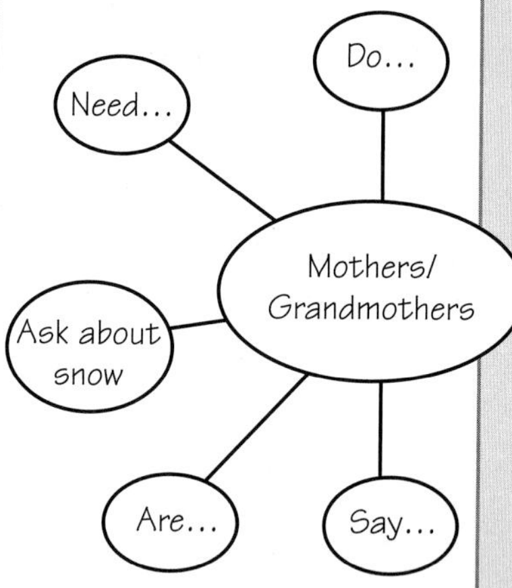

MEET THE AUTHORS

COFER

Judith Ortiz Cofer (b. 1952) was a small child when she emigrated from Puerto Rico to the United States with her family. Ortiz Cofer says that family is one of the main topics of her poetry: "The place of birth itself becomes a metaphor for the things we must all leave behind; the assimilation of a new culture is the coming into maturity by accepting the terms necessary for survival. My poetry is a study of this process of change, assimilation, and transformation."

Pat Mora (b. 1943) was born in El Paso, Texas, where her grandparents had moved from Mexico during the Mexican Revolution. Mora grew up speaking both English and Spanish in a household where "books were an important part of my life." Mora has received numerous awards, including the 2006 National Hispanic Cultural Center Literary Award, and has written more than twenty-five poetry, nonfiction, and children's books.

MORA

Cold as Heaven

A Lyric Poem by **Judith Ortiz Cofer**

Before there is a breeze again
before the cooling days of Lent, she may be gone.
My grandmother asks me to tell her
again about the snow.
We sit on her white bed
In this white room, while outside
the Caribbean sun winds up the world
like an old alarm clock. I tell her
about the enveloping blizzard I lived through
that made everything and everyone the same;
how we lost ourselves in drifts so tall
we fell through our own footprints;
how wrapped like mummies in layers of wool
that almost immobilized us, we could only
take hesitant steps like toddlers
toward food, warmth, shelter.
I talk winter real for her,
as she would once conjure for me to dream
at sweltering siesta[1] time,
cool stone castles in lands far north.
Her eyes wander to the window,
to the teeming scene of children
pouring out of a yellow bus, then to the bottle
dripping minutes through a tube
into her veins. When her eyes return to me,
I can see she's waiting to hear more
about the purifying nature of ice,
how snow makes way for a body,
how you can make yourself an angel
by just lying down and waving your arms
as you do when you say
good-bye. ❖

USE READING STRATEGIES

Ask Questions Pay attention to the details that involve things that are white or cold. What is the significance of these details?

teem • ing (tē´ miŋ) *adj.*, active with many beings; swarming

1. **siesta** (sē es´ tə). [Spanish] A two- to four-hour rest time

Is it possible to know heaven or to describe it for someone else? What images might you use to describe heaven or a similar "perfect" location? What purpose or purposes does the idea of heaven serve for society?

Gentle Communion

A Lyric Poem by **Pat Mora**

Even the long-dead are willing to move.
Without a word, she came with me from the desert.
Mornings she wanders through my rooms
making beds, folding socks.

Since she can't hear me anymore,
Mamande[1] ignores the questions I never knew
to ask, about her younger days, her red
hair, the time she fell and broke her nose
in the snow. I will never know.

When I try to make her laugh,
to disprove her sad album face, she leaves
the room, resists me as she resisted
grinning for cameras, make-up, English.

While I write, she sits and prays,
feet apart, legs never crossed,
the blue housecoat buttoned high
as her hair dries white, girlish
around her head and shoulders.

She closes her eyes, bows her head,
and like a child presses her hands together,
her patient flesh steeple, the skin
worn, like the pages of her prayer book.

Sometimes I sit in her wide-armed
chair as I once sat in her lap.

USE READING SKILLS

Important Details Why might the first sentence at the beginning of this poem be an important detail?

USE READING STRATEGIES

Make Inferences What does this description of Mamande suggest about how the speaker feels about her?

1. **Mamande (mä män´ dā).** [Spanish] A child's version of *mama grande,* Spanish for "grandmother"

Alone, we played a quiet I Spy.
She peeled grapes I still taste.

She removes the thin skin, places
the <u>luminous</u> coolness on my tongue.
I know not to bite or chew. I wait
for the thick melt,
our private green honey. ❖

lu • mi • nous (lü´ mə nəs) *adj.*, having a glowing quality

How would you define the word *communion?* How might communion be connected to memories? How might memories relate to forgiveness and the relationships between grandparents, parents, and children?

AFTER READING

REFER TO TEXT ▶▶▶▶	▶ REASON WITH TEXT	
1a. Recall what the speaker in "Cold as Heaven" tells the grandmother about.	1b. Discuss why the grandmother might have wanted to hear about this topic.	**Understand** Find meaning
2a. Referring to "Cold as Heaven," describe how to "make yourself an angel."	2b. Apply what you know about the grandmother's situation to determine the significance of the title "Cold as Heaven."	**Apply** Use information
3a. Identify what the grandmother in "Cold as Heaven" used to "conjure" for the speaker when he or she was young.	3b. Compare the effects of the grandmother's conjuring with those of the grandchild "talk[ing] winter real."	**Analyze** Take things apart
4a. Identify how the speaker in "Gentle Communion" and Mamande are different from one another.	4b. Explain the "gentle communion" referred to in the title of this poem. Compare generational differences based on this poem and your own experiences.	**Evaluate** Make judgments
5a. How does the speaker in "Gentle Communion" feel about Mamande's presence?	5b. Compare the grandparent/grandchild relationship in "Cold as Heaven" with the relationship in "Gentle Communion." How does death or the possibility of death affect the relationships?	**Create** Bring ideas together

COMPARE LITERATURE: Speaker and Tone

Both Mora and Ortiz Cofer come from Latino immigrant families. Ortiz Cofer came to America as a small child, whereas Mora is a third-generation American. Discuss with a partner or small group how the immigrant experience comes into play between the speaker and the grandmother in each poem. How are the experiences of the speakers and the grandmothers different? How in these poems did immigration affect each character's experience?

EXTEND THE TEXT

Writing Options

Creative Writing Write a **descriptive-setting poem** for a friend that describes a place you have been that your friend hasn't. Be sure to use descriptive details in order to create a vivid picture of the place for the reader. Use a chart of sensory details describing things that appeal to sight, sound, taste, smell, and touch to assist you in creating imagery to include in your poem. For an example of a Sensory Details Chart, see page 107.

Expository Writing Write a **compare-and-contrast paragraph** of both speaker and tone in "Cold as Heaven" and in "Gentle Communion." Compare what is revealed about the speaker in each poem, the tone of each poem, and the techniques the author uses to convey the tone. You may arrange your comparison by poem (one at a time) or by the aspect being compared.

Collaborative Learning

Ask the Authors With your small group, brainstorm and jot down questions you would like to ask the authors about these selections. For example, you might want to know if the poems are autobiographical, or you might want to know more about the grandmothers' backgrounds. Then use the Internet and the library to find more information about these poems and the poets. Try to find answers to as many of your questions as you can. Share your questions and answers with the class.

Critical Literacy

Role-play a Conversation What if the grandmother in "Cold as Heaven" had the opportunity to talk with the grandmother in "Gentle Communion" before she died? What do you think she would want to ask "Mamande" about what happens after one dies? What do you think Mamande would tell her? With a partner, role-play a conversation between the two grandmothers in which you explore these questions.

 Go to **www.mirrorsandwindows.com** for more.

READING ASSESSMENT

1. Which phrase best describes what the speaker is doing in "Cold as Heaven"?
   A. remembering playing in the snow with his or her grandmother
   B. planning a trip to a cold place with his or her grandmother
   C. nursing the grandmother back to health
   D. telling the grandmother what snow is like
   E. trying to comfort his or her grandmother

2. How would you describe what the speaker is doing in "Gentle Communion"?
   A. praying with his or her grandmother
   B. remembering his or her dead grandmother
   C. eating grapes with his or her grandmother
   D. making his or her grandmother laugh
   E. looking at photos of his or her grandmother

3. What do the two grandmothers share in common?
   A. They both immigrated to the United States.
   B. They are both at the end of their lives.
   C. Neither has ever seen snow.
   D. All of the above
   E. None of the above

4. Both speakers describe an aspect of their grandmothers that is
   A. childlike.
   B. stubborn.
   C. weak.
   D. proud.
   E. secretive.

5. On line 22 of "Cold as Heaven," the word *teeming* most nearly means
   A. shocking.
   B. tiring.
   C. underwhelming.
   D. significant.
   E. crowded.

6. Each of these poems explores the process of saying goodbye to a grandparent. Write a brief exploratory essay that compares and contrasts how each author gives a particular perspective on saying goodbye.

Oral History

A Lyric Poem by **Pat Mora**

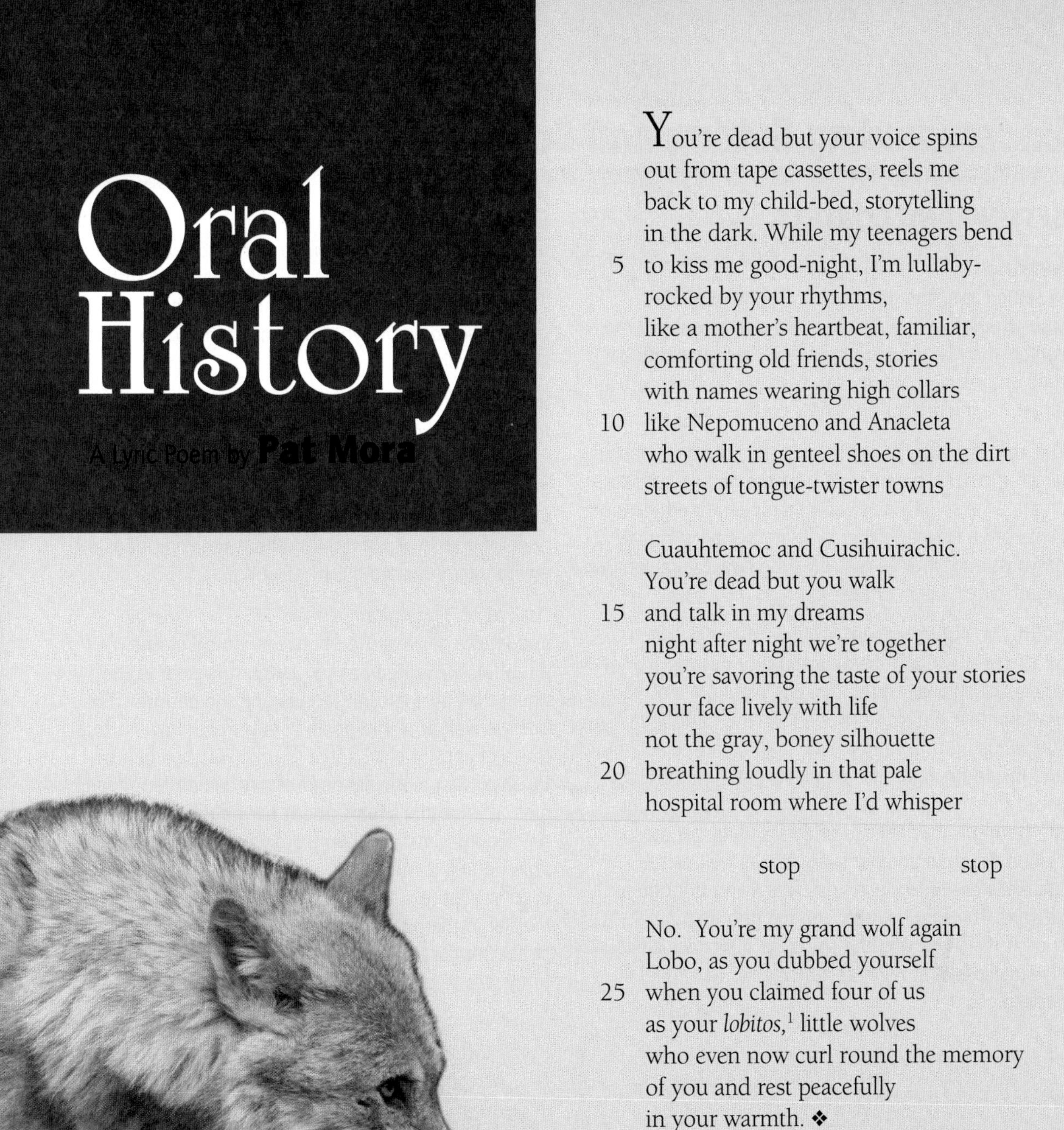

You're dead but your voice spins
out from tape cassettes, reels me
back to my child-bed, storytelling
in the dark. While my teenagers bend
to kiss me good-night, I'm lullaby-
rocked by your rhythms,
like a mother's heartbeat, familiar,
comforting old friends, stories
with names wearing high collars
like Nepomuceno and Anacleta
who walk in genteel shoes on the dirt
streets of tongue-twister towns

Cuauhtemoc and Cusihuirachic.
You're dead but you walk
and talk in my dreams
night after night we're together
you're savoring the taste of your stories
your face lively with life
not the gray, boney silhouette
breathing loudly in that pale
hospital room where I'd whisper

stop stop

No. You're my grand wolf again
Lobo, as you dubbed yourself
when you claimed four of us
as your *lobitos*,[1] little wolves
who even now curl round the memory
of you and rest peacefully
in your warmth. ❖

1. ***lobitos.*** [Spanish] Wolf cubs

Understanding Setting and Context

SETTING AND CONTEXT

Setting

In some cases, the geographical, cultural, and chronological (time) location of a poem's subject or composition is of great importance. Understanding time and place in poetry can help you to construct a larger meaning from the words on the page.

The **setting** of a literary work is the time and place in which it occurs, together with all the details used to create a sense of a particular time period and location. Poets often create setting by using **sensory details,** or words and phrases that describe how things look, sound, smell, taste, or feel.

Judith Ortiz Cofer's poem "Cold as Heaven" (page 367) is set in a Caribbean hospital or nursing home where the speaker of the poem is visiting his or her grandmother. Outside the window "the Caribbean sun winds up the world / like an old alarm clock" and inside the room the speaker's grandmother has asked the speaker to describe snow. Understanding the setting is pertinent to understanding the reason behind the grandmother's request, as well as the speaker's desire to clearly describe living through a blizzard. The contrast between the grandmother's current residence and the speaker's memories creates an atmosphere of relief at a moment when relief is needed.

> I can see she's waiting to hear more
> about the purifying nature of ice,
> how snow makes way for a body,
> how you can make yourself an angel
> by just lying down and waving your arms
> as you do when you say good-bye.
>
> —from "Cold as Heaven"
> by Judith Ortiz Cofer

Context

In literature, **context** refers to the conditions in which the poem occurs. Context is closely related to setting but focuses more on the environment of the time and place. Two common types of context include historical and cultural.

Interpreting a poem within its **historical context** requires that you have some knowledge of the time period in which it was written or of the events it describes. For example, if a poem is set during the Civil War, you would be better able to interpret the poem if you knew something about the conditions or environment created by the Civil War.

"Ballad of Birmingham" (page 375), for example, imagines a conversation between a mother and daughter on September 15, 1963. It is clear in the poem that an explosion occurs and the daughter dies, but the weight of the poem comes from knowing that the Sixteenth Street Baptist Church was bombed by Ku Klux Klan members on that day, killing four young girls. The mother's fears about her daughter attending a Freedom March are completely justified for that time period; it was common for violent methods to be used to suppress protesters in the 1960s. Little did the mother in the poem, nor the members of the Sixteenth Street Baptist Church, know that their place of sanctuary was to become the site of a heinous crime.

> "Mother dear, may I go downtown
> Instead of out to play,
> And march the streets of Birmingham
> In a Freedom March today?"
>
> "No, baby, no, you may not go,
> For the dogs are fierce and wild,
> And clubs and hoses, guns and jails
> Aren't good for a little child."
>
> —from "Ballad of Birmingham"
> by Dudley Randall

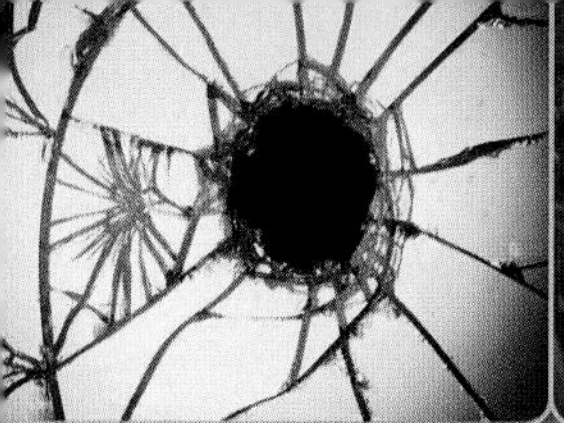

Cultural context is less dependent on a time period than on the culture of the poet, speaker, or subject of the poem. For instance, in "Local Sensibilities" (page 379), the speaker shows how certain references in the mainstream, popular culture do not mean the same thing to native Hawaiians. The speaker's point of view of being a native Hawaiian allows the reader the ability to see Hawaii both from outside and inside the culture.

> When I see a pineapple,
> I do not think of an exotic fruit sliced in
> rings to be served with ham,
> more the summer jobs at the cannery
> driving a forklift or packing wedges on
> the line.
>
> —from "Local Sensibilities"
> by Wing Tek Lum

Whereas "Local Sensibilities" is clearly about the writer's culture, a poem may yet transcend cultural definitions to take on a universal or general significance. Shu Ting's "Gifts" (page 363), for example, is grounded in the poet's experience of struggling for democracy and self-expression in communist China. Though there is nothing in the poem that is explicitly Chinese, the speaker expresses the movement of struggle and sacrifice that may not bear fruit immediately but will hopefully flourish in generations to come. The poem speaks to the experience of the Misty Poets of China (see page 362 for more information on the Misty Poets), but its message and imagery can be understood and enjoyed without that knowledge.

> My grief is the grief of birds.
> The Spring will understand:
> Flying from hardship and failure
> To a future of warmth and light.
> There my blood-stained pinions
> Will scratch hieroglyphics
> On every human heart
> For every year to come.
>
> —from "Gifts" by Shu Ting

USING READING STRATEGIES WITH SETTING AND CONTEXT

Use these strategies to help you determine the setting and the historical or cultural context of a poem:

- **Visualize** Consider whether the poem is set in a particular place or at a particular time. Try to picture the images presented in the poem.
- **Use Background Information** Sometimes, reading the comments about a historical era or about the author's life can provide information that further explains the work.
- **Write Things Down** After reading through the poem, read it again while writing down words and references that are unknown or confusing to you. Look up these words in a dictionary or try to find a translation if they are not in a language you know.
- **Ask Questions** Determine what you need to know about the setting or context to help you understand the poem. Form questions to help you research the subject. Use the library or Internet to find out more.

BALLAD OF BIRMINGHAM

BEFORE READING

A Ballad by Dudley Randall

BUILD BACKGROUND

Historical Context On September 15, 1963, the Sixteenth Street Baptist Church—the largest African-American church in Birmingham, Alabama—was bombed by Ku Klux Klan members. Four young girls were killed in the mid-morning attack: Carole Robertson, Cynthia Wesley, Addie Mae Collins, and Denise McNair. Dudley Randall wrote **"Ballad of Birmingham"** in response to this tragic event. The poem was set to music and recorded, and then published in 1965 by Dudley Randall's Broadside Press.

Reader's Context Have you ever been denied something for your own protection or because someone else was frightened? How did you react?

ANALYZE LITERATURE: Context and Setting

The **context** of a literary work is the circumstances or events that form the environment in which an event takes place. The **setting** of a literary work is the time and place in which events take place. Recognizing the context and setting is important to understanding "Ballad of Birmingham." Use the information in the Build Background section to help you understand the context and setting of "Ballad of Birmingham."

SET PURPOSE

Irony of situation is when an event occurs that violates the expectations of the characters, the reader, or the audience of a literary work. Randall uses irony of situation to enhance the tragedy of the bombing. As you read, look for an example of irony of situation and determine its effect on the poem.

MEET THE AUTHOR

Dudley Randall (1914–2000) was born in Washington, DC, and moved to Detroit, Michigan, in 1920. He published his first poem at the age of thirteen in the *Detroit Free Press* but did not publish another poem for many years. Instead, he went to work in an automotive plant for Ford and eventually became a postal worker. He served in the U.S. Army during World War II and, upon his return, earned degrees in English and Library Science. He worked as a librarian throughout much of the 1950s and in 1965, he established Broadside Press, a publishing house devoted to publishing the work of African-American poets. Broadside Press began with the publication of Randall's "Ballad of Birmingham" on a single sheet of paper, or broadside. According to Randall, Broadside Press grew by "hunches, intuition, trial and error," eventually publishing ninety titles of poetry and printing 500,000 books.

USE READING SKILLS

Cause and Effect When you evaluate cause and effect, you are looking for a logical relationship between a cause or causes and one or more effects. Transitional or signal words and phrases that indicate cause and effect include *one cause, another effect, as a result, consequently,* and *therefore.* As a reader, you determine whether the causes and effects in a text are reasonable. Recognizing causes and effects will also give you insight into a character or speaker's motivation and the reasoning behind his or her decisions. Use a Cause-and-Effect Chart, like the one below, to recognize relationships between causes and effects.

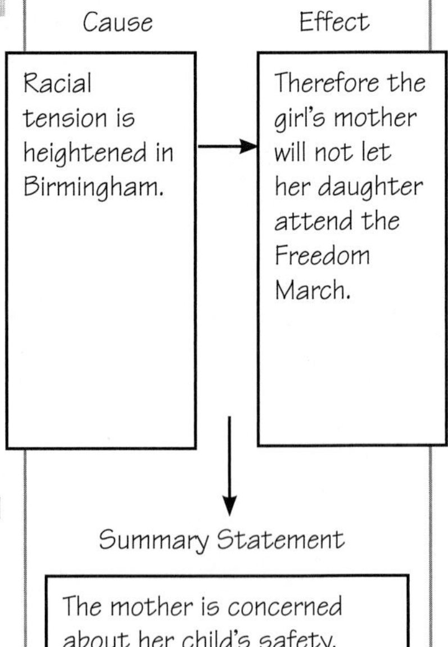
Cause
Effect
Racial tension is heightened in Birmingham.
Therefore the girl's mother will not let her daughter attend the Freedom March.
Summary Statement
The mother is concerned about her child's safety.

Sixteenth Street Baptist Church, Birmingham, Alabama.

Ballad of BIRMINGHAM

A Ballad by **Dudley Randall**

On the bombing of a church in Birmingham, Alabama, 1963

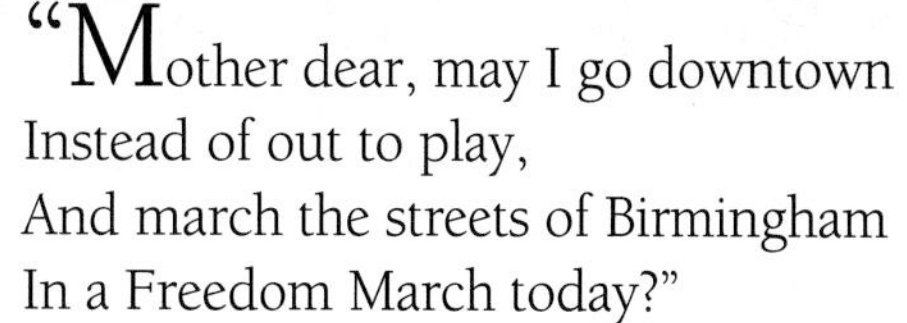

"Mother dear, may I go downtown
Instead of out to play,
And march the streets of Birmingham
In a Freedom March today?"

"No, baby, no, you may not go,
For the dogs are fierce and wild,
And clubs and hoses, guns and jails
Aren't good for a little child."

"But, mother, I won't be alone.
Other children will go with me,
And march the streets of Birmingham
To make our country free."

"No, baby, no, you may not go,
For I fear those guns will fire.
But you may go to church instead
And sing in the children's choir."

She has combed and brushed her night-dark hair,
And bathed rose petal sweet,
And drawn white gloves on her small brown hands,
And white shoes on her feet.

The mother smiled to know her child
Was in the sacred place,
But that smile was the last smile
To come upon her face.

For when she heard the explosion,
Her eyes grew wet and wild.
She raced through the streets of Birmingham
Calling for her child.

She clawed through bits of glass and brick,
Then lifted out a shoe.
"Oh, here's the shoe my baby wore,
But, baby, where are you?" ❖

What places do people consider sacred or safe? Is the bombing of a church worse than other acts of violence? What other action(s) might be worse or might compare?

Primary Source CONNECTION

From the mid-1950s until the late 1960s, the African-American Civil Rights movement gained national attention because of its determination to end racial discrimination. During the period when the Sixteenth Street Baptist Church was bombed, Birmingham, Alabama, had experienced many racially charged acts of violence, including more than a dozen bombings. While activists and community leaders strove to end the hostilities, many of those who supported segregation continued to commit acts of violence.

The New York Times **September 16, 1963**

BIRMINGHAM BOMB KILLS 4 NEGRO GIRLS IN CHURCH

A News Article by **Claude Sitton**

BIRMINGHAM, Ala., Sept. 15 – A bomb severely damaged a Negro church today during Sunday school services, killing four Negro girls and setting off racial rioting and other violence in which two Negro boys were shot to death.

Fourteen Negroes were injured in the explosion. One Negro and five whites were hurt in the disorders that followed.

The bombing came five days after the desegregation of three previously all-white schools in Birmingham. The way had been cleared for the desegregation when President Kennedy federalized the Alabama National Guard and the Federal courts issued a sweeping order against Governor Wallace, thus ending his defiance toward the integration step.

The four girls killed in the blast had just heard Mrs. Ella C. Demand, their teacher, complete the Sunday School lesson for the day. The subject was "The Love That Forgives."

During the period between the class and an assembly in the main auditorium, they went to the women's lounge in the basement, at the northeast corner of the church.

The blast occurred at about 10:25 A.M. (12:25 P.M. New York time).

Church members said they found the girls huddled together beneath a pile of masonry debris.

• • •

The blast blew gaping holes through walls in the church basement. Floors of offices in the rear of the sanctuary appeared near collapse. Stairways were blocked by splintered window frames, glass and timbers.

Chief Police Inspector W. J. Haley said the impact of the blast indicated that at least 15 sticks of dynamite might have caused it. He said the police had talked to two witnesses who reported having seen a car drive by the church, slow down and then speed away before the blast. ❖

AFTER READING

REFER TO TEXT ▶▶▶▶	▶ REASON WITH TEXT	
1a. Quote the question the child asks the mother.	1b. Summarize the mother's reasons for not granting her child's request. According to the news article, what events had taken place prior to the bombing?	**Understand** **Find meaning**
2a. State the child's reason for wanting to go to the Freedom March. Indicate why the child feels she will be safe.	2b. Examine the child's reasons for wanting to join the march. Is freedom worth risking life and limb? Explain.	**Apply** **Use information**
3a. List things the mother fears will happen if her child goes to the Freedom March.	3b. How are the mother's expectations violated? What details in the news article echo this violation?	**Analyze** **Take things apart**
4a. Recall what the mother found after the explosion and what question she asked.	4b. Evaluate whether the mother made a sound decision based on the information she had at hand. Explain.	**Evaluate** **Make judgments**
5a. Identify the details that show how the mother felt knowing her child was at church and not at the freedom march.	5b. Write a journal entry or monologue that reflects how the mother may have felt after the church bombing. Consider how the event might have changed her feelings about the civil rights movement.	**Create** **Bring ideas together**

ANALYZE LITERATURE: Context and Setting

What techniques does the author use to reveal the context and setting of this poem? If you did not have any background information on this poem, do you think you would understand it as well?

EXTEND THE TEXT

Writing Options

Creative Writing Imagine that you were a resident of Birmingham, Alabama, during the Sixteenth Street Baptist Church bombing. Write a two- to three-paragraph **reaction letter** to your local newspaper. In the letter, describe your own reaction to the bombing and offer advice for members of your community. Consider how your response might be different if you were a parent or a member of the Civil Rights movement.

Expository Writing "Ballad of Birmingham" was written about specific events in history. Nonetheless, the ideas about activism, responsibility, and safety can apply to many other contexts. Write a three-paragraph **historical analysis** that examines whether or not the historical context was crucial to this poem, or if the poem extends beyond the specific event.

Collaborative Learning

Research the 1963 Church Bombing With a partner or small group, generate research questions that would help you learn more about this period in history and the impact of the 1963 church bombing. For example, you might ask questions such as "What events led up to the bombing?" and "What was the reaction of the African-American community after the bombing?" When you have generated a list of five research questions, use the Internet and the library to find answers to them.

Media Literacy

Compare and Contrast Media Coverage It wasn't until 1977 that anyone was convicted for the bombing of the Sixteenth Street Baptist Church. In 2001 and 2002, two more men were convicted in the crime. Using the Internet and the library, find examples of news coverage of the bombing from 1963, 1977, and 2001. Create a tri-fold board presentation that compares and contrasts the media's coverage of this event over these four decades. Or compare the coverage of the 1963 church bombing between a local Birmingham newspaper and a newspaper in a different location, to analyze how the same event was covered in a different part of the country.

Go to **www.mirrorsandwindows.com** for more.

Local Sensibilities

BEFORE READING **A Lyric Poem by Wing Tek Lum**

DIRECTED READING

BUILD BACKGROUND

Cultural Context It is believed that travelers from Polynesia in the South Pacific became the first Hawaiians when they arrived on the islands between 500 and 1000 CE. The population of Hawaii now, however, is largely comprised of descendants of the early immigrants from China, Japan, and the Philippines. Popular with vacationers for sandy beaches, palm trees, and beautiful scenery, the Hawaiian Islands offer much more in terms of rich, diverse culture. In **"Local Sensibilities,"** Wing Tek Lum paints a living portrait of his native Hawaii through a series of vignettes, or descriptive scenes. He gives us a look at the industry, characters, animal life, vocabulary, and history that create the "unique universe" that he calls home.

Reader's Context How would you describe the community in which you live? How might a tourist describe that community? What might he or she miss when describing your community?

ANALYZE LITERATURE: Context

The **context** of a literary work is the circumstances or events that form the environment in which an event takes place. As you read "Local Sensibilities," consider how the speaker's Hawaiian background affects his point of view.

SET PURPOSE

Before you read, make a list of images and ideas that come to your mind when you think of Hawaii. As you read, look for images the writer uses to create a picture of Hawaii. Think about how those images engage your senses and help you see things from the poet's perspective. Compare the images in your list to the images in the poem.

MEET THE AUTHOR

Wing Tek Lum lives in Hawaii. His poem "Local Sensibilities" was originally published in *Expounding the Doubtful Points* (1987), a collection of poems that explores the author's Chinese-American identity and examines his family in Hawaii and his ancestors in China. In 1988, the book won both the Before Columbus Foundation American Book Award and the Association for Asian American Studies National Book Award. The author declined to provide biographical information about himself, saying that readers should "let the poem speak for itself."

USE READING SKILLS

Context Clues The context of a word is the setting or environment in which it is used. Read each of the following sentences containing a word from "Local Sensibilities." Each contains a **restatement context clue,** which restates an idea or explains it in a different way. After you have read the sentences below, write a sentence of your own using the underlined word in a real-life context—that is, a situation that actually exists or has existed. Next, use a thesaurus to learn some new synonyms for each word. Try substituting those words in the sentences you wrote.

PREVIEW VOCABULARY

Read the following sentences and determine the meanings of the underlined words by using the restatement clues provided.

1. The plant and animal exhibit from Ecuador was the most <u>exotic</u> exhibit the family had ever seen, being much more strikingly different from the local wildlife.
2. He does not fancy himself lolling under palm trees against a backdrop of <u>verdant</u> cliffs, no matter how scenic and green.
3. The balmy breezes <u>caressed</u> the tourists lounging in their hammocks like a loving mother rubbing a child's back.
4. Hawaii is a <u>unique</u> place with a diverse population, unusual wildlife, and an interesting history; it's unlike anything I have experienced before.

Local SENSIBILITIES

The monument to Duke Kahanamoku, the father of modern surfing, in Waikiki, Hawaii.

A Lyric Poem by **Wing Tek Lum**

When I see a pineapple,
I do not think of an exotic fruit sliced in rings
to be served with ham,
more the summer jobs at the cannery
driving a forklift or packing wedges on the line.

When I hear the name "Duke,"[1]
I envision someone other than that movie cowboy,
gravel-voiced, a true grit idol of the late night set;
instead I see a white-haired surfer by his long board,
palms so large, flashing smiles along the beach.

1. **"Duke."** Nickname of American movie actor John Wayne, who starred in *True Grit* and many other Westerns and war films

ex • ot • ic (ig zä´ tik) *adj.,* not native to the place where found; foreign; strikingly different or mysterious

When I think of a man-of-war,[2]
it is not the name of a Triple Crown horse
pacing a stud farm that comes to mind first;
rather I picture the Portuguese kind
whose stings must be salved by rubbing sand.

When I use the word "packages,"
it is usually not a reference to the parcels
waiting for me at the post office,
rather the paper sacks I get
from the supermarket to lug my groceries home.

When I read the term "Jap,"
the image of a kamikaze[3] pilot now turned to Sony exports
is not what I see;
mainly it is the Sand Island roundup[4] and those old men
who still wince long after the 442nd[5] has marched back.

When I think of Hawaii,
I do not fancy myself lolling under palm trees,
a backdrop of verdant cliffs, caressed by a balmy breeze;
instead I give thanks for classmates and our family graves,
this unique universe that we have called our home. ❖

2. **man-of-war.** Portuguese man of war. A jelly-like marine animal located in tropical and subtropical waters and known for its highly painful sting.

3. **kamikaze** (kä' mi kä´ zē). [Japanese] Member of a Japanese fighter crew that flew suicide missions on targets in World War II

4. **Sand Island roundup.** Roundup of Japanese Americans who were sent to relocation detention centers during World War II

5. **442nd.** The 442nd Regimental Combat Team (RCT), a segregated force consisting only of Nisei (first-generation Japanese-American) volunteers from Hawaii and the mainland. The 442nd joined forces with the 100th Infantry Battalion in Europe during World War II to become the most decorated unit in U.S. military history.

ver • dant (vʉr´ d'nt) *adj.*, green
ca • ress (kə res´) *v.*, to touch in a loving manner
u • nique (yü nēk´) *adj.*, being without a like or equal

Why might a non-native have a different impression of a location or community if he or she visited as a tourist? Why are tourists often perceived negatively in the eyes of local residents?

Critical Viewing

How does this advertisement promote stereotypes about Hawaii and its inhabitants?

Informational Text CONNECTION

After Japan bombed Pearl Harbor, the United States War Department called for the removal of soldiers of Japanese ancestry from active duty. In Hawaii, however, more than thirteen hundred Japanese-American soldiers in the Hawaii National Guard were kept in active service. These soldiers were sent to the mainland where they formed the 100th Infantry Battalion. The battalion's success prompted the government to allow Japanese Americans to serve in active duty. In 1943, the United States called for 1,500 volunteers from Hawaii, and more than 10,000 men volunteered. The government inducted nearly 3,000 men from Hawaii and 800 men from the mainland. These volunteers joined with the 100th Infantry Battalion to become the 442nd Infantry Regimental Combat Team.

442ND REGIMENTAL COMBAT TEAM

An informational text by the National Japanese American Historical Society

When the United States entered World War II in 1941, there were 5,000 Japanese Americans in the U.S. armed forces. Many were summarily discharged. Those of draft age were classified as 4-C, "enemy aliens," despite being U.S. citizens.

In Hawaii, however, a battalion of Nisei[1] volunteers was formed in May 1942. As the 100th Infantry Battalion, they were sent to North Africa in June of 1943 where they joined the 34th Division in combat. By September 1943, they were sent to Italy where they saw fierce combat and came to be known as the "Purple Heart Battalion" due to their high casualty rate.

In January 1943, the U.S. War Department announced the formation of the segregated 442nd Regimental Combat Team (RCT) made up of Nisei volunteers from Hawaii and the mainland. In June of 1944, the 442nd joined forces with the 100th Infantry Battalion in Europe and incorporated the 100th into the 442nd. Due to the stunning success of Nisei in combat, the draft was reinstated in January 1944 for Nisei in the detention camps to bolster the ranks of the 442nd. Eventually, the 442nd RCT consisted of the 2nd, 3rd, and 100th Battalions; the 522nd Field Artillery Battalion; the 232nd Engineering Company; the 206th Army Band; Anti-Tank Company; Cannon Company; and Service Company.

Due to their outstanding bravery and the heavy combat duty they faced, the 100/442nd RCT became the most decorated unit in U.S. military history for its size and length of service. There were over 18,000 individual decorations for bravery, 9,500 Purple Hearts, and seven Presidential Distinguished Unit Citations. ❖

1. **Nisei.** A term used to describe a son or daughter born outside of Japan to parents who emigrated from Japan in the years preceding World War II.

TEXT TO TEXT CONNECTION

What theme is present in both the poem and the informational text? According to these two selections, what hardships did Japanese Americans face? What perceptions and misconceptions of Japanese Americans are presented in each, and how are Japanese Americans depicted by the writers?

AFTER READING

REFER TO TEXT	REASON WITH TEXT	
1a. State what the speaker thinks of when he or she sees a pineapple.	1b. Infer who thinks of pineapples as "exotic fruit sliced in rings / to be served with ham."	Understand **Find meaning**
2a. Draw the Hawaii the speaker does *not* picture according to stanza 6.	2b. Produce a description of Hawaii for an "insider's" travel brochure. Show how insiders' and outsiders' views of the island might differ.	Apply **Use information**
3a. What happened to many Japanese men on the island during World War II?	3b. How might the informational text fit into stanza 5 of the poem? What contrast does Wing Tek Lum make in each stanza?	Analyze **Take things apart**
4a. Name things the speaker sees himself or herself doing.	4b. Interpret the title "Local Sensibilities." Decide whether "Hawaiian Sensibilities" would be equally effective as a title. Explain your decision.	Evaluate **Make judgments**
5a. List words or images the speaker associates with Hawaii.	5b. Using "Local Sensibilities" as a model, write one or more stanzas of a free verse poem that describes where you live.	Create **Bring ideas together**

ANALYZE LITERATURE: Context

What techniques does the author use to put ideas about Hawaii in a local context in the poem? How does he contrast a tourist's perspective of Hawaii with a resident's?

EXTEND THE TEXT

Writing Options

Creative Writing Imagine you are visiting Hawaii for an expedition, such as surfing, parasailing, scuba diving, or hiking. Write a **descriptive postcard** to a family member in which you describe a scene from your chosen activity—for example, that of a surfer riding a large wave. Explain the surrounding environment and action in thirty words or less.

Persuasive Writing Imagine that you live in Hawaii or another popular tourist destination. Like the speaker in "Local Sensibilities," you have observed the impact on the area by its many tourists, such as the use of more land for hotels and recreation and an increase in the number of jobs related to tourism. Write a **persuasive speech** arguing whether tourism is beneficial or damaging for your homeland.

Collaborative Learning

Prepare a Sensory Reading An image is a picture in words. Poets frequently choose images that appeal to the reader's senses. Review the poem, looking for examples of images. Then meet with a small group to discuss the following questions: What images in this poem appeal to the sense of sight? What images appeal to other senses? How did these images affect your enjoyment of this poem? Prepare a "sensory reading" in which the poem is read aloud while demonstrating the sensory images that are featured.

Media Literacy

Research Relocation Centers Use the Internet or books to research the relocation, or detention, camps that were set up for Japanese Americans during World War II. Explore questions such as the following: Where were the camps? Why were Japanese Americans relocated to them? How many people were detained? What were the living conditions of the camps? What did people in the camps do? Create a poster that summarizes your research. Include both text and visuals, such as a map, a statistical table, or photographs.

Go to **www.mirrorsandwindows.com** for more.

Understanding Figurative Language

FIGURATIVE LANGUAGE

Have you ever read a poem that you simply didn't comprehend? Though the text may be written in your native language, the poet may be using poetic, or figurative, language to describe an image, a scene, or a feeling.

TYPES OF FIGURATIVE LANGUAGE

Simile and Metaphor

One of the most frequently used techniques in poetry is to make a comparison between two dissimilar items, such as between a poem and a tree. How the comparison is made determines whether the writer is using a simile or a metaphor. **Similes** make the comparison by using the word *like* or *as*. For example, the poem-tree comparison written in simile would be "a poem is like a tree." Judith Ortiz Cofer uses simile in her poem "Cold as Heaven" (page 367).

> how wrapped like mummies in layers of wool
> that almost immobilized us, we could only
> take hesitant steps like toddlers
> toward food, warmth, shelter.
>
> —from "Cold as Heaven"
> by Judith Ortiz Cofer

Metaphors, on the other hand, make a comparison without using *like* or *as,* thus making the stated comparison seem stronger: "a poem is a tree." In a metaphor, the two objects being compared are called the *tenor* and the *vehicle.* The tenor is the actual object being discussed, and the vehicle is the object used to describe it. In the example above, the tenor is a poem and the vehicle is a tree. In Eve Merriam's poem "Metaphor" (page 387), the tenor is morning and the vehicle is a new sheet of paper.

> Morning is
> a new sheet of paper
> for you to write on.
>
> —from "Metaphor"
> by Eve Merriam

Analogy

Similarly, an **analogy** is a comparison between two things that are alike in some ways but otherwise quite different. Similes are *expressed analogies;* metaphors are *implied analogies.* In Shakespeare's "The Seven Ages of Man" (page 626), the speaker makes an implied analogy between life and a theatrical show.

> All the world's a stage,
> And all the men and women merely
> players,
> They have their exits and entrances,
> And one man in his time plays many parts,
> His acts being seven ages.
>
> —from "The Seven Ages of Man"
> by William Shakespeare

Personification

Another type of figurative language is personification. **Personification** is a figure of speech in which a nonhuman thing, such as an animal, an object, or an idea, is described as if it were a person. In "The Bells" (page 393), for instance, the alarm bells act as such:

> In the startled ear of night
> How they [bells] scream out their affright!
> Too much horrified to speak,
> They can only shriek, shriek,...
>
> —from "The Bells" by Edgar Allan Poe

The night is characterized as having a "startled ear," while the bells "scream out" in horror—actions and emotions that do not, of course, relate to inanimate objects. The use of personification here allows the reader to perceive the emotional overtones of the sound of the jangling bells; contrast this potent figurative language with the uninspired paraphrase, "The bells rang loudly."

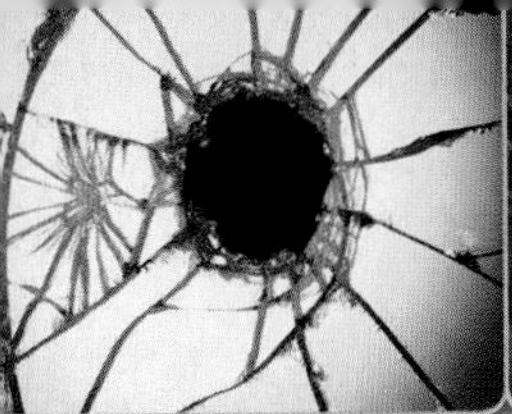

Symbolism

Symbolism is another type of literary device that falls into the category of figurative language. A **symbol** is anything that stands for or represents both itself and something else. For example, in "Caged Bird" (page 406), the cage represents oppression and slavery. The bird, a conventional symbol of physical, mental, or spiritual freedom, appears frequently in literature, as in "Caged Bird" and "'Hope' is the thing with feathers" (page 408).

> And sweetest—in the Gale—is heard—
> And sore must be the storm—
> That could abash the little Bird—
> That kept so many warm—
> —from "'Hope' is the thing with feathers"
> by Emily Dickinson

When every element of a poem or story symbolizes something else, the work is then considered an **allegory.**

Hyperbole

Another type of figurative language is **hyperbole,** in which overstatement, or exaggeration, is used for dramatic effect. The sayings "a flood of tears" or "muscles of steel" are hyperboles.

READING POETRY WITH FIGURATIVE LANGUAGE

If you find the language of poetry confusing, take a moment to consider these strategies. You also may want to jot down notes about your reading of the poem and ask yourself these questions:

- What is the main thing or idea being described?
- What images are used to describe it?
- What feelings or ideas do I associate with those images?
- How might the concepts in the poem relate to a familiar aspect of life?

Another way to better understand figurative language is to use a **graphic organizer,** such as a Figurative Language Chart like the following. As you read, identify examples of figurative language. Write down the examples in the first column of the chart. In the second column, write down the comparison being made by the figurative language, and in the third column, describe what the figurative language makes you visualize in your mind.

The following chart contains examples of the figurative language used within Marge Piercy's poem "To be of use" (page 448).

Figurative Language Chart

Example of Figurative Language	What Is Compared	What You Envision
"I love people who harness themselves, an ox to a heavy cart, who pull like water buffalo, with massive patience..."	The line compares a hard worker to an ox pulling a heavy cart.	I picture a strong, determined person working on a difficult task.

Metaphor

A Lyric Poem by Eve Merriam

A Simile

A Lyric Poem by N. Scott Momaday

COMPARING LITERATURE

BEFORE READING

BUILD BACKGROUND

Literary Context In **"Metaphor,"** Eve Merriam uses a metaphor to explore the idea that every day offers the reader the opportunity to act, speak, and live in ways he or she finds fulfilling. "Metaphor" was first published in *A Sky Full of Poems* (1986).

In **"A Simile,"** N. Scott Momaday uses a simile to explore what can happen to body language when people become tense because they aren't getting along well. "A Simile" has been published in a number of Native American anthologies, including *Carriers of the Dream* (1975).

Reader's Context Do you have any tense or uncomfortable relationships? What figurative language would you use to describe your attitude toward these relationships?

COMPARE LITERATURE: Figurative Language

Figurative language is writing or speech meant to be understood imaginatively instead of literally. Simile and metaphor are two examples of figurative language. A **simile** is a comparison using *like* or *as*. In a **metaphor,** one thing is spoken of or written about as if it were another. Similes and metaphors encourage you to make comparisons between two things. The writer's actual subject is called the *tenor,* and the thing to which the subject is likened is called the *vehicle.* As you read, note how the two poems use figurative language in their titles.

USE READING SKILLS

Meaning of Words
Brainstorming words is also called **wordstorming.** When you wordstorm, your goal is to think of as many words as you can related to a particular topic. In a two-column chart, list words from "Metaphor" and "A Simile" that are associated with the following topics: "Conflicts and arguments" and "Forgiving or being forgiven." Share your list with a partner, and add other words related to each topic.

Topic 1	Topic 2
Conflicts and arguments	Forgiving or being forgiven

MEET THE AUTHORS

MERRIAM

Eve Merriam (1916–1992) was so fascinated with language that she felt she had no choice but to become a poet. Her love of language is reflected in the hundreds of poems she wrote for young adults and children. While many of her poems explore how poetry works, she also wrote poems on social issues such as pollution, war, sexism, and television addiction. "Whatever you do, find ways to read poetry," Merriam urged. "Eat it, drink it, enjoy it, and share it."

N. Scott Momaday (b. 1934) is a poet, novelist, playwright, and nonfiction writer who has spent his life teaching and writing about Native American folklore, history, and mythology. Proud of his Native American heritage, the author grew up on Kiowa, Navajo, Apache, and Pueblo Indian reservations. In 1969, Momaday won the Pulitzer Prize for his novel *House Made of Dawn,* which tells the story of a young Native American torn between his ancestral roots and mainstream society.

MOMADAY

Metaphor

A Lyric Poem by **Eve Merriam**

Morning is
a new sheet of paper
for you to write on.

Whatever you want to say,
all day,
until night
folds it up
and files it away.

The bright words and the
dark words are gone
until dawn
and a new day
to write on. ❖

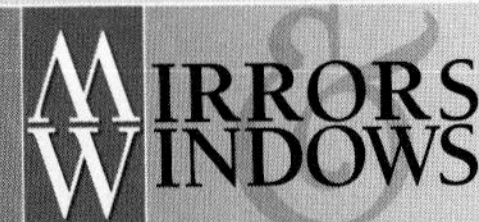

Is there freedom in starting over? Is the prospect of starting over every morning invigorating, frightening, or tedious?

A Simile

A Lyric Poem by **N. Scott Momaday**

What did we say to each other
that now we are as the deer
who walk in single file
with heads high
with ears forward
with eyes watchful
with hooves always placed on firm
ground
in whose limbs there is latent flight ❖

Under what circumstances might it be better to avoid confrontation and when might it be better to meet it head on? Can relationships sometimes benefit from avoidance?

AFTER READING

REFER TO TEXT	REASON WITH TEXT	
1a. According to the speaker in "Metaphor," what is morning? Quote stanza 1.	1b. Determine what point the writer is trying to make with this comparison.	Understand **Find meaning**
2a. Recall what dawn brings in "Metaphor" and how deer walk in "A Simile."	2b. What experiences have you had with new beginnings? What do you know about deer? Explain why the authors might have chosen the images of dawn and deer for their poems.	Apply **Use information**
3a. State what night does according to the speaker in "Metaphor" and what lies in the limbs of deer in "A Simile."	3b. Infer what the poet in "Metaphor" meant by "the bright words and the dark words." Analyze the significance of the deer's limbs. Determine what it means in the situation expressed in "A Simile."	Analyze **Take things apart**
4a. Identify the *tenor* and *vehicle* within these two poems.	4b. Critique whether the *vehicles* used in each poem are most effective options. What other *vehicles* could be used? Explain your responses.	Evaluate **Make judgments**
5a. List words and phrases that describe the *vehicles* of "Metaphor" and "A Simile."	5b. Compose your own metaphor and simile using the same *tenors*.	Create **Bring ideas together**

COMPARE LITERATURE: Figurative Language

These poems both use figurative language in different ways. What other features of these poems are similar? How are they different? Try rewriting "Metaphor" using a simile, and "A Simile" using a metaphor.

EXTEND THE TEXT

Writing Options

Creative Writing Write an **extended metaphor** about a friendship or other relationship you have with someone. An extended metaphor is a point-by-point presentation of one thing as though it were another. Eve Merriam's poem is an extended metaphor. Your metaphor can be in the form of a poem or prose paragraph.

Expository Writing Write a short **compare-and-contrast essay** about "Metaphor" and "A Simile." Compare the themes, styles, and literary techniques of each poem. You may arrange your comparison by poem (one at a time) or by aspect, such as themes or tones. The first paragraph should be a short introduction; the body paragraphs should focus on the comparison and contrast of the two poems; the final paragraph should summarize your points.

Collaborative Learning

Create Alternate Titles Eve Merriam and N. Scott Momaday both titled their poems for the type of figurative language used in the poems. Form a group of four to five students and discuss the following questions: Why do you think the writers chose to use these titles? Would it be more effective to give the poems titles that indicate what the poems are about? If they had chosen other titles, what titles do you think would be appropriate?

Critical Literacy

Write a Dialogue Imagine that the speaker in "Metaphor" is helping the speaker and the person being addressed in "A Simile" to resolve their conflict. Think about what he or she would say to them, and how they would respond. Write a brief dialogue among the three characters. Share your dialogue with the class. Discuss how the different dialogues are similar and different.

Go to **www.mirrorsandwindows.com** for more.

Understanding Sight and Sound

SIGHT AND SOUND

One of the reasons people have enjoyed poetry over the centuries is that poems can depict physical and emotional states so precisely, not only through visual imagery but through sound devices. Poets have many techniques at their disposal to make their words work for them, just as a painter has paints or a musician has notes.

TECHNIQUE OF SIGHT

Imagery

Imagery is the descriptive language that creates a vivid picture in the mind of the reader and appeals to one of the senses. Imagery uses concrete objects to represent a scene, an emotion, or an experience. For example, the captive birds in the poems "Sympathy" (page 405) and "Caged Bird" (page 406) represent the miserable condition of oppression and slavery. The reader responds to the imagery empathetically, recognizing the frustration of the imprisoned creatures. Imagery can also paint a scene so vividly that the reader will understand the feeling evoked in the speaker by the scene.

> When the first bird sings and the first bud opes,
> And the faint perfume from its chalice steals—
> —from "Sympathy"
> by Paul Laurence Dunbar

What Great Writers Do

In Pat Mora's poem "Gentle Communion" (page 368), the speaker describes his or her deceased grandmother in terms of an old prayer book and in a way that offers the reader a glimpse into the speaker's memories.

> She closes her eyes, bows her head,
> and like a child presses her hands together,
> her patient flesh steeple, the skin
> worn, like the pages of her prayer book.
> —from "Gentle Communion" by Pat Mora

TECHNIQUES OF SOUND

Rhyme

The first sound device you associate with poetry is very likely to be **rhyme.** The most common type of rhyme is the repetition of sounds at the ends of words that occur at the ends of lines, such as "In the jangling, / And the wrangling," from Edgar Allan Poe's poem "The Bells" (page 393). Such a rhyme is called **end rhyme.** If the rhyming words appear within the lines instead of at the ends of lines, the pattern is called **internal rhyme.** If the rhyme is not exact, meaning that the sounds are somewhat similar but not quite rhyming, it is considered a **slant rhyme.** In "'Hope' is the thing with feathers" (page 408), the words *soul* and *all* are matched in the rhyme scheme as a slant rhyme.

> "Hope" is the thing with feathers—
> That perches in the soul—
> And sings the tune—without the words—
> And never stops—at all—
> —from "'Hope' is the thing with feathers"
> by Emily Dickinson

A **rhyme scheme** is the pattern of end rhyme designated by assigning a different letter of the alphabet to each rhyme, such as *abab.* The rhyme scheme in Theodore Roethke's poem "My Papa's Waltz" (page 458) is *abab.*

> The whiskey on your breath *a*
> Could make a small boy dizzy; *b*
> But I hung on like death: *a*
> Such waltzing was not easy. *b*

Assonance, Consonance, and Alliteration

The sounds of letters in other parts of words can also be used for effect. **Assonance** is the repetition of vowel sounds. In "The Bells," for instance, the speaker mentions the bells' "molten-golden notes." The long *o* (ō) sound in those three words conveys a sense of smooth roundness, which is the sound image Poe seeks to create in that part of the poem.

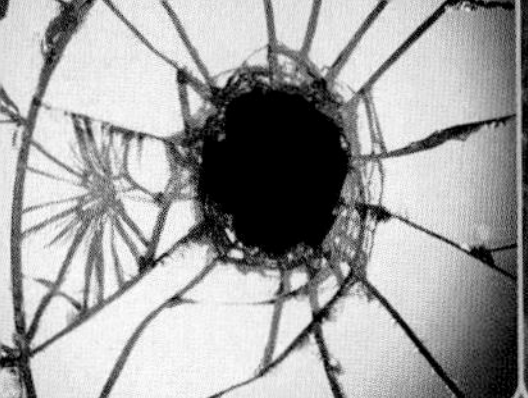

Consonance, on the other hand, is a similarity in consonant sounds in words that otherwise do not rhyme. The words "strike" and "lucky" have consonance with the *k* sound. When you notice that a consonant sound is repeated at the beginnings of several words, you have found an example of **alliteration.** An example of alliteration can be found in Pablo Neruda's poem "Poetry" (page 402).

> planets,
> palpitating plantations,
> the darkness perforated
> —from "Poetry" by Pablo Neruda

Onomatopoeia

Onomatopoeia is the use of words or phrases that sound like things to which they refer. For example, in "The Bells," the verbs *tinkle, clang,* and *moaning* all describe a particular sound, but they also imitate the sound that is being made. The word *tinkle* sounds light, delicate, and high-pitched, whereas the word *clang* sounds as harsh and grating as the sound it describes.

Repetition

The use of **repetition** can add emphasis to an idea. By repeating the word *bells,* Poe conjures a sense of the pervasive, overwhelming impression made by the tolling bells. Repetition of entire lines or stanzas also emphasizes ideas, as in "Caged Bird," where both the line "so he opens his throat to sing" and stanza 3 are repeated.

Rhythm and Meter

By paying attention to the syllables and stresses in words and lines of poetry, poets can create **rhythm** within a verse. The rhythm of a poem is determined by the **meter,** which is based on the number of beats, or stresses, in a line. These are the syllable patterns, often called *feet,* with an example of each pattern:

iambic	unstressed, stressed	trom • bone'
trochaic	stressed, unstressed	ap' • ple
anapestic	two unstressed, one stressed	en • ter • tain'
dactylic	one stressed, two unstressed	mys' • ter • y
spondaic	two stressed	bird' • house'

Below are the terms used to designate the number of feet, or stresses, in a line of verse:

- *monometer* (one-foot line)
- *dimeter* (two-foot line)
- *trimeter* (three-foot line)
- *tetrameter* (four-foot line)
- *pentameter* (five-foot line)
- *hexameter* (six-foot line, also called *Alexandrine*)
- *heptameter* (seven-foot line)
- *octameter* (eight-foot line)

Therefore, a line of poetry with five iambs would be called iambic pentameter. An example of iambic pentameter can be found in the poem "Sonnet" (page 427) by C. S. Lewis.

> ˘ / ˘ / ˘ / ˘ / ˘ /
> The stars come out; the fragrant shadows fall
> ˘ / ˘ / ˘ / ˘ / ˘ /
> About a dreaming garden still and sweet,
> ˘ / ˘ / ˘ / ˘ / ˘ /
> I hear the unseen bats above me bleat
> ˘ / ˘ / ˘ / ˘ / ˘ /
> Among the ghostly moths their hunting call
> —from "Sonnet" by C. S. Lewis

The Bells

BEFORE READING

A Lyric Poem by Edgar Allan Poe

DIRECTED READING

BUILD BACKGROUND

Literary Context A friend of Poe, Marie Louise Shew, suggested the idea for **"The Bells."** Poe was in poor mental and physical health, and the ringing of many church bells near Shew's house disturbed him greatly. Poe wrote a brief poem that was later expanded into the poem that exists today. Through the use of literary techniques, the poem creates a rendering of the sounds of four types of bells and the emotional responses that they evoke.

Reader's Context What sounds do you particularly like or dislike? Do certain sounds remind you of specific events or memories?

ANALYZE LITERATURE: Onomatopoeia

Onomatopoeia is the use of words or phrases to capture the sounds or actions to which they refer. Some examples are the words *hum, buzz,* and *chop*. As you read "The Bells," look for words that refer to sounds. Say them out loud to see if they are onomatopoeic. Does reading the poem aloud enhance your understanding?

SET PURPOSE

"The Bells" is famous for its use of **repetition**—the writer's intentional reuse of a sound, word, phrase, or sentence. As you read, note how repetition and onomatopoeia add to the mood of "The Bells."

MEET THE AUTHOR

Edgar Allan Poe (1809–1849) led a short, troubled life but managed to make major contributions to literary form and criticism. Considered the co-creator (with Nathaniel Hawthorne) of the modern short story, Poe also invented detective fiction, wrote lyric poetry, and pioneered the psychological horror story. Orphaned at age two, Poe was raised by John Allan, a prosperous Virginia merchant, who gave him a classical education. In his twenties, Poe began to write poems and stories while working at various editorial jobs. Although briefly famous for his poem "The Raven," he spent most of his adult life in poverty. Even so, Poe was committed to writing. Among his best-known poems are "Annabel Lee" and "The Bells." Both embody Poe's own definition of poetry as "the Rhythmical Creation of Beauty."

USE READING SKILLS

Text Organization Sound devices such as repetition, rhythm, and meter can assist you in understanding the meaning of a poem by revealing what the writer is trying to emphasize within the poem. As you read "The Bells," list any sound devices you encounter and try to determine what the writer meant to accomplish by using these devices.

PREVIEW VOCABULARY

A **mnemonic device** is a catchy phrase, image, or trick that helps you remember information. Mnemonic devices can often help you remember the meaning or spelling of a word. There are no rules about what mnemonics should be; they can be jingles, rhymes, images, word associations, or whatever works for you.

EXAMPLE

Balmy means mild because it rhymes with *palmy,* and palm trees grow in places where the weather is warm and mild.

For each word below, think of a mnemonic device that could help you remember the meaning or spelling of each of the words from the poem.

voluminously
clamor
melancholy
knell

The Bells

A Lyric Poem by **Edgar Allan Poe**

Church Bells Ringing, Rainy Winter Night, 1917. Charles Burchfield. The Cleveland Museum of Art.

Critical Viewing

What mood does this artwork create? Does the mood of the artwork reflect the mood of the poem?

I

Hear the sledges[1] with the bells—
Silver bells!
What a world of merriment their melody foretells!
How they tinkle, tinkle, tinkle,
In the icy air of night!
While the stars that oversprinkle
All the heavens seem to twinkle
With a crystalline delight;
Keeping time, time, time,
In a sort of Runic rhyme,[2]
To the tintinnabulation[3] that so musically wells
From the bells, bells, bells, bells,
Bells, bells, bells—
From the jingling and the tinkling of the bells.

II

Hear the mellow wedding bells,
Golden bells!
What a world of happiness their harmony foretells!
Through the balmy air of night
How they ring out their delight!
From the molten-golden notes,
And all in tune,

1. **sledges.** Sleds or sleighs
2. **Runic rhyme.** Ancient verse written in one of several alphabets used by Germanic peoples
3. **tintinnabulation.** Ringing sound

bal • my (bä´ mē *or* bäl´ mē) *adj.,* soothing; mild; pleasant

What a liquid ditty floats
To the turtle-dove that listens, while she gloats
On the moon!
Oh, from out the sounding cells
What a gush of euphony[4] voluminously wells!
How it swells!
How it dwells
On the Future! how it tells
Of the rapture that impels
To the swinging and the ringing
Of the bells, bells, bells,
Of the bells, bells, bells, bells,
Bells, bells, bells—
To the rhyming and the chiming of the bells!

III

Hear the loud alarum bells[5]—
Brazen bells!
What a tale of terror, now, their turbulency[6] tells!
In the startled ear of night
How they scream out their affright![7]
Too much horrified to speak,
They can only shriek, shriek,
Out of tune,
In a clamorous appealing to the mercy of the fire,
In a mad expostulation[8] with the deaf and frantic fire,
Leaping higher, higher, higher,
With a desperate desire,
And a resolute endeavor
Now—now to sit, or never,
By the side of the pale-faced moon.
Oh, the bells, bells, bells!
What a tale their terror tells
Of despair!
How they clang, and clash, and roar!
What a horror they outpour
On the bosom of the palpitating air!
Yet the ear it fully knows,
By the twanging,
And the clanging,
How the danger ebbs and flows;
Yet the ear distinctly tells,
In the jangling,
And the wrangling,
How the danger sinks and swells,

4. **euphony.** Pleasing sound
5. **alarum bells.** Alarm bells (archaic)
6. **turbulency.** Violent agitation
7. **affright.** Great fright or terror (archaic)
8. **expostulation.** Objection; disagreement

vo • lu • mi • nous • ly (və lü´ mə nəs lē) *adv.,* largely; fully

By the sinking or the swelling in the anger of the bells—
Of the bells—
Of the bells, bells, bells, bells,
Bells, bells, bells—
In the clamor and the clangor of the bells!

IV

Hear the tolling of the bells
Iron bells!
What a world of solemn thought their melody compels!
In the silence of the night,
How we shiver with affright
At the melancholy menace of their tone!
For every sound that floats
From the rust within their throats
Is a groan.
And the people—ah, the people—
They that dwell up in the steeple,
All alone,
And who tolling, tolling, tolling,
In that muffled monotone,
Feel a glory in so rolling
On the human heart a stone—
They are neither man nor woman—
They are neither brute nor human—
They are Ghouls:[9]
And their king it is who tolls;
And he rolls, rolls, rolls,
Rolls
A pæan[10] from the bells!
And his merry bosom swells
With the pæan of the bells!
And he dances, and he yells;
Keeping time, time, time,
In a sort of Runic rhyme,
To the pæan of the bells—
Of the bells:
Keeping time, time, time,
In a sort of Runic rhyme,
To the throbbing of the bells—

9. **Ghouls.** Evil spirits
10. **pæan.** Song of joy, triumph, or praise

clam • or (kla´ mər) *n.*, loud, continuous noise
mel • an • cho • ly (me´ lən kä' lē) *adj.*, sad; gloomy; depressed

Of the bells, bells, bells—
To the sobbing of the bells;
Keeping time, time, time,
As he knells, knells, knells,
In a happy Runic rhyme,
To the rolling of the bells—
Of the bells, bells, bells—
To the tolling of the bells,
Of the bells, bells, bells, bells—
Bells, bells, bells—
To the moaning and the groaning of the bells. ❖

knell (nel) *v.*, sounds ominously or mournfully

What reminds people of the passing of time? Why might these reminders be irritating or upsetting? Why might members of our society fear or worry about growing older?

AFTER READING

REFER TO TEXT	REASON WITH TEXT	
1a. List the types of bells that are described in the poem.	1b. Which bells does the speaker enjoy listening to? How can you tell?	Understand **Find meaning**
2a. Note the sounds the wedding bells make.	2b. Use what you know about weddings to list other images Poe might have used in this stanza.	Apply **Use information**
3a. State the message the alarum bells send. Identify the noise they use to convey this message.	3b. Identify the different meanings that bells communicate within the poem. Infer why the sounds of the bells are so significant to the speaker.	Analyze **Take things apart**
4a. Count how long the stanzas are in each part.	4b. Interpret the significance of the stanza lengths in this poem. Do you think stanza length adds any meaning to the poem? Why?	Evaluate **Make judgments**
5a. Identify the type of bells featured in the final stanza.	5b. What images does Poe use to create the mood of this final stanza? Using Poe's style, write a stanza that describes a school bell.	Create **Bring ideas together**

ANALYZE LITERATURE: Onomatopoeia

Which words in the poem sound like small, light bells? Which words sound like large, heavy bells? What repeated phrases in the poem have the rhythmic quality of ringing bells?

EXTEND THE TEXT

Writing Options

Creative Writing Consider the way Poe uses the sounds of words to recreate the sounds of and moods created by different bells. Then choose another object or animal that produces different sounds. For example, a dog might make a welcoming bark, a pained yelp, or a menacing growl. Write a **sound poem** about that object to read to a classmate. Try to use the techniques of onomatopoeia and repetition. You may find it useful to consult a thesaurus to find synonyms with appropriate sounds.

Persuasive Writing Write a three-paragraph **position statement** that argues which of the stanzas in Poe's "The Bells" is the most interesting and insightful. Use examples from the selection to support your arguments.

Collaborative Learning

Perform a Dramatic Recitation In a group of four, prepare a reading of "The Bells." Consider each person's vocal qualities as you decide which stanzas or lines should be read by individual readers and which by the group as a whole. Also discuss how you will use pitch, pace, and articulation to create the sounds and dramatic effects of the bells. As you rehearse, offer constructive suggestions for making the reading effective. Then present your reading to the class. As your classmates present their recitations, keep notes on which performances you enjoy and why you enjoyed them. When the class is finished, take a moment to discuss what elements worked the best for each presentation. Once you have finished, take a vote to decide which recitation was the most entertaining.

Media Literacy

Research Poe on the Internet Imagine that you want to apply for a grant of money to research places associated with Edgar Allan Poe's life. In order to receive a grant, you must present your ideas in a way that will persuade others to fund your project. Use the Internet to find locations that you would want to visit. Then write a grant proposal to a local business, organization, or university stating what places you need to visit and why, as well as why it should fund your trip.

Go to **www.mirrorsandwindows.com** for more.

READING ASSESSMENT

1. The sounds of sleigh bells, referred to as *sledge* bells in the poem, foretell
   - A. snowy weather.
   - B. hilarity.
   - C. sadness.
   - D. merriment.
   - E. tintinnabulation.

2. Alarm bells, referred to as *alarum* bells in the poem, give a sense of
   - A. elation.
   - B. terror.
   - C. sadness.
   - D. orderliness.
   - E. All of the above

3. As it is used on line 106, the term *knells* most closely means
   - A. sings.
   - B. whispers.
   - C. wails.
   - D. pounds.
   - E. tolls.

4. Which of these phrases from the poem does *not* include onomatopoeia?
   - A. How they clang, and clash, and roar!
   - B. How we shiver with affright
   - C. To the swinging and the ringing
   - D. How they tinkle, tinkle, tinkle,
   - E. To the moaning and the groaning of the bells.

5. What does the king of the Ghouls do?
   - A. shrieks out of tune
   - B. announces weddings
   - C. tolls the iron bells
   - D. groans and moans
   - E. rings the alarum bells

6. What effect does the repetition of the word *bells* have throughout the poem? Why do you think the author did this? Is the repetition appropriate, or overdone? Explain.

GRAMMAR & STYLE

UNDERSTAND THE CONCEPT

APPLY THE SKILL

Verb Tense

Verbs carry a concept of time, called tense. The **simple tenses** express simple past, present, and future. The **perfect tenses** give information about actions that take place over time. Each of the simple and perfect tenses has a **progressive tense** that shows continuing action. The progressive form is made by using a tense of the helping verb *be* with the present participle.

Simple Tenses Present tense verbs show that something is happening now. Past tense verbs talk about something that happened before now, and future tense verbs talk about something that will happen in the future. Using the progressive form of the simple tense allows for continuing action.

EXAMPLES

simple present: Today, I eat/do eat chocolate ice cream.
present progressive: I am eating chocolate ice cream.
simple past: Yesterday, I ate/did eat strawberry ice cream.
past progressive: I was eating strawberry ice cream.
simple future: Tomorrow, I will eat vanilla ice cream.
future progressive: I will be eating vanilla ice cream.

Perfect Tenses The perfect tenses express past, present, and future, but they add information about actions that continued over a period of time and were completed in the past or will be completed in the present or future. All perfect tenses use some form of the helping verb *to have*.

EXAMPLES

present perfect: The school has created a dance specifically for underclassmen.
present perfect progressive: Jaden has been bragging about his dance moves.
past perfect: Maria had seen Jaden dance last summer, and she wasn't impressed.
past perfect progressive: Tyler had been planning to invite Shana, but Devin asked her first.
future perfect: By the end of the week, Tyler will have arranged to go with Alison.
future perfect progressive: When the dance finally arrives, we will have been talking about it for almost two months.

Combinations It is possible to combine different verb tenses within the same sentence, as long as the sentence contains two independent clauses joined with a coordinating conjunction.

EXAMPLES

simple past, future progressive: I didn't sleep very well last night, so I won't be staying up late tonight.
past perfect, simple past: Samit had taken the wrong bus, but he got to his appointment on time anyway.
present perfect, simple present: Loraine has tried on many dresses, but she doesn't like any of them.

REVIEW TERMS

- **tense:** the sense of time carried by a verb
- **simple tenses:** tenses that express simple past, present, and future
- **perfect tenses:** tenses that give information about actions that take place over time in the past, present, or future
- **progressive tenses:** tenses that shows continuing action

UNDERSTAND THE CONCEPT

Identify Verb Tenses

Identify the verb tense in each of the following sentences as *simple present, simple past, simple future, present perfect, past perfect,* or *future perfect.*

1. Our teacher is speaking to the class about Poe's poetry.
2. Poe had written many poems and stories.
3. Poe wrote more than ninety poems.
4. I will read "The Bells" many more times so that I can understand it fully.
5. The church bells have been ringing for hours.
6. The fire alarm rings every night.
7. The wedding bells had already begun ringing when Joe arrived.
8. Edgar Allan Poe invented detective fiction.
9. Poe has been credited with co-creating the modern short story.
10. By the time she has graduated, Logeni will have read all of Poe's work.

Use Verb Tense Correctly in Your Own Writing

Fill in the missing words in this blog entry according to the directions in parentheses. Choose your own verbs to make the entry either accurate or humorous.

A Day in the Life of (your name)
This morning, after I got up, I (simple past verb) and (simple past verb). That's fairly normal for me—I usually (simple present verb) most days. After I (present perfect verb), I occasionally (simple present verb), but today was different; I (simple past verb) instead. Later, I met up with my friend (friend's name), who (either simple present, present progressive, present perfect, or simple past verb). We (present progressive verb), but soon we (simple future verb). I look forward to that day! I (future perfect progressive verb) for (length of time). As for the rest of the day, I (simple future verb).

APPLY THE SKILL

Make Verb Tense Consistent

Revise the following paragraph to use consistent verb tense throughout.

The bells began to ring at dawn. Jared comes outside to find out why they were ringing. When he saw smoke coming from a nearby house, he walks down the street to see if anyone needed help. The family has been standing outside the house, waiting for the fire department. Nobody is hurt, but Jared decided to stay with the family until help will arrive. After a few minutes, they have heard the fire truck come down the street, and Jared will have helped the family flag down the truck.

EXTEND THE SKILL

Write a set of twenty or more fortunes for fortune cookies. Keep in mind that these fortunes sometimes give information about the person, such as "You have a great sense of grace and style" or "Lately you have not been treating your friends well," and sometimes they make predictions about the future, such as "You will win the lottery later this year." Your fortunes may also combine different tenses: "People have noticed your lovely smile, so you will soon meet an admirer." Use your imagination to come up with fortunes that are fun and specific to your community or school. With a partner or group, select the ten best fortunes from each person's list. Print out a sheet of these fortunes and cut them into thin strips. Fold them up and have everybody in your group draw a new fortune each day.

The Secret

A Lyric Poem by Denise Levertov

Poetry

A Lyric Poem by Pablo Neruda

BEFORE READING

BUILD BACKGROUND

Literary Context In the following poems, Denise Levertov and Pablo Neruda write about the powerful effects of poetry. In Levertov's **"The Secret,"** the speaker considers the poet's relationship with his or her readers. In Neruda's **"Poetry,"** the speaker tells about discovering a talent for writing poetry.

Levertov and Neruda both began writing poems as children. "The Secret" and "Poetry" are lyric poems; that is, they use highly musical verse to express the emotions of a speaker.

Reader's Context Has any type of literature or visual art ever made you feel excited or emotional? Have you had a strong positive or negative reaction to someone else's creation?

COMPARE LITERATURE: Free Verse

Free verse is poetry that avoids the use of regular rhyme, rhythm, or stanza divisions. Poets writing in free verse often use line breaks or spaces between groups of lines to emphasize certain words or ideas. As you read, consider the following questions: How do the two poems differ in style, including format, word choice, and use of grammar? What feelings about poetry are expressed in each poem?

USE READING SKILLS

Compare and Contrast
Consider the similarities and differences between how Levertov and Neruda describe poetry. What effect does poetry have on the speaker's life? What effect does it have on the lives of others? How and where does poetry appear in the world? How does poetry connect people and ideas? Consider using a Venn diagram to organize your thoughts.

"The Secret"	Both	"Poetry"
Poetry shares a secret with the reader	Poetry promotes discovery	Poetry shares knowledge with the writer

MEET THE AUTHORS

LEVERTOV

Denise Levertov (1923–1997) published over twenty collections of poems during her lifetime. Born in England, she developed a spare and visionary style that was influenced by her mentor, American poet William Carlos Williams. Levertov, who was schooled at home, learned her craft by "writing and a lot of reading." Attentive to the sound of poetry, she noted, "One has to have a good ear, but you also have to read what you're working on aloud." "The Secret" is from Levertov's collection *O Taste and See,* published in 1964.

Born Neftali Ricardo Reyes Basoalto in the small town of Parral, Chile, **Pablo Neruda** (1904–1973) grew into an avid reader and began writing poetry at the age of ten. A precocious writer, by age twenty he had published two books of poems. Neruda's first book, *Crepuscalario,* was published in 1923, followed by *Twenty Love Poems and a Song of Despair* in 1924. Admired around the world, he was awarded the Nobel Prize for Literature in 1971. Known as the people's poet, he wrote about political and social struggle as well as love, loneliness, and the details of everyday life. "All paths lead to the same goal," he said, "to convey to others what we are."

NERUDA

Secret Ripple #2, 1994. Gerrit Greve.

A Lyric Poem by **Denise Levertov**

Two girls discover
the secret of life
in a sudden line of
poetry.

I who don't know the
secret wrote
the line. They
told me

(through a third person)
they had found it
but not what it was,
not even

what line it was. No doubt
by now, more than a week
later, they have forgotten
the secret,

the line, the name of
the poem. I love them
for finding what
I can't find,

and for loving me
for the line I wrote,
and for forgetting it
so that

a thousand times, till death
finds them, they may
discover it again, in other
lines,

in other
happenings. And for
wanting to know it,
for

assuming there is
such a secret, yes,
for that
most of all. ❖

Getting "lost" in a book or piece of writing is a common adage. What does it mean? Can people judge the quality of the writing by the effect it has on the reader?

POETRY

A Lyric Poem by **Pablo Neruda**

And it was at that age…poetry arrived
in search of me. I don't know, I don't know where
it came from, from winter or a river.
I don't know how or when,
no, they were not voices, they were not
words, not silence,
but from a street it called me,
from the branches of night,
abruptly from the others,
among raging fires
or returning alone,
there it was, without a face,
and it touched me.
I didn't know what to say, my mouth
had no way
with names,
my eyes were blind.
Something knocked in my soul,
fever or forgotten wings,
and I made my own way,
deciphering
that fire,
and I wrote the first, faint line,
faint, without substance, pure
nonsense,
pure wisdom
of someone who knows nothing;
and suddenly I saw
the heavens
unfastened
and open,
planets,
palpitating plantations,
the darkness perforated,
riddled
with arrows, fire, and flowers,
the overpowering night, the universe.

And I, tiny being,
drunk with the great starry
void,
likeness, image of
mystery,
felt myself a pure part
of the abyss.
I wheeled with the stars.
My heart broke loose with the wind. ❖

a • brupt • ly (ə brup[t]´ lē) *adv.*, suddenly
de • ci • pher (dē sī´ fər) *v.*, interpret
pal • pi • tat • ing (pal´ pə tāt' iŋ) *adj.*, beating rapidly; fluttering
per • fo • rat • ed (pʉr fə rāt´ əd) *adj.*, punctured
rid • dled (ri´ d'ld) *adj.*, pierced many times
a • byss (ə bis´ *or* a´ bis[']) *n.*, huge empty space or depth

What is inspiration? Can inspiration be found in everyday objects and occurrences? Can beauty be found in everyday things?

AFTER READING

REFER TO TEXT	REASON WITH TEXT	
1a. State what the two girls in "The Secret" discover and where they discover it.	1b. In your own words, explain where the speaker believes the girls will discover this secret again.	Understand **Find meaning**
2a. State what happened when the speaker in "Poetry" began writing.	2b. Is the speaker's experience with writing poetry similar to your own experience with writing? Explain. How do these experiences compare with the girls' experience in "The Secret"?	Apply **Use information**
3a. Identify what the speaker in "The Secret" loves most about the girls.	3b. Use the speaker's response to the girls to detect the theme of the poem.	Analyze **Take things apart**
4a. Recall what the speakers in both "The Secret" and "Poetry" feel themselves to be a part of.	4b. Select the words and images in the poems that are most striking to you. Explain your reactions to them.	Evaluate **Make judgments**
5a. Identify words and phrases the speaker in "Poetry" uses to describe himself in the last stanza.	5b. Think about a time when you had feelings like those the speaker describes in the last stanza of "Poetry." Generate a list of words and images you would use to describe your own experience.	Create **Bring ideas together**

COMPARE LITERATURE: Free Verse

Compare whether or not Levertov and Neruda use free verse in the same way. Do both poets use line breaks to emphasize ideas within the poem? If so, how have they done this, and to what effect?

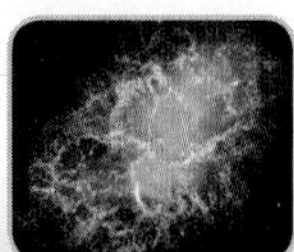

EXTEND THE TEXT

Writing Options

Creative Writing Think about the choices each poet made in using free verse, including elements such as line breaks, punctuation, and section divisions. Then compose your own **free verse poem** about writing or reading poetry. You may wish to use one or both poems as a model. Another option is to take a paragraph from a favorite story of yours and reorganize the sentences into a free verse poem by adding line breaks and section divisions.

Expository Writing What ideas about poetry are expressed in the two poems? Consider what each selection has to say about both writers and readers of poems. Write a **compare-and-contrast essay** in which you explain at least one idea from each poem. You may organize your essay either by ideas or by poems.

Lifelong Learning

Write an Author Résumé Locate an interview with the poets Denise Levertov or Pablo Neruda. Read the interview from start to finish. Use the information in the article to write a one-page résumé of the author. As you read, take notes from the article under headings such as Career, Achievements, and Awards. Then use your notes to plan and write the résumé. Trade résumés with another student to compare facts and to learn more about the author.

Collaborative Learning

Participate in a Poetry Reading Pablo Neruda published a wide variety of poetry. Select one of his poems and practice reading it aloud. Pay attention to volume, pitch, stress, tone, and gestures as you find a way to present the poem effectively. Perform your selection for the class. When it is your turn to listen, take notes on imagery or language that appeals to you. As a class, discuss responses to the poems.

Go to **www.mirrorsandwindows.com** for more.

Sympathy
A Lyric Poem by Paul Laurence Dunbar

Caged Bird
A Lyric Poem by Maya Angelou

BEFORE READING

BUILD BACKGROUND

Historical Context Paul Laurence Dunbar's poem **"Sympathy"** was published in 1899 in the book *Lyrics of the Hearthside.* Written during a time in America when a good-paying job and a college education were unavailable to most African Americans, it echoes the frustration of a talented young black poet. Credited for capturing the true voice of the African American in his poetry, Dunbar set the stage for the emergence of black artists and writers living in Harlem in the 1920s and 1930s, an era known as the Harlem Renaissance.

Maya Angelou's poem **"Caged Bird"** was published eighty-four years after "Sympathy" in a collection titled *Shaker, Why Don't You Sing?* Angelou, who is also African American, was influenced by Dunbar and a number of other writers, including William Shakespeare. Angelou chose the title *I Know Why the Caged Bird Sings* for the first book in her five-book collection of autobiographical works.

Reader's Context Both poems explore the topic of freedom. Has there ever been a time when you did not feel free to be yourself? How did you feel? What did you do?

USE READING SKILLS

Use Text Organization
Traditional poems are often arranged into stanzas, or groups of lines. In these poems, the stanza sometimes functions as a paragraph does in prose: It may explore a single idea related to the subject of the poem. Details in the stanza help to bring out the main idea. Make two charts, one for each poem, and then use them to keep notes about each stanza in the two poems.

Stanza	Main Idea	Details
Sympathy, stanza 2	Struggle for freedom	"blood is red on the cruel bars"

COMPARE LITERATURE: Rhetorical Devices

The following two poems contain examples of **rhetorical devices**—techniques that a writer uses to achieve a particular effect on the reader. Rhetorical devices may include the **repetition** of words, phrases, and passages and the use of **figurative language**—wording meant to be understood imaginatively, not literally (example: "but a caged bird stands on the grave of dreams"). As you read the two poems, take note of the repetition used. Look for not only repeated words and phrases, but also repeated imagery. Also, consider the similarities between the poems and their use of figurative language.

MEET THE AUTHORS

DUNBAR

Paul Laurence Dunbar (1872–1906), the son of former slaves, was born in Dayton, Ohio. Encouraged by his mother's love of poetry, Dunbar was writing and reciting poems by the age of six and published his first collection of poetry when he was twenty-one. Before his death at the age of thirty-four, he published twelve books of poetry, four books of short stories, a play, and five novels.

Maya Angelou (b. 1928) spent much of her childhood in the segregated South. Abused and lonely as a child, Angelou turned her painful experiences into a series of autobiographical works that includes the widely read *I Know Why the Caged Bird Sings.* Also well known for her poetry, Angelou stresses, "We need language to tell us who we are, how we feel, what we're capable of—to explain the pains and glory of our existence."

ANGELOU

Sympathy

A Lyric Poem by

Paul Laurence Dunbar

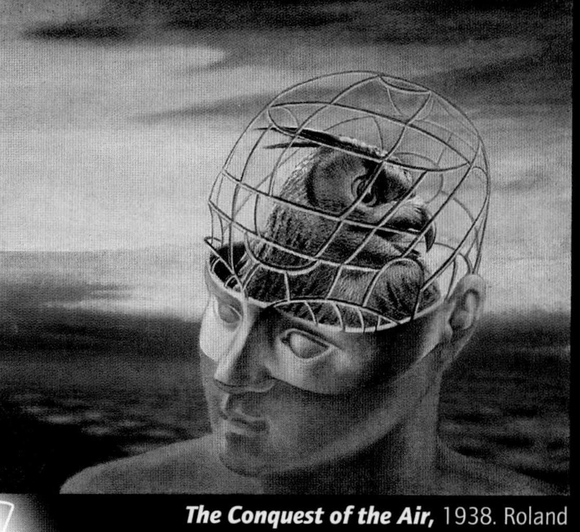

The Conquest of the Air, 1938. Roland Penrose. Southhampton City Art Gallery, England.

I know what the caged bird feels, alas![1]
When the sun is bright on the upland slopes;
When the wind stirs soft through the springing grass,
And the river flows like a stream of glass;
When the first bird sings and the first bud opes,[2]
And the faint perfume from its chalice[3] steals—
I know what the caged bird feels!

I know why the caged bird beats his wing
Till its blood is red on the cruel bars;
For he must fly back to his perch and cling
When he fain[4] would be on the bough a-swing;[5]
And a pain still throbs in the old, old scars
And they pulse again with a keener sting—
I know why he beats his wing!

I know why the caged bird sings, ah me,
When his wing is bruised and his bosom sore,—
When he beats his bars and he would be free;
It is not a carol of joy or glee,
But a prayer that he sends from his heart's deep core,
But a plea, that upward to Heaven he flings—
I know why the caged bird sings! ❖

keen (kēn) *adj.,* sharp; more intense

1. **alas.** Word used to express unhappiness, pity, or concern
2. **opes.** Opens
3. **chalice.** Cup-shaped interior of a flower
4. **fain.** With pleasure; gladly; by desire; by preference
5. **a-swing.** Swinging

Many small animals are kept in cages in order to keep them protected. Which is more important, security or freedom? What problems could arise for each?

A Lyric Poem by **Maya Angelou**

A free bird leaps
on the back of the wind
and floats downstream
till the current ends
and dips his wing
in the orange sun rays
and dares to claim the sky.

But a bird that stalks
down his narrow cage
can <u>seldom</u> see through
his bars of rage
his wings are clipped and
his feet are tied
so he opens his throat to sing.

The caged bird sings
with a fearful <u>trill</u>
of things unknown
but longed for still
and his tune is heard
on the distant hill
for the caged bird
sings of freedom.

The free bird thinks of another breeze
and the trade winds[1] soft through the sighing trees
and the fat worms waiting on a dawn-bright lawn
and he names the sky his own.

But a caged bird stands on the grave of dreams
his shadow shouts on a nightmare scream
his wings are clipped and his feet are tied
so he opens his throat to sing.

1. **trade winds.** Winds blowing almost constantly in one direction; especially a wind blowing almost continually toward the equator from the northeast or from the southeast

sel • dom (sel′dəm) *adv.*, rarely; infrequently
trill (tril) *n.*, trembling, vibrating sound

The caged bird sings
with a fearful trill
of things unknown
but longed for still
and his tune is heard
on the distant hill
for the caged bird
sings of freedom. ❖

Can people truly appreciate something that they have had all their lives and have never gone without? How might a newly independent person act compared with someone who has always had his or her independence?

REFER TO TEXT ▶▶▶▶	▶ REASON WITH TEXT	
1a. Identify what the two birds in "Sympathy" and "Caged Bird" long for and dream about.	1b. Interpret how the caged bird and the speaker feel in stanza 2 of "Sympathy"; contrast the caged bird's situation and that of the free bird in "Caged Bird."	**Understand** **Find meaning**
2a. List images that the bird notices in stanza 1 of "Sympathy."	2b. Apply what you know about the two authors to explain how the images of freedom and confinement refer to humans.	**Apply** **Use information**
3a. State how the caged birds in the two poems respond to their imprisonment.	3b. Analyze how being caged has affected the birds. What does the phrase "old, old scars" in "Sympathy" suggest about the bird's situation?	**Analyze** **Take things apart**
4a. Aside from the cage, list two other restrictions of the imprisoned bird in "Caged Bird."	4b. Judge which poem—"Sympathy" or "Caged Bird"—does a better job of depicting what it is like not to be free. Support your opinion.	**Evaluate** **Make judgments**
5a. List phrases from the two poems that illustrate the feelings of both the imprisoned birds and the free bird.	5b. Integrate the ideas about freedom from both "Sympathy" and "Caged Bird." What message do the poems have when read together? Does this differ from the meaning of each poem read individually? Explain.	**Create** **Bring ideas together**

COMPARE LITERATURE: Rhetorical Devices

Rhetorical devices used in both poems are figurative language and repetition. Consider how each poem uses figurative language and why the authors may have chosen to use figurative language in that way. Why might repetition be used in these poems? Do you think the caged bird in Angelou's poem represents the same thing that it does in Dunbar's poem? Discuss with a partner or group the use of these rhetorical devices.

CONNECTION

Emily Dickinson (1830–1886) wrote over 1,700 poems, only seven of which were published in her lifetime. Fame was not important to Dickinson. She kept her writing to herself and shared poems only with close family members and friends. Dickinson's poems frequently dealt with things in nature. The poem "'Hope' is the thing with feathers" exemplifies her highly original style, which is in a category all its own. Notice how the poet uses punctuation and grammatical structure in unusual ways and varies her rhythms abruptly in jazz-like ways.

"Hope" is the thing with feathers

A Lyric Poem by **Emily Dickinson**

"Hope" is the thing with feathers—
That perches in the soul—
And sings the tune without the words—
And never stops—at all—

And sweetest—in the Gale—is heard—
And sore must be the storm—
That could abash the little Bird
That kept so many warm—

I've heard it in the chilliest land—
And on the strangest sea—
Yet, never, in Extremity,
It asked a crumb—of Me. ❖

TEXT TO TEXT CONNECTION

How do Dunbar, Angelou, and Dickinson make use of bird imagery? Compare the tones of the poems. Is there hope in the Dunbar and Angelou poems? How might the speaker in Dickinson's poem respond to the other two poems?

EXTEND THE TEXT

Writing Options

Creative Writing Imagine that you meet the person who has caged the bird in "Sympathy" or "Caged Bird." Write a short **dialogue** in which the person explains his or her reasoning, and you counter the reasoning with an argument to convince that person to free the bird. Before writing, jot down ideas about what freedom might mean for a bird.

Descriptive Writing Write a one- to two-page **descriptive letter** to Paul Laurence Dunbar that describes the social changes that have occurred since he wrote his poem. Describe the challenges that face African Americans today. Check resources in your library or online for information about major movements, crises, and legislation that have affected issues of race in the United States. Researching the lives of Angelou and Dunbar may also give you a good indication of which topics to include in your letter.

Collaborative Learning

Write Song Lyrics In small groups, brainstorm with classmates about what freedom means. Develop a varied list of ideas about freedom. Your list could include words, phrases, quotations, names of people, or activities. You might develop examples by using a frame sentence: "One is free when ______." Use the ideas from your list to write song lyrics. Make sure the lyrics include ideas from all the members in your groupage Develop a plan for consensus building and set ground rules for decision-making. Then set your agreed upon lyrics to music using the melody of an existing song, or make up your own melody. As a group, perform your song for the class or make a recording.

Lifelong Learning

Research an Issue Use library sources, newspaper or magazine articles, or the Internet to research both sides of a current or past struggle for human or animal rights. Once you've collected enough information to understand the issue, summarize the struggle in your own words and offer your opinion. Submit your summary, your opinion, and copies of your background materials to your teacher to review and share with the class.

Go to **www.mirrorsandwindows.com** for more.

READING ASSESSMENT

1. In "Sympathy," the caged bird sings
   A. a song of happiness.
   B. a sad melody.
   C. a prayer for freedom.
   D. nothing.
   E. of things unknown but longed for still.

2. In "Caged Bird," the caged bird sings because
   A. it is the only thing left for him to do.
   B. he wants to join voices with the song of the free bird.
   C. his captors force him.
   D. he desires to feel free.
   E. he wishes to send a prayer from his heart's deep core.

3. As it is used on line 13 in "Sympathy," the term *keener* most closely means
   A. lackluster.
   B. numbing.
   C. stronger.
   D. bitter.
   E. powerful.

4. The speaker in both poems
   A. identifies with the caged bird.
   B. identifies with the free bird.
   C. feels contempt for the caged bird.
   D. envies the caged bird.
   E. despises the free bird.

5. According to the poem "Caged Bird," a free bird
   A. sings of freedom.
   B. dares to claim the sky.
   C. stands on the grave of dreams.
   D. sings when the first bud opens.
   E. All of the above

6. Does the caged bird in either poem have any hope for freedom? Write a brief essay in which you explore this question, citing lines from the poem to support your conclusions.

GRAMMAR & STYLE

UNDERSTAND THE CONCEPT | APPLY THE SKILL

Active and Passive Voice

A verb is in the **active voice** when the subject performs the action of the verb. A verb is in the **passive voice** when someone or something else performs the action of the verb, and the subject receives the action.

EXAMPLES

active voice: Paul Laurence Dunbar published *Oak and Ivy* in 1893. [Subject: Paul Laurence Dunbar; Agent (performer) of the action: Paul Laurence Dunbar]

passive voice: *Oak and Ivy* was published by Paul Laurence Dunbar in 1893. [Subject: *Oak and Ivy;* Agent (performer) of the action: Paul Laurence Dunbar]

The active voice is used more frequently than the passive voice. Using the active voice will generally make your writing stronger and clearer. Sometimes, however, the passive voice is appropriate. Use the passive voice when you want the focus to be on the receiver of the action or on the action itself, or when you do not know who performed the action.

EXAMPLES

passive voice: Air is taken into the lungs and then exhaled. [The focus is on "air," not on the person or people doing the action.]

passive voice: A mysterious package was left on the front steps. [The agent of the action is unknown.]

passive voice: Serious mistakes were made. [The agent is unnamed, thus avoiding the placing of blame.]

What Great Writers Do

Great writers alternate between active and passive voice when appropriate. Their use of passive voice still manages to be lively and interesting. Examine this excerpt from Angelou's autobiography *I Know Why the Caged Bird Sings*. Identify which sentences are active and which are passive.

> The sound of the empty cotton sacks dragging over the floor and the murmurs of waking people were sliced by the cash register as we rang up the five-cent sales.
>
> If the morning sounds and smells were touched with the supernatural, the late afternoon had all the features of the normal Arkansas life. In the dying sunlight the people dragged, rather than their empty cotton sacks.

General Store, Moundville, Alabama, 1936.
Walker Evans. Library of Congress.

REVIEW TERMS

- **subject:** the focus of the sentence
- **verb:** the action
- **agent:** the doer or performer of the action, usually the subject in active voice sentences
- **active voice:** when the subject performs the action of the verb
- **passive voice:** when someone or something else performs the action of the verb, and the subject receives the action

UNDERSTAND THE CONCEPT

APPLY THE SKILL

Identify Active and Passive Voice

Read each of the following sentences. Note which sentences are in the active voice, and which sentences are in the passive voice. Then discuss whether the active or passive voice is more appropriate in a given sentence.

1. Dunbar is considered by many critics to be the first professional African-American poet.
2. Dunbar's fiction and verse were read mainly by a white audience.
3. Six poems had been written by Dunbar by the time he was six years old.
4. Angelou was raised by her grandmother in rural Arkansas.
5. Angelou's lecture was heard by a large audience.
6. Angelou's autobiography was published in 1970.
7. Emily Dickinson had written over 1,700 poems.
8. Dickinson's poems contain images of nature.
9. The style of Emily Dickinson is regarded as very unique.
10. She would show her poetry to friends and family.

Improve Passive Sentences

Determine whether the following sentences use an active or passive voice. Rewrite any passive sentences using an active voice.

1. The caged bird was found beating his wings against the bars.
2. The winds were stirring through the grass.
3. Throughout the house, the caged bird was heard singing.
4. The caged bird would not be allowed out of his cage.
5. Through his singing, his prayers were sent to heaven.
6. A free bird would dare to claim the sky.
7. The free bird was seen on the back of the wind.
8. The fat worms are picked by the free bird.
9. The caged bird would sing with a fearful trill.
10. The caged bird will stand on the grave of dreams.

Use Passive and Active Verbs in Your Writing

Write a description to be shared with classmates about a place where you liked to spend time as a child. Use sensory details (details about how things look, smell, sound, taste, and feel) to paint a picture for the readers. You can either describe a specific occasion in that location or describe actions that normally took place. Use at least three passive verbs and three active verbs in your description of this childhood place. When finished, exchange papers with a classmate and examine how the active and passive voices are used. Make suggestions for change if the sentences would sound better in the other voice and explain why.

EXTEND THE SKILL

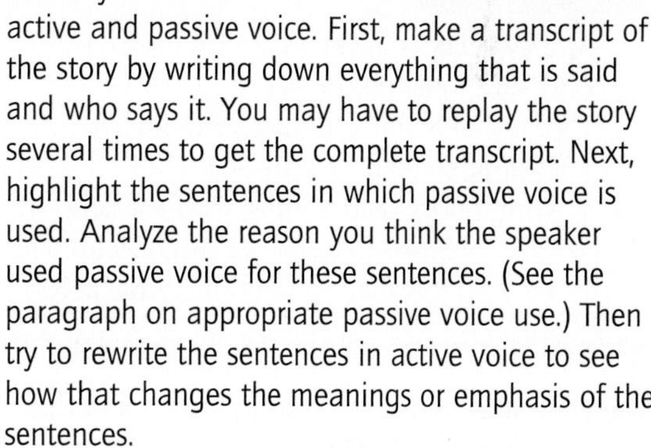

Record a segment of a news broadcast, either on television or radio. Select one story of interest to you to analyze for the use of active and passive voice. First, make a transcript of the story by writing down everything that is said and who says it. You may have to replay the story several times to get the complete transcript. Next, highlight the sentences in which passive voice is used. Analyze the reason you think the speaker used passive voice for these sentences. (See the paragraph on appropriate passive voice use.) Then try to rewrite the sentences in active voice to see how that changes the meanings or emphasis of the sentences.

To compare the use of active and passive voice in different types of media, record or read and then analyze segments of these items: newspaper article, comedy television show, history textbook, novel excerpt, magazine article.

Understanding Structure and Form

STRUCTURE AND FORM

We make meaning of a poem through identifying its organization of lines and stanzas, through studying its meter and rhyme, and in a larger sense, through analyzing its content and purpose. In other words, we look at the overall structure and form of the poem to see what that can tell us about the author's intention in creating the text.

Structures of Poetry

Whereas stories and essays are divided into paragraphs, poems can be divided into **stanzas,** or groups of lines. The type of stanza is determined by the number of lines. Two lines are a **couplet,** three a **tercet** or **triplet,** four a **quatrain,** five a **quintet** or **quintain,** six a **sestet,** seven a **septet,** and eight an **octave.** It is sometimes possible to determine the type of poem by the stanza type, if the poem is not in free verse.

"Hope" is the thing with feathers—
That perches in the soul—
And sings the tune without the words—
And never stops—at all—

And sweetest—in the Gale—is heard—
And sore must be the storm—
That could abash the little Bird
That kept so many warm—
—from "'Hope' is the thing with feathers" by
Emily Dickinson
(page 408)

The briefest of formal structures presented in this unit is the haiku. A **haiku** is a traditional Japanese poem consisting of three lines. The first and third lines contain five syllables each, and the second line contains seven. A haiku usually presents one image or picture. Matsuo Bashō's haiku (page 435) represents the traditional Japanese form. The haiku by Virgilio (page 435) and Pizzarelli (page 435) show modern versions of the haiku form.

Poems that consist of four- to six-line, rhyming stanzas (usually *abcb*) that tell a story are called **ballads.** Ballads are quite popular in folk literature and are very often sung. "Ballad of Birmingham" by Dudley Randall (page 375) is a ballad that does not so much tell a story as it portrays a detail of a historical event. W. B. Yeats used the ballad form to relate Irish folklore.

And when white moths were on the wing, *a*
And moth-like stars were flickering out, *b*
I dropped the berry in a stream *c*
And caught a little silver trout. *b*
—from "The Song of Wandering Aengus"
by W. B. Yeats
(page 415)

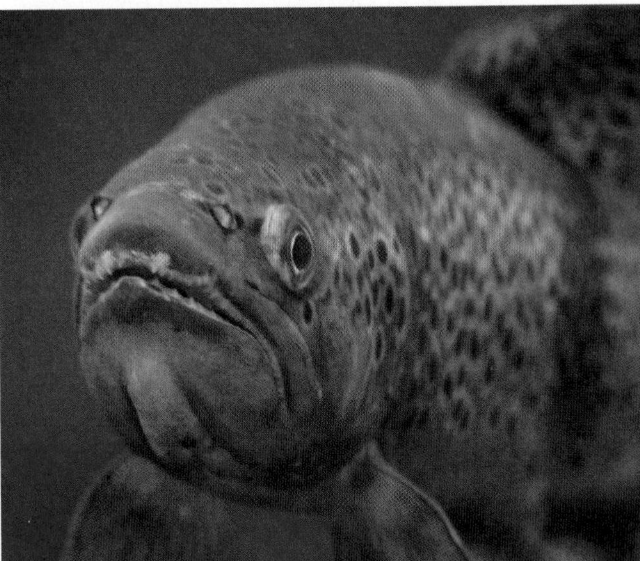

A **sonnet** is a fourteen-line poem, usually in iambic pentameter (five sets of an unstressed-stressed syllable pattern per line). There are two main types of sonnets: *Shakespearean* (or *Elizabethan* or *English*) and *Petrarchan* (or *Italian*). The Shakespearean sonnet is divided into four parts: three quatrains and a final couplet. The rhyme scheme is usually *abab cdcd efef gg*. The Petrarchan sonnet is divided into two parts: an octave and a sestet with a rhyme scheme of *abbaabba cdecde* (or *cdedce* or *cdcdcd*). C. S. Lewis's "Sonnet" (page 427) is a combination of the Shakespearean and Petrarchan sonnets with a rhyme scheme of *abbaabba cdcd ee*.

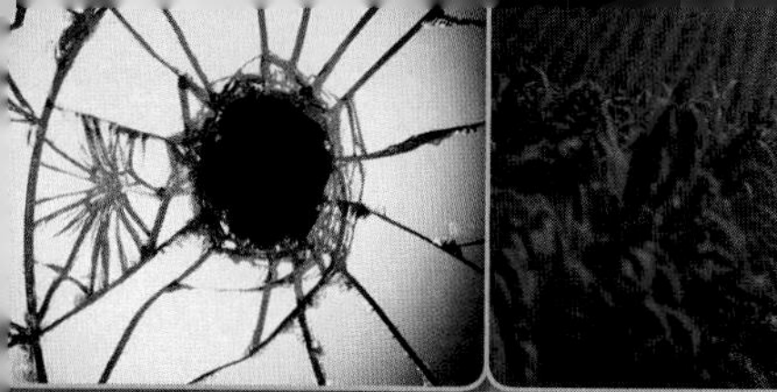

FORMS OF POETRY

The form of a poem must suit its content. If a poet wants to tell a story, for instance, the chosen form would probably be a **narrative poem.** A special type of narrative poem is the **dramatic poem,** which relies on elements of drama, such as monologue or dialogue, to tell the story. (See the Introduction to Drama on page 486 for more about monologues and dialogues.) "The Song of Wandering Aengus" and "Patterns" (page 467) are narrative poems.

> Underneath the fallen blossom
> In my bosom,
> Is a letter I have hid.
>
> It was brought to me this morning by a
> rider from the Duke.
> "Madam, we regret to inform you that Lord
> Hartwell
> Died in action Thursday se'nnight."
> As I read it in the white, morning sunlight,
> The letters squirmed like snakes.
> "Any answer, Madam," said my footman.
> "No," I told him.
> "See that the messenger takes some
> refreshment.
> No, no answer."
>
> —from "Patterns" by Amy Lowell

A **lyric poem,** on the other hand, expresses the emotions of a speaker and tends to be musical in style. "The Bells" (page 393) and "Sympathy" (page 405) are lyric poems. A common type of lyric poetry is called **free verse.** As you can tell by its name, free verse is poetry that is free from regular rhyme, meter, or stanza division.

> It is not a carol of joy or glee,
> But a prayer that he sends from his heart's
> deep core,
> But a plea, that upward to Heaven he
> flings—
> I know why the caged bird sings!
>
> —from "Sympathy"
> by Paul Laurence Dunbar

Two other forms are based on the purpose of the poem. An **ode** is a poem to honor or praise someone or something. An **elegy** can usually be recognized by its formal tone that laments the death of someone. A **prose poem** is a passage of prose that makes such extensive use of poetic language that the line between prose and poetry is blurred. Margaret Atwood's piece "Bread" (page 431) is an example of a prose poem.

> Imagine a famine. Now imagine a piece of bread. Both of these things are real but you happen to be in the same room with only one of them. Put yourself into a different room, that's what the mind is for. You are now lying on a thin mattress in a hot room. The walls are made of dried earth and your sister, who is younger than you are, is in the room with you. She is starving, her belly is bloated, flies land on her eyes; you brush them off with your hand. You have a cloth too, filthy but damp, and you press it to her lips and forehead.
>
> —from "Bread" by Margaret Atwood

RECOGNIZING STRUCTURE AND FORM

You can determine the structure and form of a poem (if it is not free verse) by looking for these elements:

- **Text organization** Is the poem divided into stanzas? How many lines are in the poem or in each stanza?
- **Rhyme scheme** Does the poem rhyme? Is there a pattern of a recurring rhyme?
- **Content** Is the poem telling a story, expressing an emotion, or presenting an image?
- **Style** Is the poem more musical or narrative in style? What tone does it take?

The Song of Wandering Aengus

BEFORE READING

A Narrative Poem by W. B. Yeats

DIRECTED READING

BUILD BACKGROUND

Literary Context "The Song of Wandering Aengus" was published in *The Wind Among the Reeds* (1899). In this poem, as in many others, Yeats drew inspiration from the myths of the ancient Celts of Ireland. Aengus was the Celtic god of love, who spent much of his life wandering. Aengus fell in love with a fairy woman and spent his life fruitlessly trying to find her again. Yeats's poem, which explores the subject of creativity, was written when the artist was still young, but it looks ahead to old age.

Reader's Context Did someone ever disappear from your life whom you would like to see again? Describe that person and what interested you about him or her.

ANALYZE LITERATURE: Ballad

A **ballad** is a simple narrative poem in four-line stanzas, usually meant to be sung. *Folk ballads,* which have been popular since the Middle Ages, are composed orally and passed by word of mouth. Written *literary ballads,* in imitation of folk ballads, have also been popular. "The Song of Wandering Aengus" is a literary ballad. It is also a narrative poem, or a poem that tells a story.

SET PURPOSE

As you read, pay attention to the structure of the ballad. Summarize the story of Aengus as told in the poem. Try to relate elements of the story to the concept of creativity.

MEET THE AUTHOR

William Butler (W. B.) Yeats (1865–1939) received the Nobel Prize for Literature in 1923. Recognized as one of the greatest poets of the twentieth century, Yeats (pronounced yāts) was also a major playwright and an important Irish cultural leader. Born in Dublin, he grew up in London and County Sligo, Ireland, studying art before leaving school to pursue writing. As a young man, he became involved with the Irish nationalist movement for independence from Great Britain. Yeats believed that his poems and plays could help to foster national pride and unity in his troubled homeland. His poetry is rich with images, many of which come from Irish folklore. Yeat's fascinating body of work reflects not only his passion and joy in life but a lifelong quest for wisdom.

USE READING SKILLS

Take Notes Taking notes as you read can help you remember what you've read. Organize the information in a way that will be easily accessible to you later. For narrative poems, making an Imagery Chart like the one below will help you literally see the poem. Fill in the chart by making quick sketches or writing brief descriptions of your visualizations (images created in your mind) as you read. Under each sketch or description, note the line or lines that you are describing.

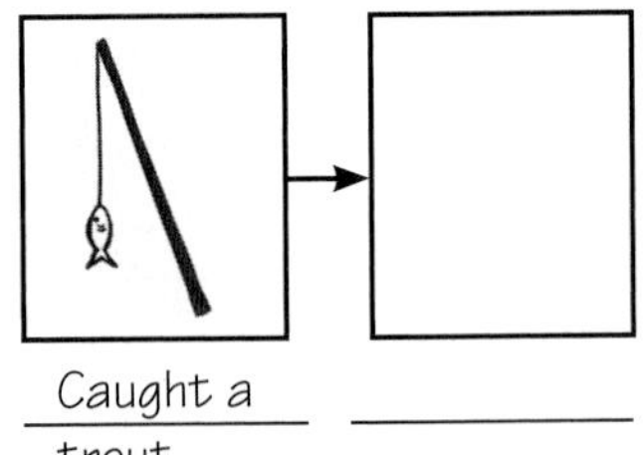

PREVIEW VOCABULARY

Analyze the meaning of the words below from the textual context of the poem. Then look up each word in the dictionary and distinguish between the denotative (dictionary) and connotative (emotional) meaning of the words.

fire
blow
old
hollow
dappled
pluck

The Song of Wandering Aengus

A Narrative Poem by **W. B. Yeats**

I went out to the hazel wood,[1]
Because a fire was in my head,
And cut and peeled a hazel wand,
And hooked a berry to a thread;
And when white moths were on the wing,
And moth-like stars were flickering out,
I dropped the berry in a stream
And caught a little silver trout.

When I had laid it on the floor
I went to blow the fire aflame,
But something rustled on the floor,
And some one called me by my name:
It had become a glimmering girl
With apple blossom in her hair
Who called me by my name and ran
And faded through the brightening air.

Though I am old with wandering
Through hollow lands and hilly lands,
I will find out where she has gone,
And kiss her lips and take her hands;
And walk among long <u>dappled</u> grass,
And pluck till time and times are done
The silver apples of the moon,
The golden apples of the sun. ❖

Plaque, c. 100. Celtic artist. National Museum of Wales.

1. **hazel wood.** Woods made up of hazel trees, from the birch family

dap • pled (da´pəld) *adj.,* spotted

MIRRORS & WINDOWS

How might devotion and obsession be similar? Is searching for what you've lost important? When might it be foolish?

Primary Source CONNECTION

Knowledge of Celtic mythology is limited. What is known comes from folk traditions and tales passed down through generations, as well as from archaeological finds, and a few ancient texts. Celtic mythology contains many gods and goddesses. The most powerful was Dagda, a Celtic father figure, similar to Zeus and Jupiter of Greek and Roman mythology. One of Dagda's children was Aengus, to whom the poem "The Song of Wandering Aengus" refers.

Aengus

A Celtic Myth Retold by **Deedra Jackson**

Also known as "Angus the young," he was considered the Irish god of love. He was a young handsome god that had four birds flying about his head—some say they symbolize kisses—who inspired love in all who heard them. He was the son of Dagda and Boann ("the wife of Elcmar").

Once, Aengus was troubled by the dream of a young maiden. He instantly fell in love with her and became love sick. He told his mother Boann and she searched the whole of Ireland for the maiden, but after a year she still had not found the maiden. Then Dagda was called and he searched Ireland for a year, and still did not find the maiden. Finally Bov the Red, king of the Dananns in Munster and Dagda's aide, was called to search and after a year he found the maiden.

Aengus was taken to the lake of the Dragon's Mouth, and there he saw 150 maidens all chained with gold into pairs. He spied her at once and her name was Caer, the daughter of Ethal and Anubal, a prince of the Dananns of Connact. On November 1 she and all the other maidens are transformed into swans for a year. He was told if he could identify her as a swan he could marry her. On November 1 Aengus went out to the lake and called to his love, and once he had found her he then turned into a swan himself and joined her. They flew off together singing such a beautiful song that all who heard them fell asleep for three days and nights.

Aengus had a son called, "Diarmuid Ua Duibhne" or Diarmuid of the Love Spot. One night while hunting Diarmuid met a maiden who made a magic love spot appear on his head, and from then on no woman ever looked upon him with out falling in love with him.

His palace was Brugh na Boinne on the River Boyne (modern New Grange). ❖

TEXT TO TEXT CONNECTION

Compare and contrast the experiences of the speaker in "The Song of Wandering Aengus" and the myth of Aengus, the Irish god of love. Who or what is being sought in each selection? What images appear in the two selections? How are these images related to one another?

AFTER READING

REFER TO TEXT	REASON WITH TEXT	
1a. Quote the reason that the speaker in "The Song of Wandering Aengus" went out to the hazel wood.	1b. Interpret what that reason might represent. Explain.	Understand **Find meaning**
2a. Recall what the girl does in stanza 2 of "The Song of Wandering Aengus."	2b. What might the girl represent? Predict what would happen if the speaker actually found the "glimmering girl." What effect would it have on the speaker? Explain.	Apply **Use information**
3a. Identify the verb tenses used in each stanza of "The Song of Wandering Aengus."	3b. Diagram how time passes from the beginning of the poem to the end. Recognize the significance time has in the poem.	Analyze **Take things apart**
4a. Indicate what the speaker of the poem will do "till time and times are done."	4b. Describe how the speaker has changed by the end of this poem. What might the last stanza be saying about imagination or creativity?	Evaluate **Make judgments**
5a. List activities the speaker does in each stanza of the poem.	5b. How are youth, adulthood, and old age portrayed in popular culture? Construct a list that describes these life stages. Compare these descriptions with those in the poem. Discuss your findings.	Create **Bring ideas together**

ANALYZE LITERATURE: Ballad

What elements of a literary ballad are present in "The Song of Wandering Aengus"? How many lines are in each stanza? What story does this ballad tell? Which elements of the poem do you think could be representative of a folk tale?

EXTEND THE TEXT

Writing Options

Creative Writing Imagine that you are the old Aengus. Write an **advice column** for adolescents about how to make the most out of life, regardless of age or physical limitations. What kind of advice do you think Aengus would give? Has he learned lessons the hard way, or has he been wise all along? Would he make different choices if given the opportunity? Before you write, discuss these ideas with a partner to determine the nature of the advice to be given.

Expository Writing Imagine you have been invited to present an essay on allegory to the editors of your literary magazine. An allegory is a work in which each element represents, or symbolizes, something else. Research this term on the Internet or in reference books at the library. Then write a short **literary research essay** explaining how "The Song of Wandering Aengus" could be described as an allegory.

Collaborative Learning

Perform a Role-Play Imagine that the old man Aengus meets the glimmering girl again. With a partner, play the roles of Aengus and the girl. Ask each other questions that are based on underlying ideas in the poem. For example, Aengus might ask, "Why did you call out my name?" The girl might ask, "Why was I turned into a girl?"

Media Literacy

Listen to Yeats Set to Music Many singers have set Yeats's poems to music. Locate recordings of such songs at the library or on the Internet. If the words are not included with the audio source, look them up in a collection of Yeats's poems. Listen to several songs on their own. Then listen again as you read the words. Share your reactions to the songs with the class. Did the musicians adapt Yeats's poems to music to help express the values of a particular culture? Discuss whether the performers adapted Yeats's words and why they might have done so.

Go to **www.mirrorsandwindows.com** for more.

UNDERSTAND THE CONCEPT | APPLY THE SKILL

Literal and Figurative Meanings

Many words and expressions have both literal and figurative meanings. A **literal meaning** is the concrete or common meaning of a word. A **figurative meaning** suggests a meaning that goes beyond the literal or concrete meaning of a word. A **figure of speech** is meant to be understood imaginatively instead of literally. Many writers, especially poets, use figures of speech to create vivid, memorable images and to help readers see and understand things in new ways.

EXAMPLES

literal meaning: A graceful hawk soared across the sky.
figurative meaning: The image of the graceful hawk soared in her heart.

In the first example, the hawk is literally soaring, or flying high. In the second example, the image of the hawk makes her feel elated; it is not literally flying in her heart.

Metaphors, similes, idioms, and personification are examples of figures of speech. **Metaphors** and **similes** compare one thing with another. Similes do so by using the word *like* or *as;* metaphors do not. **Idioms** are commonly acknowledged metaphors used by speakers of a language. Idioms differ from slang in that they survive over the years; slang terms go in and out of use. **Personification** is a figure of speech in which something not human—an animal, object, place, or idea—is given human qualities and characteristics.

EXAMPLES

metaphor: Your smile melts my heart.
simile: My love is like a red, red rose.
idiom: He fell head over heels in love with her.
personification: Misery, an unwelcome guest, walked through our front door.

What Great Writers Do

Using a mix of literal and figurative meanings or language can add vibrancy and interest to the writing. Notice how W. B. Yeats uses both literal and figurative language in these excerpts from "The Song of Wandering Aengus" (page 415).

I went out to the hazel wood,
Because a fire was in my head,
And cut and peeled a hazel wand,
And hooked a berry to a thread…

Though I am old with wandering …
I will find out where she has gone, …
And pluck till time and times are done
The silver apples of the moon,
The golden apples of the sun.

REVIEW TERMS

- **literal meaning:** concrete or common meaning
- **figurative meaning:** a meaning beyond the obvious or literal
- **figure of speech:** a term or phrase meant to be understood imaginatively, not literally
- **metaphor:** a comparison between two dissimilar items
- **simile:** a comparison between two dissimilar items using *like* or *as*
- **idiom:** an expression specific to a particular language that cannot be understood literally
- **personification:** the description of a nonhuman object as if it were human

UNDERSTAND THE CONCEPT

APPLY THE SKILL

Exercise A

Analyze each of the following pairs of sentences to decide if the underlined word is used literally or figuratively. Discuss what is really meant in the sentence that uses the word figuratively. Write an alternative, literal version of the figurative language sentence while still retaining the original meaning.

1. The field was a carpet of flowers.
   The carpet was dappled with sunlight.
2. It is often said that the pen is mightier than the sword.
   At the yard sale, Li bought an old pen and a rusty sword.
3. Petra walked through the field.
   She was lost in a field of dreams.
4. Letitia purchased a green wool coat.
   Her friend was green with envy when she saw the coat.
5. All hands on deck!
   Please wash your hands.
6. Bruno fell for the trick.
   My neighbor slipped and fell on the icy pavement.
7. The snails created holes in the leaves of the garden plants.
   Time ticked by at a snail's pace in the doctor's waiting room.
8. The autumn leaves were caught up in a little whirlwind that scattered them.
   The jet-setting couple set off for a whirlwind vacation around the world.
9. Amanda's blue eyes were rimmed with red after she cried.
   Amanda was feeling blue after her best friend moved away.
10. The coach's speech got the team fired up for the second half.
    The engineer fired up the engine on the steam train.

Exercise B

Make a list of three words that could be used literally or figuratively. Create a pair of sentences—one that uses the word literally and one that uses the word figuratively. (See Exercise A.) Then try to incorporate those same words into a paragraph in which you describe a humorous or mystical encounter (as in "The Song of Wandering Aengus") with a common household object, such as a bar of soap, a toaster, or a dishwasher. Exchange paragraphs with a classmate and try to identify which uses of those words are figurative and which are literal.

SPELLING PRACTICE

Homophones

Homophones are words that sound alike but are spelled differently and have different meanings. Homophones can pose a problem for spelling because, if you use the wrong spelling, a spell-checker program on your computer will not flag the word as being misspelled. Be sure you know the proper use of the homophones listed below from "The Song of Wandering Aengus."

air—heir	find—fined	to—too, two
are–our	hair—hare	walk—wok
berry—bury	one—won	where—ware, wear
by—buy	some—sum	wood—would
caught—cot	through—threw	
done—dun	time—thyme	

BUILD BACKGROUND

Literary Context As a poet, May Swenson is known for her love of complex wordplay. Her poems often take the form of riddles or assume a shape on the printed page that resembles the poem's subject. **"The Universe"** poses a number of intertwining questions about the universe and our role within it.

Reader's Context When you think about the universe, what goes through your mind? Do you feel any particular emotion? What do you think the universe contains?

ANALYZE LITERATURE: Concrete Poem

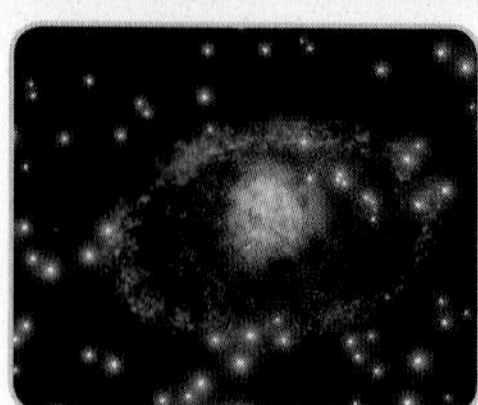

A **concrete poem,** or *shape poem,* is one printed or written in a shape that suggests its subject matter. "The Universe" is a concrete poem, but the shape is not obvious. Many poems are written in complete sentences, though sentences may extend beyond the end of a line. In poems with sentences, end punctuation marks, such as periods and question marks, help organize the text.

SET PURPOSE

As you read, think about what the poet may be trying to suggest by arranging the words on the page the way she has. Consider the reason for the author's choice in punctuation marks and what effect it has on your reading.

MEET THE AUTHOR

May Swenson (1913–1989) received numerous honors and awards for her poetry during her lifetime. The daughter of Swedish immigrants, she was born in Utah but spent her adult life in the state of New York. Before she began writing full time in 1966, she worked as a reporter and an editor. Swenson once explained that her purpose in writing poetry was "to get through the curtains of things as they appear, to things as they are, and then into the larger, wilder space of things as they are becoming." Swenson published ten volumes of poetry during her life, including *Another Animal* (1954), *In Other Words* (1987), and *Poems to Solve* (1966), a book of poems for children. She received numerous grants and fellowships during her lifetime and served as chancellor of the Academy of American Poets from 1980 until her death in 1989.

USE READING SKILLS

Text Organization When writers intentionally reuse a sound, word, phrase, or sentence it is called **repetition.** Many words are repeated in this poem, and some of those words are more important than others. As you read, make a list of the phrases in the poem that contain repetition and underline the repeated words.

PREVIEW VOCABULARY

The word "universe" contains the common prefix "uni–" which means "one." Knowing common prefixes can assist you in determining the meanings of unknown words. Brainstorm other words that use this same prefix and use each one in a sentence. Then brainstorm words with other common prefixes from the following list and create a new group of words and sentences.

Prefix	Meaning
anti–	against
hyper–	above
inter–	among
mis–	wrongly
pre–	before
trans–	across
ultra–	extreme

THE UNIVERSE

A Concrete Poem by **May Swenson**

What
is it about,
the universe,
the universe about us stretching out?
We, within our brains,
within it,
think
we must unspin
the laws that spin it.
We think *why*
because we think
because.
Because we think,
we think
the universe about us.

But does it think,
the universe?
Then what about?
About us?
If not,
must there be cause
in the universe?
Must it have laws?

And what
if the universe
is not about us?
Then what?
What
is it about?
And what
about *us*? ❖

Where do humans fit in the universe? Is it more natural for people to think that humans are significant within the universe or insignificant? Why might thinking about your place in the universe be uncomfortable?

AFTER READING

REFER TO TEXT	REASON WITH TEXT	
1a. Indicate where "we" are located.	1b. Restate in your own words the speaker's explanation of how we create the world around us.	**Understand** **Find meaning**
2a. Recall why we think "why."	2b. Produce a list of things you think about and questions you ask when you are "just thinking."	**Apply** **Use information**
3a. Quote questions the speaker asks in lines 24–31.	3b. Analyze exactly what the speaker is asking in lines 24–31. Consider whether the emphasis on the word *us* affects your understanding.	**Analyze** **Take things apart**
4a. List questions the speaker poses in lines 16–19.	4b. Consider why the poet chose to put so many questions in her poem. Assess whether the use of multiple questions is effective.	**Evaluate** **Make judgments**
5a. State what "we, within our brains" think we must do.	5b. Create a time line and document how people have done this throughout time.	**Create** **Bring ideas together**

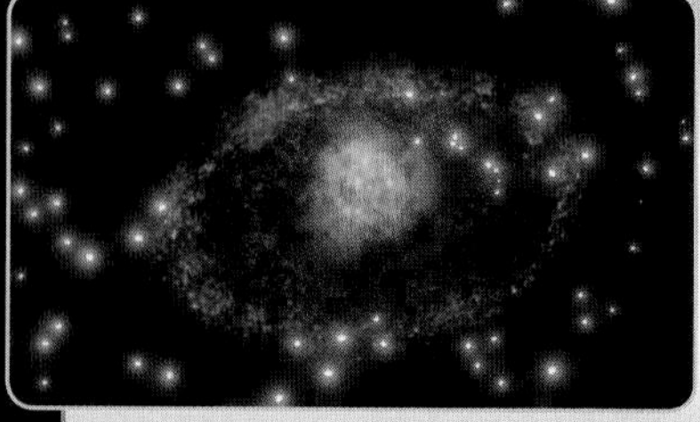

ANALYZE LITERATURE: Concrete Poem

Think about photographs you have seen of the Milky Way, the galaxy or star system in which the planet Earth is located. How would you describe its shape? Do you think the arrangement of the words in "The Universe" suggests this shape, or another shape?

EXTEND THE TEXT

Writing Options

Creative Writing Imagine someone you know has a birthday or special occasion approaching. Write a **greeting card** for a friend or relative in which the shape of your printed message resembles the subject of the card. You may want to brainstorm some subjects and their possible shapes before you begin. You can perform an Internet search for the words "shape poem" to get other examples of such poems.

Descriptive Writing Write a two- to three-paragraph **summary** of "The Universe" for someone who hasn't read the poem. Comment on the topic, form, theme, and appearance of the poem. You may organize your comments into a graphic organizer similar to the one below. Think about who might be interested in this kind of poem, such as someone interested in astronomy, philosophy, or art. Other than a language arts class, where else could this poem have relevance? Consider presenting your summary to one of the people or groups of people you've identified.

Topic	Form	Theme	Appearance
Humans and the universe			

Critical Literacy

Discuss the Poem's Questions Review the poem and identify the main questions the speaker asks about the universe in the poem. Write these down in your notebook. Below each question, jot down your thoughts on each one. Then meet with a small group and discuss each question.

Media Literacy

Analyze a Media Product The Internet opens up a universe of news, information, and entertainment to us each day. Usually, we get to the Internet through a gateway managed by an Internet service provider, or ISPAGE The ISP's welcome screen is packed with information and links to websites. Topics can range from serious news and weather to celebrity gossip and shopping tips. Evaluate the welcome screen at one of these gateways. Analyze how messages are conveyed through visual or sound techniques. What audience do the images, sound effects, or background music appeal to? What does this media product say about us and the culture we live in? Discuss your findings as a class.

Go to **www.mirrorsandwindows.com** for more.

READING ASSESSMENT

1. The speaker wonders if the universe is about us because
   A. its laws are all about us.
   B. it is not as large as we believe.
   C. we think.
   D. All of the above
   E. None of the above

2. Each of the following sentences from the poem includes repeated words. In which sentence below could the repeated word be simply crossed out without losing any meaning?
   A. We think *why* because we think *because.*
   B. What is it about, the universe, the universe about us stretching out?
   C. We, within our brains, within it, think we must unspin the laws that spin it.
   D. Because we think, we think the universe about us.
   E. None of the above

3. In lines 14–15, the phrase "we think the universe about us" most likely means
   A. We think we are the purpose of the universe.
   B. We are surrounded by the universe.
   C. We have the power to shape the universe.
   D. We create the universe by our thoughts.
   E. Our understanding of the universe equals the limits of our thoughts.

4. The speaker in this poem believes that
   A. the universe revolves around humans.
   B. humans wrote the laws of the universe.
   C. understanding the laws of the universe is the most important thing in life.
   D. we are insignificant compared to the universe.
   E. None of the above

5. Analyze the speaker's viewpoint on the relationship between the universe and humanity. Does the speaker seem to view humans as central to the universe, or as inconsequential? Explain your response.

VOCABULARY & SPELLING

UNDERSTAND THE CONCEPT

APPLY THE SKILL

Use Spelling Rules Correctly

Always check your writing for spelling errors, and try to recognize the words that give you more trouble than others. Use a dictionary when you find you have misspelled a word. Keep a list in a notebook of words that are difficult for you to spell. Write the words several times until you have memorized the correct spelling. Break down the word into syllables and carefully pronounce each individual syllable.

Prefixes and Suffixes

Prefixes and suffixes (also called affixes) are groups of letters added to the beginnings or ends of words. Most prefixes and suffixes come from Greek and Latin, although some come from Old English and other languages. Adding prefixes and suffixes to words often causes spelling errors. A **prefix** is a letter or a group of letters added to the beginning of a word to change its meaning.

When adding a prefix, do not change the spelling of the word itself.

EXAMPLES

anti– + slavery = antislavery
bene– + factor = benefactor
dis– + similar = dissimilar
ir– + relevant = irrelevant
mal– + practice = malpractice
pro– + gress = progress
sym– + pathy = sympathy

A **suffix** is a letter or a group of letters added to the end of a word to change its meaning. Remember these rules about suffixes:

- The spelling of most words is not changed when the suffix *–ness* or *–ly* is added.
- If you are adding a suffix to a word that ends with *y*, and that *y* follows a vowel, you should usually leave the *y* in place.
- If you are adding a suffix to a word that ends with *y*, and that *y* follows a consonant, you should usually change the *y* to *i*.
- If you are adding a suffix that begins with a vowel to a word that ends with a silent *e*, you should usually drop the *e*.
- If you are adding a suffix that begins with a consonant to a word that ends with a silent *e*, you should usually leave the *e* in place.
- If you are adding a suffix beginning with a vowel to a word that ends with a consonant, you should double the final consonant (such as *–ed*, *–en*, *–ance*, and so on).

EXAMPLES

even + *–ness* = evenness
employ + *–ment* = employment
silly + *–est* = silliest
shave + *–ing* = shaving
tire + –less = tireless
pity + *–ful* = pitiful
happy + *–ness* = happiness
fan + *–ed* = fanned

The ie/ei Spelling Pattern

Knowing spelling patterns can also assist you in spelling correctly. A common spelling pattern is the ie/ei rule. Words spelled with the letters *i* and *e* that have a long *e* sound are usually spelled *ie* except after the letter *c*.

EXAMPLES

belief
piece
field
conceive
receive
deceit

Note that words that contain *i* and *e* but have a long *a* sound (as in the word *eight*) are spelled *ei*.

EXAMPLES

weight
neigh
feign
vein

UNDERSTAND THE CONCEPT

APPLY THE SKILL

Exercise A

Identify Incorrect Spelling with Prefixes and Suffixes Read the following words containing prefixes and suffixes and correct any misspelled words. Mark any correctly spelled words *correct*.

1. irreplacable
2. supplied
3. missunderstood
4. buryed
5. imppatient
6. emploied
7. antisocial
8. quiter
9. ploting
10. acheivment

Exercise B

Recognize ie/ei Spelling Errors Remembering the rule "*i* before *e* except after *c* and when the sound is long *a*," identify and correct the misspelled words in the following sentences. Remember that there are exceptions to the rule. If the sentence contains no errors, write the word *correct*.

1. May Swenson recieved numerous awards for her poetry.
2. Her poem "The Universe" questions the way humans percieve the universe.
3. I was releived to be finished with my essay on "The Universe."
4. We argued for quite a while about the meaning of the universe, but he finally yeilded the point to me.
5. The two freinds read the poem in unison.
6. They didn't agree on what they believe about the universe.
7. My nieghbor thinks the universe should act in accordance to his sleep and work schedules.
8. My parents wieghed in on the issue.
9. The clerk in the store forgot to give me a receipt.
10. Don't be decieved by poems with simple language; they can still be complex.

Exercise C

Correct Spelling Errors Identify the words that are spelled incorrectly from the following list and spell them correctly. Mark any correctly spelled words *correct*.

1. stickyness
2. cried
3. unecessary
4. valueable
5. cheerily
6. definitly
7. dutifully
8. mispelled
9. judgment
10. dissatisfied
11. changable
12. existence
13. influencial
14. outragous
15. resistance

Exercise D

Use Correct Spelling in Your Own Writing

Write a poem or an essay that explores your questions about the universe. Use some of the following commonly misspelled words in your poem or essay. By memorizing these and other commonly misspelled words, you can avoid many errors in your writing. Use a dictionary to look up the meanings you do not know.

abundant
accommodate
acquaintance
apparent
beautiful
beginning
camouflage
cemetery
changeable
conscious
definitely
desirable
discipline
eighth
embarrass
environment
fascinating
fulfill
independent
irresistible
leisure
maneuver
mischievous
necessity
noticeable
occurrence
privilege
recommend
separate
susceptible
weird

EXTEND THE SKILL

Define Words with Prefixes and Suffixes

The following technical words contain prefixes or suffixes from Latin, Greek, or other languages. Determine the origin and meaning of each prefix and suffix and the meaning of each word.

bioscience
chloroform
streptococcus
dermatology
telescope
ambidextrous

Sonnet

A Sonnet by C. S. Lewis

American Sonnet

A Sonnet by Billy Collins

BEFORE READING

BUILD BACKGROUND

Literary Context "Sonnet" was printed in C. S. Lewis's first published book, *Spirits in Bondage,* a poetry collection that was published in 1919 under the pseudonym Clive Hamilton. In this poem, the speaker talks about leaving his garden for his bed, where he finds comfort, silence, and peace.

According to Billy Collins, **"American Sonnet"** is "...a rejection of the Italian and English sonnet models in favor of the American postcard...." The poem was first published in *Sailing Alone Around the Room* (2001).

Reader's Context What do you like to think about before you sleep?

COMPARE LITERATURE: Sonnet

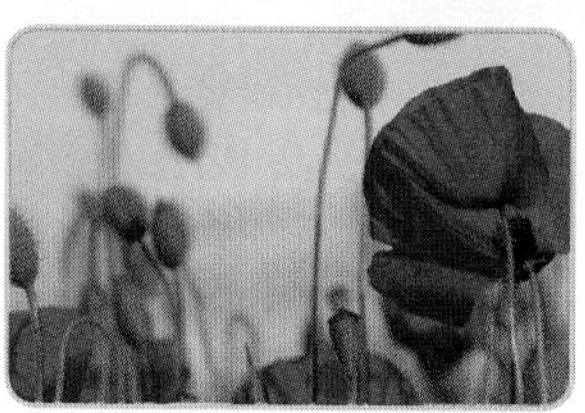

A **sonnet** is a fourteen-line poem that follows one of a number of different rhyme schemes. Sonnets are typically written in iambic pentameter. **Iambic pentameter** means that the lines are formed using five iambs. An *iamb* is an unstressed syllable followed by a stressed syllable, as in the word "insist." C. S. Lewis's sonnet is an *Italian* or a *Petrarchan* sonnet. This type of sonnet is divided into two parts: an *octave* and a *sestet*. The rhyme scheme of the octave is *abbaabba*. The rhyme scheme of the sestet varies; it may be *cdecde, cdcdcd, cdedce, cdcdee,* or a similar variation. As you read, pay attention to the images Lewis uses in the octave and those he uses in the sestet. Also consider how Collins addresses this scheme in "American Sonnet."

USE READING SKILLS

Monitor Your Progress All readers occasionally have difficulty as they read. It may be that the vocabulary is too difficult; the selection is confusing or dry in tone; or the reader is distracted by an outside source, losing focus.

As you read the following two poems, monitor your progress and use appropriate reading skills to help your understanding.

- You may need to find a dictionary or read at a slower pace.
- If you are having trouble keeping your focus, try reading aloud to yourself.
- Go to a place where you won't be disturbed and read aloud, putting emphasis and expression in your voice.
- Reading aloud also helps you decipher difficult text by talking your way through it.

MEET THE AUTHORS

LEWIS

C. S. Lewis (1898–1963) grew up in Belfast, Ireland. His mother died when he was nine years old, and Lewis said, "With my mother's death all settled happiness disappeared from my life." After her death, Lewis's father became withdrawn with grief and sent Lewis and his brother to boarding school. Lewis wrote his first novel at the age of twelve and, over the course of his life, published many works of poetry, fiction for children and adults, and essays. He is perhaps best known for his series of children's fantasy books, *The Chronicles of Narnia*.

Billy Collins (b. 1941), one of the most highly regarded poets today, graduated from the College of the Holy Cross and from the University of California, Riverside. His work has been selected several times for inclusion in the annual *Best American Poetry* series, and he was chosen as an editor for the series in 2006. He served as poet laureate of the United States (2001–2003) and was named New York State Poet for 2004. His collections of poetry include *Video Poems* (1980), *Questions About Angels* (1991), and *The Trouble with Poetry and Other Poems* (2005), among others.

COLLINS

Sonnet

A Sonnet by **C. S. Lewis**

The stars come out; the fragrant shadows fall
About a dreaming garden still and sweet,
I hear the unseen bats above me bleat
Among the ghostly moths their hunting call,
And twinkling glow-worms all about me crawl.
Now for a chamber[1] dim, a pillow meet
For slumbers deep as death, a faultless sheet,
Cool, white and smooth. So may I reach the hall
With poppies[2] strewn where sleep that is so dear
With magic sponge can wipe away an hour
Or twelve and make them naught.[3] Why not a year,
Why could a man not loiter in that bower[4]
Until a thousand painless cycles wore,
And then—what if it held him evermore?[5] ❖

La Luna, 2001. Lou Wall.

Critical Viewing

How do the images in *La Luna* compare with the images presented in the written work? Do they match your own impression of the poem's theme?

1. **chamber.** Room
2. **poppies.** Plants that are used to produce opium, a substance that induces a drug-like sleep
3. **naught.** Nothing
4. **bower.** A shady, leafy shelter
5. **evermore.** Forever

Death has been described as "the big sleep." Why might people assume or believe that death is similar to sleeping? Why might people find that idea comforting or upsetting?

AMERICAN SONNET

A Sonnet by **Billy Collins**

We do not speak like Petrarch or wear a hat like Spenser
and it is not fourteen lines
like furrows in a small, carefully plowed field

but the picture postcard, a poem on vacation,
that forces us to sing our songs in little rooms
or pour our sentiments into measuring cups.

We write on the back of a waterfall or lake,
adding to the view a caption as conventional
as an Elizabethan woman's heliocentric eyes.

We locate an adjective for the weather.
We announce that we are having a wonderful time.
We express the wish that you were here

and hide the wish that we were where you are,
walking back from the mailbox, your head lowered
as you read and turn the thin message in your hands.

A slice of this place, a length of white beach,
a piazza or carved spires of a cathedral
will pierce the familiar place where you remain,

and you will toss on the table this reversible display:
a few square inches of where we have strayed
and a compression of what we feel. ❖

Is it necessary or desirable to stay connected to "home" and the familiar? Why might some strive to keep a connection whereas others might avoid one?

AFTER READING

REFER TO TEXT	▶ REASON WITH TEXT	
1a. Make a list of images that appear in each poem.	1b. Based on these images, determine the tone of each poem in relation to setting the speaker's purpose.	**Understand** **Find meaning**
2a. What does the speaker wish for in line 7 of "Sonnet"?	2b. Based on what you learned in the Build Background information on page 426, do you think C. S. Lewis might have been writing about his father's grief in this poem? Explain why or why not.	**Apply** **Use information**
3a. What wish is hidden from the recipient of the postcard in "American Sonnet"?	3b. What does this line imply? Analyze the final three lines of the poem and state what you believe is the meaning of the poem.	**Analyze** **Take things apart**
4a. Identify the simile used in line 7 of "Sonnet" to describe sleep.	4b. What other images suggest death? Conclude whether or not this is a poem about death. Support your response.	**Evaluate** **Make judgments**
5a. Recall what the magic sponge can do.	5b. Explain why somebody might want to use the "magic sponge." Write a response to the sonnet suggesting why somebody should not "loiter in that bower."	**Create** **Bring ideas together**

COMPARE LITERATURE: Sonnet

What rhyme scheme does Lewis follow in the sestet? Is the form of the poem appropriate for the subject matter and language? Why or why not? Despite the rejection of traditional sonnet forms in "American Sonnet," do similarities of form still exist between the two poems?

EXTEND THE TEXT

Writing Options

Creative Writing Write a **sonnet** that describes a part of your daily routine, whether it's going to bed, getting ready for school, or something completely different. Choose whether you will use the English or Italian rhyme scheme. (For a review on sonnet forms, see page 412.) In your sonnet, describe what you do to prepare for the routine, your surroundings, and how the experience makes you feel.

Expository Writing Imagine that you are trying to explain one of these poems to someone who doesn't understand it. Write an **informative paragraph** that explains the poem's speaker, its setting, and what happens in the poem. Who do you think would make a good audience for a recitation of this poem? Add that information to your informative paragraph.

Collaborative Learning

Perform a Role-Play In "Sonnet," the speaker appears to be trying to escape pain with sleep. With a partner, role-play a dialogue between the speaker in "Sonnet" and a friend. The person playing the speaker should tell the friend how he or she felt on the night described in this poem. The friend should respond to the speaker, trying to show that life is worth staying awake for.

Lifelong Learning

Make a Chronology Use the Internet and the library to research C. S. Lewis's biography and publications. In your research, identify the events in the writer's life that seem to help define his life and career. On poster board, create a time line that outlines these key events in chronological order. Include illustrations, photographs, and other visuals as appropriate. Compare your time line with those of your classmates to see if you have identified similar "key events."

Go to **www.mirrorsandwindows.com** for more.

BREAD

BEFORE READING

A Prose Poem by Margaret Atwood

DIRECTED READING

BUILD BACKGROUND

Literary Context Margaret Atwood's poetry is often short, terse, written in everyday language, and filled with sharp or witty observations. Her longer, interconnected poems, like her novels, are rich with symbolism and irony. **"Bread"** is a prose poem taken from *Murder in the Dark,* a 1984 collection of short experimental pieces. Like several other of her works, this poem reflects Atwood's personal concern with human-rights abuses and oppression everywhere.

Reader's Context Does bread, or any other food, have a significant meaning for you or your family? Can you think of objects in your own life that represent something besides themselves?

ANALYZE LITERATURE: Prose Poem

A **prose poem** is a work of prose that makes such extensive use of poetic language that the line between prose and poetry becomes blurred. Unlike conventional poetry, prose poems are usually written in paragraph form, with no formal rhyme or meter. They have other characteristics that set them apart from ordinary prose, including the use of rich imagery, metaphor, repetition, and indirect or implied meaning.

SET PURPOSE

As you read, look for elements that set "Bread" apart from ordinary prose. How might the selection change if it were written in regular prose? Also consider why Atwood chose to write in *second-person point of view.* In other words, the speaker refers to the reader or audience directly, indicated by the use of "you."

MEET THE AUTHOR

Although she first became famous as a poet, Canadian **Margaret Atwood** (b. 1939) is also well known for her intense, ironic, and sometimes disturbing novels and stories, such as *Surfacing* (1972), *The Handmaid's Tale* (1986), *Cat's Eye* (1988), and *The Robber Bride* (1993). She grew up in Ottawa and Toronto, Ontario, but came to know the Canadian wilderness during summers spent in northern Quebec. She graduated from the University of Toronto and received a master's degree at Radcliffe (Cambridge, MA) in 1962. Her first book of poetry, *The Circle Game,* won a Governor General's Award in 1966, and she has won many other awards since. Atwood's writing probes varied subjects, including male-female relationships, the Canadian pioneer spirit, the influence of myth, and international human rights.

USE READING SKILLS

Context Clues One type of context clue requires the reader to make an assumption based on **cause and effect.** This type of clue tells you that something happened as a result of something else. Some words that signal cause and effect include *if...then, when...then, thus, therefore, because, so, due to, as a result of,* and *consequently.* As you read, use cause-and-effect clues to help you understand the meanings of unfamiliar words.

PREVIEW VOCABULARY

Determine the meanings of the underlined words based on the cause-and-effect context clues and your own assumptions. Create a list of synonyms for each term. Rewrite each sentence by replacing the vocabulary word with its synonym.

1. If the house is <u>infested</u> with termites, then we'd have to tear it down.
2. As a result of his <u>subversive</u> behavior within the group, his team didn't make it past the quarterfinals.
3. He has proven to be a <u>treacherous</u> lab partner, so I wouldn't trust him with the final project.
4. If the woman can <u>conjure</u> a dove out of thin air, then I'll believe she's a magician.
5. Alan <u>duped</u> his sister into staying home; therefore, we have the car all to ourselves.

Breadstuffs, 1912. Ilya Maskov. State Russian Museum, St. Petersburg, Russia.

BREAD

A Prose Poem by **Margaret Atwood**

Imagine a piece of bread. You don't have to imagine it, it's right here in the kitchen, on the bread board, in its plastic bag, lying beside the bread knife. The bread knife is an old one you picked up at an auction; it has the word BREAD carved into the wooden handle. You open the bag, pull back the wrapper, cut yourself a slice. You put butter on it, then peanut butter, then honey, and you fold it over. Some of the honey runs out onto your fingers and you lick it off. It takes you about a minute to eat the bread. This bread happens to be brown, but there is also white bread, in the refrigerator, and a heel of rye you got last week, round as a full stomach then, now going mouldy. Occasionally you make bread. You think of it as something relaxing to do with your hands.

Imagine a famine. Now imagine a piece of bread. Both of these things are real but you happen to be in the same room with only one of them. Put yourself into a different room, that's what the mind is for. You are now lying on a thin mattress in a hot room. The walls are made of dried earth and your sister, who is younger than you are, is in the room with you. She is starving, her belly is bloated, flies land on her eyes; you brush them off with your hand. You have a cloth too, filthy but damp, and you press it to her lips and forehead. The piece of bread is the bread you've been saving, for days it seems. You are as hungry as she is, but not yet as weak. How long does this take? When will someone come with more bread? You think of going out to see if you might find something that could be eaten, but outside the streets are infested with scavengers and the stink of corpses is everywhere.

Should you share the bread or give the whole piece to your sister? Should you eat the piece of bread yourself? After all, you have a better chance of living, you're stronger. How long does it take to decide?

Imagine a prison. There is something you know that you have not yet told. Those in control of the prison know that you know. So do those not in control. If you tell, thirty or forty or a hundred of your friends, your comrades, will be caught and will die. If you refuse to tell, tonight will be like last night. They always choose the night. You don't think about the night however, but about the piece of bread they offered you. How long does it take? The piece of bread was brown and fresh and reminded you of sunlight falling across a wooden floor. It reminded you of a bowl, a yellow bowl that was once in your home. It held apples and pears; it stood on a table you can also remember. It's not the hunger or the pain that is killing you but the absence of the yellow bowl. If you could only hold the bowl in your hands, right here, you could withstand anything, you tell yourself. The bread they offered you is subversive, it's treacherous, it does not mean life.

There were once two sisters. One was rich and had no children, the other had five children and was a widow, so poor that she no longer had any food left. She went to her sister and asked her for a mouthful of bread. "My children are dying," she said. The rich sister said, "I do not have enough for myself," and drove her away from the door. Then the husband of the rich sister came home and wanted to cut himself a piece of bread; but when he made the first cut, out flowed red blood.

Everyone knew what that meant.

This is a traditional German fairy-tale.

The loaf of bread I have conjured for you floats about a foot above your kitchen table. The table is normal, there are no trap doors in it. A blue tea towel floats beneath the bread, and there are no strings attaching the cloth to the bread or the bread to the ceiling or the table to the cloth, you've proved it by passing your hand above and below. You didn't touch the bread though. What stopped you? You don't want to know whether the bread is real or whether it's just a hallucination I've somehow duped you into seeing. There's no doubt that you can see the bread, you can even smell it, it smells like yeast, and it looks solid enough, solid as your own arm. But can you trust it? Can you eat it? You don't want to know, imagine that. ❖

in • fest (in fest´) *v.*, overrun in large numbers
sub • ver • sive (səb vʉr´ siv *or* səb vʉr´ ziv) *adj.*, with a goal to undermine or corrupt
treach • er • ous (tre´ chə rəs *or* trech´ rəs) *adj.*, traitorous; disloyal
con • jure (kän´ jər) *v.*, appeared as if by magic
dupe (düp *or* dyüp) *v.*, deceived by trickery

"Ignorance is bliss" is a common expression. How does it apply to the selection? Why are some decisions avoided and even feared? Would you argue that being smart and being faced with a difficult decision is better or worse than being happily ignorant?

AFTER READING

REFER TO TEXT	▶ REASON WITH TEXT	
1a. Identify the setting of the first section. List what you do.	1b. Describe the mood of the first section. Explain why the writer started with this scenario.	**Understand** **Find meaning**
2a. Recall what decision you are asked to make in the second section.	2b. Predict how you would react in a similar situation. Is it possible to know how you would react? Is it possible to judge the actions of others?	**Apply** **Use information**
3a. Identify the three scenes the speaker asks you to imagine.	3b. Analyze the meaning of the bread in each scene.	**Analyze** **Take things apart**
4a. State what happens as a result of the sister's selfishness in the fairy tale included in section 4.	4b. Assess which of the imagined scenes is most provocative. Support your opinion.	**Evaluate** **Make judgments**
5a. Quote the questions the speaker asks in the final section.	5b. Explain how bread is used symbolically in this selection. Write another scenario, using bread, which encourages the reader to question how they would react in a similar situation.	**Create** **Bring ideas together**

ANALYZE LITERATURE: Prose Poem

Give three examples of poetic techniques you find in "Bread." How might the selection be different if it were written as "pure prose" or "pure poetry"? Which technique would you have used if you were the writer? Why?

EXTEND THE TEXT

Writing Options

Creative Writing Think of an ordinary object in your own life that you take for granted, and brainstorm how different your life would be without it. Write your own **prose poem** relating to this object and its role in your life, how you imagine your life would be without it, and its role in the life of others. Use vivid imagery and examples.

Persuasive Writing In "Bread," Margaret Atwood reflects her personal concern with human-rights abuses and oppression. In a one-page **persuasive essay,** argue whether the prose poem raises your concern in the issue or whether it failed to grab your attention. Support your argument using examples from the text or include your own suggestions as to how the author could have been more effective.

Collaborative Learning

Conduct a Poetry Discussion With a partner or small group, discuss the scenarios that the author presents in the poem. Put yourself in each person's place (the two sets of sisters, the prisoner and his friends) and decide how you would respond to the situation. What would you want to do, and what would you want the others to do? Discuss the possible repercussions of each decision. Finally, decide whether you would try to touch the bread in the last paragraph. Discuss why or why not.

Media Literacy

Research Human Rights Issues Choose a country and use the Internet or library to find out what the key human-rights issues are in that country. You might start by visiting Amnesty International's website. Prepare a presentation for your class that outlines an important human-rights issue in that country; what the government is, or is not, doing about it; and what actions students can take to help improve the situation.

Go to **www.mirrorsandwindows.com** for more.

Three Haiku

Haiku Poems by Matsuo Bashō, Nicholas Virgilio, and Alan Pizzarelli

BEFORE READING

BUILD BACKGROUND

Literary Context An ancient form of lyric poetry, haiku is still the most popular form of poetry in Japan, a form that people all over the world enjoy reading and writing. A **haiku** is a traditional Japanese poem consisting of three lines. The first and third lines contain five syllables each, and the second line contains seven. A haiku usually presents one image or picture. Regardless of the language it is written in, haiku is not about the number of syllables but rather the sharp perception or significant emotion that is captured in just a few words. As you read each poem, think about where it takes you.

Reader's Context Have you ever heard the expression "Less is more"? What do you think this expression means? Give an example.

COMPARE LITERATURE: Imagery

An **image** is a picture in words. Writers create images through the use of vivid *sensory details,* words and phrases that evoke the five senses (primarily sight, but also sound, touch, taste, and smell). The images in a literary work are referred to collectively as the work's **imagery.** As you read, notice the central image that each poet uses. To what sense or senses does the imagery of each poem appeal?

USE READING SKILLS

Compare and Contrast When you compare several things, you describe their similarities. When you contrast those things, you describe their differences. Writing things down can help you compare and contrast things. Use a Venn Diagram like the one below to make notes about similarities and differences in the three poems. Record similarities in the overlapping parts and differences in the separate parts. Be sure to compare and contrast images, ideas, feelings, structures, and sounds.

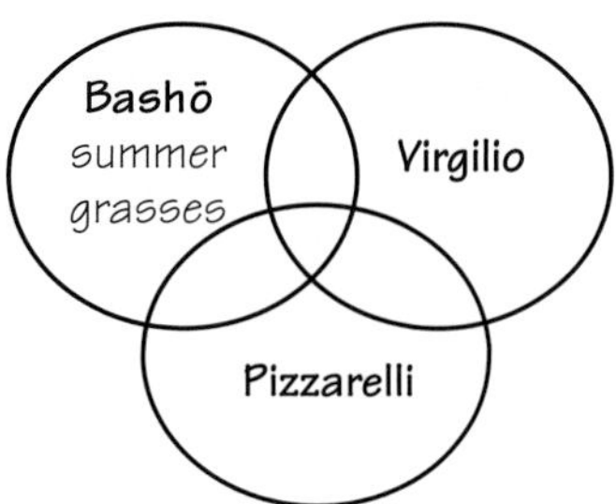

MEET THE AUTHORS

Matsuo Bashō (1644–1694) is regarded as Japan's greatest haiku poet. Bashō became interested in haiku as a young boy, wrote brilliant work in his twenties, and went on to become a professional teacher of poetry. His poems, often set in nature, are infused with the spirit of Zen Buddhism, which he studied.

Nicholas Virgilio (1928–1989) was one of the first major haiku poets in the United States. His work began appearing in haiku magazines first published in the 1960s. Virgilio believed that haiku can help us "get in touch with the real." His own haiku cover a thousand topics from nature to city life to the death of a loved one.

Alan Pizzarelli (b. 1950) is known for his playful haiku. He has written haiku about baseball, amusement parks, and throwing a stick to his dog. No subject is off-limits, he says, but a haiku must say something about human beings "within the world." Pizzarelli is also a musician and an artist.

Statue of Matsuo Bashō in Hiraizumi, Japan.

three HAIKU

Haiku Poems by **Matsuo Bashō, Nicholas Virgilio,** and **Alan Pizzarelli**

summer grasses
where stalwart soldiers
once dreamed a dream ❖

—Bashō

the blind musician
extending an old tin cup
collects a snowflake ❖

— Nicholas Virgilio

driving
out of the car wash

clouds move
across the hood ❖

—Alan Pizzarelli

#87. Gerrit Greve.

If you were to set one of the three haiku to music, which would you choose? What music would you select to accompany it? What type of music is most like a haiku?

The Great Wave off Kanagawa.
Katsushika Hokusai.

Informational Text CONNECTION

Some people assume that a haiku is just a short lyric poem. Haiku, however, is a very specific art form with many distinct features. The following text excerpt from *How to Haiku: A Writer's Guide to Haiku and Related Forms* by **Bruce Ross** explains not only how to write a haiku, but notes important rules to consider when doing so. As you read the following guidelines, consider how haiku diverges from other forms of poetry.

from HOW TO HAIKU

How-to Writing by **Bruce Ross**

There are a number of important points to consider when you write haiku. The first point is: *Haiku takes place in the present.* This is its special feature. Unlike most poetry, which exists in the mind of its author, haiku embodies a feeling experienced in a moment of time. You write the haiku because you want to share that feeling with others.

* * *

A haiku, however, is not merely a description of something that is happening in the present. This is the second point: *A haiku is a moment of awareness, insight, surprise, or delight.* This is what adds depth of feeling to haiku. For example, you might find delight in the inner life of a caterpillar's existence or gain philosophic insight into the meaning of death by watching the falling autumn leaves.

* * *

The idea is to open your mind to experience and not let it be filled with your emotions. This is what makes haiku different from other poetry.

* * *

Haiku is *most usually connected with nature.* A season word or a concrete representation connects us to a world of which we are a part but is greater than us. This connection adds depth to our experience. It also, as in most poetry, offers us an experience of beauty and, beyond that, insight.

* * *

When we actually write down our haiku they are in three lines of about twelve to fourteen syllables in a *short-long-short pattern.*

* * *

A haiku usually contains one or two images. If there were more, a haiku would be cluttered.

* * *

Remember that haiku is not merely description. You are not taking a snapshot of an object or a scene. Rather, you are expressing the feeling that you had while experiencing that object or scene. Your choice of words, phrasing, and tone make a haiku far more than a description. ❖

TEXT TO TEXT CONNECTION

Examine the three haiku. Do Bashō, Virgilio, and Pizzarelli follow the guidelines described in the *How to Haiku* excerpt? Examine the three haiku. Do Bashō, Virgilio, and Pizzarelli follow the guidelines described in the *How to Haiku* excerpt? How have the three haiku satisfied the expectations and fulfilled the desired outcomes? Analyze how the characteristics of the classical Japanese haiku by Bashō may have influenced the guidelines for modern haiku.

AFTER READING

REFER TO TEXT	REASON WITH TEXT	
1a. Identify an image you find compelling in one of the haiku.	1b. In your own words, describe the feelings evoked by that image. According to the informational text, what type of moment might you have experienced?	**Understand** Find meaning
2a. List things the three poems have in common. Consider subject and form.	2b. Develop your own definition for *haiku* based on these examples.	**Apply** Use information
3a. Identify a natural image in each haiku.	3b. Analyze whether or not the haiku connect the reader to the world, as described in the fourth paragraph of the informational text. Why or why not?	**Analyze** Take things apart
4a. Identify the person or people referenced in each haiku.	4b. Test Alan Pizzarelli's comment that a haiku must say something about human beings "within the world" using these haiku as examples.	**Evaluate** Make judgments
5a. List any descriptive words that are included in the three haiku.	5b. Write a paragraph that provides more information about the image depicted in each haiku. Discuss whether your additions add anything or if "less is more."	**Create** Bring ideas together

COMPARE LITERATURE: Imagery

What specific image or overall imagery does each poet use in these haiku? What feeling does each evoke? How does the imagery used in the three haiku accentuate the experiences being described?

EXTEND THE TEXT

Writing Options

Creative Writing Write a **memo** to each poet, describing your response to his haiku. Begin your memo with a header that includes to whom the memo is addressed, from whom it is written, what it is about, and the date. Alternatively, write a haiku in response to one of the haiku and include it in a memo to the poet, along with an explanation of how you decided to respond.

Expository Writing Write down the **instructions** to perform a specific procedure such as writing a haiku, fixing a flat tire, or making an omelet. Working in pairs, verbally explain the instructions to your partner while he or she takes notes. Then switch roles and have your partner explain his or her procedure to you while you take notes.

Collaborative Learning

Research the Nature of Haiku The Haiku Society of America has defined haiku to be a "poem in which nature is linked to human nature." Scholar Alan Watts called it "wordless" poems. On the Internet or in introductions to books about haiku, find other descriptions of haiku. Choose the one that you think best captures the essence of this form of poetry. In your small group, share and discuss the descriptions of haiku. Then consider this question: Why is haiku a form of poetry that attracts so many people?

Critical Literacy

Create a Haiku Anthology Working in a group of six to eight students, compile a haiku anthology that includes published haiku as well as student work. You may include multiple themes or pick a single theme such as urban life, sports and hobbies, or the seasons. Have each student submit five haiku for possible inclusion in the anthology. Each of these should be printed on a single sheet of paper for sharing. As a group, decide how many haiku you will include in the anthology and how you will select them. After you've made selections, come up with an imaginative way to share your anthology with the class.

Go to **www.mirrorsandwindows.com** for more.

READING POETRY INDEPENDENTLY

Theme: What We Keep

"Like a shroud my past surrounds me,
but I will cut it and stitch it,
to make good shoes with it,
shoes that fit my feet."

—Ha Jin,
from "The Past"

As we move through life, we tend to acquire things to carry with us. Sometimes, these things are physical objects: a beloved toy, a favorite pair of sneakers, jewelry passed down from your grandmother. Most often, though, we bring along a store of intangible items: memories, knowledge, traditions, the results of decisions we've made. To some extent, what we keep with us helps shape who we are. Other times, it is what we discard that says the most. As you read the selections in this part, try to determine what is being kept.

USING READING SKILLS WITH POETRY

Use Context Clues

Using **context clues** to find the meaning of an unfamiliar word involves taking a closer look at the context, or the surrounding text, for clues that can help you guess the meaning of the word. There are five main types of context clues:

- **Restatement Clues:** This type is found when an author restates an idea, or explains it in a different way. *Apposition* is a direct type of restatement that renames something. Some of the signals for restatement are *that is, in other words,* and *or.*
- **Cause-and-Effect Clues:** This type requires the reader to make an assumption based on cause and effect. Some words that signal cause and effect are *if...then, when...then, thus, therefore, because,* and *so.*
- **Examples:** Sometimes, a writer will provide examples to help clarify the meaning of a difficult word. These examples may be introduced by expressions like *including, such as, especially,* and *particularly.*
- **Comparison Clues:** Words and phrases including *such as, like, also, similarly, just as,* and *in the same way* signal comparisons and indicate that the unfamiliar word is like something that might be more familiar to you.
- **Contrast Clues:** Words and phrases such as *however, but, not, except, although,* and *on the other hand* signal that something contrasts, or differs in meaning, from something else.

Understand Denotation and Connotation

A word's **denotation** is its dictionary definition. A word's **connotations** are all the positive or negative associations it has, in addition to its literal meaning. For example, the words *dirty* and *soiled* both denote "unclean." However, the word *dirty* has negative connotations. It is associated with low morals (as in "a dirty business deal") and unpleasant tasks (as in "a dirty job"). *Soiled,* on the other hand, is rather neutral—neither positive nor negative.

Words may have different connotations for different people. For example, the word *ocean* has a positive connotation for many people. They may hear it and think peaceful thoughts. However, if you are afraid of water due to a near-drowning incident when you were a child, the word *ocean* may have a negative association for you.

In poetry, the word choices the poets make are intentional to conjure certain images or feelings. Be aware of the connotations of words as you read. One way to do that is to substitute a word that means (denotes) the same thing and see if the feeling of the sentence holds true. Use a Connotation Chart like the one below. Decide whether a word is negative, neutral, or positive and put it in the correct column. Then write in other words with the same denotation but different connotations.

Connotation Chart

Negative	Neutral	Positive
weird freakish bizarre abnormal strange	unusual different uncommon rare curious	unique remarkable extraordinary unequaled phenomenal

Determine the Appropriate Meaning for the Context

In certain contexts, a word might mean one thing, but in another, it might change. In poetry, that is especially true as poets may use figurative language and rely on connotations to carry the meanings of the words, and thus the poem. One way to keep track of a poem's meaning is to sort words and phrases from a poem into categories by type, such as images of nature and descriptions of people, or by stanzas. Next, classify each item in the chart as having a positive, neutral, or negative connotation based on its use in the poem.

Framework for Poetry

When reading poetry, you need to be aware of the form, imagery, rhythm, and sound devices of the poem. The following checklist of questions offers a framework for approaching poetry.

As you start to read...

- ❑ In what form is the poem?
- ❑ What images stand out?
- ❑ Which words are unfamiliar to me or are used in an unfamiliar way?

As you continue reading...

- ❑ What is the mood that the images create in the poem?
- ❑ What sound devices has the poet used?
- ❑ What is the meter of the poem?

After you've finished reading...

- ❑ How will reading this poem aloud bring more poetic elements to light?
- ❑ What is the message or theme of the poem?
- ❑ Of what does this poem remind me?

What Good Readers Do

Tackle Difficult Vocabulary

Difficult words in a poem can get in the way of your ability to follow the events in a work of writing. Use aids that a text provides, consult a dictionary, or ask someone about words you do not understand. When you come across a word you do not know, say to yourself

- The context tells me that this word means...
- A dictionary definition provided in the selection shows that the word means...
- My work with the word before class helps me know that the word means...
- A classmate said that the word means...
- I can skip knowing the exact meaning of this word because...

THE PAST

A Lyric Poem by **Ha Jin**

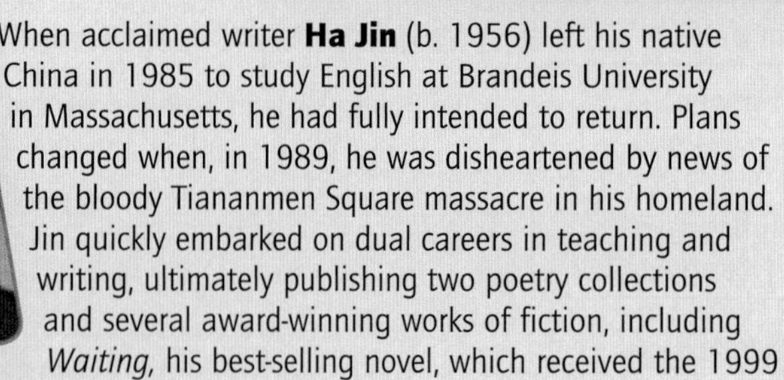

When acclaimed writer **Ha Jin** (b. 1956) left his native China in 1985 to study English at Brandeis University in Massachusetts, he had fully intended to return. Plans changed when, in 1989, he was disheartened by news of the bloody Tiananmen Square massacre in his homeland. Jin quickly embarked on dual careers in teaching and writing, ultimately publishing two poetry collections and several award-winning works of fiction, including *Waiting,* his best-selling novel, which received the 1999 National Book Award.

From his collection *Facing Shadows* (1996), Ha Jin's poem **"The Past"** demonstrates many of the elements typical of his writing style. Known for his insightful reflections on the human experience, Jin uses only the words he needs. In this poem, the author observes how the role and importance of one's past can be determined only by the individual. Although most of his stories are set in China, Jin says he's now at home in the United States. "China is distant," he says. "What's meaningful to me is the immigrant experience, the American life."

How do you regard your past experiences? Do you see them as hindrances or guides for your future?

I have supposed my past is a part of myself.
As my shadow appears whenever I'm in the sun
the past cannot be thrown off and its weight
must be borne,[1] or I will become another man.

But I saw someone wall his past into a garden
whose produce is always in fashion.
If you enter his property without permission
he will welcome you with a watchdog or a gun.

I saw someone set up his past as a harbor.
Wherever it sails, his boat is safe—
if a storm comes, he can always head for home.
His voyage is the adventure of a kite.

I saw someone drop his past like trash.
He buried it and shed it altogether.
He has shown me that without the past
one can also move ahead and get somewhere.

Like a shroud[2] my past surrounds me,
but I will cut it and stitch it,
to make good shoes with it,
shoes that fit my feet. ❖

1. **borne.** Past perfect tense of *bear,* meaning to carry (a burden)
2. **shroud.** A long, loose garment used to cover a body for burial; sometimes used, as it is here, to mean something that covers or hides

How important is the past? Can it affect a person's present strengths or weaknesses? What types of experiences are more significant than others?

Refer and Reason

1. List the three things the speaker has seen other people do with their pasts. Contrast the way the speaker will deal with his past with the ways others deal with the past.
2. Quote what the speaker says cannot be done to the past. Assess this claim. Explain why you agree or disagree with it.
3. Develop a brief profile of one of the individuals described in the poem. Based on his attitude toward the past, what kind of personality, background, or family might he have?

Writing Options

1. Imagine your descendants are going to write a biography of your life. Create a brief sketch on what you would want them to include, including your future.
2. Choose a grandparent or other older adult in your life whom you admire or find interesting. Write a brief biographical essay about the person to pass on to your future children or grandchildren.

Go to **www.mirrorsandwindows.com** for more.

FIFTEEN

A Narrative Poem by **William Stafford**

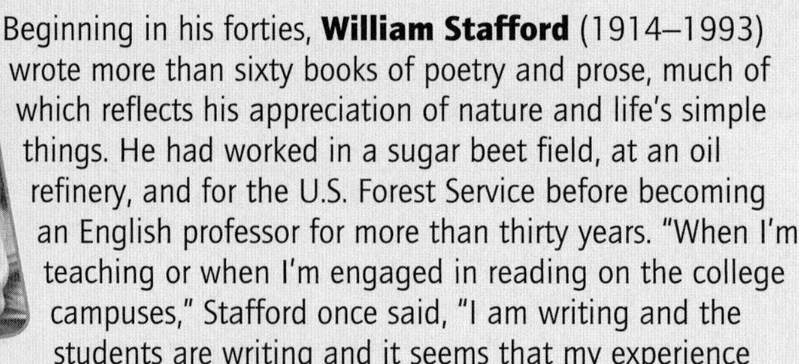

Beginning in his forties, **William Stafford** (1914–1993) wrote more than sixty books of poetry and prose, much of which reflects his appreciation of nature and life's simple things. He had worked in a sugar beet field, at an oil refinery, and for the U.S. Forest Service before becoming an English professor for more than thirty years. "When I'm teaching or when I'm engaged in reading on the college campuses," Stafford once said, "I am writing and the students are writing and it seems that my experience makes me more perceptive and humane about what they are doing."

"Fifteen" was published in William Stafford's 1966 collection *The Rescued Year*. In the poem, the speaker remembers an event—what actually took place and what was imagined—that happened when he was fifteen years old.

What opportunity or dream might compel you to abandon everything else in your life?

South of the bridge on Seventeenth
I found back of the willows one summer
day a motorcycle with engine running
as it lay on its side, ticking over
slowly in the high grass. I was fifteen.

I admired all that pulsing gleam, the
shiny flanks,[1] the demure[2] headlights
fringed where it lay; I led it gently
to the road and stood with that
companion, ready and friendly. I was fifteen.

We could find the end of a road, meet
the sky on out Seventeenth. I thought about
hills, and patting the handle got back a
confident opinion. On the bridge we indulged
a forward feeling, a tremble. I was fifteen.

Thinking, back farther in the grass I found
the owner, just coming to, where he had flipped
over the rail. He had blood on his hand, was pale—
I helped him walk to his machine. He ran his hand
over it, called me a good man, roared away.

I stood there, fifteen. ❖

1. **flanks.** Right and left sides of an object
2. **demure.** Modest; shy; indifferent

How might a child's perspective of the world differ from an adult's perspective? Why might there be a difference? How does one truly become an adult?

Refer and Reason

1. Recall what the boy finds. Separate sections of text that refer to the boy's real actions from those referring to imagined actions. In what ways do his real actions contrast with his imagined ones?
2. Identify words and phrases throughout the poem that indicate how the boy feels about the motorcycle. Interpret what the motorcycle represents to him.
3. Indicate the condition of the rider when the boy found him. Explain how helping the rider and the rider's response affected the boy's life. Write another stanza showing what you think would have happened if the speaker had carried out his imagined actions.

Writing Options

1. Imagine that the boy in "Fifteen" had taken the bike. Write a police log entry for the local newspaper, based on the way the bike owner might have reported the incident to law enforcement.
2. Create a character sketch of the speaker in "Fifteen." Note that some facts—such as his age—are spelled out in the poem, whereas others must be inferred.

 Go to **www.mirrorsandwindows.com** for more.

Hanging Fire

A Lyric Poem by

Audre Lorde

I am fourteen
and my skin has betrayed me
the boy I cannot live without
still sucks his thumb
in secret
how come my knees are
always so ashy
what if I die
before morning
and momma's in the bedroom
with the door closed.

Audre Lorde (1934–1992) grew up in New York City and started writing poetry when she was only twelve. She later worked as a librarian and a teacher and published more than eighteen books of poetry and prose. Lorde was an activist against oppression and said, "I want my poems to empower people to speak, to strengthen themselves into who they most want and need to be and then to act, to do what needs being done."

In **"Hanging Fire,"** a girl discusses her worries. The expression *to hang fire* originated during the time when firearms were loaded with gunpowder by hand and then ignited with a spark created by striking a flint against an iron plate. The gunpowder didn't always explode when the gun was fired; sometimes, it would smolder or *hang fire,* inside the gun. It could explode at any time, and so the expression *hanging fire* came to mean a delay filled with dread.

What events in your own life fill you with a sense of dread? Are they usually as bad as you imagine?

I have to learn how to dance
in time for the next party
my room is too small for me
suppose I die before graduation
they will sing sad melodies
but finally
tell the truth about me
There is nothing I want to do
and too much
that has to be done
and momma's in the bedroom
with the door closed.

Nobody even stops to think
about my side of it
I should have been on Math Team
my marks were better than his
why do I have to be
the one
wearing braces
I have nothing to wear tomorrow
will I live long enough
to grow up
and momma's in the bedroom
with the door closed. ❖

Why might people have difficulty expressing their fears and concerns? Does society encourage the expression of true emotion, or are people expected to keep their private affairs private?

Refer and Reason

1. Quote the line that is repeated in each stanza. Infer what kind of relationship the speaker has with her mother and what the speaker wants from her mother.
2. Recall how old the speaker is. Determine ways in which the speaker in this poem and the speaker's teenage self in "Fifteen" (page 443) are typical of people their ages. Do you think gender also plays a role in their worries and desires? Explain.
3. List problems and worries the speaker has. Create a dialogue between the speaker and you or one of your peers.

Writing Options

1. Imagine you are this character's friend. Write a letter to her or her mother with advice about her situation and concerns.
2. Write a brief essay analyzing how the speaker in "Hanging Fire" and the speaker in "Fifteen" by William Stafford—both teenagers—differ in their concerns and values. As prewriting, brainstorm a list of at least ten similarities and ten differences between the speakers.

Go to **www.mirrorsandwindows.com** for more.

THEME FOR English B

A Lyric Poem by **Langston Hughes**

Harlem Street Scene, 1942. Jacob Lawrence. Private collection.

Langston Hughes (1902–1967) came from a family of abolitionists, people who fought for the end of slavery in the United States. Hughes began writing poetry in eighth grade and is now considered one of the most influential writers of the Harlem Renaissance, a time between 1920 and the late 1930s that saw a flourish in African-American music, art, and literature in New York. Hughes wrote poetry, short stories, plays, and novels and said, "No great poet has ever been afraid of being himself."

"Theme for English B" allows readers to delve into the mind of an African-American college student during the first half of the twentieth century, when not many African Americans went to college or shared the same rights as whites. In the poem, the speaker reflects on the undeniable bonds shared by Americans despite racial disparities.

How do you voice your own opinion in everyday situations?

The instructor said,

Go home and write
a page tonight.
And let that page come out of you—
Then, it will be true.

I wonder if it's that simple?

I am twenty-two, colored, born in Winston-Salem.[1]
I went to school there, then Durham,[2] then here
to this college on the hill above Harlem.[3]
I am the only colored student in my class.

The steps from the hill lead down into Harlem,
through a park, then I cross St. Nicholas,
Eighth Avenue, Seventh, and I come to the Y,
the Harlem Branch Y, where I take the elevator
up to my room, sit down, and write this page:

It's not easy to know what is true for you or me
at twenty-two, my age. But I guess I'm what
I feel and see and hear. Harlem, I hear you:
hear you, hear me—we two—you, me talk on this
page.
(I hear New York, too.) Me—who?

Well, I like to eat, sleep, drink, and be in love.
I like to work, read, learn, and understand life.
I like a pipe for a Christmas present,
or records—Bessie,[4] bop,[5] or Bach.[6]

I guess being colored doesn't make me not like
the same things other folks like who are other races.
So will my page be colored that I write?
Being me, it will not be white.
But it will be

a part of you, instructor.
You are white—
yet a part of me, as I am a part of you.
That's American.
Sometimes perhaps you don't want to be a part of me.
Nor do I often want to be a part of you.
But we are, that's true!
As I learn from you,
I guess you learn from me—
although you're older—and white—
and somewhat more free.

This is my page for English B. ❖

---

1. **Winston-Salem.** A city in North Carolina
2. **Durham.** A city in North Carolina
3. **this college on the hill above Harlem.** Refers to Columbia University in New York City; Harlem is a section of Manhattan known as a center of African-American culture
4. **Bessie.** Bessie Smith (c. 1894–1937), famous American blues singer of the late 1920s
5. **bop.** Refers to bebop, a style of jazz that emerged during the 1940s and that is characterized by harmonic complexity, convoluted melodies, and often very rapid tempos
6. **Bach.** Johann Sebastian Bach (1685–1750), German composer of classical music

What can we learn from people of other cultures? What things do we all have in common?

Refer and Reason

1. Identify lines from the poem in which the speaker connects himself to others. Differentiate between the connection he draws between himself and Harlem and between himself and New York.
2. Quote what the instructor said to do. Assess whether the speaker's completed assignment will meet the instructor's expectations. Explain.
3. State how the speaker is different from others in his class and from the instructor. Consider how effective this poem is at giving readers insight into the lives of African Americans before the Civil Rights movement. Compose your own response to the instructor's question.

Writing Options

1. Imagine you are the instructor who receives Langston Hughes's poem. Write a response with either a brief paragraph or poem that you would return to him.
2. Research more about what life was like for African Americans in the first half of the twentieth century, particularly those pursuing higher education. Write a brief editorial expressing the extent to which you think opportunities for young African Americans have changed since that time.

Go to **www.mirrorsandwindows.com** for more.

To be of use

A Lyric Poem by **Marge Piercy**

Marge Piercy (b. 1936) was born in Detroit, Michigan, during the Great Depression (1929–1939). She grew up listening to the stories of her mother and grandmother and began writing poetry at age fifteen. She credits her mother with making her a poet by encouraging her to read, develop her imagination, and observe carefully. Piercy once said that she "can never imagine living without poetry." Piercy has written fourteen poetry collections and is also a novelist.

"To be of use" is a poem that celebrates people who work hard at whatever they do. **"For the young who want to"** is a poem about how society values the work of artists. In the latter, Piercy wants young aspiring writers to understand that the writing life must be driven by one's own love of writing and not by external acknowledgment of talent. Both poems express value of acts traditionally undervalued in our society.

Are people always appreciative of your talents and efforts? When are they the most appreciative? When are they the least appreciative?

The people I love the best
jump into work head first
without dallying in the shallows
and swim off with sure strokes almost out of sight.
They seem to become natives of that element,
the black sleek heads of seals
bouncing like half-submerged balls.

I love people who harness themselves, an ox to a heavy cart,
who pull like water buffalo, with massive patience,
who strain in the mud and the muck to move things forward,
who do what has to be done, again and again.

I want to be with people who submerge
in the task, who go into the fields to harvest
and work in a row and pass the bags along,
who are not parlor generals and field deserters
but move in a common rhythm
when the food must come in or the fire be put out.

The work of the world is common as mud.
Botched, it smears the hands, crumbles to dust.
But the thing worth doing well done
has a shape that satisfies, clean and evident.
Greek amphoras for wine or oil,
Hopi vases that held corn, are put in museums
but you know they were made to be used.
The pitcher cries for water to carry
and a person for work that is real. ❖

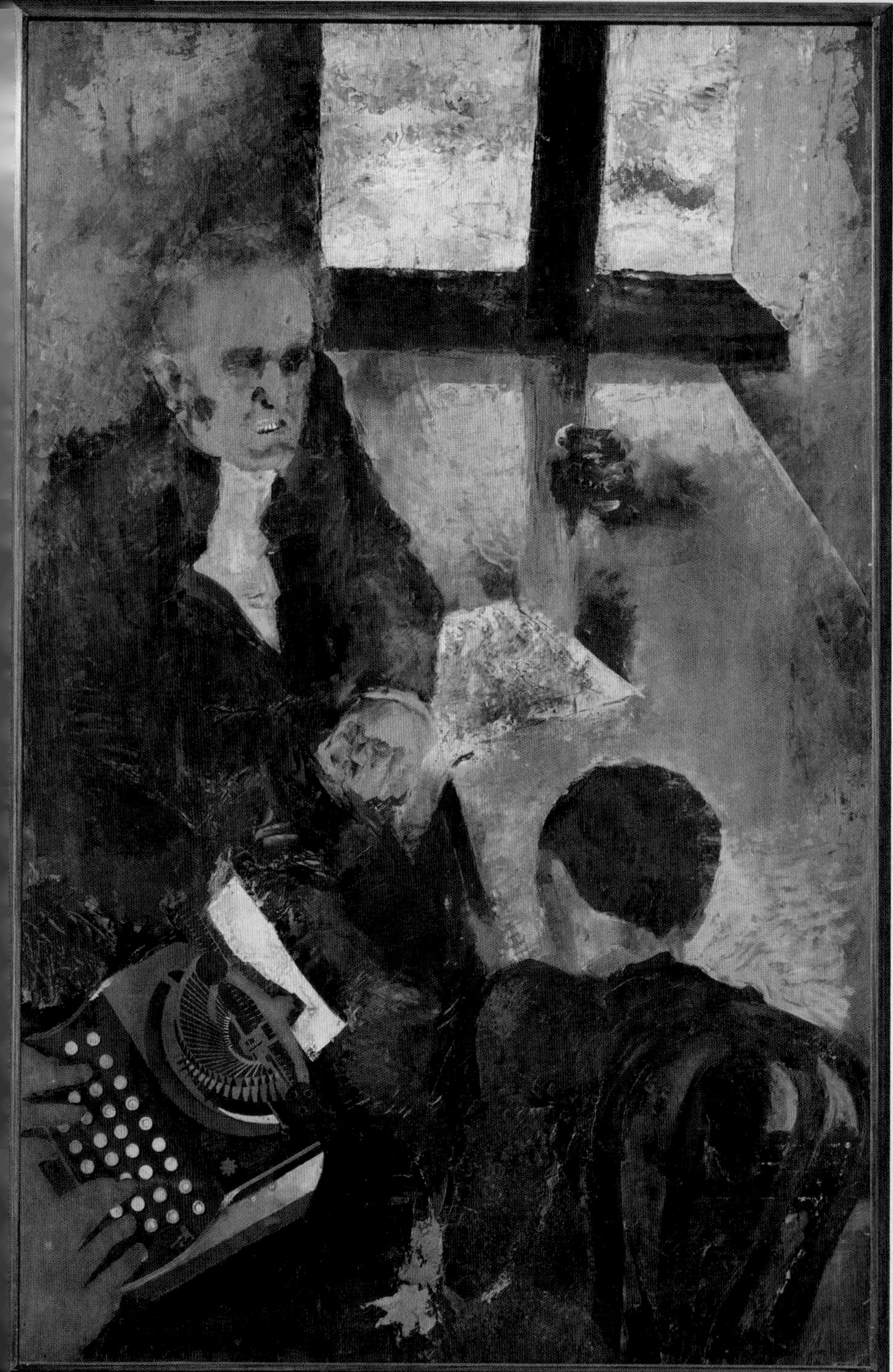

Interrogation, 1934–1938. Friedl Dicker. Jewish Museum, Prague.

Critical Viewing

How does the title of the artwork correspond with the ideas presented in the poem?

For the young who want to

A Lyric Poem by **Marge Piercy**

Talent is what they say
you have after the novel
is published and favorably
reviewed. Beforehand what
you have is a tedious
delusion, a hobby like knitting.

Work is what you have done
after the play is produced
and the audience claps.
Before that friends keep asking
when you are planning to go
out and get a job.

Genius is what they know you
had after the third volume
of remarkable poems. Earlier
they accuse you of withdrawing,
ask why you don't have a baby,
call you a bum.

The reason people want M.F.A.'s,[1]
take workshops with fancy names
when all you can really
learn is a few techniques,
typing instructions and somebody else's mannerisms

is that every artist lacks
a license to hang on the wall
like your optician, your vet
proving you may be a clumsy sadist[2]
whose fillings fall into the stew
but you're certified a dentist.

The real writer is one
who really writes. Talent
is an invention like phlogiston[3]
after the fact of fire.
Work is its own cure. You have to
like it better than being loved. ❖

1. **M.F.A.** Master of Fine Arts degree
2. **sadist.** Someone who enjoys pain and suffering
3. **phlogiston.** An imaginary element once believed to be released when objects burn

How does our society define success? Is a job worth doing if the worker receives no public recognition? Why might people work at something, despite criticism or lack of support?

Refer and Reason

1. State what you have before your novel is published. Analyze how people perceive a writer's work before and after success.
2. Identify what a person cries for according to the poem "To be of use." Judge whether Piercy finds satisfaction in her work. Use examples from both poems to support your answers.
3. What do the people that Piercy loves best do? Why? Quote the description of talent from the final stanza of "For the young who want to."

Writing Options

1. Write an introduction for an anthology and explain how these two poems are related. Identify the shared theme of the poems, and give examples from both poems to illustrate the theme.
2. Write a compare-and-contrast essay addressing Piercy's feelings about work, art, and talent reflected in her poems with Annie Dillard's ideas about the same subjects in her essay on page 306.

Go to **www.mirrorsandwindows.com** for more.

What Are Friends For

Rosellen Brown (b. 1939) is widely recognized as a gifted contemporary novelist, essayist, and poet. Her work has earned her several awards and fellowships from such organizations as the American Academy and Institute of Arts and Letters, the Guggenheim Foundation, and the National Endowment for the Arts. She currently teaches in the graduate creative writing program at the Art Institute of Chicago.

"What Are Friends For" appears in Brown's poetry collection *Cory Frye's Pillow Book,* published in 1994. It describes, in simple terms, one of life's most important gifts—friendship.

Describe a time in your life when you felt lonely or alone.

A Lyric Poem by **Rosellen Brown**

What are friends for, my mother asks.
A duty undone, visit missed,
casserole unbaked for sick Jane.
Someone has just made her bitter.

Nothing. They are for nothing, friends,
I think. All they do in the end—
they touch you. They fill you like music. ❖

How would you answer the question, "What are friends for?" List the ways friends can have a positive influence on your life.

Girls Walking, 1891–1892. Edouard Vuillard. Collection of Samuel Josefowitz, Paris, France./ Lausanne, Switzerland.

Refer and Reason

1. Quote the question the mother asks in line 1. Compare and contrast the way the speaker and her mother appear to feel about friends and friendship.
2. Decide whether the mother or the speaker is right about friends. Give examples to support your response.
3. Recall what the speaker says about friends in line 5. Explain how the speaker almost seems to "trick" the reader with her choice of language.

Writing Options

1. Write a poem of your own, similar in length to Brown's poem, expressing your personal philosophy about the roles of important people in our lives.
2. Write two to three sentences defining friendship and what friends are for.

Go to **www.mirrorsandwindows.com** for more.

Women

A Lyric Poem by **Alice Walker**

They were women then
My mama's generation
Husky of voice—Stout of
Step
With fists as well as
Hands
How they battered down
Doors
And ironed

The Wash. Maria Blanchard. Musée d'Art Moderne de la Ville de Paris.

For Pulitzer Prize-winning author **Alice Walker** (b. 1944), something extraordinary seemed to begin with something tragic. Becoming depressed at age eight after a stray BB pellet destroyed her sight in one eye, "I retreated into solitude," Walker says, "and read stories and began to write poems." But her retreat didn't last long. In the years that followed, the Georgia-born Walker became a prominent Civil Rights activist as well as a celebrated writer. Her poetry, essays, and novels, including the modern classic *The Color Purple,* are widely read by people of all backgrounds. "I never have an intended audience," Walker admits. "I just write...and I'm very happy."

In the poetry collection *In Search of Our Mothers' Gardens,* from which **"Women"** is taken, Alice Walker explores the effects of denying education to a group of people. She suggests that many great African-American writers were lost to the world because they did not have the opportunity to learn to write.

For what are you especially grateful that your parents, grandparents, or older generations provided?

Starched white
Shirts
How they led
Armies
Headragged Generals
Across mined
Fields
Booby-trapped
Ditches
To discover books
Desks
A place for us
How they knew what we
Must know
Without knowing a page
Of it
Themselves. ❖

In what ways has a parent, other family member, or guardian worked to make things better for you? How have you shown your appreciation? What privileges might your generation take for granted?

Refer and Reason

1. Quote what the speaker says about her mother's generation in line 1. Infer what the speaker thinks of her own generation. Point out possible reasons for the differences between the two groups.
2. Identify details that describe the women. Include details about things the women accomplished. Determine what the speaker admires about the women.
3. Recall what generation the speaker describes. Make a list of things you think the speaker would want her generation to pass on to their children.

Writing Options

1. Write a one-page letter from the speaker of the poem to her mother or to a woman of her mother's generation. What might the speaker say, and for what might she thank her?
2. Imagine you have been invited to present a paper on figurative language at a poetry conference. Prepare a brief three-paragraph analysis of "Women" in which you identify and analyze the meanings of the metaphors Walker uses in this poem.

 Go to **www.mirrorsandwindows.com** for more.

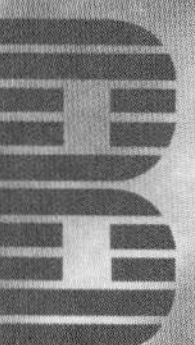

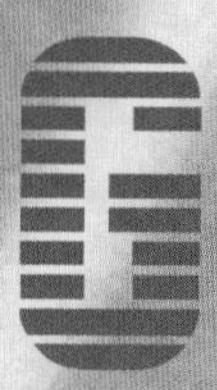

A Lyric Poem by
Gladys Cardiff

Bending, I bow my head
And lay my hand upon
Her hair, combing, and think
How women do this for
Each other. My daughter's hair
Curls against the comb,
Wet and fragrant—orange
Parings. Her face, downcast,
Is quiet for one so young.

I take her place. Beneath
My mother's hands I feel
The braids drawn up tight
As a piano wire and singing,
Vinegar-rinsed. Sitting
Before the oven I hear

When poet **Gladys Cardiff** (b. 1942) writes, she has something very valuable from which to draw: her rich cultural heritage. Her work often reflects her ancestry, particularly on her father's side—the Owl clan of the North Carolina Cherokee. From her mother's side, she is Irish and Welsh. A winner of the Governor's Writer's Award for her first book of poetry, *To Frighten a Storm,* in 1976, Cardiff has since had work published in several notable collections of Native American writings. She currently teaches in the English Department at Oakland University in Michigan.

Published in 1976, Gladys Cardiff's **"Combing"** observes a simple, special way women in families care for each other—and how that caring is passed down through generations. Cardiff uses figurative language and sensory details to create vivid images in this poem.

Who has cared for you more than anyone else?

The orange coils tick
The early hour before school.

She combed her grandmother
Mathilda's hair using
A comb made out of bone.
Mathilda rocked her oak wood
Chair, her face downcast,
Intent on tearing rags
In strips to braid a cotton
Rug from bits of orange
And brown. A simple act,

Preparing hair. Something
Women do for each other,
Plaiting the generations. ❖

In what simple ways do members of your family show they care for one another? Why do small things sometimes mean the most?

Refer and Reason

1. Identify the color mentioned in each of the first three stanzas of "Combing." Infer what this color represents for the speaker.
2. List words used to describe women in the poem. Note what the women do. Compare and contrast the women in "Combing" with the women in "Women" on page 454.
3. According to the poem, what does preparing hair do for a family? In two paragraphs, summarize a tradition followed in your own family that brings different generations together.

Writing Options

1. Write a brief personal narrative from your own childhood, noting similarities and differences among your childhood memory, the one Alice Walker describes, and the one Gladys Cardiff describes.
2. Write an expository essay describing the tone used by the speaker in "Combing." Explain how the tone may reflect the speaker's attitude toward her topic about which she is writing. Share your essay with your classmates.

Go to **www.mirrorsandwindows.com** for more.

My Papa's *Waltz*

A Lyric Poem by **Theodore Roethke**

Father and Son Dancing, 1992. Brian Kershisnik.

The whiskey on your breath
Could make a small boy dizzy;
But I hung on like death:
Such waltzing was not easy.

Critical Viewing

What feelings are depicted in the artwork? How do these emotions relate to the poem?

Like many literary greats before him, **Theodore Roethke** (1908–1963) is perhaps best known for poetry that reflects a keen sense of nature and its meaning for human life. Roethke's signature use of plant imagery as a metaphor for human experience was inspired by the greenhouse his family owned during his boyhood in Saginaw, Michigan. Among his collections are *Open House* (1941), *The Lost Son and Other Poems* (1948), and *Waking,* for which he won the Pulitzer Prize in 1954.

"My Papa's Waltz" appears in *The Lost Son and Other Poems,* Theodore Roethke's second book. Through a single childhood memory, the poem seems to paint a picture of Roethke's relationship with his father, whom he lost to cancer when Roethke was a teenager.

In your own family, with whom do you have the best relationship? What factors make this relationship the best?

We romped until the pans
Slid from the kitchen shelf;
My mother's countenance
Could not unfrown itself.

The hand that held my wrist
Was battered on one knuckle;
At every step you missed
My right ear scraped a buckle.

You beat time on my head
With a palm caked hard by dirt,
Then waltzed me off to bed
Still clinging to your shirt. ❖

Think of a childhood memory involving your parent or guardian and you. Why might certain memories stand out in our minds?

Refer and Reason

1. Quote the lines that show how the mother feels. Point out details that indicate why she might feel this way.
2. Identify details in the poem that imply physical discomfort for the speaker. Then find an example that implies comfort and warmth for the speaker. Decide whether the speaker has effectively communicated his feelings about his father. Explain your response.
3. Most young children have unconditional love for their parents, but relationships often become more complicated as a child grows. Rewrite the poem. Assume the father acts the same way, but the speaker is a teenager, not a young boy.

Writing Options

1. Imagine you are the speaker in the poem and write a personal note to your father. Explain how you feel toward him and why. Your note should touch on the father's life, nature, and personal characteristics.
2. Imagine a classmate asks you whether you think this poem represents a positive or a negative memory of the speaker's father. Write a paragraph in which you answer this question. Use specific examples and evidence from the selection to support your position.

Go to **www.mirrorsandwindows.com** for more.

MY FATHER'S Song

A Lyric Poem by **Simon Ortiz**

Wanting to say things,
I miss my father tonight.
His voice, the slight catch,
the depth from his thin chest,
the tremble of emotion
in something he has just said
to his son, his song:

We planted corn one Spring at Acu[1]—
we planted several times
but this one particular time
I remember the soft damp sand
in my hand.

My father had stopped at one point
to show me an overturned furrow;[2]
the plowshare[3] had unearthed
the burrow nest of a mouse
in the soft moist sand.

Very gently, he scooped tiny pink animals
into the palm of his hand
and told me to touch them.
We took them to the edge
of the field and put them in the shade
of a sand moist clod.

I remember the very softness
of cool and warm sand and tiny alive mice
and my father saying things. ❖

1. **Acu.** In Acoma culture, "the place where life happens"
2. **furrow.** Plowed land
3. **plowshare.** Part of the plow that cuts into the earth

Simon Ortiz (b. 1941) knew he loved language at an early age. A member of the Acoma Pueblo Nation, Ortiz says his first language, Acoma, became "the basis and source of all I would do later in poetry, short fiction, essay, and other work...." Born in Albuquerque, New Mexico, Ortiz earned degrees from the University of New Mexico and the University of Iowa Writers' School, going on to teach Native American literature and creative writing at several colleges and universities.

Like "My Papa's Waltz" (page 458), the speaker in Simon Ortiz's **"My Father's Song"** also recounts a single, yet very telling, memory of his father. Ortiz uses *flashback* to present events that happened prior to the time when the poem is taking place.

How would you describe the personality of your parent or guardian?

Campesino, 1976. Daniel Desiga. Collection of Alfredo Aragon.

What are some poignant, or emotional, moments from your own life that truly reflect your character and the characters of those around you? How do the actions of our role models make lasting impressions?

Refer and Reason

1. Recall what the speaker's father does when he sees the mice in the field. Analyze the father's actions. What do they tell you about the speaker's father?
2. Identify the emotion the speaker expresses in line 2. Determine whether you have a better idea of how the speaker feels about his father in "My Papa's Waltz" or in "My Father's Song." Explain your response.
3. State what the speaker wants to do in line 1. Write what you think the speaker would say if he could.

Writing Options

1. Write a five-stanza poem of your own, telling about a time when you learned an important lesson about life from a parent or guardian.
2. What do you think Ortiz's purpose was in writing this poem? Write a two-paragraph analysis of what you believe to be Ortiz's purpose, and how that purpose was made apparent to you in the poem.

Go to **www.mirrorsandwindows.com** for more.

The Funeral

A Lyric Poem by **Gordon Parks**

After many snows I was home again.
Time had whittled down to mere hills
The great mountains of my childhood.
Raging rivers I once swam trickled now
like gentle streams.
And the wide road curving on to China or
Kansas City or perhaps Calcutta,[1]
had withered to a crooked path of dust
Ending abruptly at the county burying ground.
Only the giant who was my father
remained the same.
A hundred strong men strained beneath his coffin
When they bore him to his grave. ❖

1. **Calcutta.** A city in India

Gordon Parks (1912–2006) was a photographer, poet, and screenwriter. His photography exhibition on a South Side black ghetto in Chicago in 1941 won Parks a photography fellowship with the Farm Security Administration. Parks moved on to work at *Life* magazine for twenty years. After leaving *Life,* Parks wrote novels, poetry, essays, and his autobiography; composed music, including the score and lyrics for a tribute to Martin Luther King Jr.; and directed films.

In **"The Funeral,"** the speaker eulogizes his deceased father, not by listing the man's accomplishments or qualities, but rather by using a poetic technique called *hyperbole* (an exaggeration made for effect).

Have you ever seen or attended a funeral or burial? What do you remember most?

Funeral in Zebegeny, 1928. Istvan Szonyi.

As people age, why might they begin to view the world differently? How does time change things? What, if anything, can be counted on to remain the same?

Refer and Reason

1. Indicate what line shows the speaker has not been home for some time. Analyze how things changed since the speaker was last home.
2. Quote what the speaker says about the men who carried his father's coffin. Evaluate the author's use of hyperbole, or exaggeration, to communicate his feelings about his father. Explain whether it is effective.
3. Recall what had stayed the same. Why might our ideas about people and places change over time?

Writing Options

1. Imagine you are profiling the speaker for his hometown newspaper. Using what you know and can infer about the speaker from the poem, write a character sketch that describes what he is like and in what ways he has changed since leaving home.
2. Write an essay comparing the point of view (first person vs. second person) used in "The Funeral," "My Papa's Waltz" (page 458), and "My Father's Song" (page 460) and evaluate the effectiveness of each point of view. How would each poem differ if it were written from another point of view?

 Go to **www.mirrorsandwindows.com** for more.

since feeling is first

A Lyric Poem by
E. E. Cummings

Critical Viewing

How would you describe the look on the young woman's face in this image? Is this the expression you would expect from the recipient of this poem?

Born in Cambridge, Massachusetts, and educated at Harvard University, poet **Edward Estlin (E. E.) Cummings** (1894–1962) quickly became famous for his signature style—simple and playful, yet highly unconventional. Among his favorite poetry themes were love, nature, and antiauthoritarianism. Two of his best-known publications include the novel *The Enormous Room* (1922) and the poetry collection *Tulips and Chimney* (1923).

Cummings is known for his unconventional syntax and form (an inclination illustrated by his refusal to capitalize his own name). The following poem, **"since feeling is first,"** explores the inadequacy of language to fully express the speaker's love for another. In both subject matter and form, "since feeling is first" epitomizes Cummings's distinct style.

How would you describe love or the love you feel for someone else?

since feeling is first
who pays any attention
to the syntax[1] of things
will never wholly kiss you;

wholly to be a fool
while Spring is in the world

my blood approves,
and kisses are a better fate
than wisdom
lady i swear by all flowers. Don't cry
—the best gesture of my brain is less than
your eyelids' flutter which says

we are for each other:then
laugh,leaning back in my arms
for life's not a paragraph

And death i think is no parenthesis ❖

1. **syntax.** Arrangement of language; order of words in phrases or sentences

Is it more important to act using common sense or instinct? How important is a person's "gut reaction" compared to his or her logical reasoning? When should experiencing something new take priority over caution?

Refer and Reason

1. Identify words and phrases that are related to language or writing. How does the subject of the poem relate to its form?
2. List words and phrases related to love. Critique this as a love poem. How would you feel if it were written for you?
3. Quote what the speaker says about life and death. Explain your interpretation of the last two lines of the poem.

Writing Options

1. Write a three-paragraph or four-stanza response to the speaker of this poem, as though he or she had sent the poem to you.
2. Write a two- to three-paragraph literary review that explains the meaning of the poem to a newspaper's audience. Be sure to explain the techniques the poet uses in the poem to express his ideas about love.

 Go to **www.mirrorsandwindows.com** for more.

Flowering Trees, 1912 (Bloeiende Bomen), Piet Mondrian 1872–1944, © 2008 Mondrian/Holtzman Trust c/o, HCR International, Virginia.

Patterns

A Lyric Poem by **Amy Lowell**

Amy Lowell (1874–1925) was born in Brookline, Massachusetts, into one of the state's wealthiest families, whose members had played prominent roles in public life since the American Revolution. While Amy Lowell understood the importance of being a Lowell, temperamentally she was miscast for the role assigned to her simply by gender. She wanted an independent life, which fortunately she had the money to achieve.

"Patterns," from *The Collected Poems of Amy Lowell,* presents a poetic counterpoint, the news of death against a backdrop of formulated beauty. Without preaching, the poem becomes a compelling antiwar statement. As an Imagist, Lowell sought to break from the tyranny of traditional poetic form by using free verse and clear language to express emotions and ideas; this poem portrays war as another type of devastating form.

Have you ever received unexpected bad news? How did you conduct yourself?

I walk down the garden-paths,
And all the daffodils
Are blowing, and the bright blue squills.
I walk down the patterned garden-paths
In my stiff, brocaded[1] gown.
With my powdered hair and jeweled fan,
I too am a rare
Pattern. As I wander down
The garden-paths.

My dress is richly figured,[2]
And the train[3]
Makes a pink and silver stain
On the gravel, and the thrift
Of the borders.
Just a plate of current fashion,
Tripping by in high-heeled, ribboned shoes.
Not a softness anywhere about me,
Only whalebone[4] and brocade.
And I sink on a seat in the shade
Of a lime-tree. For my passion
Wars against the stiff brocade.
The daffodils and squills
Flutter in the breeze
As they please.
And I weep;
For the lime-tree is in blossom
And one small flower had dropped upon my bosom.

And the plashing of waterdrops
In the marble fountain
Comes down the garden-paths.
The dripping never stops.
Underneath my stiffened gown
Is the softness of a woman bathing in a marble basin,[5]
A basin in the midst of hedges grown
So thick, she cannot see her lover hiding,
But she guesses he is near,
And the sliding of the water
Seems the stroking of a dear
Hand upon her.
What is Summer in a fine brocaded gown!

1. **brocaded.** Embroidered
2. **figured.** Patterned
3. **train.** The trailing fabric on a gown
4. **whalebone.** Substance used as a base for corsets
5. **basin.** Sink

I should like to see it lying in a heap upon the ground.
All the pink and silver crumpled up on the ground.

I would be the pink and silver as I ran along the paths,
And he would stumble after,
Bewildered by my laughter.
I should see the sun flashing from his sword hilt[6] and the buckles on his shoes. I would choose
To lead him in a maze along the patterned paths,
A bright and laughing maze for my heavy-booted lover.
Till he caught me in the shade,
And the buttons of his waistcoat bruised my body as he clasped me
Aching, melting, unafraid.
With the shadows of the leaves and the sundrops,
And the plopping of the waterdrops,
All about us in the open afternoon—
I am very like to swoon
With the weight of this brocade,
For the sun sifts through the shade.

Underneath the fallen blossom
In my bosom,
Is a letter I have hid.
It was brought to me this morning by a rider from the Duke.[7]
"Madam, we regret to inform you that Lord Hartwell
Died in action Thursday se'nnight."[8]
As I read it in the white, morning sunlight,
The letters squirmed like snakes.
"Any answer, Madam," said my footman.
"No," I told him.
"See that the messenger takes some refreshment.
No, no answer."
And I walked into the garden,
Up and down the patterned paths,
In my stiff, correct brocade.
The blue and yellow flowers stood up proudly in the sun,
Each one.
I stood upright too,
Held rigid to the pattern
By the stiffness of my gown.
Up and down I walked,
Up and down.

---

6. **hilt.** Handle
7. **the Duke.** John Churchill, Duke of Marlborough (1650–1722), military commander in the War of Spanish Succession (1701–1714)
8. **se'nnight.** Seven days and nights

In a month he would have been my husband.
In a month, here, underneath this lime,
We would have broke the pattern;
He for me, and I for him,
He as Colonel, I as Lady,
On this shady seat.
He had a whim
That sunlight carried blessing.
And I answered, "It shall be as you have said."
Now he is dead.

In Summer and in Winter I shall walk
Up and down
The patterned garden-paths
In my stiff, brocaded gown.
The squills and daffodils
Will give place to pillared roses, and to asters, and to snow.
I shall go
Up and down,
In my gown.
Gorgeously arrayed,
Boned and stayed.
And the softness of my body will be guarded from embrace
By each button, hook, and lace.
For the man who should loose me is dead,
Fighting with the Duke in Flanders,
In a pattern called a war.
Christ! What are patterns for? ❖

Are we expected to act a certain way when we grieve? In what situations are specific behaviors or reactions ever required or expected of people? What are the consequences of these expectations?

Refer and Reason

1. List patterns described in the poem. Use examples from the poem to illustrate how the patterns confine the speaker.
2. Identify the last "pattern" the speaker mentions. What theme is expressed in the last three lines? Assess how the rest of the poem supports this theme.
3. In the last line of the poem, what does the speaker mean by *patterns*? Distinguish between the denotative (dictionary) and connotative (emotional) meaning of the word derived from the context of the poem.

Writing Options

1. Imagine you are related to the speaker of the poem. Write a personal letter to the speaker, attempting to comfort her in her grief.
2. In a paragraph to be shared with classmates, analyze how the patterns of nature, love, and death portrayed in the poem are interconnected. Consider how the poem reflects Lowell's own sense of confinement and attitude toward war.

Go to **www.mirrorsandwindows.com** for more.

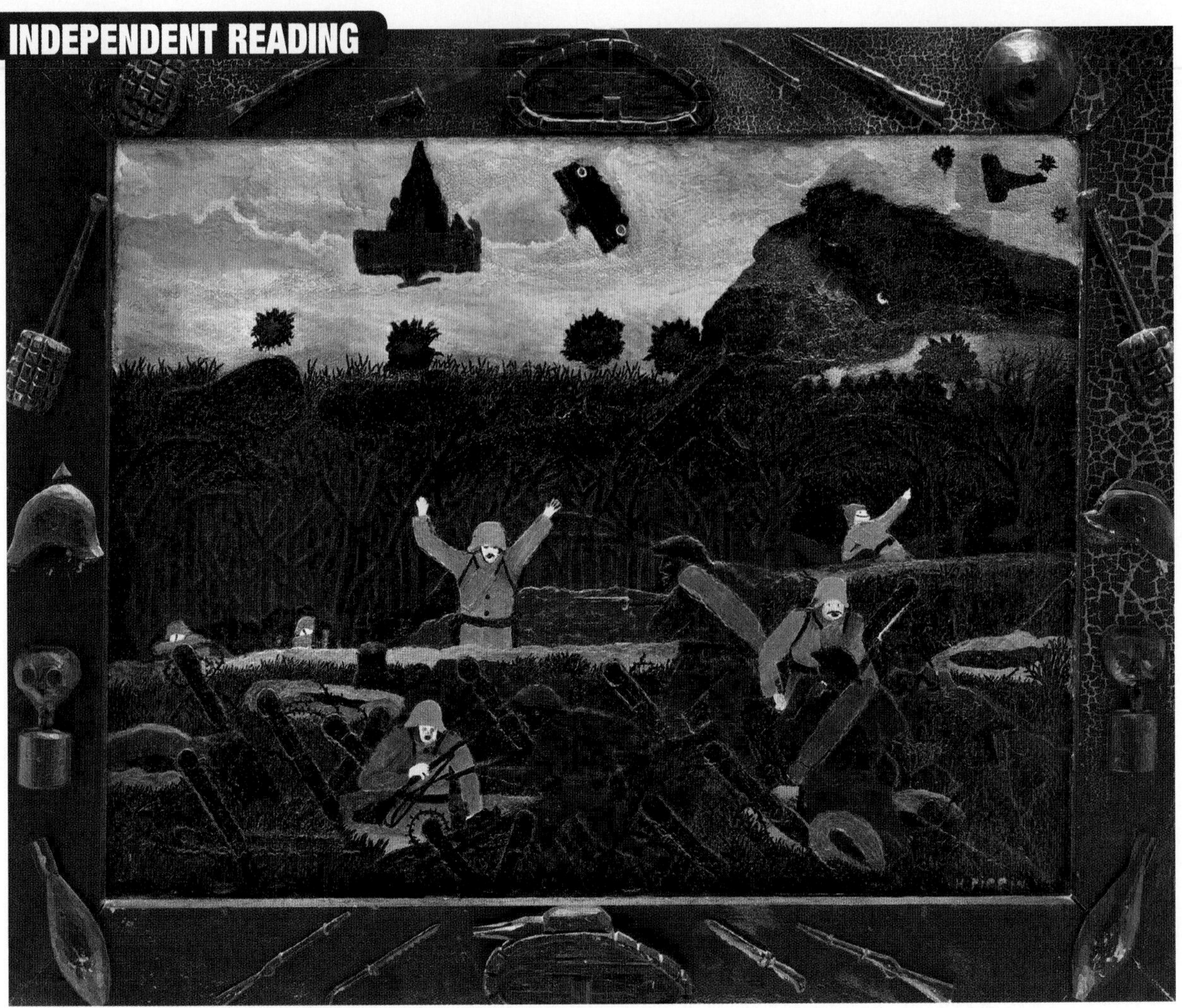

The End of the War, c. 1931. Horace Pippin. Philadelphia Museum of Art.

Anne Sexton (1928–1974) wrote in an intensely personal, "confessional" style, shining harsh light on the emotional anguish that characterized her life. She shocked readers by addressing controversial topics that "just weren't talked about" during her day. Sexton wrote about her stay in a mental institution in *To Bedlam and Part Way Back.* She was awarded a Pulitzer Prize in 1967 for her collection *Live or Die.*

In this poem, Anne Sexton looks at the little acts of courage. **"Courage"** can be seen as representing four stages in a person's life and talks about the courage one needs to face adversity and painful experiences throughout life. Sexton may be revealing some of the pain and despair she herself felt during her long struggle with depression.

What comes to mind when you think of courage? Grandiose acts of bravery? Major feats of overcoming obstacles? Everyday acts of strength?

COURAGE

A Lyric Poem by
Anne Sexton

It is in the small things we see it.
The child's first step,
as awesome as an earthquake.
The first time you rode a bike,
wallowing up the sidewalk.
The first spanking when your heart
went on a journey all alone.
When they called you crybaby
or poor or fatty or crazy
and made you into an alien,
you drank their acid
and concealed it.

Later,
if you faced the death of bombs and bullets
you did not do it with a banner,
you did it with only a hat to
cover your heart.
you did not fondle the weakness inside you
though it was there.
Your courage was a small coal
that you kept swallowing.
If your buddy saved you,
and died himself in so doing,
then his courage was not courage,
it was love; love as simple as shaving soap.

Later,
if you have endured a great despair,
then you did it alone,
getting a transfusion from the fire,
picking the scabs off your heart,
then wringing it out like a sock.
Next, my kinsman, you powdered your sorrow,
you gave it a back rub
and then you covered it with a blanket
and after it had slept a while
it woke to the wings of the roses
and was transformed.

Later,
when you face old age and its natural conclusion
your courage will still be shown in the little ways,
each spring will be a sword you'll sharpen,
those you love will live in a fever of love,
and you'll bargain with the calendar
and at the last moment
when death opens the back door
you'll put on your carpet slippers
and stride out. ❖

How does society usually define bravery? What types of courage tend to go unnoticed? Why might smaller acts of courage be the most important?

Refer and Reason

1. Quote what the speaker says about courage in lines 22–25. Do you agree with this statement? Why or why not?
2. List some of the small things the speaker identifies as courageous acts. Document a situation from your own life or an observance that Sexton might classify as courageous.
3. Identify the act of courage in the final stanza. Classify the situations in the poem into groups, such as situations that provoke fear or could cause physical harm. Write Sexton's definition of courage.

Writing Options

1. In stanza 3, Sexton personifies sorrow. If sorrow were a person, what would it look like? How would it act? Write your own personification of sorrow in a paragraph or two.
2. Choose one of the metaphors in the poem and write a brief essay for your teacher in which you analyze that metaphor. Discuss why you think Sexton chose that particular metaphor, and how it helps to express her ideas.

Go to **www.mirrorsandwindows.com** for more.

AMERICANS' FAVORITE POEMS: THE FAVORITE POEM PROJECT ANTHOLOGY

edited by Robert Pinsky and Maggie Dietz

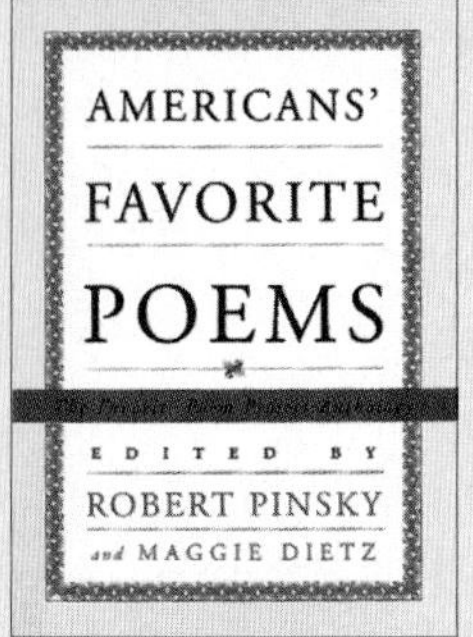

Poet laureate Robert Pinsky invited Americans to submit their favorite poems along with brief descriptions of the reasons for their choices. The thoughts of teenagers and grandparents, prisoners and artists, housewives and executives who chose the poems help to make this book not just a collection of poetry but a portrait of America as well.

VISIONS OF WAR, DREAMS OF PEACE: WRITINGS OF WOMEN IN THE VIETNAM WAR

edited by Lynda Van Devanter and Joan A. Furey

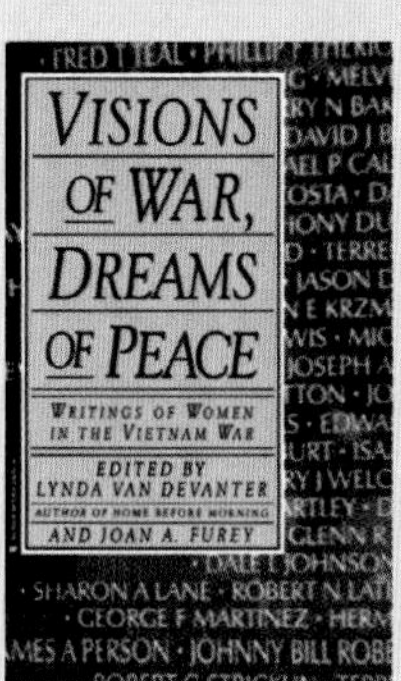

They were the U.S. nurses, entertainers, and journalists, as well as Vietnamese mothers, whose lives were forever changed by the war. All found in poetry's telegraphic format a voice for the cry of their hearts. These poems raise up timeless questions and provide insight into the experience of the forgotten women of the Vietnam War.

GOOD POEMS

selected by Garrison Keillor

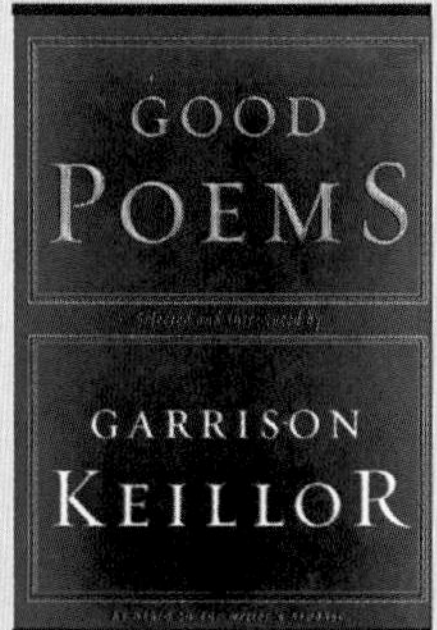

Arranged by topics such as Beasts, A Day's Work, Snow, and Yellow, they all have a narrative line, or at least a shadow of a story, which Keillor believes gives a poem "stickiness," or makes it memorable. But most importantly, says Keillor, "They give us a truer picture of life than we're used to getting."

SONG OF THE SKY: VERSIONS OF NATIVE AMERICAN SONG-POEMS

by Brian Swann and Barry O'Connell

The songs in this collection capture Native American verbal and musical art. Dating back to the seventeenth century and originally gathered by such renowned anthropologists as Frances Densmore, the song-poems have been newly worded by the editors, and some are accompanied by musical scores based on site recordings.

YOU COME TOO: FAVORITE POEMS FOR ALL AGES

by Robert Frost

Robert Frost created this collection of poems, pulling together many of the most easily read. The collection was designed for young adults and has become a great introduction to the famous poet's work. The work includes "The Death of the Hired Man," "Birches," and "Mending Wall."

19 VARIETIES OF GAZELLE: POEMS OF THE MIDDLE EAST

by Naomi Shihab Nye

Poet Naomi Shihab Nye, an Arab American, created this collection of sixty new and previously published poems after the events of September 11. The collection, which focuses on the Middle East and Arab-American experience, includes thoughts, moments, and memories of Jerusalem, Palestine, and Nye's own family.

Present a Poem

When you read a poem to others, you use your voice to bring out the special qualities of the piece. Your goal is to help the audience understand the poem and enjoy the words, sounds, or images in it. In this lesson, you will present a poem of your choice to your classmates.

1. Select a poem

Choose a poem that interests you, and that is not too short or overly long. Remember that a lyric poem is one in which a single speaker reports on his or her own emotions, and a narrative poem tells a story. Most of the poems in this unit are lyric poems.

2. Read the poem carefully

Read the poem several times. Make sure you understand it thoroughly. (See Pronunciation Tip.) To check your understanding, restate its ideas line by line in your own words.

3. Analyze the poem

In addition to its meaning, what literary elements make the poem special? Is the speaker's diction unusual? Are visual images, sound, or rhythm important? Is there a key statement or phrase? Are certain words or lines repeated? What is the mood or tone? Think about what stands out about the poem—and what you enjoy about it! Then decide how you might convey those features while you read the poem out loud.

4. Make performance notes

On a copy of the poem, make notes to guide you in performing the poem. For example, will you slow down or speed up at any point? What tone of voice will you use? Will you raise or lower your voice at times? Where might you use facial expressions for emphasis?

5. Rehearse

Read the poem aloud several times. Read first for fluency, or smoothness and clarity. Then focus on expression as you refer to your performance notes. Practice in front of a mirror, a single listener, or a video camera. Critique your presentation using the rubric provided.

6. Write an introduction

In the introduction, give the title of the poem, the name of the author, and, if appropriate, the name of the translator. If needed, add a brief comment about the author or topic to orient the audience.

7. Present the poem

By now, you should be able to look up from the poem as you read aloud. If you are feeling nervous before your presentation, take some deep, slow breaths. Then begin the poem.

Pronunciation Tip

If you come across unfamiliar or difficult words in the poem, look them up in a dictionary. Practice pronouncing the words until you can say them easily.

Speaking and Listening Rubric

Your presentation will be evaluated on these elements:

Content

- appropriate introduction
- appropriate length

Delivery and Presentation

- clear enunciation
- correct pronunciations
- effective tone, volume, pace, pitch, and stress
- appropriate facial expressions, gestures, and body movements
- good eye contact

WRITING WORKSHOP Expository Writing

Compare-and-Contrast Essay

- **Assignment**
  Compare and contrast two websites in terms of quality
- **Purpose**
  To determine the websites' quality, using a set of standards you design as the basis for your informed opinion
- **Audience**
  Your teacher, classmates, poetry lovers, and Internet users

This book includes the work of many respected poets, some of whom have written hundreds, even thousands of poems. How could you learn about a poet, read more poems, and study the poet's background? The Internet has a vast amount of research right at your fingertips. Author websites contain biographical information, critical essays, links to other works, and media features like graphics, photographs, and sound. With so many websites to choose from, how can you determine the best website for your purposes?

When you **compare and contrast** two things, you find out how they are alike and different. When you evaluate the quality of two similar websites, side by side, based on a set of criteria that you establish, you can determine which one is best for your purposes. You will also learn more about the poet.

Assignment

Choose a poet you like, one published in this book. Write an essay comparing and contrasting two author websites on the poet. Follow the three stages of the writing process: Prewrite, Draft, and Revise.

❶ PREWRITE

Writing Rubric

A successful compare-and-contrast essay has these qualities:

- ☑ includes an **introduction** naming the poet and the two websites to be examined
- ☑ includes a **thesis statement** expressing an opinion about the sites
- ☑ in the **body,** establishes standards or criteria for evaluating the websites
- ☑ strengthens an argument with evidence
- ☑ provides strong organization of information
- ☑ presents a **conclusion** that summarizes the results and restates the thesis

Select Your Topic

Consider the poets represented in this book. Select a poet whose work you enjoy. Be sure to confirm your choice with your instructor.

Gather Information

Enter your poet's name into a search engine like Yahoo or Google. (See Web Search Tip.) Choose two websites from the resulting list. Because a careful compare-and-contrast essay examines items closely, the quality differences should not be immediately obvious. Pick two websites that seem equally complete.

Next, record your observations in a chart like the one on page 475, with website choices across the top row and categories down the left column. These categories (you need at least three) are your criteria for comparing and contrasting the two websites. Use the ones provided, or establish a set of your own that serves your purpose.

Organize Your Ideas

Organization is key to a compare-and-contrast essay. There are two methods to choose from:

- **Block organization** discusses all criteria for the first website, then the next website.
- **Point-by-point organization** discusses one criterion at a time for both websites.

Website Compare-and-Contrast Chart

	Websites	
Categories:	1. Yeats Society of New York http://www.yeatssociety.org	2. Yeats Society Sligo in Ireland http://www.yeats-sligo.com
2 Content	• Info on society's programs • Yeats discography • No biographical information	• Detailed information about career, works, and influences • Several photos and drawings
1 Layout	• Small photo • Scrolling banner—green and red • Purple links • Audio file with tune	• Medium-sized photo • Blue banner at top • Small, black links
3 Links	• Extensive list of other web resources, such as sound recordings and biographies	• Links to information on visiting Sligo and Society activities • No outside web resources about Yeats

Number the categories in your table in the order you will present them in your essay. Decide whether you will use block or point-by-point organization.

Web Search Tip

Before you select your websites, consider using several search engines — for example, Lycos, AltaVista, and Yahoo! — because each one will offer slightly different results.

Write Your Thesis Statement

Your table should help you establish an opinion about the research value of each website. Write a sentence that reflects your opinion about which is better. This is your **thesis statement.** One student, Latasha Green, wrote this thesis statement in favor of one of two websites she chose about W. B. Yeats:

> Though each has its advantages, the second website, Sligo in Ireland, provided the information I needed to research Yeats.

❷ DRAFT

Write your essay by following the three-part framework described on page 476: **introduction, body,** and **conclusion.**

Draft Your Introduction

In this compare-and-contrast essay, the **introduction** should name the poet and state the two research websites and their addresses that you will compare. The introduction should also state your thesis, your opinion about which website best suits your purposes.

Read the introduction Latasha wrote during the Draft stage, shown in the first column of the chart on page 477. Her first sentence shows her appreciation for Yeats, providing a reason for her further research. The next sentence establishes the two websites she chose to compare and contrast. The last sentence, her thesis statement, states her opinion of which site is better.

- **Introduction**
  Name the poet and the two websites you will examine, including web addresses. State your thesis, your opinion of which site is better.
- **Body**
  Provide parallel information for the two websites you are comparing and contrasting. Use block or point-by-point organization.
- **Conclusion**
  Summarize your findings and re-emphasize your thesis.

Draft Your Body

In the **body,** state your detailed observations about the two websites, either criterion by criterion, or website by website. If your websites are similar, use point-by-point organization. If they are less comparable, block organization may work better. In either case, the paragraphs should parallel or mirror each other. Try to list the information in the same order in each paragraph.

Latasha used block organization to compare and contrast two websites on Yeats. She spent two paragraphs discussing each website, covering her criteria in the same order. Look at the draft of her third body paragraph, where she starts discussing the second website, in the left-hand column of the chart on page 477. Notice how she describes the website in terms of her criteria, and refers back to the first website to strengthen her comparison.

Use the method of essay organization you chose to structure your essay. Discuss the two websites and list of three criteria, using your thesis statement to focus your writing. Support your points with examples from your own observations.

Draft Your Conclusion

As in the introduction, the **conclusion** should mention both websites. Your conclusion should expand on information from the introduction and summarize the points made in the body of the essay. A good conclusion restates the thesis, provides closure, and makes readers feel they have learned something.

Does Latasha accomplish these things in her conclusion? Look at the draft of her conclusion in the chart on page 477.

What Great Writers Do

Stating complex thought in clear language, though challenging, is key to effective revision. The poet Billy Collins (b. 1941) said,

"[Poets] are writing clear, direct, amusing sometimes, poems that, even though the language might be simple, the poems still provide imaginative thrills and language pleasure."

❸ REVISE

Evaluate Your Draft

You can evaluate your own essay or exchange papers with a classmate and read each other's work. If you trade essays, review the websites your classmate used.

Focus on the essay's content, organization, and language. Make sure the essay has a solid sense of organization, covers all criteria points, and supports the thesis. Use the Revision Checklist on page 478 to guide you. You can catch mechanical errors, such as grammar and spelling, in the proofreading stage. (See the following section.)

To give positive feedback and suggest changes, use the Revision Checklist, and write your notes on the essay. Make sure content and organization are strong. One way to verify this is to refer back to your Website Compare-and-Contrast Table. The essay should be a well-developed version of your table.

Revise for Content, Organization, and Style

Latasha discovered ways to improve her first draft. Look at the chart on page 477 (right-hand column) to see how she revised the three paragraphs we studied earlier.

DRAFT STAGE		REVISE STAGE	
Introduction After I read a poem by William Butler Yeats, I searched the Internet to learn about the man and his poetry. Two websites is the W. B. Yeats Society of New York (http://www.yeatssociety.org) and the Yeats Society Sligo in Ireland (http://www.yeats-sligo.com). Though each has advantages, the second website, Sligo in Ireland, provided what I needed.	Identifies the poet and states websites to be compared Makes sure to include web addresses States thesis	When I read "Song of Wandering Aengus" by William Butler Yeats, I was struck by the poem's vivid language. Wanting more, I searched the Internet to learn about the man and his poetry. The two best websites were the W. B. Yeats Society of New York (http://www.yeatssociety.org) and the Yeats Society Sligo in Ireland (http://www.yeats-sligo.com). Though each has advantages, the second website, Sligo in Ireland, provided the information I needed to research Yeats.	Develops 1st line to add interest; uses passive voice effectively; Includes a transition Qualifies websites; makes verb agree with subject Thesis includes purpose
Body Paragraph The second site is the one from the Yeats Society in Sligo, Ireland. Like the New York society's website, it contains a photo of Yeats and information about the society's activities. Now to discuss the web design. It looks polished and professional. Unlike the New York Yeats site, the Sligo site did not offer any audio files.	Introduces next website Refers to first website Describes site in terms of criteria	The second site, the one from the Yeats Society in Sligo, Ireland, is much different. Like the New York society's website, the home page for the Irish site contains a photo of Yeats and information about the society's activities. ~~Now to discuss~~ The web design, with its blue heading, is polished and professional. However, unlike the New York Yeats site, the Sligo site does not offer any audio files.	Strengthens first line Clarifies website Combines sentences; includes descriptive evidence; adds transition Puts all verbs in present tense
Conclusion The website of the W. B. Yeats Society of New York has lots of links. The Yeats Society Sligo website contains lots of information. Now I see that both quality content and resource links are important. Both sites inspired enthusiasm for this great poet, but I preferred the Sligo website.	Brings discussion to end of story Summarizes; restates thesis	The website of the W. B. Yeats Society of New York has little information but lots of links. The Yeats Society Sligo website contains lots of information but no links for further research. ~~Now I see that~~ Examining these two websites has shown me that both quality content and resource links are important. Both sites inspire~~d~~ enthusiasm for this great poet, but, for the purposes of my research, I prefer~~red~~ the Sligo website over the New York website.	Summarizes completely using parallel information Strengthens idea Uses spelling rules correctly Strengthens ending by more fully restating thesis

- **Introduction:** By opening with a line describing a specific poem by Yeats, Latasha demonstrated passion for Yeats and generated her readers' interest.
- **Body:** In discussing the second website, Latasha strengthened her comparison by referring back to the first website. She also heightened the flow of her writing by combining sentences and adding descriptive details.
- **Conclusion:** Latasha summarized each point in a parallel order. She checked her subject-verb agreement and tense consistency. She restated her thesis, more clearly identifying her purpose in studying the websites.

REVISION CHECKLIST

Content and Organization

- ❑ Does the **introduction** include a **thesis** statement showing a preference for one website?
- ❑ Are the titles and addresses of the poet's websites to be compared clearly identified?
- ❑ What standards or criteria are used to evaluate the websites in the **body?** Are the same criteria used to judge both websites? Are the points in a parallel order?
- ❑ Is the organization strong?
- ❑ Are specific examples given about each website?
- ❑ Are the main points summarized and is the thesis restated in the **conclusion?**

Grammar and Style

- ❑ Are all **verbs** in the same **tense,** past or present? (page 398)
- ❑ Do you use active and passive voice appropriately? (page 410)
- ❑ Are words spelled correctly? (page 424)

Review the evaluation notes you or your partner made on your draft. Respond to each comment as you revise your essay.

Proofread for Errors

When you proofread, you check for remaining errors. This step is crucial. Even if your essay looks finished, to complete the assignment, print out a final draft and read the entire essay once more before turning it in. Check your essay for errors in capitalization, spelling, punctuation, and grammar. Make sure that all the subjects agree with their verbs. Use proofreader's symbols to mark any errors you find. (See Language Arts Handbook 4.1 for a list of proofreader's symbols.)

Take a look at Latasha's clean, final version on the next page. Review how she worked through the three stages of the writing process: Prewrite, Draft, and Revise.

WRITING FOLLOW-UP

Publish and Present

- Most websites value feedback from visitors. Look for a "Contact Us" button on the website you preferred. Send an e-mail to the webmaster describing why you like the site. If you wish, attach a copy of your essay. If and when you receive a return message, report your experience to your classmates.
- Ask class members to collect two or three favorite poems written by the poets they studied. Ask each student to read the poems aloud and offer some brief comments, based on his or her online research.

Reflect

- E-mail the links to the two websites you examined to a few of your classmates. Ask them to look at the websites you compared and contrasted and tell you which one they like better and why. Do they agree with your assessment? Via e-mail, discuss what set of criteria most effectively evaluates the quality of a website. How might this help you judge other Internet information you come across?

STUDENT MODEL

Travels With Yeats: A Comparison/Contrast of Two Poet Websites
by Latasha Green

When I read "Song of Wandering Aengus" by William Butler Yeats, I was struck by the poem's vivid language. Wanting more, I searched the Internet to learn about the man and his poetry. The two best websites were for the W. B. Yeats Society of New York (http://www.yeatssociety.org) and the Yeats Society Sligo in Ireland (http://www.yeats-sligo.com). Though each has its advantages, the second website, Sligo in Ireland, provided the information I needed to research Yeats.

How does the writer introduce her poet and the websites?

What is the writer's thesis statement?

The New York Yeats Society website has a clean layout, but the green banner, purple colors, and font style make it look amateurish. The homepage features a small photo of Yeats, a scrolling banner of society activities, a brief introduction, and links to other pages.

Which method of organization does the writer use?

As for the content of the New York site, most of it concerns the programs of the society, such as poetry competitions and readings. There is little information about Yeats himself, and some of the "Yeats Discography" links are broken. The site was fun to navigate, however. I found a hyperlink to a script from the television show *Seinfeld* containing a reference to Yeats, and I was able to listen to audio files of Yeats' poetry being read by various people, including Yeats himself! However, for serious research on the poet, this site does not fit the purpose.

What set of standards does the writer evaluate each website against?

The second site, the one from the Yeats Society in Sligo, Ireland, is much different. Like the New York society's website, the home page for the Irish site contains information about the society's activities. The web design, with its blue heading, is polished and professional. However, unlike the New York Yeats site, the Sligo site does not offer any audio files.

What support does the writer provide to prove each point?

The content about Yeats's life on the Sligo site is much more comprehensive. A menu links visitors to pages about Yeats's career, discussions of his literature and his influences, and quotations about his Nobel Prize. Although this website does not provide links to other web resources, overall, the site's information seemed more scholarly.

The website of the W. B. Yeats Society of New York has little information but lots of links. It does not really help people learn more about Yeats's life. The Yeats Society Sligo website contains lots of information but no links for further research. Examining these two websites has shown me that both quality content and resource links are important. Both sites inspire enthusiasm for this great poet, but, for the purposes of my research, I prefer the Sligo website over the New York website.

How does the writer rephrase her thesis statement in her conclusion?

TEST PRACTICE WORKSHOP

Reading Skills

COMPARE AND CONTRAST

Test-Taking Tip
Read the selections carefully and take notes. When you compare and contrast two separate pieces of writing, it is helpful to note the similarities you discover as you read. Underline repeated or emphasized words or phrases either directly in your text or on scratch paper.

Comparing and contrasting are closely related processes. When you **compare** one text with another, you describe similarities between the two. When you **contrast** two texts, you describe their differences. You can compare and contrast various aspects of a text, depending on its type, including subjects, main idea, organization, mood, tone, language, style, point of view, characterizations, plot development, setting, and literary techniques.

For an example of comparing and contrasting, read the following lines from the first and last stanzas, respectively, of Edgar Allan Poe's "The Bells" and think about what is the same and what is different.

Hear the <u>sledges with</u> the bells—
<u>Silver</u> bells!
What a world of <u>merriment</u> their melody <u>foretells</u>!

Hear the <u>tolling</u> of the bells
<u>Iron</u> bells!
What a world of <u>solemn thought</u> their melody <u>compels</u>!

These two stanzas are alike in many aspects. The subject matter in both is the sound of the bells. The rhyme scheme and meter are the same. Many of the same words and phrases are repeated. The differences in language have been underlined. These differences indicate a marked change in atmosphere: The first is cheery; the last is ominous.

PRACTICE

Assignment: Read the following two poems by Jane Kenyon and Donald Hall. The questions that come after the poems will ask you to compare and contrast various aspects of them.

Otherwise
by Jane Kenyon

I got out of bed
on two strong legs.
It might have been
otherwise. I ate
cereal, sweet
milk, ripe, flawless
peach. It might
have been otherwise.
I took the dog uphill
to the birch wood.
All morning I did
the work I love.

At noon I lay down
with my mate. It might
have been otherwise.
We ate dinner together
at a table with silver
candlesticks. It might
have been otherwise.
I slept in a bed
in a room with paintings
on the walls, and
planned another day
just like this day.
But one day, I know,
it will be otherwise.

The Old Life
by Donald Hall

Snow fell in the night.
At five-fifteen I woke to a bluish
mounded softness where
the Honda was. Cat fed and coffee made,
I broomed snow off the car
and drove to the Kearsarge Mini-Mart
before Amy opened
to yank my Globe out of the bundle.
Back, I set my cup of coffee
beside Jane, still half-asleep,
murmuring stuporous
thanks in the aquamarine morning.
Then I sat in my blue chair
with blueberry bagels and strong
black coffee reading news,
the obits, the comics, and the sports.
Carrying my cup twenty feet,
I sat myself at the desk
for this day's lifelong
engagement with the one task and desire.

Multiple Choice

1. Both of these poems _______.
   A. use metaphors
   B. use repetition
   C. are lyric poems
   D. are imagist poems

2. What does one of the poems have that the other one does not?
   F. sensory imagery
   G. end-of-line assonance
   H. interpretations
   J. similes

3. As it is used in line 11 of Donald Hall's poem, the term *stuporous* most nearly means
   A. idiotic.
   B. energetic.
   C. sluggish.
   D. uncommon.

4. What idea do these two poems share?
   F. Life is often dull and methodic.
   G. Be thankful for what you are able to do.
   H. The early bird gets the worm.
   J. It's better to care more for others than yourself.

5. As it is used in line 6 of Jane Kenyon's poem, the term *flawless* most nearly means
   A. flawed.
   B. consistent.
   C. unblemished.
   D. sound.

6. What reason might both poets have for including images of everyday objects and events within these two poems?
   F. to balance the underlying concern of the future
   G. to show how life is beautiful in a simple way
   H. to illustrate how tedious life can be
   J. to show how people rarely notice such objects

Constructed Response

7. Discuss similarities and differences between the subjects and main ideas of these two poems.

Writing Skills

Test-Taking Tip
Develop a thesis statement by asking yourself "What do I want people to understand when they finish reading my essay?" Your answer becomes your thesis statement.

DESCRIPTIVE WRITING

Some high-stakes tests, including one of the college entrance exams, ask you to read a quotation and write a response to the idea it expresses. In order to receive a passing score, you must write on the ideas conveyed by the quotation. Essays must be completed within a specified period of time, sometimes as little as twenty-five minutes. Descriptive writing should explain your idea in a clear way, yet use descriptive words and images. An example of descriptive writing is from Margaret Atwood's prose poem, "Bread."

> Imagine a piece of bread. You don't have to imagine it, it's right here in the kitchen, on the bread board, in its plastic bag, lying beside the bread knife. The bread knife is an old one you picked up at an auction; it has the word BREAD carved into the wooden handle. You open the bag, pull back the wrapper, cut yourself a slice. You put butter on it, then peanut butter, then honey, and you fold it over. Some of the honey runs out onto your fingers and you lick it off. It takes you about a minute to eat the bread. This bread happens to be brown, but there is also white bread, in the refrigerator, and a heel of rye you got last week, round as a full stomach then, now going mouldy. Occasionally you make bread. You think of it as something relaxing to do with your hands.

The response you express will not affect your score. What will be assessed is how well you support your ideas. Scorers will evaluate your ability to

- communicate a response and support it with examples
- organize ideas logically and progress from one idea to another smoothly
- add sensory details or imagery
- employ varied, precise, and appropriate vocabulary
- use a variety of sentence structures
- avoid errors in grammar, usage, and mechanics

PRACTICE

Timed Writing: 30 minutes

Read the following quotation from Oscar Wilde, and then consider the assignment. Allow 30 minutes to write your response to the prompt.

> "Mere color, unspoiled by meaning, and unallied with definite form, can speak to the soul in a thousand different ways."

Assignment: Do you agree that color can affect your mood or express certain properties or emotions? Write an essay in which you support your response by discussing one or more examples from your personal experience, your observations, your reading, or your knowledge of popular culture, the arts, science and technology, or current events.

Revising and Editing Skills

Some standardized tests ask you to read a draft of a text and answer questions about how to improve it. As you read the draft, think about the corrections and improvements you would make to the text. Then read each question, and consider each answer to determine which one is best.

Revising and Editing Tips

To answer the questions that accompany the draft passage, note what sentences need to be corrected and think about how the sentences relate to one another and to the passage as a whole. Follow these steps to answer the questions.

- Read the entire passage quickly to determine its overall meaning.
- Keep in mind that the passage is intended as a draft—pay attention to errors that you notice as you read.
- In answering each question, make sure that your answer about a particular sentence or group of sentences makes sense in the context of the passage as a whole.
- Choose the best answer from the choices given, even if you can think of another correct response.

PRACTICE

Zoe wrote the following draft paragraph as part of a response to the writing prompt on page 482. Imagine that you were Zoe and that you had time to review this rough draft and improve it. Read the draft and answer the questions that follow.

(1) The dinner table looks cheerful and inviting. (2) <u>There are</u> bright blue plates on yellow placemats, brightening up this dreary day <u>a lot.</u> (3) March where I live is always dreary. (4) In the center of the <u>table, a bunch of red tulips give hope to my family and me.</u> (5) Spring will soon be here. (6) The dinner table makes me feel like a little kid again. (7) <u>Life is very simple when your four years old.</u> (8) You have only red and blue and yellow. (9) Soon it gets messy and complicated with all kinds of choices.

1. What change, if any, should you make to sentence 2?
   A. Make no change.
   B. Change *are* to *is.*
   C. Change *a lot* to *alot.*
   D. Change *There are* to *They're.*

2. Where should you start a new paragraph?
   F. before sentence 3
   G. before sentence 5
   H. before sentence 6
   J. before sentence 7

3. What change, if any, should you make to sentence 4?
   A. Make no change.
   B. Change *give* to *gives.*
   C. Change *me* to *I.*
   D. Delete the comma.

4. What change, if any, should you make to sentence 7?
   F. Make no change.
   G. Change *your* to *you're.*
   H. Change *four years old* to *four-years-old.*
   J. Delete *very.*

UNIT 4

Drama

SHAKESPEARE

BANDELLO

"Drama is immensely durable; after a thousand critical disputes, it is still there, undiminished, ready for the next wranglers."

—Robertson Davies

No two performances are exactly the same; you could see the same play performed a dozen times and encounter as many different variations. Actors and directors can represent the play in a multitude of different ways, allowing this literature form to adapt to each new generation. As you read the following selections, note variations on themes, wordplay and, most of all, connections the play strikes with your own experience.

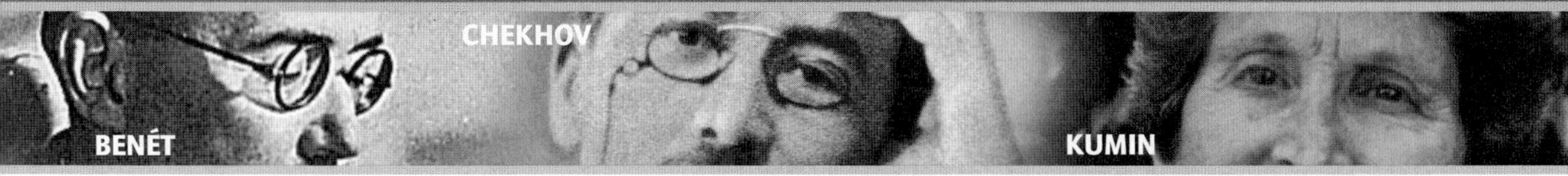

INTRODUCTION TO DRAMA

"All the world's a stage,
And all the men and women merely players..."

—William Shakespeare, from *As You Like It*

No one knows for certain how drama originated, but we do know that ritual performances have been held by people around the globe since long before the beginning of recorded history. The first dramas were created long ago in ancient Greece and may have developed from reenactments of ritual sacrifices. In fact, the ancient Greek word *tragôdia,* from which our word *tragedy* derives, meant "song of the goats." Whether you read a humorous one-act play such as *The Inspector-General,* or the five-act tragedy *Romeo and Juliet* by William Shakespeare, you will find yourself immersed in the genre of drama.

THE GENRE OF DRAMA

A **drama** is a story told through characters played by actors. That makes a drama, or play, different from other types of literature. Drama is meant to be spoken, acted out, given movement. When you read the script of a play, try to visualize the actions as they might unfold on a stage or a movie screen. Use the playwright's stage directions and notes to help you imagine a live production of the play.

Most dramas can be classified as either comedy or tragedy:

- A **comedy,** in its original sense, was an entertainment with a happy ending. Today, the term is widely used to refer to any lighthearted or humorous literary work, especially one prepared for the stage or the screen.
- A **tragedy** was originally a drama that told the story of the fall of a person of high status. In more recent times, the word *tragedy* has been used both to describe a play about the downfall of a sympathetic character, or protagonist, and a story with an unhappy ending.

ELEMENTS OF DRAMA

Like the author of a work of fiction, the playwright must combine a number of elements to successfully craft a drama. Those elements compose the **script,** or written form of the play.

Structure

In creating a drama, the playwright organizes the story into acts and scenes:

- An **act** is a major division of a play. Most plays written in Shakespeare's time, including *The Tragedy of Romeo and Juliet* (page 504), have five acts. Today, three-act and one-act plays are common. *The Devil and Daniel Webster* by Stephen Vincent Benét (page 628) is a one-act play.

- Acts are often divided into **scenes,** shorter sections that usually mark changes of time and place.

Characters

We get to know a dramatic character largely through his or her actions and speech. As you read, look for clues to a character's motivations and emotional state. Consider how one character plays off of another. The characters in drama, as in prose fiction, can be classified as protagonists or antagonists, flat or round, and major or minor. (See page 68 for more information on these types of characters.)

In drama, particularly classic drama, there are certain character creations that are quite common. These character types were fairly standard in ancient Greek dramas and in Shakespearean drama and may sometimes appear in modern plays.

In tragedies, such as Shakespeare's *Romeo and Juliet,* the main character (or characters, in this case) is frequently a **tragic hero.** Such heroes have a **tragic flaw,** or a weakness of personality, that causes them to make unfortunate choices. They are thus doomed to a tragic end. Early on in *Romeo and Juliet,* it is possible to see the lovers' tragic flaws.

A **foil** is a character who contrasts with a central character in order to highlight each other's strengths and, more usually, weaknesses.

To relieve the seriousness or emotional intensity of tragedy, playwrights often introduce a humorous character for **comic relief.** The flustered Nurse in *Romeo and Juliet* provides the comic relief with her rambling speech about raising Juliet. The Nurse also serves as a counterpoint to Friar Lawrence: Both adults aid and advise the teenage lovers, though neither truly succeeds.

Analyzing Characters Keeping a Character Chart can help you remember the key figures in a drama. In a notebook, write down the names of the important characters. Note only characters with significant appearances in the play. Next, write down a brief description of what each character says or does in a scene. Limit each description to three sentences. Add your own comments about a character, such as "funny" or "arrogant," in the designated column. When you are finished, go back over your notes to see if there are similarities or striking differences among the characters. Identify the protagonists, antagonists, flat characters, round characters, comic relief, foils (if there are any), and tragic heroes.

Character Chart

Character	Scene	What Character Says	What Character Does	Comments
Romeo	Act I, Scene i	"O, teach me how I should forget to think."	tells Benvolio about the object of his desire	obsessed with his new love

Famous Characters from Plays

- Hamlet, from *Hamlet* by William Shakespeare
- Eliza Doolittle, from *Pygmalion* by George Bernard Shaw
- Willy Loman, from *Death of a Salesman* by Arthur Miller
- Peter Pan, from *Peter Pan* by J. M. Barrie
- Blanche DuBois, from *A Streetcar Named Desire* by Tennessee Williams

Mel Gibson as Hamlet.

Dramatic Speech

Unlike a written story where all the necessary descriptions and thoughts are there for you to read, drama relies primarily on the speech of the characters to tell the story. One of the elements that makes a drama memorable is the **dialogue,** the words spoken by the actors. Badly written dialogue can make a movie or play seem silly or forced; good dialogue will impress the audience with its eloquence or emotional power.

In most cases, dialogue refers to what the actors (or characters) say aloud to one another. Sometimes, however, characters speak to themselves or to the audience directly. These are the main types of dramatic speech in a play, all of which are found in *The Tragedy of Romeo and Juliet:*

- A **dialogue** is a conversation between two or more characters. This example is from Act I, Scene i, where Romeo complains about his relationship with Rosaline:

> ROMEO. Ay me, sad hours seem long.
> Was that my father that went hence so fast?
> BENVOLIO. It was. What sadness lengthens Romeo's hours?
> ROMEO. Not having that which, having, makes them short.
> BENVOLIO. In love?
> ROMEO. Out—
> BENVOLIO. Of love?
> ROMEO. Out of her favor where I am in love.

- A **monologue** is a long speech made by one character. This example is from Act I, Scene ii, where Lord Capulet tells Paris how best to approach his daughter:

> CAPULET. And too soon marr'd are those so early made.
> Earth hath swallowed all my hopes but she;
> She's the hopeful lady of my earth.
> But woo her, gentle Paris, get her heart,
> My will to her consent is but a part;
> And she agreed, within her scope of choice
> Lies my consent and fair according voice.
> This night I hold an old accustom'd feast,
> Whereto I have invited many a guest,
> Such as I love, and you, among the store
> One more, most welcome, makes my number more. [...]

- A **soliloquy** is a speech delivered by a character alone on stage that reveals the character's thoughts and feelings. Here, Friar Lawrence is talking alone about natural remedies in Act II, Scene iii:

> FRIAR LAWRENCE. The grey-ey'd morn smiles on the frowning night,
> Check'ring the eastern clouds with streaks of light,
> And fleckled darkness like a drunkard reels
> From forth day's path and Titan's fiery wheels.
> Now ere the sun advance his burning eye,
> The day to cheer and night's dank dew to dry,
> I must up-fill this osier cage of ours
> With baleful weeds and precious-juiced flowers.
> The earth that's nature's mother is her tomb;
> What is her burying grave, that is her womb;
> And from her womb children of divers kind
> We sucking on her natural bosom find:
> Many for many virtues excellent,
> None but for some, and yet all different.
> [...]

- An **aside** is a statement made by a character in a play that's intended to be heard by the audience but not by other characters on the stage. In this moment in Act II, Scene ii, Romeo makes an aside to the audience as he listens to Juliet speaking on the balcony:

> JULIET. O Romeo, Romeo wherefore art thou Romeo?
> Deny thy father and refuse thy name;
> Or, if thou wilt not, be but sworn my love,
> And I'll no longer be a Capulet.
> ROMEO. [*Aside.*] Shall I hear more, or shall I speak at this?

Stage Directions

Stage directions are the notes provided by the playwright to describe how the play should be presented or performed. They are usually printed in italics and may be enclosed in brackets or parentheses. Stage directions may describe these aspects of the drama:

- The **setting,** or when and where a scene takes place, as well as any related background information

- The **action,** or how the actors should move and behave, including when they should enter and exit the stage and how they should employ facial expressions, gestures, and tones of voice
- The **special effects,** such as the lighting, music, sound effects, costumes, properties (called *props*), and set design

EXAMPLES

(Stage directions from Romeo and Juliet)
Enter TYBALT, PETRUCHIO, *and others.*
They fight.
Exit PAGE.
Exeunt MERCUTIO and BENVOLIO.

In stage directions, the parts of the stage are often described using the terms *up, down, right, left,* and *center,* which designate stage areas from the point of view of the actors. (See the Parts of the Stage Diagram below.)

Parts of the Stage Diagram

Up Right	Up Center	Up Left
Right Center	Center	Left Center
Down Right	Down Center	Down Left

The playwright who wants a scene to achieve a particular visual effect will often include stage directions that describe the setting, lighting, and costumes to be used in the performance. These directions not only can help the wardrobe coordinator and set designer, but can also assist a reader in visualizing the play. The following stage directions are from Anton Chekhov's *The Inspector-General.*

> The curtain goes up to reveal falling snow and a cart facing away from us. Enter the Storyteller, who begins to read the story. Meanwhile, the Traveler enters. He is a middle-aged man of urban appearance, wearing dark glasses and a long overcoat with its collar turned up. He is carrying a small traveling bag. He climbs into the cart and sits facing us.
>
> —from *The Inspector-General*
> by Anton Chekhov

Another type of stage direction gives the reader and actor an indication of how the line should be delivered. Unlike fiction, which can describe an emotional state at great length or develop a character so that the reader understands the nuances of speech, live drama must rely on the way each actor interprets emotion. To make sure the appropriate tone of the play is achieved, the playwright will add directions regarding the delivery of the lines. Below is an example of directions within the lines of Stephen Vincent Benét's *The Devil and Daniel Webster.*

> THE OLD MAN (*starting to whisper*). Let me tell you something—
> THE OLD WOMAN (*quickly*). Henry, Henry, don't you start to gossip. (*She drags him away.*)
>
> —from *The Devil and Daniel Webster*
> by Stephen Vincent Benét

Famous Plays Made Into Movies

- *The Tragedy of Romeo and Juliet,* by William Shakespeare
- *Pygmalion,* by George Bernard Shaw (Movie title: *My Fair Lady*)
- *Peter Pan,* by J. M. Barrie
- *The Miracle Worker,* by William Gibson
- *Death of a Salesman,* by Arthur Miller
- *Cyrano de Bergerac,* by Edmond Rostand (Movie title: *Roxanne*)
- *A Streetcar Named Desire,* by Tennessee Williams

DRAMA READING MODEL

BEFORE READING | DURING READING | AFTER READING

BUILD BACKGROUND

- **Connect** your own knowledge and experiences to what you read. Even though a drama may be set in a different time or place, some themes or character types may seem familiar.
- Read the information in the **Build Background** and **Meet the Author** sections. Have you read any other stories or plays by this playwright?

ANALYZE LITERATURE

- The **Analyze Literature** feature will focus on one or more literary techniques used in the selection. As you read, note how the playwright uses these elements.

SET PURPOSE

- **Set a purpose** for reading. A purpose for reading drama could be reading to discover how the writer sets up each scene of the play.
- **Preview** the text. Skim the stage directions and see how many characters are in the play. Can you guess what sort of action this play might involve?

USE READING SKILLS

- **Apply reading skills,** such as finding the theme or main idea, determining the sequence of events, identifying the author's purpose, and drawing conclusions.

BEFORE READING | DURING READING | AFTER READING

USE READING STRATEGIES

- **Make inferences,** or guesses, about the personalities or motivations of the characters based on their actions and the stage directions.
- **Visualize** the scenes and characters. Dramas are meant to be performed, so try to picture the stage in your mind and the characters as they speak.
- **Make predictions** about what will happen next. For example, what obstacles will the characters encounter?
- **Clarify** your understanding of the play by reading it aloud and paying attention to the stage directions that explain how the lines are delivered and the actions the characters take.

ANALYZE LITERATURE

- Consider the literary devices that appear within each selection and how the author utilizes them. How would the selection change without the use of these devices?

MAKE CONNECTIONS

- When a play is set in the past, consider what you know about that time period, including the overall social climate.

BEFORE READING | DURING READING | AFTER READING

REFER TO TEXT

- **Determine cause-and-effect** relationships between events in the drama.
- **Summarize** the story in two or three sentences.
- **Recall details** that may be significant to the story.

REASON WITH TEXT

- **Apply** your understanding of the elements of drama to see if they help you answer any questions.
- **Analyze** the play by breaking down information into smaller units, such as stage directions or the roles of the characters, and figuring out how each piece fits into the story as a whole.
- **Evaluate** the drama. Do you think the playwright was successful in creating a script that conveys a worthwhile story?

ANALYZE LITERATURE

- **Review** how the author uses literary elements in the play.

EXTEND THE TEXT

- **Expand** your reading beyond the page by exploring ideas through acting, designing costumes, or tackling other creative projects.

The Inspector-General

A One-Act Play by Anton Chekhov
Adapted by Michael Frayn

BEFORE READING

BUILD BACKGROUND

Historical Context Prior to the 1917 Communist Revolution in Russia, the country was ruled by a czar, similar to an emperor. As Russia was the largest country in the world, the czar couldn't rule effectively without the help of inspectors-general. They reported to him about conditions in various towns. These inspectors-general, however, were not well received by the populace.

In ***The Inspector-General,*** the newly appointed official travels in disguise to a town he's to inspect. This play is a version of the age-old stories in which a god or a king disguises himself as a common person, hoping to hear first-hand what his subjects think about him.

Reader's Context What do you consider to have been your most embarrassing moment? How did you handle the embarrassment?

ANALYZE LITERATURE: Irony

Irony is the difference between appearance and reality. *Dramatic irony* occurs when something is known by the reader or audience but is unknown to the characters. **Irony of situation** is when an event occurs that violates the expectations of the characters, and **verbal irony** occurs when a character says one thing but means another. *The Inspector-General* contains examples of irony that add to the humorous nature of the play.

SET PURPOSE

As you read the play, keep track of your impressions of the Traveler. Pay attention to how the Storyteller sets up the dramatic irony and how the dialogue between the Traveler and the Driver heightens the irony.

MEET THE AUTHOR

Playwright and short-story writer **Anton Chekhov** (1860–1904) was born in Taganrog, Russia, to a struggling grocer and his wife. The Chekhovs moved to Moscow in 1884, where Anton worked as a doctor and a writer to help support his family. After a long and difficult journey across Siberia in 1890, complications of tuberculosis caused Chekhov to move to the coastal resort of Yalta, where he wrote many dramas. In 1901, he married a famous Russian actress named Olga Knipper. He died of tuberculosis three years later. Michael Frayn (b. 1933) translated and adapted the short play *The Inspector-General* from Chekhov's *An Awl in a Sack,* a short novel published in 1885.

USE READING SKILLS

Summarize The ability to **summarize** a selection, or restate its main ideas or events in your own words, is an important reading skill. As you read "The Inspector-General," use a graphic organizer to summarize each part of the selection.

The Storyteller introduces the Traveler, who is really the Inspector-General in disguise.

PREVIEW VOCABULARY

Read the sentences below and identify the restatement clues of the underlined words in the sentences:

1. The bag of toys for the orphanage was from an <u>anonymous</u> donor. We had no clue about the identity of the kind gift-giver.
2. The farmers finished loading the wagon as it began to <u>trundle</u> toward the road. It rolled away slowly over the field so as not to spill the vegetables piled inside.
3. Vera <u>discreetly</u> removed the toilet paper from her shoe so that she wouldn't draw attention to herself.
4. The <u>cunning</u> cat showed its skill in deception by letting the mouse think it was asleep.

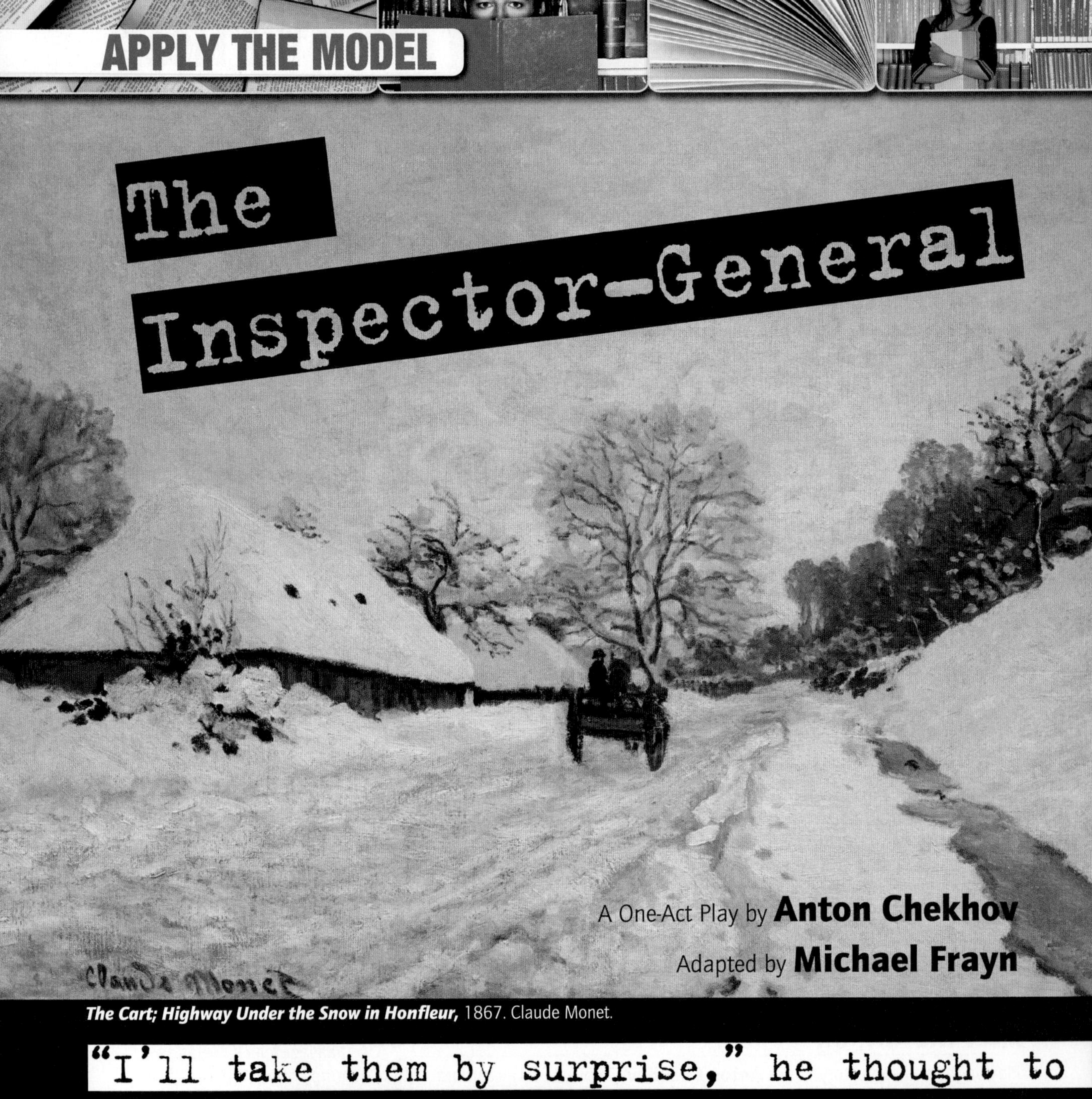

The Inspector-General

A One-Act Play by **Anton Chekhov**

Adapted by **Michael Frayn**

The Cart; Highway Under the Snow in Honfleur, 1867. Claude Monet.

"I'll take them by surprise," he thought to himself.

The curtain goes up to reveal falling snow and a cart facing away from us. Enter the STORYTELLER, *who begins to read the story. Meanwhile, the* TRAVELER *enters. He is a middle-aged man of urban appearance, wearing dark glasses and a long overcoat with its collar turned up. He is carrying a small traveling bag. He climbs into the cart and sits facing us.*

Storyteller. The Inspector-General. In deepest incognito,[1] first by express train, then along back roads, Pyotr Pavlovich Posudin was hastening toward the little town of N, to which he had been summoned by an anonymous letter. "I'll take them by surprise," he thought to himself. "I'll come down on them like a thunderbolt out of the blue. I can just imagine their faces when they hear who I am..." [*Enter the* Driver, *a peasant, who climbs onto the cart, so that he is sitting with his back to us, and the cart begins to trundle slowly away from us.*] And when he'd thought to himself for long enough, he fell into conversation with the driver of the cart. What did he talk about? About himself, of course. [*Exit the* Storyteller.]

Traveler. I gather you've got a new Inspector-General in these parts.

Driver. True enough.

Traveler. Know anything about him? [*The* Driver *turns and looks at the* Traveler, *who turns his coat collar up a little higher.*]

Driver. Know anything about him? Of course we do! We know everything about all of them up there! Every last little clerk—we know the color of his hair and the size of his boots! [*He turns back to the front, and the* Traveler *permits himself a slight smile.*]

Traveler. So, what do you reckon? Any good, is he? [*The* Driver *turns around.*]

Driver. Oh, yes, he's a good one, this one.

Traveler. Really?

Driver. Did one good thing straight off.

Traveler. What was that?

Driver. He got rid of the last one. Holy terror he was! Hear him coming five miles off! Say he's going to this little town. Somewhere like we're going, say. He'd let all the world know about it a month before. So now he's on his way, say, and it's like thunder and lightning coming down the road. And when he gets where he's going he has a good sleep, he has a good eat and drink—and then he starts. Stamps his feet, shouts his head off. Then he has another good sleep, and off he goes.

DURING READING

USE READING STRATEGIES

Make Predictions After reading the Inspector-General's plans, what do you think will happen?

DURING READING

ANALYZE LITERATURE

Irony How does the Storyteller set up the irony?

a • non • y • mous (ä nän´ ə məs) *adj.*, unknown; not identified

trun • dle (trun´ dl') *v.*, to move or roll slowly

DURING READING

USE READING STRATEGIES

Make Inferences What can you infer about the Traveler from the fact that he "permits himself a slight smile"?

DURING READING

USE READING SKILLS

Summarize How might you summarize the beginning of this one-act play?

1. **incognito.** In disguise

Traveler. But the new one's not like that?

Driver. Oh, no, the new one goes everywhere on the quiet, like. Creeps around like a cat. Don't want no one to see him, don't want no one to know who he is. Say he's going to this town down the road here. Someone there sent him a letter on the sly, let's say. "Things going on here you should know about." Something of that kind. Well, now, he creeps out of his office, so none of them up there see him go. He hops on a train just like anyone else, just like you or me. Then when he gets off he don't go jumping into a cab or nothing fancy. Oh, no. He wraps himself up from head to toe so you can't see his face, and he wheezes away like an old dog so no one can recognize his voice.

DURING READING

ANALYZE LITERATURE

Irony What is ironic about the Driver's description of the new Inspector-General?

Traveler. Wheezes? That's not wheezing! That's the way he talks! So I gather.

Driver. Oh, is it? But the tales they tell about him. You'd laugh till you burst your tripes![2]

Traveler. [*Sourly.*] I'm sure I would.

Driver. He drinks, mind!

Traveler. [*Startled.*] Drinks?

Driver. Oh, like a hole in the ground. Famous for it.

Traveler. He's never touched a drop! I mean, from what I've heard.

Driver. Oh, not in public, no. Goes to some great ball—"No thank you, not for me." Oh, no, he puts it away at home! Wakes up in the morning, rubs his eyes, and the first thing he does, he shouts, "Vodka!" So in runs his valet[3] with a glass. Fixed himself up a tube behind his desk, he has. Leans down, takes a pull on it, no one the wiser.

Traveler. [*Offended.*] How do you know all this, may I ask?

Driver. Can't hide it from the servants, can you? The valet and the coachman have got tongues in their heads. Then again, he's on the road, say, going about his business, and he keeps the bottle in his little bag. [*The* Traveler *discreetly pushes the traveling bag out of the* Driver's *sight.*] And his housekeeper…

Traveler. What about her?

DURING READING

USE READING STRATEGIES

Visualize Based on the stage directions, visualize the Traveler's actions. Imagine the facial expressions of the characters.

dis • creet • ly (di skrēt´ lē) *adv.*, with care not to be noticed

2. **tripes.** Stomach parts of a cow or a sheep that are eaten
3. **valet.** A male servant

DRIVER. Runs circles around him, she does, like a fox round his tail. She's the one who wears the trousers. The people aren't half so frightened of him as they are of her.

TRAVELER. But at least he's good at his job, you say?

DRIVER. Oh, he's a blessing from heaven, I'll grant him that.

TRAVELER. Very cunning—you were saying.

cun • ning (kun´ niŋ) *adj.,* clever; sly

DRIVER. Oh, he creeps around all right.

TRAVELER. And then he pounces, yes? I should think some people must get the surprise of their life, mustn't they?

"Then again, he's on the road, say, going about his business, and he keeps the bottle in his little bag."

Driver. No, no—let's be fair, now. Give him his due. He don't make no trouble.

Traveler. No, I mean, if no one knows he's coming…

Driver. Oh, that's what he thinks, but we all know.

Traveler. You know?

Driver. Oh, some gentleman gets off the train at the station back there with his greatcoat up to his eyebrows and says, "No, I don't want a cab, thank you, just an ordinary horse and cart for me." Well, we'd put two and two together, wouldn't we! Say it was you, now, creeping along down the road here. The lads would be down there in a cab by now! By the time you got there the whole town would be as regular as clockwork! And you'd think to yourself, "Oh, look at that! As clean as a whistle! And they didn't know I was coming!" No, that's why he's such a blessing after the other one. This one believes it!

> DURING READING
>
> **ANALYZE LITERATURE**
>
> **Irony** What is ironic about the Driver's explanation of why the town's citizens know when the new Inspector-General is coming?

Traveler. Oh, I see.

Driver. What, you thought we wouldn't know him? Why, we've got the electric telegraph these days! Take today, now. I'm going past the station back there this morning, and the fellow who runs the buffet comes out like a bolt of lightning. Arms full of baskets and bottles. "Where are you off to?" I say. "Doing drinks and refreshments for the Inspector-General!" he says, and he jumps into a carriage and goes flying off down the road here. So there's the old Inspector-General, all muffled up like a roll of carpet, going secretly along in a cart somewhere—and when he gets there, nothing to be seen but vodka and cold salmon!

> DURING READING
>
> **USE READING STRATEGIES**
>
> **Clarify** Ask yourself what the significance is in the Traveler's decision to turn around. What does his decision reveal?

Traveler. [*Shouts.*] Right—turn around, then…!

Driver. [*To the horse.*] Whoa, boy! Whoa! [*To the* Traveler.] Oh, so what's this, then? Don't want to go running into the Inspector-General, is that it? [*The* Traveler *gestures impatiently for the* Driver *to turn the cart around.*]

[Driver *to the horse.*] Back we go, then, boy. Home we go. [*He turns the cart around, and the* Traveler *takes a swig from his traveling bag.*] Though if I know the old devil, he's like as not turned around and gone home again himself. [*Blackout.*] ❖

What type of criticism is the most difficult to accept? What does it mean to be "brutally honest," and why might this action be offensive to other people?

APPLY THE MODEL

AFTER READING

REFER TO TEXT ▶ ▶ ▶ ▶	▶ REASON WITH TEXT	
1a. Why is the Inspector-General going to the town of N? How was he summoned?	1b. Describe what the problem was with the former Inspector-General. How does the new Inspector-General differ?	Understand **Find meaning**
2a. Indicate how it is known that the Inspector-General drinks too much in private.	2b. Knowing what you do about the Traveler's purpose, why is this information significant?	Apply **Use information**
3a. Who started the conversation about the Inspector-General? How does the Traveler react to the Driver's conversation?	3b. Infer what type of personality the Traveler would have were he not in disguise. How can you tell?	Analyze **Take things apart**
4a. Repeat why the Driver considers the new Inspector-General to be "such a blessing."	4b. How does the use of sarcasm add to the humor in this play? Decide if you think the sarcasm is effective. Why or why not?	Evaluate **Make judgments**
5a. How does the Traveler attempt to keep his identity hidden? What, according to the Driver, would give him away?	5b. Do you think the Driver realizes the identity of his passenger? Why or why not? Create an alternate ending in which the Traveler continues to the town of N.	Create **Bring ideas together**

ANALYZE LITERATURE: Irony

This play is a dramatic comedy, a humorous and light literary work prepared for the stage or the screen. How does the author's use of irony help to create the comedy? What is ironic about the last line of the play? How is this situation a paradox (a statement or situation that contradicts itself)?

EXTEND THE TEXT

Writing Options

Creative Writing Stories have been around for centuries about powerful or famous people who hide their identities in order to find out what ordinary people think—usually with negative results. Select a famous person to include in your own tale of this nature. Consider how to add irony as Chekhov did in his play. In a one-page **plot outline,** describe the plot and briefly explain the main interactions of your character with the people he or she encounters.

Descriptive Writing Write a one- to two-page **detailed summary** of *The Inspector-General* to be included in a collection of play descriptions for youth. In addition to describing what happens in the play, comment on the characters, tone, use of irony, elements of comedy, and stage directions.

Critical Literacy

Analyze Author's Approach With a partner or small group, research the duties of the inspectors-generals of imperial Russia and analyze the author's approach to the subject. What criticism might Chekhov have been expressing in this play? Present your findings and analysis as a panel discussion.

Lifelong Learning

Research Author's Life The name "Chekhov" is more commonly associated with serious dramas than with comedic farces like *The Inspector-General.* Research Chekhov's life to find his influences and inspirations. Propose a theory about the elements of his life that are expressed in his writing. Write your findings in a brief essay for your school's literary magazine.

Go to **www.mirrorsandwindows.com** for more.

Understanding Shakespeare

SHAKESPEARE'S LIFE AND TIMES

William Shakespeare (1564–1616) is widely considered the greatest dramatist the world has known. Despite this, little is known about his personal life. We do know that he was born around April 23, 1564, in Stratford, a small English village on the banks of the river Avon. His mother, Mary Arden Shakespeare, was from a well-to-do, well-connected family, and his father, John Shakespeare, was a prosperous glove maker and local politician. As a boy, Shakespeare likely attended the local grammar school, studying classical literature in Latin and Greek, as was typical for that era. At the age of eighteen, he married Anne Hathaway, eight years his senior. The couple's first child, Susanna, was born soon after, followed in 1585 by twins, Hamnet and Judith.

By 1592, Shakespeare had moved to London, leaving his family behind while he pursued a career as an actor and a playwright. His history plays *Henry the Sixth* and *The Tragedy of Richard the Third* were produced to great success and established him as a significant force in London theater. In 1594, the year ***The Tragedy of Romeo and Juliet*** had its debut onstage, Shakespeare became a partner in a theater company known as the Lord Chamberlain's Men. The acting troupe soon became the most popular in London and performed regularly at the court of Queen Elizabeth I. The company was wealthy enough by 1599 to build its own playhouse, the Globe Theatre. When Queen Elizabeth died in 1603, Shakespeare's company found a new patron in her successor, King James I, and changed its name to the King's Men.

Shakespeare's birthplace, located in the small English village of Stratford.

Although Shakespeare continued to act in the troupe, writing its material became his primary vocation. In the span of twenty years, he penned at least thirty-seven plays, including comedies such as *A Midsummer Night's Dream* and *Twelfth Night;* tragedies such as *Romeo and Juliet, Hamlet, Julius Caesar, King Lear, Othello,* and *Macbeth;* romances such as *The Tempest* and *The Winter's Tale;* and histories such as *The Life of Henry the Fifth* and *The Life of King Henry the Eighth.* Today, nearly four hundred years after his death, his plays are still performed for audiences all over the world. As fellow poet Ben Jonson famously said, Shakespeare's art is "not of an age, but for all time."

When he died at age fifty-two, survived by his wife and his two daughters, Shakespeare was a wealthy man. He was buried in Holy Trinity Church in Stratford-upon-Avon. Carved in stone above his grave are the following lines, believed to have been written by Shakespeare himself:

> Good frend for Jesus sake forbeare,
> To digg the dust encloased heare:
> Blest be ye man yt spares thes stones,
> And curst be he yt moves my bones.

Theater in Shakespeare's Day

In Shakespeare's England, the theater was not well respected as it is today. In fact, it was considered a somewhat vulgar and rowdy place, a place where disease and low morals were spread. Theaters were often located on the outskirts of the city and were routinely shut down because of outbreaks of the plague. City officials also sometimes arrested actors as vagabonds or shut down theaters because they objected to the content of the plays. Only by earning the support of a wealthy patron could a theater troupe survive.

Luckily for Shakespeare, Queen Elizabeth I was a great patron of the theater and all the arts. During her reign, from 1558 to 1603—a period known as the **Elizabethan Age**—English literature reached what many people consider its zenith, and theater was allowed to flourish. Shakespeare wrote and produced his plays at the height of the Elizabethan period and during the early half of the **Jacobean period,** which lasted from 1603 to 1625, when King James I ruled England. Shakespeare's acting troupe enjoyed sponsorship from both Queen Elizabeth and King James.

Queen Elizabeth I.

The Theatre and the Globe

The first permanent theater in England, called simply the Theatre [British spelling] was built by James Burbage in 1576 outside the city walls of London. Some of Shakespeare's earlier plays were performed there, including *Romeo and Juliet,* which debuted in 1594. In 1599, the Theatre was torn down and rebuilt in a new place and with a new name: the Globe. This was the location where most of Shakespeare's plays were performed.

The Globe, like the Theatre before it, was octagonal in shape. It is referred to in one of Shakespeare's plays as the "wooden O." It had eight sides and was open in the middle. The stage jutted into the center of this open area. Poorer theatergoers called groundlings, who paid a penny apiece for admission, stood around three sides of the stage. Wealthier playgoers could pay an additional penny or two to sit in one of the three galleries set in the walls of the theater.

The stage itself was partially covered with a canopy supported by two pillars. Trapdoors in the stage floor made it possible for actors to appear or disappear. Backstage center was an area known as the tiring house, in which actors could change costumes. This area could be opened for interior scenes. A second-story playing area above the tiring house could be used to represent a hilltop, a castle turret, or a balcony, such as the balcony in Juliet's house. A third level provided a space for musicians and sound effects technicians.

If you were to go back in time to see a performance of *Romeo and Juliet* at the original Theatre or the Globe, you would probably notice that the stage looked quite bare. Theaters in Shakespeare's day used little scenery and few props. The audience had to imagine the setting according to characters' descriptions of it. Another difference you would notice is that the actors were all men or boys. In Shakespeare's time, it was considered improper for women to act in plays. The part of Juliet would have been played by a boy actor in a costume.

The Globe Theatre. Illustration by Carol O'Malia.

Shakespeare's Audience

Audiences at the Globe and similar theaters included people from all stations of society: laboring people from the lower classes, middle-class merchants, members of Parliament, and lords and ladies. Pickpockets mingled among the noisy, raucous groundlings crowding around the stage. Noblemen and noblewomen sat on cushioned seats in the first-tier balcony. The fanfare of trumpets that signaled the beginning of a play was heard by some twenty-five hundred spectators, a cross-section of the Elizabethan population. As noted in the preface to the *First Folio* (the first collection of Shakespeare's plays, published in 1623), Shakespeare's plays were written for everyone, from "the most able, to him that can but spell." That may explain why they have such a universal appeal even today.

Comedies and Tragedies

The two most common types of drama during Shakespeare's day were **comedies** and **tragedies.** The key difference between the two is that comedies have happy endings and tragedies have unhappy ones. (It is sometimes said that comedies end with wedding bells and tragedies with funeral bells.)

Traditionally, a tragedy presents a sad tale of the fall of a noble character, often brought about by a personal failing called a **tragic flaw.** In *The Tragedy of Romeo and Juliet,* there are two characters who suffer a downfall—the two young people whose names appear in the title. As you read this famous play, think about what actions of the central characters lead them into trouble. Doing so will help you identify their tragic flaws.

READING SHAKESPEARE

Shakespeare's Language

Shakespeare used one of the largest vocabularies ever employed by an author. In fact, according to the *Oxford English Dictionary,* Shakespeare actually introduced an estimated three thousand new words into the English language, many of which are in common use today, including *bedazzle, silliness, critical, obscene, hurry,* and *lonely*. Numerous well-known phrases come from his plays, such as "wear my heart upon my sleeve" (*Othello*), "at one fell swoop" (*Macbeth*), "fair play" (*The Tempest*), and "the world is my oyster" (*The Merry Wives of Windsor*).

Shakespeare wrote his plays about four hundred years ago. Since that time, the English language has been altered considerably, so you will find that reading Shakespeare presents some special challenges. The meanings and spellings of some of the words he used have changed over the years, and some of the words in his writings are no longer used at all. As you read, refer to the footnotes for definitions of those archaic words. Here are some examples:

ere (before)

hie (hurry)

Marry (oath originally taken from "By the Virgin Mary")

Soft! (Hush up; wait a moment!)

want (lack)

wherefore (why)

anon (soon)

You will also find that Shakespeare used many contractions that we would not use today, such as *i'* for *in, 'tis* for *it is,* and *veil'd* for *veiled.* Often, too, the order of his words is different from the usual order of ours—as in "know you not" instead of "don't you know."

Shakespeare loved wordplay, and you will find that much of the humor in the play is based on **puns,** or plays on words that have similar sounds but different meanings. For example, in Act I, Scene i, a pun is made with the words *colliers, choler,* and *collar.* Use the footnotes to help you understand these puns.

Although the footnotes will help you, try not to get bogged down in them. Remember that a play is a dramatic action and should move quickly. First, try reading through each scene without looking at the footnotes, so that you can get a general sense of what is happening. Then reread each scene, referring to the footnotes to get the details.

If you are having trouble understanding a scene, you might try **paraphrasing** the lines, translating them into more modern language, as shown below:

Original

JULIET. How camest thou hither, tell me, and wherefore?

Paraphrase

JULIET. How did you get here, and why?

As dramas are meant to be performed, you may find that **reading the play aloud** aids your understanding of its content and language. You may also more readily notice the rhyme schemes that appear not only in monologues but also in the dialogues between certain characters.

Shakespeare's Poetic Technique

Shakespeare wrote his plays in **blank verse,** or unrhymed **iambic pentameter.** Each line of iambic pentameter consists of five *iambs,* or rhythmic units, each made up of an unstressed syllable followed by a stressed syllable, as in the word *forget.* A simpler way of describing this type of verse is to say that it contains ten syllables in each line, and every other syllable is stressed. For example:

˘ / ˘ / ˘ / ˘
But soft, | what light | through yon | der
/ ˘ /
win | dow breaks?

To maintain this pattern, the lines are sometimes split between two or more characters. This accounts for the unusual line numbering and formatting in Shakespeare's plays. In the following example, the words spoken by Benvolio and Romeo are counted as one line:

BENVOLIO. Good morrow, cousin.

ROMEO. Is the day so young?

If you scan the dialogue in *Romeo and Juliet,* you will find that most of it is written in blank verse, with some variations in stress and syllable count. Shakespeare and other playwrights of his time favored the use of blank verse in drama. They believed that it captured the natural rhythms of English speech yet still had a more noble, heroic quality that would be present in ordinary prose. You will notice that when Shakespeare does use prose, it is because the characters are speaking informally or are from the lower class.

Plot and Action

Like most plays in Shakespeare's time, *Romeo and Juliet* has five acts divided into various scenes. The action of the plot develops as follows:

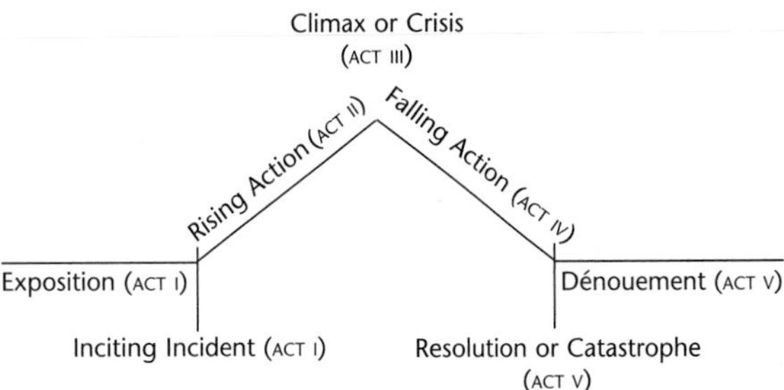

- **Act I** contains the **exposition,** or introduction. The **inciting incident** (the event that sets in motion the play's **central conflict,** or struggle) is introduced.
- **Act II** presents the **rising action,** or **complication,** a series of events that complicate the plot. The suspense builds as the plot "thickens."
- In **Act III,** suspense peaks in the **climax,** when something decisive happens to determine the future course of events. This event is also known as the **crisis,** or **turning point.** In a tragedy, the turning point marks the place where the character's fortunes begin to spiral downward, leading to a tragic ending. In a comedy, the turning point is the place where events begin to straighten out, leading to a happy ending.

- **Act IV** presents the **falling action**—the consequences, or results, of the action taken in the turning point.
- **Act V** presents the **resolution or dénouement**—the event that resolves, or ends, the central conflict. In a tragedy, this event is called the **catastrophe** because it marks the fall of the central character or characters.

Theme

Theme is the central idea in a literary work. Some works may have more than one theme, with some themes being more dominant than others. Do not confuse theme with plot. Plot indicates the story; it is the answer to the question, "What happens?" Theme, on the other hand, is the answer to the question "What is the point?"

When many people think of *The Tragedy of Romeo and Juliet,* the first thing that comes to mind is passion and romance. Although romantic love is one of its dominant themes, this drama is characterized as a tragedy, not a romance. (Shakespearean romances, such as *Cymbeline, The Winter's Tale,* and *The Tempest,* employ elements of both tragedy and comedy and are often concerned with fantasy and the imagination.) However, simply noting that love is a theme is not sufficient. What does the story tell us about love?

Another theme in *Romeo and Juliet* is that ancient grudges and war cause heartbreak and waste, a theme exemplified by the feud between the Capulets and the Montagues. This theme is set before the reader or audience in the Prologue to Act I with the speech of the Chorus. It is later echoed several times by the Prince and even by Mercutio, who cries out, "A plague a' both your houses!" as he dies in Act III, Scene i.

Yet another theme springs from a motif in this tragedy. A **motif** is any element that recurs in one or more works of literature or art. The motif of a star occurs in the prologue and in Act I, Scene iv. Romeo and Juliet are known as "star-cross'd lovers." The star motif touches on the concept of fate and destiny. As you read, decide for yourself what role fate (or "the stars") has on the events, and which events were merely caused by the decisions the characters made.

Discovering Themes

In dramas, the theme can only be conveyed through the dialogue. Therefore, pay attention to any recurring concepts that the characters discuss. The theme may not be all that obvious, however. You may find that asking yourself these questions, in addition to "What's the point?" could help you discover the theme:

- ❑ What does the playwright want me to think about?
- ❑ What seems to motivate the characters?
- ❑ What causes situations to change or events to happen?
- ❑ What is the main idea being communicated?

After you find a general theme, consider refining it. For example, saying that tragic love is a theme of *Romeo and Juliet* is a good place to start, but it doesn't explain enough about the perspective it offers on love. The movie *Casablanca* also has ill-fated love as one of its themes, but its perspective is quite different. A closer look at the theme of love in *Romeo and Juliet* could take into account the impetuousness of youth, the deathly seriousness of romantic choices, or the interference of adults in the lives of young couples.

Author's Tone

Tone is the emotional attitude toward the reader or toward the subject implied by a literary work. How can you determine the personality of a character or the attitude of an author toward a subject? You would analyze the writer's choice of language, consider the general feeling or mood of the work, and then make inferences about tone. In drama, the playwright speaks through characters to set the tone.

First, examine this passage from Act IV, Scene i, where Juliet seeks advice from Friar Lawrence about how to avoid her impending marriage to Paris:

> O, bid me leap, rather than marry Paris,
>
> From off the battlements of any tower,
>
> Or walk in thievish ways, or bid me lurk
>
> Where serpents are; chain me with roaring bears,
>
> Or hide me nightly in a charnel-house,
>
> O'ercover'd quite with dead men's rattling bones,
>
> With reeky shanks and yellow chapless skulls

Here, Juliet's conjuring of frightening images serves to reveal a tone of strong determination; she will do anything to avoid violating her vows to Romeo. The string of negative adjectives— *thievish, roaring, rattling, reeky*—demonstrates Juliet's fierce resistance to the marriage her father urges upon her.

Now, compare this speech to a later passage in Act IV, Scene iii where, alone, Juliet contemplates the dangers in what she is about to do:

> Shall I not then be stifled in the vault,
>
> To whose foul mouth no healthsome air breathes in,
>
> And there die strangled ere my Romeo comes?
>
> Or if I live, is it not very like
>
> The horrible conceit of death and night,
>
> Together with the terror of the place—
>
> As in a vault, an ancient receptacle,
>
> Where for this many hundred years the bones
>
> Of all my buried ancestors are pack'd,
>
> Where bloody Tybalt, yet but green in earth,
>
> Lies fest'ring in his shroud, where, as they say,
>
> At some hours in the night spirits resort—

This string of adjectives sets a tone of repulsion: *foul, strangled, horrible, bloody, fest'ring.* Here the words convey a sense of fear rather than of simple resistance. In this passage, Juliet's tone has changed; her love of Romeo does not make her fearless but gives her need to overcome those fears.

As you read, notice how each character's tone shifts throughout the action. What do these various tones reveal about the character's feelings and attitudes? How does tone work within the drama overall?

VIEWING AND PERFORMING SHAKESPEARE

Shakespeare never meant for his plays to be read in a book; he intended for them to be performed. All drama comes alive when it is presented by actors and is best experienced as a performance. If possible, listen to an audio version of the play or, better yet, view a production of the play on film or on a stage.

You can make *Romeo and Juliet* come to life in the classroom by reading or performing it with other students. Here are some tips to keep in mind as you read aloud or act out the play:

- Although the play is in verse, read naturally, as though you are speaking to a friend. Don't worry about placing stress on every other syllable.
- Pause or stop only when you see a punctuation mark—not at the end of each line.
- Before acting out your lines, go over them with a classmate to be sure you understand what they mean. Once you understand your lines, you can work on giving your performance the right expression and rhythm.

The Tragedy of Romeo and Juliet

BEFORE READING **A Play by William Shakespeare**

DIRECTED READING

BUILD BACKGROUND

Literary Context ***The Tragedy of Romeo and Juliet*** is set in "fair Verona," a city in northern Italy, and in the neighboring town of Mantua, during the Renaissance (1300s–1600s). Romeo and Juliet are the children of the Montague (mon´ tə gyü') and Capulet (kap´ yə let) families, noble families who have a long-standing and bitter feud. When the two supposed enemies fall in love, it can only lead to disaster.

The play begins with a **prologue,** or introduction, written in the form of a Shakespearean or Elizabethan **sonnet,** a fourteen-line poem with the rhyme scheme *abab cdcd efef gg.* It is in the Prologue that we learn the outcome of the tragedy.

Reader's Context Has your family ever disapproved of one of your friends? What problems did this situation present?

ANALYZE LITERATURE: Dramatic Speech

One of the reasons that people enjoy reading Shakespeare is the clever wordplay and sharp **dialogue,** or conversation, among characters. The humorous exchange between Sampson and Gregory at the beginning of the play does more than entertain; it sets the stage for the rivalry between the houses of Capulet and Montague. In Act I, Scene i, Romeo and Benvolio also have a brief exchange in the midst of their longer conversation about being in and out of love.

SET PURPOSE

In the Prologue, Romeo and Juliet are referred to as "star-cross'd." Taken literally, this means that they are opposed by the stars, which were believed to control people's fates. As you read *Romeo and Juliet,* decide what aspect of the tragedy is brought about by bad decisions, and what part can be blamed on fate, or the stars. Also look for instances where short but clever dialogue serves to explain situations in just a few words.

SHAKESPEARE'S SOURCE

Critics agree that *Romeo and Juliet* is timeless. It may surprise some to learn that the plot is not original to Shakespeare. Shakespeare based his play on a narrative poem by Arthur Brooke, published in 1562 with the title *The Tragicall Historye of Romeus and Juliet.* Brooke's poem, in turn, was based on earlier stories coming from Italy, including Matteo Bandello's novella *Giulietta e Romeo*. Some say that the tale was inspired by a true story of feuding families in medieval Verona, the Montecchi and Cappelletti families, who were mentioned by the author Dante in the 1300s. Although doubtful, this legend is alive and well in Verona today. If you visit the city, you can tour the homes of the "real Romeo and Juliet" and see "Juliet's Tomb."

USE READING SKILLS

Meaning of Words Knowing how to tackle difficult vocabulary will lead to improved reading comprehension. You may want to identify and define new vocabulary words before you begin reading. Possible techniques include using context clues, finding definitions in a dictionary, and decoding words by recognizing common word parts to find meanings on your own. Remember to check footnotes as you read the selection.

PREVIEW VOCABULARY

The questions below contain multiple underlined vocabulary words and no context clues. With a partner, answer each of these questions by tackling unfamiliar vocabulary words. Then confirm the meanings of the words by looking them up in the Glossary of Vocabulary Words in the back of your textbook.

1. Why are things that are put asunder not usually adjacent?
2. Do you flourish in times of strife or repose?
3. How may you discern that someone is feeling peevish?
4. Would you slander an adversary to augment your social status?
5. Is it possible to procure eloquence and dexterity? Why or why not?
6. Do you chide or dote on haughty people?
7. How would you address a grievance with a person who has a loathsome disposition?
8. Which do you prefer: discord or discourse?

Leonard Whiting and Olivia Hussey, stars of Franco Zeffirelli's 1968 film *Romeo and Juliet*.

The Tragedy of *Romeo and Juliet*

A Play by **William Shakespeare**

Characters in the Play

Chorus

Escalus, *Prince of Verona*

Paris, *a young nobleman, kinsman to the Prince*

Montague
Capulet — *heads of two houses at variance with each other*

An Old Man, *of the Capulet family*

Romeo, *son to Montague*

Mercutio, *kinsman to the Prince, and friend to Romeo*

Benvolio, *nephew to Montague, and friend to Romeo*

Tybalt, *nephew to Lady Capulet*

Petruchio, *a (mute) follower of Tybalt*

Friar Lawrence
Friar John — *Franciscans*

Balthasar, *servant to Romeo*

Abram, *servant to Montague*

Sampson
Gregory
Clown — *servants to Capulet*

Peter, *servant to Juliet's nurse*

Page *to Paris*

Apothecary

Three Musicians

Lady Montague, *wife to Montague*

Lady Capulet, *wife to Capulet*

Juliet, *daughter to Capulet*

Nurse *to Juliet*

Citizens *of Verona; several* Gentlemen *and* Gentlewomen *of both houses;* Maskers, Torchbearers, Pages, Guards, Watchmen, Servants, *and* Attendants

The Prologue

Enter Chorus.

Two households, both alike in dignity,[1]
In fair Verona, where we lay our scene,
From ancient grudge break to new mutiny,
Where civil blood makes civil hands unclean.[2]
From forth the fatal loins of these two foes
A pair of star-cross'd[3] lovers take their life;
Whose misadventur'd piteous overthrows
Doth with their death bury their parents' strife.
The fearful passage of their death-mark'd love,
And the continuance of their parents' rage,
Which, but their children's end, nought could remove,
Is now the two hours' traffic[4] of our stage;
The which if you with patient ears attend,
What here shall miss, our toil shall strive to mend.[5]

Exit.

The Prologue

1. **alike in dignity.** Of the same rank (both noble)

2. **civil blood...civil hands unclean.** Citizens are guilty of shedding one another's blood

3. **star-cross'd.** Opposed by the stars, which were believed to control fate

mu • ti • ny (myü´ t'n ē) *n.*, revolt against authority

strife (strīf) *n.*, a fight or quarrel

4. **traffic.** Business; action

5. **What here...to mend.** What we do not do well in tonight's performance, we shall correct in the future, based on your reactions.

Act I

Scene i: A Public Place in Verona

Enter Sampson *and* Gregory, *with swords and bucklers, of the house of Capulet.*

Sampson. Gregory, on my word, we'll not carry coals.[6]

Gregory. No, for then we should be colliers.[7]

Sampson. I mean, and we be in choler,[8] we'll draw.

Gregory. Ay, while you live, draw your neck out of collar.[9]

Sampson. I strike quickly, being mov'd.

Gregory. But thou art not quickly mov'd to strike.

Sampson. A dog of the house of Montague moves me.

Gregory. To move is to stir, and to be valiant is to stand; therefore, if thou art mov'd, thou run'st away.

Sampson. A dog of that house shall move me to stand! I will take the wall[10] of any man or maid of Montague's.

Act I, Scene i

6. **carry coals.** Perform menial work; figuratively, put up with insults

7. **colliers.** Coal miners

8. **be in choler.** Be angry

9. **draw your neck...collar.** Keep from being hanged; note the play on words in "colliers," "choler," and "collar"

10. **take the wall.** The inner part of a sidewalk, near the wall, was cleaner, so people allowed their superiors to walk there as a matter of courtesy.

Gregory. That shows thee a weak slave, for the weakest goes to the wall.[11]

Sampson. 'Tis true, and therefore women, being the weaker vessels, are ever thrust to the wall; therefore I will push Montague's men from the wall, and thrust his maids to the wall.

Gregory. The quarrel is between our masters, and us their men.

Sampson. 'Tis all one; I will show myself a tyrant: when I have fought with the men, I will be civil with the maids; I will cut off their heads.

Gregory. The heads of the maids?

Sampson. Ay, the heads of the maids, or their maidenheads, take it in what sense thou wilt.

Gregory. They must take it in sense that feel it.

Sampson. Me they shall feel while I am able to stand, and 'tis known I am a pretty piece of flesh.

Gregory. 'Tis well thou art not fish; if thou hadst, thou hadst been poor-John.[12] Draw thy tool, here comes two of the house of Montagues.

Enter two other servingmen Abram *and* Balthasar.

Sampson. My naked weapon is out. Quarrel, I will back thee.[13]

Gregory. How, turn thy back and run?

Sampson. Fear me not.

Gregory. No, marry, I fear thee!

Sampson. Let us take the law of our sides,[14] let them begin.

Gregory. I will frown as I pass by, and let them take it as they list.[15]

Sampson. Nay, as they dare. I will bite my thumb[16] at them, which is disgrace to them if they bear it.

Abram. Do you bite your thumb at us, sir?

Sampson. I do bite my thumb, sir.

Abram. Do you bite your thumb at us, sir?

Sampson. [*Aside to* Gregory.] Is the law of our side if I say ay?

Gregory. [*Aside to* Sampson.] No.

Sampson. No, sir, I do not bite my thumb at you, sir, but I bite my thumb, sir.

Gregory. Do you quarrel, sir?

11. **weakest...wall.** The weakest gives way.

12. **poor-John.** Inexpensive fish

13. **back thee.** Assist you

14. **take the law of our sides.** Have the law on our side

15. **list.** Wish

16. **bite my thumb.** Gesture of contempt or insult

Abram. Quarrel, sir? No, sir.

Sampson. But if you do, sir, I am for you. I serve as good a man as you.

Abram. No better?

Sampson. Well, sir.

Enter Benvolio.

Gregory. Say "better," here comes one of my master's kinsmen.

Sampson. Yes, better, sir.

Abram. You lie.

Sampson. Draw, if you be men. Gregory, remember thy washing[17] blow.

They fight.

Benvolio. Part, fools!
Put up your swords, you know not what you do.

Beats down their swords.

Enter Tybalt.

17. **washing.** Slashing

A brawl breaks out on the streets of Verona.

TYBALT. What, art thou drawn among these heartless hinds?[18]
Turn thee, Benvolio, look upon thy death.

BENVOLIO. I do but keep the peace. Put up thy sword,
Or manage it to part these men with me.

TYBALT. What, drawn and talk of peace? I hate the word
As I hate hell, all Montagues, and thee.
Have at thee, coward! *They fight.*

Enter three or four CITIZENS *with clubs or partisans.*[19]

CITIZENS. Clubs, bills,[20] and partisans! Strike! Beat them down!
Down with the Capulets! Down with the Montagues!

Enter old CAPULET *in his gown, and his wife* LADY CAPULET.

CAPULET. What noise is this? Give me my long sword ho!

LADY CAPULET. A crutch, a crutch! why call you for a sword?

CAPULET. My sword, I say! Old Montague is come,
And flourishes his blade in spite of me.

Enter old MONTAGUE *and his wife* LADY MONTAGUE.

MONTAGUE. Thou villain Capulet!—Hold me not, let me go.

LADY MONTAGUE. Thou shalt not stir one foot to seek a foe.

Enter PRINCE ESCALUS *with his* TRAIN.

PRINCE. Rebellious subjects, enemies to peace,
Profaners of this neighbor-stained steel[21] —
Will they not hear?—What ho, you men, you beasts!
That quench the fire of your pernicious rage
With purple fountains issuing from your veins—
On pain of torture, from those bloody hands
Throw your mistempered[22] weapons to the ground,
And hear the sentence of your moved prince.
Three civil brawls, bred of an airy word,
By thee, old Capulet, and Montague,
Have thrice[23] disturb'd the quiet of our streets,
And made Verona's ancient citizens
Cast by their grave beseeming ornaments[24]
To wield old partisans, in hands as old,
Cank'red[25] with peace, to part your cank'red hate;
If ever you disturb our streets again
Your lives shall pay the forfeit of the peace.
For this time all the rest depart away.
You, Capulet, shall go along with me,
And, Montague, come you this afternoon,

18. **heartless hinds.** Cowardly creatures

19. **partisans.** Broad-bladed spears
20. **bills.** Hooked blades attached to long shafts

flour • ish (flʉr´ ish) *v.*, wave in the air

21. **Profaners...steel.** People who profane, or make contemptible, their weapons by staining them with their neighbors' blood

per • ni • cious (pər nish´ əs) *adj.*, fatal; deadly

22. **mistempered.** Hardened for an improper use

23. **thrice.** Three times

24. **Cast...ornaments.** Throw aside those objects, like canes, appropriate for old age
25. **Cank'red.** Malignant

World History Connection

Renaissance Society As Italy moved from the Middle Ages into the Renaissance, society was changing rapidly. More and more people were living in cities as the merchant, or burgher, class gained wealth. Families of nobility began to share social status with the burghers. Social classes became less distinguishable, and a noble birth and inherited wealth became less important. Nobles and burghers alike benefited from heightened culture and from education. Fashion, music, art, and literature became important to people who had the means to enjoy them. Homes were graced with architectural details, elegant linens and tapestries, and elaborate gardens. Women used makeup, perfume, hairpieces, and jewelry. Men's swords and daggers were much more elegant than the utilitarian weapons of years past. People enjoyed good food, music, and entertainment. The world of Romeo and Juliet reflected the appreciation of beauty and refinement evident in Renaissance society.

To know our farther pleasure in this case,
To old Free-town, our common judgment-place.
Once more, on pain of death, all men depart.

Exeunt all but MONTAGUE, LADY MONTAGUE, *and* BENVOLIO.

MONTAGUE. Who set this ancient quarrel new abroach?[26]
Speak, nephew, were you by when it began?

BENVOLIO. Here were the servants of your adversary,
And yours, close fighting ere[27] I did approach.
I drew to part them. In the instant came
The fiery Tybalt, with his sword prepar'd,
Which, as he breath'd defiance to my ears,
He swung about his head and cut the winds,
Who, nothing hurt withal,[28] hiss'd him in scorn.
While we were interchanging thrusts and blows,
Came more and more, and fought on part and part,
Till the Prince came, who parted either part.

LADY MONTAGUE. O, where is Romeo? Saw you him today?
Right glad I am he was not at this fray.

26. **abroach.** Open and flowing freely

ad • ver • sar • y (ad´ vər ser' ē) *n.,* opponent; enemy

27. **ere.** Before

28. **nothing hurt withal.** Not harmed as a result

fray (frā) *n.,* noisy quarrel or fight

BENVOLIO. Madam, an hour before the worshipp'd sun
Peer'd forth the golden window of the east,
A troubled mind drive[29] me to walk abroad,
Where, underneath the grove of sycamore
That westward rooteth from this city side,
So early walking did I see your son.
Towards him I made, but he was ware[30] of me,
And stole into the covert[31] of the wood.
I, measuring his affections by my own,
Which then most sought where most might not be found,
Being one too many by my weary self,
Pursued my humor not pursuing his,[32]
And gladly shunn'd who gladly fled from me.

MONTAGUE. Many a morning hath he there been seen,
With tears augmenting the fresh morning's dew,
Adding to clouds more clouds with his deep sighs,
But all so soon as the all-cheering sun
Should in the farthest east begin to draw
The shady curtains from Aurora's[33] bed,
Away from light steals home my heavy son,
And private in his chamber pens himself,
Shuts up his windows, locks fair daylight out,
And makes himself an artificial night.
Black and portendous[34] must this humor[35] prove,
Unless good counsel may the cause remove.

BENVOLIO. My noble uncle, do you know the cause?

MONTAGUE. I neither know it, nor can learn of him.

BENVOLIO. Have you importun'd[36] him by any means?

MONTAGUE. Both by myself and many other friends,
But he, his own affections' counsellor,
Is to himself (I will not say how true)
But to himself so secret and so close,
So far from sounding[37] and discovery,
As is the bud bit with an envious[38] worm,
Ere he can spread his sweet leaves to the air
Or dedicate his beauty to the sun.
Could we but learn from whence[39] his sorrows grow,
We would as willingly give cure as know.

Enter ROMEO.

BENVOLIO. See where he comes. So please you step aside,
I'll know his grievance, or be much denied.

29. **drive.** Drove

30. **ware.** Wary

31. **covert.** Cover; hiding place

32. **Pursued...his.** Followed my own mood by not following him

aug • ment (ôg ment´) *v.*, add to

33. **Aurora's.** Of the Roman goddess of dawn

34. **portendous.** Ominous; portentous

35. **humor.** Moody behavior

36. **importun'd.** Questioned

37. **sounding.** Being understood

38. **envious.** Vicious

39. **whence.** What place

griev • ance (grē´ vəns) *n.*, complaint; cause of suffering

MONTAGUE. I would thou wert[40] so happy by thy stay
To hear true shrift.[41] Come, madam, let's away.

Exeunt MONTAGUE *and* LADY.

BENVOLIO. Good morrow, cousin.

ROMEO. Is the day so young?

BENVOLIO. But new strook[42] nine.

ROMEO. Ay me, sad hours seem long.
Was that my father that went hence[43] so fast?

BENVOLIO. It was. What sadness lengthens Romeo's hours?

ROMEO. Not having that which, having, makes them short.

BENVOLIO. In love?

ROMEO. Out—

BENVOLIO. Of love?

ROMEO. Out of her favor where I am in love.

BENVOLIO. Alas that love, so gentle in his view,
Should be so tyrannous and rough in proof!

ROMEO. Alas that love, whose view is muffled still,[44]
Should, without eyes, see pathways to his will!
Where shall we dine? O me! what fray was here?
Yet tell me not, for I have heard it all:
Here's much to do with hate, but more with love.
Why then, O brawling love! O loving hate!
O any thing, of nothing first create![45]
O heavy lightness, serious vanity,
Misshapen chaos of well-seeming forms,
Feather of lead, bright smoke, cold fire, sick health,
Still-waking sleep, that is not what it is!
This love feel I, that feel no love in this.[46]
Dost thou not laugh?

BENVOLIO. No, coz,[47] I rather weep.

ROMEO. Good heart, at what?

BENVOLIO. At thy good heart's oppression.

ROMEO. Why, such is love's <u>transgression</u>.
Griefs of mine own lie heavy in my breast,
Which thou wilt propagate to have it press'd
With more of thine.[48] This love that thou hast shown
Doth add more grief to too much of mine own.

40. **wert.** Were

41. **shrift.** Confession

42. **strook.** Struck

43. **hence.** From here

44. **whose view...still.** Love is conventionally pictured as blind.

45. **O any thing...create!** All things created (by God) out of nothing

46. **O brawling love...no love in this.** Romeo's string of contradictions shows the confused state he is in. He feels good because he is in love and also feels bad because his love is not returned. His language suggests that he is in love with love.

47. **coz.** Cousin (said of any relative)

trans • gres • sion (trans gresh´ ən) *n.*, offense

48. **Griefs of mine own...of thine.** The grief in my heart will multiply if it feels the further weight of your grief.

Love is a smoke made with the fume of sighs,
Being purg'd, a fire sparkling in lovers' eyes,
Being vex'd, a sea nourish'd with loving tears.
What is it else? a madness most discreet,
A choking gall, and a preserving sweet.
Farewell, my coz.

BENVOLIO. Soft,[49] I will go along;
And if you leave me so, you do me wrong.

ROMEO. Tut, I have lost myself, I am not here:
This is not Romeo, he's some other where.

BENVOLIO. Tell me in sadness,[50] who is that you love?

ROMEO. What, shall I groan and tell thee?

BENVOLIO. Groan? why, no;
But sadly tell me, who?

ROMEO. Bid a sick man in sadness make his will—
A word ill urg'd to one that is so ill!
In sadness, cousin, I do love a woman.

BENVOLIO. I aim'd so near when I suppos'd you lov'd.

ROMEO. A right good mark-man![51] And she's fair I love.

BENVOLIO. A right fair mark,[52] fair coz, is soonest hit.

ROMEO. Well, in that hit you miss: she'll not be hit
With Cupid's arrow, she hath Dian's wit;[53]
And in strong proof[54] of chastity well arm'd,
From Love's weak childish bow she lives uncharm'd.[55]
She will not stay[56] the siege of loving terms,
Nor bide th' encounter of assailing eyes,
Nor ope her lap to saint-seducing gold.[57]
O, she is rich in beauty, only poor
That, when she dies, with beauty dies her store.[58]

BENVOLIO. Then she hath sworn that she will still[59] live chaste?

ROMEO. She hath, and in that sparing[60] makes huge waste;
For beauty starv'd with her severity
Cuts beauty off from all posterity.
She is too fair, too wise, wisely too fair,
To merit bliss by making me despair.
She hath forsworn to love, and in that vow
Do I live dead that live to tell it now.

BENVOLIO. Be rul'd by me, forget to think of her.

49. **Soft.** One moment; used as an interjection

50. **in sadness.** With gravity or seriousness

51. **mark-man.** Marksman, one who shoots well
52. **mark.** Target
53. **Dian's wit.** Ideas or beliefs of Diana, the Roman goddess of chastity and of the hunt
54. **proof.** Armor
55. **uncharm'd.** Not under the spell of
56. **stay.** Abide
57. **Nor ope...gold.** The reference is to Danaë, in Roman mythology, whom Jupiter visited in the form of a shower of gold.
58. **dies her store.** Her beauty will die with her, for she left no children.
59. **still.** Always
60. **sparing.** Thriftiness

pos • ter • i • ty
(päs ter´ ə tē) *n.,* all future generations

Romeo. O, teach me how I should forget to think.

Benvolio. By giving liberty unto thine eyes:
Examine other beauties.

Romeo. 'Tis the way
To call hers, exquisite, in question more.[61]
These happy masks that kiss fair ladies' brows,
Being black, puts us in mind they hide the fair.
He that is strooken[62] blind cannot forget
The precious treasure of his eyesight lost.
Show me a mistress that is passing[63] fair,
What doth her beauty serve but as a note
Where I may read who pass'd that passing fair?
Farewell, thou canst not teach me to forget.

Benvolio. I'll pay that doctrine, or else die in debt.[64]

Exeunt.

61. **'Tis the way...more.** That's the way to make her great beauty even more evident.

62. **strooken.** Struck

63. **passing.** Extremely; surpassing others

64. **pay that...debt.** Teach you that lesson or die still under obligation to you

Scene ii: A Street in Verona

Enter Capulet, County Paris, *and the Clown,* Capulet's Servant.

Capulet. But Montague is bound as well as I,
In penalty alike, and 'tis not hard, I think,
For men so old as we to keep the peace.

Paris. Of honorable reckoning[1] are you both,
And pity 'tis you liv'd at odds so long.
But now, my lord, what say you to my suit?[2]

Capulet. But saying o'er what I have said before:
My child is yet a stranger in the world,
She hath not seen the change of fourteen years;
Let two more summers wither in their pride,
Ere we may think her ripe to be a bride.

Paris. Younger than she are happy mothers made.

Capulet. And too soon marr'd are those so early made.
Earth hath swallowed all my hopes but she;
She's the hopeful lady of my earth.[3]
But woo her, gentle Paris, get her heart,
My will to her consent is but a part;
And she agreed, within her scope of choice
Lies my consent and fair according voice.

Act I, Scene ii

1. **Of honorable reckoning.** With a favorable reputation

2. **suit.** Pleading

3. **hopeful...earth.** The one who will inherit my land, and the one who makes my world seem hopeful

This night I hold an old accustom'd feast,
Whereto I have invited many a guest,
Such as I love, and you, among the store
One more, most welcome, makes my number more.
At my poor house look to behold this night
Earth-treading stars that make dark heaven light.
Such comfort as do lusty young men feel
When well-apparell'd April on the heel
Of limping winter treads, even such delight
Among fresh fennel[4] buds shall you this night
Inherit[5] at my house; hear all, all see;
And like her most whose merit most shall be;
Which on more view of many, mine, being one,
May stand in number, though in reck'ning none.[6]
Come go with me. [*To* SERVANT.] Go, sirrah,[7] trudge about
Through fair Verona, find those persons out
Whose names are written there, and to them say,
My house and welcome on their pleasure stay.[8] *Exit with* PARIS.

SERVANT. Find them out whose names are written here! It is written that the shoemaker should meddle with his yard and the tailor with his last, the fisher with his pencil and the painter with his nets; but I am sent to find those persons whose names are here writ, and can never find what names the writing person hath here writ. I must to the learned. In good time!

Enter BENVOLIO *and* ROMEO.

BENVOLIO. Tut, man, one fire burns out another's burning,
One pain is less'ned by another's anguish;
Turn giddy, and be holp[9] by backward turning;
One desperate grief cures with another's languish:[10]
Take thou some new infection to thy eye,
And the rank poison of the old will die.

ROMEO. Your plantan leaf[11] is excellent for that.

BENVOLIO. For what, I pray thee?

ROMEO. For your broken shin.

BENVOLIO. Why, Romeo, art thou mad?

ROMEO. Not mad, but bound more than a madman is;
Shut up in prison, kept without my food,
Whipt and tormented and—God-den,[12] good fellow.

SERVANT. God gi' god-den. I pray, sir, can you read?

ROMEO. Ay, mine own fortune in my misery.

4. **fennel.** Plant with yellow flowers and a sweet aroma
5. **Inherit.** Experience
6. **May stand...none.** She may be one of a number of women, but when you reckon, or make calculations, about which is the best, you will find that none compares to her.
7. **sirrah.** Form of address used by a person of higher rank when speaking to a person of a lesser social rank
8. **on their pleasure stay.** Wait to see what will be their pleasure
9. **holp.** Helped; cured
10. **languish.** State of depression
11. **plantan leaf.** Leaf of the plantain, applied to soothe minor wounds
12. **God-den.** Good evening

Servant. Perhaps you have learn'd it without book.
But I pray, can you read any thing you see?

Romeo. Ay, if I know the letters and the language.

Servant. Ye say honestly, rest you merry!

Romeo. Stay, fellow, I can read.

[*He reads the letter.*] "Signior Martino and his wife and daughters; County Anselme and his beauteous sisters; the lady widow of Vitruvio; Signior Placentio and his lovely nieces; Mercutio and his brother Valentine; mine uncle Capulet, his wife, and daughters; my fair niece Rosaline, and Livia; Signior Valentio and his cousin Tybalt; Lucio and the lively Helena." A fair assembly. Whither should they come?

Servant. Up.

Romeo. Whither? to supper?

Servant. To our house.

Romeo. Whose house?

Servant. My master's.

Romeo. Indeed I should have ask'd thee that before.

Servant. Now I'll tell you without asking. My master is the great rich Capulet, and if you be not of the house of Montagues, I pray come and crush[13] a cup of wine. Rest you merry! *Exit.*

Benvolio. At this same ancient feast of Capulet's
Sups the fair Rosaline whom thou so loves,
With all the admired beauties of Verona.
Go thither,[14] and with unattainted[15] eye
Compare her face with some that I shall show,
And I will make thee think thy swan a crow.

Romeo. When the devout religion of mine eye
Maintains such falsehood, then turn tears to fires;
And these,[16] who, often drown'd, could never die,
Transparent heretics, be burnt for liars!
One fairer than my love! The all-seeing sun
Ne'er saw her match since first the world begun.

Benvolio. Tut, you saw her fair, none else being by,
Herself pois'd with herself in either eye;
But in that crystal scales let there be weigh'd
Your lady's love against some other maid

13. **crush.** Drink

14. **thither.** There

15. **unattainted.** Untainted; not with preconceived ideas

16. **these.** These eyes

That I will show you shining at this feast,
And she shall scant show well that now seems best.

Romeo. I'll go along no such sight to be shown,
But to rejoice in splendor of mine own. *Exeunt.*

Scene iii: Capulet's House

Enter Capulet's Wife, *and* Nurse.

Lady Capulet. Nurse, where's my daughter? Call her forth to me.

Nurse. Now by my maidenhead at twelve year old,
I bade her come. What, lamb! What, ladybird!
God forbid! Where's this girl? What, Juliet!

Lady Capulet has news for her daughter, Juliet.

Critical Viewing

What can you infer about Juliet's relationships with her mother and Nurse from the body language in this photo?

Enter Juliet.

Juliet. How now, who calls?

Nurse. Your mother.

Juliet. Madam, I am here,
What is your will?

Lady Capulet. This is the matter. Nurse, give leave[1] a while,
We must talk in secret. Nurse, come back again,
I have rememb'red me, thou s'[2] hear our counsel.
Thou knowest my daughter's of a pretty age.

Act I, Scene iii

1. **give leave.** Leave us

2. **thou s'.** You shall or you should

Nurse. Faith, I can tell her age unto an hour.

Lady Capulet. She's not fourteen.

Nurse. I'll lay fourteen of my teeth—
And yet, to my teen[3] be it spoken, I have but four—
She's not fourteen. How long is it now
To Lammas-tide?[4]

Lady Capulet. A fortnight[5] and odd days.

Nurse. Even or odd, of all days in the year,
Come Lammas-eve at night shall she be fourteen,
Susan and she—God rest all Christian souls!—
Were of an age. Well, Susan is with God,
She was too good for me. But as I said,
On Lammas-eve at night shall she be fourteen,
That shall she, marry, I remember it well.
'Tis since the earthquake now aleven[6] years,
And[7] she was wean'd—I never shall forget it—
Of all the days of the year, upon that day;
For I had then laid wormwood to my dug,[8]
Sitting in the sun under the dove-house wall.
My lord and you were then at Mantua—
Nay, I do bear a brain—but as I said,
When it did taste the wormwood on the nipple
Of my dug and felt it bitter, pretty fool,
To see it teachy[9] and fall out wi' th' dug!
Shake, quoth the dove-house;[10] 'twas no need, I trow,[11]
To bid me trudge.
And since that time it is aleven years,
For then she could stand high-lone;[12] nay, by th' rood,[13]
She could have run and waddled all about;
For even the day before, she broke her brow,
And then my husband—God be with his soul!
'A[14] was a merry man—took up the child.
"Yea," quoth he, "dost thou fall upon thy face?
Thou wilt fall backward when thou hast more wit,
Wilt thou not, Jule?" and by my holidam,[15]
The pretty wretch left crying and said, "Ay."[16]
To see now how a jest shall come about![17]
I warrant,[18] and I should live a thousand years,
I never should forget it: "Wilt thou not, Jule?" quoth he;
And, pretty fool, it stinted[19] and said, "Ay."

Lady Capulet. Enough of this, I pray thee hold thy peace.

3. **teen.** Sorrow
4. **Lammas-tide.** First of August
5. **fortnight.** Fourteen nights
6. **aleven.** Eleven
7. **And.** Since
8. **laid wormwood to my dug.** Applied the bitter herb called wormwood to her breast to wean the child
9. **teachy.** Touchy
10. **Shake...dove-house.** The dove-house shook because of the earthquake.
11. **trow.** Believe
12. **stand high-lone.** Stand upright
13. **rood.** Cross
14. **'A.** He
15. **holidam.** Holiness, sometimes referring to the Virgin Mary
16. **Ay.** Aye, or yes
17. **To see...about!** The nurse is expressing pleasure at seeing her husband's joke come true.
18. **warrant.** Swear or guarantee
19. **stinted.** Stopped (crying)

Nurse. Yes, madam, yet I cannot choose but laugh
To think it should leave crying and say, "Ay."
And yet I warrant it had upon it[20] brow
A bump as big as a young cock'rel's stone[21]—
A perilous knock—and it cried bitterly.
"Yea," quoth my husband, "fall'st upon thy face?
Thou wilt fall backward when thou comest to age,
Wilt thou not, Jule?" It stinted and said, "Ay."

Juliet. And stint thou too, I pray thee, nurse, say I.

Nurse. Peace, I have done. God mark thee to his grace![22]
Thou wast the prettiest babe that e'er I nurs'd.
And I might live to see thee married once,
I have my wish.

Lady Capulet. Marry, that "marry" is the very theme
I came to talk of. Tell me, daughter Juliet,
How stands your dispositions to be married?

Juliet. It is an honor that I dream not of.

Nurse. An honor! were not I thine only nurse,
I would say thou hadst suck'd wisdom from thy teat.

Lady Capulet. Well, think of marriage now; younger than you,
Here in Verona, ladies of esteem,
Are made already mothers. By my count,
I was your mother much upon these years
That you are now a maid. Thus then in brief:
The valiant Paris seeks you for his love.

Nurse. A man, young lady! Lady, such a man
As all the world—why, he's a man of wax.[23]

Lady Capulet. Verona's summer hath not such a flower.

Nurse. Nay, he's a flower, in faith, a very flower.

Lady Capulet. What say you? can you love the gentleman?
This night you shall behold him at our feast;
Read o'er the volume of young Paris' face,
And find delight writ there with beauty's pen;
Examine every married[24] lineament,
And see how one another lends content;
And what obscur'd in this fair volume lies
Find written in the margent[25] of his eyes.
This precious book of love, this unbound[26] lover,
To beautify him, only lacks a cover.
The fish lives in the sea, and 'tis much pride

20. **it.** Its

21. **cock'rel's stone.** Part of a young male chicken

22. **God mark...grace!** God grant grace to you!

23. **he's a man of wax.** He is as handsome as a wax figure of a man. The nurse means this as a compliment, but a wax figure is less than a real person, so the compliment is unintentionally an insult.

24. **married.** Well-matched or put together; also a pun on the usual sense of the word

25. **margent.** Margin, as in a book

26. **unbound.** Like a book unbound, he is unbound by marriage.

For fair without the fair within to hide.[27]
That book in many's eyes doth share the glory,
That in gold clasps locks in the golden story;
So shall you share all that he doth possess,
By having him, making yourself no less.

Nurse. No less! nay, bigger: women grow by men.

Lady Capulet. Speak briefly, can you like of Paris' love?[28]

Juliet. I'll look to like, if looking liking move;
But no more deep will I endart[29] mine eye
Than your consent gives strength to make it fly.

Enter Servingman.

Servingman. Madam, the guests are come, supper serv'd up, you call'd, my young lady ask'd for, the nurse curs'd in the pantry,[30] and every thing in extremity. I must hence to wait; I beseech you follow straight. *Exit.*

Lady Capulet. We follow thee. Juliet, the County stays.[31]

Nurse. Go, girl, seek happy nights to happy days. *Exeunt.*

Scene iv: In Front of Capulet's House

Enter Romeo, Mercutio, Benvolio, *with five or six other* Maskers;[1] Torch-bearers.

Romeo. What, shall this speech be spoke for our excuse?
Or shall we on without apology?

Benvolio. The date is out of such prolixity:[2]
We'll have no Cupid hoodwink'd with a scarf,[3]
Bearing a Tartar's painted bow of lath,[4]
Scaring the ladies like a crow-keeper,[5]
Nor no without-book prologue,[6] faintly spoke
After the prompter,[7] for our entrance;
But let them measure us by what they will,
We'll measure them a measure[8] and be gone.

Romeo. Give me a torch, I am not for this ambling;[9]
Being but heavy, I will bear the light.

Mercutio. Nay, gentle Romeo, we must have you dance.

Romeo. Not I, believe me. You have dancing shoes
With nimble soles, I have a soul of lead
So stakes me to the ground I cannot move.

27. **The fish...hide.** It is as appropriate for a good man to be handsome as it is for a fish to live in the sea.

28. **like of Paris' love.** Love someone like Paris

29. **endart.** Shoot like a dart

30. **the nurse...pantry.** The kitchen help are cursing because the nurse is not there to help.

31. **the County stays.** The Count (Paris) waits.

Act I, Scene iv

1. **Maskers.** People wearing masks, dressed in costumes for the party
2. **The date...prolixity.** Such a speech, given by maskers arriving at a party, is out of fashion.
3. **Cupid hoodwink'd with a scarf.** Cupid was the Roman god of love, said to pierce lovers with his arrows. To be hoodwinked meant, literally, to be blindfolded with a scarf tied around the head.
4. **Bearing...lath.** Carrying, like Cupid or like a Tartar, a small bow of painted strips of wood
5. **crow-keeper.** Scarecrow
6. **without-book prologue.** Memorized introduction
7. **After the prompter.** Repeating lines given by a prompter, a person whose job it is to help an actor who has forgotten the lines
8. **measure them a measure.** Give them a dance
9. **Give me...ambling.** Romeo wishes to carry a torch because he wants to avoid ambling, or dancing, being too heavy-hearted for such frivolity.

Romeo on his way to Capulet's party.

Mercutio. You are a lover, borrow Cupid's wings,
And soar with them above a common bound.[10]

Romeo. I am too sore enpierced with his shaft
To soar with his light feathers, and so bound
I cannot bound a pitch above dull woe;
Under love's heavy burthen[11] do I sink.

Mercutio. And, to sink in it, should you burthen love—
Too great oppression for a tender thing.

Romeo. Is love a tender thing? It is too rough,
Too rude, too boist'rous, and it pricks like thorn.

Mercutio. If love be rough with you, be rough with love;
Prick love for pricking, and you beat love down.
Give me a case to put my visage in, [*Puts on a mask.*]
A visor for a visor![12] what care I
What curious eye doth cote[13] deformities?
Here are the beetle brows[14] shall blush for me.

Benvolio. Come knock and enter, and no sooner in,
But every man betake him to his legs.[15]

Romeo. A torch for me. Let wantons light of heart
Tickle the senseless rushes[16] with their heels.

10. **a common bound.** Ordinary leap as might be made by an ordinary, untalented dancer

11. **burthen.** Burden

12. **visor for a visor!** A visor is a mask. Mercutio is suggesting that his face is also a mask, because he is a jester, one who hides his feelings behind his wit.
13. **cote.** See; notice
14. **beetle brows.** Bushy eyebrows
15. **betake him to his legs.** Begin dancing
16. **rushes.** Plants used as a floor covering

For I am proverb'd with a grandsire phrase,[17]
I'll be a candle-holder and look on:[18]
The game was ne'er so fair, and I am done.

Mercutio. Tut, dun's the mouse, the constable's own word.[19]
If thou art Dun, we'll draw thee from the mire
Of this sir-reverence love, wherein thou stickest
Up to the ears. Come, we burn daylight,[20] ho!

Romeo. Nay, that's not so.

Mercutio. I mean, sir, in delay
We waste our lights in vain, like lights by day!
Take our good meaning, for our judgment sits
Five times in that ere once in our five wits.

Romeo. And we mean well in going to this mask,
But 'tis no wit to go.

Mercutio. Why, may one ask?

Romeo. I dreamt a dream tonight.

Mercutio. And so did I.

Romeo. Well, what was yours?

Mercutio. That dreamers often lie.[21]

Romeo. In bed asleep, while they do dream things true.

Mercutio. O then I see Queen Mab[22] hath been with you.
She is the fairies' midwife, and she comes
In shape no bigger than an agot-stone[23]
On the forefinger of an alderman,
Drawn with a team of little atomi[24]
Over men's noses as they lie asleep.
Her chariot is an empty hazel-nut,
Made by the joiner squirrel or old grub,
Time out a' mind the fairies' coachmakers.
Her waggon-spokes made of long spinners' legs,
The cover of the wings of grasshoppers,
Her traces of the smallest spider web,
Her collars of the moonshine's wat'ry beams,
Her whip of cricket's bone, the lash of film,
Her waggoner a small grey-coated gnat,
Not half so big as a round little worm
Prick'd from the lazy finger of a maid.[25]
And in this state she gallops night by night
Through lovers' brains, and then they dream of love;

17. **grandsire phrase.** Proverb, or phrase known to our grandfathers

18. **I'll be…look on.** Romeo recalls the proverb, "A good candle-holder or spectator makes a good gamester."

19. **dun's…word.** A mouse is dun—a dull, grayish brown. Romeo has just suggested that he will be an onlooker, which makes Mercutio think of a hidden, quiet mouse. A constable, or police officer, might describe a stealthy criminal in that way.

20. **burn daylight.** Waste time

21. **lie.** Mercutio puns on the word *lie,* implying both "rest" and "tell falsehoods."

22. **Queen Mab.** Fairy creature

23. **agot-stone.** Agate used as a stone in a ring

24. **atomi.** Tiny beings

25. **Not half…maid.** According to a folk belief, worms grew in the fingers of lazy girls.

O'er courtiers' knees, that dream on cur'sies[26] straight;
O'er lawyers' fingers, who straight dream on fees;
O'er ladies' lips, who straight on kisses dream,
Which oft the angry Mab with blisters plagues,
Because their breath with sweetmeats tainted are.
Sometime she gallops o'er a courtier's nose,
And then dreams he of smelling out a suit;[27]
And sometime comes she with a tithe-pig's[28] tail
Tickling a parson's nose as 'a lies asleep,
Then he dreams of another benefice.[29]
Sometime she driveth o'er a soldier's neck,
And then dreams he of cutting foreign throats,
Of breaches, ambuscadoes,[30] Spanish blades,
Of healths five fadom deep;[31] and then anon[32]
Drums in his ear, at which he starts and wakes,
And being thus frighted, swears a prayer or two,
And sleeps again. This is that very Mab
That plats the manes of horses in the night,
And bakes the elf-locks in foul sluttish hairs,
Which, once untangled, much misfortune bodes.[33]
This is the hag, when maids lie on their backs,
That presses them and learns them first to bear,
Making them women of good carriage.[34]
This is she—

Romeo. Peace, peace, Mercutio, peace!
Thou talk'st of nothing.

Mercutio. True, I talk of dreams,
Which are the children of an idle brain,
Begot of nothing but vain fantasy,
Which is as thin of substance as the air,
And more inconstant than the wind, who woos
Even now the frozen bosom of the north,
And, being anger'd, puffs away from thence,
Turning his side to the dew-dropping south.

Benvolio. This wind you talk of blows us from ourselves:
Supper is done, and we shall come too late.

Romeo. I fear, too early, for my mind misgives
Some consequence yet hanging in the stars
Shall bitterly begin his fearful date
With this night's revels, and expire the term
Of a despised life clos'd in my breast
By some vile forfeit of untimely death.
But He that hath the steerage of my course

26. **on cur'sies.** Of curtsies, or bows

27. **smelling out a suit.** Thinking of something to request for oneself of a high-born or noble person

28. **tithe-pig.** Pig given as payment of tithes, dues owed to a parish

29. **benefice.** Church office that provides a living for its holder

30. **breaches, ambuscadoes.** Breaching, or breaking through fortifications; ambushes

31. **healths five fadom deep.** Drinks five fathoms deep. A fathom is a unit of measure of water equal to six feet in depth.

32. **anon.** At once

33. **bakes...bodes.** A folk belief was that elves matted the hair of lazy or slovenly people and that to unmat this hair was to bring bad luck.

34. **good carriage.** Pun, one sense of which is "women who are carrying (babies)"

Direct my sail! On, lusty gentlemen!

Benvolio. Strike, drum.

They march about the stage and stand to one side.

Scene v: A Hall in Capulet's House

And Servingmen *come forth with napkins.*

1. Servingman. Where's Potpan, that he helps not to take away? He shift a trencher?[1] he scrape a trencher?

2. Servingman. When good manners shall lie all in one or two men's hands, and they unwash'd too, 'tis a foul thing.

1. Servingman. Away with the join-stools,[2] remove the court-cupboard, look to the plate. Good thou, save me a piece of marchpane,[3] and, as thou loves me, let the porter let in Susan Grindstone and Nell. [*Exit* Second Servant.] Anthony and Potpan!

Enter Anthony *and* Potpan.

Anthony. Ay, boy, ready.

1. Servingman. You are look'd for and call'd for, ask'd for and sought for, in the great chamber.

Potpan. We cannot be here and there too. Cheerly, boys, be brisk a while, and the longer liver take all.

Exeunt.

Enter Capulet, Lady Capulet, Juliet, Tybalt, Nurse, Servingmen, *and all the* Guests *and* Gentlewomen *to the* Maskers.

Capulet. Welcome, gentlemen! Ladies that have their toes
Unplagu'd with corns will walk a bout with you.
Ah, my mistresses, which of you all
Will now deny to dance? She that makes dainty,[4]
She I'll swear hath corns. Am I come near ye now?
Welcome, gentlemen! I have seen the day
That I have worn a visor and could tell
A whispering tale in a fair lady's ear,
Such as would please; 'tis gone, 'tis gone, 'tis gone.
You are welcome, gentlemen! Come, musicians, play.

Music plays, and they dance.

A hall, a hall! give room! and foot it, girls.
More light, you knaves, and turn the tables up;

Act I, Scene v

1. **trencher.** Platter

2. **join-stools.** Wooden stools, made by carpenters called joiners

3. **marchpane.** Marzipan, a type of candy

4. **makes dainty.** Behaves shyly by refusing to dance

CULTURAL CONNECTION

Deutsch: Stilleben, 1613. Floris Claesz van Dyck.

Renaissance Feasts Wealthy people in Renaissance Italy took great pride in holding feasts and parties for friends. The feasts were elaborate affairs hosting many guests. The guests would sit at a long narrow table covered in fine linens. The meal began with appetizers and would follow with a number of different entrees featuring boiled and roasted meats, vegetables, fishes, and cheeses, accompanied by bread and wine. Dessert consisted of fruits, honey, torten, and pies. Although people used knives and spoons to dine, forks were just making an appearance in Europe and had not yet become very popular.

And quench the fire, the room is grown too hot.
Ah, sirrah, this unlook'd-for sport comes well.
Nay, sit, nay, sit, good cousin Capulet,
For you and I are past our dancing days.
How long is't now since last yourself and I
Were in a mask?

2. CAPULET. By'r lady, thirty years.

CAPULET. What, man? 'tis not so much, 'tis not so much:
'Tis since the nuptial of Lucentio,
Come Pentecost[5] as quickly as it will,
Some five and twenty years, and then we mask'd.

2. CAPULET. 'Tis more, 'tis more. His son is elder,[6] sir;
His son is thirty.

CAPULET. Will you tell me that?
His son was but a ward two years ago.

ROMEO. [*To a* SERVINGMAN.] What lady's that which doth enrich the hand
Of yonder knight?

SERVINGMAN. I know not, sir.

5. **Pentecost.** A Christian festival occurring on the seventh Sunday after Easter, marking the descent of the Holy Ghost on the disciples after the resurrection of Jesus
6. **elder.** Older

Romeo. O, she doth teach the torches to burn bright!
It seems she hangs upon the cheek of night
As a rich jewel in an Ethiop's[7] ear—
Beauty too rich for use, for earth too dear!
So shows a snowy dove trooping with crows,
As yonder lady o'er her fellows shows.
The measure done, I'll watch her place of stand,
And touching hers, make blessed my rude hand.
Did my heart love till now? Forswear it, sight!
For I ne'er saw true beauty till this night.

7. **Ethiop's.** Of a person from Ethiopia, a country in Africa

Tybalt. This, by his voice, should be a Montague.
Fetch me my rapier, boy. What dares the slave
Come hither, cover'd with an antic face,
To fleer[8] and scorn at our solemnity?
Now, by the stock and honor of my kin,
To strike him dead I hold it not a sin.

8. **fleer.** Mock

Capulet. Why, how now, kinsman, wherefore storm you so?

Tybalt. Uncle, this is a Montague, our foe;
A villain that is hither come in spite
To scorn at our solemnity this night.

Capulet. Young Romeo is it?

Tybalt. 'Tis he, that villain Romeo.

Capulet. Content thee, gentle coz, let him alone,
'A bears him like a portly gentleman;[9]
And to say truth, Verona brags of him
To be a virtuous and well-govern'd youth.
I would not for the wealth of all this town
Here in my house do him disparagement;
Therefore be patient, take no note of him;
It is my will, the which if thou respect,
Show a fair presence and put off these frowns,
An ill-beseeming semblance for a feast.

9. **portly gentleman.** Well-mannered nobleman

Tybalt. It fits when such a villain is a guest.
I'll not endure him.

Capulet. He shall be endured.
What, goodman boy?[10] I say he shall, go to!
Am I the master here, or you? go to!
You'll not endure him! God shall mend my soul,
You'll make a mutiny among my guests!
You will set cock-a-hoop![11] you'll be the man!

10. **goodman boy.** The term *goodman* was used to address non-nobles. *Goodman boy* is an insult because Tybalt is being called both common and a boy.
11. **set cock-a-hoop.** Act wildly

Romeo and Juliet meet during Capulet's party.

Critical Viewing

This picture shows Romeo and Juliet as they meet for the first time. What emotions are conveyed in the photo?

TYBALT. Why, uncle, 'tis a shame.

CAPULET. Go to, go to,
You are a saucy boy. Is't so indeed?
This trick may chance to scath you,[12] I know what.
You must contrary me![13] Marry, 'tis time—
Well said, my hearts!—You are a princox,[14] go,
Be quiet, or—More light, more light!—For shame,
I'll make you quiet, what! —Cheerly, my hearts!

12. **trick...you.** Behavior will hurt you
13. **contrary me.** Go contrary to me, or contradict me
14. **princox.** Sassy boy

Tybalt. Patience perforce with willful choler meeting
Makes my flesh tremble in their different greeting.
I will withdraw, but this intrusion shall,
Now seeming sweet, convert to bitt'rest gall.[15] *Exit.*

Romeo. [*To* Juliet.] If I profane with my unworthiest hand
This holy shrine, the gentle sin[16] is this,
My lips, two blushing pilgrims, ready stand
To smooth that rough touch with a tender kiss.

Juliet. Good pilgrim, you do wrong your hand too much,
Which mannerly devotion shows in this:
For saints have hands that pilgrims' hands do touch,
And palm to palm is holy palmers'[17] kiss.

Romeo. Have not saints lips, and holy palmers too?

Juliet. Ay, pilgrim, lips that they must use in pray'r.

Romeo. O then, dear saint, let lips do what hands do,
They pray—grant thou, lest faith turn to despair.

Juliet. Saints do not move, though grant for prayers' sake.

Romeo. Then move not while my prayer's effect I take.
Thus from my lips, by thine, my sin is purg'd. *Kissing her.*

Juliet. Then have my lips the sin that they have took.

Romeo. Sin from my lips? O trespass sweetly urg'd!
Give me my sin again. *Kissing her again.*

Juliet. You kiss by th' book.

Nurse. Madam, your mother craves a word with you.

Romeo. What is her mother?

Nurse. Marry, bachelor,
Her mother is the lady of the house,
And a good lady, and a wise and virtuous.
I nurs'd her daughter that you talk'd withal;[18]
I tell you, he that can lay hold of her
Shall have the chinks.[19]

Romeo. Is she a Capulet?
O dear account! my life is my foe's debt.[20]

Benvolio. Away, be gone, the sport is at the best.[21]

Romeo. Ay, so I fear, the more is my unrest.

15. **gall.** Something bitter to endure

16. **sin.** Fine or penalty

17. **palmers'.** Of pilgrims

18. **withal.** With

19. **chinks.** Money

20. **my foe's debt.** Owed to my enemy; in that enemy's power

21. **sport...best.** Benvolio cautions Romeo to quit while he is ahead.

Capulet. Nay, gentlemen, prepare not to be gone,
We have a trifling foolish banquet towards.[22] *They whisper in his ear.*
Is it e'en so? Why then I thank you all.
I thank you, honest gentlemen, good night.
More torches here! Come on, then let's to bed.
[*To Second Capulet.*] Ah, sirrah, by my fay,[23] it waxes late,
I'll to my rest. *Exeunt all but* Juliet *and* Nurse.

Juliet. Come hither, nurse. What is yond gentleman?

Nurse. The son and heir of old Tiberio.

Juliet. What's he that now is going out of door?

Nurse. Marry, that, I think, be young Petruchio.

Juliet. What's he that follows here, that would not dance?

Nurse. I know not.

Juliet. Go ask his name.—If he be married,
My grave is like to be my wedding-bed.

Nurse. His name is Romeo, and a Montague,
The only son of your great enemy.

Juliet. My only love sprung from my only hate!
Too early seen unknown, and known too late!
Prodigious[24] birth of love it is to me
That I must love a loathed enemy.

Nurse. What's tis? what's tis!

Juliet. A rhyme I learnt even now
Of one I danc'd withal. *One calls within,* "Juliet!"

Nurse. Anon, anon!
Come let's away, the strangers all are gone. *Exeunt.*

22. **towards.** Coming

23. **fay.** Faith

24. **Prodigious.** Ominous

What causes people to fall in love? Is there a difference between true love and infatuation?

REFER TO TEXT	REASON WITH TEXT	
1a. Name the person whom Romeo is in love with at the beginning of the play.	1b. Differentiate between love and marriage in today's world and how they were in Renaissance times. In what ways are they the same?	**Understand** **Find meaning**
2a. Identify the character who intervenes during the opening fight between the Capulets and the Montagues.	2b. Reread Capulet's words on page 515 to predict what kind of a person he is. How does he feel about feuding with Montague?	**Apply** **Use information**
3a. Recall where Romeo first sees Juliet. What are their first reactions to one another?	3b. Compare their mixed emotions regarding one another at the end of Act I. What are their concerns?	**Analyze** **Take things apart**
4a. In the Prologue, state what the Chorus reveals about the outcome of the play.	4b. What might have been Shakespeare's purpose for revealing the outcome of the play at the beginning? Critique whether it lessens or heightens the dramatic tension.	**Evaluate** **Make judgments**
5a. How do Romeo and Juliet react when they discover the identity of the other?	5b. What do the emotions they experience tell you about the two main characters? Deduce what struggles or conflicts the two will experience.	**Create** **Bring ideas together**

ANALYZE LITERATURE: Dramatic Speech

Find the monologues, or long speeches, by the Prince, Capulet, Nurse, and Mercutio in this act. What information do they give about the situation in Verona or the characters? Do they advance the story or give background information? Also note in Act I, Scene i, where Romeo uses paradoxes, or ideas that seem to contradict themselves, to explain his emotions:

O loving hate!
O any thing, of nothing first create!
O heavy lightness, serious vanity,
Misshapen chaos of well-seeming forms,
Feather of lead, bright smoke, cold fire, sick health,
Still-waking sleep, that is not what it is!

What do these paradoxes suggest about Romeo's state of mind?

UNDERSTAND THE CONCEPT

APPLY THE SKILL

Word Origins

Most English words derive from older words in other languages. A good dictionary provides the origins of words. For example, here is an entry for the word *devil:*

dev • il [ME *devel,* fr. OE *deofol,* fr. LL *diabolus,* fr. Gk *diabolos,* lit, slanderer]

According to this entry, *devil* originally came from the Greek (Gk) word *diabolos,* meaning "a slanderer." The word passed through Late Latin (LL), Old English (OE), and Middle English (ME) before becoming our Modern English word *devil. Diabolos* is also the root of the adjective *diabolical,* meaning "wicked."

Many words in English come from ancient Greek and from Latin, the language of the ancient Romans. For example, the following words come from the word root *fract,* which comes from the Latin word *fractio,* meaning the act of breaking:

fraction — what you get when you break something into pieces or portions
infraction — the breaking of a law
fracture — a broken bone

Notice that all these words have a form of "break" as part of their meaning. They are all part of the same **root family.** Knowing the meanings of common Greek and Latin roots can help you decode many unfamiliar words. Here are some common roots:

Word Root	Meaning and Examples
Latin	
am	to love (amicable, amateur)
bene	good, well (benefit)
centr	center (concentrate)
duc/duct	to lead (seduce, conduct)
fer	to carry (transfer, refer)
lum/luc	light (luminous, translucent)
mal/male	bad, badly (malnutrition)
Greek	
acr	highest point (acrobat, acme)
astr, aster	star (astrology, asteroid)
chron	time (chronological)
phil	love, fondness (Anglophile)
psych	mind (psychology)

Another language which has had considerable influence on English is French. In 1066, England was conquered by the Normans, inhabitants of northern France. In the centuries that followed this so-called Norman Conquest, many French words entered English. Since the Normans were the ruling class, many of the words they introduced were related to power and prestige, as well as art, fashion, and food. French, as a Romance language, also contains many words originally derived from Latin.

Some Words Borrowed from French	
politics	crown, government, reign
power relationships	allegiance, authority, servant
law	accuse, felony, justice, verdict
war	defense, siege, surrender
manners	courteous, dignity, loyalty
religion	devotion, faith, virtue
architecture	balcony, dungeon
clothing	attire, costume, dress, gown

Spelling Tip: Commonly Misspelled English Words

While knowing word roots will help you to better understand the meaning of a word, knowing how to spell the word is also important. Some English words are often misspelled. Knowing some of the most commonly misspelled words will help you avoid many errors in your spelling.

attendance
beautiful
breathe
calendar
eighth
embarrass
finally
forfeit
independent
judgment
league
license
misspell
naïve
niece
parallel
privilege
rhythm
succeed
tomorrow
weird
yield

UNDERSTAND THE CONCEPT

APPLY THE SKILL

Exercise A

Look up the following words from *The Tragedy of Romeo and Juliet* and record their origins and roots. Use your dictionary's key to decipher abbreviations. Name other words you find that share the same origins or roots.

1. adversary
2. augment
3. courtier
4. devout
5. forfeit
6. languish
7. nuptial
8. propagate
9. transgression
10. vex

Exercise B

Look up the meaning and origin of each of these words. Then write down the connection between the word's origin and its current meaning. For example, the word *siege* means "a military blockade of a city or fortress," and it comes from the Old French for "seat, settle," which comes from the Latin *sedere,* meaning "to sit." The connection between "sit" and "siege" is that a siege is an extended blockade where the attackers camp around the city and try to starve out their enemies—they "sit out" their enemies. Investigate the origins and connections for these words:

1. assail
2. counsel
3. flourish
4. fray
5. kinsmen
6. mire (*v.*)
7. profane
8. purge
9. visage
10. wax (*v.*)

Exercise C

Many technical terms in different subject areas are derived from other languages such as Latin, Greek, and French. Look up the origin and the meaning of each of the words below. Then write down the connection between the word's origin and its current meaning.

EXAMPLE

hyperbole
Origin: from Greek hyperbolē, meaning excess.
Current Meaning: extravagant exaggeration (exaggeration that is in excess)

1. mathematics
2. anthropology
3. barometer
4. participle
5. organism
6. metric
7. statute
8. synthesis
9. physics
10. gestation

SPELLING PRACTICE

Words with *ei* or *ie*

Whether to spell a word with the vowel combination *ei* or *ie* is one of the most troublesome issues in spelling. Many people repeat the saying taught to them in grade school: "*I* before *e,* except after *c* or when sounded long *a* as in *neighbor* or *weigh.*" However, that saying does not cover every situation in which one is faced with the *ei* or *ie* question. Additional rules state that if the vowel combination is pronounced with a long *e,* it should be spelled with *ie,* as in the word *piece.* However, if the syllable starts with the sound "see," it should be spelled *ei,* as in the words *receipt* or *seize.* Moreover, if the syllable has the "shuh" sound in it, the word will be spelled with *ie,* as in *ancient.* Some words, such as *weird,* are exceptions to the rules. Examine this list of words from *The Tragedy of Romeo and Juliet* to see which rule the word follows.

ancient	bier	chiefly
believe	briefly	

EXTEND THE SKILL

Romeo and Juliet are known as "star-cross'd lovers." The motif of a star occurs in the prologue and in Act I, Scene iv. A **motif** is any element that recurs in one or more works of literature or art. The science of the stars is called *astronomy,* which originated in around 1205, from Old French *astronomie,* Latin *astronomia,* and Greek *astronomia,* The meaning comes from the Greek root *astr* which means "star" plus the suffix *nomia* which means "arranging or regulating." Examine these words associated with astronomy to determine if they contain a Greek, Latin, or other language root, prefix, or suffix. Underline the word part and identify its origin. Then define the word using the meaning of the word part in your definition.

telescope	ultraviolet	galaxy
meteorology	solar	cosmology
celestial	planetarium	

Act II

Enter Chorus.

Now old desire doth in his death-bed lie,
And young affection gapes[1] to be his heir;
That fair[2] for which love groan'd for and would die,
With tender Juliet match'd[3] is now not fair.
Now Romeo is belov'd and loves again,[4]
Alike[5] bewitched by the charm of looks;
But to his foe suppos'd he must complain,[6]
And she steal love's sweet bait from fearful[7] hooks.
Being held a foe, he may not have access
To breathe such vows as lovers use to[8] swear,
And she as much in love, her means much less
To meet her new-beloved any where.
But passion lends them power, time means,
to meet, Temp'ring[9] extremities[10] with
extreme sweet.

Exit.

Scene i: Capulet's Orchard

Enter Romeo *alone.*

Romeo. Can I go forward when my heart is here?
Turn back, dull earth,[11] and find thy center[12] out.

Enter Benvolio *with* Mercutio. Romeo *withdraws.*

Benvolio. Romeo! my cousin Romeo! Romeo!

Mercutio. He is wise,
And, on my life, hath stol'n him home to bed.

Benvolio. He ran this way and leapt this orchard[13] wall.
Call, good Mercutio.

Mercutio. Nay, I'll conjure[14] too.
Romeo! humors! madman! passion! lover!
Appear thou in the likeness of a sigh!
Speak but one rhyme, and I am satisfied;
Cry but "Ay me!", pronounce but "love" and "dove,"
Speak to my gossip[15] Venus one fair word,
One nickname for her purblind[16] son and heir,
Young Abraham[17] Cupid he that shot so trim,[18]
When King Cophetua lov'd the beggar-maid![19]

Act II, Scene i

1. **gapes.** Desires
2. **fair.** Beauty
3. **match'd.** Compared
4. **loves again.** Loves back
5. **Alike.** Both
6. **complain.** Speak (of his love)
7. **fearful.** Dangerous
8. **use to.** Usually
9. **Temp'ring.** Lessening or making bearable
10. **extremities.** Difficulties
11. **dull earth.** The body, made of earth
12. **center.** Romeo is saying that Juliet is the center of his life. He turns back to her as things on Earth fall toward its center.
13. **orchard.** Garden
14. **conjure.** Cause a spirit to appear
15. **gossip.** Busybody or crone
16. **purblind.** Weak-sighted
17. **Abraham.** Beggar
18. **trim.** Precisely; accurately
19. **King...maid.** Love story from a popular ballad

He heareth not, he stirreth not, he moveth not,
The ape is dead, and I must conjure him.
I conjure thee by Rosaline's bright eyes,
By her high forehead and her scarlet lip,
By her fine foot, straight leg, and quivering thigh,
And the demesnes[20] that there adjacent lie,
That in thy likeness thou appear to us!

BENVOLIO. And if[21] he hear thee, thou wilt anger him.

MERCUTIO. This cannot anger him; 'twould anger him
To raise a spirit in his mistress' circle,[22]
Of some strange nature, letting it there stand
Till she had laid it and conjur'd it down.
That were some spite.[23] My invocation
Is fair and honest; in his mistress' name
I conjure only but to raise up him.

BENVOLIO. Come, he hath hid himself among these trees
To be consorted with the humorous[24] night.
Blind is his love and best befits the dark.

MERCUTIO. If love be blind, love cannot hit the mark.
Now will he sit under a medlar[25] tree,
And wish his mistress were that kind of fruit
As maids call medlars, when they laugh alone.
O, Romeo, that she were, O that she were
An open-arse,[26] thou a pop'rin pear![27]
Romeo, good night, I'll to my truckle-bed,[28]
This field-bed is too cold for me to sleep.
Come, shall we go?

BENVOLIO. Go then, for 'tis in vain
To seek him here that means not to be found. *Exit with* MERCUTIO.

20. **demesnes.** Regions

ad • ja • cent (ə jā´ sənt) *adj.,* near

21. **And if.** If

22. **To raise...circle.** To call up a spirit as in a seance

23. **spite.** Vexation

24. **consorted...humorous.** In harmony with the wet or mood-provoking

25. **medlar.** Fruit

26. **open-arse.** Another name for the medlar fruit

27. **pop'rin pear.** Kind of fruit

28. **truckle-bed.** Small bed that fits under a larger bed

SCENE II: CAPULET'S ORCHARD

ROMEO *advances.*

ROMEO. He jests at scars that never felt a wound.

Enter JULIET *above at her window.*

ROMEO. But soft, what light through yonder window breaks?
It is the east, and Juliet is the sun.
Arise, fair sun, and kill the envious moon,
Who is already sick and pale with grief
That thou, her maid,[1] art far more fair than she.

ACT II, SCENE II

1. **maid.** Servant

Be not her maid, since she is envious;
Her vestal livery[2] is but sick and green,
And none but fools do wear it; cast it off.
It is my lady, O, it is my love!
O that she knew she were!
She speaks, yet she says nothing; what of that?
Her eye discourses, I will answer it.
I am too bold, 'tis not to me she speaks.
Two of the fairest stars in all the heaven,
Having some business, do entreat her eyes
To twinkle in their spheres[3] till they return.
What if her eyes were there, they in her head?
The brightness of her cheek would shame those stars,
As daylight doth a lamp; her eyes in heaven
Would through the airy region stream[4] so bright
That birds would sing and think it were not night.
See how she leans her cheek upon her hand!
O that I were a glove upon that hand,
That I might touch that cheek!

Juliet. Ay me!

Romeo. She speaks!
O, speak again, bright angel, for thou art
As glorious to this night, being o'er my head,
As is a winged messenger of heaven
Unto the white-upturned[5] wond'ring eyes
Of mortals that fall back to gaze on him,
When he bestrides the lazy puffing clouds,
And sails upon the bosom of the air.

Juliet. O Romeo, Romeo, wherefore art thou Romeo?
Deny thy father and refuse thy name;
Or, if thou wilt not, be but sworn my love,
And I'll no longer be a Capulet.

Romeo. [*Aside.*] Shall I hear more, or shall I speak at this?

Juliet. 'Tis but thy name that is my enemy;
Thou art thyself, though not a Montague.[6]
What's Montague? It is nor hand nor foot,
Nor arm nor face, nor any other part
Belonging to a man. O, be some other name!
What's in a name? That which we call a rose
By any other word would smell as sweet;
So Romeo would, were he not Romeo call'd,
Retain that dear perfection which he owes[7]
Without that title. Romeo, doff thy name,

2. **vestal livery.** Uniform belonging to a servant of Vestia, the virgin Roman goddess

dis • course (dis kôrs´) *v.*, talk; converse

3. **spheres.** Places in the heavens

4. **stream.** Shine

5. **white-upturned.** When the eyes look up, more of the whites of them show.

6. **Thou...Montague.** If you were to change your name, it would not change who you are.

7. **owes.** Owns; has

And for[8] thy name, which is no part of thee,
Take all myself.

Romeo. I take thee at thy word.
Call me but love, and I'll be new baptiz'd;
Henceforth I never will be Romeo.

Juliet. What man art thou that thus bescreen'd in night
So stumblest on my counsel?[9]

Romeo. By a name
I know not how to tell thee who I am.
My name, dear saint, is hateful to myself,
Because it is an enemy to thee;
Had I it written, I would tear the word.

Juliet. My ears have yet not drunk a hundred words
Of thy tongue's uttering, yet I know the sound.
Art thou not Romeo, and a Montague?

Romeo. Neither, fair maid, if either thee dislike.

Juliet. How camest thou hither, tell me, and wherefore?
The orchard walls are high and hard to climb,
And the place death, considering who thou art,
If any of my kinsmen find thee here.

Romeo. With love's light wings did I o'erperch[10] these walls,
For stony limits cannot hold love out,
And what love can do, that dares love attempt;
Therefore thy kinsmen are no stop to me.

Juliet. If they do see thee, they will murther[11] thee.

Romeo. Alack, there lies more peril in thine eye
Than twenty of their swords! Look thou but sweet,
And I am proof[12] against their enmity.

Juliet. I would not for the world they saw thee here.

Romeo. I have night's cloak to hide me from their eyes,
And but thou love me,[13] let them find me here;
My life were better ended by their hate,
Than death prorogued,[14] wanting of[15] thy love.

Juliet. By whose direction foundst thou out this place?[16]

Romeo. By love, that first did prompt me to inquire;
He lent me counsel, and I lent him eyes.
I am no pilot, yet, wert thou as far
As that vast shore wash'd with the farthest sea,
I should adventure for such merchandise.[17]

8. **for.** In payment for

9. **counsel.** Meditations; private musings

10. **o'erperch.** Fly over

11. **murther.** Murder

12. **proof.** Protected

en • mi • ty (en´ mə tē) *n.*, hostility; hate; bitterness

13. **And but thou love me.** If you do not love me

14. **prorogued.** Postponed

15. **wanting of.** Lacking

16. **By whose...place?** Who gave you directions to this place?

17. **I am...merchandise.** Romeo compares his willingness to work for her love to the willingness of sailors to risk dangerous voyages.

Romeo climbs the balcony to greet Juliet.

Juliet. Thou knowest the mask of night is on my face,
Else would a maiden blush bepaint my cheek
For that which thou hast heard me speak tonight.
Fain[18] would I dwell on form,[19] fain deny
What I have spoke, but farewell compliment![20]
Dost thou love me? I know thou wilt say, "Ay,"
And I will take thy word; yet, if thou swear'st,
Thou mayest prove false: at lovers' perjuries
They say Jove laughs. O gentle Romeo,
If thou dost love, pronounce it faithfully,
Or if thou thinkest I am too quickly won,
I'll frown and be perverse, and say thee nay,
So thou wilt[21] woo, but else not for the world.
In truth, fair Montague, I am too fond,[22]
And therefore thou mayest think my behavior light,
But trust me, gentleman, I'll prove more true
Than those that have more coying[23] to be strange.[24]
I should have been more strange, I must confess,
But that thou overheardst, ere I was ware,
My true-love passion; therefore pardon me,
And not impute this yielding to light love,
Which the dark night hath so discovered.[25]

18. **Fain.** Gladly
19. **dwell on form.** Act formally
20. **compliment.** Etiquette; social graces

21. **So thou wilt.** So that you will
22. **fond.** Silly

23. **coying.** Coyness; skill at coquetry
24. **strange.** Distant; stand-offish

25. **discovered.** Shown

Romeo. Lady, by yonder blessed moon I vow,
That tips with silver all these fruit-tree tops—

Juliet. O, swear not by the moon, th' inconstant moon,
That monthly changes in her circled orb,[26]
Lest that thy love prove likewise variable.[27]

26. **circled orb.** Orbit

27. **Lest...variable.** Because of its changes, the moon is a traditional symbol of inconsistency, or fickleness.

Romeo. What shall I swear by?

Juliet. Do not swear at all;
Or if thou wilt, swear by thy gracious self,
Which is the god of my idolatry,
And I'll believe thee.

Romeo. If my heart's dear love—

Juliet. Well, do not swear. Although I joy in thee,
I have no joy of this contract tonight,
It is too rash, too unadvis'd, too sudden,
Too like the lightning, which doth cease to be
Ere one can say it lightens. Sweet, good night!
This bud of love, by summer's ripening breath,
May prove a beauteous flow'r when next we meet.
Good night, good night! as sweet repose and rest
Come to thy heart as that within my breast!

re • pose (ri pōz´) *n.,* peace; rest; sleep

Romeo. O, wilt thou leave me so unsatisfied?

Juliet. What satisfaction canst thou have tonight?

Romeo. Th' exchange of thy love's faithful vow for mine.

Juliet. I gave thee mine before thou didst request it;
And yet I would it were to give again.

Romeo. Wouldst thou withdraw it? for what purpose, love?

Juliet. But to be frank[28] and give it thee again,
And yet I wish but for the thing I have.
My bounty is as boundless as the sea,
My love as deep; the more I give to thee,
The more I have, for both are infinite. *Nurse calls within.*
I hear some noise within; dear love, adieu!
Anon,[29] good nurse! Sweet Montague, be true.
Stay but a little, I will come again. *Exit above.*

28. **frank.** Generous

29. **Anon.** Now; at once

Romeo. O blessed, blessed night! I am afeard,
Being in night, all this is but a dream,
Too flattering-sweet to be substantial.

Enter Juliet *above.*

JULIET. Three words, dear Romeo, and good night indeed.
If that thy bent of love[30] be honorable,
Thy purpose marriage, send me word tomorrow,
By one that I'll procure to come to thee,
Where and what time thou wilt perform the rite,
And all my fortunes at thy foot I'll lay,
And follow thee my lord throughout the world.

NURSE. [*Within.*] Madam!

JULIET. I come, anon.—But if thou meanest not well,
I do beseech thee—

NURSE. [*Within.*] Madam!

JULIET. By and by,[31] I come—
To cease thy strife,[32] and leave me to my grief.
Tomorrow will I send.

ROMEO. So thrive my soul—

JULIET. A thousand times good night! *Exit above.*

ROMEO. A thousand times the worse, to want thy light.
Love goes toward love as schoolboys from their books,
But love from love, toward school with heavy looks. *Retiring.*

Enter JULIET *again above.*

JULIET. Hist,[33] Romeo, hist! O, for a falc'ner's voice,
To lure this tassel-gentle[34] back again!
Bondage is hoarse, and may not speak aloud,
Else would I tear the cave where Echo lies,
And make her airy tongue more hoarse than mine,
With repetition of my Romeo's name. Romeo!

ROMEO. It is my soul that calls upon my name.
How silver-sweet sound lovers' tongues by night,
Like softest music to attending ears!

JULIET. Romeo!

ROMEO. My niesse?[35]

JULIET. What a' clock tomorrow
Shall I send to thee?

ROMEO. By the hour of nine.

JULIET. I will not fail, 'tis twenty year till then.
I have forgot why I did call thee back.

ROMEO. Let me stand here till thou remember it.

30. **thy...love.** The purpose or inclination of your love

pro • cure (prō kyür´) *v.*, get or bring about by some effort

31. **By and by.** Now, at this moment

32. **strife.** Striving; endeavor. Other texts use the word "suit" here.

33. **Hist.** Falconer's call

34. **tassel-gentle.** Male falcon of a type reserved to princes

35. **niesse.** Nestling hawk

Juliet. I shall forget, to have thee still[36] stand there,
Rememb'ring how I love thy company.

Romeo. And I'll still stay, to have thee still forget,
Forgetting any other home but this.

Juliet. 'Tis almost morning, I would have thee gone—
And yet no farther than a wanton's bird,
That lets it hop a little from his hand,
Like a poor prisoner in his twisted gyves,[37]
And with a silken thread plucks it back again,
So loving-jealous of his liberty.

Romeo. I would I were thy bird.

Juliet. Sweet, so would I,
Yet I should kill thee with much cherishing.
Good night, good night! Parting is such sweet sorrow
That I shall say good night till it be morrow. *Exit above.*

Romeo. Sleep dwell upon thine eyes, peace in thy breast!
Would I were sleep and peace, so sweet to rest!
Hence will I to my ghostly sire's close cell,[38]
His help to crave, and my dear hap[39] to tell. *Exit.*

36. **still.** Always

37. **gyves.** Chains around ankles

38. **ghostly sire's close cell.** Priest's (or confessor's) secluded room

39. **hap.** Fortune

Scene iii: Friar Lawrence's Cell

Enter Friar Lawrence *alone, with a basket.*

Friar Lawrence. The grey-ey'd morn smiles on the frowning night,
Check'ring the eastern clouds with streaks of light,
And fleckled[1] darkness like a drunkard reels
From forth day's path and Titan's fiery wheels.[2]
Now ere the sun advance his burning eye,
The day to cheer and night's dank dew to dry,
I must up-fill this osier cage[3] of ours
With baleful weeds and precious-juiced flowers.
The earth that's nature's mother is her tomb;
What is her burying grave, that is her womb;
And from her womb children of divers kind
We sucking on her natural bosom find:
Many for many virtues excellent,
None but for some,[4] and yet all different.
O, mickle[5] is the powerful grace that lies
In plants, herbs, stones, and their true qualities;
For nought so vile that on the earth doth live
But to the earth some special good doth give;

Act II, Scene iii

1. **fleckled.** Flecked; spotted with color
2. **Titan's fiery wheels.** Wheels of the chariot belonging to the sun god, Helios, one of the Titans
3. **osier cage.** Willow basket
4. **None…some.** None without some valuable property
5. **mickle.** Great

Nor aught so good but, strain'd from that fair use,
Revolts from true birth,[6] stumbling on abuse.
Virtue itself turns[7] vice, being misapplied
And vice sometime by action dignified.[8]

Enter ROMEO.

Within the infant rind of this weak flower
Poison hath residence and medicine power;
For this, being smelt, with that part cheers each part,
Being tasted, stays all senses with the heart.[9]
Two such opposed kings encamp them still
In man as well as herbs, grace and rude will;
And where the worser is predominant,
Full soon the canker[10] death eats up that plant.

ROMEO. Good morrow, father.

FRIAR LAWRENCE. *Benedicite!*[11]
What early tongue so sweet saluteth me?
Young son, it argues a distempered[12] head
So soon to bid good morrow to thy bed.
Care keeps his watch in every old man's eye,
And where care lodges, sleep will never lie;
But where unbruised youth with unstuff'd brain
Doth couch his limbs, there golden sleep doth reign.
Therefore thy earliness doth me assure
Thou art up-rous'd with some distemp'rature;
Or if not so, then here I hit it right—
Our Romeo hath not been in bed tonight.

ROMEO. That last is true—the sweeter rest was mine.

FRIAR LAWRENCE. God pardon sin! Wast thou with Rosaline?

ROMEO. With Rosaline? my ghostly father, no;
I have forgot that name, and that name's woe.

FRIAR LAWRENCE. That's my good son, but where hast thou been then?

ROMEO. I'll tell thee ere thou ask it me again.
I have been feasting with mine enemy,
Where on a sudden one hath wounded me
That's by me wounded; both our remedies
Within thy help and holy physic[13] lies.
I bear no hatred, blessed man, for lo
My intercession[14] likewise steads[15] my foe.

FRIAR LAWRENCE. Be plain, good son, and homely in thy drift,[16]
Riddling confession finds but riddling shrift.[17]

6. **true birth.** Its nature
7. **turns.** Becomes
8. **vice...dignified.** Vice may sometimes be made worthy by particular circumstances.

9. **For this...heart.** Being smelled, it improves health; being tasted, it kills.

pre • dom • i • nant (prē däm´ ə nənt) *adj.,* dominant; ruling; controlling

10. **canker.** Worm in the bud of a plant
11. ***Benedicite!*** Bless you

12. **distempered.** Disordered; disturbed

13. **physic.** Healing power
14. **intercession.** Petition; request
15. **steads.** Helps
16. **homely...drift.** Plain in your speech
17. **shrift.** Forgiveness; absolution of sin

Romeo. Then plainly know my heart's dear love is set
On the fair daughter of rich Capulet.
As mine on hers, so hers is set on mine,
And all combin'd, save what thou must combine
By holy marriage. When and where and how
We met, we woo'd, and made exchange of vow,
I'll tell thee as we pass, but this I pray,
That thou consent to marry us today.

Friar Lawrence. Holy Saint Francis, what a change is here!
Is Rosaline, that thou didst love so dear,
So soon forsaken? Young men's love then lies
Not truly in their hearts, but in their eyes.
Jesu Maria, what a deal of brine[18]
Hath wash'd thy sallow[19] cheeks for Rosaline!
How much salt water thrown away in waste,
To season love, that of it doth not taste!
The sun not yet thy sighs from heaven clears,
Thy old groans yet ringing in mine ancient ears;
Lo here upon thy cheek the stain doth sit
Of an old tear that is not wash'd off yet.
If e'er thou wast[20] thyself and these woes thine,
Thou and these woes were all for Rosaline.
And art thou chang'd? Pronounce this sentence then:
Women may fall, when there's no strength in men.

Romeo. Thou chidst me oft for loving Rosaline.

Friar Lawrence. For doting, not for loving, pupil mine.

Romeo. And badst me[21] bury love.

Friar Lawrence. Not in a grave,
To lay one in, another out to have.

Romeo. I pray thee chide me not. Her I love now
Doth grace for grace and love for love allow;
The other did not so.

Friar Lawrence. O, she knew well
Thy love did read by rote that could not spell.[22]
But come, young waverer, come go with me,
In one respect I'll thy assistant be;
For this alliance may so happy prove
To turn your households' rancor to pure love.

Romeo. O, let us hence, I stand on[23] sudden haste.

Friar Lawrence. Wisely and slow, they stumble that run fast.

Exeunt.

18. **brine.** Salt water; tears

19. **sallow.** Of a sickly, pale yellow color

20. **wast.** Was

chide (chīd) *v.*, scold
dote (dōt) *v.*, adore; spoil; make much of

21. **badst me.** Bade me; told me to

22. **Thy love...spell.** Your love was recited from memory, not really understood or felt.

ran • cor (raŋ´ kər) *n.*, bitter hate; ill will

23. **stand on.** Require

SCENE IV: A STREET IN VERONA

Enter BENVOLIO *and* MERCUTIO.

MERCUTIO. Where the dev'l should this Romeo be?
Came he not home tonight?

BENVOLIO. Not to his father's, I spoke with his man.

MERCUTIO. Why, that same pale hard-hearted wench, that Rosaline,
Torments him so, that he will sure run mad.

BENVOLIO. Tybalt, the kinsman to old Capulet,
Hath sent a letter to his father's house.

MERCUTIO. A challenge, on my life.

BENVOLIO. Romeo will answer it.

MERCUTIO. Any man that can write may answer a letter.

BENVOLIO. Nay, he will answer the letter's master, how he dares, being dar'd.

MERCUTIO. Alas, poor Romeo, he is already dead, stabb'd with a white wench's black eye, run through the ear with a love-song, the very pin[1] of his heart cleft with the blind bow-boy's butt-shaft;[2] is he a man to encounter Tybalt?

BENVOLIO. Why, what is Tybalt?

MERCUTIO. More than Prince of Cats.[3] O, he's the courageous captain of compliments.[4] He fights as you sing prick-song,[5] keeps time, distance, and proportion; he rests his minim[6] rests, one, two, and the third in your bosom: the very butcher of a silk button,[7] a duellist, a duellist; a gentle-man of the very first house, of the first and second cause. Ah, the immortal *passado,* the *punto reverso,* the *hay!*[8]

BENVOLIO. The what?

MERCUTIO. The pox of such antic, lisping, affecting phantasimes, these new tuners of accent![9] "By Jesu, a very good blade! a very tall[10] man! a very good whore!" Why, is not this a lamentable thing, grandsire, that we should be thus afflicted with these strange flies, these fashion-mongers, these pardon-me's,[11] who stand so much on the new form,[12] that they cannot sit at ease on the old bench? O, their bones, their bones!

Enter ROMEO.

BENVOLIO. Here comes Romeo, here comes Romeo.

ACT II, SCENE IV

1. **pin.** Bull's eye
2. **butt-shaft.** Blunt, non-barbed arrow used for practice by the love god Cupid
3. **Prince of Cats.** Tybalt is the name of the Prince of Cats in a series of medieval tales about Reynard the Fox.
4. **captain of compliments.** Dueling master
5. **prick-song.** Printed music
6. **minim.** A short note in music
7. **butcher...button.** Swordsman good enough to pierce a particular button on an opponent's clothing
8. **a gentle-man...*hay.*** Superb swordsman, knowledgeable about the rules and techniques of swordplay
9. **The pox...accent.** The sickness of smart, young people with their modern speech
10. **tall.** Large; intimidating
11. **pardon-me's.** Overly polite, affected people
12. **form.** Contemporary fashions or fads

Mercutio. Without his roe,[13] like a dried herring: O flesh flesh, how art thou fishified! Now is he for the numbers[14] that Petrarch flow'd in. Laura to his lady was a kitchen wench (marry, she had a better love to berhyme her), Dido a dowdy, Cleopatra a gipsy, Helen and Hero hildings[15] and harlots, Thisby[16] a gray eye or so, but not to the purpose. Signior Romeo, *bon jour!* there's a French salutation to your French slop.[17] You gave us the counterfeit fairly last night.

Romeo. Good morrow to you both. What counterfeit did I give you?

Mercutio. The slip,[18] sir, the slip, can you not conceive?[19]

Romeo. Pardon, good Mercutio, my business was great, and in such a case as mine a man may strain courtesy.

Mercutio. That's as much as to say, such a case as yours constrains a man to bow in the hams.

Romeo. Meaning to cur'sy.

Mercutio. Thou hast most kindly hit it.

Romeo. A most courteous exposition.

Mercutio. Nay, I am the very pink[20] of courtesy.

Romeo. Pink for flower.

Mercutio. Right.

Romeo. Why then is my pump[21] well flower'd.[22]

Mercutio. Sure wit! Follow me this jest now, till thou hast worn out thy pump, that when the single[23] sole of it is worn, the jest may remain, after the wearing, soly <u>singular</u>.

Romeo. O single-sol'd jest, soly singular for the singleness![24]

Mercutio. Come between us, good Benvolio, my wits faints.

Romeo. Swits and spurs,[25] swits and spurs, or I'll cry a match.[26]

Mercutio. Nay, if our wits run the wild-goose chase, I am done; for thou hast more of the wild goose in one of thy wits than, I am sure, I have in my whole five. Was I with you there for the goose?

Romeo. Thou wast never with me for any thing when thou wast not there for the goose.

Mercutio. I will bite thee by the ear for that jest.

Romeo. Nay, good goose, bite not.

Mercutio. Thy wit is a very bitter sweeting,[27] it is a most sharp sauce.

13. **Without his roe.** Thin from not eating
14. **numbers.** Verses of poetry
15. **hildings.** Good-for-nothings
16. **Laura...Thisby.** Famous women in love stories
17. **French slop.** Pants
18. **The slip.** Counterfeit coins were called *slips.*
19. **conceive.** Understand
20. **pink.** Flower
21. **pump.** Shoe
22. **flower'd.** Decorated by pinking, or punching with holes
23. **single.** Thin

sin • gu • lar
(siŋ´ gyə lər) *adj.*, one-of-a-kind; exceptional; unique

24. **O single-sol'd...singleness.** Feeble jest, unequaled in its silliness
25. **Swits and spurs.** Switches and spurs
26. **cry a match.** Claim victory
27. **sweeting.** Kind of apple

ROMEO. And is it not then well serv'd in to a sweet goose?

MERCUTIO. O, here's a wit of cheverel,[28] that stretches from an inch narrow to an ell[29] broad!

ROMEO. I stretch it out for that word "broad," which, added to the goose, proves thee far and wide a broad[30] goose.

MERCUTIO. Why, is not this better now than groaning for love? Now art thou sociable, now art thou Romeo; now art thou what thou art, by art as well as by nature, for this drivelling love is like a great natural[31] that runs lolling up and down to hide his bable[32] in a hole.

BENVOLIO. Stop there, stop there.

MERCUTIO. Thou desirest me to stop in my tale against the hair.[33]

BENVOLIO. Thou wouldst else have made thy tale large.

MERCUTIO. O, thou art deceiv'd; I would have made it short, for I was come to the whole depth of my tale, and meant indeed to occupy the argument no longer.

ROMEO. Here's goodly gear!

Enter NURSE *and her man* PETER.

A sail, a sail!

MERCUTIO. Two, two: a shirt and a smock.[34]

NURSE. Peter!

PETER. Anon!

NURSE. My fan, Peter.

MERCUTIO. Good Peter, to hide her face, for her fan's the fairer face.

NURSE. God ye good morrow, gentlemen.

MERCUTIO. God ye good den,[35] fair gentlewoman.

NURSE. Is it good den?

MERCUTIO. 'Tis no less, I tell ye, for the bawdy hand of the dial is now upon the prick[36] of noon.

NURSE. Out upon you, what a man[37] are you?

ROMEO. One, gentlewoman, that God hath made, himself to mar.

NURSE. By my troth,[38] it is well said; "for himself to mar," quoth 'a![39] Gentlemen, can any of you tell me where I may find the young Romeo?

28. **cheverel.** Easily stretched kind of leather

29. **ell.** Measure equal to forty-five inches

30. **broad.** Large or obvious

31. **natural.** Fool; jester

32. **bable.** Bauble; stick carried by a court jester

33. **against the hair.** Against my wish

34. **shirt...smock.** Man and a woman

35. **good den.** Good after-noon

36. **prick.** Mark on a sundial or clock

37. **what a man.** What sort of person

38. **troth.** Faith

39. **quoth 'a.** Says he

Romeo. I can tell you, but young Romeo will be older when you have found him than he was when you sought him. I am the youngest of that name, for fault of a worse.

Nurse. You say well.

Mercutio. Yea, is the worst well? Very well took, i' faith, wisely, wisely.

Nurse. If you be he, sir, I desire some confidence with you.

Benvolio. She will indite[40] him to some supper.

Mercutio. A bawd, a bawd, a bawd! So ho![41]

Romeo. What hast thou found?

Mercutio. No hare,[42] sir, unless a hare, sir, in a lenten pie,[43] that is something stale and hoar[44] ere it be spent.[45]

He walks by them and sings.

An old hare hoar,
And an old hare hoar,
Is very good meat in Lent;
But a hare that is hoar
Is too much for a score,[46]
When it hoars ere it be spent.

Romeo, will you come to your father's? We'll to dinner thither.

Romeo. I will follow you.

Mercutio. Farewell, ancient lady, farewell, *singing* "lady, lady, lady."

Exeunt Mercutio *and* Benvolio.

Nurse. I pray you, sir, what saucy merchant[47] was this, that was so full of his ropery?[48]

Romeo. A gentleman, nurse, that loves to hear himself talk, and will speak more in a minute than he will stand to in a month.

Nurse. And 'a speak any thing against me, I'll take him down, and 'a were lustier than he is, and twenty such Jacks; and if I cannot, I'll find those that shall. Scurvy knave, I am none of his flirt-gills,[49] I am none of his skains-mates.[50] [*She turns to* Peter, *her man.*] And thou must stand by too and suffer every knave to use me at his pleasure!

Peter. I saw no man use you at his pleasure; if I had, my weapon should quickly have been out. I warrant you, I dare draw as soon as another man, if I see occasion in a good quarrel, and the law on my side.

40. **indite.** Invite

41. **So ho.** Hunter's cry

42. **hare.** A rabbit. There is a double meaning here, as well. *Hare* was a term used to refer to a woman of loose character. Mercutio is referring to the Nurse.

43. **lenten pie.** Meatless pie prepared during Lent, into which, Mercutio suggests, one might place an old rabbit left over from before the Lenten season

44. **hoar.** Moldy

45. **spent.** Eaten

46. **Is...score.** Costs too much

47. **saucy merchant.** Jesting, vulgar man

48. **ropery.** Vulgar jokes

49. **flirt-gills.** Flirtatious, loose women

50. **skains-mates.** Outlaw women

Nurse. Now, afore God, I am so vex'd that every part about me quivers. Scurvy knave! Pray you, sir, a word: and as I told you, my young lady bid me inquire you out; what she bid me say, I will keep to myself. But first let me tell ye, if ye should lead her in a fool's paradise, as they say, it were a very gross kind of behavior, as they say; for the gentlewoman is young; and therefore, if you should deal double[51] with her, truly it were an ill thing to be offred to any gentlewoman, and very weak[52] dealing.

51. **deal double.** Speak untruly or equivocally
52. **weak.** Poor; mean

Romeo. Nurse, commend me to thy lady and mistress. I protest unto thee—

Nurse. Good heart, and, i' faith, I will tell her as much.[53] Lord, Lord, she will be a joyful woman.

53. **I will...much.** The nurse has not allowed Romeo to say anything.

Romeo. What wilt thou tell her, nurse? Thou dost not mark[54] me.

54. **mark.** Listen to

Nurse. I will tell her, sir, that you do protest, which, as I take it, is a gentleman-like offer.

Romeo. Bid her devise
Some means to come to shrift[55] this afternoon,
And there she shall at Friar Lawrence' cell
Be shriv'd and married. Here is for thy pains.

55. **shrift.** Confession

Nurse. No, truly, sir, not a penny.

Romeo. Go to, I say you shall.

Nurse. This afternoon, sir? Well, she shall be there.

Romeo. And stay, good nurse—behind the abbey wall
Within this hour my man shall be with thee,
And bring thee cords made like a tackled stair,[56]
Which to the high top-gallant[57] of my joy
Must be my convoy[58] in the secret night.
Farewell, be trusty, and I'll quit[59] thy pains.
Farewell, commend me to thy mistress.

56. **tackled stair.** Rope ladder
57. **top-gallant.** Highest mast of a ship
58. **convoy.** Means of passage
59. **quit.** Reward

Nurse. Now God in heaven bless thee! Hark you, sir.

Romeo. What say'st thou, my dear nurse?

Nurse. Is your man secret?[60] Did you ne'er hear say,
"Two may keep counsel,[61] putting one away"?[62]

60. **secret.** Discreet
61. **keep counsel.** Keep a secret
62. **putting one away.** If one of them is away

Romeo. 'Warrant thee, my man's as true as steel.

Nurse. Well, sir, my mistress is the sweetest lady—Lord, Lord! when 'twas a little prating thing—O, there is a nobleman in town, one Paris, that would fain lay knife aboard;[63] but she, good soul, had as lieve[64]

63. **lay knife aboard.** Lay siege, or claim
64. **lieve.** Willingly

see a toad, a very toad, as see him. I anger her sometimes and tell her that Paris is the properer[65] man, but I'll warrant you, when I say so, she looks as pale as any clout[66] in the versal[67] world. Doth not rosemary and Romeo begin both with a letter?[68]

65. **properer.** Handsomer
66. **clout.** Cloth
67. **versal.** Universal; whole
68. **a letter.** The same letter

Romeo. Ay, nurse, what of that? Both with an *R.*

Nurse. Ah, mocker, that's the dog's name.[69] *R* is for the—no, I know it begins with some other letter—and she hath the prettiest sententious[70] of it, of you and rosemary, that it would do you good to hear it.

69. **the dog's name.** Because an *r* sounds like the growl of a dog
70. **sententious.** Sayings (The Nurse is misusing a big word.)

Romeo. Commend me to thy lady.

Nurse. Ay, a thousand times. [*Exit* Romeo.] Peter!

Peter. Anon!

Nurse. [*Handing him her fan.*] Before, and apace.

Exit after Peter.

Scene v: Capulet's Orchard

Enter Juliet.

Juliet. The clock strook nine when I did send the nurse;
In half an hour she promised to return.
Perchance she cannot meet him—that's not so.
O, she is lame! Love's heralds should be thoughts,
Which ten times faster glides than the sun's beams,
Driving back shadows over low'ring hills;
Therefore do nimble-pinion'd doves draw Love,[1]
And therefore hath the wind-swift Cupid wings.
Now is the sun upon the highmost hill
Of this day's journey, and from nine till twelve
Is three long hours, yet she is not come.
Had she affections and warm youthful blood,
She would be as swift in motion as a ball;
My words would bandy[2] her to my sweet love,
And his to me.
But old folks—many feign as they were dead,
Unwieldy, slow, heavy, and pale as lead.

Act II, Scene v
1. **draw Love.** Pull the chariot of Venus
2. **bandy.** Toss

Enter Nurse *and* Peter.

O God, she comes! O honey nurse, what news?
Hast thou met with him? Send thy man away.

Nurse. Peter, stay at the gate. *Exit* Peter.

Juliet. Now, good sweet nurse—O Lord, why lookest thou sad?
Though news be sad, yet tell them merrily;
If good, thou shamest the music of sweet news
By playing it to me with so sour a face.

Nurse. I am a-weary, give me leave a while.
Fie, how my bones ache! What a jaunce[3] have I!

Juliet. I would thou hadst my bones, and I thy news.
Nay, come, I pray thee speak, good, good nurse, speak.

Nurse. Jesu, what haste! Can you not stay[4] a while?
Do you not see that I am out of breath?

Juliet. How art thou out of breath, when thou hast breath
To say to me that thou art out of breath?
The excuse that thou dost make in this delay
Is longer than the tale thou dost excuse.
Is thy news good or bad? Answer to that.
Say either, and I'll stay the circumstance.[5]
Let me be satisfied, is't good or bad?

Nurse. Well, you have made a simple[6] choice, you know not how to choose a man. Romeo! no, not he. Though his face be better than any man's, yet his leg excels all men's, and for a hand and a foot and a body, though they be not to be talk'd on,[7] yet they are past compare. He is not the flower of courtesy, but I'll warrant him, as gentle as a lamb. Go thy ways, wench, serve God. What, have you din'd at home?

Juliet. No, no! But all this did I know before.
What says he of our marriage? what of that?

Nurse. Lord, how my head aches! What a head have I!
It beats as it would fall in twenty pieces.
My back a' t'[8] other side—ah, my back, my back!
Beshrew your heart[9] for sending me about
To catch my death with jauncing up and down!

Juliet. I' faith, I am sorry that thou art not well.
Sweet, sweet, sweet nurse, tell me, what says my love?

Nurse. Your love says, like an honest gentleman,
An' a courteous, and a kind, and a handsome,
And, I warrant, a virtuous—Where is your mother?

Juliet. Where is my mother! why, she is within,
Where should she be? How oddly thou repliest!

3. **jaunce.** Bounce; difficult journey

4. **stay.** Wait

5. **stay the circumstance.** Wait for details

6. **simple.** Foolish

7. **be not…on.** Aren't worth talking about

8. **a' t'.** On the

9. **Beshrew your heart.** (Mild oath)

"Your love says, like an honest gentleman,
'Where is your mother?'"

Nurse. O God's lady dear!
Are you so hot?[10] Marry,[11] come up,[12] I trow;
Is this the poultice for my aching bones?
Henceforward do your messages yourself.

Juliet. Here's such a coil![13] Come, what says Romeo?

Nurse. Have you got leave to go to shrift today?

Juliet. I have.

Nurse. Then hie[14] you hence to Friar Lawrence' cell,
There stays a husband to make you a wife.
Now comes the wanton[15] blood up in your cheeks,
They'll be in scarlet straight at any news.[16]
Hie you to church, I must another way,
To fetch a ladder, by the which your love
Must climb a bird's nest soon when it is dark.
I am the drudge, and toil in your delight;
But you shall bear the burthen soon at night.
Go, I'll to dinner, hie you to the cell.

Juliet. Hie to high fortune! Honest nurse, farewell. *Exeunt.*

10. **hot.** Impatient
11. **Marry.** (Interjection)
12. **come up.** Stop now
13. **coil.** Fuss
14. **hie.** Hurry
15. **wanton.** Unrestrained
16. **They'll...news.** Any little thing makes you blush.

Scene vi: Friar Lawrence's Cell

Enter Friar Lawrence *and* Romeo.

Friar Lawrence. So smile the heavens upon this holy act,
That after-hours with sorrow chide us not!

Romeo. Amen, amen! but come what sorrow can,
It cannot countervail[1] the exchange of joy
That one short minute gives me in her sight.
Do thou but close our hands with holy words,
Then love-devouring death do what he dare,
It is enough I may but call her mine.

Friar Lawrence. These violent delights have violent ends,
And in their triumph die, like fire and powder,
Which as they kiss consume. The sweetest honey
Is loathsome in his own deliciousness,
And in the taste confounds[2] the appetite.
Therefore love moderately: long love doth so;
Too swift arrives as tardy as too slow.

Act II, Scene vi
1. **countervail.** Match; equal
2. **confounds.** Destroys

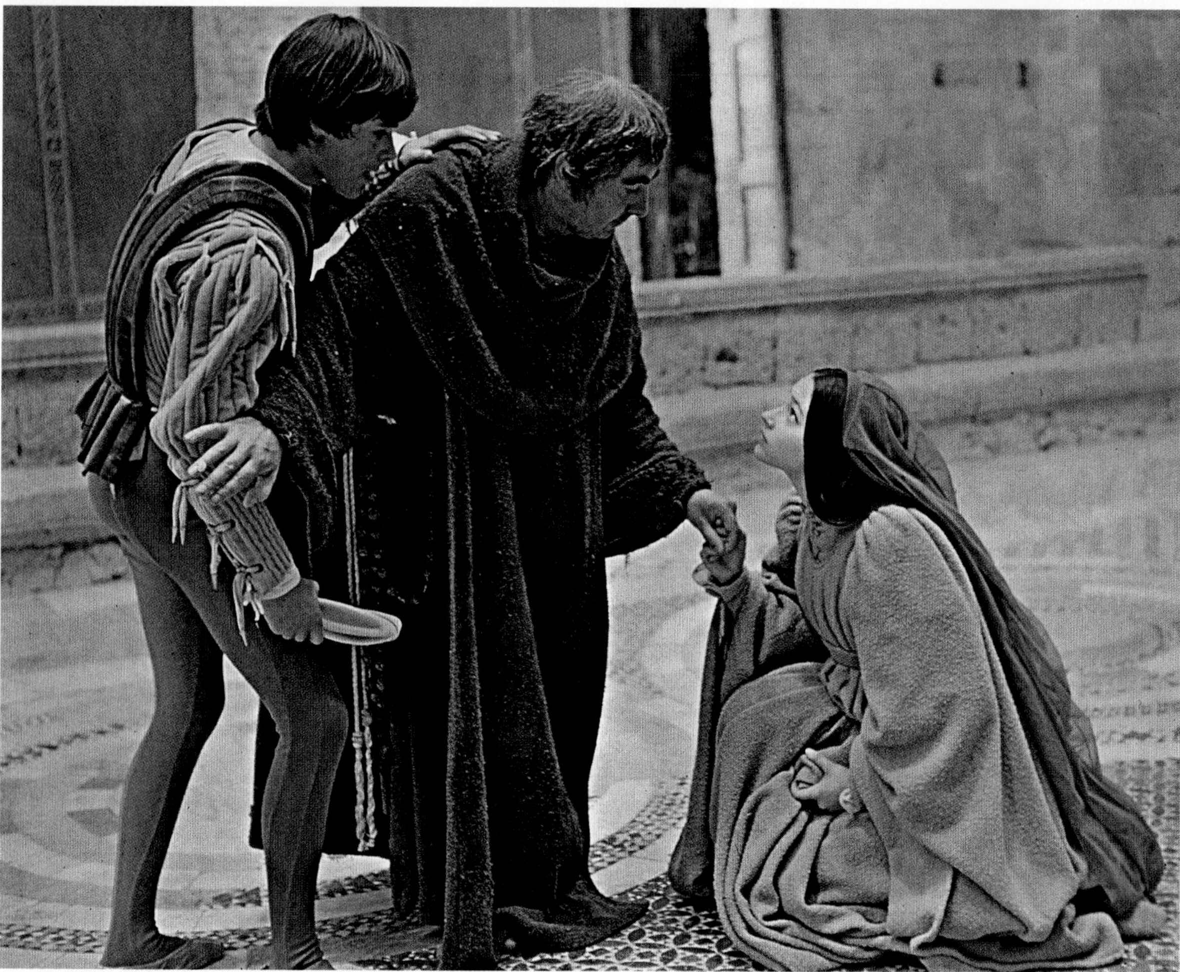

Romeo and Juliet ask the Friar to marry them.

Enter JULIET.

Here comes the lady. O, so light a foot
Will ne'er wear out the everlasting flint;
A lover may bestride the gossamers[3]
That idles in the wanton[4] summer air,
And yet not fall; so light is vanity.[5]

JULIET. Good even to my ghostly confessor.

FRIAR LAWRENCE. Romeo shall thank thee, daughter, for us both.

JULIET. As much[6] to him, else is his thanks too much.

ROMEO. Ah, Juliet, if the measure of thy joy
Be heap'd like mine, and that[7] thy skill be more
To blazon[8] it, then sweeten with thy breath
This neighbor air, and let rich music's tongue
Unfold the imagin'd happiness[9] that both
Receive in either by this dear encounter.

3. **gossamers.** Delicate threads like those spun by spiders
4. **wanton.** Sportive
5. **vanity.** Temporary joy of life
6. **As much.** A return of Romeo's greeting and kiss
7. **that.** If
8. **blazon.** Proclaim
9. **imagin'd happiness.** Unexpressed emotion

JULIET. Conceit,[10] more rich in matter than in words,
Brags of[11] his substance, not of ornament;
They are but beggars that can count their worth,
But my true love is grown to such excess
I cannot sum up sum[12] of half my wealth.

FRIAR LAWRENCE. Come, come with me, and we will make short work,
For by your leaves, you shall not stay alone
Till Holy Church incorporate two in one. *Exeunt.*

10. **Conceit.** Understanding

11. **Brags of.** Prides himself on

12. **sum up sum.** Determine the total

Why might it be important to consider the advice of those around you before acting on impulses and feelings? During what instances should people ignore the advice of others?

REFER TO TEXT	REASON WITH TEXT	
1a. Where does young men's love lie, according to Friar Lawrence?	1b. Explain why Friar Lawrence might question Romeo's sincerity.	**Understand** Find meaning
2a. List the obstacles that stand in the way of Romeo and Juliet.	2b. Calculate how the difficulty of their situation makes Romeo and Juliet's relationship seem more intense.	**Apply** Use information
3a. Name the two characters who know about the relationship between Romeo and Juliet.	3b. Compare the roles of these two characters. How are they similar? How are they different? How do they feel about Romeo and Juliet's relationship?	**Analyze** Take things apart
4a. Define why Romeo and Juliet are in such a hurry to meet with the Friar.	4b. Consider the obstacles that stand in the way of Romeo and Juliet being together. Judge whether they've chosen the course of action that will give them the best chance of being together. Explain your answer.	**Evaluate** Make judgments
5a. Identify the concerns that the Friar and the Nurse share with Romeo and Juliet.	5b. Propose why you think they helped Romeo and Juliet. Do you think it is wise of them to do so? Explain.	**Create** Bring ideas together

ANALYZE LITERATURE: Motivation

A **motivation** is a force that moves a character to think, feel, or behave in a certain way. What do you learn about Romeo and Juliet from their actions and dialogue in Act II? What are their strengths and weaknesses? What motivates their behavior? For example, why does Romeo climb the wall into the Capulets' garden, despite the danger? What motivates Juliet in her responses to Romeo?

GRAMMAR & STYLE

UNDERSTAND THE CONCEPT | APPLY THE SKILL

Capitalization

The first word of a sentence is always capitalized, but it is important to pay attention to the other words in a sentence that may also need to be capitalized.

Proper nouns, which name specific people, places, or things, should be capitalized as should **proper adjectives,** adjectives formed from proper nouns.

EXAMPLES

Proper nouns:	William Shakespeare
	Queens College
	Mexico
	San Diego Zoo
	African American
	Catholicism
Proper adjectives:	Italian village
	Christmas candles
	Georgian architecture
	Mexican food

Geographical names of specific places are capitalized, but words such as *lake, mountain,* and *river* are not when used on their own.

EXAMPLES

Jefferson County	the county
Lake Erie	a lake
Sierra Mountains	the mountains
Mississippi River	a river

Geographical directions are capitalized if they are part of a specific name of a commonly recognized region. Do not capitalize such words as east(ern), west(ern), north(ern), and south(ern) if they are used only to indicate direction.

EXAMPLES

Middle East	east end of town
West Africa	west of the highway
South Florida	southern states

Historical events, special events, and **recognized periods of time** are capitalized.

EXAMPLES

Great Depression	World Series
the Victorian Age	Civil War

Months, days, and **holidays** are capitalized, but seasons are not.

EXAMPLES

December	Sunday	Memorial Day
winter	spring	autumn

In **titles of art** or **literary works,** the first and last words and all major words in between are capitalized. Articles and prepositions are not capitalized in titles unless they are the first word in a title or they follow a colon.

EXAMPLES

The Tragedy of Romeo and Juliet
Mona Lisa
"Blues Ain't No Mockin' Bird"
My Life: The True Story
Anne Frank: The Diary of a Young Girl

Titles or **abbreviations** that come before people's names are capitalized. **Titles** are also capitalized when used as proper names.

EXAMPLES

Dr. Lewis — Friar Lawrence
Can you help, Senator?

Family relationships are only capitalized when they are used as a title or as a substitute for a name.

EXAMPLES

What can I get for you, Mother?

Grandma Moses	my grandma
Uncle Joe	your uncle

REVIEW TERMS

- **Proper nouns:** formal names of people, places, or things
- **Proper adjectives:** adjectives formed from proper nouns

UNDERSTAND THE CONCEPT

APPLY THE SKILL

Identify Proper Nouns and Proper Adjectives

Identify the proper nouns and proper adjectives in these sentences from *Romeo and Juliet* that need to be capitalized.

1. It is the east, and juliet is the sun.
2. Holy saint francis, what a change is here!
3. An old hare hoar is very good meat in lent.
4. And therefore hath the wind-swift cupid wings.
5. The english in a shakespearean drama may be difficult at first, but it's beautiful.
6. The lexington community players performed this play last spring.
7. The part of lady capulet was played by aunt linda.
8. The monday crowds were small due to memorial day.
9. However, mayor branigan and doctor mwabe were in attendance.
10. During intermission, they presented the theater with a replica of "winged victory of samothrace," the original of which can be found in the louvre museum in paris.

Correct Capitalization

Rewrite the following paragraph correcting any errors in capitalization.

> *The Tragedy Of Romeo and juliet* is set in the city of verona, in Northern italy during the renaissance. A feud between the Noble families of the montagues and the capulets leads the young Star-crossed lovers to hide their Marriage from their parents. Their wise counselor, friar Lawrence, however, marries them, even though he thinks Young People, especially romeo, are too quick to change their minds and their Passions—he recalls how enamored of rosaline Romeo was before he met lord Capulet's Daughter. The story isn't all Tragedy, however, as nurse adds Comic Relief and mercutio's lines are quite witty. This famous love story has inspired countless works, including *West side story*, which takes place in New York city and involves two rival Puerto rican gangs; a few film versions; and ballets by russian composers Tchaikovsky and prokofiev.

Use Capitalization in Your Writing

Compare the advice, suggestions, and criticisms that Friar Lawrence and Nurse give to Romeo and Juliet with advice you may have received from your parents or other adults in authority. Do these adults in *Romeo and Juliet* give sound advice? Do they seem to understand what the young lovers are going through? What kind of advice do you think friends of the couple would have given them? Write a brief essay discussing this issue of generational differences in advice for teens in love.

EXTEND THE SKILL

In a time of text-messaging and e-mail, the norms of capitalization are often relaxed for casual correspondence, since it takes slightly longer to capitalize and the words are still legible in lowercase. Over the course of a week, collect messages that do not use capitalization. First, see whether the writer avoided using capital letters altogether or if there are certain words that are still capitalized. Try to figure out the pattern behind the choice of capitalization, if there are some capital letters. Next, rewrite the messages with proper capitalization. Does the register, or tone in terms of formality, change when you follow rules of capitalization? Why or why not?

Act III

Scene i: A Public Place in Verona

Enter Mercutio, Benvolio, Page, *and* Men.

Benvolio. I pray thee, good Mercutio, let's retire.
The day is hot, the Capels are abroad,
And if we meet we shall not scape a brawl,
For now, these hot days, is the mad blood stirring.

Mercutio. Thou art like one of these fellows that, when he enters the confines of a tavern, claps me[1] his sword upon the table, and says, "God send me no need of thee!" and by the operation of the second cup draws him on the drawer,[2] when indeed there is no need.

Benvolio. Am I like such a fellow?

Mercutio. Come, come, thou art as hot a Jack in thy mood as any in Italy, and as soon mov'd to be moody,[3] and as soon moody to be mov'd.

Benvolio. And what to?

Mercutio. Nay, and there were two[4] such, we should have none shortly, for one would kill the other. Thou? why, thou wilt quarrel with a man that hath a hair more or a hair less in his beard than thou hast. Thou wilt quarrel with a man for cracking nuts, having no other reason but because thou hast hazel eyes. What eye but such an eye would spy out such a quarrel? Thy head is as full of quarrels as an egg is full of meat,[5] and yet thy head hath been beaten as addle[6] as an egg for quarrelling. Thou hast quarrell'd with a man for coughing in the street, because he hath waken'd thy dog that hath lain asleep in the sun. Didst thou not fall out with a tailor for wearing his new doublet[7] before Easter? with another for tying his new shoes with old riband?[8] and yet thou wilt tutor me from[9] quarrelling!

Benvolio. And I were so apt to quarrel as thou art, any man should buy the fee-simple[10] of my life for an hour and a quarter.

Mercutio. The fee-simple! O simple!

Enter Tybalt, Petruchio, *and others.*

Act III, Scene i

1. **claps me.** Throws down
2. **draws...drawer.** Prepares to sword fight with the bartender
3. **moody.** Irritable
4. **two.** Retort to Benvolio's *to*
5. **meat.** Matter that can be eaten
6. **addle.** Confused; rotten (with reference to eggs)
7. **doublet.** Close-fitting jacket, with or without sleeves
8. **riband.** Shoelace
9. **tutor me from.** Instruct me not to be
10. **fee-simple.** Complete ownership

Benvolio. By my head, here comes the Capulets.

Mercutio. By my heel, I care not.

Tybalt. Follow me close, for I will speak to them.
Gentlemen, good den, a word with one of you.

Mercutio. And but one word with one of us?
Couple it with something, make it a word and a blow.

Tybalt. You shall find me apt enough to that, sir, and you will give me occasion.

Mercutio. Could you not take some occasion without giving?

Tybalt. Mercutio, thou consortest with Romeo—

Mercutio. Consort![11] what, dost thou make us minstrels? And thou make minstrels of us, look to hear nothing but discords. Here's my fiddlestick,[12] here's that shall make you dance. 'Zounds,[13] consort!

Benvolio. We talk here in the public haunt of men.
Either withdraw unto some private place;
Or reason coldly of[14] your grievances,
Or else depart;[15] here all eyes gaze on us.

Mercutio. Men's eyes were made to look, and let them gaze;
I will not budge for no man's pleasure, I.

Enter Romeo.

Tybalt. Well, peace be with you, sir, here comes my man.

Mercutio. But I'll be hang'd, sir, if he wear your livery.[16]
Marry, go before to field,[17] he'll be your follower;
Your worship in that sense may call him man.[18]

Tybalt. Romeo, the love I bear thee can afford
No better term than this: thou art a villain.

Romeo. Tybalt, the reason that I have to love thee
Doth much excuse the appertaining rage[19]
To such a greeting. Villain am I none;
Therefore farewell, I see thou knowest me not.

Tybalt. Boy, this shall not excuse the injuries
That thou hast done me, therefore turn and draw.

Romeo. I do protest[20] I never injuried[21] thee,
But love thee better than thou canst devise,[22]
Till thou shalt know the reason of my love,
And so, good Capulet—which name I tender[23]
As dearly as mine own—be satisfied.

11. **Consort.** Mercutio means to "play music with." *Consort* refers to a group of musicians.
12. **fiddlestick.** Rapier, a type of sword
13. **'Zounds.** By God's (Christ's) wounds

14. **reason coldly of.** Speak about dispassionately
15. **depart.** Separate

16. **livery.** Mercutio responds as if Tybalt used "my man" to mean "my servant."
17. **field.** Setting for a duel
18. **man.** One deserving to be described as a man

19. **excuse...rage.** Lessen the appropriate anger

20. **protest.** Assert
21. **injuried.** Harmed
22. **devise.** Imagine

23. **tender.** Cherish

MERCUTIO. O calm, dishonorable, vile submission!
Alla stoccato[24] carries it away. *Draws.*
Tybalt, you rat-catcher,[25] will you walk?[26]

sub • mis • sion
(səb mi´ shən) *n.*, yielding; surrendering

TYBALT. What wouldst thou have with me?

MERCUTIO. Good King of Cats, nothing but one of your nine lives; that I mean to make bold withal, and as you shall use me hereafter,[27] dry-beat[28] the rest of the eight. Will you pluck your sword out of his pilcher[29] by the ears?[30] Make haste, lest mine be about your ears ere it be out.

TYBALT. I am for you. *Drawing.*

ROMEO. Gentle Mercutio, put thy rapier up.

MERCUTIO. Come, sir, your *passado.*[31] *They fight.*

ROMEO. Draw, Benvolio, beat down their weapons.
Gentlemen, for shame, forbear this outrage!
Tybalt, Mercutio, the Prince expressly hath
Forbid this bandying[32] in Verona streets.
ROMEO *steps between them.*
Hold, Tybalt! Good Mercutio!

TYBALT *under* ROMEO'S *arm thrusts* MERCUTIO *in.*

Away TYBALT *with his followers.*

MERCUTIO. I am hurt.
A plague a' both houses! I am sped.[33]
Is he gone and hath nothing?

BENVOLIO. What, art thou hurt?

MERCUTIO. Ay, ay, a scratch,[34] a scratch, marry, 'tis enough.
Where is my page? Go, villain,[35] fetch a surgeon. *Exit* PAGE.

ROMEO. Courage, man, the hurt cannot be much.

MERCUTIO. No, 'tis not so deep as a well, nor so wide as a church-door, but 'tis enough, 'twill serve. Ask for me tomorrow, and you shall find me a grave man.[36] I am pepper'd, I warrant, for this world. A plague a' both your houses! 'Zounds, a dog, a rat, a mouse, a cat, to scratch a man to death! a braggart, a rogue, a villain, that fights by the book of arithmetic! Why the dev'l came you between us? I was hurt under your arm.

ROMEO. I thought all for the best.

MERCUTIO. Help me into some house, Benvolio,
Or I shall faint. A plague a' both your houses!

24. ***Alla stoccato.*** Literally, "at the thrust" (fencing term). Mercutio suggests that Tybalt's attack has unarmed Romeo.
25. **rat-catcher.** Reference to his name
26. **walk.** Leave the premises
27. **as...hereafter.** Depending on how you treat me in the future
28. **dry-beat.** Beat up (without drawing blood)
29. **his pilcher.** Its sheath
30. **by the ears.** Implying that the sword resists being unsheathed
31. ***passado.*** Thrust
32. **bandying.** Fighting
33. **sped.** Spent; finished
34. **a scratch.** Another reference to Tybalt's name
35. **villain.** Person of lower class; boy
36. **grave man.** Pun stating that he may be found in a grave tomorrow

They have made worms' meat of me. I have it,
And soundly too. Your houses!

Exeunt MERCUTIO *and* BENVOLIO.

ROMEO. This gentleman, the Prince's near ally,[37]
My very[38] friend, hath got this mortal hurt
In my behalf; my reputation stain'd
With Tybalt's slander—Tybalt, that an hour
Hath been my cousin! O sweet Juliet,
Thy beauty hath made me effeminate,
And in my temper[39] soft'ned valor's steel!

Enter BENVOLIO.

BENVOLIO. O Romeo, Romeo, brave Mercutio is dead!
That gallant spirit hath aspir'd[40] the clouds,
Which too untimely here did scorn the earth.

ROMEO. This day's black fate on moe days doth depend,[41]
This but begins the woe others must end.

Enter TYBALT.

BENVOLIO. Here comes the furious Tybalt back again.

ROMEO. He gone in triumph, and Mercutio slain!
Away to heaven, respective[42] lenity,
And fire-ey'd fury be my conduct[43] now!

37. **ally.** Relative
38. **very.** Absolute
39. **temper.** Nature
40. **aspir'd.** Ascended to
41. **on...depend.** Affects days in the future
42. **respective.** Thoughtful
43. **conduct.** Guide

Romeo duels with Tybalt.

Now, Tybalt, take the "villain" back again
That late thou gavest me, for Mercutio's soul
Is but a little way above our heads,
Staying for thine to keep him company.
Either thou or I, or both, must go with him.

Tybalt. Thou wretched boy, that didst consort him here,
Shalt with him hence.

Romeo. This shall determine that.

They fight; Tybalt *falls.*

Benvolio. Romeo, away, be gone!
The citizens are up,[44] and Tybalt slain.
Stand not amazed,[45] the Prince will doom thee death
If thou art taken. Hence be gone, away!

44. **up.** Have taken arms

45. **amazed.** Bewildered; astounded

Romeo. O, I am fortune's fool!

Benvolio. Why dost thou stay? *Exit* Romeo.

Enter Citizens.

1. Citizen. Which way ran he that kill'd Mercutio?
Tybalt, that murtherer, which way ran he?

Benvolio. There lies that Tybalt.

1. Citizen. Up, sir, go with me;
I charge thee in the Prince's name, obey.

Enter Prince, *old* Montague, Capulet, *their* Wives, *and all.*

Prince. Where are the vile beginners of this fray?

Benvolio. O noble Prince, I can discover[46] all
The unlucky manage[47] of this fatal brawl:
There lies the man, slain by young Romeo,
That slew thy kinsman brave Mercutio.

46. **discover.** Uncover; divulge

47. **manage.** Process

Lady Capulet. Tybalt, my cousin! O my brother's child!
O Prince! O husband! O, the blood is spill'd
Of my dear kinsman! Prince, as thou art true,
For blood of ours, shed blood of Montague.
O cousin, cousin!

Prince. Benvolio, who began this bloody fray?

Benvolio. Tybalt, here slain, whom Romeo's hand did slay!
Romeo that spoke him fair, bid him bethink
How nice[48] the quarrel was, and urg'd withal
Your high displeasure; all this, uttered

48. **nice.** Slight

With gentle breath, calm look, knees humbly bowed,
Could not take truce with the unruly spleen
Of Tybalt deaf to peace, but that he tilts
With piercing steel at bold Mercutio's breast,
Who, all as hot, turns deadly point to point,
And, with a martial scorn, with one hand beats
Cold death aside, and with the other sends
It back to Tybalt, whose dexterity
Retorts it. Romeo he cries aloud,
"Hold, friends! friends, part!" and swifter than his tongue,
His agile arm beats down their fatal points,
And 'twixt them rushes; underneath whose arm
An envious[49] thrust from Tybalt hit the life
Of stout[50] Mercutio, and then Tybalt fled;
But by and by comes back to Romeo,
Who had but newly entertain'd[51] revenge,
And to't they go like lightning, for, ere I
Could draw to part them, was stout Tybalt slain;
And as he fell, did Romeo turn and fly.
This is the truth, or let Benvolio die.

dex • ter • i • ty (dek ster´ ə tē) *n.,* skill in using one's hands or body

ag • ile (a´ jəl) *adj.,* able to move with quick and easy grace; coordinated; nimble

49. **envious.** Spiteful
50. **stout.** Brave

51. **entertain'd.** Considered

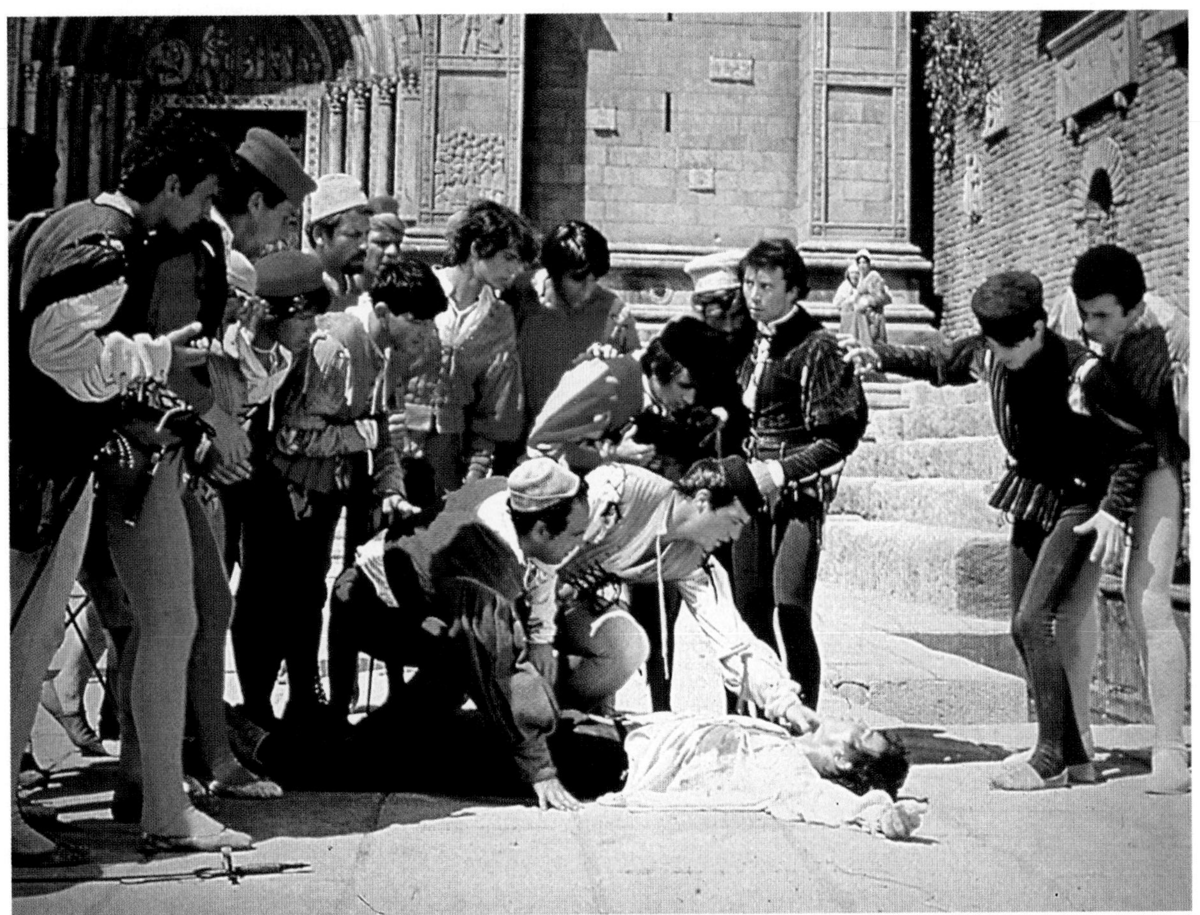

Tybalt is dead.

Lady Capulet. He is a kinsman to the Montague,
Affection makes him false, he speaks not true.
Some twenty of them fought in this black strife,
And all those twenty could but kill one life.
I beg for justice, which thou, Prince, must give:
Romeo slew Tybalt, Romeo must not live.

Prince. Romeo slew him, he slew Mercutio;
Who now the price of his dear blood doth owe?

Montague. Not Romeo, Prince, he was Mercutio's friend;
His fault concludes but what the law should end,
The life of Tybalt.

Prince. And for that offense
Immediately we do exile him hence.
I have an interest[52] in your heart's proceeding;
My blood [53] for your rude brawls doth lie a-bleeding;
But I'll amerce[54] you with so strong a fine
That you shall all repent the loss of mine.
I will be deaf to pleading and excuses,
Nor tears nor prayers shall purchase out[55] abuses;
Therefore use none. Let Romeo hence in haste,
Else, when he is found, that hour is his last.
Bear hence this body and attend our will;[56]
Mercy but murders,[57] pardoning those that kill. *Exeunt.*

52. **interest.** Concern
53. **My blood.** Mercutio and the prince are related.
54. **amerce.** Inflict a fine
55. **purchase out.** Make amends for
56. **attend our will.** Listen to my judgment
57. **murders.** Encourages future murders

Scene ii: Capulet's House

Enter Juliet *alone.*

Juliet. Gallop apace, you fiery-footed steeds,[1]
Towards Phoebus' lodging;[2] such a waggoner
As Phaëton[3] would whip you to the west,
And bring in cloudy night immediately.
Spread thy close[4] curtain, love-performing night,
That th' runaway's[5] eyes may wink,[6] and Romeo
Leap to these arms untalk'd of and unseen!
Lovers can see to do their amorous rites
By their own beauties, or, if love be blind,
It best agrees with night. Come, civil[7] night,
Thou sober-suited matron all in black,
And learn me how to lose a winning match,
Play'd for a pair of stainless maidenhoods.
Hood[8] my unmann'd blood, bating[9] in my cheeks,

Act III, Scene ii

1. **steeds.** Horses that pull the chariot of the sun-god
2. **Phoebus' lodging.** Beyond the western horizon
3. **Phaëton.** Phaëthon, son of the sun-god, who lost control of the sun-chariot and was killed by Zeus
4. **close.** Protective
5. **runaway's.** Meaning is unclear, word possibly changed
6. **wink.** Close and so not see
7. **civil.** Solemn
8. **Hood.** Hide
9. **bating.** Beating

With thy black mantle; till strange[10] love grow[11] bold,
Think true love acted simple modesty.[12]
Come, night, come, Romeo, come, thou day in night,
For thou wilt lie upon the wings of night,
Whiter than new snow upon a raven's back.
Come, gentle night, come, loving, black-brow'd night,
Give me my Romeo, and, when I shall die,
Take him and cut him out in little stars,
And he will make the face of heaven so fine
That all the world will be in love with night,
And pay no worship to the garish sun.
O, I have bought the mansion of a love,
But not possess'd it, and though I am sold,
Not yet enjoy'd. So tedious is this day
As is the night before some festival
To an impatient child that hath new robes
And may not wear them. O, here comes my nurse,

Enter NURSE *wringing her hands, with the ladder of cords in her lap.*

And she brings news; and every tongue that speaks
But Romeo's name speaks heavenly eloquence.
Now, nurse, what news? What hast thou there? the cords
That Romeo bid thee fetch?

NURSE. Ay, ay, the cords. *Throws them down.*

JULIET. Ay me, what news? Why dost thou wring thy hands?

NURSE. Ah, weraday,[13] he's dead, he's dead, he's dead!
We are undone, lady, we are undone!
Alack the day, he's gone, he's kill'd, he's dead!

JULIET. Can heaven be so envious?[14]

NURSE. Romeo can,
Though heaven cannot. O Romeo, Romeo!
Who ever would have thought it? Romeo!

JULIET. What devil art thou that dost torment me thus?
This torture should be roar'd in dismal hell.
Hath Romeo slain himself? Say thou but ay,
And that bare vowel *I* shall poison more
Than the death-darting eye of cockatrice.[15]
I am not I, if there be such an ay,
Or those eyes shut,[16] that makes thee answer ay.
If he be slain, say ay, or if not, no.
Brief sounds determine my weal or woe.[17]

10. **strange.** Restrained
11. **grow.** Becomes
12. **modesty.** Virtuousness

el • o • quence
(el′ ə kwən[t]s) *n.,* speech or writing that is vivid, forceful, and persuasive

13. **weraday.** Pity

14. **envious.** Spiteful

15. **cockatrice.** Basilisk, mythical serpent that could kill with a glance
16. **Or…shut.** If Romeo dies

17. **determine…woe.** Decide whether I am happy or sad

Nurse. I saw the wound, I saw it with mine eyes—
God save the mark![18]—here on his manly breast.
A piteous corse,[19] a bloody piteous corse,
Pale, pale as ashes, all bedaub'd in blood,
All in gore blood; I sounded[20] at the sight.

Juliet. O, break, my heart, poor bankrout,[21] break at once!
To prison, eyes, ne'er look on liberty!
Vile earth,[22] to earth resign,[23] end motion here,
And thou and Romeo press one heavy bier!

Nurse. O Tybalt, Tybalt, the best friend I had!
O courteous Tybalt, honest gentleman,
That ever I should live to see thee dead!

Juliet. What storm is this that blows so contrary?
Is Romeo slaught'red? and is Tybalt dead?
My dearest cousin, and my dearer lord?
Then, dreadful trumpet,[24] sound the general doom,
For who is living, if those two are gone?

Nurse. Tybalt is gone, and Romeo banished,
Romeo that kill'd him, he is banished.

Juliet. O God, did Romeo's hand shed Tybalt's blood?

Nurse. It did, it did, alas the day, it did!

Juliet. O serpent heart, hid with a flow'ring[25] face!
Did ever dragon keep[26] so fair a cave?
Beautiful tyrant! fiend angelical!
Dove-feather'd raven! wolvish ravening lamb!
Despised substance[27] of divinest show![28]
Just opposite to what thou justly seem'st,[29]
A damned saint, an honorable villain!
O nature, what hadst thou to do in hell
When thou didst bower[30] the spirit of a fiend
In mortal paradise of such sweet flesh?
Was ever book containing such vile matter
So fairly bound? O that deceit should dwell
In such a gorgeous palace!

Nurse. There's no trust,
No faith, no honesty in men, all perjur'd,
All forsworn, all naught,[31] all dissemblers.
Ah, where's my man? Give me some aqua-vitae;[32]
These griefs, these woes, these sorrows make me old.
Shame come to Romeo!

18. **God...mark.** Expression used to ward off bad omens
19. **corse.** Dead body
20. **sounded.** Fainted
21. **bankrout.** Emptiness
22. **Vile earth.** Body
23. **resign.** Relinquish yourself
24. **trumpet.** Signal of Judgment Day
25. **flow'ring.** Young and attractive
26. **keep.** Reside in
27. **substance.** Contemptible being
28. **show.** Appearance
29. **Just...seem'st.** Exactly the opposite of what you appear to be
30. **bower.** Enclose
31. **naught.** Evil
32. **aqua-vitae.** Strong liquor

JULIET. Blister'd be thy tongue
For such a wish! he was not born to shame:
Upon his brow shame is asham'd to sit;
For 'tis a throne where honor may be crown'd
Sole monarch of the universal earth.
O, what a beast was I to chide at him!

NURSE. Will you speak well of him that kill'd your cousin?

JULIET. Shall I speak ill of him that is my husband?
Ah, poor my lord, what tongue shall smooth thy name,
When I, thy three-hours wife, have mangled it?
But wherefore, villain, didst thou kill my cousin?
That villain cousin would have kill'd my husband.
Back, foolish tears, back to your native spring,
Your tributary drops belong to woe,[33]
Which you, mistaking, offer up to joy.[34]
My husband lives that Tybalt would have slain,
And Tybalt's dead that would have slain my husband.
All this is comfort, wherefore weep I then?
Some word there was, worser than Tybalt's death,
That murd'red me; I would forget it fain,
But O, it presses to my memory
Like damned guilty deeds to sinners' minds:
"Tybalt is dead, and Romeo banished."
That "banished," that one word "banished,"
Hath slain ten thousand Tybalts. Tybalt's death
Was woe enough if it had ended there;
Or if sour woe delights in fellowship,
And needly[35] will be rank'd[36] with other griefs,
Why followed not, when she said, "Tybalt's dead,"
Thy father or thy mother, nay, or both,
Which modern[37] lamentation might have moved?
But with a rearward[38] following Tybalt's death,
"Romeo is banished," to speak that word,
Is father, mother, Tybalt, Romeo, Juliet,
All slain, all dead: "Romeo is banished"!
There is no end, no limit, measure, bound,
In that word's death, no words can that woe sound.[39]
Where is my father and my mother, nurse?

NURSE. Weeping and wailing over Tybalt's corse.
Will you go to them? I will bring you thither.

JULIET. Wash they his wounds with tears? Mine shall be spent,
When theirs are dry, for Romeo's banishment.
Take up those cords. Poor ropes, you are beguil'd,[40]

33. **belong to woe.** Indicate sadness
34. **joy.** Romeo's survival
35. **needly.** Inevitably
36. **rank'd.** Grouped
37. **modern.** Customary
38. **rearward.** Rear guard
39. **sound.** Define; measure
40. **beguil'd.** Deceived

Both you and I, for Romeo is exil'd.
He made you for a highway to my bed,
But I, a maid, die maiden-widowed.
Come, cords, come, nurse, I'll to my wedding-bed,
And death, not Romeo, take my maidenhead!

Nurse. Hie to your chamber. I'll find Romeo
To comfort you, I wot[41] well where he is.
Hark ye, your Romeo will be here at night.
I'll to him, he is hid at Lawrence' cell.

Juliet. O, find him! Give this ring to my true knight,
And bid him come to take his last farewell. *Exeunt.*

41. **wot.** Know

Scene iii: Friar Lawrence's Cell

Enter Friar Lawrence.

Friar Lawrence. Romeo, come forth, come forth, thou fearful[1] man:
Affliction is enamor'd of thy parts,[2]
And thou art wedded to calamity.

Enter Romeo.

Romeo. Father, what news? What is the Prince's doom?[3]
What sorrow craves acquaintance at my hand,
That I yet know not?

Friar Lawrence. Too familiar
Is my dear son with such sour company!
I bring thee tidings of the Prince's doom.

Romeo. What less than dooms-day[4] is the Prince's doom?

Friar Lawrence. A gentler judgment vanish'd[5] from his lips—
Not body's death, but body's banishment.

Romeo. Ha, banishment? Be merciful, say "death";
For exile hath more terror in his look,
Much more than death. Do not say "banishment"!

Friar Lawrence. Here from Verona art thou banished.
Be patient,[6] for the world is broad and wide.

Romeo. There is no world without[7] Verona walls,
But purgatory, torture, hell itself.
Hence "banished" is banish'd from the world,
And world's exile[8] is death;[9] then "banished"
Is death misterm'd. Calling death "banished,"

Act III, Scene iii
1. **fearful.** Frightened
2. **parts.** Traits
3. **doom.** Judgment
4. **dooms-day.** Death
5. **vanish'd.** Uttered without possibility of recall
6. **Be patient.** Calm yourself
7. **without.** Beyond
8. **world's exile.** Banishment from the world
9. **death.** Capital offense

Thou cut'st my head off with a golden axe,
And smilest upon the stroke that murders me.

Friar Lawrence. O deadly sin! O rude unthankfulness!
Thy fault our law calls death, but the kind Prince,
Taking thy part, hath rush'd[10] aside the law,
And turn'd that black word "death" to "banishment."
This is dear[11] mercy, and thou seest it not.

Romeo. 'Tis torture, and not mercy. Heaven is here
Where Juliet lives, and every cat and dog
And little mouse, every unworthy thing,
Live here in heaven and may look on her,
But Romeo may not. More validity,[12]
More honorable state, more courtship[13] lives
In carrion flies than Romeo; they may seize
On the white wonder of dear Juliet's hand,
And steal immortal blessing from her lips,
Who, even in pure and vestal modesty
Still blush, as thinking their own kisses sin;
But Romeo may not, he is banished.
Flies may do this, but I from this must fly;
They are free men, but I am banished:
And sayest thou yet that exile is not death?
Hadst thou no poison mix'd, no sharp-ground knife,
No sudden mean of death, though ne'er so mean,[14]
But "banished" to kill me? "Banished"?
O friar, the damned use that word in hell;
Howling attends it. How hast thou the heart,
Being a divine, a ghostly confessor,
A sin-absolver, and my friend profess'd,
To mangle me with that word "banished"?

Friar Lawrence. Thou fond[15] mad man, hear me a little speak.

Romeo. O, thou wilt speak again of banishment.

Friar Lawrence. I'll give thee armor to keep off that word:
Adversity's sweet milk, philosophy,
To comfort thee though thou art banished.

Romeo. Yet "banished"? Hang up philosophy!
Unless philosophy can make a Juliet,
Displant[16] a town, reverse a prince's doom,
It helps not, it prevails not.[17] Talk no more.

Friar Lawrence. O then I see that madmen have no ears.

Romeo. How should they when that wise men have no eyes?

10. **rush'd.** Pushed

11. **dear.** Unusual

12. **validity.** Honor; worth

13. **courtship.** Courtliness

14. **mean...mean.** Means...ignoble

15. **fond.** Naïve

ad • ver • si • ty
(ad vʉr´ sə tē) *n.*, misfortune; hardship; suffering

16. **Displant.** Relocate

17. **prevails not.** Has no effect

Friar Lawrence. Let me dispute[18] with thee of thy estate.[19]

18. **dispute.** Talk
19. **estate.** Situation

Romeo. Thou canst not speak of that thou dost not feel.
Wert thou as young as I, Juliet thy love,
An hour but married, Tybalt murdered,
Doting like me, and like me banished,
Then mightst thou speak, then mightst thou tear thy hair,
And fall upon the ground, as I do now,
Taking the measure of an unmade grave.

Enter Nurse *within and knock.*

Friar Lawrence. Arise, one knocks. Good Romeo, hide thyself.

Romeo. Not I, unless the breath of heart-sick groans
Mist-like infold me from the search of eyes. *Knock.*

Friar Lawrence. Hark how they knock!—Who's there?—
Romeo, arise,
Thou wilt be taken.—Stay a while![20]—Stand up; *Loud knock.*
Run to my study.—By and by!—God's will,
What simpleness[21] is this?—I come, I come! *Knock.*
Who knocks so hard? Whence come you? What's your will?

20. **Stay a while.** Wait
21. **simpleness.** Absurdity

Nurse. [*Within.*] Let me come in, and you shall know my errant.[22]
I come from Lady Juliet.

22. **errant.** Purpose

Friar Lawrence. Welcome then. *Unlocks the door.*

Enter Nurse.

Nurse. O holy friar, O, tell me, holy friar,
Where's my lady's lord? where's Romeo?

Friar Lawrence. There on the ground, with his own tears made
drunk.

Nurse. O, he is even in my mistress' case,
Just in her case. O woeful sympathy![23]
Piteous predicament! Even so lies she,
Blubb'ring and weeping, weeping and blubb'ring.
Stand up, stand up, stand, and you be a man.
For Juliet's sake, for her sake, rise and stand;
Why should you fall into so deep an O?[24]

23. **sympathy.** Piteous suffering
24. **O.** State of despair

Romeo. Nurse! *He rises.*

Nurse. Ah sir, ah sir, death's the end of all.

Romeo. Spakest thou of Juliet? How is it with her?
Doth not she think me an old[25] murtherer,
Now I have stain'd the childhood of our joy

25. **old.** Experienced

With blood removed but little from her own?
Where is she? and how doth she? and what says
My conceal'd lady[26] to our cancell'd love?

NURSE. O, she says nothing, sir, but weeps and weeps,
And now falls on her bed, and then starts up,
And Tybalt calls, and then on Romeo cries,
And then down falls again.

ROMEO. As if that name,
Shot from the deadly level[27] of a gun,
Did murther her, as that name's cursed hand
Murder'd her kinsman. O, tell me, friar, tell me,
In what vile part of this anatomy
Doth my name lodge? Tell me, that I may sack
The hateful mansion.

He offers to stab himself, and the NURSE *snatches the dagger away.*

FRIAR LAWRENCE. Hold thy desperate hand!
Art thou a man? Thy form cries out thou art;
Thy tears are womanish, thy wild acts denote
The unreasonable[28] fury of a beast.
Unseemly woman[29] in a seeming man,
And ill-beseeming beast in seeming both,
Thou hast amaz'd me! By my holy order,
I thought thy disposition better temper'd.[30]
Hast thou slain Tybalt? Wilt thou slay thyself,
And slay thy lady that in thy life lives,
By doing damned hate upon thyself?
Why railest thou on thy birth? the heaven and earth?[31]
Since birth, and heaven, and earth, all three do meet
In thee at once, which thou at once wouldst lose.
Fie, fie, thou shamest thy shape, thy love, thy wit,[32]
Which[33] like a usurer[34] abound'st in all,
And usest none in that true use indeed
Which should bedeck thy shape, thy love, thy wit.
Thy noble shape is but a form of wax,[35]
Digressing from the valor of a man;
Thy dear love sworn but hollow perjury,
Killing that love which thou hast vow'd to cherish;
Thy wit, that ornament to shape and love,
Misshapen[36] in the conduct[37] of them both,
Like powder in a skilless soldier's flask,[38]
Is set afire by thine own ignorance,
And thou dismemb'red with thine own defense.
What, rouse thee, man! thy Juliet is alive,

26. **conceal'd lady.** Secret wife

27. **level.** Aim

28. **unreasonable.** Irrational

de • note (di nōt´) *v.,* indicate

dis • po • si • tion (dis' pə zi´ shən) *n.,* nature; frame of mind; temperament

29. **Unseemly woman.** Romeo's behavior is like that of a woman who offends good taste.

30. **temper'd.** Composed; controlled

31. **heaven and earth.** Soul and body

32. **wit.** Mind

33. **Which.** Who

34. **usurer.** One who misuses possessions

35. **form of wax.** Lifeless figure

36. **Misshapen.** Badly trained

37. **conduct.** Use

38. **flask.** Powder horn; container for gunpowder

For whose dear sake thou wast but lately dead:
There art thou happy.[39] Tybalt would kill thee,
But thou slewest Tybalt: there art thou happy.
The law that threat'ned death becomes thy friend,
And turns it to exile: there art thou happy.
A pack of blessings light upon thy back,
Happiness courts thee in her best array,
But like a mishaved[40] and sullen wench,
Thou pouts upon thy fortune and thy love.
Take heed, take heed, for such die miserable.
Go get thee to thy love as was decreed,[41]
Ascend her chamber, hence and comfort her.
But look thou stay not till the watch be set,[42]
For then thou canst not pass to Mantua,
Where thou shalt live till we can find a time
To blaze[43] your marriage, reconcile your friends,[44]
Beg pardon of the Prince, and call thee back
With twenty hundred thousand times more joy
Than thou went'st forth in lamentation.
Go before, nurse; commend me to thy lady,
And bid her hasten all the house to bed,
Which heavy sorrow makes them apt unto.
Romeo is coming.

Nurse. O Lord, I could have stay'd here all the night
To hear good counsel. O, what learning is!
My lord, I'll tell my lady you will come.

Romeo. Do so, and bid my sweet prepare to chide.

Nurse *offers to go in, and turns again.*

Nurse. Here, sir, a ring she bid me give you, sir.
Hie you, make haste, for it grows very late.

Romeo. How well my comfort is reviv'd by this!

Exit Nurse.

Friar Lawrence. Go hence, good night; and here stands all your state:[45]
Either be gone before the watch be set,
Or by the break of day disguis'd from hence.
Sojourn in Mantua. I'll find out your man,
And he shall signify from time to time
Every good hap to you that chances here.
Give me thy hand. 'Tis late; farewell, good night.

39. **happy.** Lucky

40. **mishaved.** Misbehaved

41. **decreed.** Ordered

42. **watch be set.** Guard is posted

43. **blaze.** Announce

44. **friends.** Family

45. **here...state.** Your situation is this

Romeo. But that a joy past joy calls out on me,
It were a grief, so brief[46] to part with thee.
Farewell. *Exeunt.*

46. **brief.** Quickly

Scene iv: Capulet's House

Enter old Capulet, *his* Wife, *and* Paris.

Capulet. Things have fall'n out, sir, so unluckily
That we have had no time to move our daughter.
Look you, she lov'd her kinsman Tybalt dearly,
And so did I. Well, we were born to die.
'Tis very late, she'll not come down tonight.
I promise you, but for your company,
I would have been a-bed an hour ago.

Paris. These times of woe afford no times to woo.
Madam, good night, commend me to your daughter.

Lady Capulet. I will, and know her mind early tomorrow;
To-night she's mewed up to[1] her heaviness.[2]

Paris *offers to go in, and* Capulet *calls him again.*

Capulet. Sir Paris, I will make a desperate tender[3]
Of my child's love. I think she will be rul'd
In all respects by me; nay more, I doubt it not.
Wife, go you to her ere you go to bed,
Acquaint her here of my son Paris' love,
And bid her—mark you me?—on We'n'sday next—
But soft, what day is this?

Paris. Monday, my lord.

Capulet. Monday! ha, ha![4] Well, We'n'sday is too soon,
A'[5] Thursday let it be—a' Thursday, tell her,
She shall be married to this noble earl.
Will you be ready? do you like this haste?
We'll keep no great ado—a friend or two,
For hark you, Tybalt being slain so late,
It may be thought we held him carelessly,
Being our kinsman, if we revel much:
Therefore we'll have some half a dozen friends,
And there an end. But what say you to Thursday?

Paris. My lord, I would that Thursday were tomorrow.

Act III, Scene iv
1. **mewed up to.** Shut up with (falconry term)
2. **heaviness.** Sadness
3. **desperate tender.** Daring offer
4. **ha, ha.** Sound he mutters as he thinks
5. **A'.** On

CAPULET. Well, get you gone, a' Thursday be it then.—
Go you to Juliet ere you go to bed,
Prepare her, wife, against[6] this wedding-day.
Farewell, my lord. Light to my chamber ho!
Afore me,[7] it is so very late that we
May call it early by and by. Good night. *Exeunt.*

6. **against.** For

7. **Afore me.** I say

SCENE V: CAPULET'S ORCHARD

Enter ROMEO *and* JULIET *aloft at the window.*

JULIET. Wilt thou be gone? it is not yet near day.
It was the nightingale, and not the lark,
That pierc'd the fearful hollow of thine ear;
Nightly she sings on yond pomegranate tree.
Believe me, love, it was the nightingale.

ROMEO. It was the lark, the herald of the morn,
No nightingale. Look, love, what envious streaks
Do lace the severing clouds in yonder east.
Night's candles are burnt out, and jocund day
Stands tiptoe on the misty mountain tops.
I must be gone and live, or stay and die.

JULIET. Yond light is not day-light, I know it, I;
It is some meteor that the sun exhal'd[1]
To be to thee this night a torch-bearer
And light thee on thy way to Mantua.
Therefore stay yet, thou need'st not to be gone.

ACT III, SCENE V
1. **exhal'd.** Meteors were believed to be vapors from earth that were ignited by the sun's heat.

ROMEO. Let me be ta'en, let me be put to death,
I am content, so thou wilt have it so.
I'll say yon grey is not the morning's eye,
'Tis but the pale reflex[2] of Cynthia's[3] brow;
Nor that is not the lark whose notes do beat
The vaulty heaven so high above our heads.
I have more care[4] to stay than will to go.
Come, death, and welcome! Juliet wills it so.
How is't, my soul? Let's talk, it is not day.

2. **reflex.** Reflection
3. **Cynthia's.** The moon's

4. **care.** Wish

JULIET. It is, it is! Hie hence, be gone, away!
It is the lark that sings so out of tune,
Straining harsh discords and unpleasing sharps.[5]
Some say the lark makes sweet division;[6]
This doth not so, for she divideth us.
Some say the lark and loathed toad change[7] eyes;

5. **sharps.** High-pitched sounds
6. **division.** Melodic variations

dis • cord (dis´ kôrd) *n.,* harsh or unpleasant sound; lack of agreement or harmony

7. **change.** Exchange

Critical Viewing

Which lines from the play might this photo illustrate? What might Romeo and Juliet be thinking and feeling at this point in the play?

Romeo and Juliet say goodbye as Romeo prepares to leave for Mantua.

O now I would they had chang'd voices too,
Since arm from arm[8] that voice doth us affray,[9]
Hunting thee hence with hunt's-up[10] to the day.
O now be gone, more light and light it grows.

Romeo. More light and light, more dark and dark our woes!

Enter Nurse *hastily.*

Nurse. Madam!

Juliet. Nurse?

Nurse. Your lady mother is coming to your chamber.
The day is broke, be wary, look about. *Exit.*

Juliet. Then, window, let day in, and let life out.

Romeo. Farewell, farewell! One kiss, and I'll descend. *He goeth down.*

Juliet. Art thou gone so, love, lord, ay, husband, friend![11]
I must hear from thee every day in the hour,
For in a minute there are many days.
O, by this count I shall be much in years[12]
Ere I again behold my Romeo!

Romeo. [*From below.*] Farewell!
I will omit no opportunity
That may convey my greetings, love, to thee.

Juliet. O, think'st thou we shall ever meet again?

Romeo. I doubt it not, and all these woes shall serve
For sweet discourses in our times to come.

Juliet. O God, I have an ill-divining[13] soul!
Methinks I see thee now, thou art so low,
As one dead in the bottom of a tomb.
Either my eyesight fails, or thou lookest pale.

Romeo. And trust me, love, in my eye so do you;
Dry sorrow drinks our blood.[14] Adieu, adieu! *Exit.*

Juliet. O Fortune, Fortune, all men call thee fickle;
If thou art fickle, what dost thou[15] with him
That is renown'd for faith? Be fickle, Fortune:
For then I hope thou wilt not keep him long,
But send him back.

Lady Capulet. [*Within.*] Ho, daughter, are you up?

Juliet. Who is't that calls? It is my lady mother.

8. **arm from arm.** From each other's arms
9. **affray.** Startle; scare
10. **hunt's-up.** Song to waken hunters
11. **friend.** Dear one; sweetheart
12. **much in years.** Old
13. **ill-divining.** Sensing evil
14. **Dry...blood.** Sorrow was thought to deplete the blood.
15. **what dost thou.** What do you have to do

Is she not down[16] so late, or up so early?
What unaccustom'd cause procures her hither?
She goeth down from the window.[17]

Enter Mother LADY CAPULET.

LADY CAPULET. Why, how now, Juliet?

JULIET. Madam, I am not well.

LADY CAPULET. Evermore weeping for your cousin's death?
What, wilt thou wash him from his grave with tears?
And if thou couldst, thou couldst not make him live;
Therefore have done. Some grief shows much of love,
But much of grief shows still some want of wit.

JULIET. Yet let me weep for such a feeling[18] loss.

LADY CAPULET. So shall you feel the loss, but not the friend
Which you weep for.

JULIET. Feeling so the loss,
I cannot choose but ever weep the friend.

LADY CAPULET. Well, girl, thou weep'st not so much for his death,
As that the villain lives which slaughter'd him.

JULIET. What villain, madam?

LADY CAPULET. That same villain Romeo.

JULIET. [*Aside.*] Villain and he be many miles asunder.—
God pardon him! I do with all my heart;
And yet no man like[19] he doth grieve my heart.

LADY CAPULET. That is because the traitor murderer lives.

JULIET. Ay, madam, from the reach of these my hands.
Would none but I might venge my cousin's death!

LADY CAPULET. We will have vengeance for it, fear thou not.
Then weep no more. I'll send to one in Mantua,
Where that same banish'd runagate[20] doth live,
Shall give him such an unaccustom'd dram[21]
That he shall soon keep Tybalt company;
And then I hope thou wilt be satisfied.

JULIET. Indeed I never shall be satisfied
With Romeo, till I behold him—dead—
Is my poor heart, so for a kinsman vex'd.
Madam, if you could find out but a man
To bear a poison, I would temper[22] it,

16. **not down.** Still awake

17. ***She...window.*** Apparently she descends and re-enters the main stage, which is no longer the garden but a room in the house.

18. **feeling.** Deep

a • sun • der
(ə sun´ dər) *adv.*, far apart; widely separated

19. **like.** So much as

20. **runagate.** Renegade

21. **dram.** A unit of weight for apothecaries or druggists; a measure of some drug or drink

22. **temper.** Prepare

That Romeo should, upon receipt thereof,
Soon sleep in quiet. O how my heart abhors
To hear him nam'd, and cannot come to him
To wreak the love I bore my cousin
Upon his body that[23] hath slaughter'd him!

ab • hor (əb hôr′) *v.,* hate; detest

23. **his body that.** Body of the person who

LADY CAPULET. Find thou the means, and I'll find such a man.
But now I'll tell thee joyful tidings, girl.

JULIET. And joy comes well in such a needy time.
What are they, beseech your ladyship?

LADY CAPULET. Well, well, thou hast a careful[24] father, child,
One who, to put thee from thy heaviness,
Hath sorted out a sudden[25] day of joy,
That thou expects not, nor I look'd not for.

24. **careful.** Caring

25. **sudden.** Fast-approaching

JULIET. Madam, in happy time, what day is that?

LADY CAPULET. Marry, my child, early next Thursday morn,
The gallant, young, and noble gentleman,
The County Paris, at Saint Peter's Church,
Shall happily make thee there a joyful bride.

JULIET. Now, by Saint Peter's Church and Peter too,
He shall not make me there a joyful bride.
I wonder at this haste, that I must wed
Ere he that should be husband comes to woo.
I pray you tell my lord and father, madam,
I will not marry yet, and when I do, I swear
It shall be Romeo, whom you know I hate,
Rather than Paris. These are news indeed!

LADY CAPULET. Here comes your father, tell him so yourself;
And see how he will take it at your hands.

Enter CAPULET *and* NURSE.

CAPULET. When the sun sets, the earth doth drizzle dew,
But for the sunset of my brother's son
It rains downright.
How now, a conduit,[26] girl? What, still in tears?
Evermore show'ring? In one little body
Thou counterfeits a bark, a sea, a wind:
For still thy eyes, which I may call the sea,
Do ebb and flow with tears; the bark thy body is,
Sailing in this salt flood; the winds, thy sighs,
Who, raging with thy tears, and they with them,
Without a sudden calm,[27] will overset

26. **conduit.** Fountain

27. **Without...calm.** Unless they stop soon

Thy tempest-tossed body. How now, wife?
Have you delivered to her our decree?

LADY CAPULET. Ay, sir, but she will none, she gives you thanks.[28]
I would the fool were married to her grave!

CAPULET. Soft, take me with you,[29] take me with you, wife.
How, will she none? Doth she not give us thanks?
Is she not proud?[30] Doth she not count her blest,
Unworthy as she is, that we have wrought[31]
So worthy a gentleman to be her bride?[32]

JULIET. Not proud you have, but thankful[33] that you have.
Proud can I never be of what I hate,
But thankful even for hate that is meant love.

CAPULET. How how, how how, chopp'd logic![34] What is this?
"Proud," and "I thank you," and "I thank you not,"
And yet "not proud," mistress minion[35] you?
Thank me no thankings, nor proud me no prouds,
But fettle[36] your fine joints 'gainst Thursday next,

28. **but...thanks.** She declines with thanks.

29. **take...you.** Tell me what you mean

30. **proud.** Happy
31. **wrought.** Obtained
32. **bride.** Bridegroom

33. **thankful.** Politely grateful

34. **chopp'd logic.** Misleading but clever argument
35. **minion.** Spoiled child

36. **fettle.** Ready (term usually used for horses)

HISTORY CONNECTION

Wedding portrait of King Ferdinand of Aragón and Queen Isabella of Castile.

European Nobility and Arranged Marriages Arranged marriages among European nobility were common until the eighteenth century. Families arranged marriages to protect their economic or political interests. The young man and woman usually did not know each other well and were not expected to have a strong emotional attachment, even after marriage. Often, these marriages were arranged by the parents when the children were no more than ten or eleven years old, with the marriage taking place a few years later. Some famous arranged marriages include Ferdinand and Isabella of Spain (uniting two separate kingdoms, Aragón and Castile, into one country), Marie Antoinette of Austria and Louis XVI of France (married at the ages of fourteen and fifteen, respectively), and Mary II of England and William III of Orange.

To go with Paris to Saint Peter's Church,
Or I will drag thee on a hurdle[37] thither.
Out,[38] you green-sickness[39] carrion! Out, you baggage![40]
You tallow-face!

LADY CAPULET. Fie, fie, what, are you mad?

JULIET. Good father, I beseech you on my knees,
Hear me with patience but to speak a word.

She kneels down.

CAPULET. Hang thee, young baggage! disobedient wretch!
I tell thee what: get thee to church a' Thursday,
Or never after look me in the face.
Speak not, reply not, do not answer me!
My fingers itch. Wife, we scarce thought us blest
That God had lent us but this only child,
But now I see this one is one too much,
And that we have a curse in having her.
Out on her, hilding!

NURSE. God in heaven bless her!
You are to blame, my lord, to rate[41] her so.

CAPULET. And why, my Lady Wisdom? Hold your tongue,
Good Prudence, smatter[42] with your gossips, go.

NURSE. I speak no treason.

CAPULET. O, God-i-goden![43]

NURSE. May not one speak?

CAPULET. Peace, you mumbling fool!
Utter your gravity o'er a gossip's bowl,
For here we need it not.

LADY CAPULET. You are too hot.

CAPULET. God's bread, it makes me mad! Day, night, work, play,
Alone, in company, still my care hath been
To have her match'd; and having now provided
A gentleman of noble parentage,
Of fair demesnes,[44] youthful and nobly lien'd,[45]
Stuff 'd, as they say, with honorable parts,
Proportion'd as one's thought would wish a man,
And then to have a wretched puling[46] fool,
A whining mammet,[47] in her fortune's tender,[48]
To answer, "I'll not wed, I cannot love;
I am too young, I pray you pardon me."
But and you will not wed, I'll pardon you.

37. **hurdle.** Sled on which prisoners were taken
38. **Out.** Exclamation of rebuke
39. **green-sickness.** Pale
40. **baggage.** Worthless being
41. **rate.** Scold
42. **smatter.** Chatter
43. **God-i-goden.** Exclamation of impatience meaning "for God's sake"
44. **demesnes.** Domain
45. **nobly lien'd.** Of good standing
46. **puling.** Whining
47. **mammet.** Doll
48. **in...tender.** When good fortune comes

Graze where you will, you shall not house with me.
Look to't, think on't, I do not use[49] to jest.
Thursday is near, lay hand on heart, advise.[50]
And you be mine, I'll give you to my friend;
And you be not, hang, beg, starve, die in the streets,
For, by my soul, I'll ne'er acknowledge thee,
Nor what is mine shall never do thee good.
Trust to't, bethink you, I'll not be forsworn. *Exit.*

Juliet. Is there no pity sitting in the clouds,
That sees into the bottom of my grief?
O sweet my mother, cast me not away!
Delay this marriage for a month, a week,
Or if you do not, make the bridal bed
In that dim monument where Tybalt lies.

Juliet learns that she is to wed Paris.

49. **do not use.** Don't usually

50. **advise.** Think carefully

LADY CAPULET. Talk not to me, for I'll not speak a word.
Do as thou wilt, for I have done with thee. *Exit.*

JULIET. O God!—O nurse, how shall this be prevented?
My husband is on earth, my faith in heaven;[51]
How shall that faith return again to earth,[52]
Unless that husband send it me from heaven
By leaving earth? Comfort me, counsel me!
Alack, alack, that heaven should practice[53] stratagems
Upon so soft a subject as myself!
What say'st thou? Hast thou not a word of joy?
Some comfort, nurse.

NURSE. Faith, here it is.
Romeo is banished, and all the world to nothing[54]
That he dares ne'er come back to challenge[55] you;
Or if he do, it needs must be by stealth.
Then, since the case so stands as now it doth,
I think it best you married with the County.
O he's a lovely gentleman!
Romeo's a dishclout to[56] him. An eagle, madam,
Hath not so green, so quick, so fair an eye
As Paris hath. Beshrow[57] my very heart,
I think you are happy in this second match,
For it excels your first; or if it did not,
Your first is dead, or 'twere as good he were
As living here[58] and you no use of him.

JULIET. Speak'st thou from thy heart?

NURSE. And from my soul too, else beshrew them both.

JULIET. Amen![59]

NURSE. What?

JULIET. Well, thou hast comforted me marvellous much.
Go in, and tell my lady I am gone,
Having displeas'd my father, to Lawrence' cell,
To make confession and to be absolv'd.

NURSE. Marry, I will, and this is wisely done. *Exit.*

JULIET. [*She looks after* NURSE.] Ancient damnation![60] O most wicked fiend!
Is it more sin to wish me thus forsworn,
Or to dispraise my lord with that same tongue
Which she hath prais'd him with above compare

51. **my...heaven.** I swore my marriage vow before God.
52. **How...earth?** How can I remarry unless Romeo dies?
53. **practice.** Invent; contrive
54. **all...nothing.** It is a safe bet; the odds are
55. **challenge.** Claim
56. **to.** Compared to
57. **Beshrow.** Beshrew; curse
58. **here.** On earth
59. **Amen.** So be it.
60. **Ancient damnation.** Damned old woman

So many thousand times? Go, counsellor,
Thou and my bosom[61] henceforth shall be twain.[62]
I'll to the friar to know his remedy;
If all else fail, myself have power to die. *Exit.*

61. **bosom.** Inner thoughts
62. **twain.** Separate

Is avenging someone's death honorable? Under what circumstances might it be or not be acceptable?

REFER TO TEXT	REASON WITH TEXT	
1a. Recall what happens during the duel between Tybalt and Romeo in Act III, Scene i.	1b. Who started the duel? Explain what Romeo's actions during the duel reveal. What makes Romeo a sympathetic character?	**Understand** **Find meaning**
2a. List the arguments that Capulet uses to suggest that Juliet should obey him.	2b. Relate whether or not generational conflicts have changed since that time. Why or why not?	**Apply** **Use information**
3a. How do Juliet's parents respond to her refusals?	3b. Compare the judgment the Prince imposes on Romeo to the punishment with which Capulet threatens Juliet if she refuses to marry Paris. What seems to motivate these men to make the decisions they do?	**Analyze** **Take things apart**
4a. Define the events that are driving Romeo and Juliet further apart.	4b. What tragic mistakes have been made and by whom so far in the play? How might Romeo and Juliet's problems have been avoided? Determine where you think the blame lies. Explain.	**Evaluate** **Make judgments**
5a. Repeat the Nurse's advice to Juliet.	5b. What might resolve the conflict and complications that have taken place? What would the main characters have to be willing to do? Propose a plan for the characters and assess the likelihood of their following it.	**Create** **Bring ideas together**

ANALYZE LITERATURE: Stage Directions and Understatement

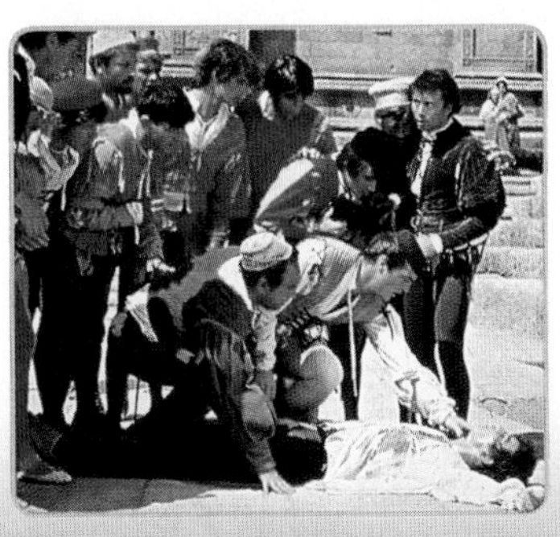

Stage directions are notes included in a play, in addition to the dialogue, for the purpose of describing how something should be performed on stage. How are the stage directions in this act crucial to understanding the action? What other stage directions would you add if you were to produce this play?

An **understatement** is an ironic statement that de-emphasizes something important. Notice in Act III, Scene i, when Mercutio is slain by Tybalt, Mercutio uses understatement to express his condition: "Ay, ay, a scratch, a scratch, marry, 'tis enough." What does this use of understatement say about Mercutio's character?

UNDERSTAND THE CONCEPT | APPLY THE SKILL

Modifiers

Adjectives and adverbs—two kinds of **modifiers**—add meaning to nouns, adjectives, verbs, and adverbs. An **adjective** modifies a noun or a pronoun. An **adverb** modifies a verb, an adjective, or another adverb.

EXAMPLES

adjective O *calm, dishonorable, vile* submission! (The adjectives in italics modify the noun *submission.*)

adverb Either withdraw unto some private place; / Or reason *coldly* of your grievances. (The adverb *coldly* modifies the verb *reason.*)

I do protest I *never* injuried thee, / But love thee *better* than thou canst devise. (The adverb *never* modifies the verb *injuried,* and the adverb *better* modifies the verb *love.*)

But I'll amerce you with *so* strong a fine / That you shall all repent the loss of mine. (The adverb *so* modifies the adjective *strong.*)

To determine whether a modifier is an adjective or an adverb, you can follow these steps:

1. Look at the word that is modified.
2. Ask yourself, "Is this modified word a noun or a pronoun?" If the answer is yes, the modifier is an adjective. If the answer is no, the modifier is an adverb.

Modifiers can also come in the form of a phrase or clause that, because of its placement in a sentence, describes another word. A **dangling modifier** is a phrase or clause that, because of its placement in a sentence, describes a word it is not intended to describe or modify.

EXAMPLES

Smelling the gas leak, the restaurant was emptied. (The restaurant can't smell.)

Wrapped in a blanket stuffed into a trash can, the mayor found his mother's sapphire. (What was the mayor doing wrapped in a blanket inside a trash can?)

If a modifier is too far away from the word it should describe, this is a **misplaced modifier.**

EXAMPLES

Jeannine has many books about tornados *in her study*. (This sentence makes it sound as if tornados are actually in Jeannine's study.)

I found a coupon for a free Thanksgiving turkey *in the newspaper*. (The coupon, not the turkey, was found in the newspaper.)

To eliminate dangling or misplaced modifiers, add words, change words, or reword. Notice how the simple changes below correct the problems:

EXAMPLES

Smelling the gas leak, we left the restaurant.

The mayor found his mother's stolen sapphire wrapped in a blanket inside a trash can.

Jeannine's study houses several books about tornados.

I found a coupon in the newspaper for a free Thanksgiving turkey.

REVIEW TERMS

- **modifiers:** words that add meaning to nouns, adjectives, verbs, and adverbs
- **adjective:** a word that modifies a noun or a pronoun
- **adverb:** a word that modifies a verb, an adjective, or another adverb
- **dangling modifier:** a phrase or clause that describes a word it is not intended to describe or modify
- **misplaced modifier:** a modifier placed too far away from the word it is meant to modify

UNDERSTAND THE CONCEPT

APPLY THE SKILL

Identify Modifiers

Read the following sentences. Identify the modifiers in each sentence, whether they are adjectives, adverbs, or modifying phrases.

1. Not wanting to fight with his new wife's cousin, Romeo tries to stop the argument between Tybalt and Mercutio.
2. Mercutio calls for a plague upon both of the rival houses as he dies.
3. With a stroke, Romeo kills Tybalt and realizes how very unfortunate the circumstances are.
4. Juliet dreamily anticipates her wedding night with Romeo, unaware that Romeo has killed her cousin.
5. Initially, Juliet believes that Romeo is the one for whom Nurse is crying so pitifully.
6. Friar Lawrence chastises Romeo for acting so foolishly when there is still hope for a life with Juliet.
7. Wanting to cheer up his grieving daughter, Lord Capulet has arranged for County Paris to make Juliet his joyful bride.
8. Lord Capulet angrily declares that he will throw Juliet out unless she shows herself an obedient and grateful daughter.
9. The Nurse compares Romeo unfavorably with the "lovely gentleman" called Paris.
10. Juliet firmly resolves either to get Friar Lawrence's advice on how to avoid this unexpected marriage or to kill herself.

Fix Problems with Modifiers

Revise the following paragraph to fix any problem modifiers.

> Not realizing it is Tybalt who is dead, the Nurse's words cause Juliet to start mourning for Romeo. Now banished, the Nurse explains finally that Romeo killed Tybalt. At first, Juliet curses Romeo complete for being a vile fiend in such a fairly package. However, when the Nurse cries "Shame come to Romeo," she is scolded by Juliet, coming to the defense of her new husband. Hiding in Friar Lawrence's cell, the Nurse finds Romeo to bid him go quick to Juliet's room.

Use Modifiers in Your Writing

In Act III, Juliet at first feels anger toward Romeo for killing Tybalt but then feels guilty for momentarily losing faith in her husband. She knows her family's grief but cannot completely share in it. Write about a time when you felt your loyalties were torn. The conflict could be one between two arguing friends, between your family and your friends, or between a friend and your own sense of right and wrong. Use adjectives, adverbs, and modifying phrases to explain the situation, how you felt about it, and what finally happened.

EXTEND THE SKILL

One of the most frequent problems with modifiers is using an adjective in place of an adverb. Quite often this happens in spoken English, for example, when a person might wish someone a safe return home by saying, "Drive safe," or when wishing good-night by saying, "Sleep good." In both cases, an adjective is used in place of the correct adverb forms *safely* and *well.* As you watch television or listen to the radio, pay attention to how adverbs are used and keep track of the mistakes. Programs with unscripted interviews, such as local news broadcasts, may yield the most mistakes. Next to where you have jotted down the mistake, write the correct form.

ACT IV

SCENE I: FRIAR LAWRENCE'S CELL

Enter FRIAR LAWRENCE *and* COUNTY PARIS.

FRIAR LAWRENCE. On Thursday, sir? The time is very short.

PARIS. My father Capulet will have it so,
And I am nothing slow to slack his haste.[1]

FRIAR LAWRENCE. You say you do not know the lady's mind?
Uneven is the course, I like it not.

PARIS. Immoderately she weeps for Tybalt's death,
And therefore have I little talk'd of love,
For Venus smiles not in a house of tears.
Now, sir, her father counts it dangerous
That she do give her sorrow so much sway;
And in his wisdom hastes our marriage,
To stop the inundation of her tears,
Which, too much minded by herself alone,
May be put from her by society.[2]
Now do you know the reason of this haste.

FRIAR LAWRENCE. [*Aside.*] I would[3] I knew not why it should be slowed.—
Look, sir, here comes the lady toward my cell.

Enter JULIET.

PARIS. Happily met, my lady and my wife!

JULIET. That may be, sir, when I may be a wife.

PARIS. That may be must be, love, on Thursday next.

JULIET. What must be shall be.

FRIAR LAWRENCE. That's a certain text.

PARIS. Come you to make confession to this father?

JULIET. To answer that, I should confess to you.

PARIS. Do not deny to him that you love me.

JULIET. I will confess to you that I love him.

PARIS. So will ye, I am sure, that you love me.

JULIET. If I do so, it will be of more price,

ACT IV, SCENE I

1. **I am...haste.** I have no desire to cause him to act less hastily.

in • un • da • tion
(in' ən dā´ shən) *n.*, flood; deluge

2. **too much...society.** Paris suggests that Juliet's sorrow is worse because she is alone and that she would feel better in the company of others.
3. **would.** Wish

Being spoke behind your back, than to your face.

Paris. Poor soul, thy face is much abus'd with tears.

Juliet. The tears have got small victory by that,
For it was bad enough before their spite.

Paris. Thou wrong'st it more than tears with that report.

Juliet. That is no slander, sir, which is a truth,
And what I spake, I spake it to my face.[4]

Paris. Thy face is mine, and thou hast sland'red it.

Juliet. It may be so, for it is not mine own.
Are you at leisure, holy father, now,
Or shall I come to you at evening mass?

Friar Lawrence. My leisure serves me, pensive[5] daughter, now.
My lord, we must entreat the time alone.

Paris. God shield[6] I should disturb devotion!
Juliet, on Thursday early will I rouse ye;
Till then adieu, and keep this holy kiss. *Exit.*

Juliet. O, shut the door, and when thou hast done so,
Come weep with me, past hope, past cure, past help!

Friar Lawrence. O Juliet, I already know thy grief,
It strains[7] me past the compass[8] of my wits.
I hear thou must, and nothing may prorogue[9] it,
On Thursday next be married to this County.

Juliet. Tell me not, friar, that thou hearest of this,
Unless thou tell me how I may prevent it.
If in thy wisdom thou canst give no help,
Do thou but call my resolution wise,
And with this knife I'll help it presently.[10]
God join'd my heart and Romeo's, thou our hands,
And ere this hand, by thee to Romeo's seal'd,
Shall be the label[11] to another deed,
Or my true heart with treacherous revolt
Turn to another, this shall slay them both.
Therefore, out of thy long-experienc'd time,
Give me some present counsel, or, behold,
'Twixt my extremes and me this bloody knife
Shall play the umpeer,[12] arbitrating[13] that
Which the commission[14] of thy years and art[15]
Could to no issue of true honor bring.
Be not so long to speak, I long to die,
If what thou speak'st speak not of remedy.

slan • der (slan´ dər) *n.,* false statement damaging another person's character or reputation

4. **to my face.** About my own face

5. **pensive.** Sad and thoughtful

6. **shield.** Forbid

7. **strains.** Forces
8. **compass.** Boundaries or borders
9. **prorogue.** Argue against or prevent

res • o • lu • tion (rez' ə lʉ´ shün) *n.,* expression of will or intent; determination

10. **presently.** At this moment

11. **label.** Seal

12. **umpeer.** Umpire
13. **arbitrating.** Deciding
14. **commission.** Authority
15. **art.** Ability

FRIAR LAWRENCE. Hold, daughter! I do spy a kind of hope,
Which craves as desperate an execution
As that is desperate which we would prevent.
If rather than to marry County Paris,
Thou hast the strength of will to slay thyself,
Then is it likely thou wilt undertake
A thing like death to chide away this shame,
That cop'st with Death himself to scape from it;[16]
And if thou darest, I'll give thee remedy.

JULIET. O, bid me leap, rather than marry Paris,
From off the battlements of any tower,
Or walk in thievish ways, or bid me lurk
Where serpents are; chain me with roaring bears,
Or hide me nightly in a charnel-house,[17]
O'ercover'd quite with dead men's rattling bones,
With reeky[18] shanks and yellow chapless[19] skulls;
Or bid me go into a new-made grave,
And hide me with a dead man in his shroud[20]—
Things that, to hear them told, have made me tremble—
And I will do it without fear or doubt,
To live an unstain'd wife to my sweet love.

FRIAR LAWRENCE. Hold then. Go home, be merry, give consent
To marry Paris. We'n'sday is tomorrow;
Tomorrow night look that thou lie alone,
Let not the nurse lie with thee in thy chamber.
Take thou this vial, being then in bed,
And this distilling liquor drink thou off,
When presently through all thy veins shall run
A cold and drowsy humor;[21] for no pulse
Shall keep his native progress,[22] but surcease;[23]
No warmth, no breath shall testify thou livest;
The roses in thy lips and cheeks shall fade
To wanny[24] ashes, thy eyes' windows[25] fall,
Like death when he shuts up the day of life;
Each part, depriv'd of supple government,[26]
Shall, stiff and stark and cold, appear like death,
And in this borrowed likeness of shrunk death
Thou shalt continue two and forty hours,
And then awake as from a pleasant sleep.
Now when the bridegroom in the morning comes
To rouse thee from thy bed, there art thou dead.
Then, as the manner of our country is,
In thy best robes, uncovered on the bier,
Thou shall be borne to that same ancient vault

16. **That cop'st...from it.** You who would have dealings with death in order to escape the death of a marriage to one whom you do not love

17. **charnel-house.** House where corpses are kept
18. **reeky.** Reeking; smelly
19. **chapless.** Jawless

20. **shroud.** Cloth used to wrap a corpse for burial

21. **humor.** Fluid
22. **keep...progress.** Occur as usual
23. **surcease.** Cease

24. **wanny.** Pale
25. **windows.** Lids
26. **supple government.** Control over movements

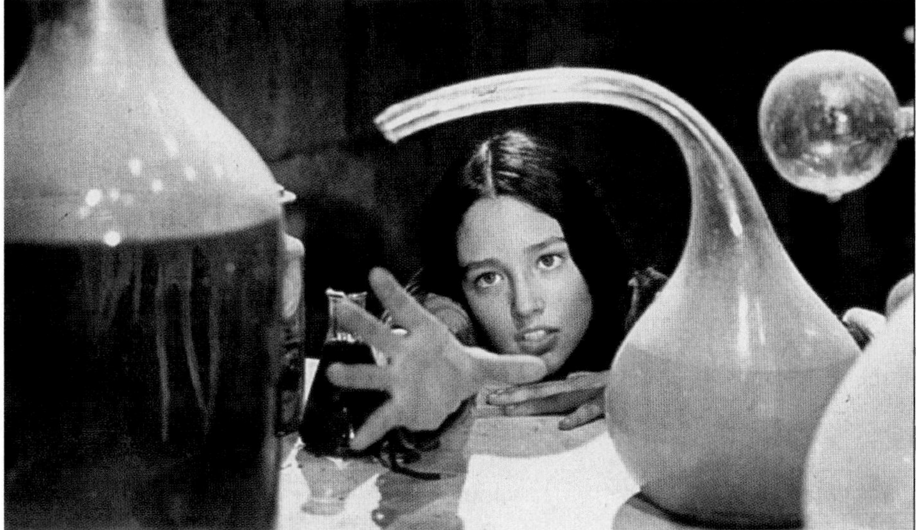

Juliet reaches for the Friar's potion.

Where all the kindred of the Capulets lie.
In the mean time, against[27] thou shalt awake,
Shall Romeo by my letters know our drift,[28]
And hither shall he come, an' he and I
Will watch thy waking, and that very night
Shall Romeo bear thee hence to Mantua.
And this shall free thee from this present shame,
If no inconstant toy,[29] nor womanish fear,
Abate thy valor in the acting it.

27. **against.** To prepare for the moment when
28. **drift.** Intentions

29. **inconstant toy.** Change of mind

JULIET. Give me, give me! O, tell not me of fear!

FRIAR LAWRENCE. Hold, get you gone. Be strong and prosperous
In this resolve. I'll send a friar with speed
To Mantua, with my letters to thy lord.

JULIET. Love give me strength! and strength shall help afford.
Farewell, dear father! *Exeunt.*

SCENE II: CAPULET'S HOUSE

Enter Father CAPULET, *Mother* LADY CAPULET, NURSE, *and* SERVINGMEN, *two or three.*

CAPULET. So many guests invite as here are writ.

Exit FIRST SERVANT.

Sirrah, go hire me twenty cunning cooks.

2. SERVANT. You shall have none ill, sir, for I'll try if they can lick their fingers.

CAPULET. How canst thou try them so?[1]

2. SERVANT. Marry, sir, 'tis an ill cook that cannot lick his own fingers;[2] therefore he that cannot lick his fingers goes not with me.

CAPULET. Go, be gone. *Exit* SECOND SERVANT.
We shall be much unfurnish'd[3] for this time.
What, is my daughter gone to Friar Lawrence?

NURSE. Ay forsooth.

CAPULET. Well, he may chance to do some good on her.
A peevish self-will'd harlotry it is.

Enter JULIET.

NURSE. See where she comes from shrift with merry look.

CAPULET. How now, my headstrong, where have you been gadding?[4]

JULIET. Where I have learnt me to repent the sin
Of disobedient opposition
To you and your behests, and am enjoin'd
By holy Lawrence to fall prostrate[5] here
To beg your pardon. [*She kneels down.*] Pardon, I beseech you!
Henceforward I am ever rul'd by you.

CAPULET. Send for the County, go tell him of this.
I'll have this knot knit up tomorrow morning.

JULIET. I met the youthful lord at Lawrence' cell,
And gave him what becomed[6] love I might,
Not stepping o'er the bounds of modesty.

CAPULET. Why, I am glad on't, this is well, stand up.
This is as't should be. Let me see the County;
Ay, marry, go, I say, and fetch him hither.
Now, afore God, this reverend holy friar,
All our whole city is much bound to him.

JULIET. Nurse, will you go with me into my closet[7]
To help me sort such needful ornaments
As you think fit to furnish me tomorrow?

LADY CAPULET. No, not till Thursday, there is time enough.

CAPULET. Go, nurse, go with her, we'll to church tomorrow.

Exeunt JULIET *and* NURSE.

LADY CAPULET. We shall be short in our provision,
'Tis now near night.

ACT IV, SCENE II

1. **try them so.** By that means tell whether they can cook
2. **lick...fingers.** The servant is suggesting that a good cook will be willing to taste his own cooking by licking his fingers.
3. **unfurnish'd.** Unprepared

pee • vish (pē´ vish) *adj.*, hard to please; irritable

4. **gadding.** Going in a purposeless manner

5. **prostrate.** Lying face-down in demonstration of great humility

6. **becomed.** Fitting

7. **closet.** Room

Capulet. Tush, I will stir about,
And all things shall be well, I warrant thee, wife;
Go thou to Juliet, help to deck up her.
I'll not to bed tonight; let me alone,
I'll play the huswife[8] for this once. What ho!
They are all forth. Well, I will walk myself
To County Paris, to prepare up him
Against tomorrow. My heart is wondrous light,
Since this same wayward girl is so reclaim'd. *Exeunt.*

8. **huswife.** Housewife

Scene III: Capulet's House

Enter Juliet *and* Nurse.

Juliet. Ay, those attires are best, but, gentle nurse,
I pray thee leave me to myself tonight,
For I have need of many orisons[1]
To move the heavens to smile upon my state,
Which, well thou knowest, is cross and full of sin.

Act IV, Scene III
1. **orisons.** Prayers

Enter Mother Lady Capulet.

Lady Capulet. What, are you busy, ho? Need you my help?

Juliet. No, madam, we have cull'd such necessaries
As are behoofeful[2] for our state[3] tomorrow.
So please you, let me now be left alone,
And let the nurse this night sit up with you,
For I am sure you have your hands full all,
In this so sudden business.

2. **behoofeful.** Needed
3. **state.** Ceremony

Lady Capulet. Good night.
Get thee to bed and rest, for thou hast need.

Exeunt Lady Capulet *and* Nurse.

Juliet. Farewell! God knows when we shall meet again.
I have a faint cold fear thrills through my veins,
That almost freezes up the heat of life.
I'll call them back again to comfort me.
Nurse!—What should she do here?
My dismal scene I needs must act alone.
Come, vial.
What if this mixture do not work at all?
Shall I be married then tomorrow morning?
No, no, this shall forbid it. Lie thou there.

Laying down her dagger.

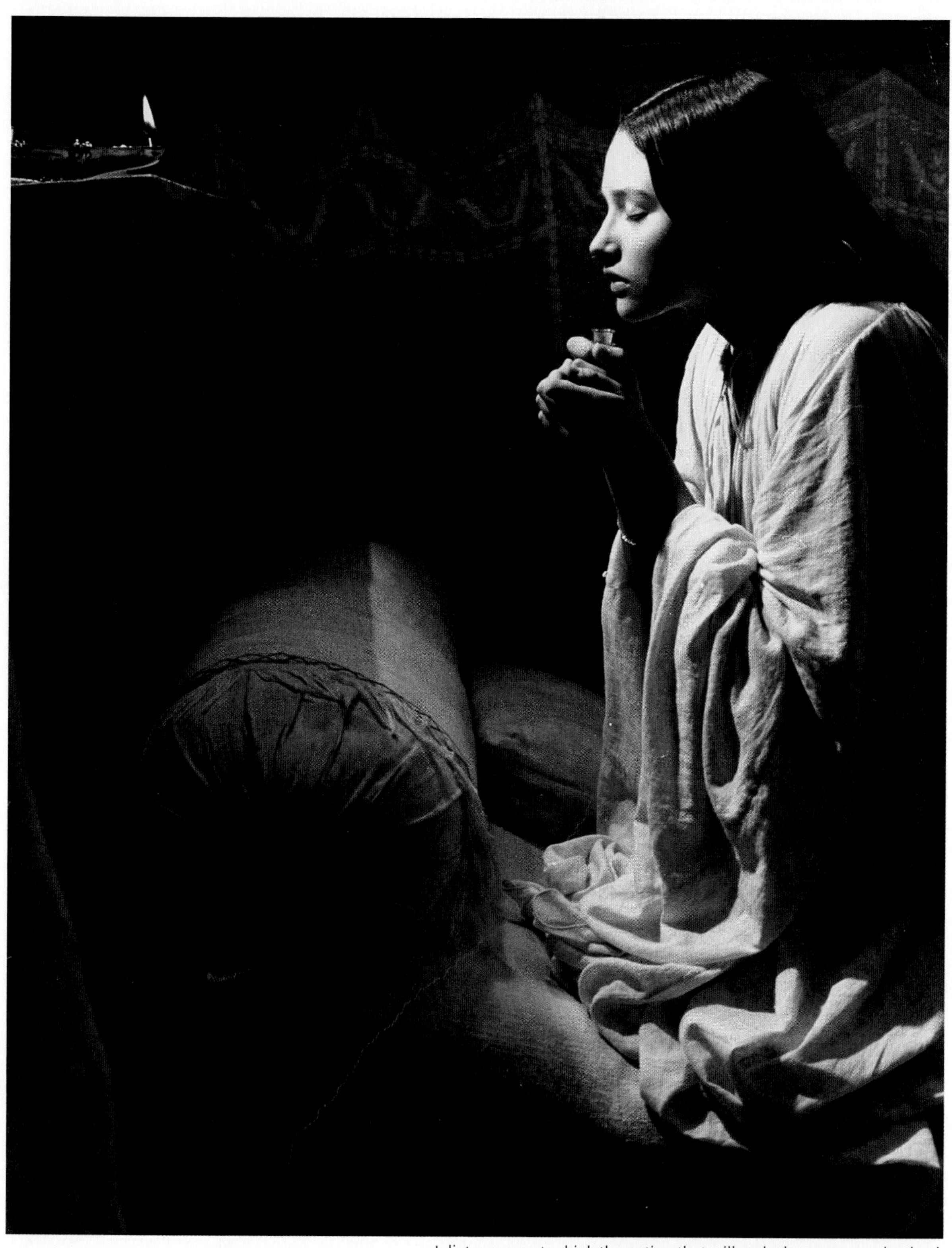

Juliet prepares to drink the potion that will make her appear to be dead.

What if it be a poison which the friar
Subtilly hath minist'red to have me dead,
Lest in this marriage he should be dishonor'd
Because he married me before to Romeo?
I fear it is, and yet methinks it should not,
For he hath still[4] been tried[5] a holy man.
How if, when I am laid into the tomb,
I wake before the time that Romeo
Come to redeem me? there's a fearful point!
Shall I not then be stifled in the vault,
To whose foul mouth no healthsome air breathes in,
And there die strangled ere my Romeo comes?
Or if I live, is it not very like
The horrible conceit[6] of death and night,
Together with the terror of the place—
As in a vault, an ancient receptacle,
Where for this many hundred years the bones
Of all my buried ancestors are pack'd,
Where bloody Tybalt, yet but green in earth,[7]
Lies fest'ring in his shroud, where, as they say,
At some hours in the night spirits resort—
Alack, alack, is it not like that I,
So early waking—what with loathsome smells,
And shrikes like mandrakes'[8] torn out of the earth,
That living mortals, hearing them, run mad—
O, if I wake, shall I not be distraught,
Environed with all these hideous fears,
And madly play with my forefathers' joints,
And pluck the mangled Tybalt from his shroud,
And in this rage, with some great kinsman's bone,
As with a club, dash out my desp'rate brains?
O, look! methinks I see my cousin's ghost
Seeking out Romeo, that did spit his body
Upon a rapier's point. Stay, Tybalt, stay!
Romeo, Romeo, Romeo! Here's drink—I drink to thee.

She falls upon her bed, within the curtains.

4. **still.** Always
5. **been tried.** Been shown to be
6. **conceit.** Idea
7. **green in earth.** Newly buried

loath • some (lōth´ səm) *adj.,* disgusting; detestable

8. **shrikes like mandrakes'.** Shrieks like those made by mandrakes. The mandrake root, used in magic because of its supposed resemblance to a human being, was believed to shriek when pulled out of the ground.

Scene iv: Continues in Capulet's House

Enter lady of the house Lady Capulet *and* Nurse *with herbs.*

Lady Capulet. Hold, take these keys and fetch more spices, nurse.

Nurse. They call for dates and quinces in the pastry.[1]

Act IV, Scene iv
1. **pastry.** Pastry-room

Enter old CAPULET.

CAPULET. Come, stir, stir, stir! the second cock hath crowed,
The curfew-bell hath rung, 'tis three a' clock.
Look to the bak'd meats, good Angelica,[2]
Spare not for cost.

NURSE. Go, you cot-quean,[3] go,
Get you to bed. Faith, you'll be sick tomorrow
For this night's watching.[4]

CAPULET. No, not a whit. What, I have watch'd ere now
All night for lesser cause, and ne'er been sick.

LADY CAPULET. Ay, you have been a mouse-hunt[5] in your time,
But I will watch you from such watching now.

Exeunt LADY CAPULET *and* NURSE.

CAPULET. A jealous hood, a jealous hood![6]

Enter three or four SERVINGMEN *with spits and logs and baskets.*

Now, fellow, what is there?

1. SERVANT. Things for the cook, sir, but I know not what.

CAPULET. Make haste, make haste. Sirrah, fetch drier logs.

Exit FIRST SERVANT.

Call Peter, he will show thee where they are.

2. SERVANT. I have a head, sir, that will find out logs,
And never trouble Peter for the matter.

CAPULET. Mass, and well said, a merry whoreson, ha!
Thou shalt be logger-head.[7] Good faith, 'tis day.

Exit SECOND SERVANT.

The County will be here with music straight,
For so he said he would. [*Play music within.*] I hear him near.
Nurse! Wife! What ho! What, nurse, I say!

Enter NURSE.

Go waken Juliet, go and trim her up,
I'll go and chat with Paris. Hie, make haste,
Make haste, the bridegroom he is come already,
Make haste, I say. *Exit.*

2. **Angelica.** The Nurse

3. **cot-quean.** Male house-keeper

4. **watching.** Wakefulness

5. **mouse-hunt.** Mouse-hunter; one who is up all night, like a cat

6. **jealous hood.** Jealous person

7. **logger-head.** Blockhead

Scene v: Continues in Capulet's House

Nurse. Mistress! what, mistress! Juliet!—Fast,[1] I warrant her, she.—
Why, lamb! why, lady! fie, you slug-a-bed!
Why, love, I say! madam! sweet heart! why, bride!
What, not a word? You take your pennyworths[2] now;
Sleep for a week, for the next night, I warrant,
The County Paris hath set up his rest
That you shall rest but little. God forgive me!
Marry and amen! How sound is she asleep!
I needs must wake her. Madam, madam, madam!
Ay, let the County take you in your bed,
He'll fright you up, i' faith. Will it not be? *Draws back the curtains.*
What, dress'd, and in your clothes, and down again?
I must needs wake you. Lady, lady, lady!
Alas, alas! Help, help! my lady's dead!
O, weraday, that ever I was born!
Some aqua-vitae ho! My lord! my lady!

Enter Mother, Lady Capulet.

Lady Capulet. What noise is here?

Nurse. O lamentable[3] day!

Lady Capulet. What is the matter?

Nurse. Look, look! O heavy day!

Lady Capulet. O me, O me, my child, my only life!
Revive, look up, or I will die with thee!
Help, help! Call help.

Enter Father Capulet.

Capulet. For shame, bring Juliet forth, her lord is come.

Nurse. She's dead, deceas'd, she's dead, alack the day!

Lady Capulet. Alack the day, she's dead, she's dead, she's dead!

Capulet. Hah, let me see her. Out alas, she's cold,
Her blood is settled, and her joints are stiff;
Life and these lips have long been separated.
Death lies on her like an untimely frost
Upon the sweetest flower of all the field.

Nurse. O lamentable day!

Lady Capulet. O woeful time!

Act IV, Scene v

1. **Fast.** Fast asleep

2. **pennyworths.** Small amounts (of sleep)

3. **lamentable.** Grievous; deplorable; distressing

Capulet. Death, that hath ta'en her hence to make me wail,
Ties up my tongue and will not let me speak.

Enter Friar Lawrence *and the* County Paris *with the* Musicians.

Friar Lawrence. Come, is the bride ready to go to church?

Capulet. Ready to go, but never to return.—
O son, the night before thy wedding-day
Hath Death lain with thy wife. There she lies,
Flower as she was, deflowered by him.
Death is my son-in-law, Death is my heir,
My daughter he hath wedded. I will die,
And leave him all; life, living, all is Death's.

Paris. Have I thought long to see this morning's face,
And doth it give me such a sight as this?

Lady Capulet. Accurs'd, unhappy, wretched, hateful day!
Most miserable hour that e'er time saw
In lasting labor of his pilgrimage![4]
But one, poor one, one poor and loving child,
But one thing to rejoice and solace in,
And cruel Death hath catch'd[5] it from my sight!

Nurse. O woe! O woeful, woeful, woeful day!
Most lamentable day, most woeful day
That ever, ever, I did yet behold!
O day, O day, O day, O hateful day!
Never was seen so black a day as this.
O woeful day, O woeful day!

Paris. Beguil'd, divorced, wronged, spited, slain!
Most detestable Death, by thee beguil'd,
By cruel cruel thee quite overthrown!
O love, O life! not life, but love in death!

Capulet. Despis'd, distressed, hated, martyr'd, kill'd!
Uncomfortable time, why cam'st thou now
To murther, murther our solemnity?[6]
O child, O child! my soul, and not my child!
Dead art thou! Alack, my child is dead,
And with my child my joys are buried.

Friar Lawrence. Peace ho, for shame! Confusion's cure lives not
In these confusions. Heaven and yourself
Had part in this fair maid, now heaven hath all,
And all the better is it for the maid.
Your part in her you could not keep from death,

4. **Most miserable...pilgrimage.** The worst hour since the beginning of time's long journey

5. **catch'd.** Stolen; taken

6. **solemnity.** Festivity; ceremony

But heaven keeps his part in eternal life.
The most you sought was her promotion,
For 'twas your heaven she should be advanc'd,
And weep ye now, seeing she is advanc'd
Above the clouds, as high as heaven itself?
O, in this love, you love your child so ill
That you run mad, seeing that she is well.
She's not well married that lives married long,
But she's best married that dies married young.
Dry up your tears, and stick your rosemary[7]
On this fair corse, and as the custom is,
And in her best array, bear her to church;
For though fond nature bids us all lament,[8]
Yet nature's tears are reason's merriment.[9]

Capulet. All things that we ordained festival,
Turn from their office[10] to black funeral:
Our instruments to melancholy bells,
Our wedding cheer to a sad burial feast;
Our solemn hymns to sullen dirges change;
Our bridal flowers serve for a buried corse;[11]
And all things change them to the contrary.

Friar Lawrence. Sir, go you in, and, madam, go with him;
And go, Sir Paris. Every one prepare
To follow this fair corse unto her grave.
The heavens do low'r upon you for some ill;
Move them no more by crossing[12] their high will.

They all, but the Nurse *and the* Musicians, *go forth, casting rosemary on her, and shutting the curtains.*

1. Musician. Faith, we may put up our pipes and be gone.

Nurse. Honest good fellows, ah, put up, put up,
For well you know this is a pitiful case. *Exit.*

1. Musician. Ay, by my troth, the case may be amended.[13]

Enter Peter.

Peter. Musicians, O musicians, "Heart's ease,"[14] "Heart's ease"! O, and you will have me live, play "Heart's ease."

1. Musician. Why "Heart's ease"?

Peter. O musicians, because my heart itself plays "My heart is full."
O, play me some merry dump[15] to comfort me.

1. Musician. Not a dump we, 'tis no time to play now.

Peter. You will not then?

7. **rosemary.** Herb associated with remembrance

8. **lament.** Express deep sorrow

9. **nature's...merriment.** Human nature weeps at things that reason considers joyful.

10. **office.** Purpose or function

11. **corse.** Corpse; dead body

12. **crossing.** Going against; challenging

13. **amended.** Mended; fixed; repaired

14. **"Heart's ease."** Title of a popular ballad

15. **dump.** Song

CULTURAL CONNECTION

Elizabethan Music The Elizabethans were particularly fond of music, and Shakespeare included many songs in his plays. A popular form of music was the madrigal, which several people sang without accompaniment. A solo singer accompanied by the lute was also popular. Though the lute was held in the highest esteem during the Renaissance, the viol family was quickly taking shape. The viol da gamba, a six-stringed instrument smaller than a cello but played between the legs or on the lap, was frequently taken up in courtly circles. For the common folk, however, instruments tended to be of a simpler construction. Between scene changes of Shakespeare's plays, a pipe and tabor (a type of drum) would be played to entertain the audience. Usually just one person would play both instruments, requiring a good amount of coordination.

1. MUSICIAN. No.

PETER. I will then give it you soundly.

1. MUSICIAN. What will you give us?

PETER. No money, on my faith, but the gleek;[16] I will give you the minstrel.[17]

1. MUSICIAN. Then will I give you the serving-creature.

PETER. Then will I lay the serving-creature's dagger on your pate.[18] I will carry no crotchets,[19] I'll *re* you, I'll *fa* you.[20] Do you note[21] me?

1. MUSICIAN. And[22] you *re* us and *fa* us, you note us.[23]

2. MUSICIAN. Pray you put up your dagger, and put out[24] your wit.

PETER. Then have at you with my wit! I will drybeat you with an iron wit, and put up my iron dagger. Answer me like men:

"When griping griefs the heart doth wound,
And doleful dumps the mind oppress,
Then music with her silver sound"—

why "silver sound"? Why "music with her silver sound"? What say you, Simon Catling?

1. MUSICIAN. Marry, sir, because silver hath a sweet sound.

PETER. Pretty! What say you, Hugh Rebeck?

16. **gleek.** Jest; insult
17. **give...minstrel.** Call you names
18. **pate.** Head
19. **carry no crotchets.** Pun meaning both "sing no quarter notes" and "endure no gibes"
20. **I'll *re*...you.** Pun meaning both "I'll sing the notes *re* and *fa* to you" and "I'll mess you up and clean you up," from *ray*, "to befoul," and *fay*, "to clean up"
21. **note.** Hear; listen to
22. **And.** If
23. **note us.** Set us to music
24. **put out.** Bring out

2. Musician. I say, "silver sound," because musicians sound for silver.

Peter. Pretty too! What say you, James Soundpost?

3. Musician. Faith, I know not what to say.

Peter. O, I cry you mercy,[25] you are the singer; I will say for you; it is "music with her silver sound," because musicians have no gold for sounding:

"Then music with her silver sound
With speedy help doth lend redress." *Exit.*

1. Musician. What a pestilent knave is this same!

2. Musician. Hang him, Jack! Come, we'll in here, tarry for the mourners, and stay[26] dinner. *Exeunt.*

25. **cry you mercy.** Beg your pardon

26. **stay.** Wait for

How does the saying "love is blind" relate to the story of Romeo and Juliet? Could the same be said for hatred? How do blind love and blind hate appear in today's world? What effect do they have on people and the world?

REFER TO TEXT	REASON WITH TEXT	
1a. Why does Juliet visit the Friar after her father demands that she marry Paris?	1b. Explain why Juliet would return to her family home with "a merry look."	**Understand** **Find meaning**
2a. State why the Nurse can't stay in Juliet's room the night before the wedding.	2b. Generalize how Juliet's relationship with her family and the Nurse has changed. Why?	**Apply** **Use information**
3a. Recall what Juliet does prior to drinking the Friar's potion.	3b. Analyze Juliet's soliloquy in Scene iii, lines 14–58, in which she weighs the pros and cons of carrying out the Friar's plan. List the various concerns or fears that she considers in these lines.	**Analyze** **Take things apart**
4a. Distinguish between how the Friar and the Nurse respond to Juliet upon hearing about the unhappy engagement. What was their advice?	4b. Critique Friar Lawrence's actions. What have his motivations been? Has he acted wisely? How do his actions compare with those of the Nurse's?	**Evaluate** **Make judgments**
5a. Quote the reason Friar Lawrence gives for saying that Juliet's family should not grieve too much.	5b. Can you summarize what the outcome of the play would have been, thus far, had Friar Lawrence not become involved? Should he be punished and, if so, what might the punishment be?	**Create** **Bring ideas together**

ANALYZE LITERATURE: Mood

Mood, or atmosphere, is the emotion created in the reader by part or all of a literary work. Discuss the dramatic shifts in mood that occur throughout Act IV. Which scenes are the most intense and serious? Which scenes provide comic relief? Do you find the comic scenes in Act IV to be effective, or would the play be stronger without them? Explain.

GRAMMAR & STYLE

UNDERSTAND THE CONCEPT

APPLY THE SKILL

Complete Sentences

A complete sentence contains both a subject and a predicate. The **subject** tells who or what the sentence is about. The **predicate** gives information about the subject—what the subject is, what the subject does, or what happens to the subject. The essential part of the predicate is the *verb,* which must agree with the subject. More information on subject-verb agreement can be found in Unit 1 on page 24.

EXAMPLES

complete sentence

The wise old friar	concocts a tricky scheme.
subject	**predicate**
The young woman	would not obey her parents.
subject	**predicate**

A **sentence fragment** is a phrase that is punctuated like a sentence but does not have both a subject and a predicate. To correct a sentence fragment, add the missing subject or predicate, or combine the fragment with another sentence.

EXAMPLES

sentence fragment A vial of sleeping potion.

complete sentence A vial of sleeping potion is Juliet's escape route from marriage with Paris.

sentence fragment Turned into funeral plans instead.

complete sentence The wedding festivities turned into funeral plans instead.

sentence fragment Romeo interfering with the fight.

complete sentence Mercutio was slain as a result of Romeo interfering with the fight.

Sentence fragments should be avoided in formal writing, such as the essays you write in class. However, writers sometimes use fragments intentionally for stylistic reasons. Fragments can be used effectively to add emphasis or to make an exclamation.

EXAMPLES

Fragment to add emphasis:
A jealous hood, a jealous hood!

Fragment as an exclamation:
Accurs'd, unhappy, wretched, hateful day!
Most miserable hour that e'er time saw
In lasting labor of his pilgrimage!

Fragment as a response in dialogue:
Things for the cook, sir, but I know not what.

REVIEW TERMS

- **complete sentence:** a group of words that has both a subject and a predicate
- **subject:** who or what the sentence is about
- **predicate:** the part of a sentence that includes the verb and gives information about the subject
- **sentence fragment:** a phrase that is punctuated like a sentence but does not have both a subject and a predicate

UNDERSTAND THE CONCEPT

APPLY THE SKILL

Identify Complete Sentences

Identify which of these sentences are complete and which are sentence fragments.

1. The marriage of Paris and Juliet is planned for Thursday.
2. To stop Juliet from excessive grief.
3. Threatens to kill herself if she must wed Paris.
4. Friar Lawrence has a remedy.
5. After drinking the potion, Juliet will appear dead.
6. Happy now that she has a way to remain faithful to her vows to Romeo.
7. After being contacted by letter, Romeo will arrive at Juliet's cell and take her to Mantua.
8. Having already separated from her mother and the Nurse.
9. Juliet, in her clothes and still in her bed.
10. The joyful wedding day becomes a sorrowful funeral day.

Fix Errors in Sentence Completion

Find the sentence fragments in this paragraph. Rewrite the paragraph so that all of the sentences are complete.

> Strange that no one thought to tell Capulet that Juliet was already married. Friar Lawrence obviously would not have been able to perform the ceremony because it would have gone against his religious practices. Scared of Capulet's anger, I think. He would've thrown Juliet out, but why would that be so bad? Either planning to kill herself or run off with Romeo, anyway. Friar Lawrence, respected in Verona and sought by both Capulets and Montagues. He should have told Capulet the truth. Instead, a dangerous and complicated scheme to fool the Capulets and Paris. Why Juliet preferred death over being banished by her father? Makes no sense to me. The Nurse was not very helpful, either. At first, she supports Juliet's secret marriage. Then acts as though the vows are meaningless. Not a problem to be married to two men? You'd think the adults would behave in a more mature manner.

Use Complete Sentences in Your Writing

Write a paragraph about a time you tried to get out of doing something. What were you required to do? Why didn't you want to do it? Answer these questions in your paragraph in addition to explaining your plan for avoiding it, why you thought the plan would work, and whether or not it did. When you finish your paragraph, exchange it with a classmate. First, read the paragraph for understanding. If you have any questions about the situation, write those in the margin. Next, reread the paragraph checking to make sure that the majority of the sentences are complete sentences and that any fragments are used for emphasis or in dialogue.

EXTEND THE SKILL

Read a variety of magazine articles, editorials, and personal essays to look for any sentence fragments. Copy or write down the instances of fragments that you find, including the surrounding sentences. Determine the reason for the fragment use and write a brief explanation of why the author made the choice to use a fragment.

Next, rewrite the fragment as a complete sentence and compare it with the original. Determine from this comparison what the effect of fragment use is.

ACT V

SCENE I: A STREET IN MANTUA

Enter ROMEO.

ROMEO. If I may trust the flattering[1] truth of sleep,
My dreams presage some joyful news at hand.
My bosom's lord[2] sits lightly in his throne,[3]
And all this day an unaccustom'd spirit
Lifts me above the ground with cheerful thoughts.
I dreamt my lady came and found me dead—
Strange dream, that gives a dead man leave to think!—
And breath'd such life with kisses in my lips
That I reviv'd and was an emperor.
Ah me, how sweet is love itself possess'd,
When but love's shadows are so rich in joy!

Enter ROMEO'S *man* BALTHASAR, *booted.*

News from Verona! How now, Balthasar?
Dost thou not bring me letters from the friar?
How doth my lady? Is my father well?
How doth my Juliet? That I ask again,
For nothing can be ill if she be well.

BALTHASAR. Then she is well and nothing can be ill:
Her body sleeps in Capel's monument,
And her immortal part with angels lives.
I saw her laid low in her kindred's vault,
And presently[4] took post[5] to tell it you.
O, pardon me for bringing these ill news,
Since you did leave it for my office,[6] sir.

ROMEO. Is it e'en so? Then I defy you, stars!
Thou knowest my lodging, get me ink and paper,
And hire post-horses; I will hence tonight.

BALTHASAR. I do beseech you, sir, have patience.
Your looks are pale and wild, and do import
Some misadventure.

ROMEO. Tush, thou art deceiv'd.
Leave me, and do the thing I bid thee do.
Hast thou no letters to me from the friar?

BALTHASAR. No, my good lord.

ACT V, SCENE I
1. **flattering.** Favorable
2. **My bosom's lord.** Love
3. **his throne.** Romeo's heart
4. **presently.** Immediately
5. **took post.** Traveled by horse
6. **office.** Duty

mis • ad • ven • ture
(mis' əd ven´ chər) *n.,* unlucky accident; mishap

Romeo. No matter, get thee gone,
And hire those horses; I'll be with thee straight. *Exit* Balthasar.
Well, Juliet, I will lie with thee tonight.
Let's see for means.[7] O mischief, thou art swift
To enter in the thoughts of desperate men!
I do remember an apothecary—
And hereabouts 'a dwells—which late I noted
In tatt'red weeds,[8] with overwhelming[9] brows,
Culling of simples;[10] meagre were his looks,
Sharp misery had worn him to the bones;
And in his needy shop a tortoise hung,
An alligator stuff 'd and other skins
Of ill-shap'd fishes, and about his shelves
A beggarly account[11] of empty boxes,
Green earthen pots, bladders, and musty seeds,
Remnants of packthread, and old cakes of roses[12]
Were thinly scattered, to make up a show.
Noting this penury,[13] to myself I said,
"An' if[14] a man did need a poison now,
Whose sale is present death[15] in Mantua,
Here lives a caitiff[16] wretch would sell it him."
O, this same thought did but forerun my need,
And this same needy man must sell it me.
As I remember, this should be the house.
Being holiday, the beggar's shop is shut.
What ho, apothecary!

Enter Apothecary.

Apothecary. Who calls so loud?

Romeo. Come hither, man. I see that thou art poor.
Hold, there is forty ducats;[17] let me have
A dram of poison, such soon-speeding gear[18]
As will disperse itself through all the veins
That the life-weary taker may fall dead,
And that the trunk may be discharg'd of breath
As violently as hasty powder fir'd
Doth hurry from the fatal cannon's womb.

Apothecary. Such mortal drugs I have, but Mantua's law
Is death to any he[19] that utters[20] them.

Romeo. Art thou so bare and full of wretchedness,
And fearest to die? Famine is in thy cheeks,
Need and oppression starveth in thy eyes,
Contempt and beggary hangs upon thy back;
The world is not thy friend, nor the world's law,

7. **see for means.** See how

8. **weeds.** Clothes

9. **overwhelming.** Overhanging; large

10. **simples.** Medicines

11. **beggarly account.** Small number

12. **cakes of roses.** Rose petals made into cakes for their scent

13. **penury.** Extreme poverty

14. **An' if.** If

15. **present death.** Capital offense

16. **caitiff.** Cowardly

17. **ducats.** Gold coins

18. **soon-speeding gear.** Fast-acting stuff

19. **any he.** Anyone

20. **utters.** Dispenses

The world affords no law to make thee rich;
Then be not poor, but break it, and take this.

Apothecary. My poverty, but not my will, consents.

Romeo. I pay thy poverty, and not thy will.

Apothecary. Put this in any liquid thing you will
And drink it off, and if you had the strength
Of twenty man, it would dispatch[21] you straight.

Romeo. There is thy gold, worse poison to men's souls,
Doing more murther in this loathsome world,
Than these poor compounds that thou mayest not sell.
I sell thee poison, thou hast sold me none.
Farewell! Buy food, and get thyself in flesh.[22]

Exit Apothecary.

Come, cordial[23] and not poison, go with me
To Juliet's grave, for there must I use thee. *Exit.*

21. **dispatch.** Kill

22. **get...flesh.** Become fat (i.e., prosper)

23. **cordial.** Medicine

Scene ii: Friar Lawrence's Cell

Enter Friar John.

Friar John. Holy Franciscan friar! brother, ho!

Enter Friar Lawrence.

Friar Lawrence. This same should be the voice of Friar John.
Welcome from Mantua! What says Romeo?
Or, if his mind be writ, give me his letter.

Friar John. Going to find a barefoot brother out,
One of our order, to associate[1] me,
Here in this city visiting the sick,
And finding him, the searchers[2] of the town,
Suspecting that we both were in a house
Where the infectious pestilence did reign,
Seal'd up the doors and would not let us forth,
So that my speed to Mantua there was stay'd.

Friar Lawrence. Who bare my letter then to Romeo?

Friar John. I could not send it—here it is again—
Nor get a messenger to bring it thee,
So fearful were they of infection.

Friar Lawrence. Unhappy fortune! By my brotherhood,
The letter was not nice[3] but full of charge,[4]

Act V, Scene ii
1. **associate.** Accompany
2. **searchers.** Health officials
3. **nice.** About small matters
4. **full of charge.** Important

History Connection

The Black Death At the end of the Middle Ages and during the beginning of the Renaissance, the bubonic plague—known as the Black Death—hit Europe hard, killing one third of the continent's population. People had little understanding of the plague or how it spread (we know today that it was spread by fleas and rats), so many people resorted to talismans, charms, scent therapy, and other ineffective means. Quarantine, like that which affected Friar John, was one of the more effective ways of controlling the disease.

Of dear[5] import, and the neglecting it
May do much danger. Friar John, go hence,
Get me an iron crow,[6] and bring it straight
Unto my cell.

Friar John. Brother, I'll go and bring it thee. *Exit.*

Friar Lawrence. Now must I to the monument alone,
Within this three hours will fair Juliet wake.
She will beshrew[7] me much that Romeo
Hath had no notice of these accidents;[8]
But I will write again to Mantua,
And keep her at my cell till Romeo come—
Poor living corse, clos'd in a dead man's tomb! *Exit.*

5. **dear.** Extreme; great

6. **crow.** Crowbar

7. **beshrew.** Censure

8. **accidents.** Events

Scene iii: The Churchyard Wherein Lies the Capulet Family Tomb

Enter Paris *and his* Page *with flowers and sweet[1] water and a torch.*

Paris. Give me thy torch, boy. Hence, and stand aloof.[2]
Yet put it out, for I would not be seen.
Under yond yew trees lay thee all along,[3]
Holding thy ear close to the hollow ground,
So shall no foot upon the churchyard tread,
Being[4] loose, unfirm, with digging up of graves,

Act V, Scene iii

1. ***sweet.*** Perfumed
2. **aloof.** Away from here; distant
3. **all along.** Flat against the ground
4. **Being.** Because the ground is

But thou shalt hear it. Whistle then to me
As signal that thou hearest something approach.
Give me those flowers. Do as I bid thee, go.

Page. [*Aside.*] I am almost afraid to stand[5] alone
Here in the churchyard, yet I will adventure.[6]

5. **stand.** Stay

6. **adventure.** Try

Retires. Paris *strews the tomb with flowers.*

Paris. Sweet flower, with flowers thy bridal bed I strew—
O woe, thy canopy is dust and stones!—
Which with sweet water nightly I will dew,
Or wanting that, with tears distill'd by moans.
The obsequies[7] that I for thee will keep
Nightly shall be to strew thy grave and weep.

7. **obsequies.** Prayers or rites for dead persons

Whistle Boy.

The boy gives warning, something doth approach.
What cursed foot wanders this way tonight,
To cross[8] my obsequies and true love's rite?
What, with a torch? Muffle me, night, a while. *Retires.*

8. **cross.** Interrupt; go against

Enter Romeo *and* Balthasar *with a torch, a mattock, and a crow of iron.*

Romeo. Give me that mattock and the wrenching iron.
Hold, take this letter; early in the morning
See thou deliver it to my lord and father.
Give me the light. Upon thy life I charge thee,
What e'er thou hearest or seest, stand all aloof,
And do not interrupt me in my course.
Why I descend into this bed of death
Is partly to behold my lady's face,
But chiefly to take thence from her dead finger
A precious ring—a ring that I must use
In dear employment—therefore hence be gone.
But if thou, jealous, dost return to pry
In what I farther shall intend to do,
By heaven, I will tear thee joint by joint,
And strew this hungry churchyard with thy limbs.
The time and my intents are savage-wild,
More fierce and more inexorable[9] far
Than empty tigers or the roaring sea.

9. **inexorable.** Not to be persuaded or moved by entreaty

Balthasar. I will be gone, sir, and not trouble ye.

Romeo. So shalt thou show me friendship. Take thou that;
Live and be prosperous, and farewell, good fellow.

Balthasar. [*Aside.*] For all this same, I'll hide me hereabout,

His looks I fear, and his intents I doubt. *Retires.*

Romeo. Thou detestable maw,[10] thou womb of death,
Gorg'd with the dearest morsel of the earth,
Thus I enforce thy rotten jaws to open,
And in despite I'll cram thee with more food.
Romeo *begins to open the tomb.*

10. **maw.** Mouth

Paris. This is that banish'd haughty Montague,
That murd'red my love's cousin, with which grief
It is supposed the fair creature died,
And here is come to do some villainous shame
To the dead bodies. I will apprehend him. *Steps forth.*
Stop thy unhallowed toil, vile Montague!
Can vengeance be pursued further than death?
Condemned villain, I do apprehend thee.
Obey and go with me, for thou must die.

haugh • ty (hô´ tē) *adj.,* proud; arrogant; self-important; conceited

Romeo. I must indeed, and therefore came I hither.
Good gentle youth, tempt not a desp'rate man.
Fly hence and leave me, think upon these gone,
Let them affright thee. I beseech thee, youth,
Put not another sin upon my head,
By urging me to fury: O, be gone!
By heaven, I love thee better than myself,
For I come hither arm'd against myself.
Stay not, be gone; live, and hereafter say
A madman's mercy bid thee run away.

Paris. I do defy thy conjuration,
And apprehend thee for a felon here.

Romeo. Wilt thou provoke me? Then have at thee, boy! *They fight.*

Page. O Lord, they fight! I will go call the watch. *Exit.*

Paris. O, I am slain! [*Falls.*] If thou be merciful,
Open the tomb, lay me with Juliet. *Dies.*

Romeo. In faith, I will. Let me peruse this face.
Mercutio's kinsman, noble County Paris!
What said my man, when my betossed soul
Did not attend him as we rode? I think
He told me Paris should have married Juliet.
Said he not so? or did I dream it so?
Or am I mad, hearing him talk of Juliet,
To think it was so? O, give me thy hand,
One writ with me in sour misfortune's book!
I'll bury thee in a triumphant grave.

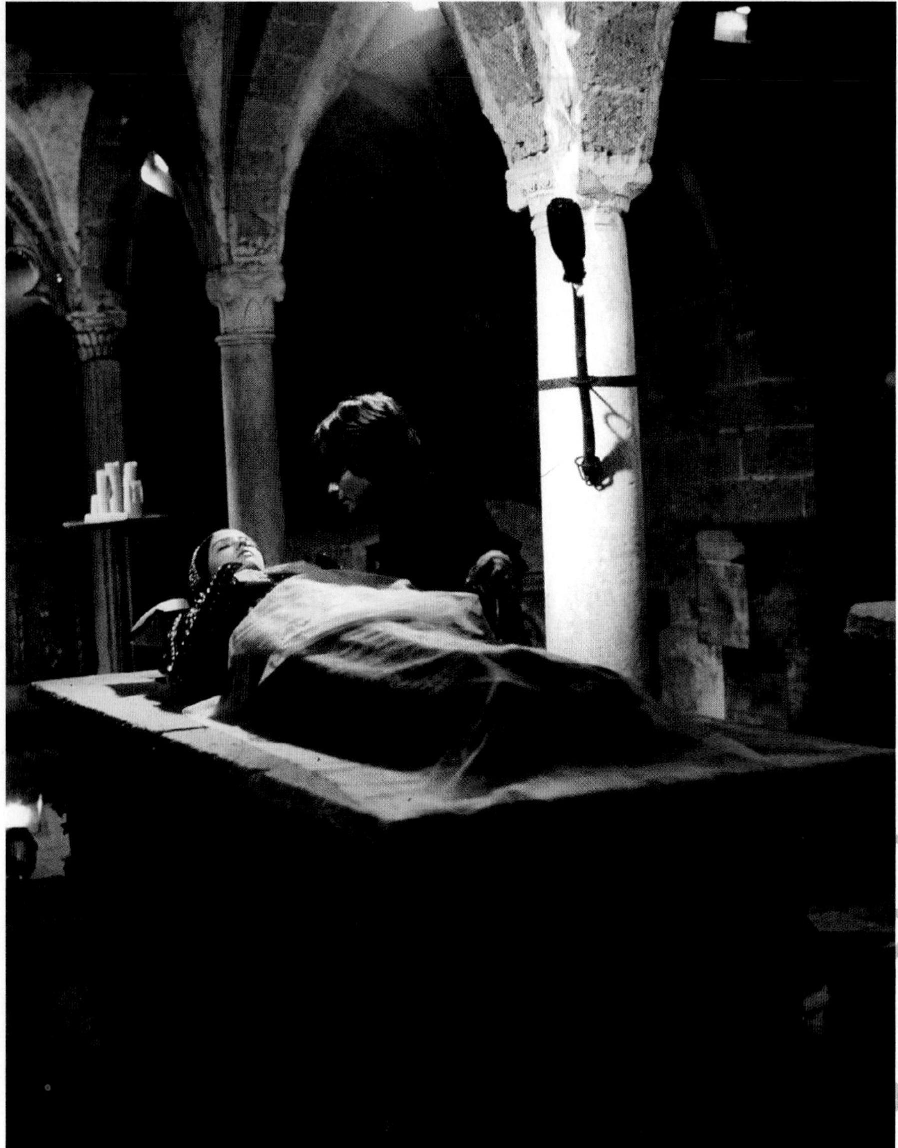

Romeo finds Juliet in the tomb.

A grave? O no, a lanthorn,[11] slaught'red youth;
For here lies Juliet, and her beauty makes
This vault a feasting presence[12] full of light.
Death, lie thou there, by a dead man interr'd.

Laying PARIS *in the tomb.*

How oft when men are at the point of death
Have they been merry, which their keepers call
A lightning before death! O how may I
Call this a lightning? O my love, my wife,
Death, that hath suck'd the honey of thy breath,
Hath had no power yet upon thy beauty:
Thou art not conquer'd, beauty's ensign yet

11. **lanthorn.** Lantern (a tower room with glass on all sides)
12. **feasting presence.** Appear like a place decorated for a feast

Is crimson in thy lips and in thy cheeks,
And death's pale flag is not advanced[13] there.
Tybalt, liest thou there in thy bloody sheet?
O, what more favor can I do to thee,
Than with that hand that cut thy youth in twain
To sunder[14] his that was thine enemy?
Forgive me, cousin! Ah, dear Juliet,
Why art thou yet so fair? Shall I believe
That unsubstantial Death is amorous,
And that the lean abhorred monster keeps
Thee here in dark to be his paramour?
For fear of that, I still will stay with thee,
And never from this palace of dim night
Depart again. Here, here will I remain
With worms that are thy chambermaids; O, here
Will I set up my everlasting rest,
And shake the yoke of inauspicious stars
From this world-wearied flesh. Eyes, look your last!
Arms, take your last embrace! and, lips, O you
The doors of breath, seal with a righteous kiss
A dateless bargain to engrossing death!
Come, bitter conduct,[15] come, unsavory guide!
Thou desperate pilot, now at once run on
The dashing rocks thy sea-sick weary bark!
Here's to my love! [*Drinks.*] O true apothecary!
Thy drugs are quick. Thus with a kiss I die. *Dies.*

Enter FRIAR LAWRENCE *with lanthorn, crow, and spade.*

FRIAR LAWRENCE. Saint Francis be my speed! how oft tonight
Have my old feet stumbled at graves! Who's there?

BALTHASAR. Here's one, a friend, and one that knows you well.

FRIAR LAWRENCE. Bliss be upon you! Tell me, good my friend,
What torch is yond, that vainly lends his light
To grubs and eyeless skulls? As I discern,
It burneth in the Capels' monument.

BALTHASAR. It doth so, holy sir, and there's my master,
One that you love.

FRIAR LAWRENCE. Who is it?

BALTHASAR. Romeo.

FRIAR LAWRENCE. How long hath he been there?

BALTHASAR. Full half an hour.

13. **advanced.** Raised

14. **sunder.** Cut

in • aus • pi • cious (in' ô spi´ shəs) *adj.*, unfavorable; unlucky

15. **conduct.** Guide

dis • cern (di sʉrn´) *v.*, recognize; identify

Friar Lawrence. Go with me to the vault.

Balthasar. I dare not, sir.
My master knows not but I am gone hence,
And fearfully did menace me with death
If I did stay to look on his intents.

Friar Lawrence. Stay then, I'll go alone. Fear comes upon me.
O, much I fear some ill unthrifty[16] thing.

Balthasar. As I did sleep under this yew tree here,
I dreamt my master and another fought,
And that my master slew him.

Friar Lawrence. Romeo!

Friar stoops and looks on the blood and weapons.

Alack, alack, what blood is this, which stains
The stony entrance of this sepulchre?
What mean these masterless and gory swords
To lie discolor'd by this place of peace? *Enters the tomb.*
Romeo, O, pale! Who else? What, Paris too?
And steep'd in blood? Ah, what an unkind[17] hour
Is guilty of this lamentable chance!
The lady stirs. *Juliet rises.*

Juliet. O comfortable friar! where is my lord?
I do remember well where I should be,
And there I am. Where is my Romeo?

Noise within.

Friar Lawrence. I hear some noise, lady. Come from that nest
Of death, contagion, and unnatural sleep.
A greater power than we can contradict
Hath thwarted our intents. Come, come away.
Thy husband in thy bosom there lies dead;
And Paris too. Come, I'll dispose of thee
Among a sisterhood of holy nuns.
Stay not to question, for the watch is coming.
Come go, good Juliet [*noise again*], I dare no longer stay. *Exit.*

Juliet. Go get thee hence, for I will not away.
What's here? A cup clos'd in my true love's hand?
Poison, I see, hath been his timeless[18] end.
O churl,[19] drunk all, and left no friendly drop
To help me after?[20] I will kiss thy lips,
Haply some poison yet doth hang on them,
To make me die with a restorative.[21]
Thy lips are warm.

16. **unthrifty.** Unlucky

17. **unkind.** Unnatural; cruel

18. **timeless.** Untimely; premature
19. **churl.** Low person
20. **help me after.** Help me to come after or follow you
21. **restorative.** Romeo's kiss will restore Juliet.

1. **Watch.** [*Within.*] Lead, boy, which way?

Juliet. Yea, noise? Then I'll be brief. O happy dagger,
Taking Romeo's *dagger.*
This is thy sheath [*stabs herself*]; there rust, and let me die.
Falls on Romeo's *body and dies.*

Enter Paris's Boy *and* Watch.

Page. This is the place, there where the torch doth burn.

1. **Watch.** The ground is bloody, search about the churchyard.
Go, some of you, whoe'er you find attach.[22] *Exeunt some.*
Pitiful sight! here lies the County slain,
And Juliet bleeding, warm, and newly dead,
Who here hath lain this two days buried.
Go tell the Prince, run to the Capulets,
Raise up the Montagues; some others search. *Exeunt others.*
We see the ground whereon these woes do lie,
But the true ground of all these piteous woes
We cannot without circumstance descry.

22. **attach.** Stop; detain

Juliet stabs herself.

Enter some of the WATCH *with Romeo's man* BALTHASAR.

2. WATCH. Here's Romeo's man, we found him in the churchyard.

1. WATCH. Hold him in safety till the Prince come hither.

Enter FRIAR LAWRENCE *and another* WATCHMAN.

3. WATCH. Here is a friar, that trembles, sighs, and weeps.
We took this mattock[23] and this spade from him,
As he was coming from this churchyard's side.

23. **mattock.** Digging tool

1. WATCH. A great suspicion. Stay the friar too.

Enter the PRINCE *and* ATTENDANTS.

PRINCE. What misadventure is so early up,
That calls our person from our morning rest?

Enter Capels CAPULET, LADY CAPULET, *and others.*

CAPULET. What should it be that is so shrik'd abroad?

LADY CAPULET. O, the people in the street cry "Romeo,"
Some "Juliet," and some "Paris," and all run
With open outcry toward our monument.

PRINCE. What fear is this which startles in your ears?

1. WATCH. Sovereign, here lies the County Paris slain,
And Romeo dead, and Juliet, dead before,
Warm and new kill'd.

PRINCE. Search, seek, and know how this foul murder comes.

1. WATCH. Here is a friar, and slaughter'd Romeo's man,
With instruments upon them, fit to open
These dead men's tombs.

CAPULET. O heavens! O wife, look how our daughter bleeds!
This dagger hath mista'en, for lo, his house
Is empty on the back of Montague,
And it mis-sheathed in my daughter's bosom!

LADY CAPULET. O me, this sight of death is as a bell
That warns my old age to a sepulchre.

Enter MONTAGUE *and others.*

PRINCE. Come, Montague, for thou art early up
To see thy son and heir now early down.

MONTAGUE. Alas, my liege,[24] my wife is dead tonight;
Grief of my son's exile hath stopp'd her breath.
What further woe conspires against mine age?

24. **liege.** Lord or master

PRINCE. Look and thou shalt see.

MONTAGUE. O thou untaught! what manners is in this,
To press before thy father to a grave?

PRINCE. Seal up the mouth of outrage[25] for a while,
Till we can clear these ambiguities,
And know their spring, their head,[26] their true descent,
And then will I be general of[27] your woes,
And lead you even to death.[28] Mean time forbear,
And let mischance be slave to patience.
Bring forth the parties of suspicion.[29]

FRIAR LAWRENCE. I am the greatest, able to do least,
Yet most suspected, as the time and place
Doth make against me, of this direful murther;
And here I stand both to impeach and purge
Myself condemned and myself excus'd.

PRINCE. Then say at once what thou dost know in this.

FRIAR LAWRENCE. I will be brief, for my short date of breath[30]
Is not so long as is a tedious tale.
Romeo, there dead, was husband to that Juliet,
And she, there dead, that Romeo's faithful wife.
I married them, and their stol'n marriage-day
Was Tybalt's dooms-day, whose untimely death
Banish'd the new-made bridegroom from this city,
For whom, and not for Tybalt, Juliet pin'd.
You, to remove that siege of grief from her,
Betroth'd and would have married her perforce
To County Paris. Then comes she to me,
And with wild looks bid me <u>devise</u> some mean
To rid her from this second marriage,
Or in my cell there would she kill herself.
Then gave I her (so tutor'd by my art)
A sleeping potion, which so took effect
As I intended, for it wrought on her
The form of death. Mean time I writ to Romeo,
That he should hither come as[31] this dire night
To help to take her from her borrowed grave,
Being the time the potion's force should cease.
But he which bore my letter, Friar John,
Was stayed by accident, and yesternight
Return'd my letter back. Then all alone,
At the prefixed hour of her waking,
Came I to take her from her kindred's vault,

25. **outrage.** Impassioned grief
26. **their spring, their head.** Their source
27. **be general of.** Learn about
28. **death.** The execution of guilty persons
29. **parties of suspicion.** Suspects

30. **my...breath.** The little time left to me in this life

de • vise (di vīz´) *v.,* work out or create; plan; invent

31. **as.** On

Meaning to keep her closely at my cell,
Till I conveniently could send to Romeo.
But when I came, some minute ere the time
Of her awakening, here untimely lay
The noble Paris and true Romeo dead.
She wakes, and I entreated her come forth
And bear this work of heaven with patience.
But then a noise did scare me from the tomb,
And she, too desperate, would not go with me,
But as it seems, did violence on herself.
All this I know, and to the marriage
Her nurse is privy; and if aught in this
Miscarried by my fault, let my old life
Be sacrific'd some hour before his time,
Unto the rigor of severest law.

Prince. We still[32] have known thee for a holy man.
Where's Romeo's man? what can he say to this?

32. **still.** Always

Balthasar. I brought my master news of Juliet's death,
And then in post he came from Mantua
To this same place, to this same monument.
This letter he early bid me give his father,
And threat'ned me with death, going in the vault,
If I departed not and left him there.

Prince. Give me the letter, I will look on it.
Where is the County's page that rais'd the watch?
Sirrah, what made[33] your master in this place?

33. **made.** Wanted; did

Page. He came with flowers to strew his lady's grave,
And bid me stand aloof, and so I did.
Anon comes one with light to ope the tomb,
And by and by my master drew on him,
And then I ran away to call the watch.[34]

34. **watch.** Watchman

Prince. This letter doth make good the friar's words,
Their course of love, the tidings of her death;
And here he writes that he did buy a poison
Of a poor 'pothecary, and therewithal
Came to this vault, to die and lie with Juliet.
Where be these enemies? Capulet! Montague!
See what a scourge is laid upon your hate,
That heaven finds means to kill your joys with love.
And I for winking at your discords too
Have lost a brace[35] of kinsmen. All are punish'd.

35. **a brace.** Two

All mourn the tragic deaths of Romeo and Juliet.

Capulet. O brother Montague, give me thy hand.
This is my daughter's jointure,[36] for no more
Can I demand.

Montague. But I can give thee more,
For I will raise her statue in pure gold,
That whiles Verona by that name is known,
There shall no figure at such rate be set
As that of true and faithful Juliet.

Capulet. As rich shall Romeo's by his lady's lie,
Poor sacrifices of our enmity!

Prince. A glooming[37] peace this morning with it brings,
The sun, for sorrow, will not show his head.

36. **jointure.** Dowry

37. **glooming.** Gloomy

Go hence to have more talk of these sad things;
Some shall be pardon'd, and some punished:
For never was a story of more woe
Than this of Juliet and her Romeo. *Exeunt omnes.*[38] ❖

38. ***Exeunt omnes.*** Exit all

Pride and hatred have the capacity to create great unhappiness. What combats these feelings? What other emotions or beliefs have the ability to change things for the worse? for the better?

REFER TO TEXT ▶ ▶ ▶ ▶	▶ REASON WITH TEXT	
1a. Define what the apothecary needs. What does Romeo need?	1b. How does Romeo think the apothecary should feel about the world and death? Describe the differences between Romeo's and the apothecary's feelings about death.	**Understand** **Find meaning**
2a. Identify why Paris is in the graveyard.	2b. Examine why Romeo says to Paris, "I love thee better than myself."	**Apply** **Use information**
3a. For what reason does the Prince command that the vault be sealed? What must be discovered?	3b. Point out the causes of Romeo and Juliet's tragedy. In what ways are they themselves or their families to blame? What other factors seem to play a part in this tragedy?	**Analyze** **Take things apart**
4a. Recall which characters have a change of heart or opinion during the play.	4b. Evaluate the motivations and intentions behind each of the following actions: Capulet decides Juliet will marry Paris; the Nurse advises Juliet to marry Paris; Friar Lawrence creates the plan that ultimately leads to the deaths of Romeo and Juliet; Juliet fakes her own death; Romeo takes his own life.	**Evaluate** **Make judgments**
5a. Indicate what finally happens after all the deaths.	5b. What does this play communicate about feuds and grudges? Generate possible messages communicated within this play. What might the main message be? What other themes, or major ideas, can you identify in this play?	**Create** **Bring ideas together**

ANALYZE LITERATURE: Irony

Irony is the difference between appearance and reality. For what purpose did Shakespeare use dramatic irony? Scan the text for examples. In each case, do you think the character or characters who were unaware would have acted differently if they had known what the audience knew? Explain your answer for each case.

Literature CONNECTION

Very little is known about **Arthur Brooke.** The narrative poem *"The Tragicall Historye of Romeus and Juliet"* was first published in 1562, two years before Shakespeare was born. This sonnet, **"The Argument,"** which appears at the beginning of Brooke's narrative poem, summarizes the story of Romeo and Juliet. It is widely thought that Brooke created his free paraphrase of the story of Romeo and Juliet from a French version of a novel by the Italian novelist Matteo Bandello (c. 1485–c. 1561). Bandello lived in Mantua, Italy, for many years before taking up residence in France. Many historians believe that Brooke died in a shipwreck in 1561.

THE ARGUMENT

from THE TRAGICALL HISTORYE OF ROMEUS AND JULIET

A Poem by **Arthur Brooke**

Love hath inflamed twayne by sodayn sight.[1]
And both do graunt the thing that both desyre.
They wed in shrift by counsell of a frier.
Yong Romeus clymes fayre Juliets bower by night.
Three monthes he doth enjoy his cheefe delight.
By Tybalts rage, provoked unto yre,[2]
He payeth death to Tybalt for his hyre.
A banisht man he scapes by secret flight.
New mariage is offred to his wyfe:
She drinkes a drinke that seemes to reve her breath.
They bury her, that sleping yet hath lyfe.
Her husband heares the tydinges of her death.
He drinkes his bane. And she with Romeus knyfe,
When she awakes, her selfe (alas) she sleath.[3] ❖

1. **Love hath...sight.** Love has inflamed the two (twain) by sudden sight.
2. **yre.** Ire; anger
3. **sleath.** Slayeth (slays)

TEXT TO TEXT CONNECTION

Compare and contrast the excerpt from *The Tragicall Historye of Romeus and Juliet* with the Prologue that appears in Shakespeare's *The Tragedy of Romeo and Juliet.* What does this poetic version of the play leave out of the story? Evaluate which piece is the most successful in describing the underlying theme of the story. How does "The Argument" compare with Shakespeare's play?

KUMIN

Literature CONNECTION

"Purgatory," by poet **Maxine Kumin** (b. 1925), offers the reader a picture of what the lives of Romeo and Juliet might have been like had they managed to carry out Friar Lawrence's plan and escape to Mantua. The word *purgatory* refers to a place or state of suffering and misery. Kumin received the Pulitzer Prize in Poetry for her collection *Up Country: Poems of New England* (1972). She served as the Consultant in Poetry to the Library of Congress (the former title of the Poet Laureate) from 1981–1982.

PURGATORY

A Poem by **Maxine Kumin**

And suppose the darlings get to Mantua,
suppose they cheat the crypt, what next? Begin
with him, unshaven. Though not, I grant you, a
displeasing cockerel,[1] there's egg yolk on his chin.
His seedy robe's aflap,[2] he's got the rheum.[3]
Poor dear, the cooking lard has smoked her eye.
Another Montague is in the womb
although the first babe's bottom's not yet dry.
She scrolls a weekly letter to her Nurse
who dares to send a smock[4] through Balthasar,
and once a month, his father posts a purse.[5]
News from Verona? Always news of war.
Such sour years it takes to right this wrong!
The fifth act runs unconscionably[6] long. ❖

Dante's Purgatorio 18, Gustave Doré.

1. **cockerel.** Young male rooster; young man
2. **his seedy...aflap.** His shabby robe hangs open
3. **rheum.** Watery discharge from the eyes or nose
4. **smock.** Item of women's clothing
5. **posts a purse.** Sends money
6. **unconscionably.** Excessively; unreasonably

TEXT ◄TO► TEXT CONNECTION

- Consider if Shakespeare had allowed Romeo and Juliet to survive their ordeal. Might he have imagined their ending as similar to Kumin's "Purgatory"? What questions does Maxine Kumin's poem "Purgatory" raise about the nature of Romeo and Juliet's relationship?
- If the speaker in Kumin's poem could give advice to Romeo and Juliet, what do you think she or he would say?
- Compare "Purgatory" to the final act of Shakespeare's *The Tragedy of Romeo and Juliet*. What are the greatest losses and the greatest gains in each ending?

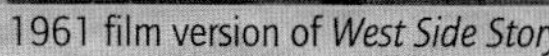

1961 film version of *West Side Story.*

Claire Danes and Leonardo DiCaprio in the 1996 film *Romeo + Juliet.*

Informational Text CONNECTION

Is reading *Romeo and Juliet* in this textbook your first encounter with the story of these ill-fated lovers? Before you read the play, had you ever heard anyone quote lines from it? If so, which lines? **"Romeo and Juliet Over the Centuries,"** by **Dorothy May,** is a brief informative article that chronicles the history of the famous story of the two star-crossed lovers from before Shakespeare into modern times. This article explores the different versions of the story of Romeo and Juliet that have been presented over time.

Do you think that the story of Romeo and Juliet is still relevant to high school students today? Why or why not?

Olivia Hussey and Leonard Whiting.

Romeo and Juliet OVER THE CENTURIES

An Article by **Dorothy May**

Romeo and Juliet is probably the best known and best loved of all William Shakespeare's plays. Generations of audiences have been able to relate to the two "star-cross'd" young lovers, whose passion is doomed from the start by the bitter feuding between their families. Since Elizabethan times, the play has been interpreted in many forms, inspiring operas, ballets, musicals, and poetry. It has been translated into nearly every language and has been updated in such modern contexts as gangland New York City, the Israeli-Palestinian conflict in Jerusalem, and war-torn Sarajevo.

The power of the story itself is evident in that it has been told for centuries; in fact, it was not even new to Shakespeare's audience. According to legend, the real story of Romeo and Juliet took place in Verona in 1303, although similar stories were told in Greece dating back to the second century. Shakespeare's source for the play is thought to be *The Tragicall Historye of Romeus and Juliet,* a long poem written by Englishman Arthur Brooke in 1562. Brooke himself based his poem on an earlier Italian work that had been translated into French.

The timeless story of two lovers found its most treasured and enduring form in the unparalleled poetry of Shakespeare. His version of *Romeo and Juliet* is exceptional for its wit and wordplay, its soaring poetic descriptions, and its frenetic pace. Many lines from *Romeo and Juliet,* like so many others from Shakespeare's body of work, have entered the common lexicon. Everyone knows "a rose by any other name would smell as sweet" and understands the term "Romeo" to mean a lover. The unforgettable balcony scene in Act II has become an archetype of romantic love.

Shakespeare's plays were meant to be performed, not read. *Romeo and Juliet* in particular, because of its explosive emotion and lack of subtle, introspective brooding, is especially suited for musical interpretations such as those of famous composers like Berlioz and Tchaikovsky. Following are some of the many ways *Romeo and Juliet* has been performed.

- Charles Francois Gounod's **opera** *Romeo and Juliet,* composed in 1867, is the most famous operatic version of Shakespeare's ultimate love story. It continues to be performed in opera houses worldwide.
- Leonard Bernstein's 1957 **musical** *West Side Story* moved the setting from Verona to New York City and changed the warring families into rival street gangs. Juliet became "Maria," sister of the leader of the Puerto Rican gang, the Sharks. She falls in love with the leader of the rival Anglo gang, the Jets. The show incorporated modern music and dance. *West Side Story* is also a 1961 movie directed by Robert Wise and starring Natalie Wood as Maria.
- *Romeo and Juliet,* a **ballet** in three acts composed by Serge Prokofiev, had its world premiere in 1965 and starred Margot Fonteyn and Rudolf Nureyev. A 1966 video is available, as well as a 1982 version choreographed by Nureyev.
- The romantic **film** version of *Romeo and Juliet,* directed by Franco Zeffirelli in 1968 and starring teenagers Olivia Hussey as Juliet, and Leonard Whiting as Romeo, is the most popular Shakespearean movie of all time.
- Director Baz Luhrmann's 1996 **film** *Romeo + Juliet,* starring Leonardo DiCaprio and Claire Danes, changed the scene to fictional Verona Beach, in an otherworldly Los Angeles. The characters and setting are updated to an almost futuristic time, but the language is the original verse of Shakespeare. The movie's lush visuals, modern music, and cutting-edge style have led some to call this "Shakespeare for the MTV generation."
- A new **rock musical** of *Romeo and Juliet,* composed by Jerome Korman and Terrence Mann, and directed by Mann, had its debut onstage in 1999. The musical incorporates modern dance and ballet and puts Shakespeare's verse into contemporary pop/rock for the new millennium. ❖

REFER TO TEXT ▶▶▶▶	▶ REASON WITH TEXT	
1a. State where, other than Verona, Italy, the story has been set.	1b. Determine what about the story of Romeo and Juliet lends itself to other forms of performance art, such as ballets and musical productions.	**Understand** **Find meaning**
2a. Identify the earliest known date for the written story of Romeo and Juliet.	2b. It is often said that the story of Romeo and Juliet is timeless. Conclude whether the story really is timeless. Could culture ever evolve in a way that makes the story seem implausible? Explain your answer.	**Evaluate** **Make judgments**
3a. Define what about *Romeo and Juliet* makes it suitable for performance.	3b. Relate whether you can think of any stories that have been recently written that might have the kind of lasting and worldwide appeal that *Romeo and Juliet* has had. Explain.	**Create** **Bring ideas together**

TEXT TO TEXT CONNECTION

An **archetype** is a type of character, image, theme, symbol, plot, or other element that has appeared in the literature of the world from ancient times until today. What elements of Shakespeare's *The Tragedy of Romeo and Juliet* easily apply to more contemporary settings? View one or more of the film versions of *Romeo and Juliet* and compare how these archetypal elements are presented.

AFTER READING

EXTEND THE TEXT

Writing Options

Creative Writing An *epitaph* is an inscription or a verse written to be used on a tomb or written in commemoration of someone who has died. Write an **epitaph** for Romeo, Juliet, Paris, or Lady Montague. You might write your verse in iambic pentameter, in free verse, or in prose. Try to express the personal traits of the character you choose in your epitaph. Write at least ten lines.

Expository Writing Write a one-page **character analysis** examining a character in *Romeo and Juliet.* Do not simply describe the character, but make a statement about his or her role in the play. For instance, you might state that Friar Lawrence chastises yet cares for Romeo, and his decisions unintentionally led to the tragedy. Explain how his or her particular traits made the character behave in certain ways. Include evidence from the play, and share your character analysis with the class.

Collaborative Learning

Counsel Romeo Work with a partner to role-play a counseling session between Friar Lawrence and Romeo on Romeo's plans to marry Juliet or when he learns of his banishment. Think about the motivation of Friar Lawrence and of Romeo. What is each most interested in? What points would each want to make? After practicing with your partner, perform your role-play for the class. Then, as a class, discuss whether or not events would have turned out differently if Friar Lawrence had held such a counseling session with Romeo.

Media Literacy

View a Film and Write a Film Review View a film adaptation of Romeo and Juliet, such as the 1968 version directed by Franco Zeffirelli. Then, write a review of the film for your classmates. Your review should include the following: the title and director of the film, names of the lead actors, your overall impression of the film, a plot summary that notes differences between the film and the play, an analysis of how visual and sound techniques are used, and an evaluation of how well the actors acted their parts.

Go to **www.mirrorsandwindows.com** for more.

READING ASSESSMENT

1. Which of these lines does *not* express a theme of the play?
   - A. "See what a scourge is laid upon your hate, / That heaven finds means to kill your joys with love." (Act V, Scene iii, lines 292–293)
   - B. "I fear, too early, for my mind misgives / Some consequence yet hanging in the stars / Shall bitterly begin his fearful date / With this night's revels" (Act I, Scene iv, lines 106–109)
   - C. "Virtue itself turns vice, being misapplied / And vice sometime by action dignified." (Act II, Scene iii, lines 21–22)
   - D. All of the above
   - E. None of the above
2. What does the word *presage* mean when Romeo says in Act V, Scene i, "If I may trust the flattering truth of sleep, / My dreams presage some joyful news at hand"?
   - A. declare wisely
   - B. suppress
   - C. invent
   - D. predict
   - E. represent
3. Which of the following is the main idea of the article "Romeo and Juliet Over the Centuries"?
   - A. *Romeo and Juliet* is the best loved of all Shakespeare's plays.
   - B. *Romeo and Juliet* is a timeless story that has been told and retold in many forms throughout the world since before Shakespeare's time to the present.
   - C. *Romeo and Juliet* was meant to be performed on the stage and is especially suited to musical interpretations.
   - D. The story of Romeo and Juliet found its most enduring form in the poetry of Shakespeare's play *Romeo and Juliet.*
   - E. Recreating *Romeo and Juliet* in a new form robs it of its original meaning.
4. There are several themes in *Romeo and Juliet.* Choose one theme to explore. Cite lines from the play that express the theme you have chosen and explain how the lines develop it.

UNDERSTAND THE CONCEPT

APPLY THE SKILL

Reference Materials for Vocabulary Words

You can use a number of different reference books to investigate words. Each type offers certain information about words, such as variations on the definitions, synonyms and antonyms, or origins. Vocabulary reference works include dictionaries and thesauri.

Dictionaries

Standard dictionaries of English provide the spellings, pronunciations, definitions, and other information about most words you will encounter in your reading and listening.

It is important to understand how to make sense of a dictionary entry. A standard dictionary entry will usually contain these parts:

(1) [1]**keen** (2) (kēn´) (3) *adj.* (4) [ME *kene* brave, sharp, fr. OE *cēne* brave; akin to OHG *kuoni* brave] (13c) **1** : having a sharp edge or point ⟨a *keen* sword⟩ **2** : having a sharp or piercing effect ⟨a *keen* insult⟩ **3 a** (5) : having or showing a sharp mind **b** : being particularly perceptive or sensitive ⟨a *keen* eye; a *keen* sense of smell⟩ **4** (6) : showing great enthusiasm ⟨she is very *keen* on horses⟩. (7) *syn* see *sharp, eager.* (8) —**keen • ly** *adv.* — **keen • ness** (kēn´ nəs) *n.*

(1) [2]**keen** (kēn´) *n.* [Ir *caoinim,* or "lament"] **1** : a wailing cry of mourning —*v.* **2** : to make wailing cries of mourning for the dead

1. **Main entry.** A word may have one or more main entries if it has more than one possible meaning. The main entry shows how a word is spelled and how it may be divided into syllables.
2. **Pronunciation.** The pronunciation is shown by the use of phonetic symbols. A key to the symbols can be found in your dictionary.
3. **Part-of-speech label.** The part-of-speech labels indicate whether a word might be used as a noun (*n.*), verb (*v.*), adjective (*adj.*), or another part of speech.
4. **Etymology.** The etymology gives the origins and history of the word, telling how and approximately when the word came into English.
5. **Definitions.** Each definition of a word is numbered. Some definitions are broken down into two or more sub-definitions that are lettered.
6. **Example phrase.** Example phrases are sometimes given to show how the word may be used.
7. **Synonyms.** Synonyms and antonyms of a word may be given. Some dictionaries may also explain the different shades of meaning carried by each.
8. **Other forms.** Related forms of the word, such as an adjective form of a noun, may be given at the end of the entry.

Thesauruses

A **thesaurus** is a reference book that contains lists of synonyms and antonyms for words. When you look up a word, you get a short, general definition and, typically, an extensive list of synonyms and antonyms. The **synonyms** all will have the same basic meaning as the primary word and **antonyms** will mean the opposite of the primary word. In general, these words will vary from one another in connotation. A word's connotation is all the associations it has in addition to its literal meaning.

Other Tools

Encyclopedias, atlases, history time lines, and other specialized reference books can also be helpful when looking for information about references to dates, events, obscure places, literary works, or mythology. Technology allows readers to use the Internet to quickly find meaning in such references online.

UNDERSTAND THE CONCEPT | APPLY THE SKILL

Exercise A

Decide which type of reference book you would use to determine the meaning of each of the following terms from *The Devil and Daniel Webster.*

1. John C. Calhoun
2. deprecatory
3. Salem witch trials
4. Congo
5. telea polyphemus
6. Whig
7. Concord
8. Simon Girty
9. "as Ruth unto Naomi"
10. knave

Exercise B

Use a dictionary to find the meaning of each of the following words from *The Devil and Daniel Webster.* Describe the denotation (dictionary definition), the connotation (emotional associations), and etymology (word origin).

1. mirth
2. deprecatory
3. homage
4. insinuatingly
5. placidly
6. livery
7. inexorably
8. plaintiff
9. immaterial

Use a thesaurus to find a synonym for each of the following words from *The Devil and Daniel Webster.*

1. prosperity
2. feigned
3. doleful
4. bias
5. denounce
6. ominous
7. toil
8. treachery
9. exultantly
10. asunder

Use the Glossary of Vocabulary Words in your textbook to determine the meaning of the following words from *The Tragedy of Romeo and Juliet.*

abhor
denote
enmity
fray
inauspicious
mutiny
pernicious
rancor
submission
transgression

EXTEND THE SKILL

Use reference works from your classroom, library, or computer to answer the following questions. You will need to look up the italicized words.

- Where is *Mantua?* How far is it from Verona? What is another name for *Mantua?*
- What does Arthur Brooke mean by "Love hath inflamed *twayne* by *sodayn* sight"?
- What is the meaning of *purgatory*, the title of Maxine Kumin's poem?
- What does the author of "Romeo and Juliet Over the Centuries" mean by "*explosive* emotion" when describing the play? What synonym could be used in place of *explosive?*

SPELLING PRACTICE

Silent Letters

Silent letters can pose a problem in spelling unless you are familiar with the word or can recognize a common form. For instance, if you know that the *b* in *comb* is silent, you will know how to pronounce *lamb* when you see it and may be able to remember to spell it with the silent letter. Group these words from the excerpt from "The Devil and Daniel Webster" by patterns in their silent letters.

answer
blight
brought
business
candlelight
condemning
doubts
foreigner
honest
lightning
mortgage
neighborhood
straighten
wrestling
wretch
wriggled
wryly

GRAMMAR & STYLE

UNDERSTAND THE CONCEPT | APPLY THE SKILL

Compound Sentences and Clauses

Knowing how to write and correctly punctuate compound sentences is an important skill.

A **compound sentence** consists of two clauses joined by a semicolon or by a coordinating conjunction and a comma. A **clause** is a group of words that contains both a subject and a verb. The most common coordinating conjunctions are *and, or, nor, for, but, yet,* and *so.*

EXAMPLES

Gwen enjoys her family's canoe trips, but her sister isn't as fond of the outdoors. ("Gwen enjoys her family's canoe trips" is one clause. "Her sister isn't as fond of the outdoors" is the other clause. The word *but* is the coordinating conjunction.)

Basketball is my favorite sport; baseball is yours. ("Basketball is my favorite sport" is one clause. "Baseball is yours" is the other clause.)

If a sentence does not include two complete clauses, the inclusion of a semicolon or a comma is not necessary. A sentence may have a compound subject or a compound predicate, but that doesn't make it a compound sentence.

EXAMPLES

Incorrect:
I love to watch movies, but rarely go to the theater.

Arthur jumped in his sports car, and sped down the street.

Correct:
I love to watch movies but rarely go to the theater. (This sentence has a compound predicate. It has two verbs, *love* and *go,* but it isn't a compound sentence.)

Arthur jumped in his sports car and sped down the street. (This sentence also has a compound predicate with two verbs, but it doesn't have two independent clauses, each with a subject and a verb.)

One common mistake in combining clauses to form a sentence is the comma splice. A **comma splice** is a flawed sentence that combines two clauses with a comma and no coordinating conjunction.

EXAMPLES

Incorrect:
John went downtown for the weekend, Alicia traveled to the shore.
Choose the prize you want, I'll take the other one.

Correct:
John went downtown for the weekend; Alicia traveled to the shore.
John went downtown for the weekend, but Alicia traveled to the shore.

Choose the prize you want; I'll take the other one.
Choose the prize you want, and I'll take the other one.

KEY TERMS

coordinating conjunction: a word used to join words or groups of words of equal importance in a sentence, usually *and, or, nor, for, but, yet,* and *so*
compound subject: has two or more simple subjects that have the same predicate, joined by the conjunction *and, or,* or *but*
compound predicate: contains two or more simple predicates, or verbs, that share the same subject; verbs are connected by the conjunction *and, or,* or *but*
independent clause: sometimes called a *main clause*; has a subject and a verb and expresses a complete thought

UNDERSTAND THE CONCEPT | APPLY THE SKILL

Identify Compound Sentences

Identify which of these sentences from *The Tragedy of Romeo and Juliet* are compound sentences and which are not.

1. If I may trust the flattering truth of sleep, my dreams presage some joyful news at hand.
2. Her body sleeps in Capel's monument, and her immortal part with angels lives.
3. Your looks are pale and wild, and do import some misadventure.
4. Such mortal drugs I have, but Mantua's law is death to any he that utters them.
5. I do defy thy conjuration, and apprehend thee for a felon here.
6. This is thy sheath; there rust, and let me die.
7. We see the ground whereon these woes do lie, but the true ground of all these piteous woes we cannot without circumstance descry.
8. Romeo, there dead, was husband to that Juliet, and she, there dead, that Romeo's faithful wife.
9. Then gave I her a sleeping potion, which so took effect as I intended, for it wrought on her the form of death.
10. At the prefixed hour of her waking, came I to take her from her kindred's vault, meaning to keep her closely at my cell, till I conveniently could send to Romeo.

Fix Errors in Compound Sentences

Read the following sentences. Determine whether they are written correctly as compound sentences or if they contain errors. If you find an error, rewrite the sentence, correcting the error. Write the word "correct" when a sentence needs no rewriting.

1. Friar Lawrence wrote to Romeo of the plan, but he did not get the letter on time.
2. Paris was at the tomb to grieve, Romeo was there to kill himself.
3. Friar Lawrence tried to get Juliet out of the tomb yet he did not insist that she follow him.
4. Friar John was delayed by quarantine, so he could not deliver the letter to Romeo.
5. Romeo sought a poor apothecary from which to buy poison; only a man desperate for money would risk Mantua's death sentence against selling poison.
6. Juliet attempts to use Romeo's poison; but finding it used up, stabs herself instead.
7. The Capulets were surprised to see Juliet newly dead; and Romeo and Paris both dead in her tomb.
8. The Prince declares that "all are punish'd" for the long-standing feud, for he, too, lost kinsmen.
9. Friar Lawrence stated he was prepared to receive a death sentence but the Prince forgave him, claiming he was always known as a holy man.
10. The Montagues will raise a gold statue of Juliet and the Capulets will raise one of Romeo.

Use Compound Sentences in Your Writing

Compound sentences can make your writing flow more smoothly. Write a summary of *Romeo and Juliet* that uses compound sentences. Practice for your summary by combining each of the following pairs of sentences to make either a compound sentence (two independent clauses) or a simple sentence (only one independent clause; it may have a compound subject or predicate).

1. The wedding day of Juliet and Romeo was marred by tragedy. It was the day that Romeo killed Tybalt and was banished.
2. Romeo blocked Mercutio from attacking Tybalt. Tybalt was then able to stab Mercutio from around Romeo.
3. At first, Nurse was supportive of Juliet's marriage to Romeo. Later, Juliet felt betrayed when Nurse told her to forget him.
4. Capulet thought his daughter was too upset by Tybalt's death. He thought that marrying Paris would cheer her up.
5. Friar Lawrence gives Juliet a sleeping potion to appear dead. She will then be able to avoid having to marry Paris.

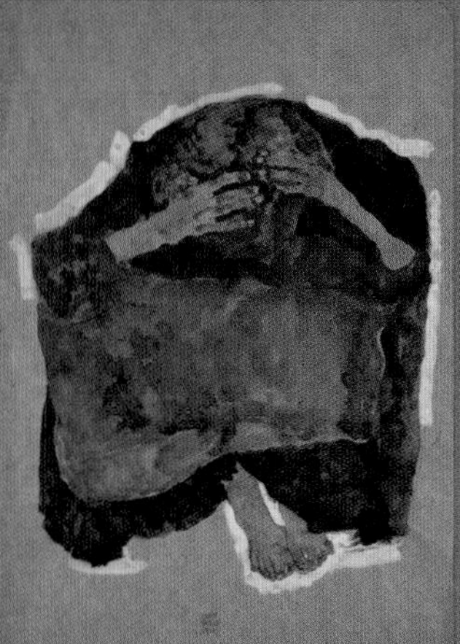

READING DRAMA INDEPENDENTLY

Theme: Temptation and Loss

"We are tricked and trapped—we stumble into the pit—but, out of the pit, we rise again."

—Daniel Webster, from *The Devil and Daniel Webster*

The desire for something better in life is part of being human. Sometimes, however, that desire is for something that may not be good for us or that comes at a cost. How we handle the temptation to take the easier path or get something that is not rightly ours is part of defining character. So, too, is dealing with the eventual loss of what we do have. Loss is a natural part of life, which ends in death, but, especially in drama, it can also be a punishment for giving in to greed and temptation. As you read the selections in this section, decide which of these two aspects of life the characters confront, if not both. How are characters shaped by this confrontation?

USING READING SKILLS WITH DRAMA

Recognize the Sequence of Events

Sequence refers to the order in which things happen. When you read a drama, keep track of the sequence of events. You might do this by making a Time Line or Sequence Map.

To make a Time Line, draw a line and divide it into equal parts. Label each part with a date or a time. Then add key events at the right places along the Time Line.

To make a Sequence Map, draw a series of boxes. In each box, draw pictures that represent key events in a selection. Then write a caption under each box that explains each event. Draw the events in the order in which they occur. Alternatively, write brief statements under the boxes about the major events. An example has been done for you based on *The Tragedy of Romeo and Juliet.*

Sequence Map

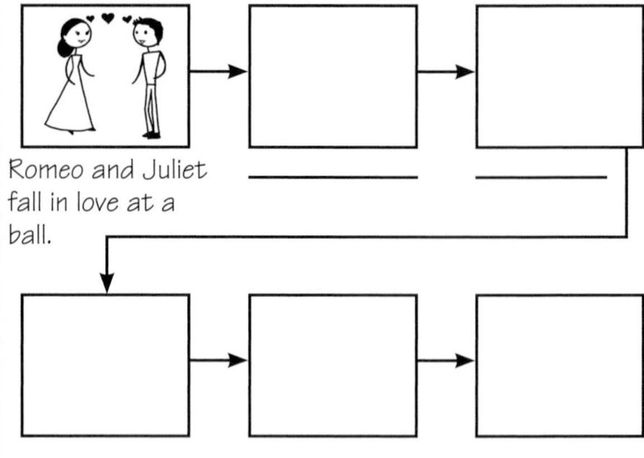

Romeo and Juliet fall in love at a ball.

Identify Relationships

Understanding the relationships between characters and between ideas is important in understanding drama. To keep track of the relationships between characters, it may help to make a family tree if the characters are related or a diagram with arrows making the connections if the characters are connected through some other relationship. In dramas with many characters, such as Shakespearean plays, understanding these relationships can help explain the characters' actions.

To keep track of the relationships between ideas or parts of the text, you could evaluate cause and effect. When you evaluate **cause and effect,** you are looking for a logical relationship between an event or events and one or more results. A graphic organizer like the one below will help you to recognize relationships between causes and effects.

Cause-and-Effect Chart

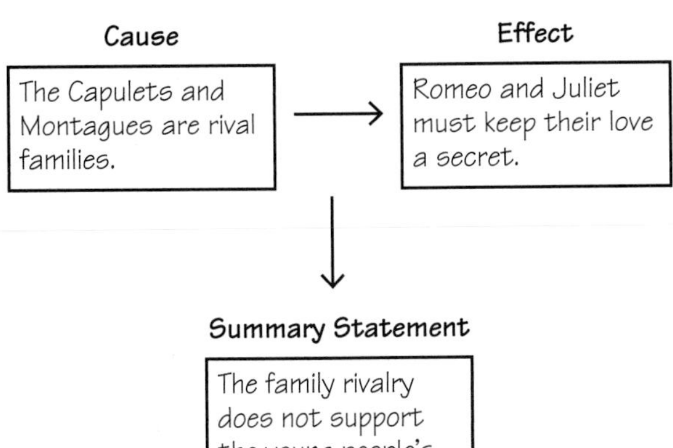

Cause
The Capulets and Montagues are rival families.
Effect
Romeo and Juliet must keep their love a secret.
Summary Statement
The family rivalry does not support the young people's love.

Understand Rhetorical Devices

When reading a drama, you will come across various **rhetorical devices,** or techniques used by the playwright to convey the sense of the play to the audience. Such devices include stage directions, dialogue, monologue, soliloquies, and asides. Pay attention to these devices, as they tell the story of the drama.

Framework for Drama

When reading drama, you need to be aware of the stage directions, dialogue, and other rhetorical devices, as well as the relationships between characters and parts of the text. The following checklist of questions offers a framework for understanding drama.

As you start to read...

- ❑ Who are the characters?
- ❑ Where is the drama set? How would the stage look?
- ❑ What events occur?

As you continue reading...

- ❑ What are the relationships between the characters?
- ❑ What mood is set by the dialogue and the setting (in the stage directions)?
- ❑ What events are caused by earlier events?

After you've finished reading...

- ❑ What is the theme of the drama?
- ❑ Which scenes stand out to me? Why?
- ❑ How would I stage this drama as a live performance?

What Good Readers Do

Ask Your Own Questions

Think about what you want to know about the selection and make notes as you read. Asking questions helps you to pinpoint parts of the text that are confusing. You can ask questions in your head, or you may write them down. Say to yourself:

- ❑ What does the character mean when he or she says...?
- ❑ What motivated the character to...?
- ❑ Do I agree with what the character or narrator says...?
- ❑ What emotions am I experiencing as I read...?
- ❑ How can I put this in my own words...?

The Seven

A Dramatic Monologue by

William Shakespeare

All the world's a stage,
And all the men and women merely players;[1]
They have their exits and their entrances,
And one man in his time plays many parts,
His acts being seven ages. At first, the infant,
Mewling[2] and puking in the nurse's arms.
Then the whining schoolboy, with his satchel
And shining morning face, creeping like snail
Unwillingly to school. And then the lover,
Sighing like furnace, with a woeful ballad
Made to his mistress' eyebrow. Then a soldier,
Full of strange oaths and bearded like the pard,[3]
Jealous in honor, sudden and quick in quarrel,
Seeking the bubble reputation
Even in the cannon's mouth. And then the justice,
In fair round belly with good capon lined,[4]

1. **players.** Actors
2. **mewling.** Crying
3. **bearded like the pard.** Having a beard like a leopard
4. **justice...capon lined.** Judge, whose belly is filled with fine roasted chicken (alluding to the fact that judges were often bribed with gifts such as capons)

A **dramatic monologue** is a poem written in the form of a speech of a single character to an imaginary audience. The following monologue **"The Seven Ages of Man"** is an excerpt from **William Shakespeare's** comedy *As You Like It* (Act II, Scene vii, lines 139–166). In this play, the brothers Duke Senior and Duke Frederick are rivals, as are brothers Oliver and Orlando. When Rosalind flees the court of Duke Frederick and disguises herself as a boy, a comedic pursuit begins. Jaques, the character who delivers this speech, is known for his pessimism. In the speech, he compares the world to a stage and describes the progression of a person's life as acts in a play.

Ages of Man

With eyes severe and beard of formal cut,
Full of wise saws[5] and modern instances;
And so he plays his part. The sixth age shifts
Into the lean and slippered pantaloon,[6]
With spectacles on nose and pouch on side;
His youthful hose, well saved, a world too wide
For his shrunk shank,[7] and his big manly voice,
Turning again toward childish treble, pipes
And whistles in his sound. Last scene of all,
That ends this strange eventful history,
Is second childishness and mere oblivion,
Sans[8] teeth, sans eyes, sans taste, sans everything. ❖

5. **wise saws.** Maxims or sayings
6. **pantaloon.** A foolish old man who was a stock character in the Italian comedy
7. **hose...shank.** Stockings...too wide for his shrunken *shank,* or leg
8. **Sans.** French for "without"

How does society view aging? How might these attitudes be changed? What about aging do people look forward to? What concerns people most about aging?

Refer and Reason

1. Explain how the last age brings people "full circle" to the first age.
2. Identify the speaker's tone, or attitude, toward each stage.
3. What analogy or comparison does Shakespeare make about life? Write a brief analogy describing another object that life could be compared to. Include the function of the object.

Writing Options

1. In the form of a dramatic monologue or poem, write your own version of the stages of life using more modern images. Try to use iambic pentameter. (Refer to Understanding Sight and Sound on page 390 for more information on iambic pentameter.)
2. Write the stage directions for the actor performing this piece. Include your directions for the emotions and actions he should portray for each of life's "stages."

MW Go to **www.mirrorsandwindows.com** for more.

The Devil & Daniel Webster

Eagle Cliff, Franconia Notch, New Hampshire, 1858. Jasper Cropsey. North Carolina Museum of Art, Raleigh.

A One-Act Play by
Stephen Vincent Benét

Poet and novelist **Stephen Vincent Benét** (1898–1943) was born in Bethlehem, Pennsylvania. He won Pulitzer Prizes for his book-length narrative poem *John Brown's Body* (1928) and *Western Star* (1943). Benét was fiercely patriotic, and much of his writing reflects an enthusiasm for American politics and history. He once said, "We have our own folk gods and giants and figures of earth in this country. It's always seemed to me...that legends and yarns and folktales are as much a part of the real history of a country as proclamations and provisos and constitutional amendments...."

Based upon Benét's short story, ***The Devil and Daniel Webster*** presents the fictional tale of a man who makes a bargain with the devil. It features as one of its main characters Daniel Webster, a real figure from American history. Daniel Webster (1782–1852) was one of the greatest orators in the history of American politics. He argued many cases before the Supreme Court and served as a congressman, senator, and secretary of state.

Have you ever desired something so badly you put yourself in danger in order to get it?

CAST

Jabez Stone
Mary Stone
Daniel Webster
Mr. Scratch
Men and Women of Cross Corners, New Hampshire
Justice Hathorne's Clerk
Justice Hathorne
The Fiddler
King Philip
Walter Butler
Simon Girty
Teach

Scene—Jabez Stone's farmhouse.
Time—1841.

The scene is the main room of a New Hampshire farmhouse in 1841, a big comfortable room that hasn't yet developed the stuffiness of a front parlor. A door, right, leads to the kitchen—a door, left, to the outside. There is a fireplace, right. Windows, in center, show a glimpse of summer landscape. Most of the furniture has been cleared away for the dance which follows the wedding of Jabez *and* Mary Stone, *but there is a settee or bench by the fireplace, a table, left, with some wedding presents upon it, at least three chairs by the table, and a cider barrel on which the* Fiddler *sits, in front of the table. Near the table, against the sidewall, there is a cupboard where there are glasses and a jug. There is a clock.*

A country wedding has been in progress—the wedding of Jabez *and* Mary Stone. *He is a husky young farmer, around twenty-eight or thirty. The bride is in her early twenties. He is dressed in stiff, store clothes but not ridiculously—they are of good quality and he looks important. The bride is in a simple white or cream wedding dress and may carry a small, stiff bouquet of country flowers.*

Now the wedding is over and the guests are dancing. The Fiddler *is perched on the cider barrel. He plays and calls square-dance figures. The guests include the recognizable types of a small New England town, doctor, lawyer, storekeeper, old maid, schoolteacher, farmer, etc. There is an air of prosperity and hearty country mirth about the whole affair.*

At rise, Jabez *and* Mary *are up left center, receiving the congratulations of a few last guests who talk to them and pass on to the dance. The others are dancing. There is a buzz of conversation that follows the tune of the dance music.*

First Woman. Right nice wedding.

First Man. Handsome couple.

Second Woman [*passing through crowd with dish of oyster stew*]. Oysters for supper!

Second Man [*passing cake*]. And layer cake—layer cake—

An Old Man [*hobbling toward cider barrel*]. Makes me feel young again! Oh, by jingo!

An Old Woman [*pursuing him*]. Henry, Henry, you've been drinking cider!

Fiddler. Set to your partners! Do-si-do![1]

Women. Mary and Jabez.

Men. Jabez and Mary.

A Woman. Where's the State Senator?

A Man. Where's the lucky bride?

[*With cries of "Mary—Jabez—strike it up, fiddler—make room for the bride and groom," the* Crowd *drags* Mary *and* Jabez, *pleased but embarrassed, into the center of the room and* Mary *and* Jabez *do a little solo dance, while the* Crowd *claps, applauds and makes various remarks.*]

1. **Do-si-do.** Square dance move. Other square dance terms follow, including "cut a pigeon-wing," "scratch for corn," and "grand chain."

A MAN. Handsome steppers!

A WOMAN. She's pretty as a picture.

A SECOND MAN. Cut your pigeon-wing, Jabez!

THE OLD MAN. Young again, young again, that's the way I feel! [*He tries to cut a pigeon-wing himself.*]

THE OLD WOMAN. Henry, Henry, careful of your rheumatiz![2]

A THIRD WOMAN. Makes me feel all teary—seeing them so happy.

[*The solo dance ends, the music stops for a moment.*]

THE OLD MAN [*gossiping to a neighbor*]. Wonder where he got it all—Stones was always poor.

HIS NEIGHBOR. Ain't poor now—makes you wonder just a mite.

A THIRD MAN. Don't begrudge it to him—but I wonder where he got it.

THE OLD MAN [*starting to whisper*]. Let me tell you something—

THE OLD WOMAN [*quickly*]. Henry, Henry, don't you start to gossip. [*She drags him away.*]

FIDDLER [*cutting in*]. Set to your partners! Scratch for corn!

[*The dance resumes, but as it does so, the* CROWD *chants back and forth.*]

WOMEN. Gossip's got a sharp tooth.

MEN. Gossip's got a mean tooth.

WOMEN. She's a lucky woman. They're a lucky pair.

MEN. That's true as gospel. But I wonder where he got it.

WOMEN. Money, land and riches.

MEN. Just came out of nowhere.

WOMEN AND MEN [*together*]. Wonder where he got it all.—But that's his business.

FIDDLER. Left and right—grand chain!

[*The dance rises to a pitch of ecstasy with the final figure—the fiddle squeaks and stops. The dancers mop their brows.*]

FIRST MAN. Whew! Ain't danced like that since I was knee-high to a grasshopper!

SECOND MAN. Play us "The Portland Fancy," fiddler!

THIRD MAN. No, wait a minute, neighbor. Let's hear from the happy pair! Hey, Jabez!

FOURTH MAN. Let's hear from the State Senator!

[*They crowd around* JABEZ *and push him up on the settee.*]

OLD MAN. Might as well. It's the last time he'll have the last word!

OLD WOMAN. Now, Henry Banks, you ought to be ashamed of yourself!

OLD MAN. Told you so, Jabez!

THE CROWD. Speech!

JABEZ [*embarrassed*]. Neighbors—friends—I'm not much of a speaker—spite of your 'lecting me to State Senate—

THE CROWD. That's the ticket, Jabez. Smart man, Jabez. I voted for ye. Go ahead, Senator, you're doing fine.

JABEZ. But we're certainly glad to have you here—me and Mary. And we want to thank you for coming and—

A VOICE. Vote the Whig[3] ticket!

ANOTHER VOICE. Hooray for Daniel Webster!

JABEZ. And I'm glad Hi Foster said that, for those are my sentiments, too. Mr. Webster has promised to honor us with his presence here tonight.

THE CROWD. Hurray for Dan'l! Hurray for the greatest man in the U.S.!

JABEZ. And when he comes, I know we'll give him a real New Hampshire welcome.

THE CROWD. Sure we will—Webster forever—and to hell with Henry Clay![4]

2. **rheumatiz.** Rheumatism, inflammation of or pain in the muscles or joints

3. **Whig.** The American political party formed around 1834 in opposition to the Jacksonian Democrats; it was associated chiefly with manufacturing, commercial, and financial interests. Daniel Webster was one of its leaders.

4. **Henry Clay.** Well-known American politician and member of the Whigs like Daniel Webster

Jabez. And meanwhile—well, there's Mary and me [*takes her hand*]—and, if you folks don't have a good time, well, we won't feel right about getting married at all. Because I know I've been lucky—and I hope she feels that way, too. And, well, we're going to be happy or bust a trace!

[*He wipes his brow to terrific applause. He and* Mary *look at each other.*]

A Woman [*in kitchen doorway*]. Come and get the cider, folks!

[*The* Crowd *begins to drift away—a few to the kitchen—a few toward the door that leads to the outside. They furnish a shifting background to the next little scene, where* Mary *and* Jabez *are left alone by the fireplace.*]

Jabez. Mary.

Mary. Mr. Stone.

Jabez. Mary.

Mary. My husband.

Jabez. That's a big word, husband.

Mary. It's a good word.

Jabez. Are you happy, Mary?

Mary. Yes. So happy, I'm afraid.

Jabez. Afraid?

Mary. I suppose it happens to every girl—just for a minute. It's like spring turning into summer. You want it to be summer. But the spring was sweet. [*Dismissing the mood*] I'm sorry. Forgive me. It just came and went, like something cold. As if we'd been too lucky.

Jabez. We can't be too lucky, Mary. Not you and me.

Mary [*rather mischievously*]. If you say so, Mr. Stone. But you don't even know what sort of housekeeper I am. And Aunt Hepsy says—

Jabez. Bother your Aunt Hepsy! There's just you and me and that's all that matters in the world.

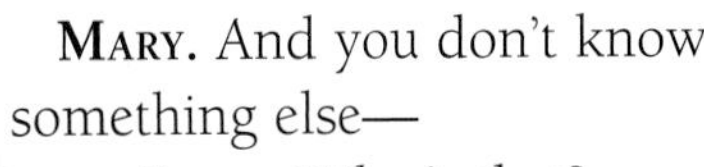

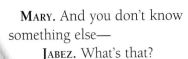

Daniel Webster.

Mary. And you don't know something else—

Jabez. What's that?

Mary. How proud I am of you. Ever since I was a little girl. Ever since you carried my books. Oh, I'm sorry for women who can't be proud of their men. It must be a lonely feeling.

Jabez [*uncomfortably*]. A man can't always be proud of everything, Mary. There's some things a man does, or might do—when he has to make his way.

Mary [*laughing*]. I know—terrible things—like being the best farmer in the county and the best State Senator—

Jabez [*quietly*]. And a few things, besides. But you remember one thing, Mary, whatever happens. It was all for you. And nothing's going to happen. Because he hasn't come yet—and he would have come if it was wrong.

Mary. But it's wonderful to have Mr. Webster come to us.

Jabez. I wasn't thinking about Mr. Webster. [*He takes both her hands.*] Mary, I've got something to tell you. I should have told you before, but I couldn't seem to bear it. Only, now that it's all right, I can. Ten years ago—

A Voice [*from off stage*]. Dan'l! Dan'l Webster!

[Jabez *drops* Mary's *hands and looks around. The* Crowd *begins to mill and gather toward the door. Others rush in from the kitchen.*]

Another Voice. Black Dan'l![5] He's come!

Another Voice. Three cheers for the greatest man in the U.S.!

Another Voice. Three cheers for Daniel Webster!

5. **Black Dan'l.** Nickname for Daniel Webster

[*And, to the cheering and applause of the crowd,* DANIEL WEBSTER *enters and stands for a moment upstage, in the familiar pose, his head thrown back, his attitude leonine.*[6] *He stops the cheering of the crowd with a gesture.*]

WEBSTER. Neighbors—old friends—it does me good to hear you. But don't cheer me—I'm not running for President this summer. [*a laugh from the* CROWD] I'm here on a better errand—to pay my humble respects to a most charming lady and her very fortunate spouse.

[*There is the twang of a fiddlestring breaking.*]

FIDDLER. 'Tarnation! Busted a string!

A VOICE. He's always bustin' strings.

[WEBSTER *blinks at the interruption but goes on.*]

WEBSTER. We're proud of State Senator Stone in these parts—we know what he's done. Ten years ago he started out with a patch of land that was mostly rocks and mortgages[7] and now—well, you've only to look around you. I don't know that I've ever seen a likelier farm, not even at Marshfield[8]—and I hope, before I die, I'll have the privilege of shaking his hand as Governor of this State. I don't know how he's done it—I couldn't have done it myself. But I know this—Jabez Stone wears no man's collar. [*At this statement there is a discordant*[9] *squeak from the fiddle, and* JABEZ *looks embarrassed.* WEBSTER *knits his brows.*] And what's more, if I know Jabez, he never will. But I didn't come here to talk politics—I came to kiss the bride. [*He does so among great applause. He shakes hands with* JABEZ.] Congratulations, Stone—you're a lucky man. And now, if our friend in the corner will give us a tune on his fiddle—

[*The* CROWD *presses forward to meet the great man. He shakes hands with several.*]

A MAN. Remember me, Mr. Webster? Saw ye up at the State House at Concord.

ANOTHER MAN. Glad to see ye, Mr. Webster. I voted for ye ten times.

[WEBSTER *receives their homage politely, but his mind is still on music.*]

WEBSTER [*a trifle irritated*]. I said, if our friend in the corner would give us a tune on his fiddle—

FIDDLER [*passionately, flinging the fiddle down*]. Hell's delight—excuse me, Mr. Webster. But the very devil's got into that fiddle of mine. She was doing all right up to just a minute ago. But now I've tuned her and tuned her and she won't play a note I want.

"But the very devil's got into that fiddle of mine."

[*And, at this point,* MR. SCRATCH *makes his appearance. He has entered, unobserved, and mixed with the crowd while all eyes were upon* DANIEL WEBSTER. *He is, of course, the devil—a New England devil, dressed like a rather shabby attorney but with something just a little wrong in clothes and appearance. For one thing, he wears black gloves on his hands. He carries a large black tin box, like a botanist's collecting box, under one arm. Now he slips through the crowd and taps the* FIDDLER *on the shoulder.*]

SCRATCH [*insinuatingly*]. Maybe you need some rosin[10] on your bow, fiddler?

FIDDLER. Maybe I do and maybe I don't. [*Turns and confronts the stranger*] But who are you? I don't remember seeing you before.

6. **leonine.** Like a lion, i.e., proud and regal
7. **mortgages.** Agreements held with a bank or other money-lender that allow land to be used as security for a loan
8. **Marshfield.** Massachusetts town where Daniel Webster had a farm
9. **discordant.** Unpleasant to hear; shrill
10. **rosin.** Substance used to treat the bows of stringed instruments

SCRATCH. Oh, I'm just a friend—a humble friend of the bridegroom's. [*He walks toward* JABEZ. *Apologetically.*] I'm afraid I came in the wrong way, Mr. Stone. You've improved the place so much since I last saw it that I hardly knew the front door. But, I assure you, I came as fast as I could.

JABEZ [*obviously shocked*]. It—it doesn't matter. [*With a great effort*] Mary—Mr. Webster—this is a—a friend of mine from Boston—a legal friend. I didn't expect him today but—

SCRATCH. Oh, my dear Mr. Stone—an occasion like this—I wouldn't miss it for the world. [*He bows.*] Charmed, Mrs. Stone. Delighted, Mr. Webster. But—don't let me break up the merriment of the meeting. [*He turns back toward the table and the* FIDDLER.]

FIDDLER [*with a grudge, to* SCRATCH]. Boston lawyer, eh?

SCRATCH. You might call me that.

FIDDLER [*tapping the tin box with his bow*]. And what have you got in that big tin box of yours? Law papers?

SCRATCH. Oh—curiosities for the most part. I'm a collector, too.

FIDDLER. Don't hold much with Boston curiosities, myself. And you know about fiddling, too, do you? Know all about it?

SCRATCH. Oh—[*a deprecatory shrug*]

FIDDLER. Don't shrug your shoulders at me—I ain't no Frenchman. Telling me I needed more rosin!

MARY [*trying to stop the quarrel*]. Isaac—please—

FIDDLER. Sorry, Mary—Mrs. Stone. But I been playing the fiddle at Cross Corners weddings for twenty-five years. And now here comes a stranger from Boston and tells me I need more rosin!

SCRATCH. But, my good friend—

FIDDLER. Rosin indeed! Here—play it yourself then and see what you can make of it! [*He thrusts the fiddle at* SCRATCH. *The latter stiffens, slowly lays his black collecting box on the table, and takes the fiddle.*]

SCRATCH [*with feigned embarrassment*]. But really, I— [*He bows toward* JABEZ.] Shall I—Mr. Senator? [JABEZ *makes a helpless gesture of assent.*]

MARY [*to* JABEZ]. Mr. Stone—Mr. Stone—are you ill?

JABEZ. No—no—but I feel—it's hot—

WEBSTER [*chuckling*]. Don't you fret, Mrs. Stone. I've got the right medicine for him. [*He pulls a flask from his pocket.*] Ten-year-old Medford, Stone—I buy it by the keg down at Marshfield. Here—[*He tries to give some of the rum to* JABEZ.]

JABEZ. No—[*he turns*]—Mary—Mr. Webster—[*But he cannot explain. With a burst.*] Oh, let him play—let him play! Don't you see he's bound to? Don't you see there's nothing we can do?

[*A rustle of discomfort among the guests.* SCRATCH *draws the bow across the fiddle in a horrible discord.*]

FIDDLER [*triumphantly*]. I told you so, stranger. The devil's in that fiddle!

SCRATCH. I'm afraid it needs special tuning. [*Draws the bow in a second discord*] There—that's better [*grinning*]. And now for this happy—this very happy occasion—in tribute to the bride and groom—I'll play something appropriate—a song of young love—

MARY. Oh, Jabez—Mr. Webster—stop him! Do you see his hands? He's playing with gloves on his hands.

[WEBSTER *starts forward, but, even as he does so,* SCRATCH *begins to play, and all freeze as* SCRATCH *goes on with the extremely inappropriate song that follows. At first his manner is oily and mocking—it is not till he reaches the line "The devil took the words away" that he really becomes terrifying and the crowd starts to be afraid.*]

SCRATCH [*accompanying himself fantastically*].
Young William was a thriving boy.
[Listen to my doleful tale.]
Young Mary Clark was all his joy.
[Listen to my doleful tale.]

He swore he'd love her all his life.
She swore she'd be his loving wife.
But William found a gambler's den
And drank with livery-stable men.

He played the cards, he played the dice
He would not listen to advice.

And when in church he tried to pray,
The devil took the words away.

[SCRATCH, *still playing, starts to march across the stage.*]

The devil got him by the toe
And so, alas, he had to go.

"Young Mary Clark, young Mary Clark,
I now must go into the dark."

[*These last two verses have been directed at* JABEZ. SCRATCH *continues, now turning on* MARY.]

Young Mary lay upon her bed.
"Alas my Will-i-am is dead."

He came to her a bleeding ghost—

[*He rushes at* MARY *but* WEBSTER *stands between them.*]

WEBSTER. Stop! Stop! You miserable wretch—can't you see that you're frightening Mrs. Stone? [*He wrenches the fiddle out of* SCRATCH'S *hands and tosses it aside.*] And now, sir—out of this house!

SCRATCH [*facing him*]. You're a bold man, Mr. Webster. Too bold for your own good, perhaps. And anyhow, it wasn't my fiddle. It belonged to—[*He wheels and sees the* FIDDLER *tampering with the collecting box that has been left on the table.*] Idiot! What are you doing with my collecting box? [*He rushes for the* FIDDLER *and chases him round the table, but the* FIDDLER *is just one jump ahead.*]

FIDDLER. Boston lawyer, eh? Well, I don't think so. I think you've got something in that box of yours you're afraid to show. And, by jingo—[*He throws open the lid of the box. The lights wink and there is a clap of thunder. All eyes stare upward. Something has flown out of the box. But what?* FIDDLER, *with relief.*] Why, 'tain't nothing but a moth.

MARY. A white moth—a flying thing.

WEBSTER. A common moth—telea polyphemus—

THE CROWD. A moth—just a moth—a moth—

FIDDLER [*terrified*]. But it ain't. It ain't no common moth! I seen it! And it's got a death's-head[11] on it! [*He strikes at the invisible object with his bow to drive it away.*]

VOICE OF THE MOTH. Help me, neighbors! Help me!

WEBSTER. What's that? It wails like a lost soul.

MARY. A lost soul.

THE CROWD. A lost soul—lost—in darkness—in the darkness.

VOICE OF THE MOTH. Help me, neighbors!

FIDDLER. It sounds like Miser Stevens.

JABEZ. Miser Stevens!

THE CROWD. The Miser—Miser Stevens—a lost soul—lost.

FIDDLER [*frantically*]. It sounds like Miser Stevens—and you had him in your box. But it can't be. He ain't dead.

JABEZ. He ain't dead—I tell you he ain't dead! He was just as spry and mean as a woodchuck Tuesday.

11. **death's-head.** Refers to the death's-head hawkmoth, which has markings resembling a human skull on the back of its thorax

The Crowd. Miser Stevens—soul of Miser Stevens—but he ain't dead.

Scratch [*dominating them*]. Listen!

[*A bell off stage begins to toll a knell, slowly, solemnly.*]

Mary. The bell—the church bell—the bell that rang at my wedding.

Webster. The church bell—the passing bell.

Jabez. The funeral bell.

The Crowd. The bell—the passing bell—Miser Stevens—dead.

Voice of the Moth. Help me, neighbors, help me! I sold my soul to the devil. But I'm not the first or the last. Help me. Help Jabez Stone!

Scratch. Ah, would you! [*He catches the moth in his red bandanna, stuffs it back into his collecting box, and shuts the lid with a snap.*]

Voice of the Moth [*fading*]. Lost—lost forever, forever. Lost, like Jabez Stone.

[*The* Crowd *turns on* Jabez. *They read his secret in his face.*]

The Crowd. Jabez Stone—Jabez Stone—answer us—answer us.

Mary. Tell them, dear—answer them—you are good—you are brave—you are innocent.

[*But the* Crowd *is all pointing hands and horrified eyes.*]

The Crowd. Jabez Stone—Jabez Stone. Who's your friend in black, Jabez Stone? [*They point to* Scratch.]

Webster. Answer them, Mr. State Senator.

The Crowd. Jabez Stone—Jabez Stone. Where did you get your money, Jabez Stone?

[Scratch *grins and taps his collecting box,* Jabez *cannot speak.*]

Jabez. I—I—[*He stops.*]

"He's sold his soul to the devil! The devil himself!"

The Crowd. Jabez Stone—Jabez Stone. What was the price you paid for it, Jabez Stone?

Jabez [*looking around wildly*]. Help me, neighbors! Help me!

[*This cracks the built-up tension and sends the* Crowd *over the edge into fanaticism.*[12]]

A Woman's Voice [*high and hysterical*]. He's sold his soul to the devil! [*She points to* Jabez.]

Other Voices. To the devil!

The Crowd. He's sold his soul to the devil! The devil himself! The devil's playing the fiddle! The devil's come for his own!

Jabez [*appealing*]. But, neighbors—I didn't know—I didn't mean—oh, help me!

The Crowd [*inexorably*[13]]. He's sold his soul to the devil!

Scratch [*grinning*]. To the devil!

The Crowd. He's sold his soul to the devil! There's no help left for him, neighbors! Run, hide, hurry, before we're caught! He's a lost soul—Jabez Stone—he's the devil's own. Run, hide, hasten! [*They stream across the stage like a flurry of bats, the cannier picking up the wedding presents they have given to take along with them.*]

[Mr. Scratch *drives them out into the night, fiddle in hand, and follows them.* Jabez *and* Mary *are left with* Webster. Jabez *has sunk into a chair, beaten, with his head in his hands.* Mary *is trying to comfort him.* Webster *looks at them for a moment and shakes his head, sadly. As he crosses to exit to the porch, his hand drops for a moment on* Jabez' *shoulder, but* Jabez *makes no sign.* Webster *exits.* Jabez *lifts his head.*]

12. **fanaticism.** State of crazed enthusiasm

13. **inexorably.** Relentlessly

Mary [*comforting him*]. My dear—my dear—

Jabez. I—it's all true, Mary. All true. You must hurry.

Mary. Hurry?

Jabez. Hurry after them—back to the village—back to your folks. Mr. Webster will take you—you'll be safe with Mr. Webster. You see, it's all true and he'll be back in a minute. [*With a shudder*] The other one. [*He groans.*] I've got until twelve o'clock. That's the contract. But there isn't much time.

Mary. Are you telling me to run away from you, Mr. Stone?

Jabez. You don't understand, Mary. It's true.

Mary. We made some promises to each other. Maybe you've forgotten them. But I haven't. I said, it's for better or worse. It's for better or worse. I said, in sickness or in health. Well, that covers the ground, Mr. Stone.

Jabez. But, Mary, you must—I command you.

Mary. "For thy people shall be my people and thy God my God." [*Quietly*] That was Ruth, in the Book.[14] I always liked the name of Ruth—always liked the thought of her. I always thought—I'll call a child Ruth, some time. I guess that was just a girl's notion. [*She breaks.*] But, oh, Jabez—why?

Jabez. It started years ago, Mary. I guess I was a youngster then—guess I must have been. A youngster with a lot of ambitions and no way in the world to get there. I wanted city clothes and a big white house—I wanted to be State Senator and have people look up to me. But all I got on the farm was a crop of stones. You could work all day and all night, but that was all you got.

Mary [*softly*]. It was pretty—that hill farm, Jabez. You could look all the way across the valley.

Jabez. Pretty? It was fever and ague[15]—it was stones and blight. If I had a horse, he got colic—if I planted garden truck, the woodchucks ate it. I'd lie awake nights and try to figure out a way to get somewhere—but there wasn't any way. And all the time you were growing up, in the town. I couldn't ask you to marry me and take you to a place like that.

Mary. Do you think it's the place makes the difference to a woman? I'd—I'd have kept your house. I'd have stroked the cat and fed the chickens and seen you wiped your shoes on the mat. I wouldn't have asked for more. Oh, Jabez—why didn't you tell me?

Jabez. It happened before I could. Just an average day—you know—just an average day. But there was a mean east wind and a mean small rain. Well, I was plowing, and the share broke clean off on a rock where there hadn't been any rock the day before. I didn't have money for a new one—I didn't have money to get it mended. So I said it and I said loud, "I'll sell my soul for about two cents," I said. [*He stops.* Mary *stares at him.*] Well, that's all there is to it, I guess. He came along that afternoon—that fellow from Boston—and the dog looked at him and ran away. Well, I had to make it more than two cents, but he was agreeable to that. So I pricked my thumb with a pin and signed the paper. It felt hot when you touched it, that paper. I keep remembering that. [*He pauses.*] And it's all come true and he's kept his part of the bargain. I got the riches

14. **Ruth, in the Book.** According to the Book of Ruth in the Bible, these words were spoken by Ruth to her mother-in-law, Naomi.

15. **ague.** Fit of shivering; chill

and I've married you. And, oh, God Almighty, what shall I do?

Mary. Let us run away! Let us creep and hide!

Jabez. You can't run away from the devil—I've seen his horses. Miser Stevens tried to run away.

Mary. Let us pray—let us pray to the God of Mercy that He redeem us.

Jabez. I can't pray, Mary. The words just burn in my heart.

Mary. I won't let you go! I won't! There must be someone who could help us. I'll get the judge and the squire—

Jabez. Who'll take a case against old Scratch? Who'll face the devil himself and do him brown? There isn't a lawyer in the world who'd dare do that.

[Webster *appears in the doorway.*]

Webster. Good evening, neighbors. Did you say something about lawyers—

Mary. Mr. Webster!

Jabez. Dan'l Webster! But I thought—

Webster. You'll excuse me for leaving you for a moment. I was just taking a stroll on the porch, in the cool of the evening. Fine summer evening, too.

Jabez. Well, it might be, I guess, but that kind of depends on the circumstances.

Webster. H'm. Yes I happened to overhear a little of your conversation. I gather you're in trouble, Neighbor Stone.

Jabez. Sore trouble.

Webster [*delicately*]. Sort of law case, I understand.

Jabez. You might call it that, Mr. Webster. Kind of a mortgage case, in a way.

Mary. Oh, Jabez!

> *"So I said it and I said loud, 'I'll sell my soul for about two cents'"* . . .

Webster. Mortgage case. Well, I don't generally plead now, except before the Supreme Court, but this case of yours presents some very unusual features, and I never deserted a neighbor in trouble yet. So, if I can be of any assistance—

Mary. Oh, Mr. Webster, will you help him?

Jabez. It's a terrible lot to ask you. But—well, you see, there's Mary. And, if you could see your way to it—

Webster. I will.

Mary [*weeping with relief*]. Oh, Mr. Webster!

Webster. There, there, Mrs. Stone. After all, if two New Hampshire men aren't a match for the devil, we might as well give the country back to the Indians. When is he coming, Jabez?

Jabez. Twelve o'clock. The time's getting late.

Webster. Then I'd better refresh my memory. The—er—mortgage was for a definite term of years?

Jabez. Ten years.

Webster. And it falls due—?

Jabez. Tonight. Oh, I can't see how I came to be such a fool!

Webster. No use crying over spilt milk, Stone. We've got to get you out of it, now. But tell me one thing. Did you sign this precious document of your own free will?

Jabez. Yes, it was my own free will. I can't deny that.

Webster. H'm, that's a trifle unfortunate. But we'll see.

Mary. Oh, Mr. Webster, can you save him? Can you?

Webster. I shall do my best, madam. That's all you can ever say till you see what the jury looks like.

Mary. But even you, Mr. Webster—oh, I know you're Secretary of State—I know you're a great man—I know you've done wonderful things. But it's different—fighting the devil!

Webster [*towering*]. I've fought John C. Calhoun, madam. And I've fought Henry Clay. And, by the great shade of Andrew Jackson,[16] I'd fight ten thousand devils to save a New Hampshire man!

Jabez. You hear, Mary?

Mary. Yes. And I trust Mr. Webster. But—oh, there must be some way that I can help!

Webster. There is one, madam, and a hard one. As Mr. Stone's counsel, I must formally request your withdrawal.

Mary. No.

Webster. Madam, think for a moment. You cannot help Mr. Stone—since you are his wife, your testimony would be prejudiced. And frankly, madam, in a very few minutes this is going to be no place for a lady.

Mary. But I can't—I can't leave him—I can't bear it!

Jabez. You must go, Mary. You must.

Webster. Pray, madam—you can help us with your prayers. Are the prayers of the innocent unavailing?[17]

Mary. Oh, I'll pray—I'll pray. But a woman's more than a praying machine, whatever men think. And how do I know?

Webster. Trust me, Mrs. Stone.

[Mary *turns to go, and, with one hand on* Jabez' *shoulder, as she moves to the door, says the following prayer:*]

Mary.

Now may there be a blessing and a light betwixt[18] thee and me, forever.

For, as Ruth unto Naomi, so do I cleave unto thee.

Set me as a seal upon thy heart, as a seal upon thine arm, for love is strong as death.

Many waters cannot quench love, neither can the floods drown it.

As Ruth unto Naomi, so do I cleave unto thee.

The Lord watch between thee and me when we are absent, one from the other.

Amen. Amen. [*She goes out.*]

Webster. Amen.

Jabez. Thank you, Mr. Webster. She ought to go. But I couldn't have made her do it.

Webster. Well, Stone—I know ladies—and I wouldn't be surprised if she's still got her ear to the keyhole. But she's best out of this night's business. How long have we got to wait?

Jabez [*beginning to be terrified again*]. Not long—not long.

Webster. Then I'll just get out the jug, with your permission, Stone. Somehow or other, waiting's wonderfully shorter with a jug. [*He crosses to the cupboard, gets out jug and glasses, pours himself a drink.*] Ten-year-old Medford. There's nothing like it. I saw an inchworm take a drop of it once, and he stood right up on his hind legs and bit a bee. Come—try a nip.

Jabez. There's no joy in it for me.

Webster. Oh, come, man, come! Just because you've sold your soul to the devil, that needn't make you a teetotaller.[19] [*He laughs and passes the jug to* Jabez, *who tries to pour from it. But at that moment the clock whirs and begins to strike the three-quarters, and* Jabez *spills the liquor.*]

Jabez. Oh, God!

Webster. Never mind—it's a nervous feeling, waiting for a trial to begin. I remember my first case—

Jabez. 'Tain't that. [*He turns to* Webster.] Mr. Webster—Mr. Webster—for God's sake

16. **John C. Calhoun...Andrew Jackson.** Political opponents of Webster. Calhoun was vice president of the United States from 1825–1832; Jackson was president from 1829–1837.

17. **unavailing.** Futile; useless

18. **betwixt.** Between

19. **teetotaller.** One who does not drink alcoholic beverages

harness your horses and get away from this place as fast as you can!

Webster [*placidly*]. You've brought me a long way, neighbor, to tell me you don't like my company.

Jabez. I've brought you the devil's own way. I can see it all, now. He's after both of us—him and his damn collecting box! Well, he can have me, if he likes—I don't say I relish it, but I made the bargain. But you're the whole United States! He can't get you, Mr. Webster—he mustn't get you!

Webster. I'm obliged to you, neighbor Stone. It's kindly thought of. But there's a jug on the table and a case in hand. And I never left a jug or a case half-finished in my life. [*There is a knock at the door.* Jabez *gives a cry.*] Ah, I thought your clock was a trifle slow, neighbor Stone. Come in!

[Scratch *enters from the night.*]

Scratch. Mr. Webster! This is a pleasure!

Webster. Attorney of record for Jabez Stone. Might I ask your name?

Scratch. I've gone by a good many. Perhaps Scratch will do for the evening. I'm often called that in these regions. May I? [*He sits at the table and pours a drink from the jug. The liquor steams as it pours into the glass while* Jabez *watches, terrified.* Scratch *grins, toasting* Webster *and* Jabez *silently in the liquor. Then he becomes businesslike. To* Webster.] And now I call upon you, as a law-abiding citizen, to assist me in taking possession of my property.

Webster. Not so fast, Mr. Scratch. Produce your evidence, if you have it.

[Scratch *takes out a black pocketbook and examines papers.*]

Scratch. Slattery—Stanley—Stone. [*takes out a deed*] There, Mr. Webster. All open and aboveboard and in due and legal form. Our firm has its reputation to consider—we deal only in the one way.

Webster [*taking deed and looking it over*]. H'm. This appears—I say, it appears—to be properly drawn. But, of course, we contest the signature [*tosses it back, contemptuously*].

Scratch [*suddenly turning on* Jabez *and shooting a finger at him*]. Is that your signature?

Jabez [*wearily*]. You know damn well it is.

Webster [*angrily*]. Keep quiet, Stone. [*To* Scratch] But that is a minor matter. This precious document isn't worth the paper it's written on. The law permits no traffic in human flesh.

Scratch. Oh, my dear Mr. Webster! Courts in every State in the Union have held that human flesh is property and recoverable. Read your Fugitive Slave Act.[20] Or, shall I cite Brander versus McRae?

Webster. But, in the case of the State of Maryland versus Four Barrels of Bourbon—

Scratch. That was overruled, as you know, sir. North Carolina versus Jenkins and Co.

Webster [*unwillingly*]. You seem to have an excellent acquaintance with the law, sir.

Scratch. Sir, that is no fault of mine. Where I come from, we have always gotten the pick of the Bar.[21]

Webster [*changing his note, heartily*]. Well, come now, sir. There's no need to make hay and oats of a trifling matter when we're both sensible men. Surely we can settle this little difficulty out of court. My client is quite prepared to offer a compromise. [Scratch *smiles.*] A very substantial compromise. [Scratch *smiles more broadly, slowly shaking his head.*] Hang it, man, we offer ten thousand dollars! [Scratch *signs "No."*] Twenty thousand—thirty—name your figure! I'll raise it if I have to mortgage Marshfield!

Scratch. Quite useless, Mr. Webster. There is only one thing I want from you—the execution of my contract.

Webster. But this is absurd. Mr. Stone is now a State Senator. The property has greatly increased in value!

20. **Fugitive Slave Act.** Law that required that runaway slaves be captured and returned to their owners
21. **pick of the Bar.** Choice of the best lawyers

Scratch. The principle of *caveat emptor*[22] still holds, Mr. Webster. [*He yawns and looks at the clock.*] And now, if you have no further arguments to adduce—I'm rather pressed for time—[*He rises briskly as if to take* Jabez *into custody.*]

Webster [*thundering*]. Pressed or not, you shall not have this man. Mr. Stone is an American citizen, and no American citizen may be forced into the service of a foreign prince. We fought England for that, in '12,[23] and we'll fight all hell for it again!

Scratch. Foreign? And who calls me a foreigner?

Webster. Well, I never yet heard of the dev—of your claiming American citizenship?

Scratch. And who with better right? When the first wrong was done to the Indian, I was there. When the first slaver put out for the Congo, I stood on her deck. Am I not in your books and stories and beliefs, from the first settlements on? Am I not spoken of, still, in every church in New England? 'Tis true, the North claims me for a Southerner and the South for a Northerner, but I am neither. I am merely an honest American like yourself—and of the best descent—for, to tell the truth, Mr. Webster, though I don't like to boast of it, my name is older in the country than yours.

Webster. Aha! Then I stand on the Constitution! I demand a trial for my client!

Scratch. The case is hardly one for an ordinary jury—and indeed, the lateness of the hour—

Webster. Let it be any court you choose, so it is an American judge and an American jury. Let it be the quick[24] or the dead, I'll abide the issue.

Scratch. The quick or the dead! You have said it! [*He points his finger at the place where the jury is to appear. There is a clap of thunder and a flash of light. The stage blacks out completely. All that can be seen is the face of* Scratch, *lit with a ghastly green light as he recites the invocation that summons the* Jury. *As, one by one, the important* Jurymen *are mentioned, they appear.*]

I summon the jury Mr. Webster demands.
From churchyard mold and gallows grave,
Brimstone pit and burning gulf,
I summon them!
Dastard, liar, scoundrel, knave,
I summon them! Appear!
There's Simon Girty, the renegade,
The haunter of the forest glade
Who joined with Indian and wolf
To hunt the pioneer.
The stains upon his hunting shirt
Are not the blood of the deer.
There's Walter Butler,[25] the loyalist,
Who carried a firebrand in his fist
Of massacre and shame.
King Philip's[26] eye is wild and bright.
They slew him in the great Swamp Fight,
But still, with terror and affright,
The land recalls his name.
Blackbeard Teach, the pirate fell,
Smeet the strangler, hot from hell,
Dale, who broke men on the wheel,
Morton,[27] of the tarnished steel,
I summon them, I summon them
From their tormented flame!
Quick or dead, quick or dead,
Broken heart and bitter head,
True Americans, each one,
Traitor and disloyal son,
Cankered earth and twisted tree,
Outcasts of eternity,
Twelve great sinners, tried and true,
For the work they are to do!

---

22. ***caveat emptor*** **(ka´ vē ät' em[p]´ tôr).** [Latin] "Let the buyer beware." Refers to the idea, in business, that the buyer is responsible for any risks involved in buying something without a warranty.
23. **in '12.** During the War of 1812
24. **quick.** Living
25. **Walter Butler.** Loyalist officer in the American Revolution who fought against the patriots
26. **King Philip.** Chief of the Wampanoag people, a Native American group who lived around Rhode Island and Massachusetts. He led a war against white settlers in 1675.
27. **Blackbeard Teach...Morton.** Edward Teach, nicknamed Blackbeard, was an English pirate who targeted American ships in the early 1700s. Sir Thomas Dale was a governor of the colony of Virginia in the early 1600s known for being a severe ruler. Thomas Morton was a poet and lawyer who looked down on the Puritans and sought to live in harmony with the Native Americans.

I summon them, I summon them!

Appear, appear, appear!

[*The* JURY *has now taken its place in the jury box*—WALTER BUTLER *in the place of foreman. They are eerily lit and so made-up as to suggest the unearthly. They sit stiffly in their box. At first, when one moves, all move, in stylized gestures. It is not till the end of* WEBSTER'S *speech that they begin to show any trace of humanity. They speak rhythmically, and, at first, in low, eerie voices.*]

JABEZ [*seeing them, horrified*]. A jury of the dead!

JURY. Of the dead!

JABEZ. A jury of the damned!

JURY. Of the damned!

SCRATCH. Are you content with the jury, Mr. Webster?

WEBSTER. Quite content. Though I miss General Arnold[28] from the company.

SCRATCH. Benedict Arnold is engaged upon other business. Ah, you asked for a justice, I believe. [*He points his finger and* JUSTICE HATHORNE, *a tall, lean, terrifying Puritan, appears, followed by his* CLERK.] Justice Hathorne is a jurist of experience. He presided at the Salem witch trials.[29] There were others who repented of the business later. But not he, not he!

HATHORNE. Repent of such notable wonders and undertakings? Nay, hang them, hang them all! [*He takes his place on the bench.*]

[*The* CLERK, *an ominous little man with clawlike hands, takes his place. The room has now been transformed into a courtroom.*]

CLERK [*in a gabble of ritual*]. Oyes, oyes, oyes. All ye who have business with this honorable court of special session this night, step forward!

HATHORNE [*with gavel*]. Call the first case.

CLERK. The World, the Flesh and the Devil versus Jabez Stone.

HATHORNE. Who appears for the plaintiff?

SCRATCH. I, Your Honor.

HATHORNE. And for the defendant?

WEBSTER. I.

JURY. The case—the case—he'll have little luck with this case.

HATHORNE. The case will proceed.

WEBSTER. Your Honor, I move to dismiss this case on the grounds of improper jurisdiction.[30]

HATHORNE. Motion denied.

WEBSTER. On the grounds of insufficient evidence.

HATHORNE. Motion denied.

JURY. Motion denied—denied. Motion denied.

WEBSTER. I will take an exception.

HATHORNE. There are no exceptions in this court.

JURY. No exceptions—no exceptions in this court. It's a bad case, Daniel Webster—a losing case.

WEBSTER. Your Honor—

HATHORNE. The prosecution will proceed—

28. **General Arnold.** Benedict Arnold, general of the American Revolutionary War who rejoined British forces and was regarded as a traitor.

29. **Salem witch trials.** In 1692, trials were held in Massachusetts, in which women and girls were accused of being witches. Often, those found guilty were killed.

30. **jurisdiction.** The power, right, or authority to interpret and apply the law; the territory within which authority may be exercised

Scratch. Your Honor—gentlemen of the jury. This is a plain, straightforward case. It need not detain us long.

Jury. Detain us long—it will not detain us long.

Scratch. It concerns one thing alone—the transference, barter and sale of a certain piece of property, to wit, his soul, by Jabez Stone, farmer, of Cross Corners, New Hampshire. That transference, barter or sale is attested by a deed. I offer that deed in evidence and mark it Exhibit A.

Webster. I object.

Hathorne. Objection denied. Mark it Exhibit A.

[Scratch *hands the deed—an ominous and impressive document—to the* Clerk, *who hands it to* Hathorne. Hathorne *hands it back to the* Clerk, *who stamps it. All very fast and with mechanical gestures.*]

Jury. Exhibit A—mark it Exhibit A. [Scratch *takes the deed from the* Clerk *and offers it to the* Jury, *who pass it rapidly among them, hardly looking at it, and hand it back to* Scratch.] We know the deed—the deed—it burns in our fingers—we do not have to see the deed. It's a losing case.

Scratch. It offers incontestable[31] evidence of the truth of the prosecution's claim. I shall now call Jabez Stone to the witness stand.

Jury [*hungrily*]. Jabez Stone to the witness stand, Jabez Stone. He's a fine, fat fellow, Jabez Stone. He'll fry like a battercake, once we get him where we want him.

Webster. Your Honor, I move that this jury be discharged for flagrant and open bias!

Hathorne. Motion denied.

Webster. Exception.

Hathorne. Exception denied.

"We know the deed – the deed – it burns in our fingers..."

Jury. His motion's always denied. He thinks himself smart and clever—lawyer Webster. But his motion's always denied.

Webster. Your Honor! [*He chokes with anger.*]

Clerk [*advancing*]. Jabez Stone to the witness stand!

Jury. Jabez Stone—Jabez Stone.

[Webster *gives* Jabez *an encouraging pat on the back, and* Jabez *takes his place in the witness stand, very scared.*]

Clerk [*offering a black book*]. Do you solemnly swear—testify—so help you—and it's no good, for we don't care what you testify?

Jabez. I do.

Scratch. What's your name?

Jabez. Jabez Stone.

Scratch. Occupation?

Jabez. Farmer.

Scratch. Residence?

Jabez. Cross Corners, New Hampshire.

[*These three questions are very fast and mechanical on the part of* Scratch. *He is absolutely sure of victory and just going through a form.*]

Jury. A farmer—he'll farm in hell—we'll see that he farms in hell.

Scratch. Now, Jabez Stone, answer me. You'd better, you know. You haven't got a chance, and there'll be a cooler place by the fire for you.

Webster. I protest! This is intimidation! This mocks all justice!

Hathorne. The process is irrelevant, incompetent and immaterial. We have our own justice. The protest is denied.

Jury. Irrelevant, incompetent and immaterial—we have our own justice—oh,

31. **incontestable.** Unquestionable

ho, Daniel Webster! [*The* JURY'S *eyes fix upon* WEBSTER *for an instant, hungrily.*]

SCRATCH. Did you or did you not sign this document?

JABEZ. Oh, I signed it! You know I signed it. And, if I have to go to hell for it, I'll go!

[*A sigh sweeps over the* JURY.]

JURY. One of us—one of us now—we'll save a place by the fire for you, Jabez Stone.

SCRATCH. The prosecution rests.

HATHORNE. Remove the prisoner.

WEBSTER. But I wish to cross-examine—I wish to prove—

HATHORNE. There will be no cross-examination. We have our own justice. You may speak, if you like. But be brief.

JURY. Brief—be very brief—we're weary of earth—incompetent, irrelevant and immaterial—they say he's a smart man, Webster, but he's lost his case tonight—be very brief—we have our own justice here.

[WEBSTER *stares around him like a baited bull. Can't find words.*]

MARY'S VOICE [*from off stage*]. Set me as a seal upon thy heart, as a seal upon thine arm, for love is strong as death—

JURY [*loudly*]. A seal!—ha, ha—a burning seal!

MARY'S VOICE. Love is strong—

JURY [*drowning her out*]. Death is stronger than love. Set the seal upon Daniel Webster—the burning seal of the lost. Make him one of us—one of the damned—one with Jabez Stone!

[*The* JURY'S *eyes all fix upon* WEBSTER. *The* CLERK *advances as if to take him into custody. But* WEBSTER *silences them all with a great gesture.*]

WEBSTER. Be still!

I was going to thunder and roar. I shall not do that.

I was going to denounce and defy. I shall not do that.

You have judged this man already with your abominable justice. See that you defend it. For I shall not speak of this man.

You are demons now, but once you were men. I shall speak to every one of you.

Of common things I speak, of small things and common.

The freshness of morning to the young, the taste of food to the hungry, the day's toil, the rest by the fire, the quiet sleep.

These are good things.

But without freedom they sicken, without freedom they are nothing.

Freedom is the bread and the morning and the risen sun.

It was for freedom we came in the boats and the ships. It was for freedom we came.

It has been a long journey, a hard one, a bitter one.

But, out of the wrong and the right, the sufferings and the starvations, there is a new thing, a free thing.

The traitors in their treachery, the wise in their wisdom, the valiant in their courage—all, all have played a part.

It may not be denied in hell nor shall hell prevail against it.

Have you forgotten this? [*He turns to the* JURY.] Have you forgotten the forest?

GIRTY [*as in a dream*]. The forest, the rustle of the forest, the free forest.

WEBSTER [*to* KING PHILIP]. Have you forgotten your lost nation?

KING PHILIP. My lost nation—my fires in the wood—my warriors.

WEBSTER [*to* TEACH]. Have you forgotten the sea and the way of ships?

TEACH. The sea—and the swift ships sailing—the blue sea.

JURY. Forgotten—remembered—forgotten yet remembered.

WEBSTER. You were men once. Have you forgotten?

JURY. We were men once. We have not thought of it nor remembered. But we were men.

WEBSTER. Now here is this man with good and evil in his heart.

Do you know him? He is your brother. Will you take the law of the oppressor[32] and bind him down?

It is not for him that I speak. It is for all of you.

There is sadness in being a man, but it is a proud thing, too.

There is failure and despair on the journey—the endless journey of mankind.

We are tricked and trapped—we stumble into the pit—but, out of the pit, we rise again.

No demon that was ever foaled[33] can know the inwardness of that—only men—bewildered men.

They have broken freedom with their hands and cast her out from the nations—yet shall she live while man lives.

She shall live in the blood and the heart—she shall live in the earth of this country—she shall not be broken.

When the whips of the oppressors are broken and their names forgotten and destroyed,

I see you, mighty, shining, liberty, liberty! I see free men walking and talking under a free star.

God save the United States and the men who have made her free.

The defense rests.

Jury [*exultantly*]. We were men—we were free—we were men—we have not forgotten—our children—our children shall follow and be free.

Hathorne [*rapping with gavel*]. The jury will retire to consider its verdict.

Butler [*rising*]. There is no need. The jury has heard Mr. Webster. We find for the defendant, Jabez Stone!

Jury. Not guilty!

Scratch [*in a screech, rushing forward*]. But, Your Honor—

[*But, even as he does so, there is a flash and a thunderclap, the stage blacks out again, and when the lights come on,* Judge *and* Jury *are gone. The yellow light of dawn lights the windows.*]

Jabez. They're gone and it's morning—Mary, Mary!

Mary [*in doorway*]. My love—my dear. [*She rushes to him.*]

[*Meanwhile* Scratch *has been collecting his papers and trying to sneak out. But* Webster *catches him.*]

Webster. Just a minute, Mr. Scratch. I'll have that paper first, if you please. [*He takes the deed and tears it.*] And, now, sir, I'll have you!

Scratch. Come, come, Mr. Webster. This sort of thing is ridic—ouch—is ridiculous. If you're worried about the costs of the case, naturally, I'd be glad to pay.

Webster. And so you shall! First of all, you'll promise and covenant[34] never to bother Jabez Stone or any other New Hampshire man from now till doomsday. For any hell we want to raise in this State, we can raise ourselves, without any help from you.

Scratch. Ouch! Well, they never did run very big to the barrel but—ouch—I agree!

Webster. See you keep to the bargain! And then—well, I've got a ram named Goliath. He can butt through an iron door. I'd like to turn you loose in his field and see what he could do to you. [Scratch *trembles.*] But that would

32. **oppressor.** One who torments or uses his or her power unfairly; in this case, refers to the devil
33. **foaled.** Born
34. **covenant.** Agree by signing a written contract

be hard on the ram. So we'll just call in the neighbors and give you a shivaree.[35]

Scratch. Mr. Webster—please—oh—

Webster. Neighbors! Neighbors! Come in and see what a long-barreled, slab-sided, lantern-jawed, fortune-telling note-shaver I've got by the scruff of the neck! Bring on your kettles and your pans! [*a noise and murmur outside*] Bring on your muskets and your flails!

Jabez. We'll drive him out of New Hampshire!

Mary. We'll drive old Scratch away!

[*The* Crowd *rushes in, with muskets, flails, brooms, etc. They pursue* Scratch *around the stage, chanting.*]

The Crowd.

We'll drive him out of New Hampshire!
We'll drive old Scratch away!
Forever and a day, boys,
Forever and a day!

[*They finally catch* Scratch *between two of them and fling him out of the door, bodily.*]

A Man. Three cheers for Dan'l Webster!

Another Man. Three cheers for Daniel Webster! He's licked the devil!

Webster [*moving to center stage, and joining* Jabez' *hands and* Mary's]. And whom God hath joined let no man put asunder. [*He kisses* Mary *and turns, dusting his hands.*] Well, that job's done. I hope there's pie for breakfast, neighbor Stone.

[*And, as some of the women, dancing, bring in pies from the kitchen*]

THE CURTAIN FALLS ❖

35. **shivaree.** Noisy mock serenade to a newly married couple

Do you agree that every American is connected by the love of freedom? What other desires and goals might connect all of humankind?

Refer and Reason

1. The events of this play take place in 1841, more than fifty years after the United States declared its independence from Great Britain, and twenty years before the start of the Civil War. Look back through the play, and identify references to events that took place in America from the time of its independence to the time during which the play takes place.
2. Judge whether the jury made the correct decision. Support your opinion with facts from the story.
3. Toward the end of his speech, Webster says that men have "broken freedom with their hands and cast her out from the nations." Infer what "nations" he might be talking about. Explain the connection between the references to specific events in American history and the argument that Daniel Webster makes to the jury.

Writing Options

1. Write a narrative paragraph as if you were part of the prosecution and were allowed to respond to Daniel Webster's closing remarks. What might you say to keep the jury on your side?
2. Write a two-paragraph step-by-step explanation of the strategy that Webster uses to accomplish his persuasion of a jury of the dead and damned.

Go to **www.mirrorsandwindows.com** for more.

OTHELLO

by William Shakespeare

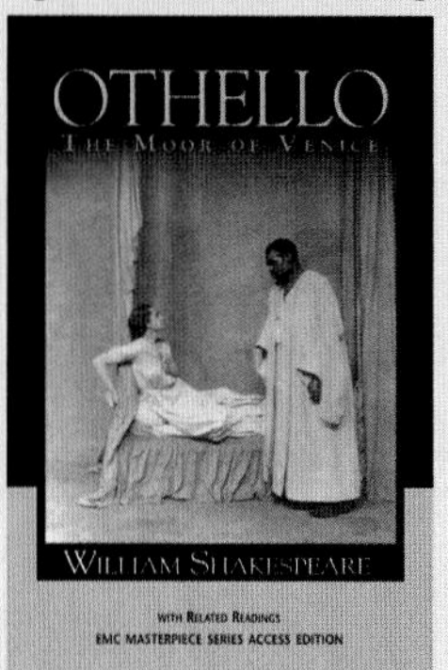

Iago serves the Moorish general Othello but secretly schemes to make Othello jealous and distrusting of his new wife, Desdemona. When Othello is called to fend off a Turkish attack in Cyprus, Iago unleashes his plans to poison the newlyweds' happiness—leaving a wake of destruction too tragic to comprehend.

ROMEO AND JULIET AND WEST SIDE STORY

by William Shakespeare
Norris Houghton (editor)

This book provides the scripts of both Shakespeare's *Romeo and Juliet* and its modern adaptation, *West Side Story*. One is set in Renaissance Verona, the other in the gang environment of New York City's West Side, but both tell the story of young lovers who refuse to allow prejudice and feuding to keep them apart.

SHAKING HANDS WITH SHAKESPEARE: A TEENAGER'S GUIDE TO READING AND PERFORMING THE BARD

by Allison Wedell Schumacher

Written especially for students, this introduction to Shakespeare's plays presents historical background, information on the four main categories of plays and types of characters, tips on understanding their language, great moments in their plotting, and the basics of performing Shakespeare.

A RAISIN IN THE SUN

by Lorraine Hansberry

When Willie Younger squanders a $10,000 insurance payment reserved for his sister's medical school tuition, he's offered a way to make it up. The Clybourne Park Improvement Association will pay the family *not* to move into its white neighborhood. Will he take the bribe?

AN ENEMY OF THE PEOPLE

by Henrik Ibsen

When Dr. Stockton discovers the newly-built baths in his small town are contaminated, he assumes the baths will be closed. But some fear the economic cost involved and form an alliance against Stockton, who is declared "an enemy of the people." Soon, Stockton must choose whether to stand alone or submit to the majority's will.

THE MIRACLE WORKER

by William Gibson

Twelve-year-old Helen Keller was deaf, blind, and mute. Having no true form of communication, she was left in a world of darkness. Helen was wild and afraid, fighting anyone who attempted to help her. All seemed hopeless until Annie Sullivan, a half-blind teacher, came to help the family.

SPEAKING & LISTENING WORKSHOP

Present a Dramatic Scene

In this lesson, you will present a scene from *The Tragedy of Romeo and Juliet* for your classmates.

1. Select a scene

With a group of your classmates, select a scene from the play and assign parts. Some scenes, such as the balcony scene (Act II, Scene ii), require only two actors; others, such as Act I, Scene ii, require many. Be sure that everyone who wants one has a speaking role.

2. Read through and mark up scripts

Make copies of the scene for each actor to use as a script. Read the scene together as a group. As you read, mark up your scripts with notes about how to perform the scene. For example, you might note places where you should pause, speak more loudly or softly, or use particular facial expressions and gestures.

3. Choreograph and rehearse

Next, plan the choreography—that is, the movement onstage, including entrances and exits and interaction such as fighting. As you rehearse, avoid blocking other actors. Face the audience as much as possible and project your voice so that your lines are heard clearly. Have your teacher or another student act as director, giving pointers as you rehearse the scene.

4. Add props and costumes

Gather any props needed for your scene (for example, swords, torches, or a vial). Consider using simple costumes—for example, tights and long, belted T-shirts for the male characters, and long dresses for the women.

5. Present the scene

Finally, present the dramatic scene in front of the class. Your classmates may evaluate your performance using the performance rubric shown.

Speaking Tip

Although the play is mostly in verse, read your lines naturally. Do not pause at the end of each line, but only where you see a comma, semicolon, or period.

Performance Rubric

A good dramatic performance includes the following:

Delivery and Presentation

- ☑ voice projection (volume)
- ☑ accurate line interpretation and expression
- ☑ appropriate facial expressions and gestures
- ☑ smooth choreography
- ☑ interesting use of props and costumes

Dramatic Scene

Assignment
Write a scene based on a theme and characters from *Romeo and Juliet.*

Purpose
To explore, through dramatic writing, a theme that interests you

Audience
Your teacher and classmates, possibly others in the school or community

A play tells a story through characters. The script of a play consists of characters, dialogue, and stage directions. It's broken into **dramatic scenes** that move the play forward. Each scene has a striking opening and conclusion, or resolution, even if the problem is not solved. At the heart of the story is some kind of conflict. Shakespeare wrote *The Tragedy of Romeo and Juliet* more than four hundred years ago, yet his play's themes—love, defiance, commitment, and family strife—never grow old.

What would those themes look like in a contemporary version of *Romeo and Juliet?* The characters, in an updated, recognizable setting, might express the same passionate grief, longing, anger, desire, or love as Shakespeare's characters. By carrying themes from *Romeo and Juliet* into the twenty-first century, you may further appreciate the timeless quality of Shakespeare's work.

❶ PREWRITE

Select Your Topic

To write your scene, you need a theme, a conflict, and characters. Jot down a list of the themes from *Romeo and Juliet.* Choose the one you like best. Brainstorm basic conflicts that would illustrate the theme. Again, choose the one you like best.

Gather Information

Once you establish a conflict, or situation, you can develop characters. Often, your characters' personalities drive the plot. The way characters interact heightens the conflict. To get to know your characters, ask yourself core questions about them: What do they want? What are their strengths and weaknesses? What prevents them from getting what they want?

Create a Character Cluster Chart, like the one on page 649, and jot down everything you can think of about your main characters. This will give you a strong foundation for writing dialogue that reveals their distinct personalities and motives.

Organize Your Ideas

For each character you wrote about, highlight material that is most directly relevant to your conflict and theme. Transfer this material to a clean page in your notebook or the computer, perhaps in bullet-point format, and side-by-side, in columns.

When you put your characters together, their personalities may clash or bond in ways that will start to develop your conflict. Begin to think about what happens when they come together. How will they talk, respond, and react to each other?

Writing Rubric

A successful dramatic script:

- ☑ creates a **scene opening** for the reader/viewer, introducing characters and setting
- ☑ develops **dialogue,** including **stage directions,** true to characters' personalities
- ☑ creates a **central conflict,** which, in this case, illuminates a theme from *Romeo and Juliet*
- ☑ has an **introduction,** a **body,** and a **conclusion** (a beginning, a middle, and an end)
- ☑ follows the format for script-writing and logic

Character Cluster Chart

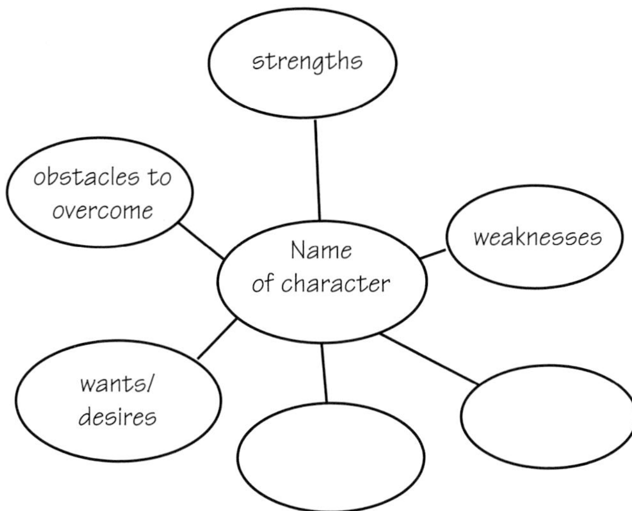

Write Your Thesis Statement, or Central Conflict

It will help you write your scene if you are clear about its **central idea,** the core conflict. Summarize your scene in one sentence. One student, Kristy Cady, summarized her scene this way (see Student Model on page 653):

> When Chris and George (based on Mercutio and Tybalt) are assigned to the same debate team, their personal rivalry interferes with the debate.

What Great Writers Do

Stating simple information in fresh, unique ways brightens a dramatic scene. Russian playwright Anton Chekhov (1860–1904), who adapted *The Inspector-General* (page 498), has this advice:

"Don't tell me the moon is shining; show me the glint of light on broken glass."

❷ DRAFT

Write your dramatic scene by following the three-part framework described at right: **introduction, body,** and **conclusion.**

- **Introduction**
  Sets the stage and introduces the characters
- **Body**
  Enacts the drama, heightens the conflict, and moves the story forward
- **Conclusion**
  Closes the scene and clarifies the conflict as to whether or not it gets resolved

Draft Your Introduction, or Scene Opening

In a play, the **scene opening** orients the audience. It describes the setting, props, and characters. It directs the cast so that when a scene opens, the audience knows where and when the action is happening. Good stage directions explain the situation, but they don't spoil the outcome.

Kristy drafted her scene opening, as shown in the first column of the chart on page 651. The audience won't read these words but will see the result of them on stage. Kristy's words need to explain, for the cast and stage crew, how she wants the stage to look. However, in her draft, she assumes her crew knows what a debate setup looks like. How could she make her description more clear?

Draft Your Body, or Dialogue

Once you know your characters, their conflict, and your theme, you are ready to write the **body** of your script. Unlike expository writing, there is usually no explanatory prose in a play. The characters tell the story and reveal the conflict through dialogue.

Kristy's characters, Rose and Chris, reveal a potential conflict as they talk casually, prior to the debate. Look at the draft of Kristy's dialogue in the left-hand column of the chart on page 651. As Rose and Chris talk, they show the audience who they are and reveal Chris's looming confrontation with George. Later, the conflict will reach a climax, or turning point.

Review your Character Chart. Your characters' personalities will motivate them to say certain things. How would a character with a short temper speak? What about the class clown? Use dialogue that will distinguish your characters. Your language should be natural, consistent to the characters' personalities but still appropriate for a school audience.

Draft Your Conclusion, or Resolution

End your scene with a strong **conclusion** or resolution. Whether or not it has been resolved, make sure your conflict is heightened and clarified. Your characters have committed irreversible actions; consequences have resulted. A good scene satisfies the audience yet encourages them to predict what will happen next.

Look at the draft of Kristy's conclusion, the resolution of her scene on page 651. Does she accomplish those things as she closes her scene?

❸ REVISE

Evaluate Your Draft

After you finish drafting your script, it's time to evaluate it. You can evaluate your own writing or exchange papers with a classmate and read each other's work. Think carefully about what's done well and what can be improved.

Refer back to the drafted statement of your central conflict. Does the scene focus on it? As you check content and organization, make sure the scene opening, dialogue, and conclusion work together to highlight the conflict and to illuminate the theme. Use the Revision Checklist on page 652 to make this evaluation. Make notes on the script suggesting changes that could be made.

Next, check your draft and give attention to the guidelines in the Grammar & Style workshops in this unit. Again, refer to the Revision Checklist to evaluate the writing. Think about making the dialogue even more interesting. A good trick is to read the words aloud, revising them so they sound the way the characters would really speak.

Revise for Content, Organization, and Style

Kristy evaluated her draft and found a number of things to improve. Look at the chart on page 651 (the right-hand column) to see how she revised the sections:

- **Opening:** Kristy replaced vague setting directions with specific, visual instructions. She made sure to provide only the character information needed to understand the scene.

What Great Writers Do

Shakespeare's plays thrive today not only for the ingenious plots, but for the poetry in his language. In Romeo's brief cry, "Oh, I am fortune's fool!" the audience hears the depths of his grief. Juliet's passionate line of longing, "Romeo, Romeo, wherefore art thou, Romeo," is memorable because of its poetic rhythm.

DRAFT STAGE		REVISE STAGE	
Introduction Setting: A high school debate.	Identifies place setting	Setting: A high school debate, classroom desks arranged, a table with two chairs on each side of the room, and a speaking podium at the front.	Strengthens direction with specific details
Props: Four containers filled with evidence; papers; pens.	Provides prop information	Props: Four containers filled with evidence; papers; pens.	
Characters: Debaters Chris (Mercutio) with a sense of humor and a basketball trophy; George (Tybalt) with a short temper; Rose (Benvolio), former teammate; Coach White (the Prince)	Describes characters without spoiling the plot	Characters: Debaters Chris (Mercutio) with a sense of humor ~~and a basketball trophy~~; George (Tybalt) with a short temper; Rose (Benvolio), former teammate; Coach White (the Prince).	Deletes irrelevant information
Body Paragraph **Chris:** I still can't believe I got put me with George for Districts! What was Coach thinking?	Uses dialogue to set up the conflict	**Chris:** ~~I still can't believe~~ Preposterous – ~~I got put~~ me partnered with George for Districts! Mr. Perfect over there. What was Coach White thinking?	Heightens word choice; uses good action verbs; adds details showing why Chris feels the way he does
Rose: He was thinking that you're both strong debaters.	Provides background through dialogue	**Rose:** ~~He was thinking~~ That you're both strong debaters?	Deletes wordiness
		Rose: This is your big chance, lucky dogs.	Adds dialogue to show Chris's sense of humor and his friendship with Rose
		Chris: Dogs who need you, Rose. Arf, arf.	
Conclusion **Coach White:** [barely controlling his anger] Unbelievable! Your attitudes have cost us the competition. [storms out]	Shows character's response Uses effective last lines that provide closure	**Coach White:** [~~barely controlling his anger~~ clenched fist, tight lips] Unbelievable! Your attitudes have cost us the competition. You are both suspended from this team. [storms out]	Replaces vague stage direction with specific action Adds information about their consequences
[Chris and George hate each other even more now]		[Chris and George ~~hate each other even more now~~ look down at the floor]	Replaces explanatory line with active stage direction
		Rose: [shakes her head] That's bad. But you deserve it. [she exits, leaving Chris and George alone]	

REVISION CHECKLIST

Content and Organization

- ❑ Does the **setting** make clear where and when the scene takes place?
- ❑ Do the **characters** parallel specific characters from *Romeo and Juliet?*
- ❑ Where does **conflict** occur in the scene? Where does the conflict reach its peak or climax?
- ❑ What **theme** does the scene explore?
- ❑ Is the **dialogue** true to the characters' personalities?
- ❑ What consequences result? What provides **closure** for the scene?
- ❑ Is your script formatted correctly? Does it follow standard script-writing **format?**

Grammar and Style

- ❑ Has capitalization been used correctly? (page 554)
- ❑ Are modifiers used correctly? (page 582)
- ❑ Are sentence fragments avoided or used for stylistic reasons? (page 598)
- ❑ Are compound sentences and clauses used correctly? (page 622)

- **Dialogue:** Kristy made changes in dialogue that would better convey each character's personality. She used good action verbs and eliminated empty words, making the language concise.
- **Conclusion:** Kristy added stage directions for Rose. She also changed Rose's final speech, making it clear to the audience that Chris and George would suffer heavy consequences as a result of their rivalry.

Review the notes you or your partner made as you reviewed your draft. Respond to those notes and effectively revise your scene.

Proofread for Errors

Proofread to check solely for mechanical errors in capitalization, spelling, punctuation, and grammar. You may have fixed some errors as you evaluated and revised your scene but focus intently on them now. Use proofreader's symbols to mark any errors you find. (See Language Arts Handbook 4.1 for a list of proofreader's symbols.) Format your dramatic scene like the Student Model. Print out your final draft and read the entire thing once more before turning it in.

Read Kristy's script on the next page. Notice how she moved through the three stages of the writing process–prewrite, draft, and revise–to create her finished piece.

WRITING FOLLOW-UP

Publish and Present

- Perform your scene for your class. Ask classmates to act your roles. Rehearse the scene. As director, choreograph action (such as dancing or fighting), entrances and exits, timing, sound effects, and so on. Use simple costumes and props.
- Design a playbill advertising your scene. It should briefly explain the scene, announce the actors' names, and include illustrations. Post it or distribute copies to your classmates.

REFLECT

- Writing a scene involves many skills: imagining, planning, writing, staging, and collaborating with others. What did you learn as you progressed through these stages? Which skills were easiest for you? Which were difficult?
- What were the challenges and rewards of trying to update Shakespeare's language, themes, and characters?

STUDENT MODEL

The Debate
by Kristy Cady

Setting: A high school debate, a table with two chairs on each side of the classroom, and a speaking podium at the front.

Props: Four containers filled with evidence; papers; pens.

Characters: Debaters Chris (Mercutio) with a sense of humor; George (Tybalt) with a short temper; Rose (Benvolio), their former teammate; Coach White (the Prince); the judge and two negative debaters (Citizens).

[scene opens; Chris and Rose talk in back; George, at a table, sorts through his papers, the negative debaters are at the opposite table]

Chris: Preposterous – me partnered with George for Districts! Mr. Perfect over there. What was Coach White thinking?

Rose: That you're both strong, capable, and worthy debaters? This is your big chance, lucky dogs.

Chris: Dogs who need you, Rose. Arf, arf.

Rose: [laughs] You're better than I ever was.

Chris: True. [grins] Rose, lend your expertise – read a new case I wrote? [holds a folder out to her] It will shock the other team.

Rose: [puzzled] Have you shown it to George yet?

[George glares at Chris from the table, taps his watch.]

Chris: [laughing] Too late. [walks over to George and places the folder on the table]

George: [angrily] About time! You're going to cost us this debate.

Chris: [in a mocking tone] If only I could be as prepared as you! [George scowls, Chris approaches the podium] Negatives ready? [they nod] Judge ready? [she nods] Resolved: That the federal government should establish an education policy to increase academic achievement in secondary schools. [pauses; opens the file in his hand] Studies show that the addition of Mozart into the classroom increases academic achievement.

George: [shocked, whispers angrily to Chris] Stick to what we've worked on!

Chris: [smiles smugly] My partner will extend upon these arguments. Thank you, vote Affirmative. [Chris returns to his seat, whispers to George] Can you handle that?

George: [slams his fist on the table; stands] This isn't funny! You're on your own. [leaves the room; everyone else stares wide-eyed at Chris]

How is the stage set up?

On which characters from Romeo and Juliet are these characters based?

What is the central conflict of this scene?

What does the dialogue reveal about the characters' personalities?

Which part of the scene could be considered the climax?

Reading Skills

EVALUATE CAUSE AND EFFECT

Cause and effect is the relationship between two things when one thing makes something else happen. For example, if we eat too much food and do not exercise, we gain weight. Eating too much food combined with a failure to exercise is the cause; weight gain is the effect. Recognizing cause-and-effect relationships is necessary in understanding how the world works.

Test-Taking Tip
If you don't know the answer to a multiple-choice question, see how many of the choices you can eliminate. Once you have narrowed down your options, the odds are better that you will choose the correct answer.

The writer may present the cause(s) and effect(s) in any order. Sometimes, the cause comes first; in other passages, the effect is mentioned first. In a more complicated structure, one effect may become the cause of another effect. It's a chain reaction—for example, if you tripped over a cat and fell against a table, in turn knocking off a vase. Your tripping is first an effect and then a cause.

Transitional, or signal, words and phrases that indicate a cause-and-effect relationship include the following: *as a result, because, since, consequently,* and *therefore.* However, signal words are not always present in a text explaining a cause-and-effect relationship. For example, read the following excerpts from "Romeo and Juliet Over the Centuries."

> *Romeo and Juliet* is probably the best known and best loved of all William Shakespeare's plays. Generations of audiences have been able to relate to the two "star-cross'd" young lovers, whose passion is doomed from the start by the bitter feuding between their families.

A more subtle cause-and-effect relationship is presented in this excerpt. One of the reasons why *Romeo and Juliet* is so well known and loved (the effect) is because "generations of audiences have been able to relate" to the main characters (the cause).

When you, the reader, evaluate cause and effect, you determine whether the causes and effects in a text are reasonable. Keep track of what happens in a passage and the reasons given. Then think about whether what happens could have resulted for these reasons.

PRACTICE

Directions: Read the following excerpt from the Knight Ridder Tribune News Service. The questions that come after it will ask you to evaluate cause and effect.

Light-struck or star-struck?
Knight Ridder Tribune News Service
Washington, March 23, 2004

The following editorial appeared in the *Hartford Courant* on Monday, March 22:

With fossil fuel-burning vehicles multiplying like fruit flies and the planet steadily warming, the subject of light pollution may not appear to be an environmental priority.

It should be. Brightly lit civilization is creeping across the landscape as inexorably as urban sprawl. It is keeping most Americans from ever enjoying the nuances of the night sky.

Except for people in remote areas, most of us live as if a faraway flashlight were trained on our eyes, preventing us from viewing celestial surroundings. An estimated two-thirds of the population has never looked heavenward to witness the wonder of their own galaxy, the Milky Way, as subtle as milkweed silk.

That's sad from an aesthetic point of view. But it also prevents the light-struck from experiencing the cosmic connection that is both a source of inspiration and a humbling thing.

When lying on one's back in the dark looking up at a sky full of stars, there's a feeling of communion with those distant points of light. We can imagine others like ourselves looking up from other galaxies. We are inspired to learn and explore. This is an experience worth protecting just as we do mountain ridges and beautiful vistas.

Light pollution also affects plants and wildlife, as any egg farmer who keeps hens in perpetual daylight can tell you.

Some states have taken measures to regulate excessive lighting, from billboards to ballparks. New Mexico has a Night Sky Protection Act banning streetlights with high-powered mercury vapor bulbs. Maine and Arizona have adopted energy efficiency and glare standards.

In lieu of federal environmental standards, all states should adopt suitable measures to reduce light pollution, which actually saves money in the long run. Here's an illuminating fact from Tucson: Officials replaced streetlights with hooded fixtures forcing the light to shine down, rather than toward the sky. The result was 50 percent more illumination at half the wattage.

Next time there's a celestial event like a comet or a meteor shower, remember that it can actually cost less to improve everyone's view.

Multiple Choice

1. Which is *not* an effect of stargazing?
   A. measures to regulate excessive lighting
   B. a cosmic connection
   C. inspiration to learn more about the universe
   D. a desire to explore other galaxies
   E. All of the above

2. The result of Tucson's change of streetlights is
   A. cost savings.
   B. increased wattage.
   C. a replacement with hooded fixtures.
   D. a new federal environmental regulation.
   E. more pollution.

3. According to this excerpt, what produces inspiration to learn and explore?
   A. being humbled
   B. an aesthetic point of view
   C. experiencing the cosmic connection
   D. looking at beautiful vistas
   E. replacing lightbulbs

4. Based on the information presented, which of the following is *both* a cause and an effect?
   A. urban sprawl
   B. light pollution
   C. fossil fuel-burning vehicles
   D. hens laying fewer eggs
   E. noise pollution

5. Which of the following *most* directly states the cause-and-effect relationships in the first sentence of the next to the last paragraph?
   A. If states adopted suitable measures that would result in decreased light pollution, it would, in turn, result in an actual savings of money.
   B. All states should adopt suitable measures to reduce light pollution because it would actually save money in the long run.
   C. States would save money if they adopted suitable measures to reduce light pollution.
   D. Therefore, all should adopt suitable measures to reduce light, and in so doing, save.
   E. None of the above

Constructed Response

6. Discuss the results of attempts to regulate excessive lighting.

Writing Skills

EXPOSITORY WRITING

Writing Tip
Between planning and outlining your essay and the actual writing, reexamine your thesis. Ask yourself these two questions: (1) Is it logical? (2) Will readers find the supporting evidence you offer convincing? If the answer to either is "no," take a few minutes more to rethink your position.

Many standardized tests include sections that ask you to demonstrate your writing ability by composing an essay in response to a prompt, or topic. Sometimes, you are asked to write an expository, or informative, piece. The purpose of this common mode of writing is to inform, explain, or instruct in a straightforward manner. Examples of informative pieces include news articles, research reports, book reviews, expository essays, and instruction manuals.

When you write an informative essay, keep the following tips in mind:

- Include only relevant information.
- Choose words that the reader will be able to readily understand.
- Write clearly and concisely.
- Include an introduction (in which you identify your narrowed topic), a body (in which you explain the topic), and a conclusion (in which you sum up the information that you have covered).

Remember that in an expository essay, you are just describing or explaining, not trying to convince the reader to share your opinion.

To prepare effectively for the essay-writing section of standardized tests, you should practice the following:

- using the allotted time effectively
- analyzing the prompt
- planning your response
- writing a good introduction
- staying focused on the task
- writing a good conclusion

Because you will be evaluated in part on your ability to use standard English, you should also pay attention to grammar, usage, capitalization, spelling, and punctuation. Be sure that your language and tone are appropriate for the audience.

PRACTICE

Timed Writing: 30 minutes

Read the following quotations by Michelangelo Antonioni and Steve McQueen, respectively. Then consider the assignment below them. Allow 30 minutes to write your response to the prompt.

> "I have never felt salvation in nature. I love cities above all."
> —Michelangelo Antonioni

> "I'd rather wake up in the middle of nowhere than in any city on earth."
> —Steve McQueen

Assignment: Is it better to live in a city, in the country, or in a small town? Write an essay about where you'd prefer to live based on what you've experienced, read, seen, or heard.

Revising and Editing Skills

Some standardized tests ask you to read a draft of an essay and then answer questions about how to improve it. As you read the draft, think about the corrections and improvements you would make to the essay. Watch for the following errors:

- misspellings
- disagreement between subject and verb
- incorrect forms for irregular verbs
- inconsistent verb tense
- incorrect pronoun forms
- missing or incorrect punctuation
- incorrect capitalization
- double negatives
- incorrect use of frequently confused words, such as *affect* and *effect*
- sentence fragments and run-ons
- inappropriate language or tone

Then read each question, and consider each answer to determine which one is best.

PRACTICE

Directions: In the passage that follows, each sentence is numbered, and certain phrases are underlined. The questions below the passage correspond to the sentence in the passage. In the questions, you will find alternatives for each underlined phrase. Choose the alternative that makes the text correct according to the conventions of standard written English. If you think the original version is best, choose the first alternative, MAKE NO CHANGE.

(1) Amherst<u>, Massachusetts, is located in the Pioneer Valley, which is in the western</u> part of the state. (2) <u>There's hills nearby, and</u> you can see mountains in the distance. (3) <u>It's population is about 30,000, and it would seem like a small town except for the presence</u> of the huge University of Massachusetts. (4) Two other colleges are located in Amherst, Amherst College and Hampshire <u>College, two more are nearby: Smith College and</u> Mt. Holyoke.

1. A. MAKE NO CHANGE.
   B. Massachusetts is located in the Pioneer Valley, which is in the western
   C. Massachusetts, is located in the Pioneer Valley which is in the western
   D. Massachusetts, is located in the Pioneer Valley, which is in the Western
   E. Massachusetts is the Western

2. A. MAKE NO CHANGE.
   B. There's hills nearby and
   C. Theirs hills nearby, and
   D. There are hills nearby, and
   E. There is hills nearby, and

3. A. MAKE NO CHANGE.
   B. It's population is about 30,000 and it would seem like a small town except for the presence
   C. Its population is about 30,000, and it would seem like a small town except for the presence
   D. It's population is about 30,000, and it would seem like a small town except for the presense
   E. It's population is 30,000 with the inclusion of

4. A. MAKE NO CHANGE.
   B. College; two more are nearby: Smith College and
   C. College, two more are nearby: Smith College, and
   D. College, two more are nearby; Smith College and
   E. College two more are nearby: Smith College, and

UNIT 5

Folk Literature

MAUGHAM

YOUNG

ATWOOD

"Myths and legends die hard in America. We love them for the extra dimension they provide, the illusion of near-infinite possibility to erase the narrow confines of most men's reality."

—Hunter S. Thompson

How might you explain something that you don't understand? If you were to describe the most amazing thing you have ever witnessed, how would you describe it? In the following unit, you will encounter a variety of tales that attempt to teach an important lesson, describe events, or explain the reasoning behind certain aspects of life.

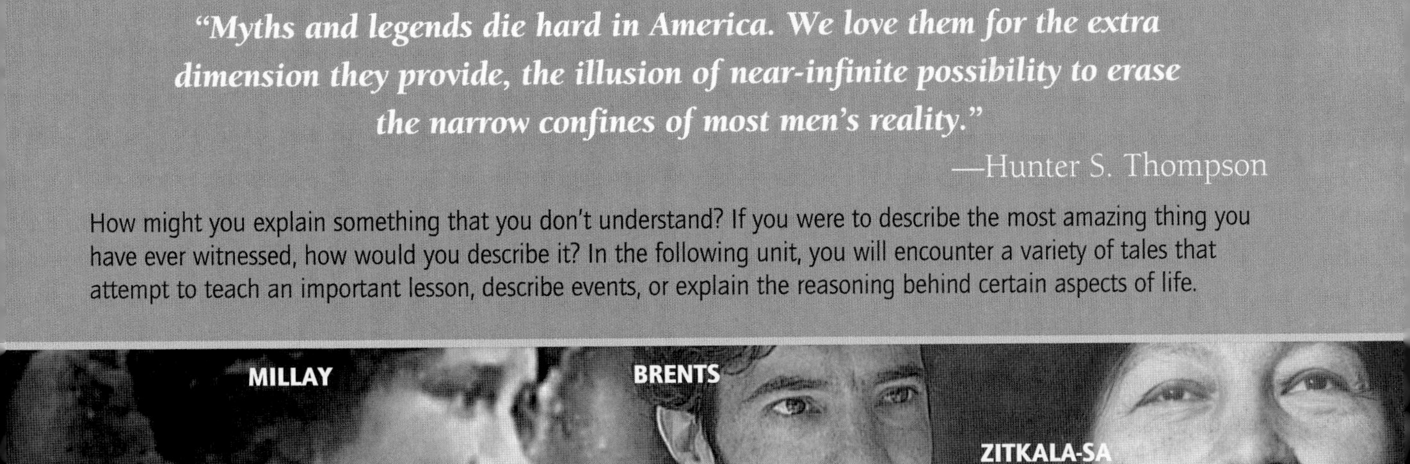

MILLAY

BRENTS

ZITKALA-SA

INTRODUCTION TO FOLK LITERATURE

"You want great fortunes yet each of you is rich already in words of beauty and imagination."

—"The Golden Lamb"
by Jean Russell Larson

Human beings are storytellers. Long before people invented writing, they were handing down stories about their gods and heroes and experiences. The best of these stories survived from generation to generation to form the basis of the literature that we know today. The following selections are products of this storytelling tradition.

THE GENRE OF FOLK LITERATURE

Folk literature is the traditional knowledge and beliefs of cultures that are transmitted by word of mouth. Some early stories were told in the form of poems or songs. Others were in the form of prose tales, the first type of fiction. The passing of stories, poems, and songs transmitted verbally from one generation to the next comprises a culture's oral tradition.

TYPES OF FOLK LITERATURE

Myths and Legends

Myths are traditional stories, rooted in a particular culture, that deal with gods, goddesses, and other supernatural beings, as well as human heroes. Myths often embody religious beliefs and values and explain natural phenomena. Every early culture around the globe has produced its own myths. Two Greek myths appear in this unit: "The Story of Dædalus and Icarus" by Ovid, translated by Rolfe Humphries (page 664), and "Echo & Narcissus" retold by Walker Brents (page 671).

Legends are stories that are passed down through generations and are often based on real events or characters from long ago. Unlike myths, legends are usually regarded as having a historical basis; however, they may contain fantastic or unverifiable elements. An example of a legend is the story of George Washington chopping down the cherry tree. "The Silver Pool" (page 679) tells a story of the legendary Irish, or Celtic, hero Fionn MacCumhail.

Epics

Epics are long stories, often told in verse, involving heroes and gods. Epics have often been passed on orally and may have anonymous authors. Grand in length and scope, an epic provides a portrait of an entire culture—of the legends, beliefs, values, laws, arts, and ways of life of a people. Homer's *The Odyssey* (page 713) is an example of an epic poem.

Folk Tales

Folk tales are brief stories passed by word of mouth from generation to generation. "The Golden Lamb" (page 699) is an Iraqi folk tale.

Tall tales are lighthearted or humorous folk tales that often contain highly exaggerated, unrealistic elements. The stories of Paul Bunyan and Pecos Bill are tall tales.

Fairy tales are stories that deal with mischievous spirits and other supernatural occurrences, often in medieval settings. The name is generally applied to stories of the kind collected by Charles Perrault in France and the Brothers Grimm in Germany or told by Hans Christian Andersen of Denmark. "Cinderella" and "The Little Mermaid" are famous examples. "The White Snake" (page 691) is another famous fairy tale from the European oral tradition.

> As soon as he had fastened the door securely, he lifted the cover, and there he saw a white snake lying on the dish. After seeing it he could not resist the desire to taste it, and so he cut off a small piece and put it in his mouth. As soon as it touched his tongue he heard outside his window a strange chorus of delicate voices. He went and listened, and found that it was the sparrows talking together, and telling each other all they had seen in the fields and woods. The virtue of the snake had given him power to understand the speech of animals.
>
> —from "The White Snake"
> by Jacob and Wilhelm Grimm

Other Folk Literature

Parables are very brief stories told to teach moral lessons. The most famous parables are those told by Jesus in the Bible. "The Prodigal Son," a famous story from the Bible, is one such parable.

Fables are brief stories, often with animal characters, told to express morals. Famous fables include those of Aesop and Jean de La Fontaine.

Folk songs are traditional or composed songs typically made up of stanzas, a refrain, and a simple melody. A form of folk literature, folk songs are expressions of commonly shared ideas or feelings and may be narrative or lyric in style. Traditional folk songs are anonymous works that have been transmitted orally, such as the ballad "John Henry." **Spirituals** are religious songs from the African-American folk tradition. Examples include "Steal Away" and "Go Down, Moses."

Proverbs, or *adages*, are traditional sayings, such as "You can lead a horse to water, but you can't make it drink" and the title of Shakespeare's play *All's Well That Ends Well.*

Memorable Characters of Folk Literature

The following are well-known folk literature characters. Consider why these tales continue to be enjoyed today.

Beauty and the Beast (fairy tale)
Br'er Rabbit (fable)
Cinderella (fairy tale)
Coyote (fable)
Davy Crockett (legend)
Hercules (myth)
King Arthur (legend)
Paul Bunyan and Babe the Blue Ox (tall tale)
Zeus (myth)

FOLK LITERATURE READING MODEL

BEFORE READING | DURING READING | AFTER READING

BUILD BACKGROUND

- **Connect** your own knowledge and experiences to what you read. Many myths and folk tales explain natural phenomena, such as the changing seasons or the origins of thunder and lightning. How would you explain those natural phenomena?
- Read the **Build Background** and **Meet the Author** sections. Based on these sections, what elements do you think the story will involve?

ANALYZE LITERATURE

- Note the **literary technique** that is introduced.

SET PURPOSE

- **Preview** the text for its form, vocabulary, footnotes, and art. What can you learn about the story from these elements?
- Much folk literature has a moral or a lesson in it. Try to anticipate what the point of this tale will be.

USE READING SKILLS

- Before reading, **apply reading skills** such as determining the author's purpose, analyzing text structure, previewing new vocabulary, and using context clues.

BEFORE READING | DURING READING | AFTER READING

USE READING STRATEGIES

- **Visualize** or form pictures in your mind to help you see the characters, actions, or other elements, such as Dædalus's invention.
- **Make predictions** about what's going to happen next. As you read, gather more clues that will either confirm or change your predictions.
- **Ask questions** about things that you don't understand or that seem unusual or interesting. For instance, you may want to know more about the references to other Greek gods or islands.
- **Clarify** events in the story for better understanding. Take notes about what seems odd or confusing and reread the story to try to figure those things out.
- **Make inferences,** or educated guesses, about what is not stated directly.

ANALYZE LITERATURE

- Note what literary elements stand out as you read the story. How does the author achieve his or her purpose?

MAKE CONNECTIONS

- Notice where there are **connections** between the story and your life or the world beyond the story. Have you encountered references to this myth or folk tale in other places? How can the lesson or moral be applied to modern life?

BEFORE READING | DURING READING | AFTER READING

REFER TO TEXT

- **Recall** the facts. **Remember** details like characters' names, locations or settings, and events.
- **Determine the sequence of events,** or the order in which things happened.
- Try to **summarize** the story in a sentence or two based on the events.

REASON WITH TEXT

- **Apply** your ideas about the story's elements to see if they help you answer any additional questions.
- **Analyze** the text by breaking down information into smaller units and figuring out how those pieces fit into the story as a whole.
- **Evaluate** the text. **Draw conclusions** by bringing together what you have read and using this material to make a decision or form an opinion.

ANALYZE LITERATURE

- **Review** how the author's use of literary elements enhanced your understanding or enjoyment of the story. How effective is the author in expressing meaning through the folk literature?

EXTEND THE TEXT

- **Expand** your reading beyond the story by exploring ideas through writing or doing other creative projects.

The Story of Dædalus and Icarus

from **the Metamorphoses, an Epic Poem by Ovid**
Translated by Rolfe Humphries

BEFORE READING

BUILD BACKGROUND

Literary Context "The Story of Dædalus and Icarus" is about the brilliant mythical inventor Dædalus and his son, who escape from captivity in Crete, an island ruled by King Minos. According to Greek mythology, Minos ordered Dædalus to design a labyrinth (a building of many passageways) to hold the half-bull, half-human monster, the Minotaur, that belonged to the king. Minos was pleased with the labyrinth but feared that Dædalus would reveal its secret, so he prevented him from leaving the island.

The works of Ovid include Roman myths, many of them borrowed from the Greeks. Singers (sometimes called troubadours) and bards, or reciters of narratives, traveled among the peoples of the ancient world, offering these memorable tales, which were later written down by poets such as Ovid.

Reader's Context Think about an improbable invention you would like to experience. How long before you think your improbable invention could become reality?

ANALYZE LITERATURE: Foreshadowing

The act of presenting hints to events that will occur later in a story is called **foreshadowing.** Foreshadowing may be obvious or subtle. Often, it includes the appearance of an object or a symbol, but it can also include warnings or predictions.

SET PURPOSE

Many myths and folk tales were created with the purpose of explaining a phenomenon in nature or giving a lesson about how to live (a moral). As you read "The Story of Dædalus and Icarus," consider what the purpose of the myth is.

Be aware of moments when the fates of the characters are foreshadowed. Is the foreshadowing obvious or subtle?

MEET THE AUTHOR

Ovid is the pen name of Publius Ovidius Naso (43 BCE–c. 17 CE), one of the greatest of the Latin poets. Ovid lived at the time of the emperor Augustus, when the Roman Empire was in its golden age. Popular in his time, he was best known for his love poetry, including *Ars amatoria (The Art of Love)*. Ovid's masterpiece is now considered to be the *Metamorphoses*. An epic poem in fifteen books, it covers the history of the world and focuses on changes, especially on the transformation of beings into different forms. In the *Metamorphoses,* Ovid retold many myths of the ancient world.

USE READING SKILLS

Context Clues Look at the three vocabulary words from the selection:

dominion
traverse
plumage

First, guess at their meanings. If you cannot guess, find the words underlined in the text and try to determine their meanings based on the context of the sentences in which you find them. Check your guesses against the definitions provided next to the selection.

Once you have the definitions of the words, consider what significance they may have in the story. Make up a brief summary of a story (no more than three sentences) that uses the three words. Summarize your own story using the three vocabulary words from the selection listed above. For example, if the three words were *serpent, levitating,* and *astonished,* you could write this summary of a story: "The snake charmer was able to get the serpent into a trance while levitating above his mat. The crowd was astonished by his feats."

APPLY THE MODEL

Landscape with the Fall of Icarus, c. 1558. Pieter Bruegel. Musées Royaux des Beaux-Arts, Brussels.

The Story of Dædalus and Icarus

from the Metamorphoses

An Epic Poem by **Ovid**

Translated by

Rolfe Humphries

Homesick for homeland, Dædalus[1] hated Crete[2]
And his long exile there, but the sea held him.
"Though Minos[3] blocks escape by land or water,"
Dædalus said, "surely the sky is open,
And that's the way we'll go. Minos' dominion
Does not include the air." He turned his thinking
Toward unknown arts, changing the laws of nature.
He laid out feathers in order, first the smallest,
A little larger next it, and so continued,
The way that pan-pipes[4] rise in gradual sequence.
He fastened them with twine and wax, at middle,
At bottom, so, and bent them, gently curving,
So that they looked like wings of birds, most surely.
And Icarus,[5] his son, stood by and watched him,
Not knowing he was dealing with his downfall,
Stood by and watched, and raised his shiny face
To let a feather, light as down, fall on it,
Or stuck his thumb into the yellow wax,

DURING READING

USE READING STRATEGIES

Make Inferences What does it suggest about Dædalus's scheme that he "...turned his thinking / Toward unknown arts, changing the laws of nature"?

do • min • ion (də min´ yən) *n.,* governed territory

DURING READING

ANALYZE LITERATURE

Foreshadowing What do lines 14–20 foreshadow? How does this passage affect your reading of the rest of the myth?

1. **Dædalus (ded´ ə ləs).** Inventor
2. **Crete (krēt).** Greek island
3. **Minos (mē´ nōs).** King of Crete
4. **pan-pipes.** Instruments made of reeds of various lengths
5. **Icarus (i´ kə rəs).** Son of Dædalus

Fooling around, the way a boy will, always,
Whenever a father tries to get some work done.
Still, it was done at last, and the father hovered,
Poised, in the moving air, and taught his son:
"I warn you, Icarus, fly a middle course:
Don't go too low, or water will weigh the wings down;
Don't go too high, or the sun's fire will burn them.
Keep to the middle way. And one more thing,
No fancy steering by star or constellation,
Follow my lead!" That was the flying lesson,
And now to fit the wings to the boy's shoulders.
Between the work and warning the father found
His cheeks were wet with tears, and his hands trembled.
He kissed his son (*Good-bye,* if he had known it),
Rose on his wings, flew on ahead, as fearful
As any bird launching the little nestlings[6]
Out of high nest into thin air. *Keep on,*
Keep on, he signals, *follow me!* He guides him
In flight—O fatal art!—and the wings move
And the father looks back to see the son's wings moving.
Far off, far down, some fisherman is watching
As the rod dips and trembles over the water,
Some shepherd rests his weight upon his crook,
Some ploughman on the handles of the ploughshare,
And all look up, in absolute amazement,
At those air-borne above. They must be gods!
They were over Samos, Juno's sacred island,
Delos and Paros toward the left, Lebinthus
Visible to the right, and another island,
Calymne,[7] rich in honey. And the boy
Thought *This is wonderful!* and left his father,
Soared higher, higher, drawn to the vast heaven,
Nearer the sun, and the wax that held the wings
Melted in that fierce heat, and the bare arms
Beat up and down in air, and lacking oarage[8]
Took hold of nothing. *Father!* he cried, and *Father!*
Until the blue sea hushed him, the dark water
Men call the Icarian now. And Dædalus,
Father no more, called "Icarus, where are you!

DURING READING

USE READING STRATEGIES

Make Predictions What will happen to Dædalus and Icarus? Will Icarus follow his father's warnings?

DURING READING

ANALYZE LITERATURE

Character From what you have read so far about Icarus, what can you say about his character?

6. **nestlings.** Young birds that have not left the nest yet
7. **Samos...Calymne** (kä lim´ nā). Greek islands in the Aegean Sea
8. **oarage.** Ability to propel

Where are you, Icarus? Tell me where to find you!"
And saw the wings on the waves, and cursed his talents,
Buried the body in a tomb, and the land
Was named for Icarus.
During the burial
A noisy partridge, from a muddy ditch,
Looked out, drummed with her wings in loud approval.
No other bird, those days, was like the partridge,
Newcomer to the ranks of birds; the story
Reflects no credit on Dædalus. His sister,
Ignorant of the fates, had sent her son
To Dædalus as apprentice, only a youngster,
Hardly much more than twelve years old, but clever,
With an inventive turn of mind. For instance,
Studying a fish's backbone for a model,
He had notched a row of teeth in a strip of iron,
Thus making the first saw, and he had bound
Two arms of iron together with a joint
To keep them both together and apart,
One standing still, the other traversing
In a circle, so men came to have the compass.
And Dædalus, in envy, hurled the boy
Headlong from the high temple of Minerva,
And lied about it, saying he had fallen
Through accident, but Minerva, kind protectress
Of all inventive wits, stayed him in air,
Clothed him with plumage; he still retained his aptness
In feet and wings, and kept his old name, Perdix,
But in the new bird-form, Perdix, the partridge,
Never flies high, nor nests in trees, but flutters
Close to the ground, and the eggs are laid in hedgerows.
The bird, it seems, remembers, and is fearful
Of all high places. ❖

DURING READING

USE READING STRATEGIES

Visualize How is a fish's backbone like a saw?

tra • verse (trə vʉrs´) *v.*, turn; travel across

plum • age (plüm´ ij) *n.*, bird's feathers

DURING READING

USE READING SKILLS

Context Clues What might be the meaning of the word *aptness?*

Why may young people disregard the advice of their parents or other adults? How does envy or jealousy motivate people? Is this type of motivation negative, or can it have positive outcomes?

AFTER READING

REFER TO TEXT ▶	REASON WITH TEXT	
1a. Name the island that Dædalus and Icarus are stranded on. What is their reason for wanting to leave?	1b. Describe Dædalus's skill, what this skill achieves for him, and how it causes problems.	**Understand** **Find meaning**
2a. Quote the advice that Dædalus provides to Icarus before they attempt to escape. What happens to Icarus?	2b. Examine whether or not Icarus's death can be blamed on someone other than himself. Who is responsible?	**Apply** **Use information**
3a. Why does Icarus disobey his father and fly too high?	3b. Conclude what lesson the ancient Romans may have drawn from Icarus's fate.	**Analyze** **Take things apart**
4a. How would you state the moral of the tale?	4b. "The Story of Dædalus and Icarus" is one of the most familiar stories in Western literature. Determine why it may have remained so popular.	**Evaluate** **Make judgments**
5a. Name the inventions created by Dædalus's nephew. What happens to the nephew because of these inventions?	5b. Based on the example of Minerva, summarize what you think the people of the ancient world believed about their gods. Explain your reasoning.	**Create** **Bring ideas together**

ANALYZE LITERATURE: Foreshadowing

The obvious foreshadowing of Icarus's death means that there really isn't much suspense in this story; most readers could have predicted that either Icarus or Dædalus would perish in their attempts to escape. What other purpose, then, do you think the author had in making the foreshadowing so evident?

EXTEND THE TEXT

Writing Options

Creative Writing Create a three-paragraph **myth** that explains the origin of something in the world around you. You might describe the origin of a natural object or a technological innovation, such as television or computers. If you wish, include supernatural elements such as the gods who intervene in the process.

Expository Writing In the library or from the Internet, choose a myth that is not in this textbook. Write a one-page **literary analysis** explaining the moral, or lesson about life, that this tale offers. Use details from the story to support your conclusion. If you need help in selecting a myth to analyze, ask your teacher or a librarian to assist you.

Collaborative Learning

Perform Reader's Theater Working in small groups, select gods and goddesses from Greek or Roman mythology. Make a poster that includes the names, descriptions, and reproductions of traditional images of these deities. Locate a myth in which a particular god or goddess plays a major role. Retell the story dramatically to the class as the group displays its poster.

Media Literacy

Find Media References to Mythology References to mythological characters or occurrences are often found in contemporary media. With a partner, find three 20th or 21st century references to Greek or Roman mythology in entertainment, advertising, or popular literature. Photocopy or clip any articles and advertisements. Analyze the influences of Greek and Roman mythology you found in each example.

Go to **www.mirrorsandwindows.com** for more.

Understanding Myths and Legends

MYTHS AND LEGENDS

Nearly every day, we encounter examples of the influence of ancient myths and age-old legends on our modern world. Did you eat *cereal* this morning? Perhaps you heard on the news that an unmanned research vehicle landed on *Mars.* If it's Valentine's Day, you may see cards decorated with a *Cupid,* a mischievous child with a bow and arrow. Or maybe it's just a *Thursday* in the month of *May* or *June.* Each of these situations or references contain an allusion to a myth or a legend, a story told and retold over decades or centuries. (See below.)

Cereal: from Cerealia, a festival for Ceres, the Roman goddess of the harvest
Mars: Roman god of war
Cupid: young Roman god, and the son of Venus, the goddess of love
Thursday: named after Thor, the Norse god of thunder
May: named after Maia, Greek goddess of the fields
June: named after Juno, the Roman goddess of marriage and women

Originally, myths and legends were used to explain the cause and occurrence of phenomena in the natural world. Since the advance of science, however, these tales are more often read or told to entertain rather than to instruct. Myths and legends do more than provide names for days and planets, however; they form a common point of reference and understanding within, and occasionally across, cultures.

Myths

Myths are traditional stories, rooted in particular cultures, that deal with gods and other supernatural beings as well as with human heroes. Myths often embody religious beliefs and values and explain natural phenomena. Every early culture around the globe has produced its own myths. In the Greek myth "Echo & Narcissus" (page 671), natural events are explained by the relationships or lack thereof among the many gods and goddesses in ancient Greece.

Legends

Legends are stories that often have mythic qualities and sometimes serve as morality lessons or tellers of cultural customs. Some are based on real historical figures, whereas others have a less certain origin. Even the legends about real people, however, are embellished with fantastic and sometimes superhuman aspects. As the stories are told over the years, they often change to reflect the cultures of the storytellers. For instance, the stories of King Arthur of England show him to be a good Christian king who sends his knights on a quest for the Holy Grail, the drinking vessel used by Christ. It is widely believed, however, that the real Arthur was probably a Welsh chieftain who lived during the pre-Christian era.

ELEMENTS OF MYTHS AND LEGENDS

Archetypes

Have you heard this story? A young lad goes on a quest for adventure. At first, the idea seems thrilling, but soon the adventures turn more dangerous and challenging. Along the way, the lad is aided by a wise old mentor who teaches him the skills he will need. However, the forces of evil eventually kill the mentor, leaving the young man to finish the quest on his own. Through many trials, the lad succeeds and realizes he has become a mature, capable man.

Perhaps you know that story as the movie *Star Wars.* Maybe you thought of the *Lord of the Rings* trilogy by J. R. R. Tolkien. Maybe Harry Potter or *Eragon* came to mind. The reason this plot sounds so familiar is that it is the basis of an archetypal story.

An **archetype** is a story, character, motif, or theme that represents a familiar pattern repeated throughout literature and across cultures. The psychologist Carl Jung popularized the term to refer to the idea of a "collective unconscious," which refers to the way in which certain compelling experiences become part of human consciousness and are passed down through generations. Perhaps that is why today's readers can so readily grasp the universal meaning of traditional forms of literature. We respond emotionally to familiar symbols—the hero, the mentor, the quest—precisely because our minds are ready to understand their significance.

For example, the sample story above involves the archetypal themes of a quest and of growing up. It also includes the archetypal characters of the boy hero becoming a man and the wise old mentor who must die before the boy can truly become the hero. Other archetypal topics, themes, characters, and symbols include death and rebirth, initiation, "boy-meets-girl," the thief who aids the poor, the damsel in distress, the trickster, and the dove as a symbol for peace.

Many myths and legends are based on archetypes that we immediately recognize, even though our actual experiences do not involve noble quests, talking animals, or magical beings.

Tricksters

The mythical character known as a **trickster** can be found in many cultures across the globe. The trickster, who is either an animal or a shape-shifter, is more than an annoyance to the mythical gods: He or she is often responsible for bringing important gifts to humanity, such as fire. In some instances, the trickster is also a creator, though he or she may bring disease, war, or other problems. These are some of the most famous tricksters in folk literature:

Eris.

- Hare (African; becomes Br'er Rabbit in the *Uncle Remus* stories and is the basis for Bugs Bunny)
- Coyote (Southwestern Native American)
- Loki (Norse)
- Anansi (West African; usually in spider form)
- Eshu (African, particularly Yoruba)
- Eris (Greek; the goddess of discord)
- Maui (Hawaiian)

Words from Mythology

Many words in the English language came from mythology. Do you recognize any of the following words?

- **narcissism:** This word means "To love oneself." It comes from the story of Narcissus, who fell in love with himself after seeing his own reflection in a pool.
- **nemesis:** This word means "someone who wants to bring about vengeance." It comes from the name of the goddess of vengeance.
- **meander:** This word is derived from the ancient Greek river Maiandros or Maeander, which was known for its crooked and winding course, and means "a bend in a river." The verb form of *meander* means "to wander aimlessly."
- **stoical:** This word comes from a school of Greek philosophy that believed that people hoping to be wise should be free of joy, grief, and passions. As it is used today, *stoical* typically means "impassive" or "not showing emotion or pain."

Modern Versions of Myths and Legends

Myths and legends endure in the modern world because they capture ideas about universal aspects of life. The stories have remained popular over the ages for their ability to entertain as well as to create a common understanding. These are but a few of the references you may find in speech and in writing:

- **Achilles' heel:** a person's weak spot
- **Siren:** an alluring singer who may lead listeners astray
- **Herculean effort or Herculean task:** something requiring incredible amounts of strength
- ***The Odyssey:*** modernized in the film *O Brother, Where Art Thou?*
- **characters named from Greek mythology:** (Morpheus, Niobe, the Oracle) as seen in the movie *The Matrix*
- **Cerberus:** the creature who guards the entrance to the Underworld, referenced in the three-headed dog in *Harry Potter and the Sorcerer's Stone*
- **Poseidon:** god of the sea, in the film *The Poseidon Adventure*

What 20th or 21st century literature can you think of that has been influenced by mythic literature?

Echo & Narcissus

BEFORE READING

A Myth Retold by Walker Brents

BUILD BACKGROUND

Literary Context The world of the ancient Greeks and Romans was populated with gods and goddesses. Although these supernatural beings had more authority than people, they were portrayed as experiencing human emotions such as jealousy and passion. In **"Echo & Narcissus,"** gods and other characters with special powers play a significant part in the lives of men and women and of other gods. As you read, consider how the myths may have helped young people become useful members of their community. In which ways did the ancient religions have a purpose similar to that of faiths today?

Reader's Context If you were at a loss for words or unable to get your point across, how might you handle the situation?

ANALYZE LITERATURE: Myth

A **myth** is a traditional story, rooted in a particular culture and dealing with gods, goddesses, and other supernatural beings, as well as with human heroes. Many myths are based on religious beliefs and helped the Greeks explain natural events. The story "Echo & Narcissus" explains the origin of two natural occurrences.

SET PURPOSE

As you read, look for the features that make "Echo & Narcissus" a myth. When you have finished the story, consider the purpose of such tales in a society that had little understanding of science and in which most people could not read or write. Think, too, of why the myths appeal to modern readers.

MEET THE AUTHOR

Walker Brents (b. 1959) is a poet and storyteller who has studied myths since, at age five, he discovered the tales of Hercules and the Greek gods. After majoring in English and philosophy at Drury College in Springfield, Missouri, Brents worked with the Jesuit Volunteer Corps. While working at a refugee center in southern California, he listened to the many stories of Vietnamese, Romanian, Laotian, and Cambodian emigrants. More recently, Brents has delighted listeners by narrating Hindu, Japanese, and Chinese myths and folk tales at the Asian Art Museum in San Francisco. He lectures each month on literary, historical, and mythological subjects at the Bird and Beckett Bookstore in San Francisco.

USE READING SKILLS

Evaluate Cause and Effect
Looking for a cause-and-effect connection between events in a story can help you understand motivation—the reasons the characters behave as they do. Realizing that one event causes another enables you to follow the narrative and to appreciate the unity of the tale. In tracking cause-and-effect connections, you might create a chart like the one below.

Cause	Effect	Summary
Narcissus's beauty	Everyone fell in love with him.	Unwanted attention made him scorn others.

PREVIEW VOCABULARY

Choose the best word from this list to complete the sentences: *oblivious, beguile, curtailed, disintegrated, enigmatic.* You may need to change the tenses of the verbs to fit the sentences.

1. The note _____ into tiny pieces after it had accidentally gone through the wash.
2. Peter turned up the volume on the TV, _____ to the fact that he was disturbing everyone's sleep.
3. Julia's answer was so _____ that I couldn't understand it at all.
4. After the army was defeated, the general's authority was _____.
5. When my nephew wouldn't stop crying, I _____ him by reading his favorite stories.

Echo & Narcissus

A Myth Retold by **Walker Brents**

"How is it that when I find my love, his very nearness keeps us far apart?"

Liriope the river nymph gave birth to a beautiful child. She brought him to the blind seer Tiresias to ask his destiny. Tiresias predicted that the boy would live a long life, but only if he never "came to know himself."

The child was named Narcissus. As he grew, his beauty increased. His dazzling looks had a strange effect upon the woodland spirits, the naiads and the dryads,[1] around whom he spent his days. They all fell in love with him, but he was oblivious, interested only in hunting in the hills with his companions. His pride in his beauty grew so great that he had nothing but scorn for the feelings of others.

There was one nymph, Echo by name, who saw Narcissus chasing deer into nets in the hills. Echo was instantly seized by love and could not overcome it. Secretly, she followed

1. **the naiads and the dryads.** Nymphs of the water and of trees

obliv • i • ous (ə bli´ vē əs) *adj.,* unaware; not paying attention

> **ANALYZE LITERATURE**
>
> **Myth** What elements in paragraphs 1–3 indicate that "Echo & Narcissus" is a myth?

him through the wilderness, waiting for her chance to make herself known to him—but one thing held her back: she could not initiate speech on her own. She could only repeat what was said to her. This was her condition, and it had come about because one day the goddess Hera was questioning the nymphs about her husband Zeus. She asked them where Zeus was, suspecting that the unfaithful god had been chasing the lovely nymphs and dwelling among them. Indeed he had, and while he was making his escape Echo distracted Hera with a flow of entertaining conversation. When Hera learned she had been fooled, she cursed Echo, saying, "From now on your words will not be your own. You will only be able to repeat what is said to you. That way your powers to beguile and distract will be curtailed."

Thereafter Echo could only repeat the words she heard. She could not announce herself to Narcissus. She trailed him silently, hoping for the right circumstance to meet him and declare her love. One day Narcissus had wandered away from his companions, and was in the forest looking for them. Echo was nearby, but Narcissus did not see her. "Is anyone here?" he cried. "Here," she answered. "Come to me," he called out. "Come to me," she replied. "Do not avoid me," he chided. She said the same to him. "Let us meet," he announced. This was her chance. She stepped out of hiding and stood before him smiling, saying, "Let us meet." He fell back from her scornfully. "You are not the one I seek. I would die before I would be near you." Echo advanced toward him, pleading, "I would be near you." But he ran from her.

> **USE READING STRATEGIES**
>
> **Clarify** Who is Narcissus expecting when Echo approaches him in the forest?

Haunted by his rejection and crushed by shame, Echo hid herself in caves and covered herself with leaves. She began to waste away and disappear. In the end only her bones were left, and these became rocks. But her voice remained. Travelers and wanderers heard it sometimes, answering them with their own words. Still Echo did not forget Narcissus.

Meanwhile, Narcissus too fell victim to a curse. Another nymph had fallen in love with him, but was also spurned. This one cried to the heavens for vengeance: "May Narcissus fall into a love that is not returned!" The goddess of righteous anger, Nemesis, heard these words. And so it happened that on a sunny and hot day Narcissus found himself at a pond to which no shepherd's flocks had been, from which no goats had drunk. It was a wild place. A green meadow surrounded it, and tall trees shaded it from the sun and sheltered it from winds. Putting his face to the waters in order to quench his thirst, Narcissus caught

be • guile (bi gī[ə]l´) *v.,* lead by deception; distract
cur • tail (ker['] tāl´) *v.,* make less, as if by cutting away a part

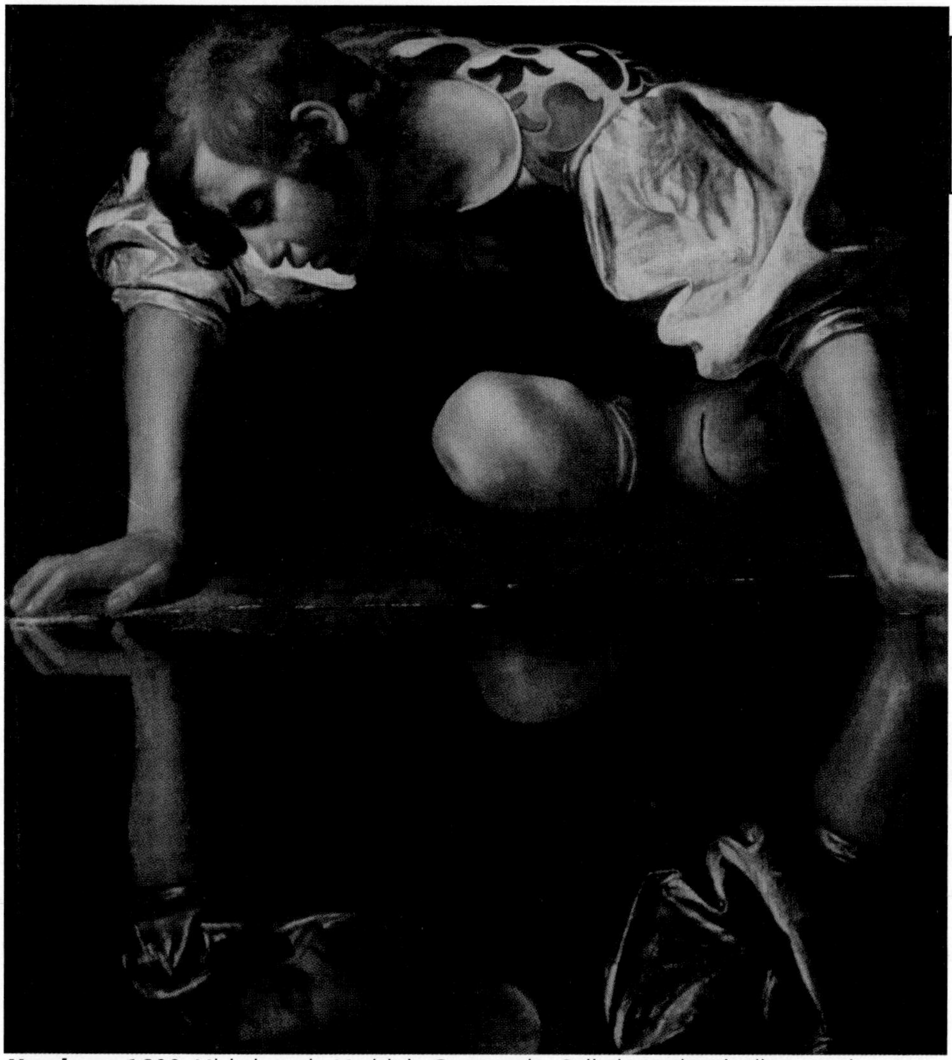

Critical Viewing

How does Caravaggio's painting illustrate Narcissus's plight?

Narcissus, 1600. Michelangelo Merisi da Caravaggio. Galleria Nazionale d'Arte Antica, Rome.

sight for the first time of his own reflection. He was astonished by the beautiful face that met his eye.

"What star-like eyes are these; what smooth skin! That forehead, that jaw, that gorgeous flowing hair! Who are you? Draw near to me!" He reached his hands to the water but the reflected image disintegrated. He waited for it to reappear. "Only the surface of these waters parts us. No fortress gates nor city walls; no long rocky highway, no impenetrable forest nor unclimbable mountain stands between us. Yet I cannot reach you! How can this be?" He cried to the endless skies, "How is it that when I find my love, his very nearness keeps us far apart?" But there was no answer.

Narcissus could not leave this place. Entranced by his own reflection he began to waste away from hunger and thirst. His strength and his life ebbed[2] away and did not return. Echo hovered around him, invisible and unforgetting. Her

USE READING SKILLS

Evaluate Cause and Effect How does Nemesis's punishment of Narcissus result from Tiresias's prediction (in paragraph 1) of the boy's fate?

2. **ebbed.** Fell to a lower or worse condition

dis • in • te • grate (dis['] in´ tə grāt') *v.*, to break or fall apart disembodied voice repeated his final word, which was "Alas." He died and his spirit left his body. Even on the boat of souls, crossing the river between this world and the other one, Narcissus leaned over the edge, looking into those waters, trying to catch a glimpse of the image that so captivated him.

The nymphs heard of his death and went to the pond to retrieve his body for the funeral ceremony. But when they got there they found no corpse, only a new blossom with snowy petals and a yellow corona.[3] The flower came to be called "Narcissus," in honor of one who, in the <u>enigmatic</u> words of Tiresias, "came to know himself," and fell in love. ❖

3. **corona.** The trumpet-shaped cup of flowers such as the daffodil

enig • mat • ic (e' nig['] ma´ tik *or* ē' nig['] ma´ tik) *adj.*, mysterious; hard to figure out

What does the expression "Let the punishment fit the crime" mean? Do people usually agree with the idea?

AFTER READING

REFER TO TEXT	▶ REASON WITH TEXT	
1a. Recall what Echo had done to anger Hera.	1b. Describe what motivates Hera as she chooses a punishment for Echo.	Understand **Find meaning**
2a. What remains of Echo at the end of the myth?	2b. Employing what you have learned about Greek mythology, how do you think these stories might be used by the ancient Greeks?	Apply **Use information**
3a. Identify why Narcissus is mesmerized by the image in the pond. What replaces his body?	3b. Analyze why this object would be chosen as a replacement for Narcissus.	Analyze **Take things apart**
4a. Indicate why Echo and Narcissus have been punished. What are the punishments?	4b. Justify whether or not you think the punishment Echo and Narcissus each receive is fair.	Evaluate **Make judgments**
5a. Recognize whether Nemesis's choice of punishment for Narcissus "fits the crime."	5b. Imagine if this type of justice were possible in today's society. Generate and describe punishments you might see among your peers, yourself, and society as a whole. Try to think of punishments that would leave a lasting impression on those around you.	Create **Bring ideas together**

ANALYZE LITERATURE: Myth

Which elements of "Echo & Narcissus" make it a myth? What does the story indicate about acceptable and unacceptable behavior in ancient Greek culture? In which way might these standards contribute to society as a whole?

EXTEND THE TEXT

Writing Options

Creative Writing The magazine *Poetry for Youth* is having a contest and would like you to write and submit a one-page **poem** about Echo and Narcissus. You can write a *narrative poem,* one that tells the characters' story (include *dialogue,* or conversation). Or you can write a *lyric poem,* in which you express feelings (the characters' or an observer's) about the events.

Expository Writing You have been asked to meet with a group of psychology students who are examining the behaviors of characters in Greek myths. Write a one-page **compare-and-contrast essay** of Echo and Narcissus (either one or both) to today's youth. Focus on the similarities and differences between the personality traits of the Greek character(s) and personal qualities that psychologists might observe in young people today.

Collaborative Learning

Teach a Science Lesson With a partner or in a small group, prepare a science lesson for elementary school students on the echo. Do simple research, if you need to, in the library or on the Internet, on where and why echoes occur. You can display your findings on a chart or a poster board. Be prepared to answer questions from the young students.

Media Literacy

Create a Modern Myth Imagine that a community has suffered from a natural disaster. Ordinary laws and regulations cannot be enforced because newspapers, radio, and TV are not functioning. With a small group, create a myth that will provide a sense of order and of respect among citizens, and develop innovative ways to circulate the myth in the community. Explain how your myth will provide a sense of order without limiting the rights of individuals.

Go to **www.mirrorsandwindows.com** for more.

READING ASSESSMENT

1. Number these events in the correct sequence, with 1 being the first one to happen and 5 being the last.
   ___ Echo falls in love with Narcissus.
   ___ Nemesis, the goddess of righteous anger, punishes Narcissus.
   ___ Echo is punished by Hera for deception.
   ___ The nymphs find only a yellow-and-white flower by the pond.
   ___ Another nymph shouts a curse against Narcissus.

2. On page 674, the term *enigmatic* most nearly means
   A. ancient.
   B. unfathomable.
   C. sinister.
   D. energetic.
   E. huge.

3. Which of the following reasons does *not* cause Narcissus to die young?
   A. He falls in love with his reflection in the water.
   B. He rejects Echo and the other nymphs who love him.
   C. He is excessively proud of his beauty.
   D. He realizes how cruel he has been to Echo.
   E. He cannot see past his own beauty.

4. In which ways are Echo and Narcissus similar?
   A. Neither is able to love another human nor to speak clearly.
   B. Both are punished by the gods and goddesses, and both die of a broken heart.
   C. Both are respectful of the gods but disrespectful of nature.
   D. Both try to trick the gods and to ignore those who are less attractive.
   E. Neither obeys the laws of society and instead does whatever he or she wishes.

5. What provides Echo with the opportunity to finally "speak" with Narcissus?
   A. Narcissus's friends organize their meeting without his knowledge.
   B. Narcissus notices Echo among the trees and initiates the conversation.
   C. She sends him a beautifully written letter.
   D. Narcissus has lost his friends in the forest and is calling for them to reappear.
   E. The gods change Narcissus into a flower.

6. Why might societies in early human history have developed myths? What is the benefit of myths in a society?

GRAMMAR & STYLE

UNDERSTAND THE CONCEPT

APPLY THE SKILL

Coordination, Subordination, and Apposition

Coordinating conjunctions join words, phrases, or clauses of equal importance in a sentence. Common coordinating conjunctions are *and, or, nor, for, but, yet,* and *so.* A comma is used before a coordinating conjunction to join two complete sentences.

EXAMPLES

Echo was instantly seized by love and could not overcome it. [joins a compound verb]
They all fell in love with him, but he was oblivious. [connects two complete thoughts to form a compound sentence]

Subordinating conjunctions join two phrases or clauses that are not of equal importance. Examples of subordinating conjunctions are *after, before, if, than, since, unless, when,* and *while.* A comma is used after a subordinating phrase or clause at the beginning of a sentence.

EXAMPLES

When Hera learned she had been fooled, she cursed Echo.
Tiresias predicted that the boy would live a long life if he never came to know himself.
After Hera placed the curse, Echo was unable to speak on her own.

An **appositive** is a noun that is placed next to another noun to identify or clarify it.

EXAMPLES

Hera was searching for her husband, Zeus. [The noun *Zeus* identifies the noun *husband.*]
Echo, a nymph, distracted Hera long enough for Zeus to escape. [The noun *nymph* clarifies who *Echo* is.]

An **appositive phrase** includes an appositive and other words that modify it; the whole phrase modifies or clarifies the noun.

EXAMPLE

Narcissus's love, his own reflection in a calm pond, made it so he would not leave the water's edge. [The appositive phrase renames the noun *love.*]

Essential or **restrictive appositives** specifically identify the noun that precedes them. **Nonessential** or **nonrestrictive appositives** are not necessary to identify the noun and are set off by commas.

EXAMPLES

The myth "Echo & Narcissus" explains the origins of the echo. [restrictive]
"Echo & Narcissus," a myth retold by Walker Brents, shows the perils of self-obsession. [nonrestrictive]

REVIEW TERMS

- **coordinating conjunction:** a word that joins words, phrases, or clauses of equal importance in a sentence
- **subordinating conjunction:** a word that joins two phrases or clauses that are not of equal importance
- **appositive:** a noun placed next to another noun to identify or clarify it
- **essential** or **restrictive appositive:** a phrase or clause that specifically identifies the noun that precedes it
- **nonessential** or **nonrestrictive appositive:** a phrase or clause that is not necessary to identify the noun
- **appositive phrase:** a group of words made up of an appositive and all its modifiers. The phrase renames or identifies a noun or a pronoun.
- **clause:** a group of words that contain both a subject and a verb

UNDERSTAND THE CONCEPT

APPLY THE SKILL

Identify Coordination, Subordination, and Apposition

Identify whether the following sentences use coordination, subordination, apposition, or a combination thereof.

1. The river nymph Liriope gave birth to Narcissus.
2. She went to Tiresias, the blind seer, to ask about his destiny.
3. His beauty made the naiads and the dryads fall in love with him.
4. The woodland spirits swooned, but Narcissus ignored them.
5. When Narcissus chased deer in the hills, Echo saw him and fell in love.
6. Although Echo longed to meet him, she could not introduce herself, for she had been cursed by Hera.
7. Echo had distracted Hera, Zeus's wife, by her conversation while Zeus made his escape.
8. Narcissus called out for his companions, so Echo was able to repeat his words back to him and show herself to him.
9. After Narcissus rejected her, Echo wasted away and disappeared.
10. The goddess of righteous anger, Nemesis, heard the other nymph's cry for vengeance.

Improve the Use of Conjunctions

Rewrite each of the following sentences, filling the blank with an appropriate coordinating or subordinating conjunction.

1. Echo was haunted by Narcissus's rejection ___ crushed by shame.
2. ____ she had dwindled to nothing but a voice, Echo still remembered Narcissus.
3. Another nymph then fell in love with him, ____ she was likewise spurned.
4. ____ the nymph cried for vengeance, Nemesis responded by granting her wish.
5. A green meadow surrounded the pond, ___ tall trees shaded it from the sun.
6. It was here that Narcissus met his destiny ___ he saw his own reflection in the pond.
7. He fell in love with his reflection ___ would not leave the spot.
8. Echo repeated his final word _____ he died.
9. The nymphs went to retrieve his body, ___ they only found a flower.
10. The flower was named after the man who "came to know himself" ___ he fell in love.

Use Conjunctions and Appositives in Your Writing

Write a paragraph in which you describe a time when either you experience unrequited love (love that is not returned) or "righteous anger," as the nymphs experience in "Echo & Narcissus." Describe the circumstance as though you and the other people involved are mythic characters. Use coordinating and subordinating conjunctions, as well as appositives, to make connections between ideas and to make your writing flow more smoothly.

EXTEND THE SKILL

Find a picture of a group of people. You can use a photograph of your own or a picture from a magazine. Write one or two sentences about each person, such as what he or she does and how he or she is related to the other people in the picture. You will need to indicate which person in the photo is being described in the sentence, so appositives may help you do that; for example, you could write, "Miriam, the woman in the green dress, is the oldest daughter of my next-door neighbor." You can write factual information about the people or invent background information for them. To put the most information into each sentence, try to use coordination, subordination, and appositives.

The Silver Pool

BEFORE READING

A Legend Retold by Ella Young

GUIDED READING

BUILD BACKGROUND

Cultural Context The main character in **"The Silver Pool"** is Fionn MacCumhail (pronounced "Finn McCool" by English speakers), a famous Irish hero. According to tradition, Fionn followed in his father's footsteps to become chief of the king of Ireland's army, a band of warriors known as the *Fianna.* Irish legends have been passed on orally since ancient times. The stories of Fionn MacCumhail, collectively called the Fionn Saga, reflect a period, before the eighth century, when Ireland was organized into clans, which paid homage to the high king of Ireland, at Tara. Each clan chief or king kept an official poet, or Druid. In "The Silver Pool," Fionn seeks out the Druid Finnegas to learn the ancient poetry and tales of Ireland.

Reader's Context What are your long-term dreams or goals? What obstacles do you expect to encounter in meeting those goals?

ANALYZE LITERATURE: Legend

A **legend** is a story that comes down from the past and is often based on real events or characters from ancient times. Unlike myths, legends are popularly regarded as historical; however, they may contain fantastic or difficult-to-prove elements. Consider which characters, descriptions, or events in "The Silver Pool" are generally realistic and which have been embroidered by the imaginations of the narrators over the generations.

SET PURPOSE

While reading "The Silver Pool," notice the flowery language and special names for Irish traditions, such as the *Pool of the Star-Dance.* How are a society's values and beliefs expressed through the legends it creates?

MEET THE AUTHOR

Ella Young (1867–1956) was born in the small village of Feenagh, in County Antrim, Ireland. After she grew older and moved to Dublin, Ireland's capital city, Young met a group of Irish literature scholars and began collecting legends. Young said, "I read every translation I could get, learned Irish, and betook myself to Gaelic Ireland where, by turf fires, I could hear the poems of the Fianna recited by folk who had heard the faery music and danced in faery circles." In *The Tangle-Coated Horse,* Young retells many of the old tales of Fionn and the Fianna.

USE READING SKILLS

Draw Conclusions When you **draw conclusions,** you take clues from the text and combine them with other information, either from your prior knowledge or from the text, to draw a conclusion. A conclusion is a theory about what is happening, has happened, or will happen and why. For example, when the man in "The Silver Pool" says there is only one fish he wishes to catch, you might conclude that this fish will play an important role in the story. To help you draw conclusions, create a chart like the one below. As you read the story, fill in the statement or action and the conclusion you came to based on it.

Statement or Action	Conclusion

PREVIEW VOCABULARY

Preview vocabulary words from this selection as they are used in the sentences below. Look for context clues that help you unlock the meanings of the words.

1. Amorous of legends, I enjoy reading about Finn McCool.
2. If you consort with storytellers, you may end up telling interesting stories.
3. The writer's stratagem for writing the best folk tale seemed clever, but it failed.
4. Today, most people accept that they cannot know the future; in ancient times, people often relied on prophecy.
5. Wanting to hear the legend, we made a foray into the room.

The Silver Pool

Still Life of a Salmon on a Riverbank in a Mountainous Landscape, c. 1700s.
John Russell. Bonhams, London.

A Legend Retold by **Ella Young**

Fionn leaped to his feet, flung the sword into the air, caught it midway and whirled it about his head.

Fionn walked sturdily forward. Birds were singing in leafy branches. The river Boyne showed a gleam of silver between tree-trunks; it made a soft plashing sound among its reeds. Fionn whistled a little tune as he walked. He had no plan in his mind, save to meet what happened: and day by day to grow tall and strong so that some day he might wrest the Treasure-Wallet from Lia of Luachra; avenge his father's wrong; and win to the headship of the Fianna. Many moons had withered in the sky since he had said farewell to Bovemall and Liath[1] and the kindly oak forest. Many a buffet[2] fate had dealt him since then: many a sharp and evil chance he had known; many a good happening. He had set eyes on many a hill, many a valley since then: he had seen many a proud chieftain's lime-washed dune.[3] Sun had tanned him. His bright hair was cropped like the hair of a churl,[4] chariot-dust of the roadway had grimed his deerskin tunic: save for the pride

USE READING STRATEGIES

Visualize What details used in describing Fionn indicate how long he has been traveling?

1. **Bovemall and Liath.** Two old women who raised Fionn in the forest
2. **buffet** (bʉˊ fət). A blow, especially by the hand
3. **dune.** Hill or ridge of sand piled up by the wind
4. **churl.** A rude, vulgar, or unsophisticated person

of his walk there was little to betray the chief's son in him.

The morning was hot, and the plashy sound of the Boyne drew Fionn to the river side. Picking his way between alder and willow and flowering rush he came to where the water swirled in silvery singing reaches in the pool that is called the Pool of the Star-Dance. By the pool was a man in the garb[5] of the fisher-folk drawing to land a small casting-net. There were silver-gleaming trout spotted with crimson in the net, but the man took them one by one and threw them into the pool again.

"One fish alone I am eager to snare," said the man, "and that is the purple-finned crimson-banded Salmon of Knowledge…."

"Greeting to you," said Fionn, as he drew near, "and luck on your fishing."

"I have no luck on my fishing," said the man.

"It is a strange thing, indeed," said Fionn, "that you make naught[6] of the red-spotted trout of the Boyne. There's few but yourself would grumble at so good a catch."

"One fish alone I am eager to snare," said the man, "and that is the purple-finned crimson-banded Salmon of Knowledge that has gold of the sun and silver of the moon in every scale of him."

"A wise woman taught me," said Fionn, "that the Salmon of Knowledge swims in the Heaven-World in the pool of the Sacred Hazels."

"She might have taught you, to boot," said the man, "that whatever happens in the Heaven-World makes a shadow of itself here. It is in this pool, they say, that the shadow-self of the Salmon of Knowledge swims. I would snare it."

"I have heard that men of learning and poets can snare the Salmon in a net made of their dreams," said Fionn, "and have thereafter one shining scale of him. You that are the Flower of Poets and the Jewel of Learning should have more than one scale."

"Why do you use this manner of speech to me, that am naught but a plain fisherman?"

"I know you for the King's Poet," said Fionn. "In the year of the Great Assembly I saw you riding on a white stallion with the mane and tail dyed purple; you were wearing the singing robe and the head-dress of a royal poet, and you had fifty princes in your train. I was crouching in the thickness of an oak-bough when you rode past the Wood of the Golden Hawks, and I thought that if I had choice of speech with any one man that went by me there in a flashing chariot, or on a proud-stepping horse, I would choose to have speech with you."

USE READING STRATEGIES

Clarify Why does Fionn wish to assist the fisherman? What does the fisherman have to offer?

"What help is there in words?" said the man. "You could not teach me how to snare the Salmon: I could not teach you more wood-craft than you know already."

"You could teach me poetry," said Fionn; "and I could serve you: cut rushes for your bed; bring you eggs of the wild duck; and deer from the mountain, with swift hares of the valley."

5. **garb.** Style of clothing
6. **naught.** Nothing

Critical Viewing

How does the accompanying art reflect the emotions and experiences of Fionn?

"What learning and what arts and what weapon-knowledge have you come by?" asked the man.

"Sword-craft I had from a robber that forced me to consort with him. I herded cows for a herb-leech[7] and learned the virtues of herbs. The ways of horses I learned among horse-boys. The forest taught me wood-craft; but he who is ignorant of poetry is but a churl!"

"You shall serve me," said the man, "what name have you? I am, as is known to you, Finnegas the Poet."

USE READING SKILLS

Draw Conclusions When Fionn says his name is Demna, the narrator notes that "Fionn" is a nickname. Why might this fact be significant?

"Demna is my name," said Fionn, and in this he spake truth, for the name Fionn, which means Beautiful One, was a nickname.

So it came to pass that Fionn abode with the King's Poet. He plaited[8] mats of rushes, he snared wild fowl, he culled[9] water-cress and sweet and bitter herbs of the field such as go with savory meats, he pounded acorns and made bread as he had seen Bovemall do in the forest. And the King's Poet talked with him of heroes and kings and of the art of verse and the ceremonial of palaces. Fionn stored these conversations in his mind: and always he practised with his sling at casting stones, and with a sword of wood at thrusting and parrying,[10] and with a pole cut from an ash tree he practised the hurling of spears. He ran, and jumped, and wrestled with tough boughs and saplings, so that he might grow in strength and hardihood. He put words together in praise of forest things and in praise of the small blossoms of the field and the songs of the blackbird and thrush: the King's Poet taught him how to shape them till he could make good well-hammered verse.

7. **herb-leech.** Healer that specializes in herbs and other plants
8. **plaited.** Braided or woven
9. **culled.** Selected from a group; chose
10. **parrying.** Warding off a weapon or a blow

con • sort (kən sôrt´ *or* kän´ sôrt *or* kän' sôrt´) *v.*, to keep company (typically with undesirable people; usually followed by the word *with*)

Finn McCool, 1928. Vera Bock.

USE READING STRATEGIES

Ask Questions What has Fionn learned from Finnegas?

On a day of the days it chanced that Fionn had been praised for a poem, and in lightness of heart he set off to search for eggs of the plover[11] that are delicate to the taste, for he had in mind to make festival for the King's Poet: that had naught himself in mind but the swirling of the Boyne and the Salmon that might lurk in the shallows, or in deep melodious reaches of the waters.

Fionn got the eggs and turned homeward. As he went, his foot struck on something hard, and stooping he saw a piece of strangely shaped greenish metal that had thrust from the marsh-soil. There was something familiar in the curve of it, and his hands dug eagerly into the grass-roots; more and more eagerly as the treasure unbared itself. At last he drew it forth—a bronze sword, double-edged and perfect! A sword that Gobniu the Smith might have fashioned: a sword that Lugh might have reddened in the battle of Moytirra. Fionn rubbed it with a bunch of grass till it shone greenly, he fingered the finely tapered edges, he gripped the hilt: and all the while the tears ran down his face.

"My Treasure," he cried, "If Uail could see you; or Bovemall that had no sword to give me! If Crimmall[12] knew I had you, his heart would be glad. I will show you to the sunlight. I will take you where you can hear loud battle-shouts—loud as those you heard before the man that had you flung you from him lest his slayers should boast of you! Flame of Battle be glad of me—be glad of me!"

Fionn leaped to his feet, flung the sword into the air, caught it midway and whirled it about his head. Then he gathered up his plover eggs and set off at a run.

As he neared the pool where the King's Poet fished, day in and day out, he saw that something must have happened. The King's Poet was coming hastily to him gesticulating and shouting. Fionn hurried a little more and caught the words.

"I have snared him! I have snared him," the King's Poet was shouting, "I have snared the Salmon of Knowledge!"

And sure enough a small salmon, all silver-scaled and blue and carmine[13] spotted, lay glinting on the bank.

"By what token do you know it for the Salmon of Knowledge?" asked Fionn.

"Never have I snared the like of it," said the King's Poet, "and there is a prophecy that the Salmon of Knowledge will be snared in this pool, and eaten by a poet named Finnegas or Fionn. Now I am Finnegas and I will eat this Salmon."

"Indeed you shall eat it with heartiness and enjoyment," said Fionn, "and I will broil it for you as Bovemall taught me to broil the salmon

11. **plover.** Shore bird similar to a sandpiper
12. **Crimmall.** Fionn's uncle, the brother of his father, Uail
13. **carmine.** Vivid red

proph • e • cy (prä´ fə sē) *n.,* prediction; foretelling of later event

> **ANALYZE LITERATURE**
>
> **Legend** Identify two or three features of a legend in the passage describing Fionn's trip homeward after he gathers the plover eggs.

of the Shannon[14] that are kings' food. I have plover eggs too, and sharptasting herbs: sweet and bitter."

"I will touch naught but the Salmon, that I may have wisdom through it," said Finnegas.

Fionn made ready an oven and broiled the Salmon: but sitting by it, his mind wandered to the sword, and a flame licked the salmon-scales. Fionn turned the fish hastily and as he did so, a little bit of scale stuck to his thumb and burned him. He thrust his thumb into his mouth without thinking and so tasted the Salmon. He watched his work carefully after that, and when the fish was cooked through and through he brought it to Finnegas. Finnegas prepared to eat it as one should eat a sacred fish.

Fionn sat by the river bank and his thoughts were on his sword. Suddenly he was aware that the King's Poet stood beside him.

"A strange thing has happened, Demna," said the Poet, "the savor and virtue[15] of the Salmon have gone. It is as any other fish. Can it be that you have tricked me and have eaten of it?"

"Nay," said Fionn, "I have not tasted of it, save for a scale that clung, burning, to my thumb."

"That scale has taken the virtue of the fish," said the Poet, "and yet it is strange that a prophecy could be so easily broken. The Salmon was for a poet called Fionn, or Finnegas—and you are Demna!"

"Demna is my name, but I am called Fionn: it is a nickname that stuck to me."

"Fionn, henceforth, will be your true name: for now I see that the Salmon was meant for you. It is not to one who is weary of mart[16] and court and battleground that the Salmon of Knowledge will give himself, but to one who is eager for the sword-hilt and amorous of life."

"I have a sword," cried Fionn, "a sword for a king it is! a luck-bringer, a battle-queller, a singer of war-songs!"

He held up the sword, his eyes caressing it.

Finnegas took it in his hands.

"May luck be with it," he said, "it is indeed a royal sword. How came you by it?"

Fionn told the story of its finding.

"Some Lord of the Shining Folk[17] has blessed this day for you," said Finnegas. "Salmon and Sword! What have you in mind to do with your fortune?"

"I have in mind to avenge my father that was treacherously slain."

"What man was your father?" asked Finnegas, "I know well you are no churl's son."

"I would name my father," said Fionn, "only to one that had loved him, or to the High King of Ireland on that day when I win back my heritage. I am no churl's son, Finnegas, and if I live I will set poetry as a craft for warriors. I will come, too—if I win out—to seek you in whatever place you may be!"

"I know not in what place I may be," said Finnegas, "mayhap at Tara with the High King; mayhap in some mountain wilderness; mayhap in this hut by the river, if I be not under the sod—but tell me what way of life do you plan for yourself: for I know you will not tarry[18] with me longer."

"I purpose to join with myself other lads, as I find them," said Fionn, "and practise feats and stratagems till we can make ourselves felt in some foray and come by weapons: then we will seek a warrior that is kin to me—outlawed

14. **Shannon.** River that flows in western Ireland
15. **virtue.** The beneficial quality or power of something
16. **mart.** Market
17. **Shining Folk.** Gods
18. **tarry.** Delay or be tardy; to remain in or at a place

am • o • rous (a´ mə rəs *or* am´ rəs) *adj.,* being in love; enamored (usually followed by the word *of*)
strat • a • gem (stra´ tə jəm *or* stra´ tə jem') *n.,* a trick or scheme to achieve an aim
for • ay (fôr´ ā' *or* fär´ ā *or* fô rā´ *or* fə rā´) *n.,* sudden invasion or attack

USE READING SKILLS

Draw Conclusions
Based on what you know about legends, decide whether or not Finnegas's prediction is possible.

now and in hiding—and do as his wisdom counsels."

"I dare predict that you will win your heritage," said the King's Poet. "Eat now the Salmon, and we will spend the hours that remain to us in the telling of tales and the recital of poems and in sound sleep: that tomorrow may be fortunate for your setting forth."

So Fionn ate the Salmon, and wondered if its wisdom would help him to find lads like himself, eager to venture; comrades of the Sword and the Treasure-Wallet. And the King's Poet ate the plover eggs with the sweet and bitter herbs; and wondered whether it would be wise to go back again to the bright-colored loud-sounding life of palaces; or wiser to stay in the little hut by the Boyne, watching cloud-shadows: and herons brooding on reedy pools. ❖

Do most people appear to believe that the future is open to possibilities or already determined? Would knowing whether or not it was open or predetermined be a relief or a discouragement?

AFTER READING

REFER TO TEXT ▶▶▶▶	▶ REASON WITH TEXT	
1a. Write a brief outline of Fionn's goals at the start of his journey. Whom is he seeking?	1b. Explain why he seeks this person. How will this person help him reach his goals?	**Understand** **Find meaning**
2a. Fionn tells Finnegas that he will reveal his father's name only under certain conditions. List these conditions.	2b. Knowing what you do about Fionn and his quest, examine why you think these conditions are important.	**Apply** **Use information**
3a. Recall how Fionn came to eat the fish before Finnegas.	3b. Analyze why Finnegas, who has been eager to catch the fish, would agree so quickly that the Salmon "was meant for" Fionn.	**Analyze** **Take things apart**
4a. Identify what Fionn has gained from staying with Finnegas.	4b. Decide whether or not you agree that leaders must begin as poets (or as educated people) and must learn survival skills. Explain.	**Evaluate** **Make judgments**
5a. State what Fionn decides to do after he mistakenly eats the Salmon.	5b. Document how you believe Fionn will fare in his upcoming journey. What events support your deduction?	**Create** **Bring ideas together**

ANALYZE LITERATURE: Legend

Which incidents, details, character traits, and descriptions in the legend "The Silver Pool" seem realistic, and which seem fantastic? How do realism and fantasy appeal to the audience? What does the presence of the two approaches in a work suggest about its creators' view of life?

EXTEND THE TEXT

Writing Options

Creative Writing A field guide is a book used by naturalists and botanists (scientists who study plants) to identify animals and plants found in nature. The book includes descriptions and, usually, drawings or photographs of various species. Write a **field guide entry** for the Salmon of Knowledge. How would you describe the magical fish so that visitors to the area can recognize it? If you like, you may also draw or paint the fish to illustrate the entry.

Expository Writing A classmate has several questions about "The Silver Pool." Why, for instance, is the Salmon given a key role in the tale, and why would eating it provide knowledge? Why was poetry of such importance to the ancient Irish? And what happens to the hero in other tales in the Fionn Saga? Research the answers to these questions (or others you may have) on the Internet or in the library and write a three- to four-paragraph **informative essay.**

Collaborative Learning

Create a News Segment Imagine that you are a television reporter in Fionn MacCumhail's day. The news has reached you that the Salmon of Knowledge has been caught, and you would like to do a feature story on Fionn. Work in small groups. One of you can play the news anchor; another, the on-site reporter; others, Fionn, Finnegas, and other characters who would add to the impact. The anchor can introduce the story; the reporter can provide details about when and how the Salmon was caught.

Critical Literacy

Compare Legends and Myths The legend "The Silver Pool" and the myth "Echo & Narcissus" have certain motifs and elements in common. With a partner, read the entries for *motif, myth,* and *legend* in the Handbook of Literary Terms found in the back of this textbook. Which motifs do the stories have in common? Why is one of the works considered a legend and the other a myth? Could the labels be interchanged? Explain.

Go to **www.mirrorsandwindows.com** for more.

READING ASSESSMENT

1. Number these events in the correct chronological sequence, with 1 being the first to happen and 6 being the last.
   ___ Fionn refuses to tell his father's name.
   ___ In speaking to the King's Poet, Fionn refers to himself as Demna.
   ___ Finnegas says that the shadow-self of the Salmon swims in the pool.
   ___ Finnegas predicts that Fionn will regain his heritage.
   ___ Fionn finds a bronze sword in the marshland.
   ___ "I have snared him!" the King's Poet was shouting.

2. As it is used on page 683, the term *amorous* most closely means
   A. watched over.
   B. tolerate.
   C. indifferent.
   D. loathe.
   E. fascinated with.

3. Which of the following are *not* features of a legend?
   A. unexpected or coincidental happenings
   B. predictions of events
   C. events based on historical documents
   D. heroes based on historical figures
   E. fantastic and hard-to-prove elements

4. Fionn probably introduces himself to the King's Poet as Demna, a name he rarely uses, because
   A. Fionn doesn't like his nickname.
   B. Fionn wants to trick the King's Poet.
   C. Fionn is still seeking his true identity.
   D. Fionn thinks it is more proper not to use his nickname.
   E. Fionn thinks that the King's Poet will laugh at his nickname.

5. Why does Finnegas accept that the Salmon of Knowledge was not meant for himself?
   A. He learns that Demna is also known as Fionn.
   B. He no longer yearns, as Fionn does, for a life of adventure.
   C. He does not want to question a prophecy.
   D. A and B
   E. B and C

6. "The Silver Pool" includes several instances in which appearance differs from reality. For instance, Fionn looks like a churl but is, in fact, the son of a chief. Give other examples of appearance versus reality from the tale.

GRAMMAR & STYLE

UNDERSTAND THE CONCEPT APPLY THE SKILL

Semicolons and Colons

A **semicolon** joins two closely related sentences; the mark of punctuation is also used between items in a series when the items contain internal commas.

EXAMPLES

His foot struck something in the soil**;** he felt a piece of metal on his boot.
The young man would hunt rabbits, gather eggs, and cut grass**;** run, jump, and wrestle with branches**;** and write poetry.

- Use a semicolon to join the independent clauses of a compound sentence if no coordinating conjunction, such as *and, but, so, or, nor, for,* and *yet* appears. Semicolons can also be used in place of the comma and the coordinating conjunction.

EXAMPLES

The legends may be based on a warrior in early Britain**, and** they are similar in some ways to the Fionn Saga.
The legends may be based on a warrior in early Britain**;** they are similar in some ways to the Fionn Saga.

- Use a semicolon between independent clauses joined by a conjunction if either clause contains commas.

EXAMPLE

Fionn finds a sword in the marshland**; and** Arthur, for his part, pulls a sword from a stone.

- Use a semicolon between items in a series if the items contain commas.

EXAMPLE

The Arthurian tales include the settling of Britain by a Roman hero named Brutus**;** characters like Lear and Cymbeline, familiar to readers of Shakespeare**;** and Merlin, the famous magician.

- Use a semicolon between independent clauses joined by a conjunctive adverb or a transitional phrase.

EXAMPLE

Arthur is believed to have fought against the invading Saxons**; however,** the German tribe later conquered the island nation.

A **colon** is a punctuation mark that tells the reader to "note what follows."

EXAMPLE

While Fionn lived with the King's Poet, he completed many daily chores**:** plaiting mats of rushes, culling water-cress, and snaring wild fowl.

- Use a colon to introduce a list of items.

EXAMPLE

In the legends, you'll observe several themes**:** loyalty and disloyalty, heroic valor, treachery and deceit, and the role of warfare in society.

- Use a colon to introduce a quotation or a long or formal statement, or between two independent clauses when the second clause explains or summarizes the first. Always capitalize the first word following a colon if the word begins a complete sentence.

EXAMPLES

To his knights, Arthur expressed himself clearly**:** "You are to act in the best interests of the king and of the people."
There may be a reason why the Arthurian legends are better known than the Fionn Saga**:** Unlike the Irish tales, the stories of Arthur were narrated in many languages.

- Use a colon between numbers that tell hours and minutes, and after the greeting in a business letter.

EXAMPLES

The performance of *Camelot,* based on the Arthurian tales, starts at 8**:**00 PM.
Dear Ms. Guinevere**:**

- Do not use a colon after a verb, between a preposition and its object(s), or after *because* or *as*.

EXAMPLES

Layamon wrote the first narration of the Arthurian tales in English. [not "wrote**:** the first"]
Before him, Geoffrey had written his version in Latin. [not "in**:** Latin"]
The troubadours were admired because their verses were sung to music. [not "because**:** their verses were sung]

UNDERSTAND THE CONCEPT

APPLY THE SKILL

Identify Correct and Incorrect Use of Colons

Rewrite the following sentences by correctly using colons.

1. One of the legends' ironies concerns the betrayal of Arthur the king is defeated by his nephew, Modred.
2. Life in Arthurian times included: brave knights but no organized army, and a king but no sense of nationhood.
3. Among other aspects of medieval Europe were the following a population of mostly poor farmers, education only for noble children, and few periods of peace.
4. The letter to the head of the Medieval Players Group began, "Dear Mr. President Can you meet us at tonight's concert of troubadour music, which starts at 715?"
5. A modern-day British knight, Sir Paul McCartney, might declare to his fans: "Remember the Beatles, the troubadours of the 1960s."
6. Fionn was able to work for Finnegas: in exchange for an education in poetry.
7. Fianna were remarkable warriors, they could jump as high as their own head, pull thorns from their feet while they ran, and duck as low as their knee height.
8. The Fionn Saga reflects a specific period in Irish history, literature and art flourished and all clans paid homage to the king of Ireland at Tara.
9. Ella Young was introduced to Irish folk tales at an early age "From childhood I heard tales of ghosts, banshees, haunted castles, mischievous and friendly sprites, snatches of ballads and political arguments."
10. Prior to the 1700s, Ireland was: organized into clans that often waged war against one another.

Insert Semicolons Correctly

Correctly insert a semicolon to combine each pair of independent clauses or to separate items in a series containing commas.

1. The first English version of the Arthurian legend, by the poet Layamon, describes the knights' bitter rivalries indeed, the famous Round Table was constructed so that no one would be seated at the head of the table.
2. In one of the many conflicts in the legends, Arthur's wife, Guinevere, is in love with Lancelot both the queen and the knight are troubled by their disloyalty to the king.
3. You may enjoy the legends of King Arthur for their adventure, heroism, and warfare for the range of characters, including magicians, evil-doers, and knights and for the vivid depiction of a long-ago society.
4. In the European versions, the emphasis is on flowery speeches, religious disputes, and melodrama on complicated events involving many characters and on long-winded discussions of philosophical issues.
5. The twentieth-century author T. H. White imagined Arthur's life as a novel consequently, *The Once and Future King* used modern techniques to relate an ancient tale.

EXTEND THE SKILL

Work with a partner. One partner will write a letter of application for a job (either for a real job or an imagined one). The other partner will write a response as an employee of the company or other organization that received the letter. In both of the letters, use colons where needed, and make sure all punctuation is correct.

Understanding Folk Tales

FOLK TALES

The names of Cinderella, Snow White, Paul Bunyan, and Pecos Bill may be familiar to you from stories you heard in your childhood. Children often delight in these stories of magical beings, fantastic creatures, and larger-than-life characters; in fact, folk tales and fairy tales have charmed listeners for centuries.

Folk tales are brief stories passed by word-of-mouth from generation to generation. Many folk tales can also be considered legends. **Fairy tales** are stories that deal with mischievous spirits and other supernatural occurrences, often in medieval settings.

ORIGINS OF FOLK TALES

No one knows for sure who first told these stories or when the tales originated. It is believed that workers passed these along to each other to while away the hours of tedious tasks, such as spinning thread or carding wool, and the stories passed in turn from parents to their children. Some tales spread across cultures, with each region adding its own particular touch to the retelling.

You may be surprised when you read some of the original versions of folk tales and fairy tales collected by the Brothers Grimm, as they called themselves. Jacob and Wilhelm Grimm were well-educated and patriotic Germans who wanted to preserve their culture. Their first book of tales, *Children's and Household Tales,* was published in 1812. Despite the title, the stories were not especially appropriate for young children. Violent and sinister, these early versions of the tales would not pass the approval of many modern parents.

The Brothers Grimm considered themselves folklorists and cultural researchers rather than authors of children's literature. Their original tales, however, authentically reflect the hard lives of the common folk of earlier days, when hunger and poverty were widespread. The brothers themselves experienced such hardships, which may account for the number of tales that include these elements.

Another famous recorder of folklore was Denmark's Hans Christian Andersen (1805–1875). Andersen's early years were marked by poverty and limited education. When his father died in 1816, Andersen had to learn how to make his way in the world. He turned to the arts, theater in particular. Though he did not succeed as an actor, a singer, or a dancer, he drew the attention of wealthy people who paid for his education. Writing became Andersen's creative outlet. His works show the influences of the fantastic stories he had read and been told as a child.

Although Andersen became the most celebrated Danish author of his time, he still felt like an outsider in the world of the upper class—a theme that appears many times in his fairy tales. "The Little Mermaid" and "The Ugly Duckling," the most famous of his fairy tales, are thought to reflect themes from his life, such as the desire for a different life, the alienation of the outsider, and the loss of love.

The Origin of Folk Tales

Some of these nineteenth-century tales originated or were influenced by folk tales from as far away as Ireland, Russia, and Japan. In fact, scholars believe that the story of Cinderella, also known as "Ashgirl," may be Chinese in origin. Today, collections of folk tales from around the world are growing in popularity. Browse through the children's picture book section of a library and find folk tales from another part of the world, such as the Middle East, Latin America, Africa, or Asia. How have these traditional folk tales influenced 20th and 21st century folk tales?

Cinderella, 1897. Gustave Doré.

ELEMENTS OF FOLK TALES

Symbols

Symbolism became a major element of the folk tradition: A well-chosen representation or image, such as an apple, more easily conveyed beliefs than did wordy explanations. Even a century ago, a significant number of people did not know how to read. Thus, the ideas represented by the recurring symbols in folk tales and fairy tales, such as beasts (especially wolves); dark, scary woods; fruit (especially apples); and articles of clothing (capes and shoes in particular), were more universally understood.

Motifs

A **motif** is any element that occurs in one or more works of literature or art. Themes and circumstances that occur frequently:

- transformation ("The Frog-King," "Beauty and the Beast," and "The Ugly Duckling," to name a few)
- abandonment by parents, either by death or by intention ("Hop o' My Thumb" and "Hansel and Gretel")
- incredible strength or size ("Paul Bunyan" and "John Henry")

Twisted Tales

The familiarity of many folk tales and fairy tales provides authors with the chance to twist and change the stories to suit their tastes. The results can be amusing or thought-provoking. Check out these twists on age-old tales:

- *Cinderella (As If You Didn't Already Know the Story)* by Barbara Ensor
- *Politically Correct Bedtime Stories* by James Finn Garner
- *Don't Bet on the Prince* by Jack David Zipes
- *The True Story of the Three Little Pigs* by Jon Scieszka
- *Cinder Edna* by Ellen Jackson
- *The Three Little Wolves and the Big Bad Pig* by Eugene Trivizas
- The musical *Into the Woods* with music and lyrics by Stephen Sondheim

READING FOLK TALES

When reading folk tales, record in your notebook the symbols and the magical elements that you observe. Doing so can help you dig more deeply into the tale, to reveal its likely significance to the early storytellers and their audiences. First, create a graphic organizer like the one below. On the left side, list the symbols and magical or unreal elements. In the middle, list the location of similar elements you may have encountered, whether in another story, in a comic book, or in a movie. On the right side, speculate, or make guesses, about what the symbolic or magical feature meant to the early storytellers or why they created such magical or fantastic characters.

Symbol or Element	Similar to...	Meaning or Importance
Three hungry crows	The less fortunate in other fairy tales	You will be rewarded or punished, based on how you treat those around you.

THE WHITE SNAKE

BEFORE READING

A Fairy Tale Retold by Jacob and Wilhelm Grimm
Translated by Lucy Crane

DIRECTED READING

BUILD BACKGROUND

Literary Context Many of the fairy tales you may be familiar with began as folk songs and stories from the European oral tradition and were later written down. The Grimm brothers, Jacob and Wilhelm, collected word-of-mouth tales, including **"The White Snake"** and "Rapunzel," in their native Germany. In France, Charles Perrault (1628–1703) created written versions of other folk stories—among them, "Cinderella" and "Sleeping Beauty." A century later, the Danish writer Hans Christian Andersen (1805–1875) retold such tales as "The Princess and the Pea," "The Ugly Duckling," and "The Emperor's New Clothes."

Reader's Context Do you remember any fairy tales from your childhood? If so, which features were the most appealing to you?

ANALYZE LITERATURE: Fairy Tale

A **fairy tale** is a story that deals with mischievous spirits and other supernatural occurrences, often in medieval settings. Many fairy tales contain more than just playful or mean-spirited creatures. In fairy tales, humans usually have some kind of magical experience that changes them in significant ways. In this tale, the spirits represent good; but in others, they are evil.

SET PURPOSE

What features of the fairy tale can you identify in "The White Snake"? What forms do the spirits take? Consider how the servant's curiosity sets him on a surprising journey. What does he learn from his adventures? What might the lesson for the reader be? In which ways can humans learn from well-meaning creatures and from troublemaking ones?

MEET THE AUTHORS

Jacob Grimm (1785–1863) and his brother **Wilhelm** (1786–1859) were German scholars. Among young people around the globe, the Grimm brothers are famous for collecting folk songs and folk tales from the European oral tradition. The writers, who transcribed these tales as they heard them narrated, gave the stories a readable form without changing their traditional quality. The two hundred tales they collected express the spirit and imagination of generations of storytellers.

USE READING SKILLS

Classify Information When you **classify information,** you separate it into groups according to significant qualities. For example, you might classify characters in "The White Snake" into groups: ordinary humans, humans with supernatural abilities, and talking animals. Classifying helps you understand a story's major ideas. As you read the selection, use a chart like the one below to list other classifications.

Group 1: Ordinary Humans	Group 2: Supernatural Humans	Group 3: Talking Animals
Characters: Queen	Characters: King	Characters:

PREVIEW VOCABULARY

Examine the following vocabulary words:

abroad
anxiety
contrive
superintendence
plume

Classify them according to their parts of speech in the story. Then determine which of the words can, in different contexts or forms, be used as another part of speech. Write a sentence using each of these words as another part of speech. Be sure to provide a context that helps indicate the meaning of each word. To review the parts of speech, refer to the Parts of Speech Chart in the Language Arts Handbook 3.2, The Parts of Speech.

The Keepsake, 1901. Kate Elizabeth Bunce. Birmingham Museums and Art Gallery, Birmingham, England.

The virtue of the snake had given him power to understand the speech of animals.

THE WHITE

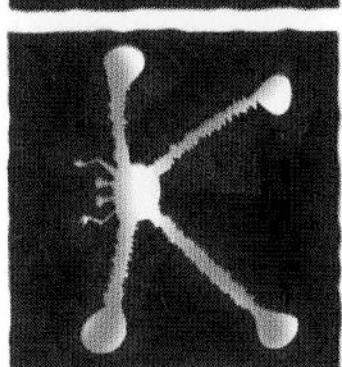

A Fairy Tale Retold by

Jacob and Wilhelm Grimm

Translated by **Lucy Crane**

A long time ago there lived a King whose wisdom was noised abroad in all the country. Nothing remained long unknown to him, and it was as if the knowledge of hidden things was brought to him in the air. However, he had one curious custom. Every day at dinner, after the table had been cleared and every one gone away, a trusty servant had to bring in one other dish. But it was covered up, and the servant himself did not know what was in it, and no one else knew, for the King waited until he was quite alone before he uncovered it. This had gone on a long time, but at last there came a day when the servant could restrain his curiosity no longer, but as he was carrying the dish away he took it into his own room. As soon as he had fastened the door securely, he lifted the cover, and there he saw a white snake lying on the dish. After seeing it he could not resist the desire to taste it, and so he cut off a small piece and put it in his mouth. As soon as it touched his tongue he heard outside his window a strange chorus of delicate voices. He went and listened, and found that it was the sparrows talking together, and telling each other all they had seen in the fields and

a • broad (ə brôd′) *adv.*, far and wide

woods. The virtue of the snake had given him power to understand the speech of animals.

Now it happened one day that the Queen lost her most splendid ring, and suspicion fell upon the trusty servant, who had the general superintendence, and he was accused of stealing it. The King summoned him to his presence, and after many reproaches told him that if by the next day he was not able to name the thief he should be considered guilty, and punished. It was in vain that he protested his innocence; he could get no better sentence. In his uneasiness and anxiety he went out into the courtyard, and began to consider what he could do in so great a necessity. There sat the ducks by the running water and rested themselves, and plumed themselves with their flat bills, and held a comfortable chat. The servant stayed where he was and listened to them. They told how they had waddled about all yesterday morning and found good food; and then one of them said pitifully, "Something lies very heavy in my craw,[1] it is the ring that was lying under the Queen's window; I swallowed it down in too great a hurry."

Then the servant seized her by the neck, took her into the kitchen, and said to the cook,

"Kill this one, she is quite ready for cooking."

"Yes," said the cook, weighing it in her hand; "there will be no trouble of fattening this one—it has been ready ever so long."

She then slit up its neck, and when it was opened the Queen's ring was found in its craw. The servant could now clearly prove his innocence, and in order to make up for the injustice he had suffered the King permitted him to ask some favour for himself, and also promised him the place of greatest honour in the royal household.

But the servant refused it, and only asked for a horse and money for travelling, for he had a fancy to see the world, and look about him a little. So his request was granted, and he set out on his way; and one day he came to a pool of water, by which he saw three fishes who had got entangled in the rushes, and were panting for water. Although fishes are usually considered dumb creatures, he understood very well their lament that they were to perish so miserably; and as he had a compassionate heart he dismounted from his horse, and put the three fishes back again into the water. They quivered all over with joy, stretched out their heads, and called out to him,

"We will remember and reward thee, because thou hast delivered us." He rode on, and after a while he heard a small voice come up from the sand underneath his horse's feet. He listened, and understood how an ant-king was complaining,

"If only these men would keep off, with their great awkward beasts! Here comes this stupid horse treading down my people with his hard hoofs!" The man then turned his horse to the side-path, and the ant-king called out to him, "We will remember and reward thee!"

The path led him through a wood, and there he saw a father-raven and mother-raven standing by their nest and throwing their young ones out.

"Off with you! young gallows-birds!"[2] cried they; "we cannot stuff you any more; you are big enough to fend for yourselves!" The poor young ravens lay on the ground, fluttering, and beating the air with their pinions, and crying,

"We are poor helpless things, we cannot fend for ourselves, we cannot even fly! we can only die of hunger!"

Then the kind young man dismounted, killed his horse with his dagger, and left it to the young ravens for food. They came hopping up, feasted away at it, and cried,

1. **craw.** Stomach of an animal
2. **gallows-birds.** Creatures that deserve to be hanged

su • per • in • ten • dence (sü' p[ə]rin ten´ dən[t]s) *n.,* supervision; management
anx • i • ety (aŋ zī´ ə tē) *n.,* worry; sense of unease or dread
plume (plüm) *v.,* preen, or clean and arrange one's feathers

"We will remember and reward thee!"

So now he had to use his own legs, and when he had gone a long way he came to a great town. There was much noise and thronging in the streets, and there came a man on a horse, who proclaimed,

"That the King's daughter seeks a husband, but he who wishes to marry her must perform a difficult task, and if he cannot carry it through successfully, he must lose his life."

Many had already tried, but had lost their lives, in vain. The young man, when he saw the King's daughter, was so dazzled by her great beauty, that he forgot all danger, went to the King and offered himself as a wooer.

Then he was led to the sea-side, and a gold ring was thrown into the water before his eyes. Then the King told him that he must fetch the ring up again from the bottom of the sea, saying,

"If you come back without it, you shall be put under the waves again and again until you are drowned."

Every one pitied the handsome young man, but they went, and left him alone by the sea. As he was standing on the shore and thinking of what he should do, there came three fishes swimming by, none other than those he had set free. The middle one had a mussel in his mouth, and he laid it on the strand at the young man's feet; and when he took it up and opened it there was the gold ring inside! Full of joy he carried it to the King, and expected the promised reward; but the King's daughter, proud of her high birth,[3] despised him, and set him another task to perform. She went out into the garden, and strewed about over the grass ten sacks full of millet seed.[4]

"By the time the sun rises in the morning you must have picked up all these," she said, "and not a grain must be wanting."

The young man sat down in the garden and considered how it was possible to do this task, but he could contrive nothing, and stayed there, feeling very sorrowful, and expecting to be led to death at break of day. But when the first beams of the sun fell on the garden he saw that the ten sacks were all filled, standing one by the other, and not even a grain was missing. The ant-king had arrived in the night with his thousands of ants, and the grateful creatures had picked up all the millet seed, and filled the sacks with great industry. The King's daughter came herself into the garden and saw with astonishment that the young man had performed all that had been given him to do. But she could not let her proud heart melt, but said, "Although he has completed the two tasks, he shall not be my bridegroom unless he brings me an apple from the tree of life."

LITERARY CONNECTION

Julie Andrews as Mary Poppins

Fantastic Elements in Literature
Traditional and classical literature for children and young adults often contains fantastic elements that have captured the imaginations of young people for generations. Kenneth Grahame, for instance, set his novel *The Wind in the Willows* (1908) in the forest; his characters include Mr. Toad and Water Rat. Popular series include the *Mary Poppins* books, written in the 1930s by PAGE L. Travers, and the *Dr. Dolittle* volumes, of a decade earlier, featuring a veterinarian who converses with his patients. In *The Hobbit* (1937) and other works by J. R. R. Tolkien, the imaginary creatures of the title—as well as elves, dragons, and people—exist in a world that reflects the challenges and joys of human society. What 20th or 21st century literature can you think of that has been influenced by traditional or classical literature?

3. **high birth.** Being born into a noble family
4. **millet seed.** Seed of a grain grown for food

con • trive (kən trīv´) *v.*, plan; scheme; bring about by strategy or with difficulty

The young man did not know where the tree of life was to be found, but he set out and went on and on, as long as his legs could carry him, but he had no hope of finding it. When he had gone through three kingdoms he came one evening to a wood, and seated himself under a tree to go to sleep; but he heard a rustling in the boughs, and a golden apple fell into his hand. Immediately three ravens flew towards him, perched on his knee, and said,

"We are the three young ravens that you delivered from starving; when we grew big, and heard that you were seeking the golden apple, we flew over the sea to the end of the earth, where the tree of life stands, and we fetched the apple."

Full of joy the young man set off on his way home, and brought the golden apple to the King's beautiful daughter, who was without any further excuse.

So they divided the apple of life, and ate it together; and their hearts were filled with love, and they lived in undisturbed happiness to a great age. ❖

Do most people do good deeds purely to benefit others or do they hope to gain something in return? Have you ever performed an act of kindness without letting the other person know about it? What do you think is the greatest reward for doing good deeds?

AFTER READING

REFER TO TEXT	REASON WITH TEXT	
1a. Recall how the young man responds when he is offered a place of honor in the royal household.	1b. Infer other reasons the young man may have for his decision to travel.	**Understand** Find meaning
2a. Identify whom the young man helps during his travels.	2b. What do the servant's encounters with the animals show about his character?	**Apply** Use information
3a. Write down the tasks that the young man must perform before he can win the princess's hand.	3b. Explain whether or not you think the young man could have performed these tasks without the help of the animals.	**Analyze** Take things apart
4a. State the reason why the princess adds more tasks for the young man to perform. Do you think she is worthy of him? Explain.	4b. What motivates the young man to continue despite the unlikelihood of success? Conclude whether or not he is foolish or is to be admired for his determination. Explain.	**Evaluate** Make judgments
5a. It is common in fairy tales for events to occur in threes. List the events in "The White Snake" that follow this pattern.	5b. Create one more incident in which the man assists animals and must complete a fourth task. Try to write in the style of "The White Snake."	**Create** Bring ideas together

ANALYZE LITERATURE: Fairy Tale

Among the characters in fairy tales are mischievous spirits (such as elves, imps, ogres, and fairies) and magical elements. What are the mischievous spirits or magical elements in "The White Snake"? How do these unusual beings affect the story?

EXTEND THE TEXT

Writing Options

Creative Writing Fairy tales have traditional settings, such as castles and forests, and old-fashioned characters. Prepare a **modern-day retelling** of "The White Snake" in a setting of your choice, such as a suburb or a big city. You can replace the old-fashioned characters with modern ones, too, if you wish. Your version can be one or two pages long.

Persuasive Writing In a story, *flat characters* remain the same from beginning to end: They don't change at all. Write a one- to two-page **character analysis** in which you argue whether or not the young man is a flat character. Support your opinion with details from "The White Snake."

Collaborative Learning

Create a Collection of Fairy Tales Fairy tales are often gathered together and published as a volume. Working with a partner or in a small group, collect several fairy tales from different cultures (European, Native American, Asian, African), different time periods, and different media—some may be narrated on tape; others may take the form of wall paintings or other visual art; some may be musical (for instance, Tchaikovsky's *Peter and the Wolf*). List and briefly describe the items in your collection, and share them with the class.

Lifelong Learning

Bring Medieval Europe to Life In general, fairy tales from Europe had their start in medieval times, when a population that was mostly illiterate (unable to read and write) depended on the oral presentation of the stories. On the Internet or in the library, find out what daily life was like during the Middle Ages. Except for the nobility, most families struggled to plant crops and raise a few animals. Look, in particular, for information on the role of fairy tales in easing the peasants' difficult, mostly unrewarding lives.

Go to **www.mirrorsandwindows.com** for more.

READING ASSESSMENT

1. Number these events in the correct sequence, with 1 being the first thing to happen and 6 being the last.
   ___ The ants fill sacks with millet.
   ___ The servant asks the cook to kill the duck.
   ___ The princess had no more excuses.
   ___ The King offers the servant a place of honor in the household.
   ___ The young man kills his horse as food for the baby ravens.
   ___ "We will remember and reward thee!" the ant-king called out.

2. As it is used on page 693, the term *contrive* most closely means
   A. see.
   B. arrange.
   C. remember.
   D. foresee.
   E. None of the above

3. Twice in the story a ring is lost and then found, having been eaten by a duck and a mussel. The repetition suggests all but which of the following?
   A. The restatement of details helps oral narrators recall the tale.
   B. The narrators may have run out of ideas.
   C. The recurrence of the event adds to its significance.
   D. The repetition links the two parts of the story.
   E. The recurrence evokes the man's earlier troubles.

4. Which of the following statements best expresses the meaning of the fairy tale?
   A. A person who is given a special ability will be rewarded for using it compassionately and generously.
   B. A person with a special ability will be aided in a time of trouble.
   C. Animals know as much about humans as humans know about them.
   D. People can rise in the world by showing curiosity and determination.
   E. Wisdom is wasted among those who are afraid of adventure.

5. For what reason does the Princess refuse to marry the young man after he completes the first task?
   A. The rules demanded that he complete three tasks.
   B. The princess didn't approve of the young man's methods.
   C. Her father didn't approve of the young man.
   D. She did not want to marry a commoner.
   E. She suspected that he had cheated on the first task.

6. To show kindness to some animals, the young man must display cruelty to other animals. What does this contradiction suggest about life?

GRAMMAR & STYLE

UNDERSTAND THE CONCEPT | APPLY THE SKILL

Hyphens, Ellipses, and Italics

Hyphens are used in making compound words. **Ellipses** are spaced dots showing that material has been omitted from a quoted passage. **Italics** are used for titles of certain works, for words referred to as words, and for emphasis.

Many *compound words* and *compound expressions* consist of two or more words connected by a hyphen.

EXAMPLES

cease-fire, great-grandson, self-confidence, father-in-law [Hyphens link words that form a noun.]
war-torn city, *fat-free* food, *stop-and-go* traffic, *once-in-a-lifetime* deal [Hyphens link words that form an adjective.]
ninety-nine, one-half inch, *two-thirds* of the students, *seven-day* vacation [Hyphens are used in spelled-out compound numbers and fractions and in numerals used as adjectives.]

Ellipses, or spaced points, show where one or more words or sentences have been omitted from a quoted passage. To indicate material left out at the beginning or the middle of a sentence, use three spaced dots. To indicate material left out at the end of a sentence, place the period at the new end and add three spaced dots. To indicate the omission of one or more sentences in a passage, use three spaced dots after the last period.

In this passage, the underlined material is omitted and replaced with ellipses in the second model:

EXAMPLE

Modern literature that contains elements <u>of fairy tales, folk tales, and other features</u> of the oral tradition suggests that readers still respond to fantasy and magic, even in our science-oriented world. <u>They may feel that</u> the emphasis on technology has lessened our appreciation of nature <u>and of the poetic</u>. Readers are looking for an escape from <u>the predictability and</u> the lack of imagination in today's culture. <u>What would happen if a mischievous creature replaced a robot and offered three wishes instead of a car off the assembly line?</u>

Modern literature that contains elements...of the oral tradition suggests that readers still respond to fantasy and magic, even in our science-oriented world....
[T]he emphasis on technology has lessened our appreciation of nature.... Readers are looking for an escape from...the lack of imagination in today's culture....

Italics are used in writing the names of books, plays, long poems, movies, and musical works; magazines, radio and TV series, computer games, comic strips; trains, ships, aircraft, and spacecraft. In handwriting, use underlining instead of italics.

EXAMPLES

The Odyssey; The Hobbit; The Miracle Worker; Atlantic Monthly; Morning News; Mozart's *Jupiter* Symphony [long poem; novel; play; magazine; TV series; musical work]
Whistlestop; Queen Elizabeth II; Challenger [train; ship; spacecraft]

Italics are also used in referring to words, letters, symbols, and numerals as such.

EXAMPLES

The word *mischievous* is hard to spell. Does it have an *ie* or *ei* vowel combination?
An apostrophe is added for the plural form of a number: two *6*'s.

REVIEW TERMS

- **hyphens:** punctuation marks that are shorter than dashes and that are used in making compound words and compound expressions
- **ellipses:** spaced points that indicate where one or more words or sentences have been omitted from a quoted passage
- **italics:** a style type that slants slightly to the right and that is used for certain titles of works, for words referred to as words, and for emphasis

UNDERSTAND THE CONCEPT | APPLY THE SKILL

Use Hyphens Correctly

In the following sentences, insert hyphens where they are needed. If you aren't sure how to spell a word, consult a dictionary.

1. While watching closed circuit TV, I noticed an advertisement for a free eight day vacation to Europe.
2. Twenty five people were guaranteed free travel and lodgings in a beautiful high rise apartment.
3. The trip included a tour of famous locations in European folklore and a day of sight seeing in an all terrain vehicle.
4. A self appointed on the scene photographer would document our trip.
5. I applied for the vacation but realized that, if I won, I would need to replace my two piece luggage set and dyed to match jacket.

Use Ellipses Correctly

Read the following sentences from "The White Snake" and rewrite each of the sentences, correctly adding ellipses in place of the underlined material.

1. A long time ago there lived a King <u>whose wisdom was noised abroad in all the country</u>.
2. Nothing remained long unknown to him, and it was as if the knowledge of hidden things was brought to him in the air. <u>However, he had one curious custom.</u>
3. <u>Every day at dinner,</u> after the table had been cleared <u>and every one gone away</u>, a trusty servant had to bring in one other dish.
4. <u>But it was covered up, and</u> the servant himself did not know what was in it, and no one else knew<u>, for the King waited until he was quite alone before he uncovered it</u>.
5. This had gone on a long time, but <u>at last there came a day when</u> the servant could restrain his curiosity no longer<u>, but as he was carrying the dish away he took it into his own room</u>.

Use Italics (Underlining) Correctly

In the following sentences, underline the items that should be in italics.

1. The novel Harriet Dishwater may sound dull, but the review in Books Weekly says reading it is as exciting as a ride on the Zipper Express.
2. Harriet begins her mysterious journey by examining clues in Leonardo da Vinci's Mona Lisa and in Beethoven's Eroica Symphony.
3. According to the would-be sleuth, the word dishwater may indicate the style of her journey, and a figure 8 may suggest its form.
4. A book-length poem about Harriet's success aboard the space traveler Cosmic Reach might be called Adventures Among the Stars.
5. "I will not be kept from my plans," she forcefully announced, "even if my first task is to wash tonight's pots and pans."

EXTEND THE SKILL

Work with a partner. Individually, find a paragraph from a book, a magazine, or a newspaper article, or write your own paragraph. Underline words, phrases, or sentences that you'd like replaced by ellipses. Select text for removal carefully, so that when the items are replaced by ellipses, the paragraph still makes sense. Exchange papers with your partner and replace the indicated passages with ellipses.

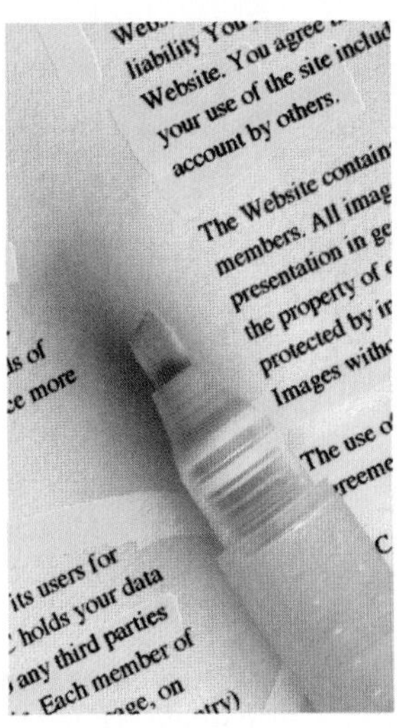

The Golden Lamb

BEFORE READING

A Folk Tale by Jean Russell Larson

DIRECTED READING

BUILD BACKGROUND

Cultural Context In **"The Golden Lamb,"** set in what is now Iraq, three young men are each promised a lamb as payment for their shepherding. When one of the lambs turns out to have a golden fleece, an argument results over who should rightly own the lamb. The men travel to Baghdad and there receive an answer from the Caliph Haroun-al-Rashid. A *caliph* is a Muslim political leader, believed to be a descendant of the prophet Muhammad. Haroun-al-Rashid (763–809 CE) was the fifth caliph and ruled for approximately twenty-three years. He is considered one of the great caliphs for promoting science, art, music, and religion during his reign, making Baghdad a cultural seat and inspiring tales that eventually ended up in the *Book of One Thousand and One Nights.*

Reader's Context Which skills, abilities, and qualities do you think are most important in the modern world?

ANALYZE LITERATURE: Folk Tale

A **folk tale** is a brief story passed by word of mouth from generation to generation. Certain details of the story may change over time or as the tale passes from one region to another. Furthermore, the various storytellers, who may belong to different cultural groups, often add features, such as characters and descriptions, to make the story more relevant to their experiences.

SET PURPOSE

Many of the folk tales from the Middle East involve a wise man revealing a truth to others, even a truth about the question-seekers themselves. As you are reading the selection, try to predict what the caliph's answer will be and what truth he will reveal. Note details in "The Golden Lamb" that you think would appeal to a Middle Eastern audience. What features would capture the imagination of any audience?

MEET THE AUTHOR

Jean Russell Larson (b. 1930) was born in Marshalltown, Iowa, and has been interested in folk tales for much of her life. She attended Winthrop College from 1948–1949, received her undergraduate degree from Buena Vista University, and received her master's degree from Iowa State University. Larson has published several books, including *Palace in Baghdad,* the collection in which "The Golden Lamb" appears; *The Glass Mountain and Other Arabian Tales;* and *The Silkspinners.* She has received many awards, including an American Library Association Award and a Lewis Carroll Shelf Award.

USE READING SKILLS

Identify Sequence of Events

The **sequence of events** is the order in which events happen in a story. Paying attention to the order in which incidents occur helps you understand the connection, the cause-and-effect link, between the actions. Make a chart like the one below to record the events in "The Golden Lamb." In each box, draw a picture or jot down words or phrases that will help you remember what happens in the story.

Sequence Chart

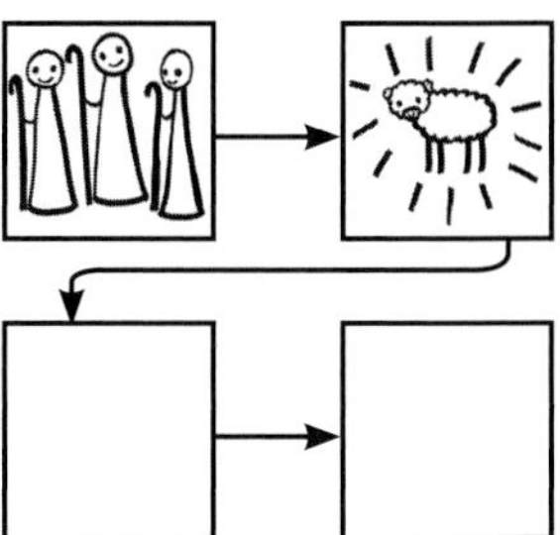

PREVIEW VOCABULARY

Look at vocabulary words from the selection and answer the following questions.

quarrel *dispute*
haste *ferocious*
astonished

1. Which two words are synonyms (have the same meaning)?
2. Which vocabulary word describes a reaction an individual might have?
3. Which word is always used as an adjective? What is the noun form of this word?
4. What happens to the sound of *haste* when the word is changed to a verb?

The Golden Lamb

A Folk Tale by **Jean Russell Larson**

But then the trouble began, for one of the lambs had fleece of purest gold.

There lived in a far land, in the days of the great caliph Haroun-al-Rashid, three young men whose names were Haboul, Kerim, and Zeid. The three longed to set forth to seek their fortunes, but hard times had come down upon the village in which they lived and there was no money with which to begin their travels. The only work to be found in all of the countryside was that of tending sheep for an aged widow.

"I can offer you no wages," she said, "but in the spring three lambs will be born. Those you may take and sell, keeping the money for yourselves."

"We will get little for the lambs in times like these, I suppose," said Haboul.

"You need not suppose, you may be quite sure," replied Kerim crossly. "Still I will take the work and welcome. Someday, when I am a wealthy merchant, I shall laugh at my humble beginnings."

Then the three fell to dreaming and spinning grand tales of the lives they would one day lead.

Through the long dreary winter Haboul, Kerim, and Zeid watched over the small flock of sheep. A blustery wind blew and dark clouds scudded through the sky, but the young men kept up their spirits by making plans for the spring. Then three lambs would be theirs. How quickly they would sell those lambs and with coins jingling, be off to the city.

Spring came at last, bringing white clouded skies, gentle breezes, and three tiny lambs. But then the trouble began, for one of the lambs had fleece of purest gold.

"I'll have that lamb!" declared Haboul.

"You'll not have him!" Kerim shouted, stomping hard on Haboul's foot. "He's mine!"

"Oh, my foot! My foot!" cried Haboul, hopping up and down.

"The beast belongs to me," Zeid announced, drawing himself up grandly, "since I am the eldest."

"The eldest, is it?" hooted Kerim. "Well I am the one who would put the money to the best use, for I am the smartest."

So the three fell to quarreling and disputing among themselves about the fate of the golden lamb. Night came down on them and still the argument was not settled. At length it was decided that they would travel to Bagdad, to the great caliph himself, to seek an answer to the problem.

"It will be a waste of your time," warned Zeid, "for he is sure to decide in my favor."

The young men were up early the next morning and leaving the flock in the care of a friend, set out for Bagdad with the golden lamb. Resuming the disagreement of the night before, they quarreled on, across the plains and over the hills, right up to the gates of the great palace.

Kerim's knees shook as a royal attendant escorted the shepherds to the caliph's council chamber. Zeid's teeth chattered and Haboul was uncommonly pale. Quickly they stated their problem, interrupting each other rudely in their haste. They were anxious to have the matter settled and be gone.

When they had finished, the caliph was silent. He stroked his beard thoughtfully. Each young man had set forth good reasons why he should be allowed the profits from the golden lamb. In fact, so well had each of them spoken, that the caliph was unable to decide the matter at once.

"Sleep in the stable and return to me in the morning," he told them, "and I will have an answer for you."

Having spent their strength in the trip to Bagdad, Haboul, Kerim, and Zeid were glad for the soft beds of straw which were prepared for them in the stable. Soon sleep swept down on them.

The following day was full of sunshine. The three shepherds arose in high spirits and went eagerly to the palace to learn the caliph's decision.

"So troublesome is this puzzle that I have asked my grand vizier[1] to attend me in judging it," the caliph told them. "He is a wise and remarkable man."

The grand vizier bowed low.

"I have noticed that each of you has a gift with words," the caliph continued, "and so it has been decided that each will tell a brief story. He whose tale is found to be the most interesting shall be proclaimed winner of the lamb. Would you like time to prepare?"

Kerim stepped forward.

"I've no need to wait," he said. "I am ready with a story of adventure."

The people of the royal court whispered excitedly for a moment and then were still.

"Please relate it," said the caliph, and Kerim began.

It was a splendid tale concerning a land of towering mountains and deep, wooded valleys. A huge ferocious beast called a gorgo dwelled in a mountain cave there and ranged forth nightly, stealing children from their homes. He hid the children in his damp dark cave. Daud, a young man of great courage, volunteered to capture the gorgo. After much difficulty, Daud succeeded in taking the gorgo prisoner with a silken sash which he had looped at one end and flung round the beast's neck. The children were returned to their homes and there was peace in the land once more. All of this seemed

1. **vizier.** A high executive officer in some Muslim countries

quar • rel (kwôr´ əl) *v.*, to argue
dis • pute (dis pyüt´) *v.*, to debate
haste (hāst) *n.*, state of hurry
fe • ro • cious (fə rō´ shəs) *adj.*, fierce; violent

real to Kerim's listeners, so skillfully did he tell it.

As Kerim ended his story the people of the court remained still, as though cast under a spell. At last the caliph broke the silence.

"That was well done and difficult to equal. Who will go next?"

Haboul cleared his throat noisily and stepped forward.

"It was a first-class tale, but I have a better one."

His listeners leaned forward, waiting eagerly.

"Pray, tell it" said the caliph, and Haboul began.

His voice was low and silky as he told of a tiny bird which had become separated from its parents. It flew about frantically, searching everywhere for them, and encountering great danger. A tawny[2] cat stole toward it as it rested in a treetop. Only the snapping of a twig warned the little bird of the cat's presence, thus saving his life.

Seventeenth-century miniature painting.

On the shore of a silver-blue lake the bird met a man carrying a wooden cage. Before the little bird could think twice, he had been imprisoned in the cage and transported to a large city. There the cage was placed in a bazaar. Many people passed, laying down coins in payment for viewing the bird, and though they praised him, calling him a bird of rare beauty, his small heart ached with loneliness.

At last a kind young man, seeing the plight of the bird, took pity upon it and set it free. After flying for many days, across land and water, it came upon the spot where its mother and father sat, mourning their lost child. Following a joyful reunion, the three set off together through the clear blue sky.

The gentlemen of the court clapped their hands in delight when Haboul had finished.

2. **tawny.** A sandy, light brown to brownish-orange color

The ladies sighed with pleasure at so sweet a tale.

"Wait," said the caliph, raising his hand for silence. "We have yet another story to hear. Are you ready?" he asked Zeid.

"I am," declared Zeid, coming to the center of the room. "The lamb is as good as mine."

"Please begin," said the caliph.

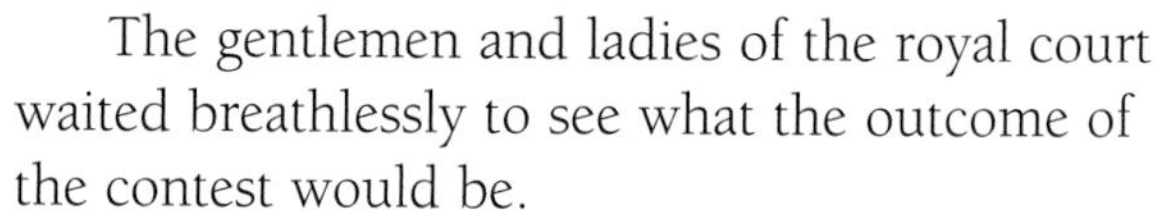

Zeid's story was filled with suspense. A merchant, thinking to catch the thief who came each night and took goods from his shop, concealed himself behind a curtain and kept watch. In the hour after midnight a man slipped through a window of the shop and began to fill a large bag with silks and sweets. The merchant, realizing the thief might be but the tool of another, yet more powerful man, remained in his hiding place till the bag was filled, then followed the thief from the shop. Through the dark winding streets went the thief, the merchant after him. At length they reached a dwelling and the thief entered. Peeping in the window, the merchant was astonished to see a dozen men, each more terrible than the other, emptying bags of ill-gotten goods on a carpet in the center of the room. Quickly the merchant summoned the authorities, witnessed the arrest of the robber band, and received the praise of honest men throughout the city.

When Zeid had finished his story he stepped back beside Haboul and Kerim.

The caliph and his grand vizier sat talking quietly, nodding from time to time and motioning in the direction of the three shepherds.

The gentlemen and ladies of the royal court waited breathlessly to see what the outcome of the contest would be.

"Step forward," said the caliph at last, and the three young men approached the throne.

"The grand vizier has a question to ask and I would like your answers."

The three nodded their agreement.

Rising, the grand vizier addressed the shepherds.

"What will you do with the money from the sale of the lamb?" he asked.

"Why, I'll rent a small space in the bazaar," Kerim replied, "and sell silks and spices. Soon I shall have enough money to open a shop of my own and then I will build a fortune."

"And you?" asked the grand vizier, looking at Haboul.

"I shall use the money to keep a room and buy food while I learn to do figuring and keep accounts. The services of an account keeper

as • ton • ished (ä stän′ ish ed) *adj.*, surprised

come high and one day I will be a wealthy man."

"And now you." The vizier turned to Zeid.

"I shall use the money to buy passage on a ship. I will sail to a far-off port and gather strange wares to bring back here. I'll sell them at a profit, then go back for more. That is the way to make a real fortune."

The grand vizier sat down and consulted with the caliph once more. Then the caliph stood up.

"Since the stories you told were of equal quality, it has been decided that the grand vizier will take the lamb from you and change it to profit which can be divided three ways. Is that agreeable to you?"

"But one of us should get it all, not just one third," objected Haboul. "How can we carry out our plans if we don't have what we need?"

"I promise that each of you will have what you need," said the vizier, smiling.

The people of the court watched excitedly.

Taking up the golden lamb, the vizier turned around three times, crooned a strange rhyme, and threw the lamb up into the air.

But the lamb did not come down. It changed in the twinkling of an eye to a shower of peculiar objects which rained down at the feet of Haboul, Kerim, and Zeid.

The ladies of the court gasped. The gentlemen of the court laughed loudly.

Haboul, Kerim, and Zeid bent down to see what their precious lamb had become. There on the floor were three loaves of bread, three coarse cloaks, and three pairs of sandals.

"What have you done with our lamb?" Haboul demanded, his face crimson. "And where is the money you promised us?"

"I said nothing about money," said the grand vizier sweetly. "I promised you those things which you would need and that is what you see before you."

"But what can we do with bread and cloaks and sandals?" Zeid shouted.

"You can walk far in the sandals for they are sturdy. The cloaks will keep you warm. As for the bread, it will keep you from hunger until you reach the next town. The people there will be happy to feed you in return for what you will give to them."

"What will we give them?" asked Kerim.

"Why, stories," said the caliph, smiling. "You want great fortunes yet each of you is rich already in words of beauty and imagination."

"But why can we not have money?" Haboul demanded.

"There can be no money in order that there will be something better," said the vizier. "If you had money you would become merchants and account keepers. While merchants are

CULTURAL CONNECTION

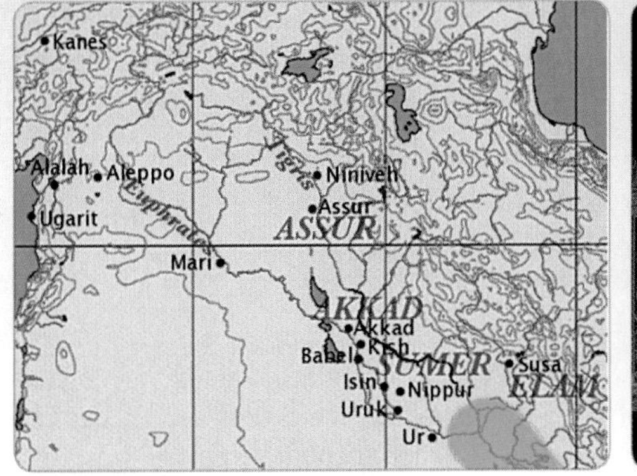

Mesopotamia The region that is now Iraq was once known as Mesopotamia, from the Greek for "between two rivers," the Tigris and the Euphrates. In the seventh century CE, the Arabs, whose religion is Islam, occupied the land and brought with them an interest in education and the arts. Cultural elements introduced to Europe include *algebra* (the original Arabic means "reduction") and the *arabesque* style of art, notable for its small-scale geometric designs. From the early seventeenth century to World War I, the region was controlled by the Ottoman Empire (named for its founder, Othman I). Mehmed II, pictured above, assisted in the continuation of the Ottoman Empire's rule.

needed and account keepers too, clearly you were meant for something else. Do not mourn for what you have not, rather rejoice for what you have to give."

The gentlemen of the court pressed around the young men, declaring them fine fellows and praising the wisdom of the caliph's decision. The ladies went to search out delicacies[3] to tuck into the cloaks along with the bread.

For long years Haboul, Kerim, and Zeid roamed from south to north and from west to east giving pleasure to the people of their land with stories of beauty and excitement. The three young men were much loved and were rich in friends and contentment. ❖

3. **delicacies.** Something to eat that is considered rare or luxurious

In your opinion, how valued are storytellers in society? How are they rewarded compared to "merchants and account keepers"? Do you think that artists, including writers, are adequately paid?

AFTER READING

REFER TO TEXT	REASON WITH TEXT	
1a. Identify the task that the caliph assigns the three men. What else does he require of them?	1b. Determine how their responses assisted the caliph in deciding what to do.	**Understand** **Find meaning**
2a. Recall why each man believes that he alone should be awarded the lamb.	2b. Relate why you think the three men cannot decide who gets the golden lamb. To whom would you have awarded the lamb?	**Apply** **Use information**
3a. Record what each man would do with the profits if he was awarded the lamb.	3b. The story begins with the men setting out to "seek their fortunes"—a frequent literary device in folklore. Distinguish whether or not the ending fulfills the expectations that the device suggests.	**Analyze** **Take things apart**
4a. Repeat what the three men receive from the caliph.	4b. Assess whether or not the simple gifts that the caliph gave the men served their intended purpose. Explain.	**Evaluate** **Make judgments**
5a. State how the three men feel about the caliph's decision.	5b. Reconstruct this story as a modern-day narrative. Consider changes such as the following: What character might replace the caliph? What would replace the golden lamb as the prize? How would you resolve the dispute among the three men?	**Create** **Bring ideas together**

ANALYZE LITERATURE: Folk Tale

What features make the story a folk tale? Which of the caliph's statements best express his values? In which way is the story both entertaining and educational? Review the items you entered on your Sequence Chart (see page 698). Try retelling the story just by using your chart.

EXTEND THE TEXT

Writing Options

Creative Writing Imagine that you have a young friend or relative who dreams of making a great deal of money, but you think this young person should think about other goals besides becoming wealthy. Write a one- to two-page **letter** to the person, explaining your feelings about preparing for the future. Provide examples of other people who achieved happiness or success in life without pursuing money.

Expository Writing "The Golden Lamb" is similar, in some ways, to the story of King Solomon in the Old Testament. Read the story of Solomon, or find a similar folk tale, and then write a three- to four-paragraph **compare-and-contrast essay** in which you examine the likenesses and differences between the two narratives. Be sure to discuss the values that are promoted in each story. Share your work with classmates. Use a Venn Diagram, like the one below, to assist you.

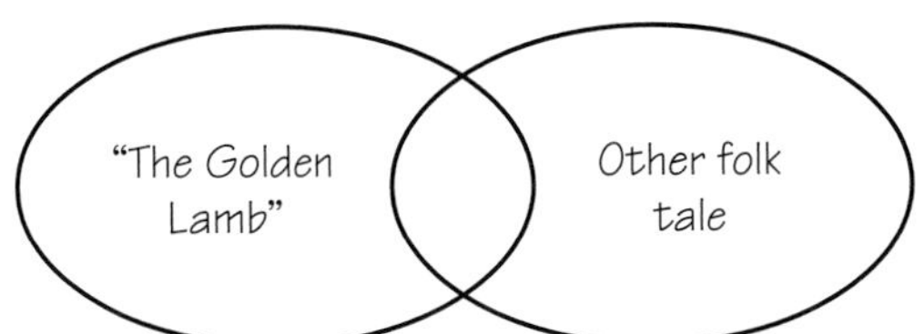

Collaborative Learning

Explore Job Opportunities In "The Golden Lamb," a gift for narration is more prized than business sense. Today, people with financial skills play an important role in a complex economy. Working with a partner or in a small group, do research to find out about well-paying or interesting jobs in business and finance and also about the educational requirements for these positions. Present your findings as a panel discussion; be prepared to answer classmates' questions.

Media Literacy

Prepare a Public Health Announcement In recent years, diseases transmitted from farm animals to humans have become a public health concern. If you were going to raise sheep, what should you know about keeping them, and yourself, healthy? Do some research on the subject, and prepare a brochure or a poster displaying the information. If you prefer, you can research diseases that spread from other animals, such as cats, birds, or dogs, to humans.

Go to **www.mirrorsandwindows.com** for more.

READING ASSESSMENT

1. Number these events in the correct sequence, with 1 being the first event to happen and 6 being the last.
   ___ All three men say they would use the money to set themselves up in business.
   ___ The three friends go to Baghdad to seek advice.
   ___ The caliph says that each man speaks well.
   ___ Three friends, before they can seek their fortune, work as shepherds.
   ___ The three men do not end up wealthy, but they gain wisdom and contentment.
   ___ The young men are dismayed at the caliph's gifts.

2. At first, the three men don't understand
   A. the worth of the golden lamb.
   B. the cost of setting up a business.
   C. the value of storytelling.
   D. the art of persuasion.
   E. the importance of friendship.

3. As it is used on page 702, the term *astonished* most nearly means
   A. angered.
   B. frightened.
   C. irritated.
   D. saddened.
   E. surprised.

4. Which statement best expresses the story's message?
   A. A wise ruler is a great blessing to a people.
   B. Small gifts can motivate people to follow their dreams.
   C. Understanding what is of true value and what is not has its rewards.
   D. People who choose commerce instead of art are foolish.
   E. Fighting will get you nowhere.

5. The caliphs were considered the successors of Muhammad, the founder of Islam. After reading "The Golden Lamb," how would you describe the ideal, or expected, role of the caliph in early days? Who would fill this role in your own culture?

VOCABULARY & SPELLING

UNDERSTAND THE CONCEPT APPLY THE SKILL

Prefixes, Roots, and Suffixes

The words *impossible, postponement,* and many other ordinary words consist of three parts: a **prefix,** a letter or group of letters added to the *beginning* of a word to change its meaning; the **root,** or base word; and a **suffix,** a letter or group of letters added to the *end* of a word to change its meaning or its part of speech. Recognizing the word parts and their meanings can help you figure out the definitions of unfamiliar words. The chart shows a few of the many prefixes, roots, and suffixes in English.

Other common prefixes include *sub-* ("under, below, less" as in *<u>sub</u>stitution*); *re-* ("again, back" as in *<u>re</u>petitive*); *un-* ("not" as in *<u>un</u>specific*).

Suffixes include *-ial* ("relating to" as in *president<u>ial</u>*); *-icity* ("state of" as in *domest<u>icity</u>*); *-hood* ("state of" as in *bachelor<u>hood</u>*). As you can see from the chart, the primary function of suffixes is often to indicate the part of speech.

Because there are so many root words—mostly from Old or Middle English, French, Greek, and Latin—it's a good idea to keep a notebook of unfamiliar root words you come across in literature and in science, social studies, and other subjects.

In using your knowledge of prefixes, roots, and suffixes to unlock the meaning of an unfamiliar word, be sure you have the correct definition of the word part and the correct spelling of the word itself. In fact, knowing how prefixes and roots work together should be useful when you are not sure how to spell a challenging word. Keep in mind that many words have a prefix and a root, or a root and a suffix—not necessarily all three parts.

Prefix/ Meaning	**Root/ Meaning**	**Suffix/ Meaning (Function)**	**Word Meaning**
dis- (the opposite of)	*enchant* (charm, attract)	*-ment* (state of; turns verb into noun)	*disenchantment* (act of disappointing)
pre- (before)	*dict* (say, tell)	*-able* (able to, capable of being; turns verb into adjective)	*predictable* (able to be foretold; able to be seen in advance)
col- (with)	*labor* (work, toil)	*-ation* (state of; turns verb into noun)	*collaboration* (act of working together; cooperation)
hyper- (over, above, beyond)	*therm* (heat)	*-ia* (state of)	*hyperthermia* (state of being over-heated)
se- (apart, aside, without)	*greg* (flock, herd)	*-ate* (to make or cause to be)	*segregate* (to set apart from others or from the general mass)

UNDERSTAND THE CONCEPT

APPLY THE SKILL

Exercise A

Use your knowledge of prefixes, roots, and suffixes—and a dictionary if needed—to define the following words. Then use each word in a sentence whose context helps indicate the word's meaning.

1. malodorous
2. retroactive
3. prognosis
4. unmindful
5. intercontinental
6. circumstantial
7. contingency
8. geosynchronous
9. luminosity
10. epigraph
11. prevalence
12. respiration
13. perquisite
14. delineate
15. colleague
16. counterproductive
17. ventriloquist
18. decelerate
19. anticipatory
20. intangible

Exercise B

Work with a partner. Individually, make a chart like the one on the previous page but fill in only the right-hand column. List three to five words that have a prefix, root, and suffix. Then exchange papers. Your partner can fill in the empty boxes to complete the chart.

Prefix/ Meaning	Root/ Meaning	Suffix/ Meaning (Function)	Word Meaning

EXTEND THE SKILL

The words we use for numbers, such as *five, twenty, hundred,* and *thousand,* are primarily from Old English, the earliest known form of the language. Nevertheless, many prefixes and roots that refer to numbers are from Latin or ancient Greek.

Examples are *mono-* ("one"), *deca-* ("ten"), and *mille-* ("thousand"). English terms that incorporate these word parts include *monologue* ("conversation in which only one person speaks"), *decathlon* ("athletic contest with ten parts"), and *millennium* ("a period of one thousand years"). Other numerical prefixes and roots include *bi-, tri-, quad-, penta-, hecta-, octa-,* and *cent-.*

Imagine that you are a sports correspondent covering the Olympics. Write a brief report of the competitive events you observe. Use numerical prefixes and roots to make your story more authentic; explain the terms to readers.

SPELLING PRACTICE

Words with Prefixes and Suffixes

Being able to recognize common prefixes and suffixes will help to make you a better speller because you will know how to spell the affix when you hear it. Some affixes you will recognize immediately, such as adding *-s* or *-es* to the end of a noun to make it plural; others are less common. Examine this list of spelling words from "The Golden Lamb" to determine which affixes have been used.

agreeable
anxious
argument
attendant
beginning
breathlessly
decision
delicacies
difficulty
disagreement
excitedly
ferocious
frantically
imprisoned
loneliness
remarkable
reunion
skillfully
succeeded
terrible
thoughtfully
troublesome
uncommonly
wealthy

Understanding Epics

THE EPIC

Thousands of years ago, before history had been written down in books, the people of ancient Greece turned to the poets to hear tales of the past. These poets, or bards, were masterful storytellers who would travel from village to village, singing or reciting long poetic **epics**—partly memorized, partly improvised—about the gods and heroes of days gone by. According to legend, the greatest of the ancient Greek bards was Homer. His two famous works, *The Iliad* (iˊ lē əd) and *The Odyssey* (äˊ də sē), are considered the most important and influential in all epic literature.

Since Homer's time, the epic has been recognized as a distinct *genre,* or type, of literature and, accordingly, imitated by other authors. **Epics** share the following characteristics:

- They are narrative poems—that is, they tell a story in verse, typically one taken from history or legend.
- They are grand in length and scope and provide a portrait of a culture—its beliefs, values, laws, arts, and ways of life.
- Their tone and style are serious and formal.
- Their subject is a battle or a great journey undertaken by a hero. Gods or other supernatural beings participate in the action.

ELEMENTS OF EPICS

The Epic Hero

At the center of the epic is a larger-than-life hero, a character of great, even superhuman, strength and courage who undertakes a difficult journey or quest. Often the hero does the following:

- travels to diverse, exotic settings around the world or the universe in the course of a quest or journey.
- is aided by gods or other supernatural beings.
- struggles against gods, monsters, or other antagonists that test his or her strength and wit, and must complete several formidable tasks before returning home.

The hero of *The Odyssey* is Odysseus, a Greek general who led his men to victory in the Trojan War. *The Odyssey* is about Odysseus's journey home from the war. During this ten-year journey, Odysseus faces many antagonists, including the Cyclops, Scylla and Charybdis, and the witch Circe. Like most epic heroes, Odysseus demonstrates heroic qualities—strength, courage, leadership, and craftiness—as well as a devotion to the home and family he has left behind. Odysseus's voyage can be seen as a metaphor or an allegory for the journey we go through in life, with its triumphs and heartbreaks.

The Epic Narrator

Epics like *The Odyssey* were not written but narrated by a poet who would chant or sing the tales to the tune of a lyre, a stringed instrument. The poet-narrator often improvised, or changed details, but generally followed these conventions:

- The narrator started with an **invocation**—a plea to the Muse, or goddess of poetry, for inspiration.
- The narrator began telling the tale ***in medias res,*** or "in the middle of things," filling in earlier details later, often in the form of speeches given by the main characters.
- The narrator used many stock expressions, or "word formulas," such as epithets and epic similes. **Epithets** are brief descriptive phrases that emphasize an important characteristic of a person or thing. These stock expressions were easy to remember and helped the oral poets improvise on a poem as it was sung. **Epic similes,** also known as *Homeric similes,* are extended comparisons that go on for several lines. Like the epithets, these long descriptive passages were probably memorized and repeated by the oral poets each time they told the story. In *The Odyssey,* Homer continually refers to "versatile Odysseus," "that man [Odysseus] skilled in all ways of contending," and "Dawn with finger tips of rose."

> A man in a distant field, no hearthfires
> near,
> will hide a fresh brand in his bed of embers
> to keep a spark alive for the next day;
> so in the leaves Odysseus hid himself,
> while over him Athena showered sleep…
> —from *The Odyssey,* Book 5, by Homer

ORIGIN OF EPICS

The oldest epic poem in the world dates back to ancient Mesopotamian cultures, in what is modern-day Iraq. The epic tale of *Gilgamesh* is based on a real king who ruled the city-state of Uruk around 2600 BCE. In a quest for immortality, he has a series of adventures battling monsters and defending himself against the goddess Inanna (Ishtar), whom he has offended. In a sense, Gilgamesh may be considered the first superhero (or anti-hero—he was not always a just ruler) in literature.

A Familiar Story?

Gilgamesh visits his relative Utnapishtim, who gives him a special water plant that can provide immortality. Utnapishtim is immortal himself, because he and his wife were told by the god Enki about a flood that would destroy humanity. They put a sample of every living thing on a boat and survived the flood to repopulate the earth. Scholars widely believe that this story is the basis for the story of Noah in the Bible. Interestingly, stories of world-destroying floods and the repopulating of the earth can also be found in the myths of the Aztecs, the Norse, the Chinese, the Incas, the Greeks, and the Hindus.

Illustration of the story of Noah's Ark.

The longest epic comes from India. The *Mahabharata* describes the feud between the Pandavas and the Kauravas, two families descended from King Bharata. These families supposedly lived in northern India around 1200 BCE and, like most epics, the tale involves the intervention of a god, Krishna. The *Mahabharata* is seven times the length of both *The Iliad* and *The Odyssey.*

GODS AND GODDESSES AT WORK

Like the epic tale of *Gilgamesh* and the *Mahabharata*, Homer's epics also involve the supernatural and the fantastic. To the ancient Greeks, the gods and goddesses were an important part of everyday life. They were believed to intervene in human affairs and could influence people's lives—for better or for worse. The Greeks feared their gods and offered prayers and sacrifices to win their protection. Zeus, the ruler of the sky, was the most powerful god (to the Romans he was known as Jupiter). Zeus's brother Poseidon (known by the Romans as Neptune) ruled the oceans. Frequently in *The Odyssey,* Poseidon creates threatening conditions at sea to hinder Odysseus's journey. In contrast, the goddess of wisdom, Athena, comes to the hero's aid when he is most in need of help.

Other Famous Epics

- *Ramayana:* second major Indian epic, written around 500 BCE. Like *The Iliad,* it describes a battle over a man's wife who is taken away.
- *Aeneid:* written by the Roman Virgil around 25 BCE. It involves the hero Aeneas relating his story of the trick of the Trojan horse and the fall of Troy.
- *El Cid:* The tale of a real soldier who fought for both the Christians and the Moors in eleventh-century Spain.

Sita-Rama: Hero and Heroine of the *Ramayana.*

Understanding Homer's Epics

THE ILIAD AND *THE ODYSSEY*

The legendary bard **Homer** is credited with composing *The Iliad* and *The Odyssey,* the two greatest epic poems of ancient Greece.

The Iliad and *The Odyssey,* two of the greatest narrative poems in the Western tradition, provide us with insight into the world of the ancient Greeks. (In *The Odyssey,* they are referred to as Achaeans.) The epics are exciting, suspenseful stories, told in memorable, poetic language that has appealed to readers since Homer's day. The questions they raise and the themes they explore are at the core of the human experience.

The Iliad tells the story of the Trojan War, a battle fought around 1200 BCE by the Greeks and the Trojans (inhabitants of Troy, now part of Turkey). According

to legend, the war started when the Trojan prince Paris kidnapped Helen, the wife of the king of the Greek city-state Sparta. Helen was fabled to be the most beautiful woman in the world, and her husband was determined to get her back. After declaring war on Troy, Menelaus recruited kings and soldiers from all around Greece to help him fight. (Troy was also known as Ilion, the origin of the name *Iliad.*) Odysseus, king of Ithaca (a small Ionian Island off the coast of western Greece),

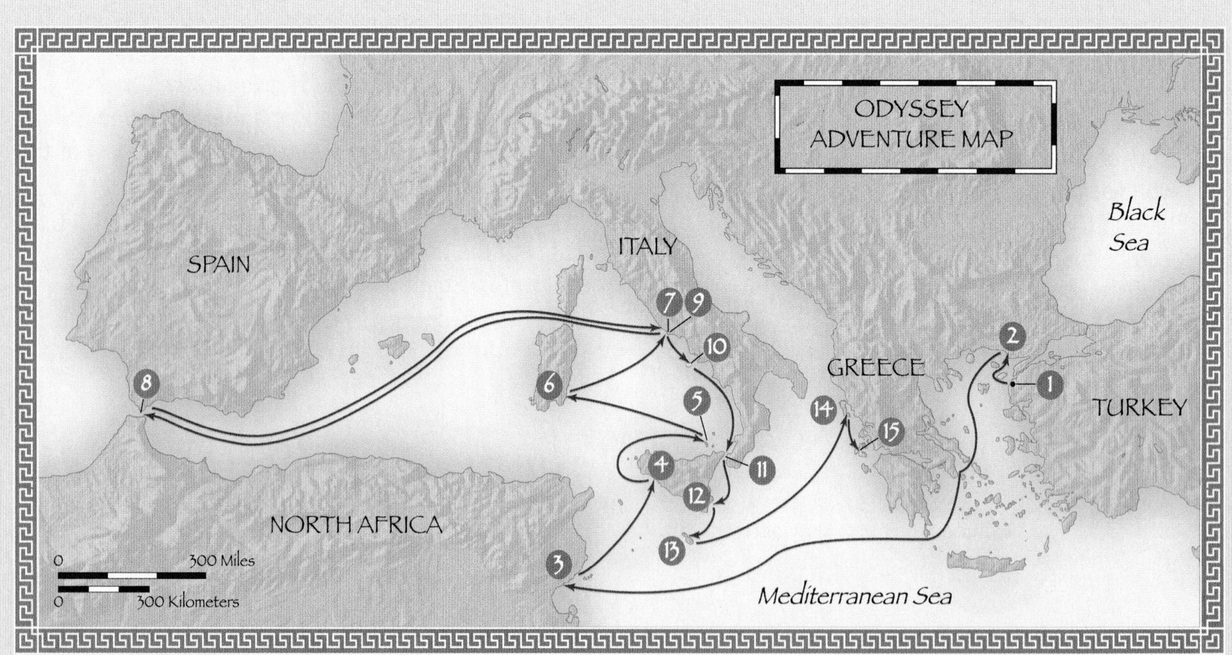

KEY

1. Troy (also called Ilion)
2. Cicones
3. Lotus Eaters
4. Cyclopes
5. Aeolia, the Island of Winds
6. Laestrygonians
7. Circe
8. Land of the Dead
9. Circe again
10. Sirens
11. Scylla and Charybdis
12. Thrinakia, the Island of Helios
13. Calypso
14. Phaeacia
15. Ithaca

did not want to leave his family and his homeland. In order to avoid fighting, he acted as though he had gone mad. He did this by plowing his fields night and day and planting salt instead of grain. His sanity was revealed, however, when his son was put before the plow. Odysseus revealed his sanity when he swerved, missing the boy.

THE EPIC VOYAGE TO ITHACA

For ten years, the Greeks laid siege to Troy but could not penetrate the city walls—until "clever Odysseus," as Homer calls him, devised a plan. His companions erected a giant wooden horse, a number of soldiers crept inside it, and what has become known as the Trojan horse was left outside the city. Then the Greeks pretended to sail homeward. Believing that the impressive structure was a gift from their defeated enemy, the Trojans wheeled it through the city gates. That night, the soldiers crawled out, opened the gates to admit their waiting comrades, and together they conquered the Trojans.

After the defeat of the Trojans, Odysseus set sail for Ithaca. During the ten-year voyage described in *The Odyssey*, the hero and his companions are confronted by vicious monsters and deadly temptations. Their ship is tossed about by Poseidon, the god of the sea, who holds a grudge against the "wily Odysseus." When, at long last, Odysseus reaches Ithaca, after an absence of twenty years, he finds that his faithful wife, Penelope, and their son, Telemachus, have been besieged by suitors eager to marry Penelope and become king of Ithaca. With the aid of Athena, Odysseus eventually slaughters the suitors. Husband, wife, and son are reunited.

Pronunciation Guide

Characters and Places in *The Odyssey*

Achaeans (ə kē´ ənz): Greeks
Agamemnon (a' gə mem´ nän' *or* a' gə mem´ nən): Greek king and husband of Helen, whose kidnapping by the Trojans set off the Trojan War
Alcinous (al sin´ ō əs): king of the island of Phaeacia, where Odysseus is shipwrecked near the end of his journey
Antinous (an tin ō´ əs): one of Penelope's suitors
Argos (är´ gəs): Odysseus's dog
Cicones (sī kō´ nes): allies of the Trojans and enemies of the Greeks
Erebus (er´ ə bəs): place of darkness in the Underworld
Eumaeus (yü´ mē əs): Odysseus's swineherd
Eurycleia (yü´ ri klē ə): Odysseus's nurse
Eur'ylochus (yü ri´ lō kəs): member of Odysseus's crew
Eurymachus (yü rim´ ə kəs): one of Penelope's suitors
Laertes (lā ʉr´ tēz): Odysseus's father
Laestrygonians (les trig ō´ nē ənz): cannibals who lived on a distant island
Lotus (lō´ təs) Eaters: people who live off the intoxicating lotus plant
Odysseus (ō di´ sē əs): king of Ithaca, hero of the Trojan War, and main character in *The Odyssey*
Penelope (pə ne´ lə pē): wife of Odysseus
Perimêdês (pe ri me´ des): a member of Odysseus's crew
Phaeacia (fē ā´ shə): island kingdom ruled by Alcinous
Philoeteus (fil oi´ tē əs): Odysseus's cowherd
Pieria (pī ir ē´ ə): a location in central Greece not far from Olympus; a favorite location of Hermes
Pylos (pi´ lōs): home of Nestor, a soldier who fought with Odysseus in the Trojan War
Teiresias (tī rē´ sē əs): blind prophet
Telemachus (tə le´ mə kəs): son of Odyssey and Penelope
Telemus (tel´ə məs): wizard who foretold Polyphemus's future
Thrinakia (thri nä´ kē ä): island filled with grazing farm animals owned by Helios, the sun god

Gods, Goddesses, and Mythical Creatures

Athena (ə thē´ nə): goddess of wisdom and protector of Odysseus
Calypso (kə lip´ sō[']): sea nymph who holds Odysseus captive on her island for seven years
Charybdis (kə rib´ dəs *or* shə rib´ dəs *or* chə rib´ dəs): female monster who lives underwater and forms a deadly whirlpool
Circe (sʉr´ sē[']): goddess and sorceress (witch) who lives on the island of Aeaea
Cyclopes (sī klō´ pēz[']): one-eyed giants; plural of *Cyclops*
Hades (hā´ dēz[']): god of the Underworld
Helios (hē´ lē əs *or* hē´ lē ōs[']): sun god
Hermes (hʉr´ mēz[']): messenger god
Muse (myüz): goddess of epic poetry
Persephone (pər se´ fə nē): daughter of Zeus whom Pluto kidnapped
Polyphemus (pä' lə fē´ məs): the Cyclops who eats some of Odysseus's crew; son of Poseidon (pə sī´ d'n), god of the sea and earthquakes
Scylla (si´ lə): six-headed female sea monster
Sirens (sī´ rənz): group of singing nymphs who lure men to their deaths
Zeus (züs): ruler of all the gods

from The Odyssey: PART ONE

BEFORE READING **An Epic Poem by Homer, Translated by Robert Fitzgerald**

DIRECTED READING

BUILD BACKGROUND

Literary Context Homer's ***The Odyssey,*** like many epics, is told in a lofty style that employs a number of literary conventions, or traditional features. The epic opens with the speaker's **invocation,** or plea, to the goddess of poetry for inspiration. Like many epics, Odysseus' story starts ***in medias res,*** or "in the middle of things"—seven years after the hero's arrival on Calypso's island, where he remains against his will. The selection from Book 5, still in the speaker's voice, explains how the gods rescue him from the sea nymph Calypso. When Odysseus reaches the island of Phaeacia, he narrates the story of his troubled journey from the beginning, since leaving Troy (Book 9). As you read Part One, consider why Homer introduces Odysseus' tale in a flashback near the end of his travels. A flashback interrupts the chronological sequence of a literary work and presents an event that occurred earlier. In *The Odyssey,* the hero describes the events that have brought him to Phaeacia.

Reader's Context If you were treated rudely when you were a guest in someone's home, how might you handle the situation?

ANALYZE LITERATURE: Epic Poem

Thousands of years ago, the people of ancient Greece turned to the poets to hear tales from the past. These poets, or bards, were masterful storytellers who traveled from village to village, singing or reciting **epic poems.** Epics provide a portrait of a culture; interwoven in the majestic tales are a society's legends, beliefs, values, laws, arts, and customs.

SET PURPOSE

Keep in mind that *The Odyssey* is told from two **points of view**—much of the narration is from Odysseus' perspective *(first person),* but some of it is from the viewpoint of the speaker, who remains outside the events *(third person).* Try to determine why Homer switches points of view when he does. Visualize the characters and settings that Homer describes, and consider what the hero's thoughts and actions suggest about the culture of ancient Greece.

MEET THE AUTHOR

The facts of Homer's life are shrouded in legend, and nobody knows if Homer actually existed. Some ancient accounts, not necessarily reliable, say that the poet was blind and lived on the Greek island of Chios in the Aegean Sea. According to other sources, Homer was from Ionia, an ancient region in Asia Minor (modern-day Turkey). If Homer was a historical figure, he probably composed and recited his poems around 800 BCE. Because, like most of his listeners, Homer could neither read nor write, he recited his poems to appreciative listeners. His masterpieces, therefore, were probably not written down until several hundred years after his death.

USE READING SKILLS

Identify Text Organization Being alert to text organization helps you notice changes in a story's point of view. As you read the selections from Books 1, 5, and 9 of *The Odyssey,* observe the link between shift in narrator and change in setting (time and place). You can keep track of point of view by using a graphic organizer like the one below.

Event	Narrator
Calypso releases Odysseus	Homer
War in Ísmaros	Odysseus

PREVIEW VOCABULARY

Examine the vocabulary words listed and answer the questions that follow.

plunder *adversity*
valor *ponderous*
mandate *cordial*
exile *sage*
versatile *adversary*

1. Which of the adjectives have a primarily positive meaning, and which are primarily negative?
2. Which words are always used as nouns?
3. Which words have similar etymologies (histories)?
4. Which two adjectives can also be nouns with entirely different meanings?

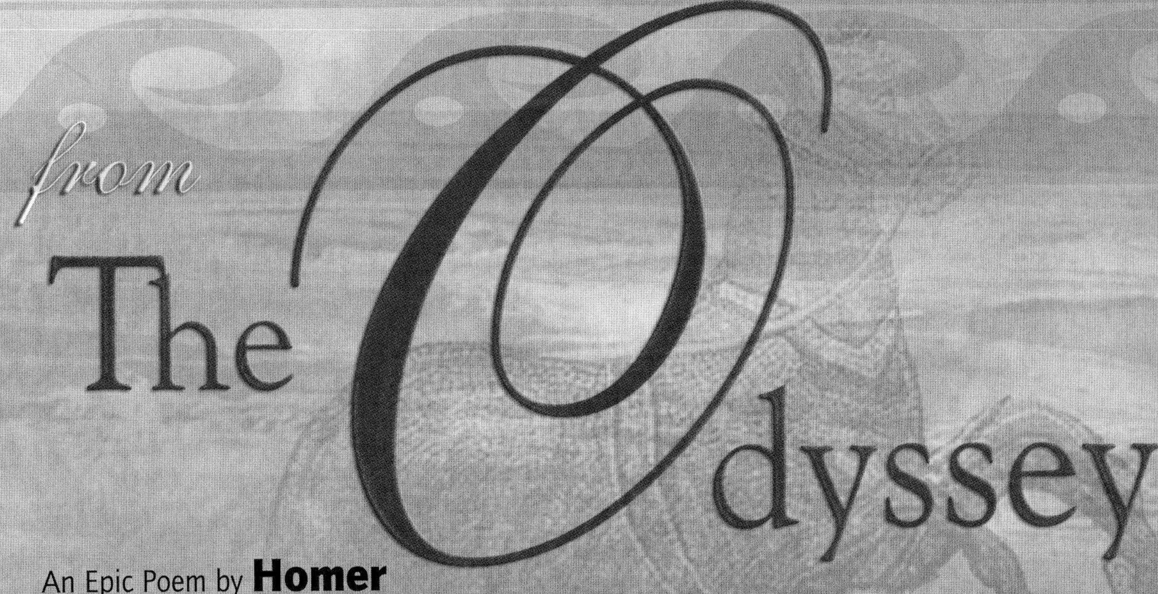

from The Odyssey

An Epic Poem by **Homer**

Translated by **Robert Fitzgerald**

Part One: from Books 1, 5, and 9

Yet all the gods had pitied Lord Odysseus, all but Poseidon, raging cold and rough against the brave king till he came ashore at last on his own land....

Homer Begins His Tale (from Book 1)

Homer begins with an invocation, or prayer, in which he calls upon a Muse—the goddess of epic poetry—for help and inspiration in telling his tale. In the invocation, he also gives his listeners a brief outline of the story that is to come.

Sing in me, Muse, and through me tell the story
of that man skilled in all ways of contending,
the wanderer, harried for years on end,
after he plundered the stronghold
on the proud height of Troy.
                    He saw the townlands
and learned the minds of many distant men,

plun • der (plʉn´ dər) *v.*, steal or take by trickery or by force

CULTURAL CONNECTION

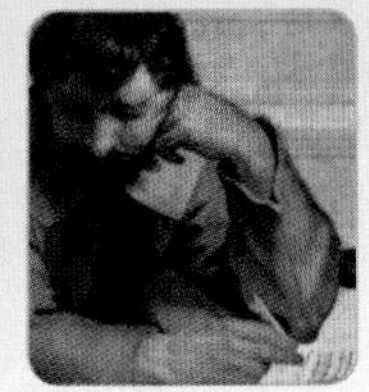

Education Homer's epics, *The Iliad* and *The Odyssey,* became well known beyond his homeland of Asia Minor. By the sixth century CE, schoolboys in the city of Athens could recite the poems, often by heart. Unfortunately, schoolboys constituted a tiny minority of children in the Mediterranean world at that time. Even among the wealthy, girls were taught mostly how to fulfill their obligations as wives and mothers. Few children of slaves received any schooling. Indeed, until relatively recently in the United States and Europe, most young girls, and most sons and daughters of servants, received only the most basic education.

and weathered many bitter nights and days
in his deep heart at sea, while he fought only
to save his life, to bring his shipmates home.
But not by will nor valor could he save them,
for their own recklessness destroyed them all—
children and fools, they killed and feasted on
the cattle of Lord Helios, the Sun,
and he who moves all day through heaven
took from their eyes the dawn of their return.

Of these adventures, Muse, daughter of Zeus,
tell us in our time, lift the great song again.
Begin when all the rest who left behind them
headlong death in battle or at sea
had long ago returned, while he alone still hungered
for home and wife. Her ladyship Calypso
clung to him in her sea-hollowed caves—
a nymph, immortal and most beautiful,
who craved him for her own.

And when long years and seasons
wheeling brought around that point of time
ordained for him to make his passage homeward,
trials and dangers, even so, attended him
even in Ithaca, near those he loved.

val • or (va´ lər) *n.,* personal bravery

Yet all the gods had pitied Lord Odysseus,
all but Poseidon, raging cold and rough
against the brave king till he came ashore
at last on his own land....

The Sweet Nymph Calypso (from Book 5)

Books 1–4 tell about the travels of Telemachus (tə lem′ ə kəs), *Odysseus' son, who has been searching unsuccessfully for his missing father. Nearly ten years after the Greeks' victory at Troy, the hero Odysseus still has not returned home to Ithaca. For seven of those years, he has been held prisoner by the sea nymph Calypso* (kə lip′ sō). *Now the goddess Athena, feeling sorry for Odysseus, appeals to her father, Zeus, to intervene. Zeus sends Hermes* (hʉr′ mēz′), *the messenger god, to Calypso with an order: She must release Odysseus and help him to return home.*

Calypso and Telemachus, 1809. Benjamin West.

No words were lost on Hermes the Wayfinder,
who bent to tie his beautiful sandals on,
ambrosial, golden, that carry him over water
or over endless land in a swish of the wind,
and took the wand with which he charms asleep—
or when he wills, awake—the eyes of men.
So wand in hand he paced into the air,
shot from Pieria down, down to sea level,
and veered to skim the swell. A gull patrolling
between the wave crests of the desolate sea
will dip to catch a fish, and douse his wings;
no higher above the whitecaps Hermes flew
until the distant island lay ahead,
then rising shoreward from the violet ocean
he stepped up to the cave. Divine Calypso,
the mistress of the isle, was now at home.
Upon her hearthstone a great fire blazing
scented the farthest shores with cedar smoke
and smoke of thyme, and singing high and low
in her sweet voice, before her loom a-weaving,
she passed her golden shuttle to and fro.
A deep wood grew outside, with summer leaves
of alder and black poplar, pungent cypress.
Ornate birds here rested their stretched wings—
horned owls, falcons, cormorants—long-tongued
beachcombing birds, and followers of the sea.
Around the smoothwalled cave a crooking vine
held purple clusters under ply of green;
and four springs, bubbling up near one another
shallow and clear, took channels here and there
through beds of violets and tender parsley.
Even a god who found this place
would gaze, and feel his heart beat with delight:
so Hermes did; but when he had gazed his fill
he entered the wide cave. Now face to face
the magical Calypso recognized him,
as all immortal gods know one another
on sight—though seeming strangers, far from home.
But he saw nothing of the great Odysseus,
who sat apart, as a thousand times before,
and racked his own heart groaning, with eyes wet
scanning the bare horizon of the sea....

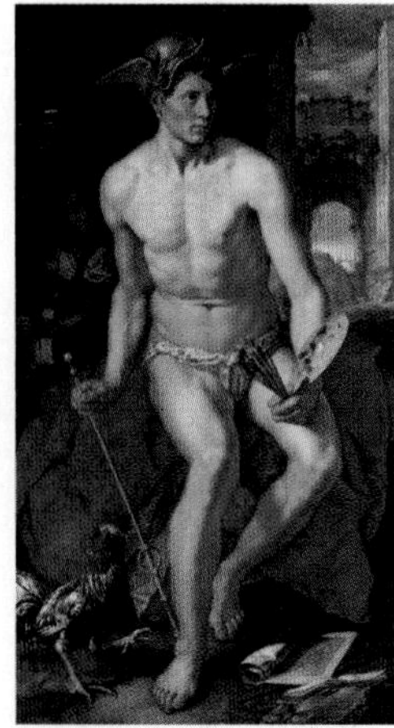

Mercury, 1611.
Hendrick Goltzius.

As Calypso serves him ambrosia and nectar, Hermes delivers the message that she must release Odysseus.

The strong god glittering left her as he spoke,
and now her ladyship, having given heed
to Zeus' mandate, went to find Odysseus
in his stone seat to seaward—tear on tear
brimming his eyes. The sweet days of his life time
were running out in anguish over his exile,
for long ago the nymph had ceased to please.
Though he fought shy of her and her desire,
he lay with her each night, for she compelled him.
But when day came he sat on the rocky shore
and broke his own heart groaning, with eyes wet
scanning the bare horizon of the sea.
Now she stood near him in her beauty, saying:

"O forlorn man, be still.
Here you need grieve no more; you need not feel
your life consumed here; I have pondered it,
and I shall help you go. . . ."

Calypso tells Odysseus to make a raft for his journey home. He expresses disbelief at her willingness to help him, but she insists that it is not a trick—he really will be free to go at last.

Swiftly she turned and led him to her cave,
and they went in, the mortal and immortal.
He took the chair left empty now by Hermes,
where the divine Calypso placed before him
victuals[1] and drink of men; then she sat down
facing Odysseus, while her serving maids
brought nectar and ambrosia to her side.
Then each one's hands went out on each one's feast
until they had had their pleasure; and she said:

"Son of Laertes, versatile Odysseus,
after these years with me, you still desire
your old home? Even so, I wish you well.
If you could see it all, before you go—

1. **victuals.** Food

man • date (man´ dāt') *n.,* formal order; command
ex • ile (eg´ zīl' *or* eg´ zī' əl) *n.,* period of forced absence from one's country
ver • sa • tile (vʉr´ sə t'l) *adj.,* able to perform a variety of functions

all the adversity you face at sea—
you would stay here, and guard this house, and be
immortal—though you wanted her forever,
that bride for whom you pine each day.
Can I be less desirable than she is?
Less interesting? Less beautiful? Can mortals
compare with goddesses in grace and form?"

To this the strategist Odysseus answered:

"My lady goddess, here is no cause for anger.
My quiet Penelope—how well I know—
would seem a shade before your majesty,
death and old age being unknown to you,
while she must die. Yet, it is true, each day
I long for home, long for the sight of home...."

Odysseus sets out on the sea, but Poseidon sends a storm that destroys his raft. With the help of Athena he is saved, but just barely. Exhausted and swollen with seawater, he is washed up on the shore of a strange island.

A man in a distant field, no hearthfires near,
will hide a fresh brand in his bed of embers
to keep a spark alive for the next day;
so in the leaves Odysseus hid himself,
while over him Athena showered sleep
that his distress should end, and soon, soon.
In quiet sleep she sealed his cherished eyes.

Ulysses at the Court of Alcinous, 1813–1815. Francesco Hayez.

ad • ver • si • ty (ad vʉr´ sə tē) *n.,* a state of continued misfortune

I AM LAERTES' SON (from Book 9)

The island on which Odysseus lands turns out to be Phaeacia (fē ā´ shə), *an island kingdom ruled by King Alcinous* (al sin´ ō əs). *In Books 6–8, the shipwrecked Odysseus is found by the king's daughter and brought to the royal palace. The king and queen offer to assist him on his journey home. At a banquet at their palace, a poet sings stories about the Trojan War, which sadden the hero. Odysseus then reveals his identity and tells the story of what happened to him after he left Troy.*

Now this was the reply Odysseus made:...

"I am Laertes' son, Odysseus.
                                                  Men hold me
formidable for guile in peace and war:
this fame has gone abroad to the sky's rim.
My home is on the peaked sea-mark of Ithaca
under Mount Neion's wind-blown robe of leaves,
in sight of other islands—Doulíkhion,
Samê, wooded Zakynthos—Ithaca
being most lofty in that coastal sea,
and northwest, while the rest lie east and south.
A rocky isle, but good for a boy's training;
I shall not see on earth a place more dear,
though I have been detained long by Calypso,
loveliest among goddesses, who held me
in her smooth caves, to be her heart's delight,
as Circe of Aeaea, the enchantress,
desired me, and detained me in her hall.
But in my heart I never gave consent.
Where shall a man find sweetness to surpass
his own home and his parents? In far lands
he shall not, though he find a house of gold.

What of my sailing, then, from Troy?
                                                  What of those years
of rough adventure, weathered under Zeus?
The wind that carried west from Ilion
brought me to Ísmaros, on the far shore,
a strongpoint on the coast of the Cicones.
I stormed that place and killed the men who fought.
Plunder we took, and we enslaved the women,
to make division, equal shares to all—
but on the spot I told them: 'Back, and quickly!
Out to sea again!' My men were mutinous,

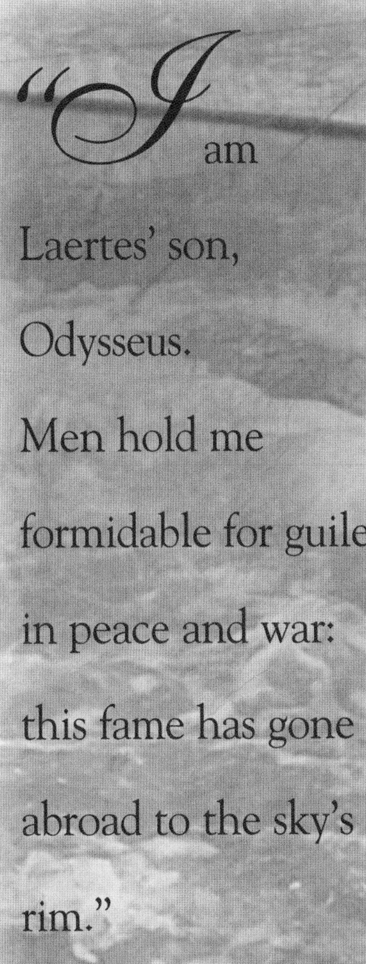
"I am
Laertes' son,
Odysseus.
Men hold me
formidable for guile
in peace and war:
this fame has gone
abroad to the sky's
rim."

HISTORY CONNECTION

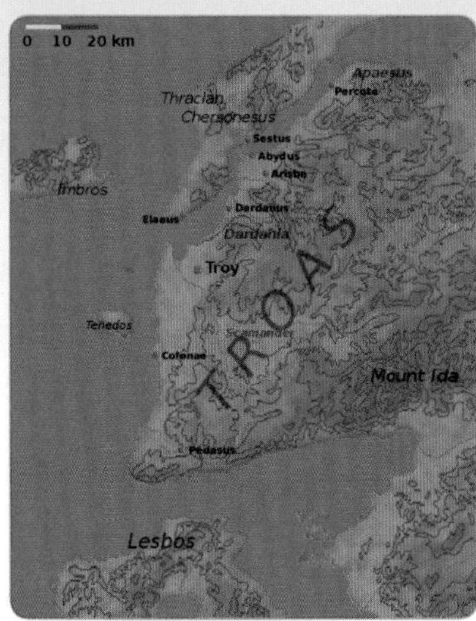

Excavation of Troy In the nineteenth century, a German excavator, Heinrich Schliemann, sailed to Troy (in modern-day Turkey). Schliemann dug into a hill overlooking the Aegean Sea, at what he thought was the site of the famous war. He and his followers discovered not one but nine cities—layer upon layer of long-ago civilizations. As one culture suffered defeat in war or was toppled by an earthquake, the next group of settlers constructed their city on top of the walls, buildings, and other relics of the ruins. According to some archaeologists, the layer identified as VIIA might be the Troy of *The Iliad.* The location probably attracted so many societies because of its strategic setting near the trade routes between Europe and Asia.

fools, on stores of wine. Sheep after sheep
they butchered by the surf, and shambling cattle,
feasting,—while fugitives went inland, running
to call to arms the main force of Cicones.
This was an army, trained to fight on horseback
or, where the ground required, on foot. They came
with dawn over that terrain like the leaves
and blades of spring. So doom appeared to us,
dark word of Zeus for us, our evil days.
My men stood up and made a fight of it—
backed on the ships, with lances kept in play,
from bright morning through the blaze of noon
holding our beach, although so far outnumbered;
but when the sun passed toward unyoking time,
then the Achaeans, one by one, gave way.
Six benches were left empty in every ship
that evening when we pulled away from death.
And this new grief we bore with us to sea:
our precious lives we had, but not our friends.
No ship made sail next day until some shipmate
had raised a cry, three times, for each poor ghost
unfleshed by the Cicones on that field.

Now Zeus the lord of cloud roused in the north
a storm against the ships, and driving veils
of squall moved down like night on land and sea.
The bows went plunging at the gust; sails

cracked and lashed out strips in the big wind.
We saw death in that fury, dropped the yards,
unshipped the oars, and pulled for the nearest lee:
then two long days and nights we lay offshore
worn out and sick at heart, tasting our grief,
until a third Dawn came with ringlets shining.
Then we put up our masts, hauled sail, and rested,
letting the steersmen and the breeze take over.

The Lotus Eaters (from Book 9)

I might have made it safely home, that time,
but as I came round Malea the current
took me out to sea, and from the north
a fresh gale drove me on, past Cythera.
Nine days I drifted on the teeming sea
before dangerous high winds. Upon the tenth
we came to the coastline of the Lotus Eaters,
who live upon that flower. We landed there
to take on water. All ships' companies
mustered alongside for the mid-day meal.
Then I sent out two picked men and a runner
to learn what race of men that land sustained.
They fell in, soon enough, with Lotus Eaters,
who showed no will to do us harm, only
offering the sweet Lotus to our friends—
but those who ate this honeyed plant, the Lotus,
never cared to report, nor to return:
they longed to stay forever, browsing on
that native bloom, forgetful of their homeland.
I drove them, all three wailing, to the ships,
tied them down under their rowing benches,
and called the rest: 'All hands aboard;
come, clear the beach and no one taste
the Lotus, or you lose your hope of home.'
Filing in to their places by the rowlocks
my oarsmen dipped their long oars in the surf,
and we moved out again on our sea faring...."

Land of the Cyclopes

The next land Odysseus and his men visit in Book 9 is the land of the Cyclopes (sī´ klō pēz), *one-eyed giants who dwell in mountain caves. Odysseus disembarks with twelve of his best men to investigate the cave of the Cyclops named Polyphemus* (päl i fē´ məs), *who happens to be the son of Poseidon, god of the sea. Once they reach the cave, Odysseus' men suggest that they steal the giant's cheeses and livestock and flee as quickly as possible back to the waiting ship. Odysseus, however, wants to wait so he can see the giant for himself. His curiosity puts him and his men in grave danger, and the hero must use some of his famed wiliness in order to escape with his life.*

"We lit a fire, burnt an offering,
and took some cheese to eat; then sat in silence
around the embers, waiting. When he came
he had a load of dry boughs on his shoulder
to stoke his fire at suppertime. He dumped it
with a great crash into that hollow cave,
and we all scattered fast to the far wall.
Then over the broad cavern floor he ushered
the ewes he meant to milk. He left his rams
and he-goats in the yard outside, and swung
high overhead a slab of solid rock
to close the cave. Two dozen four-wheeled wagons,
with heaving wagon teams, could not have stirred
the tonnage of that rock from where he wedged it
over the doorsill. Next he took his seat
and milked his bleating ewes. A practiced job
he made of it, giving each ewe her suckling;
thickened his milk, then, into curds and whey,
sieved out the curds to drip in withy[2] baskets,
and poured the whey to stand in bowls
cooling until he drank it for his supper.
When all these chores were done, he poked the fire,
heaping on brushwood. In the glare he saw us.

'Strangers,' he said, 'who are you? And where from?
What brings you here by sea ways—a fair traffic?[3]
Or are you wandering rogues,[4] who cast your lives
like dice, and ravage other folk by sea?'

2. **withy.** Made of willow twigs
3. **fair traffic.** Honest trade
4. **rogues.** Wicked or rascally persons

We felt a pressure on our hearts, in dread
of that deep rumble and that mighty man.
But all the same I spoke up in reply:

'We are from Troy, Achaeans, blown off course
by shifting gales on the Great South Sea;
homeward bound, but taking routes and ways
uncommon; so the will of Zeus would have it.
We served under Agamemnon, son of Atreus—
the whole world knows what city
he laid waste, what armies he destroyed.
It was our luck to come here; here we stand,
beholden for your help, or any gifts
you give—as custom is to honor strangers.[5]
We would entreat you, great Sir, have a care
for the gods' courtesy; Zeus will avenge
the unoffending guest.'

He answered this
from his brute chest, unmoved:

'You are a ninny,
or else you come from the other end of nowhere,
telling me, mind the gods! We Cyclopes
care not a whistle for your thundering Zeus
or all the gods in bliss; we have more force by far.
I would not let you go for fear of Zeus—
you or your friends—unless I had a whim to.
Tell me, where was it, now, you left your ship—
around the point, or down the shore, I wonder?'

He thought he'd find out, but I saw through this,
and answered with a ready lie:

'My ship?
Poseidon Lord, who sets the earth a-tremble,
broke it up on the rocks at your land's end.
A wind from seaward served him, drove us there.
We are survivors, these good men and I.'

Neither reply nor pity came from him,
but in one stride he clutched at my companions
and caught two in his hands like squirming puppies

"We would entreat you, great Sir, have a care for the gods' courtesy; Zeus will avenge the unoffending guest."

5. **as custom...strangers.** Among the ancient Greeks, treating visitors well was considered a sacred obligation.

to beat their brains out, spattering the floor.
Then he dismembered them and made his meal,
gaping and crunching like a mountain lion—
everything: innards, flesh, and marrow bones.
We cried aloud, lifting our hands to Zeus,
powerless, looking on at this, appalled;
but Cyclops went on filling up his belly
with manflesh and great gulps of whey,
then lay down like a mast among his sheep.
My heart beat high now at the chance of action,
and drawing the sharp sword from my hip I went
along his flank to stab him where the midriff
holds the liver. I had touched the spot
when sudden fear stayed me: if I killed him
we perished there as well, for we could never
move his ponderous doorway slab aside.
So we were left to groan and wait for morning.

When the young Dawn with finger tips of rose
lit up the world, the Cyclops built a fire
and milked his handsome ewes, all in due order,
putting the sucklings to the mothers. Then,
his chores being all dispatched, he caught
another brace[6] of men to make his breakfast,
and whisked away his great door slab
to let his sheep go through—but he, behind,
reset the stone as one would cap a quiver.[7]
There was a din[8] of whistling as the Cyclops
rounded his flock to higher ground, then stillness.
And now I pondered how to hurt him worst
if but Athena granted what I prayed for.
Here are the means I thought would serve my turn:

a club, or staff, lay there along the fold—
an olive tree, felled green and left to season
for Cyclops' hand. And it was like a mast
a lugger of twenty oars, broad in the beam—
a deep-sea-going craft—might carry:
so long, so big around, it seemed. Now I
chopped out a six-foot section of this pole

6. **brace.** A pair or couple, set of two similar things considered as a unit
7. **cap a quiver.** Put the top on a container for arrows
8. **din.** Noise

pon • der • ous (pän´ d[ə] rəs) *adj.*, heavy; bulky; massive

and set it down before my men, who scraped it;
and when they had it smooth, I hewed again
to make a stake with pointed end. I held this
in the fire's heart and turned it, toughening it,
then hid it, well back in the cavern, under
one of the dung piles in profusion there.
Now came the time to toss for it: who ventured
along with me? whose hand could bear to thrust
and grind that spike in Cyclops' eye, when mild
sleep had mastered him? As luck would have it,
the men I would have chosen won the toss—
four strong men, and I made five as captain.

At evening came the shepherd with his flock,
his woolly flock. The rams as well, this time,
entered the cave: by some sheep-herding whim—
or a god's bidding—none were left outside.
He hefted[9] his great boulder into place
and sat him down to milk the bleating ewes
in proper order, put the lambs to suck,
and swiftly ran through all his evening chores.
Then he caught two more men and feasted on them.
My moment was at hand, and I went forward
holding an ivy bowl of my dark drink,
looking up, saying:

'Cyclops, try some wine.
Here's liquor to wash down your scraps of men.
Taste it, and see the kind of drink we carried
under our planks. I meant it for an offering
if you would help us home. But you are mad,
unbearable, a bloody monster! After this,
will any other traveller come to see you?'

He seized and drained the bowl, and it went down
so fiery and smooth he called for more:

'Give me another, thank you kindly. Tell me,
how are you called? I'll make a gift will please you.
Even Cyclopes know the wine-grapes grow
out of grassland and loam in heaven's rain,
but here's a bit of nectar and ambrosia!'[10]

9. **hefted.** Lifted
10. **ambrosia.** Food of the gods

Ulysses Overcoming Polyphemus, 1640.
Theodor van Thulden.

Three bowls I brought him, and he poured them down.
I saw the fuddle and flush come over him,
then I sang out in <u>cordial</u> tones:

'Cyclops,
you ask my honorable name? Remember
the gift you promised me, and I shall tell you.
My name is Nohbdy: mother, father, and friends,
everyone calls me Nohbdy.'

cor • dial (kôr´ jəl) *adj.,* friendly

And he said:
'Nohbdy's my meat, then, after I eat his friends.
Others come first. There's a noble gift, now.'

Even as he spoke, he reeled and tumbled backward,
his great head lolling to one side: and sleep
took him like any creature. Drunk, hiccupping,
he dribbled streams of liquor and bits of men.

Now, by the gods, I drove my big hand spike
deep in the embers, charring it again,
and cheered my men along with battle talk
to keep their courage up: no quitting now.
The pike of olive, green though it had been,
reddened and glowed as if about to catch.
I drew it from the coals and my four fellows
gave me a hand, lugging it near the Cyclops
as more than natural force nerved them; straight
forward they sprinted, lifted it, and rammed it
deep in his crater eye, and I leaned on it
turning it as a shipwright turns a drill
in planking, having men below to swing
the two-handled strap that spins it in the groove.
So with our brand we bored that great eye socket
while blood ran out around the red hot bar.
Eyelid and lash were seared; the pierced ball
hissed broiling, and the roots popped.

In a smithy
one sees a white-hot axehead or an adze[11]
plunged and wrung in a cold tub, screeching steam—
the way they make soft iron hale and hard—:
just so that eyeball hissed around the spike.
The Cyclops bellowed and the rock roared round him,
and we fell back in fear. Clawing his face
he tugged the bloody spike out of his eye,
threw it away, and his wild hands went groping;
then he set up a howl for Cyclopes
who lived in caves on windy peaks nearby.
Some heard him; and they came by divers[12] ways
to clump around outside and call:

'What ails you,

11. **adze.** Axe-like tool with a curved blade
12. **divers.** Various; several

Polyphemus? Why do you cry so sore
in the starry night? You will not let us sleep.
Sure no man's driving off your flock? No man
has tricked you, ruined you?'

Out of the cave
the mammoth Polyphemus roared in answer:

'Nohbdy, Nohbdy's tricked me, Nohbdy's ruined me!'

To this rough shout they made a <u>sage</u> reply:

'Ah well, if nobody has played you foul
there in your lonely bed, we are no use in pain
given by great Zeus. Let it be your father,
Poseidon Lord, to whom you pray.'

So saying
they trailed away. And I was filled with laughter
to see how like a charm the name deceived them.
Now Cyclops, wheezing as the pain came on him,
fumbled to wrench away the great doorstone
and squatted in the breach with arms thrown wide
for any silly beast or man who bolted—
hoping somehow I might be such a fool.
But I kept thinking how to win the game:
death sat there huge; how could we slip away?
I drew on all my wits, and ran through tactics,
reasoning as a man will for dear life,
until a trick came—and it pleased me well.
The Cyclops' rams were handsome, fat, with heavy
fleeces, a dark violet.

Three abreast
I tied them silently together, twining
cords of willow from the ogre's bed;
then slung a man under each middle one
to ride there safely, shielded left and right.
So three sheep could convey each man. I took
the woolliest ram, the choicest of the flock,
and hung myself under his kinky belly,
pulled up tight, with fingers twisted deep
in sheepskin ringlets for an iron grip.
So, breathing hard, we waited until morning.

sage (sāj) *adj.*, wise

Ulysses in the Cave of Polyphemus, 1630. Jacob Jordaens.

Critical Viewing

Compare the artwork to that on page 726. Which most successfully depicts the suspenseful nature of Odysseus' encounter with Polyphemus?

When Dawn spread out her finger tips of rose
the rams began to stir, moving for pasture,
and peals of bleating echoed round the pens
where dams[13] with udders full called for a milking.
Blinded, and sick with pain from his head wound,
the master stroked each ram, then let it pass,
but my men riding on the pectoral[14] fleece
the giant's blind hands blundering never found.
Last of them all my ram, the leader, came,
weighted by wool and me with my meditations.
The Cyclops patted him, and then he said:

'Sweet cousin ram, why lag behind the rest
in the night cave? You never linger so,
but graze before them all, and go afar
to crop sweet grass, and take your stately way
leading along the streams, until at evening

13. **dams.** Female sheep
14. **pectoral.** Located in or near the chest

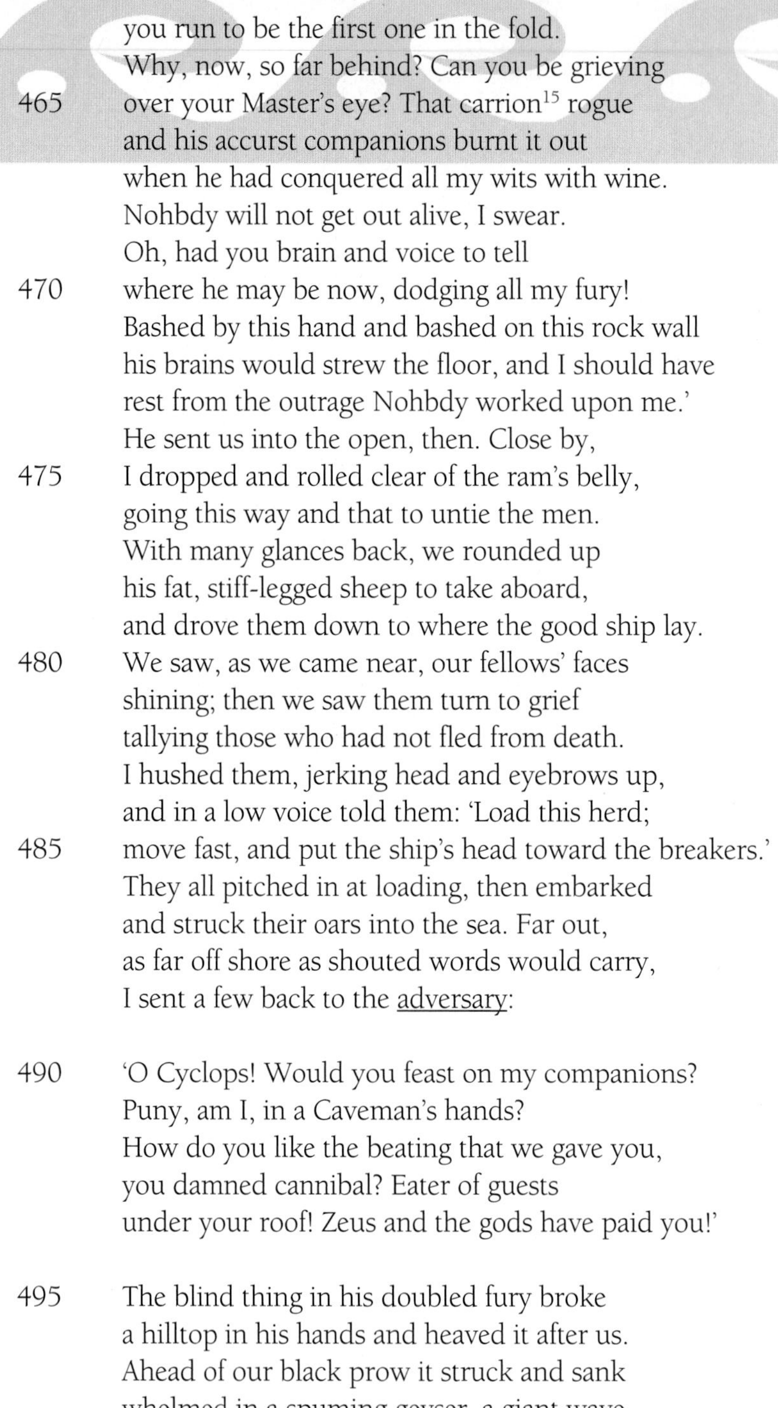

you run to be the first one in the fold.
Why, now, so far behind? Can you be grieving
over your Master's eye? That carrion[15] rogue
and his accurst companions burnt it out
when he had conquered all my wits with wine.
Nohbdy will not get out alive, I swear.
Oh, had you brain and voice to tell
where he may be now, dodging all my fury!
Bashed by this hand and bashed on this rock wall
his brains would strew the floor, and I should have
rest from the outrage Nohbdy worked upon me.'
He sent us into the open, then. Close by,
I dropped and rolled clear of the ram's belly,
going this way and that to untie the men.
With many glances back, we rounded up
his fat, stiff-legged sheep to take aboard,
and drove them down to where the good ship lay.
We saw, as we came near, our fellows' faces
shining; then we saw them turn to grief
tallying those who had not fled from death.
I hushed them, jerking head and eyebrows up,
and in a low voice told them: 'Load this herd;
move fast, and put the ship's head toward the breakers.'
They all pitched in at loading, then embarked
and struck their oars into the sea. Far out,
as far off shore as shouted words would carry,
I sent a few back to the adversary:

'O Cyclops! Would you feast on my companions?
Puny, am I, in a Caveman's hands?
How do you like the beating that we gave you,
you damned cannibal? Eater of guests
under your roof! Zeus and the gods have paid you!'

The blind thing in his doubled fury broke
a hilltop in his hands and heaved it after us.
Ahead of our black prow it struck and sank
whelmed in a spuming geyser, a giant wave
that washed the ship stern foremost back to shore.
I got the longest boathook out and stood
fending us off, with furious nods to all
to put their backs into a racing stroke—

15. **carrion.** Literally, like a piece of dead meat; figuratively, disgusting or repulsive

ad • ver • sary (ad´ və[r] ser' ē *or* ad´ və[r] se' rē) *n.,* enemy; opponent

Polyphemus Attacking Odysseus' Ship, 1855. Alexandre Gabriel DeCamps. Musée des Beaux-Arts, Rouen, France.

row, row, or perish. So the long oars bent
kicking the foam sternward,[16] making head
until we drew away, and twice as far.
Now when I cupped my hands I heard the crew
in low voices protesting:

'Godsake, Captain!
Why bait the beast again? Let him alone!'
'That tidal wave he made on the first throw
all but beached us.'

'All but stove us in!'

'Give him our bearing with your trumpeting,
he'll get the range and lob a boulder.'

'Aye
He'll smash our timbers and our heads together!'

16. **sternward.** Toward the rear of a ship

I would not heed them in my glorying spirit,
but let my anger flare and yelled:

'Cyclops,
if ever mortal man inquire
how you were put to shame and blinded, tell him
Odysseus, raider of cities, took your eye:
Laertes' son, whose home's on Ithaca!'

At this he gave a mighty sob and rumbled:

'Now comes the weird[17] upon me, spoken of old.
A wizard, grand and wondrous, lived here—Telemus,
a son of Eurymus; great length of days
he had in wizardry among the Cyclopes,
and these things he foretold for time to come:
my great eye lost, and at Odysseus' hands.
Always I had in mind some giant, armed
in giant force, would come against me here.
But this, but you—small, pitiful and twiggy—
you put me down with wine, you blinded me.
Come back, Odysseus, and I'll treat you well,
praying the god of earthquake to befriend you—
his son I am, for he by his avowal
fathered me, and, if he will, he may
heal me of this black wound—he and no other
of all the happy gods or mortal men.'

Few words I shouted in reply to him:

'If I could take your life I would and take
your time away, and hurl you down to hell!
The god of earthquake[18] could not heal you there!'

At this he stretched his hands out in his darkness
toward the sky of stars, and prayed Poseidon:

'O hear me, lord, blue girdler of the islands,
if I am thine indeed, and thou art father:
grant that Odysseus, raider of cities, never
see his home: Laertes' son, I mean,
who kept his hall on Ithaca. Should destiny

17. **weird.** Fate or destiny

18. **god of earthquake.** Poseidon, god of the seas, who could cause earthquakes and tidal waves with his trident, or three-pronged spear

intend that he shall see his roof again
among his family in his father land,
far be that day, and dark the years between.
Let him lose all companions, and return
under strange sail to bitter days at home.'...

Can a hero be both a larger-than-life figure and a flawed human being? Do flaws make someone more appealing or less so?

REFER TO TEXT ▶▶▶▶	▶ REASON WITH TEXT	
1a. Name the person for whom Odysseus "pine[s] each day" while being held captive in Calypso's cave.	1b. An *analogy* is a comparison of two things. Odysseus is compared to a hot iron after he washes up on shore. Write a brief analogy describing another object that Odysseus could be compared to. Include the function of the object.	**Understand** **Find meaning**
2a. Quote what the other Cyclopes ask Polyphemus when they arrive at his cave after he is attacked. What is his answer?	2b. In *dramatic irony,* characters may accidentally hurt themselves because they don't have information that the reader or audience does. Relate what dramatic irony occurs when the other Cyclopes dismiss Polyphemus' calls for help (lines 406–420).	**Apply** **Use information**
3a. Identify the goddess who serves as Odysseus' protector.	3b. Analyze why Homer selects that specific goddess as his hero's protector.	**Analyze** **Take things apart**
4a. Recall what Odysseus says to the Cyclopes as his ship escapes.	4b. Critique Odysseus' leadership skills and determine what kind of leader he is. Why does Odysseus gloat about his escape? Does he protect his crew to the best of his ability? Explain.	**Evaluate** **Make judgments**
5a. As the mariners leave the land of the Cyclopes, what and to whom does Polyphemus call out?	5b. Explain how Homer's listeners might have responded to this incident. How might modern readers respond?	**Create** **Bring ideas together**

ANALYZE LITERATURE: Epic Poem

Like many epics, Odysseus' story starts *in medias res.* Describe the origin and meaning of the phrase *in medias res.* How does the story enfold? What does the epic suggest about the customs and values of ancient Greek culture? How do the supernatural characters influence the characters in the story and determine the events?

BRENTS

Neptune's Horses, 1910. Walter Crane.

Primary Source CONNECTION

In **"Poseidon, God of the Sea," Walker Brents** has created a Greek myth for our time. Thus the characters, setting, and some of the events are from Greek mythology. The writing style (especially the choice of words) and some of the actions are distinctly modern, however. For instance, how many lawyers, angry or otherwise, existed in Poseidon's day? Overall, the new myth has a present-day *sensibility,* or perspective. For more information about the author, Walker Brents, see "Echo & Narcissus," page 670.

What is the strangest animal you know? What animal, in your opinion, is the most beautiful?

POSEIDON, GOD OF THE SEA

A Myth Retold by **Walker Brents**

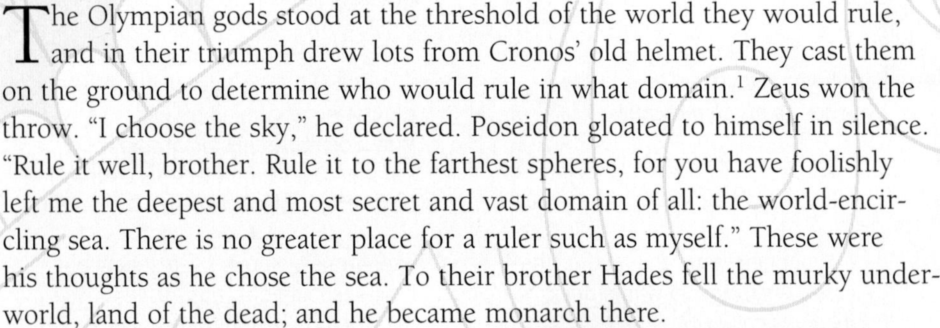

The Olympian gods stood at the threshold of the world they would rule, and in their triumph drew lots from Cronos' old helmet. They cast them on the ground to determine who would rule in what domain.[1] Zeus won the throw. "I choose the sky," he declared. Poseidon gloated to himself in silence. "Rule it well, brother. Rule it to the farthest spheres, for you have foolishly left me the deepest and most secret and vast domain of all: the world-encircling sea. There is no greater place for a ruler such as myself." These were his thoughts as he chose the sea. To their brother Hades fell the murky underworld, land of the dead; and he became monarch there.

Poseidon's qualities and the qualities of the ocean soon became one. Sometimes tranquil, sometimes stormy. Now a calm reflector, now a turbid[2] engulfer. As the sea forever encroaches upon the land, Poseidon constantly pressed his case in the courts of Olympus: arguing, threatening, challenging, blustering. He felt slighted by Zeus' dominant position in the Olympian hierarchy, and when he couldn't stand it he abruptly retreated to his ornate and

1. **drew lots...in what domain.** Used the chance selection of markers to decide on the gods' areas of influence
2. **turbid.** Foul; muddy

remote hermitage beneath the sea, a palace of coral and pearl, whose inner chambers held his throne of gold and seashell and sealskin. There were stables there, full of magnificent creatures, as well as Poseidon's golden chariot, at the approach of which turbulent storms ceased, and sea-monsters rose playfully from the depths all around it.

Nothing brought a brighter smile to his otherwise dour face than his creation of grotesque creatures. A spirit of amusement would seize him, and he would swirl his godly hands, out of which appeared some strange new monstrosity: a bird-beaked and cyclopean-eyed octopus of pulsating tentacles, a trumpet-snouted seahorse, a translucent writhing squid, a glowing jellyfish, a spiny spherical sea urchin, and a scorpion fish with scales of quilted armor, dangerous and flaring. Laughter carries a long way undersea; and the deepest darkness resounded with his mirth when he was in such creative moods.

One morning Poseidon woke up with the need for a consort. "I must find a queen!" he declared. The seashells resounded with the echo of his resolution. He eyed Thetis the Nereid lasciviously,[3] but when he heard the prophecy that any son she bore would be more magnificent than his father, he turned away. It was just as well, for time proved it true—eventually she married Peleus, and bore the great Achilles.

"A queen, I say. A queen!" This longing spurred one of his greater creations: Poseidon's hands swirled, the depths whorled, spinning into being an animal never before seen—a sleek and beautiful dolphin, smiling and graceful, chattering with the joy of being born from a god's need. "I send you forth to bring me back my empress," commanded Poseidon. Thus he commissioned

3. **lasciviously.** Lewdly; flirtatiously

or • nate (ôr nāt´) *adj.*, elaborately or excessively decorated
trans • lu • cent (tran[t]s lü´ sənt) *adj.*, clear; transparent

the dolphin as his romantic messenger, and away it sped. Time passed, and when it returned, who stood there in its bubbly wake but Amphitrite, nymph-goddess of the emerald waters. Now Poseidon's chariot had a new passenger, and what a pair they made as they came and went, looming and beckoning, submerging and emerging in the sea.

Poseidon could be vengeful, and persistent in his grudges. After being blinded by Odysseus, Poseidon's son Polyphemus shouted out through the fathomless brine to his father, demanding that Odysseus and his men be cursed, that if they return home at all, it be only after the most extreme and severe tribulations. Poseidon, of course, was only too glad to oblige. Despite his dominion in the vast salt sea, he nourished a rancor[4] and a thirst to expand his kingdom however he might. Like an angry lawyer, he issued suit after suit before the council of the gods. He clashed with Dionysus for possession of the island Naxos. With Zeus he contested the land of Aegina, with Helius he fought for Corinth, and with Hera for Argolis. Regardless of his truculence,[5] he tended to be unsuccessful.

Sometimes he went to extremes. Once he plunged his trident into the rocks at the base of the Acropolis. "I claim the land of Attica!" he shouted as a salty fountain erupted from the abyss he had opened up. The people of Athens were frightened at this furious oceanic roaring. They had no desire to be under the sway of such an angry and vengeful god, known to sweep away entire fleets of sailing ships in waves as arbitrary as they were immense. And so the goddess Athena made her epiphany.[6] She manifested[7] her wisdom by causing an olive tree to appear one morning alongside the salty cataract.[8] The people of Athens knew then that they wanted Athena, not Poseidon, to rule over them, and they pleaded with all their collective might to gain the attention of the denizens[9] of Olympus and make their claim. The gods and goddesses appeared in the sky above Athens, holding court, weighing the competing claims of Poseidon and Athena. They ruled in Athena's favor, in light of the usefulness of the olive to humans, its fruitful reward to the labor of their cultivation. Poseidon was infuriated, and vented his rage upon fleets and islands, but the divine judgment was not to be gainsaid.[10] He fled to his underwater refuge, nursing his grudge.

It was only after Poseidon encountered the goddess Demeter that he forgot his anger. Once, they met on a high mountain pass and he vehemently demanded her favor. Unable to brush aside his entreaties any other way, Demeter posed a bargain: she said she would accompany him if he

4. **rancor.** Bitterness; resentment; deep-seated ill will
5. **truculence.** Shrill insistence
6. **epiphany.** Appearance of a supernatural being
7. **manifested.** Displayed; showed
8. **cataract.** Waterfall
9. **denizens.** Inhabitants
10. **gainsaid.** Contradicted; opposed

trib • u • la • tion (tri' byə lā´shən) *n.*, suffering caused by oppression or persecution
do • mi • nion (də mi´ nyən) *n.*, domain; absolute ownership

could create for her a beautiful animal. She believed her freedom was secure, knowing only of his penchant for producing bizarre creatures. For his part, Poseidon was fired not only with desire for Demeter, but also the realization of the power and grace of his creative and godly aptitude. He straight away began making creature after creature. One and then another proceeded from nothingness: the camel, the hippopotamus, the giraffe, the zebra, and the donkey; all emerged full-blown and capering, but they were not quite what he wanted to bring forth. He dismissed them all into free passage, then took a deep breath, gathered his thoughts in a spirit of profound calm, and manifested the creature of his dreams: the horse.

Both he and Demeter were enraptured to behold such a sublime and unique form. Poseidon, satisfied beyond all expectation, expressed his joyful fascination headlong by leaping upon the horse's back and riding away. As the animal galloped and neighed and reared, more horses emerged from its pores, filling the canyons and ledges with their prancing silhouettes. This was the origin of the first earthly horse-herd, fed by Demeter from that time on. Their descendants still gallop today. Poseidon decamped[11] to his undersea castle, eager to create more horses. He fashioned some with bronze hooves and golden manes to fill his stables and pull his chariot.

No other creature satisfied his creative urge more fully. Poseidon adopted the horse as his symbol, its surging strength and rippling unpredictable grace a reminder and echo of the waves of the sea. ❖

11. **decamped.** Departed suddenly

pen • chant (pen´ chənt) *n.*, a strong and continued inclination; liking

REFER TO TEXT ▶▶▶▶	▶ REASON WITH TEXT	
1a. Identify Poseidon's most beloved creation.	1b. Determine how this creation, like the sea, reflects the character of Poseidon.	**Understand** **Find meaning**
2a. Recall why Poseidon chose to rule the sea.	2b. Appraise whether or not Poseidon used sound reasoning when choosing his domain. Why might he not be satisfied with his decision?	**Analyze** **Take things apart**
3a. State which domains Poseidon's brothers chose.	3b. Formulate what may have happened if Poseidon had ruled the other two domains instead of the sea. What monstrosities would he have created? What consequences would Poseidon's moods have had on humans?	**Evaluate** **Make judgments**

TEXT ◄TO► TEXT CONNECTION

Compare this selection with Books 1, 5, and 9 of *The Odyssey*. Analyze how Homer's depiction of gods and goddesses may have influenced Walker's modern retelling. How do the gods and goddesses appear to humans, and

Informational Text Connection

Many animals that once lived on Earth are now extinct. Evidence that they did exist is found in the *fossil record*—the remains, impressions, or traces of plants and animals that have been preserved in the earth's crust. Many fossils of prehistoric creatures were formed at the bottom of bodies of water. An animal's bones, teeth, or shell was covered by sediment, made up of sand and other matter, which hardened around the remains and preserved them. In this article from nationalgeographic.com, the journalist Hillary Mayell explores a possible link between real fossils and the imaginary Cyclops of Homer's *The Odyssey.* As you read the article, decide which passages include facts and which passages offer opinions. On what basis can you make this distinction?

Cyclops Myth Spurred by "One-Eyed" Fossils?

Hillary Mayell for *National Geographic News* February 5, 2003

Ever wonder where our worst nightmares come from? For the ancient Greeks, it may have been the fossils of giant prehistoric animals.

The tusk, several teeth, and some bones of a *Deinotherium giganteum,* which, loosely translated, means really huge terrible beast, have been found on the Greek island Crete. A distant relative to today's elephants, the giant mammal stood 15 feet (4.6 meters) tall at the shoulder, and had tusks that were 4.5 feet (1.3 meters) long. It was one of the largest mammals ever to walk the face of the Earth.

"This is the first finding in Crete and the south Aegean in general," said Charalampos Fassoulas, a geologist with the University of Crete's Natural History Museum. "It is also the first time that we found a whole tusk of the animal in Greece. We haven't dated the fossils yet, but the sediment[1] where we found them is of 8 to 9 million years in age."

1. **sediment.** Material carried and deposited in water by water, wind, or ice; matter that settles at the bottom of a liquid

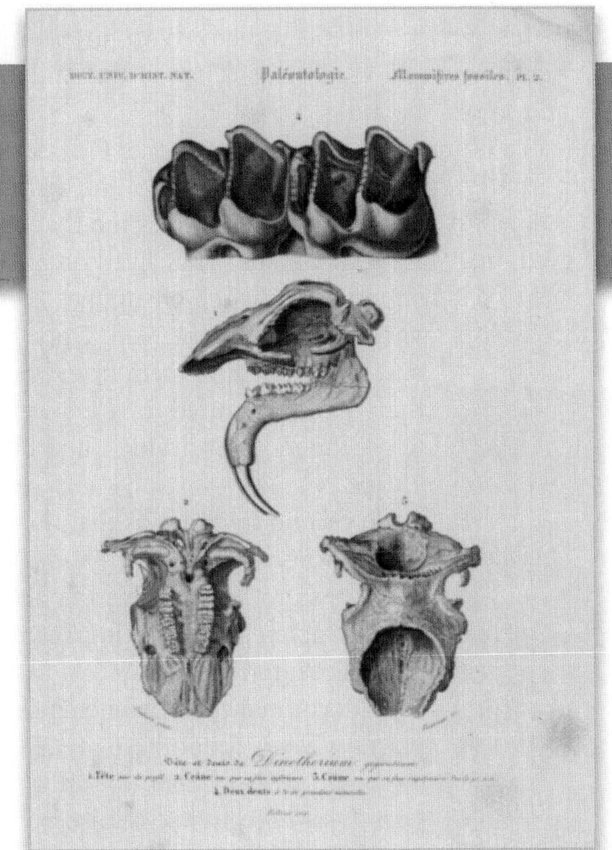

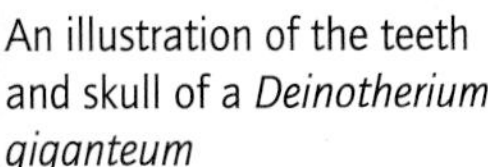
An illustration of the teeth and skull of a *Deinotherium giganteum*

Skulls of *Deinotherium giganteum* found at other sites show it to be more primitive, and the bulk a lot more vast, than today's elephant, with an extremely large nasal opening in the center of the skull.

To paleontologists today, the large hole in the center of the skull suggests a pronounced trunk. To the ancient Greeks, *Deinotherium* skulls could well be the foundation for their tales of the fearsome one-eyed Cyclops.

Explaining the Natural World

In her book *The First Fossil Hunters: Paleontology in Greek and Roman Times,* Adrienne Mayor argues that the Greeks and Romans used fossil evidence—the enormous bones of long-extinct species—to support existing myths and to create new ones.

"The idea that mythology explains the natural world is an old idea," said Thomas Strasser, an archaeologist at California State University, Sacramento, who has done extensive work in Crete. "You'll never be able to test the idea in a scientific fashion, but the ancient Greeks were farmers and would certainly come

pa • le • on • tol • o • gist (pā' lē än' tä´ lə jist *or* pā' lē ən tä´ lə jist) *n.,* scientist who studies Earth's geological periods by using fossil remains
ar • chae • ol • o • gist (är' kē ä´ lə jist) *n.,* scientist who studies ancient societies by examining fossils, artifacts (including tools and other objects), and monuments

across fossil bones like this and try to explain them. With no concept of evolution, it makes sense that they would reconstruct them in their minds as giants, monsters, sphinxes,[2] and so on," he said.

Homer, in his epic tale of the trials and tribulations[3] of Odysseus during his 10-year return trip from Troy to his homeland, tells of the traveler's encounter with the Cyclops. In *The Odyssey,* he describes the Cyclops as a band of giant, one-eyed, man-eating shepherds. They lived on an island that Odysseus and some of his men visited in search of supplies. They were captured by one of the Cyclops, who ate several of the men. Only brains and bravery saved all of them from becoming dinner. The captured travelers were able to get the monster drunk, blind him, and escape.

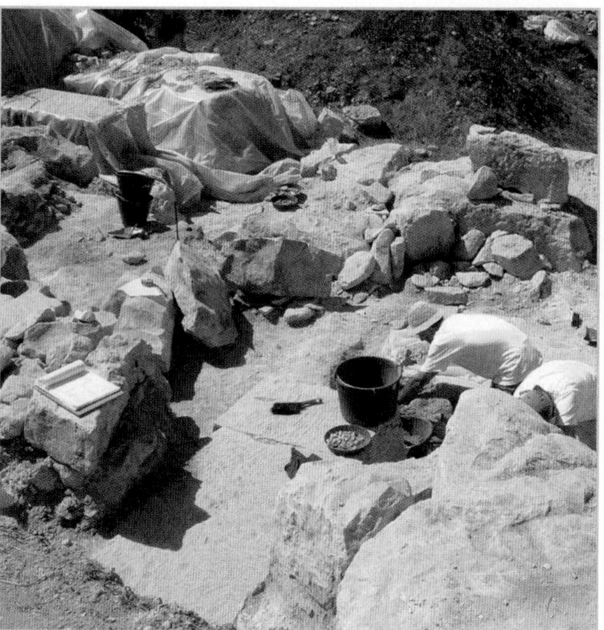

A second myth holds that the Cyclops are the sons of Gaia (earth) and Uranus (sky). The three brothers became the blacksmiths of the Olympian gods, creating Zeus' thunderbolts, Poseidon's trident.[4]

"Mayor makes a convincing case that the places where a lot of these myths originate occur in places where there are a lot of fossil beds,"[5] said Strasser. "She also points out that in some myths monsters emerge from the ground after big storms, which is just one of those things I had never thought about, but it makes sense, that after a storm the soil has eroded and these bones appear."

Wandering the Earth

A cousin to the elephant, deinotheres roamed Europe, Asia, and Africa during the Miocene (23 to 5 million years ago) and Pliocene (5 to 1.8 million years ago) eras[6] before becoming extinct.

Finding the remains on Crete suggests the mammal moved around larger areas of Europe than previously believed, Fassoulas said. Fassoulas is in charge of the museum's paleontology division, and oversaw the excavation.

He suggests that the animals reached Crete from Turkey, swimming and island hopping across the southern Aegean Sea during periods when sea

2. **sphinxes.** In Greek mythology, monsters with the head of a woman, the wings of an eagle, and the body of a lion
3. **trials and tribulations.** A series of challenges and difficulties
4. **Poseidon's trident.** A three-pronged spear that was the symbol of the god of the sea
5. **fossil beds.** Collections of fossils in certain locations
6. **Miocene...Pliocene eras.** Two of the epochs, or long periods of time, in the development of planet Earth

ex • ca • va • tion (ek' skə vā´ shən) *n.,* the process of digging up or unearthing objects, especially historical remains levels were lower. Many herbivores, including the elephants of today, are exceptionally strong swimmers.

"We believe that these animals came probably from Turkey via the islands of Rhodes and Karpathos to reach Crete," he said.

The *Deinotherium's* tusks, unlike the elephants of today, grew from its lower jaw and curved down and slightly back rather than up and out. Wear marks on the tusks suggest they were used to strip bark from trees, and possibly to dig up plants.

...in some myths monsters emerge from the ground after big storms...

"According to what we know from studies in northern and eastern Europe, this animal lived in a forest environment," said Fassoulas. "It was using his ground-faced tusk to dig, settle the branches and bushes, and in general to find his food in such an ecosystem."

The fossils were uncovered when land was being cleared for an olive orchard; Fassoulas is encouraging farmers to be on the lookout for more. ❖

her • bi • vore ([h]ʉr´ bə vôr') *n.*, plant-eating animal

REFER TO TEXT ▶▶▶▶	▶ REASON WITH TEXT	
1a. Identify what suggestion is made regarding fossils and ancient myths.	1b. Point out whether or not Adrienne Mayor and Charalampos Fassoulas, in their works discussed in the article, present mostly fact, mostly opinion, or some of each. Explain your response.	**Analyze** **Take things apart**
2a. List the examples that are given to support the connection between fossils and ancient myths.	2b. Decide how valuable such theories are in our efforts to understand historical development. If these theories were to be established as fact, how might our view of human history be likely to change?	**Evaluate** **Make judgments**
3a. According to Mayell, recall what literary creature could have originated from the skull of a *Deinotherium giganteum*. How are the creature and the skull similar?	3b. Think of other historic monsters and mysteries. Explain where these might have originated.	**Create** **Bring ideas together**

TEXT ◄TO► TEXT CONNECTION

In what way might archaeological findings help readers appreciate Homer's epics? Are there any ways in which being aware of scientific evidence might lessen the readers' enjoyment of *The Odyssey?* Explain your responses.

from The Odyssey: PART TWO

BEFORE READING **An Epic Poem by Homer, Translated by Robert Fitzgerald**

DIRECTED READING

BUILD BACKGROUND

Literary Context In a famous episode from Book 11, Odysseus and his crew must navigate their ships between two threats at sea: Charybdis, a maelstrom, or violent whirlpool; and Scylla, a many-legged sea monster on the prowl for dolphins and other animals. What underwater creature might Scylla represent? What do you think the modern-day expression "between Scylla and Charybdis" means? What does Odysseus' handling of the tricky navigation reveal about him as a captain?

Reader's Context Have you ever put yourself or your friends in danger or had to decide between two equally unpleasant tasks? What were the results?

ANALYZE LITERATURE: Mood

Atmosphere, or **mood,** is the emotion created in the reader by a work of literature. Atmosphere can be created using specific word choices, developing a specific setting (location), and using vivid imagery (descriptions that appeal to the five senses). The dominant mood of Part Two is sadness, loss, destruction, and death. What does the mood suggest about the epic hero's role?

SET PURPOSE

As you go through the selections from Books 10–12, examine how word choice, setting, characterization, imagery, and events help create the mood. Consider how Odysseus responds to the challenges he faces and what he learns from them. Create a Sensory Details Chart like the one that appears on page 282.

USE READING SKILLS

Cause and Effect You can use what you learned from Part One of *The Odyssey* to understand Part Two. Identifying cause and effect helps you see the long, sometimes complicated epic as a unified work. For example, as you follow Odysseus' adventures, remember Polyphemus' curse from Part One. A chart like the one below provides a way to keep track of cause and effect to better understand the events of Part Two.

Cause	Effect
Eurylochus is afraid of Circe.	He is able to avoid her snare.

PREVIEW VOCABULARY

Examine the vocabulary words from the selection: *beguiling, stealth, assuage, implacable, rancor, insolent, tumult, provision, insidious, restitution.* Like text passages, individual words can convey mood. Which nouns and adjectives in the list suggest a feeling of unpleasantness? For each of these words, list a synonym with a more positive **connotation,** or emotional association. Which verb and which noun indicate movement from unpleasantness to pleasantness? Which word expresses no particular mood?

from The Odyssey

An Epic Poem by **Homer**

Translated by **Robert Fitzgerald**

PART TWO: from Books 10–12

"The lovely voices in ardor appealing over the water made me crave to listen, and I tried to say 'Untie me!' to the crew, jerking my brows."

Ulysses and the Sirens, 1891. John Waterhouse. National Gallery of Victoria, Melbourne, Australia.

THE ENCHANTRESS CIRCE (from Book 10)

After escaping the Cyclopes' island, Odysseus and his men land on the island of Aeolus (ē´ ə ləs), *king of the winds. Aeolus assists him by putting all of the unfavorable winds in a bag, which he gives to Odysseus. His curious crew, however, rip open the bag, and the hurricane-like winds blow the ships far off course. In the days that follow, Odysseus and his men fight a battle with cannibals on Laestrygonia* (les trig ō´ nē ə), *in which they lose many men and all but one of their ships. Odysseus and his remaining men then arrive on the island of the goddess and sorceress Circe* (sʉr´ sē). *Though his men are fearful of what they may find there, Odysseus sends out a scouting party.*

"In the wild wood they found an open glade
around a smooth stone house—the hall of Circe—
and wolves and mountain lions lay there, mild
in her soft spell, fed on her drug of evil.
None would attack—oh, it was strange, I tell you—
but switching their long tails they faced our men
like hounds, who look up when their master comes
with tidbits for them—as he will—from table.
Humbly those wolves and lions with mighty paws
fawned on our men—who met their yellow eyes
and feared them.
In the entrance way they stayed
to listen there: inside her quiet house
they heard the goddess Circe.
Low she sang
in her beguiling voice, while on her loom
she wove ambrosial fabric sheer and bright,
by that craft known to the goddesses of heaven.
No one would speak, until Polites—most
faithful and likable of my officers, said:

'Dear friends, no need for stealth: here's a young weaver
singing a pretty song to set the air
a-tingle on these lawns and paven courts.
Goddess she is, or lady. Shall we greet her?'

So reassured, they all cried out together,
and she came swiftly to the shining doors
to call them in. All but Eurylochus—
who feared a snare—the innocents went after her.
On thrones she seated them, and lounging chairs,
while she prepared a meal of cheese and barley
and amber honey mixed with Pramnian wine,
adding her own vile pinch, to make them lose
desire or thought of our dear father land.
Scarce had they drunk when she flew after them
with her long stick and shut them in a pigsty—

be • guil • ing (bi gī [ə]liŋ) *adj.*, outwardly charming but inwardly deceptive
stealth (stelth) *n.*, sneakiness; secretiveness

Circe Pouring Poison Into a Vase and Awaiting the Arrival of Ulysses. Sir Edward Burne-Jones.

bodies, voices, heads, and bristles, all
swinish now, though minds were still unchanged.
So, squealing, in they went. And Circe tossed them
acorns, mast, and cornel berries—fodder
for hogs who rut and slumber on the earth.
Down to the ship Eurylochus came running
to cry alarm, foul magic doomed his men![1]
But working with dry lips to speak a word
he could not, being so shaken; blinding tears
welled in his eyes; foreboding filled his heart.
When we were frantic questioning him, at last
we heard the tale: our friends were gone. . . ."

Odysseus leaves the ship at once to confront Circe himself. Protected from her spells with help from Hermes, Odysseus convinces the goddess to restore his shipmates to their human form. Odysseus and his crew dally on Circe's island for a year. When Odysseus decides they must head home, Circe tells him he will not return safely unless he goes to the Land of the Dead to seek advice from the blind seer Teiresias.

1. **magic doomed his men.** Crew members enslaved by Circe's tricks

A GATHERING OF SHADES[2] (from Book 11)

Odysseus and his men sail to the Land of the Dead to consult with the blind prophet Teiresias. Upon entering the land, they make offerings to the ghosts of the dead.

"Then I addressed the blurred and breathless dead,
vowing to slaughter my best heifer for them
before she calved, at home in Ithaca,
and burn the choice bits on the altar fire;
as for Teiresias, I swore to sacrifice
a black lamb, handsomest of all our flock.
Thus to assuage the nations of the dead
I pledged these rites, then slashed the lamb and ewe,
letting their black blood stream into the wellpit.
Now the souls gathered, stirring out of Erebus,
brides and young men, and men grown old in pain,
and tender girls whose hearts were new to grief;
many were there, too, torn by brazen lanceheads,
battle-slain, bearing still their bloody gear.
From every side they came and sought the pit
with rustling cries; and I grew sick with fear.
But presently I gave command to my officers
to flay those sheep the bronze cut down, and make
burnt offerings of flesh to the gods below—
to sovereign Death, to pale Persephone.
Meanwhile I crouched with my drawn sword to keep
the surging phantoms from the bloody pit
till I should know the presence of Teiresias....

Among the ghosts of the dead who gather around, Odysseus sees one of his shipmates who died on the island of Circe. He also sees his mother, who had still been alive when he left for Troy. Odysseus grieves upon learning that she has died. Through his tears, he holds the spirits back, still waiting for Teiresias to appear.

Soon from the dark that prince of Thebes[3] came forward
bearing a golden staff; and he addressed me:
'Son of Laertes and the gods of old,
Odysseus, master of land ways and sea ways,

2. **Shades.** Ghosts
3. **prince of Thebes.** Another name for Teiresias

as • suage (ə swāj´ *or* ə swāzh´ *or* ə swäzh´) *v.,* lessen the intensity of; ease; relieve

CULTURAL CONNECTION

Land of the Dead When Odysseus goes to the Land of the Dead, he visits a place that the ancient Greeks considered an important part of their world. In fact, the ruler of the Underworld was the brother of Zeus, whose realm was the earth and the sky, and of Poseidon, king of the seas. The name *Hades*—perhaps a politer term, in English, for *Hell*—comes from that of the third brother, better known as Pluto. Burial customs of the time included the practice, among women, of placing a lock of hair by the dead body. As they snipped their tresses, they may have been sacrificing a cherished aspect of their beauty to assuage their grief.

why leave the blazing sun, O man of woe,
to see the cold dead and the joyless region?
Stand clear, put up your sword;
let me but taste of blood, I shall speak true.'

At this I stepped aside, and in the scabbard
let my long sword ring home to the pommel silver,
as he bent down to the sombre blood. Then spoke
the prince of those with gift of speech:[4]

'Great captain,
a fair wind and the honey lights of home
are all you seek. But anguish lies ahead;
the god who thunders on the land prepares it,
not to be shaken from your track, implacable,
in rancor for the son whose eye you blinded.
One narrow strait may take you through his blows:

4. **gift of speech.** Ability to predict the future

im • pla • ca • ble (im' pla´ kə bəl) *adj.*, resisting change; stubborn
ran • cor (raŋ´ kər) *n.*, deep anger or ill will

denial of yourself, restraint of shipmates.
When you make landfall on Thrinakia first
and quit the violet sea, dark on the land
you'll find the grazing herds of Helios
by whom all things are seen, all speech is known.
Avoid those kine, hold fast to your intent,
and hard seafaring brings you all to Ithaca.
But if you raid the beeves, I see destruction
for ship and crew. Though you survive alone,
bereft of all companions, lost for years,
under strange sail shall you come home, to find
your own house filled with trouble: insolent men
eating your livestock as they court your lady.
Aye, you shall make those men atone in blood!
But after you have dealt out death—in open
combat or by stealth—to all the suitors,
go overland on foot, and take an oar,
until one day you come where men have lived
with meat unsalted, never known the sea,
nor seen seagoing ships, with crimson bows
and oars that fledge light hulls for dipping flight.
The spot will soon be plain to you, and I
can tell you how: some passerby will say,
"What winnowing fan is that upon your shoulder?
Halt, and implant your smooth oar in the turf
and make fair sacrifice to Lord Poseidon:
a ram, a bull, a great buck boar; turn back,
and carry out pure hecatombs[5] at home
to all wide heaven's lords, the undying gods,
to each in order. Then a seaborne death
soft as this hand of mist will come upon you
when you are wearied out with rich old age,
your country folk in blessed peace around you.
And all this shall be just as I foretell. . . . '"

Beware the Sirens and Scylla and Charybdis (from Book 12)

On their way back from the Land of the Dead, Odysseus and his men stop again at the Island of Aeaea, where Circe and her handmaids welcome them with food and wine. Circe prepares them for the dangers they will encounter as they continue on their journey.

5. **hecatombs.** A kind of sacrifice

in • so • lent (in[t]´ s[ə] lənt) *adj.*, rude and nasty

Third-century Roman mosaic depicting Odysseus and the Sirens.

"'Listen with care
to this, now, and a god will arm your mind.
Square in your ship's path are Sirens, crying
beauty to bewitch men coasting by;
woe to the innocent who hears that sound!
He will not see his lady nor his children
in joy, crowding about him, home from sea;
the Sirens will sing his mind away
on their sweet meadow lolling. There are bones
of dead men rotting in a pile beside them
and flayed skins shrivel around the spot.
Steer wide;
keep well to seaward; plug your oarsmen's ears
with beeswax kneaded soft; none of the rest
should hear that song.
But if you wish to listen,
let the men tie you in the lugger, hand
and foot, back to the mast, lashed to the mast,
so you may hear those harpies' thrilling voices;
shout as you will, begging to be untied,
your crew must only twist more line around you
and keep their stroke up, till the singers fade. . . .'"

Next, Circe describes a perilous passageway between high cliffs, through which Odysseus' ship must pass.

"'...[T]hat is the den of Scylla, where she yaps
abominably, a newborn whelp's cry,
though she is huge and monstrous. God or man,
no one could look on her in joy. Her legs—
and there are twelve—are like great tentacles,
unjointed, and upon her serpent necks
are borne six heads like nightmares of ferocity,
with triple serried rows of fangs and deep
gullets of black death. Half her length, she sways
her heads in air, outside her horrid cleft,
hunting the sea around that promontory
for dolphins, dogfish, or what bigger game
thundering Amphitrite feeds in thousands.
And no ship's company can claim
to have passed her without loss and grief; she takes,
from every ship, one man for every gullet.

The opposite point seems more a tongue of land
you'd touch with a good bowshot, at the narrows.
A great wild fig, a shaggy mass of leaves,
grows on it, and Charybdis lurks below
to swallow down the dark sea tide. Three times
from dawn to dusk she spews it up
and sucks it down again three times, a whirling
maelstrom;[6] if you come upon her then
the god who makes earth tremble could not save you.
No, hug the cliff of Scylla, take your ship
through on a racing stroke. Better to mourn
six men than lose them all, and the ship, too....'

Then you will coast Thrinakia, the island
where Helios' cattle graze, fine herds, and flocks
of goodly sheep. The herds and flocks are seven,
with fifty beasts in each.
No lambs are dropped,
or calves, and these fat cattle never die....

Now give those kine a wide berth, keep your thoughts
intent upon your course for home,
and hard seafaring brings you all to Ithaca.

6. **maelstrom.** Whirlpool

But if you raid the beeves, I see destruction
for ship and crew. . . .'"

Circe concludes her warnings by giving Odysseus one final, somber prediction: he, Odysseus, will be the only one to arrive home safely. As Dawn breaks, Odysseus and his men prepare to set sail. He tells his crew of Circe's warnings, but leaves out her dire prediction.

"The crew being now silent before me, I
addressed them, sore at heart:

'Dear friends,
more than one man, or two, should know those things
Circe foresaw for us and shared with me,
so let me tell her forecast: then we die
with our eyes open, if we are going to die,
or know what death we baffle[7] if we can. Sirens
weaving a haunting song over the sea
we are to shun, she said, and their green shore
all sweet with clover; yet she urged that I
alone should listen to their song. Therefore
you are to tie me up, tight as a splint,
erect along the mast, lashed to the mast,
and if I shout and beg to be untied,
take more turns of the rope to muffle me.'

I rather dwelt on this part of the forecast,
while our good ship made time, bound outward down
the wind for the strange island of Sirens.
Then all at once the wind fell, and a calm
came over all the sea, as though some power
lulled the swell.

The crew were on their feet
briskly, to furl the sail, and stow it; then,
each in place, they poised the smooth oar blades
and sent the white foam scudding by. I carved
a massive cake of beeswax into bits
and rolled them in my hands until they softened—
no long task, for a burning heat came down
from Helios, lord of high noon. Going forward
I carried wax along the line, and laid it
thick on their ears. They tied me up, then, plumb

"'. . . you are to tie me up . . . and if I shout and beg to be untied, take more turns of the rope to muffle me.'"

7. **baffle.** Barely escape from

amidships, back to the mast, lashed to the mast,
and took themselves again to rowing. Soon,
as we came smartly within hailing distance,
the two Sirens, noting our fast ship
off their point, made ready, and they sang....
The lovely voices in ardor[8] appealing over the water
made me crave to listen, and I tried to say
'Untie me!' to the crew, jerking my brows;
but they bent steady to the oars. Then Perimedes
got to his feet, he and Eurylochus,
and passed more line about, to hold me still.
So all rowed on, until the Sirens
dropped under the sea rim, and their singing
dwindled away.
My faithful company
rested on their oars now, peeling off
the wax that I had laid thick on their ears;
then set me free.
But scarcely had that island
faded in blue air than I saw smoke
and white water, with sound of waves in tumult—
a sound the men heard, and it terrified them.
Oars flew from their hands; the blades went knocking
wild alongside till the ship lost way,
with no oarblades to drive her through the water.

Well, I walked up and down from bow to stern,
trying to put heart into them, standing over
every oarsman, saying gently,

'Friends,
have we never been in danger before this?
More fearsome, is it now, than when the Cyclops
penned us in his cave? What power he had!
Did I not keep my nerve, and use my wits
to find a way out for us?

Now I say
by hook or crook this peril too shall be
something that we remember.
Heads up, lads!
We must obey the orders as I give them.

8. **ardor.** Eagerness; passion

tu • mult (tü´ məlt' *or* tyü´ məlt' *or* tʉ´ məlt') *n.*, loud confusion

Critical Viewing

What does the image of Odysseus suggest within this particular scene? What do you think the artist is trying to convey?

Odysseus in Front of Scylla and Charybdis, 1794–1796. Johann Heinrich Füssli.

Get the oarshafts in your hands, and lay back
hard on your benches; hit these breaking seas.
Zeus help us pull away before we founder.
You at the tiller, listen, and take in
all that I say—the rudders are your duty;
keep her out of the combers and the smoke;
steer for that headland; watch the drift, or we
fetch up in the smother, and you drown us.'

That was all, and it brought them round to action.
But as I sent them on toward Scylla, I
told them nothing, as they could do nothing.
They would have dropped their oars again, in panic,
to roll for cover under the decking. Circe's
bidding against arms had slipped my mind,
so I tied on my cuirass[9] and took up
two heavy spears, then made my way along
to the foredeck—thinking to see her first from there,
the monster of the grey rock, harboring
torment for my friends. I strained my eyes
upon that cliffside veiled in cloud, but nowhere

9. **cuirass.** Armor, often made of leather, covering the chest

could I catch sight of her.
And all this time,
in travail, sobbing, gaining on the current,
we rowed into the strait—Scylla to port
and on our starboard beam Charybdis, dire
gorge of the salt sea tide. By heaven! when she
vomited, all the sea was like a cauldron
seething over intense fire, when the mixture
suddenly heaves and rises.
The shot spume
soared to the landside heights, and fell like rain.
But when she swallowed the sea water down
we saw the funnel of the maelstrom, heard
the rock bellowing all around, and dark
sand raged on the bottom far below.
My men all blanched against the gloom, our eyes
were fixed upon that yawning mouth in fear
of being devoured.
Then Scylla made her strike,
whisking six of my best men from the ship.
I happened to glance aft at ship and oarsmen
and caught sight of their arms and legs, dangling
high overhead. Voices came down to me
in anguish, calling my name for the last time.
A man surfcasting on a point of rock
for bass or mackerel, whipping his long rod
to drop the sinker and the bait far out,
will hook a fish and rip it from the surface
to dangle wriggling through the air:
so these
were borne aloft in spasms toward the cliff.

She ate them as they shrieked there, in her den,
in the dire grapple, reaching still for me—
and deathly pity ran me through
at that sight—far the worst I ever suffered,
questing the passes of the strange sea.
We rowed on.
The Rocks were now behind; Charybdis, too,
and Scylla dropped astern.
Then we were coasting
the noble island of the god, where grazed
those cattle with wide brows, and bounteous flocks
of Helios, lord of noon, who rides high heaven.

Print depicting Odysseus' ship maneuvering between the Scylla and the Charybdis.

From the black ship, far still at sea, I heard
the lowing of the cattle winding home
and sheep bleating; and heard, too, in my heart
the words of blind Teiresias of Thebes
and Circe of Aeaea: both forbade me
the island of the world's delight, the Sun...."

Helios' Cattle (from Book 12)

As the ship sails alongside the Island of the Sun God, Odysseus warns his men to steer the ship away, as both Teiresias and Circe predicted they would find fatal trouble on the island. The men, who are weary and hungry, insist that they stop and stay the night. Finally, Odysseus gives in. They will stop on the island, but, he insists, they must not touch any of the god's sacred cattle or sheep.

"In the small hours of the third watch, when stars
that shone out in the first dusk of evening

had gone down to their setting, a giant wind
blew from heaven, and clouds driven by Zeus
shrouded land and sea in a night of storm;
so, just as Dawn with finger tips of rose
touched the windy world, we dragged our ship
to cover in a grotto, a sea cave
where nymphs had chairs of rock and sanded floors.
I mustered all the crew and said:

'Old shipmates,
our stores are in the ship's hold, food and drink;
the cattle here are not for our provision,
or we pay dearly for it.

Fierce the god is
who cherishes these heifers and these sheep:
Helios; and no man avoids his eye.'

To this my fighters nodded. Yes. But now
we had a month of onshore gales, blowing
day in, day out—south winds, or south by east.
As long as bread and good red wine remained
to keep the men up, and appease their craving,
they would not touch the cattle. But in the end,
when all the barley in the ship was gone,
hunger drove them to scour the wild shore
with angling hooks, for fishes and sea fowl,
whatever fell into their hands; and lean days
wore their bellies thin.

The storms continued.
So one day I withdrew to the interior
to pray the gods in solitude, for hope
that one might show me some way of salvation.
Slipping away, I struck across the island
to a sheltered spot, out of the driving gale.
I washed my hands there, and made supplication[10]
to the gods who own Olympus, all the gods—
but they, for answer, only closed my eyes
under slow drops of sleep.

Now on the shore Eurylochus
made his insidious plea:

---

10. **supplication.** Act of pleading

pro • vi • sion (prə vi´ zhən) *n.,* food and other supplies
in • sid • i • ous (in si´ dē əs) *adj.,* having a gradual but serious effect

Upland Pasture, 1905. Julian Alden Weir.

'Comrades,' he said,
You've gone through everything; listen to what I say.
All deaths are hateful to us, mortal wretches,
but famine is the most pitiful, the worst
end that a man can come to.
Will you fight it?
Come, we'll cut out the noblest of these cattle
for sacrifice to the gods who own the sky;
and once at home, in the old country of Ithaca,
if ever that day comes—
we'll build a costly temple and adorn it
with every beauty for the Lord of Noon.
But if he flares up over his heifers lost,
wishing our ship destroyed, and if the gods
make cause with him, why, then I say: Better
open your lungs to a big sea once for all
than waste to skin and bones on a lonely island!'

Thus Eurylochus; and they murmured 'Aye!'

trooping away at once to round up heifers.
Now, that day tranquil cattle with broad brows
were grazing near, and soon the men drew up
around their chosen beasts in ceremony.
They plucked the leaves that shone on a tall oak—
having no barley meal—to strew the victims,
performed the prayers and ritual, knifed the kine
and flayed each carcass, cutting thighbones free
to wrap in double folds of fat. These offerings,
with strips of meat, were laid upon the fire.
Then, as they had no wine, they made libation
with clear spring water, broiling the entrails first;
and when the bones were burnt and tripes shared,
they spitted the carved meat.

Just then my slumber
left me in a rush, my eyes opened,
and I went down the seaward path. No sooner
had I caught sight of our black hull, than savory
odors of burnt fat eddied around me;
grief took hold of me, and I cried aloud:

'O Father Zeus and gods in bliss forever,
you made me sleep away this day of mischief!
O cruel drowsing, in the evil hour!
Here they sat, and a great work they contrived.'

Lampetia in her long gown meanwhile
had borne swift word to the Overlord of Noon:

'They have killed your kine.'[11]

And the Lord Helios
burst into angry speech amid the immortals:

'O Father Zeus and gods in bliss forever,
punish Odysseus' men! So overweening,
now they have killed my peaceful kine, my joy
at morning when I climbed the sky of stars,
and evening, when I bore westward from heaven.
Restitution or penalty they shall pay—
and pay in full—or I go down forever
to light the dead men in the underworld.... '"

11. **kine.** Cattle (archaic plural of *cow*)

res • ti • tu • tion (res' tə tü´ shən) *n.,* repayment, especially for wrongdoing

For six days the men feast on Helios' cattle. When they set sail again, Zeus delivers his punishment in the form of a thunderbolt that destroys their ship. All the men are drowned but Odysseus. Clinging to pieces of timber from the ship, he drifts on the sea for nine days until he reaches the island of Calypso. Now Odysseus has finished telling his tale to Alcinous' court.

"But as I sent them on toward Scylla, I told them nothing, as they could do nothing." Does Odysseus' reasoning make sense? Is it acceptable to withhold important information or details because you know it will upset others?

REFER TO TEXT ▶▶▶▶	▶ REASON WITH TEXT	
1a. Repeat Circe's recommendation regarding Odysseus' ship passing Scylla and Charybdis.	1b. Determine why Odysseus chooses not to tell his men about Scylla.	**Understand** **Find meaning**
2a. State why Odysseus' men, after they have vowed otherwise, decide to kill one of Helios' cows.	2b. Knowing what you do about myths and prophecies, examine whether or not Odysseus was foolish to assume that his men could escape the fate foretold by both Circe and Teiresias.	**Apply** **Use information**
3a. Identify the advantage Odysseus has over his men in Part Two.	3b. Differentiate between the role of Odysseus and his shipmates. What do the contrasts suggest about the role of the hero in an epic?	**Analyze** **Take things apart**
4a. Indicate what Odysseus and his crew must do while waiting for Teiresias in the Land of the Dead.	4b. Describe the effect on you, as a reader, of the mood of disgust and despair. Do you think the mood enriches or detracts from the narrative? Explain.	**Evaluate** **Make judgments**
5a. Recall the choice the crew members make regarding their deaths.	5b. The episodes of Scylla and Charybdis and of the Cattle of the Sun God raise timeless concerns regarding thoughtful choices and resistance to temptation. Choose one of these incidents and rewrite it in a modern setting.	**Create** **Bring ideas together**

ANALYZE LITERATURE: Mood

How does the mood impact the story and how did it reflect on Odysseus? Why might Homer have chosen to create this atmosphere while describing his epic hero's adventure? Return to the story and find details that support the atmosphere Homer has created. How might other details have changed the story?

ATWOOD

Literature CONNECTION

Margaret Atwood (b. 1939) is a highly acclaimed poet, novelist, and critic who grew up in Toronto and in the wild areas of northern Quebec and Ontario. Her writing probes many facets of human behavior, usually from a woman's perspective. For whom might **"Siren Song"** be written? In what way is the message *ironic*, or not what you would expect after reading about the Sirens in *The Odyssey?*

Siren Song

Odysseus and the Sirens, c. 470 BCE. Greek artist. British Museum, London.

A Poem by **Margaret Atwood**

This is the one song everyone
would like to learn: the song
that is irresistible:

the song that forces men
to leap overboard in squadrons
even though they see the beached skulls

the song nobody knows
because anyone who has heard it
is dead, and the others can't remember

Shall I tell you the secret
and if I do, will you get me
out of this bird suit?

I don't enjoy it here
squatting on this island
looking picturesque and mythical

with these two feathery maniacs,
I don't enjoy singing
this trio, fatal and valuable.

I will tell the secret to you,
to you, only to you.
Come closer. This song

is a cry for help: Help me!
Only you, only you can,
you are unique

at last. Alas
it is a boring song
but it works every time. ❖

REFER TO TEXT ▶▶▶▶	▶ REASON WITH TEXT	
1a. Identify the speaker of the poem.	1b. Recognize the difference of perspective in this poem compared with Homer's *The Odyssey.* Whom does the speaker seem to be addressing? Why might this be significant?	**Analyze** **Take things apart**
2a. Define the "secret" that the Siren shares with the listener.	2b. Determine why a song such as this might lure sailors.	**Evaluate** **Make judgments**
3a. Recall what the Siren reveals to the listener in the final stanza.	3b. Formulate a possible comment that the speaker in Atwood's poem might be making about the relationship between men and women.	**Create** **Bring ideas together**

TEXT ◄TO► TEXT CONNECTION

- Compare Margaret Atwood's and Homer's depiction of Sirens and the effect they have on passing sailors. Do the texts complement or contrast one another in these depictions?
- Brainstorm possible reasons for the authors to depict Sirens in their respective ways. What effect does each description have on their listeners?

Literature CONNECTION

Constantine Cavafy (1863–1933), who lived most of his life in Alexandria, Egypt, is a major Greek poet of the early twentieth century. **"Ithaca"** offers an ironic look at Odysseus' shattering experiences during his ten-year voyage home. Such details as "pleasurable perfumes" seem to mock the heartbreaking struggles the hero endures. What is the difference in **tone,** or author's attitude, between "Ithaca" and the selection from *The Odyssey?* What view of life, whether of a hero or an average citizen, does the poem suggest?

ITHACA

A Poem by **Constantine Cavafy**

When you start on your journey to Ithaca,
then pray that the road is long,
full of adventure, full of knowledge.
Do not fear the Lestrygonians[1]
and the Cyclopes and the angry Poseidon.
You will never meet such as these on your path,
if your thoughts remain lofty, if a fine
emotion touches your body and your spirit.
You will never meet the Lestrygonians,
the Cyclopes and the fierce Poseidon,
if you do not carry them within your soul,
if your soul does not raise them up before you.

Then pray that the road is long.
That the summer mornings are many,
that you will enter ports seen for the first time

1. **Lestrygonians.** Tribe of cannibals who devour many of Odysseus' crew members

with such pleasure, with such joy!
Stop at Phoenician markets,
and purchase fine merchandise,
mother-of-pearl and corals, amber and ebony,
and pleasurable perfumes of all kinds,
buy as many pleasurable perfumes as you can;
visit hosts of Egyptian cities,
to learn and learn from those who have knowledge.

Always keep Ithaca fixed in your mind.
To arrive there is your ultimate goal.
But do not hurry the voyage at all.
It is better to let it last for long years;
and even to anchor at the isle when you are old,
rich with all that you have gained on the way,
not expecting that Ithaca will offer you riches.

Ithaca has given you the beautiful voyage.
Without her you would never have taken the road.
But she has nothing more to give you.

And if you find her poor, Ithaca has not defrauded[2] you.
With the great wisdom you have gained, with so much experience,
You must surely have understood by then what Ithaca means. ❖

2. **defrauded.** Cheated

REFER TO TEXT	REASON WITH TEXT	
1a. List the characters from *The Odyssey* that are mentioned in the poem.	1b. Compare the mentioned characters. What do they have in common? What might they symbolize in Cavafy's poem?	Analyze **Take things apart**
2a. Indicate why travelers won't encounter Cyclopes, Lestrygonians, and Poseidon on their own journey.	2b. Consider what that fact might imply about Odysseus.	Evaluate **Make judgments**
3a. What point does the speaker make about Ithaca and about the journey in the last three lines?	3b. Would Odysseus have agreed with that idea? Explain. If Odysseus could include his own examples within the poem, propose which events he might include.	Create **Bring ideas together**

TEXT TO TEXT CONNECTION

- Compare the voyages described in *The Odyssey* and "Ithaca." What is the purpose of each journey? How are these purposes similar and how are they different? Explain.
- How do the texts describe challenges within the journey? How are these challenges to be avoided or handled?
- How do gods of *The Odyssey* and "lofty" thoughts of "Ithaca" assist in these journeys? What might have Cavafy intended with this advice?

from The Odyssey: PART THREE

BEFORE READING

An Epic Poem by Homer, Translated by Robert Fitzgerald

BUILD BACKGROUND

Literary Context Part Three, which recounts the dramatic events of Odysseus' return to Ithaca, is narrated in the *third person.* As you read, consider how the speaker creates **suspense,** or readers' curiosity to know what happens next. Note the caution with which Odysseus reveals himself to servants and family members. What does the behavior of Penelope and of her suitors, in her husband's absence, indicate about both loyalty and disloyalty?

Reader's Context Have you ever been reunited with an old friend or a family member? Has anyone ever disappointed you or surprised you in your absence? How did you respond to the situation?

ANALYZE LITERATURE: Dramatic Irony

In **dramatic irony,** the reader (or audience) and some of the characters have information that other characters do not. Because of their ignorance, the uninformed characters may say or do ridiculous and even self-destructive things. Odysseus' care in revealing himself to other characters leads to instances of dramatic irony.

SET PURPOSE

The selections in Part Three take a revealing look at the falsity that may lie beneath the social structure. Why, on his return, does Athena transform Odysseus into a beggar? He is, after all, king of Ithaca. As you read the passages, consider how the disguises help Odysseus size up his opponents and how their foolishness makes his task easier.

Athena with spear and shield.

USE READING SKILLS

Compare and Contrast As you are reading Part Three of *The Odyssey,* you can draw comparisons and contrasts—for example, between the hero and the suitors, and between expectations about Penelope's reaction to Odysseus and her actual response. Observing differences—between two events, two characters, two ideas—helps you understand what *both* contribute to the story. You can organize your comparisons and contrasts in a grid like the one below.

Element 1 of Comparison	Element 2 of Comparison	What Comparison Suggests About Each
Suitors: Lazy, having a good time at Penelope's expense	Odysseus: Determined, has a plan	Odysseus deserves his kingdom and the love of Penelope.

PREVIEW VOCABULARY

Examine the list of vocabulary words and the list of antonyms, words or phrases with opposite meanings. Match the vocabulary words with their opposites from the antonym list.

Vocabulary	Antonyms
candor	*unmanageable*
lithe	*straight shooter*
revelry	*smile*
glower	*narrow space*
lavish	*awkward*
aloof	*silence*
pliant	*dishonesty*
imposter	*withhold*
abyss	*friendly*

from The Odyssey

An Epic Poem by **Homer**

Translated by **Robert Fitzgerald**

Part Three: from Books 16–17, 21–23

Penelope with the Suitors, 1509. Bernardino Pintoricchio.

Now shrugging off his rags the wiliest fighter of the islands leapt and stood on the broad door sill, his own bow in his hand.

Homecoming (from Book 16)

In Books 13–15, Odysseus finishes telling his tale to the Phaeacians, and returns to Ithaca on one of their ships. As he arrives in his homeland at last, Athena appears to him and warns him that it is not safe to go home just yet. His house has been overrun by suitors, men who want to marry Queen Penelope. Penelope has been able to put them off for several years by pretending that she will choose a husband when she finishes weaving a shroud, or burial cloth, for her father-in-law Laertes. However, each night, Penelope undoes the weaving that she has completed during the day. While the suitors wait impatiently for Penelope to finish her never-complete weaving, they are eating and drinking all the stores in the household, wasting all the money that is meant for Telemachus' inheritance.

Odysseus naturally wants to return to his house at once to set things right, but Athena advises him to proceed with caution. She transforms him into a shriveled beggar. Rather than go directly to his manor, he first stops at the home of Eumaeus, a swineherd, or herder of pigs, who has been a long and faithful servant of Odysseus' household. Eumaeus offers the "beggar" warm hospitality. The two men are seated in the swineherd's hut when Telemachus, Odysseus' son, arrives unexpectedly, back from a yearlong journey in search of his father.

But there were two men in the mountain hut—
Odysseus and the swineherd. At first light
blowing their fire up, they cooked their breakfast
and sent their lads out, driving herds to root
in the tall timber.
When Telemachus came,
the wolvish troop of watchdogs only fawned on him
as he advanced. Odysseus heard them go
and heard the light crunch of a man's footfall—
at which he turned quickly to say:

"Eumaeus,
here is one of your crew come back, or maybe
another friend: the dogs are out there snuffling
belly down; not one has even growled.
I can hear footsteps—"

But before he finished
his tall son stood at the door.
The swineherd
rose in surprise, letting a bowl and jug
tumble from his fingers. Going forward,
he kissed the young man's head, his shining eyes
and both hands, while his own tears brimmed and fell.
Think of a man whose dear and only son,
born to him in exile, reared with labor,
has lived ten years abroad and now returns:
how would that man embrace his son! Just so
the herdsman clapped his arms around Telemachus
and covered him with kisses—for he knew
the lad had got away from death. He said:

"Light of my days, Telemachus,
you made it back! When you took ship for Pylos
I never thought to see you here again.
Come in, dear child, and let me feast my eyes;
here you are, home from the distant places!
How rarely anyway, you visit us,
your own men, and your own woods and pastures!
Always in the town, a man would think
you loved the suitors' company, those dogs!"

Telemachus with his clear candor said:

"I am with you, Uncle.[1] See now, I have come
because I wanted to see you first, to hear from you
if Mother stayed at home—or is she married
off to someone and Odysseus' bed
left empty for some gloomy spider's weaving?"

Gently the forester replied to this:

"At home indeed your mother is, poor lady,
still in the women's hall. Her nights and days
are wearied out with grieving."

Stepping back
he took the bronze-shod lance, and the young prince
entered the cabin over the worn door stone.
Odysseus moved aside, yielding his couch,
but from across the room Telemachus checked him:

"Friend, sit down; we'll find another chair
in our own hut. Here is the man to make one!"

The swineherd, when the quiet man sank down,
built a new pile of evergreens and fleeces—
a couch for the dear son of great Odysseus—
then gave them trenchers of good meat, left over
from the roast pork of yesterday, and heaped up
willow baskets full of bread, and mixed
an ivy bowl of honey-hearted wine.

1. **Uncle.** A term used to show respect for an elder or a longtime servant

can • dor (kan´ dər *or* kan´ dôr') *n.,* openness; honesty; frankness

Then he in turn sat down, facing Odysseus,
their hands went out upon the meat and drink
as they fell to, ridding themselves of hunger....

Athena.

As the men eat, Telemachus talks despairingly about the suitors who have taken over his home. Odysseus, still in disguise, listens attentively. After dinner, Eumaeus goes to the manor house to give Penelope the news that Telemachus has returned. Father and son are left alone together, and Athena decides it is time for Odysseus to reveal himself.

...[S]he tipped her golden wand upon the man,
making his cloak pure white and the knit tunic
fresh around him. Lithe and young she made him,
ruddy with sun, his jawline clean, the beard
no longer grew upon his chin. And she
withdrew when she had done.

Then Lord Odysseus

reappeared—and his son was thunderstruck.
Fear in his eyes, he looked down and away
as though it were a god, and whispered:

"Stranger,

you are no longer what you were just now!
Your cloak is new; even your skin! You are
one of the gods who rule the sweep of heaven!
Be kind to us, we'll make you fair oblation[2]
and gifts of hammered gold. Have mercy on us!"

The noble and enduring man replied:

"No god. Why take me for a god? No, no.
I am that father whom your boyhood lacked
and suffered pain for lack of. I am he."

Held back too long, the tears ran down his cheeks
as he embraced his son.

Only Telemachus,

uncomprehending, wild
with incredulity,[3] cried out:

"You cannot

2. **oblation.** Something offered in worship
3. **incredulity.** Disbelief

lithe (līth *or* līth) *adj.,* graceful

be my father Odysseus! Meddling spirits
conceived this trick to twist the knife in me!
No man of woman born could work these wonders
by his own craft, unless a god came into it
with ease to turn him young or old at will.
I swear you were in rags and old,
and here you stand like one of the immortals!"

Odysseus brought his ranging mind to bear
and said:

"This is not princely, to be swept
away by wonder at your father's presence.
No other Odysseus will ever come,
for he and I are one, the same; his bitter
fortune and his wanderings are mine.
Twenty years gone, and I am back again
on my own island…."

Then, throwing
his arms around this marvel of a father
Telemachus began to weep. Salt tears
rose from the wells of longing in both men,
and cries burst from both as keen and fluttering
as those of the great taloned hawk,
whose nestlings farmers take before they fly.
So helplessly they cried, pouring out tears,
and might have gone on weeping so till sundown….

Odysseus and Telemachus continue talking, and together they formulate a plan for getting rid of the suitors.

The Beggar at the Manor (from Book 17)

In the morning, Telemachus goes to see his mother, who is overjoyed that he has returned safely from his year-long journey. As they talk, a soothsayer, or person who predicts the future, tells them that Odysseus has returned and is present on the island. Penelope wants to believe but has almost given up all hope. Telemachus does not yet reveal that he has seen his father.
Later that day, disguised again as a beggar and accompanied by Eumaeus, Odysseus himself approaches the manor. Although Odysseus has not been home in twenty years, he is recognized by one old and faithful friend.

While he spoke
an old hound, lying near, pricked up his ears

and lifted up his muzzle. This was Argos,
trained as a puppy by Odysseus,
but never taken on a hunt before
his master sailed for Troy. The young men, afterward,
hunted wild goats with him, and hare, and deer,
but he had grown old in his master's absence.
Treated as rubbish now, he lay at last
upon a mass of dung before the gates—
manure of mules and cows, piled there until
fieldhands could spread it on the king's estate.
Abandoned there, and half destroyed with flies,
old Argos lay.
But when he knew he heard
Odysseus' voice nearby, he did his best
to wag his tail, nose down, with flattened ears,
having no strength to move nearer to his master.
And the man looked away,
wiping a salt tear from his cheek; but he
hid this from Eumaeus. Then he said:

"I marvel that they leave this hound to lie
here on the dung pile;
he would have been a fine dog, from the look of him,
though I can't say as to his power and speed
when he was young. You find the same good build
in house dogs, table dogs landowners keep
all for style."

And you replied, Eumaeus:

"A hunter owned him—but the man is dead
in some far place. If this old hound could show
the form he had when Lord Odysseus left him,
going to Troy, you'd see him swift and strong.
He never shrank from any savage thing
he'd brought to bay in the deep woods; on the scent
no other dog kept up with him. Now misery
has him in leash. His owner died abroad,
and here the women slaves will take no care of him.
You know how servants are: without a master
they have no will to labor, or excel.
For Zeus who views the wide world takes away
half the manhood of a man, that day
he goes into captivity and slavery."

Eumaeus crossed the court and went straight forward
into the mégaron among the suitors;
but death and darkness in that instant closed
the eyes of Argos, who had seen his master,
Odysseus, after twenty years....

When Odysseus and Eumaeus enter the palace, the suitors are feasting. Telemachus has food brought to Odysseus, still disguised as a beggar, but he is mistreated by several of the suitors and even some of Odysseus' servants. In Book 18, one of the suitors goads another beggar into a fight with Odysseus. Penelope appears and reprimands the suitors for starting the fight and for eating up the household's food.

In Book 19, after everyone has gone to bed, Odysseus and Telemachus remove all of the weapons from the hall. Penelope comes down to speak to the "beggar." She talks about her loneliness for her husband and how she has tried to put off the suitors. Odysseus is deeply moved by her story. Penelope orders that the beggar be treated kindly as a guest of the household. When Odysseus' old nurse, Eurycleia, bathes his feet, she recognizes a scar on his leg and almost gives him away. Then Penelope describes the contest she will hold in the morning to choose her new husband.

Odysseus spends a restless night, but Athena appears before him and promises he will defeat his enemies. Meanwhile, Penelope prays for rescue from marriage to another man. When the suitors return the next day, a soothsayer warns them that they face grave danger.

The Test of the Bow (from Book 21)

Penelope goes to a storeroom to bring out the great bow Odysseus had set aside before going to war at Troy. She plans to use it in a test for the suitors.

...Now the queen reached the storeroom door and halted.
Here was an oaken sill, cut long ago
and sanded clean and bedded true. Foursquare
the doorjambs and the shining doors were set
by the careful builder. Penelope untied the strap
around the curving handle, pushed her hook
into the slit, aimed at the bolts inside,
and shot them back. Then came a rasping sound
as those bright doors the key had sprung gave way—
a bellow like a bull's vaunt in a meadow—
followed by her light footfall entering
over the plank floor. Herb-scented robes
lay there in chests, but the lady's milkwhite arms
went up to lift the bow down from a peg
in its own polished bowcase.

Now Penelope
sank down, holding the weapon on her knees,
and drew her husband's great bow out, and sobbed
and bit her lip and let the salt tears flow.
Then back she went to face the crowded hall,
tremendous bow in hand, and on her shoulder hung
the quiver spiked with coughing death.[4] Behind her
maids bore a basket full of axeheads, bronze
and iron implements for the master's game.
Thus in her beauty she approached the suitors,
and near a pillar of the solid roof
she paused, her shining veil across her cheeks,
her maids on either hand and still,
then spoke to the banqueters:

"My lords, hear me:
suitors indeed, you commandeered this house
to feast and drink in, day and night, my husband
being long gone, long out of mind. You found
no justification for yourselves—none
except your lust to marry me. Stand up, then:
we now declare a contest for that prize.
Here is my lord Odysseus' hunting bow.
Bend and string it if you can. Who sends an arrow
through iron axe-helve sockets,[5] twelve in line?
I join my life with his, and leave this place, my home,
my rich and beautiful bridal house, forever
to be remembered, though I dream it only."...

"Here is my lord Odysseus' hunting bow.
Bend and string it if you can."

Many suitors try to string Odysseus' bow, but none is strong enough to accomplish the task.

Two men had meanwhile left the hall:
swineherd and cowherd, in companionship,

4. **coughing death.** Poisoned arrows
5. **axe-helve sockets.** The hole in an axe handle

one downcast as the other. But Odysseus
followed them outdoors, outside the court,
and coming up said gently:

"You, herdsman,
and you, too, swineherd, I could say a thing to you,
or should I keep it dark?

No, no; speak,
my heart tells me. Would you be men enough
to stand by Odysseus if he came back?
Suppose he dropped out of a clear sky, as I did?
Suppose some god should bring him?
Would you bear arms for him, or for the suitors?"

The cowherd said:

"Ah, let the master come!
Father Zeus, grant our old wish! Some courier
guide him back! Then judge what stuff is in me
and how I manage arms!"

Likewise Eumaeus
fell to praying all heaven for his return,
so that Odysseus, sure at least of these,
told them:

"I am at home, for I am he.
I bore adversities, but in the twentieth year
I am ashore in my own land. I find
the two of you, alone among my people,
longed for my coming. Prayers I never heard
except your own that I might come again.
So now what is in store for you I'll tell you:
If Zeus brings down the suitors by my hand
I promise marriages to both, and cattle,
and houses built near mine. And you shall be
brothers-in-arms of my Telemachus.
Here, let me show you something else, a sign
that I am he, that you can trust me, look:
this old scar from the tusk wound that I got
boar hunting on Parnassus—. . ."

CULTURAL CONNECTION

Early Olympic Games The original Olympic Games (named for Mount Olympus, the traditional home of the gods) were, as they are today, held every four years. For over a thousand years, from the eighth century BCE to the fourth century CE, Greek citizens—men who were not slaves—competed in such events as chariot racing, discus throwing, and wrestling. Indeed, one of the events in the modern Olympics is Greek- and Roman-style wrestling. Not only were women forbidden to participate; they were not allowed to sit on the bleachers and cheer for the contestants.

Shifting his rags
he bared the long gash. Both men looked, and knew,
and threw their arms around the old soldier, weeping,
kissing his head and shoulders. He as well
took each man's head and hands to kiss, then said—
to cut it short, else they might weep till dark—

"Break off, no more of this.
Anyone at the door could see and tell them.
Drift back in, but separately at intervals
after me.
Now listen to your orders:
when the time comes, those gentlemen, to a man,
will be dead against giving me bow or quiver.
Defy them. Eumaeus, bring the bow
and put it in my hands there at the door.
Tell the women to lock their own door tight.
Tell them if someone hears the shock of arms
or groans of men, in hall or court, not one
must show her face, but keep still at her weaving.
Philoeteus, run to the outer gate and lock it.
Throw the cross bar and lash it."...

When the leader of the suitors asks that the contest continue the next day, the beggar asks for the chance to try to string the bow. The suitors protest, but the swineherd, Eumaeus, hands Odysseus the bow. Meanwhile, the cowherd Philoeteus locks the gates so none of them can leave.

And Odysseus took his time,
turning the bow, tapping it, every inch,
for borings that termites might have made
while the master of the weapon was abroad.
The suitors were now watching him, and some
jested among themselves:

"A bow lover!"

"Dealer in old bows!"

"Maybe he has one like it
at home!"

"Or has an itch to make one for himself."

"See how he handles it, the sly old buzzard!"

And one disdainful suitor added this:

"May his fortune grow an inch for every inch he bends it!"

But the man skilled in all ways of contending,
satisfied by the great bow's look and heft,
like a musician, like a harper, when
with quiet hand upon his instrument
he draws between his thumb and forefinger
a sweet new string upon a peg: so effortlessly
Odysseus in one motion strung the bow.
Then slid his right hand down the cord and plucked it,
so the taut gut vibrating hummed and sang
a swallow's note.
In the hushed hall it smote the suitors
and all their faces changed. Then Zeus thundered
overhead, one loud crack for a sign.
And Odysseus laughed within him that the son
of crooked-minded Cronus had flung that omen down.

omen (ō´ mən) *n.*, symbol or sign of future misfortune

He picked one ready arrow from his table
where it lay bare: the rest were waiting still
in the quiver for the young men's turn to come.
He nocked it, let it rest across the handgrip,
and drew the string and grooved butt of the arrow,
aiming from where he sat upon the stool.
                                        Now flashed
arrow from twanging bow clean as a whistle
through every socket ring and grazed not one,
to thud with heavy brazen head beyond.
                                        Then quietly
Odysseus said:

                                "Telemachus, the stranger
you welcomed in your hall has not disgraced you.
I did not miss, neither did I take all day
stringing the bow. My hand and eye are sound,
not so contemptible as the young men say.
The hour has come to cook their lordships' mutton—
supper by daylight. Other amusements later,
with song and harping that adorn a feast."

He dropped his eyes and nodded, and the prince
Telemachus, true son of King Odysseus,
belted his sword on, clapped hand to his spear,
and with a clink and glitter of keen bronze
stood by his chair, in the forefront near his father.

Death in the Great Hall (from Book 22)

There are more than one hundred suitors in the great hall. Earlier, Telemachus had removed their weapons. Now, these men watch in disbelief as Odysseus takes off his beggar's rags and faces them, bow in hand.

Now shrugging off his rags the wiliest fighter of the islands
leapt and stood on the broad door sill, his own bow in his hand.
He poured out at his feet a rain of arrows from the quiver
and spoke to the crowd:

                "So much for that. Your clean-cut game is over.
Now watch me hit a target that no man has hit before,
if I can make this shot. Help me, Apollo."

He drew to his fist the cruel head of an arrow for Antinous
just as the young man leaned to lift his beautiful drinking cup,

embossed, two-handled, golden: the cup was in his fingers:
the wine was even at his lips: and did he dream of death?
How could he? In that revelry amid his throng of friends
who would imagine a single foe—though a strong foe indeed—
could dare to bring death's pain on him and darkness on his eyes?
Odysseus' arrow hit him under the chin
and punched up to the feathers through his throat.

Backward and down he went, letting the winecup fall
from his shocked hand. Like pipes his nostrils jetted
crimson runnels, a river of mortal red,
and one last kick upset his table
knocking the bread and meat to soak in dusty blood.

Now as they craned to see their champion where he lay
the suitors jostled in uproar down the hall,
everyone on his feet. Wildly they turned and scanned
the walls in the long room for arms; but not a shield,
not a good ashen spear was there for a man to take and throw.
All they could do was yell in outrage at Odysseus:

"Foul! to shoot at a man! That was your last shot!"

"Your own throat will be slit for this!"

"Our finest lad is down!
You killed the best on Ithaca."

"Buzzards will tear your eyes out!"

For they imagined as they wished—that it was a wild shot,
an unintended killing—fools, not to comprehend
they were already in the grip of death.
But glaring under his brows Odysseus answered:

"You yellow dogs, you thought I'd never make it
home from the land of Troy. You took my house to plunder,
twisted my maids to serve your beds. You dared
bid for my wife while I was still alive.
Contempt was all you had for the gods who rule wide heaven,
contempt for what men say of you hereafter.
Your last hour has come. You die in blood."

rev • el • ry (re´ vəl rē) *n.*, noisy partying or merrymaking

As they all took this in, sickly green fear
pulled at their entrails, and their eyes flickered
looking for some hatch or hideaway from death.
Eurymachus alone could speak. He said:

"If you are Odysseus of Ithaca come back,
all that you say these men have done is true.
Rash actions, many here, more in the countryside.
But here he lies, the man who caused them all.
Antinous was the ringleader; he whipped us on
to do these things. He cared less for a marriage
than for the power Cronion[6] has denied him
as king of Ithaca. For that
he tried to trap your son and would have killed him.
He is dead now and has his portion. Spare
your own people. As for ourselves, we'll make
restitution of wine and meat consumed,
and add, each one, a tithe of twenty oxen
with gifts of bronze and gold to warm your heart.
Meanwhile we cannot blame you for your anger."

Odysseus glowered under his black brows
and said:

"Not for the whole treasure of your fathers,
all you enjoy, lands, flocks, or any gold
put up by others, would I hold my hand.
There will be killing till the score is paid.
You forced yourselves upon this house. Fight your way out,
or run for it, if you think you'll escape death.
I doubt one man of you skins by."…

Odysseus kills the suitor Eurymachus with another arrow. A chaotic battle follows in which Odysseus and Telemachus, aided by their two faithful servants, slay many of the suitors. Athena has been standing by, secretly helping Odysseus' men. Now, at the climax of the fight, the goddess makes her presence known...

At this moment that unmanning thunder cloud,
the aegis, Athena's shield,
took form aloft in the great hall.

"You forced yourselves upon this house. Fight your way out, or run for it, if you think you'll escape death."

6. **Cronion.** Another name for Zeus or descendant of Cronus

glow • er (glau̇r *or* glau̇´ ər *or* glō[ə]r) *v.*, look at with anger

And the suitors mad with fear
at her great sign stampeded like stung cattle by a river
when the dread shimmering gadfly strikes in summer,
in the flowering season, in the long-drawn days.
After them the attackers wheeled, as terrible as falcons
from eyries in the mountains veering over and diving down
with talons wide unsheathed on flights of birds,
who cower down the sky in chutes and bursts along the valley—
but the pouncing falcons grip their prey, no frantic wing avails,
and farmers love to watch those beakèd hunters.
So these now fell upon the suitors in that hall,
turning, turning to strike and strike again,
while torn men moaned at death, and blood ran smoking
over the whole floor....

Odysseus Reunited with Penelope (from Book 23)

All of the suitors are killed. Odysseus has his nurse, Eurycleia, identify the maidservants who had been disloyal to him by entertaining the suitors. After being ordered to remove the dead bodies from the hall, the disloyal servants are taken outside and hanged. Odysseus then purifies the hall by burning brimstone. Eurycleia goes to Penelope and tells her that Odysseus has returned and killed all the men who had taken over his household. Penelope responds at first with joy but then disbelief.

Crossing the door sill she sat down at once
in firelight, against the nearest wall,
across the room from the lord Odysseus.
There
leaning against a pillar, sat the man
and never lifted up his eyes, but only waited
for what his wife would say when she had seen him.
And she, for a long time, sat deathly still
in wonderment—for sometimes as she gazed
she found him—yes, clearly—like her husband,
but sometimes blood and rags were all she saw.
Telemachus' voice came to her ears:

"Mother,
cruel mother, do you feel nothing,
drawing yourself apart this way from Father?
Will you not sit with him and talk and question him?

What other woman would remain so cold?
Who shuns her lord, and he come back to her
from wars and wandering, after twenty years?
Your heart is hard as flint and never changes!"

Penelope answered:

"I am stunned, child.
I cannot speak to him. I cannot question him.
I cannot keep my eyes upon his face.
If really he is Odysseus, truly home,
beyond all doubt we two shall know each other
better than you or anyone. There are
secret signs we know, we two."

A smile
came now to the lips of the patient hero, Odysseus,
who turned to Telemachus and said:

"Peace: let your mother test me at her leisure.
Before long she will see and know me best.
These tatters, dirt—all that I'm caked with now—
make her look hard at me and doubt me still."

The Sign of the Olive Tree

Telemachus, the swineherd, and the cowherd bathe and put on fresh clothing, while Odysseus prepares to do the same.

Greathearted Odysseus, home at last,
was being bathed now by Eurynome
and rubbed with golden oil, and clothed again
in a fresh tunic and a cloak. Athena
lent him beauty, head to foot. She made him
taller, and massive, too, with crisping hair
in curls like petals of wild hyacinth
but all red-golden. Think of gold infused
on silver by a craftsman, whose fine art
Hephaestus taught him, or Athena: one
whose work moves to delight: just so she lavished
beauty over Odysseus' head and shoulders.
He sat then in the same chair by the pillar,
facing his silent wife, and said:

lav • ish (la´ vish) *v.*, provide, as with gifts, praise, and the like

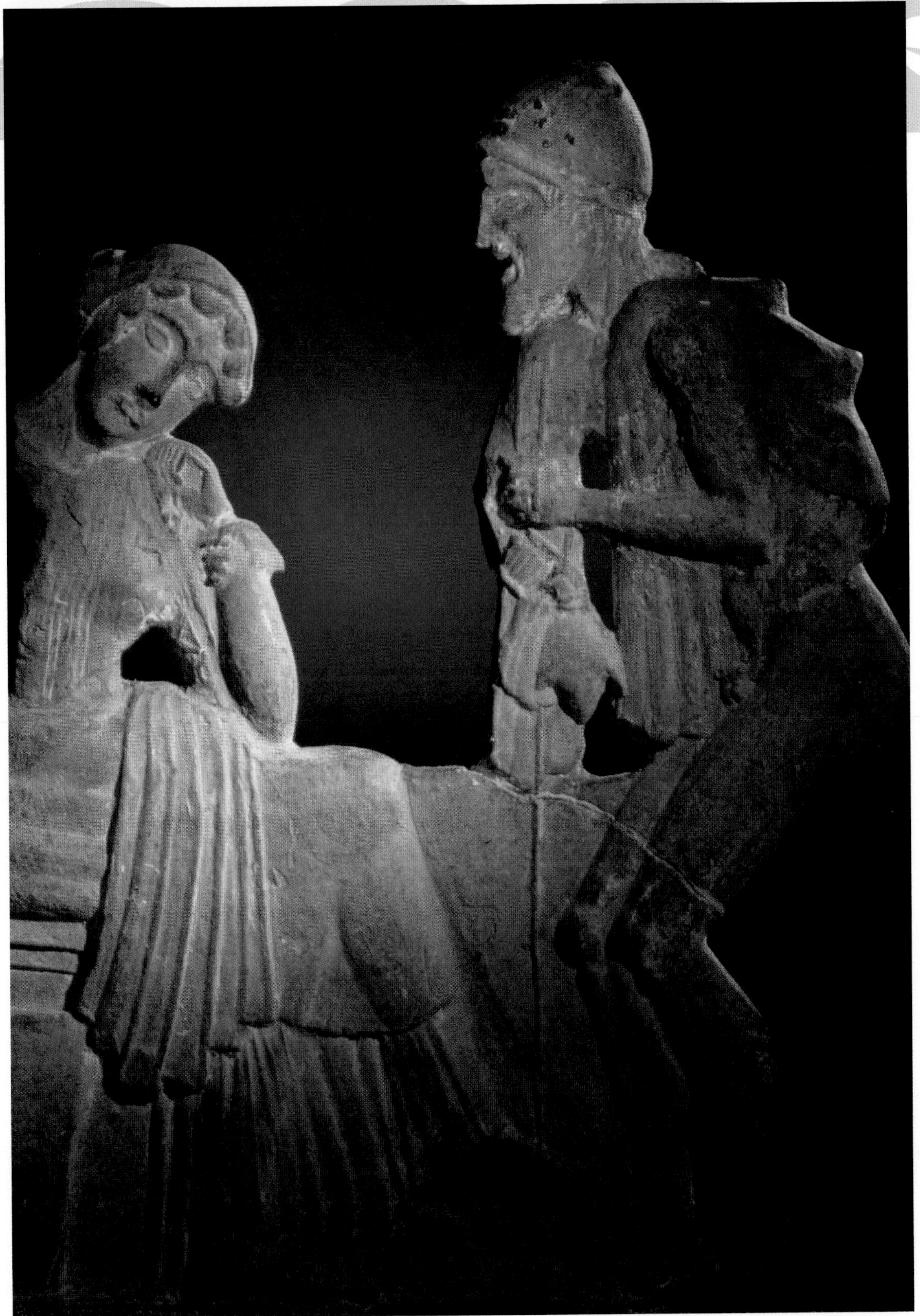

Odysseus and Penelope reunited.

"Strange woman,
the immortals of Olympus made you hard,
harder than any. Who else in the world
would keep aloof as you do from her husband
if he returned to her from years of trouble,
cast on his land in the twentieth year?

Nurse, make up a bed for me to sleep on.
Her heart is iron in her breast."

Penelope
spoke to Odysseus now. She said:

"Strange man,
if man you are...This is no pride on my part
nor scorn for you—not even wonder, merely.
I know so well how you—how he—appeared
boarding the ship for Troy. But all the same...

Make up his bed for him, Eurycleia.
Place it outside the bedchamber my lord
built with his own hands. Pile the big bed
with fleeces, rugs, and sheets of purest linen."

With this she tried him to the breaking point,
and he turned on her in a flash raging:

"Woman, by heaven you've stung me now!
Who dared to move my bed?
No builder had the skill for that—unless
a god came down to turn the trick. No mortal
in his best days could budge it with a crowbar.
There is our pact and pledge, our secret sign,
built into that bed—my handiwork
and no one else's!

An old trunk of olive
grew like a pillar on the building plot,
and I laid out our bedroom round that tree,
lined up the stone walls, built the walls and roof,
gave it a doorway and smooth-fitting doors.
Then I lopped off the silvery leaves and branches,

aloof (ə lüf´) *adj.,* unfriendly

hewed and shaped that stump from the roots up
into a bedpost, drilled it, let it serve
as model for the rest. I planed them all,
inlaid them all with silver, gold and ivory,
and stretched a bed between—a pliant web
of oxhide thongs dyed crimson.

There's our sign!
I know no more. Could someone else's hand
have sawn that trunk and dragged the frame away?"

Their secret! as she heard it told, her knees
grew tremulous and weak, her heart failed her.
With eyes brimming tears she ran to him,
throwing her arms around his neck, and kissed him,
murmuring:

"Do not rage at me, Odysseus!
No one ever matched your caution! Think
what difficulty the gods gave: they denied us
life together in our prime and flowering years,
kept us from crossing into age together.
Forgive me, don't be angry. I could not
welcome you with love on sight! I armed myself
long ago against the frauds of men,
imposters who might come—and all those many
whose underhanded ways bring evil on!...

But here and now, what sign could be so clear
as this of our own bed?
No other man has ever laid eyes on it—
only my own slave, Actoris, that my father
sent with me as a gift—she kept our door.
You make my stiff heart know that I am yours."

Now from his breast into his eyes the ache
of longing mounted, and he wept at last,
his dear wife, clear and faithful, in his arms,
longed for
as the sunwarmed earth is longed for by a swimmer
spent in rough water where his ship went down
under Poseidon's blows, gale winds and tons of sea.

"Do not rage at me, Odysseus! No one ever matched your caution! Think what difficulty the gods gave: they denied us life together in our prime and flowering years"

pli • ant (plī´ ənt) *adj.*, easy to handle; capable of being reshaped
im • pos • ter (im päs´ tər) *n.*, person pretending to be what he or she is not

Few men can keep alive through a big surf
to crawl, clotted with brine, on kindly beaches
in joy, in joy, knowing the abyss behind:
and so she too rejoiced, her gaze upon her husband,
her white arms round him pressed as though forever.... ❖

abyss (ə bis´ *or* a bis´ *or* a´ bis[']) *n.,* bottomless gulf or pit; immeasurable space

"This is not princely, to be swept / away by wonder at your father's presence." Why do you think the king of Ithaca scolds his son at this tender moment? What reasoning might other parents or guardians have for discouraging the show of emotion or affection?

REFER TO TEXT ▶▶▶▶	▶ REASON WITH TEXT	
1a. How is Odysseus disguised when he arrives in Ithaca?	1b. Explain why Athena might choose to disguise Odysseus.	**Understand** **Find meaning**
2a. Identify what the suitors must accomplish to win Penelope's hand in marriage.	2b. Show in which ways the suitors' ridicule of the beggar's participation in the test (Book 21) is an example of dramatic irony. How does the outcome of the contest, in Book 22, make their ridicule even more ironic?	**Apply** **Use information**
3a. Recall what the suitors tell Odysseus after he reveals himself. How does he respond?	3b. Identify why Homer has Odysseus kill the suitors before revealing his identity to Penelope.	**Analyze** **Take things apart**
4a. What does it take for Penelope to believe that Odysseus is indeed her husband?	4b. Evaluate whether Penelope is justified in remaining unfriendly to Odysseus (Book 23). Explain.	**Evaluate** **Make judgments**
5a. Repeat what Penelope is compared to at the end of the selection.	5b. Reread Book 11. In lines 100–123, Teiresias tells Odysseus what he must do after regaining his kingdom and his wife. Summarize how these events relate to the selections you have read.	**Create** **Bring ideas together**

ANALYZE LITERATURE: Dramatic Irony

What condition sets up the dramatic irony in Book 16, in which Odysseus meets the swineherd and Telemachus? Under what conditions would the scene not have included dramatic irony?

Edna St. Vincent Millay (1892–1950) was born in Rockland, Maine. In 1917, Millay's first book, *Renaissance and Other Poems,* was published. In 1923, *The Harp Weaver and Other Poems* earned her a Pulitzer Prize. Like many other American writers of her time, Millay is remembered for her artistic experimentation and her rebelliousness. As you read **"An Ancient Gesture,"** compare and contrast the character Penelope in the poem with her counterpart in *The Odyssey.*

An Ancient Gesture

A Poem by **Edna St. Vincent Millay**

I thought, as I wiped my eyes on the corner of my apron:
Penelope did this too.
And more than once: you can't keep weaving all day
And undoing it all through the night;
Your arms get tired, and the back of your neck gets tight;

And along towards morning, when you think it will never be light,
And your husband has been gone, and you don't know where, for years,
Suddenly you burst into tears;
There is simply nothing else to do.

And I thought, as I wiped my eyes on the corner of my apron:
This is an ancient gesture, authentic, antique,
In the very best tradition, classic, Greek;
Ulysses[1] did this too.
But only as a gesture,—a gesture which implied
To the assembled throng that he was much too moved to speak.
He learned it from Penelope...
Penelope, who really cried. ❖

1. **Ulysses.** Roman name for Odysseus

REFER TO TEXT ▶▶▶▶	▶ REASON WITH TEXT	
1a. According to the speaker, how is Penelope's gesture different from that of Ulysses?	1b. Infer what this difference implies about Penelope and Odysseus.	**Analyze** **Take things apart**
2a. Define how the poem describes Penelope's life while her husband is away.	2b. How does Penelope's experience compare with Odysseus' journey? Evaluate which was the better experience.	**Evaluate** **Make judgments**
3a. Identify the emotional state of the poem's speaker. Explain.	3b. If Penelope had comforted the speaker of the poem, compose the advice she might have offered.	**Create** **Bring ideas together**

TEXT TO TEXT CONNECTION

Compare Homer's treatment of Penelope and the depiction of Penelope within "An Ancient Gesture." How is Penelope's strength and wit shown in each text? How is her sadness and grief depicted?

Literature CONNECTION

Katerina Anghelaki-Rooke was born in Athens, Greece, in 1939. At colleges in France, Greece, and Switzerland, she studied foreign languages and literature. Today, she is a leading poet in Greece as well as a translator of poetry, including the works of Dylan Thomas, Seamus Heaney, and Samuel Beckett. In 1985, Anghelaki-Rooke received the National Prize for Poetry in her native Greece. As you read the poem, consider how its Penelope is similar to and different from Odysseus' wife in Homer's epic.

Penelope weaving a shroud for Laertes her father-in-law while she awaits the return of her husband Odysseus, 1895. Max Klinger.

Says Penelope

A Poem by

Katerina Anghelaki-Rooke

I was not weaving or knitting
a story I was writing, rewriting
stifling
under the burden of words,
unable to reach perfection
with grief crushing my center.
Absence, always the subject of my life
—absence from life—
tears spring from the paper
and the natural anguish
of a deprived body.

Rewriting, tearing
stifling my living cries
Where are you, come, I'm waiting
this spring is not like others
and every morning I begin all over
with new birds and white linen
drying in the sun.
You will never be here
with the hose to water the flowers
the old ceiling dripping
soaked with rain,
and I, dissolving inside you
quietly, autumnlike…
Your exquisite heart
—exquisite because I've chosen it—
will always be elsewhere
and with words I will break
the threads binding me
to that certain man
for whom I long
until Odysseus becomes a symbol of longing
sailing the seas
of our brain.
I forget you with passion
every day
until washed from sweet smelling sin
and entirely clean at last
you'll enter immortality.
A hard and thankless task,
my only reward if finally I can understand
the meaning of existence
of absence
how the self can go on
in all that loneliness, endlessly,
how the body always renews itself
it falls and it rises
as if axed down
afflicted or in love,
hoping
to gain the essence
of that which it can no longer touch. ❖

REFER TO TEXT ▶▶▶	▶ REASON WITH TEXT	
1a. Repeat how the speaker of the poem describes her grief.	1b. Determine how the hopes and worries of Penelope in the poem differ from those of Penelope in *The Odyssey*.	**Analyze** **Take things apart**
2a. Identify what the speaker of the poem was doing instead of weaving or knitting.	2b. After reading these three selections—Part Three of *The Odyssey*, "An Ancient Gesture," and "Says Penelope"—rank which Penelope you admire or sympathize with more. Explain.	**Evaluate** **Make judgments**
3a. In the poems by Millay and Anghelaki-Rooke, Penelope is the first-person speaker. Recall in which passages from Homer does Penelope explain her actions.	3b. The two twentieth-century poets presented here use Homer's epic as a springboard from which to express modern ideas. Specify what that fact suggests about *The Odyssey*.	**Create** **Bring ideas together**

TEXT TO TEXT CONNECTION

What actions do the Penelopes of these three texts utilize and for what purpose? Do the three have similar or different purposes for their actions? Compare and contrast what these actions serve and whether or not they are accomplishing the intended goal.

AFTER READING

EXTEND THE TEXT

Writing Options

Creative Writing Penelope from *The Odyssey* and the speaker in Millay's poem "An Ancient Gesture" have formed a support group for women whose husbands have been gone for many years. Imagine that you are a reporter who has interviewed the two women. Create a brief **broadcast script** of your questions and the women's responses.

Descriptive Writing A friend who is unfamiliar with modern poetry asks you to explain the difference between Penelope in *The Odyssey* and the speaker in Anghelaki-Rooke's poem, "Says Penelope." Prepare a brief **character description** in which you describe the similarities and the differences between the two Penelopes.

Collaborative Learning

Explore the Technology of Ancient Greece Work with a partner or in a small group to find out more about ancient Greek ships and navigation, weapons (including the bow and arrow), carpentry, or other technical achievements. Do research on the Internet or in the library; then consider how advanced (or how primitive) Greek know-how was. Look for inventions or discoveries that have application in modern technology.

Lifelong Learning

Present a Living Pantheon From *The Odyssey* selections and other sources, prepare a *pantheon,* or list of gods and goddesses of ancient Greece or ancient Rome. In a presentation, each student plays the role of a deity by providing "autobiographical" details. Students may want to display features associated with their deities, such as Hermes' winged feet.

Go to **www.mirrorsandwindows.com** for more.

READING ASSESSMENT

1. Number these events, which occur in the Land of the Cyclopes (Book 9), in the correct sequence, with 1 being the first event to happen and 5 being the last.
   - ______ Odysseus' plan is to have crew members cling to the underside of the sheep.
   - ______ Odysseus prays to Athena for assistance.
   - ______ Odysseus realizes that if he kills the one-eyed giant, he and the crew will be unable to escape from the cave.
   - ______ When asked to identify himself to Polyphemus, Odysseus answers falsely.
   - ______ Polyphemus prays to his father, Poseidon, to cause Odysseus to return to Ithaca alone.

2. In Helios' Cattle (Book 12), the crew promises to build a temple to Helios as punishment for killing his livestock. Which passage does this "bargaining" scene foreshadow?
   - A. the description of the crew butchering livestock in Book 9, lines 457–458
   - B. the passage in Book 21 in which Penelope announces the contest
   - C. the passage in Book 21 in which the suitors ridicule the beggar
   - D. the scene in Book 22 from Death in the Great Hall
   - E. the scene in Book 23 in which Penelope tells Telemachus why she is unfriendly to his father

3. Which of the following is an incorrect statement about *The Odyssey?*
   - A. For the Greeks, the sea represented both life and death.
   - B. Odysseus is in no hurry to return to Ithaca.
   - C. In a cycle of evil, a wrongdoing is revenged by further violence.
   - D. Odysseus' return to Ithaca is marked by violence.
   - E. Warnings and omens were to be heeded.

4. Which of the following lessons about life can probably not be drawn from Odysseus' homecoming?
   - A. Returning home does not guarantee peace.
   - B. Even in familiar surroundings, people faced with challenges must use caution.
   - C. People returning home must be prepared to kill their enemies.
   - D. People cannot assume that loved ones will recognize them after a long absence.
   - E. Returning home is not as joyous as you may imagine it.

5. An **archetype** is a type of character, image, theme, symbol, plot, or other element that has appeared in the literature of the world from ancient times until today. Choose two key incidents from the selections and explain their timeless, universal relevance to human society.

READING FOLK LITERATURE INDEPENDENTLY

Theme: Pass It On

"Once upon a time, in a far country, there lived a king whose daughter was the prettiest princess in the world."

—James Thurber, from "The Princess and the Tin Box"

Stories, poems, and songs that are passed by word of mouth are important elements of a group's culture. The stories serve to instruct children on appropriate behavior and the values of their community. Over time, the stories may change form, focus, or meaning; however, people still retain the basic desire to pass them on. The following selections encompass a variety of cultures and times, yet all provide a glimpse into the beliefs and customs of their people.

USING READING SKILLS WITH FOLK LITERATURE

Make Generalizations and Draw Conclusions

When you **make generalizations,** you look at the information provided and **synthesize** it, or piece it together, to develop a general principle or an idea about the selection. This synthesis may draw information from various parts of a text. To make generalizations, you need to identify the supporting details. For example, in folk literature, you may want to keep track of the details that describe a character or statements about the land or culture of the people in the tale. A Generalizations Chart, like the one below for "The Story of Dædalus and Icarus," will help:

Generalizations Chart

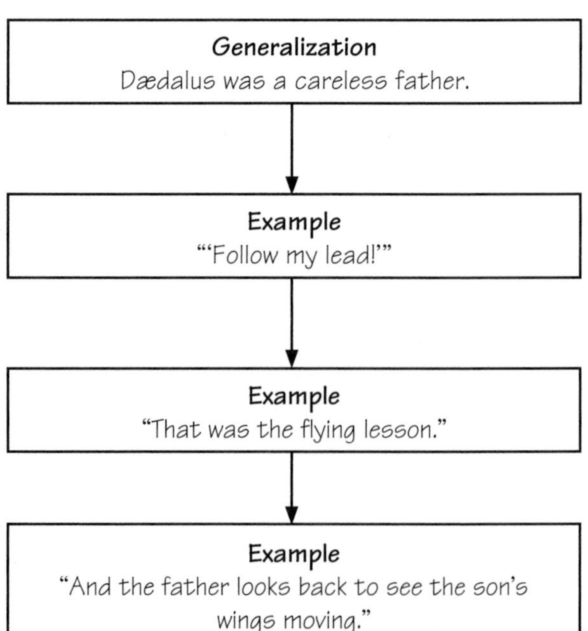
Generalization
Dædalus was a careless father.
Example
"'Follow my lead!'"
Example
"That was the flying lesson."
Example
"And the father looks back to see the son's wings moving."

Similarly, when you **draw conclusions,** you are gathering pieces of information and then deciding what that information means. The information you gather can be supporting details or even the generalizations that you make based on those details.

Drawing conclusions is an essential part of reading. It may be helpful to use a graphic organizer such as a chart or log to keep track of the information you find while you are reading and the conclusions you draw. You could arrange the information from your generalizations into a chart like the following that leads to a conclusion:

Drawing Conclusions Chart

Key Idea	Key Idea
Dædalus was a careless father.	
Supporting Details	**Supporting Details**
"'Follow my lead!'" "That was the flying lesson." "And the father looks back to see the son's wings moving."	
Overall Conclusion	**Overall Conclusion**
Dædalus was too focused on "changing the laws of nature" to recognize that he was putting his son's life in danger.	

What Good Readers Do

Write Things Down

As you read stories, folk tales, and other forms of folk literature, writing things down is a helpful practice. Possible ways to write things down include:

- Underline characters' names.
- Write messages on sticky notes.
- Highlight the setting.
- Create a graphic organizer to keep track of plot elements.
- Use a code in the margin that shows how you respond to the characters, setting, or events. For instance, you can mark a description you enjoy with a "+."

Framework for Folk Literature

In the stories, poems, and songs that are a part of folk literature, storytellers want to entertain their audience and to pass along cultural ideas and beliefs. The following checklists offer strategies for reading folk literature.

As you start to read...

- ❑ From which culture does this tale come?
- ❑ Who are the characters in this tale?
- ❑ What do the characters do?

As you continue reading...

- ❑ Which supporting details describe the characters?
- ❑ Where does the narrator or author seem to make judgments about the characters or their actions?
- ❑ What generalizations can you make based on the details?

After you've finished reading...

- ❑ What is the final result of the tale?
- ❑ What conclusions can you draw about the story by synthesizing the evidence?
- ❑ What seems to be the main message or moral of the tale?

PERSEUS

A Myth Retold by **Edith Hamilton**

Edith Hamilton (1867–1963), who was born in Germany but lived most of her life in the United States, is admired for her numerous books on ancient society. Some of her works are scholarly; others, like the retelling of various myths, appeal to all readers. **"Perseus"** is of particular interest because it sheds light on ancient Greek religion. Throughout the main character's life—even from before his birth—the gods intervene to determine his fate.

As you are reading the tale, ask yourself what Perseus's challenging quest may have signified to the Greeks and what he learns from it. How might you feel if you were sent on a difficult, perhaps frustrating mission to achieve your goals?

Persus and Athena.

NO MAN UNAIDED COULD KILL MEDUSA.

King Acrisius[1] of Argos had only one child, a daughter, Danaë.[2] She was beautiful above all the other women of the land, but this was small comfort to the King for not having a son. He journeyed to Delphi to ask the god if there was any hope that some day he would be the father of a boy. The priestess told him no, and added what was far worse: that his daughter would have a son who would kill him.

The only sure way to escape that fate was for the King to have Danaë instantly put to death—taking no chances, but seeing to it himself. This Acrisius would not do. His fatherly affection was not strong, as events proved, but his fear of the gods was. They visited with terrible punishment those who shed the blood of kindred.

Acrisius did not dare slay his daughter. Instead, he had a house built all of bronze and sunk underground, but with part of the roof open to the sky so that light and air could come through. Here he shut her up and guarded her.

> So Danaë endured, the beautiful,
> To change the glad daylight for
> brass-bound walls,
> And in that chamber secret as the grave

1. **Acrisius.** (a kris´ ē əs)
2. **Danaë.** (dan´ ā ē)

She lived a prisoner. Yet to her came
Zeus in the golden rain.

As she sat there through the long days and hours with nothing to do, nothing to see except the clouds moving by overhead, a mysterious thing happened, a shower of gold fell from the sky and filled her chamber. How it was revealed to her that it was Zeus who had visited her in this shape we are not told, but she knew that the child she bore was his son.

For a time she kept his birth secret from her father, but it became increasingly difficult to do so in the narrow limits of that bronze house and finally one day the little boy—his name was Perseus—was discovered by his grandfather. "Your child!" Acrisius cried in great anger. "Who is his father?" But when Danaë answered proudly, "Zeus," he would not believe her. One thing only he was sure of, that the boy's life was a terrible danger to his own. He was afraid to kill him for the same reason that had kept him from killing her, fear of Zeus and the Furies who pursue such murderers. But if he could not kill them outright, he could put them in the way of tolerably certain death. He had a great chest made, and the two placed in it. Then it was taken out to sea and cast into the water.

In that strange boat Danaë sat with her little son. The daylight faded and she was alone on the sea.

When in the carven chest the winds and
waves
Struck fear into her heart she put her arms,
Not without tears, round Perseus tenderly
She said, "O son, what grief is mine.
But you sleep softly, little child,
Sunk deep in rest within your cheerless
home,
Only a box, brass-bound. The night, this
darkness visible,
The scudding waves so near to your soft
curls,
The shrill voice of the wind, you do not
heed,
Nestled in your red cloak, fair little face."

Through the night in the tossing chest she listened to the waters that seemed always about to wash over them. The dawn came, but with no comfort to her for she could not see it. Neither could she see that around them there were islands rising high above the sea, many islands. All she knew was that presently a wave seemed to lift them and carry them swiftly on and then, retreating, leave them on something solid and motionless. They had made land; they were safe from the sea, but they were still in the chest with no way to get out.

Fate willed it—or perhaps Zeus, who up to now had done little for his love and his child—that they should be discovered by a good man, a fisherman named Dictys. He came upon the great box and broke it open and took the pitiful cargo home to his wife who was as kind as he. They had no children and they cared for Danaë and Perseus as if they were their own. The two lived there many years, Danaë content to let her son follow the fisherman's humble trade, out of harm's way. But in the end more trouble came. Polydectes,[3] the ruler of the little island, was the brother of Dictys, but he was a cruel and ruthless man. He seems to have taken no notice of the mother and son for a long time, but at last Danaë attracted his attention. She was still radiantly beautiful even though Perseus by now was full grown, and Polydectes fell in love with her. He wanted her, but he did not want her son, and he set himself to think out a way of getting rid of him.

There were some fearsome monsters called Gorgons who lived on an island and were known far and wide because of their deadly power. Polydectes evidently talked to Perseus about them; he probably told him that he would rather have the head of one of them

3. **Polydectes.** (pol i dek′ tez)

than anything else in the world. This seems practically certain from the plan he devised for killing Perseus. He announced that he was about to be married and he called his friends together for a celebration, including Perseus in the invitation. Each guest, as was customary, brought a gift for the bride-to-be, except Perseus alone. He had nothing he could give. He was young and proud and keenly mortified. He stood up before them all and did exactly what the King had hoped he would do, declared that he would give him a present better than any there. He would go off and kill Medusa and bring back her head as his gift. Nothing could have suited the King better. No one in his senses would have made such a proposal. Medusa was one of the Gorgons,

> And they are three, the Gorgons, each with wings
> And snaky hair, most horrible to mortals.
> Whom no man shall behold and draw again

The breath of life, for the reason that whoever looked at them were turned instantly into stone. It seemed that Perseus had been led by his angry pride into making an empty boast. No man unaided could kill Medusa.

But Perseus was saved from his folly. Two great gods were watching over him. He took ship as soon as he left the King's hall, not daring to see his mother first and tell her what he intended, and he sailed to Greece to learn where the three monsters were to be found. He went to Delphi, but all the priestess would say was to bid him seek the land where men eat not Demeter's golden grain, but only acorns. So he went to Dodona, in the land of oak trees, where the talking oaks were which declared Zeus's will and where the Selli lived who made their bread from acorns. They could tell him, however, no more than this, that he was under the protection of the gods. They did not know where the Gorgons lived.

When and how Hermes and Athena came to his help is not told in any story, but he must have known despair before they did so. At last, however, as he wandered on, he met a strange and beautiful person. We know what he looked like from many a poem, a young man with the first down upon his cheek when youth is loveliest, carrying, as no other young man ever did, a wand of gold with wings at one end, wearing a winged hat, too, and winged sandals. At sight of him hope must have entered Perseus' heart, for he would know that this could be none other than Hermes, the guide and the giver of good.

This radiant personage told him that before he attacked Medusa he must first be properly equipped, and that what he needed was in the possession of the nymphs of the North. To find the nymphs' abode, they must go to the Gray Women who alone could tell them the way. These women dwelt in a land where all was dim and shrouded in twilight. No ray of sun looked ever on that country, nor the moon by night. In that gray place the three women lived, all gray themselves and withered as in extreme old age. They were strange creatures, indeed, most of all because they had but one eye for the three, which it was their custom to take turns with, each removing it from her forehead when she had had it for a time and handing it to another.

All this Hermes told Perseus and then he unfolded his plan. He would himself guide Perseus to them. Once there Perseus must keep hidden until he saw one of them take the eye out of her forehead to pass it on. At that moment, when none of the three could see, he must rush forward and seize the eye and refuse to give it back until they told him how to reach the nymphs of the North.

He himself, Hermes said, would give him a sword to attack Medusa with—which could not be bent or broken by the Gorgon's scales, no matter how hard they were. This was a wonderful gift, no doubt, and yet of what use was a sword when the creature to be struck by it could turn the swordsman into stone before

Study for Perseus and the Graiae, 1880. Sir Edward Burne-Jones.

him full directions at once; they would have done anything to get their eye back. He returned it to them and went on the way they had pointed out to him. He was bound, although he did not know it, to the blessed country of the Hyperboreans,[4] at the back of the North Wind, of which it is said: "Neither by ship nor yet by land shall one find the wondrous road to the gathering place of the Hyperboreans." But Perseus had Hermes with him, so that the road lay open to him, and he reached that host of happy people who are always banqueting and holding joyful revelry. They showed him great kindness: they welcomed him to their feast, and the maidens dancing to the sound of flute and lyre paused to get for him the gifts he sought. These were three: winged sandals, a magic wallet which would always become the right size for whatever was to be carried in it, and, most important of all, a cap which made the wearer invisible. With these and Athena's shield and Hermes' sword Perseus was ready for the Gorgons. Hermes knew where they lived, and leaving the happy land the two flew back across Ocean and over the sea to the Terrible Sisters' island.

By great good fortune they were all asleep when Perseus found them. In the mirror of the bright shield he could see them clearly, creatures with great wings and bodies covered with golden scales and hair a mass of twisting snakes. Athena was beside him now as well as Hermes. They told him which one was Medusa and that was important, for she alone of the three could be killed; the other two were immortal. Perseus on his winged sandals hovered above them, looking, however, only at the shield. Then he aimed a stroke down

he was within striking distance? But another great deity was at hand to help. Pallas Athena stood beside Perseus. She took off the shield of polished bronze which covered her breast and held it out to him. "Look into this when you attack the Gorgon," she said. "You will be able to see her in it as in a mirror, and so avoid her deadly power."

Now, indeed, Perseus had good reason to hope. The journey to the twilight land was long, over the stream of Ocean and on to the very border of the black country where the Cimmerians dwell, but Hermes was his guide and he could not go astray. They found the Gray Women at last, looking in the wavering light like gray birds, for they had the shape of swans. But their heads were human and beneath their wings they had arms and hands. Perseus did just as Hermes had said, he held back until he saw one of them take the eye out of her forehead. Then before she could give it to her sister, he snatched it out of her hand. It was a moment or two before the three realized they had lost it. Each thought one of the others had it. But Perseus spoke out and told them he had taken it and that it would be theirs again only when they showed him how to find the nymphs of the North. They gave

4. **Hyperboreans.** (hī per bō´ rē anz)

at Medusa's throat and Athena guided his hand. With a single sweep of his sword he cut through her neck and, his eyes still fixed on the shield with never a glance at her, he swooped low enough to seize the head. He dropped it into the wallet which closed around it. He had nothing to fear from it now. But the two other Gorgons had awakened and, horrified at the sight of their sister slain, tried to pursue the slayer. Perseus was safe; he had on the cap of darkness and they could not find him.

Perseus with the Head of Medusa, 1705–1710. Sebastiano Ricci.

So over the sea rich-haired Danaë's son,
Perseus, on his winged sandals sped,
Flying swift as thought.
In a wallet of silver,
A wonder to behold,
He bore the head of the monster,
While Hermes, the son of Maia,
The messenger of Zeus,
Kept ever at his side.

On his way back he came to Ethiopia and alighted there. By this time Hermes had left him. Perseus found, as Hercules was later to find, that a lovely maiden had been given up to be devoured by a horrible sea serpent. Her name was Andromeda and she was the daughter of a silly vain woman,

That starred Ethiop queen who strove
To set her beauty's praise above
The sea-nymphs, and their power offended.

She had boasted that she was more beautiful than the daughters of Nereus, the Sea-god. An absolutely certain way in those days to draw down on one a wretched fate was to claim superiority in anything over any deity'; nevertheless people were perpetually doing so. In this case the punishment for the arrogance the gods detested fell not on Queen Cassiopeia,[5] Andromeda's mother, but on her daughter. The Ethiopians were being devoured in numbers by the serpent; and, learning from the oracle that they could be freed from the pest only if Andromeda were offered up to it, they forced Cepheus,[6] her father, to consent. When Perseus arrived the maiden was on a rocky ledge by the sea, chained there to wait for the coming of the monster. Perseus saw her and on the instant loved her. He waited beside her until the great snake came for its prey; then he cut its head off just as he had the Gorgon's. The headless body dropped back into the water; Perseus took Andromeda to her parents and asked for her hand, which they gladly gave him.

5. **Cassiopeia.** (kas´ ē ō pē' ə)
6. **Cepheus.** (sē´ fəs)

With her he sailed back to the island and his mother, but in the house where he had lived so long he found no one. The fisherman Dictys' wife was long since dead, and the two others, Danaë and the man who had been like a father to Perseus, had had to fly and hide themselves from Polydectes, who was furious at Danaë's refusal to marry him. They had taken refuge in a temple, Perseus was told. He learned also that the King was holding a banquet in the palace and all the men who favored him were gathered there. Perseus instantly saw his opportunity. He went straight to the palace and entered the hall. As he stood at the entrance, Athena's shining buckler on his breast, the silver wallet at his side, he drew the eyes of every man there. Then before any could look away he held up the Gorgon's head; and at the sight one and all, the cruel King and his servile courtiers, were turned into stone. There they sat, a row of statues, each, as it were, frozen stiff in the attitude he had struck when he first saw Perseus.

When the islanders knew themselves freed from the tyrant it was easy for Perseus to find Danaë and Dictys. He made Dictys king of the island, but he and his mother decided that they would go back with Andromeda to Greece and try to be reconciled to Acrisius, to see if the many years that had passed since he had put them in the chest had not softened him so that he would be glad to receive his daughter and grandson. When they reached Argos, however, they found that Acrisius had been driven away from the city, and where he was no one could say. It happened that soon after their arrival Perseus heard that the King of Larissa, in the North, was holding a great athletic contest, and he journeyed there to take part. In the discus-throwing when his turn came and he hurled the heavy missile, it swerved and fell among the spectators. Acrisius was there on a visit to the King, and the discus struck him. The blow was fatal and he died at once.

So Apollo's oracle was again proved true. If Perseus felt any grief, at least he knew that his grandfather had done his best to kill him and his mother. With his death their troubles came to an end. Perseus and Andromeda lived happily ever after. Their son, Electryon, was the grandfather of Hercules.

Medusa's head was given to Athena, who bore it always upon the aegis, Zeus's shield, which she carried for him. ❖

What kinds of difficult quests or journeys might people today challenge themselves to pursue? What might be their motivations? What might be the results?

Refer and Reason

1. Why is King Acrisius told to kill his daughter, Danaë? Identify the ironical consequences of his refusal to obey.
2. Assess why Polydectes wants to kill Perseus.
3. Summarize the differences and similarities between Perseus's journey and Odysseus's.

Writing Options

1. Imagine that you are King Acrisius when he hears the priestess at the oracle of Delphi tell him what he must do to avoid the dreadful prediction. Create a diary entry to describe your dilemma.
2. Perseus is sent to meet the Gray Women, who will tell him how to find Medusa. What do you think the Gray Women suggest about the ancient Greeks' view of aged females? Write your historical analysis in a paragraph or two.

Go to **www.mirrorsandwindows.com** for more.

In **"Iya, the Camp-Eater,"** a group of hunters comes upon an abandoned baby, who is quickly adopted by the chief's daughter. Ignoring one hunter's word of caution, the people celebrate the addition to the tribe. The author, Gertrude Bonnin, was known more commonly as **Zitkala-Sa.** Like many Native Americans who receive a Western-style education, Zitkala-Sa was torn between two cultures—the Yankton Nakota tribe and the mainstream community of the United States. As you read the legend, look for the literary elements foreshadowing and symbolism.

Suppose you were to ignore someone's warning and then, later on, regret your action. How might you handle the situation?

Iya, the Camp-Eater

A Native American Legend by **Zitkala-Sa**

From the tall grass came the voice of a crying babe. The huntsmen who were passing nigh heard and halted.

The tallest one among them hastened toward the high grass with long, cautious strides. He waded through the growth of green with just a head above it all. Suddenly exclaiming "Hunhe!" he dropped out of sight. In another instant he held up in both his hands a tiny little baby, wrapped in soft brown buckskins.

"Oh ho, a wood-child!" cried the men, for they were hunting along the wooded river bottom where this babe was found.

While the hunters were questioning whether or not they should carry it home, the wee Indian baby kept up his little howl.

"His voice is strong!" said one.

"At times it sounds like an old man's voice!" whispered a superstitious fellow, who feared some bad spirit hid in the small child to cheat them by and by.

"Let us take it to our wise chieftain," at length they said; and the moment they started toward the camp ground the strange wood-child ceased to cry.

Beside the chieftain's teepee waited the hunters while the tall man entered with the child.

"How! how!" nodded the kind-faced chieftain, listening to the queer story. Then rising, he took the infant in his strong arms; gently he laid the black-eyed babe in his daughter's lap. "This is to be your little son!" said he, smiling.

"Yes, father," she replied. Pleased with the child, she smoothed the long black hair fringing his round brown face.

"Tell the people that I give a feast and dance this day for the naming of my daughter's little son," bade the chieftain.

In the meanwhile among the men waiting by the entrance way, one said in a low voice: "I have heard that bad spirits come as little children into a camp which they mean to destroy."

"I have heard that bad spirits come as little children into a camp which they mean to destroy."

"No! no! Let us not be overcautious. It would be cowardly to leave a baby in the wild wood where prowl the hungry wolves!" answered an elderly man.

The tall man now came out of the chieftain's teepee. With a word he sent them to their dwellings half running with joy.

"A feast! a dance for the naming of the chieftain's grandchild!" cried he in a loud voice to the village people.

"What? what?" asked they in great surprise, holding a hand to the ear to catch the words of the crier.

There was a momentary silence among the people while they listened to the ringing voice of the man walking in the center ground. Then broke forth a rippling, laughing babble among the cone-shaped teepees. All were glad to hear of the chieftain's grandson. They were happy to attend the feast and dance for its naming. With excited fingers they twisted their hair into glossy braids and painted their cheeks with bright red paint. To and fro hurried the women, handsome in their gala-day dress. Men in loose deerskins, with long tinkling metal fringes, strode in small numbers toward the center of the round camp ground.

Here underneath a temporary shade-house of green leaves they were to dance and feast. The children in deerskins and paints, just like their elders, were jolly little men and women. Beside their eager parents they skipped along toward the green dance house.

Here seated in a large circle, the people were assembled, the proud chieftain rose with the little baby in his arms. The noisy hum of voices was hushed. Not a tinkling of a metal fringe broke the silence. The crier came forward to greet the chieftain, then bent attentively over the small babe, listening to the words of the chieftain. When he paused the crier spoke aloud to the people:

"This woodland child is adopted by the chieftain's eldest daughter. His name is Chaske. He wears the title of the eldest son. In honor of Chaske the chieftain gives this feast and dance! These are the words of him you see holding a baby in his arms."

"Yes! Yes! Hinnu! How!" came from the circle. At once the drummers beat softly and slowly their drum while the chosen singers hummed together to find the common pitch. The beat of the drum grew louder and faster. The singers burst forth in a lively tune. Then the drumbeats subsided and faintly marked the rhythm of the singing. Here and there bounced up men and women, both young and old. They danced and sang with merry light hearts. Then came the hour of feasting.

Late into the night the air of the camp ground was alive with the laughing voices of women and the singing in unison of young men. Within her father's teepee sat the chieftain's daughter. Proud of her little one, she watched over him asleep in her lap.

Gradually a deep quiet stole over the camp ground, as one by one the people fell into pleasant dreams. Now all the village was still. Alone sat the beautiful young mother watching the babe in her lap, asleep with a gaping little mouth. Amid the quiet of the night, her ear heard the far-off hum of many voices. The faint sound of murmuring people was in the air. Upward she glanced at the smoke hole of the wigwam and saw a bright star peeping down upon her. "Spirits in the air above?" she wondered. Yet there was no sign to tell her of their nearness. The fine small sound of voices grew larger and nearer.

"Father! rise! I hear the coming of some tribe. Hostile or friendly—I cannot tell. Rise and see!" whispered the young woman.

"Yes, my daughter!" answered the chieftain, springing to his feet.

Though asleep, his ear was ever alert. Thus rushing out into the open, he listened for strange sounds. With an eagle eye he scanned the camp ground for some sign.

Returning he said: "My daughter, I hear nothing and see no sign of evil nigh."

"Oh! the sound of many voices comes up from the earth about me!" exclaimed the young mother.

Bending low over her babe she gave ear to the ground. Horrified was she to find the mysterious sound came out of the open mouth of her sleeping child!

"Why so unlike other babes!" she cried within her heart as she slipped him gently from her lap to the ground. "Mother, listen and tell me if this child is an evil spirit come to destroy our camp!" she whispered loud.

Placing an ear close to the open baby mouth, the chieftain and his wife, each in turn heard the voices of a great camp. The singing of men and women, the beating of the drum, the rattling of deer-hoofs strung like bells on a string, these were the sounds they heard.

"We must go away," said the chieftain, leading them into the night. Out in the open he whispered to the frightened young woman: "Iya, the camp-eater, has come in the guise of a babe. Had you gone to sleep, he would have jumped out into his own shape and would have devoured our camp. He is a giant with spindling legs. He cannot fight, for he cannot run. He is powerful only in the night with his tricks. We are safe as soon as day breaks." Then moving closer to the woman, he whispered: "If he wakes now, he will swallow the whole tribe with one hideous gulp! Come, we must flee with our people."

Thus creeping from teepee to teepee a secret alarm signal was given. At midnight the teepees were gone and there was left no sign of the village save heaps of dead ashes. So quietly had the people folded their wigwams and bundled their tent poles that they slipped away unheard by the sleeping Iya babe.

When the morning sun arose, the babe awoke. Seeing himself deserted, he threw off his baby form in a hot rage.

Wearing his own ugly shape, his huge body toppled to and fro, from side to side, on a pair of thin legs far too small for their burden. Though with every move he came dangerously nigh to falling, he followed in the trail of the fleeing people.

"I shall eat you in the sight of a noon-day sun!" cried Iya in his vain rage, when he spied them encamped beyond a river.

By some unknown cunning he swam the river and sought his way toward the teepees.

"Hin! hin!" he grunted and growled. With perspiration beading his brow he strove to wiggle his slender legs beneath his giant form.

"Ha! ha!" laughed all the village people to see Iya made foolish with anger. "Such spindle legs cannot stand to fight by daylight!" shouted the brave ones who were terror-struck the night before by the name "Iya."

Warriors with long knives rushed forth and slew the camp-eater.

Lo! there rose out of the giant a whole Indian tribe: their camp ground, their teepees in a large circle, and the people laughing and dancing.

"We are glad to be free!" said these strange people.

Thus Iya was killed; and no more are the camp grounds in danger of being swallowed up in a single night time. ❖

How does the saying "Don't judge a book by its cover" relate to understanding new people and things? Why might it be easier to ignore the principles behind this saying?

Refer and Reason

1. Identify why the voice of warning in the story is ignored. What may the sudden shift from celebration to despair indicate about the tribe's experience?
2. Evaluate what you think the baby symbolizes. Is the representation convincing? Explain.
3. What are the similarities and differences between "Iya, the Camp-Eater" and the Trojan horse incident in *The Iliad?* (See page 711.) Specify what may be the reason for the difference in outcome.

Writing Options

1. Think of an incident, real or imaginary, that could be the basis of a legend, and narrate the legend as a one- to two-page tale. Your story can take place in a long-ago time and faraway place. In the characters and actions in your legend, try to express some of the values, customs, or other features of the society you are portraying.
2. Is "Iya, the Camp-Eater" a typical Native American legend? Do research, in the library or on the Internet, to learn what the tale has in common with other Native American legends. Write up your findings in a brief literary research paper.

Go to **www.mirrorsandwindows.com** for more.

The Mosquito

"I want to grant your wishes, but I fear that you will regret it later."

A Vietnamese Legend Retold by

George F. Schultz

Ngoc Tam, a modest farmer, had married Nhan Diep. The two young people were poor but in excellent health, and they seemed destined to enjoy the happiness of a simple rural life. The husband worked in the paddy and cultivated a small field of mulberry trees, and the wife engaged in raising silkworms.

But Nhan Diep was a coquette at heart. She was lazy, and dreamed of luxury and pleasures. She was also clever enough to hide her desires and ambitions from her husband, whose love was genuine, but neither demanding nor discerning. He supposed his wife to be content with her lot and happy in her daily chores.

The Vietnamese legend **"The Mosquito"** appears in the collection *Asian-Pacific Folktales and Legends*, edited by Jeannette L. Faurot. Grouped under the heading "How Things Came to Be," the brief tale narrates the origin of that pesky insect. As you are reading the story, consider what the tale says about such human feelings and behavior as loyalty, grief, foolishness, and betrayal, and about the conflict between a loving husband and his wife, who is motivated more by greed than by devotion.

If you discovered that placing your trust in someone was a mistake, how would you deal with the situation?

Ngoc Tam toiled diligently, hoping to ease their poverty and improve their station in life.

Suddenly Nhan Diep was carried away by death. Ngoc Tam was plunged into such deep sorrow that he would not leave his wife's body and opposed its burial.

One day, after having sold his possessions, he embarked in a sampan with the coffin and sailed away.

One morning he found himself at the foot of a fragrant, green hill which perfumed the countryside.

He went ashore and discovered a thousand rare flowers and orchards of trees laden with the most varied kinds of fruit.

There he met an old man who supported himself with a bamboo cane. His hair was white as cotton and his face wrinkled and sunburned, but under his blond eyelashes his eyes sparkled like those of a young boy. By this last trait, Ngoc Tam recognized the genie of medicine, who traveled throughout the world on his mountain, Thien Thai, to teach his science to the men of the earth and to alleviate their ills.

Ngoc Tam threw himself at the genie's feet.

Then the genie spoke to him: "Having learned of your virtues, Ngoc Tam, I have

stopped my mountain on your route. If you wish, I will admit you to the company of my disciples."

Ngoc Tam thanked him profusely but said that he desired only to live with his wife. He had never thought of any life other than the one he would lead with her, and he begged the genie to bring her back to life.

The genie looked at him with kindness mixed with pity and said, "Why do you cling to this world of bitterness and gall? The rare joys of this life are only a snare. How foolish you were to entrust your destiny to a weak and inconstant being! I want to grant your wishes, but I fear that you will regret it later."

Then, on the genie's order, Ngoc Tam opened the coffin; he cut the tip of his finger and let three drops of blood fall on Nhan Diep's body. The latter opened her eyes slowly, as if awakening from a deep sleep. Then her faculties quickly returned.

"Do not forget your obligations," the genie said to her. "Remember your husband's devotion. May you both be happy."

On the voyage home Ngoc Tam rowed day and night, eager to reach his native land again. One evening he went ashore in a certain port to buy provisions. During his absence a large ship came alongside the wharf, and the owner, a rich merchant, was struck by Nhan Diep's beauty. He entered into conversation with her and invited her to have refreshments aboard his vessel. As soon as she was aboard, he gave the order to cast off and sailed away.

Ngoc Tam searched an entire month for his wife before locating her aboard the merchant's vessel.

She answered his questions without the least hesitation, but had grown accustomed to her new life. It satisfied her completely and she refused to return home with him. Then for the first time, Ngoc Tam saw her in her true light. Suddenly he felt all love for her vanish, and he no longer desired her return.

"You are free," he said to her. "Only return to me the three drops of blood that I gave to bring you back to life. I do not want to leave the least trace of myself in you."

Happy to be set free so cheaply, Nhan Diep took a knife and cut the tip of her finger. But, as soon as the blood began to flow, she turned pale and sank to the ground. An instant later she was dead.

Even so, the lighthearted frivolous woman could not resign herself to leave this world forever. She returned in the form of a small insect and followed Ngoc Tam relentlessly, in order to steal the three drops of blood from him, which would restore her to human life. Day and night she worried her former husband, buzzing around him incessantly, protesting her innocence, and begging his pardon. Later, she received the name of *mosquito*. Unfortunately for us, her race has multiplied many times. ❖

What is the appeal of stories about humans and animals? In which ways do such tales help humans gain self-knowledge?

Refer and Reason

1. The genie fears that if he brings Nhan Diep back to life, her husband will later regret his doing so. Relate whether the genie's prediction turns out to be correct. Explain.
2. Justify why the story is an appropriate (if unscientific) explanation of the origin of the mosquito.
3. Explain in which ways the legend is more than a "how it came to be" tale.

Writing Options

1. Think of a species of animal whose traits remind you of the behavior, good or bad, of humans. Then write a brief narrative explaining the origins of this species. In your story, try to suggest how the explanation applies to human nature.
2. Choose a legend from a culture other than your own (for example, Asian, African, Inuit, Native American, or Caribbean). Write a brief compare-and-contrast essay, to point out the similarities and differences between that legend and "The Mosquito."

Go to **www.mirrorsandwindows.com** for more.

The *Princess* and the *Tin Box*

A Fable by **James Thurber**

Even before the amusing twist at the end of **"The Princess and the Tin Box,"** you will probably realize that this story of a wealthy princess seeking a husband is not an ordinary fable. Although the tale ends with a moral, or lesson about life, the story is not your everyday fable. No wonder, because it was written by **James Thurber** (1894–1961), one of the twentieth-century's greatest humorists. As a child, Thurber lost his sight in one eye while playing with his brothers. The disability didn't stop him from attending public schools and, later, Ohio State University. Although celebrated for his witty cartoons as well as for his written works, Thurber was modest about his gift for illustration. "I'm a painstaking writer who doodles for relaxation," he observed. As you are reading the story, consider whom the target of Thurber's good-natured humor is.

If you were to write an amusing tale, at whom might you choose to poke gentle fun?

Young Princess, 1930. Guirand de Scevola, Lucien.

"Now," the king said to his daughter, "you must select the gift you like best and marry the prince that brought it."

Once upon a time, in a far country, there lived a king whose daughter was the prettiest princess in the world. Her eyes were like the cornflower, her hair was sweeter than the hyacinth, and her throat made the swan look dusty.

From the time she was a year old, the princess had been showered with presents. Her nursery looked like Cartier's window.[1] Her toys were all made of gold or platinum or diamonds

1. **Cartier's window.** Refers to the display window of the well-known French jeweler and watchmaker

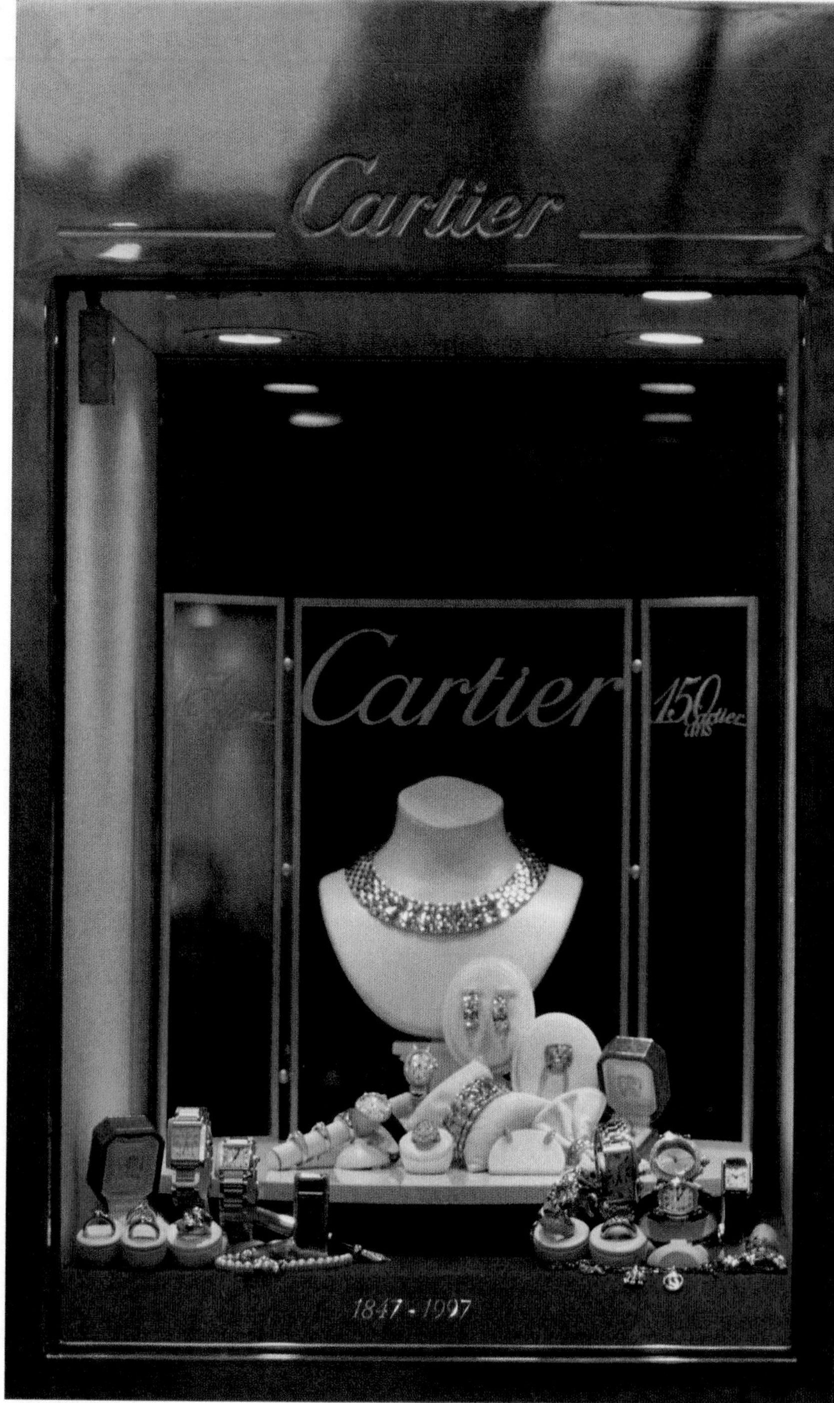

or emeralds. She was not permitted to have wooden blocks or china dolls or rubber dogs or linen books, because such materials were considered cheap for the daughter of a king.

When she was seven, she was allowed to attend the wedding of her brother and throw real pearls at the bride instead of rice. Only the nightingale, with his lyre of gold, was permitted to sing for the princess. The common blackbird, with his boxwood flute, was kept out of the palace grounds. She walked in silver-and-samite slippers to a sapphire-and-topaz bathroom and slept in an ivory bed inlaid with rubies.

On the day the princess was eighteen, the king sent a royal ambassador to the courts of five neighboring kingdoms to announce that he would give his daughter's hand in marriage to the prince who brought her the gift she liked the most.

The first prince to arrive at the palace rode a swift white stallion and laid at the feet of the princess an enormous apple made of solid gold which he had taken from a dragon who had guarded it for a thousand years. It was placed on a long ebony table set up to hold the gifts of the princess's suitors. The second prince, who came on a gray charger, brought her a nightingale made of a thousand diamonds, and it was placed beside the golden apple. The third prince, riding on a black horse, carried a great jewel box made of platinum and sapphires, and it was placed next to the diamond nightingale. The fourth prince, astride a fiery yellow horse, gave the princess a gigantic heart made of rubies and pierced by an emerald arrow. It was placed next to the platinum-and-sapphire jewel box.

Now the fifth prince was the strongest and handsomest of all the five suitors, but he was the son of a poor king whose realm had been overrun by mice and locusts and wizards and mining engineers so that there was nothing much of value left in it. He came plodding up to the palace of the princess on a plow horse and he brought her a small tin box filled with mica and feldspar and hornblende[2] which he had picked up on the way.

The other princes roared with disdainful laughter when they saw the tawdry gift the fifth prince had brought to the princess. But she examined it with great interest and squealed with delight, for all her life she had been glutted with precious stones and priceless metals, but she had never seen tin before or mica or feldspar or hornblende. The tin box was placed next to the ruby heart pierced with an emerald arrow.

"Now," the king said to his daughter, "you must select the gift you like best and marry the prince that brought it."

The princess smiled and walked up to the table and picked up the present she liked the most. It was the platinum-and-sapphire jewel box, the gift of the third prince.

"The way I figure it," she said, "is this. It is a very large and expensive box, and when I am married, I will meet many admirers who will give me precious gems with which to fill it to the top. Therefore, it is the most valuable of all the gifts my suitors have brought me and I like it the best."

The princess married the third prince that very day in the midst of great merriment and high revelry. More than a hundred thousand pearls were thrown at her and she loved it.

Moral: All those who thought the princess was going to select the tin box filled with worthless stones instead of one of the other gifts will kindly stay after class and write one hundred times on the blackboard "I would rather have a hunk of aluminum silicate than a diamond necklace. ❖

2. **mica and feldspar and hornblende.** Common, rock-forming minerals

What does society appear to value most when looking for a significant other? What characteristics would you value?

Refer and Reason

1. Outline the descriptions of each prince, including details of his arrival and his gift for the princess. How are they different from the poor young man?
2. Evaluate whether or not you think the author does an effective job of setting up the reader to be surprised. Explain.
3. **Sarcasm** is sharp and satirical or ironic language designed to cut or give pain to another. Explain why the moral at the end of the fable is an example of sarcasm.

Writing Options

1. Imagine that the princess's cherished pet has run away, and the man who finds and returns the animal alive shall marry the princess. Write a lost-and-found advertisement describing the princess's predicament and reward.
2. Just what is it about "The Princess and the Tin Box" that makes the tale so amusing? Is it the over-the-top description of the wealthy princess, or the allusion to a fancy store on Fifth Avenue in New York City? Write a two-paragraph literary analysis of the techniques Thurber uses in making the reader laugh.

Go to **www.mirrorsandwindows.com** for more.

The Appointment in Samarra

A Fable by

W. Somerset Maugham

"The Appointment in Samarra" is a retelling of an ancient fable—a short story that teaches a moral or a lesson about life. The author, **William Somerset Maugham** (1874–1965), included the fable in his comic play *Sheppey,* about a man who wins the Irish Sweepstakes and decides to give all the prize money to the poor, much to his family's dismay. When Death comes to visit the man, he recounts this tale.

In addition to writing, Maugham served as an ambulance driver in 1914 and was an intelligence officer in World Wars I and II. He also worked as a secret agent in Switzerland and Russia. His adventures and his extensive world travels are reflected in his writing. Maugham said of himself: "I have never pretended to be anything but a story teller." As you are reading the selection, consider what its moral is.

Have you ever gone out of your way to avoid someone? What was the result?

Death speaks:

There was a merchant in Bagdad who sent his servant to market to buy provisions and in a little while the servant came back, white and trembling, and said, Master, just now when I was in the market-place I was jostled by a woman in the crowd and when I turned I saw it was Death that jostled me. She looked at me and made a threatening gesture, now, lend me your horse, and I will ride away from this city and avoid my fate. I will go to Samarra and there death will not find me. The merchant lent him his horse, and the servant mounted it, and he dug his spurs in its flanks and as fast as the horse could gallop he went. Then the merchant went down to the market-place and he saw me standing in the crowd and he came to me and said, Why did you make a threatening gesture to my servant when you saw him this morning? That was not a threatening gesture, I said, it was only a start of surprise. I was astonished to see him in Bagdad, for I had an appointment with him to-night in Samarra. ❖

Is it possible to alter destiny? Do most people believe in fate or that they have the ability to alter their own destiny?

Informational Text CONNECTION

The city of Samarra, where Death will meet the merchant's servant, is located in Iraq and was founded by the Abbasid caliphs, a family of Muslim leaders descended from an uncle of the Prophet Muhammad. **"History of Samarra"** provides additional information about this ancient city. As you read the article, consider what light the material sheds on a region that has been much in the news since the early 1990s but that many people in the United States know little about.

History of Samarra

An Informational Article from

Encyclopedia of the Orient

City in central Iraq with about 200,000 inhabitants (2002 estimate). Samarra lies on the east bank of the Tigris River.

Samarra is a trade center of its region. There is some industry and small crafts, as well as local administration.

While Samarra today is a modest regional center, it was the capital of the Muslim world for 56 years in the 9th century, when the Abbasid caliphate was moved here from Baghdad. At the most, the royal palaces and gardens stretched out for a distance of 30 km along the river.

The most prominent remains of this past is the famous Great Friday Mosque from 852 with the unique spiral minaret. This mosque itself is predominantly in ruins, with only the outer walls standing. The plan of the mosque is 240 x 160 meters, i.e. more than 38,000 m^2. The walls are about 10 meters high, 2.65 meters thick and supported by 44 towers. An ambitious restoration process began in the late 1990s, aiming at rebuilding the columns and eventually the roof.

The spiral minaret, "Malwiya" in Arabic, is a separate structure from the main congregation hall, 27 meters north of the main hall. It is 52 meters high, and 33 meters in diameter. It is easily entered by a staircase spiralling up on the outside of the round walls. At the summit, the staircase penetrates the structure for the first time, giving access to a flat platform on the top, about 3.5 meters wide. It is believed by many that the minaret was built about 15 years before the main structure.

About 22 km south of Samarra lies a replica of the Great Friday Mosque, the Abu Duluf Mosque. The main hall is almost as big, 215 x

138 meters, but the minaret spiral, once again, is only 19 meters high.

Samarra holds the remains of the Caliph's residence. It used to be 700 meters long, along the Tigris river, but today only 3 huge gates towards the river stand. According to the stories, the Caliph sat in these gates to hear complaints and suggestions from his subjects.

Samarra holds the tomb of two imams, the 10th, Ali al-Hadi and the 11th, Hassan al-Askari. They are placed in the same sanctuary, a structure that closely resembles the ones of Karbala and Najaf. In addition to the two imams, there [are] two other tombs of prominent female Muslims.

The second shrine of Samarra is meant to indicate where the 12th imam went into concealment. The shrine is quite different from the other Shi'i shrines of Iraq, as it doesn't have a golden dome, but one covered with blue tiles. Underneath the dome there is a cellar, said to be the last place the 12th imam dwelled.

HISTORY

836: Caliph al-Mu'tasim buys the land of a Christian monastery, and builds a military camp here. He gives it the name "surra man ra'a" (English: "he who sees it, rejoices"), a pun based upon the nearby town of Samarra. It is turned into the new residence of the Caliph, after he is pressured to move from Baghdad. This made it the capital of the entire Muslim world, which by now extended from Spain in the west to India in the east.

852: The Great Friday Mosque is inaugurated, being the largest mosque of its time.

892: The Caliph moves back to Baghdad, and Samarra loses most of its importance.

1905: The golden dome of the sanctuary of the two imams is completed.

2006 February 22: The shrine and mosque of the two imams, Ali al-Hadi and Hassan al-Askari, is destroyed in a bomb explosion. Immediate reactions suggest that militant Sunni groups are behind. ❖

Refer and Reason

1. According to the article, where was the Abbasid caliphate originally located? Where was it moved to? Analyze how this information adds to your appreciation of Maugham's fable.
2. Determine what role the merchant plays in the story. How would the tale be different if this character were not in the tale?
3. Explain the effect of having this first-person story narrated by Death.

Writing Options

1. Write your own fable that expresses your view of fate or destiny. You may want to read other fables to get a sense of their tone, characters, and structure.
2. Think about how the servant and the merchant react to Death. How might their approaches to Death affect their approaches to life? How might their lives affect their reaction to Death? Write a thesis for a compare-and-contrast essay about the servant and the merchant.

Go to **www.mirrorsandwindows.com** for more.

TEXT ←TO→ TEXT CONNECTION

Compare and contrast the role of Samarra in the text from the *Encyclopedia of the Orient* and in the passage from Maugham's fable. How might the fable differ if it included some of the details from the encyclopedia? Which details from the fable might be appropriate to include in the nonfiction material?

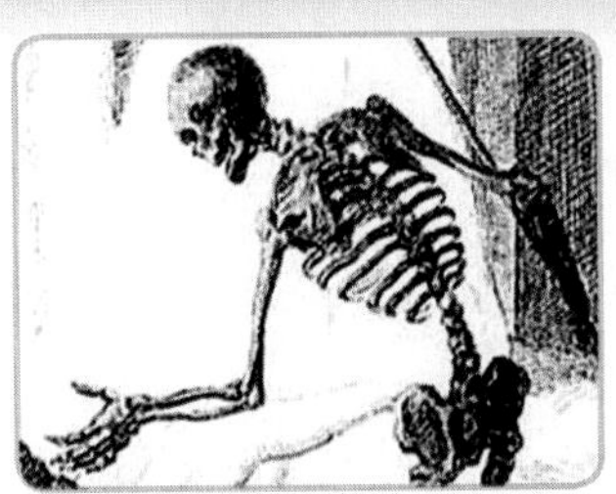

FOR YOUR READING LIST

THE CHILDREN OF ODIN: THE BOOK OF NORTHERN MYTHS

by Padraic Colum

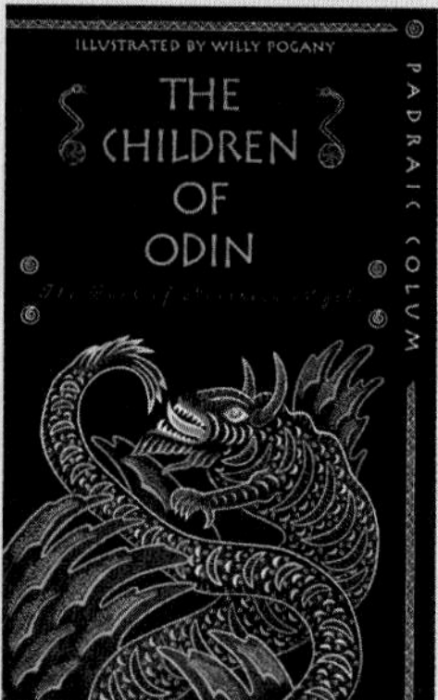

Before the beginning of time, the Norse gods and goddesses lived in Asgard. They were Odin, the father god; Thor, the defender of Asgard; mischievous Loki; and lovely Freya. In poet Padraic Colum's retelling of the old Norse sagas, the stories of their exploits flow smoothly from one to the next.

FOLKLORE, MYTHS, AND LEGENDS: A WORLD PERSPECTIVE

by Donna Rosenberg

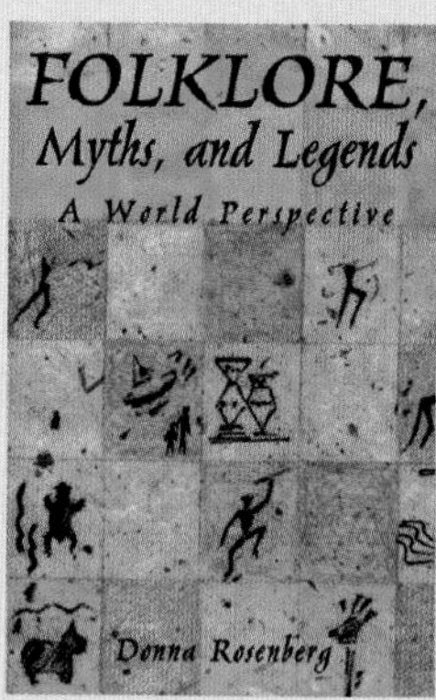

This collection retells thirty tales from all over the world. Selections range from the familiar Doctor Faust legend to a trickster tale from the Ashanti people of Ghana to a Japanese Ainu water goddess myth. Each contains historical and cultural background material and is followed by questions for understanding.

OEDIPUS REX

by Sophocles

Thebes is in trouble: Its crops have failed, and its citizens are dying of the plague. When King Oedipus seeks advice from the god Apollo, he learns the city's woes are related to the unsolved murder of the previous king. A man of action, Oedipus sets out to find the murderer—with horrific consequences.

MYTHOLOGY

by Edith Hamilton

The gods of ancient peoples were often fearsome, monstrous creations. The Greeks were the first to transform this worldview. Endowing their gods with human qualities, they used stories to explain the natural world. In simple prose, classics scholar Hamilton relates the earliest creation stories and heroic adventure tales.

THE ODYSSEY

by Homer

After the Trojan War has been won, Odysseus attempts to return to his home in Ithaca. The gods, however, had other plans. The complete story of Odysseus's perilous journey also includes the story of Penelope and Telemachus, who must defend and maintain authority over Ithaca.

THE ILIAD

by Homer

Before Odysseus began his ten-year voyage, he fought in the Trojan War. *The Iliad* begins in the middle of a battle during that war. The battle wages not just between the Trojans and the Greeks, but also their heroes and gods. With the gods protecting and attacking different sides of the fight, who will prevail?

Gathering Information from an Interview

In this lesson, you will conduct and gather information from an **interview.** In an interview, you meet with someone and ask him or her questions. Interviewing experts or individuals with unique experiences is an excellent way to gain information about a particular topic. Prior to meeting with your subject, do some background research on the topic and think carefully about the questions you would like to ask.

1. Contact the person you want to interview in advance.

Set aside a time to meet in a quiet place. Explain the purpose of the interview—this will give the person an idea of questions you may ask and allow him or her to answer them effectively.

2. Ask mostly open-ended questions.

These require more than a simple "yes" or "no" answer. They allow the person to elaborate and express personal views. Be sure to write your questions out in advance.

3. Take notes during the interview.

Write down the main points the person makes. Write his or her most important statements word for word. You may also want to tape-record the interview, if the person allows it.

4. Clarify spelling and get permission for quotations.

Be sure to get the correct spelling of the person's name and to ask permission to quote his or her statements.

5. End the interview on time and thank the person.

The person was courteous enough to give you his or her time. Be certain that you return this courtesy by being punctual and by limiting your interview to an allotted time. Before leaving, show your appreciation by thanking the person for his or her help. Send a thank-you note afterward.

6. Write up the results of the interview soon after you conduct it.

Over time, what seemed like a very clear note may become unclear or confusing. Contact the person if you need any clarification. Give the person a finished copy of the interview publication.

Speaking and Listening Tips

- Watch **tone.** It is important to come across as friendly, courteous, and interested.
- Try to use **clear, simple wording** when explaining the purpose of your interview and when asking questions.
- Be sure to **listen actively.** Show through **eye contact, gestures** (such as nodding), and **facial expressions** that you are listening.

Speaking and Listening Rubric

Preparation

- ☑ set up time to meet with person
- ☑ explained purpose of interview
- ☑ wrote out clearly-worded questions (mostly open-ended)

Interview

- ☑ maintained friendly, courteous tone
- ☑ took notes throughout
- ☑ confirmed spelling and got permission for quotations
- ☑ listened actively, shown through eye contact, gestures, and facial expressions

Post-interview

- ☑ thanked person
- ☑ wrote out results of interview soon after conducting

Assignment
Record and document an oral history
Purpose
To illustrate a family history or a human experience through a specific oral history
Audience
Your classmates and teacher, your family and friends

Oral History

As a child, most likely you listened to someone tell you spellbinding tales of heroes and heroines. Ella Young, author of "The Silver Pool," went to Ireland to sit by turf fires and listen, as she says, to poems "recited by folk who had heard the faery music and danced in faery circles." Folk tales, fables, and legends have profound reverberations; they allow us to deeply investigate life's mysteries. They tell stories of decision and consequence that are both personal and universal, both literal and symbolic. In *The Odyssey,* readers relate to the lessons Odysseus learns on his journey, even though such things could never happen to them.

You also have heard the spellbinding stories your parents and grandparents tell about their parents and grandparents. These **oral histories** explain who you are and where you come from. They may be the foundation of an entire lineage. Besides their personal relevance, these episodes from people's lives are history—family and cultural history. Capturing oral histories preserves them for generations to come.

ASSIGNMENT

Interview an older relative or a wise family friend, and document a story of special meaning. Prewrite, draft, and revise the oral history.

❶ PREWRITE

Select Your Topic

You may wish to conduct pre-interviews with several people. Choose one person to interview, and then settle on one story—about an event, a memory, or an important heirloom or object—that has great meaning or interest.

Writing Rubric

A successful oral history:

- **introduces** the subject being interviewed
- includes a **thesis** that states the focus of the story he or she will tell
- records the person's narrative in chronological order in the **body,** using direct quotations, paraphrasing, and summary
- finishes with a **conclusion** that provides closure to the story and that reflects on the significance of the story, both to the subject and to the writer

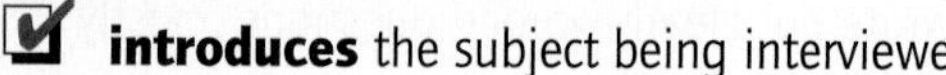

Gather Information

Your task in this phase is to listen to the story. Be respectful of your subject; take careful notes. If you can, record the story, with your subject's permission, so you can work with it later. Though you may wish to have a list of questions handy as a guide, be open to the story your subject wants to tell.

Writing your notes in an oral history chart, like the one on page 815, will help you stay alert to the important relevance of this oral history.

Organize Your Ideas

Your subject will most likely tell the story **chronologically,** in the order things happened. You can organize your writing the same way. Ask yourself, what information is extraneous or irrelevant? What details are most important? As you work with your subject's narrative, you may gain insight into its significance. Did you observe something he or she did not recognize or respond to?

Oral History Chart

Interview with: my grandfather, Dennis Neil Johnson

Date: September 28

Time: 2 PM

Place: Grandpa's home at 186 S. Oak St. See if we can meet in his study, where he keeps all those old photos and souvenirs

Permission to take notes, tape-record, and print: Yes

My goal for the interview: learn about his cross-country trip in the family Buick

The event, memory, or object: cross-country trip in 1949 with his parents and five siblings

Questions for the interview:

Who?	What?	Where?	When?	Why?	How?
1. Who went on the trip? 2. Whom did you meet or see on the trip?	1. What did you do on the trip? 2. What did your parents and siblings do?	1. Where did you start? 2. Where did the trip end?	1. When, or what time of year, did you go on the trip? 2. When during the day did you travel?	1. Why did you go on the trip? 2. Why especially do you remember the trip?	1. How did the trip affect you at the time? 2. How did the trip change the way you saw things?

Mementos: (newspaper clippings, photographs, scrapbooks, clothing, jewelry)

Direct quotations:

Main ideas, key words, and observations:

Gestures and expressions worth noting:

Review the notes you took while listening to your subject. Highlight the most striking and interesting aspects. Delete details that sidetrack or veer from the story's focus. You can always conduct a follow-up interview to get more information.

Write Your Thesis Statement

After listening to the oral history, write a single sentence summarizing the main point. This is your **thesis statement.** One student, Neil Hebbert, wrote this thesis statement about the conversation he recorded:

> One summer, in 1949, when my grandpa was 15, he left the farm behind and went on a family adventure to see the West.

❷ DRAFT

Write your oral history by following the three-part framework described at left: **introduction, body,** and **conclusion.**

Draft Your Introduction

In an oral history, the **introduction** should introduce your subject to the reader. Describe the person whose oral history you are capturing. The introduction should also include a thesis statement, one sentence specifying the focus of the story and the time period.

- **Introduction**
  Identify your subject and the story he or she told. Include a thesis statement summarizing the focus of the story.
- **Body**
  Accurately tell the person's story, using direct quotations, paraphrasing, and summary.
- **Conclusion**
  Finish the story and reflect on the significance of the oral history.

The introduction that Neil wrote during the Draft stage is shown in the first column of the chart on page 817. In his first few sentences, Neil introduced his grandfather and provided general background information. The last sentence, his thesis, tells what story the essay will focus on. Neil doesn't stress its significance, however. What could he do to increase the relevance of his oral history in his thesis statement?

Draft Your Body

The **body** of your oral history tells the story surrounding your thesis and will most likely unfold chronologically. Determine how best to divide the information into coherent paragraphs. Present the information using a combination of direct quotations, paraphrasing, and summary. Tell your subject's story in your writer's voice. Decide when to quote and when to paraphrase.

Neil began the body of his oral history with the start of his grandfather's trip West. Neil described the rest of the trip in three more body paragraphs. Look at the draft of his first body paragraph in the left-hand column of the chart on page 817. He stayed true to his grandfather's story by paraphrasing information and using direct quotations.

Review the highlighted information on your Oral History Chart. Drawing from your notes and the recorded interview, tell your subject's story in an effective, interesting, and logical way. Include the most relevant pieces of information.

What Great Writers Do

Bruno Bettelheim (1903–1990), an American developmental psychologist, wrote a ground-breaking book called *The Uses of Enchantment: The Meaning and Importance of Fairy Tales*. He was a great believer in the power of story to transform people. His book's opening line is this: "If we hope to live not just from moment to moment, but in true consciousness to our existence, then our greatest need and most difficult achievement is to find meaning in our lives."

Draft Your Conclusion

To finish your oral history, write your **conclusion.** Summarize or finish the story itself. You might choose to briefly touch on the years following the story, even up to present time. Referring back to your thesis statement, emphasize the story's focus and reflect on its significance. State how the story is meaningful to both you and your subject. Finally, end with a sentence that provides a satisfying closure for the reader.

Does Neil successfully accomplish these things in his conclusion? Look at the draft of his conclusion in the chart on page 817.

❸ REVISE

Evaluate Your Draft

Evaluate your own writing or exchange papers with a classmate and evaluate each other's work. In either case, think carefully about what's done well and what can be improved. Use the Revision Checklist on page 818 to make this evaluation. Make notes directly on the essay about what changes need to be made.

Think of ways to make the writing clear and interesting. One way, in an oral history, is to establish a warm, familiar tone with your own voice. Relate the oral history using the devices of good storytelling.

DRAFT STAGE		REVISE STAGE	
Introduction My grandfather, Dennis Neil Johnson, grew up on a farm in South Dakota, in 1935. He jokes that cows and horses earned him a Ph.D. in Earth Science working on the farm was his life. One summer my grandpa went out west with his family.	Identifies and introduces subject Provides background information States thesis, what the oral history is about	My grandfather, Dennis Neil Johnson, grew up on a farm in South Dakota, in 1935. A simple farm boy, he never considered leaving, even for college. He jokes that cows and horses earned him a Ph.D. in Earth Science. Working on the farm was his life. One summer ~~my grandpa went out west with his family~~, however, in 1949, when my grandpa was 15, he left the farm behind and went on a family adventure to see the West.	Adds details to provide a picture of his subject Corrects fused sentences Gives thesis a stronger sense of the story's relevance.
Body Paragraph They camped the first night just outside Presho, South Dakota. "We pulled the car over and threw our sleeping bags on the ground," Grandpa said. "Driving to Wyoming up on some highway…The back roads without any rails. When I saw those mountains emerge, I was speechless," Grandpa said. "I learned why they're called majestic."	Continues the narrative in chronological order Uses direct quotations	They camped the first night just outside Presho, South Dakota, a small town 213 miles west of Sioux Falls. "We pulled the car over and threw our sleeping bags on the ground," Grandpa said. ~~"Driving to Wyoming up on some highway … The back roads without any rails.~~ The next day, they traveled to Wyoming. "When I saw those mountains emerge, I was speechless," Grandpa said. He smiled as if he could see them in his mind. "I learned why they're called majestic."	Adds information readers might not know Deletes irrelevant details; paraphrases Adds writer's observation
Conclusion The family got home at the end of August. "I never imagined this old place would look so good to me," he said. Grandpa finished high school. He got married. He raised children. He inherited the farm when Great-Grandpa died. I asked him if he regrets his life as a farmer. "Not for a minute," he said, squeezing my knee.	Concludes the story Touches on what happened after the story Reflects on the story's relevance Provides closure	The family ~~got~~, including my grandfather, returned home at the end of August. "I never imagined this old place would look so good to me," he said. "I was glad to go, gladder to get back." Grandpa finished high school, got married, and raised children. He inherited the farm when Great-Grandpa died. Sixty years later, he still talks about his trip west. I asked him if he regrets his life as a farmer. "Not for a minute," he said, squeezing my knee.	Develops sentence Inserts interesting quotation Combines sentences to vary length Emphasizes the significance to both the writer and the subject

Revise for Content, Organization, and Style

Neil evaluated his draft and found some ways to improve his writing. Look at the chart on page 817 (this time, the right-hand column) to see how he revised the three paragraphs we looked at earlier:

- **Introduction:** Neil added details to characterize his grandfather and to provide context for the relevance of the story. He also improved his writing style and clarified his thesis statement.
- **Body:** Neil added important details and deleted an irrelevant detail from his subject's narrative. He paraphrased when the direct quotation didn't seem that special and included an observation he made while listening to his subject tell the story.
- **Conclusion:** Neil developed sentences with better word choices. He inserted a quotation that showed his grandfather's character and combined choppy sentences to vary the sentence length. Lastly, Neil emphasized the significance of this oral history.

Review the notes you or your partner made as you evaluated your draft. Then respond to each comment and effectively revise your essay.

Proofread for Errors

The purpose of proofreading is to check for remaining errors. Use proofreader's symbols to mark any errors you find. (See the Language Arts Handbook 4.1 for a list of proofreader's symbols.) To complete the assignment, print a final draft and read it through once more before turning it in.

WRITING FOLLOW-UP

Publish and Present

- Oral histories are meant to be shared. Your class may wish to compile these histories in a booklet, or to post them online for others to read.
- Replay a section of the original recording for your classmates. Discuss the differences between listening to a story and reading it.

REFLECT

- What did you learn about the importance of oral history? How might you continue to capture important personal oral histories?
- How is listening to or reading your classmates' oral histories valuable? How do stories that don't seem to directly apply to you have a universal appeal?

REVISION CHECKLIST

Content and Organization

- ❑ Do you identify your subject in the **introduction?** Do you include enough background to provide context and generate interest for your readers?
- ❑ Does the **thesis statement** in the **introduction** communicate the focus of the oral history?
- ❑ Are the **body** paragraphs coherent? Are they organized chronologically? Do paragraph transitions provide a seamless flow?
- ❑ In the **body,** do you effectively quote, paraphrase, or summarize the information?
- ❑ Does the **conclusion** complete the narrative, touch on years beyond the specific story, reflect on the significance of the oral history, and provide closure for the reader?

Grammar & Style

- ❑ Do you use the correct subordinating and coordinating conjunctions within your sentences? (page 676)
- ❑ Are colons and semicolons properly placed within your draft? (page 686)
- ❑ Do you use hyphens, ellipses, and italics correctly? (page 696)

STUDENT MODEL

One Man's Journey
by Neil Hebbert

My grandfather, Dennis Neil Johnson, grew up on a farm in South Dakota, in 1935. A simple farm boy, he never considered leaving, even for college. He jokes that cows and horses earned him a Ph.D. in Earth Science. Working on the farm was his life. One summer, however, in 1949, when he was 15, Grandpa left the farm behind and went on a family adventure to see the West.

Who is the writer's subject and what is their relationship? What is the writer's thesis statement?

Great-Grandpa had broken his ankle. Great-Grandma Ovida decided they needed a vacation. Leaving the farm in the care of good farmhands, they packed their six children into the Buick. "Pa couldn't drive with his bad ankle. He plunked me behind the wheel and that was it," Grandpa said, laughing. "I drove the whole way. It was an adventure from the moment we left the farm."

How does the story begin? What methods does the writer use to convey it?

They camped the first night just outside Presho, South Dakota, a small town 213 miles west of Sioux Falls. "We just pulled the car over and put our sleeping bags on the ground," Grandpa said. The next day, they traveled to Wyoming. "When I saw those mountains emerge, I was speechless," Grandpa said. He smiled as if he could see them in his mind. "I learned why they're called majestic."

Why are the details relevant?

They stopped in Yellowstone National Park. "Your great-grandmother was afraid one of us kids would fall into a geyser," Grandpa remembered. At that time, he explained, geysers were not fenced off. Later, a bear stuck its head into an open window of the Buick. My great-grandpa threw food out another window and shouted, "Step on it!" when the bear moved away. Grandpa said he never drove so fast in his life. They drove to Idaho, Oregon, and Washington.

How effectively does the writer use direct quotations, paraphrasing, and summary?

They drove through sequoia forests and past waterfalls until they reached the ocean. "We stayed two days. Never in my life had I seen such a thing," Grandpa said. "It opened my soul. I swam in the waves, walked on the sand, and stared at the water. My mother had to drag me away." Grandpa paused. "I sincerely thought about staying. If I hadn't been needed to drive, I'd have let the family go home without me." He looked at me. "Mighta turned out different for you if I had."

How is this story relevant universally and culturally?

The family returned home at the end of August. "I never imagined this old place would look so good to me," he said. "I was glad to go, gladder to get back." Grandpa finished high school, got married, and raised children. He later inherited the farm. Sixty years later, he still talks about his trip West. I asked him if he regrets his life as a farmer. "Not for a minute," he said, squeezing my knee.

How does the writer reflect on the story's significance?

Reading Skills

IDENTIFYING THE MAIN IDEA

The **main idea** is a brief statement of what you think the author wants you to know, think, or feel after reading the text. In a literary work, this main idea is called the *theme.*

In some cases, the main idea will actually be stated directly. The first and last paragraphs are the most common locations for a sentence that sums up the entire passage, but it can come anywhere in the text.

Usually, however, the author will not tell you directly what the main idea is; thus, you will have to infer it. To infer the main idea, ask yourself the following questions:

- Who or what is this text about?
- What does the author want me to know, think, feel, or do about this "who" or "what"?
- If I had to tell someone in one sentence what this text is about, what would I say?

For an example of identifying the main idea, read the following poem, "The Funeral," by Gordon Parks.

After many snows I was home again.
Time had whittled down to mere hills
The great mountains of my childhood.
Raging rivers I once swam trickled now
like gentle streams.
And the wide road curving on to China or
Kansas City or perhaps Calcutta,
had withered to a crooked path of dust
Ending abruptly at the county burying ground.
Only the giant who was my father
remained the same.
A hundred strong men strained beneath his coffin
When they bore him to his grave.

Test-Taking Tip
A good way to find the main idea of a text is to gather important details. It can be helpful to list them. Then see what these details have in common or seem to say as a whole.

Here, the supporting details include the following:

- The speaker has been gone a long time.
- The mountains now appeared to be mere hills.
- Raging rivers now were like gentle streams.
- The wide road that once seemed to lead anywhere you wanted to go was just a path to the cemetery.
- The speaker's father alone remained the same—a giant.
- The father is dead.

The main idea is that everything (the hills, the rivers, the road) seems smaller except the speaker's father, who is dead.

PRACTICE

Directions: Read the following North African folk tale, as retold by Mahmoud Ibrahim Mostafa, and answer the questions that follow. These questions deal with identifying the main idea.

Goha and the Pot

One day, many, many years ago, Goha wanted to fix a meal for his family. He found that he needed a big pot, so he went to his next door neighbor to ask if he might borrow a big brass pot. The neighbor was reluctant to lend him the pot, but Goha promised that he would return it to his neighbor the following day.

To the surprise of his neighbor, Goha returned the next day with the big brass pot that he had borrowed and another one, smaller than the first. The neighbor felt that Goha must have made a mistake since he had lent Goha one pot, but Goha said that there was no mistake at all. He explained that overnight the pot he had borrowed went into labor and gave birth to this nice, shiny, little pot, and Goha insisted that the small pot also belonged to his neighbor!

A few days later, Goha returned to the same neighbor and asked if he could borrow another pot. This time the neighbor did not have any trouble giving him two big pots, thinking that Goha would return with more pots anyway. And indeed, when Goha returned the two big pots, he also brought two smaller, shining pots, much to the delight of his neighbor.

The next time Goha knocked on his neighbor's door, before he could even say a word, the neighbor gave him a basket full of big pots. In fact he gave Goha all the pots he had in his possession. His neighbor did not stop there, however, he even helped to carry the pots to Goha's house.

Days passed, then weeks, and the neighbor began to worry, but he did not mention his concern to Goha, hoping that Goha would come by some day soon with a whole room full of pots. After three whole months had gone by, the neighbor decided to go to Goha to inquire about his pots. Upon his inquiry, Goha with a very sad face said to his neighbor, "My dear neighbor, I'm saddened to tell you that your pots are all dead!"

The neighbor was furious, and he shouted, "Are you a madman? Pots don't die!"

Then Goha quietly said, "My dear neighbor, you were very willing to accept the fact that pots can have babies, weren't you? Why for goodness' sake don't you accept that they can also die?"

Multiple Choice

1. What is the main idea of the first four paragraphs?
   A. Goha often needs pots for cooking.
   B. The pots give birth to babies at Goha's house.
   C. It is important to have good neighbors.
   D. The neighbor is greedy although he appears generous.

2. Which paragraph provides the most clues to the main idea of the entire passage?
   F. the second paragraph
   G. the fourth paragraph
   H. the fifth paragraph
   J. the seventh paragraph

3. Which of the following details in paragraph 1 is most important to the main idea?
   A. Goha needed a big pot.
   B. Goha didn't have the kind of pot he needed.
   C. Goha's neighbor is reluctant to lend him a pot.
   D. This story happened a long time ago.

4. The neighbor went wrong in
   F. lending Goha a pot in the first place.
   G. lending Goha two pots the second time.
   H. inquiring about the unreturned pots.
   J. accepting the extra pots, and thereby, seeming to accept the explanation.

Constructed Response

5. What is this passage's moral, or the lesson that it teaches?

Writing Skills

NARRATIVE WRITING

Many standardized tests include sections that ask you to demonstrate your writing ability by composing an essay in response to a prompt, or topic. Some writing prompts ask you to tell a story or narrate a series of events to make a point. This type of writing is called **narrative writing.** Short stories, biographies, legends, historical accounts, and myths are forms of narrative writing.

Test-Taking Tip
It is important to use your time wisely if you have only an allotted number of minutes in which to write an essay. Practice writing an essay in 25 or 30 minutes.

When you respond to a narrative prompt, keep the following tips in mind:

- Narrow the topic to one specific series of events about which you want to make a point.
- Don't just tell what happened, but explain the lesson learned.
- Include an introduction (in which you identify your narrowed topic), a body (in which you tell about the event or series of events), and a conclusion (in which you summarize what happened and tell about what was learned).

As you write, make sure that you
- include a thesis statement
- write clearly
- keep your purpose in mind and stay focused on it
- organize the information and provide transitions to help the reader go from one thought to the next
- use a variety of sentence structures to make the writing interesting
- proofread your writing for errors in grammar, usage, spelling, punctuation, and capitalization

PRACTICE

Timed Writing: 25 minutes

Think carefully about the issue presented in the following quotation and assignment.

You've probably heard the saying "you learn more from your mistakes than from your successes." But, in general, is that indeed true?

Assignment: Do we tend to learn more from the mistakes that we make than from our successes? Plan and write a narrative essay in which you address this question. Include a story or narrate a series of events to support or illustrate your response.

Revising and Editing Skills

As part of the Writing section, some standardized tests ask you to improve sentences. The items in this section focus on your ability to recognize and write clear, effective, and precise sentences. They assess correctness, effectiveness, and conciseness of expression—without ambiguity and awkwardness.

PRACTICE

Directions: In this section, students must choose the best possible replacement for the underlined portion of the provided sentences. Beneath each sentence are four ways of saying the same thing as the underlined material. Choice *A* repeats the way it was in the original sentence. The other three choices are ways to rephrase the underlined text. If you think the original phrasing is better than any of the alternatives offered, select choice *A*. If not, circle one of the other choices.

Multiple Choice

1. The poet W. B. Yeats, who lived from 1865 to 1939, he often wrote about Ireland.
   A. Yeats, who lived from 1865 to 1939, he often wrote
   B. Yeats, living from 1865 to 1939, he often wrote
   C. Yeats, who lived from 1865 to 1939, he often did write
   D. Yeats, who lived from 1865 to 1939, often wrote

2. After fixing breakfast and glancing at the morning paper, the baby went to daycare.
   F. After fixing breakfast and glancing at the morning paper, the baby went
   G. After fixing breakfast and glancing at the morning paper, the baby goes
   H. After fixing breakfast and glancing at the morning paper, Dad took the baby
   J. After fixing breakfast and glancing at the morning paper, the baby was taken

3. Michael usually walks to work instead of driving or taking the bus because it's good exercise, doesn't harm the environment, and it doesn't cost anything.
   A. bus because it's good exercise, doesn't harm the environment, and it doesn't cost anything
   B. bus because it's good for his health, his financial situation, and the environment
   C. bus, the reason being that it's good exercise, doesn't harm the environment, and it doesn't cost anything
   D. bus because it's good exercise, doesn't harm the environment, and he doesn't have to spend anything

4. The increasing number of casualties in the war have resulted in its decreased popularity.
   F. have resulted in its
   G. have resulted in their
   H. has resulted in its
   J. have resulted in it's

5. Luca learned to play tennis last summer; he was nine years old at the time.
   A. summer; he was nine years old at the time
   B. summer, at which time he was nine years old
   C. summer at the age of nine
   D. summer; he had been nine years old at the time

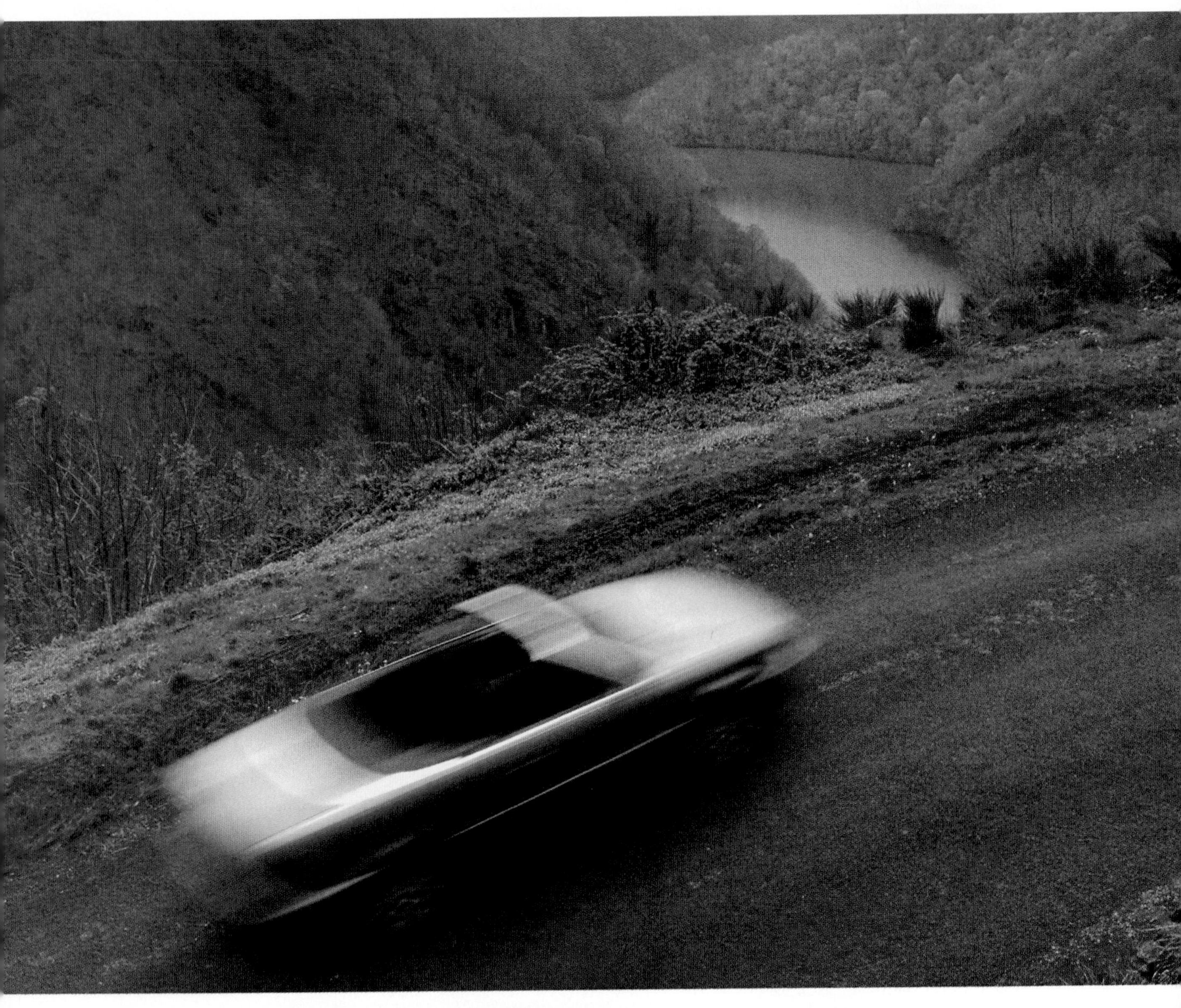

UNIT 6
Independent Reading

QUINDLEN

ANGELOU

BRADBURY

"Literature is my Utopia. Here I am not disenfranchised. No barrier of the senses shuts me out from the sweet, gracious discourses of my book friends. They talk to me without embarrassment or awkwardness." —Helen Keller

As a reader, you read for different purposes. Whether you read for enjoyment, to learn, or for information, applying reading strategies and skills will help you to become an active, independent reader. The selections in this unit are organized thematically to include the different genres you have studied in this textbook. Apply the strategies and skills you've practiced in Units 1–5 as you read the following selections.

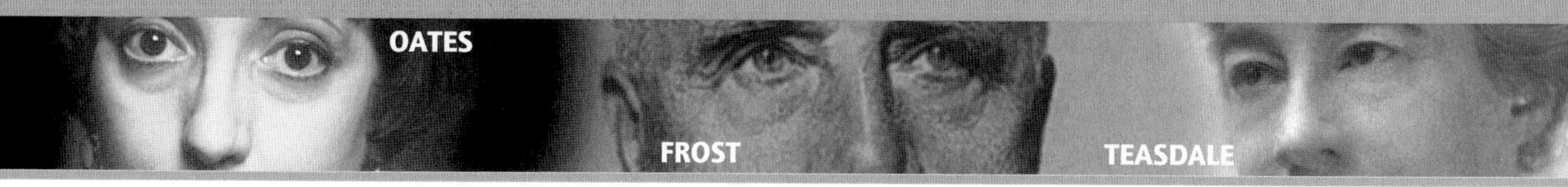

READING INDEPENDENTLY

Theme: Journeys

"You discover on the map a smaller road, not exactly parallel to the highway and not as direct, but one that leads to the same city."

—Joyce Carol Oates
from "Journey"

A journey can be as simple as going from point A to point B, but what happens to the traveler between those two points fills volumes of literature. The concept of "journey" signals a progression—not just from one place to another, but also between one level of awareness or maturity and another. Of the archetypes in literature (an archetype is an element that has appeared in the literature of the world from ancient times until today), the journey is one of the most important, as the hero usually must undergo a journey to complete his or her quest and gain self-knowledge. As you read these selections, consider what type of journey is described and what the characters or speakers gain from it in the end.

USE READING STRATEGIES

As you read the selections on your own, use the following guidelines:

Before Reading

- **Preview** by reading the title of the piece; scanning any art, quotations, subheads, and sidebars in the selection; and reading the footnotes for the selection.
- Find and **make connections** to the selections by reading the introductory information. What is familiar to you?
- Set your own **purpose for reading,** and remember that you can modify that purpose as you read.

During Reading

- **Ask questions** about things that puzzle you, and make notes about things you want to remember.
- **Visualize** the setting, characters, and images while you read.
- **Make predictions** about what might happen next in the text. Adjust your predictions as you get more information.
- **Make inferences** about the information that is not specifically stated.
- **Clarify** the information you read by writing things down, such as comments about the literary techniques or elements the author uses and difficult vocabulary. Also try reading the selection aloud, especially if it's poetry.

After Reading

- **Reread** the story if you have time. Everybody benefits from rereading a story because there are always details that may have been missed or forgotten in the first reading. If there are questions following the story, read those first to set a new purpose for reading.

- **Summarize** the story or poem on paper or in your head. If you can't remember a part of the story or poem, go back and **skim** or **scan** it to find the part you need to reread.
- **Review vocabulary words** that you found difficult. Try to use the words in your own sentences.
- **Draw conclusions** by asking questions about what you just read, such as what the "point" of the story is. The answer to that question will likely be the theme.

What Good Readers Do

Make Connections

Being aware of what you already know and thinking about it as you read can help you keep track of what's happening in the selection and increase your knowledge. As you read, say to yourself:

- ❑ I already know this about the story...
- ❑ This part of the story reminds me of...
- ❑ I think this part of the story is like...
- ❑ My experience tells me that...
- ❑ I like this description because...

Student Model

Note how this student applied reading strategies to the essay "Homeless" by Anna Quindlen (page 833).

Ask Questions
Who is Ann? Why doesn't she think she should be interviewed? Hopefully, this information will be revealed as I keep reading.

Visualize
I can imagine Ann pulling these papers from her tote bag, carefully, as she finds them very important.

Make Inferences
Infer what having a home may mean to Ann. Perhaps she equates having a house with having security or comfort.

Her name was Ann, and we met in the Port Authority Bus Terminal several Januarys ago. I was doing a story on homeless people. She said I was wasting my time talking to her; she was just passing through, although she'd been passing through for more than two weeks. To prove to me that this was true, she rummaged through a tote bag and a manila envelope and finally unfolded a sheet of typing paper and brought out her photographs.

They were not pictures of family, or friends, or even a dog or cat, its eyes brown-red in the flashbulb's light. They were pictures of a house. It was like a thousand houses in a hundred towns, not suburb, not city, but somewhere in between, with aluminum siding and a chain-link fence, a narrow driveway running up to a one-car garage and a patch of backyard. The house was yellow. I looked on the back for a date or a name, but neither was there. There was no need for discussion. I knew what she was trying to tell me, for it was something I had often felt. She was not adrift, alone, anonymous, although her bags and her raincoat with the grime shadowing its creases had made me believe she was. She had a house, or at least once upon a time had had one. Inside were curtains, a couch, a stove, potholders. You are where you live. She was somebody.

Clarify
The narrator's point seems important here. The lines, "You are where you live. She was somebody," imply that a home means more than a shelter.

Make Predictions
I predict that the narrator will explore these themes of homes vs. houses and focus on the need of homes for people like Ann.

INDEPENDENT READING

from Song of the Open Road

A Poem by **Walt Whitman**

Walt Whitman (1819–1892) was born on Long Island, New York. His work celebrates the beauty of the ordinary, often using natural imagery. The speaker in Walt Whitman's **"Song of the Open Road"** is setting out on a journey represented by not only the road before him or her, but also by a feeling that life will be full of new possibilities. This poem first appeared in Whitman's most famous work, *Leaves of Grass,* a collection of experimental free verse poetry which Whitman paid to have published in 1855. Although it received very little attention, it was later expanded and republished in 1864 and was revised several times before his death in 1892. Whitman wrote, "Now I see the secret of the making of the best persons. It is to grow in the open air and to eat and sleep with the earth."

How do you feel at the start of a journey or vacation?

1

Afoot and light-hearted I take to the open road,
Healthy, free, the world before me,
The long brown path before me leading wherever I choose.

Henceforth I ask not good fortune, I myself am good fortune,
Henceforth I whimper no more, postpone no more, need nothing,
Done with indoor complaints, libraries, querulous criticisms,
Strong and content I travel the open road.

The earth, that is sufficient,
I do not want the constellations any nearer,
I know they are very well where they are,
I know they suffice for those who belong to them.

9

Allons! whoever you are come travel with me!
Traveling with me you find what never tires.

The earth never tires,
The earth is rude, silent, incomprehensible at first, Nature is rude and
incomprehensible at first,
Be not discouraged, keep on, there are divine things well envelop'd,
I swear to you there are divine things more beautiful than words can tell.

15

Camerado, I give you my hand!
I give you my love more precious than money,
I give you myself before preaching or law;
Will you give me yourself? will you come travel with me?
Shall we stick by each other as long as we live? ❖

Many people claim "life is a journey." How might one's perspective affect his or her journey? What choices might affect this journey? Where, or what, is the "open road"?

Refer and Reason

1. Identify what the speaker is leaving behind. Infer what kind of life he or she is seeking.
2. Consider what might have prompted the speaker to start on this new path.
3. Focus on the line "Henceforth I ask not good fortune, I myself am good fortune." How can a change in attitude of this sort affect a person's life?

Writing Options

1. Using evidence from the text, identify a theme Whitman expresses. Then continue the theme in another stanza as the speaker continues his or her journey down the road.
2. Work with a partner to find evidence from the text to create a character profile of the speaker. Speculate on the speaker's life before and after setting off on the journey.

Go to **www.mirrorsandwindows.com** for more.

I Wandered Lonely as a CLOUD

A Poem by **William Wordsworth**

I wandered lonely as a cloud
That floats on high o'er vales and hills,
When all at once I saw a crowd,
A host, of golden daffodils,
Beside the lake, beneath the trees,
Fluttering and dancing in the breeze.

Continuous as the stars that shine
And twinkle on the Milky Way,
They stretched in never-ending line
Along the margin of a bay;
Ten thousand saw I at a glance,
Tossing their heads in sprightly dance.

The waves beside them danced, but they
Outdid the sparkling waves in glee;
A poet could not but be gay,
In such a jocund[1] company;
I gazed—and gazed—but little thought
What wealth the show to me had brought:

For oft, when on my couch I lie
In vacant or in pensive mood,
They flash upon that inward eye
Which is the bliss of solitude;
And then my heart with pleasure fills,
And dances with the daffodils. ❖

1. **jocund.** Jolly; high-spirited merriment

William Wordsworth (1770–1850) was born in the Lake District of England. Though he was formally educated and graduated from Cambridge University, his grades were only average. His interest lay more in poetry and the natural world, inspiring him to write, "Come forth into the light of things, / Let Nature be your teacher." The speaker in Wordsworth's **"I Wandered Lonely as a Cloud"** experiences rapture, or great joy, upon witnessing a scene in nature. This feeling stays with him or her long after the return home. Like Whitman's "Song of the Open Road" (page 828), this poem expresses the idea that the journey has the power to change the traveler. Compare Wordsworth's poem with "Song of the Open Road."

What do you enjoy most about nature? Have you ever witnessed an awe-inspiring scene?

"They flash upon that inward eye / Which is the bliss of solitude." How might past experiences assist in everyday life?

WORDSWORTH

Primary Source

CONNECTION

In 1795, **Dorothy Wordsworth** (1771–1855) moved in with her brother William and took care of his household. She began keeping a series of journals, including ***The Grasmere Journals,*** written from 1800 to 1803 while she lived in Grasmere. This journal, along with her *Alfoxden Journal,* which she wrote in 1798, are still read today. These journals often provide insight into her brother's work. Compare the description of daffodils along the shore in her April 15, 1802, entry with William Wordsworth's "I Wandered Lonely as a Cloud."

from The Grasmere Journals

A Journal by **Dorothy Wordsworth**

April 15, 1802: It was a threatening misty morning—but mild. We set off after dinner from Eusemere. Mrs Clarkson went a short way with us but turned back. The wind was furious and we thought we must have returned. We first rested in the large boat-house, then under a furze bush opposite Mr Clarkson's. Saw the plough going in the field. The wind seized our breath the lake was rough. There was a boat by itself floating in the middle of the bay below Water Millock.[1] *We rested again in the Water Millock lane. The hawthorns are black and green, the birches here and there greenish but there is yet more of purple to be seen on the twigs. We got over into a field to avoid some cows—people working, a few primroses by the roadside, wood-sorrel flowers, the anemone, scentless violets, strawberries, and that*

1. **Water Millock.** Refers to Watermillock, a village located near Grasmere, in the Lake District National Park region of England

starry yellow flower which Mrs C. calls pile wort. When we were in the woods beyond Gowbarrow Park we saw a few daffodils close to the waterside. We fancied that the lake had floated the seeds ashore, and that the little colony had so sprung up. But as we went along there were more and yet more and at last under the boughs of the trees, we saw that there was a long belt of them along the shore, about the breadth of a country turnpike road. I never saw daffodils so beautiful they grew among the mossy stones about and about them, some rested their heads upon these stones as on a pillow for weariness and the rest tossed and reeled and danced and seemed as if they verily laughed with the wind that blew upon them over the lake, they looked so gay ever glancing ever changing. This wind blew directly over the lake to them. There was here and there a little knot and a few stragglers a few yards higher up but they were so few as not to disturb the simplicity and unity and life of that one busy highway. We rested again and again. The bays were stormy, and we heard the waves at different distances and in the middle of the water like the sea.... ❖

Refer and Reason

1. Analyze how the speaker's mood changes over the course of the poem. Give specific examples from the poem that show how the writer created each mood.
2. Decide what kind of lifestyle the speakers in the selections lead. What details lead you to this conclusion?
3. Both "Song of the Open Road" and "I Wandered Lonely as a Cloud" show us a speaker who is on a journey. Compare and contrast how the speakers are affected by their journeys.

Writing Options

1. Write a brief dialogue between Walt Whitman and William Wordsworth in which they discuss their journeys and the meanings of their journeys.
2. Wordsworth uses dance imagery in every stanza. Write a paragraph analyzing the use of the image of dance in "I Wandered Lonely as a Cloud."

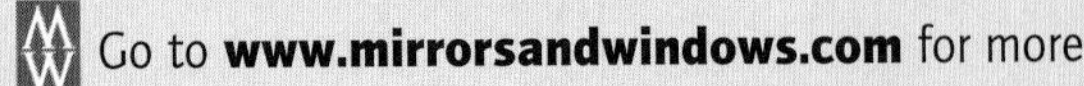
Go to **www.mirrorsandwindows.com** for more.

TEXT TO TEXT CONNECTION

Think about the ideas expressed by William and Dorothy Wordsworth, and Walt Whitman. What kind of scenery does each prefer? What imagery do they use to describe these scenes and how are these images similar and different? Do you think these three authors would have similar travel habits?

HOMELESS

An Essay by **Anna Quindlen**

They are not the homeless. They are people who have no homes.

Philadelphia native **Anna Quindlen** (b. 1952) is perhaps best known for her regular columns in the *New York Times* and *Newsweek.* She has earned several prestigious awards, including the 1992 Pulitzer Prize for Commentary for her *Times* column "Public & Private." "I think of a column as having a conversation with a person that it just so happens I can't see," she once said. **"Homeless,"** an insightful take on a pervasive societal issue, was published in a 1988 collection of Anna Quindlen's columns called *Living Out Loud.* In the reflective essay, Quindlen explains what home means to her and then examines what it means to people who lack one of their own.

What do you know about homeless people? Have you ever met someone who didn't have a home of his or her own?

Her name was Ann, and we met in the Port Authority Bus Terminal several Januarys ago. I was doing a story on homeless people. She said I was wasting my time talking to her; she was just passing through, although she'd been passing through for more than two weeks. To

prove to me that this was true, she rummaged through a tote bag and a manila envelope and finally unfolded a sheet of typing paper and brought out her photographs.

They were not pictures of family, or friends, or even a dog or cat, its eyes brown-red in the flashbulb's light. They were pictures of a house. It was like a thousand houses in a hundred towns, not suburb, not city, but somewhere in between, with aluminum siding and a chain-link fence, a narrow driveway running up to a one-car garage and a patch of backyard. The house was yellow. I looked on the back for a date or a name, but neither was there. There was no need for discussion. I knew what she was trying to tell me, for it was something I had often felt. She was not adrift, alone, anonymous, although her bags and her raincoat with the grime shadowing its creases had made me believe she was. She had a house, or at least once upon a time had had one. Inside were curtains, a couch, a stove, potholders. You are where you live. She was somebody.

I've never been very good at looking at the big picture, taking the global view, and I've always been a person with an overactive sense of place, the legacy of an Irish grandfather. So it is natural that the thing that seems most wrong with the world to me right now is that there are so many people with no homes. I'm not simply talking about shelter from the elements, or three square meals a day or a mailing address to which the welfare people can send the check—although I know that all these are important for survival. I'm talking about a home, about precisely those kinds of feelings that have wound up in cross-stitch and French knots on samplers over the years.

Home is where the heart is. There's no place like it. I love my home with a ferocity totally out of proportion to its appearance or location. I love dumb things about it: the hot-water heater, the plastic rack you drain dishes in, the roof over my head, which occasionally leaks. And yet it is precisely those dumb things that make it what it is—a place of certainty, stability, predictability, privacy, for me and for my family. It is where I live. What more can you say about a place than that? That is everything.

Yet it is something that we have been edging away from gradually during my lifetime and the lifetimes of my parents and grandparents. There was a time when where you lived often was where you worked and where you grew the food you ate and even where you were buried. When that era passed, where you lived at least was where your parents had lived and where you would live with your children when you became enfeebled. Then, suddenly, where you lived was where you lived for three years, until you could move on to something else and something else again.

And so we have come to something else again, to children who do not understand what it means to go to their rooms because they have never had a room, to men and women whose fantasy is a wall they can paint a color of their own choosing, to old people reduced to sitting on molded plastic chairs, their skin blue-white in the lights of a bus station, who pull pictures of houses out of their bags. Homes have stopped being homes. Now they are real estate.

People find it curious that those without homes would rather sleep sitting up on benches or huddled in doorways than go to shelters. Certainly some prefer to do so because they are emotionally ill, because they have been locked in before and they are damned if they will be locked in again. Others are afraid of the violence and trouble they may find there. But some seem to want something that is not available in shelters, and they will not compromise, not for a cot, or oatmeal, or a shower with special soap that kills the bugs. "One room," a woman with a baby who was sleeping on her sister's floor, once told me, "painted blue." That was the crux of it; not size or location, but pride of ownership. Painted blue.

This is a difficult problem, and some wise and compassionate people are working hard at it. But in the main I think we work around it, just as we walk around it when it is lying on the sidewalk or sitting in the bus terminal—the problem, that is. It has been customary to take people's pain and lessen our own participation in it by turning it into an issue, not a collection of human beings. We turn an adjective into a noun: the poor, not poor people; the homeless, not Ann or the man who lives in the box or the woman who sleeps on the subway grate.

Sometimes I think we would be better off if we forgot about the broad strokes and concentrated on the details. Here is a woman without a bureau. There is a man with no mirror, no wall to hang it on. They are not the homeless. They are people who have no homes. No drawer that holds the spoons. No window to look out upon the world. My God. That is everything. ❖

What purpose does it serve to "lessen our own participation" in the troubles of others? Why does this happen and what does it say about the people who allow this to happen? How might people resist this habit?

Refer and Reason

1. Summarize the essay and identify why Quindlen says she is better at looking at the details than at the big picture. Which has she tried to do in this essay?
2. Critique how successful Quindlen has been in debunking stereotypes about homeless people. Explain.
3. Do you think Quindlen's essay might influence your future thoughts about and actions toward people who are homeless? Why or why not?

Writing Options

1. Write a first-person account of three waking hours in the life of a homeless person.
2. Write a critical analysis of "Homeless," in which you touch on some of the elements that have likely contributed to the popularity of Anna Quindlen's writing. Consider subject matter, language, tone, and other aspects that stand out for you.

Go to **www.mirrorsandwindows.com** for more.

from Learning Joy from Dogs Without Collars

A Memoir by **Lauralee Summer**

Lauralee Summer (b. 1976) first came to fame in 1994 when she won a wrestling scholarship and then a scholarship to Harvard University. With her mother, Summer had moved twenty times before the age of twelve, going from homeless shelter to homeless shelter. Ultimately settling in Boston, Summer earned her bachelor's degree from Harvard and went on to the University of California, Berkeley, for a master's degree.

In her 2003 memoir, ***Learning Joy from Dogs Without Collars,*** Lauralee Summer recounts her experience of being homeless for much of her childhood. The following excerpt describes several of the homeless shelters Summer had stayed in over the years—and her longing for a home of her own.

What do you remember from your childhood home? What do you enjoy the most about your current home?

I wanted an address so badly, just to have a spot where I could get mail and magazines.

The year I was to enter fourth grade, my mother decided that we should move. She hoped to find a job in the Industrial Belt of Southern California, and she preferred the warm weather there to the cold rains of Northern Oregon. I didn't realize what moving would mean. I don't remember being especially sad about moving. We had to move out of our apartment anyway. We had been evicted[1] because the landlord didn't make repairs necessary for the building to pass the housing authority's inspection.

We held the rummage sale inside our apartment of the past three years. We displayed our possessions around the edges of the rooms and stuck price tags made of bits of masking tape to them. Piles of things were stacked on the edges of the brown shag carpet where I had built forts out of blankets and couch pillows and chairs. This was the rug that I had fallen asleep on every winter afternoon, reading books in front of the wall heater, the warm air making me languorous[2] and dreamy. My bike and my Lite-Brite and my giant stuffed raccoon sat outside on the porch for passersby to speculate on. My mom had stacked her plants high on a multitiered plant stand. The layers of sunny green were among the few things we had that sold for more than their original price, since most of my mom's seeds and seedlings were free, transplanted from people's overflowing gardens or from friends. All of my books—the Ramona books by Beverly Cleary, The Chronicles of Narnia by C. S. Lewis, *Harriet the Spy, The Borrowers,* Nancy Drew mysteries, the Great Brain books, *Charlotte's Web, The Hobbit,* a whole collection of Golden Books whose spines made a long golden rectangle on my shelf, *Lady and the Tramp* and *The Aristocats,* which had records with them, Lloyd Alexander books (fantasy adventures), and many others—were sold. We made fifty dollars from selling my books and toys. My mother told me that she'd put the money in the bank for me to save for a bicycle.

The next morning we boarded the bus to California. I didn't get to say good-bye to any of my friends. That is always the way on journeys and leave-takings. You think there will be time or occasion for one final good-bye, but there never is. There is only time for countless unofficial good-byes. *I'm sure I'll see you again so I won't say good-bye now.*

Things did not go as expected when we arrived in California. The rents were high, we had little money, and finding a job without recent training and experience was harder than my mother had anticipated. For a month we lived in a shelter in San Jose, located off of the edges of town in a large institutional building. The inside was made up of cinder-block cubicles. In the basement was a cafeteria and lounge. The rooms had no windows. They were coded by color and number; each had two sets of bunk beds with bare mattresses. My mom and I lived for a month in Yellow Number 3. I remember one day clearly—being sick, puking and hanging over the edge of the bottom bunk and looking at the doorway, the yellow paint and stenciled number. Two children at the shelter gave me a get-well note. On the outside of the card a childish script scrawls: To Yellow Number 3....

One windy day in San Jose, my mother sat on a park bench, waiting for the bus. She

1. **evicted.** Forced out
2. **languorous.** Sleepy; slow-moving; relaxed

felt cold, even though it was August. So she thought, Forget about this, we're moving farther south. So we moved on to Santa Barbara.

In Santa Barbara we lived in the Wings of Love shelter for a few weeks. It was a small religious shelter that looked like someone's home. I became friends with a fifteen-year-old girl named Star. Tall, thin, and muscular, Star had deep brown sparkling eyes and dark brown skin and braided hair. She and her mother and brother Chris and my mom and I all stayed in one carpeted room. Star and her mom were in the bunks across from us. Her brother Chris—who was in eighth grade—was in the bunk above me. My mom and I were stuck sharing a bunk because I was small for my age.

The first night we were there, Chris repeatedly sang the "Revenge of the Nerds" song, face upside down from where he was sprawled in his upper bunk, teasing me because I was so nerdy with my glasses and my shyness. I hunched in a corner of the bunk, my nose in a book. It was one of the last times I read in a long while.

When I think about our brief stay at the Wings of Love, I see bright-colored walls and blankets, and thick carpets everywhere. The colors of Star's and Chris's faces blend in with the dark brown wood and flashy colors of the room. The woman running the place wore a cloth headdress like a nun, and she made us go to church all the time. She cooked grits and other food I wasn't used to, but I was hungry so I ate it. After a few weeks, we moved to the Salvation Army shelter. I didn't give Chris and Star much thought because by now I was used to leaving people behind. I expected the faces around me to change every few weeks. At the Salvation Army, I saw the crazy woman who ran the Wings of Love on the news. It turned out she had been keeping all the money she was given for the shelter for herself instead of using it to help the people who lived there.

We stayed at the Salvation Army for a few months, maybe half a year. In stark contrast to the Wings of Love shelter, it was big, institutional, and bleak,[3] with rows and rows of cots in a large room lit brightly by white fluorescent

3. **bleak.** Dismal; lacking warmth

lights. The room had linoleum floors like a schoolroom, and white cinder-block walls with high windows along one side.

There was no place to be alone, no place to be by myself. I woke up at six each morning to bright lights, a long cement room, strange people scurrying, rows of cots. I felt myself dispersing[4] into the wide whiteness of the shelter's walls and the noise of strangers' words.

Each night before bed, I put clean clothes and a small towel at the bed's foot. When I woke, I would jump up before I could begin to lose myself in the confusion. I grabbed my bundle of clothes and scooted to the showers. There were only a few for many women.

Inside the shower, I rested my knee, shoulder, and face against the warm yellow tiles. It was the only place I felt alone and undisturbed. I folded myself into the corner, standing on one leg like a stork, the other knee pushing into the corner. The warm water wrung itself over me, and I would begin to feel at home, no cold spots. The door to this yellow cubicle was shut tight, and the glass grew cloudy with steam.

I wanted to stay in that warm womb forever. I couldn't, it wasn't my own home. But before I left for the day I could daydream and imagine. My imaginings resonated[5] around me, reverberating off the yellow tiles and enveloping me. I shut my eyes, pressed my forehead into the corner. I thought of a rectangle shape cut into a door. This was the mail slot in the door of my new house. *Swoosh-plop,* a magazine fell through onto the floor inside.

I wanted an address so badly, just to have a spot where I could get mail and magazines. Sometimes at newsstands in California I looked at the subscription cards in kids' and teen magazines—"only $10 a year—six issues." How easy life would be if only I could fill out that little card. I could fill in the address and have a home as well as a year's subscription sent back to me. A year to sleep in the same place.... ❖

4. **dispersing.** Evaporating; scattering
5. **resonated.** Vibrated; resounded

How does it feel to be out of your own element? Is solitude an important part of life? Do people need to be alone on occasion?

Refer and Reason

1. Identify the different places where Summer and her mother stay in this excerpt, noting how long they stay in each one. Why might Summer not express a lot of emotion about leaving each shelter or city?
2. Decide who you think would have a harder time adjusting to the sort of life described in this excerpt, a child or an adult. Why?
3. Both Quindlen in "Homeless" on page 833 and Summer focus on details that make a place a home and that create a sense of "normal life." Specify what things you think you could do without while still maintaining feelings of home and normalcy. What is needed to create those feelings?

Writing Options

1. Given the situation outlined in the essays, write an op-ed piece to express your opinion on how mayors could improve the conditions of their cities and how homeless shelters could improve their facilities. An op-ed piece is a newspaper editorial, written by a guest writer, that expresses an opinion.
2. Point of view is the vantage point from which a story is told. Write a critical analysis on how the authors of "Homeless" and *Learning Joy from Dogs Without Collars* use point of view to achieve their purposes.

Go to **www.mirrorsandwindows.com** for more.

from Blue Highways: A Journey into America

A Travelogue by **William Least Heat-Moon**

William Least Heat-Moon (b. 1939) was born William Trogdon in Kansas City, Missouri. He later changed his name to reflect his Osage heritage. In 1978, he set out from Missouri in a truck named Ghost Dancing and followed 13,000 miles of rural roads. Least Heat-Moon describes his journey of self-discovery in ***Blue Highways: A Journey into America.*** He named his book after the small roads he traveled on his journey. He called these backroads "blue highways" because they were marked in blue on a road map, unlike larger interstate highways or freeways. Least Heat-Moon says, "Americans have developed the notion that when your life goes wrong, what you do is hit the road.... We're a restless people and the way we solve things is to start moving."

If you could go anywhere, where would you go, and whom would you talk to along the way?

CHAPTER 14

Had it not been raining hard that morning on the Livingston square, I never would have learned of Nameless, Tennessee. Waiting for the rain to ease, I lay on my bunk and read the atlas to pass time rather than to see where I might go. In Kentucky were towns with fine names like Boreing, Bear Wallow, Decoy, Subtle, Mud Lick, Mummie, Neon; Belcher was just down the road from Mouthcard, and Minnie only ten miles from Mousie.

I looked at Tennessee. Turtletown eight miles from Ducktown. And also: Peavine, Wheel, Milky Way, Love Joy, Dull, Weakly, Fly, Spot, Miser Station, Only, McBurg, Peeled Chestnut, Clouds, Topsy, Isoline. And the best of all, Nameless. The logic! I was heading east, and Nameless lay forty-five miles west. I decided to go anyway.

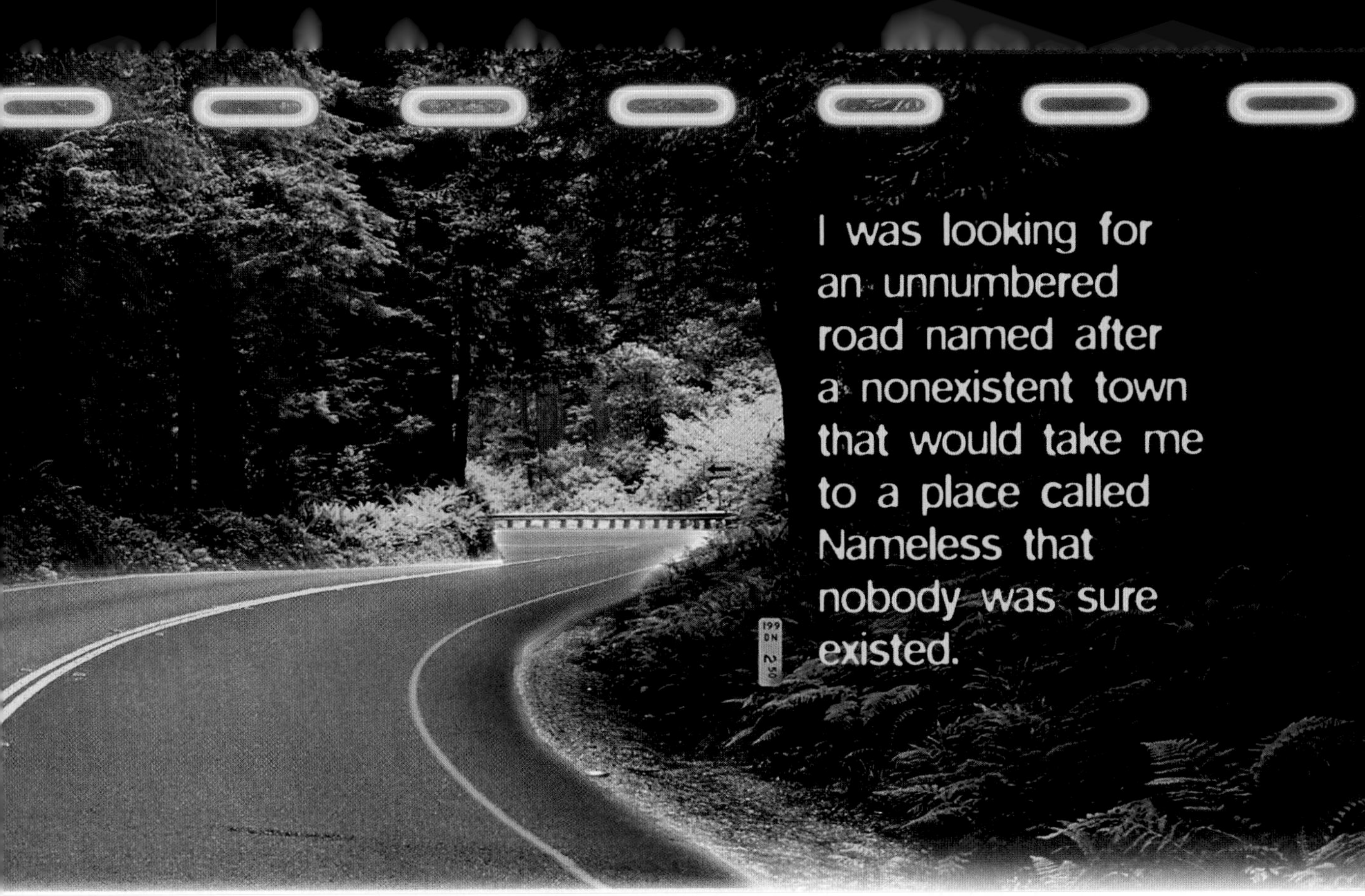

I was looking for an unnumbered road named after a nonexistent town that would take me to a place called Nameless that nobody was sure existed.

The rain stopped, but things looked saturated, even bricks. In Gainesboro, a hill town with a square of businesses around the Jackson County Courthouse, I stopped for directions and breakfast. There is one almost infallible way to find honest food at just prices in blue-highway America: count the wall calendars in a cafe.

No calendar: Same as an interstate pit stop.
One calendar: Preprocessed food assembled in New Jersey.
Two calendars: Only if fish trophies present.
Three calendars: Can't miss on the farm-boy breakfasts.
Four calendars: Try the ho-made pie too.
Five calendars: Keep it under your hat, or they'll franchise.

One time I found a six-calendar cafe in the Ozarks, which served fried chicken, peach pie, and chocolate malts, that left me searching for another ever since. I've never seen a seven-calendar place. But old-time travelers—road men in a day when cars had running boards and lunchroom windows said AIR COOLED in blue letters with icicles dripping from the tops—those travelers have told me the golden legends of seven-calendar cafes.

To the rider of back roads, nothing shows the tone, the voice of a small town more quickly than the breakfast grill or the five-thirty tavern. Much of what the people do and believe and share is evident then. The City Cafe in Gainesboro had three calendars that I could see from the walk. Inside were no interstate refugees with full bladders and empty tanks, no wild-eyed children just released from the glassy cell of a stationwagon backseat, no long-haul truckers talking in CB numbers.[1] There were only townspeople wearing overalls, or catalog-

1. **CB numbers.** CB radios were the only way drivers could communicate before cell phones became available.

order suits with five-and-dime ties, or uniforms. That is, here were farmers and mill hands, bank clerks, the dry goods merchant,[2] a policeman, and chiropractor's receptionist. Because it was Saturday, there were also mothers and children.

I ordered my standard on-the-road breakfast: two eggs up, hashbrowns, tomato juice. The waitress, whose pale, almost translucent skin shifted hue in the gray light like a thin slice of mother of pearl,[3] brought the food. Next to the eggs was a biscuit with a little yellow Smiley button stuck in it. She said, "You from the North?"

"I guess I am." A Missourian gets used to Southerners thinking him a Yankee, a Northerner considering him a cracker,[4] a Westerner sneering at his effete Easternness, and the Easterner taking him for a cowhand.

"So whata you doin' in the mountains?"

"Talking to people. Taking some pictures. Looking mostly."

"Lookin' for what?"

"A three-calendar cafe that serves Smiley buttons on the biscuits."

"You needed a smile. Tell me really."

"I don't know. Actually, I'm looking for some jam to put on this biscuit now that you've brought one."

She came back with grape jelly. In a land of quince jelly, apple butter, apricot jam, blueberry preserves, pear conserves, and lemon marmalade, you always get grape jelly.

"Whata you lookin' for?"

Like anyone else, I'm embarrassed to eat in front of a watcher, particularly if I'm getting interviewed. "Why don't you have a cup of coffee?"

"Cain't right now. You gonna tell me?"

"I don't know how to describe it to you. Call it harmony."

She waited for something more. "Is that it?" Someone called her to the kitchen. I had managed almost to finish by the time she came back. She sat on the edge of the booth. "I started out in life not likin' anything, but then it grew on me. Maybe that'll happen to you." She watched me spread the jelly. "Saw your van." She watched me eat the biscuit. "You sleep in there?" I told her I did. "I'd love to do that, but I'd be scared spitless."

"I don't mind being scared spitless. Sometimes."

"I'd love to take off cross country. I like to look at different license plates. But I'd take a dog. You carry a dog?"

"No dogs, no cats, no budgie birds. It's a one-man campaign to show Americans a person can travel alone without a pet."

"Cain't travel without a dog!"

"I like to do things the hard way."

"Shoot! I'd take me a dog to talk to. And for protection."

"It isn't traveling to cross the country and talk to your pug instead of people along the way. Besides, being alone on the road makes you ready to meet someone when you stop. You get sociable traveling alone."

She looked out toward the van again. "Time I get the nerve to take a trip, gas'll cost five dollars a gallon."

"Could be. My rig might go the way of the steamboat." I remembered why I'd come to Gainesboro. "You know the way to Nameless?"

"Nameless? I've heard of Nameless. Better ask the amlance driver in the corner booth." She pinned the Smiley on my jacket. "Maybe I'll see you on the road somewhere. His name's Bob, by the way."

"The ambulance driver?"

"The Smiley. I always name my Smileys—otherwise they all look alike. I'd talk to him before you go."

"The Smiley?"

"The amlance driver."

2. **dry goods merchant.** Seller of cloth or clothing products

3. **mother of pearl.** Shiny inner layer of certain marine shells (for example, the pearl oyster or abalone)

4. **cracker.** Insulting term applied to an uneducated white person, especially from the rural South

And so I went looking for Nameless, Tennessee, with a Smiley button named Bob.

CHAPTER 15

I don't know if I got directions for where you're goin'," the ambulance driver said.

"I *think* there's a Nameless down the Shepardsville Road."

"When I get to Shepardsville, will I have gone too far?"

"Ain't no Shepardsville."

"How will I know when I'm there?"

"Cain't say for certain."

"What's Nameless look like?"

"Don't recollect."

"Is the road paved?"

"It's possible."

Those were the directions. I was looking for an unnumbered road named after a nonexistent town that would take me to a place called Nameless that nobody was sure existed.

Clumps of wild garlic lined the county highway that I hoped was the Shepardsville Road. It scrimmaged[5] with the mountain as it tried to stay on top of the ridges; the hillsides were so steep and thick with oak, I felt as if I were following a trail through the misty treetops. Chickens, doing more work with their necks than legs, ran across the road, and, with a battering of wings, half leapt and half flew into the lower branches of oaks. A vicious pair of mixed-breed German shepherds raced along trying to eat the tires. After miles, I decided I'd missed the town—assuming there truly *was* a Nameless, Tennessee. It wouldn't be the first time I'd qualified for the Ponce de Leon[6] Believe Anything Award.

I stopped beside a big man loading tools in a pickup. "I may be lost."

5. **scrimmaged.** Wrestled or struggled

6. **Ponce de Leon.** Spanish explorer (1460–1521) who sought in vain for the "fountain of youth"

Knoxville, Tennessee, 1971. Lee Friedlander. Montclair Art Museum, Montclair, New Jersey.

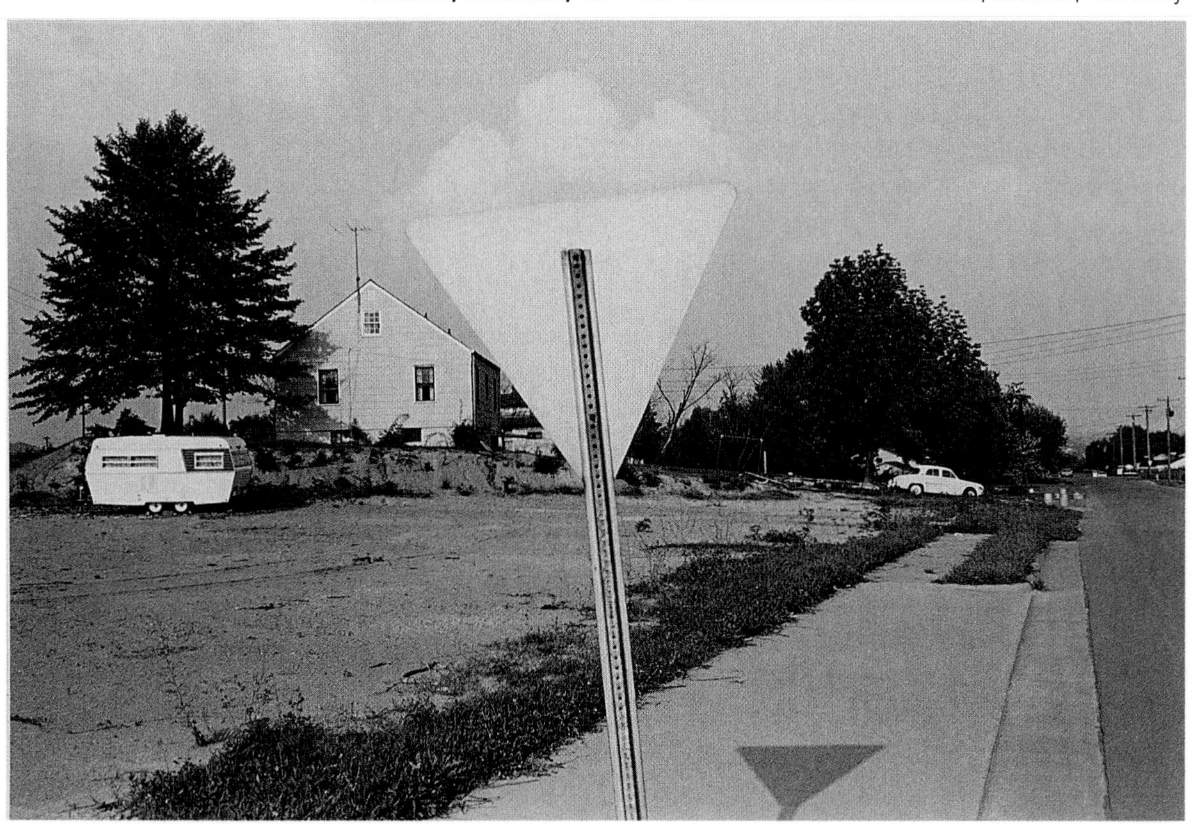

"Where'd you lose the right road?"

"I don't know. Somewhere around nineteen sixty-five."

"Highway fifty-six, you mean?"

"I came down fifty-six. I think I should've turned at the last junction."

"Only thing down that road's stumps and huckleberries, and the berries ain't there in March. Where you tryin' to get to?"

"Nameless. If there is such a place."

"You might not know Thurmond Watts, but he's got him a store down the road. That's Nameless at his store. Still there all right, but I might not vouch you that tomorrow." He came up to the van. "In my Army days, I wrote Nameless, Tennessee, for my place of birth on all the papers, even though I lived on this end of the ridge. All these ridges and hollers got names of their own. That's Steam Mill Holler over yonder. Named after the steam engine in the gristmill. Miller had him just one arm but done a good business."

"What business you in?"

"I've always farmed, but I work in Cookeville now in a heatin' element factory. Bad back made me go to town to work." He pointed to a wooden building not much bigger than his truck. By the slanting porch, a faded Double Cola sign said J M WHEELER STORE. "That used to be my business. That's me—Madison Wheeler. Feller came by one day. From Detroit. He wanted to buy the sign because he carried my name too. But I didn't sell. Want to keep my name up." He gave a cigarette a good slow smoking. "Had a decent business for five years, but too much of it was in credit. Then them supermarkets down in Cookeville opened, and I was buyin' higher than they was sellin'. With these hard roads now, everybody gets out of the hollers to shop or work. Don't stay up in here anymore. This tar road under my shoes done my business in, and it's likely to do Nameless in."

"Do you wish it was still the old way?"

"I got no debts now. I got two boys raised, and they never been in trouble. I got a brick house and some corn and tobacco and a few Hampshire hogs and Herefords. A good bull. Bull's pumpin' better blood than I do. Real generous man in town let me put my cow in with his stud. I couldna paid the fee on that specimen otherwise."[7] He took another long, meditative pull on his filtertip. "If you're satisfied, that's all they are to it. I'll tell you, people from all over the nation—Florida, Mississippi—are comin' in here to retire because it's good country. But our young ones don't stay on. Not much way to make a livin' in here anymore. Take me. I been beatin' on these stumps all my life, tryin' to farm these hills. They don't give much up to you. Fightin' rocks and briars all the time. One of the first things I recollect is swingin' a briar blade—filed out of an old saw it was. Now they come in with them crawlers and push out a pasture in a day. Still, it's a grudgin' land—like the gourd. Got to hard cuss gourd seed, they say, to get it up out of the ground."

The whole time, my rig sat in the middle of the right lane while we stood talking next to it and wiped at the mist. No one else came or went. Wheeler said, "Factory work's easier on the back, and I don't mind it, understand, but a man becomes what he does. Got to watch that. That's why I keep at farmin', although the crops haven't ever throve.[8] It's the doin' that's important." He looked up suddenly. "My apologies. I didn't ask what you do that gets you into these hollers."

I told him. I'd been gone only six days, but my account of the trip already had taken on some polish.

He nodded. "Satisfaction is doin' what's important to yourself. A man ought to honor

7. **Bull's...otherwise.** Wheeler means that his bull is the offspring of a fine bull belonging to the generous man.

8. **throve.** Thrived; grown vigorously

other people, but he's got to honor what he believes in too."

As I started the engine, Wheeler said, "If you get back this way, stop in and see me. Always got beans and taters and a little piece of meat."

Down along the ridge, I wondered why it's always those who live on little who are the ones to ask you to dinner.

CHAPTER 16

Nameless, Tennessee, was a town of maybe ninety people if you pushed it, a dozen houses along the road, a couple of barns, same number of churches, a general merchandise store selling Fire Chief gasoline, and a community center with a lighted volleyball court. Behind the center was an open-roof, rusting metal privy with PAINT ME on the door; in the hollow of a nearby oak lay a full pint of Jack Daniel's Black Label. From the houses, the odor of coal smoke.

Next to a red tobacco barn stood the general merchandise store with a poster of Senator Albert Gore, Jr.,[9] smiling from the window. I knocked. The door opened partway. A tall, thin man said, "Closed up. For good," and started to shut the door.

"Don't want to buy anything. Just a question for Mr. Thurmond Watts."

The man peered through the slight opening. He looked me over. "What question would that be?"

"If this is Nameless, Tennessee, could he tell me how it got that name?"

The man turned back into the store and called out, "Miss Ginny! Somebody here wants to know how Nameless come to be Nameless."

Miss Ginny edged to the door and looked me and my truck over. Clearly, she didn't approve. She said, "You know as well as I do, Thurmond. Don't keep him on the stoop in the damp to tell him." Miss Ginny, I found out, was Mrs. Virginia Watts, Thurmond's wife.

I stepped in and they both began telling the story, adding a detail here, the other correcting a fact there, both smiling at the foolishness of it all. It seems the hilltop settlement went for years without a name. Then one day the Post Office Department told the people if they wanted mail up on the mountain they would have to give the place a name you could properly address a letter to. The community met; there were only a handful, but they commenced debating. Some wanted patriotic names, some names from nature, one man recommended in all seriousness his own name. They couldn't agree, and they ran out of names to argue about. Finally, a fellow tired of the talk; he didn't like the mail he received anyway. "Forget the durn Post Office," he said. "This here's a nameless place if I ever seen one, so leave it be." And that's just what they did.

Watts pointed out the window. "We used to have signs on the road, but the Halloween boys keep tearin' them down."

"You think Nameless is a funny name," Miss Ginny said. "I see it plain in your eyes. Well, you take yourself up north a piece to Difficult or Defeated or Shake Rag. Now them are silly names."

The old store, lighted only by three fifty-watt bulbs, smelled of coal oil and baking bread. In the middle of the rectangular room, where the oak floor sagged a little, stood an iron stove. To the right was a wooden table with an unfinished game of checkers and a stool made from an apple-tree stump. On shelves around the walls sat earthen jugs with corncob stoppers, a few canned goods, and some of the two thousand old clocks and clockworks Thurmond Watts owned. Only one was ticking; the others he just looked at. I asked how long he'd been in the store.

9. **Senator Albert Gore, Jr.** Former senator from Tennessee who became vice president in 1992 and later ran for president

"Thirty-five years, but we closed the first day of the year. We're hopin' to sell it to a churchly couple. Upright people. No athians."[10]

"Did you build this store?"

"I built this one, but it's the third general store on the ground. I fear it'll be the last. I take no pleasure in that. Once you could come in here for a gallon of paint, a pickle, a pair of shoes, and a can of corn."

"Or horehound candy," Miss Ginny said. "Or corsets and salves. We had cough syrups and all that for the body. In season, we'd buy and sell blackberries and walnuts and chestnuts, before the blight got them. And outside, Thurmond milled corn and sharpened plows. Even shoed a horse sometimes."

"We could fix up a horse or a man or a baby," Watts said.

"Thurmond, tell him we had a doctor on the ridge in them days."

"We had a doctor on the ridge in them days. As good as any doctor alivin'. He'd cut a crooked toenail or deliver a woman. Dead these last years."

"I got some bad ham meat one day," Miss Ginny said, "and took to vomitin'. All day, all night. Hangin' on the drop edge of yonder. I said to Thurmond, 'Thurmond, unless you want shut of me, call the doctor.' "

"I studied on it,"[11] Watts said.

"You never did. You got him right now. He come over and put three drops of iodeen

10. **churchly couple...athians.** Religious couple with a strong sense of morality, not atheists.

11. **I studied on it.** I thought about it.

in half a glass of well water. I drank it down and the vomitin' stopped with the last swallow. Would you think iodeen could do that?"

"He put Miss Ginny on one teaspoon of spirits of ammonia in well water for her nerves. Ain't nothin' works better for her to this day."

"Calms me like the hand of the Lord."

Hilda, the Wattses' daughter, came out of the backroom. "I remember him," she said. "I was just a baby. Y'all were talkin' to him, and he lifted me up on the counter and gave me a stick of Juicy Fruit and a piece of cheese."

"Knew the old medicines," Watts said. "Only drugstore he needed was a good kitchen cabinet. None of them antee-beeotics that hit you worsen your ailment. Forgotten lore now, the old medicines, because they ain't profit in iodeen."

Miss Ginny started back to the side room where she and her sister Marilyn were taking apart a duck-down mattress to make bolsters. She stopped at the window for another look at Ghost Dancing. "How do you sleep in that thing? Ain't you all cramped and cold?"

"How does the clam sleep in his shell?" Watts said in my defense.

"Thurmond, get the boy a piece of buttermilk pie afore he goes on."

"Hilda, get him some buttermilk pie." He looked at me. "You like good music?" I said I did. He cranked up an old Edison phonograph, the kind with the big morning-glory blossom for a speaker, and put on a wax cylinder. "This will be 'My Mother's Prayer,'" he said.

While I ate buttermilk pie, Watts served as disc jockey of Nameless, Tennessee. "Here's 'Mountain Rose.'" It was one of those moments that you know at the time will stay with you to the grave: the sweet pie, the gaunt man playing the old music, the coals in the stove glowing orange, the scent of kerosene and hot bread. "Here's 'Evening Rhapsody.'" The music was so heavily romantic we both laughed. I thought: It is for this I have come.

Feathered over and giggling, Miss Ginny stepped from the side room. She knew she was a sight. "Thurmond, give him some lunch. Still looks hungry."

Hilda pulled food off the woodstove in the backroom: home-butchered and canned whole-hog sausage, home-canned June apples, turnip greens, cole slaw, potatoes, stuffing, hot cornbread. All delicious.

Watts and Hilda sat and talked while I ate. "Wish you would join me."

"We've ate," Watts said. "Cain't beat a woodstove for flavorful cookin'."

He told me he was raised in a one-hundred-fifty-year-old cabin still standing in one of the hollows. "How many's left," he said, "that grew up in a log cabin? I ain't the last surely, but I must be climbin' on the list."

Hilda cleared the table. "You Watts ladies know how to cook."

"She's in nursin' school at Tennessee Tech. I went over for one of them football games last year there at Coevul." To say *Cookeville,* you let the word collapse in upon itself so that it comes out "Coevul."

"Do you like football?" I asked.

"Don't know. I was so high up in that stadium, I never opened my eyes."

Watts went to the back and returned with a fat spiral notebook that he set on the table. His expression had changed. "Miss Ginny's *Deathbook*."

The thing startled me. Was it something I was supposed to sign? He opened it but said nothing. There were scads of names written in a tidy hand over pages incised to crinkliness by a ballpoint. Chronologically, the names had piled up: wives, grandparents, a stillborn infant, relatives, friends close and distant. Names, names. After each, the date of the unknown finally known and transcribed. The last entry bore yesterday's date.

"She's wrote out twenty years' worth. Ever day she listens to the hospital report on the radio and puts the names in. Folks come by to check a date. Or they just turn through the books. Read them like a scrapbook."

Hilda said, "Like Saint Peter at the gates inscribin' the names."

Watts took my arm. "Come along." He led me to the fruit cellar under the store. As we went down, he said, "Always take a newborn baby upstairs afore you take him downstairs, otherwise you'll incline him downwards."

The cellar was dry and full of cobwebs and jar after jar of home-canned food, the bottles organized as a shopkeeper would: sausage, pumpkin, sweet pickles, tomatoes, corn relish, blackberries, peppers, squash, jellies. He held a hand out toward the dusty bottles. "Our tomorrows."

Upstairs again, he said, "Hope to sell the store to the right folk. I see now, though, it'll be somebody offen the ridge.[12] I've studied on it, and maybe it's the end of our place." He stirred the coals. "This store could give a comfortable livin', but not likely get you rich. But just gettin' by is dice rollin' to people nowadays. I never did see my day guaranteed."

When it was time to go, Watts said, "If you find anyone along your way wants a good store—on the road to Cordell Hull Lake—tell them about us."

I said I would. Miss Ginny and Hilda and Marilyn came out to say goodbye. It was cold and drizzling again. "Weather to give a man the weary dismals," Watts grumbled. "Where you headed from here?"

"I don't know."

"Cain't get lost then."

Miss Ginny looked again at my rig. It had worried her from the first as it had my mother. "I hope you don't get yourself kilt in that durn thing gallivantin' around the country."

"Come back when the hills dry off," Watts said. "We'll go lookin' for some of them round rocks all sparkly inside."

I thought a moment. "Geodes?"

"Them's the ones. The country's properly full of them." ❖

12. **offen the ridge.** Watts means from beyond his community on the ridge.

"It's the doin' that's important." What exactly does this statement mean? How might someone "become what he does"? And if that's true, what effect would this have on how people choose to spend their time?

Refer and Reason

1. Write down what Madison Wheeler values and finds satisfaction in and what the Watts value. Compare and contrast these values.
2. The author claims that "being alone on the road makes you ready to meet someone when you stop. You get sociable traveling alone." Evaluate the truth of this statement and judge to what extent living away from people has affected rural dwellers' sociability.
3. Madison Wheeler says that people are retiring to the "hollers," but the young people are leaving. Why do you think they are leaving? Explain what effect their departure will have on the region.

Writing Options

1. Many of the people whom Least Heat-Moon encounters show concern for his safety. Write a safety manual for people who wish to travel cross-country and combine your own advice with the advice of Least Heat-Moon.
2. Write a summary of what Least Heat-Moon learned from his search for and visit to Nameless, Tennessee.

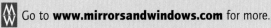

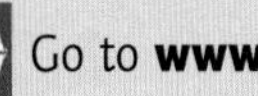
Go to **www.mirrorsandwindows.com** for more.

Journey

A Short Story by
Joyce Carol Oates

Joyce Carol Oates (b. 1938) is a prolific writer whose works include novels, short-story collections, plays, children's books, criticism, essays, and poetry collections. Of her work Oates states, "Writing and teaching have always been, for me, so richly rewarding that I don't think of them as work in the usual sense of the word."

In **"Journey,"** which was first published in *The Poisoned Kiss and Other Stories* in 1975, Joyce Carol Oates talks directly to the reader about the paths we take in life and the choices we make on our way to individuality. Oates shows that rarely do we follow a straight path to our future goals. Instead, life offers us many opportunities to take detours and make changes. As you read, think about your goals and expectations for your own life.

What choices do you make on a daily basis? Which are the most rewarding?

You begin your journey on so high an elevation that your destination is already in sight—a city that you have visited many times and that, moreover, is indicated on a traveler's map you have carefully folded up to take along with you. You are a lover of maps, and you have already committed this map to memory, but you bring it with you just the same.

The highway down from the mountains is broad and handsome, constructed after many years of ingenious blasting and leveling and paving. Engineers from all over the country aided in the construction of this famous highway. Its cost is so excessive that many rumors have circulated about it—you take no interest in such things, sensing that you will never learn the true cost anyway, and that this will make no difference to your journey.

After several hours on this excellent highway, where the sun shines ceaselessly and where there is a moderate amount of traffic, cars like your own at a safe distance from you, as if to assure you that there are other people in the world, you become sleepy from the monotony and wonder if perhaps there is another, less perfect road parallel to this. You discover on the map a smaller road, not exactly parallel to the highway and not as direct, but one that leads to the same city.

You turn onto this road, which winds among foothills and forests and goes through several small villages. You sense by the attitude of the villagers that traffic on this road is infrequent but nothing to draw special attention. At some curves the road shrinks, but you are fortunate enough to meet no oncoming traffic.

The road leads deep into a forest, always descending in small cramped turns. Your turning from left to right and from right to left, in a slow hypnotic passage, makes it impossible for you to look out at the forest and discover that for some time you have not been able to see the city you are headed for, though you know it is still somewhere ahead of you.

By mid-afternoon you are tired of this road, though it has served you well, and you come upon a smaller, unpaved road that evidently leads to your city, though in a convoluted way. After only a moment's pause you turn onto this road, and immediately your automobile registers the change, the chassis[1] bounces, something begins to vibrate, something begins to rattle. This noise is disturbing, but after a while you forget about it in your interest in the beautiful countryside. Here the trees are enormous. There are no villages or houses. For a while the dirt road runs alongside a small river, dangerously close to the river's steep bank, and you begin to feel apprehension. It is necessary for you to drive very slowly. At times your speedometer registers less than five miles an hour. You will not get to the city before dark.

The road narrows until it is hardly more than a lane. Grass has begun to grow in its center. As the river twists and turns, so does the road twist and turn, curving around hills that consist of enormous boulders, bare of all trees and plants, covered only in patches by a dull, brown lichen[2] that is unfamiliar to you. Along one stretch rocks of varying sizes have fallen down onto the road, so that you are forced to drive around them with great caution.

Navigating these blind turns, you tap your horn to give warning in case someone should be approaching. But it is all unnecessary, since you come upon no other travelers. Late in the afternoon, your foot numb from its constant pressure on the accelerator, your body jolted by the constant bumps and vibrations of the car, you decide to make the rest of your journey on foot, since you must be close to your destination by now.

A faint path leads through a tumble of rocks and bushes and trees, and you follow it enthusiastically. You descend a hill, slipping a little, so that a small rock slide is released; but you are able to keep your balance. At the back of your head is the precise location of your parked car, and behind that the curving dirt road, and behind that the other road, and the magnificent highway itself; you understand that it would be no difficult feat to make your way back to any of these roads, should you decide that going by foot is unwise. But the path, though overgrown, is through a lovely forest, and then through a meadow in which yellow flowers are blooming, and you feel no inclination to turn back.

By evening you are still in the wilderness and you wonder if perhaps you have made a mistake. You are exhausted, your body aches, your eyes are seared[3] by the need to stare so intently at everything around you. Now that the sun has nearly set, it is getting cold; evenings here in the mountains are always chilly.

You find yourself standing at the edge of a forest, staring ahead into the dark. Is that a field ahead, or a forest of small trees? Your path has long since given way to wild grass. Clouds obscure the moon, which should give you some light by which to make your way and you wonder if you dare continue without this light.

Suddenly you remember the map you left back in the car, but you remember it as a blank sheet of paper.

You resist telling yourself you are lost. In fact, though you are exhausted and it is almost night, you are not lost. You have begun to shiver, but it is only with cold, not with fear. You are really satisfied with yourself. You are not lost. Though you can remember your map only as a blank sheet of paper, which can tell you nothing, you are not really lost.

If you had the day to begin again, on that highway which was so wide and clear, you would not have varied your journey in any way: in this is your triumph. ❖

1. **chassis.** Frame and working parts of a car, exclusive of the body
2. **lichen.** Fungus and algae that form a scaly or spongelike growth on rocks or trees
3. **seared.** Dried up; shriveled; burned

"...[Y]ou would not have varied your journey in any way: in this is your triumph." During moments of uncertainty, what qualities are needed to be triumphant? What qualities might hinder success?

Literature CONNECTION

OLIVER

Mary Oliver (b. 1935) writes poetry that reflects a deep communion with the natural world. She published her first collection of poems, *No Voyage, and Other Poems,* in 1963 and continued to write many other collections of poetry and prose. Awarded Guggenheim and National Endowment for the Arts grants, Oliver won a Pulitzer Prize with her collection *American Primitive* (1983). Oliver has also written books about reading and writing poetry, such as *A Poetry Handbook,* published in 1994. **"The Journey"** was published in Oliver's poetry collection *Dream Work* in 1996.

The Journey

A Poem by **Mary Oliver**

One day you finally knew
what you had to do, and began,
though the voices around you
kept shouting
their bad advice—
though the whole house
began to tremble
and you felt the old tug
at your ankles.
"Mend my life!"
each voice cried.
But you didn't stop.
You knew what you had to do,
though the wind pried
with its stiff fingers
at the very foundations—
though their melancholy
was terrible.

It was already late
enough, and a wild night,
and the road full of fallen
branches and stones.
But little by little,
as you left their voices behind,
the stars began to burn
through the sheets of clouds,
and there was a new voice,
which you slowly
recognized as your own,
that kept you company
as you strode deeper and deeper
into the world,
determined to do
the only thing you could do—
determined to save
the only life you could save. ❖

Refer and Reason

1. Break down the journey described in "Journey" into four stages. What allegorical meanings do the changing roads have? Does the journey within Oliver's poem belong in any of these stages? Explain.
2. In the beginning of the story, "You are a lover of maps." What does it mean when you are well into your journey and you see the map "as a blank sheet of paper"? Judge whether that is a positive change.
3. Identify differences and similarities between the kinds of journeys represented in these two selections. Classify each journey as an inward or outward journey and explain your reasoning.

Writing Options

1. Imagine you are the person described in "Journey." Write several brief entries for your travel journal. In each entry, describe the environment around you, including a variety of sensory details, and explain how and why you decide on your course.
2. What might the setting of this short story represent? Consider the sights, smells, and any other sensory details that are provided. Using these details, write a two-paragraph setting analysis for "Journey."

Go to **www.mirrorsandwindows.com** for more.

TEXT ←TO→ TEXT CONNECTION

Compare and contrast how Joyce Carol Oates and Mary Oliver depict independence and individuality. What imagery do they use to portray fears, self-doubt, choices, and the triumphant realization of self?

NEW DIRECTIONS

Women working in a southern sawmill.

"I LOOKED UP THE ROAD I WAS GOING AND BACK THE WAY I COME, AND SINCE I WASN'T SATISFIED, I DECIDED TO STEP OFF THE ROAD AND CUT ME A NEW PATH."

An Essay by **Maya Angelou**

In 1903 the late Mrs. Annie Johnson of Arkansas found herself with two toddling sons, very little money, a slight ability to read and add simple numbers. To this picture add a disastrous marriage and the burdensome fact that Mrs. Johnson was a Negro.

When she told her husband, Mr. William Johnson, of her dissatisfaction with their marriage, he conceded that he too found it to be less than he expected, and had been secretly hoping to leave and study religion. He added that he thought God was calling him not only to preach but to do so in Enid, Oklahoma. He did not tell her that he knew a minister in Enid with whom he could study and who had a friendly, unmarried daughter. They parted amicably, Annie keeping the one-room house and William taking most of the cash to carry himself to Oklahoma.

Annie, over six feet tall, big-boned, decided that she would not go to work as a domestic and leave her "precious babes" to anyone else's care. There was no possibility of being hired at the town's cotton gin or lumber mill, but maybe there was a way to make the two

Maya Angelou (b. 1928) was born Marguerite Johnson in St. Louis, Missouri. Throughout her life, she has had many professions, including poet, dramatist, actor, editor, and San Francisco cable car conductor—the first African American to do so. A friend of both Martin Luther King Jr. and Malcolm X, she is also a civil rights activist.

Like the speaker in "The Road Not Taken (page 856)," Mrs. Annie Johnson in **"New Directions"** has to choose a path. The essay was published in the collection *Wouldn't Take Nothing for My Journey Now.*

Are you able to see where you're headed in life? In what ways could you "step off the road"?

Critical Viewing

Based on this photograph, what reasons might Miss Annie Johnson have had for deciding to find a different job?

Workers outside a cotton gin, circa 1879.

factories work for her. In her words, "I looked up the road I was going and back the way I come, and since I wasn't satisfied, I decided to step off the road and cut me a new path." She told herself that she wasn't a fancy cook but that she could "mix groceries well enough to scare hungry away and from starving a man."

She made her plans meticulously and in secret. One early evening to see if she was ready, she placed stones in two five-gallon pails and carried them three miles to the cotton gin. She rested a little, and then, discarding some rocks, she walked in the darkness to the saw mill five miles farther along the dirt road. On her way back to her little house and her babies, she dumped the remaining rocks along the path.

That same night she worked into the early hours boiling chicken and frying ham. She made dough and filled the rolled-out pastry with meat. At last she went to sleep.

The next morning she left her house carrying the meat pies, lard, an iron brazier,[1] and coals for a fire. Just before lunch she appeared in an empty lot behind the cotton gin. As the dinner noon bell rang, she dropped the savors into boiling fat and the aroma rose and floated over to the workers who spilled out of the gin, covered with white lint, looking like specters.

Most workers had brought their lunches of pinto beans and biscuits or crackers, onions and cans of sardines, but they were tempted by the hot meat pies which Annie ladled out of the fat. She wrapped them in newspapers, which soaked up the grease, and offered them for sale at a nickel each. Although business was slow, those first days Annie was determined. She balanced her appearances between the two hours of activity.

So, on Monday if she offered hot fresh pies at the cotton gin and sold the remaining cooled-down pies at the lumber mill for three cents, then on Tuesday she went first to the lumber mill presenting fresh, just-cooked pies as the lumbermen covered in sawdust emerged from the mill.

For the next few years, on balmy spring days, blistering summer noons, and cold, wet, and wintry middays, Annie never disappointed her customers, who could count on seeing the tall, brown-skin woman bent over her brazier, carefully turning the meat pies. When she felt certain that the workers had become dependent on her, she built a stall between the two hives of industry and let the men run to her for their lunchtime provisions.She had indeed stepped from the road which seemed to have been chosen for her and cut herself a brand-new path. In years that stall became a store where customers could buy cheese, meal, syrup, cookies, candy, writing tablets, pickles, canned goods, fresh fruit, soft drinks, coal, oil, and leather soles for worn-out shoes.

Each of us has the right and the responsibility to assess the roads which lie ahead, and those over which we have traveled, and if the future road looms ominous or unpromising, and the roads back uninviting, then we need to gather our resolve and, carrying only the necessary baggage, step off that road into another direction. If the new choice is also unpalatable, without embarrassment, we must be ready to change that as well. ❖

1. **brazier.** A pan for holding burning coals, allows food to be exposed to heat through a wire grill

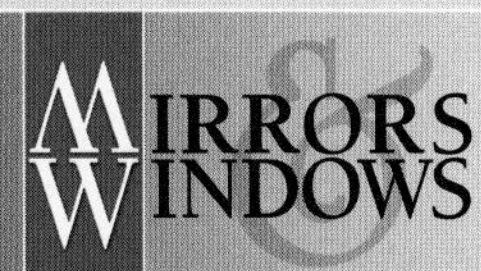

What does the ability to create a "new path" imply about a person? The essay states that if the new path "is also unpalatable, without embarrassment, we must be ready to change that as well." How is creating a new path similar to perseverance?

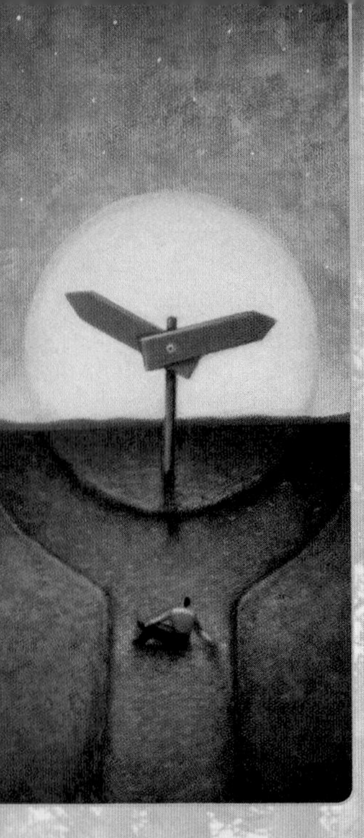

Literature
CONNECTION

Robert Frost (1874–1963) was born in San Francisco, but as a child moved to New England. He attended Dartmouth and Harvard but didn't finish a degree. Nevertheless, Frost has been honored with four Pulitzers and in 1961 was invited to read a poem at President Kennedy's inauguration. In **"The Road Not Taken,"** the speaker contemplates the choice he must make about the different roads before him while on a walk in the woods. Many people read the poem as one that celebrates individualism. Frost himself noted, "It's a trick poem—very tricky." "The Road Not Taken" was published in *Mountain Intervals,* one of Frost's many collections.

THE ROAD NOT TAKEN

A Poem by **Robert Frost**

Two roads diverged in a yellow wood,
And sorry I could not travel both
And be one traveler, long I stood
And looked down one as far as I could
To where it bent in the undergrowth;

Then took the other, as just as fair,
And having perhaps the better claim,
Because it was grassy and wanted wear;
Though as for that, the passing there
Had worn them really about the same,

And both that morning equally lay
In leaves no step had trodden black.
Oh, I kept the first for another day!
Yet knowing how way leads on to way,
I doubted if I should ever come back.

I shall be telling this with a sigh
Somewhere ages and ages hence:
Two roads diverged in a wood, and I—
I took the one less traveled by,
And that has made all the difference. ❖

Refer and Reason

1. What is the speaker of "The Road Not Taken" sorry about in line 2? What does the speaker wish that he or she could do in life?
2. Predict what kind of life Annie in "New Directions" would have likely led if she hadn't "cut herself a brand-new path." Explain your reasoning.
3. If you were to write a moral for "New Directions," what would it be? In what way can the story of Annie Johnson serve as an example for others?

Writing Options

1. Imagine you are Annie and are trying to get a loan from the bank. Write a business letter to support your application. Describe your plan for the store and how you would make it a success. Use proper business letter format for your letter.
2. Imagine you are going to speak at a symposium on Robert Frost for high school students. Write a summary of your key points on the significance of the choice made in "The Road Not Taken."

Go to **www.mirrorsandwindows.com** for more.

TEXT TO TEXT CONNECTION

The speaker in "The Road Not Taken" decides on the road "less traveled by." Annie from "New Directions" cuts her own path. How do you think they each came to the decision they did? Compare the way the speaker and Annie react to their decisions. How are each of their options similar and how are they different?

THE ROAD and the End

A Poem by **Carl Sandburg**

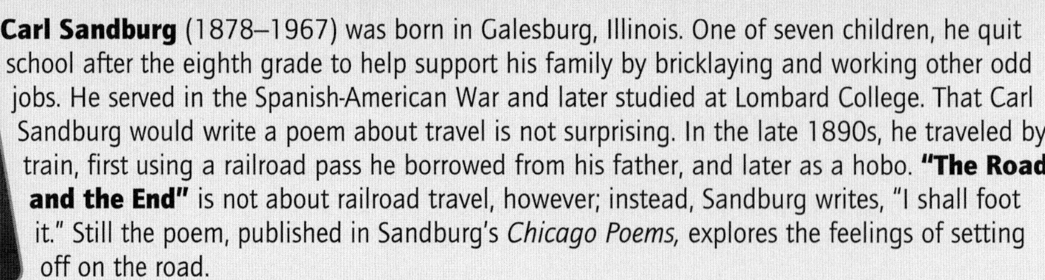

Carl Sandburg (1878–1967) was born in Galesburg, Illinois. One of seven children, he quit school after the eighth grade to help support his family by bricklaying and working other odd jobs. He served in the Spanish-American War and later studied at Lombard College. That Carl Sandburg would write a poem about travel is not surprising. In the late 1890s, he traveled by train, first using a railroad pass he borrowed from his father, and later as a hobo. **"The Road and the End"** is not about railroad travel, however; instead, Sandburg writes, "I shall foot it." Still the poem, published in Sandburg's *Chicago Poems*, explores the feelings of setting off on the road.

What do you notice most when you travel from place to place?

Untitled from the *Seen and Not Seen* series. Ken Rosenthal.

I shall foot it
Down the roadway in the dusk,
Where shapes of hunger wander
And the fugitives of pain go by.
I shall foot it
In the silence of the morning,
See the night slur into dawn,
Hear the slow great winds arise
Where tall trees flank the way
And shoulder toward the sky.

The broken boulders by the road
Shall not commemorate[1] my ruin.
Regret shall be the gravel under foot.
I shall watch for
Slim birds swift of wing
That go where wind and ranks of thunder
Drive the wild processionals of rain.

The dust of the traveled road
Shall touch my hands and face. ❖

1. **commemorate.** Serve as a memorial, to remember

"The dust of the traveled road / Shall touch my hands and face." What remains when a journey is completed? What do journeys provide to the traveler?

Refer and Reason

1. How does the speaker appear to regard regret? Visualize the setting and analyze the mood of the poem. What details create this mood?
2. Think about other poems or stories in which the road is symbolic. Assess whether the road in this poem is symbolic. Explain your answer.
3. Compare the speaker's thoughts on travel to the thoughts of another author you've read about in this unit.

Writing Options

1. Write a stanza or two of a poem about walking on a road you have traveled before. What would you notice as you walked on this road? How would you feel? Your poem may have symbolic meaning, or it may simply capture the time and place.
2. Write a symbolism analysis on "The Road and the End" in which you examine Sandburg's use of symbolism within the poem. Be prepared to present your findings to your classmates.

Go to **www.mirrorsandwindows.com** for more.

READING INDEPENDENTLY

Theme: Visions of the Future

"And I see something even beyond this. It may be fantastic now, a mere dream..."

—Isaac Asimov,
from "The Feeling of Power"

When you think of the future, do you feel afraid or hopeful? Many writers have contemplated the future of humanity in light of advances in technology and political conflicts between nations. For such writers, the future holds grim promise, unless humans change their ways. Other writers may take a more optimistic view of the future, believing that technology will allow people to do amazing things. The stories in this section could be read as either a warning or a promise.

USE READING SKILLS

When you read independently, you use various reading skills without thinking about it. Each of these excerpts from "A Sound of Thunder" by Ray Bradbury (page 882) are followed by a model for applying the reading skills you have practiced in Units 1–5.

> A warm phlegm gathered in Eckels's throat; he swallowed and pushed it down. The muscles around his mouth formed a smile as he put his hand slowly out upon the air, and in that hand waved a check for ten thousand dollars to the man behind the desk.
>
> "Does this safari guarantee I come back alive?"

- **Determine Author's Approach:** The story is told from the third-person limited point of view, meaning that we're able to see things from Eckels's perspective. This helps us experience what he experiences and to understand his feelings.

> Eckels glanced across the vast office at a mass and tangle, a snaking and humming of wires and steel boxes, at an aurora that flickered now orange, now silver, now blue. There was a sound like a gigantic bonfire burning all of Time, all the years and all the parchment calendars, all the hours piled high and set aflame.

- **Determine Importance of Details:** The description of what Eckels sees here shows that he is in the presence of a powerful machine. The description emphasizes that not only is the object difficult to comprehend, but it's unlike anything with which Eckels is familiar.

> The Machine howled. Time was a film run backward. Suns fled and ten million moons fled after them. "Think," said Eckels. "Every hunter that ever lived would envy us today. This makes Africa seem like Illinois."

- **Compare and Contrast:** Eckels is making a comparison between Africa and Illinois. His point being that hunting in another time period will be a much greater feat than any kind of hunting he has experienced before. This comparison implies that their hunting ground will be extremely dangerous and exciting.

> "We don't want to change the Future. We don't belong here in the Past. The government doesn't *like* us here. We have to pay big graft to keep our franchise."

- **Use Context Clues:** From this short section, I can tell by the clues that the word *graft* means taxes or bribes. This means that the Time Machine owners are paying off the government so they aren't prevented from running their business. This also implies that, since the government is uncomfortable with the business, traveling through time is dangerous.

> "A Time Machine is finicky business. Not knowing it, we might kill an important animal, a small bird, a roach, a flower even, thus destroying an important link in a growing species."

- **Determine Author's Purpose:** It seems here that the author is warning his readers to respect technology and is also advising them to avoid playing with things that they don't understand completely.

> "Destroy this one man, and you destroy a race, a people, an entire history of life.... The stomp of your foot, on one mouse, could start an earthquake, the effects of which could shake our earth and destinies down through Time, to their very foundations."

- **Find the Main Idea:** I think the main idea of this story is that one creature, no matter how small and seemingly insignificant, can affect many things.

> "Who knows? Who really can say he knows? We don't know. We're guessing. But until we do know for certain whether our messing around in Time *can* make a big roar or a little rustle in history, we're being careful."

- **Draw Conclusions:** I come to the conclusion that the time travelers will discover the answer to this question.

What Good Readers Do

Code the Text

Taking notes is a helpful tool for reading. You may agree or disagree with a selection or an idea, really enjoy or dislike the text, or you may not understand something and decide to reread it later. Instead of writing short responses to each selection, use a symbol or short word to indicate your reactions. Use codes like the ones listed below.

+	I like this.
–	I don't like this.
√	This is important.
Yes	I agree with this.
No	I disagree with this.
?	I don't understand this.
!	This is like something I know.
_	I need to come back to this later.

All Watched Over by Machines of Loving Grace

A Poem by **Richard Brautigan**

I like to think (and
the sooner the better!)
of a cybernetic[1] meadow
where mammals and computers
live together in mutually
programming harmony
like pure water
touching clear sky.

I like to think
(right now, please!)
of a cybernetic forest
filled with pines and electronics
where deer stroll peacefully
past computers
as if they were flowers
with spinning blossoms.

I like to think
(it has to be!)
of a cybernetic ecology
where we are free of our labors
and joined back to nature,
returned to our mammal
brothers and sisters,
and all watched over
by machines of loving grace. ❖

1. **cybernetic.** Relating to cybernetics, the comparative study of the control and communication systems of humans and electronics

Richard Brautigan (1935–1984) is best known for his first novel, *Trout Fishing in America,* a darkly humorous work that explores the deterioration of both the American landscape and its populace. Brautigan began his career by writing poetry, and he continued to write poetry throughout his life. He once said, "I wrote poetry for seven years to learn how to write a sentence because I really wanted to write novels and I figured that I couldn't write a novel until I could write a sentence." His poem, **"All Watched Over by Machines of Loving Grace,"** refers to an imagined cybernetic world where people and machines live side by side. As you read, consider how the speaker of this poem views the role of machines in our society.

Do you trust technology? Do you think the advancement of technology will help mankind?

Why was technology created? Might mankind prefer to return to nature? What would be the benefits? Would people ever allow themselves to be cared for by something other than another human?

Refer and Reason

1. Scan the visual images in the art that accompanies this poem. Identify how they help to illustrate the speaker's vision of a cybernetic ecology.
2. Evaluate whether there is any truth to the speaker's vision of a "cybernetic ecology" in today's society. Do computers and other technology have any power over mankind? Do they have the potential to reduce humans to the same level as other mammals? Why or why not?
3. Imagine that someone tried to create Brautigan's cybernetic ecology by placing a lot of computers throughout a forest. Propose how society would react. How might it affect plants and animals?

Writing Options

1. Choose a machine that you use often. Write a simile that describes it from the perspective of the speaker in "All Watched Over by Machines of Loving Grace." A simile is a comparison of two unlike objects using *like* or *as*.
2. What ideas about technology are expressed in this poem? Do you agree with these ideas? Write a two- to three-paragraph persuasive essay in which you argue for or against the speaker's beliefs.

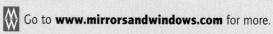

Go to **www.mirrorsandwindows.com** for more.

MINISTER WITHOUT PORTFOLIO

A Short Story by
Mildred Clingerman

GEOGRAPHY HAD ALWAYS BEEN HER WEAK POINT.

Mrs. Chriswell's little roadster came to a shuddering halt. Here was the perfect spot. Only one sagging wire fence to step over and not a cow in sight. Mrs. Chriswell was terrified of cows, and if the truth were told, only a little less afraid of her daughter-in-law Clara. It was all Clara's idea that her mother-in-law should now be lurking in meadows peering at birds. Clara had been delighted with the birdwatching idea, but frankly, Mrs. Chriswell was bored with birds. They *flew* so much. And as for their colours,[1] it was useless for her to speculate. Mrs. Chriswell was one of those rare women who are quite, quite colour-blind.

"But, Clara," Mrs. Chriswell had pleaded, "what's the point if I can't tell what colour they are?"

1. **colours.** British spelling for "colors"

Mildred Clingerman (1918–1997) published many science fiction and fantasy stories in magazines such as *Harper's* and *Collier's* as well as in anthologies. In this short story, **"Minister Without Portfolio,"** Clingerman writes about an elderly woman's encounter with men from outer space. The main character's innocent and trusting view of the world, combined with her color blindness, make for a far different encounter than one might expect. The author uses *dramatic irony,* in which something is known by the reader or audience but unknown to the characters, to make this an amusing science fiction tale. "Minister Without Portfolio" was first published in 1952 and was also included in her short-story collection *A Cupful of Space* (1960).

How do you interact with strangers? Think about the kinds of strangers to whom you would feel most comfortable talking.

"Well, but, darling," Clara had said crisply, "how much cleverer if you get to know them just from the distinctive markings!"

Mrs. Chriswell, sighing a little as she recalled the firm look of Clara's chin, manoeuvred[2] herself and her burdens over the sagging wire fence. She successfully juggled the binoculars, the heavy bird book, and her purse, and thought how ghastly it was at sixty to be considered so useless that she must be provided with harmless occupations to keep her out of the way.

Since Mr. Chriswell's death she had moved in with her son and his wife to face a life of enforced idleness. The servants resented her presence in the kitchen, so cooking was out. Clara and the snooty nursemaid would brook no interference with the nursery routine, so Mrs. Chriswell had virtually nothing to do. Even her crocheted doilies[3] disappeared magically soon after their presentation to Clara and the modern furniture.

Mrs. Chriswell shifted the heavy bird book and considered rebelling. The sun was hot and her load was heavy. As she toiled on across the field she thought she saw the glint of sun on water. She would sit and crochet in the shade nearby and remove the big straw cartwheel hat Clara termed "just the thing."

Arrived at the trees, Mrs. Chriswell dropped her burdens and flung the hat willy-nilly. Ugly, ridiculous thing. She glanced around for the water she thought she'd seen, but there was no sign of it. She leaned back against a tree trunk and sighed blissfully. A little breeze had sprung up and was cooling the damp tendrils on her forehead. She opened her big purse and scrambled through the muddle of contents for her crochet hook and the ball of thread attached to a half-finished doily. In her search she came across the snapshots of her granddaughters—in colour, they were, but unfortunately Mrs. Chriswell saw them only in various shades of grey. The breeze was getting stronger now, very pleasant, but the dratted old cartwheel monstrosity was rolling merrily down the slight grade to the tangle of berry bushes a few yards away. Well, it would catch on the brambles. But it didn't. The wind flirted it right around the bushes, and the hat disappeared.

"Fiddle!" Mrs. Chriswell dared not face Clara without the hat. Still hanging on to the bulky purse, she got up to give chase. Rounding the tangle of bushes, she ran smack into a tall young man in uniform.

"Oh!" Mrs. Chriswell said. "Have you seen my hat?"

The young man smiled and pointed on down the hill. Mrs. Chriswell was surprised to see her hat being passed from hand to hand among three other tall young men in uniform. They were laughing at it, and she didn't much blame them. They were standing beside a low, silvery aircraft of some unusual design. Mrs. Chriswell studied it a moment, but, really, she knew nothing about such things.... The sun glinted off it, and she realized this was what she had thought was water. The young man beside her touched her arm. She turned towards him and saw that he had put a rather lovely little metal hat on his head. He offered her one with grave courtesy. Mrs. Chriswell smiled up at him and nodded. The young man fitted the hat carefully, adjusting various little ornamental knobs on the top of it.

"Now we can talk," he said. "Do you hear well?"

"My dear boy," Mrs. Chriswell said, "of course I do. I'm not so old as all that." She found a smooth stone and sat down to chat. This was much nicer than birdwatching, or even crochet.

The tall young man grinned and signalled excitedly to his companions. They too put on little metal hats and came bounding up the hill. Still laughing, they deposited the cartwheel in Mrs. Chriswell's lap. She patted the stone by

2. **manoeuvred.** British spelling of "maneuvered"

3. **doilies.** Small ornamental mats made of cotton or linen that are placed beneath dishes or bowls

like one note from the Harmony Hills of home!" He passed the handkerchief all around the circle, and the young men sniffed at it and smiled.

Mrs. Chriswell tried to remember if she had ever read of the Harmony Hills, but Mr. Chriswell had always told her she was lamentably weak in geography, and she supposed that this was one of her blank spots, like where on earth was Timbuktu? Or the Hellandgone people were always talking about? But it was rude not to make some comment. Wars shifted people about such a lot, and these boys must be homesick and weary of being strangers, longing to talk of home. She was proud of herself for realizing that they were strangers. But there was something.... Hard to say, really. The way they had bounded up the hill? Mountain people, perhaps, to whom hills were mere springboards to heights beyond.

"Tell me about your hills," she said.

"Wait," Jord said. "I will show you." He glanced at his leader as if for approval. The young man who had fitted her hat nodded. Jord drew a fingernail across the breast of his uniform. Mrs. Chriswell was surprised to see a pocket opening where no pocket had been before. Really, the Air Force did amazing things with its uniforms, though, frankly, Mrs. Chriswell thought the cut of these a bit extreme.

Carefully, Jord was lifting out a packet of gossamer material. He gently pressed the centre[4] of the packet and it blossomed out into voluminous clouds of featherweight threads, held loosely together in a wave like a giant spider web. To Mrs. Chriswell's eyes the mesh of threads was the colour of fog, and almost as insubstantial.

way of invitation, and the youngest looking one of the four dropped down beside her.

"What is your name, Mother?" he asked.

"Ida Chriswell," she said. "What's yours?"

"My name is Jord," the boy said.

Mrs. Chriswell patted his hand. "That's a nice, unusual name." The boy grabbed Mrs. Chriswell's hand and rubbed it against the smoothness of his cheek.

"You are like my Mother's Mother," the boy explained, "whom I have not seen in too long." The other young men laughed, and the boy looked abashed and stealthily wiped with his hands at a tear that slid down his nose.

Mrs. Chriswell frowned warningly at the laughter and handed him her clean pocket handkerchief, scented with lavender. Jord turned it over and over in his hands, and then tentatively sniffed at it.

"It's all right," Mrs. Chriswell said. "Use it. I have another." But Jord only breathed more deeply of the faint perfume in its fold.

"This is only the thinnest thread of melody," he said, "but, Mother Ida, it is very

4. **centre.** British spelling of "center"

"Do not be afraid," Jord said softly, stepping closer to her. "Bend your head, close your eyes, and you shall hear the lovely Harmony Hills of home."

There was one quick-drawn breath of almost-fear, but before she shut her eyes Mrs. Chriswell saw the love in Jord's, and in that moment she knew how rarely she had seen this look, anywhere...anytime. If Jord had asked it of her, it was all right. She closed her eyes and bowed her head, and in that attitude of prayer she felt a soft weightlessness descend upon her. It was as if twilight had come down to drape itself on her shoulders. And then the music began. Behind the darkness of her eyes it rose in majesty and power, in colours she had never seen, never guessed. It blossomed like flowers—giant forests of them. Their scents were intoxicating and filled her with joy. She could not tell if the blending perfumes made the music, or if the music itself created the flowers and the perfumes that poured forth from them. She did not care. She wanted only to go on forever listening to all this colour. It seemed odd to be listening to colour, perhaps, but after all, she told herself, it would seem just as odd to me to *see* it.

She sat blinking at the circle of young men. The music was finished. Jord was putting away the gossamer threads in the secret pocket, and laughing aloud at her astonishment.

"Did you like it, Mother Ida?" he dropped down beside her again and patted her wrinkled face, still pink with excitement.

"Oh, Jord," she said, "how lovely...Tell me..."

But the leader was calling them all to order. "I'm sorry, Mother Ida, we must hurry about our business. Will you answer some questions? It is very important."

"Of course," Mrs. Chriswell said. She was still feeling a bit dazed.

"If I can...If it's like the quizzes on the TV, though, I'm not very good at it."

The young man shook his head. "We," he said, "have been instructed to investigate and report on the true conditions of this...of the world." He pointed at the aircraft glittering in the sunlight. "We have travelled all around in that slow machine, and our observations have been accurate...." He hesitated, drew a deep breath and continued. "...and perhaps we shall be forced to give an unfavourable[5] report, but this depends a great deal on the outcome of our talk with you. We are glad you stumbled upon us. We were about to set out on a foray[6] to secure some individual for questioning. It is our last task." He smiled. "And Jord, here, will not be sorry. He is sick for home and loved ones." He sighed, and all the other young men echoed the sigh.

"Every night," Mrs. Chriswell said, "I pray for peace on earth. I cannot bear to think of boys like you fighting and dying, and the folks at home waiting and waiting..." She glanced all around at their listening faces. "And I'll tell you something else," she said, "I find I can't really hate anybody, even the enemy." Around the circle the young men nodded at each other. "Now ask me your questions." She fumbled in her purse for her crochet work and found it.

Beside her Jord exclaimed with pleasure at the sight of the half-finished doily. Mrs. Chriswell warmed to him even more.

The tall young man began his grave questioning. They were very simple questions, and Mrs. Chriswell answered them without hesitation. Did she believe in God? Did she believe in the dignity of man? Did she truly abhor war? Did she believe that man was capable of love for his neighbour?[7] The questions went on and on, and Mrs. Chriswell crocheted while she gave her answers.

At last, when the young man had quite run out of questions, and Mrs. Chriswell had

5. **unfavourable.** British spelling of "unfavorable"
6. **foray.** Brief excursion; invasion; raid
7. **neighbour.** British spelling of "neighbor"

finished the doily, Jord broke the sun-lazy silence that had fallen upon them.

"May I have it, Mother?" He pointed to the doily. Mrs. Chriswell bestowed it upon him with great pleasure, and Jord, like a very small boy, stuffed it greedily into another secret pocket. He pointed at her stuffed purse.

"May I look, Mother?"

Mrs. Chriswell indulgently passed him her purse. He opened it and poured the litter of contents on the ground between them. The snapshots of Mrs. Chriswell's grandchildren stared up at him. Jord smiled at the pretty little-girl faces. He groped in the chest pocket and drew out snapshots of his own. "These," he told Mrs. Chriswell proudly, "are my little sisters. Are they not like these little girls of yours? Let us exchange, because soon I will be at home with them, and there will be no need for pictures. I would like to have yours."

Mrs. Chriswell would have given Jord the entire contents of the purse if he had asked for them. She took the snapshots he offered and looked with pleasure at the sweet-faced children. Jord still stirred at the pile of possessions from Mrs. Chriswell's purse. By the time she was ready to leave he had talked her out of three illustrated recipes torn from magazines, some swatches of material, and two pieces of peppermint candy.

The young man who was the leader helped her to remove the pretty little hat when Mrs. Chriswell indicated he should. She would have liked to keep it, but she didn't believe Clara would approve. She clapped the straw monstrosity on her head, kissed Jord's cheek, waved goodbye to the rest, and groped her way around the berry bushes. She had to grope because her eyes were tear-filled. They had saluted her so grandly as she left.

Clara's usually sedate household was in an uproar when Mrs. Chriswell returned. All the radios in the house were blaring. Even Clara sat huddled over the one in the library. Mrs. Chriswell heard a boy in the street crying

"EXTRA! EXTRA!"[8] and the upstairs maid almost knocked her down getting out the front door to buy one. Mrs. Chriswell, sleepy and somewhat sunburned, supposed it was something about the awful war.

She was just turning up the stairs to her room when the snooty nursemaid came rushing down to disappear kitchenwards with another newspaper in her hand. Good, the children were alone. She'd stop in to see them. Suddenly she heard the raised voices from the back of the house. The cook was yelling at somebody. "I tell you, I saw it! I took out some garbage and there it was, right over me!" Mrs. Chriswell lingered at the foot of the stairway puzzled by all the confusion. The housemaid came rushing in with the extra edition. Mrs. Chriswell quietly reached out and took it. "Thank you, Nadine," she said. The nursemaid was still staring at her as she climbed the stairs.

Edna and Evelyn were sitting on the nursery floor, a candy box between them, and shrieking at each other when their grandmother opened the door. They were cramming chocolates into their mouths between shrieks. Their faces and pinafores[9] were smeared with the candy. Edna suddenly yanked Evelyn's hair, hard. "Pig!" she shouted. "You got three more than I did!"

8. **"EXTRA! EXTRA!"** A call announcing an additional edition of a newspaper.

9. **pinafores.** Sleeveless dresses that resemble aprons; used to protect other clothing

"Children! Children! Not fighting?" Mrs. Chriswell was delighted. Here was something she could cope with. She led them firmly to the bathroom and washed their faces. "Change your frocks," she said, "and I'll tell you my adventure."

There were only hissing accusals and whispered countercharges behind her as she turned her back on the children to scan the newspaper. The headlines leapt up at her.

Mysterious broadcast interrupts programmes[10] *on all wave lengths*

Unknown woman saves world, say men from space

One sane human found on earth

Cooking, needlework, home, religious interests sway space judges

Every column of the paper was crowded with the same unintelligible nonsense. Mrs. Chriswell folded it neatly, deposited it on the table, and turned to tie her granddaughters' sashes and tell her adventure.

"...And then he gave me some lovely photographs. In colour, he said...Good little girls, just like Edna and Evelyn. Would you like to see them?"

Edna made a rude noise with her mouth pursed. Evelyn's face grew saintlike in retaliation. "Yes, show us," she said.

Mrs. Chriswell passed them the snapshots, and the children drew close together for the moment before Evelyn dropped the pictures as if they were blazing. She stared hard at her grandmother while Edna made a gagging noise.

"Green!" Edna gurgled. "Gaaa...green skins!"

"Grandmother!" Evelyn was tearful. "Those children are frog-coloured!"

Mrs. Chriswell bent over to pick up the pictures. "Now, now, children," she murmured absently. "We don't worry about the colour of people's skins. Red...yellow...black...we're all God's children. Asia or Africa, makes no difference..." But before she could finish her thought, the nursemaid loomed disapprovingly in the doorway. Mrs. Chriswell hurried out to her own room, while some tiny worry nagged at her mind. "Red, yellow, black, white," she murmured over and over, "and brown...but green...?" Geography had always been her weak point. Green...Now where on earth...? ❖

10. **programmes.** British spelling of "programs"

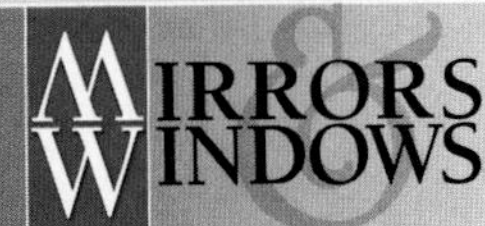

How do fears and prejudices affect everyday life? Is there a purpose for fears? for prejudices? How can judgments help or hinder a person's understanding of something?

Refer and Reason

1. Identify what characteristics of Mrs. Chriswell's the narrator makes fun of. In what ways did these characteristics help save the world?
2. Determine whether this story has a main idea that applies to the real world. If so, what is that idea?
3. Imagine how Mrs. Chriswell would have reacted to Jord and the other man had she not been colorblind. What might have been the consequences?

Writing Options

1. Pretend you are Jord. Write a letter to your family back home about your meeting with Mrs. Chriswell. Explain what your impressions were about life on Earth before you met Mrs. Chriswell, and how she changed your view.
2. In a one-page descriptive essay, describe the type of experiences and people that the aliens must have encountered prior to meeting Mrs. Chriswell. Use examples from the text to support these inferences. Include descriptions of this fictional society and how it is similar to today's society.

 Go to **www.mirrorsandwindows.com** for more.

THE TEST

A Short Story by

Theodore L. Thomas

It was a good day for driving.

Robert Proctor was a good driver for so young a man. The Turnpike curved gently ahead of him, lightly traveled on this cool morning in May. He felt relaxed and alert. Two hours of driving had not yet produced the twinges of fatigue that appeared first in the muscles in the base of the neck. The sun was bright, but not glaring, and the air smelled fresh and clean. He breathed it deeply, and blew it out noisily. It was a good day for driving.

He glanced quickly at the slim, gray-haired woman sitting in the front seat with him. Her mouth was curved in a quiet smile. She watched the trees and the fields slip by on her side of the pike. Robert Proctor immediately looked back at the road. He said, "Enjoying it, Mom?"

"Yes, Robert." Her voice was as cool as the morning. "It is very pleasant to sit here. I was thinking of the driving I did for you when you were little. I wonder if you enjoyed it as much as I enjoy this."

Theodore L. Thomas (b. 1920) has published many stories and articles in anthologies and magazines. Though employed in fields as diverse as chemical engineering and patent law, he has always found time for his writing. Thomas originally intended **"The Test"** to show only what a driver's test of the future might be like. The test was created to judge not only technical driving skills, but moral and emotional fitness as well. The conclusion did not satisfy Thomas, however, and one night before falling asleep he realized the meaning behind the scenes of his story. With this new idea in mind, he was able to write the last two paragraphs of the story.

Consider why Thomas altered the world the way he did. What might he be trying to say? What worries you the most about driving or learning to drive?

He smiled, embarrassed. "Sure I did."

She reached over and patted him gently on the arm, and then turned back to the scenery.

He listened to the smooth purr of the engine. Up ahead he saw a great truck, spouting a geyser of smoke as it sped along the Turnpike. Behind it, not passing it, was a long blue convertible, content to drive in the wake of the truck. Robert Proctor noted the arrangement and filed it in the back of his mind. He was slowly overtaking them, but he would not reach them for another minute or two.

He listened to the purr of the engine, and he was pleased with the sound. He had tuned that engine[1] himself over the objections of the mechanic. The engine idled rough now, but it ran smoothly at high speed. You needed a special feel to do good work on engines, and Robert Proctor knew he had it. No one in the world had a feel like his for the tune of an engine.

It was a good morning for driving, and his mind was filled with good thoughts. He pulled nearly abreast of the blue convertible and began to pass it. His speed was a few miles per hour above the Turnpike limit, but his car was under perfect control. The blue convertible suddenly swung out from behind the truck. It swung out without warning and struck his car near the right front fender, knocking his car to the shoulder on the left side of the Turnpike lane.

Robert Proctor was a good driver, too wise to slam on the brakes. He fought the steering wheel to hold the car on a straight path. The left wheels sank into the soft left shoulder, and the car tugged to pull to the left and cross the island and enter the lanes carrying the cars heading in the opposite direction. He held it, then the wheel struck a rock buried in the soft dirt, and the left front tire blew out. The car slewed, and it was then that his mother began to scream.

The car turned sideways and skidded part of the way out into the other lanes. Robert Proctor fought against the steering wheel to straighten the car, but the drag of the blown tire was too much. The scream rang steadily in his ears, and even as he strained at the wheel one part of his mind wondered coolly how a scream could so long be sustained without a breath. An oncoming car struck his radiator from the side and spun him viciously, full into the left-hand lanes.

He was flung into his mother's lap, and she was thrown against the right door. It held. With his left hand he reached for the steering wheel and pulled himself erect against the force of the spin. He turned the wheel to the left, and tried to stop the spin and careen out of

1. **tuned that engine.** Set the timing and replaced the spark plugs, for example, to improve the engine's running condition

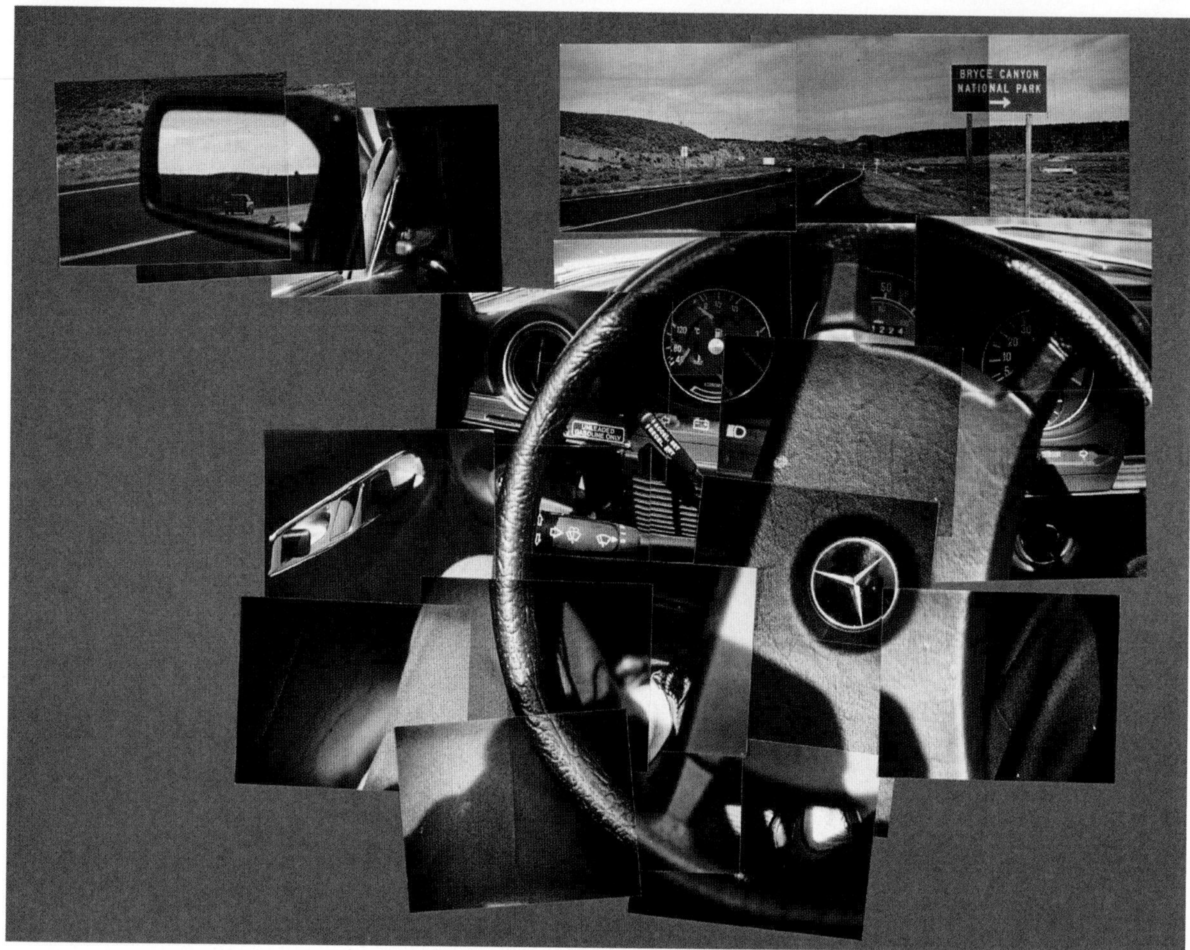

Steering Wheel, 1982. David Hockney.

the lanes of oncoming traffic. His mother was unable to right herself; she lay against the door, her cry rising and falling with the eccentric spin of the car.

The car lost some of its momentum. During one of the spins he twisted the wheel straight, and the car wobblingly stopped spinning and headed down the lane. Before Robert Proctor could turn it off the pike to safety a car loomed ahead of him, bearing down on him. There was a man at the wheel of that other car, sitting rigid, unable to move, eyes wide and staring and filled with fright. Alongside the man was a girl, her head against the back of the seat, soft curls framing a lovely face, her eyes closed in easy sleep. It was not the fear in the man that reached into Robert Proctor; it was the trusting helplessness in the face of the sleeping girl. The two cars sped closer to each other, and Robert Proctor could not change the direction of his car. The driver of the other car remained frozen at the wheel. At the last moment Robert Proctor sat motionless staring into the face of the onrushing, sleeping girl, his mother's cry still sounding in his ears. He heard no crash when the two cars collided head-on at a high rate of speed. He felt something push into his stomach, and the world began to go gray. Just before he lost consciousness he heard the scream stop, and he knew then that he had been hearing a single, short-lived scream that had only seemed to drag on and on. There came a painless wrench,[2] and then darkness.

2. **wrench.** Jolt; sharp, pulling motion

Robert Proctor seemed to be at the bottom of a deep black well. There was a spot of faint light in the far distance, and he could hear the rumble of a distant voice. He tried to pull himself toward the light and the sound, but the effort was too great. He lay still and gathered himself and tried again. The light grew brighter and the voice louder. He tried harder, again, and he drew closer. Then he opened his eyes full and looked at the man sitting in front of him.

"You all right, Son?" asked the man. He wore a blue uniform, and his round, beefy face was familiar.

Robert Proctor tentatively moved his head, and discovered he was seated in a reclining chair, unharmed, and able to move his arms and legs with no trouble. He looked around the room, and he remembered.

The man in the uniform saw the growing intelligence in his eyes and he said, "No harm done, Son. You just took the last part of your driver's test."

Robert Proctor focused his eyes on the man. Though he saw the man clearly, he seemed to see the faint face of the sleeping girl in front of him.

The uniformed man continued to speak. "We put you through an accident under hypnosis—do it to everybody these days before they can get their driver's licenses. Makes better drivers of them, more careful drivers the rest of their lives. Remember it now? Coming in here and all?"

Robert Proctor nodded, thinking of the sleeping girl. She never would have awakened; she would have passed right from a sweet, temporary sleep into the dark heavy sleep of death, nothing in between. His mother would have been bad enough; after all, she was pretty old. The sleeping girl was downright waste.

The uniformed man was still speaking. "So you're all set now. You pay me the ten dollar fee, and sign this application, and we'll have your license in the mail in a day or two." He did not look up.

Robert Proctor placed a ten dollar bill on the table in front of him, glanced over the application and signed it. He looked up to find two white-uniformed men, standing one on each side of him, and he frowned in annoyance. He started to speak, but the uniformed man spoke first. "Sorry, Son. You failed. You're sick; you need treatment. "

The two men lifted Robert Proctor to his feet, and he said, "Take your hands off me. What is this?"

The uniformed man said, "Nobody should want to drive a car after going through what you just went through. It should take months before you can even think of driving again, but you're ready right now. Killing people doesn't bother you. We don't let your kind run around loose in society any more. But don't you worry now, Son. They'll take good care of you, and they'll fix you up." He nodded to the two men, and they began to march Robert Proctor out.

At the door he spoke, and his voice was so urgent the two men paused. Robert Proctor said, "You can't really mean this. I'm still dreaming, aren't I? This is still part of the test, isn't it?"

The uniformed man said, *"How do any of us know?"* And they dragged Robert Proctor out the door, knees stiff, feet dragging, his rubber heels sliding along the two grooves worn into the floor. ❖

Should the government or other officials be allowed to judge an individual's mental health in the name of public safety? Is it possible to judge a person's mental health based on his or her reaction to surroundings?

SHAPIRO

Literature CONNECTION

Karl Shapiro (1913–2000) was born in Baltimore, Maryland. He believed in using common, everyday language in his poems, which were raw expressions of sensations. Shapiro received a Pulitzer Prize in 1944 for his first successful poetry collection, *V-Letter and Other Poems,* written while he was serving in the U.S. Army in the South Pacific during World War II. In **"Auto Wreck,"** Shapiro writes about witnessing a car crash and the questions that arise from such a tragedy.

Auto Wreck

A Poem by **Karl Shapiro**

Its quick soft silver bell beating, beating,
And down the dark one ruby flare
Pulsing out red light like an artery,
The ambulance at top speed floating down
Past beacons and illuminated clocks
Wings in a heavy curve, dips down,
And brakes speed, entering the crowd.
The doors leap open, emptying light;
Stretchers are laid out, the mangled lifted
And stowed into the little hospital.
Then the bell, breaking the hush, tolls once,
And the ambulance with its terrible cargo
Rocking, slightly rocking, moves away,
As the doors, an afterthought, are closed.

We are deranged, walking among the cops
Who sweep glass and are large and composed.
One is still making notes under the light.
One with a bucket douches ponds of blood
Into the street and gutter.

One hangs lanterns on the wrecks that cling,
Empty husks of locusts, to iron poles.

Our throats were tight as tourniquets,
Our feet were bound with splints, but now,
Like convalescents intimate and gauche,[1]
We speak through sickly smiles and warn
With the stubborn saw of common sense,
The grim joke and the banal resolution.
The traffic moves around with care,
But we remain, touching a wound
That opens to our richest horror.
Already old, the question Who shall die?
Becomes unspoken Who is innocent?

For death in war is done by hands;
Suicide has cause and stillbirth, logic;
And cancer, simple as a flower, blooms.
But this invites the occult mind,[2]
Cancels our physics with a sneer,
And spatters all we knew of dénouement[3]
Across the expedient and wicked stones. ❖

White Burning Car III, 1963. Andy Warhol.

1. **gauche.** Lacking social experience or grace
2. **occult mind.** Having thoughts that focus on the supernatural
3. **dénouement.** The resolution, or point at which the central conflict is resolved

Refer and Reason

1. Identify the details that make the crashes in "The Test" and "Auto Wreck" seem real to you. How important are these details for each selection? Are there details that make them seem unreal?
2. What do you think of the driving test that Robert was given? Judge whether it is an accurate way to determine if somebody is fit to drive. Do you think the test serves other purposes? What do you think it says about the people who created it?
3. Explain how you think people in our society would react if moral fitness became a criterion for getting a driver's license. What would be the advantages and disadvantages for adopting such a criterion?

Writing Options

1. Write an alternative ending for "The Test" (page 878) that begins after the paragraph that ends, "...and then darkness."
2. The short story "The Test" and the related reading "Auto Wreck" describe a car accident from two different perspectives. Write a brief compare-and-contrast essay of these two selections in terms of point of view, imagery, and effectiveness.

Go to **www.mirrorsandwindows.com** for more.

TEXT TO TEXT CONNECTION

Compare how the first two selections, "The Test" and "Auto Wreck," address death and destruction. Is judgment passed on the people involved? Who is to blame for the accidents? What questions are posed at the end of the story and the poem?

"Every hunter that ever lived would envy us today."

A SOUND OF Thunder

A Short Story by
Ray Bradbury

The sign on the wall seemed to quaver under a film of sliding warm water. Eckels felt his eyelids blink over his stare, and the sign burned in this momentary darkness:

TIME SAFARI, INC.
Safaris to any year in the past.
You name the animal.
We take you there.
You shoot it.

A warm phlegm gathered in Eckels's throat; he swallowed and pushed it down. The muscles around his mouth formed a smile as he put his hand slowly out upon the air, and in that hand waved a check for ten thousand dollars to the man behind the desk.

"Does this safari guarantee I come back alive?"

Ray Bradbury (b. 1920) was born in Waukegan, Illinois, and has been writing since 1943. Bradbury has published more than thirty books, including novels, children's books, and collections of short stories, poetry, and plays. Bradbury's science fiction stories offer social criticism and warnings against the dangers of uncontrolled technological development.

"A Sound of Thunder" opens in the year 2055 as a group of time travelers prepare to travel to prehistoric times to hunt dinosaurs. An important theme in "A Sound of Thunder" is how killing one animal, be it large or small, can drastically affect the balance of nature and the course of history.

Where would you go and what would you do if you could travel to the past?

"We guarantee nothing," said the official, "except the dinosaurs." He turned. "This is Mr. Travis, your Safari Guide in the Past. He'll tell you what and where to shoot. If he says no shooting, no shooting. If you disobey instructions, there's a stiff penalty of another ten thousand dollars, plus possible government action, on your return."

Eckels glanced across the vast office at a mass and tangle, a snaking and humming of wires and steel boxes, at an aurora that flickered now orange, now silver, now blue. There was a sound like a gigantic bonfire burning all of Time, all the years and all the parchment calendars, all the hours piled high and set aflame.

A touch of the hand and this burning would, on the instant, beautifully reverse itself. Eckels remembered the wording in the advertisements to the letter. Out of chars and ashes, out of dust and coals, like golden salamanders, the old years, the green years, might leap; roses sweeten the air, white hair turn Irish-black, wrinkles vanish; all, everything fly back to seed, flee death, rush down to their beginnings, suns rise in western skies and set in glorious easts, moons eat themselves opposite to the custom, all and everything cupping one in another like Chinese boxes, rabbits into hats, all and everything returning to the fresh death, the seed death, the green death, to the time before the beginning. A touch of a hand might do it, the merest touch of a hand.

"Unbelievable." Eckels breathed, the light of the Machine on his thin face. "A real Time Machine." He shook his head. "Makes you think. If the election had gone badly yesterday, I might be here now running away from the results. Thank God Keith won. He'll make a fine President of the United States."

"Yes," said the man behind the desk. "We're lucky. If Deutscher had gotten in, we'd have the worst kind of dictatorship. There's an anti-everything man for you, a militarist, anti-Christ, anti-human, anti-intellectual. People called us up, you know, joking but not joking. Said if Deutscher became President they wanted to go live in 1492. Of course it's not our business to conduct Escapes, but to form Safaris. Anyway, Keith's President now. All you got to worry about is—"

"Shooting my dinosaur," Eckels finished it for him.

"A *Tyrannosaurus rex*. The Tyrant Lizard, the most incredible monster in history. Sign this release. Anything happens to you, we're not responsible. Those dinosaurs are hungry."

Eckels flushed angrily. "Trying to scare me!"

"Frankly, yes. We don't want anyone going who'll panic at the first shot. Six Safari leaders were killed last year, and a dozen hunters. We're here to give you the severest thrill a *real* hunter ever asked for. Traveling you back sixty million years to bag the biggest game in all of Time. Your personal check's still there. Tear it up."

Mr. Eckels looked at the check. His fingers twitched.

"Good luck," said the man behind the desk. "Mr. Travis, he's all yours."

They moved silently across the room, taking their guns with them, toward the Machine, toward the silver metal and the roaring light.

First a day and then a night and then a day and then a night, then it was day-night-day-night-day. A week, a month, a year, a decade! A.D. 2055. A.D. 2019. 1999! 1957! Gone! The Machine roared.

They put on their oxygen helmets and tested the intercoms.

Eckels swayed on the padded seat, his face pale, his jaw stiff. He felt the trembling in his arms, and he looked down and found his hands tight on the new rifle. There were four other men in the Machine. Travis, the Safari Leader; his assistant, Lesperance; and two other hunters, Billings and Kramer. They sat looking at each other, and the years blazed around them.

"Can these guns get a dinosaur cold?" Eckels felt his mouth saying.

"If you hit them right," said Travis on the helmet radio. "Some dinosaurs have two brains, one in the head, another far down the spinal column. We stay away from those. That's stretching luck. Put your first two shots into the eyes, if you can, blind them, and go back into the brain."

The Machine howled. Time was a film run backward. Suns fled and ten million moons fled after them. "Think," said Eckels. "Every hunter that ever lived would envy us today. This makes Africa seem like Illinois."

The Machine slowed; its scream fell to a murmur. The Machine stopped.

The sun stopped in the sky.

The fog that had enveloped the Machine blew away and they were in an old time, a very old time indeed, three hunters and two Safari Heads with their blue metal guns across their knees.

"Christ isn't born yet," said Travis. "Moses has not gone to the mountain to talk with God. The Pyramids are still in the earth, waiting to be cut out and put up. *Remember* that. Alexander, Caesar, Napoleon, Hitler—none of them exists."

The men nodded.

"That"—Mr. Travis pointed—"is the jungle of sixty million two thousand and fifty-five years before President Keith."

He indicated a metal path that struck off into green wilderness, over streaming swamp, among giant ferns and palms.

"And that," he said, "is the Path, laid by Time Safari for your use. It floats six inches above the earth. Doesn't touch so much as one grass blade, flower, or tree. It's an anti-gravity metal. Its purpose is to keep you from touching this world of the Past in any way. Stay on the Path. Don't go off it. I repeat. *Don't go off*. For *any* reason! If you fall off, there's a penalty. And don't shoot any animal we don't okay."

"Why?" asked Eckels.

They sat in the ancient wilderness. Far birds' cries blew on a wind, and the smell of tar and an old salt sea, moist grasses, and flowers the color of blood.

"We don't want to change the Future. We don't belong here in the Past. The government doesn't *like* us here. We have to pay big graft to keep our franchise. A Time Machine is finicky business. Not knowing it, we might kill an important animal, a small bird, a roach, a flower even, thus destroying an important link in a growing species."

"That's not clear," said Eckels.

"All right," Travis continued, "say we accidentally kill one mouse here. That means all the future families of this one particular mouse are destroyed, right?"

"Right."

"And all the families of the families of the families of that one mouse! With a stamp of your foot, you annihilate first one, then a dozen, then a thousand, a million, a *billion* possible mice!"

"So they're dead," said Eckels. "So what?"

"So what?" Travis snorted quietly. "Well, what about the foxes that'll need those mice to survive? For want of ten mice, a fox dies. For want of ten foxes, a lion starves. For want of a lion, all manner of insects, vultures, infinite billions of life forms are thrown into chaos and destruction. Eventually it all boils down to this: Fifty-nine million years later, a cave man, one of a dozen in the *entire world,* goes hunting wild boar or saber-toothed tiger for food. But you, friend, have *stepped* on all the tigers in that region. By stepping on *one* single mouse. So the cave man starves. And the cave man, please note, is not just *any* expendable man, no! He is an *entire future nation*. From his loins would have sprung ten sons. From *their* loins one hundred sons, and thus onward to a civilization. Destroy this one man, and you destroy a race, a people, an entire history of life. It is comparable to slaying some of Adam's grandchildren. The stomp of your foot, on one mouse, could start an earthquake, the effects of which could shake our earth and destinies down through Time, to their very foundations. With the death of that one cave man, a billion others yet unborn are throttled in the womb. Perhaps Rome never rises on its seven hills. Perhaps Europe is forever a dark forest, and only Asia waxes healthy and teeming. Step on a mouse and you crush the Pyramids. Step on a mouse and you leave your print, like a Grand Canyon, across Eternity. Queen Elizabeth might never be born, Washington might not cross the Delaware, there might never be a United States at all. So be careful. Stay on the Path. *Never* step off!"

"I see," said Eckels. "Then it wouldn't pay for us even to touch the *grass?*"

"Correct. Crushing certain plants could add up infinitesimally. A little error here would multiply in sixty million years, all out of proportion. Of course maybe our theory is wrong. Maybe Time *can't* be changed by us. Or maybe it can be changed only in little subtle ways. A dead mouse here makes an insect imbalance there, a population disproportion later, a bad harvest further on, a depression, mass starvation, and, finally, a change in *social* temperament in far-flung countries. Something much more subtle, like that. Perhaps only a soft breath, a whisper, a hair, pollen on the air, such a slight, slight change that unless you looked close you wouldn't see it. Who knows? Who really can say he knows? We don't know. We're guessing. But until we do know for certain whether our messing around in Time *can* make a big roar or a little rustle in history, we're being careful. This Machine, this Path, your clothing and bodies, were sterilized, as you know, before the journey. We wear these oxygen helmets so we can't introduce our bacteria into an ancient atmosphere."

"How do we know which animals to shoot?"

"They're marked with red paint," said Travis. "Today, before our journey, we sent Lesperance here back with the Machine. He came to this particular era and followed certain animals."

"Studying them?"

"Right," said Lesperance. "I track them through their entire existence, noting which of them lives longest. Very few. How many times they mate. Not often. Life's short. When I find one that's going to die when a tree falls on him, or one that drowns in a tar pit, I note the exact hour, minute, and second. I shoot a paint bomb. It leaves a red patch on his side. We can't miss it. Then I correlate our arrival in the Past so that we meet the Monster not more than two minutes before he would have died anyway. This way, we kill only animals with no future, that are never going to mate again. You see how *careful* we are?"

"But if you came back this morning in Time," said Eckels eagerly, "you must've bumped into *us*, our Safari! How did it turn out? Was it successful? Did all of us get through—alive?"

Travis and Lesperance gave each other a look.

"That'd be a paradox," said the latter. "Time doesn't permit that sort of mess—a man meeting himself. When such occasions threaten, Time steps aside. Like an airplane hitting an air pocket. You felt the Machine jump just before we stopped? That was us passing ourselves on the way back to the Future. We saw nothing. There's no way of telling *if* this expedition was a success, *if we* got our monster, or whether all of us—meaning *you,* Mr. Eckels—got out alive." Eckels smiled palely.

"Cut that," said Travis sharply. "Everyone on his feet!"

They were ready to leave the Machine.

The jungle was high and the jungle was broad and the jungle was the entire world forever and forever. Sounds like music and sounds like flying tents filled the sky, and those were pterodactyls soaring with cavernous gray wings, gigantic bats of delirium and night fever. Eckels, balanced on the narrow Path, aimed his rifle playfully.

"Stop that!" said Travis. "Don't even aim for fun, blast you! If your guns should go off—"

Eckels flushed. "Where's our *Tyrannosaurus?*"

Lesperance checked his wristwatch. "Up ahead. We'll bisect his trail in sixty seconds. Look for the red paint! Don't shoot till we give the word. Stay on the Path. *Stay on the Path!*"

They moved forward in the wind of morning.

"Strange," murmured Eckels. "Up ahead, sixty million years, Election Day over. Keith made President. Everyone celebrating. And here we are, a million years lost, and they don't exist. The things we worried about for months, a lifetime, not even born or thought of yet."

"Safety catches off, everyone!" ordered Travis. "You, first shot, Eckels. Second, Billings. Third, Kramer."

"I've hunted tiger, wild boar, buffalo, elephant, but now, this is *it,*" said Eckels. "I'm shaking like a kid."

"Ah," said Travis.

Everyone stopped.

Travis raised his hand. "Ahead," he whispered. "In the mist. There he is. There's His Royal Majesty now."

The jungle was wide and full of twitterings, rustlings, murmurs, and sighs.

Suddenly it all ceased, as if someone had shut a door.

Silence.

A sound of thunder.

Out of the mist, one hundred yards away, came *Tyrannosaurus rex.*

"It," whispered Eckels. "It..."

"Sh!"

It came on great oiled, resilient, striding legs. It towered thirty feet above half of the

Out of the mist, one hundred yards away, came Tyrannosaurus rex.

trees, a great evil god, folding its delicate watchmaker's claws close to its oily reptilian chest. Each lower leg was a piston, a thousand pounds of white bone, sunk in thick ropes of muscle, sheathed over in a gleam of pebbled skin like the mail of a terrible warrior. Each thigh was a ton of meat, ivory, and steel mesh. And from the great breathing cage of the upper body those two delicate arms dangled out front, arms with hands which might pick up and examine men like toys, while the snake neck coiled. And the head itself, a ton of sculptured stone, lifted easily upon the sky. Its mouth gaped, exposing a fence of teeth like daggers. Its eyes rolled, ostrich eggs, empty of all expression save hunger. It closed its mouth in a death grin. It ran, its pelvic bones crushing aside trees and bushes, its taloned feet clawing damp earth, leaving prints six inches deep wherever it settled its weight. It ran with a gliding ballet step, far too poised and balanced for its ten tons. It moved into a sunlit arena warily, its beautifully reptilian hands feeling the air.

"Why, why," Eckels twitched his mouth. "It could reach up and grab the moon."

"Sh!" Travis jerked angrily. "He hasn't seen us yet."

"It can't be killed." Eckels pronounced this verdict quietly, as if there could be no argument. He had weighed the evidence and this was his considered opinion. The rifle in his hands seemed a cap gun. "We were fools to come. This is impossible."

"Shut up!" hissed Travis.

"Nightmare."

"Turn around," commanded Travis. "Walk quietly to the Machine. We'll remit one half your fee."

"I didn't realize it would be this *big,*" said Eckels. "I miscalculated, that's all. And now I want out."

"It *sees* us!"

"There's the red paint on its chest!"

The Tyrant Lizard raised itself. Its armored flesh glittered like a thousand green coins. The coins, crusted with slime, steamed. In the slime, tiny insects wriggled, so that the entire body seemed to twitch and undulate, even while the monster itself did not move. It exhaled. The stink of raw flesh blew down the wilderness.

"Get me out of here," said Eckels. "It was never like this before. I was always sure I'd come through alive. I had good guides, good safaris, and safety. This time, I figured wrong. I've met my match and admit it. This is too much for me to get hold of."

"Don't run," said Lesperance. "Turn around. Hide in the Machine."

"Yes." Eckels seemed to be numb. He looked at his feet as if trying to make them move. He gave a grunt of helplessness.

"Eckels!"

He took a few steps, blinking, shuffling.

"Not *that* way!"

The Monster, at the first motion, lunged forward with a terrible scream. It covered one hundred yards in six seconds. The rifles jerked up and blazed fire. A windstorm from the beast's mouth engulfed them in the stench of slime and old blood. The Monster roared, teeth glittering with sun.

Eckels, not looking back, walked blindly to the edge of the Path, his gun limp in his arms, stepped off the Path, and walked, not knowing it, in the jungle. His feet sank into green moss. His legs moved him, and he felt alone and remote from the events behind.

The rifles cracked again. Their sound was lost in shriek and lizard thunder. The great level of the reptile's tail swung up, lashed sideways. Trees exploded in clouds of leaf and branch. The Monster twitched its jeweler's hands down to fondle at the men, to twist them in half, to crush them like berries, to cram them into its teeth and its screaming throat. Its boulder-stone eyes leveled with the men. They saw themselves mirrored. They fired at the metallic eyelids and the blazing black iris.

Like a stone idol, like a mountain avalanche, *Tyrannosaurus* fell. Thundering, it clutched trees, pulled them with it. It wrenched and tore the metal Path. The men flung themselves back and away. The body hit, ten tons of cold flesh and stone. The guns fired. The Monster lashed its armored tail, twitched its snake jaws, and lay still. A fount of blood spurted from its throat. Somewhere inside, a sac of fluids burst. Sickening gushes drenched the hunters. They stood, red and glistening.

The thunder faded.

The jungle was silent. After the avalanche, a green peace. After the nightmare, morning.

Billings and Kramer sat on the pathway and threw up. Travis and Lesperance stood with smoking rifles, cursing steadily.

In the Time Machine, on his face, Eckels lay shivering. He had found his way back to the Path, climbed into the Machine.

Travis came walking, glanced at Eckels, took cotton gauze from a metal box, and returned to the others, who were sitting on the Path.

"Clean up."

They wiped the blood from their helmets. They began to curse too. The Monster lay, a hill of solid flesh. Within, you could hear the sighs and murmurs as the furthest chambers of it died, the organs malfunctioning, liquids running a final instant from pocket to sac to spleen, everything shutting off, closing up forever. It was like standing by a wrecked locomotive or a steam shovel at quitting time, all valves being released or levered tight. Bones cracked; the tonnage of its own flesh, off balance, dead weight, snapped the delicate forearms, caught underneath. The meat settled, quivering.

Another cracking sound. Overhead, a gigantic tree branch broke from its heavy mooring, fell. It crashed upon the dead beast with finality.

"There." Lesperance checked his watch. "Right on time. That's the giant tree that was scheduled to fall and kill this animal originally." He glanced at the two hunters. "You want the trophy picture?"

"What?"

"We can't take a trophy back to the Future. The body has to stay right here where it would have died originally, so the insects, birds, and bacteria can get at it, as they were intended to. Everything in balance. The body stays. But we *can* take a picture of you standing near it."

The two men tried to think, but gave up, shaking their heads.

They let themselves be led along the metal Path. They sank wearily into the Machine cushions. They gazed back at the ruined Monster, the stagnating mound, where already strange reptilian birds and golden insects were busy at the steaming armor.

A sound on the floor of the Time Machine stiffened them. Eckels sat there, shivering.

"I'm sorry," he said at last.

"Get up!" cried Travis.

Eckels got up.

"Go out on that Path alone," said Travis. He had his rifle pointed. "You're not coming back in the Machine. We're leaving you here!"

Lesperance seized Travis's arm. "Wait—"

"Stay out of this!" Travis shook his hand away. "This fool nearly killed us. But it isn't *that* so much, no. It's his *shoes!* Look at them! He ran off the Path. That *ruins* us! We'll forfeit! Thousands of dollars of insurance! We guarantee no one leaves the Path. He left it. Oh, the fool! I'll have to report to the government. They might revoke our license to travel. Who knows *what* he's done to Time, to History!"

"Take it easy, all he did was kick up some dirt."

"How do we *know?*" cried Travis. "We don't know anything! It's all a mystery! Get out of here, Eckels!"

Eckels fumbled his shirt. "I'll pay anything. A hundred thousand dollars!"

Travis glared at Eckels's checkbook and spat. "Go out there. The Monster's next to the Path. Stick your arms up to your elbows in his mouth. Then you can come back with us."

"That's unreasonable!"

"The Monster's dead, you idiot. The bullets! The bullets can't be left behind. They don't belong in the Past; they might change anything. Here's my knife. Dig them out!"

The jungle was alive again, full of the old tremorings and bird cries. Eckels turned slowly to regard the primeval garbage dump, that hill of nightmares and terror. After a long time, like a sleepwalker he shuffled out along the Path.

He returned, shuddering, five minutes later, his arms soaked and red to the elbows. He held out his hands. Each held a number of steel bullets. Then he fell. He lay where he fell, not moving.

"You didn't have to make him do that," said Lesperance.

"Didn't I? It's too early to tell." Travis nudged the still body. "He'll live. Next time he won't go hunting game like this. Okay." He jerked his thumb wearily at Lesperance. "Switch on. Let's go home."

1492. 1776. 1812.

They cleaned their hands and faces. They changed their caking shirts and pants. Eckels was up and around again, not speaking. Travis glared at him for a full ten minutes.

"Don't look at me," cried Eckels. "I haven't done anything."

"Who can tell?"

"Just ran off the Path, that's all, a little mud on my shoes—what do you want me to do—get down and pray?"

"We might need it. I'm warning you, Eckels, I might kill you yet. I've got my gun ready."

"I'm innocent. I've done nothing!"

1999. 2000. 2055.

The Machine stopped.

"Get out," said Travis.

The room was there as they had left it. But not the same as they had left it. The same man sat behind the same desk. But the same man did not quite sit behind the same desk.

Travis looked around swiftly. "Everything okay here?" he snapped.

"Fine. Welcome home!"

Travis did not relax. He seemed to be looking at the very atoms of the air itself, at the way the sun poured through the one high window.

"Okay, Eckels, get out. Don't ever come back."

Eckels could not move.

"You heard me," said Travis. "What're you *staring* at?"

Eckels stood smelling of the air, and there was a thing to the air, a chemical taint so subtle, so slight, that only a faint cry of his subliminal senses warned him it was there. The colors, white, gray, blue, orange, in the wall, in the furniture, in the sky beyond the window, were... were...And there was a *feel*. His flesh twitched. His hands twitched. He stood drinking the oddness with the pores of his body. Somewhere, someone must have been screaming one of those whistles that only a dog can hear. His body screamed silence in return. Beyond this room, beyond this wall, beyond this man who was not quite the same man seated at this desk that was not quite the same desk...lay an entire world of streets and people. What sort of world it was now, there was no telling. He could feel them moving there, beyond the walls, almost, like so many chess pieces blown in a dry wind....

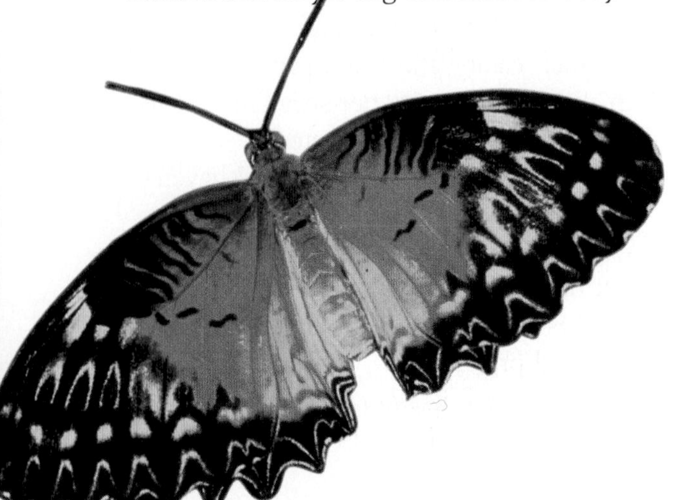

But the immediate thing was the sign painted on the office wall, the same sign he had read earlier today on first entering.

Somehow, the sign had changed:

TYME SEFARI INC.
Sefaris tu any yeer en the past.
Yu naim the animall.
Wee taekyuthair.
Yu shoot itt.

Eckels felt himself fall into a chair. He fumbled crazily at the thick slime on his boots. He held up a clod of dirt, trembling, "No, it *can't* be. Not a *little* thing like that. No!"

Embedded in the mud, glistening green and gold and black, was a butterfly, very beautiful and very dead.

"Not a little thing like *that!* Not a butterfly!" cried Eckels.

It fell to the floor, an exquisite thing, a small thing that could upset balances and knock down a line of small dominoes and then big dominoes and then gigantic dominoes, all down the years across Time. Eckels's mind whirled. It *couldn't* change things. Killing one butterfly couldn't be *that* important! Could it?

His face was cold. His mouth trembled, asking: "Who—who won the presidential election yesterday?"

The man behind the desk laughed. "You joking? You know very well. Deutscher, of course! Who else? Not that fool weakling Keith. We got an iron man now, a man with guts!" The official stopped. "What's wrong?"

Eckels moaned. He dropped to his knees. He scrabbled at the golden butterfly with shaking fingers. "Can't we," he pleaded to the world, to himself, to the officials, to the Machine, "can't we take it *back*, can't we *make* it alive again? Can't we start over? Can't we—"

He did not move. Eyes shut, he waited, shivering. He heard Travis breathe loud in the room; he heard Travis shift his rifle, click the safety catch, and raise the weapon.

There was a sound of thunder. ❖

SCIENCE CONNECTION

The Butterfly Effect The butterfly effect is the theory that small variations in an initial system can produce large variations in the same system over a period of time. The term "butterfly effect" was derived from the most commonly used example of this theory. The idea is that a butterfly flapping its wings might create a tiny change in the atmosphere that could ultimately cause a tornado to form. The theory appears within "A Sound of Thunder," as the hunters realize that a small alteration in the past has led to an enormous change in the present. While Bradbury didn't create the theory for his story, he could be credited with popularizing the connection between the butterfly effect and the concept of time travel.

Do you agree with the idea that killing a single butterfly could affect the course of history as portrayed in this story? Could altering the past ever be justified?

Refer and Reason

1. What causes Eckels to step off the Path?
2. Identify the differences in the setting before and after the expedition.
3. Imagine that Eckels had been left behind on the safari. Explain how his inhabiting the ancient world might have affected the other living things of that time and, in turn, the course of history.

Writing Options

1. Write a narrative description of a time when you felt so nervous or scared that you could not think rationally. Mimic Bradbury's writing style from "A Sound of Thunder." For example, write in the third person and use lots of figurative language.
2. Imagine you are Mr. Travis and you have to write an incident report to your employer. Write a cause-and-effect analysis explaining what lead to the changes in the Present at the end of the story.

 Go to **www.mirrorsandwindows.com** for more.

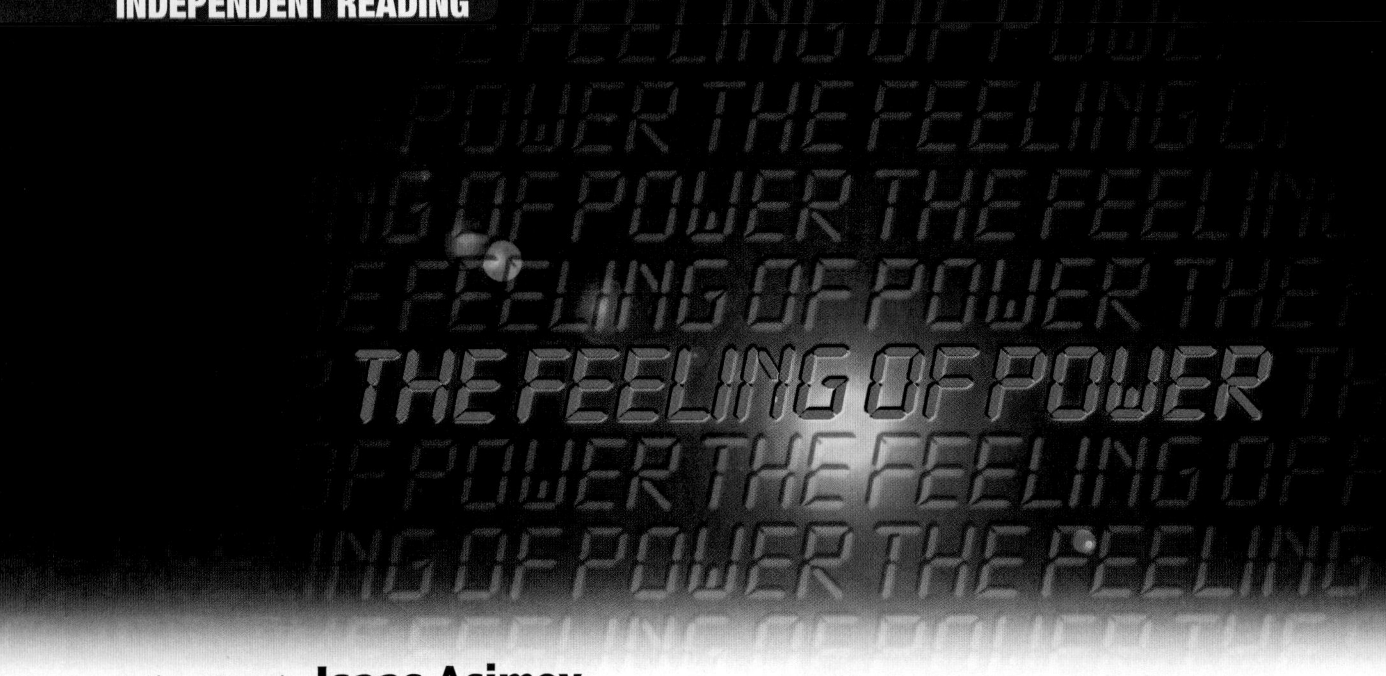

A Short Story by **Isaac Asimov**

"BUT HOW FAR CAN HUMAN COMPUTATION GO?"

Jehan Shuman was used to dealing with the men in authority on long-embattled Earth. He was only a civilian, but he originated programming patterns that resulted in self-directing war computers of the highest sort. Generals consequently listened to him. Heads of congressional committees, too.

There was one of each in the special lounge of New Pentagon. General Weider was space-burnt and had a small mouth puckered almost into a cipher. Congressman Brant was smooth cheeked and clear eyed. He smoked Denebian[1] tobacco with the air of one whose patriotism was so notorious, he could be allowed such liberties.

Shuman, tall, distinguished, and Programmer-first-class, faced them fearlessly.

He said, "This, gentlemen, is Myron Aub."

"The one with the unusual gift that you discovered quite by accident," said Congressman Brant placidly. "Ah." He inspected the little man with the egg-bald head with amiable curiosity.

The little man, in return, twisted the fingers of his hands anxiously. He had never been near such

1. **Denebian.** Fictional alien race

Isaac Asimov (1920–1992) has been called one of the "Big Three" of science fiction, along with authors Robert Heinlein and Arthur C. Clarke. These writers ushered in the "Golden Age" of science fiction, when for the first time it was widely accepted by the reading public. One of the great abilities of science fiction is its tendency to look ahead at new possibilities for science and technology. **"The Feeling of Power"** gives a different twist to this science fiction tradition. Instead of creating a new science or technology, Asimov shows what might happen if an old science, such as mathematics, is forgotten and then regained.

What invention would you want to see in the future? Why?

great men before. He was only an aging, low-grade Technician who had long ago failed all tests designed to smoke out the gifted ones among mankind and had settled into the rut of unskilled labor. There was just this hobby of his that the great Programmer had found out about and was now making such a frightening fuss over.

General Weider said, "I find this atmosphere of mystery childish."

"You won't in a moment," said Shuman. "This is not something we can leak to the first comer.—Aub!" There was something imperative about his manner of biting off that one-syllable name, but then he was a great Programmer speaking to a mere Technician. "Aub! How much is nine times seven?"

Aub hesitated a moment.

His pale eyes glimmered with a feeble anxiety. "Sixty-three," he said.

Congressman Brant lifted his eyebrows. "Is that right?"

"Check it for yourself, Congressman."

The congressman took out his pocket computer, nudged the milled edges twice, looked at its face as it lay there in the palm of his hand, and put it back. He said, "Is this the gift you brought us here to demonstrate. An illusionist?"

"More than that, sir. Aub has memorized a few operations and with them he computes on paper."

"A paper computer?" said the general. He looked pained.

"No, sir," said Shuman patiently. "Not a paper computer. Simply a sheet of paper. General, would you be so kind as to suggest a number?"

"Seventeen," said the general.

"And you, Congressman?"

"Twenty-three."

"Good! Aub, multiply those numbers and please show the gentlemen your manner of doing it."

"Yes, Programmer," said Aub, ducking his head. He fished a small pad out of one shirt pocket and an artist's hairline stylus out of the other. His forehead corrugated as he made painstaking marks on the paper.

General Weider interrupted him sharply. "Let's see that."

Aub passed him the paper, and Weider said, "Well, it looks like the figure seventeen."

Congressman Brant nodded and said, "So it does, but I suppose anyone can copy figures off a computer. I think I could make a passable seventeen myself, even without practice."

"If you will let Aub continue, gentlemen," said Shuman without heat.

Aub continued, his hand trembling a little. Finally he said in a low voice, "The answer is three hundred and ninety-one."

Congressman Brant took out his computer a second time and flicked it, "By Godfrey, so it is. How did he guess?"

"No guess, Congressman," said Shuman. "He computed that result. He did it on this sheet of paper."

"Humbug," said the general impatiently. "A computer is one thing and marks on paper are another."

"Explain, Aub," said Shuman.

"Yes, Programmer. —Well, gentlemen, I write down seventeen and just underneath it, I write twenty-three. Next, I say to myself: seven times three—"

The congressman interrupted smoothly, "Now, Aub, the problem is seventeen times twenty-three."

"Yes, I know," said the little Technician earnestly, "but I *start* by saying seven times three because that's the way it works. Now seven times three is twenty-one."

"And how do you know that?" asked the congressman.

"I just remember it. It's always twenty-one on the computer. I've checked it any number of times."

"That doesn't mean it always will be, though, does it?" said the congressman.

"Maybe not," stammered Aub. "I'm not a mathematician. But I always get the right answers, you see."

"Go on."

"Seven times three is twenty-one, so I write down twenty-one. Then one times three is three, so I write down a three under the two of twenty-one."

"Why under the two?" asked Congressman Brant at once.

"Because— " Aub looked helplessly at his superior for support. "It's difficult to explain."

Shuman said, "If you will accept his work for the moment, we can leave the details for the mathematicians."

Brant subsided.

Aub said, "Three plus two makes five, you see, so the twenty-one becomes a fifty-one. Now you let that go for a while and start fresh. You multiply seven and two, that's fourteen, and one and two, that's two. Put them down like this and it adds up to thirty-four. Now if you put the thirty-four under the fifty-one this way and add them, you get three hundred and ninety-one and that's the answer."

There was an instant's silence and then General Weider said, "I don't believe it. He goes through this rigmarole[2] and makes up numbers and multiplies and adds them this way and that, but I don't believe it. It's too complicated to be anything but hornswoggling."

"Oh no, sir," said Aub in a sweat. "It only *seems* complicated because you're not used to it. Actually, the rules are quite simple and will work for any numbers."

"Any numbers, eh?" said the general. "Come then." He took out his own computer (a severely styled GI model) and struck it at random. "Make a five seven three eight on the paper. That's five thousand seven hundred and thirty-eight."

"Yes, sir," said Aub, taking a new sheet of paper.

"Now," (more punching of his computer), "seven two three nine. Seven thousand two hundred and thirty-nine."

"Yes, sir."

"And now multiply those two."

"It will take some time," quavered Aub.

"Take the time," said the general.

"Go ahead, Aub," said Shuman crisply.

Aub set to work, bending low. He took another sheet of paper and another. The general took out his watch finally and stared at it. "Are you through with your magic-making, Technician?"

"I'm almost done, sir. —Here it is, sir. Forty-one million, five hundred and thirty-seven thousand, three hundred and eighty-two." He showed the scrawled figures of the result.

General Weider smiled bitterly. He pushed the multiplication contact on his computer and let the numbers whirl to a halt. And then he stared and said in a surprised squeak, "Great Galaxy, the fella's right."

The President of the Terrestrial Federal had grown haggard in office, and, in private, he allowed a look of settled melancholy to appear on his sensitive features. The Denebian war, after its early start of vast movement and great popularity, had trickled down into a sordid matter of maneuver and countermaneuver, with discontent rising steadily on Earth. Possibly, it was rising on Deneb, too.

2. **rigmarole.** Confused or meaningless talk

Amorous Figures, c. 1900s. Giacomo Balla. Private collection.

And now Congressman Brant, head of the important Committee on Military Appropriations, was cheerfully and smoothly spending his half-hour appointment spouting nonsense.

"Computing without a computer," said the president impatiently, "is a contradiction in terms."

"Computing," said the congressman, "is only a system for handling data. A machine might do it, or the human brain might. Let me give you an example." And, using the new skills he had learned, he worked out sums and products until the president, despite himself, grew interested.

"Does this always work?"

"Every time, Mr. President. It is foolproof."

"Is it hard to learn?"

"It took me a week to get the real hang of it. I think you would do better."

"Well," said the president, considering, "it's an interesting parlor game, but what is the use of it?"

"What is the use of a newborn baby, Mr. President? At the moment there is no use, but don't you see that this points the way toward liberation from the machine? Consider, Mr. President"—the congressman rose and his deep voice automatically took on some of the cadences he used in public debate— "that the Denebian war is a war of computer against computer. Their computers forge an impenetrable shield of countermissiles against our missiles, and ours forge one against theirs. If we advance the efficiency of our computers, so do they theirs, and for five years a precarious and profitless balance has existed.

"Now we have in our hands a method for going beyond the computer, leapfrogging it, passing through it. We will combine the mechanics of computation with human thought; we will have the equivalent of intelligent computers; billions of them. I can't predict what the consequences will be in detail, but they will be incalculable. And if Deneb beats us to the punch, they may be unimaginably catastrophic."

The president said, troubled, "What would you have me do?"

"Put the power of the administration behind the establishment of a secret project on human computation. Call it Project Number, if you like. I can vouch for my committee, but I will need the administration behind me."

"But how far can human computation go?"

"There is no limit. According to Programmer Shuman, who first introduced me to this discovery—"

"I've heard of Shuman, of course."

"Yes. Well, Dr. Shuman tells me that in theory there is nothing the computer can do that the human mind cannot do. The computer merely takes a finite amount of data and performs a finite number of operations upon them. The human mind can duplicate the process."

The president considered that. He said, "If Shuman says this, I am inclined to believe him—in theory. But, in practice, how can anyone know how a computer works?"

Brant laughed genially. "Well, Mr. President, I asked the same question. It seems that at one time computers were designed directly by human beings. Those were simple computers, of course, this being before the time of the rational use of computers to design more advanced computers."

"Yes, yes. Go on."

"Technician Aub apparently had, as his hobby, the reconstruction of some of these ancient devices, and in so doing he studied the details of their workings and found he could imitate them. The multiplication I just performed for you is an imitation of the workings of a computer."

"Amazing!"

The congressman coughed gently. "If I may make another point, Mr. President—the further we can develop this thing, the more we can divert our Federal effort from computer production and computer maintenance. As the human brain takes over, more of our energy can be directed into peacetime pursuits, and the impingement of war on the ordinary man will be less. This will be most advantageous for the party in power, of course."

"Ah," said the president, "I see your point. Well, sit down, Congressman, sit down. I want some time to think about this.—But meanwhile, show me that multiplication trick again. Let's see if I can't catch the point of it."

Programmer Shuman did not try to hurry matters. Loesser was conservative, very conservative, and liked to deal with computers as his father and grandfather had. Still, he controlled the West European computer combine, and if he could be persuaded to join Project Number in full enthusiasm, a great deal would be accomplished.

But Loesser was holding back. He said, "I'm not sure I like the idea of relaxing our hold on computers. The human mind is a capricious thing. The computer will give the same answer to the same problem each time. What guarantee have we that the human mind will do the same?"

"The human mind, Computer Loesser, only manipulates facts. It doesn't matter whether the human mind or a machine does it. They are just tools."

"Yes, yes. I've gone over your ingenious demonstration that the mind can duplicate the computer, but it seems to me a little in the air. I'll grant the theory, but what reason have we for thinking that theory can be converted to practice?"

"I think we have reason, sir. After all, computers have not always existed. The cave men with their triremes, stone axes, and railroads had no computers."

"And possibly they did not compute."

"You know better than that. Even the building of a railroad or a ziggurat called for some computing, and that must have been without computers as we know them."

"Do you suggest they computed in the fashion you demonstrate?"

"Probably not. After all, this method—we call it 'graphitics,' by the way, from the old European word *grapho,* meaning 'to write'—is developed from the computers themselves, so it cannot have antedated them. Still, the cave men must have had *some* method, eh?"

"Lost arts! If you're going to talk about lost arts—"

"No, no. I'm not a lost art enthusiast, though I don't say there may not be some. After all, man was eating grain before hydroponics,[3] and if the primitives ate grain, they must have grown it in soil. What else could they have done?"

"I don't know, but I'll believe in soil-growing when I see someone grow grain in soil. And I'll believe in making fire by rubbing two pieces of flint together when I see that, too."

3. **hydroponics.** Growing plants without soil, as with a nutrient solution or other material

Shuman grew placative. "Well, let's stick to graphitics. It's just part of the process of etherealization. Transportation by means of bulky contrivances is giving way to direct mass-transference. Communications devices become less massive and more efficient constantly. For that matter, compare your pocket computer with the massive jobs of a thousand years ago. Why not, then, the last step of doing away with computers altogether? Come, sir, Project Number is a going concern; progress is already headlong. But we want your help. If patriotism doesn't move you, consider the intellectual adventure involved."

Loesser said skeptically, "What progress? What can you do beyond multiplication? Can you integrate a transcendental[4] function?"

"In time, sir. In time. In the last month I have learned to handle division. I can determine, and correctly, integral quotients and decimal quotients."

"Decimal quotients? To how many places?"

Programmer Shuman tried to keep his tone casual. "Any number!"

Loesser's lower jaw dropped. "Without a computer?"

"Set me a problem."

"Divide twenty-seven by thirteen. Take it to six places."

Five minutes later, Shuman said, "Two point oh seven six nine two three."

Loesser checked it. "Well, now, that's amazing. Multiplication didn't impress me too much because it involved integers after all, and I thought trick manipulation might do it. But decimals—"

"And that is not all. There is a new development that is, so far, top secret and that, strictly speaking, I ought not to mention. Still—we may have made a breakthrough on the square root front."

"Square roots?"

"It involves some tricky points and we haven't licked the bugs yet, but Technician Aub, the man who invented the science and who has an amazing intuition in connection with it, maintains he has the problem almost solved. And he is only a Technician. A man like yourself, a trained and talented mathematician, ought to have no difficulty."

"Square roots," muttered Loesser, attracted.

"Cube roots, too. Are you with us?"

Loesser's hand thrust out suddenly, "Count me in."

General Weider stumped his way back and forth at the head of the room and addressed his listeners after the fashion of a savage teacher

"WHY NOT, THEN, THE LAST STEP OF DOING AWAY WITH COMPUTERS ALTOGETHER?"

facing a group of recalcitrant students. It made no difference to the general that they were the civilian scientists heading Project Number. The general was the overall head, and he so considered himself at every waking moment.

He said, "Now square roots are all fine. I can't do them myself and I don't understand the methods, but they're fine. Still, the Project will not be sidetracked into what some of you call the fundamentals. You can play with graphitics any way you want to after the war is over, but right now we have specific and very practical problems to solve."

In a far corner, Technician Aub listened with painful attention. He was no longer a Technician, of course, having been relieved of his duties and assigned to the Project, with a fine-sounding title and good pay. But, of course, the social distinction remained and the highly placed scientific leaders could never bring themselves to admit him to their ranks

4. **transcendental.** A function, such as sine, cosine, or tangent, that cannot be separated into a finite number of calculations

on a footing of equality. Nor, to do Aub justice, did he, himself, wish it. He was as uncomfortable with them as they with him.

The general was saying, "Our goal is a simple one, gentlemen; the replacement of the computer. A ship that can navigate space without a computer on board can be constructed in one-fifth the time and at one-tenth the expense of a computer-laden ship. We could build fleets five times, ten times as great as Deneb could if we could but eliminate the computer.

"And I see something even beyond this. It may be fantastic now, a mere dream, but in the future I see the manned missile!"

There was an instant murmur from the audience.

The general drove on. "At the present time, our chief bottleneck is the fact that missiles are limited in intelligence. The computer controlling them can only be so large, and for that reason they can meet the changing nature of antimissile defenses in an unsatisfactory way. Few missiles, if any, accomplish their goal, and missile warfare is coming to a dead end—for the enemy, fortunately, as well as for ourselves.

"On the other hand, a missile with a man or two within, controlling flight, by graphitics, would be lighter, more mobile, more intelligent. It would give us a lead that might well mean the margin of victory. Besides which, gentlemen, the exigencies of war compel us to remember one thing. A man is much more dispensable than a computer. Manned missiles could be launched in numbers and under circumstances that no good general would care to undertake as far as computer-directed missiles are concerned—"

He said much more, but Technician Aub did not wait.

Technician Aub, in the privacy of his quarters, labored long over the note he was leaving behind. It read finally as follows:

"When I began the study of what is now called graphitics, it was no more than a hobby. I saw no more in it than an interesting amusement, an exercise of mind.

"When Project Number began, I thought that others were wiser than I; that graphitics might be put to practical use as a benefit to mankind, to aid in the production of really practical mass-transference devices perhaps. But now I see it is to be used only for death and destruction.

"I cannot face the responsibility involved in having invented graphitics."

He then deliberately turned the focus of a protein-depolarizer on himself and fell instantly and painlessly dead.

They stood over the grave of the little Technician while tribute was paid to the greatness of his discovery.

Programmer Shuman bowed his head along with the rest of them but remained unmoved. The Technician had done his share and was no longer needed, after all. He might have started graphitics, but now that it had started, it would carry on by itself overwhelmingly, triumphantly, until manned missiles were possible with who knew what else.

Nine times seven, thought Shuman with deep satisfaction, is sixty-three, and I don't need a computer to tell me so. The computer is in my own head.

And it was amazing the feeling of power that gave him. ❖

As technology becomes more advanced, would you expect human life to be worth more or less? What fears do people have concerning advancing technology today? Are these concerns justified?

Refer and Reason

1. Compare the story's society, with its attitudes on technology and advancement, with today's real human society. What similarities and differences do you notice?
2. Assess whether Asimov's criticism or praise is justified. Does he create an accurate picture of society, or is he wrong about human nature? Explain.
3. Does Asimov seem to be suggesting any solutions to societal problems? If so, explain what they are and why you think they would or would not work. If not, generate solutions of your own to any problems Asimov raises.

Writing Options

1. Imagine that you live in this time period and create a short, persuasive pamphlet describing to people what the government wants to use graphitics for and why this is wrong. Use strong emotional language to influence readers.
2. For a presentation at a conference on science fiction literature, write a one-page persuasive essay explaining what point you think Asimov was trying to make in this story. Be sure to give examples from the story that help support your argument.

 Go to **www.mirrorsandwindows.com** for more.

Harrison Bergeron

A Short Story by **Kurt Vonnegut**

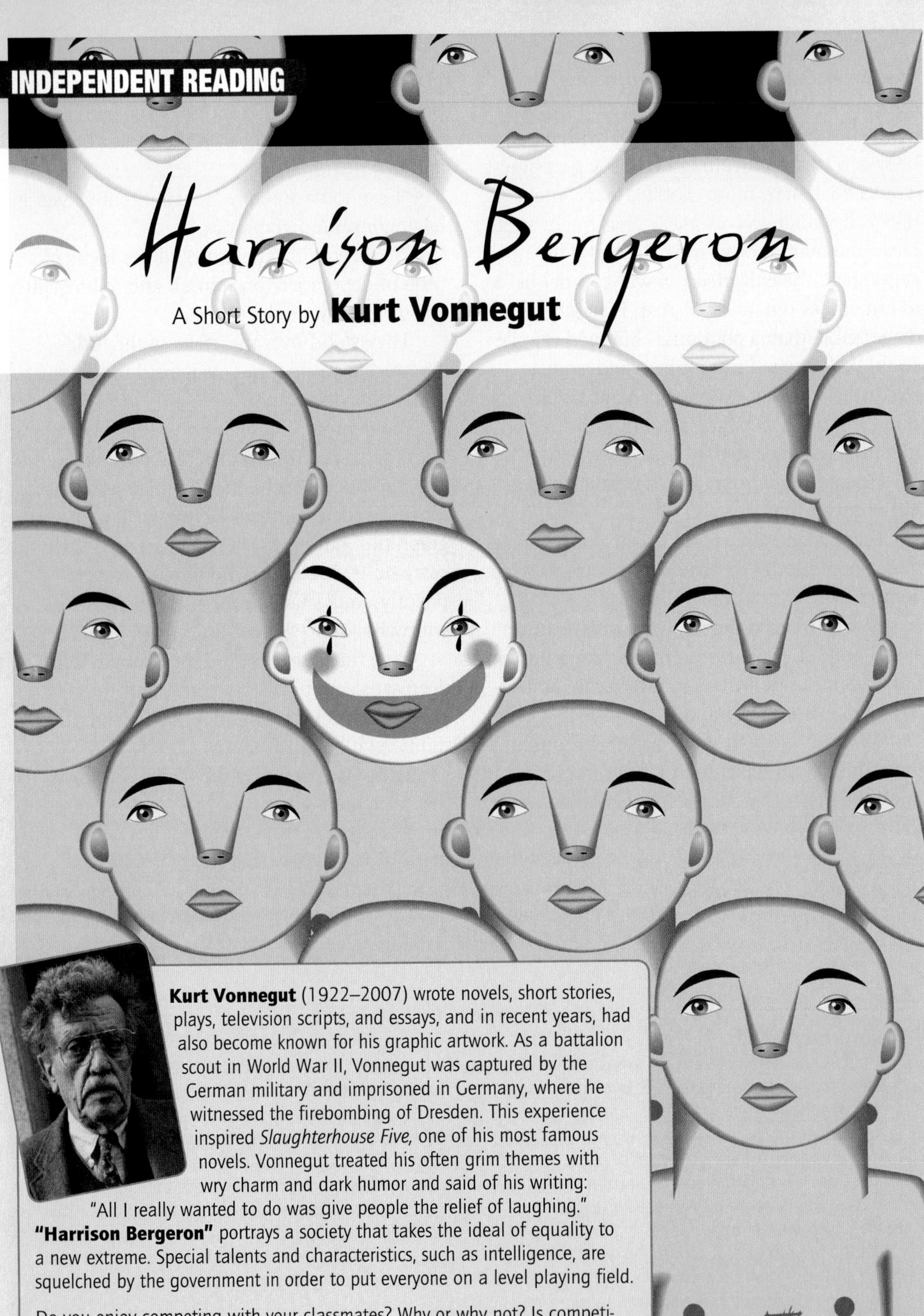

Kurt Vonnegut (1922–2007) wrote novels, short stories, plays, television scripts, and essays, and in recent years, had also become known for his graphic artwork. As a battalion scout in World War II, Vonnegut was captured by the German military and imprisoned in Germany, where he witnessed the firebombing of Dresden. This experience inspired *Slaughterhouse Five,* one of his most famous novels. Vonnegut treated his often grim themes with wry charm and dark humor and said of his writing: "All I really wanted to do was give people the relief of laughing."

"Harrison Bergeron" portrays a society that takes the ideal of equality to a new extreme. Special talents and characteristics, such as intelligence, are squelched by the government in order to put everyone on a level playing field.

Do you enjoy competing with your classmates? Why or why not? Is competition positive or negative?

The year was 2081, and everybody was finally equal. They weren't only equal before God and the law. They were equal every which way. Nobody was smarter than anybody else. Nobody was better looking than anybody else. Nobody was stronger or quicker than anybody else. All this equality was due to the 211th, 212th, and 213th Amendments to the Constitution, and to the unceasing vigilance of agents of the United States Handicapper General.

Some things about living still weren't quite right, though. April, for instance, still drove people crazy by not being springtime. And it was in that clammy month that the H-G men took George and Hazel Bergeron's fourteen-year-old son, Harrison, away.

The year was 2081, and everybody was finally equal.

It was tragic all right, but George and Hazel couldn't think about it very hard. Hazel had a perfectly average intelligence, which meant she couldn't think about anything except in short bursts. And George, while his intelligence was way above normal, had a little mental handicap radio in his ear. He was required by law to wear it at all times. It was tuned to a government transmitter. Every twenty seconds or so, the transmitter would send out some sharp noise to keep people like George from taking unfair advantage of their brains.

George and Hazel were watching television. There were tears on Hazel's cheeks, but she'd forgotten for the moment what they were about.

On the television screen were ballerinas.

A buzzer sounded in George's head. His thoughts fled in panic, like bandits from a burglar alarm.

"That was a real pretty dance, that dance they just did," said Hazel.

"Huh?" said George.

"That dance—it was nice," said Hazel.

"Yup," said George. He tried to think a little about the ballerinas. They weren't really very good—no better than anybody else would have been, anyway. They were burdened with sash-weights and bags of birdshot, and their faces were masked, so that no one, seeing a free and graceful gesture or a pretty face, would feel like something the cat drug in. George was toying with the vague notion that maybe dancers shouldn't be handicapped. But he didn't get very far with it before another noise in his ear radio scattered his thoughts.

George winced. So did two out of the eight ballerinas.

Hazel saw him wince. Having no mental handicap herself, she had to ask George what the latest sound had been.

"Sounded like somebody hitting a milk bottle with a ball peen hammer," said George.

"I'd think it would be real interesting, hearing all the different sounds," said Hazel, a little envious. "All the things they think up."

"Um," said George.

"Only, if I was Handicapper General, you know what I would do?" said Hazel. Hazel, as a matter of fact, bore a strong resemblance to the Handicapper General, a woman named Diana Moon Glampers. "If I was Diana Moon Glampers," said Hazel, "I'd have chimes on Sunday—just chimes. Kind of in honor of religion."

"I could think, if it was just chimes," said George.

"Well—maybe make 'em real loud," said Hazel. "I think I'd make a good Handicapper General."

"Good as anybody else," said George.

"Who knows better'n I do what normal is?" said Hazel.

"Right," said George. He began to think glimmeringly about his abnormal son who was now in jail, about Harrison, but a twenty-one-gun salute in his head stopped that.

"Boy!" said Hazel, "that was a doozy, wasn't it?"

It was such a doozy that George was white and trembling, and tears stood on the rims of his red eyes. Two of the eight ballerinas had collapsed to the studio floor, were holding their temples.

"All of a sudden you look so tired," said Hazel. "Why don't you stretch out on the sofa, so's you can rest your handicap bag on the pillows, honeybunch." She was referring to the forty-seven pounds of birdshot in a canvas bag, which was padlocked around George's neck. "Go on and rest the bag for a little while," she said. "I don't care if you're not equal to me for a while."

George weighed the bag with his hands. "I don't mind it," he said. "I don't notice it any more. It's just a part of me."

"You been so tired lately—kind of wore out," said Hazel. "If there was just some way we could make a little hole in the bottom of the bag, and just take out a few of them lead balls. Just a few."

"Two years in prison and two thousand dollars fine for every ball I took out," said George. "I don't call that a bargain."

"If you could just take a few out when you came home from work," said Hazel. "I mean—you don't compete with anybody around here. You just set around."

"If I tried to get away with it," said George, "then other people'd get away with it—and pretty soon we'd be right back to the dark ages again, with everybody competing against everybody else. You wouldn't like that, would you?"

"I'd hate it," said Hazel.

"There you are," said George. "The minute people start cheating on laws, what do you think happens to society?"

If Hazel hadn't been able to come up with an answer to this question, George couldn't have supplied one. A siren was going off in his head.

"Reckon it'd fall all apart," said Hazel.

"What would?" said George blankly.

"Society," said Hazel uncertainly. "Wasn't that what you just said?"

"Who knows?" said George.

The television program was suddenly interrupted for a news bulletin. It wasn't clear at first as to what the bulletin was about, since the announcer, like all announcers, had a serious speech impediment. For about half a minute, and in a state of high excitement, the announcer tried to say, "Ladies and gentlemen—"

He finally gave up, handed the bulletin to a ballerina to read.

"That's all right—" Hazel said of the announcer, "he tried. That's the big thing. He tried to do the best he could with what God gave him. He should get a nice raise for trying so hard."

"Ladies and gentlemen—" said the ballerina, reading the bulletin. She must have been extraordinarily beautiful, because the mask she wore was hideous. And it was easy to see that she was the strongest and most graceful of all the dancers, for her handicap bags were as big as those worn by two-hundred-pound men.

And she had to apologize at once for her voice, which was a very unfair voice for a woman to use. Her voice was a warm, luminous, timeless melody. "Excuse me—" she said, and she began again, making her voice absolutely uncompetitive.

"Harrison Bergeron, age fourteen," she said in a grackle squawk, "has just escaped from jail, where he was held on suspicion of plotting to overthrow the government. He is a genius and an athlete, is under-handicapped, and should be regarded as extremely dangerous."

A police photograph of Harrison Bergeron was flashed on the screen—upside down, then sideways, upside down again, then right side up. The picture showed the full length of Harrison against a background calibrated in feet and inches. He was exactly seven feet tall.

The rest of Harrison's appearance was Halloween and hardware. Nobody had ever born heavier handicaps. He had outgrown hindrances faster than the H-G men could think them up. Instead of a little ear radio for a mental handicap, he wore a tremendous

pair of earphones, and spectacles with thick wavy lenses. The spectacles were intended to make him not only half blind, but to give him whanging headaches besides.

Scrap metal was hung all over him. Ordinarily, there was a certain symmetry, a military neatness to the handicaps issued to strong people, but Harrison looked like a walking junkyard. In the race of life, Harrison carried three hundred pounds.

And to offset his good looks, the H-G men required that he wear at all times a red rubber ball for a nose, keep his eyebrows shaved off, and cover his even white teeth with black caps at snaggle-tooth random.

"If you see this boy," said the ballerina, "do not—I repeat, do not—try to reason with him."

There was the shriek of a door being torn from its hinges.

Screams and barking cries of consternation came from the television set. The photograph of Harrison Bergeron on the screen jumped again and again, as though dancing to the tune of an earthquake.

George Bergeron correctly identified the earthquake, and well he might have—for many was the time his own home had danced to the same crashing tune. "My God—" said George, "that must be Harrison!"

The realization was blasted from his mind instantly by the sound of an automobile collision in his head.

When George could open his eyes again, the photograph of Harrison was gone. A living, breathing Harrison filled the screen.

Clanking, clownish, and huge, Harrison stood in the center of the studio. The knob of the uprooted studio door was still in his hand. Ballerinas, technicians, musicians, and announcers cowered on their knees before him, expecting to die.

"I am the Emperor!" cried Harrison. "Do you hear? I am the Emperor! Everybody must do what I say at once!" He stamped his foot and the studio shook.

"Even as I stand here—" he bellowed, "crippled, hobbled, sickened—I am a greater ruler than any man who ever lived! Now watch me become what I *can* become!"

Harrison tore the straps of his handicap harness like wet tissue paper, tore straps guaranteed to support five thousand pounds.

Harrison's scrap-iron handicaps crashed to the floor.

Harrison thrust his thumbs under the bar of the padlock that secured his head harness. The bar snapped like celery. Harrison smashed his headphones and spectacles against the wall.

He flung away his rubber-ball nose, revealed a man that would have awed Thor, the god of thunder.

"I shall now select my Empress!" he said, looking down on the cowering people. "Let the first woman who dares rise to her feet claim her mate and her throne!"

A moment passed, and then a ballerina arose, swaying like a willow.

Harrison plucked the mental handicap from her ear, snapped off her physical handicaps with marvelous delicacy. Last of all, he removed her mask.

She was blindingly beautiful.

"Now—" said Harrison, taking her hand, "shall we show the people the meaning of the word dance? Music!" he commanded.

The musicians scrambled back into their chairs, and Harrison stripped them of their handicaps, too. "Play your best," he told them, "and I'll make you barons and dukes and earls."

The music began. It was normal at first—cheap, silly, false. But Harrison snatched two musicians from their chairs, waved them like batons as he sang the music as he wanted it played. He slammed them back into their chairs. The music began again and was much improved.

Harrison and his Empress merely listened to the music for a while—listened gravely, as though synchronizing their heartbeats with it.

They shifted their weights to their toes.

Harrison placed his big hands on the girl's tiny waist, letting her sense the weightlessness that would soon be hers.

And then, in an explosion of joy and grace, into the air they sprang!

Not only were the laws of the land abandoned, but the law of gravity and the laws of motion as well.

They reeled, whirled, swiveled, flounced, capered, gamboled, and spun.

They leaped like deer on the moon.

The studio ceiling was thirty feet high, but each leap brought the dancers nearer to it.

It became their obvious intention to kiss the ceiling.

They kissed it.

And then, neutralizing gravity with love and pure will, they remained suspended in air inches below the ceiling, and they kissed each other for a long, long time.

It was then that Diana Moon Glampers, the Handicapper General, came into the studio with a double-barreled ten-gauge shotgun. She fired twice, and the Emperor and the Empress were dead before they hit the floor.

Diana Moon Glampers loaded the gun again. She aimed it at the musicians and told them they had ten seconds to get their handicaps back on.

It was then that the Bergerons' television tube burned out.

Hazel turned to comment about the blackout to George. But George had gone out into the kitchen for a can of beer.

George came back in with the beer, paused while a handicap signal shook him up. And then he sat down again. "You been crying?" he said to Hazel.

"Yup," she said.

"What about?" he said.

"I forget," she said. "Something real sad on television."

"What was it?" he said.

"It's all kind of mixed up in my head," said Hazel.

"Forget sad things," said George.

"I always do," said Hazel.

"That's my girl," said George. He winced. There was the sound of a rivetting gun in his head.

"Gee—I could tell that one was a doozy," said Hazel.

"You can say that again," said George.

"Gee—" said Hazel, "I could tell that one was a doozy." ❖

How does our society value equality? What characteristics does our society strive to "equalize"? Do we value certain abilities and characteristics more than others?

Refer and Reason

1. Identify and record specific incidents in the story that reveal the societal effects of the equalizing process.
2. Summarize how the society in Vonnegut's story attempts to eliminate competition. Judge whether this attempt is an effective approach to creating equality. Why or why not?
3. Consider how our society might function if it were the complete opposite of Vonnegut's "Harrison Bergeron." What might occur if those who are less fortunate were completely ignored or unsupported in society?

Writing Options

1. Pretend that you are Harrison Bergeron. Write a letter to the Handicapper General in which you present your arguments against the current system of handicapping individuals.
2. Write a three- to five-paragraph compare-and-contrast essay comparing Vonnegut's imagined society to your own. Consider how they are most related.

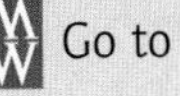 Go to **www.mirrorsandwindows.com** for more.

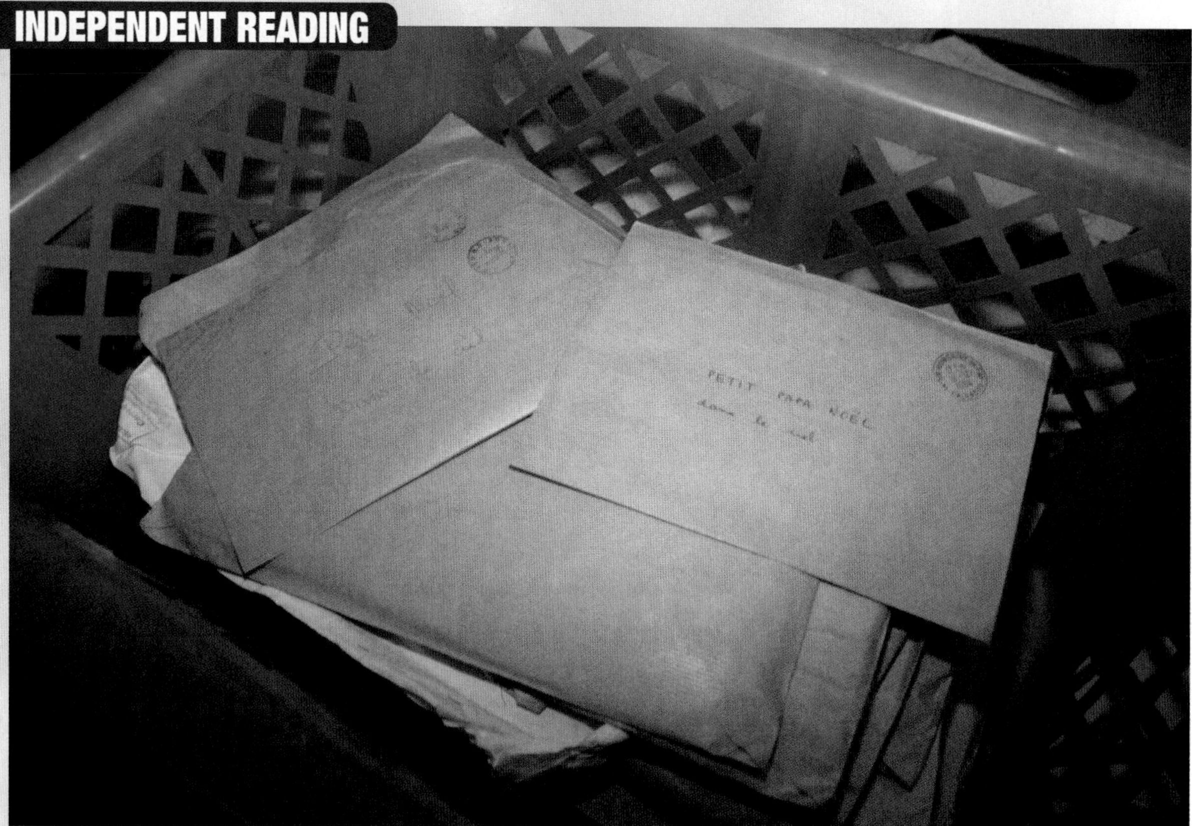

the censors

A Short Story by **Luisa Valenzuela**

He had a truly patriotic task, both self-denying and uplifting.

Luisa Valenzuela (b. 1938) was born in Argentina. Her father was a physician, and her mother, Luisa Mercedes Levinson, was a noted writer in Argentina. The author of several novels, Valenzuela has written for magazines, newspapers, and radio in Argentina. Much of Valenzuela's fiction is written in a style known as magical realism, blending magical and realistic elements.

This satirical tale, **"The Censors,"** follows the career path of a young man living in a highly censored society. The man applies for a job as a censor in order to intercept a letter he wrote to a loved one.

Have you ever gotten wrapped up in something you originally resisted? Why or why not?

Poor Juan! One day they caught him with his guard down before he could even realize that what he had taken as a stroke of luck was really one of fate's dirty tricks. These things happen the minute you're careless, as one often is. Juancito let happiness—a feeling you can't trust—get the better of him when he received from a confidential source Mariana's new address in Paris and knew that she hadn't forgotten him. Without thinking twice, he sat down at his table and wrote her a letter. *The* letter that now keeps his mind off his job during the day and won't let him sleep at night (what had he scrawled, what had he put on that sheet of paper he sent to Mariana?).

Juan knows there won't be a problem with the letter's contents, that it's irreproachable, harmless. But what about the rest? He knows that they examine, sniff, feel, and read between the lines of each and every letter, and check its tiniest comma and most accidental stain. He knows that all letters pass from hand to hand and go through all sorts of tests in the huge censorship offices and that, in the end, very few continue on their way. Usually it takes months, even years, if there aren't any snags; all this time the freedom, maybe even the life, of both sender and receiver is in jeopardy. And that's why Juan's so troubled: thinking that something might happen to Mariana because of his letters. Of all people, Mariana, who must finally feel safe there where she always dreamt she'd live. But he knows that the *Censor's Secret Command* operates all over the world and cashes in on the discount in air fares; there's nothing to stop them from going as far as that hidden Paris neighborhood, kidnapping Mariana, and returning to their cozy homes, certain of having fulfilled their noble mission.

Well, you've got to beat them to the punch, do what everyone tries to do: sabotage the machinery, throw sand in its gears, get to the bottom of the problem so as to stop it.

This was Juan's sound plan when he, like many others, applied for a censor's job—not because he had a calling or needed a job: no, he applied simply to intercept his own letter, a consoling albeit unoriginal idea. He was hired immediately, for each day more and more censors are needed and no one would bother to check on his references.

Ulterior motives couldn't be overlooked by the *Censorship Division,* but they needn't be too strict with those who applied. They knew how hard it would be for the poor guys to find the letter they wanted and even if they did, what's a letter or two when the new censor would snap up so many others? That's how Juan managed to join the *Post Office's Censorship Division,* with a certain goal in mind.

The building had a festive air on the outside that contrasted with its inner staidness. Little by little, Juan was absorbed by his job, and he felt at peace since he was doing everything he could to get his letter for Mariana. He

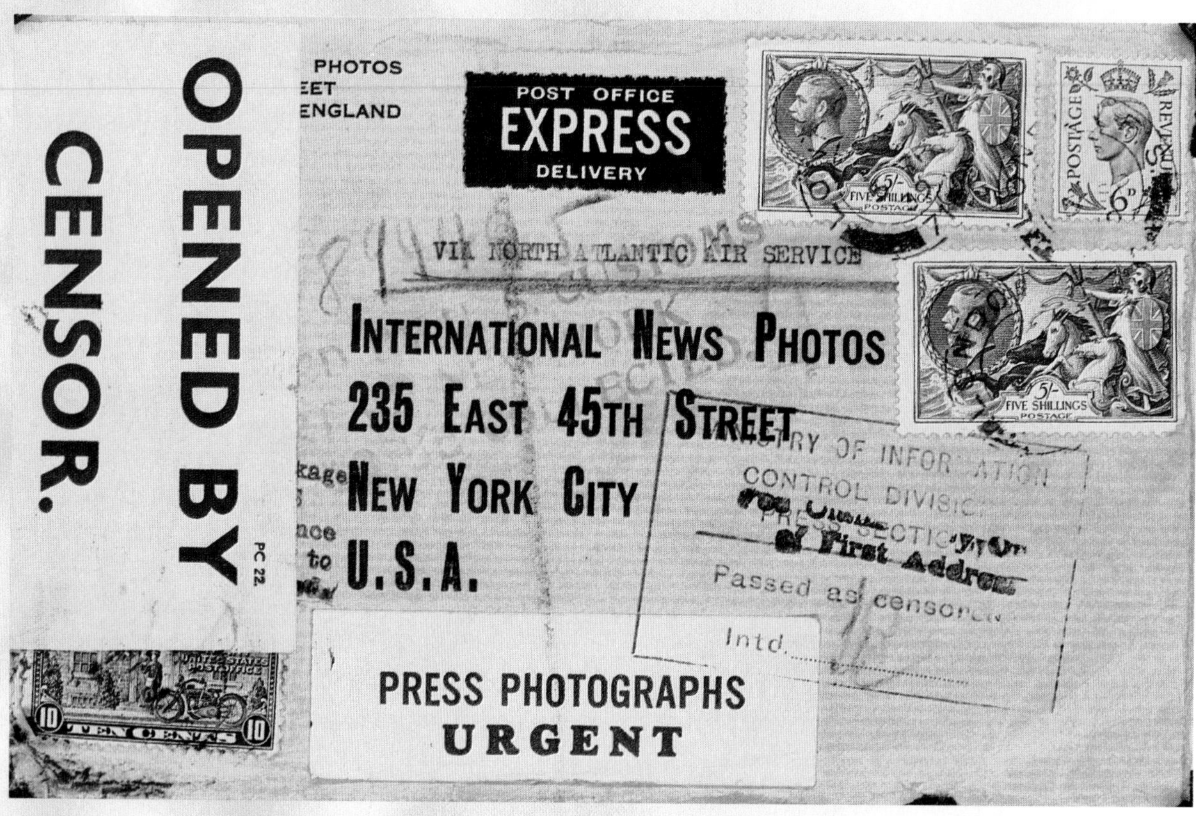

didn't even worry when, in his first month, he was sent to *Section K* where envelopes are very carefully screened for explosives.

It's true that on the third day, a fellow worker had his right hand blown off by a letter, but the division chief claimed it was sheer negligence on the victim's part. Juan and the other employees were allowed to go back to their work, though feeling less secure. After work, one of them tried to organize a strike to demand higher wages for unhealthy work, but Juan didn't join in; after thinking it over, he reported the man to his superiors and thus got promoted.

You don't form a habit by doing something once, he told himself as he left his boss's office. And when he was transferred to *Section J*, where letters are carefully checked for poison dust, he felt he had climbed a rung in the ladder.

By working hard, he quickly reached *Section E* where the job became more interesting, for he could now read and analyze the letters' contents. Here he could even hope to get hold of his letter, which, judging by the time that had elapsed, had gone through the other sections and was probably floating around in this one.

Soon his work became so absorbing that his noble mission blurred in his mind. Day after day he crossed out whole paragraphs in red ink, pitilessly chucking many letters into the censored basket. These were horrible days when he was shocked by the subtle and conniving ways employed by people to pass on subversive messages; his instincts were so sharp that he found behind a simple "the weather's unsettled" or "prices continue to soar" the wavering hand of someone secretly scheming to overthrow the Government.

His zeal brought him swift promotion. We don't know if this made him happy. Very few letters reached him in *Section B*—only a handful passed the other hurdles—so he read them over and over again, passed them under a magnifying glass, searched for microprint with an electronic microscope, and tuned his sense of smell so that he was beat by the time he made it home. He'd barely manage to warm up his soup, eat some fruit, and fall into bed, satisfied with having done his duty. Only his darling mother worried, but she couldn't get him back on the right track. She'd say, though it wasn't always true: Lola called, she's at the bar with the girls, they miss you, they're waiting for you. Or else she'd leave a bottle of red wine on the table. But Juan wouldn't overdo it: any distraction could make him lose his edge and the perfect censor had to be alert, keen, attentive, and sharp to nab cheats. He had a truly patriotic task, both self-denying and uplifting.

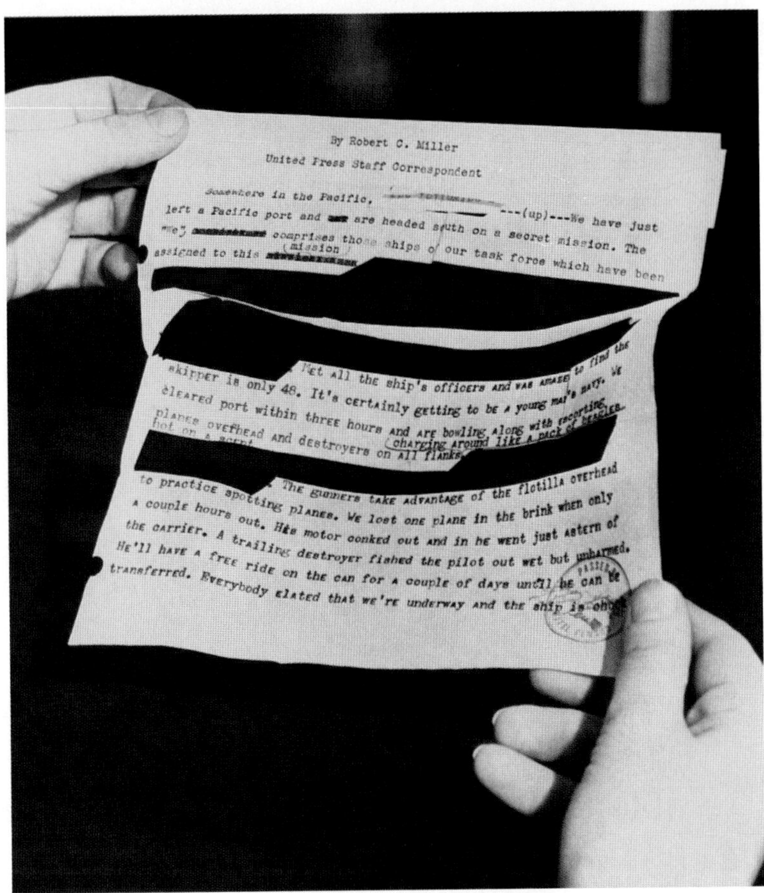
By Robert C. Miller
United Press Staff Correspondent

Somewhere in the Pacific, ---(up)---We have just left a Pacific port and are headed south on a secret mission. The comprises those ships of our task force which have been assigned to this (mission)

met all the ship's officers and was amazed to find the skipper is only 48. It's certainly getting to be a young man's navy. We cleared port within three hours and are bowling along with escorting planes overhead and destroyers on all flanks (charging around like a pack of beagles)

to practice spotting planes. The gunners take advantage of the flotilla overhead a couple hours out. We lost one plane in the brink when only the carrier. A trailing destroyer fished the pilot out wet but unharmed. He'll have a free ride on the can for a couple of days until he can be transferred. Everybody elated that we're underway and the ship is

His basket for censored letters became the best fed as well as the most cunning basket in the whole *Censorship Division*. He was about to congratulate himself for having finally discovered his true mission, when his letter to Mariana reached his hands. Naturally, he censored it without regret. And just as naturally, he couldn't stop them from executing him the following morning, another victim of his devotion to his work. ❖

Explain what you think the author is saying in this story about censorship and government control. Are there times when government security justifies violation of individual rights to privacy? At what point should a political system be questioned?

Refer and Reason

1. Describe how Juan changes during the course of the story.
2. How does the author's choice in perspective affect the story?
3. At the end of the story, Juan himself gets executed because of the letter he wrote to Mariana. What do you think might have happened if he had not gotten a job as a censor?

Writing Options

1. Write Juan's letter to Mariana based on what you imagine it might have said. Try to include phrasing that could be considered subversive or code by the censors.
2. Pretend you are a historian studying the society that Juan lived in. Write a brief critique of the censorship practices of this society. Explain why you think the censorship practices limited or helped the society and what can be learned from such a society.

Go to **www.mirrorsandwindows.com** for more.

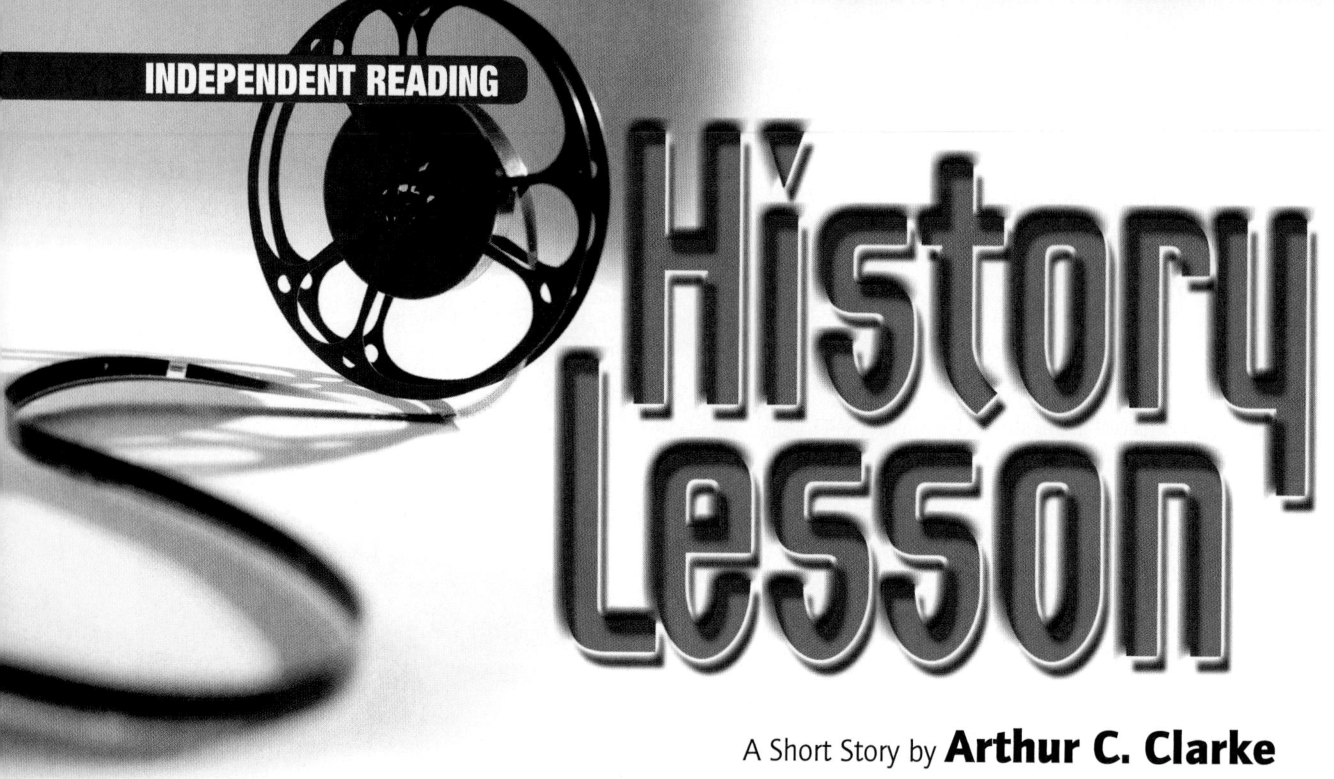

History Lesson

A Short Story by **Arthur C. Clarke**

It was the story of a civilization that had passed beyond recall.

No one could remember when the tribe had begun its long journey. The land of great rolling plains that had been its first home was now no more than a half-forgotten dream.

For many years, Shann and his people had been fleeing through a country of low hills and sparkling lakes, and now the mountains lay ahead. This summer they must cross them to the southern lands. There was little time to lose. The white terror that had come down from the Poles, grinding continents to dust and freezing the very air before it, was less than a day's march behind.

Shann wondered if the glaciers could climb the mountains ahead, and within his heart he dared to kindle a little flame of hope. This might prove a barrier against which even the remorseless ice would batter in vain. In the southern lands of which the legends spoke his people might find refuge at last.

It took weeks to discover a pass through which the tribe and the animals could travel. When midsummer came, they had camped in a lonely valley where the air was thin and the stars shone with a brilliance no one had ever seen before.

Arthur C. Clarke (1917–2008) was born in Somerset, England, and graduated with honors in physics and mathematics from King's College in London. In the Royal Air Force, he worked with radar. Combining his interest in science with a skilled narrative style, he has created numerous entertaining, instructive stories and novels. His science fiction works often focus on exploration and the place of humans in the universe. Clarke's amusing and thought-provoking tale, **"History Lesson,"** covers themes of world destruction, exploration, and mankind's place in the universe. The story makes us question our society: what values it promotes, how powerful it is, and what weaknesses it possesses. It also offers an unusual "history lesson."

Do you believe in life on other planets? Why or why not?

Critical Viewing

How well does this image depict the landscape of Shann and his people? Does it seem uninhabitable?

The summer was waning when Shann took his two sons and went ahead to explore the way. For three days they climbed, and for three nights slept as best they could on the freezing rocks, and on the fourth morning there was nothing ahead but a gentle rise to a cairn[1] of gray stones built by other travelers, centuries ago.

Shann felt himself trembling, and not with cold, as they walked toward the little pyramid of stones. His sons had fallen behind. No one spoke, for too much was at stake. In a little while they would know if all their hopes had been betrayed.

To east and west, the wall of mountains curved away as if embracing the land beneath. Below lay endless miles of undulating plain, with a great river swinging across it in tremendous loops. It was a fertile land, one in which the tribe could raise crops knowing that there would be no need to flee before the harvest came.

Then Shann lifted his eyes to the south, and saw the doom of all his hopes. For there at the edge of the world glimmered that deadly light he had seen so often to the north—the glint of ice below the horizon.

There was no way forward. Through all the years of flight, the glaciers from the south had been advancing to meet them. Soon they would be crushed beneath the moving walls of ice....

Southern glaciers did not reach the mountains until a generation later. In that last summer the sons of Shann carried the sacred treasures of the tribe to the lonely cairn overlooking the plain. The ice that had once gleamed below the horizon was now almost at their feet. By spring it would be splintering against the mountain walls.

No one understood the treasures now. They were from a past too distant for the understanding of any man alive. Their origins were lost in the mists that surrounded the Golden Age, and how they had come at last into the possession of this wandering tribe was a story that now would never be told. For it was the story of a civilization that had passed beyond recall.

Once, all these pitiful relics had been treasured for some good reason, and now they had become sacred though their meaning had

1. **cairn.** Heap of stones piled up as a memorial or landmark

long been lost. The print in the old books had faded centuries ago though much of the lettering was still visible—if there had been any to read it. But many generations had passed since anyone had had a use for a set of seven-figure logarithms, an atlas of the world, and the score of Sibelius's Seventh Symphony printed, according to the flyleaf, by H. K. Chu and Sons, at the City of Pekin in the year 2371 AD.

The old books were placed reverently in the little crypt that had been made to receive them. There followed a motley collection of fragments—gold and platinum coins, a broken telephoto lens, a watch, a cold-light lamp, a microphone, the cutter from an electric razor, some midget radio tubes, the flotsam[2] that had been left behind when the great tide of civilization had ebbed forever.

All these treasures were carefully stowed away in their resting place. Then came three more relics, the most sacred of all because the least understood.

The first was a strangely shaped piece of metal, showing the coloration of intense heat. It was, in its way, the most pathetic of all these symbols from the past, for it told of man's greatest achievement and of the future he might have known. The mahogany stand on which it was mounted bore a silver plate with the inscription

Auxiliary Igniter from Starboard Jet Spaceship
"Morning Star"
Earth-Moon, AD 1985

Next followed another miracle of the ancient science—a sphere of transparent plastic with strangely shaped pieces of metal imbedded in it. At its center was a tiny capsule of synthetic radio-element, surrounded by the converting screens that shifted its radiation far down the spectrum. As long as the material remained active, the sphere would be a tiny radio transmitter, broadcasting power in all directions. Only a few of these spheres had ever been made. They had been designed as perpetual beacons to mark the orbits of the asteroids. But man had never reached the asteroids and the beacons had never been used.

Last of all was a flat, circular tin, wide in comparison with its depth. It was heavily sealed, and rattled when shaken. The tribal lore predicted that disaster would follow if it was ever opened, and no one knew that it held one of the great works of art of nearly a thousand years before.

The work was finished. The two men rolled the stones back into place and slowly began to descend the mountainside. Even to the last, man had given some thought to the future and had tried to preserve something for posterity.

That winter the great waves of ice began their first assault on the mountains, attacking from north and south. The foothills were overwhelmed in the first onslaught, and the glaciers ground them into dust. But the mountains stood firm, and when the summer came the ice retreated for a while.

So, winter after winter, the battle continued, and the roar of the avalanches, the grinding of rock and the explosions of splintering ice filled the air with tumult. No war of man's had been fiercer than this, and even man's battles had not quite engulfed the globe as this had done.

At last the tidal waves of ice began to subside and to creep slowly down the flanks of the mountains they had never quite subdued. The valleys and passes were still firmly in their grip. It was stalemate. The glaciers had met their match, but their defeat was too late to be of any use to man.

So the centuries passed, and presently there happened something that must occur once at least in the history of every world in the universe, no matter how remote and lonely it may be.

The ship from Venus came five thousand years too late, but its crew knew nothing of this. While still many millions of miles away, the telescopes had seen the great shroud of ice

2. **flotsam.** Floating debris

that made Earth the most brilliant object in the sky next to the sun itself.

Here and there the dazzling sheet was marred by black specks that revealed the presence of almost buried mountains. That was all. The rolling oceans, the plains and forests, the deserts and lakes—all that had been the world of man was sealed beneath the ice, perhaps forever.

The ship closed in to Earth and established an orbit less than a thousand miles away. For five days it circled the planet, while cameras recorded all that was left to see and a hundred instruments gathered information that would give the Venusian scientists many years of work.

An actual landing was not intended. There seemed little purpose in it. But on the sixth day the picture changed. A panoramic monitor, driven to the limit of its amplification, detected the dying radiation of the five-thousand-year-old beacon. Through all the centuries, it had been sending out its signals with ever-failing strength as its radioactive heart steadily weakened.

The monitor locked on the beacon frequency. In the control room, a bell clamored for attention. A little later, the Venusian ship broke free from its orbit and slanted down toward Earth, toward a range of mountains that still towered proudly above the ice, and to a cairn of gray stones that the years had scarcely touched....

The great disk of the sun blazed fiercely in a sky no longer veiled with mist, for the clouds that had once hidden Venus had now completely gone. Whatever force had caused the change in the sun's radiation had doomed one civilization, but had given birth to another. Less than five thousand years before, the half-savage people of Venus had seen sun and stars for the first time. Just as the science of Earth had begun with astronomy, so had that of Venus, and on the warm, rich world that man had never seen progress had been incredibly rapid.

Perhaps the Venusians had been lucky. They never knew the Dark Age that held man enchained for a thousand years. They missed the long detour into chemistry and mechanics but came at once to the more fundamental laws of radiation physics. In the time that man had taken to progress from the Pyramids to the rocket-propelled spaceship, the Venusians had passed from the discovery of agriculture to antigravity itself—the ultimate secret that man had never learned.

The warm ocean that still bore most of the young planet's life rolled its breakers languidly against the sandy shore. So new was this continent that the very sands were coarse and gritty. There had not yet been time enough for the sea to wear them smooth.

The scientists lay half in the water, their beautiful reptilian bodies gleaming in the sunlight. The greatest minds of Venus had gathered on this shore from all the islands of the planet. What they were going to hear they did not know, except that it concerned the Third World and the mysterious race that had peopled it before the coming of the ice.

The Historian was standing on the land, for the instruments he wished to use had no love of water. By his side was a large machine which attracted many curious glances from his colleagues. It was clearly concerned with optics, for a lens system projected from it toward a screen of white material a dozen yards away.

The Historian began to speak. Briefly he recapitulated what little had been discovered concerning the Third Planet and its people.

He mentioned the centuries of fruitless research that had failed to interpret a single word of the writings of Earth. The planet had been inhabited by a race of great technical ability. That, at least, was proved by the few pieces of machinery that had been found in the cairn upon the mountain.

"We do not know why so advanced a civilization came to an end," he observed. "Almost certainly, it had sufficient knowledge to survive an Ice Age. There must have been some other factor of which we know nothing. Possibly disease or racial degeneration may have been responsible. It has even been suggested that the tribal conflicts endemic[3] to our own species in prehistoric times may have continued on the Third Planet after the coming of technology.

"Some philosophers maintain that knowledge of machinery does not necessarily imply a high degree of civilization, and it is theoretically possible to have wars in a society possessing mechanical power, flight, and even radio. Such a conception is alien to our thoughts, but we must admit its possibility. It would certainly account for the downfall of the lost race.

"It has always been assumed that we should never know anything of the physical form of the creatures who lived on Planet Three. For centuries our artists have been depicting scenes from the history of the dead world, peopling it with all manner of fantastic beings. Most of these creations have resembled us more or less closely, though it has often been pointed out that because *we* are reptiles it does not follow that all intelligent life must necessarily be reptilian.

"We now know the answer to one of the most baffling problems of history. At last, after hundreds of years of research, we have discovered the exact form and nature of the ruling life on the Third Planet."

There was a murmur of astonishment from the assembled scientists. Some were so taken aback that they disappeared for a while into the comfort of the ocean, as all Venusians were apt to do in moments of stress. The Historian waited until his colleagues reemerged into the element they so disliked. He himself was quite comfortable, thanks to the tiny sprays that were continually playing over his body. With their help he could live on land for many hours before having to return to the ocean.

The excitement slowly subsided and the lecturer continued:

"One of the most puzzling of the objects found on Planet Three was a flat metal container holding a great length of transparent plastic material, perforated at the edges and wound tightly into a spool. This transparent tape at first seemed quite featureless, but an examination with the new subelectronic microscope has shown that this is not the case. Along the surface of the material, invisible to our eyes but perfectly clear under the correct radiation, are literally thousands of tiny pictures. It is believed that they were imprinted on the material by some chemical means, and have faded with the passage of time.

"These pictures apparently form a record of life as it was on the Third Planet at the height of its civilization. They are not independent. Consecutive pictures are almost identical, differing only in the detail of movement. The purpose of such a record is obvious. It is

3. **endemic.** Belonging to a particular group or place

only necessary to project the scenes in rapid succession to give an illusion of continuous movement. We have made a machine to do this, and I have here an exact reproduction of the picture sequence.

"The scenes you are now going to witness take us back many thousands of years, to the great days of our sister planet. They show a complex civilization, many of whose activities we can only dimly understand. Life seems to have been very violent and energetic, and much that you will see is quite baffling.

"It is clear that the Third Planet was inhabited by a number of different species, none of them reptilian. That is a blow to our pride, but the conclusion is inescapable. The dominant type of life appears to have been a two-armed biped. It walked upright and covered its body with some flexible material, possibly for protection against the cold, since even before the Ice Age the planet was at a much lower temperature than our own world. But I will not try your patience any further. You will now see the record of which I have been speaking."

A brilliant light flashed from the projector. There was a gentle whirring, and on the screen appeared hundreds of strange beings moving rather jerkily to and fro. The picture expanded to embrace one of the creatures, and the scientists could see that the Historian's description had been correct.

The creature possessed two eyes, set rather close together, but the other facial adornments were a little obscure. There was a large orifice in the lower portion of the head that was continually opening and closing. Possibly it had something to do with the creature's breathing.

The scientists watched spellbound as the strange being became involved in a series of fantastic adventures. There was an incredibly violent conflict with another, slightly different creature. It seemed certain that they must both be killed, but when it was all over neither seemed any the worse.

Then came a furious drive over miles of country in a four-wheeled mechanical device which was capable of extra-ordinary feats of locomotion. The ride ended in a city packed with other vehicles moving in all directions at breathtaking speeds. No one was surprised to see two of the machines meet head on with devastating results.

After that, events became even more complicated. It was now quite obvious that it would take many years of research to analyze and understand all that was happening. It was also clear that the record was a work of art, somewhat stylized, rather than an exact reproduction of life as it actually had been on the Third Planet.

Most of the scientists felt themselves completely dazed when the sequence of pictures came to an end. There was a final flurry of motion, in which the creature that had been the center of interest became involved in some tremendous but incomprehensible catastrophe. The picture contracted to a circle, centered on the creature's head.

The last scene of all was an expanded view of its face, obviously expressing some powerful emotion. But whether it was rage, grief, defiance, resignation or some other feeling could not be guessed. The picture vanished. For a moment some lettering appeared on the screen, then it was all over.

For several minutes there was complete silence, save for the lapping of the waves upon the sand. The scientists were too stunned to speak. The fleeting glimpse of Earth's civilization had had a shattering effect on their minds. Then little groups began to start talking together, first in whispers and then more and more loudly as the implications of what they had seen became clearer. Presently the Historian called for attention and addressed the meeting again.

"We are now planning," he said, "a vast program of research to extract all available knowledge from this record. Thousands of copies are being made for distribution to all workers. You will appreciate the problems involved. The psychologists in particular have an immense task confronting them.

"But I do not doubt that we shall succeed. In another generation, who can say what we may not have learned of this wonderful race? Before we leave, let us look again at our remote cousins, whose wisdom may have surpassed our own but of whom so little has survived."

Once more the final picture flashed on the screen, motionless this time, for the projector had been stopped. With something like awe, the scientists gazed at the still figure from the past, while in turn the little biped stared back at them with its characteristic expression of arrogant bad temper.

For the rest of time it would symbolize the human race. The psychologists of Venus would analyze its actions and watch its every movement until they could reconstruct its mind. Thousands of books would be written about it. Intricate philosophies would be contrived to account for its behavior.

But all this labor, all this research, would be utterly in vain. Perhaps the proud and lonely figure on the screen was smiling sardonically at the scientists who were starting on their age-long fruitless quest.

Its secret would be safe as long as the universe endured, for no one now would ever read the lost language of Earth. Millions of times in the ages to come those last few words would flash across the screen, and none could ever guess their meaning.

A Walt Disney Production. ❖

"Some philosophers maintain that knowledge of machinery does not necessarily imply a high degree of civilization, and it is theoretically possible to have wars in a society possessing mechanical power, flight, and even radio." What is civilization, and has today's world succeeded or failed to be civilized?

Literature CONNECTION

TEASDALE

Sara Teasdale was a popular lyrical poet in the early twentieth century. She was born in St. Louis, Missouri, in 1884. Her first book of poetry, *Sonnets to Duse and Other Poems,* was published in 1907, and in 1918, she won the Columbia University Poetry Society prize for *Love Songs*. Teasdale wrote several collections of poems, including *Strange Victory* that was printed after her death in 1933. Her poem **"There Will Come Soft Rains"** deals with the possibility that people might completely destroy themselves.

There Will Come Soft Rains

A Poem by **Sara Teasdale**

There will come soft rains and the smell
of the ground,
And swallows circling with their
shimmering sound;

And frogs in the pools singing at night,
And wild plum-trees in tremulous white;

Robins will wear their feathery fire
Whistling their whims on a low fence-wire;
And not one will know of the war, not one
Will care at last when it is done.

Not one would mind, neither bird nor tree
If mankind perished utterly;

And Spring herself, when she woke at dawn,
Would scarcely know that we were gone. ❖

Refer and Reason

1. Point out what the Venusians in "History Lesson" hope to gain by studying the film record. What don't they understand about this record?
2. Reread the passages that describe the film. Upon viewing this film, what misconceptions might the Venusians have about humans? Describe the ways in which it is an accurate portrayal of life as we know it on Earth.
3. Imagine that the Venusians had found some footage from the evening news as well as the cartoon. Explain how the two films would compare and contrast.

Writing Options

1. Imagine that the Venusians have set up an exhibit about life on the Third Planet based on the items left in the cairn. Write a museum guide to this exhibit that includes a short description of each piece including its possible function. Explain these items from a Venusian point of view.
2. Write a compare-and-contrast essay comparing Venusian society to today's human society. Compare the differences in the values of each society, and any other elements that you noticed in the story.

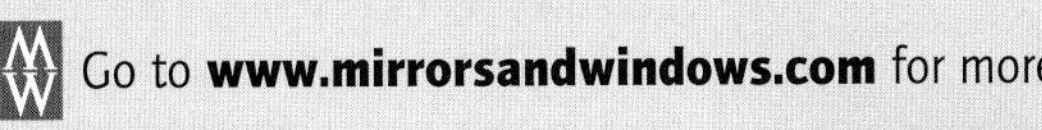
Go to **www.mirrorsandwindows.com** for more.

TEXT TO TEXT CONNECTION

Compare and contrast how each selection depicts the end of human civilization. What causes the destruction of mankind in "History Lesson" and in "There Will Come Soft Rains"? How does the earth respond to these events and the final outcome? What remains of the human race at the end of each selection?

Designing

Anne Underwood has been a reporter for *Newsweek* magazine since 1996. In 1987, she earned a George Polk Award for Foreign Reporting for her coverage of terrorism in the Middle East. In this selection, Underwood interviews **William McDonough,** an architect and industrial designer who founded McDonough Braungart Design Chemistry. McDonough is working with Fortune 500 companies and the Chinese government to develop unique ways to make buildings, factories, products—even cities—environmentally sustainable. McDonough has received three U.S. presidential awards for his work in environmentally sustainable design.

MCDONOUGH

In your opinion, just how important is recycling and using recycled products?

the Future

An Interview by
Anne Underwood

"Our job is to dream—and to make those dreams happen."

In a new interview series, NEWSWEEK talks to a leading ecological architect whose goal is nothing less than eliminating waste and pollution.

NEWSWEEK, May 16, 2005

Imagine buildings that generate more energy than they consume and factories whose waste water is clean enough to drink. William McDonough has accomplished these tasks and more. Architect, industrial designer and founder of McDonough Braungart Design Chemistry in Charlottesville, Va., he's not your traditional environmentalist. Others may expend their energy fighting for stricter environmental regulations and repeating the mantra "reduce, reuse, recycle." McDonough's vision for the future includes factories so safe they *need* no regulation, and novel, safe materials that can be totally reprocessed into new goods, so there's no reason to scale back consumption (or lose jobs). In short, he wants to overhaul the Industrial Revolution—which would sound crazy if he weren't working with Fortune 500 companies and the government of China to make it happen. The recipient of two U.S. presidential honors and the National Design Award, McDonough is the former dean of architecture at the University of Virginia and co-chair of the China-U.S. Center for Sustainable Development. He spoke in New York recently with NEWSWEEK's Anne Underwood.

UNDERWOOD: Why do we need a new industrial revolution?

MCDONOUGH: The Industrial Revolution as a whole was not designed. It took shape gradually as industrialists and engineers figured out how to make things. The result is that we put billions of pounds of toxic materials in the air, water and soil every year and generate gigantic amounts of waste. If our goal is to destroy the world—to produce global warming and toxicity and endocrine disruption—we're doing great. But if the goal isn't global warming, what is? I want to crank the wheel of industry in a different direction to produce a world of abundance and good design—a delightful, safe world that our children can play in.

You say that recycling, as it's currently practiced, is "downcycling."

What we call recycling is typically the product losing its quality. Paper gets mixed with other papers, re-chlorinated and contaminated with toxic inks. The fiber length gets shorter, allowing more particles to abrade into the air, where they get into your lungs and nasal passages, and cause irritation. And you end up with gray, fuzzy stuff that doesn't really work for you. That's downcycling.

[My mentor and colleague] Michael Braungart and I coined the term upcycling, meaning that the product could actually get better as it comes through the system. For example, some plastic bottles contain the residues of heavy-metal catalysts. We can remove those residues as the bottles come back to be upcycled.

Not all products lend themselves to that.

Most manufacturers take resources out of the ground and convert them to products that are designed to be thrown away or incinerated within months. We call these "cradle to grave" product flows. Our answer to that is "cradle to cradle" design. Everything is reused—either returned to the soil as nontoxic "biological nutrients" that will biodegrade safely, or returned to industry as "technical nutrients" that can be infinitely recycled. Aluminum is a technical nutrient. It takes tremendous energy to make, but it's easy to recapture and reuse. Since 1880, the human species has made 660 million tons of it. We still know where 440 million tons are today.

Are there products already that meet cradle-to-cradle goals? If so, how do we find them?

Within the month, we will be branding cradle to cradle. Products that meet our criteria for biological and technical nutrients can be certified to use our logo. A note on the packaging will tell you how to recycle it. You'll know: this one goes into my tomato plot when I'm finished or this one goes back to industry forever. We have already approved a nylon, some polyester textiles, running tracks, window shades, chairs from Herman Miller and Steelcase, and carpets from Shaw, which is part of Berkshire Hathaway. The first was a Steelcase fabric that can go back to the soil. We're now working on electronics on a global scale.

How do paper products like magazines fit into this picture?

Why take something as exquisite as a tree and knock it down? Trees make oxygen, sequester carbon, distill water, build soils, convert solar energy to fuel, change colors with the seasons, create microclimates and provide habitat.

My book "Cradle to Cradle," which I wrote with Michael Braungart, is printed on pages made of plastic resins and inorganic fillers that are infinitely recyclable. They're too heavy, but we're working with companies now to develop lightweight plastic papers. We have safe, lightweight inks designed to float off the paper in a bath of 180 degrees—hotter than you would encounter under normal circumstances. We can recapture the inks and reuse them without adding chlorine and dioxins to the environment. And the pages are clean, smooth and white.

Cradle to Cradle by William McDonough and Michael Braungart.

So we can keep our trees and have newspapers, too.

Most environmentalists feel guilty about how society behaves, so they say we should make longer-lasting products—for example, a car that lasts 25 years. That car will still use compound epoxies and toxic adhesives, but the ecological footprint is reduced because you've amortized it over a longer time. But what's the result? You lose jobs because people aren't buying as much, and you're using the wrong technology longer. I want five-year cars. Then you can always be getting the newest car—more solar-powered, cleaner, with the newest air bags and safety features. The old car gets upcycled into new cars, so there are still plenty of jobs. And you don't feel guilty about throwing the old one away. People want new technology. You're not typing on an Underwood, if you know what I mean.

So growth is good?

Yes, if you use nature as a model and mentor, if you use modern designs and chemicals that are safe. Growth is destructive if you use energy not from the sun and a system of chemicals that is toxic, so it's anti-life.

Given that industry today fits your definition of anti-life, why aren't you fighting for stricter environmental regulations?

If coal plants release mercury—and mercury is a neurotoxin that damages children's brains—then reducing the amount of mercury in emissions doesn't stop that. It just says, "We'll tell you at what rate you can dispense death." Being less bad is not being good. Our idea is to make production so clean, there's nothing bad left to regulate. This is extremely interesting to people of all political persuasions—those who love the environment and those who want commerce free of regulation.

Can you really have industry so clean it requires no controls?

[At the Rohner textile plant in Switzerland] we designed a fabric safe enough to eat. The manufacturing process uses no mutagens, carcinogens, endocrine disrupters, heavy-metal contaminants or chemicals that cause ozone depletion, allergies, skin desensitization or plant and fish toxicity. We screened 8,000 commonly used chemicals and ended up with 38. When inspectors measured the effluent water, they thought their instruments were broken. The water was as clean as Swiss drinking water. A garden club started using the waste trimmings as mulch. Workers no longer had to wear protective clothing. And it eliminated regulatory paperwork, so they've reduced the cost of production by 20 percent. Why spend money on paperwork, when you can spend it delivering service or paying your workers a living wage?

Where would I find this fabric?

It was selected for upholstery on the new Airbus 380. It's made of worsted wool to keep you at the right temperature—cool when it's hot and warm when it's cold—and [a plant fiber called] ramie to wick away moisture. It's a high-performance-design product. Going ecological doesn't mean downgrading performance criteria.

How do you get more industries to adopt these ideals?

Industries don't change unless they have to or there's some commercial benefit. At Herman Miller [the furniture company], we designed a factory full of daylight and fresh air. Productivity soared. And because of all the natural light, they cut lighting costs by 50 percent—overall energy by 30 percent. We've been doing this a long time. But now that China has taken it up, it portends exciting things.

"Why take something as exquisite as a tree and knock it down?"

What are you doing in China?

The China Housing Industry Association has the responsibility for building housing for 400 million people in the next 12 years. We're working with them to design seven new cities. We're identifying building materials of the future, such as a new polystyrene from BASF [with no noxious chemicals]. It can be used to build walls that are strong, lightweight and superinsulating. The building can be heated and cooled for next to nothing. And it's silent. If there are 13 people in the apartment upstairs, you won't hear them.

We've designed a luxurious new toilet. The bowl is like a lotus leaf—so smooth, axle grease slips right off. Nothing sticks to it, including

Pudong skyline in Shanghai, China.

bacteria. A light mist when you're done will be enough to flush it, so you won't use lots of water. We'll have bamboo wetlands nearby to purify the waste—and the bamboo, which grows a foot a day, can be harvested and used for wood.

The Chinese are afraid urbanization will reduce productive farmland, so we'll move farms onto rooftops. At least, that's what I'm proposing. The farmers can live downstairs. And when you look at the city from a distance, it will look like part of the landscape.

Is it practical to put farms on roofs?

Traditional roofs aren't practical. They degrade from thermal shock and ultraviolet radiation and have to be replaced in 20 years. For the Gap's corporate campus in San Bruno, Calif., we planted a "green roof" of ancient grasses. The roof now damps the sounds of jets from the San Francisco airport. It absorbs storm water, which is important because they have serious issues with storm water there. It makes oxygen, provides habitat, and it's beautiful. We also made a green roof for Ford Motor Co.'s River Rouge plant. It saved Ford millions of dollars in storm-water equipment.

How will you fuel the Chinese cities?

I want to see solar power cheaper than coal, but to get the speed and scale to do that fast, you need a place like China. We're not talking about dinky solar collectors on roofs. Think of square miles of marginal land covered with them. This could drop the cost of solar energy an order of magnitude. And for every job making solar panels, there are four jobs putting them in place and maintaining them. We could import these panels, and for every job the Chinese give themselves, we get four. What a gift. And I guarantee you, China will never be able to capture an American photon. We would have indigenous energy and energy security. And we wouldn't be throwing our money into holes in the ground.

And we wouldn't need nuclear energy.

I love nuclear energy. I just want to make sure it stays where God put it—93 million miles away, in the sun.

Your ideas are really catching on.

It's an amazing moment in history. We also have two huge new projects in England—working with the cities of Greenwich and Wembley. The developer, Adrian Wyatt, has asked us to conceive the meta-framework for the project.

We won't get everything right the first time. Change requires experimentation. But no problem can be solved by the same consciousness that created it. Our job is to dream—and to make those dreams happen. ❖

According to William McDonough, "...no problem can be solved by the same consciousness that created it." Assuming this is true, what does that imply about the rest of the world's problems? How might the world go about solving these problems?

Refer and Reason

1. Differentiate between McDonough's views and those of a "traditional" environmentalist. Evaluate to what extent McDonough's opinions are substantiated in the text.
2. Paraphrase McDonough's main ideas or goals, and decide whether his ideas have the potential to affect our environment in a positive way. Why or why not?
3. Relate how you think traditional environmentalists view McDonough's philosophy and work. Do you think some might support it, and others see it as a threat? Explain your answer.

Writing Options

1. Imagine that McDonough Braungart Design Chemistry is having an open house to present the company's latest innovations to the public. Write a letter of invitation to the event in which you try to entice potential investors to attend.
2. Write an editorial in which you comment on Anne Underwood's interview with McDonough. In your editorial, summarize McDonough's work and explain how you think he could impact today's environmental challenges.

Go to **www.mirrorsandwindows.com** for more.

THE STAR

By H. G. Wells
Art by Brad Teare

British author **H. G. (Herbert George) Wells** (1866–1946), one of the fathers of science fiction, wrote the original version of the short story "The Star" in 1897. This story was the first of a science fiction subgenre depicting a planet or star colliding, or near-colliding with earth. Utah artist **Brad Teare's** graphic version of "The Star" was published in 2005.

It is amazing what little damage the Earth has sustained. The masses of the seas remain intact. The only difference seems to be a shrinkage of polar ice.

The End

What other apocalyptic (end of the world) works of literature or films have you seen? What similarities or differences do they have with this depiction?

Refer and Reason

1. What does the astronomer see through his telescope?
2. What effect did the absence of captions or text in this graphic portrayal have on your interpretation of the story?
3. **Irony** is the difference between appearance and reality. How is the comment made by the aliens at the end of the story ironic?

Writing Options

1. Write a plot summary of the story based on the illustrations showing the events.
2. Write a short essay discussing how Wells' fictional vision of the future in 1897 compares with environmental concerns today.

 Go to **www.mirrorsandwindows.com** for more.

FOR YOUR READING LIST

THE OLD MAN AND THE SEA
by Ernest Hemingway

After Santiago goes eighty-four days without catching a single fish, he decides to row his little boat far out into the ocean. Soon, he has hooked the largest marlin he has ever seen. How will old Santiago manage to kill the fish and bring him back to the harbor? This classic tale narrates Santiago's battle with the sea.

BLUE HIGHWAYS: A JOURNEY INTO AMERICA
by William Least Heat-Moon

After losing his job and his wife, Least Heat-Moon sets off on a 13,000 mile trip on the back roads of America. His personal account describes not only his journey through forgotten towns and highways, but also the stories of the people he encounters along the way.

LEAVING HOME
selected by Hazel Rochman and Darlene Z. McCampbell

Leaving Home contains a collection of short stories about personal growth and tragedy, childhood experiences, and other personal journeys. The collection includes the work of fifteen well-known authors, including Amy Tan, Sandra Cisneros, Tim O'Brien, and Toni Morrison.

MEMORY BOY
by Will Weaver

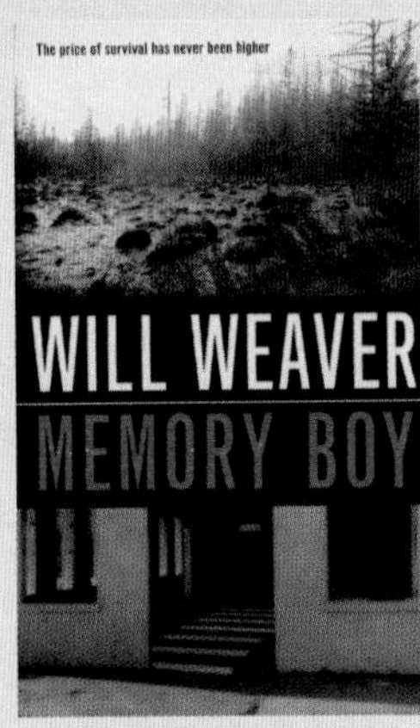

Since Washington's Mount Rainier erupted, volcanic ash has been falling over the United States causing food and fuel shortages. Looting and killing are now common on the streets of Minneapolis. The Newells want to leave the city, but the trip is dangerous. However, sixteen-year-old Miles has a secret weapon: an astounding memory.

FAHRENHEIT 451
by Ray Bradbury

The government has decided that reading books leads to unhappiness. Fireman Guy Montag's job is to burn books. One day, he steals a book from a fire and must seek the help of an unemployed professor to understand its contents. He soon hopes for a future where people can read and think. That is, until he is turned in.

THE EAR, THE EYE, AND THE ARM
by Nancy Farmer

After his three children sneak out of their secure home and disappear, General Matsika hires a team of mutant detectives to track them down. Set in Zimbabwe in the year 2194, the tale portrays the futuristic society as well as the eldest son's struggle to find his own identity and prove his worth to his father and himself.

SPEAKING & LISTENING WORKSHOP

Give a Descriptive Writing Presentation

In this lesson, you will present an original descriptive piece of writing to your classmates.

1. Select the subject of your descriptive piece.

Descriptive writing typically portrays a person, an object, or a scene. Decide who, what, or where (place) you are going to describe in your writing.

2. Select the form your writing will take.

You may wish to write a descriptive poem, a short descriptive personal essay, or a descriptive short story.

3. Review a few pieces of descriptive writing by other writers.

It is always good for writers to be inspired by the accomplishments of other writers. Two selections from the unit that you may want to review are "Blue Highways: A Journey into America" by William Least Heat-Moon and "A Sound of Thunder" by Ray Bradbury. Note how Least Heat-Moon describes the town of Nameless, Tennessee, in the first paragraph of Chapter 16 (page 845). Least Heat-Moon includes vivid and precise descriptions throughout his travelogue to create a strong sense of place and scene. These are the types of details that you want to incorporate in your own work.

4. Provide sensory details.

Take time to visualize the details of that which you are trying to describe in your writing. Remember, your main goal is to create a vivid picture in the listeners' minds. Make the reader see, hear, taste, smell, and feel the subject of your description.

5. Use precise language.

You can't be lazy with language when you are writing a descriptive piece. Put effort into choosing precise nouns, verbs, adverbs, and adjectives. You should have a dictionary and a thesaurus close at hand.

6. Once your writing is final, practice presenting it.

Practice reading your written work aloud in front of the mirror or with a friend or family member.

7. Deliver your descriptive piece.

Finally, deliver your descriptive piece of writing to your teacher and classmates.

Speaking Tips

- Watch **volume** and **pace.** Do not speak too softly or too quickly.
- Be sure to **enunciate,** or pronounce your words clearly.
- Vary your **pitch** (the highness or lowness of the voice) to give expression to your description, and use **stress** to emphasize important ideas.
- Maintain **eye contact** to keep your audience interested, and use **facial expressions** and **gestures,** if appropriate, to help bring your writing to life.

Speaking and Listening Rubric

Your presentation will be evaluated on these elements:

Content

- Does the descriptive work make use of a variety of sensory details?
- Does the descriptive work use precise and original language?
- Does the descriptive work accomplish creating a vivid mental picture of a person, an object, or a scene in the minds of the listeners?

Delivery and Presentation

- Are volume, enunciation, and pace appropriate?
- Does the speaker use an expressive voice, varying the pitch, stress, and tone appropriately?
- Has the speaker used eye contact, facial expressions (if appropriate), gestures, and body language effectively?

Research Paper: The I-Search

Assignment
Write an I-search essay exploring a personal talent in order to learn how to develop it and use it in the future.
Purpose
To use various sources to gain insight into this talent or interest
Audience
Teachers, classmates, family, and others interested in the same field

An **I-search** is an essay written on a topic of personal relevance. William Least Heat-Moon, author of *Blue Highways: A Journey into America,* traveled the back roads to actively explore this country and learn about himself. Dorothy Wordsworth wrote her *Grasmere Journals* to discover her heart and mind, describing her life process as she did. In an I-search essay, the author builds the story of his or her journey into the research itself.

Conduct an I-search to explore a talent you have and the career options it may provide. Do you love music, sports, or science? Do you aspire to perform in a band, play for a team, or cure cancer? Learn about your skills and that field through conducting personal interviews, visiting relevant sites, and doing research. Even though an I-search is informal, using first-person narration, sources must be documented properly.

Assignment
Plan, write, and revise an I-search paper in which you explore—and describe the process you undergo—a talent you'd like to develop and the potential careers it could lead you to.

Writing Rubric

A successful I-search essay

- ☑ provides an **introduction** that identifies a talent meaningful to you, and the assumptions you have about it
- ☑ includes a clear **thesis statement** expressing your purpose in exploring the topic
- ☑ in the **body,** supports the purpose by using appropriate and varied sources related to the topic and also describes the process of finding sources and learning information
- ☑ in the **conclusion,** reflects on and perhaps summarizes what was learned, based on the statement of purpose
- ☑ documents **sources** correctly

❶ PREWRITE

Select Your Topic
Brainstorm a list of your talents. Choose one you are best at or most interested in to explore and write about.

Gather Information
Begin with journal writing; express what you already know about your talent and assumptions you have about the kind of career it could lead to. Next, choose a variety of sources. Interview experts, visit relevant locations, and find readings and websites. You will find tips for gathering information from an interview on page 813.

Don't worry about getting too much information—you can always cut back later. As you gather information, be sure to take notes for each source and to write down all information needed to document the source correctly. It's much harder to go back and track down a source than it is to accurately identify it the first time!

Use a K-W-L Chart like the one on page 921 to track information, sources, and the process of conducting your I-search. One student, Neil Ross, used the chart to track his research, which helped him create his works-cited section.

Organize Your Ideas
Your essay should include the steps you took from beginning to end, from what you first believed, to what you discovered, to what degree your attitude changed. Use the four columns of your chart as a guide for organizing your draft. Review your K-W-L Chart. What discovery surprised you? What differences are there between the

K-W-L Chart

What do you know?	What do you want to learn?	Where will you search?	What have you learned?
I know I like music, especially guitar; had my dad's, got a new one. Girlfriend likes it too. I like the guitar shop and take lessons.	I want to know if I could make a living in music.	I will search books and the Internet; interview experts. Interview: Penske, Isaac. Personal interview. 3 February 2006.	I learned: Difficult to make it big. Don't need college degree. Have to join a union. Other jobs for musicians: floorshow band, dance bands (part-time); give lessons; write music.

first and last columns, between your assumptions and your discoveries? Highlight your insights. Think about how to present your information in a way that will allow readers to share in your journey of discovery.

Write Your Thesis Statement

Review your chart and journal writing. Draft a **thesis statement** that cites your talent or interest and summarizes why you want to research it. Neil wrote this statement to guide his essay:

> Because of the rewards of learning to play the guitar, I often wonder if being a professional musician is something I should consider as a career.

What Great Writers Do

William Least Heat-Moon knows how to include readers in his process of exploration. He says this: "In everything I write, my primary wish is to make the reader feel that he or she is there. I want the reader to feel that you are at my side. If I accomplish that, then I think I have a chance at getting some of the other things across, but if I fail in that, I'll probably fail in everything that really counts."

❷ DRAFT

Write your essay using the three-part framework described at right: **introduction, body,** and **conclusion.**

- **Introduction**
  Name the talent or interest you will explore. Include a statement of purpose as your thesis.
- **Body**
  Describe both the process (how you found your sources) and the research (what you learned from your sources and interviews).
- **Conclusion**
  Expand on your statement of purpose so it reflects what you learned.

Draft Your Introduction

The **introduction** of your I-search essay should establish the talent you have and your purpose for exploring it. Since this writing is less formal than a research paper, write in first person from your mind and heart. This point of view will help you convey insights and discoveries important to you and capture your readers' interest.

The introduction that Neil drafted is shown in the first column of the chart on page 924. In his first two sentences, Neil establishes his passion for playing guitar. Next, he describes his assumption about the field of popular music. His last sentence declares why he wants to conduct his research. How could he develop his introduction in a way that would engage readers more effectively?

Draft Your Body

In the **body,** elaborate on your research. Use statistics, information from sources, and quotations from interviews. Use **parenthetical** or **in-text citations** to identify sources when you directly quote, summarize or paraphrase, or state a fact or statistic. Write the complete citations in your bibliography, or works-cited page, at the end of your paper. (See the Language Arts Handbook 5.6, Documenting Sources.)

What Great Writers Do

William Zinsser (b. 1922), a writer and teacher, wrote a book called *On Writing Well* that has inspired college students for more than twenty-five years. A master of careful editing, he says, "With each rewrite I try to make what I have written stronger and more precise, eliminating every element that is not doing useful work. Then I go over it once more, reading it aloud, and am always amazed at how much clutter can still be cut."

In his first body paragraph, Neil paraphrases facts from a library search and uses parenthetical citations. In three following body paragraphs, he references a website, describes firsthand observation, and directly quotes from a personal interview.

Review your K-W-L Chart. The body of your essay should unfold using a similar progression as your chart. Cull the best information from your research and develop it into paragraphs that relate directly to the purpose for your inquiry.

Draft Your Conclusion

Lastly, write the **conclusion** of your I-search essay. A good conclusion reflects on the findings of the research, responds to and builds on the statement of purpose, and provides closure for readers.

Does Neil accomplish these things in his conclusion? Look at the draft of his conclusion in the chart on page 924.

USE PROPER DOCUMENTATION

You need to credit authors and sources for the information that you use in your research. Citing your sources properly allows readers to verify your research and protects you against plagiarism. Plagiarism is a serious offense that involves taking someone else's words or thoughts and pretending that they are your own.

Directly quote when passages are precise, eloquent, or unique to a source. Put the exact words in quotation marks, and, in parentheses, reference the last name of the author of the source and the page where you found those words. When using quotations, don't let them stand alone in your paper. Blend them into your writing, and show how they contribute to your overall analysis. This style of documentation is called **parenthetical citation.**

EXAMPLE

> Homelessness is not easy to solve. While some people work hard to combat it, others lessen their own participation by "turning it into an issue, not a collection of human beings. We turn an adjective into a noun: the poor, not poor people; the homeless, not Ann or the man who lives in the box..." (Quindlen 835).

When not quoting directly, you may want to **paraphrase,** or tell in your own words, an author's ideas. In paraphrasing, you must still credit the author by referencing the author's last name and the page where you found the idea. If the author's name is unavailable, use a shortened form of the title of the work.

EXAMPLE

> The idea of a home has changed. Previous generations lived, worked, and were usually buried in the same place; today, people are more likely to move multiple times (Quindlen 834–835).

When you cite information from other sources, you should include the source information for easy reference. This works-cited section at the end of your paper will include the information a reader would need to locate the original sources. (See an example of a works-cited section in the Student Model on page 927.)

Proper documentation includes the following information: author (or editor, compiler, or translator), title, place, publisher, and date of publication. The chart below shows the correct form for different types of bibliography entries, according to the *Modern Language Association Handbook for Writers of Research Papers.*

Forms for Works Cited	
Book	Douglass, Frederick. *Escape from Slavery: The Boyhood of Frederick Douglass in His Own Words.* New York: Alfred A. Knopf, 1994. Print.
Magazine article	Reston, James, Jr. "Orion: Where Stars Are Born." *National Geographic.* December 1995: 90-101. Print.
Encyclopedia entry	"Lewis and Clark Expedition." *Encyclopedia Americana.* Jackson, Donald. 1995 ed. Print.
Interview	Campbell, Silas. Personal interview. 6 February 1997.
Film	*The Big Heat.* Dir. Fritz Lang. With Glenn Ford and Gloria Grahame. Writ. Sidney Boehm. Based on the novel of the same title by William P. McGiven. 90 min. Columbia, 1953. Film.
Internet site	Armstrong, Mark. "That's 'Sir' Mick Jagger to You." 17 June 2002. E! Online, Inc. Web. 17 June 2003. <http://www.eonline.com/News/Items/0,1,10110,00.html>.

Review your own draft and make sure you have used documentation correctly.

❸ REVISE

Evaluate Your Draft

Decide whether to evaluate your own writing or trade papers with a classmate and evaluate each other's work. Either way, make notes directly on the essay about what's been done well and what can be improved.

Check the content and organization. Make sure that the three parts of the essay—the introduction, body, and conclusion—work together to support the statement of purpose. The body paragraphs should unfold in a logical progression. Use the Revision Checklist on page 925 to make this evaluation and suggest changes that could be made.

Check that sources have been documented correctly. Again, use the Revision Checklist to evaluate the essay. Think about how the writing, in first person, can be both personable and grammatically clear. One way to achieve this is to vary and polish sentences; to do so, combine information where appropriate, and separate sentences that are too long.

Revise for Content, Organization, and Style

Neil evaluated his draft and found some ways to improve his writing. Look at the chart on page 924 (this time, the right-hand column) to see how he revised the three paragraphs we looked at earlier.

DRAFT STAGE		REVISE STAGE	
Introduction The best thing I can do is play guitar. I dream of making it big. Rock stars on TV have it made—big houses, hot cars. My parents don't consider music practical. Still, because of how much I love the guitar, I want to become a professional musician.	Identifies talent States assumptions States thesis, or statement of purpose	~~The best thing I can do is play guitar.~~ My guitar teacher says I have natural talent. After a year of lessons, I can play the music of artists I love and have written a few songs of my own. I admit I dream of making it big. Rock stars on TV have it made—big houses, hot cars. My parents don't consider music practical. Still, because of how much I love the guitar, I ~~want to become~~ wonder if being a professional musician is something I should consider as a career.	Replaces flat statement with informative sentences; strengthens tone to add interest Develops statement of purpose
Body Paragraph U2 and Metallica make millions. However, making it big is rare. Shelly Field wrote that most bands bomb. Musicians play in floorshow or dance bands. They play at schools, nightclubs and hotels. They earn anywhere from $100 to $10,000 per engagement (Field 191). In order to get jobs, musicians are advised to join a union.	Uses specific information and statistics to support statement of purpose; documents sources	In the library I learned, no surprise, that groups like U2 and Metallica make millions of dollars a year. However, making it big is rare. ~~Shelly Field wrote~~ Most bands ~~bomb~~ never get a recording contract (Field 7). Musicians play in floorshow or dance bands~~. They play~~ and at schools, nightclubs, and hotels, ~~They~~ earning anywhere from $100 to $10,000 per engagement (Field 191). In order to get jobs, musicians are advised to join a union (Field 241).	Includes process Changes in-text citation to parenthetical citation; improves language choice Combines sentences for less choppy writing Makes sure to reference all information
Conclusion I've decided playing makes me happy, not some fantasy of performing. Sure, playing in a band would be fun. But I'd enjoy teaching, or working in a music store, even if it may sound boring, but it's practical. That should make my parents happy. It's nice to know I could find a way to play music and make a living.	Describes change in thinking Expands on statement of purpose Brings essay full circle by echoing the introduction	Maybe being a rock star isn't as easy, or even as appealing, as it seems. I've decided playing makes me happy, not some fantasy of performing. I'm sure that playing in a band would be fun. I now know I'd also enjoy teaching, or working in a music store. ~~even if~~ It may sound boring, but it's practical. That should make my parents happy. It's nice to know I could find a way to play music and make a living. What more could I ask for?	Reflects on the introduction Describes learning Creates separate sentences for clarity Provides closure

- **Introduction:** Neil replaced a basic statement of his interest with two sentences showing the same idea in better, more specific detail. He created a more personable tone of voice by adding simple phrases.
- **Body:** Neil made sure to describe the process he used to gather information. He improved word choice. He combined choppy sentences to create a better flow. He was careful to cite the sources of all information.
- **Conclusion:** Neil brought his essay full circle by expanding on statements he made in his introduction. He distinguished what he learned. He separated sentences for clarity. He added a final sentence to satisfy readers and provide closure.

Review the notes you or your partner made as you evaluated your draft. Then respond to each comment and revise your essay effectively.

Proofread for Errors

The purpose of proofreading is to check for remaining errors. While you may certainly correct errors as you evaluate your essay, focus on it exclusively during proofreading. Use proofreader's symbols to mark any errors you find. (See Language Arts Handbook 4.1 for a list of proofreader's symbols.) To complete the assignment, print out a final draft and read the entire thing once more before turning it in.

Read through Neil's final draft on the next page. See how he worked through the three stages of the writing process: Prewrite, Draft, and Revise.

REVISION CHECKLIST

Content and Organization

- ❑ Did the writer clearly identify a talent or an interest in the **introduction?**
- ❑ Does the **statement of purpose** accurately identify the main idea of the essay? If not, how could it be improved?
- ❑ Do the **body** paragraphs progress in a logical manner?
- ❑ Do **body** paragraphs contain both research information and the writer's process?
- ❑ Does the **conclusion** expand on the statement of purpose? Does it reflect what the writer learned? Does it provide closure?

Grammar and Style

- ❑ Are **quotations** and **paraphrasing** documented accurately? (pages 922–923)
- ❑ Is the **works-cited section** formatted correctly? (page 923)
- ❑ Have all pieces of information been referenced with a **source?** (page 922)
- ❑ Are a **variety of sentence types** used? (page 923)

WRITING FOLLOW-UP

Publish and Present

- You and your classmates may wish to publish your work in an anthology or to post a paper a month on your school's website.
- Connect with students who have similar interests as you. Share and compare research experiences (interviews and sites visited) and the information you learned.

Reflect

- How was this experience meaningful to you? In what ways might your I-search essay be useful in the future? (Hint: In a few years, you may be able to use it in a college application. Decades from now, you might read it to reflect back on your life.)
- What did you learn about research and organization as you conducted your I-search? What did you learn about your own process of researching a topic?

STUDENT MODEL

Making It Big
by Neil Ross

My guitar teacher says I have natural talent. After a year of lessons, I can play the music of artists I love and have written a few songs of my own. I admit I dream of making it big. Rock stars on TV have it made—big houses, hot cars, and sold-out shows that keep them in the spotlight. My parents don't consider playing music to be a practical career aspiration. Still, because of how much I love the guitar, I wonder if being a professional musician is something I should consider as a career.

What talent does the writer explore? What is his statement of purpose?

In the library I learned, no surprise, that groups like U2 and Metallica make millions of dollars a year. However, making it big is rare. For every success story, there are hundreds of musicians and groups who can't get a recording contract (Field 7). Most musicians play in floorshow or dance bands at schools and at nightclubs and hotels, earning anywhere from $100 to $10,000 per engagement (Field 191). Show bands travel a lot, sometimes being on the road for weeks at a time. A step below the show band is the dance band. Dance bands play in schools, bars, clubs, cafes, hotels, and for private parties (Field 194).

How would you describe the writer's voice? Is it appropriate? Explain.

Most dance bands play part time, so members usually have other jobs to support themselves. Full-time musicians often resent these part-time players because they feel that the part-timers take jobs away from them. Also, part-timers will often accept less money for gigs, which lowers the pay scale for everyone (Levine 7). In order to get jobs, musicians have to join a union (Field 241). Probably the best compromise, if you can't afford to be a full-time musician, is to find a job that is related to the music industry like teaching or working in a music store.

What problems do musicians often face? Which sources does the writer cite when explaining?

The website for Music Mates lists jobs, club schedules, bands seeking musicians, musicians seeking bands, and teachers for hire. Looking at this website was a reality check. Most of the jobs listed don't sound as glamorous as I initially expected. To make it in music, people like me play in bands no one has ever heard of. The field was beginning to sound a bit too brutal for me.

Does the paper's organization seem logical? Explain.

To boost my spirits, I went straight to the source of my excitement: the guitar shop. It's a cool place, with close to a hundred guitars hanging on the walls. Often, a customer or an employee will pick one up and start playing. I've heard some awesome music just by hanging out in the guitar shop. The employees are knowledgeable and also very friendly. It was here that I decided to find someone to interview.

One employee, Isaac Penske, was interested in telling me all about his experiences as a musician. He told me he used to be in a band called Bad Temper. "I have to tell you, a live audience is a rush. Of course, Bad Temper—let's just say we didn't make the cover of *Rolling Stone*." He laughed, even though it must have been a disappointment. "Plus, the late nights, all the travel—it was exhausting. So I started working here," he said, shrugging. "Every day, I'm around what I love most, music. I get to be around other musicians and even instruct newcomers. It's really fun teaching people about something you love." While we talked, Isaac strummed a classical guitar. I realized this was his ideal job. He's not up on stage, but he makes a decent living in the music industry.

What impact does the writer's interview with Isaac have on his paper?

Maybe being a rock star isn't as easy, or even as appealing, as it first seemed. I've decided that playing makes me happy, not some fantasy of performing. I plan to focus on the music, no matter where it takes me. I'm sure that playing in a band would be fun. I now know I'd also enjoy teaching, or working in a music store, like Isaac. It may sound boring, but it's more practical than being a rock star. That should make my parents happy. It's nice to know I could find a way to play music and make a living. What more could I ask for?

What conclusion does the writer draw about a potential career in music?

Works Cited

Field, Shelly. *Career Opportunities in the Music Industry*. New York: Facts on File, 1995. Print.

Levine, Mike. *How to Be a Working Musician*. New York: Billboard Books, 1997. Print.

Music Mates. Dec. 2005. Music Mates, LLC. Web. 4 Feb. 2006 <www.musicmates.com>.

Penske, Isaac. Personal interview, 3 Feb. 2006.

Reading Skills

SYNTHESIZING IDEAS AND DRAWING CONCLUSIONS

Synthesizing ideas and drawing conclusions are necessary steps in understanding not just texts but life itself. Bits of information by themselves don't usually mean much; they are like the pieces of a jigsaw puzzle. The more pieces you can fit together, the more of the big picture you are able to see.

Test-Taking Tip
When a test requires you to answer questions about a passage, it's a good idea to glance over the questions before reading the passage itself. That way, you know specific things to look for when reading the passage. Otherwise, you will probably end up spending a great deal of precious time going back and rereading the passage repeatedly in order to answer each question.

To **synthesize** is to combine ideas to produce a coherent whole or a higher level of understanding. When you synthesize ideas, you are somehow grouping the information in the text so that it leads to better comprehension.

When you read, you are incorporating or integrating the new information you encounter with your existing knowledge. Some synthesizing occurs automatically and subconsciously because we are accustomed to wanting to make sense of what we encounter in the world. Other synthesizing, however, takes more of an effort on the reader's part. You need to think about what pieces of a text go together and how they fit with what you already know from other sources and your experiences.

When reading and thinking about what you have read, you are dealing with lots of pieces of information that belong in different groupings. The various pieces each belong to a different part of the puzzle. Some pieces may belong to the *tone* group; others are in the *characterization* group, and so on.

Once you synthesize the ideas, you then are in a position to draw one or more conclusions. When you **draw conclusions,** you are gathering pieces of information or clues from synthesizing ideas and deciding what that information means.

Drawing conclusions is an essential part of reading. As you read, it may be helpful to use a graphic organizer to keep track of the key ideas and supporting points you find and the conclusions you draw. Once your information is organized, you can proceed to analyzing it.

PRACTICE

Directions: Read the following excerpt by Joette Lorian. The questions that follow ask you to synthesize ideas and draw conclusions.

"For the Future of Florida: Repair the Everglades!'

"If the people will it, if they enforce their will on the water managers of Florida's future, the Everglades can be restored to nature's design."

—Marjory Stoneman Douglas

The Marshall Plan

Marjory Stoneman Douglas recently turned 108 years old, but the preceding words from her book *The Everglades: River of Grass* are as true today as when she wrote them. Equally true is the headline of this newsletter. This same headline appeared in the Everglades Reporter in 1981 when Friends of the Everglades announced a plan to restore the Everglades. The repair plan was developed by ecologist Art Marshall. The message of the "Marshall Plan" was simple: To repair the Everglades ecosystem, sheetflow must be restored, to the greatest extent possible, from the Kissimmee River down through Lake Okeechobee, south through the central Everglades and into Florida Bay.

The purpose of the Plan was to protect and recover a vast array of natural resources which were quickly being degraded—drinking water, freshwater fisheries, marine fisheries and Everglades National Park. Restoration of the ecosystem called for, among other things, resolving the pollution problems of Lake Okeechobee and the vast Everglades Agricultural Area, as well as dechannelizing the lower Kissimmee River, which would provide the start of the long sheetflow of water which pass through Lake Okeechobee and into the Everglades and the Park.

Art Marshall's plan was necessary because the Central and Southern Florida Project, started in 1948, had created an 1800 mile canal and levee system to provide flood control for cities and farms. This ditching, diking, and draining of the Everglades reduced this four million acre wetland by half and resulted in a reduction of nesting wading birds by 94%. The Marshall Plan forms the basis of the plan for restoration being supported by most conservationists today and guides the efforts of Friends of the Everglades.

Marjory spoke of Art Marshall's role in her autobiography *Voice of the River*: "Although my phrase 'River of Grass' first awakened people to the notion of the Everglades as a river, it was Art Marshall who filled in the blanks…More than any other person, he stretched our idea of the Everglades and how the system interacts with everything else, which created the most powerful arguments for preserving the water. Self-interest is a more reliable motivation than environmental pity or noblesse oblige, and Marshall accomplished the extraordinary magic of taking the Everglades out of the bleeding hearts category forever."

Multiple Choice

1. Along with improving the quality of drinking water, which is also a purpose of the Marshall Plan?
   A. reducing wetlands
   B. restoring sheetflow
   C. creating a canal and levee system
   D. providing flood control for cities and farms
   E. fight crime

2. According to the excerpt, what is one thing necessary for the restoration of the ecosystem?
   A. protecting the wildlife within the Everglades
   B. channelizing the lower Kissimmee River
   C. resolving the pollution problems of Lake Okeechobee
   D. adding another levee system
   E. finding endangered plant life

3. As it is used in the second paragraph, the term *degraded* most nearly means
   A. improved.
   B. ruined.
   C. provided.
   D. cleaned.
   E. assessed.

4. Based on this excerpt, which do you think is the final conclusion?
   A. Marjory's efforts were mainly wasted.
   B. Art Marshall worked with Marjory Stoneman Douglas to deliver the message.
   C. It is difficult for people to work together.
   D. Restoring the health of the Everglades is vital to people, animals, and the land.
   E. The ecosystem is strong.

Constructed Response

5. How did you draw this conclusion in question 4? Cite specifics from the excerpt.

Writing Skills

PERSUASIVE WRITING

Test-Taking Tip
Essay prompts contain clues about what is expected of you. Sometimes, you will find key words that will help you determine exactly what is being asked. For example, are you being asked to analyze or identify, describe or discuss, evaluate or argue for or against something, or justify or explain? After drafting your essay, go back and make sure that you have addressed all parts of the prompt.

Many standardized tests include sections that ask you to demonstrate your writing ability by composing an essay in response to a prompt, or topic. Some writing prompts ask you to try to convince the audience about something, either to do something or to think in a certain way. This type of writing is called persuasive, or argumentative. Examples of persuasive writing include editorials, petitions, and political speeches.

When you respond to a persuasive prompt, keep the following in mind:

- Be as logical and objective as possible.
- Don't just tell the audience what they should do or how they should think about this subject, but provide them with convincing reasons.
- Be as concrete and specific as possible. Trying to be concise will help you think more clearly.
- In a persuasive essay especially, it is important to use strong (but not offensive) language and strong constructions. Try to use the active voice instead of the passive whenever possible. Also, try to use active verbs instead of many "there is" or "there are" constructions.

Because you will be evaluated in part on your ability to use standard English, you should also pay attention to grammar, usage, capitalization, spelling, and punctuation.

PRACTICE

Timed Writing: 30 minutes

Think carefully about the issue presented in the following excerpt and the assignment below. Allow 30 minutes to write your response to the prompt.

In *Northanger Abbey,* Jane Austen wrote the following about novels:

"[A novel is] some work in which the most thorough knowledge of human nature, the happiest delineation of its varieties, the liveliest effusions of wit and humor are conveyed to the world in the best chosen language."

Some people see truth in this statement; others think nonfiction has more to offer the reader. Does reading fiction or nonfiction teach us more about human nature? In your essay, take a position on this question. You may write about either one of the two points of view given, or you may present a different point of view on this question.

Assignment: Plan and write an essay that states and supports your opinion of whether more can be learned about human nature from fiction or nonfiction. Use details such as examples, observations, and feelings to support and clarify your position.

Revising and Editing Skills

Some standardized tests ask you to read a draft of an essay and answer questions about how to improve it. As you read the draft, watch for errors like these:

- incorrect spellings and incorrect use of frequently confused words
- disagreement between subject and verb; inconsistent verb tense; incorrect forms for irregular verbs; sentence fragments and run-ons; and double negatives
- missing end marks, incorrect comma use, and lowercased proper nouns and proper adjectives
- unclear purpose, unclear main ideas, and lack of supporting details
- confusing order of ideas and missing transitions
- language that is inappropriate to the audience and purpose, and mood that is inappropriate for the purpose

After checking for errors, read each test question and decide which answer is best.

PRACTICE

Directions: In the passage that follows, certain words and phrases are numbered and underlined. Below the passage, you will find alternatives for each underlined word or phrase. Choose the alternative that best expresses the idea, that is worded most consistently with the style and tone of the rest of the passage, or that makes the text correct according to the conventions of standard written English. If you think the original version is best, choose the first alternative, "Make no change."

(1) Although the book was written long ago, it doesn't seem outdated or inaccessable. (2) What it says about relationships and love still is true, and the troubles of the life of a teenager seem timeless. (3) Everybody can relate to the characters, every one of which seems very real and believable. (4) You'll wish that the book would never end, but of course, it does; however, it will continue to effect you forever. (5) There's nothing more I could want from any written piece regardless of its genre.

1. A. Make no change.
   B. ago, it doesn't seem outdated or inaccessible
   C. ago; it doesn't seem outdated or inaccessable
   D. ago, it doesn't seem outdated, or inaccessable
   E. ago: it doesn't seem outdated, or inaccessable

2. A. Make no change.
   B. is true; and the troubles of the life of a teenager seem
   C. are true; and the troubles of the life of a teenager seem
   D. is true; and the troubles of the life of a teenager seems
   E. are true; and troubles seem

3. A. Make no change.
   B. characters, everyone of which seems
   C. characters, every one of which seem
   D. characters every one of which seems
   E. Characters. Everyone of which seems

4. A. Make no change.
   B. never end, but of course, it does; however, it will continue to affect you forever
   C. never end but of course, it does; however, it will continue to effect you forever
   D. never end, but of course, it does; however, it continues to effect you forever
   E. never ends, but of course. It does.

5. A. Make no change.
   B. I could want from any written piece irregardless of its
   C. I could want from any written piece regardless of it's
   D. you could want from any written piece regardless of its
   E. you could want regardless of it's

Language Arts Handbook

1.1 The Reading Process

The reading process begins before you actually start to read. All readers use a reading process, even if they don't think about it. By becoming aware of this process, you can become a more effective reader. The reading process can be broken down into three stages: before reading, during reading, and after reading.

BEFORE READING | DURING READING | AFTER READING

BUILD BACKGROUND

- Think about the **context** you as a reader bring to the selection based on your knowledge and experiences. What do you know about the topic? What do you want to know?

SET PURPOSE

- **Preview** the text to set a purpose for reading. Skim the first few paragraphs and glance through the selection to figure out what it's about and who the main characters are. What can you learn from the art or photos?

USE READING SKILLS

- Apply **reading skills** such as determining the author's purpose, analyzing text structure, and previewing new vocabulary.

BEFORE READING | DURING READING | AFTER READING

USE READING STRATEGIES

- **Ask questions** about things that seem unusual or interesting, like why a character might have behaved in an unexpected way.
- **Visualize** by forming pictures in your mind to help you see the characters or actions.
- **Make predictions** about what's going to happen next. As you read, gather more clues that will either confirm or change your predictions.
- **Make inferences,** or educated guesses, about what is not stated directly. Things may be implied or hinted at, or they may be left out altogether.
- **Clarify** your understanding of what you read by rereading any difficult parts.

ANALYZE LITERATURE

- Determine what **literary elements** stand out as you read the selection. Ask whether the characters are engaging and lifelike. Determine if there is a strong central conflict or theme.

MAKE CONNECTIONS

- Notice where there are **connections** between the story and your life or the world beyond the story. Be aware of feelings or thoughts you have while reading the story.

BEFORE READING | DURING READING | AFTER READING

REFER TO TEXT

- Think about the facts. **Remember details** like characters' names, locations or settings, and any other things that you can recall.
- Determine the **sequence of events** or the order in which things happened.
- **Reread** the story to pick up any details you may have missed the first time around.
- Try to **summarize** the story in a sentence or two based on the events.

REASON WITH TEXT

- **Analyze** the text by breaking down information into smaller pieces and figuring out how those pieces fit into the story as a whole. Your knowledge of literary tools can help you analyze the author's technique.
- **Evaluate** the text. **Synthesize** and **draw conclusions** by bringing together what you have read and using it to make a decision or form an opinion. Decide if you agree with the author's views.

Framework for Reading

BEFORE READING

ASK YOURSELF

- ❑ What's my purpose for reading this?
- ❑ What is this going to be about?
- ❑ How is this information organized?
- ❑ What do I already know about the topic?
- ❑ How can I apply this information to my life?

DURING READING

ASK YOURSELF

- ❑ What is the best way to accomplish my purpose for reading?
- ❑ What do I want or need to find out while I'm reading?
- ❑ What is the essential information presented here?
- ❑ What is the importance of what I am reading?
- ❑ Do I understand what I just read?
- ❑ What can I do to make the meaning more clear?

AFTER READING

ASK YOURSELF

- ❑ What did I learn from what I have read?
- ❑ What is still confusing?
- ❑ What do I need to remember from my reading?
- ❑ What effect did this text have on me?
- ❑ What else do I want to know about this topic?

1.2 Using Reading Strategies

Reading actively means thinking about what you are reading as you read it. A **reading strategy,** or plan, helps you read actively and get more from your reading. The following strategies can be applied at each stage of the reading process: before, during, and after reading.

Reading Strategies
- Build Background
- Set Purpose
- Ask Questions
- Visualize
- Make Predictions
- Make Inferences
- Clarify
- Make Connections

BUILD BACKGROUND

Each reader brings his or her own context to a selection based on prior knowledge and experiences. What do you know about the topic? What do you want to know? Before and during reading, think about what you already know about the topic or subject matter. By connecting to your prior knowledge, you will increase your interest in and understanding of what you read. Fill in the first two columns of a K-W-L Chart before you read. Fill in the last column after you finish reading.

K-W-L Chart

What I *Know*	What I *Want* to Learn	What I Have *Learned*
A scarlet ibis is a type of red bird.	Why did the author name this story after a bird?	The image of the scarlet ibis comes to represent one of the brothers.

SET PURPOSE

Before you begin reading, think about your reason for reading the material. You might be reading from a textbook to complete a homework assignment, skimming a magazine for information about one of your hobbies, or reading a novel for your own enjoyment. Know why you are reading and what information you seek. Decide on your purpose for reading as clearly as you can. Be aware that the purpose of your reading may change as you read.

Preview the text to set a purpose for reading. Skim the first few paragraphs and glance through the selection to figure out what it's about and who the main characters are. What can you learn from the art or photos? Fill in a Reader's Purpose Chart at each stage of reading to set a purpose for reading and to help you attain it.

Reader's Purpose Chart

Before Reading
Set a purpose for reading I want to know what the "most dangerous game" might be. The pictures show an island, hunting trophies, a leopard, and an illustration of two men hunting together.
During Reading
Take notes on what you learn Our protagonist is an excellent hunter but gets stranded on an island. Our protagonist has discovered another hunter who lives there, but the General makes our protagonist uncomfortable.
After Reading
Reflect on your purpose and what you learned I was not expecting the most dangerous game to be anything other than a leopard or other wild animal. I was surprised by this turn of events and the final resolution of the story.

ASK QUESTIONS

Think and reflect by asking questions to further your understanding of what you are reading. Asking questions helps you to pinpoint parts of the text that are confusing. You can ask questions in your head, or you may write them down. Ask questions about things that seem unusual or interesting, like why a character might have behaved in an unexpected way. What do you wonder about as you read the text? Use a Generate Questions Bookmark like the following to record your questions as you read.

Generate Questions Bookmark

Generate Questions Bookmark	
Page #	What I Wonder About
6	What is the woman going to do with the boy who tried to steal her purse?

VISUALIZE

Reading is more than simply sounding out words. It is an active process that requires you to use your imagination. When you visualize, you form a picture or an image in your mind of the action and descriptions in a text. Each reader's images will be different based on his or her prior knowledge and experiences. Keep in mind that there are no "right" or "wrong" visualizations. Visualize by forming pictures in your mind to help you see the characters or actions. Use a Visualization Map to draw pictures that represent key events in a selection. Write a caption under each box that explains each event. Draw the events in the order they occur.

Visualization Map

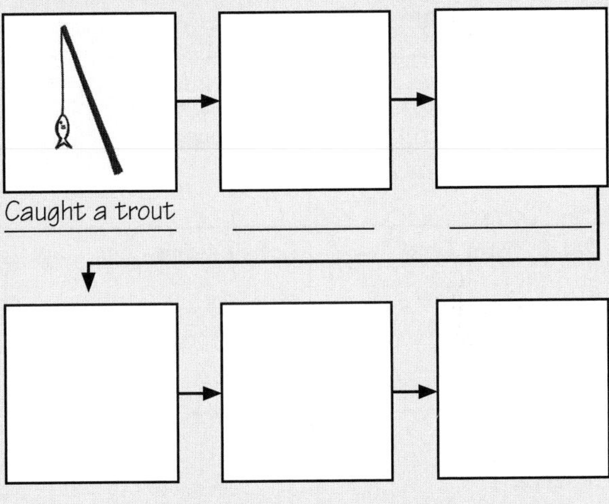

MAKE PREDICTIONS

When you **make predictions** during reading, you are making guesses about what the reading is going to be about or what might happen next. Before you read, make predictions based on clues from the page and from what you already know about the topic. Continue to make guesses as you read. The guesses do not have to be correct. When you pause during reading, gather information that helps you make more predictions and check predictions you have already made. As you read, gather more clues that will either confirm or change your predictions.

Prediction Chart

Guesses	Reasons	Evidence
I think Ulrich will find his enemy and have his revenge.	The story opens with the tale of the neighbor's feud, so I bet there will be some confrontation.	"Ulrich von Gradwitz patrolled the dark forest in quest of a human enemy."

MAKE INFERENCES

Making an inference means putting together the clues given in the text with your own prior knowledge. Make inferences, or educated guesses, about what is not stated directly. Things may be implied or hinted at, or they may be left out altogether. By paying close attention to what you read, you will be able to make inferences about what the writer is trying to communicate. Use an Inference Chart to document your conclusions.

Inference Chart

Text	What I Infer
"The best sport in the world," agreed Rainsford.	Rainsford loves to hunt.
Detail from Text	**Conclusions**
"Who cares how a jaguar feels?"	Rainsford gives little thought to the animals he hunts.

CLARIFY

Check that you understand what you read and identify text that is confusing or unclear. If you encounter problems or lose focus, it may be helpful to use **Fix-Up Ideas,** such as rereading difficult parts, reading in shorter chunks, going back and reading aloud, or changing your reading rate. (See Monitor Comprehension on page 943 for more information.)

MAKE CONNECTIONS

Notice where there are **connections** between the story and your life or the world beyond the story. Be aware of feelings or thoughts you have while reading the story.

Connections Chart

Page #	Event	Reminds Me of
71	Celestine Duval does not want to go to her son's house.	My aunt—she refuses to talk to people who annoy her.

1.3 Using Reading Skills

Using the following skills as you read helps you to become an independent, thoughtful, and active reader who can accomplish tasks evaluated on tests, particularly standardized tests.

Reading Skills
- Identify Author's Purpose and Approach
- Skim and Scan
- Find the Main Idea
- Determine Importance of Details
- Understand Literary Elements
- Meaning of Words
- Use Context Clues
- Take Notes
- Analyze Text Organization
- Identify Sequence of Events
- Compare and Contrast
- Evaluate Cause and Effect
- Classify and Reorganize Information
- Distinguish Fact from Opinion
- Identify Multiple Levels of Meaning
- Interpret Visual Aids
- Monitor Comprehension
- Summarize
- Draw Conclusions

IDENTIFY AUTHOR'S PURPOSE AND APPROACH

Author's Purpose

A writer's **purpose** is his or her aim or goal. Being able to figure out an author's purpose, or purposes, is an important reading skill. An author may write with one or more of the purposes listed in the following chart. A writer's purpose corresponds to a specific mode, or type, of writing. A writer can choose from a variety of forms while working within a mode.

Purposes of Writing

Mode of Writing	Purpose	Examples
expository	to inform	news article, research report
narrative	to express thoughts or ideas, or to tell a story	personal account, memoir
descriptive	to portray a person, place, object, or event	travel brochure, personal profile
persuasive	to convince people to accept a position and respond in some way	editorial, petition

Once you identify what the author is trying to do, you can evaluate, or judge, how well the author achieved that purpose. For example, you may judge that the author of a persuasive essay made a good and convincing argument. Or, you may decide that the novel you are reading has a boring plot.

Before Reading
Identify the author's purpose, the type of writing he or she uses, and the ideas he or she wants to communicate.
During Reading
Gather ideas that the author communicates to the readers.
After Reading
Summarize the ideas the author communicates. Explain how these ideas help fulfill the author's purpose.

Author's Approach

The literary elements, the terms and techniques used in literature, make up the **author's approach** to conveying his or her main idea or theme. Understanding the author's approach in fiction involves recognizing literary elements such as *point of view, tone,* and *mood.* What perspective, or way of looking at things, does the author have? What is his or her attitude toward the subject? Is the writing serious or playful in nature? What emotions is the writer trying to evoke in the reader? (See Understand Literary Elements on page 938.)

SKIM AND SCAN

When you **skim,** you glance through material quickly to get a general idea of what it is about. Skimming is an excellent way to get a quick overview of material. It is useful for previewing a chapter in a textbook, for surveying material to see if it contains information that will be useful to you, and for reviewing material for a test or an essay. When skimming, look at titles, headings, and words that appear in boldface or colored type. Also read topic sentences of paragraphs, first and last paragraphs of sections, and any summaries or conclusions. In addition, glance at illustrations, photographs, charts, maps, or other graphics.

When you **scan,** you look through written material quickly to locate particular information. Scanning is useful when, for example, you want to find an entry in an index or a definition in a textbook chapter. To scan, simply run your eye down the page, looking for a key word. When you find the key word, slow down and read carefully.

To **skim** a text, preview the following:

- titles
- headings
- bold or colored type
- topic sentences
- first/last paragraphs of sections
- summaries
- graphics

When you **scan** a text, you may be looking for the following:

- specific information
- key words
- main ideas
- answers to questions

FIND THE MAIN IDEA

The **main idea** is a brief statement of what you think the author wants you to know, think, or feel after reading the text. In some cases, the main idea will actually be stated. Check the first and last paragraphs for a sentence that sums up the entire passage. The author may not tell you what the main idea is, and you will have to infer it.

In general, nonfiction texts have main ideas; literary texts (poems, short stories, novels, plays, and personal essays) have themes. Sometimes, however, the term *main idea* is used to refer to the theme of a literary work, especially an essay or a poem. Both deal with the central idea in a written work.

A good way to find the main or overall idea of a whole selection (or part of a selection) is to gather important details into a Main Idea Map like the one below. Use the details to determine the main or overall thought or message.

Main Idea Map

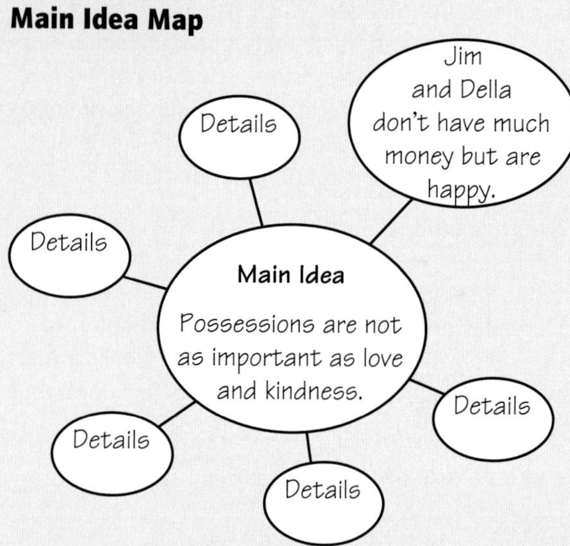

DETERMINE IMPORTANCE OF DETAILS

The main ideas are what the selection is about; the minor ideas and details provide support for the main ones. To identify supporting details, you need to do the following:

- **Locate basic facts,** such as names, dates, and events.
- **Determine the importance** of those facts to the understanding of the piece. Some facts or details will be more important than others.
- **Interpret** subtly stated details. These details can help clarify the author's stance or purpose, or they may give fuller meaning to the basic facts.
- **Understand the function** of a part of a passage. Is the author providing information, supporting a previously made point, presenting a conflicting argument, building suspense? Pay attention to how your understanding of a topic or your feelings toward it change as you read.
- **Make inferences,** or educated guesses, about how the author uses the supporting details to achieve his or her desired result. Put together clues from the text with your known prior knowledge to make inferences. A Main Idea Map or an Inference Chart can help you keep track of your ideas.

UNDERSTAND LITERARY ELEMENTS

Literary elements are the terms and techniques that are used in literature. When you read literature, you need to be familiar with the literary terms and reading skills listed below. These literary elements are explained in more detail in the Introduction to Fiction on page 2.

- **Recognize Mood and Tone** The atmosphere or emotion conveyed by a literary work is called **mood.** A writer creates mood by using concrete details to describe the setting, characters, or events. **Tone** is the writer's attitude toward the subject or toward the reader of a work. Examples of different tones that a work may have include familiar, ironic, playful, sarcastic, serious, and sincere.
- **Understand Point of View** The vantage point, or perspective, from which a story or narrative is told is referred to as **point of view.** Stories are typically written from the following points of view:
  first-person point of view: narrator uses words such as *I* and *we*
  second-person point of view: narrator uses *you*
  third-person point of view: narrator uses words such as *he, she, it,* and *they*
- **Analyze Character and Characterization** A **character** is a person (or sometimes an animal) who takes part in the action of a story. Characterization is the literary techniques writers use to create characters and make them come alive.
- **Examine Plot Development** The plot is basically what happens in a story. A **plot** is a series of events related to a central conflict, or struggle. A typical plot involves the introduction of a conflict, its development, and its eventual resolution. The elements of plot include the exposition, rising action, climax, falling action, and resolution. A graphic organizer called a Plot Diagram (page 12) can be used to chart the plot of a literature selection.

MEANING OF WORDS

To understand the **meaning of words** that are unfamiliar, use vocabulary skills, such as prior knowledge of word parts and word families, context clues (see the following section), and denotation and connotation. Other helpful resources include footnotes, glossaries, and dictionaries. For more information, refer to the Language Arts Handbook, section 2, Vocabulary & Spelling, page 944.

USE CONTEXT CLUES

You can often figure out the meaning of an unfamiliar word by using context clues. **Context clues** are words and phrases near a difficult word that provide hints about its meaning. The context in which a word is used may help you guess what it means without having to look it up in the dictionary.

Different types of context clues include the following:

- **comparison clue:** shows a comparison, or how the unfamiliar word is like something that might be familiar to you
- **contrast clue:** shows that something contrasts, or differs in meaning, from something else
- **restatement clue:** uses different words to express the same idea
- **examples clue:** gives examples of other items to illustrate the meaning of something
- **cause-and-effect clue:** tells you that something happened as a result of something else

TAKE NOTES

Taking or making notes helps you pay attention to the words on a page and remember important ideas. *Paraphrase,* or write in your own words, what you have read and put it into notes you can read later. Taking or making notes is also a quick way for you to retell what you have just read. Since you cannot write in, mark up, or highlight information in a textbook or library book, make a response bookmark like the one that follows and use it to record your thoughts and reactions. As you read, ask yourself questions, make predictions, react to ideas, identify key points, and/or write down unfamiliar words.

Response Bookmark

Page #	Questions, Predictions, Reactions, Key Points, and Unfamiliar Words
59	The narrator has vowed revenge!
59	Unfamiliar words: unredressed & redresser

Making notes in **graphic organizers** helps you organize ideas as you read. For instance, if you are reading an essay that compares two authors, you might use a Venn Diagram or a Cluster Chart to collect information about each author. If you are reading about an author's life, you may construct a Time Line. As you read a selection, create your own method for gathering and organizing information. You might use your own version of a common graphic organizer or invent a new way to show what the selection describes.

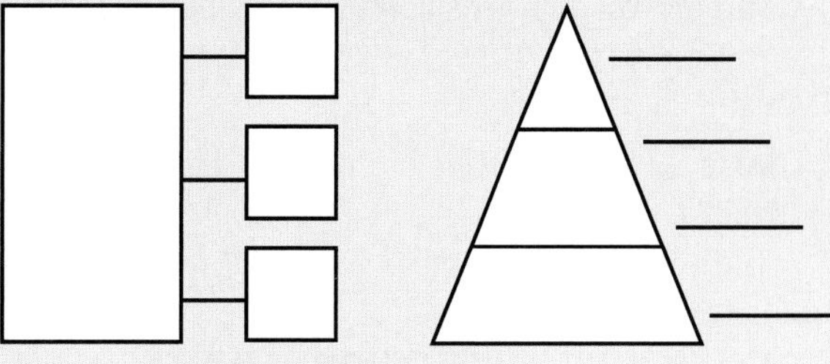

Common Graphic Organizers

ANALYZE TEXT ORGANIZATION

Text organization refers to the different ways a text may be presented or organized. If you are aware of the ways different texts are organized, you will find it easier to understand what you read. For example, familiarity with typical plot elements—the exposition, rising action, climax, falling action, and resolution—is important for understanding the events in a short story or novel. Focusing on signal words and text patterns is important for understanding nonfiction and informational text. For instance, transition words, such as *first, second, next, then,* and *finally,* might indicate that an essay is written in chronological, or time, order. Common methods of organization appear on the following page.

Methods of Organization

Chronological Order	Events are given in the order they occur.
Order of Importance	Details are given in order of importance or familiarity.
Comparison and Contrast Order	Similarities and differences of two things are listed.
Cause and Effect Order	One or more causes are presented followed by one or more effects.

IDENTIFY SEQUENCE OF EVENTS

Sequence refers to the order in which things happen. When you read certain types of writing, such as a short story, a novel, a biography of a person's life, or a history book, keep track of the sequence of events. You might do this by making a Time Line or a Sequence Map.

Time Line

To make a Time Line, draw a line and divide it into equal parts like the one below. Label each part with a date or a time. Then add key events at the right places along the Time Line.

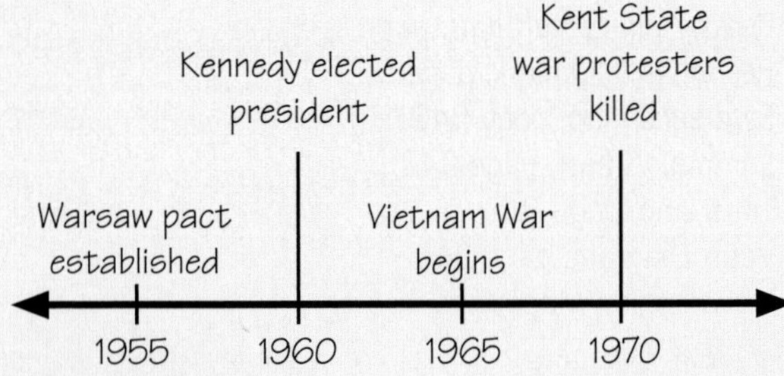

Sequence Map

In each box, draw pictures that represent key events in a selection. Then write a caption under each box that explains each event. Draw the events in the order in which they occur.

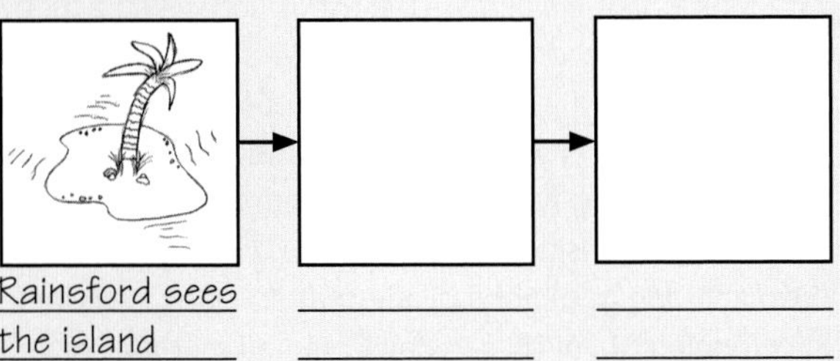

COMPARE AND CONTRAST

Comparing and contrasting are closely related processes. When you **compare** one thing to another, you describe similarities between the two things; when you **contrast** two things, you describe their differences. To compare and contrast, begin by listing the features of each subject. Then go down both lists and check whether each feature is shared or not. You can also show similarities and differences in a *Venn Diagram.* A Venn Diagram uses two slightly overlapping circles. The outer part of each circle shows what aspects of two things are different from each other. The inner, or shared, part of each circle shows what aspects the two things have in common.

Venn Diagram

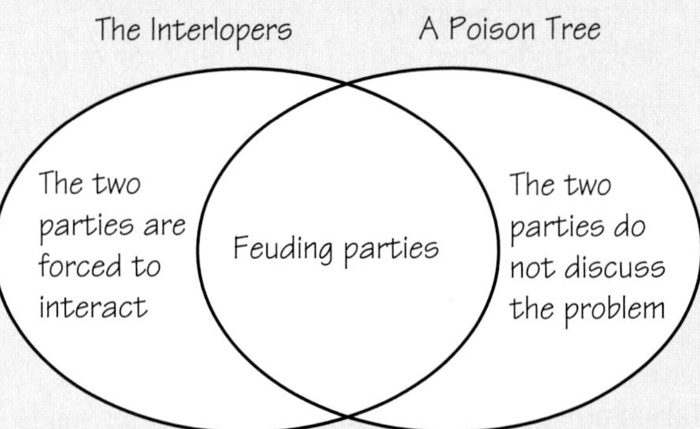

Another method for comparison and contrast is to use a Pro and Con Chart like the one below to take notes on both sides of an argument.

Pro and Con Chart

Arguments in Favor of Banning Pesticides (PRO)	**Arguments Against Banning Pesticides (CON)**
Argument 1: Chemicals are harmful to the environment. Support: Chemicals stay in the environment long after the intended effects end.	Argument 1: Chemicals help our farmers. Support: Chemically treated fields yield larger corps.
Argument 2: Support	Argument 2: Support

EVALUATE CAUSE AND EFFECT

When you evaluate **cause and effect,** you are looking for a logical relationship between a cause or causes and one or more effects. A writer may present one or more causes followed by one or more effects, or one or more effects followed by one or more causes. Transitional, or signal, words and phrases that indicate cause and effect include *one cause, another effect, as a result, consequently,* and *therefore.* As a reader, you determine whether the causes and effects in a text are reasonable. A graphic organizer like the one below will help you to recognize relationships between causes and effects. Keep track of what happens in a story and why in a chart like the one below. Use cause-and-effect signal words to help you identify causes and their effects.

Cause-and-Effect Chart

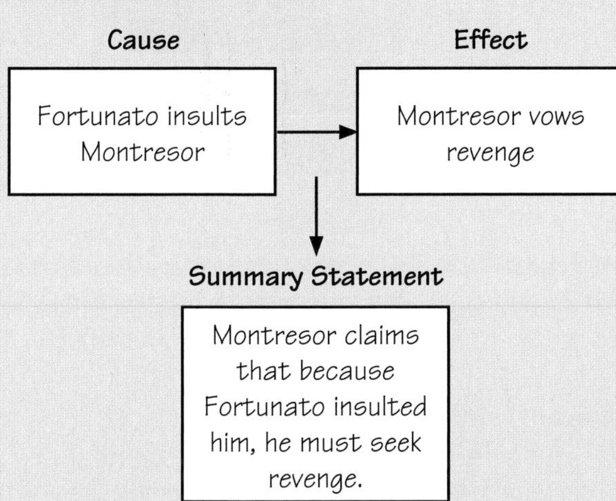

CLASSIFY AND REORGANIZE INFORMATION

To **classify** is to put into classes or categories. Items in the same category should share one or more characteristics. A writer may group things to show similarities and name the categories to clarify how one group is similar or different from another. For example, whales can be classified by their method of eating as *baleen* or *toothed*. Classifying or reorganizing the information into categories as you read increases your understanding.

The key step in classifying is choosing categories that fit your purpose. Take classification notes in a chart like the one that follows to help you organize separate types or groups and sort their characteristics.

Classification Chart

Category 1 Intense Focus	Category 2	Category 3
Items in Category Early interest in music	Items in Category	Items in Category
Details and Characteristics "He would listen to [music] for hours, . . ."	Details and Characteristics	Details and Characteristics

DISTINGUISH FACT FROM OPINION

A **fact** is a statement that can be proven by direct observation. Every statement of fact is either true or false. The following statement is an example of fact:

> Many Greek myths deal with human emotion. (This statement is a fact that can be proven by examining the content of Greek myths.)

An **opinion** is a statement that expresses an attitude or a desire, not a fact about the world. One common type of opinion statement is a *value statement.* A value statement expresses an attitude toward something.

> Ancient Greece produced some **beautiful** and **inspiring** myths. (The adjectives used to describe myths express an attitude or opinion toward something that cannot be proven.)

Fact:	Opinion:
Two thirds of households in the United States have pets.	"They're shaggy-looking. They're suffering the same emotional loss that people are."
Proof: Survey by the American Veterinary Medical Association	**Support:** Quotation by a St. Bernard Parish councilman

IDENTIFY MULTIPLE LEVELS OF MEANING

There is often more than one purpose to a story or nonfiction work. Though there is always a main idea or theme, other levels of meaning are nonetheless important in understanding the overall meaning of the selection. As you read, take note of the multiple levels of meaning, and record them in a Levels of Meaning Chart like the one below:

Levels of Meaning Chart

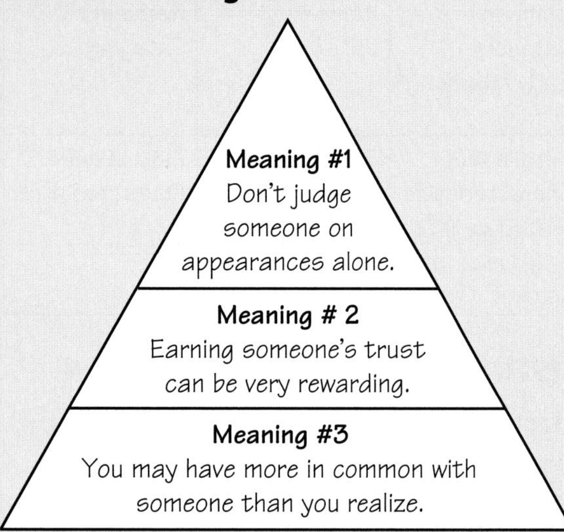

INTERPRET VISUAL AIDS

Visual aids are charts, graphs, pictures, illustrations, photos, maps, diagrams, spreadsheets, and other materials that present information. Many writers use visual aids to present data in understandable ways. Information visually presented in tables, charts, and graphs can help you find data, see trends, discover facts, and uncover patterns.

Pie Chart

A **pie chart** is a circle that stands for a whole group or set. The circle is divided into parts to show the divisions of the whole. When you look at a pie chart, you can see the relationships of the parts to one another and to the whole.

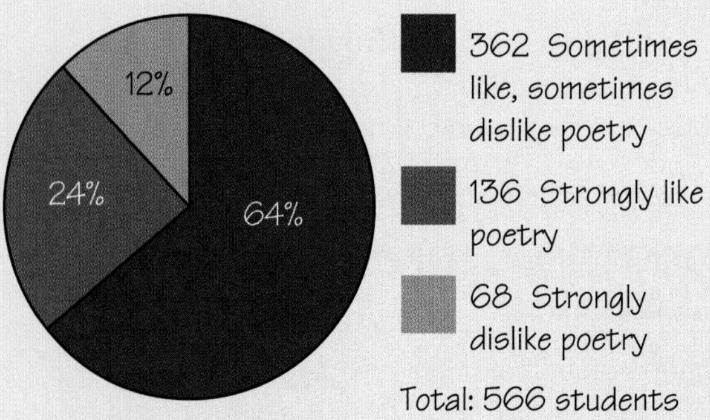

Bar Graph

A **bar graph** compares amounts of something by representing the amounts as bars of different lengths. In the bar graph below, each bar represents the value in dollars of canned goods donated by several communities to a food drive. To read the graph, simply imagine a line drawn from the edge of the bar to the bottom of the graph. Then read the number. For example, the bar graph below shows that the community of Russell Springs donated $600 worth of goods during the food drive.

DOLLAR VALUE OF DONATED GOODS TO CANNED FOOD DRIVE

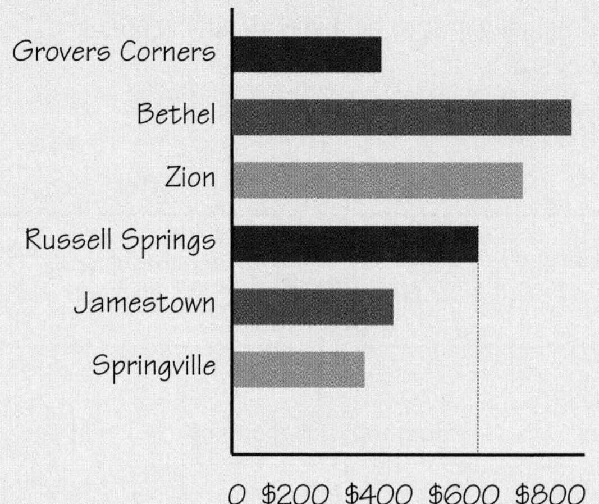

Map

A **map** is a representation, usually on a surface such as paper or a sheet of plastic, of a geographic area showing various significant features of that area.

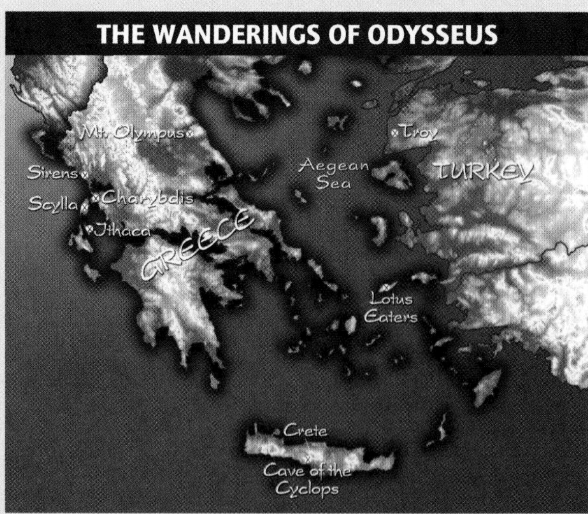

MONITOR COMPREHENSION

All readers occasionally have difficulty as they read. As you read, you should always **monitor,** or pay attention to, your progress, stopping frequently to check how well you are understanding what you are reading. If you encounter problems or lose focus, use a **fix-up idea** to get back on track. Readers who know how to apply fix-up ideas are well on the way to reading independence. They know when they are having a problem and are able to adjust and get back on track.

The following **fix-up ideas** can help you "fix up" any confusion or lack of attention you experience as you read. You probably use many of these already.

- **Reread** If you don't understand a sentence, paragraph, or section the first time through, go back and reread it. Each time you reread a text, you understand and remember more.
- **Read in shorter chunks** Break a long text into shorter chunks. Read through each "chunk." Then go back and make sure you understand that section before moving on.
- **Read aloud** If you are having trouble keeping your focus, try reading aloud to yourself. Go somewhere private and read aloud, putting emphasis and expression in your voice. Reading aloud also allows you to untangle difficult text by talking your way through it.
- **Ask questions** As you read, stop and ask yourself questions about the text. These questions may help you pinpoint things that are confusing you or things that you want to come back to later. You can ask questions in your head, or jot them down in the margins or on a piece of paper.
- **Change your reading rate** Your reading rate is how fast or slow you read. Good readers adjust their rate to fit the situation. In some cases, when you just need to get the general idea or main points of a reading, or if the reading is simple, you will want to read through it quickly and not get bogged down. Other times, such as when a text is difficult or contains a lot of description, you will need to slow down and read carefully.

SUMMARIZE

Summarizing is giving a shortened version of something that has been said or written, stating its main points. When you summarize a selection, you are **paraphrasing,** or restating something using other words in order to make it simpler or shorter. Summarizing what you have read will help you identify, understand, and remember the main and supporting points in the text. Read and summarize short sections of a selection at a time. Then write a summary of the entire work. Use a Summary Chart like the one below.

Summary Chart

Summary of Section 1: He was angry at a friend, but he discussed the issue with his friend and they resolved it.
Summary of Section 2: He was angry at someone he didn't like, and instead of discussing the issue, he allowed it to grow and fester.
Summary of Section 3: The anger grew until he had created something that his enemy couldn't ignore, or he tempted his enemy to wrong him again.
Summary of Section 4: The speaker is delighted upon the death of the enemy.
Summary of the Selection: Not discussing an issue will only make the problem worsen. Talking about problems will help you avoid unnecessary battles.

DRAW CONCLUSIONS

When you **draw conclusions,** you are gathering pieces of information and then deciding what that information means. Drawing conclusions is an essential part of reading. It may be helpful to use a graphic organizer such as a chart or log to keep track of the information you find while you are reading and the conclusions you draw.

Drawing Conclusions Log

Key Idea Swimming across the Bering Sea is tremendously difficult.
Supporting Points My hands are numb, and they ache...suddenly it occurs to me that my life is escaping through my hands.
Overall Conclusion Lynne Cox's reason for attempting this swim must be very important.

2.1 Using Context Clues

You can often figure out the meaning of an unfamiliar word by using context clues. Context clues, or hints you gather from the words and sentences around the unfamiliar word, prevent you from having to look up every unknown word in the dictionary. The chart below defines the types of context clues and gives you an example of each. It also lists words that signal each type of clue.

Context Clues	
comparison clue	shows a comparison, or how the unfamiliar word is like something that might be familiar to you
signal words	*and, like, as, just as, as if, as though*
EXAMPLE Joan was as nimble as a mountain goat as she hiked along the steep, rocky trail. (A mountain goat is extremely agile and sure on its feet. *Nimble* must mean "agile.")	
contrast clue	shows that something contrasts, or differs in meaning, from something else
signal words	*but, nevertheless, on the other hand, however, although, though, in spite of*
EXAMPLE Hsuan is very reflective, but his friend Ku Min is known for jumping into things without thinking about them. (The word *but* signals a contrast between Hsuan's and Ku Min's ways of doing things. If Ku Min jumps in without thinking, Hsuan must think things through more thoroughly. *Reflective* must mean "thoughtful, meditative.")	
restatement clue	uses different words to express the same idea
signal words	*that is, in other words, or*
EXAMPLE I know Kayesha will prevail in the student council election; I have no doubt that she's going to win! (As the information after the semicolon indicates, *prevail* means "win.")	
examples clue	gives examples of other items to illustrate the meaning of something
signal words	*including, such as, for example, for instance, especially, particularly*
EXAMPLE Trevor has always been interested in celestial bodies such as planets, stars, and moons. (If you know enough about the examples listed, you can tell that celestial bodies are visible bodies in the sky.)	
cause-and-effect clue	tells you that something happened as a result of something else
signal words	*if/then, when/then, thus, therefore, because, so, as a result of, consequently*
EXAMPLE I hadn't planned on going to the party, but the host invited me in such a cordial way that I felt welcome. (If the host's cordial invitation helped the speaker feel welcome, you can guess that *cordial* means "friendly.")	

2.2 Breaking Words Into Base Words, Word Roots, Prefixes, and Suffixes

Many words are formed by adding prefixes and suffixes to main word parts called base words (if they can stand alone) or word roots (if they can't). A prefix is a letter or group of letters added to the beginning of a word to change its meaning. A suffix is a letter or group of letters added to the end of a word to change its meaning.

Word Part	Definition	Example
base word	main word part that can stand alone	form
word root	main word part that can't stand alone	struc
prefix	letter or group of letters added to the beginning of the word	pre–
suffix	letter or group of letters added to the end of the word	–tion

Common Prefixes		
Prefix	**Meaning**	**Examples**
ambi–/amphi–	both	ambidextrous, amphibian
anti–/ant–	against; opposite	antibody, antacid
bi–	two	bicycle, biped
circum–	around; about	circumnavigate, circumstance
co–/col–/com–/con–/cor–	together	cooperate, collaborate, commingle, concentrate, correlate
counter–	contrary; complementary; opposite	counteract, counterpart
de–	opposite; remove; reduce	decipher, defrost, devalue
dia–	through; apart	dialogue, diaphanous
dis–	not; opposite of	dislike, disguise
dys–	abnormal; difficult; bad	dysfunctional, dystopia
em–/en–	into or onto; cover with; cause to be; provide with	embark, empower, enslave, enfeeble
ex–	out of; from; away	explode, export, extend
extra–/extro–	outward; outside; beyond	extraordinary, extrovert
hyper–	too much, too many, extreme; above	hyperbole, hyperactive
hypo–	under	hypodermic, hypothermic
il–, im–, in–, ir–	not	illogical, impossible, inoperable, irrational
	in; within; toward; on	illuminate, imperil, infiltrate, irrigate
inter–	among; between	international, intersect
intra–/intro–	into; within; inward	introvert, intramural

Common Prefixes *(cont.)*		
Prefix	**Meaning**	**Examples**
meta–	after; changed	metamorphosis, metaphor
mis–	wrongly	mistake, misfire
non–	not	nonsense, nonsmoker
out–	in a manner that goes beyond	outrun, outmuscle
over–	excessive	overdone, overkill
per–	through; throughout	permeate, permanent
peri–	all around	perimeter, periscope
post–	after; later	postgame, postpone
pre–	before	prefix, premature
pro–	before; forward	proceed, prologue
re–	again; back	redo, recall
retro–	back	retrospect, retroactive
semi–	half; partly	semicircle, semidry
sub–/sup–	under	substandard, subfloor, support
super–	above; over; exceeding	superstar, superfluous
sym–/syn–	with; together	sympathy, synonym, synergy
trans–	across; beyond	transatlantic, transfer, transcend
ultra–	too much; too many; extreme	ultraviolet, ultrasound
un–	not	unethical, unhappy
under–	below; short of a quantity or limit	underestimate, understaffed
uni–	one	unicorn, universe

Common Suffixes		
Noun Suffixes	**Meaning**	**Examples**
–ance/–ancy/–ence/–ency	quality; state	defiance, independence, emergency
–age	action; process	marriage, voyage
–ant/–ent	one who	defendant, assistant, resident
–ar/–er/–or	one who	lawyer, survivor, liar
–dom	state; quality of	freedom, boredom
–es/–s	plural form of noun	siblings, trees
–ion/–tion	action; process	revolution, occasion
–ism	act; state; system of belief	plagiarism, barbarism, Buddhism
–ist	one who does or believes something	ventriloquist, idealist

Common Suffixes *(cont.)*		
Noun Suffixes	**Meaning**	**Examples**
–itude, –tude	quality of; state of	multitude, magnitude
–ity/–ty	state of	longevity, piety
–ment	action or process; state or quality; product or thing	development, government, amusement, amazement, ointment, fragment
–ness	state of	kindness, happiness
Adjective Suffixes	**Meaning**	**Examples**
–able/–ible	capable of	attainable, possible
–al	having characteristics of	personal, governmental
–er	more	higher, calmer, shorter
–est	most	lowest, craziest, tallest
–ful	full of	helpful, gleeful, woeful
–ic	having characteristics of	scientific, chronic
–ish	like	childish, reddish
–ive	performs; tends toward	creative, pensive
–less	without	hapless, careless
–ous	possessing the qualities of	generous, joyous
–y	indicates description	happy, dirty, flowery
Adverb Suffixes	**Meaning**	**Examples**
–ly	in such a way	quickly, studiously, invisibly
–ward, –ways, –wise	in such a direction	toward, sideways, crosswise
Verb Suffixes	**Meaning**	**Examples**
–ate	make or cause to be	fixate, activate
–ed	past tense of verb	walked, acted, fixed
–ify/–fy	make or cause to be	vilify, magnify, glorify
–ing	indicates action in progress (present participle); can also be a noun (gerund)	running, thinking, being
–ize	bring about; cause to be	colonize, legalize

Common Word Roots		
Word Root	**Meaning**	**Examples**
acr	highest point	acrobat, acropolis
act	do	actor, reaction
ann/annu/enni	year	annual, bicentennial
aqu	water	aquarium, aquatic
aster, astr	star	asteroid, astronomy
aud	hear	audition, auditorium
bene	good	beneficial, benefactor
bibl, bibli	book	Bible, bibliography
chron	time	chronic, chronological
cosm	universe; order	cosmic, cosmos
cred	believe; trust	credit, credible
cycl	circle	bicycle, cyclone
dem/demo	people	democracy, demagogue
derm	skin	dermatologist, hypodermic
dic/dict	say	dictate, dictionary
duc/duct	lead; pull	conduct, reproduction
dyn	force, power	dynamic, dynamite
equ/equi/iqui	equal	equidistant, equitable, iniquity
fer	carry	transfer, refer
fin	end	finish, infinite
firm	firm, strong	confirm, reaffirm
flect/flex	bend	deflect, reflex, flexible
fort	strong	fortify, comfort
ge	earth	geode, geography
gress	go	progress, regress
hydra, hydro	water	hydrate, hydrogen
ign	fire	ignite, ignition, igneous
ject	throw	projector, eject
judic	judgment	prejudice, judicial
lect/leg	read; choose	lecture, election, legible
liber	free	liberate, liberal
loc	place	location, relocate
locut/loqu	speak	elocution, loquacious, colloquial
log/logue	word; speech; discourse	logic, monologue

Common Word Roots		
Word Root	**Meaning**	**Examples**
luc/lumin	shine; light	lucid, luminous
mal	bad	malevolent, malodorous
man/manu	hand	manufacture, manual
metr	measure	metric, metronome
morph	form	morpheme, metamorphosis
mot	move	motor, emotion
mut	change	mutation, transmutable
nov	new	novelty, renovate
onym	name	synonym, antonym
path	feel; suffer; disease	sympathy, pathology
ped	foot; child	pedal, pediatrics
phon/phony	sound; voice; speech	symphony, microphone
phot	light	photography, photon
physi	nature	physical, physics
pop	people	popular, populate
port	carry	transport, portable
psych	mind; soul	psychology, psychic
reg	rule	register, regulate
rupt	break	disrupt, interruption, rupture
scrib/script	write	describe, prescription
son	sound	sonic, sonar
spec/spect/spic	look	speculate, inspect, specimen
spir	breathe	spirit, inspiration
ter/terr	earth	inter, terrestrial, terrain
therm	heat	thermal, hypothermia
top	place	topography, topical
tract	draw; drag	retract, tractor, contract
typ	stamp; model	typical, type
ver	truth	veracity, verifiable
vert	turn	divert, introvert, extrovert
vid/vis	see	video, visual
viv	alive	vivacious, vivid
vol/volv	turn	evolution, revolve

2.3 Exploring Word Origins and Word Families

The English language expands constantly and gathers new words from many different sources. Understanding the source of a word can help you unlock its meaning.

One source of new words is the names of people and places associated with the thing being named. Words named for people and places are called **eponyms.**

EXAMPLES

hamburger Originally known as "Hamburg steak," the hamburger takes its name from the German city Hamburg.

spoonerism The slip of the tongue whereby the beginning sounds of words are switched is named after the Rev. William A. Spooner, who was known for such slips. For example, after a wedding, he told the groom, "It is kisstomary to cuss the bride."

Another source for new words is **acronyms.** Acronyms are words formed from the first letter or letters of the major parts of terms.

EXAMPLES

sonar, from sound navigation ranging
NATO, from North American Treaty Organization

Some words in the English language are borrowed from other languages.

EXAMPLES

deluxe (French), **Gesundheit** (German), **kayak** (Inuit)

Many words are formed by shortening longer words.

EXAMPLES

ad, from advertisement

lab, from laboratory

stereo, from stereophonic

Brand names are often taken into the English language. People begin to use these words as common nouns, even though most of them are still brand names.

EXAMPLES

Scotch tape **Xerox** **Rollerblade**

2.4 Using a Dictionary

When you can't figure out a word using the strategies already described, or when the word is important to the meaning of the text and you want to make sure you have it right, use a dictionary. There are many parts to a dictionary entry. Study the following sample. Then read the explanations of each part of an entry below.

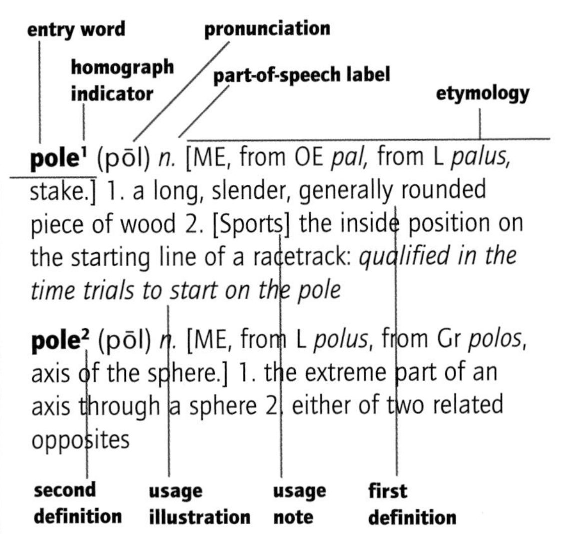

The **pronunciation** is given immediately after the entry word. The dictionary's table of contents will tell you where you can find a complete key to pronunciation symbols. In some dictionaries, a simplified pronunciation key is provided at the bottom of each page.

An abbreviation of the **part of speech** usually follows the pronunciation. This label tells how the word can be used. If a word can be used as more than one part of speech, a separate entry is provided for each part of speech.

An **etymology** is the history of the word. In the first entry, the word *pole* can be traced back through Middle English (ME) and Old English (OE) to the Latin (L) word *palus,* which means "stake." In the second entry, the word *pole* can be traced back through Middle English to the Latin word *polus,* which comes from the Greek (Gr) word *polos,* meaning "axis of the sphere."

Sometimes the entry will include a list of **synonyms,** or words that have the same or very similar meanings. The entry may also include a **usage illustration,** which is an example of how the word is used in context.

2.5 Understanding Multiple Meanings

Each definition in the entry gives a different meaning of the word. When a word has more than one meaning, the different definitions are numbered. The first definition in an entry is the most common meaning of the word, but you will have to choose the meaning that fits the context in which you have found the word. Try substituting each definition for the word until you find the one that makes the most sense. If you come across a word that doesn't seem to make sense in context, consider whether that word might have another, lesser known meaning. Can the word be used as more than one part of speech, for example, as either a noun or a verb? Does it have a broader meaning than the one that comes to your mind? For example, a line from *The Odyssey* reads "he gave me seven shining talents." The most common meaning of *talent* is "special skill or ability," but that doesn't fit here. Consulting the footnote at the bottom of the page, you would discover that the word *talent* can also refer to a type of old coin.

Keep in mind that some words not only have multiple meanings but also different pronunciations. Words that are spelled the same but are pronounced differently are called **homographs.**

2.6 Understanding Denotation and Connotation

The **denotation** of a word is its dictionary definition. Sometimes, in order to understand a passage fully, it is helpful to know the connotations of the words as well. A **connotation** of a word is an emotional association the word has in addition to its literal meaning. For example, the words *cheap* and *thrifty* both denote "tending to spend less money," but *cheap* has a negative connotation similar to "stingy," whereas *thrifty* has a positive connotation involving being responsible with money. The best way to learn the connotation of a word is to pay attention to the context in which the word appears or to ask someone more familiar with the word.

Connotation Chart

Negative	Neutral	Positive
weird	unusual	unique
freakish	different	remarkable
bizarre	uncommon	extraordinary
abnormal	rare	unequaled
mob	group	congregation

2.7 Spelling

SPELLING RULES

Always check your writing for spelling errors, and try to recognize the words that give you more trouble than others. Use a dictionary when you find you have misspelled a word. Keep a list in a notebook of words that are difficult for you to spell. Write the words several times until you have memorized the correct spelling. Break down the word into syllables and carefully pronounce each individual syllable.

Some spelling problems occur when adding prefixes or suffixes to words or when making nouns plural. Other spelling problems occur when words follow certain patterns, such as those containing *ie/ei*. The following spelling rules can help you spell many words correctly.

PREFIXES AND SUFFIXES

Prefixes

A **prefix** is a letter or a group of letters added to the beginning of a word to change its meaning. When adding a prefix, do not change the spelling of the word itself.

EXAMPLES

mis– + perception = misperception
im– + possible = impossible
in– + conceivable = inconceivable
anti– + social = antisocial
al– + mighty = almighty

Suffixes

A **suffix** is a letter or a group of letters added to the end of a word to change its meaning.

The spelling of most words is not changed when the suffix *–ness* or *–ly* is added.

EXAMPLES

shy + –ness = shyness
forgive + –ness = forgiveness
eager + –ness = eagerness
strange + –ly = strangely
bad + –ly = badly
splendid + –ly = splendidly

If you are adding a suffix to a word that ends with *y* following a vowel, usually leave the *y* in place.

EXAMPLES

employ	employs	employing	employed
defray	defrays	defraying	defrayment
buoy	buoys	buoying	buoyancy

If you are adding a suffix to a word that ends with *y* following a consonant, change the *y* to *i* before adding any ending except *–ing.*

EXAMPLES

bury	buried	burying
copy	copied	copying
supply	supplied	supplying
magnify	magnified	magnifying

Double the final consonant before adding a suffix beginning with a vowel (such as *–ed, –en, –er, –ing, –ence, –ance,* or *–y*) in words ending in a single consonant preceded by a single vowel if the word is either a single syllable or ends in a stressed syllable.

EXAMPLES

regret	regrettable	regretting
quit	quitter	quitting
fan	fanned	fanning
refer	referred	referring
plot	plotted	plotting
deter	deterrence	deterring
rot	rotten	rotting

If you are adding a suffix that begins with a vowel to a word that ends with a silent *e,* usually drop the *e.*

EXAMPLES

tune	tuning
oblige	obligation
pursue	pursuable
grieve	grievous

If you are adding a suffix that begins with a consonant to a word that ends with a silent *e,* usually leave the *e* in place.

EXAMPLES

spite	spiteful
achieve	achievement
state	stately
lame	lameness

EXCEPTIONS

awe	awful
wise	wisdom
nine	ninth
due	duly

If the word ends in a soft *c* sound (spelled *ce*) or a soft *g* sound (spelled *ge*), keep the *e* when adding the suffixes *–able* or *–ous.*

EXAMPLES

acknowledge	acknowledgeable
enforce	enforceable
outrage	outrageous

PLURAL NOUNS

Plural Nouns

Most noun plurals are formed by simply adding *–s* to the end of the word.

EXAMPLES

surface + –s = surfaces
mouthful + –s = mouthfuls
platelet + –s = platelets
refrigerator + –s = refrigerators

The plural of nouns that end in *o, s, x, z, ch,* or *sh* should be formed by adding *–es.*

EXAMPLES

tomato + –es = tomatoes
loss + –es = losses
fox + –es = foxes
buzz + –es = buzzes
inch + –es = inches
flash + –es = flashes

The exception to the rule above is that musical terms and certain other words that end in *o* are usually made plural by adding *–s.* Check a dictionary if you aren't sure whether to add *–s* or *–es.*

EXAMPLES

piano + –s = pianos
portico + –s = porticos
solo + –s = solos
soprano + –s = sopranos
vibrato + –s = vibratos

Form the plural of nouns that end in *y* following a consonant by changing the *y* to an *i* and adding *–es.*

EXAMPLES

democracy	democracies
fairy	fairies
fallacy	fallacies
fifty	fifties
filly	fillies
signatory	signatories

Nouns that end in *f* or *fe* must be modified, changing the *f* or *fe* to *v*, before adding *–es* to the plural form.

EXAMPLES

shelf	shelves
knife	knives
scarf	scarves
leaf	leaves
calf	calves

SPELLING PATTERNS

The ie/ei Spelling Pattern

A word spelled with the letters *i* and *e* and has a long *e* sound is usually spelled *ie* except after the letter *c*.

EXAMPLES

belief	conceive
piece	receive
field	deceit

EXCEPTIONS

leisure   either

Use *ei* when the sound is not long *e*.

EXAMPLES

forfeit   surfeit   foreign   height

EXCEPTIONS

science   mischief   sieve

If the vowel combination has a long *a* sound (as in *eight*), always spell it with *ei*.

EXAMPLES

weight   vein   reign

When two vowels are pronounced separately in a word, spell them in the order of their pronunciation.

EXAMPLES

siesta   patio   diode   transient

The "Seed" Sound Pattern

The "seed" ending sound has three spellings: *–sede, –ceed*, and *–cede*.

EXAMPLES

Only one word ends in *–sede: supersede*

Three words end in *–ceed: proceed, succeed, exceed*

All other words end in *–cede: accede, concede, recede, precede, secede*

Silent Letters

Some spelling problems result from letters written but not heard when a word is spoken. Becoming familiar with the patterns in letter combinations containing silent letters will help you identify other words that fit the patterns.

- Silent *b* usually occurs with *m*.

EXAMPLES

dumb   bomb   climb   lamb

- Silent *b* also appears in *debt* and *doubt*.
- Silent *c* often appears with *s*.

EXAMPLES

scissors   scent   scenic   science

- Silent *g* often appears with *n*.

EXAMPLES

design   resign   gnome   foreign

- Silent *gh* often appears at the end of a word, either alone or in combination with *t (–ght)*.

EXAMPLES

fright   freight   sought   wrought

- Silent *h* appears at the beginning of some words.

EXAMPLES

hourly   heir   honestly   honor

- Silent *h* also appears in a few other words, as in *rhythm* and *ghost*.
- Silent *k* occurs with *n*.

EXAMPLES

knack   knight   knot   kneecap
knapsack

- Silent *n* occurs with *m* at the end of some words.

EXAMPLES

condemn   solemn   column   autumn

- Silent *p* occurs with *s* at the beginning of some words.

EXAMPLES

psyche   psychosis   psaltery   psoriasis

- Silent *s* occurs with *l* in some words.

EXAMPLES

island   islet   aisle

- Silent *t* occurs with *s* in a few words.

EXAMPLES
listen hasten nestle

- Silent *w* occurs at the beginnings of some words.

EXAMPLES
wreak wrong wraith wrapper

- Silent *w* also occurs with *s* in a few words, such as *sword* and *answer.*

Letter Combinations

Some letter combinations have a different pronunciation when combined and can cause spelling problems.

- The letters *ph* produce the *f* sound.

EXAMPLES
sphinx photograph alphanumeric
phosphate

- The letters *gh* produce the *f* sound usually at the end of a word. (Otherwise, they are silent.)

EXAMPLES
cough enough neigh weigh

- The letter combination *tch* sounds the same as *ch*.

EXAMPLES
sketch pitch snitch hatch
such hunch grouch torch

If the letters *c* and *g* have soft sounds (of *s* and *j*), they will usually be followed by *e, i,* or *y*.

EXAMPLES
cyclone giant
circle gyroscope
cent region
regent outrageous

If the letters *c* and *g* have hard sounds (of *k* and *g*), they will usually be followed by *a, o,* or *u*.

EXAMPLES
candid gasket
congeal engorge
convey garland
conjugate argument
cunning gun

Spelling Patterns of Borrowed Words

Many words borrowed from other languages follow the spelling patterns of the original language. For example, some English words borrowed from French, Spanish, and Italian follow letter patterns of the language of origin.

- The final *t* is silent in many words borrowed from French.

EXAMPLES
croquet
parquet
ballet

- The letter combinations *eur* and *eau* appear at the end of many words with French origin.

EXAMPLES
amateur bureau
chauffeur plateau
grandeur tableau

- The letter combination *oo* appears in many words borrowed from the Dutch language.

EXAMPLES
roost
cooper
toot

Many plural Italian words end in *i*.

EXAMPLES
ravioli
manicotti
linguini

Many words of Spanish origin end in *o*.

EXAMPLES
machismo
tomato
patio

Compound Nouns

A **compound noun** consists of two or more nouns used together to form a single noun. Sometimes they are written as one word *(football, uptown);* other times they are written separately *(picnic table, tennis shoes)*. Some compound nouns are connected with hyphens *(great-grandfather, fly-by-night).* Consult a good dictionary when you are not sure of the form of compounds.

Numerals

Spell out numbers of *one hundred* or less and all numbers rounded to hundreds. Larger round numbers such as *seven thousand* or *three million* should also be spelled out.

EXAMPLES

Joe Morgan hit more than **twenty** home runs and stole at least **thirty** bases in the same season **four** times in his career.

Joe DiMaggio was the first baseball player to receive an annual salary of more than **a hundred thousand** dollars.

Use a hyphen to separate compound numbers from twenty-one through ninety-nine.

EXAMPLES

forty-two birds
seventy-four candles
one hundred soldiers
sixty thousand dollars

Use a hyphen in a fraction used as a modifier, but not in a fraction used as a noun.

EXAMPLES

The glass is **two-fifths full** of water.

After an hour, I had mowed **three fourths** of the backyard.

Use Arabic numerals for numbers greater than one hundred that are not rounded numbers.

EXAMPLES

Our company sent out **493,745** mailings in just **145** days this year.

My uncle boasted that he has read **1,323** books thus far in his life.

If a number appears at the beginning of a sentence, spell it out or rewrite the sentence.

EXAMPLES

incorrect
356 years ago, my ancestors moved to North America.
correct
Three hundred fifty-six years ago, my ancestors moved to North America.
correct
My ancestors moved to North America **356** years ago.

Use words to write the time unless you are writing the exact time (including the abbreviation AM or PM). When the word *o'clock* is used for time of day, express the number in words.

EXAMPLES

Our meeting will start at **a quarter after ten.**

At **eight-thirty,** the show will begin.

I was born at **5:22 PM** on a Monday.

You have until **three o'clock** to finish the proposal.

Use numerals to express dates, street numbers, room numbers, apartment numbers, telephone numbers, page numbers, exact amounts of money, scores, and percentages. Spell out the word *percent.* Round dollar or cent amounts of only a few words may be expressed in words.

EXAMPLES

May 27, 1962
(402) 555-1725
5219 Perret Street
pages 49–73
seventy cents
three hundred dollars
Apartment 655
38 percent
$1.6 billion (or $1,600,000,000)
$2,634

When you write a date, do not add *–st, –nd,* or *–th.*

EXAMPLES

incorrect	
August 17th, 1968	November 5th
correct	
August 17, 1968	November 5 or the fifth of November

COMMON SPELLING ERRORS

Pronunciation is not always a reliable guide for spelling because words are not always spelled the way they are pronounced. However, by paying attention to both letters that spell sounds and letters that are silent, you can improve some aspects of your spelling. Always check a dictionary for the correct pronunciations and spellings of words that are new to your experience.

Extra Syllables

Sometimes people misspell a word because they include an extra syllable. For example, *arthritis* is easily misspelled if it is pronounced *artheritis,* with four syllables instead of three. Pay close attention to the number of syllables in these words.

EXAMPLES

two syllables

foundry carriage lonely

three syllables

privilege boundary separate

Omitted Sounds

Sometimes people misspell a word because they do not sound one or more letters when pronouncing the word. Be sure to include the underlined letters of these words even if you don't pronounce them.

EXAMPLES

barbarous	candidate	drowned
gratitude	governor	grocery
literature	sophomore	quantity
mischievous		

Homophones

Words that have the same pronunciation but different spellings and meanings are called **homophones.** An incorrect choice can be confusing to your readers. Knowing the spelling and meaning of these groups of words will improve your spelling.

EXAMPLES

allowed/aloud	compliment/complement
sole/soul	alter/altar
hear/here	some/sum
ascent/assent	lead/led
threw/through	bear/bare
night/knight	wait/weight
brake/break	pair/pear
weak/week	buy/bye/by
peace/piece	who's/whose
capital/capitol	plain/plane
coarse/course	site/sight/cite

Commonly Confused Words

Some other groups of words are not homophones, but they are similar enough in sound and spelling to create confusion. Knowing the spelling and meaning of these groups of words will also improve your spelling.

EXAMPLES

access/excess	farther/further
nauseous/nauseated	accept/except
formally/formerly	passed/past
alternate/alternative	literal/literally
principle/principal	desert/dessert
loose/lose	stationary/stationery

COMMONLY MISSPELLED WORDS

Some words are often misspelled. Here is a list of 150 commonly misspelled words. If you master this list, you will avoid many errors in your spelling.

absence
abundant
academically
accessible
accidentally
accommodate
accurate
acknowledgment
acquaintance
adequately
adolescent
advantageous
advisable
ancient
annihilate
anonymous
answer
apparent
article
attendance
bankruptcy
beautiful
beggar
beginning
behavior
biscuit
breathe
business
calendar
camouflage
catastrophe
cellar
cemetery
changeable
clothes
colossal
column
committee
conceivable
conscientious
conscious
consistency
deceitful
descendant
desirable

disastrous
discipline
efficiency
eighth
embarrass
enormous
enthusiastically
environment
exhaust
existence
fascinating
finally
forfeit
fulfill
guerrilla
guidance
hindrance
hypocrite
independent
influential
ingenious
institution
interference
irrelevant
irresistible
judgment
league
leisure
license
lightning
liquefy
magnificent
manageable
maneuver
meadow

mediocre
miniature
mischievous
misspell
mortgage
mysterious
naïve
necessity
nickel
niece
noticeable
nucleus
nuisance
nutritious
obedience
occasionally
occurrence
orchestra
outrageous
pageant
parallel
pastime
peasant
permanent
persistent
phenomenon
physician
pneumonia
prestige
privilege
procedure
prophesy
prove
receipt
referred

rehearsal
relieve
resistance
resources
responsibility
rhythm
schedule
seize
separate
sergeant
siege
significance
souvenir
sponsor
succeed
surprise
symbol
synonymous
temperature
tomorrow
transparent
twelfth
undoubtedly
unmistakable
unnecessary
vacuum
vehicle
vengeance
villain
vinegar
weird
whistle
withhold
yacht
yield

GRAMMAR & STYLE

3.1 The Sentence

THE SENTENCE

In the English language, the sentence is the basic unit of meaning. A **sentence** is a group of words that expresses a complete thought. Every sentence has two basic parts: a subject and a predicate. The **subject** tells whom or what the sentence is about. The **predicate** tells information about the subject.

EXAMPLE

sentence
The experienced detective **[subject]** |
asked the suspect several questions **[predicate].**

A group of words that does not have both a subject and a predicate is called a **sentence fragment.** A sentence fragment does not express a complete thought.

EXAMPLES

sentence fragment
The newspaper carrier. (The fragment does not have a predicate. The group of words does not answer the question *What did the newspaper carrier do?*)
sentence fragment
Flung the morning edition. (The fragment does not have a subject. The group of words does not answer the question *Who flung the morning edition?*)
sentence fragment
Onto the front porch. (The fragment does not have a subject or a predicate. The group of words does not tell what the sentence is about or tell what the subject does.)
complete sentence
The newspaper carrier flung the morning edition onto the front porch.

FUNCTIONS OF SENTENCES

There are four different kinds of sentences: *declarative, interrogative, imperative,* and *exclamatory*. Each kind of sentence has a different purpose. You can vary the tone and mood of your writing by using the four different sentence types.

- A **declarative sentence** makes a statement. It ends with a period.

EXAMPLE
Samantha is in the backyard trying to repair the lawnmower.

- An **interrogative sentence** asks a question. It ends with a question mark.

EXAMPLE
Will she be joining you for supper later tonight?

- An **imperative sentence** gives an order or makes a request. It ends with a period or an exclamation point. An imperative sentence has an understood subject, most often *you*.

EXAMPLES
(You) Please take a glass of lemonade to her.
(You) Don't touch that sharp blade!

- An **exclamatory sentence** expresses strong feeling. It ends with an exclamation point.

EXAMPLE
Samantha is a wizard at fixing lawnmowers!

SUBJECTS AND PREDICATES

The **subject** tells whom or what the sentence is about, whereas the **predicate** tells what the subject is, what the subject does, or what happens to the subject.

EXAMPLE
The yellow-eyed owls **[subject]** |
sat quietly in the oak tree **[predicate].**

To find the subject, ask who or what performs the action of the verb.

EXAMPLE
Who or what sat quietly in the oak tree? *the yellow-eyed owls* **[subject]**

What did the yellow-eyed owls do? *sat quietly in the oak tree* **[predicate]**

SIMPLE AND COMPLETE SUBJECTS AND PREDICATES

In a sentence, the **simple subject** is the key word or words in the subject. The simple subject is usually a noun or a pronoun and does not include any modifiers. The **complete subject** includes the simple subject and all the words that modify it.

The **simple predicate** is the key verb or verb phrase that tells what the subject does, has, or is. The **complete predicate** includes the verb and all the words that modify it.

In the following sentence, a vertical line separates the complete subject and complete predicate. The simple subject is underlined once. The simple predicate is underlined twice.

EXAMPLE

Bright orange tongues of flame **[complete subject]** |
danced erratically in the center of the clearing **[complete predicate].**

Sometimes, the simple subject is also the complete subject, and the simple predicate or verb is also the complete predicate.

EXAMPLE

Falcons | swooped.

To find the simple subject and simple predicate in a sentence, first break the sentence into its two basic parts: complete subject and complete predicate. Then, identify the simple predicate by asking yourself, "What is the action of this sentence?" Finally, identify the simple subject by asking yourself, "Who or what is performing the action?" In the following sentences, the complete predicate is in parentheses. The simple predicate, or verb, appears in boldface.

EXAMPLES

one-word verb
Your friend on the track team (**runs** swiftly.)
two-word verb
Your friend on the track team (**will run** swiftly in this race.)
three-word verb
All season long, your friend on the track team (**has been running** swiftly.)
four-word verb
If he hadn't twisted his ankle last week, your friend on the track team (**would have been running** swiftly today.)

COMPOUND SUBJECTS AND PREDICATES

A sentence may have more than one subject or predicate. A **compound subject** has two or more simple subjects that have the same predicate. The subjects are joined by the conjunction *and, or,* or *but.*

A **compound predicate** has two or more simple predicates, or verbs, that share the same subject. The verbs are connected by the conjunction *and, or,* or *but.*

EXAMPLES

compound subject
Pamela and Else | read their books in the library.
compound predicate
Four maniacal crows | watched and waited while I washed the car.

The conjunctions *either* and *or* and *neither* and *nor* can also join compound subjects or predicates.

EXAMPLES

compound subject
Either Peter *or* Paul | sings the national anthem before each game.
Neither yesterday *nor* today | seemed like a good time to start the project.
compound predicate
Her dogs | *either* heard *or* smelled the intruder in the basement.
The police inspector | *neither* visited *nor* called last night.

A sentence may also have a compound subject and a compound predicate.

EXAMPLE

compound subject and compound predicate
Mandy and Eric | grilled the hamburgers and made the coleslaw.

SENTENCE STRUCTURES

A **simple sentence** consists of one independent clause and no subordinate clauses. It may have a compound subject and a compound predicate. It may also have any number of phrases. A simple sentence is sometimes called an independent clause because it can stand by itself.

EXAMPLES

Three bears emerged from the forest.

They spotted the campers and the hikers and decided to pay a visit.

The three bears enjoyed eating the campers' fish, sandwiches, and candy bars.

A **compound sentence** consists of two sentences joined by a semicolon or by a coordinating conjunction and a comma. Each part of the compound sentence has its own subject and verb. The most common coordinating conjunctions are *and, or, nor, for, but, so,* and *yet.*

EXAMPLES

Feeding bears is dangerous and unwise, **for** it creates larger problems in the long run.

Our zoo is home to two panda bears**;** they were originally captured in Asia.

A **complex sentence** consists of one independent clause and one or more subordinate clauses. The subordinate clauses in the examples below are underlined.

EXAMPLES

<u>When you finish your report</u>, remember to print it out on paper <u>that contains 25 percent cotton fiber</u>.

Jim will water the lawn <u>after he returns home from the baseball game</u>.

If you combine a compound sentence and a complex sentence, you form a **compound-complex sentence.** This kind of sentence must have two or more independent clauses and at least one subordinate clause. In the following examples, the subordinate clauses are underlined.

EXAMPLES

Rabbits, <u>which like to nibble on the flowers</u>, often visit my garden early in the morning, or they wait until early evening <u>when the dog is inside the house.</u>

Larry enthusiastically leaps out of bed each morning <u>after his alarm clock rings</u>, yet he often feels sleepy in the afternoon.

3.2 The Parts of Speech

IDENTIFYING THE PARTS OF SPEECH

Each word in a sentence performs a basic function or task. Words perform four basic tasks: they name, modify, express action or state of being, or link.

There are eight different parts of speech. Each part of speech is defined in the following chart.

Part of Speech	Definition	Example
noun	A **noun** names a person, place, thing, or idea.	**Apples, oranges,** and **potato chips** were the only **items** on the **list.**
pronoun	A **pronoun** is used in place of a noun.	Fanny whispered to **her** friend as **they** waited for **their** new teacher.
verb	A **verb** expresses action or a state of being.	Playful fox cubs **tumbled** out of the den and **chased** one another across the field.
adjective	An **adjective** modifies a noun or pronoun. The most common adjectives are the articles *a, an,* and *the.*	**Tattered** curtains hung in the **dark** windows of the **gray, sagging** house.
adverb	An **adverb** modifies a verb, an adjective, or another adverb.	**Sharply** turning to the left, the bicyclist **nearly** caused an accident.
preposition	A **preposition** shows the relationship between its object—a noun or a pronoun—and another word in a sentence. Common prepositions include *after, around, at, behind, beside, off, through, until, upon,* and *with.*	**During** winter, we often sit **by** the fireplace **in** the evening.
conjunction	A **conjunction** joins words or groups of words. Common conjunctions are *and, but, for, nor, or, so,* and *yet.*	**Neither** Grant **nor** Felix felt tired after two miles, **so** they ran another mile.
interjection	An **interjection** is a word used to express emotion. Common interjections are *oh, ah, well, hey,* and *wow.*	**Wow!** Did you see the dive he took from the high jump?

3.3 Nouns

NOUNS

A **noun** is a part of speech that names a person, place, idea, or thing. In this unit, you'll learn about the different kinds of nouns and what they name.

EXAMPLES

people Noah, editor, aunt, actor

places homeland, Wrigley Field, St. Peter's Basilica

ideas prejudice, subtraction, boredom, plot

things volleyball, song, trajectory, candle

Types of Nouns	Definition	Examples
common noun	names a person, place, idea, or thing	mother, garage, plan, flower
proper noun	names a specific person, place, or thing; begins with capital letter	John Adams, New York City, Monroe Doctrine
concrete noun	names a thing that can be touched, seen, heard, smelled, or tasted	ruler, mirror, giggle, garbage, banana
abstract noun	names an idea, a theory, a concept, or a feeling	approval, philosophy, faith, communism
singular noun	names one person, place, idea, or thing	governor, tree, thought, shoe
plural noun	names more than one thing	governors, trees, thoughts, shoes
possessive noun	shows ownership or possession of things or qualities	Jan's, Mrs. Wilson's, women's, intern's
compound noun	made up of two or more words	staircase, picnic table, brother-in-law
collective noun	names groups	organization, platoon, team

3.4 Pronouns

PRONOUNS

A **pronoun** is used in place of a noun. Sometimes a pronoun refers to a specific person or thing.

Pronouns can help your writing flow more smoothly. Without pronouns, your writing can sound awkward and repetitive.

The most commonly used pronouns are *personal pronouns*, *reflexive and intensive pronouns*, *demonstrative pronouns*, *indefinite pronouns*, *interrogative pronouns*, and *relative pronouns.*

Types of Pronouns	Definition	Examples
personal pronoun	used in place of the name of a person or thing	I, me, we, us, he, she, it, him, her, you, they, them
indefinite pronoun	points out a person, place, or thing, but not a specific or definite one	one, someone, anything, other, all, few, nobody
reflexive pronoun	refers back to a noun previously used; adds –self and –selves to other pronoun forms	myself, herself, yourself, themselves, ourselves
intensive pronoun	emphasizes a noun or a pronoun	me myself, he himself, you yourself, they themselves, we ourselves
interrogative pronoun	asks a question	who, whose, whom, what, which
demonstrative pronoun	points out a specific person, place, idea, or thing	this, these, that, those
relative pronoun	introduces an adjective clause	that, which, who, whose, whom
singular pronoun	used in place of the name of one person or thing	I, me, you, he, she, it, him, her
plural pronoun	used in place of more than one person or thing	we, us, you, they, them
possessive pronoun	shows ownership or possession	mine, yours, his, hers, ours, theirs

PRONOUNS AND ANTECEDENTS

The word that a pronoun stands for is called its **antecedent.** The antecedent clarifies the meaning of the pronoun. The pronoun may appear in the same sentence as its antecedent or in a following sentence.

EXAMPLES

Where is **Linda? Maria** thought **she** saw **her** in the garden. (*Linda* is the antecedent of *her. Maria* is the antecedent of *she.*)

The backyard **fence** is rather old, and **it** needs painting. (*Fence* is the antecedent of *it.*)

GRAMMAR & STYLE

A pronoun should agree in both number (singular or plural) and gender (masculine, feminine, or neutral) with its antecedent.

EXAMPLES

number

singular — **Robert Frost** wrote many poems. "Stopping by Woods on a Snowy Evening" is perhaps **his** most well-known poem.

plural — The visiting **poets** were asked if **they** would give a reading on Saturday night.

gender

masculine — **Robert Frost** was born in California, but **he** was raised in Massachusetts and New Hampshire.

feminine — **Toni Morrison** begins **her** writing day before dawn.

neutral — The **poem** is titled "Birches," and **it** is one of my favorites.

Singular pronouns are used with some nouns that are plural in form but singular in meaning, such as *economics, electronics, gymnastics, linguistics, mathematics, measles, news,* and *physics.*

EXAMPLES

My younger brother has the **measles.** I hope I don't catch **it.**

Would you like to try **gymnastics? It** is excellent exercise.

Plural pronouns are used with some nouns that are plural in form but refer to single items, such as *pliers, eyeglasses, pants, scissors,* and *shorts.*

EXAMPLES

I can't find my **eyeglasses.** Have you seen **them?**

The **pants** fit you well, but **they** need hemming.

Agreement between a relative pronoun—*who, whom, whose, which,* and *that*—and its antecedent is determined by the number of the antecedent.

EXAMPLES

Marie, who has always enjoyed **her** rural life, has surprisingly decided to move to the city. (*Who* is singular because it refers to the singular noun *Marie. Her* is used to agree with *who.*)

All who wish to vote by absentee ballot should complete **their** ballots and mail **them** to the county clerk's office. (*Who* is plural because it refers to the plural pronoun *All. Their* is used to agree with *who. Them* is used to agree with *ballots.*)

PRONOUN CASES

Personal pronouns take on different forms—called *cases*—depending on how they are used in sentences. Personal pronouns can be used as subjects, direct objects, indirect objects, and objects of prepositions. In the English language, there are three case forms for personal pronouns: *nominative, objective,* and *possessive.* The following chart organizes personal pronouns by case, number, and person.

Personal Pronouns

	Nominative Case	Objective Case	Possessive Case
Singular			
first person	I	me	my, mine
second person	you	you	your, yours
third person	he, she, it	him, her, it	his, her, hers, its
Plural			
first person	we	us	our, ours
second person	you	you	your, yours
third person	they	them	their, theirs

Indefinite Pronouns

An **indefinite pronoun** points out a person, place, or thing, but not a particular or definite one. The indefinite pronouns are listed below.

Singular	Plural	Singular or Plural
another	both	all
anybody	few	any
anyone	many	more
anything	others	most
each	several	none
each other		some
either		
everybody		
everyone		
everything		
much		
neither		
nobody		
no one		
nothing		
one		
one another		
somebody		
someone		
something		

EXAMPLES

singular
Something makes a ticking noise in the night.

Everyone is welcome to join us at the picnic.

plural
Many are eager to participate in the summer festival.

Several were missing the necessary information.

3.5 Verbs

VERBS—PREDICATES

Every sentence can be divided into two parts: the **subject** and the **predicate.** The following sentence is divided between the complete subject and the complete predicate.

EXAMPLE

The tardy **student** | **raced** through the maze of hallways to class.

The subject of a sentence names whom or what the sentence is about. The predicate tells what the subject does, is, or has. A **verb** is the predicate without any complements, linkers, or modifiers. In other words, the verb is the simple predicate.

Verbs are the **expressers** of the English language. Verbs are used to express action or a state of being. They tell whether the action is completed, continuing, or will happen in the future. Verbs also express all kinds of conditions for the action. Verbs in the English language can be from one to four words long. When a main verb is preceded by one or more helping verbs, it is called a **verb phrase.**

EXAMPLES

Lauren **volunteers** at the food pantry.

Lauren **is volunteering** at the food pantry.

Lauren **has been volunteering** at the food pantry.

Lauren **might have been volunteering** at the food pantry.

The following chart lists the different types of verbs and their functions, along with examples of how they are used.

Type of Verb	Definition	Examples
action verb	names an action	howl, wobble, skitter, flutter, fly
helping verb	helps a main verb express action or a state of being	My dogs will howl when a siren sounds. A butterfly has been fluttering above the daisies.
linking verb	connects a noun with another noun, pronoun, or adjective that describes or identifies it; the most common linking verbs are formed from the verb *to be*	The butterfly is a monarch. It seems to float in the breeze.
transitive verb	has a direct object	The scientist remembered the secret code.
intransitive verb	does not have a direct object	My brother snores.
irregular verb	has a different past tense form and spelling	forget/forgot think/thought write/wrote

VERB TENSES

The Simple Tenses

Verbs have different forms, called **tenses,** which are used to tell the time in which an action takes place. The **simple tenses** of the verb are **present, past,** and **future.**

The **present tense** tells that an action happens now—in present time.

EXAMPLES

present tense singular
The short-order cook **flips** pancakes on the grill.

present tense plural
The short-order cooks **flip** pancakes on the grill.

present tense singular
She **listens** carefully to the instructions.

present tense plural
They **listen** carefully to the instructions.

The **past tense** tells that an action happened in the past—prior to the present time. The past tense of a regular verb is formed by adding *–d* or *–ed* to the present verb form.

EXAMPLES

past tense singular
The short-order cook **flipped** pancakes on the grill.

past tense plural
The short-order cooks **flipped** pancakes on the grill.

past tense singular
She **listened** carefully to the instructions.

past tense plural
They **listened** carefully to the instructions.

The **future tense** tells that an action will happen in the future. The future tense is formed by adding the word *will* or *shall* before the present verb form.

EXAMPLES

future tense singular
The short order cook **will (shall) flip** pancakes on the grill.

future tense plural
The short-order cooks **will (shall) flip** pancakes on the grill.

The Perfect Tenses

The **perfect tenses** of verbs also express present, past, and future time, but they show that the action continued and was completed over a period of time or that the action will be completed in the present or future. The perfect tense is formed by using *has, have,* or *had* with the past participle.

EXAMPLES

present perfect singular
Vincent **has watered** the garden. The garden **has been watered** by Vincent.

present perfect plural
Vincent and Lena **have watered** the garden. (have or has + past participle)

past perfect singular
Vincent **had watered** the garden yesterday. The garden **had been watered** yesterday by Vincent.

past perfect plural
Vincent and Lena **had watered** the garden yesterday. (had + past participle)

future perfect singular
Vincent **will have watered** the garden by now.

future perfect plural
Vincent and Lena **will have watered** the garden by now. (will have or shall have + past participle)

THE PROGRESSIVE AND EMPHATIC VERB FORMS

Each of the six tenses has another form called the progressive form. The **progressive form** of a verb is used to express continuing action or state of being. The progressive form is made of the appropriate tense of the verb *be* and the present participle of a verb.

EXAMPLES

present progressive
I **am singing.** He **is singing.** They **are singing.**

past progressive
I **was singing.** They **were singing.**

future progressive
I **will (shall) be singing.**

present perfect progressive
He **has been singing.** They **have been singing.**

past perfect progressive
I **had been singing.**

future perfect progressive
I **will (shall) have been singing.**

The **emphatic form** of a verb is used to express emphasis. Only the present and past tenses have the emphatic form.

EXAMPLES

present emphatic
I **do try** to be punctual.
It **does matter** to me.

past emphatic
I **did clean** my room.

3.6 Complements

COMPLEMENTS FOR ACTION VERBS

A sentence must have a subject and a verb to communicate its basic meaning. In the following sentences, the subject and verb express the total concept. There is no receiver of the verb's action.

EXAMPLES

The girls shopped.

Sandra seldom shouts.

The thunder boomed.

Many sentences that include action verbs, however, need an additional word or group of words to complete the meaning.

EXAMPLES

The musicians tuned.

The musicians tuned their instruments.

The group of words *The musicians tuned* contains a subject *(musicians)* and a verb *(tuned).* Although the group of words may be considered a sentence, it does not express a complete thought. The word *instruments* completes the meaning expressed by the verb *tuned*. Therefore, *instruments* is called a **complement** or a completing word. The *completers* for action verbs are **direct objects** and **indirect objects.**

Direct Objects

A **direct object** receives the action in the sentence. It usually answers the question *what?* or *whom?* To find the direct object, find the action verb in the sentence. Then ask *what?* or *whom?* about the verb.

EXAMPLES

Sam **drove Jilly** to her mother's house. (*Drove* is the action verb. Whom did Sam drive? *Jilly* is the direct object.)

The coach **blew** her **whistle**. (*Blew* is the action verb. What did the coach blow? *Whistle* is the direct object.)

Remember to use object pronouns for a direct object.

singular me, you, him, her, it
plural us, you, them

EXAMPLES

Adam invited **us** to the party.

My dog follows **me** everywhere.

Indirect Objects

Sometimes the direct object is received by someone or something. This receiver is called the **indirect object.** It comes before the direct object and tells *to whom* the action is directed or *for whom* the action is performed. Only verbs that have direct objects can have indirect objects.

EXAMPLE

Lorelei **gave** the **teacher** her project. (*Gave* is the action verb. *Project* is the direct object because it tells what Lorelei gave. *Teacher* is an indirect object. It tells to whom Lorelei gave her project.)

To identify the indirect object: (1) Look for a noun or a pronoun that precedes the direct object. (2) Determine whether the word you think is a direct object seems to be the understood object of the preposition *to* or *for.*

COMPLEMENTS FOR LINKING VERBS

A **linking verb** connects a subject with a noun, a pronoun, or an adjective that describes it or identifies it. Linking verbs do not express action. Instead, they express state of being and need a noun, a pronoun or an adjective to complete the sentence meaning.

In each of the following sentences, the subject and verb would not be complete without the words that follow them.

EXAMPLES

Franklin D. Roosevelt **was** a popular president.

He **seemed** trustworthy and reliable.

Most linking verbs are forms of the verb *to be,* including *am, are, is, was,* and *been.* Other words that can be used as linking verbs include *appear, feel, grow, smell, taste, seem, sound, look, stay, feel, remain,* and *become*. When *to be* verbs are part of an action verb, they are helpers.

PREDICATE NOUNS AND PREDICATE PRONOUNS

A **predicate noun** is a noun that completes a sentence that uses a form of the verb *to be*. Similarly, a **predicate pronoun** is a pronoun that completes a sentence that uses a form of the verb *to be*. In fact, the relationship between the subject and the predicate noun or pronoun is so close that the sentence usually suggests an equation. Such sentences can often be reordered without changing the meaning.

EXAMPLES

predicate noun
Jacinta was the first girl to play on the boys' baseball team. (Jacinta = girl)

GRAMMAR & STYLE

The first girl to play on the boys' baseball team was Jacinta. (girl = Jacinta)

predicate pronoun
The friend who took me bowling was you. (friend = you)

You were the friend who took me bowling. (You = friend)

To find a predicate noun or pronoun, ask the same question you would ask to find a direct object.

EXAMPLES

My aunt is a great **chef.** (My aunt is a what? *Chef* is the predicate noun that renames or identifies *aunt,* the subject of the sentence.)

The first contestant will probably be **you.** (The first contestant will be who? *You* is the predicate pronoun that renames or identifies contestant, the subject of the sentence.)

The ticket taker at the booth was **she.** (Think: She was the ticket taker at the booth.)

The leaders of the hike were Sara and **he.** (Think: Sara and he were the leaders of the hike.)

PREDICATE ADJECTIVES

A **predicate adjective** completes a sentence by modifying, or describing, the subject of a sentence. To find a predicate adjective, ask the same question you would ask to find a direct object.

EXAMPLE

Your directions were **precise.** (Your directions were what? *Precise* is the predicate adjective that describes *directions,* the subject of the sentence.)

3.7 Agreement

SUBJECT AND VERB AGREEMENT

A **singular** noun describes or stands for *one* person, place, thing, or idea. A **plural noun** describes or stands for *more than one* person, place, thing, or idea.

EXAMPLES

singular nouns
beetle, mango, knife, fairy, goose
plural nouns
beetles, mangoes, knives, fairies, geese

In a sentence, a verb must be singular if its subject is singular and plural if its subject is plural. In other words, a verb must agree in number with its subject.

EXAMPLES

singular subject and verb
The **beetle chews** the flowers and stems.

plural subject and verb
The **beetles chew** the flowers and stems.

singular subject and verb
A **mango adds** a delightful flavor to the salad.

plural subject and verb
The **mangoes add** a delightful flavor to the salad.

singular subject and verb
A **goose protects** its goslings vigorously.

plural subject and verb
The **geese protect** their goslings vigorously.

COMPOUND SUBJECT AND VERB AGREEMENT

A **compound subject** consists of two or more subjects that share the same verb.

EXAMPLE

Tomatoes and sprouts make a sandwich taste better. (*Tomatoes and sprouts*—the compound subject—share the verb *make.*)

A compound subject must have either a singular or a plural verb, depending on how the parts of the subject are connected.

Use a singular verb:
- when the compound subject is made up of singular nouns or pronouns connected by *either/or* or *neither/nor.*

EXAMPLES

singular verb
Either a spoon or a fork **works** well.

Neither rice nor pasta **is** low in calories.

Use a plural verb:
- when the compound subject is connected by the coordinating conjunction *and.*
- when the compound subject is formed from plural nouns or pronouns.

EXAMPLES

plural verb

Flood and drought **alternate** in devastating Texas.

Either fruits or vegetables **provide** the necessary nutrients.

Neither the Red Sox nor the Blue Jays **have been** to the World Series recently.

When a compound subject consists of a singular subject and a plural subject connected by *or* or *nor*, use a verb that agrees in number with the subject that is closer to it in the sentence.

EXAMPLES

Either Ben or the Roses **distribute** the magazines. (*Roses distribute*—plural)

Neither the community nor the mayor **accepts** the budget as final. (*mayor accepts*—singular)

INDEFINITE PRONOUN AND VERB AGREEMENT

An **indefinite pronoun** does not refer to a specific person, place, or thing. Some indefinite pronouns are always singular and take singular verbs: *anybody, anyone, anything, each, either, everybody, everyone, everything, much, neither, nobody, no one, nothing, one, somebody, someone, something.*

EXAMPLES

singular

Nobody wants that jacket.

Something seems different about you.

Some indefinite pronouns are always plural and take plural verbs: *both, few, many, others, several.*

EXAMPLES

plural

Many of my friends **are** serious readers.

Several flights **leave** this airport every day.

Some indefinite pronouns can be either singular or plural, depending on their use in the sentence: *all, any, most, none, some.* They are singular when they refer to a portion or to a single person, place, or thing. They are plural when they refer to a number of individual persons, places, or things. Often the object of the preposition will signal whether the pronoun is singular or plural.

EXAMPLES

singular

None of their music **makes** sense to me.

plural

None of the lyrics **make** any sense.

3.8 Modifiers

ADJECTIVES AND ADVERBS

Adjectives and adverbs—two kinds of **modifiers**—add meaning to nouns, adjectives, verbs, and adverbs. An **adjective** modifies a noun or a pronoun. An **adverb** modifies a verb, an adjective, or another adverb.

EXAMPLES

adjective

The **yellow** roses have rambled up the **wooden** trellis onto the roof.
(*Yellow* modifies the noun *roses; wooden* modifies the noun *trellis.*)

adverb

The roses are **too** thorny to be trimmed.
(*Too* modifies the adjective *thorny.*)

The roses have grown **very** slowly, but they bloom **profusely** every spring.
(*Very* modifies the adverb *slowly; profusely* modifies the verb *bloom.*)

To determine whether a modifier is an adjective or an adverb, you can follow these steps.

1. Look at the word that is modified.
2. Ask yourself, "Is this modified word a noun or a pronoun?" If the answer is yes, the modifier is an adjective. If the answer is no, the modifier is an adverb.

In the following example, the word *balloonist* is modified by the word *daring*. The word *balloonist* is a noun, so the word *daring* is an adjective.

EXAMPLE

The **daring balloonist** traveled around the world.

GRAMMAR & STYLE

In the next example, the word *landed* is modified by the word *safely.* The word *landed* is a verb; therefore, the word *safely* is an adverb.

EXAMPLE

After surviving a storm at sea, the balloonist **landed safely** in Australia.

ADJECTIVES

Adjectives modify nouns by telling specific details about them.

EXAMPLES

noun	fence
a little more specific	picket fence
more specific yet	rickety picket fence
even more specific	old, rickety picket fence

Some adjectives tell *how many* or *what kind* about the nouns or pronouns they modify.

EXAMPLES

Many repairs are needed to restore the fence to its original charm.

First, we'll replace the **rotting** wood and then apply **white** paint.

Other adjectives tell *which one* or *which ones.*

EXAMPLES

Luckily, the **old** fence is in excellent condition.

These slats do not need to be replaced.

The **articles** *a, an,* and *the* are the most commonly occurring adjectives. *A* and *an* refer to any person, place, or thing in general. *The* refers to a specific person, place, or thing.

EXAMPLES

A fence can be made of wood or metal. (*A* refers to a fence in general.)

The gate on **the** fence is open. (*The* refers to a specific gate on a specific fence.)

A **proper adjective** is formed from a proper noun. Proper adjectives are capitalized and often end in *–n, –an, –ian, –ese,* or *–ish.*

EXAMPLES

African mahogany trees are valued for their hard, reddish brown wood.

Furniture and ships are often built with durable **Asian** teakwood.

Type of Adjective	Definition	Examples
adjective	modifies nouns and pronouns; answers the questions *what kind? which one? how many?* and *how much?*	**shiny** pennies **hieroglyphic** inscription **dozen** roses **one** mistake
article	*a* and *an* refer to an unspecified person, place, thing, or idea; *the* refers to a specific person, place, thing, or idea	**A** problem has developed. I peeled **an** orange. **The** tomatoes are ripe.
proper adjective	is formed from proper nouns; is capitalized; often ends in *–n, –an, –ian, –ese,* or *–ish*	**Serbian** restaurant **Victorian** England **Chinese** calendar **Jewish** tradition

ADVERBS

Adverbs modify verbs, adjectives, or other adverbs. Many times adverbs will tell us *how, when, where, why* or *to what extent.*

EXAMPLES

adverbs modify verbs
Horses galloped **swiftly** across the plains. (*Swiftly* tells how they galloped.)

Horses **usually** stay **away** from the trainer until a bond is developed. (*Usually* tells when they stay away from the trainer; *away* tells where they stay.)

adverbs modify adjectives
This young colt is **really** frightened. (*Really* tells to what extent the colt is frightened.)

The trainer has **tremendous** patience in working with the colt. (*Tremendous* tells to what extent the trainer has patience.)

adverbs modify adverbs
Finally, the colt approaches the trainer **very** slowly. (*Very* tells how slowly the colt approaches the trainer.)

The colt's movements were predicted **so** accurately by the experienced trainer. (*So* tells how accurately the colt's movements were predicted.)

POSITION OF ADVERBS

An adverb can be placed before or after a verb it modifies. Sometimes an adverb can be separated from a verb by another word or words.

EXAMPLES

The coin collector **carefully examined** the rare silver coin.

Eager to find out when it was minted, he **looked carefully** through the magnifying glass.

He **polished** the coin **carefully** to reveal the embossed date.

Note, however, in the following examples, how changing the position of an adverb changes the meaning of the sentence.

EXAMPLES

He **only** worried about money. (He did nothing else but worry about money.)

He worried **only** about money. (He worried about nothing else but money.)

3.9 Prepositions and Conjunctions

PREPOSITIONS AND CONJUNCTIONS

Prepositions and conjunctions are the linkers of the English language. They are used to join words and phrases to the rest of a sentence. They also show the relationships between ideas. Prepositions and conjunctions help writers vary their sentences by connecting sentence parts in different ways.

A **preposition** is used to show how its object, a noun or a pronoun, is related to other words in the sentence. Some commonly used prepositions include *above, after, against, among, around, at, behind, beneath, beside, between, down, for, from, in, on, off, toward, through, to, until, upon,* and *with.*

EXAMPLES

A bright beacon led them safely **to** the shore.

He placed the book **beside** the bed.

Most Commonly Used Prepositions

aboard	between	on
about	beyond	over
above	but (meaning	past
across	"except")	since
after	by	through
against	concerning	throughout
along	down	to
amid	during	under
among	except	underneath
around	for	until
at	from	up
before	in	upon
behind	into	with
below	like	within
beside	of	without
besides	off	

A **conjunction** is a word used to link related words, groups of words, or sentences. Like a preposition, a conjunction shows the relationship between the words it links. Some of the most commonly used conjunctions are *and, but, for, nor, or, yet, so, if, after, because, before, although, unless, while,* and *when.* Some conjunctions are used in pairs, such as *both/and, neither/nor,* and *not only/but also.*

EXAMPLES

We went out for dinner **and** a movie on Saturday night.

They played poorly **because** they did not warm up before the game.

Neither I **nor** my brother inherited our mother's red hair.

Certain words can function as either conjunctions or prepositions. There are two important differences between a word used as a preposition and one used as a conjunction.

1. A preposition is always followed by an *object,* but a conjunction is not.

EXAMPLES

preposition
You may have a turn **after** your sister. (The noun *sister* is the object of the preposition *after.*)

conjunction
After you arrived, we had a wonderful time. (*After* is not followed by an object. It introduces a group of words, or clause, that depends on the rest of the sentence for meaning.)

2. A preposition introduces a prepositional phrase that connects parts of a sentence. A conjunction connects words or groups of words (clauses containing a subject and verb).

EXAMPLES

preposition
I never eat breakfast **before** exercising. (*Before* introduces the prepositional phrase *before exercising.*)

conjunction
Put on sunscreen **before** the swim meet begins. (*Before* introduces a clause, that is, a subject and verb, that modifies *put,* telling when to put on the sunscreen.)

The types of conjunctions are listed below.

Type of Conjunction	Definition	Examples
coordinating conjunction	joins words or groups of words of equal importance; coordinating conjunctions are *and, but, for, nor, or, so, yet*	Holly and Max are Labrador retrievers. They are well-behaved dogs, *for* they have taken many obedience lessons.
correlative conjunction	word pairs that join words or groups of words; correlative conjunctions include *both/and, neither/nor, either/or*	*Both* Labrador retrievers *and* golden retrievers are excellent companion dogs.
subordinating conjunction	introduces a subordinate clause and joins it to an independent clause; subordinating conjunctions include *after, although, as, as if, because, before, if, since, unless, till, when,* and *while*	*Because* Holly is growing old, she has white whiskers on her chin.

3.10 Interjections

An **interjection** is a part of speech that expresses feeling, such as surprise, joy, relief, urgency, pain, or anger. Common interjections include *ah, aha, alas, bravo, dear me, goodness, great, ha, help, hey, hooray, hush, indeed, mercy, of course, oh, oops, ouch, phooey, really, say, see, ugh,* and *whew.*

EXAMPLES

Hey, that's not fair!

Goodness, you don't need to get so upset.

Hush! You'll wake the baby.

Why, of course! Please do join us for dinner.

Interjections actually indicate different degrees of emotion. They may express intense or sudden emotion, as in *Wow! That was unexpected.* Notice that the strong expression of emotion stands alone in the sentence and is followed by an exclamation point. Interjections can also express mild emotion, as in *Well, that is the best we could do.* In this sentence, the interjection is part of the sentence and is set off only with a comma. Even when interjections are part of a sentence, they do not relate grammatically to the rest of the sentence.

3.11 Phrases

A **phrase** is a group of words used as a single part of speech. A phrase lacks a subject, a verb, or both; therefore, it cannot be a sentence. There are three common kinds of phrases: prepositional phrases, verbal phrases, and appositive phrases.

PREPOSITIONAL PHRASES

A **prepositional phrase** consists of a preposition, its object, and any modifiers of that object. A prepositional phrase adds information to a sentence by relating its object to another word in the sentence. It may function as an adjective or an adverb.

EXAMPLES

adjectives
Sue planned a party **with music and dancing.** (The prepositional phrase *with music and dancing* tells what kind of party Sue planned. The phrase is used as an adjective, modifying the noun *party.*)

She found the CDs and tapes in a box **under her bed.** (The prepositional phrase *under her bed* tells in which box Sue found the CDs and tapes. The phrase is used as an adjective, modifying the object of the prepositional phrase *in a box.*)

adverbs
Albert struggled **into his jacket.** (The prepositional phrase *into his jacket* tells how Albert struggled. The phrase is used as an adverb, modifying the verb *struggled.*)

My friend is generous **with her time.** (The prepositional phrase *with her time* tells how the friend is generous. The phrase is used as an adverb, modifying the adjective *generous.*)

Use prepositional phrases to create sentence variety. When every sentence in a paragraph starts with its subject, the rhythm of the sentences becomes boring. Revise your sentences, where it is appropriate, to start some with prepositional phrases.

EXAMPLE

Chad stacked sandbags **for nearly eight hours.**

For nearly eight hours, Chad stacked sandbags.

VERBAL PHRASES

Verbals are verb forms that act as namers or modifiers. There are three kinds of verbals: participles, gerunds, and infinitives.

Participial Phrases

A **participle** is a verb form ending in *–ing, –d,* or *–ed* that acts as an adjective, modifying a noun or a pronoun. A **participial phrase** is made up of a participle and all of the words related to the participle, which may include objects, modifiers, and prepositional phrases. The entire phrase acts as an adjective.

EXAMPLES

Swimming quickly toward the shore, Diego thought eagerly about a warm shower. (The participle *swimming,* the adverb *quickly,* and the prepositional phrase *toward the shore* make up the participial phrase that modifies *Diego.*)

Jeffrey picked up the clothes **scattered around his bedroom.** (The participle *scattered* and the prepositional phrase *around his bedroom* make up the participial phrase that modifies *clothes.*)

For variety, begin some of your sentences with participial phrases. However, be sure to place the participial phrase close to the word it modifies. Otherwise, you may say something you do not mean.

EXAMPLES

misplaced participial phrase
I saw the craters on the moon looking through a telescope.

revised sentence
Looking through a telescope, I saw the craters on the moon.

Gerund Phrases

A **gerund phrase** is a phrase made up of a gerund (a verb form ending in *–ing*) and all of its modifiers and complements. The entire phrase functions as a noun. This means that the phrase may be the subject, predicate nominative, direct object, indirect object, or object of the preposition in a sentence. A gerund's modifiers include adjectives, adverbs, and prepositional phrases.

EXAMPLES

Waiting for the school bus gives Henry time to read. (The gerund phrase functions as the subject of the sentence.)

One of Henry's favorite quiet times is **waiting for the school bus.** (The gerund phrase functions as the predicate nominative of the sentence.)

Jim, however, hated **waiting for the school bus** more than anything else. (The gerund phrase functions as the direct object of the sentence.)

He always stopped for snacks before **waiting for the school bus.** (The gerund phrase functions as the object of the preposition.)

Infinitive Phrases

An **infinitive phrase** is made up of an infinitive (a verb form preceded by the word *to*) and all its modifiers and complements. Infinitive phrases can function as nouns, adjectives, or adverbs.

EXAMPLES

It's pleasant **to eat strawberries with whipped cream.** (The infinitive phrase functions as an adverb.)

The general intends **to charge at the enemy's flank.** (The infinitive phrase functions as a noun.)

Sometimes the *to* of an infinitive phrase is left out; it is understood.

EXAMPLES

Eli helped **[to]** build the deck.
I'll go **[to]** turn off the porch light.

GRAMMAR & STYLE

APPOSITIVE PHRASES

An **appositive phrase** is a group of words made up of an appositive and all its modifiers. The phrase renames or identifies a noun or a pronoun.

EXAMPLES

Sara's house, **a cabin in a remote area,** is the site for the weekend retreat. (The appositive phrase renames the noun *house*.)

The languages **English, Spanish, and French** blasted from the loudspeakers. (The appositive phrase identifies which languages blasted from the loudspeakers.)

The first example above, *a cabin in a remote area,* is a **nonessential,** or **nonrestrictive, appositive phrase.** It is not necessary to the meaning of the sentence; it is not needed to identify which particular house, since we already know that it is Sara's. Therefore, it is set off with commas.

The second example, *English, Spanish, and French,* is an **essential,** or **restrictive, appositive phrase.** It is necessary for understanding the sentence because it identifies which particular languages, since we do not already know which ones. This appositive phrase is not set off with commas.

Appositive phrases add variety to your writing because they can be placed at the beginning, in the middle, or at the end of a sentence. Using appositive phrases to combine sentences eliminates unimportant words and creates more fact-filled sentences. When you join two ideas with an appositive phrase, place the idea you wish to stress in the main clause and make the less important idea the appositive.

3.12 Clauses

A **clause** is a group of words that contains a subject and a verb and that functions as one part of speech. There are two types of clauses—independent and subordinate.

An **independent clause,** sometimes called a *main clause,* has a subject and a verb and expresses a complete thought. Since it can stand alone as a sentence, it is called *independent.*

EXAMPLE

Iceland has a misunderstood reputation as a land of ice, snow, and fog.

A **subordinate clause** or *dependent clause* has a subject and a verb, but it doesn't express a complete thought. It can't stand alone. It must be attached to or inserted into an independent clause. When you combine subordinate clauses with independent clauses, you form complete sentences.

EXAMPLES

Because the theater was sold out, the twins went to the mall. (The subordinate clause *because the film was sold out* is attached to an independent clause.)

The baby **who captured everyone's attention** got the part in the commercial. (The subordinate clause *who captured everyone's attention* is inserted into the independent clause *The baby got the part in the commercial.*)

ADJECTIVE CLAUSES

There are three types of subordinate clauses: adjective clauses, adverb clauses, and noun clauses.

An **adjective clause** is a subordinate clause that functions as an adjective. It modifies a noun or a pronoun. Adjective clauses are introduced most frequently with words like the following: *that, which, who, whom, whose, when, why,* and *where.* An adjective clause follows the word it modifies.

ADVERB CLAUSES

An **adverb clause** is a subordinate clause that functions as an adverb. It modifies a verb, an adjective, or another adverb.

EXAMPLES

Virgil used the computer **every chance he could.** (*Every chance he could* modifies the verb *used.*)

Nancy studies much harder **than her sister does.** (*Than her sister does* modifies the adverb *harder.*)

Today, Stanley played far better **than he usually does.** (*Than he usually does* modifies the adverb *better.*)

When you use an adverb clause at the beginning of a sentence, follow it with a comma. If you use an adverb clause at the end of a sentence, you do not need to use a comma before it.

EXAMPLES

If you're going to the grocery store, please bring home a gallon of milk.

Please bring home a gallon of milk *if you're going to the grocery store.*

Adverb clauses often, but not always, start with a subordinating conjunction such as *after, although, because, before, if, so that, unless, when, where, whether,* and *while.*

NOUN CLAUSES

A **noun clause** is a subordinate clause that functions as a noun. This means that it can function as a subject, predicate nominative, direct object, indirect object, object of a preposition, or appositive. Notice that noun clauses can have modifiers and complements. They can come at the beginning, middle, or end of a sentence. Words like these often introduce noun clauses: *that, what, whatever, where, whether, which, who, whoever, whom,* and *whose.*

EXAMPLES

subject
That the phone didn't ring was entirely surprising.

predicate nominative
This is **why she moved.**

direct object
The editor had no idea **where the manuscript was.**

indirect object
Tell **whomever you like** about the upcoming concert.

object of the preposition
Adele was greatly valued for **what she knew about human biology.**

appositive
The focus of the ad campaign, **that frequent brushing promotes healthy teeth,** appealed to the organization of dentists.

Too many noun clauses can make your writing sound wordy and overly formal, especially when the noun clauses are used as subjects.

3.13 Common Usage Problems

INCORRECT SUBJECT-VERB AGREEMENT

A subject and its verb must agree in number. Use singular verb forms with singular subjects and plural verb forms with plural subjects.

Intervening Words

A prepositional phrase that comes between a subject and a verb does not determine whether the subject is singular or plural.

EXAMPLES

The **tree** in the backyard **sways** with the breeze. (*tree sways,* singular)

The **governor,** along with his family, **watches** the parade. (*governor watches,* singular)

The **kids** in the neighborhood **play** baseball each night. (*kids play,* plural)

The **characters** in the movie **are** not very interesting. (*characters are,* plural)

In some cases, the *object* of the preposition controls the verb.

EXAMPLES

Some of the **pizza** was burned in the oven.

Some of the **pizzas** were burned in the oven.

Compound Subjects

Use a plural verb with most compound subjects connected by *and.*

EXAMPLES

<u>Charlotte and her boss</u> **review** the budget once a month.

<u>Otters, beavers, and alligators</u> **live** near bodies of water.

INCORRECT USE OF APOSTROPHES

Use an apostrophe to replace letters that have been left out in a contraction.

EXAMPLES

that's = that is
aren't = are not
we'll = we will

Use an apostrophe to show possession.

GRAMMAR & STYLE

GRAMMAR & STYLE

Singular Nouns

Use an apostrophe and an *s* (*'s*) to form the possessive of a singular noun, even if it ends in *s, x,* or *z.*

EXAMPLES

storm's damage
Chris's guitar
Max's spoon
jazz's history

Plural Nouns

Use an apostrophe and an *s* (*'s*) to form the possessive of a plural noun that does not end in *s.*

EXAMPLES

geese's flight
women's conference
children's laughter

Use an apostrophe alone to form the possessive of a plural noun that ends in *s.*

EXAMPLES

dolphins' migration
wheels' hubcaps
jets' engines

Do not add an apostrophe or *'s* to possessive personal pronouns: *mine, yours, his, hers, its, ours,* or *theirs.* They already show ownership.

EXAMPLES

His homework is finished; **mine** is not done yet.

The red house on the corner is **theirs.**

DOUBLE NEGATIVES

Make sure that you use only one of the following negatives in each sentence: *not, nobody, none, nothing, hardly, can't, doesn't, won't, isn't, aren't.* A **double negative** is the use of two negative words together when only one is needed. Correct double negatives by removing one of the negative words or by replacing one of the negative words with a positive word.

EXAMPLES

double negative
They can't hardly afford the plane tickets.

corrected sentence
They can hardly afford the plane tickets.
They can't afford the plane tickets.

double negative
Cassidy hasn't never read *The Call of the Wild.*

corrected sentence
Cassidy hasn't ever read *The Call of the Wild.*
Cassidy has never read *The Call of the Wild.*

DANGLING AND MISPLACED MODIFIERS

Place modifying phrases and clauses as close as possible to the words they modify; otherwise, your sentences may be unclear or unintentionally humorous.

A **dangling modifier** has nothing to modify because the word it would logically modify is not present in the sentence. In the following sentence, the modifying phrase has no logical object. The sentence says that a spider was reading.

EXAMPLE

Reading in his rocking chair, a spider was spotted on the wall.

You can eliminate dangling modifiers by rewriting the sentence so that an appropriate word is provided for the modifier to modify. You can also expand a dangling phrase into a full subordinate clause.

EXAMPLES

Reading in his rocking chair, he spotted a spider on the wall.

While Frank was reading in his rocking chair, he spotted a spider on the wall.

A **misplaced modifier** is located too far from the word it should modify.

EXAMPLE

Jennifer arrived home after the two-week training session on Friday.

You can revise a misplaced modifier by moving it closer to the word it modifies.

EXAMPLES

Jennifer arrived home on Friday after the two-week training session.

On Friday, Jennifer arrived home after the two-week training session.

FORMS OF *WHO* AND *WHOM*

Who and *whom* can be used to ask questions and to introduce subordinate clauses. Knowing what form of *who* to use can sometimes be confusing. The case of the pronoun *who* is determined by the pronoun's function in a sentence.

nominative case	who, whoever
objective case	whom, whomever

EXAMPLES

Who wrote the novel *One Hundred Years of Solitude?* (Because *who* is the subject in the sentence, the pronoun is in the nominative case.)

Did you say **who** called? (Because *who* is the subject of the subordinate clause, the pronoun is in the nominative case.)

Whoever returns my wallet will receive a reward. (Because *whoever* is the subject in the sentence, the pronoun is in the nominative case.)

Whom did you visit? (Because *whom* is the direct object in the sentence, the pronoun is in the objective case.)

SPLIT INFINITIVES

An infinitive, the base verb combined with *to,* should not be split under most circumstances. Infinitives such as *to save, to teach,* and *to hold* should not be interrupted by adverbs or other sentence components.

EXAMPLES

nonstandard
I began to seriously think about becoming a vegetarian.

standard
I began to think seriously about becoming a vegetarian.

In some cases, a modifier sounds awkward if it does not split the infinitive. In these situations, it may be best to reword the sentence to eliminate splitting the infinitive.

EXAMPLES

nonstandard
Jeff would like to nearly save the same amount of money as he did in 2001.

revised
Jeff would like to save nearly as much money as he did in 2001.

In certain cases, you may want to use a split infinitive to clarify the meaning of the sentence.

3.14 Commonly Misused Words

The following chart contains an alphabetic list of words and phrases that often cause usage problems.

Word/Phrases	Correct Use	Examples
a, an	Use *a* before words beginning with a consonant sound. Use *an* before words beginning with a vowel sound, including a silent *h*.	While walking in the woods, Jonah saw **a** coyote. **An** orangutan has a shaggy, reddish brown coat and very long arms. It is hard to find **an** honest politician in this town.
accept, except	*Accept* is a verb meaning "to receive willingly" or "to agree." *Except* is a preposition that means "leaving out" or "but."	I wish you would **accept** this token of my appreciation. Everyone has apologized for the misunderstanding **except** the mayor.
affect, effect	*Affect* is a verb that means "to influence." The noun *effect* means "the result of an action." The verb *effect* means "to cause" or "to bring about."	You can't let the audience **affect** your concentration. We saw the **effect** of last night's storm throughout the town. Peter will **effect** the proposed reorganization when he takes office.
ain't	This word is nonstandard English. Avoid using it in speaking and writing.	**nonstandard:** I ain't going to study English this semester. **standard:** I **am not** going to study English this semester.

Word/Phrases	Correct Use	Examples
all ready, already	*All ready* means "entirely ready or prepared." *Already* means "previously."	Speaking with each team member, I determined that they were **all ready** to play. Sandy **already** finished her homework before soccer practice.
all right	*All right* means "satisfactory," "unhurt," "correct," or "yes, very well." The word *alright* is not acceptable in formal written English.	**All right,** let's begin the meeting. Is your ill father going to be **all right?**
a lot	*A lot* means "a great number or amount" and is always two words. Because it is imprecise, you should avoid it except in informal usage. *Alot* is not a word.	We found **a lot** of seashells on the beach. Your brother had **a lot** of help planning the surprise party.
altogether, all together	*Altogether* is an adverb meaning "thoroughly." Something done *all together* is done as a group or mass.	He was **altogether** embarrassed after tripping on the sidewalk. The family members were **all together** when they heard the good news.
anywheres, everywheres, somewheres, nowheres	Use these words and others like them without the *s: anywhere, everywhere, somewhere, nowhere.*	The little gray dog was **nowhere** to be found. Yolanda never goes **anywhere** without her cell phone.
at	Don't use this word after *where.*	Where are your brothers hiding?
bad, badly	*Bad* is always an adjective, and *badly* is always an adverb. Use *bad* after linking verbs.	I developed a **bad** cold after shoveling the heavy, wet snow. Tom feels **bad** about losing your favorite CD. We **badly** need to find another relief pitcher.
beside, besides	*Beside* means "next to." *Besides* means "in addition to." *Besides* can also be an adverb meaning "moreover."	The yellow plant is sitting **beside** the purple vase. I bought socks and shoes **besides** a new shirt and jacket. There is nothing worth watching on TV tonight; **besides,** I have to study for a test.
between, among	Use *between* when referring to two people or things. Use *among* when you are discussing three or more people or things.	While on vacation, I divided my time **between** Paris and Brussels. The thoughtful pirate divided the loot **among** his shipmates.
bring, take	Use *bring* when you mean "to carry to." It refers to movement toward the speaker. Use *take* when you mean "to carry away." It refers to movement away from the speaker.	You need to **bring** your backpack home. Don't forget to **take** the garbage out to the curb tonight.
bust, busted	Do not use these nonstandard words as verbs to substitute for *break* or *burst.*	**nonstandard:** I busted my leg sliding into third base. The barrel busted after the extra batch was added. **standard:** I **broke** my leg sliding into third base. The barrel **burst** after the extra batch was added.
can, may	The word *can* means "able to do something." The word *may* is used to ask or give permission.	**Can** you speak a foreign language? You **may** borrow my red sweater.
choose, chose	*Choose* is the present tense, and *chose* is the past tense.	I **choose** to start work at 6:00 AM each day. Randy **chose** to quit his job after working only three days.

Word/Phrases	Correct Use	Examples
could of	Use the helping verb *have* (which may sound like *could of*) with *could, might, must, should, ought,* and *would.*	**nonstandard:** We could of won the game in overtime. **standard:** We **could have** won the game in overtime.
doesn't, don't	*Doesn't* is the contraction of *does not.* It is used with singular nouns and the pronouns *he, she, it, this,* and *that. Don't* is the contraction of *do not.* Use it with plural nouns and the pronouns *I, we, they, you, these,* and *those.*	Jason **doesn't** know what to make for lunch. We **don't** answer the phone during dinner.
farther, further	Use *farther* to refer to physical distance. Use *further* to refer to greater extent in time or degree or to mean "additional."	I walked **farther** today than I did yesterday. The board members will discuss this issue **further** at the meeting. The essay requires **further** revision before it can be published.
fewer, less	Use *fewer,* which tells "how many," to refer to things that you can count individually. *Fewer* is used with plural words. Use *less* to refer to quantities that you cannot count. It is used with singular words and tells "how much."	I see **fewer** fans coming out to the ballpark each year. Jasmine has more experience and thus needs **less** training than Phil.
good, well	*Good* is always an adjective. *Well* is an adverb meaning "ably" or "capably." *Well* is also a predicate adjective meaning "satisfactory" or "in good health." Don't confuse *feel good,* which means "to feel happy or pleased," with *feel well,* which means "to feel healthy."	Charles was a **good** pilot during the war. Leslie felt **good** [pleased] after bowling three strikes in a row. Shirley paints **well** for someone with no formal training. Not feeling **well,** Samuel stayed home from school today.
had ought, hadn't ought	The verb *ought* should never be used with the helping verb *had.*	**nonstandard:** Ted had ought to find another route into town. **standard:** Ted **ought** to find another route into town. **nonstandard:** She hadn't ought climb that tree. **standard:** She **ought** not climb that tree.
hardly, scarcely	Since both of these words have negative meanings, do not use them with other negative words such as *not, no, nothing,* and *none.*	**nonstandard:** That music is so loud I can't hardly hear myself think. **standard:** That music is so loud I can **hardly** hear myself think. **nonstandard:** Shane hadn't scarcely enough gas to make it back home. **standard:** Shane had **scarcely** enough gas to make it back home.
he, she, they	Do not use these pronouns after a noun. This error is called a double subject.	**nonstandard:** Jed's brother he is a famous actor. **standard:** Jed's brother is a famous actor.
hisself, theirselves	These are incorrect forms. Use *himself* and *themselves.*	**nonstandard:** Paul talks to hisself when mowing the lawn. **standard:** Paul talks to **himself** when mowing the lawn. **nonstandard:** The panel talked among theirselves about the Holy Roman Empire. **standard:** The panel talked among **themselves** about the Holy Roman Empire.

GRAMMAR & STYLE

Word/Phrases	Correct Use	Examples
how come	Do not use in place of *why*.	**nonstandard: How come** you didn't call me last night? **standard: Why** didn't you call me last night?
in, into	Use *in* to mean "within" or "inside." Use *into* to suggest movement toward the inside from the outside.	The children were **in** the kitchen. The children raced **into** the kitchen.
its, it's	*Its* is a possessive pronoun. *It's* is the contraction for *it is*.	The radio station held **its** annual fundraiser. **It's** too late tonight to start another game.
kind, sort, type	Use *this* or *that* to modify the singular nouns *kind, sort,* and *type*. Use *these* and *those* to modify the plural nouns *kinds, sorts,* and *types*. *Kind* should be singular when the object of the preposition following it is singular. It should be plural when the object of the preposition is plural.	This **kind** of ice cream is my favorite. These **types** of problems are difficult to solve.
kind of, sort of	Do not use these terms to mean "somewhat" or "rather."	**nonstandard:** He feels kind of sluggish today. **standard:** He feels rather sluggish today.
lay, lie	*Lay* means "to put" or "to place." *Lay* usually takes a direct object. *Lie* means "to rest" or "to be in a lying position." *Lie* never takes a direct object. (Note that the past tense of *lie* is *lay*.)	Please **lay** the blanket on the bed. I **laid** the blanket on the bed. **Lie** down on the bed and take a nap. Mary **lay** down on the bed and took a nap.
learn, teach	*Learn* means "to gain knowledge." *Teach* means "to give knowledge." Do not use them interchangeably.	Betty took lessons to **learn** how to fly a small airplane. I would like to find someone to **teach** me how to sew.
like, as	*Like* is usually a preposition followed by an object. It generally means "similar to." *As, as if,* and *as though* are conjunctions used to introduce subordinate clauses. *As* is occasionally a preposition: *He worked as a farmer.*	The alligator was motionless **like** a rock on the riverbank. The spider spun its web **as** the unsuspecting fly flew into the silky trap. Roger looks **as though** he's not feeling well.
of	This word is unnecessary after the prepositions *inside, outside,* and *off*.	The feather pillow slid **off** the bed. People gathered **outside** the stadium before the game. Please put the chattering parrot **inside** its cage.
precede, proceed	*Precede* means "to go or come before." *Proceed* means "to go forward."	The calf-roping competition will **precede** the bull-riding event. If you hear the alarm, **proceed** down the stairs and out the exit.
quiet, quite	Although these words sound alike, they have different meanings. *Quiet* is an adjective that means "making little or no noise"; *quite* is an adverb meaning "positively" or "completely."	The house became **quiet** after the baby finally fell asleep. Unfortunately, our bill for the car repairs was **quite** large.
real, really	*Real* is an adjective meaning "actual." *Really* is an adverb meaning "actually" or "genuinely." Do not use *real* to mean "very" or "extremely."	The table is very sturdy because it is made of **real** oak. Heather was **really** (not *real*) excited about trying out for the play.

Word/Phrases	Correct Use	Examples
reason...because	*Reason is because* is both wordy and redundant. Use *reason is that* or simply *because.*	**nonstandard:** The reason I am in a good mood is because today is Friday. **standard:** The reason for my good mood is that it is Friday. **standard:** The reason for my good mood is that today is Friday. **standard:** I am in a good mood because today is Friday.
regardless, irregardless	Use *regardless, unmindful, heedless,* or *anyway. Irregardless* is a double negative and should never be used.	**nonstandard:** Irregardless of the rain, the concert will still be held as scheduled. **standard: Regardless** of the rain, the concert will still be held as scheduled.
rise, raise	*Rise* is an intransitive verb that means "to move upward." It is an irregular verb that does not take a direct object. *Raise* is a transitive verb that means "to lift or make something go upward." It is a regular verb that takes a direct object.	The sun **rises** and sets every day. Perry **raised** his hand to ask a question.
scratch, itch	*Scratch* means "to scrape lightly to relieve itching." *Itch* means "to feel a tingling of the skin, with the desire to scratch."	Please do not **scratch** the mosquito bites. The mosquito bites on my leg still **itch.**
set, sit	*Set* is a transitive verb meaning "to place something." It always takes a direct object. *Sit* is an intransitive verb meaning "to rest in an upright position." It does not take a direct object.	Please **set** the pitcher of milk on the table. Let's **sit** outside on the back deck.
some, somewhat	*Some* is an adjective meaning "a certain unspecified quantity." *Somewhat* is an adverb meaning "slightly." Do not use *some* as an adverb.	**nonstandard:** The pressure on her schedule has eased some. **standard:** The pressure on her schedule has eased **somewhat.** **standard:** I need to find **some** index cards before starting my report.
than, then	*Than* is a conjunction used in comparisons. *Then* is an adverb that shows a sequence of events.	Hank's lawn is greener **than** Dale's lawn is. We went to the post office and **then** drove to the mall.
that	*That* is used to refer either to people or things. Use it to introduce essential, or restrictive, clauses that refer to things or groups of people. Do not use a comma before *that* when it introduces an essential clause.	The tree **that** fell in the storm was more than one hundred years old. An automobile **that** never needs repairs is rare.
their, there, they're	*Their* is the possessive form of *they. There* points out a place or introduces an independent clause. *They're* is the contracted form of *they are.*	Our neighbors inspected **their** roof after the hailstorm. When you arrive at the airport, I will be **there** waiting. I don't think **they're** going to be visiting us this summer.
them	*Them* is a pronoun. It should never be used as an adjective. Use *those.*	**nonstandard:** Remember to return them books to the library. **standard:** Remember to return **those** books to the library.

Word/Phrases	Correct Use	Examples
this here, that there	Do not use. Simply say *this* or *that.*	**nonstandard:** This here is the best coffee shop in town. **standard: This** is the best coffee shop in town. **nonstandard:** That there is an antique rocking chair. **standard: That** is an antique rocking chair.
to, too, two	*To* is a preposition that can mean "in the direction of." *Too* is an adverb that means both "extremely, overly" and "also." *Two* is the spelling for the number 2.	Please carry the luggage **to** the car. Leah has **too** many boxes in the attic. Tony and Liz are excellent students, **too.** I bought **two** pairs of blue jeans.
try and	Use *try to* instead.	**nonstandard:** Try and find the umbrella before you leave. **standard: Try to** find the umbrella before you leave.
use to, used to	Be sure to add the *–d* to *use* to form the past participle.	**nonstandard:** Rory use to enjoy singing in the choir. **standard:** Rory **used to** enjoy singing in the choir.
way, ways	Do not use *ways* for *way* when referring to distance.	**nonstandard:** We traveled a long ways from home. **standard:** We traveled a long **way** from home.
when, where	When you define a word, don't use *when* or *where.*	**nonstandard:** A *perfect game* is when a bowler throws twelve strikes resulting in a score of 300. **standard:** A *perfect game* is twelve strikes resulting in a score of 300.
where, that	Do not use *where* to mean "that."	**nonstandard:** I read where school will start a week earlier in August. **standard:** I read **that** school will start a week earlier in August.
which, that, who, whom	*Which* is used to refer only to things. Use it to introduce nonessential, or nonrestrictive, clauses that refer to things or to groups of people. Always use a comma before *which* when it introduces a nonessential clause.	Our garage, **which** was built last year, is already showing signs of wear. The panel, **which** was assembled to discuss the election, will publish its conclusions.
who, whom	*Who* or *whom* is used to refer only to people. Use *who* or *whom* to introduce essential and nonessential clauses. Use a comma only when the pronoun introduces a nonessential clause.	Lyle is the man **who** rescued us from the fire. Abraham Lincoln, **whom** many admired, issued the Emancipation Proclamation.
who's, whose	*Who's* is a contraction for *who is* or *who has. Whose* is the possessive form of *who.*	**Who's** going to make dinner tonight? **Whose** pig is running loose in my garden?
without, unless	Do not use the preposition *without* in place of the conjunction *unless.*	**nonstandard:** I am not leaving without I have your endorsement. **standard:** I am not leaving **without** your endorsement. **standard:** I am not leaving **unless** I have your endorsement.
your, you're	*Your* is a possessive pronoun. *You're* is a contraction for the words *you are.*	Ron repaired **your** leaky kitchen faucet. **You're** very skilled at repairing things!

3.15 Punctuation

EDITING FOR PUNCTUATION ERRORS

When editing your work, correct all punctuation errors. Several common punctuation errors to avoid are the incorrect use of end marks, commas, semicolons, and colons.

Punctuation Reference Chart

Punctuation	Function	Examples
End Marks	tell the reader where a sentence ends and show the purpose of the sentence; periods are also used for abbreviations.	Our next-door neighbor is Mrs**.** Ryan**.**
Periods	with **declarative** sentences	The weather forecast predicts rain tonight**.**
	with **abbreviations**	
	personal names	**N.** Scott Momaday, **W. W.** Jacobs, Ursula **K.** Le Guin
	titles	**Mr.** Bruce Webber, **Mrs.** Harriet Cline, **Ms.** Steinem, **Dr.** Duvall, **Sen.** Hillary Clinton, **Gov.** George Pataki, **Capt.** Horatio Hornblower, **Prof.** Klaus
	business names	Tip Top Roofing **Co.**, Green **Bros.** Landscaping, Gigantic **Corp.**
	addresses	Oak **Dr.**, Grand **Blvd.**, Main **St.**, Kennedy **Pkwy.**, Prudential **Bldg.**
	geographical terms	Kensington, **Conn.**, San Francisco, **Calif.**, Canberra, **Aus.**
	time	2 **hrs.** 15 **min.**, **Thurs.** morning, **Jan.** 20, 21st **cent.**
	units of measurement	3 **tbsp.** olive oil 1/2 **c.** peanut butter 8 **oz.** milk 5 **ft.** 4 **in.** 20 **lbs.**
	exceptions: metric measurements, state names in postal addresses, or directional elements	**metric measurements** cc, ml, km, g, L **state postal codes** MN, WI, IA, NE, CA, NY **compass points** N, NW, S, SE
Question Marks	with **interrogative** sentences	May I have another serving of spaghetti**?**
Exclamation Points	with **exclamatory** sentences	Hey, be careful**!**
Commas	to separate words or groups of words within a sentence; to tell the reader to pause at certain spots in the sentence	Casey was confident he could hit a home run**,** but he struck out.
	to separate items in a series	The magician's costume included a **silk scarf, black satin hat,** and **magic wand.**
	to combine sentences using *and, but, or, nor, yet, so,* or *for*	An infestation of beetles threatened the summer squash and zucchini crops**, yet** the sturdy plants thrived. I'll apply an organic insecticide**, or** I'll ignore the garden pest problem.
	after an introductory word, phrase, or clause	**Surprisingly,** fashions from the 1970s are making a come-back. **Frayed and tight-fitting,** denim bellbottoms remain a fashion hit.

Punctuation	Function	Examples
	to set off words or phrases that interrupt sentences	Harpers Ferry**, a town in northeastern West Virginia,** was the site of John Brown's raid in 1859. The violent raid**, however,** frightened people in the North and South. **An abolitionist leader,** Brown was captured during the raid and later executed.
	between two or more adjectives that modify the same noun and that could be joined by *and*	A **warm,** [and] **spicy** aroma enticed us to enter the kitchen. Steaming bowls of chili satisfied the **tired,** [and] **hungry** travelers.
	to set off names used in direct address	**Olivia,** the zinnias and daisies need to be watered. Please remember to turn off the back porch light**, John.**
	to separate parts of a date	The United States Stock Exchange collapsed on October **28, 1929.** The stock market crash in October 1929 precipitated a severe economic crisis.
	to separate items in addresses	Gabriel García Márquez was born in **Aracataca, Colombia.** My brother will be moving to **1960 Jasmine Avenue, Liberty, Missouri 64068.**
Semicolons	to join two closely related sentences	It was a beautiful summer morning**;** we took advantage of it by going on a picnic.
	to join the independent clauses of a compound sentence if no coordinating conjunction is used	Marjory Stoneman Douglas was a pioneer conservationist. She formed a vigorous grassroots campaign to protect and restore the Everglades. Marjory Stoneman Douglas was a pioneer conservationist**;** she formed a vigorous grassroots campaign to protect and restore the Everglades.
	between independent clauses joined by a conjunction if either clause contains commas	Douglas was a writer, editor, publisher, and tireless advocate for the protection of the Everglades**;** and President Clinton awarded her the Medal of Freedom in 1993 for her work.
	between items in a series if the items contain commas	Members of Friends of the Everglades **wrote petitions; contacted local groups, political organizations, and governmental agencies; and gathered public support** for the restoration of the Everglades.
	between independent clauses joined by a conjunctive adverb or a transitional phrase	**conjunctive adverb** Starting in 1948, the Central and Southern Florida Project ditched and drained the Everglades**; consequently,** the four million acre wetland was reduced by half. **transitional phrase** Douglas knew that restoration of the Everglades would be a daunting task**; in other words,** she knew that it would take the combined efforts of local, state, and federal groups working in unison.
Colons	to mean "note what follows"	Make sure you have all your paperwork in order**:** passport, visa, and tickets.
	to introduce a list of items	*The Tragedy of Romeo and Juliet* explores **these dominant themes:** civil strife, revenge, love, and fate. The main characters in the play are **as follows:** Romeo, Juliet, Paris, Mercutio, Tybalt, and Friar Lawrence. The role of Juliet has been played by **the following actresses:** Norma Shearer, Susan Shentall, and Olivia Hussey.

Punctuation	Function	Examples
	to introduce a long or formal statement or a quotation	Shakespeare's prologue to *Romeo and Juliet* begins with **these memorable lines:** Two households, both alike in dignity, In fair Verona, where we lay our scene, From ancient grudge break to new mutiny, Where civil blood makes civil hands unclean. John Dryden made **the following remark about Shakespeare:** "He was the man who of all modern, and perhaps ancient poets, had the largest and most comprehensive soul." Nearly everyone recognizes **this line by Shakespeare:** "All the world's a stage."
	between two independent clauses when the second clause explains or summarizes the first clause	Shakespeare deserves the greatest of praise**:** his work has influenced and inspired millions of people over the centuries. For Romeo and Juliet, their love is star-crossed**:** If they tell their feuding parents of their love, they will be forbidden from seeing each other. On the other hand, by keeping their love secret, they follow a path that leads, tragically, to their deaths.
	between numbers that tell hours and minutes, after the greeting in a business letter, and between chapter and verse of religious works	Our English class meets Tuesdays and Thursdays from **9:00** AM to **10:00** AM Dear Juliet**:** Please meet me on the balcony at midnight. Ecclesiastes **3:1–8**
	not after a verb, between a preposition and its object(s), or after *because* or *as*	**after a verb** **incorrect** Three of Shakespeare's most famous plays are: *Romeo and Juliet, Macbeth,* and *Hamlet.* **correct** These are three of Shakespeare's most famous plays: *Romeo and Juliet, Macbeth,* and *Hamlet.* **between a preposition and its object(s)** **incorrect** I have seen performances of Shakespeare's plays in: London, New York, and Chicago. **correct** I have seen performances of Shakespeare's plays in the following cities: London, New York, and Chicago. **after *because* or *as*** **incorrect** Shakespeare was a great playwright because: he had an extraordinary skill in depicting human nature and the universal struggles all people experience. **correct** Shakespeare was a great playwright because he had an extraordinary skill in depicting human nature and the universal struggles all people experience.
Ellipsis Points	to show that material from a quotation or a quoted passage has been left out	"Doing something does not require discipline**...**it creates its own discipline."
	if material is left out at the beginning of a sentence or passage	**...**The very thought of hard work makes me queasy.
	if material is left out in the middle of a sentence	The very thought**...**makes me queasy.
	if material is left out at the end of a sentence	It's hard work, doing something with your life**....**I'd rather die in peace. Here we are, all equal and alike and none of us much to write home about**....**

Punctuation	Function	Examples
Apostrophes	to form the possessive case of a singular or plural noun	the **window's** ledge, **Carlos's** father, **jazz's** beginnings, **wolves'** howls, twenty-five **cents'** worth, **countries'** treaties, **students'** textbooks
	to show joint or separate ownership	**Zack and Josh's** experiment, **Lisa and Randall's** cabin, **Sarah's** and **Jason's** schedules, **Steve's and John's** trumpets
	to form the possessive of an indefinite pronoun	**anyone's** guess, **each other's** notes, **everybody's** dream
	to form a contraction to show where letters, words, or numerals have been omitted	**I'm** = I am **you're** = you are **she's** = she is **o'clock** = of the clock **they're** = they are
	to form the possessive of only the last word in a compound noun, such as the name of an organization or a business	brother-in-**law's** sense of humor; Teller, Teller, and **Teller's** law firm; Volunteer Nursing **Association's** office
	to form the possessive of an acronym	**NASA's** flight plan, **NATO's** alliances, **UNICEF's** contributions
	to form the plural of letters, numerals, and words referred to as words	two **A's**, **ABC's**, three **7's**, twelve **yes's**
	to show the missing numbers in a date	drought of **'02**, class of **'06**
Underlining and Italics	with titles of books, plays, long poems, periodicals, works of art, movies, radio and television series, videos, computer games, comic strips, and long musical works and recordings	**books:** *To Kill a Mockingbird, Silent Spring, Black Elk Speaks* **plays:** *The Tragedy of Romeo and Juliet, The Monsters Are Due on Maple Street* **long poems:** *Metamorphoses, The Odyssey* **periodicals:** *Sports Illustrated, Wall Street Journal, The Old Farmer's Almanac* **works of art:** *The Acrobat, In the Sky, The Teacup* **movies:** *Il Postino, North by Northwest, Cast Away* **radio/television series:** *Fresh Air, West Wing, Friends, Animal Planet* **videos:** *Yoga for Strength, Cooking with Julia, Wizard of Oz* **computer games:** *Empire Earth, Age of Wonders II* **comic strips:** *Zits, Foxtrot, Overboard* **long musical works/recordings:** *Requiem, Death and the Maiden, La Traviata*
	with the names of trains, ships, aircraft, and spacecraft	**trains:** *Sunset Limited* **ships:** *Titanic* **aircraft:** *Air Force One* **spacecraft:** *Apollo 13*
	with words, letters, symbols, and numerals referred to as such	The word ***filigree*** has a Latin root. People in western New York pronounce the letter ***a*** with a harsh, flat sound. The children learned that the symbol ***+*** is used in addition. Your phone number ends with four ***7***s.
	to set off foreign words or phrases that are not common in English	Did you know the word ***amor*** means "love"? The first Italian words I learned were ***ciao*** and ***pronto***.
	to place emphasis on a word	Why is the soup ***blue***? You're not going to borrow ***my*** car.

Punctuation	Function	Examples
Quotation Marks	at the beginning and end of a direct quotation	**"**Do you want to ride together to the concert?**"** asked Margaret. **"**Don't wait for me,**"** sighed Lillian. **"**I'm running late as usual.**"**
	to enclose the titles of short works such as short stories, poems, articles, essays, parts of books and periodicals, songs, and episodes of TV series	**short stories: "**Gwilan's Harp,**" "**Everyday Use**"** **poems: "**Hanging Fire,**" "**Mirror**"** **articles: "**Where Stars Are Born,**" "**Ghost of Everest**"** **essays: "**Thinking Like a Mountain,**" "**It's Not Talent; It's Just Work**"** **parts of books: "**The Obligation to Endure,**" "**Best Sky Sights of the Next Century**"** **songs: "**At the Fair,**" "**Johnny's Garden**"** **episodes of TV series: "**The Black Vera Wang,**" "**Isaac and Ishmael**"**
	to set off slang, technical terms, unusual expressions, invented words, and dictionary definitions	We nicknamed our dog **"Monkey"** because he moves quickly and loves to play tricks. My mother says that **"groovy"** and **"cool"** were the slang words of her generation. Did you know that the word *incident* means **"a definite, distinct occurrence"**?
Hyphens	to make a compound word or compound expression	**compound nouns:** great-grandfather Schaefer, great-uncle Tom **compound adjectives used before a noun:** best-known novel, down-to-earth actor, real-life adventure **compound numbers:** ninety-nine years, twenty-five cents **spelled-out fractions:** one-half inch, three-fourths cup
	to divide an already hyphenated word at the hyphen	Finally, after much coaxing, our **great-grandfather** told his stories.
	to divide a word only between syllables	**incorrect:** After hiking in the woods, the novice ca-mpers became tired and hungry. **correct:** After hiking in the woods, the novice **camp-ers** became tired and hungry.
	with the prefixes *all-, ex-, great-, half-* and *self-,* and with all prefixes before a proper noun or proper adjective	**all-**purpose, **ex-**husband, **pre-**Industrial age, **great-**grandparent, **half-**baked, **self-**expression
	with the suffixes *-free, -elect,* and *-style*	fragrance**-free** detergent, mayor**-elect** Kingston, Southern**-style** hospitality
Dashes	to show a sudden break or change in thought	"I say it did," replied the other. "There was no thought about it; I had just**—**What's the matter?"
	to mean *namely, that is,* or *in other words*	Our puppy knows only two commands**—***sit* and *stay.* The hotel rates were surprisingly reasonable**—**less than a hundred dollars**—**for a double room.
Parentheses and Brackets	around material added to a sentence but not considered of major importance	Toni Cade Bambara **(**1939–1995**)** grew up in Harlem and Brooklyn, New York. The Taj Mahal **(**a majestic site!**)** is one man's tribute of love to his departed, beloved wife. More grocery stores are stocking natural food ingredients **(**for example, whole grains, soy products, and dried fruits**)**.

Punctuation	Function	Examples
	to punctuate a parenthetical sentence contained within another sentence.	When the quilt is dry **(**it shouldn't take long**)**, please fold it and put it in the linen closet. The piping-hot funnel cakes **(**they were covered with powdered sugar!**)** just melted in our mouths. The vitamin tablets **(**aren't you supposed to take one every morning?**)** provide high doses of vitamins A and E.
	to enclose words or phrases that interrupt the sentence and are not considered essential to meaning.	They took pasta salad and fruit **(**how could we have forgotten dessert?**)** to the summer concert.
	to enclose information that explains or clarifies a detail in quoted material	A literary critic praised the author's new book, "She **[**Martha Grimes**]** never fails to delight her devoted fans with witty dialogue, elegant prose, and a cast of characters we'd like to consider our friends." Another literary critic wrote, "**[**Martha**]** Grimes is the queen of the mystery genre."

3.16 Capitalization

EDITING FOR CAPITALIZATION ERRORS

To avoid capitalization errors, check your draft for proper nouns and proper adjectives; geographical names, directions, and historical names; and titles of artworks and literary works.

Capitalization Reference Chart

Category/Rule	Examples
Proper Nouns and Proper Adjectives	
Proper Nouns	
Names of people	**S**ojourner **T**ruth, **F**ranklin **D.** **R**oosevelt, **M**artin **L**uther **K**ing **J**r.
Months, days, and holidays	**O**ctober, **W**ednesday, **M**emorial **D**ay
Names of religions, languages, races, and nationalities	**B**aptist, **C**atholicism, **C**hilean, **B**uddhism, **F**rench, **H**ispanic, **G**reek, **A**frican **A**merican
Names of clubs, organization, businesses, and institutions	**L**ittle **L**eague, **A**merican **H**eart **A**ssociation, **P**ratt-**R**ead **C**ompany, **W**ebster **B**ank
Names of awards, prizes, and medals	**E**mmy **A**ward, **N**obel **P**eace **P**rize, **P**urple **H**eart, **P**ulitzer **P**rize
Proper Adjectives	
Proper adjectives formed from proper nouns	**J**apanese gardening, **E**nglish class, **C**aribbean music, **A**laskan oil drilling
Proper nouns used as adjectives	**S**enate bill, **A**gatha **C**hristie masterpiece, **C**alifornia coast, **F**ranklin stove
I and First Words	
The pronoun *I*.	Next week **I** will leave on my trip to Yellowstone National Park.
First word of each sentence.	**T**he oldest of the U.S. national parks is noted for its beauty, wildlife, and geysers.
First word of a direct quotation.	"**T**hat mountain stands taller than any other in the state," the guide reported with pride to his group of tourists.
First lines of most poetry. (Follow the capitalization of the original poem.)	**A**nd far as the eye of God could see **D**arkness covered everything, **B**lacker than a hundred midnights **D**own in a cypress swamp.

Category/Rule	Examples
First word in a letter salutation and the name or title of the person addressed.	**D**ear **D**ad, **M**y dear **A**unt **N**ola, **D**ear **M**adam
First word in letter closings.	**S**incerely yours, **Y**ours truly, **F**ondly, **W**arm wishes
Family Relationships and Titles of Persons	
Capitalize the titles or abbreviations that come before the names of people.	**A**dmiral Michael Chase, **M**s. Gloria Steinem, **S**enator Dodd, **M**r. and **M**rs. Douglas, **D**r. Watson, **C**hief **J**ustice Oliver Wendell Holmes
Person's title as a proper noun.	Can you meet us on Tuesday, **R**abbi? It's time to start rounds, **D**octor.
Words showing family relationships when used as titles or as substitutes for a name.	**U**ncle Fred, **G**randmother Parker, **F**ather, **C**ousin Sam
Abbreviations	
Social titles after a name.	My teacher is named **Mr.** Franks. Can't you ask **Prof.** Pardoe to help us in the soup kitchen?
Abbreviate the titles of organizations.	Northeastern **Mfg.** Connecticut Yard Workers **Assoc.**
Parts of government, and business, with the initials of each word in the title.	**NATO** (North Atlantic Treaty Organization) **USMC** (United States Marine Corps) **IBM** (International Business Machines) **SNET** (Southern New England Telephone)
Abbreviate address titles.	Stoughton **St.**, Fort **Rd.**, Park **Ave.**
Time Designations	
Time abbreviations BCE (BC), CE (AD), AM, and PM	Hatshepsut, who lived from 1503 to 1482 **BCE**, was one of five women to reign as Queen of Egypt. The cruel Caligula ruled Rome until **CE** 41. My appointment was for 9:30 **AM**, and I'm not happy about waiting. We have a 7:00 **PM** dinner reservation at my favorite restaurant.
Geographical Names, Directions, and Historical Names	
Names of cities, states, countries, islands, and continents	**cities:** **H**onolulu, **M**oscow, **G**uatemala **C**ity **states:** **G**eorgia, **I**owa, **N**ew **M**exico **countries:** **Z**imbabwe, **B**elgium, **E**cuador **islands:** **T**ahiti, **C**ayman **I**slands, **C**yprus **continents:** **N**orth **A**merica, **E**urope, **A**frica
Names of bodies of water and geographical features	**B**lack **S**ea, **S**nake **R**iver, **S**ahara **D**esert, **M**ount **M**cKinley
Names of buildings, monuments, and bridges	**W**oolsey **H**all, **E**mpire **S**tate **B**uilding, **V**ietnam **V**eterans **M**emorial, **G**olden **G**ate **B**ridge
Names of streets and highways	**R**ailroad **A**venue, **N**ew **E**ngland **T**urnpike, **P**alm **D**rive, **R**oute 153
Sections of the country	the **S**unbelt, the **P**acific **C**oast, the **S**outheast, the **M**idwest
Names of historical events, special events, documents, and historical periods	**historical events:** **B**attle of the **B**ulge, **W**orld **W**ar I **special events:** **S**ummerfest, **B**oston **M**arathon **documents:** **M**agna **C**arta, **D**eclaration of **I**ndependence **historical periods:** **R**econstruction, **I**ndustrial **A**ge
Titles of Artworks and Literary Works	
First and last words and all important words in the titles of artworks and literary works, including books, magazines, short stories, poems, songs, movies, plays, paintings, and sculpture	*Transworld Skateboarding* (magazine), ***T**oo **C**lose to the **F**alls* (book), "**T**he **C**ask of **A**montillado" (short story), **B**irches at **S**unrise (painting), "**P**olka **D**ots and **M**oonbeams" (song), ***T**he **L**ion in **W**inter* (movie)
Titles of religious works	**H**ebrew **B**ible, **K**oran, **O**ld **T**estament

3.17 Writing Effective Sentences

SENTENCE FRAGMENTS

A sentence contains a subject and a verb and should express a complete thought. A **sentence fragment** is a phrase or clause that does not express a complete thought but that has been punctuated as though it did.

EXAMPLES

complete sentence
The hungry raccoon climbed into the garbage can.

sentence fragment
Climbed into the garbage can. (The subject is missing.)

sentence fragment
The hungry raccoon. (The verb is missing.)

sentence fragment
Into the garbage can. (The subject and verb are missing.)

RUN-ON SENTENCES

A **run-on sentence** is made up of two or more sentences that have been run together as if they were one complete thought. A run-on sentence can confuse the reader about where a thought starts or ends.

In the first example, called a *fused sentence,* no punctuation mark is used between the run-on sentences. In the second run-on, called a *comma splice,* a comma is used incorrectly.

EXAMPLES

The start of the Civil War shocked the nation many Americans thought the war would be over in a matter of days. (fused sentence)

The United States had several forgettable presidents in the two decades prior to the Civil War, they were reluctant to deal with the slavery issue. (comma splice)

You can correct a run-on by dividing it into two separate sentences. Mark the end of each idea with a period, question mark, or exclamation point. Capitalize the first word of each new sentence.

EXAMPLE

The start of the Civil War shocked the nation. Many Americans thought the war would be over in a matter of days.

You can also correct a run-on by using a semicolon. The second part of the sentence is not capitalized. Use a semicolon to join two sentences only if the thoughts are closely related.

EXAMPLE

The United States had several forgettable presidents in the two decades prior to the Civil War; they were reluctant to deal with the slavery issue.

SENTENCE COMBINING AND EXPANDING

A series of short sentences in a paragraph can make your writing sound choppy and uninteresting. The reader might also have trouble understanding how your ideas are connected. By **combining and expanding sentences,** you can connect related ideas, make sentences longer and smoother, and make a paragraph more interesting to read.

One way to combine sentences is to take a key word or phrase from one sentence and insert it into another sentence.

EXAMPLES

short, choppy sentences
The squirrels scrambled up the tree trunk. They were playful.

combined sentence (with key word)
The **playful** squirrels scrambled up the tree trunk.

short, choppy sentences
We visited my grandfather in October. He lives on the West Coast.

combined sentence (with key phrase)
We visited my grandfather on the **West Coast in October.**

Another way of combining sentences is to take two related sentences and combine them by using a coordinating conjunction—*and, but, or, so, for, yet,* or *nor.* By using a coordinating conjunction, you can form a compound subject, a compound verb, or a compound sentence. Be sure to use a comma before the coordinating conjunction that links two sentences.

EXAMPLES

two related sentences
Jessica is from Upper Michigan. She often writes poetry about the landscape of that area.

combined sentence
Jessica is from Upper Michigan, and she often writes poetry about the landscape of that area. (compound sentence)

two related sentences
Cockroaches infested the abandoned warehouse. Rats lived there, too.

combined sentence
Cockroaches and rats infested the abandoned warehouse. (compound subject)

two related sentences
Snow fell throughout the night. It buried the mountain village.

combined sentence
Snow fell throughout the night and buried the mountain village. (compound verb)

VARYING SENTENCE STRUCTURE

Just as you probably wouldn't like to eat the same thing for breakfast every morning, your readers wouldn't enjoy reading the same sentence pattern in every paragraph. By **varying sentence structure,** you can give your sentences rhythm, create variety, and keep your readers engaged.

Sentences often begin with a subject. To vary sentence style, start some sentences with a one-word modifier, a prepositional phrase, a participial phrase, or a subordinate clause.

EXAMPLES

subject
She occasionally likes to fly a kite at the park.

one-word modifier
Occasionally, she likes to fly a kite at the park.

prepositional phrase
During breakfast, he always reads the sports section of the paper.

participial phrase
Recalling yesterday's game, the coach devised a new strategy

subordinate clause
Since it may rain tomorrow, Derrick mowed the lawn tonight

WORDY SENTENCES

A **wordy sentence** includes extra words and phrases that can be difficult, confusing, or repetitive to read. When you write, use only words necessary to make your meaning clear. Revise and edit your sentences so that they are not unnecessarily wordy or complicated.

Replace a group of words with one word.

EXAMPLES

wordy
Sam cleaned the car **because of the fact that** he had a date that evening.

revised
Sam cleaned his car **because** he had a date that evening.

Replace a clause with a phrase.

EXAMPLES

wordy
After Josh washed his clothes in the washing machine, he looked for the ironing board.

revised
After washing his clothes, Josh looked for the ironing board.

Delete a group of unnecessary or repetitive words.

EXAMPLES

wordy
What I believe is your house will not take long to sell after it is listed.

revised
Your house will not take long to sell after it is listed.

wordy
Mr. Jones is very frugal, **and he doesn't like to spend money**.

revised
Mr. Jones is very frugal.

GRAMMAR & STYLE

USING PARALLELISM

A sentence has **parallelism** when the same forms are used to express ideas of equal—or parallel—importance. Parallelism can add emphasis, balance, and rhythm to a sentence. Words, phrases, and clauses that have the same form and function in a sentence are called **parallel.**

EXAMPLES

not parallel
The soldiers **marched** onto the field, **loaded** their muskets, and then **had pointed** their bayonets. (The highlighted verbs are not in the same tense.)

parallel
The soldiers **marched** onto the field, **loaded** their muskets, and then **pointed** their bayonets.

not parallel
The actress is **lovely, talented,** and **sings**. (The three highlighted words include two adjectives and one verb.)

parallel
The actress is a **lovely** and **talented** singer.

MAKING PASSIVE SENTENCES ACTIVE

A verb is **active** when the subject of the verb performs the action. It is **passive** when the subject of the verb receives the action.

EXAMPLES

active
The frosty air **stung** his cheekbones.

passive
His cheekbones **were stung** by the frosty air.

USING COLORFUL LANGUAGE

When you write, use words that tell your readers exactly what you mean. **Colorful language**—such as precise and lively nouns, verbs, and modifiers—tells your readers exactly what you mean and makes your writing more interesting.

Precise nouns give your reader a clear picture of who or what is involved in the sentence.

EXAMPLES

original sentence
The **bird** sat in the **tree.**

revised sentence
The **cardinal** sat in the **elm.**

Colorful, vivid verbs describe the specific action in the sentence.

EXAMPLES

original sentence
The tiger **jumped** from behind the tree.

revised sentence
The tiger **leapt** from behind the tree.

Modifiers—adjectives and adverbs—describe the meanings of other words and make them more precise. Colorful or surprising modifiers can make your writing come alive for your readers.

EXAMPLES

original sentence
The **large** dinosaur crashed through the barrier.

revised sentence
The **massive** dinosaur crashed **forcefully** through the barrier.

4.1 The Writing Process

All writers—whether they are beginning writers, famous published writers, or somewhere in between—go through a process that leads to a complete piece of writing. The specifics of each writer's process may be unique, but for every writer, writing is a series of steps or stages.

The Writing Process	
Stage	**Tasks**
1. Prewriting	Plan your writing: choose a topic, audience, purpose, and form; gather ideas; arrange them logically.
2. Drafting	Get your ideas down on paper.
3. Revising	Evaluate, or judge, the writing piece and suggest ways to improve it. Judging your own writing is called self-evaluation. Judging a classmate's writing is called peer evaluation. Work to improve the content, organization, and expression of your ideas. Proofread your writing for errors in spelling, grammar, capitalization, and punctuation. Correct these errors, make a final copy of your paper, and proofread it again.
Writing Follow-Up: Publish and Present	Share your work with an audience.
Reflect	Think through the writing process to determine what you learned as a writer, what you accomplished, and what you would like to strengthen the next time you write.

While writing moves through these stages, it is also a continuing cycle. You might need to go back to a previous stage before going on to the next step. Returning to a previous stage will strengthen your final work. Note also that you can take time to reflect on your writing between any of the other stages. The more you reflect on your writing, the better your writing will become.

1 PREWRITE

In the prewriting stage of the writing process, you decide on a purpose, audience, topic, and form. You also begin to discover your voice and gather and organize ideas.

Prewriting Plan	
Set Your Purpose	A **purpose,** or aim, is the goal that you want your writing to accomplish.
Identify Your Audience	An **audience** is the person or group of people intended to read what you write.
Find Your Voice	**Voice** is the quality of a work that tells you that one person wrote it.
Select Your Topic	A **topic** is simply something to write about. For example, you might write about a sports hero or about a cultural event in your community.
Select a Writing Form	A **form** is a kind of writing. For example, you might write a paragraph, an essay, a short story, a poem, or a news article.

Set Your Purpose

When you choose your mode and form of writing, think about what purpose or aim you are trying to accomplish. Your purpose for writing might be to inform, to tell a story, to describe something, or to convince others to see your viewpoint. Your writing might have more than one purpose. For example, a piece of writing might inform your readers about an important event while persuading them to respond in a specific way.

Mode of Writing	Purpose	Form
expository	to inform	news article, research report
narrative	to express thoughts or ideas, or to tell a story	personal account, memoir, short story
descriptive	to portray a person, place, object, or event	travel brochure, personal profile, poem
persuasive	to convince people to accept a position and respond in some way	editorial, petition, political speech

Identify Your Audience

An **audience** is the person or group of people intended to read what you write. For example, you might write for yourself, a friend, a relative, or your classmates. The best writing usually is intended for a specific audience. Choosing a specific audience before writing will help you make important decisions about your work. For an audience of young children, for example, you would use simple words and ideas. For

WRITING

an audience of your peers in an athletic group, you would use jargon and other specialized words that your peers already know. For an adult audience, you would use more formal language.

Use the following questions to help identify your audience.

- Who will be most interested in my topic?
- What are their interests and values?
- How much do they already know about the topic?
- What background information do they need in order to understand my ideas and point of view?
- What words, phrases, or concepts will I need to define for my audience?
- How can I capture my audience's interest from the very start?

Use Appropriate Language

Formal Versus Informal English To write effectively, you must choose your language according to your audience, purpose, and the occasion or situation. **Formal English** contains carefully constructed, complete sentences; avoids contractions; follows standard English usage and grammar; uses a serious tone; and uses sophisticated vocabulary. **Informal English** contains everyday speech and popular expressions, uses contractions, and may include sentence fragments.

Formal English is appropriate for school essays, oral or written reports, interviews, and debates. Informal English is appropriate for communication with friends, personal letters or notes, and journal entries.

EXAMPLES

formal English
I am very pleased that I received a perfect score on the math exam.

informal English
I'm so pumped that I aced that math exam!

Find Your Voice

Voice is the quality of a work that tells you that one person wrote it. Voice makes a person's writing unique. In your writing, you should strive to develop your own voice, not to imitate the voices of others. Be true to your own voice, and your experience will speak directly to the experience of others.

Select Your Topic

A **topic** is simply something to write about. For example, you might write about a sports hero or about a cultural event in your community. Here are some ideas that may help you find interesting writing topics:

Ways to Find a Writing Topic	
Check your journal	Search through your journal for ideas that you jotted down in the past. Many professional writers get their ideas from their journals.
Think about your experiences	Think about people, places, or events that affected you strongly. Recall experiences that taught you important lessons or that you felt strongly about.
Look at reference works	Reference works include printed or computerized dictionaries, atlases, almanacs, and encyclopedias.
Browse in a library	Libraries are treasure houses of information and ideas. Simply looking around in the stacks of a library can suggest good ideas for writing.
Use mass media	Newspapers, magazines, radio, television, and films can suggest good topics for writing. For example, a glance at listings for public television programs might suggest topics related to the arts, to history, or to nature.
Search the Internet	Search key words in a search engine or web browser to expand on your ideas. Make sure to keep your work original and avoid plagiarizing from websites.

Select a Writing Form

Another important decision that a writer needs to make is what form his or her writing will take. A form is a kind of writing. Once you've identified your topic, your purpose for writing, and your audience, a particular form of writing may become immediately obvious as the perfect one to convey your ideas. But, sometimes, an unexpected choice of form may be even more effective in presenting your topic. The following chart lists some of the many different forms of writing.

Forms of Writing

adventure	book review
advertisement	brochure
advice column	character sketch
agenda	children's story
apology	comedy
autobiography	consumer report
biography	debate

- detective story
- dialogue
- directions
- editorial
- epitaph
- essay
- eulogy
- experiment
- fable
- family history
- fantasy
- history
- human interest story
- instructions
- interview questions
- itinerary
- journal entry
- letter
- magazine article
- memorandum
- minutes
- movie review
- mystery
- myth
- narrative
- newspaper article
- obituary
- parable
- paraphrase
- petition
- play
- police/accident report
- poster
- proposal
- radio or tv spot
- recommendation
- research report
- résumé
- science fiction
- short story
- song lyrics
- speech
- sports story
- statement of belief
- summary
- tall tale
- tour guide
- want ad

Gather Ideas

After you have identified your purpose, audience, topic, and form, the next step in the prewriting stage is to gather ideas. There are many ways to gather ideas for writing.

- **Brainstorm** When you **brainstorm,** you think of as many ideas as you can, as quickly as you can, without stopping to evaluate or criticize them. Anything goes—no idea should be rejected in the brainstorming stage.
- **Freewrite. Freewriting** is simply taking a pencil and paper and writing whatever comes into your mind. Try to write for several minutes without stopping and without worrying about spelling, grammar, usage, or mechanics.
- **Question** Ask the **reporting questions** *who, what, where, when, why,* and *how* about your topic. This questioning strategy is especially useful for gathering information about an event or for planning a story.
- **Create a Graphic Organizer** A good way to gather information is to create a **graphic organizer,** such as a Cluster Chart, Venn Diagram, Sensory Details Chart, Time Line, Story Map, or Pro-and-Con Chart. For examples, see the Language Arts Handbook, section 1, Reading Strategies and Skills, page 933.

Organize Your Ideas

Writing Paragraphs After you have gathered ideas for a piece of writing, the next step is to organize these ideas in a useful and reader-friendly way. The most basic organization of ideas occurs in forming paragraphs. A good paragraph is a carefully organized unit of writing. It develops a sequence in narrative writing or develops a particular topic in informational or persuasive writing.

Paragraphs with Topic Sentences Many paragraphs include a topic sentence that presents a main idea. The topic sentence can be placed at the beginning, middle, or end of the paragraph. Topic sentences usually appear early on in the paragraph and are commonly followed by one or more supporting sentences. Often these supporting sentences begin with transitions that relate them to the other sentences or to the topic sentence. This type of paragraph may end with a clincher sentence, which sums up what has been said in the paragraph.

EXAMPLE

Topic Sentence	*Romeo and Juliet* is probably the best known and best loved of all William Shakespeare's plays.
Supporting Details	Generations of audiences have been able to relate to the two "star-cross'd" young lovers, whose passion is doomed from the start by the bitter feuding between their families. Since Elizabethan times, the play has been interpreted in many forms, inspiring operas, ballets, musicals, and poetry. It has been translated into nearly every language and has been updated in such modern contexts as gangland New York City, the Israeli-Palestinian conflict in Jerusalem, and war-torn Sarajevo.
Clincher Sentence	The power of the story is evident in that it has been told for centuries.

Paragraphs Without Topic Sentences Most paragraphs do not have topic sentences. In a narrative piece of writing, many paragraphs state a series of events, and no sentence in the paragraph sums up the events. In good narrative writing, the sequence of events appears in chronological order. Descriptive writing may contain paragraphs organized spatially—

in the order in which the speaker or narrator sees, hears, feels, smells, and tastes things in a given situation.

Write Your Thesis Statement

One way to start organizing your writing, especially if you are writing an informative or persuasive essay, is to identify the main idea of what you want to say. Present this idea in the form of a sentence or two called a thesis statement. A **thesis statement** is simply a sentence that presents the main idea or the position you will take in your essay.

Example thesis for a persuasive essay

The development at Rice Creek Farm should be stopped because it will destroy one of the best natural areas near the city.

Example thesis for an informative essay

Wilma Rudolph was an athlete who succeeded in the elite sport of tennis before the world was willing to recognize her.

Methods of Organization

The ideas in your writing should be ordered and linked in a logical and easily understandable way. You can organize your writing in the following ways:

Methods of Organization	
Chronological Order	Events are given in the order they occur.
Order of Importance	Details are given in order of importance or familiarity.
Comparison-and-Contrast Order	Similarities and differences of two things are listed.
Cause-and-Effect Order	One or more causes are presented followed by one or more effects.

To link your ideas, use connective words and phrases. In informational or persuasive writing, *for example, as a result, finally, therefore,* and *in fact* are common connectives. In narrative and descriptive writing, words like *first, then, suddenly, above, beyond, in the distance,* and *there* are common connectives. In comparison-contrast organization, common phrases include *similarly, on the other hand,* and *in contrast.* In cause-and-effect organization, linkers include *one cause, another effect, as a result, consequently, finally,* and *therefore.*

Create an Outline An **outline** is an excellent framework for highlighting main ideas and supporting details. To create a rough outline, simply list your main ideas in some logical order. Under each main idea, list the supporting details set off by dashes.

EXAMPLE

What Is Drama?
Definition of Drama
—Tells a story
—Uses actors to play characters
—Uses a stage, properties, lights, costumes, makeup, and special effects
Types of Drama
—Tragedy
  —Definition: A play in which the main character meets a negative fate
  —Examples: *Antigone, Romeo and Juliet, Death of a Salesman*
—Comedy
  —Definition: A play in which the main character meets a positive fate
  —Examples: *A Midsummer Night's Dream, Cyrano de Bergerac, The Odd Couple*

2 DRAFT

After you have gathered your information and organized it, the next step in writing is to produce a draft. A **draft** is simply an early attempt at writing a paper. Different writers approach drafting in different ways. Some prefer to work slowly and carefully, perfecting each part as they go. Others prefer to write a discovery draft, getting all their ideas down on paper in rough form and then going back over those ideas to shape and focus them. When writing a discovery draft, you do not focus on spelling, grammar, usage, and mechanics. You can take care of those details during revision.

Draft Your Introduction

The purpose of an introduction is to capture your reader's attention and establish what you want to say. An effective introduction can start with a quotation, a question, an anecdote, an intriguing fact, or a description that hooks the reader to keep reading. An effective introduction can open with a quotation, question, anecdote, fact, or description.

EXAMPLES

"That's one small step for man, one giant leap for mankind." With these words, Neil Armstrong signaled his success as the first man to set foot on the moon...

What would it be like if all the birds in the world suddenly stopped their singing?

When my brother was nineteen, he volunteered in a homeless shelter making sure people had a safe place to spend the night. He told me once that he would never forget the time he met...

Draft Your Body

When writing the body of an essay, refer to your outline. Each heading in your outline will become the main idea of one of your paragraphs. To move smoothly from one idea to another, use transitional words or phrases. As you draft, include evidence from documented sources to support the ideas that you present. This evidence can be paraphrased, summarized, or quoted directly. For information on proper documentation, see the Language Arts Handbook 5.6, Documenting Sources, page 1005.

Draft Your Conclusion

In the conclusion, bring together the main ideas you included in the body of your essay and create a sense of closure to the issue you raised in your thesis. There is no single right way to conclude a piece of writing. Possibilities include:

- Making a generalization
- Restating the thesis and major supporting ideas in different words
- Summarizing the points made in the rest of the essay
- Drawing a lesson or moral
- Calling on the reader to adopt a view or take an action
- Expanding on your thesis or main idea by connecting it to the reader's own interests
- Linking your thesis to a larger issue or concern

3 REVISE

Evaluate Your Draft

Self- and Peer Evaluation When you evaluate something, you examine it carefully to find its strengths and weaknesses. Evaluating your own writing is called **self-evaluation.** A **peer evaluation** is an evaluation of a piece of writing done by classmates, or peers. The following tips can help you to become a helpful peer reader, to learn to give and receive criticism, and to improve your writing.

Tips for evaluating writing

- **Check for content** Is the content, including the main idea, clear? Have any important details been left out? Do unimportant or unrelated details confuse the main point? Are the main idea and supporting details clearly connected to one another?
- **Check for organization** Are the ideas in the written work presented in a logical order?
- **Check the style and language** Is the language appropriately formal or informal? Is the tone appropriate for the audience and purpose? Have any key or unfamiliar terms been defined?

Tips for delivering helpful criticism

- **Be focused** Concentrate on content, organization, and style. At this point, do not focus on proofreading matters such as spelling and punctuation; they can be corrected during the proofreading stage.
- **Be positive** Respect the writer's feelings and genuine writing efforts. Tell the writer what you like about his or her work. Answer the writer's questions in a positive manner, tactfully presenting any changes you are suggesting.
- **Be specific** Give the writer concrete ideas for improving his or her work.

Tips for benefiting from helpful criticism

- **Tell your peer evaluator your specific concerns and questions.** If you are unsure whether you've clearly presented an idea, ask the evaluator how he or she might restate the idea.
- **Ask questions to clarify comments that your evaluator makes.** When you ask for clarification, you make sure you understand your evaluator's comments.
- **Accept your evaluator's comments graciously.** Criticism can be helpful, but you don't have to use any or all of the suggestions.

Revise for Content, Organization, and Style

After identifying weaknesses in a draft through self-evaluation and peer evaluation, the next step is to revise the draft. Here are four basic ways to improve meaning and content:

- **Adding or Expanding** Sometimes writing can be improved by adding details, examples, or transitions to connect ideas. Often a single added adjective, for example, can make a piece of writing clearer or more vivid.

draft Wind whistled through the park.

revised The **bone-chilling** wind whistled through the park.

- **Cutting or Condensing** Often writing can be improved by cutting unnecessary or unrelated material.

  draft Will was firmly determined to find the structure of the DNA molecule.

  revised Will was determined to find the structure of the DNA molecule.

- **Replacing** Sometimes weak writing can be made stronger through more concrete, more vivid, or more precise details.

  draft Several things had been bothering Tanya.

  revised Several personal problems had been bothering Tanya.

- **Moving** Often you can improve the organization of your writing by moving part of it so that related ideas appear near one another.

After you've revised the draft, ask yourself a series of questions. Think of these questions as your "revision checklist."

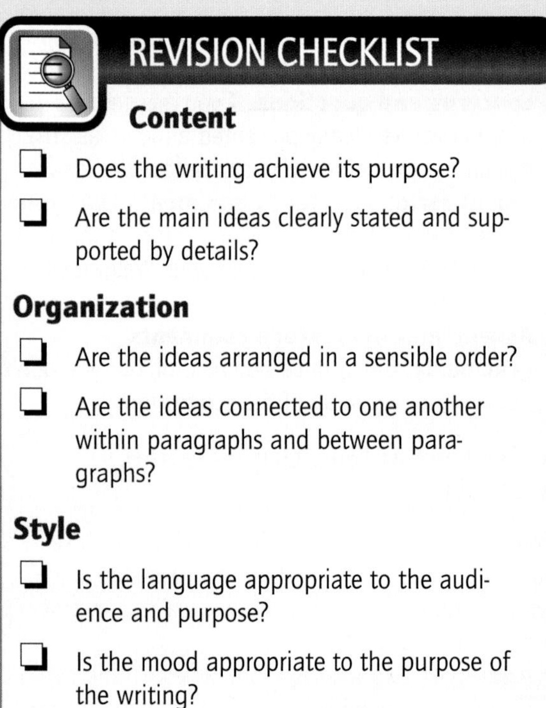

REVISION CHECKLIST

Content

- ❑ Does the writing achieve its purpose?
- ❑ Are the main ideas clearly stated and supported by details?

Organization

- ❑ Are the ideas arranged in a sensible order?
- ❑ Are the ideas connected to one another within paragraphs and between paragraphs?

Style

- ❑ Is the language appropriate to the audience and purpose?
- ❑ Is the mood appropriate to the purpose of the writing?

Proofread for Errors

When you proofread your writing, you read it through to look for errors and to mark corrections. When you mark corrections, use the standard proofreading symbols as shown in the following chart.

Proofreader's Symbols

Symbol and Example	Meaning of Symbol
The very first time	Delete (cut) this material.
dog's life	Insert (add) something that is missing.
George	Replace this letter or word.
All the horses king's	Move this word to where the arrow points.
french toast	Capitalize this letter.
the vice-President	Lowercase this letter.
housse	Take out this letter and close up space.
book keeper	Close up space.
gebril	Change the order of these letters.
end. "Watch out," she yelled.	Begin a new paragraph.
Love conquers all	Put a period here.
Welcome friends.	Put a comma here.
Getthe stopwatch	Put a space here.
Dear Madam	Put a colon here.
She walked he rode.	Put a semicolon here.
name brand products	Put a hyphen here.
cats meow	Put an apostrophe here.
cat's cradle stet	Let it stand. (Leave as it is.)

After you have revised your draft, make a clean copy of it and proofread it for errors in spelling, grammar, and punctuation. Use the following proofreading checklist.

Proofreading Checklist

Spelling

- ❑ Are all words, including names, spelled correctly?

Grammar

- ❑ Does each verb agree with its subject?
- ❑ Are verb tenses consistent and correct?
- ❑ Are irregular verbs formed correctly?
- ❑ Are there any sentence fragments or run-ons?
- ❑ Have double negatives been avoided?
- ❑ Have frequently confused words, such as affect and effect, been used correctly?

Punctuation

- ❑ Does every sentence end with an end mark?
- ❑ Are commas used correctly?
- ❑ Do all proper nouns and proper adjectives begin with capital letters?

Prepare Your Final Manuscript

After proofreading your draft, you will prepare your final manuscript. Follow the guidelines given by your teacher or the guidelines provided here. After preparing a final manuscript according to these guidelines, proofread it one last time for errors.

Guidelines for Final Manuscript Preparation

- Keyboard your manuscript using a typewriter or word processor, or write it neatly using blue or black ink.
- Double-space your writing.
- Use one side of the paper.
- Leave one-inch margins on all sides of the text.
- Indent the first line of each paragraph.
- Make a cover sheet listing the title of the work, your name, the date, and the class.
- In the upper right-hand corner of the first page, put your name, class, and date. On every page after the first, include the page number in the heading, as follows:

EXAMPLE

Sharon Turner
English 9
March 25, 2009
p. 2

WRITING FOLLOW-UP

Publish and Present

Some writing is done just for oneself—journal writing, for example. Most writing, however, is meant to be shared with others. Here are several ways in which you can publish your writing or present it to others:

- Submit your work to a local publication, such as a school literary magazine, school newspaper, or community newspaper.
- Submit your work to a regional or national publication.
- Enter your work in a contest.
- Read your work aloud to classmates, friends, or family members.
- Collaborate with other students to prepare a publication—a brochure, online literary magazine, anthology, or newspaper.
- Prepare a poster or bulletin board, perhaps in collaboration with other students, to display your writing.
- Make your own book by typing or word processing the pages and binding them together.
- Hold an oral reading of student writing as a class or school-wide project.
- Share your writing with other students in a small writers' group.

Reflect

After you've completed your writing, think through the writing process to determine what you learned as a writer, what you learned about your topic, how the writing process worked or didn't work for you, and what skills you would like to strengthen.

Reflection can be done on a self-evaluation form, in small-group discussion, or simply in silent reflection. By keeping a journal, however, you'll be able to keep track of your writing experience and pinpoint ways to make the writing process work better for you. Here are some questions to ask as you reflect on the writing process and yourself as a writer:

- Which part of the writing process did I enjoy most and least? Why? Which part of the writing process was most difficult? least difficult? Why?

- What would I change about my approach to the writing process next time?
- What have I learned in writing about this topic?
- What have I learned by using this form?
- How have I developed as a writer while writing this piece?
- What strengths have I discovered in my work?
- What aspects of my writing do I want to strengthen? How can I strengthen them?

4.2 Modes and Purposes of Writing

Types of writing generally fall within four main classifications or modes: expository, narrative, descriptive, and persuasive. Each of these modes has a specific purpose. See the Mode of Writing Chart on page 991.

Expository Writing

The purpose of **expository writing** is to inform, to present or explain an idea or a process. News articles and research reports are examples of informative expository writing. One function of expository writing is to define, since a definition explains what something is. Another function of expository writing is to analyze and interpret. For example, a book review is writing that analyzes and interprets a piece of literature to inform an audience about its worth. Similarly, a movie review evaluates and judges for its viewing audience how well a movie accomplishes its purpose.

Narrative Writing

Narrative writing tells a story or relates a series of events. It can be used to entertain, to make a point, or to introduce a topic. Narrating an event involves the dimension of action over time.

Narratives are often used in essays, reports, and other nonfiction forms because stories are entertaining and fun to read. Just as important, they are a good way to make a point. Biographies, autobiographies, and family histories are also forms of narrative writing.

Descriptive Writing

The purpose of **descriptive writing** is to entertain, enrich, and enlighten by using a form such as fiction or poetry to share a perspective. Descriptive writing is used to describe something, to set a scene, to create a mood, to appeal to the reader's senses. Descriptive writing is often creative and uses visual and other sensual details, emotional responses, and imagery. Poems, short stories, and plays are examples of descriptive writing.

Persuasive Writing

The purpose of **persuasive writing** is to persuade readers or listeners to respond in some way, such as to agree with a position, change a view on an issue, reach an agreement, or perform an action. Examples of persuasive writing are editorials, petitions, political speeches, and essays.

5.1 Critical Thinking Skills

In literature and informational texts, some things are stated as facts *(literal)* and other things are inferred or implied by the author *(inferential)*. We use **critical thinking skills** to fully understand and interpret what we read. There are six basic levels of understanding, or *cognitive domains,* which are listed below: The categories can be thought of as degrees of difficulty. That is, the first one must be mastered before the next one can take place. We apply these skills as we read a text.

Levels of Critical Thinking		
Refer to Text	**Remember**	**Recall facts:** Retrieve information presented in the text
Reason with Text	**Understand**	**Find meaning:** Interpret and explain ideas or concepts
	Apply	**Use information:** Utilize knowledge in another situation
	Analyze	**Take things apart:** Break down details to explore interpretations and relationships
	Evaluate	**Make judgments:** Justify a decision or course of action
	Create	**Bring ideas together:** Synthesize understanding to generate new ideas, products, or ways of viewing things

The paired **Refer to Text/Reason with Text** questions following the selections in this textbook are broken down into *literal* questions that refer directly to the facts in the text (Refer to Text) followed by inferential questions that ask you to apply higher levels of thinking to interpret the text (Reason with Text).

5.2 Research Skills

Learning is a lifelong process, one that extends far beyond school. Both in school and on your own, it is important to remember that your learning and growth are up to you. One good way to become an independent lifelong learner is to master research skills. Research is the process of gathering ideas and information. One of the best resources for research is the library.

How Library Materials Are Organized

Each book in a library is assigned a unique number, called a call number. The call number is printed on the spine (edge) of each book. The numbers serve to classify books as well as to help the library keep track of them. Libraries commonly use one of two systems for classifying books. Most school and public libraries use the Dewey Decimal System.

Dewey Decimal System	
Call Numbers	**Subjects**
000–099	Reference and General Works
100–199	Philosophy, Psychology
200–299	Religion
300–399	Social Studies
400–499	Language
500–599	Science, Mathematics
600–699	Technology
700–799	Arts
800–899	Literature
900–999	History, Geography, Biography[1]

1. Biographies (920s) are arranged alphabetically by the name of the person whose life is treated in each biography.

Most college libraries use the Library of Congress Classification System or the LC system, shown on the following page.

Library of Congress System	
Call Numbers	**Subjects**
A	Reference and General Works
B–BJ	Philosophy, Psychology
BK–BX	Religion
C–DF	History
G	Geography, Autobiography, Recreation
H	Social Sciences
J	Political Science
K	Law
L	Education
M	Music
N	Fine Arts
P	Language, Literature
Q	Science, Mathematics
R	Medicine
S	Agriculture
T	Technology
U	Military Science
V	Naval Science
Z	Bibliography, Library Science

How to Locate Library Materials

If you know the call number of a book or the subject classification number you want, you can usually go to the bookshelves, or stacks, to obtain the book. Use the signs at the ends of the rows to locate the section you need. Then find the particular shelf that contains call numbers close to yours.

Library collections include many other types of publications besides books, such as magazines, newspapers, audio and video recordings, and government documents. Ask a librarian to tell you where to find the materials you need. To find the call numbers of books that will help you with your research, use the library's catalog. The catalog lists all the books in the library (or a group of libraries if it is part of a larger system).

Internet Libraries It is also possible to visit the Internet Public library online at **http://www.ipl.org/.** The Internet Public Library is the first public library online of the Internet. This site provides library services to the Internet community by finding, evaluating, selecting, organizing, describing, and creating quality information resources; teaches what librarians have to contribute in a digital environment; and promotes the importance of libraries.

Computerized Catalogs Many libraries today use computerized catalogs. Systems differ from library to library, but most involve using a computer terminal to search through the library's collection. You can usually search by author, title, subject, or key word.

EXAMPLE COMPUTERIZED CATALOG SEARCHES

Search By	Example	Hints
Author	gould, stephen j	Type last name first. Type as much of the name as you know.
Title	mismeasure of man	Omit articles such as a, an, or the at the beginning of titles.
Subject	intelligence tests; ability-testing	Use the list of subjects provided by the library.
Key words	darwin; intelligence; craniology	Use related topics if you can't find anything in your subject.

If your library has a computerized catalog, you will need to learn how to use your library's particular system. A librarian can help you to master the system. The following is a sample book entry screen from a computerized catalog.

Author	Wallace, David Rains, 1945–
Title	The Quetzal and the Macaw: The Story of Costa Rica's National Parks
Publication info.	Sierra Club Books, 1992
No. of pages/size	xvi, 222 p. : maps : 24 cm.
ISBN	ISBN 0-87156-585-4
Subjects	National parks and reserves–Costa Rica–History
	Costa Rica. Servicio de Parques
	Nacionales–History
	Nature conservation–Costa Rica–History
Dewey call number	333.78

Card Catalogs Like a computerized catalog, a card catalog contains basic information about each book in the library. In a card catalog the information is typed on paper cards, which are arranged alphabetically in drawers. For each book there is a title card, one author card for each author, and at least one subject card. All of these cards show the book's title, author, and call number, so you can search for a book by title, author, or subject. The following illustration shows a typical title card.

EXAMPLE TITLE CARD

333.78 The Quetzal and the Macaw : the story of
Costa Rica's national parks.
Wallace, David Rains, 1945–
The Quetzal and the Macaw : the story of
Costa Rica's national parks.—San
Francisco: Sierra Club Books, 1992
xvi, 222 p. : maps : 24 cm.
1. National parks and reserves—Costa Rica—
History. 2. Costa Rica. Servicio de
Parques nacionales—History. 3. Nature
conservation—Costa Rica—History. I. Title.
ISBN 0-87156-585-4

When you find the entries for the books you want, write down the call number of each book and then go to the shelves. If you cannot find a particular book you need in the catalog, ask the librarian if your library can request books from another library through an interlibrary loan.

Interlibrary Loans Many libraries are part of larger library networks. In these libraries, the computerized catalog covers the collections of several libraries. If you want a book from a different library, you will need to request the book at the library's request desk or by using its computer. Ask your librarian to help you if you have questions. He or she will be able to tell you when the book will be shipped to your library.

Using Reference Works

Most libraries have an assortment of reference works in which knowledge is collected and organized so that you can find it easily. Usually, reference works cannot be checked out of the library.

Types of Dictionaries You will find many types of dictionaries in the library reference section. The most common is a dictionary of the English language. Examples include *Merriam Webster's Collegiate Dictionary,* the *American Heritage Dictionary,* and the multi-volume *Oxford English Dictionary*. Other word dictionaries focus on slang, abbreviations and acronyms, English/foreign language translation, and spelling.

Biographical, historical, scientific, and world language dictionaries are also some of the works you will find in the reference section.

Using a Thesaurus A thesaurus is a reference book that groups synonyms, or words with similar meanings. Suppose that you are writing an essay and have a word that means almost but not quite what you want, or perhaps you find yourself using the same word over and over. A thesaurus can give you fresh and precise words to use. For example, if you look up the word *sing* in a thesaurus, you might find the following synonyms listed:

sing (v.) carol, chant, croon, hum, vocalize, warble, yodel

Using Almanacs, Yearbooks, and Atlases
Almanacs and **yearbooks** are published each year. An almanac provides statistics and lists, often related to recent events. In an almanac you can find facts about current events, countries of the world, famous people, sports, entertainment, and many other subjects. An overview of the events of the year can be found in a yearbook. Some of the more widely used almanacs and yearbooks are *The Guinness Book of World Records;* the *Information Please, Almanac, Atlas, and Yearbook;* the *World Almanac and Book of Facts;* and the *World Book Yearbook of Events.*

An **atlas** is a collection of maps and other geographical information. Some atlases show natural features such as mountains and rivers; others show political features such as countries and cities. If you need to locate a particular feature on a map in an atlas, refer to the gazetteer, an index that lists every item shown on the map.

Using Biographical References and Encyclopedias A **biographical reference** contains information on the lives of famous people. Examples include *Who's Who,* the *Dictionary of American Biography,* and *Contemporary Authors.*

Encyclopedias provide a survey of knowledge. General encyclopedias, such as *World Book,* contain information on many different subjects. Specialized encyclopedias, such as the *LaRousse Encyclopedia of Mythology,* contain information on one particular area of knowledge. The topics in an encyclopedia are treated in articles, which are usually arranged in alphabetical order. If you look up a topic and do not find it, check the index (usually in the last volume).

The index will tell you where in the encyclopedia your topic is covered.

Using Indexes, Appendices, and Glossaries
An **index** lists in alphabetical order the subjects mentioned in a book or collection of periodicals and pages where these subjects are treated. Indexes help you locate possible sources of information about your topic. An index can be at the back of a book of nonfiction, or it can be a published book itself. Indexes are available as bound books, on microfilm, and online on the Internet.

An **appendix** provides additional material, often in chart or table form, at the end of a book or other writing.

A **glossary** lists key words in a book and their definitions.

Primary and Secondary Sources

Primary sources are the original unedited materials created by someone directly involved in an event or speaking directly for a group. They may include first-hand documents such as diaries, interviews, works of fiction, artwork, court records, research reports, speeches, letters, surveys, and so on.

Secondary sources offer commentary or analysis of events, ideas, or primary sources. They are often written significantly later and may provide historical context or attempt to describe or explain primary sources. Examples of secondary sources include dictionaries, encyclopedias, textbooks, and books and articles that interpret or review original works.

	Primary Source	Secondary Source
Art	Painting	Article critiquing the artist's technique
History	Prisoner's diary	Book about World War II internment camps
Literature	Poem	Literary criticism on a particular form of poetry
Science	Research report	Analysis of results

See the Language Arts Handbook, 5.4 Media Literacy, page 1004, for information on using newspapers, periodicals, and other forms of media to document your research.

5.3 Internet Research

The Internet is an enormous collection of computer networks that can open a whole new world of information. With just a couple of keystrokes, you can access libraries, government agencies, high schools and universities, nonprofit and educational organizations, museums, user groups, and individuals around the world.

Keep in mind that the Internet is not regulated and everything you read online may not be verified or accurate. Confirm facts from the Internet against another source. In addition, to become a good judge of Internet materials, do the following:

- **Consider the domain name of the resource.** Be sure to check out the sites you use to see if they are commercial (.com or .firm), educational (.edu), governmental (.gov), or organizational (.org or .net). Ask yourself questions like these: What bias might a commercial site have that would influence its presentation of information? Is the site sponsored by a special-interest group that slants or spins information to its advantage?

Key to Internet Domains	
.com	commercial entity
.edu	educational institution
.firm	business entity
.gov	government agency or department
.org or .net	organization

- **Consider the author's qualifications.** Regardless of the source, ask these questions: Is the author named? What expertise does he or she have? Can I locate other online information about this person? Evaluate the quality of information.
- **How accurate is the information?** Does it appear to be reliable and without errors? Is the information given without bias?
- **Check the date posted.** Is the information timely? When was the site last updated?

Search Tools

A number of popular and free search engines allow you to find topics of interest. Keep in mind that each service uses slightly different methods of searching, so you may get different results using the same key words.

All the Web	http://www.alltheweb.com
AltaVista	http://www.altavista.com
Go	http://www.go.com
Yahoo	http://www.yahoo.com
Excite	http://www.excite.com
HotBot	http://www.hotbot.com
WebCrawler	http://www.webcrawler.com
Google	http://www.google.com

Keep Track of Your Search Process

Because the Internet allows you to jump from one site to the next, it's easy to lose track of how you got from place to place. A research journal, kept in a separate electronic file or in a notebook, is an excellent tool for mapping how you find information.

Internet Research Checklist

- ❑ Write a brief statement of the topic of your research.
- ❑ Write key words or phrases that will help you search for this information.
- ❑ Note the search engines that you will use.
- ❑ As you conduct a search, note how many "hits" or Internet sites the search engine has accessed. Determine whether you need to narrow or expand your search. Write down new key words and the results of each new search.
- ❑ Write down all promising sites. As you access them, evaluate the source and nature of the information and jot down your assessment.
- ❑ As you find the information you need, document it carefully according to the directions in "Citing Internet Sources," page 1007.
- ❑ Keep a list of favorite websites, either in your research journal or in your browser software. This feature may be called book-mark or favorites. You can click on the name of the site in your list and return to that page without having to retype the URL (Uniform Resource Locator).

The following example shows one way to set up a research log.

Internet Research Log

Topic: ____________________
____
____
____

Key words: ____________________
____

Search engine: ____________________
____

Promising hits (titles and summary of sources): ____________________
____
____
____

New key words or phrases tried: ____________________
____

Promising hits (titles and summary of sources): ____________________
____
____
____

Complete web addresses of most promising sites: ____________________
____
____
____

Search Tips

- To make searching easier, less time consuming, and more directed, narrow your subject to a key word or a group of key words. These key words are your search terms. Key search connectors, or Boolean commands, can help you limit or expand the scope of your topic.

AND (or +) narrows a search by retrieving documents that include both terms—for example: Ulysses Grant AND Vicksburg.

OR broadens a search by retrieving documents that include any of the terms—for example: Ulysses Grant OR Vicksburg OR Civil War.

NOT narrows a search by excluding documents containing certain words—for example: Ulysses Grant NOT Civil War.

- If applicable, limit your search by specifying a geographical area by using the word *near*—for example, golf courses near Boulder, Colorado.
- When entering a group of key words, present them in order, from the most important to the least important key word.
- If the terms of your search are not leading you to the information you need, try using synonyms. For example, if you were looking for information about how to care for your garden, you might use these terms: *compost, pest control,* and *watering*.
- Avoid opening the link to every page in your results list. Search engines typically present pages in descending order of relevancy or importance. The most useful pages will be located at the top of the list. However, skimming the text of lower order sites may give you ideas for other key words.
- If you're not getting the desired results, check your input. Common search mistakes include misspelling search terms and mistyping URLs. Remember that URLs must be typed exactly as they appear, using the exact capital or lowercase letters, spacing, and punctuation.

For information on citing Internet sources, see the Language Arts Handbook 5.6, Documenting Sources.

5.4 Media Literacy

The term **media,** in most applications, is used as a plural of *medium,* which means a channel or system of communication, information, or entertainment. *Mass media* refers specifically to means of communication, such as newspapers, radio, or television, which are designed to reach the mass of the people. *Journalism* is the gathering, evaluating, and disseminating, through various media, of news and facts of current interest. Originally, journalism encompassed only such printed matter as newspapers and periodicals. Today, however, it includes other media used to distribute news, such as radio, television, documentary or newsreel films, the Internet, and computer news services.

Newspapers are publications usually issued on a daily or weekly basis, the main function of which is to report the news. Newspapers also provide commentary on the news, advocate various public policies, furnish special information and advice to readers, and sometimes include features such as comic strips, cartoons, and serialized books.

Periodicals are publications released at regular intervals, such as journals, magazines, or newsletters. Periodicals feature material of special interest to particular audiences. The contents of periodicals can be unrelated to current news stories—however, when dealing with the news, periodicals tend to do so in the form of commentaries or summaries.

Technical writing refers to scientific or process-oriented instructional writing that is of a technical or mechanical nature. Technical writing includes instruction manuals, such as computer software manuals, how-to instructional guides, and procedural memos.

Electronic media include online magazines and journals, known as webzines or e-zines; computer news services; and many web-based newspapers that are available on the Internet. The web is by far the most widely used part of the Internet.

Multimedia is the presentation of information using the combination of text, sound, pictures, animation, and video. Common multimedia computer applications include games, learning software, presentation software, reference materials, and web pages. Most multimedia applications include links that enable users to switch between media elements and topics. The connectivity provided by these links transforms multimedia from static presentations with pictures and sound into a varied and informative interactive experience.

Visual media, such as fine art, illustrations, and photographs, is used extensively in today's visually stimulating world to enhance the written word. Visual arts offer insights into our world in a different way than print does. Critical viewing or careful examination of a painting or photograph can help you to comprehend its meaning and be able to compare and contrast the visual image with a literary work or other piece of writing.

5.5 Evaluating Sources

To conduct your research efficiently, you need to evaluate your sources and set priorities among them. Ideally, a source will be:

- **Unbiased.** When an author has a personal stake in what people think about a subject, he or she may withhold or distort information. Investigate the author's background to see if she or he is liable to be biased. Using loaded language and overlooking obvious counterarguments are signs of author bias.

- **Authoritative.** An authoritative source is reliable and trustworthy. An author's reputation, especially among others who conduct research in the same field, is a sign of authority. Likewise, periodicals and publishers acquire reputations for responsible or poor editing and research.
- **Timely.** Information about many subjects changes rapidly. An astronomy text published last year may already be out of date. In other fields—for instance, algebra—older texts may be perfectly adequate. Consult with your teacher and your librarian to decide how current your sources must be.
- **Available.** Borrowing through interlibrary loan, tracing a book that is missing, or recalling a book that has been checked out to another person takes time. Make sure to allow enough time for these materials.
- **Appropriate for your level.** Find sources that present useful information that you can understand. Materials written for "young people" may be too simple to be helpful. Books written for experts may presume knowledge that you do not have. Struggling with a difficult text is often worth the effort, but if you do so, monitor your time and stay on schedule.

5.6 Documenting Sources

As you use your research in your writing, you must document your sources of information.

- Credit the sources of all ideas and facts that you use.
- Credit original ideas or facts that are expressed in text, tables, charts, and other graphic information.
- Credit all artistic property, including works of literature, song lyrics, and ideas.

Keeping a Research Journal A research journal is a notebook, electronic file, or other means to track the information you find as you conduct research. A research journal can include the following:

- A list of questions you want to research. (Such questions can be an excellent source of writing topics.)

EXAMPLES

How did the Vietnam Veterans Memorial come to be? Why is it one of the most visited memorials in America?

Where can I find more artwork by Faith Ringgold?

Why was Transcendentalism such an important literary movement in America but not in Europe?

As you conduct your research, rely on your research journal as a place to take notes on the sources you find and your evaluation of them. Keeping a research journal can be an invaluable way to track your research and to take notes.

Avoiding Plagiarizing **Plagiarism** is taking someone else's words or thoughts and presenting them as your own. Plagiarism is a very serious problem and has been the downfall of many students and professionals. Whenever you use someone else's writing to help you with a paper or a speech, you must be careful either to **paraphrase,** put the ideas in your own words; **summarize** the main ideas; or to use **quotation marks.** In any case, you must document your sources and give credit to the person whose ideas you are using. As you do research, make sure to include paraphrases, summaries, and direct quotations in your notes.

Informal and Formal Note-Taking

Informal Note-Taking Take informal notes when you want information for your own use only, and when you will not need to quote or document your sources. You would take informal notes when preparing materials to use in studying, for instance, as you watch a film or listen to a lecture.

Informal note-taking is similar to outlining. Use important ideas as headings, and write relevant details below. You will not be able to copy every word, nor is there any need to. Write phrases instead of sentences. You will also want to record information about the event or performance, including the date, time, place, speaker, and title, as applicable.

EXAMPLE

quotation
"Jerzy Kosinski came to the United States in 1957, and in 1958 he was awarded a Ford Foundation fellowship."

notes
Jerzy Kosinski
—came to US 1957
—Ford Foundation fellowship 1958

Formal Note-Taking Take formal notes when you may need to quote or document your sources. When you are keeping formal notes for a project—for instance, for a debate or a research paper—you should use 4" x 6" index cards.

Preparing Note Cards

1. Identify the source at the top right corner of the card. (Use the source numbers from your bibliography cards.)
2. Identify the subject or topic of the note on the top line of the card. (This will make it easier to organize the cards later.)
3. Use a separate card for each fact or quotation. (This will make it easier to organize the cards later.)
4. Write the pertinent source page number or numbers after the note.

EXAMPLE NOTE CARD

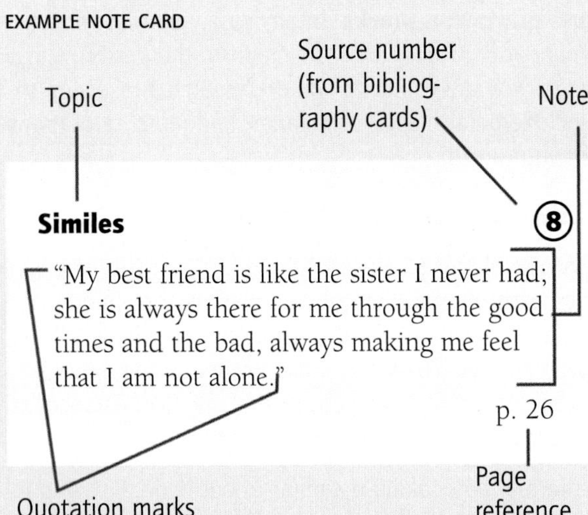
Topic
Source number (from bibliography cards)
Note
Similes
8
"My best friend is like the sister I never had; she is always there for me through the good times and the bad, always making me feel that I am not alone."
p. 26
Quotation marks
Page reference

Bibliographies and Bibliography Cards

If you are writing a research paper, your teacher will ask you to include a bibliography, or list of works cited, to tell where you got your information. A bibliography is a list of sources that you used for your writing. A source is a book, a magazine, a film, or any other written or audiovisual material that you use to get information. As you work on your paper, you should be writing down on note cards the information for each source that you use.

EXAMPLE BIBLIOGRAPHY CARD

Van Lawick-Goodall, Jane.
In the Shadow of Man
Boston: Houghton, 1971.
Peabody Institute Library
599.8

For each source used, prepare an index card with complete bibliographical information. Include all of the information in the following chart when preparing your cards.

Information to Include on a Bibliography Card	
Author(s)	Write the complete name(s) of all author(s), editor(s), and translator(s).
Title	Write the complete title. If the piece is contained in a larger work, include the title of the larger work. (For example, write the name of the encyclopedia as well as the name of the article you used.)
Publisher	Write exactly as it appears on the title page.
Place and date of publication	Copy this information from the title page or copyright page of a book. For a magazine, write the date of the issue that you used.
Location and call number	Note where you found the book. If it is in a library collection, write the call number.
Card number	Give each bibliography card that you prepare a number. Write that number in the top right-hand corner of the card and circle it. When you take notes from the source, include this number on each note card so that you will be able to identify the source of the note later on.

The following chart shows the correct form for citing different types of bibliography entries, following the *Modern Language Association (MLA) Handbook for Writers of Research Papers.* Note that all citations should include the medium of the publication, such as *print*, *film*, or *web*.

MLA Forms for Works Cited	
Book	Douglass, Frederick. *Escape from Slavery: The Boyhood of Frederick Douglass in His Own Words.* New York: Alfred A. Knopf, 1994. Print.
Magazine article	Reston, James, Jr. "Orion: Where Stars Are Born." *National Geographic* Dec. 1995: 90-101. Print.
Encyclopedia entry	"Lewis and Clark Expedition." *Encyclopedia Americana.* Jackson, Donald. 1995 ed. Print.
Interview	Campbell, Silas. Personal interview. 6 Feb. 2007.
Film	*The Big Heat.* Dir. Fritz Lang. Perf. Glenn Ford and Gloria Grahame. Screenplay by Sidney Boehm. Columbia, 1953. Film.

Citing Internet Sources

To document your Internet sources, use your research journal to record each site you visit (See the Language Arts Handbook, 5.3 Internet Research, page 1002) or make bibliography cards as you search. An Internet source entry should include the following general pieces of information:

- Name of the author, if available, last name first, followed by a period.
- Title of the source, document, file, or page in quotation marks, followed by a period.
- If available, the information about the print publication, followed by a period.
- Name of the database or online source, in italics, and followed by a period.
- The date the website was last updated, followed by a period.
- The name of the institution or organization associated with the website, followed by a period.
- Medium of publication (Web).
- Date the source was accessed (day, month, year).
- Provide an electronic address, URL, only when needed to locate the source or if required by your instructor. Enclose the URL in angle brackets (< >), followed by a period. Avoid showing network and e-mail addresses as underlined hyperlinks. Note that when line length forces you to break a Web address, always break it after a slash mark.

The *Modern Language Association Handbook for Writers of Research Papers* acknowledges that all source tracking information on the Internet may not be obtainable. Therefore, the manual recommends that if you cannot find some of this information, cite what is available.

EXAMPLE INTERNET CITATIONS

Armstrong, Mark. "That's 'Sir' Mick Jagger to You." E! Online. 17 June 2002. E! Online, Inc. Web. 17 June 2009 <http://www.eonline.com/News/Items/0,1,10110,00.html>.

For sites with no name of the database or online source:
Chachich, Mike. "Letters from Japan Vol 1" 30 Mar. 1994. Web. 17 June 2009 <http://www.chachich.com/cgi-bin/catlfj?1>.

For sites with no author:
"The Science Behind the Sod." *MSU News Bulletin*. 13 June 2002. Michigan State University. Web. 17 June 2009 <http://www.newsbulletin.msu.edu/june13/sod.html>.

For an e-mail message:
Daniel Akaka (senator@akaka.senate.gov). "Oceanic Exploration Grant." E-mail to Joseph Biden (senator@biden.senate.gov). 17 June 2003.

Parenthetical Documentation

Parenthetical documentation is currently the most widely used form of documentation. To use this method to document the source of a quotation or an idea, you place a brief note identifying the source in parentheses immediately after the borrowed material. This type of note is called a parenthetical citation, and the act of placing such a note is called citing a source.

The first part of a parenthetical citation refers the reader to a source in your List of Works Cited or Works Consulted. For the reader's ease in finding the source in your bibliography, you must cite the work according to how it is listed in the bibliography.

EXAMPLE PARENTHETICAL CITATIONS

For works listed by title, use an abbreviated title.

Sample bibliographic entry
"History." *Encyclopedia Britannica: Macropædia*. 1992 ed. Print.

Sample citation
Historians go through three stages in textual criticism ("History" 615).

For works listed by author or editor, use the author's or editor's last name.

Sample bibliographic entry
Brown, Dee. *Bury My Heart at Wounded Knee: An Indian History of the American West*. New York: Holt, 1970. Print.

Sample citation
"Big Eyes Schurz agreed to the arrest" (Brown 364).

When the listed name or title is stated in the text, cite only the page number.

Brown states that Big Eyes Schurz agreed to it (364).

For works of multiple volumes, use a colon after the volume number.

Sample bibliographic entry
Pepys, Samuel. *The Diary of Samuel Pepys.* Eds. Robert Latham and William Matthews. 10 vols. Berkeley: University of California Press, 1972. Print.

Sample citation
On the last day of 1665, Pepys took the occasion of the new year to reflect, but not to celebrate (6: 341-2).

For works quoted in secondary sources, use the abbreviation "qtd. in."

Sample citation
According to R. Bentley, "reason and the facts outweigh a hundred manuscripts" (qtd. in "History" 615).

For classic works that are available in various editions, give the page number from the edition you are using, followed by a semicolon; then identify the section of the work to help people with other editions find the reference.

Footnotes and Endnotes

In addition to parenthetical documentation, footnoting and endnoting are two other accepted methods.

Footnotes Instead of putting citations in parentheses within the text, you can place them at the bottom or foot of the page; hence the term *footnote.* In this system, a number or symbol is placed in the text where the parenthetical citation would otherwise be, and a matching number or symbol at the bottom of the page identifies the citation. This textbook, for example, uses numbered footnotes in its literature selections to define obscure words and to provide background information.

Endnotes Many books use endnotes instead of footnotes. Endnotes are like footnotes in that a number or symbol is placed within the text, but the matching citations are compiled at the end of the book, chapter, or article rather than at the foot of the page. Footnote and endnote entries begin with the author's (or editor's) name in its usual order (first name, then last) and include publication information and a page reference.

EXAMPLE FOOTNOTE OR ENDNOTE CITATIONS

Book with one author
[1]Jean Paul-Sartre, *Being and Nothingness* (New York: The Citadel Press, 1966) 149-51. Print.

Book with one editor and no single author
[2]Shannon Ravenel, ed., *New Stories from the South: The Year's Best, 1992* (Chapel Hill, NC: Algonquin Books, 1992) 305. Print.

Magazine article
[3]Andrew Gore, "Road Test: The Apple Powerbook," *MacUser,* Dec. 1996: 72. Print.

6.1 Workplace and Consumer Documents

Applied English is English in the world of work or business, or *practical* English. Entering a new school, writing a professional letter, applying for a job, reading an instructional manual—these are but a few of the many situations you may encounter that involve **workplace and consumer documents.** You can apply English skills to many real-world situations, using your reading, writing, speaking, and listening abilities to help you be successful in any field or occupation you choose to pursue.

6.2 Writing a Step-by-Step Procedure

A **step-by-step procedure** is a how-to or process piece that uses directions to teach someone something new. Written procedures include textual information and sometimes graphics. Spoken procedures can be given as oral demonstrations. They can include textual and graphic information and other props. Examples of step-by-step procedures include an oral demonstration of how to saddle a horse; instructions on how to treat a sprained ankle; a video showing how to do the perfect lay-up in basketball; and an interactive Internet site allowing the user to design and send a bouquet of flowers.

Guidelines for Writing a Step-by-Step Procedure

- Demonstrate the steps. If you are showing how to make something, create several different samples to show each step of the procedure. For example, if you are showing how to make a wooden basket, you might want to display the raw materials, the started basket, the basket halfway finished, and then the finished product.
- Be prepared. The best way to prevent problems is to anticipate and plan for them. Rehearse an oral demonstration several times. If you are preparing the procedure in written form, go through your directions as if you knew nothing about the process. Anticipate what it would be like to learn this procedure for the first time. See if you can follow your own directions, or have a friend work through the procedure and offer suggestions for improvement.
- Acknowledge mistakes. If you are sharing a procedure "live" as an oral demonstration and you can't talk around or correct a mistake, tell your audience what has gone wrong, and why. If you handle the situation in a calm, direct way, the audience may also learn from your mistake.
- Know your topic. The better you know it, the better you will be able to teach others.

6.3 Writing a Business Letter

A **business letter** is usually addressed to someone you do not know personally. Therefore, a formal tone is appropriate for such a letter. Following appropriate form is especially important when writing business letters. If you follow the correct form and avoid errors in spelling, grammar, usage, and mechanics, your letter will sound professional and make a good impression. Above the salutation, a business letter should contain the name and title of the person to whom you are writing and the name and address of that person's company or organization (see the model on the following page).

One common form for a business letter is the block form. In the **block form,** each part of the letter begins at the left margin. The parts are separated by line spaces.

Begin the salutation with the word *Dear,* followed by the courtesy or professional title used in the inside address, such as Ms., Mr., or Dr., and a colon. If you are not writing to a specific person, you may use a general salutation such as *Dear Sir or Madam.*

In the body of your letter, use a polite, formal tone and standard English. Make your points clearly, in as few words as possible.

End with a standard closing such as *Sincerely, Yours truly,* or *Respectfully yours.* Capitalize only the first word of the closing. Type your full name below the closing, leaving three or four blank lines for your signature. Sign your name below the closing in blue or black ink (never in red or green). Proofread your letter before you send it. Poor spelling, grammar, or punctuation can ruin an otherwise well-written business letter.

Guidelines for Writing a Business Letter

- Outline your main points before you begin.
- Word process your letter, if at all possible. Type or print it on clean 8 1/2" x 11" white or off-white paper. Use only one side of the paper.
- Use the block form or another standard business letter form.
- Single space, leaving a blank line between each part, including paragraphs.
- Use a standard salutation and a standard closing.
- Stick to the subject. State your main idea clearly at the beginning of the letter. Keep the letter brief and informative.
- Check your spelling, grammar, usage, and punctuation carefully.

6.4 Application Letter

One of the most frequently used types of business letters is an **application letter,** which you would write to apply to a school or for a job. In an application letter, it is important to emphasize your knowledge about the business and the skills that you can bring to the position. The following is an example of a letter written to the owner of a dive shop to apply for a summer job.

EXAMPLE APPLICATION LETTER

498 Blue Key Rd.
Charleston, SC 02716

May 3, 2008

Mr. Davy Jones, Owner
Deep Sea Divers, Inc.
73 Ocean St.
Charleston, SC 02716

Dear Mr. Jones:

Please consider me for a position as a part-time clerk in your store for the coming summer. I understand that in the summer your business increases considerably and that you might need a conscientious, hardworking clerk. I can offer you considerable knowledge of snorkeling and diving equipment and experience working in a retail shop.

I will be available for work three days per week between June 1 and August 12. I am enclosing a résumé and references. Please contact me if you wish to set up an interview.

Sincerely,

Jorge Alvarez
Jorge Alvarez

6.5 Writing a Résumé

A **résumé** is a summary of a job applicant's career objectives, previous employment experience, and education. Its purpose is to help the applicant obtain the job he or she seeks. A résumé should be accompanied by a cover letter to the employer (see 6.4 Application Letter). Many helpful books and articles are available in libraries and bookstores on writing a résumé. Here are some guidelines.

Guidelines for Writing a Résumé

- Keep your information brief—to one page if possible. The goal of the résumé is to give a potential employer a quick snapshot of your skills and abilities.
- Include all vital contact information—name, address, phone number, and e-mail address, if applicable—at the top of the page.
- Use headings to summarize information regarding job or career objective, education, work experience, skills, extracurricular activities, awards (if applicable), and references. Note that work experience should be listed starting with your most recent job and working backward.
- Key or type your résumé on white or off-white paper. Proofread it carefully for any errors; all facts must be accurate as well. Make it as neat as possible.
- You may list references, or simply state that they are available on request.

EXAMPLE RÉSUMÉ

Pat Mizos
5555 Elm Street
Anytown, NY 20111
(212) 555-5555

Objective:
To gain employment working in a summer camp program for children

Education:
Orchard High School, 2008 graduate

Major area of study: College preparatory, with concentration in science and physical education classes

Grade point average: 3.5 (B+)

Work experience:

Summer 2007	Summer youth counselor, Anytown Parks and Recreation Department
Summer 2006	Dishwasher, The Lobster Shack, Anytown, NY

Skills:
Intermediate level Spanish (3 years in high school)
Beginning level American Sign Language (1 semester at Anytown Vocational School)
Certified in CPR

Extracurricular Activities:
Swim team, tennis team, youth hot-line crisis volunteer

References:
Available on request.

6.6 Writing a Memo

In businesses, schools, and other organizations, employees, students, and others often communicate by means of *memoranda,* or **memos.** For example, the director of a school drama club might write a memo to the editor of the student newspaper announcing tryouts for a new play. Some memos will be more informal than others. If you know the person to whom you are writing well or if the memo has only a social function such as announcing a party, the tone can be fairly informal. Most memos, however, have a fairly formal tone. A memo begins with a header. Often this header contains the word *memorandum* (the singular form of memoranda) and the following words and abbreviations:

TO:
FR: (from)
DT: (date)
RE: (regarding)
cc: (copy)

In the following example, Jack Hart, the president of the drama club at Wheaton High School, wishes to have the upcoming tryouts for his club's production of *Oklahoma!* announced in the school newspaper. He decides to write a memo to the editor of the paper, Lisa Lowry.

EXAMPLE MEMORANDUM

MEMORANDUM
TO: Lisa Lowry
FR: Jack Hart
RE: Tryouts for the spring production of *Oklahoma!*
DT: February 12, 2008
cc: Ms. Wise

Please include the following announcement in the upcoming issue of the *Wheaton Crier:* Tryouts for the Wheaton Drama Club's spring production of *Oklahoma!* will be held on Friday, February 26, at 6:00 p.m. in the Wheaton High School Auditorium. Students interested in performing in this musical should come to the auditorium at that time prepared to deliver a monologue less than two minutes long and to sing one song from the musical. Copies of the music and lyrics can be obtained from the sponsor of the Wheaton Drama Club, Ms. Wise. For additional information, please contact Ms. Wise or any member of the Drama Club.

Thank you.

6.7 Writing a Proposal

A **proposal** outlines a project that a person wants to complete. It presents a summary of an idea, the reasons why the idea is important, and an outline of how the project would be carried out. Because the proposal audience is people who can help carry out the proposal, a proposal is both informative and persuasive.

EXAMPLES

- You want funding for an art project that would benefit your community.
- Your student council proposes a clothing drive for disaster relief.
- You and a group of your friends want to help organize a summer program for teens your age.

Proposal: To host a Community Arts Day at the park behind Jordan High School that would allow high school artists to try new art forms and to exhibit their works.

Rationale: The art students at Jordan High School have shown there is a lot of talent here worth sharing. A Community Arts Day would let everyone interested get involved, and build school and community pride. Art students could lead others through simple art projects, and people could learn new things. At the end, the art could be displayed in an art fair at the community park. Artwork and refreshments could be sold, with all proceeds going to the Jordan High School Art Scholarship.

Schedule/Preparation Outline

Present proposal to School Pride Committee	April 1
Meet with art students to organize event	April 6-15
Contact area businesses for donations	April 6-15
Advertise event and sell tickets	April 16-25
Have practice day to make sure art activities work	April 20
Hold Community Arts Day	April 26

BUDGET

Expenses

Posters, mailings, tickets	$30
Art supplies	$200
Refreshments	$75

Note: Expenses will be less if we ask area businesses to help sponsor event.

Total estimated expenses	$305

Income

Ticket sales (Estimated 150 tickets sold @ $3 each)	$450
Refreshment sales	$100
Earnings from art sold at exhibit	$200
Total estimated income	$750
Net proceeds	$445

Note: All proceeds will be donated to the Jordan High School Art Scholarship Fund.

Guidelines for Writing a Proposal

- Keep the tone positive, courteous, and respectful.
- State your proposal and rationale briefly and clearly.
- Give your audience all necessary information. A proposal with specific details makes it clear what you want approved, and why your audience—often a committee or someone in authority—should approve it.
- Use standard, formal English.
- Format your proposal with headings, lists, and schedules to make your proposed project easy to understand and approve.

6.8 Writing a Press Release

A **press release** is an informative piece intended for publication in local news media. A press release is usually written to promote an upcoming event or to inform the community of a recent event that promotes, or strengthens, an individual or organization.

EXAMPLES

- a brief notice from the choir director telling the community of the upcoming spring concert
- an informative piece by the district public information officer announcing that your school's art instructor has been named the state Teacher of the Year

Guidelines for Writing a Press Release

- Know your purpose. What do you want your audience to know from reading your piece?
- Use the 5 *Ws* and an *H—who, what, where, why, when,* and *how*—questioning strategy to convey the important information at the beginning of your story.
- Keep the press release brief. Local media are more likely to publish or broadcast your piece if it is short and to the point.
- Include contact information such as your name, phone number, and times you can be reached. Make this information available to the media representative or, if applicable, to the reading public.
- Type your press release using conventional manuscript form. Make sure the text is double-spaced and that you leave margins of at least an inch on all sides of the page.
- At the beginning of the press release, key the day's date and the date the information is to be released. (You can type "For immediate release" or designate the date you would like the press release to be printed in the newspaper.)
- At the end of the press release, key the word "END."
- Check a previous newspaper for deadline information or call the newspaper office to make sure you get your material there on time. Address the press release to the editor.

6.9 Writing a Public Service Announcement

A **public service announcement,** or **PSA,** is a brief, informative article intended to be helpful to the community. PSAs are written by nonprofit organizations and concerned citizens for print in local newspapers, for broadcast by television and radio stations, and for publication on the Internet.

EXAMPLES

- an article by the American Cancer Society outlining early warning signs of cancer
- an announcement promoting Safety Week
- an informative piece telling coastal residents what to do during a hurricane

Guidelines for Writing a Public Service Announcement

- Know your purpose. What do you want your audience to know from reading or hearing your piece?
- State your information as objectively as possible.
- As with most informative writing, use the 5 *Ws* and an *H—who, what, where, why, when,* and *how*—questioning strategy to get your important information at the beginning of your story.
- Keep your announcement brief. Local media are more likely to publish or broadcast your piece if it is short and to the point.
- Include contact information in case the media representative has any questions. You might also include contact information in the PSA itself.
- Key or type your PSA in conventional manuscript form. Make sure the text is double-spaced and that you leave margins of at least an inch on all sides of the page.
- At the end of the PSA, key "END" to designate the end of the announcement.
- Be aware of print and broadcast deadlines and make sure your material is sent on time.

7.1 Verbal and Nonverbal Communication

Human beings use both verbal and nonverbal communication to convey meaning and exchange ideas. When a person expresses meaning through words, he or she is using verbal communication. When a person expresses meaning without using words, for example by standing up straight or shaking his or her head, he or she is using nonverbal communication. When we speak to another person, we usually think that the meaning of what we say comes chiefly from the words we use. However, as much as sixty percent of the meaning of a message may be communicated nonverbally.

Elements of Verbal Communication

Element	Description	Guidelines for Speakers
Volume	Loudness or softness	Vary your volume, but make sure that you can be heard.
Melody, Pitch	Highness or lowness	Vary your pitch. Avoid speaking in a monotone (at a single pitch).
Pace	Speed	Vary the speed of your delivery to suit what you are saying.
Tone	Emotional quality	Suit your tone to your message, and vary it appropriately as you speak.
Enunciation	Clearness with which words are spoken	When speaking before a group, pronounce your words more precisely than you would in ordinary conversation.

Elements of Nonverbal Communication

Element	Description	Guidelines for Speakers
Eye contact	Looking audience members in the eye	Make eye contact regularly with people in your audience. Try to include all audience members.
Facial expression	Using your face to show your emotions	Use expressions to emphasize your message—raised eyebrows for a question, pursed lips for concentration, eyebrows lowered for anger, and so on.
Gesture	Meaningful motions of the arms and hands	Use gestures to emphasize points. Be careful, however, not to overuse gestures. Too many can be distracting.
Posture	Position of the body	Keep your spine straight and head high, but avoid appearing stiff. Stand with your arms and legs slightly open, except when adopting other postures to express particular emotions.
Proximity	Distance from audience	Keep the right amount of distance between yourself and the audience. You should be a comfortable distance away, but not so far away that the audience cannot hear you.

7.2 Listening Skills

Learning to listen well is essential not only for success in personal life but also for success in school and, later, on the job. It is estimated that high school and college students spend over half their waking time listening to others, yet most people are rather poor listeners.

Active Versus Passive Listening

Active listening requires skill and concentration. The mind of a good listener is focused on what a speaker is trying to communicate. In other words, an effective listener is an active listener. Ineffective listeners view listening as a passive activity, something that simply "happens" without any effort on their part. **Passive listening** is nothing more than hearing sounds. This type of listening can cause misunderstanding and miscommunication.

ADAPTING LISTENING SKILLS

Just as different situations require different types of listening, different tasks or goals may also require different listening strategies and skills.

Listening for Comprehension

Listening for comprehension means listening for information or ideas communicated by other people.

SPEAKING & LISTENING

For example, you are listening for comprehension when you try to understand directions to a friend's house or your teacher's explanation of how to conduct a classroom debate.

When listening for comprehension, your goal is to reach understanding, so it is important to recognize and remember the key information or ideas presented. Concentrate on getting the **main points or major ideas** of a message rather than all the supporting details. This can prevent you from becoming overwhelmed by the amount of information presented.

You might also use a technique called **clarifying and confirming** to help you better remember and understand information. This technique involves paraphrasing or repeating back to the speaker in your own words the key information presented to make sure that you have understood correctly. If the situation prevents you from using the technique—for instance, if there is no opportunity for you to respond directly to the speaker—it can still be helpful to rephrase the information in your own words in your head to help you remember and understand it.

Listening Critically

Listening critically means listening to a message in order to comprehend and evaluate it. When listening for comprehension, you usually assume that the information presented is true. Critical listening, on the other hand, includes **comprehending and judging** the arguments and appeals in a message in order to decide whether to accept or reject them. Critical listening is most useful when you encounter a persuasive message such as a sales pitch, advertisement, campaign speech, or news editorial.

When evaluating a persuasive message, you might consider the following:

- Is the speaker trustworthy and qualified to speak about this subject?
- Does the speaker present logical arguments supported by solid facts?
- Does the speaker use unproven assumptions to make a case?
- Does the speaker use questionable motivational appeals, such as appeals to fear or to prejudice?

These questions can help you decide whether or not to be convinced by a persuasive message.

Listening to Learn Vocabulary

Listening to learn vocabulary involves a very different kind of listening because the focus is on learning new words and how to use them properly. For instance, you have a conversation with someone who has a more advanced vocabulary and use this as an opportunity to learn new words. The key to listening in order to learn vocabulary is to **pay attention to how words are used in context.** Sometimes it is possible to figure out what an unfamiliar word means based simply on how the word is used in a sentence.

Once you learn a new word, try to use it several times so it becomes more familiar and you become comfortable using it. Also be sure to look up the word in a dictionary to find out whether it has other meanings or connotations of which you are not aware.

Listening for Appreciation

Listening for appreciation means listening purely for enjoyment or entertainment. You might listen appreciatively to a singer, a comedian, a storyteller, an acting company, or a humorous speaker. Appreciation is a very individual matter and there are no rules about how to appreciate something. However, as with all forms of listening, listening for appreciation requires attention and concentration.

7.3 Collaborative Learning and Communication

Collaboration is the act of working with one or more other people to achieve a goal. Many common learning situations involve collaboration.

- Participating in a small-group discussion
- Doing a small-group project
- Tutoring another student or being tutored
- Doing peer evaluation

Guidelines for Group Discussion

- **Listen actively.** Maintain eye contact with the speakers. Make notes on what they say. Mentally translate what they say into your own words. Think critically about whether you agree or disagree with each speaker, and why.
- **Be polite.** Wait for your turn to speak. Do not interrupt others. If your discussion has a group leader, ask to be recognized before speaking by raising your hand.

- **Participate in the discussion.** At appropriate times, make your own comments or ask questions of other speakers.
- **Stick to the discussion topic.** Do not introduce unrelated or irrelevant ideas.
- **Assign roles.** For a formal dicussion, choose a group leader to guide the discussion and a secretary to record the minutes (the main ideas and proposals made by group members). Also draw up an agenda before the discussion, listing items to be discussed.

Guidelines for Projects

- **Choose a group leader** to conduct the meetings of your project group.
- **Set a goal** for the group. This goal should be some specific outcome or set of outcomes that you want to bring about.
- **Make a list of tasks** that need to be performed.
- **Make a schedule** for completing the tasks, including dates and times for completion of each task.
- **Make an assignment sheet.** Assign certain tasks to particular group members. Be fair in distributing the work to be done.
- **Set times for future meetings.** You might want to schedule meetings to evaluate your progress toward your goal as well as meetings to actually carry out specific tasks.
- **Meet to evaluate** your overall success when the project is completed. Also look at the individual contributions of each group member.

7.4 Asking and Answering Questions

There are many situations in which you will find it useful to ask questions of a speaker, or in which you will be asked questions about a presentation. Often a formal speech or presentation will be followed by a question-and-answer period. Keep the following guidelines in mind when asking or answering questions.

Guidelines for Asking and Answering Questions

- **Wait to be recognized.** In most cases, it is appropriate to raise your hand if you have a question and to wait for the speaker or moderator to call on you.
- **Make questions clear and direct.** The longer your question, the less chance a speaker will understand it. Make your questions short and to the point.
- **Do not debate or argue.** If you disagree with a speaker, the question-and-answer period is not the time to hash out an argument. Ask to speak with the speaker privately after the presentation is over, or agree on a later time and place to meet.
- **Do not take others' time.** Be courteous to other audience members and allow them time to ask questions. If you have a follow-up question, ask the speaker if you may proceed with your follow up.
- **Do not give a speech.** Sometimes audience members are more interested in expressing their own opinion than in asking the speaker a question. Do not give in to the temptation to present a speech of your own.
- **Come prepared for a question-and-answer period.** Although you can never predict the exact questions that people will ask you, you can anticipate many questions that are likely to be asked. Rehearse aloud your answers to the most difficult questions.
- **Be patient.** It may take some time for audience members to formulate questions in response to your speech. Give the audience a moment to do so. Don't run back to your seat the minute your speech is over, or if there is an awkward pause after you invite questions.
- **Be direct and succinct.** Be sure to answer the question directly as it has been asked, and to provide a short but clear answer.

7.5 Conducting an Interview

In an interview, you meet with someone and ask him or her questions. Interviewing experts is an excellent way to gain information about a particular topic. For example, if you are interested in writing about the art of making pottery, you might interview an art teacher, a professional potter, or the owner of a ceramics shop.

When planning an interview, you should do some background research on your subject and think carefully about questions you would like to ask. Write out a list of questions, including some about the person's background as well as about your topic. Other questions might occur to you as the interview proceeds, but it is best to be prepared. For guidelines on being a good listener, see Language Arts Handbook 7.2, Listening Skills, page 1015. Guidelines for interviewing appear on the following page:

SPEAKING & LISTENING

Guidelines for Conducting an Interview

- **Set up a time in advance.** Don't just try to work questions into a regular conversation. Set aside time to meet in a quiet place where both you and the person you are interviewing can focus on the interview.
- **Explain the purpose** of the interview. Be sure the person you are interviewing knows what you want to find out and why you need to know it. This will help him or her to answer your questions in a way that is more useful and helpful to you.
- **Ask mostly open-ended questions.** These are questions that allow the person you are interviewing to express a personal point of view. They cannot be answered with a simple "yes" or "no" nor a brief statement of fact. The following are all examples of open-ended questions:
  "Why did you become a professional potter?"
  "What is the most challenging thing about owning your own ceramics shop?"
  "What advice would you give to a beginning potter?"

  One of the most valuable questions to ask at the end of the interview is, "What would you like to add that I haven't asked about?" This can provide some of the most interesting or vital information of all.
- **Tape-record the interview** (if possible). Then you can review the interview at your leisure. Be sure to ask the person you are interviewing whether or not you can tape-record the session. If the person refuses, accept his or her decision.
- **Take notes** during the interview, whether or not you are also tape-recording it. Write down the main points and some key words to help you remember details. Record the person's most important statements word for word.
- **Clarify spelling and get permission** for quotations. Be sure to get the correct spelling of the person's name and to ask permission to quote his or her statements.
- **End the interview on time.** Do not extend the interview beyond the time limits of your appointment. The person you are interviewing has been courteous enough to give you his or her time. Return this courtesy by ending the interview on time, thanking the person for his or her help, and leaving.
- **Write up the results** of the interview as soon as possible after you conduct it. Over time, what seemed like a very clear note may become unclear or confusing. If you are unclear of something important that the person said, contact him or her and ask for clarification.
- Send a thank-you note to the person you interviewed as a follow-up.

7.6 Public Speaking

The fear of speaking in public, although quite common and quite strong in some people, can be overcome by preparing a speech thoroughly and practicing positive thinking and relaxation. Learning how to give a speech is a valuable skill, one that you most likely will find much opportunity to use in the future.

The nature of a speech, whether formal or informal, is usually determined by the situation or context in which it is presented. **Formal speeches** usually call for a greater degree of preparation, might require special attire such as a suit or dress, and are often presented to larger groups who attend specifically to hear the presentation. A formal speech situation might exist when presenting an assigned speech to classmates, giving a presentation to a community group or organization, or presenting a speech at an awards ceremony. **Informal speeches** are more casual and might include telling a story among friends, giving a pep talk to your team at halftime, or presenting a toast at the dinner table.

Types of Speeches

The following are four common types of speeches:

- **Extemporaneous:** a speech in which the speaker refers to notes occasionally and that has a specific purpose and message. An example would be a speech given at a city council meeting.
- **Informative:** a speech used to share new and useful information with the audience. Informative speeches are based on fact, not opinion. Examples would include a speech on how to do something or a speech about an event.
- **Persuasive:** a speech used to convince the audience to side with an opinion and adopt a plan. The speaker tries to persuade the audience to believe something, do something, or change their behavior. Persuasive speeches use facts and research to support, analyze, and sell an opinion and plan. Martin Luther King's famous "I Have a Dream"

speech and Nelson Mandela's "Glory and Hope" speech are examples of persuasive speeches.

- **Commemorative:** a speech that honors an individual for outstanding accomplishments and exemplary character. Examples would be a speech honoring a historical figure, leader, teacher, athlete, relative, or celebrity.

Guidelines for Giving a Speech

A speech should always include a beginning, a middle, and an end. The **beginning,** or introduction, of your speech should spark the audience's interest, present your central idea, and briefly preview your main points. The **middle,** or body, of your speech should expand upon each of your main points in order to support the central idea. The **end,** or conclusion, of your speech should be memorable and should give your audience a sense of completion.

- **Be sincere and enthusiastic.** Feel what you are speaking about. Apathy is infectious and will quickly spread to your audience.
- **Maintain good but relaxed posture.** Don't slouch or lean. It's fine to move around a bit; it releases normal nervous tension. Keep your hands free to gesture naturally instead of holding on to note cards, props, or the podium so much that you will "tie up" your hands.
- **Speak slowly.** Oral communication is more difficult than written language and visual images for audiences to process and understand. Practice pausing. Don't be afraid of silence. Focus on communicating with the audience. By looking for feedback from the audience, you will be able to pace yourself appropriately.
- **Maintain genuine eye contact.** Treat the audience as individuals, not as a mass of people. Look at individual faces.
- **Speak in a genuine, relaxed, conversational tone.** Don't act or stiffen up. Just be yourself.
- **Communicate.** Focus on conveying your message, not "getting through" the speech. Focus on communicating with the audience, not speaking at or to it.
- **Use strategic pauses.** Pause briefly before proceeding to the next major point, before direct quotations, and to allow important or more complex bits of information to sink in.
- **Remain confident and composed.** Remember that listeners are generally "for you" while you are speaking, and signs of nervousness are usually undetectable. To overcome initial nervousness, take two or three deep breaths as you are stepping up to speak.

7.7 Oral Interpretation

Oral interpretation is the process of presenting a dramatic reading of a literary work or group of works. The presentation should be sufficiently dramatic to convey to the audience a sense of the particular qualities of the work. Here are the steps you need to follow to prepare and present an oral interpretation:

Guidelines for Oral Interpretation

1. **Choose a cutting,** which may be a single piece; a selection from a single piece; or several short, related pieces on a single topic or theme.
2. **Write** the introduction and any necessary transitions. The introduction should mention the name of each piece, the author, and, if appropriate, the translator. It should also present the overall topic or theme of the interpretation. Transitions should introduce and connect the parts of the interpretation.
3. **Rehearse,** using appropriate variations in volume, pitch, pace, stress, tone, gestures, facial expressions, and body language. If your cutting contains different voices (a narrator's voice and characters' voices, for example), distinguish them. Try to make your verbal and nonverbal expression mirror what the piece is saying. However, avoid movement—that's for drama. Practice in front of an audience or mirror, or use a video camera or tape recorder.
4. **Present** your oral interpretation. Before actually presenting your interpretation, relax and adopt a confident attitude. If you begin to feel stage fright, try to concentrate on the work you are presenting and the audience, not on yourself.

Interpreting Poetry

Here are some additional considerations as you prepare to interpret a poem. The way you prepare your interpretation of a poem will depend on whether the poem you have chosen is a lyric poem, a narrative poem, or a dramatic poem.

- A **lyric poem** has a single speaker who reports his or her own emotions.
- A **narrative poem** tells a story. Usually a narrative poem has lines belonging to the narrator, or person who is telling the story. The narrator may or may not take part in the action.

- A **dramatic poem** contains characters who speak. A dramatic poem may be lyrical, in which characters simply report emotions, or narrative, which tells a story. A dramatic monologue presents a single speaker at a moment of crisis or self-revelation and may be either lyrical or narrative.

Before attempting to dramatize any poem, read through the poem carefully several times. Make sure that you understand it well. To check your understanding, try to paraphrase the poem, or restate its ideas, line by line, in your own words.

7.8 Telling a Story

A story or narrative is a series of events linked together in some meaningful fashion. We use narratives constantly in our daily lives: to make a journal entry, to tell a joke, to report a news story, to recount a historical event, to record a laboratory experiment, and so on. When creating a narrative, consider all of the following elements:

Guidelines for Storytelling

- **Decide on your purpose.** Every story has a point or purpose. It may be simply to entertain or to share a personal experience, but it may have a moral or lesson.
- **Select a focus.** The focus for your narrative will depend largely on your purpose in telling it.
- **Choose your point of view.** The storyteller or narrator determines the point of view from which the story will be told. You can choose to speak in the *first person,* either as a direct participant in the events or as an observer (real or imagined) who witnessed the events firsthand, or in the *third person* voice to achieve greater objectivity.
- **Determine sequence of events.** The sequence of events refers to the order in which they are presented. Although it might seem obvious that stories should "begin at the beginning," this is not always the best approach. Some narratives begin with the turning point of the story to create a sense of drama and to capture the listeners' interest. Others begin at the end of the story and present the events leading up to this point in hindsight. Wherever you choose to begin the story, your narrative should present events in a logical fashion and establish a clear sense of direction for your listeners.
- **Determine duration of events.** Duration refers to how long something lasts. Everyone has experienced an event that seemed to last for hours, when in reality it only took minutes to occur. A good storyteller can likewise manipulate the duration of events in order to affect the way listeners experience them.
- **Select details carefully.** Make them consistent with your focus and make sure they are necessary to your purpose. A well-constructed story should flow smoothly, and should not get bogged down by irrelevant or unnecessary detail. Details can also establish the tone and style of the story and affect how listeners react to the events being described.
- **Choose characters.** All stories include characters who need to be developed so that they become real for listeners. Try to provide your listeners with vivid, concrete descriptions of the mental and physical qualities of important characters in the story. Remember that listeners need to understand and relate to the characters in order to appreciate their behavior.
- **Create dialogue.** Although it is possible to tell a story in which the characters do not speak directly, conversation and dialogue help to add life to a story. As with detail, dialogue should be used carefully. It is important that dialogue sound authentic, relate to the main action of the story, and advance the narrative.

7.9 Participating in a Debate

A debate is a contest in which two people or groups of people defend opposite sides of a proposition in an attempt to convince a judge or an audience to agree with their views. Propositions are statements of fact, value, or policy that usually begin with the word "resolved." The following are examples of typical propositions for debate:

RESOLVED	That lie detector tests are inaccurate. (proposition of fact)
RESOLVED	That imagination is more important than knowledge. (proposition of value)
RESOLVED	That Congress should prohibit the sale of handguns to private citizens. (proposition of policy)

The two sides in a debate are usually called the affirmative and the negative. The affirmative takes the "pro" side of the debate and argues in favor of the proposition, whereas the negative takes the "con" side and argues against the proposition. Using a single proposition to focus the debate ensures that the two sides argue or clash over a common topic. This allows the participants in the debate to develop their logic and ability to argue their positions persuasively.

Guidelines for Participating in a Debate

- **Be prepared.** In a debate, it will never be possible to anticipate all the arguments your opponent might make. However, by conducting careful and thorough research on both sides of the issue, you should be able to prepare for the most likely arguments you will encounter. You can prepare briefs or notes on particular issues in advance of the debate to save yourself preparation time during the debate.
- **Be organized.** Because a debate involves several speeches that concern the same basic arguments or issues, it is important that you remain organized during the debate. When attacking or refuting an opponent's argument, or when advancing or defending your own argument, be sure to follow a logical organizational pattern to avoid confusing the audience or the other team.
- **Take notes** by turning a long sheet of paper sideways. Draw one column for each speaker, taking notes on each speech going down one column, and recording notes about a particular argument or issue across the page as it is discussed in each successive speech.
- **Be audience-centered.** In arguing with your opponent, it is easy to forget the goal of the debate: to persuade your audience that your side of the issue is correct.
- **Prepare in advance** for the most likely arguments your opponents, will raise. Use time sparingly to organize your materials and think of responses to unanticipated arguments. Save time for the end of the debate, during rebuttal speeches, when it will be more valuable.

7.10 Preparing a Multimedia Presentation

Whether you use a simple overhead projector and transparencies or a PowerPoint presentation that involves graphics, video, and sound, multimedia technology can add an important visual element to a presentation. Consider the following guidelines to create a multimedia presentation:

Guidelines for a Multimedia Presentation

- **Use effective audiovisuals** that enhance understanding. The multimedia elements should add to the verbal elements, not distract from them. Be sure the content of the presentation is understandable, and that the amount of information—both verbal and visual—will not overwhelm audience members.
- **Make sure the presentation is clearly audible and visible.** Video clips or graphics may appear blurry on a projection screen or may not be visible to audience members in the back or on the sides of the room. Audio clips may sound muffled or may echo in a larger room or a room with different acoustics. When creating a multimedia presentation, be sure the presentation can be easily seen and heard from all parts of the room.
- **Become familiar with the equipment.** Well before the presentation, be sure you know how to operate the equipment you will need, that you know how to troubleshoot if the equipment malfunctions, and that the equipment you will use during the presentation is the same as that which you practiced with.
- **Check the room** to be sure it can accommodate your needs. Once you know where you will make your presentation, be sure the necessary electrical outlets and extension cords are available, that lights can be dimmed or turned off as needed, that the room can accommodate the equipment you will use, and so on.
- **Rehearse with the equipment.** Make sure that you can operate the equipment while speaking at the same time. Be sure that the multimedia elements are coordinated with other parts of your presentation. If you will need to turn the lights off in the room, make sure you can operate the equipment in the dark and can still see your note cards.

8.1 Preparing for Tests

Tests are a common part of school life. You take tests in your classes to show what you have learned in each class. In addition, you might have to take one or more standardized tests each year. Standardized tests measure your skills against local, state, or national standards and may determine whether you graduate, what kind of job you can get, or which college you can attend. Learning test-taking strategies will help you succeed on the tests you are required to take.

The following guidelines will help you to prepare for and take tests on the material you have covered in class.

Preparing for a Test

- **Know what will be covered on the test.** If you have questions about what will be covered, ask your teacher.
- **Make a study plan** to allow yourself time to go over the material. Avoid last-minute cramming.
- **Review the subject matter.** Use the graphic organizers and notes you made as you read as well as notes you took in class. Review any study questions given by your teacher.
- **Make lists** of important names, dates, definitions, or events. Ask a friend or family member to quiz you on them.
- **Try to predict questions** that may be on the test. Make sure you can answer them.
- **Get plenty of sleep** the night before the test. Eat a nutritious breakfast on the morning of the test.

Taking a Test

- **Survey the test** to see how long it is and what types of questions are included.
- **Read all directions and questions carefully.** Make sure you know exactly what to do.
- **Plan your time.** Answer easy questions first. Allow extra time for complicated questions. If a question seems too difficult, skip it and go back to it later. Work quickly, but do not rush.
- **Save time for review.** Once you have finished, look back over the test. Double-check your answers, but do not change answers too readily. Your first responses are often correct.

8.2 Strategies for Taking Standardized Tests

Standardized tests are given to large groups of students in a school district, a state, or a country. Statewide tests measure how well students are meeting the learning standards the state has set. Other tests, such as the SAT (Scholastic Aptitude Test) or ACT (American College Test), are used to help determine admission to colleges and universities. Others must be taken to enter certain careers. These tests are designed to measure overall ability or skills acquired so far. Learning how to take standardized tests will help you to achieve your goals.

You can get better at answering standardized test questions by practicing the types of questions that will be on the test. Use the Test Practice Workshop questions in this book and other sample questions your teacher gives you to practice. Think aloud with a partner or small group about how you would answer each question. Notice how other students tackle the questions and learn from what they do.

In addition, remember these points:

- **Rule out some choices** when you are not sure of the answer. Then guess from the remaining possibilities.
- **Skip questions that seem too difficult** and go back to them later. Be aware, however, that most tests allow you to go back only within a section.
- **Follow instructions exactly.** The test monitor will read instructions to you, and instructions may also be printed in your test booklet. Make sure you know what to do.

8.3 Answering Objective Questions

An **objective question** has a single correct answer. The following chart describes the kinds of questions you may see on objective tests. It also gives you strategies for tackling each kind of question.

Description	Guidelines
True/False You are given a statement and asked to tell whether the statement is true or false.	• If any part of a statement is false, then the statement is false. • Words like *all, always, never,* and *every* often appear in false statements. • Words like *some, usually, often,* and *most* often appear in true statements. • If you do not know the answer, guess. You have a 50/50 chance of being right.
Matching You are asked to match items in one column with items in another column.	• Check the directions. See if each item is used only once. Also check to see if some are not used at all. • Read all items before starting. • Match those items you know first. • Cross out items as you match them.
Short Answer You are asked to answer the question with a word, phrase, or sentence.	• Read the directions to find out if you are required to answer in complete sentences. • Use correct spelling, grammar, punctuation, and capitalization. • If you cannot think of the answer, move on. Something in another question might remind you of the answer.

8.4 Answering Multiple-Choice Questions

On many standardized tests, questions are multiple choice and have a single correct answer. The guidelines below will help you answer these kinds of questions effectively.

- **Read each question carefully.** Pay special attention to any words that are bolded, italicized, written in all capital letters, or otherwise emphasized.
- **Read all choices** before selecting an answer.
- **Eliminate** any answers that do not make sense, that disagree with what you remember from reading a passage, or that seem too extreme. Also, if two answers have exactly the same meaning, you can eliminate both.
- **Beware of distractors.** These are incorrect answers that look attractive because they are partially correct. They might contain a common misunderstanding, or they might apply the right information in the wrong way. Distractors are based on common mistakes students make.
- **Fill in circles completely** on your answer sheet when you have selected your answer.

8.5 Answering Reading Comprehension Questions

Reading comprehension questions ask you to read a passage and answer questions about it. These questions measure how well you perform the essential reading skills. Many of the Reading Assessment questions that follow each literature selection in this book are reading comprehension questions. Use them to help you learn how to answer these types of questions correctly. Work through each question with a partner using a "think aloud." Say out loud how you are figuring out the answer. Talk about how you can eliminate incorrect answers and determine the correct choice. You may want to make notes as you eliminate answers. By practicing this thinking process with a partner, you will be more prepared to use it silently when you have to take a standardized test.

The following steps will help you answer the reading comprehension questions on standardized tests.

- **Preview the passage and questions** and predict what the text will be about.
- **Use the reading strategies** you have learned to read the passage. Mark the text and make notes in the margins.
- **Reread the first question carefully.** Make sure you know exactly what it is asking.
- **Read the answers.** If you are sure of the answer, select it and move on. If not, go on to the next step.
- **Scan the passage** to look for key words related to the question. When you find a key word, slow down and read carefully.
- **Answer the question** and go on to the next one. Answer each question in this way.

8.6 Answering Synonym and Antonym Questions

Synonym or antonym questions give you a word and ask you to select the word that has the same meaning (for a synonym) or the opposite meaning (for an antonym). You must select the best answer even if none is exactly correct. For this type of question, you should consider all the choices to see which is best. Always notice whether you are looking for a synonym or an antonym. You will usually find both among the answers.

8.7 Answering Sentence Completion Questions

Sentence completion questions present you with a sentence that has one or two words missing. You must select the word or pair of words that best completes the sentence. The key to questions with two words missing is to make sure that both parts of the answer you have selected work well in the sentence.

8.8 Answering Constructed-Response Questions

In addition to multiple-choice questions, many standardized tests include **constructed-response questions** that require you to write essay answers in the test booklet. Constructed-response questions might ask you to identify key ideas or examples from the text by writing a sentence about each. In other cases, you will be asked to write a paragraph in response to a question about the selection and to use specific details from the passage to support your answer.

Other constructed-response questions ask you to apply information or ideas from a text in a new way. Another question might ask you to use information from the text in a particular imaginary situation. As you answer these questions, remember that you are being evaluated based on your understanding of the text. Although these questions may offer opportunities to be creative, you should still include ideas, details, and examples from the passage you have just read.

The following tips will help you answer constructed-response questions effectively:

- **Skim the questions first.** Predict what the passage will be about.
- **Use reading strategies** as you read. Underline information that relates to the questions and make notes. After you have finished reading, you can decide which of the details you have gathered to use in your answers.
- **List the most important points** to include in each answer. Use the margins of your test booklet or a piece of scrap paper.
- **Number the points** you have listed to show the order in which they should be included.
- **Draft your answer to fit** in the space provided. Include as much detail as possible in the space you have.
- **Revise and proofread** your answers as you have time.

8.9 Answering Essay Questions

An essay question asks you to write an answer that shows what you know about a particular subject. A simplified writing process like the one below will help you tackle questions like this.

1. Analyze the Question

Essay questions contain clues about what is expected of you. Sometimes you will find key words that will help you determine exactly what is being asked. See the chart below for some typical key words and their meanings.

Key Words for Essay Questions	
analyze; identify	break into parts, and describe the parts and how they are related
compare	tell how two or more subjects are similar; in some cases, also mention how they are different
contrast	tell how two or more subjects are different from each other
describe	give enough facts about or qualities of a subject to make it clear to someone who is unfamiliar with it
discuss	provide an overview and analysis; use details for support
evaluate; argue	judge an idea or concept, telling whether you think it is good or bad, or whether you agree or disagree with it
explain	make a subject clearer, providing supporting details and examples
interpret	tell the meaning and importance of an event or concept
justify	explain or give reasons for decisions; be persuasive
prove	provide factual evidence or reasons for a statement
summarize	state only the main points of an event, concept, or debate

2. Plan Your Answer

As soon as the essay prompt is clear to you, collect and organize your thoughts about it. First, gather ideas using whatever method is most comfortable for you. If you don't immediately have ideas, try freewriting for five minutes. When you **freewrite,** you write whatever comes into your head without letting your hand stop moving. You might also gather ideas in a cluster chart like the one on the following page. Then, organize the ideas you came up with. A simple outline or chart can help.

3. Write Your Answer

Start with a clear thesis statement in your opening paragraph. Your **thesis statement** is a single sentence that sums up your answer to the essay question. Then follow your organizational plan to provide support for your thesis. Devote one paragraph to each major point of support for your thesis. Use plenty of details as evidence for each point. Write quickly and keep moving. Don't spend too much time on any single paragraph, but try to make your answer as complete as possible. End your essay with a concluding sentence that sums up your major points.

4. Revise Your Answer

Make sure you have answered all parts of the question and included everything you were asked to include. Check to see that you have supplied enough details to support your thesis. Check for errors in grammar, spelling, punctuation, and paragraph breaks. Make corrections to your answer.

ACT. An **act** is a major division of a play. There are five acts in Shakespeare's *The Tragedy of Romeo and Juliet* (Unit 4).

ALLEGORY. An **allegory** is a work in which characters, events, or settings symbolize, or represent, something else. Yeats's poem "The Song of Wandering Aengus" in Unit 3 is traditionally read as an allegory for a person's aging.

ALLITERATION. **Alliteration** is the repetition of initial consonant sounds. Though alliteration usually refers to sounds at the beginnings of words, it can also be used to refer to sounds within words. The following line from Edgar Allan Poe's poem "The Bells," in Unit 3, contains two examples of alliteration:

> What a world of merriment their melody fore-
> tells!

ALLUSION. An **allusion** is a reference to a well-known person, event, object, or work from history or literature. For example, Martin Luther King Jr.'s speech "I Have a Dream" (Unit 2) contains several allusions to Biblical events and passages.

ANALOGY. An **analogy** is a comparison of two things that are alike in some ways but otherwise quite different. Often an analogy explains or describes something unfamiliar, by comparing it to something more familiar. In "It's Not Talent; It's Just Work" (Unit 2), Annie Dillard makes an analogy between life and a show.

ANECDOTE. An **anecdote** is usually a short account of an interesting, amusing, or biographical incident. Anecdotes are sometimes used in nonfiction writing as examples to help support an idea or opinion. In "An Ethnic Trump" (Unit 2), Gish Jen tells several anecdotes about raising her biracial son to underscore the problems that ethnicity raises in American society.

ANTAGONIST. An **antagonist** is a character or force in a literary work that is in conflict with a main character, or protagonist. The antagonist of Richard Connell's story "The Most Dangerous Game" (Unit 1) is General Zaroff. *See* Character.

APOSTROPHE. **Apostrophe,** which is common in poetry and speeches, is a method by which a speaker turns from the audience as a whole to address a single person or thing. For example, in *The Tragedy of Romeo and Juliet* (Unit 4), Juliet turns from the audience and addresses a speech to the night:

> Spread thy close curtain, love-performing
> Night,
> That th' runaway's eyes may wink, and Romeo
> Leap to these arms untalk'd of and unseen!
> Lovers can see to do their amorous rites
> By their own beauties, or, if love be blind,
> It best agrees with night. (III.ii.5–10)

ARCHETYPE. An **archetype** is a story, character, or theme that represents a familiar pattern repeated throughout literature and across cultures. For example, the story in which a character sets off on a quest or journey, experiences adventure and danger, and becomes wiser may be considered archetypal. An example of this is Graham Salisbury's story "The Ravine" (Unit 1).

ASIDE. An **aside** is a statement made by a character in a play that is intended to be heard by the audience but not by other characters on the stage. Romeo makes an aside in Act II, Scene ii, of Shakespeare's *The Tragedy of Romeo and Juliet* (Unit 4).

> **JULIET.** O Romeo, Romeo, wherefore art thou
> Romeo?
> Deny thy father and refuse thy name;
> Or, if thou wilt not, be but sworn my love,
> And I'll no longer be a Capulet.
> **ROMEO.** [*Aside.*] Shall I hear more, or shall I
> speak at this?

ASSONANCE. **Assonance** is the repetition of vowel sounds. An example is the repetition of the long *o* sound in the following line from Edgar Allan Poe's "The Bells" (Unit 3):

> From the molten-golden notes

ATMOSPHERE. *See* Mood.

AUTOBIOGRAPHY. An **autobiography** is the story of a person's life, written by that person. Maya Angelou's *I Know Why the Caged Bird Sings* (excerpted in Unit 3) is an example of an autobiography. *See* Biography *and* Memoir.

BALLAD. A **ballad** is a poem that tells a story and is written in four- to six-line stanzas, usually meant to be sung. Most ballads have regular rhythms and rhyme schemes and feature a refrain, or repetition of lines.

BIAS. **Bias** is a personal judgment about something, or a mental leaning in one direction or another.

BIOGRAPHY. A **biography** is the story of a person's life, told by someone other than that person. Lindsley Cameron's "Becoming a Composer" (Unit 2) is a biography. *See* Autobiography.

BLANK VERSE. **Blank verse** is unrhymed poetry with a rhythmic pattern known as iambic pentameter. Shakespeare used blank verse in his plays. The following are some typical lines:

> **JULIET.** 'Tis but they name that is my enemy;
> Thou art thyself, though not a Montague.
> What's Montague? It is nor hand nor foot,
> Nor arm nor face, nor any other part
> Belonging to a man. O, be some other name!

See Meter.

CHARACTER. A **character** is an individual that takes part in the action of a literary work. A character is usually a person but may also be a personified plant, animal, object, or imaginary creature. The main character, or protagonist, has the central role in a work and is in conflict with the antagonist.

Characters can also be classified in other ways. *Major characters* play significant roles in a work, and *minor characters* play lesser roles. A *flat character* shows only one quality, or character trait. A *round character* shows the multiple character traits of a real person. A *static character* does not change during the course of the action. A *dynamic character* does change.

CHARACTERIZATION. **Characterization** is the act of creating or describing a character. Writers create characters using three major techniques: showing what characters say, do, or think; showing what other characters say or think about them; and describing what physical features, dress, and personalities the characters display. The first two methods may be considered examples of *indirect characterization,* in which the writer *shows* what a character is like and allows the reader to judge the character. The third technique is considered *direct characterization,* in which the writer *tells* what the character is like. *See* Character.

CHORUS. In drama, a **chorus** is a group of actors who speak directly to the audience between scenes, commenting on the action of the play. In classical Greek drama, the chorus conveyed its message through a series of *odes,* or serious poems, which it sang throughout the play. In *The Tragedy of Romeo and Juliet* (Unit 4), a chorus opens Act II.

CHRONOLOGICAL ORDER. When telling a story in **chronological order,** the writer unfolds events in the order in which they occurred.

CLIMAX. The **climax** is the high point of interest and suspense in a literary work. The term also is sometimes used to describe the turning point of the action in a story or play, the point at which the rising action ends and the falling action begins. The climax in *The Tragedy of Romeo and Juliet* by Shakespeare (Unit 4) occurs in Act V with the deaths of both Romeo and Juliet in the Capulet tomb. *See* Plot.

COMEDY. A **comedy** is any lighthearted or humorous literary work with a happy ending, especially one prepared for the stage or the screen. Comedy is often contrasted with tragedy, in which the hero meets an unhappy fate. Comedies typically show characters with human limitations, faults, and misunderstandings. The action in a comedy usually progresses from initial order to a humorous misunderstanding or confusion and back to order again. Standard elements of comedy include mistaken identities, wordplay, satire, and exaggerated characters and events. *The Inspector-General* by Anton Chekhov (Unit 4) is an example of a comedy. *See* Tragedy.

COMIC RELIEF. **Comic relief** is a technique used to relieve the seriousness or emotional intensity of a literary work by introducing a humorous character or situation.

CONFLICT. A **conflict** is a struggle between two forces in a literary work. A plot introduces a conflict, develops it, and eventually resolves it. There are two types of conflict: external and internal. In an *external conflict,* the main character struggles against another character, against the forces of nature, against society or social norms, or against fate. In an *internal conflict,* the main character struggles against some element within himself or herself. In Richard Connell's "The Most Dangerous Game" (Unit 1), Rainsford is in an external conflict with General Zaroff who wants to kill him. Rainsford is also in an internal conflict over the decision to kill or be killed while playing General Zaroff's dangerous game. *See* Plot.

CONNOTATION. The **connotation** of a word is the set of ideas or emotional associations it suggests, in addition to its actual meaning. For example, the word *inexpensive* has a positive connotation, whereas the word *cheap* has a negative connotation, even though both words refer to "low cost." *See* Denotation.

CONSONANCE. Consonance is a kind of rhyme in which the consonant sounds of two words match, but the preceding vowel sounds do not, as in the words *wind* and *sound.* The following lines from Yeats's poem "The Song of Wandering Aengus" (Unit 3) provide an example:

> The silver apples of the moon,
> The golden apples of the sun.

COUPLET. A **couplet** is two lines of verse that rhyme. These lines from Shakespeare's *The Tragedy of Romeo and Juliet* (Unit 4) provide an example:

> But passion lends them power, time means, to meet,
> Temp'ring extremities with extreme sweet.

A *closed couplet* is a pair of rhyming lines that present a complete statement. A pair of rhyming iambic pentameter lines is also known as a *heroic couplet.*

DEDUCTIVE REASONING. Deductive reasoning is a pattern of thought that starts with a general idea and, using examples and facts, moves into a precise conclusion. *See* Inductive Reasoning.

DENOTATION. The **denotation** of a word is its dictionary meaning without any emotional associations. For example, the words *dirt* and *soil* share a common denotation. However, *dirt* has a negative connotation of uncleanliness, whereas *soil* does not. *See* Connotation.

DÉNOUEMENT. *See* Plot.

DESCRIPTION. A **description** is a picture in words. *Descriptive writing* is used to portray a character, an object, or a scene. Descriptions include *sensory details*—words and phrases that describe how things look, sound, smell, taste, or feel. In his poem "Local Sensibilities" (Unit 3), Wing Tek Lum appeals to the senses by using images to describe Hawaii in the following manner:

> When I think of Hawaii,
> I do not fancy myself lolling under palm trees,
> a backdrop of verdant cliffs, caressed by a balmy breeze;
> instead I give thanks for classmates and our family graves,

DIALECT. A **dialect** is a version of a language spoken by the people of a particular place, time, or social group. A *regional dialect* is one spoken in a particular place. A *social dialect* is one spoken by members of a particular social group or class. The following is an example of dialect from Toni Cade Bambara's story "Blues Ain't No Mockin Bird" (Unit 1):

> "Woulda," said Terry. "I woulda gone upside her head with my fist and—"
> "You woulda done whatcha always do—go cry to Mama, you big baby," said Tyrone.

DIALOGUE. Dialogue is conversation between two or more people or characters. Plays are made up of dialogue and stage directions. Fictional works are made up of dialogue, narration, and description. When dialogue is included in fiction or nonfiction, the speaker's words are enclosed in quotation marks.

DICTION. Diction, when applied to writing, refers to the author's choice of words. Much of a writer's style is determined by his or her diction—the types of words that he or she chooses. *See* Style.

DRAMA. A **drama** is a story told through characters played by actors. Dramas are divided into segments called *acts.* The script of a drama is made up of dialogue spoken by the characters and stage directions. Because it is meant to be performed before an audience, drama features elements such as lighting, costumes, makeup, properties, set pieces, music, sound effects, and the movements and expressions of actors. Two major types of drama are comedy and tragedy. *See* Comedy, Dialogue, Stage Directions, *and* Tragedy.

DRAMATIC IRONY. *See* Irony.

DRAMATIC MONOLOGUE. A **dramatic monologue** is a poem written in the form of a speech by a single character to an imaginary audience.

DRAMATIC POEM. A **dramatic poem** relies heavily on literary devices such as *monologue* (speech by a single character) or *dialogue* (conversation involving two or more characters). Often, dramatic poems tell stories. Types of dramatic poetry include the dramatic monologue and the soliloquy. *See* Dramatic Monologue *and* Soliloquy.

EPIC. An **epic** is a long story, often told in verse, involving heroes and gods. Grand in length and scope, an epic provides a portrait of an entire culture—of the legends, beliefs, values, laws, arts, and ways of life of a people. Famous epic poems include Homer's *The Odyssey* (Unit 5) and *The Iliad,* Virgil's *Aeneid,* Dante's *The Divine Comedy,* the anonymous Old English *Beowulf,* and Milton's *Paradise Lost.*

EPIPHANY. An **epiphany** is a moment of sudden insight in which the nature of a person, thing, or situation is revealed.

ESSAY. An **essay** is a short nonfiction work that presents a single main idea, or *thesis,* about a particular topic.

- An *expository,* or *informative, essay* explores a topic with the goal of informing or enlightening the reader. An example is Anna Quindlen's essay "Homeless" (Unit 6).
- A *persuasive essay* aims to persuade the reader to accept a certain point of view. Rachel Carson's *Silent Spring* (Unit 2) is an example of a persuasive essay.
- A *personal essay* explores a topic related to the life or interests of the writer. Personal essays are characterized by an intimate and informal style or tone. An example of a personal essay is "Us and Them" by David Sedaris (Unit 2).

EUPHEMISM. A **euphemism** is an indirect word or phrase used in place of a direct statement that might be considered too harsh or offensive. The phrase *pass away,* used instead of *die,* and the phrase *waste management,* used in place of *garbage collection,* are euphemisms. In *The Teacher Who Changed My Life* (Unit 2), Nicholas Gage chooses the term "reeducation camp" to describe the places communist guerrillas sent kids to indoctrinate them with communist ideas.

EXPOSITION. In a plot, the **exposition** provides background information, often about the characters, setting, or conflict. Exposition is also another word for *expository writing,* the type of writing that aims to inform or explain. *See* Plot.

EXTENDED METAPHOR. An **extended metaphor** is a point-by-point presentation of one thing as though it were another. The description is meant as an implied comparison, inviting the reader to associate the thing being described with something that is quite different from it. Eve Merriam's poem "Metaphor" (Unit 3) is an example of an extended metaphor. In this poem, morning is described as being a blank sheet of paper. Each day's activities, thoughts, and feelings are words on the paper.

FABLE. **Fables** are brief stories, often with animal characters, told to express morals. Famous fables include those of Aesop and Jean de La Fontaine.

FAIRY TALE. **Fairy tales** are stories that deal with mischievous spirits and other supernatural occurrences, often in medieval settings. "The White Snake" (Unit 5) is an example of a fairy tale.

FALLING ACTION. *See* Plot.

FANTASY. A **fantasy** is a literary work that contains highly unrealistic elements. Included as fantasy are stories that resemble fairy tales, involve the supernatural, or have imaginary characters and settings. *See* Magical Realism *and* Science Fiction.

FICTION. **Fiction** is any work of prose that tells an invented or imaginary story. The primary forms of fiction are the novel and the short story. *See* Novel *and* Short Story.

FIGURATIVE LANGUAGE. **Figurative language** is writing or speech meant to be understood imaginatively instead of literally. Many writers, especially poets, use figurative language to help readers see things in new ways. Types of figurative language, or **figures of speech,** include *hyperbole, metaphor, personification, simile,* and *understatement.*

FIGURES OF SPEECH. *See* Figurative Language.

FLASHBACK. A **flashback** interrupts the chronological sequence of a literary work and presents an event that occurred earlier. Writers use flashbacks most often to provide background information about characters or situations. In the short story "The Interlopers" (Unit 1), Saki uses flashbacks to provide readers with background information about Georg and Ulrich and their families' battle over the land.

FOIL. A **foil** is a character whose traits contrast with, and therefore highlight, the traits of another character. In Shakespeare's *The Tragedy of Romeo and Juliet* (Unit 4), Tybalt's fight-loving character acts as a foil to peace-loving Romeo.

FOLK LITERATURE. **Folk literature,** or *folklore,* refers to a body of cultural knowledge and beliefs passed from one generation to the next, both orally and in writing. Much of folk literature originated as part of the *oral tradition,* or the passing of a work, an idea, or a custom by word of mouth from generation to generation. *See* Folk Song, Folk Tale, *and* Oral Tradition.

FOLK SONG. **Folk songs** are traditional or composed songs typically made up of stanzas, a refrain, and a simple melody. A form of folk literature, folk songs are expressions of commonly shared ideas or feelings and may be narrative or lyric in style.

FOLK TALE. A **folk tale** is a brief story passed by word of mouth from generation to generation. Types of folk tales include fairy tales, tall tales, parables, and fables. "The Golden Lamb" (Unit 5) is an example of a folk tale. *See* Fable, Fairy Tale, Parable, *and* Tall Tale.

FOOT. *See* Meter.

FORESHADOWING. **Foreshadowing** is the act of presenting hints to events that will occur later in a story. In Ovid's epic poem "The Story of Dædalus and Icarus" (Unit 5), Dædalus's repeated warnings foreshadow Icarus's death.

FREE VERSE. **Free verse** is poetry that does not use regular rhyme, meter, or stanza division. Free verse may contain irregular line breaks and sentence fragments and tends to mimic the rhythm of ordinary speech. Most contemporary poetry is written in free verse. The poem "Local Sensibilities" by Wing Tek Lum (Unit 3) is an example of a poem written in free verse.

GENRE. A **genre** (zhän′ rə) is a type or category of literary composition. Major genres of literature include fiction, nonfiction, poetry, and drama. *See* Drama, Fiction, Poetry, *and* Prose.

HAIKU. A **haiku** is a traditional Japanese three-line poem containing five syllables in the first line, seven in the second, and five in the third. The syllable pattern is often lost when a haiku is translated into English. A haiku presents a single vivid image, often of nature or the seasons, intended to evoke in the reader a specific emotional or spiritual response.

HERO. A **hero** is a character whose actions are inspiring and courageous. In early literature, a hero was often part divine and had remarkable abilities, such as magical power, superhuman strength, or great courage. Odysseus in Homer's *The Odyssey* (Unit 5) is one such hero. In contemporary literature, the term *hero* often refers to any main character.

HYPERBOLE. **Hyperbole** (hī pür′ bə lē′) is an overstatement, or exaggeration, used for dramatic effect.

IAMB. *See* Meter.

IAMBIC PENTAMETER. *See* Meter.

IDIOM. An **idiom** is an expression that cannot be understood from the meanings of its separate words but must be learned as a whole.

IMAGE. An **image** is a picture formed in the mind of a reader.

IMAGERY. **Imagery** is language that creates pictures by appealing to the senses of sight, sound, touch, taste, and smell. *See* Description *and* Figurative Language.

INDUCTIVE REASONING. **Inductive reasoning** is a pattern of thought that starts with specific details and uses them to make a general, broader conclusion. Inductive reasoning is often used in persuasive writing. *See* Deductive Reasoning.

INFORMATIONAL TEXT. An **informational text** is a form of nonfiction that aims at conveying or explaining information. Examples of informational texts include reference materials, articles, editorials, and how-to writing.

INTERNAL MONOLOGUE. An **internal monologue** reveals the private thoughts and emotions of the first-person narrator of a story.

IRONY. **Irony** is the difference between appearance and reality—in other words, what seems to be and what really is. Types of irony include the following: *dramatic irony,* in which something is known by the reader or audience but unknown to the characters; *verbal irony,* in which a writer or character says one thing but means another; and *irony of situation,* in which an event occurs that violates the expectations of the characters, the reader, or the audience. Verbal irony occurs in "The Most Dangerous Game" (Unit 1) when General Zaroff states, "We do our best to preserve civilization here." This statement is ironic because his pastime of killing men for sport is the antithesis of civilization. Irony of situation occurs in the same story when Rainsford, a devoted hunter, is forced to become the hunted.

LEGEND. A **legend** is a story that is passed down through generations and is often based on real events or characters from the past. Unlike myths, legends are usually considered to be historical; however, they may contain elements that are fantastic or unverifiable.

LYRIC POEM. A **lyric poem** is a highly musical type of poetry that expresses the emotions of a speaker. Lyric poems are often contrasted with narrative poems, which have storytelling as their main purpose. Edgar Allan Poe's "The Bells" (Unit 3) is an example of lyric poetry. *See* Poetry.

MAGICAL REALISM. **Magical realism** is a kind of fiction that is for the most part realistic but that contains elements of fantasy. It originated in the works of Latin American writers and reflects the fact that

Latin American culture often accepts as everyday life incidents that Europeans would consider "fantastic occurrences."

MEMOIR. A **memoir** is a type of autobiography that focuses on one incident or period in a person's life. Memoirs are often based on a person's memories of, and reactions to, historical events. Nicholas Gage's memoir *The Teacher Who Changed My Life* (Unit 2) focuses on his school years and the teacher who pushed him to overcome his troubled past as a Greek refugee through the use of writing. *See* Autobiography.

METAPHOR. A **metaphor** is a comparison in which one thing is spoken of or written about as if it were another. This figure of speech invites the reader to make a comparison between the writer's actual subject—the *tenor* of the metaphor—and another thing to which the subject is likened—the *vehicle* of the metaphor. Eve Merriam employs this metaphor in her poem "Metaphor" (Unit 3): "Morning is / a new sheet of paper / for you to write on." The tenor of the metaphor is "morning," and the vehicle of the metaphor is "new sheet of paper." *See* Extended Metaphor *and* Figurative Language.

METER. **Meter** is a regular rhythmic pattern in poetry. The pattern is determined by the number of beats, or stresses, in each line. Stressed and unstressed syllables are divided into rhythmical units called *feet*. Feet commonly used in poetry are as follows:

Type of Foot	Stress Pattern	Example
iamb (iambic)	an unstressed syllable followed by a stressed syllable	◡ / in**sist**
trochee (trochaic)	a stressed syllable followed by an unstressed syllable	/ ◡ **free**dom
anapest (anapestic)	two unstressed syllables followed by one stressed syllable	◡ ◡ / unim**pressed**
dactyl (dactylic)	one stressed syllable followed by two unstressed syllables	/ ◡ ◡ **fe**verish
spondee (spondaic)	two stressed syllables	/ / baseball

Terms used to describe the number of feet in a line include the following:
monometer for a one-foot line
dimeter for a two-foot line
trimeter for a three-foot line
tetrameter for a four-foot line
pentameter for a five-foot line
hexameter, or *Alexandrine,* for a six-foot line
heptameter for a seven-foot line
octameter for an eight-foot line

A complete description of the meter of a line includes both the term for the type of foot used most often in the line and the term for the number of feet in the line. The most common meters are *iambic tetrameter* and *iambic pentameter*. The following are examples of each:

iambic tetrameter

◡ / ◡ / ◡ / ◡ /
O slow | ly, slow | ly rose | she up

iambic pentameter

◡ / ◡ / ◡ / ◡ / ◡ /
The cur | few tolls | the knell | of part | ing day

MOOD. **Mood,** or *atmosphere,* is the emotion created in the reader by part or all of a literary work. The writer can evoke in the reader an emotional response—such as fear, discomfort, longing, or anticipation—by working carefully with descriptive language and sensory details. "The Scarlet Ibis" (Unit 1) is characterized by a haunted, lonely mood.

MORAL. A **moral** is a lesson that relates to the principles of right and wrong and is intended to be drawn from a story or other work of literature.

MOTIF. A **motif** is any element that appears in one or more works of literature or art. Examples of common folk-tale motifs found in oral traditions throughout the world include the granting of three wishes, the trial or quest, and the magical metamorphosis or transformation of one thing into another. "Cinderella," "The Ugly Duckling," and the Arthurian "Sword in the Stone" are examples of the transformation motif, in which persons or creatures of humble station are revealed to be exceptional. Much can be revealed about a literary work by studying the motifs within it. In *The Tragedy of Romeo and Juliet* (Unit 4), the motif of the stars is significant because it underscores the importance of fate in the play.

MOTIVATION. A **motivation** is a force that moves a character to think, feel, or behave in a certain way. Juliet, in *The Tragedy of Romeo and Juliet* (Unit 4), is motivated by love to fake her own death in hopes that she will be reunited with Romeo when she awakes.

MYTH. A **myth** is a traditional story, rooted in a particular culture, that deals with gods, goddesses, and other supernatural beings, as well as human heroes. Myths often embody religious beliefs and values and explain natural phenomena. Every early culture around the globe has produced its own myths. "Echo and Narcissus" (Unit 5) is an example of a myth.

NARRATION. Narration is a type of writing that tells a story, or describes events.

NARRATIVE POEM. A **narrative poem** is one that tells a story. "The Song of Wandering Aengus" by W. B. Yeats in Unit 3 is an example of a narrative poem. *See* Poetry.

NARRATOR. A **narrator** is a character or speaker who tells a story. The writer's choice of narrator is important to the story and determines how much and what kind of information readers will be given about events and other characters. The narrator in a work of fiction may be a major or minor character or simply someone who witnessed or heard about the events being related. A *reliable narrator* gives a trustworthy account of events. An *unreliable narrator* cannot be trusted. *See* Point of View *and* Speaker.

NONFICTION. **Nonfiction** writing explores real people's lives, places, things, events, and ideas. Essays, autobiographies, biographies, and news articles are all types of nonfiction. *See* Prose.

NOVEL. A **novel** is a long work of fiction. Often, novels have involved plots, many characters, and numerous settings. An excerpt from William Least Heat-Moon's novel *Blue Highways: A Journey into America* appears in Unit 6.

OCTET. An **octet** is a stanza of poetry containing eight lines. *See* Stanza.

ODE. An **ode** is a poem to honor or praise someone or something.

ONOMATOPOEIA. **Onomatopoeia** is the use of words or phrases that sound like the things to which they refer. Examples of onomatopoeia include words such as *buzz, click,* and *pop.* In Edgar Allan Poe's "The Bells" (Unit 3), sleigh bells make the onomatopoeic sound "tinkle, tinkle, tinkle."

ORAL TRADITION. The **oral tradition** is the passing of a work, an idea, or a custom by word of mouth from generation to generation. Common works found in the oral traditions of peoples around the world include folk tales, fables, fairy tales, tall tales, nursery rhymes, proverbs, legends, myths, parables, riddles, charms, spells, and ballads. *See* Folk Tale, Legend, Myth, *and* Parable.

OXYMORON. An **oxymoron** is a word or group of words that contradict themselves. Words like *bittersweet* and *pianoforte* (literally, "soft-loud") are oxymorons.

PARABLE. A **parable** is a very brief story told to teach a moral lesson. The most famous parables are those told by Jesus in the Bible.

PARADOX. A **paradox** is a seemingly contradictory statement, idea, or event that may actually be true. Some paradoxes present unresolvable contradictory ideas. An example of such a paradox is the statement, "This sentence is a lie." If the sentence is true, then it is false; if it is false, then it is true. *See* Irony *and* Oxymoron.

PARALLELISM. **Parallelism** is a rhetorical device in which a writer emphasizes the equal value or weight of two or more ideas by expressing them in the same grammatical form. *See* Rhetorical Device.

PARODY. A **parody** is a literary work that closely imitates the style of another work for humorous purposes. Parodies often exaggerate elements of the original work to create a comic effect.

PERSONIFICATION. **Personification** is a figure of speech in which an animal, a thing, a force of nature, or an idea is described as if it were human or is given human characteristics. In *The Odyssey* (Unit 5), Homer personifies dawn by giving it hands: "Dawn spread out her finger tips of rose."

PERSUASION. **Persuasion,** or *persuasive writing,* is intended to change or influence the way a reader thinks or feels about a particular issue or idea.

PLOT. A **plot** is the series of events related to a central conflict, or struggle. A plot typically introduces a conflict, develops it, and eventually resolves it. A plot often contains the following elements, although it may not include all of them and they may not appear in precisely this order:

- The **exposition,** or introduction, sets the tone or mood, introduces the characters and setting, and provides necessary background information.
- The **rising action** occurs as the conflict is developed and intensified.
- The **climax** is the high point of interest or suspense.
- The **falling action** consists of all the events that follow the climax.
- The **resolution,** or dénouement (dā' nü män´), is the point at which the central conflict is ended, or resolved.

See Climax *and* Exposition.

POETRY. Poetry is a major type of literature. It features imaginative and musical language carefully chosen and arranged to communicate experiences, thoughts, or emotions. It differs from prose in that it compresses meaning into fewer words and often uses meter, rhyme, and imagery. Poetry is usually arranged in lines and stanzas as opposed to sentences and paragraphs, and it can be more free in the ordering of words and the use of punctuation. Types of poetry include narrative, dramatic, and lyric. *See* Dramatic Poem, Lyric Poem, Meter, Narrative Poem, *and* Rhyme.

POINT OF VIEW. Point of view is the vantage point, or perspective, from which a story is told—in other words, who is telling the story. In **first-person point of view,** the story is told by someone who participates in or witnesses the action; this person, called the narrator, uses words such as *I* and *we* in telling the story. **Second-person point of view** uses the word *you* and addresses the reader directly, positioning the reader in the story. In **third-person point of view,** the narrator usually stands outside the action and observes; the narrator uses words such as *he, she, it,* and *they.* There are two types of third-person point of view: limited and omniscient. In *limited point of view,* the thoughts of only the narrator or a single character are revealed. In *omniscient point of view,* the thoughts of all the characters are revealed. "The Scarlet Ibis" (Unit 1) is told from the omniscient point of view. *See* Narrator.

PRIMARY SOURCE. *See* Source.

PROPAGANDA. The intentional use of false arguments to persuade others is called **propaganda.** Propaganda most often appears in nonfiction writing. There are many types of propaganda:

- A **glittering generality** is a statement given to make something sound more appealing than it actually is.
- **Spin** is a technique of creating manipulative and misleading statements in order to slant public perception of the news.
- **Circular reasoning** is the error of trying to support an opinion by restating it in different words.
- Words that stir up strong feelings, both positive and negative, are called **loaded words.**
- **Bandwagon appeal** is a statement that plays to a person's desire to be part of the crowd—to be like everyone else and do what everyone else is doing.
- A **stereotype** is an overgeneralization about a group of people based on a lack of knowledge or experience.

PROSE. Prose is the broad term used to describe all writing that is not drama or poetry, including fiction and nonfiction. Types of prose writing include novels, short stories, essays, and news stories. Most biographies, autobiographies, and letters are written in prose.

PROSE POEM. A **prose poem** is a passage of prose that makes such extensive use of poetic language that the line between prose and poetry becomes blurred. "Bread" by Margaret Atwood (Unit 3) is a prose poem.

PROTAGONIST. A **protagonist** has the central role in a literary work. Sanger Rainsford is the protagonist of Richard Connell's story "The Most Dangerous Game" (Unit 1). *See* Antagonist.

PROVERBS. Proverbs, or *adages,* are traditional sayings, such as "You can lead a horse to water, but you can't make it drink."

PUN. A **pun** is a play on words that involves either two words that sound alike but have different meanings or a word with two or more meanings. In Act III of Shakespeare's *The Tragedy of Romeo and Juliet* (Unit 4), Mercutio's line, "Ask for me tomorrow, and you shall find me a grave man" is a pun. The word *grave,* in this context, means "having serious thoughts." However, he is also hinting that he might be dead and in a grave tomorrow.

PURPOSE. A writer's **purpose** is his or her aim, or goal. People usually write with one or more of the following purposes: to inform or explain (*expository writing*); to portray a person, place, object, or event (*descriptive writing*); to convince people to accept a position and respond in some way (*persuasive writing*); and to express thoughts or ideas, or to tell a story (*narrative writing*). *See* Description, Exposition, Narration, *and* Persuasion.

QUATRAIN. A **quatrain** is a stanza of poetry containing four lines. *See* Stanza.

QUINTAIN. A **quintain** is a stanza of poetry containing five lines. *See* Quintet and Stanza.

QUINTET. A **quintet** is a stanza of poetry containing five lines. *See* Quintain and Stanza.

REFRAIN. A **refrain** is a line or group of lines repeated in a poem or song. Many ballads contain refrains.

REPETITION. **Repetition** is a writer's intentional reuse of a sound, word, phrase, or sentence. Writers often use repetition to emphasize ideas or, especially in poetry, to create a musical effect. *See* Rhetorical Device.

RESOLUTION. *See* Plot.

RHETORICAL DEVICE. A **rhetorical device** is a technique used by a speaker or a writer to achieve a particular effect, especially to persuade or influence. Common rhetorical devices include parallelism, repetition, and rhetorical questions. *See* Parallelism, Repetition, *and* Rhetorical Question.

RHETORICAL QUESTION. A **rhetorical question** is a question asked for effect but not meant to be answered. In the speech "I Have a Dream" (Unit 2), Martin Luther King Jr. asks the rhetorical question, "When will you be satisfied?"

RHYME. **Rhyme** is the repetition of sounds in words. Types of rhyme include the following:

- *end rhyme* (the use of rhyming words at the ends of lines)
- *internal rhyme* (the use of rhyming words within lines)
- *exact rhyme* (in which the rhyming words end with the same sound or sounds, as in *moon* and *June*)
- *slant rhyme* (in which the rhyming sounds are similar but not identical, as in *rave* and *rove*)
- *sight rhyme* (in which the words are spelled similarly but pronounced differently, as in *lost* and *ghost* or *give* and *thrive*)

RHYME SCHEME. A **rhyme scheme** is the pattern of end rhymes designated by assigning a different letter of the alphabet to each rhyme. For example, the rhyme scheme for Theodore Roethke's poem "My Papa's Waltz" (Unit 3) is *abab.*

The whiskey on your breath	*a*
Could make a small boy dizzy;	*b*
But I hung on like death:	*a*
Such waltzing was not easy.	*b*

RHYTHM. **Rhythm** is the pattern of beats, or stresses, in a line of poetry. Rhythm can be regular or irregular. A regular rhythmic pattern in a poem is called a *meter.* *See* Meter.

RISING ACTION. *See* Plot.

ROMANCE. **Romance** is a term used to refer to the following four types of literature:

- medieval stories about the adventures and loves of knights
- novels and other fiction involving exotic locations and extraordinary or mysterious events and characters
- nonrealistic fiction in general
- in popular, modern usage, love stories of all kinds

SATIRE. **Satire** is humorous writing or speech intended to point out errors, falsehoods, foibles, or failings. It is written for the purpose of reforming human behavior or human institutions.

SCENE. A **scene** is a short section of a play that usually marks changes of time and place.

SCIENCE FICTION. **Science fiction** is highly imaginative fiction containing fantastic elements based on scientific principles, discoveries, or laws. Ray Bradbury's short story "A Sound of Thunder" in Unit 6 is an example of science fiction.

SENSORY DETAILS. *See* Description.

SEPTET. A **septet** is a stanza of poetry containing seven lines. *See* Stanza.

SESTET. *See* Stanza.

SETTING. The **setting** of a literary work is the time and place in which it occurs, together with all the details used to create a sense of a particular time period and location. Writers create setting by various means. In drama, the setting is often revealed by the stage set and the costumes, though it may be revealed through what the characters say about their environs. In fiction, setting is most often revealed by means of description of such elements as landscape, scenery, buildings, furniture, clothing, the weather, and the season. It can also be revealed by how characters talk and behave. In "The Scarlet Ibis" (Unit 1), the setting is important because it has become a part of Doodle's character.

SHORT STORY. A **short story** is a brief work of fiction. Short stories are typically crafted carefully to develop a plot, a conflict, characters, a setting, a mood, and a theme, all within relatively few pages. *See* Fiction *and* Genre.

SIMILE. A **simile** is a comparison of two seemingly unlike things using the word *like* or *as*. N. Scott Momaday uses this figure of speech in his poem "A Simile" (Unit 3):

> What did we say to each other
> that now we are as the deer....

SOLILOQUY. In drama, a **soliloquy** is a speech delivered by a character alone on stage that reveals the character's thoughts and feelings. In Shakespeare's *The Tragedy of Romeo and Juliet* (Unit 4), Juliet's speech, "Farewell! God knows when we shall meet again..." (Act IV, Scene iii, lines 14–58), is an example of a soliloquy.

SONNET. A **sonnet** is a fourteen-line poem, usually in iambic pentameter, that follows one of a number of different rhyme schemes. The *English, Elizabethan,* or *Shakespearean sonnet* is divided into four parts: three quatrains and a final couplet. The rhyme scheme of such a sonnet is *abab cdcd efef gg.* The sonnets that open Act I and Act II of Shakespeare's *The Tragedy of Romeo and Juliet* (Unit 4) are examples. The *Italian* or *Petrarchan sonnet* is divided into two parts: an octave and a sestet. The rhyme scheme of the octave is *abbaabba*. The rhyme scheme of the sestet can be *cdecde, cdcdcd,* or *cdedce. See* Meter, Rhyme Scheme, *and* Stanza.

SOURCE. A **source** is evidence of an event, an idea, or a development. A *primary source* is direct evidence, or proof that comes straight from those involved. Primary sources include official documents as well as first-hand accounts, such as diaries, letters, photographs, and paintings done by witnesses or participants. A *secondary source* offers commentary or analysis of events, ideas, or primary sources.

SPEAKER. The **speaker** is the character who speaks in, or narrates, a poem—the voice assumed by the writer. The speaker and the writer of a poem are not necessarily the same person. The speaker in Shu Ting's poem "Gifts" (Unit 3) expresses faith in the human spirit by narrating the poem through the eyes of a pond. *See* Narrator.

SPIRITUAL. **Spirituals** are religious songs from the African-American folk tradition.

STAGE DIRECTIONS. **Stage directions** are notes included in a play, in addition to the dialogue, for the purpose of describing how something should be performed on stage. Stage directions describe setting, lighting, music, sound effects, entrances and exits, properties, and the movements of characters. They are usually printed in italics and enclosed in brackets or parentheses.

STANZA. A **stanza** is a group of lines in a poem. The following are some types of stanzas:

two-line stanza	couplet
three-line stanza	triplet or tercet
four-line stanza	quatrain
five-line stanza	quintain or quintet
six-line stanza	sestet
seven-line stanza	septet
eight-line stanza	octave

STEREOTYPE. A **stereotype** is an overgeneralization about a group of people based on a lack of knowledge and experience. See *Propaganda.*

STYLE. **Style** is the manner in which something is said or written. A writer's style is characterized by such elements as word choice (or *diction*), sentence structure and length, and other recurring features that distinguish his or her work from that of another. One way to think of a writer's style is as his or her written personality.

SUSPENSE. **Suspense** is a feeling of expectation, anxiousness, or curiosity created by questions raised in the mind of a reader or a viewer.

SYMBOL. A **symbol** is anything that stands for or represents both itself and something else. Writers use two types of symbols—conventional, and personal or idiosyncratic. A *conventional symbol* is one with traditional, widely recognized associations. Such symbols include doves for peace; the color green for jealousy; winter, evening, or night for old age; wind for change or inspiration. A *personal* or *idiosyncratic symbol* is one that assumes its secondary meaning because of the special use to which it is put by a writer. In James Hurst's short story "The Scarlet Ibis" (Unit 1), the scarlet ibis becomes a symbol of the uniqueness and fragility of the character Doodle.

TALL TALE. A **tall tale** is a story, often lighthearted or humorous, that contains highly exaggerated, unrealistic elements. Stories about Paul Bunyan are tall tales.

TANKA. A **tanka** is a traditional Japanese poem consisting of five lines, with five syllables in the first and third lines and seven syllables in the other lines

(5-7-5-7-7). The syllable pattern is often lost when a tanka is translated into English. Tanka uses imagery to evoke emotions in the reader, but its images are often more philosophical and less immediate than those in a haiku. *See* Haiku.

TERCET. A **tercet** is a stanza of poetry containing three lines. *See* Triplet and Stanza.

THEME. A **theme** is a central message or perception about life that is revealed through a literary work. Themes may be stated or implied. A *stated theme* is presented directly, whereas an *implied theme* must be inferred. Most works of fiction do not have a stated theme but rather several implied themes. A *universal theme* is a message about life that can be understood by people of most cultures. The theme of Leslie Marmon Silko's story "The Man to Send Rain Clouds" (Unit 1) is that the culture of a people should be respected.

THESIS. A **thesis** is a main idea that is supported in a work of nonfiction. The thesis of "Trapped New Orleans Pets Still Being Rescued" by Laura Parker and Anita Manning (Unit 2) is that it is not too late to save the trapped animals and that their rescue is important because of the animals' impact on people's lives.

TONE. **Tone** is the emotional attitude toward the reader or toward the subject implied by a literary work. Examples of the different tones that a work may have include familiar, ironic, playful, sarcastic, serious, and sincere. In the poem "Cold as Heaven" (Unit 3), Judith Ortiz Cofer employs a wistful and reminiscent tone.

TRAGEDY. A **tragedy** is a work of literature, particularly a drama, that tells the story of the fall of a person of high status. It celebrates the courage and dignity of a tragic hero in the face of inevitable doom. Sometimes, that doom is made inevitable by a tragic flaw. Today, the term *tragedy* is used more loosely to mean any work that has an unhappy ending. *The Tragedy of Romeo and Juliet* (Unit 4) is a tragedy. *See* Comedy, Tragic Flaw, *and* Tragic Hero.

TRAGIC FLAW. A **tragic flaw** is a weakness of personality that causes the tragic hero to make unfortunate choices.

TRAGIC HERO. A **tragic hero** is the main character in a tragedy. Romeo is a tragic hero in the play *The Tragedy of Romeo and Juliet*, written by Shakespeare (Unit 4).

TRICKSTER. In folk literature, the **trickster,** who is either an animal or a shape-shifter, is a cunning or deceptive character who not only annoys the gods, but is also often responsible for bringing important gifts to humanity, such as fire.

TRIPLET. A **triplet** is a stanza of poetry containing three lines. *See* Tercet and Stanza.

UNDERSTATEMENT. An **understatement** is an ironic statement that de-emphasizes something important, as in "He's sort of dead, I think."

VOICE. **Voice** is the way a writer uses language to reflect his or her unique personality and attitude toward topic, form, and audience. A writer expresses voice through tone, word choice (diction), and sentence structure. *See* Diction *and* Tone.

Glossary of Vocabulary Words

Pronunciation Key

Vowel Sounds

a	hat	i	sit	ü	blue, stew	ə	extra
ā	play	ī	my	oi	boy		under
ä	star	ō	go	ou	wow		civil
e	then	ô	paw, born	u	up		honor
ē	me	u̇	book, put	ʉ	burn		bogus

Consonant Sounds

b	but	j	jump	p	pop	th (underlined)	the
ch	watch	k	brick	r	rod	v	valley
d	do	l	lip	s	see	w	work
f	fudge	m	money	sh	she	y	yell
g	go	n	on	t	sit	z	pleasure
h	hot	ŋ	song, sink	th	with		

A

a • bashed (ə bashd´) *adj.*, embarrassed; upset

a • broad (ə brôd´) *adv.*, far and wide

a • brupt • ly (ə brup[t]´ lē) *adv.*, suddenly

a • byss (ə bis´ *or* a´ bis[']) *n.*, huge empty space or depth

a • dorn • ment (ə dôrn´ mənt) *n.*, ornament; decoration

a • men • i • ty (ə me´ nə tē) *n.*, something that makes life easier or more pleasant

a • non • y • mous (ä nän´ ə məs) *adj.*, unknown; not identified

a • skance (ə skans´) *adv.*, with disapproval or scorn

a • sun • der (ə sun´ dər) *adv.*, far apart; widely separated

a • veng • er (ə venj´ ər) *n.*, one who gets back at someone for a wrongdoing

ab • hor (əb hôr´) *v.*, hate; detest

abyss (ə bis´ *or* a bis´ *or* a´ bis[']) *n.*, bottomless gulf or pit; immeasurable space

ac • cost (ə kôst´) *v.*, approach in a challenging or an aggressive way

ad • ja • cent (ə jā´ sənt) *adj.*, near

ad • vent (ad´ vent') *n.*, coming into being or use; arrival

ad • ver • sar • y (ad´ və[r] ser' ē *or* ad´ və[r] se' rē) *n.*, enemy; opponent

ad • ver • si • ty (ad vʉr´ sə tē) *n.*, misfortune; hardship; suffering

af • flict (ə flikt´) *v.*, distress or trouble so severely as to cause suffering

af • flu • ence (a´ flü əns) *n.*, wealth

ag • ile (a´ jəl) *adj.*, able to move with quick and easy grace; coordinated; nimble

al • le • vi • ate (ə lē´ vē āt') *v.*, relieve; make less severe

aloof (ə lüf´) *adj.*, unfriendly

am • nes • ty (am´ nə stē) *n.*, pardon for past offenses

am • o • rous (a´ mə rəs *or* am´ rəs) *adj.*, being in love; enamored (usually followed by the word *of*)

an • a • lyt • i • cal (a' nə li´ti kəl) *adj.*, skilled in breaking a whole into its parts and examining their relationships

an • i • mate (a´ nə māt´) *v.*, to give life to; to move to action

an • o • nym • i • ty (an' ə nim´ ə tē) *n.*, quality or state of not being known

anx • i • ety (aŋ zī´ ə tē) *n.*, worry; sense of unease or dread

ap•er • ture (ap´ ər chu̇r') *n.*, hole; gap; opening

ap • per • tain (a' pər tān´) *v.*, connecting to; being a part of

ar • chae • ol • o • gist (är' kē ä´ lə jist) *n.*, scientist who studies ancient societies by examining fossils, artifacts (including tools and other objects), and monuments

as • sail (ə sāl´) *v.*, attack physically

as • suage (ə swāj´ *or* ə swäzh´ *or* ə swäzh´) *v.*, lessen the intensity of; ease; relieve

as • ton • ished (ä stän´ ish ed) *adj.*, surprised

au • thor • i • tar • i • an (ə thär' ə ter´ ē ən) *adj.*, expecting or demanding strict obedience

aug • ment (ôg ment´) *v.*, add to

B

bal • my (bä´ mē *or* bäl´ mē) *adj.*, soothing; mild; pleasant

bar • ba • rous (bär´bə rəs) *adj.*, cruel; uncultured

bar • rage (bə räzh´ *or* bə räj´) *n.*, rapid outpouring of many things at once

bar • ren (bar´ən) *adj.*, lacking interest or charm

be • guil • ing (bi gī´ [ə]liŋ) *adj.*, outwardly charming but inwardly deceptive

be • guile (bi gī[ə]l´) *v.*, lead by deception; distract

C

ca • reen (kə rēn´) *v.*, lurch from side to side, especially while moving rapidly

ca • ress (kə res´) *v.*, to touch in a loving manner

can • dor (kan´ dər *or* kan´ dôr') *n.*, openness; honesty; frankness

cha • grin (shə grin´) *n.*, feeling of annoyance caused by failure or disappointment

chasm (ka´ z'm) *n.*, marked division, separation, or difference

chide (chīd) *v.*, scold

clam • or (kla´ mər) *n.*, loud, continuous noise

com • pel (kəm pel´) *v.*, force to do something

com • pro • mise (käm´prə mīz) *v.*, settle by having both sides make concessions

con • done (kən dōn´) *v.*, forgive or overlook an offense

con • fer (kən fʉr´) *v.*, grant; bestow

con • jure (kän´ jər) *v.*, appeared as if by magic

con • sci • en • tious (kän' shē en´ shəs) *adj.*, careful; thoughtfully upright

con • sort (kən sôrt´ *or* kän´ sôrt *or* kän' sôrt´) *v.*, to keep company (typically with undesirable people; usually followed by the word *with*)

con • tem • pla • tive • ly (kən tem´plə tiv´lē) *adv.*, in a thoughtful or studious way

con • trive (kən trīv´) *v.*, plan; scheme; bring about by strategy or with difficulty

cor • dial (kôr´ jəl) *adj.*, friendly

creed (krēd) *n.*, set of fundamental beliefs

cun • ning (kun´ niŋ) *adj.*, clever; sly

cur • tail (ker['] tāl´) *v.*, make less, as if by cutting away a part

D

dap • pled (da´pəld) *adj.*, spotted

de • ci • pher (dē sī´ fər) *v.*, interpret

de • note (di nōt´) *v.*, indicate

de • nounce (dē nouns´) *v.*, condemn strongly as evil or wrong

de • pre • ci • ate (di prē´ shē āt') *v.*, lower in value

de • te • ri • o • rat • ing (di tir´ ē ə rāt' ing *or* dē tir´ ē ə rāt' ing) *adj.*, worsening

de • vise (di vīz´) *v.*, work out or create; plan; invent

dep • ri • va • tion (de' prə vā´ shən) *n.*, state of having something taken away

det • ri • men • tal (de' trə men´ t'l) *adj.*, harmful

dex • ter • i • ty (dek ster´ ə tē) *n.*, skill in using one's hands or body

di • as • po • ra (dī as´ p[ə] rə) *n.*, the movement, migration, or scattering of a people away from an established or ancestral homeland

di • lap • i • dat • ed (də la´ pə dā' təd) *adj.*, decayed; fallen into partial ruin through neglect

dis • arm • ing (dis ärm´iŋ) *adj.*, friendly or harmless

dis • cern (di sʉrn´) *v.*, recognize; identify

dis • cord (dis´ kôrd) *n.*, harsh or unpleasant; a combination of musical sounds that strikes the ear harshly; lack of agreement or harmony

dis • course (dis kôrs´) *v.*, talk; converse

dis • creet (di skrēt´) *adj.*, showing careful reserve in speech or action

dis • creet • ly (di skrēt´ lē) *adv.*, with care not to be noticed

dis • in • te • grate (dis['] in´ tə grāt') *v.*, to break or fall apart

dis • po • si • tion (dis' pə zi´ shən) *n.*, nature; frame of mind; temperament

dis • pute (dis pyüt´) *v.*, to debate

dis • traught (di strôt´) *adj.*, upset by doubt or mental conflict

do • min • ion (də min´ yən) *n.*, domain; absolute ownership; governed territory

dote (dōt) *v.*, adore; spoil; make much of

drawl (drôl) *n.*, a slow manner of speech

du • pli • ca • tion (dü' pli kā´ shən) *n.*, act or process of duplicating; a copy or double

dupe (düp *or* dyüp) *v.*, deceived by trickery

E

e • la • tion (i lā´ shən) *n.*, state of great joy and pride

e • lude (ē lüd´) *v.*, avoid

ear • nest (ʉrn´ əst) *adj.*, sincere; serious

eer • ie (ir´ ē) *adj.*, frightening because of strangeness or mysteriousness

el • o • quence (el´ ə kwən[t]s) *n.*, speech or writing that is vivid, forceful, and persuasive

em • bit • ter (im bi´tər) *v.*, make resentful

ema • ci • ate (i mā´ shē āt') *v.*, to waste away physically; to lose flesh so as to become very thin

en • deav • our (in de´vər) *n.*, attempt; effort; British spelling of "endeavor"

en • mi • ty (en´ mə tē) *n.*, hostility; hate; bitterness

en • thralled (en thräld´) *adj.*, being charmed or captivated

enig • mat • ic (e' nig['] ma´ tik *or* ē' nig['] ma´ tik) *adj.*, mysterious; hard to figure out

eu • tha • nize (yü´ thə nīz') *v.*, to kill or permit the death of hopelessly sick or injured animals in a relatively painless way for reasons of mercy

ev • a • nesce (ev' ə nes´) *v.*, disappear

ex • ca • va • tion (ek' skə vā´ shən) *n.*, the process of digging up or unearthing objects, especially historical remains

ex • cru • ci • at • ing (ik skrü´ shē ā tiŋ) *adj.*, very painful

ex • ile (eg´ zīl' *or* eg´ zī' əl) *n.*, period of forced absence from one's country

ex • ot • ic (ig zä´ tik) *adj.*, not native to the place where found; foreign; strikingly different or mysterious

F

fe • ro • cious (fə rō´ shəs) *adj.*, fierce; violent

fi • nesse (fə nes´) *n.*, refinement; delicacy

flour • ish (flʉr´ ish) *v.*, wave in the air

for • ay (fôr´ ā' *or* fär´ ā *or* fô rā´ *or* fə rā´) *n.*, sudden invasion or attack

for • mal • i • ty (fôr ma´ lə tē) *n.*, behavior that follows accepted forms, rules, or customs

for • mi • da • ble (fôrm´ mə də bəl) *adj.*, causing fear or dread; inspiring awe

frail (frāl) *adj.*, weak; slight

fray (frā) *n.*, noisy quarrel or fight

fu • tile (fyü´ tl) *adj.*, having no result or effect

G

gloat (glōt) *v.*, to consider in a victorious and boastful way

glow • er (glaůr *or* glaů ər *or* glō[ə]r) *v.*, look at with anger

griev • ance (grē´ vəns) *n.*, complaint; cause of suffering

gro • tesque (grō tesk´) *adj.*, bizarre; absurdly awkward

H

haste (hāst) *n.*, state of hurry

haugh • ty (hô´ tē) *adj.*, proud; arrogant; self-important; conceited

her • bi • vore ([h]ʉr´ bə vôr') *n.*, plant-eating animal

her • e • sy (her´ i sē) *n.*, contradiction of what is generally believed to be true or right

hi • er • ar • chy (hī´ ər är' kē) *n.*, group classified by grade or rank

hom • age (ä´ mij *or* hä´ mij) *n.*, respectful admiration

hys • ter • i • cal (his ter´ i kəl) *adj.*, displaying excessive emotion, often through uncontrollable laughter or tears

I

i • con • ic (ī kä´ nik) *adj.*, having characteristics of an icon, an object of uncritical devotion

im • mi • nent (im´ ə nənt) *adj.*, likely to happen soon

im • mod • er • ate (i[m] mä´ d[ə] rət) *adj.*, excessive; unrestrained

im • ped • i • ment (im ped´ ə mənt) *n.*, obstacle; roadblock; interference

im • pla • ca • ble (im' pla´ kə bəl) *adj.*, resisting change; stubborn

im • pos • ter (im päs´ tər) *n.*, person pretending to be what he or she is not

im • pu • ta • tion (im' pyə tā´ shən) *n.*, accusation; insinuation

in • a • li • en • a • ble (i' nāl´ yə nə bəl *or* i' nā´ lē ə nə bəl) *adj.*, impossible to give up or take away

in • aus • pi • cious (in' ô spi´ shəs) *adj.*, unfavorable; unlucky

in • ces • sant • ly (in' se´ sn´[t] lē) *adv.*, constantly; endlessly

in • con • se • quen • tial (in['] kän[t]' sə kwen[t]´ shəl) *adj.*, unimportant
in • dig • nant • ly (in dig´nənt lē) *adv.*, feeling anger as a reaction to ungratefulness
in • dis • crim • i • nate (in' dis krim´ nət *or* in' dis kri´ mə nət) *adj.*, reckless; without concern for distinction
in • dis •crim • i • nate • ly (in' dis krim´ ən at lē *or* in' dis kri´ mən at lē) *adv.*, without picking and choosing
in • e • vit • a • ble (in ev´ə tə b'l) *adj.*, unavoidable
in • es • ti • ma • ble (i nes´ tə mə bəl) *adj.*, too valuable to be measured
in • ev • i • ta • ble (i ne´ və tə bəl) *adj.*, unable to be avoided
in • fal • li • bil • i • ty (in fal' ə bil´ i tē) *n.*, correctness; incapacity for error
in • fest (in fest´) *v.*, overrun in large numbers
in • flict (in flikt´) *v.*, cause something unpleasant to be endured
in • sid • i • ous (in si´ dē əs) *adj.*, having a gradual but serious effect
in • so • lent (in[t]´ s[ə] lənt) *adj.*, rude and nasty
in • un • da • tion (in' ən dā´ shən) *n.*, flood; deluge
ir • i • des • cent (ir' i de´ sənt) *adj.*, having shifting changes in color

K

keen (kēn) *adj.*, sharp; more intense
knell (nel) *v.*, sounds ominously or mournfully

L

la • ment (lə ment´) *v.*, express sadness or regret
lan • guor (laŋ´gər) *n.*, lack of interest; listlessness
las • so (la´ sō') *v.*, capture as if with rope
lat • i • tude (la´ tə tüd) *n.*, freedom of action and choice
lav • ish (la´ vish) *v.*, provide, as with gifts, praise, and the like
le • git • i • ma • cy (li ji´ tə mə sē) *n.*, authenticity
le • thal (lē´ th'l) *adj.*, deadly
leg • end • ar • y (le´ jən dār' ē) *adj.*, famous; mythical; of legend
lithe (līth *or* līth) *adj.*, graceful
loath • some (lōth´ səm) *adj.*, disgusting; detestable
lu • mi • nous (lü´ mə nəs) *adj.*, having a glowing quality

M

ma • raud • er (mə rôd´ ər) *n.*, person who raids and plunders
man • date (man´ dāt') *n.*, formal order; command
mar • tyr (mär´ tər) *n.*, person who sacrifices his or her life for the sake of a principle or cause
mel • an • cho • ly (me´ lən kä' lē) *adj.*, sad; gloomy; depressed
men • tor (men´ tôr') *n.*, a trusted teacher; a role model
mer • e • tri • cious (mer' ə tri´ shəs) *adj.*, attractive in a false, showy way
mer • it (mer´ ət *or* me´ rət) *v.*, be worthy of
mis • ad • ven • ture (mis' əd ven´ chər) *n.*, unlucky accident; mishap
mo • bil • i • ty (mō bi´ lə tē) *n.*, ability to move from place to place
mor • ti • fy (môr´ tə fī) *v.*, embarrass deeply
mu • ti • late (myü´ tə lāt') *v.*, cut or tear up; damage
mu • ti • ny (myü´ t'n ē) *n.*, revolt against authority

N

noc • tur • nal (näk tur´ n´l) *adj.*, active at night

O

o • di • ous (ō´ dē əs) *adj.*, hateful; offensive
o • rig • i • nal (ə rij´ ə n'l) *adj.*, new; fresh and unusual; inventive
ob • lig • a • to • ry (ō blig´ ə tō rē) *adj.*, required
obliv • i • ous (ə bli´ vē əs) *adj.*, unaware; not paying attention
om • i •nous (ä´ mə nəs) *adj.*, suggesting that disaster is about to occur
omen (ō´ mən) *n.*, symbol or sign of future misfortune
or • nate (ôr nāt´) *adj.*, elaborately or excessively decorated

P

pa • le • on • tol • o • gist (pā' lē än' tä´ lə jist *or* pā' lē ən tä´ lə jist) *n.*, scientist who studies Earth's geological periods by using fossil remains

pal • pa • ble (pal´pə bəl) *adj.*, able to be touched or felt

pal • pi • tat • ing (pal´ pə tāt' iŋ) *adj.*, beating rapidly; fluttering

par • si • mo • ny (pär´ sə mō' nē) *n.*, stinginess; extreme thriftiness

pee • vish (pē´ vish) *adj.*, hard to please; irritable

pen • chant (pen´ chənt) *n.*, a strong and continued inclination; liking

pen • sive • ly (pen´ siv lē) *adv.*, in a thoughtful or troubled manner

per • fo • rat • ed (pʉr fə rāt´ əd) *adj.*, punctured

per • ni • cious (pər nish´ əs) *adj.*, fatal; deadly

per • pet • u • ate (pʉr pe´ chü āt) *v.*, to continue

per • va • sive • ly (per vā´ siv lē) *adv.*, widespread; in a manner that affects many

pin • ion (pin´ yən) *v.*, bind

pli • ant (plī´ ənt) *adj.*, easy to handle; capable of being reshaped

plight (plīt) *n.*, dangerous situation

plum • age (plüm´ ij) *n.*, bird's feathers

plume (plüm) *v.*, preen, or clean and arrange one's feathers

plun • der (plʉn´ dər) *v.*, steal or take by trickery or by force

pon • der • ous (pän´ d[ə] rəs) *adj.*, heavy; bulky; massive

pos • ter • i • ty (päs ter´ ə tē) *n.*, all future generations

pre • cip • i • tous (pri si´ pə təs) *adj.*, steep

pre • clude (pri klüd´) *v.*, prevent or make impossible beforehand; rule out in advance

pre • dom • i • nant (prē däm´ ə nənt) *adj.*, dominant; ruling; controlling

pre • dom • i • nate (pri dä´ mə nāt') *v.*, holding advantage in numbers

pre • mo • ni • tion (prə mə ni´ shən) *n.*, vision of the future

pre • sent • a • ble (pri zent' ə bl) *adj.*, looking good enough to be shown to other people

pri • ma • cy (prī´ mə sē) *n.*, state of being first in time, place, or rank

pro • cure (prō kyür´) *v.*, get or bring about by some effort

pro • vi • sion (prə vi´ zhən) *n.*, food and other supplies

proph • e • cy (prä´ fə sē) *n.*, prediction; foretelling of later event

pru • dence (prü´ d'n[t]s) *n.*, sound judgment

pru • dent (prü´ d'nt) *adj.*, cautious; careful

Q

quar • rel (kwôr´ əl) *v.*, to argue

quiz • zi • cal • ly (kwiz´i kə lē) *adv.*, in a perplexed manner

R

ran • cor (raŋ´ kər) *n.*, deep anger or ill will; bitter hate

re • it • er • ate (rē it´ ə rāt') *v.*, repeat

re • pose (ri pōz´) *n.*, peace; rest; sleep

re • strain • ing (ri strān´ iŋ) *adj.*, controlling; disciplining

re • tri • bu • tion (re' trə byü´ shən) *n.*, punishment

re • vere (re vir´) *v.*, regard with deep respect and love

rec • on • cil • i • a • tion (re' kən si' lē ā´shən) *n.*, settling of problems or disputes

rep • ri • mand (re´ prə mand') *v.*, scold harshly

res • o • lu • tion (rez' ə lʉ´ shün) *n.*, expression of will or intent; determination

res • ti • tu • tion (res' tə tü´ shən) *n.*, repayment, especially for wrongdoing

rev • el • ry (re´ vəl rē) *n.*, noisy partying or merrymaking

rid • dled (ri´ d'ld) *adj.*, pierced many times

S

sage (sāj) *adj.*, wise

sal • low (sa´ lō) *adj.*, of a grayish yellow color

sear (sir) *v.*, burn; destroy

sel • dom (sel´dəm) *adv.*, rarely; infrequently

sin • gu • lar (siŋ´ gyə lər) *adj.*, one-of-a-kind; exceptional; unique

slan • der (slan´ dər) *n.*, false statement damaging another person's character or reputation

so • lace (sä´ ləs) *n.*, relief; consolation

so • lic • i • tous • ly (sə li´sə təs lē) *adv.*, showing concern

sparse (spärs) *adj.*, thin; meager

spurn (spʉrn) *v.*, reject or refused with scorn

stealth (stelth) *n.*, sneakiness; secretiveness
strat • a • gem (stra´ tə jəm *or* stra´ tə jem') *n.*, a trick or scheme to achieve an aim
strick • en (stri´ kən) *adj.*, plagued by fear, disease, or misfortune
strife (strīf) *n.*, a fight or quarrel
su • per • in • ten • dence (sü' p[ə]rin ten´ dən[t]s) *n.*, supervision; management
sub • mis • sion (səb mi´ shən) *n.*, yielding; surrendering
sub • ver • sive (səb vʉr´ siv *or* səb vʉr´ ziv) *adj.*, with a goal to undermine or corrupt
suc • ces • sion (sək se´ shən) *n.*, repeated following of one thing after another
sul • len • ly (sul´ ən lē) *adv.*, gloomily
sup • ple • ness (sʉ´ pəl nəs) *n.*, flexibility
swift (swift) *adj.*, fast
syn • the • tic (sin the´ tik) *adj.*, produced artificially

T

tan • gi • ble (tan´jə bəl) *adj.*, having substance or reality; capable of being touched
teem • ing (tē´ miŋ) *adj.*, active with many beings; swarming
ten • ant (te´ nənt) *n.*, resident
ten • ta • tive (ten´tə tiv) *adj.*, hesitant
ter • min • a • tion (tʉr' mə nā´ shən) *n.*, ending; conclusion
tra • verse (trə vʉrs´) *v.*, turn; travel across
tran • scend (tran[t] send´) *v.*, go beyond the limits of; overcome
tran • scribe (tran skrīb´) *v.*, write down; make a written copy of
trans • gres • sion (trans gresh´ ən) *n.*, offense
trans • lu • cent (tran[t]s lü´ sənt) *adj.*, clear; transparent
treach • er • ous (tre´ chə rəs *or* trech´ rəs) *adj.*, traitorous; disloyal
trib • u • la • tion (tri' byə lā´shən) *n.*, suffering caused by oppression or persecution
trill (tril) *n.*, trembling, vibrating sound
trun • dle (trun´ dl') *v.*, to move or roll slowly
tu • mult (tü´ məlt' *or* tyü´ məlt' *or* tʉ´ məlt') *n.*, loud confusion
tyr • an • ny (tir´ ə nē) *n.*, oppressive power

U

u • nique (yü nēk´) *adj.*, being without a like or equal
u • sur • er (yü´zhər ər *or* yüzh´ rər) *n.*, a person who lends money at an extremely high interest rate
un • bri • dled (ən' brī´ d'ld) *adj.*, without restraint; left free

---

V

val • or (va´ lər) *n.*, personal bravery
ver • dant (vʉr´ d'nt) *adj.*, green
ver • sa • tile (vʉr´ sə t'l) *adj.*, able to perform a variety of functions
vis • cer • al (vi´ sə rəl) *adj.*, intensely emotional; felt as if in the internal organs
vo • lu • mi • nous • ly (və lü´ mə nəs lē) *adv.*, largely; fully
vor • tex (vôr´ teks) *n.*, whirlpool; eddy

W

wal • low (wä´ lō') *v.*, allow oneself to accept a state of helplessness
wield (wēld) *v.*, carry, as with a weapon

Literary Acknowledgments

A&C Black Publishers Ltd. "The Inspector-General" by Anton Chekhov, adapted by Michael Frayn. Reprinted by permission of A&C Black Publishers Ltd.

Arte Publico Press. "Gentle Communion" is reprinted with permission from the publisher of *Communion* by Pat Mora (Houston: Arte Publico Press-University of Houston © 1991). "Oral History" is reprinted with permission from the publisher of *My Own True Name* by Pat Mora (© 2000 Arte Publico Press–University of Houston).

Associated Press. "Glory and Hope" by Nelson Mandela, Inaugural Address, May 10, 1994, Associated Press. Reprinted by permission.

Elizabeth Barnett. "An Ancient Gesture" by Edna St. Vincent Millay from *Collected Poems,* HarperCollins, copyright © 1954, 1982 by Norma Millay Ellis. All rights reserved. Used by permission of Elizabeth Barnett, literary executor.

Susan Bergholz Literary Services. "Aha Moment" by Julia Alvarez. Copyright © 2000 by Julia Alvarez. First published in *O, The Oprah Magazine* 1, no. 5 (November 2000). Reprinted by permission of Susan Bergholz Literary Services, New York. All rights reserved. "Only Daughter" by Sandra Cisneros. Copyright © 1990 by Sandra Cisneros. First published in *Glamour,* November 1990. Reprinted by permission of Susan Bergholz Literary Services, New York. All rights reserved.

Bilingual Press/Editorial Bilingüe. "Cold as Heaven" from *Reaching for the Mainland and Selected New Poems* by Judith Ortiz Cofer. Reprinted by permission of Bilingual Press/Editorial Bilingüe, Arizona State University, Tempe, AZ.

Brandt & Hochman Literary Agents, Inc. "The Devil and Daniel Webster" by Stephen Vincent Benét. Copyright © 1936 by Stephen Vincent Benét. Copyright © renewed 1964 by Thomas C. Benét, Stephanie B. Mahin and Rachel Benét Lewis. Reprinted by permission of Brandt & Hochman Literary Agents, Inc. "The Most Dangerous Game" by Richard Connell. Copyright © 1924 by Richard Connell. Copyright renewed © 1952 by Louise Fox Connell. Used by permission of Brandt & Hochman Literary Agents, Inc.

Walker Brents. "The Sea God Poseidon" retold by Walker Brents. Reprinted by permission of the author.

Brooks Permissions. "Martin Luther King, Jr." by Gwendolyn Brooks. Reprinted by Consent of Brooks Permissions.

Calyx Books. "Tears of Autumn" by Yoshiko Uchida was published in The Forbidden Stitch: An Asian American Women's Anthology (Calyx Books, 1989). Copyright © 1989, edited by Shirley Lim, et al.

Gladys Cardiff. "Combing" by Gladys Cardiff as appeared in *Puget Soundings,* March 1971. Reprinted by permission of Gladys Cardiff.

Diana Chang. "Saying Yes" by Diana Chang. Reprinted by permission of the author.

Mildred Clingerman. "Minister Without Portfolio" by Mildred Clingerman. Reprinted by permission.

Don Congdon Associates, Inc. "A Sound of Thunder" by Ray Bradbury. Reprinted by permission of Don Congdon Associates, Inc. Copyright © 1952 by Crowell Collier Publishing, renewed 1980 by Ray Bradbury.

Copper Canyon Press. "To the Oak" by Shu Ting, translated by Carolyn Kizer from *Cool, Calm, and Collected: Poems 1960–2000* by Carolyn Kizer. Reprinted by permission.

Denver Post. "TV Coverage of JFK's Death Forged Medium's Role" by Joanne Ostrow from *Denver Post,* November 16, 2003. Reprinted by permission of *Denver Post.*

Annie Dillard. "It's Not Talent; It's Just Work" by Annie Dillard from *Seventeen,* June 1979. Reprinted by permission of the author.

Eureka Productions. "The Star" by H.G. Wells from Graphic Classics: H.G. Wells. Reprinted by permission of Eureka Productions.

Farrar, Straus and Giroux, LLC. Excerpts from *The Odyssey* translated by Robert Fitzgerald. Copyright © 1961, 1963 by Robert Fitzgerald. Copyright renewed 1989 by Benedict R.C. Fitzgerald, on behalf of the Fitzgerald children. Reprinted by permission of Farrar, Straus and Giroux, LLC. "Gifts" by Shu Ting from *A Splintered Mirror: Chinese Poetry from the Democracy Movement* translated by Donald Finkel. Translation copyright © 1991 by Donald Finkel. Used by permission of North Point Press, a division of Farrar, Straus and Giroux, LLC. "Poetry" from *Isla Negra: A*

Notebook by Pablo Neruda, translated by Alastair Reid. Translation copyright © 1981 by Alastair Reid. Reprinted by permission of Farrar, Straus and Giroux, LLC. "Thank You, M'am" from *Short Stories* by Langston Hughes. Copyright © 1966 by Ramona Bass and Arnold Rampersad. Reprinted by permission of Hill and Wang, a division of Farrar, Straux and Giroux, LLC. "What Are Friends For" from *Cora Fry's Pillow Book* by Rosellen Brown. Copyright © 1994 by Rosellen Brown. Reprinted by permission of Farrar, Straus and Giroux, LLC.

Flannery Literary. "The Ravine" by Graham Salisbury from *On the Edge: Stories at the Brink,* copyright © 2000. Used by permission.

Friends of the Everglades. "For the Future of Florida: Repair the Everglades!" by Joette Lorion from *The Everglades Reporter,* copyright 1997. Reproduced by permission of the Friends of the Everglades.

Nicholas Gage. "The Teacher Who Changed My Life" by Nicholas Gage. Published in PARADE, December 17, 1989. Copyright © 1989. Reprinted by permission of the author.

Diane Glancy. "Without Title" from *Iron Woman* by Diane Glancy. Copyright © 1980, 1990 by Diane Glancy. Reprinted by permission of the author.

Graywolf Press. "Fifteen" by William Stafford. Copyright 1966, 1977, 1998 by the Estate of William Stafford. Reprinted from *The Way It Is: New & Selected Poems* with the permission of Graywolf Press, Saint Paul, Minnesota. "Otherwise" copyright 1996 by the Estate of Jane Kenyon. Reproduced from *Otherwise: New & Selected Poems* with the permission of Graywolf Press, Saint Paul, Minnesota.

Grove/Atlantic. "Indian Education" from *The Lone Ranger and Tonto Fistfight in Heaven* by Sherman Alexie. Copyright © 1993 by Sherman Alexie. Used by permission of Grove/Atlantic, Inc. "The Journey" from *Dream Work* by Mary Oliver. Copyright © 1986 by Mary Oliver. Reprinted by permission of Grove/Atlantic, Inc.

Hanging Loose Press. "The Past" from *Facing Shadows* © 1996 by Ha Jin. Used by permission of Hanging Loose Press.

Harcourt, Inc. "The Necklace" by Guy de Maupassant from *Adventures in Reading,* Laureate Edition, Grade 9, copyright © 1963 by Harcourt, Inc. and renewed 1991 by Deborah Jean Lodge, Alice Lodge, Jeanne M. Shutes, Jessica Sand, Lydia Winderman, Florence F. Potell, and Mary Rives Bowman, reprinted by permission of Harcourt, Inc. This material may not be reproduced in any form or by any means without the prior written permission of the publisher. "Sonnet" from *Spirits in Bondage: A Cycle of Lyrics* by C. S. Lewis. Copyright © 1984 by C. S. Lewis PTE Ltd. Reprinted with permission by Harcourt, Inc. "Women" from *Revolutionary Petunias & Other Poems,* © 1970 and renewed 1998 by Alice Walker. Reprinted by permission of Harcourt, Inc.

HarperCollins Publishers. From "The Burden of Expectations" from *The Girls of Summer: The U.S. Women's Soccer Team and How It Changed the World* by Jere Longman. Copyright © 2000 by Jere Longman. Reprinted by permission of HarperCollins Publishers.

Harvard University Press. "'Hope' is the thing with feathers." Reprinted by permission of the publishers and the Trustees of Amherst College from *The Poems of Emily Dickinson,* Ralph W. Franklin, ed., Cambridge, Mass.: The Belknap Press of Harvard University Press, Copyright © 1998 by the President and Fellows of Harvard College. Copyright © 1951, 1955, 1979, 1983 by the President and Fellows of Harvard College.

John Hawkins & Associates, Inc. "Journey" from *The Poison Kiss and Other Stories* by Joyce Carol Oates. Copyright © 1975 by Ontario Review. Reprinted by permission of John Hawkins & Associates, Inc.

Barbara Hogenson Agency. "The Princess and the Tin Box" from *The Beast in Me and Other Animals* by James Thurber. Copyright © 1948 by James Thurber. Copyright © renewed 1976 by Rosemary A. Thurber. Reprinted by arrangement with Rosemary A. Thurber and The Barbara Hogenson Agency. All rights reserved.

Julian Hope. From "Sheppey" from *The Collected Plays of W. Somerset Maugham* by W. Somerset Maugham. Reprinted by permission.

Houghton Mifflin Company. "All Watched Over by Machines of Loving Grace" from *Pill Versus the Springhill Mine Disaster* by Richard Brautigan. Copyright © 1965 by Richard Brautigan. Reprinted by permission of Houghton Mifflin Company. All rights reserved. "Courage," from *The Awful Rowing Toward God* by Anne Sexton. Copyright © 1975 by Loring Conant, Jr., Executor of the Estate of Anne Sexton. Reprinted by permission of Houghton Mifflin Company. All rights reserved. "Siren Song" from

Selected Poems, 1965–1975 by Margaret Atwood. Copyright © 1976 by Margaret Atwood. Reprinted by permission of Houghton Mifflin Company. All rights reserved. "The Obligation to Endure" from *Silent Spring* by Rachel Carson. Copyright © 1962 by Rachel L. Carson. Copyright © renewed 1990 by Roger Christie. Reprinted by permission of Houghton Mifflin Company. All rights reserved. "The Old Life" in *The Old Life* by Donald Hall. Copyright © 1996 by Donald Hall. Reproduced by permission of Houghton Mifflin Company. All rights reserved.

James Hurst. "The Scarlet Ibis" by James Hurst as appeared in *The Atlantic Monthly,* July 1960. Reprinted by permission of the author.

Indiana University Press. "The Story of Dædalus and Icarus" from *Metamorphoses* by Ovid, translated by Rolfe Humphries. Copyright © 1955, Indiana University Press. Reprinted by permission of Indiana University Press.

Kastaniotis Publishing. From "The Scattered Papers of Penelope" by Katerina Anghelaki-Rooke. Reprinted by permission of Kastaniotis Publishing.

Garrison Keillor. "How to Write a Letter" from *We Are Still Married.* Copyright © 1987 by International Paper Company. Reprinted by permission of Garrison Keillor.

Knight-Ridder News Service. "Light-struck or star-struck?" Knight-Ridder News Service, March 23, 2004. Reprinted by permission of Knight-Ridder News Service.

Jean Russell Larson. "The Golden Lamb" from *Palace in Bagdad: Seven Tales from Arabia* by Jean Russell Larson. Reprinted by permission of the author.

LexicOrient. "Encyclopaedia of the Orient: Samarra" from http://i-cias.com/e.o/samarra.htm. © 1996–2005 LexicOrient. All rights reserved. Reprinted by permission.

Little, Brown and Co., Inc. "Nameless, Tennessee" from *Blue Highways* by William Least Heat-Moon. Copyright © 1982, 1999 by William Least Heat-Moon. By permission of Little, Brown and Co., Inc. "Us and Them" from *Dress Your Family in Corduroy and Denim* by David Sedaris. Copyright © 2004 by David Sedaris. Reprinted by permission of Little, Brown and Company, Inc.

Liveright Publishing Corporation. "since feeling is first." Copyright 1926, 1954, © 1991 by the Trustees for the E. E. Cummings Trust. Copyright © 1985 by George James Firmage, from *Complete Poems: 1904–1962* by E. E. Cummings, edited by George J. Firmage. Used by permission of Liveright Publishing Corporation.

Lowenstein-Yost Associates, Inc. "Beware: Do Not Read This Poem" excerpted from the book, *New and Collected Poems* by Ishmael Reed. Copyright © 1989 by Atheneum. Permission granted by Lowenstein-Yost Associates, Inc.

Wing Tek Lum. "Local Sensibilities" by Wing Tek Lum. Reprinted by permission of the author.

N. Scott Momaday. "A Simile" by N. Scott Momaday from *The Gourd Dancer* (1976) by permission of Harper & Row Publishers, Inc. Reprinted by permission of the author.

National Geographic Society. "Cyclops Myth Spurred by 'One-Eyed' Fossils?" by Hillary Mayell, *National Geographic News,* February 5, 2003. Reprinted by permission.

National Japanese American Historical Society. 442nd Regimental Combat Team. Reprinted by permission.

New Directions Publishing Corp. "The Secret" by Denise Levertov from *Poems 1960–1967,* copyright © 1964 by Denise Levertov. Reprinted by permission of New Directions Publishing Corp.

Newsweek. "Designing the Future" by Anne Underwood from *Newsweek,* May 16, 2005, p. 40. Copyright © 2005 Newsweek, Inc. All rights reserved. Reprinted by permission.

The New York Times Co. "An Ethnic Trump" by Gish Jen, *The New York Times.* Copyright © 1996 by The New York Times Co. Reprinted with permission. "Birmingham Bomb Kills Negro Girls In Church; Riots Flare; 2 Boys Slain" by Claude Sitton from *New York Times*, September 16, 1963. Copyright © 1963. The New York Times all rights reserved. Used by permission and protected by the Copyright Laws of the United States. The printing, copying, redistribution, or retransmission of the Material without express written permission is prohibited. "Close Encounter of the Human Kind" by Abraham Verghese from *New York Times Magazine*, Sept. 18, 2005. Reprinted with permission.

Naomi Shihab Nye. "This Is Not Who We Are" by Naomi Shihab Nye, in *O, The Oprah Magazine,* April 2002. Used by permission of the author, Naomi Shihab Nye, 2005.

W. W. Norton & Company, Inc. "Hanging Fire," from *The Black Unicorn* by Audre Lorde. Copyright © 1978 by Audre Lorde. Used by permission of W. W. Norton & Company, Inc. "Purgatory." Copyright © 1965 by Maxine Kumin, from *Selected Poems 1960–1990* by Maxine Kumin. Used by permission of W. W. Norton & Company, Inc.

Harold Ober Associates Incorporated. "The Good Deed" from *The Good Deed and Other Stories* by Pearl S. Buck. Copyright © 1953 by Pearl S. Buck. Copyright renewed 1981. Reprinted by permission of Harold Ober Associates, Inc.

Simon Ortiz. "My Father's Song" by Simon Ortiz, as appeared in *Woven Stone,* University of Arizona Press. Used by permission of Simon Ortiz.

Penguin Group (USA) Inc. "Rules of the Game" from *The Joy Luck Club* by Amy Tan, copyright © 1989 by Amy Tan. Used by permission of G. P. Putnam's Sons, a division of Penguin Group (USA) Inc.

Peters Fraser & Dunlop Group Ltd. "The Sniper" from *Spring Sowing* by Liam O'Flaherty, (Copyright © The Estate of Liam O'Flaherty 1924) is reproduced by permission PFD (www.pfd.co.uk) on behalf of the Estate of Liam O'Flaherty.

Alan Pizzarelli. "driving out of the car wash..." by Alan Pizzarelli from *Hike.* Reprinted by permission of the author.

Princeton University Press. "Ithaca" by Constantine Cavafy from *Collected Poems* by C. P. Cavafy, translated by Edmund Keeley and Philip Sherrard. Copyright © 1975 by Edmund Keeley and Philip Sherrard. Reproduced by permission of Princeton University Press.

Dudley Randall Estate. "Ballad of Birmingham" by Dudley Randall, copyright 1963. Reprinted by permission of the Dudley Randall Estate.

Random House, Inc. "Blues Ain't No Mockin Bird" copyright © 1971 by Toni Cade Bambara, from *Gorilla, My Love* by Toni Cade Bambara. Used by permission of Random House, Inc. "Bread" from *Good Bones and Simple Murders* by Margaret Atwood, copyright © 1983, 1992, 1994, by O. W. Toad Ltd. A Nan Talese Book. Used by permission of Doubleday, a division of Random House, Inc. "Caged Bird" copyright © 1983 by Maya Angelou, from *Shaker, Why Don't You Sing?* by Maya Angelou. Used by permission of Random House, Inc. "New Directions" from *Wouldn't Take Nothing for My Journey Now* by Maya Angelou, copyright © 1993 by Maya Angelou. "Climbing Mount Fuji" from *Dave Barry Does Japan* by Dave Barry, copyright © 1992 by Dave Barry. Used by permission of Random House, Inc. "For the young who want to" from *The Moon is Always Female* by Marge Piercy, copyright © 1980 by Marge Piercy. Used by permission of Alfred A. Knopf, a division of Random House, Inc. "To be of use" from *Circles on the Water* by Marge Piercy, copyright © 1982 by Marge Piercy. Used by permission of Alfred A. Knopf, a division of Random House, Inc. "Harrison Bergeron" from *Welcome to the Monkey House* by Kurt Vonnegut, Jr., copyright © 1961 by Kurt Vonnegut, Jr. Used by permission of Dell Publishing, a division of Random House, Inc. "Homeless" copyright © 1987 by Anna Quindlen, from *Living Out Loud* by Anna Quindlen. Used by permission of Random House, Inc. "My Papa's Waltz" copyright © 1942 by Hearst Magazines, Inc., from *The Collected Poems of Theodore Roethke* by Theodore Roethke. Used by permission of Doubleday, a division of Random House, Inc. "The Feeling of Power" from *Isaac Asimov: The Complete Stories of Vol. 1* by Isaac Asimov, copyright © 1957 by Quinn Publishing Co. Copyright renewed 1985 by Isaac Asimov. Used by permission of Doubleday, a division of Random House, Inc. From *Swimming to Antarctica* by Lynne Cox. Copyright © 2004 by Lynne Cox. Used by permission of Alfred A. Knopf, a division of Random House, Inc. "Theme for English B" from *Collected Poems of Langston Hughes* by Langston Hughes, copyright © 1994 by The Estate of Langston Hughes. Used by permission of Alfred A. Knopf, a division of Random House, Inc. "Vision Quest" from *American Indian Myths and Legends* by Richard Erdoes and Alfonso Ortiz, editors. Copyright © 1984 by Richard Erdoes and Alfonso Ortiz. Reprinted by permission of Pantheon Books, a division of Random House, Inc.

Reiner Literary Agency. "Metaphor" from *It Doesn't Always Have to Rhyme* by Eve Merriam. Copyright © 1964, 1992 by Eve Merriam. Used by permission of Marian Reiner.

Scovil Chichak Galen Literary Agency, Inc. "History Lesson" by Arthur C. Clarke. Reprinted by permission of the author and the author's agents, Scovil Chichak Galen Literary Agency, Inc.

Seaver Books. "The Man to Send Rain Clouds" by Leslie Marmon Silko. Copyright © 1981 by Leslie Marmon Silko. Reprinted from *Storyteller* by Leslie

Marmon Silko, published by Seaver Books, New York, New York. Reprinted by permission of Seaver Books.

Seven Stories Press. "Furor Scribendi" by Octavia Butler. First published in *L. Ron Hubbard Presents Writers of the Future Volume IX*. Copyright © 1993 by Octavia Butler. Reprinted with permission.

Charlotte Sheedy Literary Agency. "Becoming a Composer" from *The Music of Light: The Extraordinary Story of Hikari and Kenzaburo Oe* by Lindsley Cameron. Reprinted by permission of Charlotte Sheedy Literary Agency.

Simon & Schuster, Inc. From "An 'A' in Failure" reprinted with the permission of Simon & Schuster Adult Publishing Group from *Creative Habit: Learn It and Use It for Life* by Twyla Tharp, Mark Reiter. Copyright © 2003 by W.A.T. Ltd. "There and Back Again." Reprinted with the permission of Simon & Schuster Adult Publishing Group from *Learning Joy from Dogs Without Collars* by Lauralee Summer. Copyright © 2003 by Lauralee Summer. "There Will Come Soft Rains." Reprinted with the permission of Scribner, an imprint of Simon & Schuster Adult Publishing Group, from *The Collected Poems of Sara Teasdale* by Sara Teasdale. Copyright © 1937 by The Macmillan Company.

SLL/Sterling Lord Literistic, Inc. "The Funeral" from *Whispers of Intimate Things* by Gordon Parks. Reprinted by permission of SLL/Sterling Lord Literistic, Inc. Copyright 1971 by Gordon Parks.

Smithsonian Migratory Bird Center. "When It Comes to Pesticides, Birds Are Sitting Ducks," by Mary Deinlein from *Migratory Bird Center* as appeared on nationalzoo.si.edu website. Reprinted by permission of the Smithsonian Migratory Bird Center, National Zoological Park.

Stanford University Press. From Haiku "At Takadachi in Mutsu Province" from *Basho and his Interpreters: Selected Hokku with Commentary*, translated by Makoto Ueda. Copyright © 1992 by the Board of Trustees of the Leland Stanford Jr. University. All rights reserved. Used with the permission of Stanford University Press, www.sup.org.

The Literary Estate of May Swenson. "The Universe" by May Swenson. Used with permission of The Literary Estate of May Swenson.

Theodore L. Thomas. "The Test" by Theodore L. Thomas. Reprinted by permission of the author.

Charles E. Tuttle Co., Inc. From *How to Haiku* by Bruce Ross. Copyright © 2002 by Bruce Ross. Reprinted by permission of Charles E. Tuttle Co., Inc. "The Mosquito" from *Vietnamese Legends* adapted by George F. Schultz, 1965. Used by permission of Charles E. Tuttle Co., Inc.

The University of Georgia Press. "American History" from *The Latin Deli: Prose & Poetry* by Judith Ortiz Cofer, published by The University of Georgia Press. Copyright © 1993 Judith Ortiz Cofer. Reprinted by permission of the publisher.

University of Pittsburgh Press. *American Sonnet* by Billy Collins. Copyright © 1991, Billy Collins. Reprinted with permission by University of Pittsburgh Press.

University of Virginia Press. "Sympathy" from *The Collected Poetry of Paul Lawrence Dunbar* edited by Joanne M. Braxton. Reprinted with permission of the University of Virginia Press.

USA TODAY. "Trapped New Orleans Pets Still Being Rescued" by Laura Parker and Anita Manning. *USA Today*, Oct. 6, 2005. Reprinted with permission.

Anthony Virgilio. "the blind musician..." from *Selected Haiku (Second Edition)* by Nicholas Virgilio. Reprinted by permission of Anthony Virgilio.

Wieser & Elwell, Inc. "Auto Wreck" by Karl Shapiro. Reprinted by permission of Wieser & Elwell, Inc.

Joanna H. Wos. "The One Sitting There" by Joanna H. Wos. Used by permission of the author.

Writers House, Inc. "I Have a Dream" by Martin Luther King Jr. Reprinted by arrangement with the Estate of Martin Luther King Jr., c/o Writers House, Inc. as agent for the proprietor New York, NY. Copyright 1963 by Martin Luther King Jr., copyright renewed 1991 by Coretta Scott King.

The Wylie Agency Inc. "Destiny" by Louise Erdrich from *American Stories: Fiction from the Atlantic Monthly*, edited by C. Michael Curtis. First published in the *Atlantic Monthly*, January 1985. Copyright © 1985 by Louise Erdrich. Reprinted by permission of the Wylie Agency.

Art and Photo Credits

Cover and iii (top left) © Sea World of California/CORBIS; (top right) Digital Vision Royalty Free Photograph/Fotosearch; (bottom left) © Werner Forman/CORBIS; (bottom right) © Vanni/Art Resource, NY; **viii** (top) © C Squared Studios/Getty Images; **ix** (bottom) © Kevin Fleming/CORBIS; **x** (top) Smithsonian American Art Museum, Washington, DC/Art Resource, NY; (middle) © C Squared Studios/Getty Images; (bottom) © Sea World of California/CORBIS; **xi** (middle) © Bettmann/CORBIS; (bottom) © C.I. Aguera/CORBIS; **xii** (top) © CORBIS; **xiii** (top) Jim Dandy/Stock Illustration RF/Getty Images; (bottom) AP/WIDE WORLD PHOTOS; xiv (top) Jeff Schmaltz, MODIS Rapid Response Team, NASA/GSFC; (bottom) © Tracy Kahn/CORBIS; xv (top) © Danny Lehman/CORBIS; (bottom) © Mike Segar/Reuters/CORBIS; **xvi** © Gordon Osmundson/CORBIS; **xvii** (top) © Wayne Bennett/CORBIS; **xviii** © Werner Forman/CORBIS; **xix** (top) © Peter Finger/CORBIS; (bottom) © Frank Whitney/Brand X/CORBIS; **xx** © Archivo Iconografico, S.A./CORBIS; **xxi** Courtesy of Photofest; **xxii** (bottom) GNU Free Documentation License; **xxiii** (bottom) © Catherine Karnow/CORBIS; **xxiv** © Martyn Goddard/CORBIS; **xxv** (top) © Lanny Ziering/Brand X/CORBIS; (bottom) © Jim Zuckerman/CORBIS

Unit 1

1 (top left) © E. & P. Bauer/zefa/CORBIS; (top middle) John Sloan: *The City from Greenwich Village,* 1992. © Artists Rights Society (ARS) New York; (top right) © Roy Morsch/zefa/CORBIS; (bottom left to right) © University of Georgia; Brandt and Brandt Literary Agents; Library of Congress; Library of Congress; © William J. Weber; Photo courtesy of James Hurst; **2** (top left) © E. & P. Bauer/zefa/CORBIS; (top middle) John Sloan: *The City from Greenwich Village,* 1992. © Artists Rights Society (ARS) New York; (top right) © Roy Morsch/zefa/CORBIS; (bottom) Hachette Book Group. Cover from *To Kill a Mockingbird* by Harper Lee. Copyright © 1960, 1982 Warner Books. Reprinted by permission; **4–5** (left to right) Photo by Sanja Gjenero; Stockbyte/Getty Images; Photo by Michal Koralewski; Stockbyte/Getty Images; Stockbyte Royalty Free Photograph/Fotosearch; © Tim O'Hara/CORBIS; Photo by Gary Tamin; Photo by Julia Freeman-Woolpert; **5** (middle) Smithsonian American Art Museum, Washington, DC/Art Resource, NY; (bottom) The Granger Collection, New York; **6** Smithsonian American Art Museum, Washington, DC/Art Resource, NY; **8** Smithsonian American Art Museum, Washington, DC/Art Resource, NY; **9** (left) © Bettmann/CORBIS; **10** (left) Photo by Gordon Parks; Courtesy of the Library of Congress; (right) GNU Free Documentation License; **11** Smithsonian American Art Museum, Washington, DC/Art Resource, NY; **14** Archive Photos; **15** The Bridgeman Art Library; **16** © Staffan Widstrand/CORBIS; **18** John Morgan/JupiterImages; **22** (top left) © Bettman/CORBIS; (bottom right) © Ingram Publishing/SuperStock; **24** Archive Photos; **24–25** © BananaStock/SuperStock; **26** (top) © John Wang/CORBIS; (bottom) Brandt and Brandt Literary Agents; **31** © Bob Kristi/CORBIS; **33** The Bridgeman Art Library; **40** (top left) © Bettmann/CORBIS; (bottom left) Library of Congress; (top right) © Hulton-Deutsch Collection/CORBIS; **41** © John Lund/Stone/Getty Images; **44–45** Photo by Brenton Nicholls; **48** © William J. Weber; **49** © William A. Bake/CORBIS; **50** Photo by Jendo Neversil; **51** © Rob Goldman/CORBIS; **58** Library of Congress; **59** © Todd Gipstein/CORBIS; **60** (top left) Blaine Kern's Mardi Gras World, http://www.neworleansonline.com; (top right) Library of Congress; **61** © John Nakata/CORBIS; **62** © Carl & Ann Purcell/CORBIS; **63** © Charles & Josette Lenars/CORBIS; **65** © Blue Lantern Studio/CORBIS; **69** Photo by Luca Zaninoni; **70** Courtesy of Media Bakery; **70** © Michael Dorris; **71** © Silvia Otte/Photonica/Getty Images; **73** © Douglas Schwartz/CORBIS; **75** © Angela Wyant/Stone+/Getty Images; **77** © Fabian Cevallos/CORBIS SYGMA; **79** Photo by Philip MacKenzie; **80** Courtesy of Media Bakery; **82** (bottom left) Library of Congress; (bottom right) Bancroft Library, UC Berkeley, Berkeley, CA; **83** © Catherine Karnow/CORBIS; **85** © Bojan Brecelj/CORBIS; **88** (top middle) © Royalty-Free/CORBIS; (top right) © Royalty-Free/CORBIS; **93** © CORBIS; **94** © C Squared Studios/Getty Images; **96** © Adam Woolfitt/CORBIS; **101–103** Library of Congress; **104** (bottom right) Library of Congress; **106** Brandt and Brandt Literary Agents; **107** Noah K. Strycker/www.stockxpert.com; **108** Photo courtesy James Hurst; **109** © Sea World of California/CORBIS; **111** © David Frazier/CORBIS; **115** (top left) © David Monniaux/GNU Free Documentation License; (bottom left) Library of Congress; (top right) Library of Congress; **116** © Sea World of California/CORBIS; **120** © University of Georgia; **121** © The Brett Weston

Archive/CORBIS; **122** © Owen Franken/CORBIS; **124** (left) © MAPS.com/CORBIS; (right) © Photodisc/Fotosearch; **125** © Bettmann/CORBIS; **127** © C. I. Aguera/CORBIS; **129** (top left) Library of Congress; (top right) © CORBIS; (bottom right) © CBS Photo Archive/Hulton Archive/Getty Images; **130** (top) © Bettmann/CORBIS; (bottom right) Library of Congress; **134** © University of Georgia; **135** Random House, Inc. From *Cat in the Hat* by Dr. Seuss, copyright TM and copyright © by Dr. Seuss Enterprises, L.P. 1957, renewed 1985. Used by Permission of Random House Children's Books, a division of Random House, Inc.; **138** (top right) Photo by Maciek Sliwinski; (bottom left) © Bettmann/CORBIS; (bottom right) Library of Congress; **139** Manchester City Art Galleries, England; **143** © Bettmann/CORBIS; **144** (top left) Library of Congress; (bottom left) Library of Congress; **145** Museum of Fine Arts, Boston. Zoe Oliver Sherman; **147** © Bettmann/CORBIS; **148** © CORBIS; **152** (top left) © E. & P. Bauer/zefa/CORBIS; (top middle) John Sloan: *The City from Greenwich Village,* 1992. © Artists Rights Society (ARS) New York; (top right) © Roy Morsch/zefa/CORBIS; **154** © Jeff Pfeffer; **157** © Fabio Cardoso/zefa/CORBIS; **161** (top) High Museum of Art. Purchase with funds provided by AT&T NEW ART/NEW VISIONS and funds from Alfred Austell Thornton in memory of Leila Austell Thornton and Albert Edward Thornton, Sr., and Sarah Miller Venable and William Hoyt Venable, 1995.54; (bottom) © SuperStock, Inc./SuperStock; **163** © Ed Freeman/The Image Bank/Getty Images; **165** (top) © Howard Davies/CORBIS; (bottom) AP/WIDE WORLD PHOTOS; **166** Olivier Rebbot/PictureQuest; **167** © David Turnley/CORBIS; **168** © Peter Turnley/CORBIS; **170** Photo by Robert Foothorap © 1995; **180** (bottom left) Library of Congress; (middle) Photo by Joe Zlomek; **183** Photo courtesy of Leslie Marmon Silko; **186** Smithsonian American Art Museum, Washington, DC/Art Resource, NY; **188** (top left) Photo by Brian Hill; (bottom left) Photo Courtesy of Diane Glancy; (top right) Photo by Pasqualantonio Pingue; **190** (top left to right) Jacket Illustration copyright © 2004 by Jim Tsingan, from *Finding Miracles* by Julia Alvarez. Used by permission of Alfred A. Knopf, an imprint of Random House Children's Books, a division of Random House, Inc.; Book cover from *Delta Wedding*, Harcourt Brace Modern Classic Edition, copyright 1946, 1945 and renewed 1974, 1973 by Eudora Welty, reprinted by permission of Harcourt, Inc.; Cover illustration from *Jack London, Five Great Short Stories* by Jack London, 1992. Reprinted by permission of Dover Publications; **192–193** © JLP/Deimos/CORBIS; **193** Library of Congress; **194** Library of Congress; **198** © Jeffrey Coolidge/CORBIS

Unit 2

202–203 (top left) © Philadelphia Museum of Art/CORBIS; (top middle) © Bohemian Nomad Picturemakers/CORBIS; (top right) © Images.com/CORBIS; (bottom, left to right) Library of Congress; Photo by James H. Evans; Photo courtesy of Sherman Alexie; Photo courtesy of Octavia Butler; Photo courtesy of Gish Jen; Library of Congress; **204** (left) Philadelphia Museum of Art/CORBIS; (middle) © Bohemian Nomad Picturemakers/CORBIS; (right) © Images.com/CORBIS; **207** (top) © Geoffrey Gove/CORBIS; (bottom) © Daniel Cima; **208** © CORBIS; **210** © Royalty-Free/CORBIS; **212** Photo by Am Y; **213** HarperCollins Publishers. Cover from *Hawk: Occupation: Skateboarder* by Tony Hawk. Copyright © 2000, 2001 by Tony Hawk. Reprinted by permission; **214** (top) Photo by Chrissi Nerantzi (bottom) Photo Courtesy of Nicholas Gage; **215** Eddie Adams Workshop. Photograph of Miss Hurd and Nicholas Gage by Eddie Adams, published with the article "The Teacher Who Changed My Life" by Nicholas Gage in *Parade* Magazine, 17 December 1989 (page 4). Reprinted by permission of Eddie Adams Workshop; **217** (left) © Hulton-Deutsch Collection/CORBIS; (middle) © Bettmann/CORBIS; (right) © Bettmann/CORBIS; **221** Photo by Thomas Arhelger; **222** (top) GNU Free Documentation License; (bottom) Photo courtesy of Lynne Cox; **223** © Mary Iverson/CORBIS; **224** GNU Free Documentation License; **225** (top) © Shepard Sherbell/CORBIS SABA; **227** © Bettmann/CORBIS; **230** Library of Congress; **238** www.stockxpert.com; **242** © Rollie McKenna; **244** (top) Photo by Oliver C. Grüener; (bottom) Photo courtesy of David Sedaris; **245** Jim Dandy/Stock Illustration RF/Getty Images; **249** © Hulton-Deutsch Collection/CORBIS; **252** Library of Congress; **253** © Julie Delton; **255** © CORBIS; **256** (top left) Photo by Patti Adair; (bottom left) © Bettmann/CORBIS; (top right) Photo by Steve Knight; **258** © Galen Rowell/CORBIS; **260** (top left) © Jeremy Woodhouse/CORBIS; (bottom left) Photo courtesy of Mary Deinlein; (top middle) © Stockbyte/SuperStock; (top right) © Galen Rowell/CORBIS; **266** Library of Congress; **267** The Granger Collection, New York; **268** (top and bottom) Library of Congress; **269** AP/WIDE WORLD PHOTOS; **270** (all images)

Library of Congress; **271** © Flip Schulke/CORBIS; **273** Library of Congress; **274** (top left) Library of Congress; (top right) © Reuters/CORBIS; (bottom left) Library of Congress); (bottom right) © CORBIS; **276** (top) Photo by Matthew Bowden; (bottom) AP/WIDE WORLD PHOTOS; **277** © Paul Velasco; Gallo Images/CORBIS; **278** (top right) © Peter Turnley/CORBIS; **279** © David Turnley/CORBIS; **283** © Ingram Publishing/SuperStock; **287** © LEE CELANO/Reuters/CORBIS; **289** © TOM FOX/Dallas Morning News/CORBIS; **291** Jeff Schmaltz, MODIS Rapid Response Team, NASA/GSFC; **292** (top left) AP/WIDE WORLD PHOTOS; (bottom left) Photo courtesy of Abraham Verghese; (top right) © John O'Boyle/Star Ledger/CORBIS; **296** (top right) Michaela Stejskalova/www.stockxpert.com; (bottom left) Photo courtesy of Octavia Butler; (bottom right) Photo courtesy of Garrison Keillor; **297** © 2008 Artists Rights Society (ARS), New York/ADAGP, Paris/Photo: © The Barnes Foundation, Merion Station, Pennsylvania/CORBIS; **298** © Tracy Kahn/CORBIS; **299** © Julie Delton; **300** © Thom Lang/CORBIS; **304** (top left) © Philadelphia Museum of Art/CORBIS; (top middle) © Bohemian Nomad Picturemakers/CORBIS; (top right) © Images.com/CORBIS; **306** © Rollie McKenna; **306–307** Photo by Pierre Amerlynck; **308** (bottom) Photo courtesy of Gish Jen; **309** Photo by Jon Wisbey; **311** (top left) Photo by Lynne Lancaster; (top middle) Photo by Ibon San Martin; (top right) © L. Clarke/CORBIS; (bottom left) © Lawrence Manning/CORBIS; **312** Photo courtesy of Sherman Alexie; **312–313** © Danny Lehman/CORBIS; **314** © Ed Eckstein/CORBIS; **316** Photo courtesy of Sandra Cisneros; **317** © 2007 Diego Rivera & Frida Kahlo Museums Trust/Photo: © SuperStock, Inc./Superstock; **318** © Jose Luis Pelaez, Inc./CORBIS; **320** Photo by James H. Evans; **321** © Historical Picture Archive/CORBIS; **322** © Todd Davidson PTY LTD./The Image Bank/Getty Images; **323** (left) © Miki Kratsman/CORBIS; (middle) GNU Free Documentation License; (right) Creative Commons; **325** © Petre Buzoianu/CORBIS; **326** © Geoffrey Clements/CORBIS; **328** (top) Will Mcintyre/Time & Life Pictures/Getty Images; (bottom) HarperCollins Publishers. Cover *The Girls of Summer: The U.S. Women's Soccer Team and How It Changed the World* by Jere Longman. Copyright © 2000, 2001 by Jere Longman. Reprinted by permission of HarperCollins Publishers; **330** © MARCOS BRINDICCI/Reuters/CORBIS; **332** © Mike Segar/Reuters/CORBIS; **334** (top) © Dex Image/CORBIS; (bottom) AP Photo/Lynne Sladky; **335** © Bohemian Nomad; **338** (top left to right) *Selections from the Journals* by Henry David Thoreau, 1995. Reprinted by permission of Dover Publications; Book cover of *Grand Mothers* edited by Nikki Giovanni, © 1994 by Henry Holt and Company. Reprinted by permission of Henry Holt and Company, LLC; From *Farewell to Manzanar* (Jacket Cover) by Jeanne W. Houston, James D. Houston, copyright © 1973 by James D. Houston. Used by permission of Bantam Books, a division of Random House, Inc.; Cover from *Silent Spring*, 40th Anniversary Edition by Rachel Carson (Boston: Houghton Mifflin, 2002); Cover photo by Greg Lowe from *High Exposure: An Enduring Passion for Everest and Unforgiving Places* by David Breashears, Jon Krakauer, 1999. Used by permission; "Jacket Cover," from *Swimming to Antarctica* by Lynne Cox, copyright © 2004 by Lynne Cox. Used by permission of Alfred A. Knopf, a division of Random House, Inc.; **341** Library of Congress; **342** © Bettmann/CORBIS

Unit 3

350–351 (top left) © Ron Chapple/CORBIS; (top right) © Peter Finger/CORBIS; (bottom, left to right) Library of Congress; Library of Congress; © Roger Ressmeyer/CORBIS; Library of Congress; Library of Congress; © Bettmann/CORBIS; **352** (left) © Ron Chapple/CORBIS; (right) © Peter Finger/CORBIS; **355** (top) © Andrew Unangst/CORBIS; (bottom) Photo courtesy of Ishmael Reed; **356** © Gordon Osmundson/CORBIS; **360** © Bettmann/CORBIS; **361** Photo by Jamie Brelsford; **362** (top) Photo by Paul Joseph; (bottom) Photograph by Dorothy Alexander; **364** Photo by G & A Scholiers; **366** (top left) Photo by Kathryn McCallum; (bottom left) © University of Georgia; (bottom right) Arte Pœblico Press; **367** Photo by Kathryn McCallum; **371** © age fotostock/SuperStock, Inc.; **373** Photo by Diane Groves; **374** (top) GNU Free Documentation License; **375** © Kevin Fleming/CORBIS; **376** AP/WIDE WORLD PHOTOS; **377–378** GNU Free Documentation License; **378–379** (background) © John and Lisa Merrill/CORBIS; **379** © Catherine Karnow/CORBIS; **380–381** (background) © John and Lisa Merrill/CORBIS; **381** © Swim Ink 2, LLC/CORBIS; **382** The U.S. Army Center for Military History (USACMH); **383** GNU Free Documentation License; **385** © Peter Guttman/CORBIS; **386** (bottom left) Photo by Bachrach; (bottom right) Photo courtesy of N. Scott Momaday; **387** © Chris Rogers/CORBIS; **388** ©

Wayne Bennett/CORBIS; **392** (bottom) Library of Congress; **393** Watercolor over graphite, 77x49.8cm. © The Cleveland Museum of Art, 1999, Gift of Louise Dunn in memory of Henry G. Keller, 1949.544; **399** Photo by Linnell Esler; **400** (top left) Photodisc; (top right) Photo Courtesy of NASA and the European Space Agency; (bottom left and right) AP/WIDE WORLD PHOTOS; **401** © Gerrit Greve/CORBIS; **403** (right) Photo Courtesy of NASA and the European Space Agency; **404** (bottom left) Library of Congress; (bottom right) Courtesy of Maya Angelou; **405** The Conquest of the Air, 1938 (oil on canvas), Penrose, Roland (1900–1984)/ © Southampton City Art Gallery, Hampshire, UK/The Bridgeman Art Library; **408** (top left) © Bettmann/CORBIS; (bottom left) Photo by Ziadin Givan; **410** Library of Congress; **411** Photo by Antonio Jiménez Alonso; **412** Photograph by Marcus Österberg; **414** Library of Congress; **415** © Werner Forman/CORBIS; **416** (top and bottom right) GNU Free Documentation License; **418** Library of Congress; **419** GNU Free Documentation License; **420** (bottom) © Oscar White/CORBIS; **420** (bottom) © Oscar White/CORBIS; **421** NASA, ESA, and the Hubble Heritage Team (STScI/AURA)-ESA/Hubble Collaboration Acknowledgment: B. Whitmore (Space Telescope Science Institute); **426** (top left) Photo By Marcin Łotysz; (bottom right) © Christopher Felver/CORBIS; **427** © Lou Wall/CORBIS; **428** © Lake County Museum/CORBIS; **430** (top) Photograph by Christy Thompson; (bottom) The Library of Congress; **431** © The State Russian Museum/CORBIS; **434** (top) Photo by Bianca de Blok; **435** © Gerrit Greve/CORBIS; **438** (left) © Ron Chapple/CORBIS; (right) © Peter Finger/CORBIS; **440** (top) © Images.com/CORBIS; (bottom) Photo Courtesy of Jin Ha; **442** (top) © Frank Whitney/Brand X/CORBIS; (bottom) Photo by Mike Markee; **444** (top) PhotoDisc; (bottom) Library of Congress; **446** (top) © The Jacob and Gwendolyn Lawrence Foundation, Seattle/Artists Rights Society (ARS), New York/Photo: The Jacob and Gwendolyn Lawrence Foundation/Art Resource, NY; (bottom) The Granger Collection, New York; **448** © Debi Milligan; **448–449** © Peter Finger/CORBIS; **450** Erich Lessing/Art Resource, NY; **452** Photo Courtesy of Rosellen Brown; **453** © 2008 Artists Rights Society (ARS), New York/ADAGP, Paris/Photo: Erich Lessing/Art Resource, NY; **454** (left) © Roger Ressmeyer/CORBIS; (right) Musee d'Arte Moderne de la Ville de Paris, France/Lauros-Giraudon/SuperStock; **456** Photo courtesy of Gladys Cardiff; **457** Flat Earth/Fotosearch; **458** (top) © Brian Kershisnik; (bottom) AP/WIDE WORLD PHOTOS; **460** Photo by Alison Freese; **461** Campesino, 1976. Daniel Desiga. Collection of Alfredo Aragon; **462** (background detail) © 2008 Artists Rights Society (ARS), New York/HUNGART, Budapest/Photo: © The Art Archive/CORBIS; (bottom) Library of Congress; **463** © 2008 Artists Rights Society (ARS), New York/HUNGART, Budapest/Photo: © The Art Archive/CORBIS; **464** (top) © Blue Lantern Studio/CORBIS; (bottom) Library of Congress; **466** (top) Digital file © Burstein Collection/CORBIS; (bottom) © Bettmann/CORBIS; **470** (top) © Philadelphia Museum of Art/CORBIS; (bottom) Library of Congress; **472** (top left to right) Cover illustration from *Americans' Favorite Poems: The Favorite Poem Project Anthology*, edited by Robert Pinsky & Maggie Dietz. Copyright © 2000 by Robert Pinsky and Maggie Dietz. Used by permission of W. W. Norton & Company; Cover from *Song of the Sky: Versions of Native American Song Poems* by Brian Swann. Copyright © 1985, 1993 by Brian Swann. Reprinted by permission; Cover illustration from *Visions of War, Dreams of Peace* by Joan Furey, Lynda Van Devanter, 1991. Reprinted by permission; Cover from *You Come Too: Favorite Poems for All Ages* by Robert Frost. Copyright © 1975 by Lesley Frost Ballantine. Used by permission; "Cover," from *Good Poems* by Garrison Keillor, copyright © 2002 by Garrison Keillor. Used by permission of Viking Penguin, a division of Penguin Group (USA) Inc.; Naomi Shihab Nye. Cover *19 Varieties of Gazelle: Poems of the Middle East* by Naomi Shihab Nye. Copyright © 1994, 1995, 1998, 2002 by Naomi Shihab Nye. Reprinted by permission of the author; **476** © Christopher Felver/CORBIS

Unit 4

484–485 (top left) © Geoffrey Clements/CORBIS; (top middle) Art Resource, NY; (top right) © Christie's Images/CORBIS; (bottom far left, middle, and far right) © The Art Archive/CORBIS; Archive Photos; Photo courtesy of Maxine Kumin; **486** (top left) © Geoffrey Clements/CORBIS; (top middle) Art Resource, NY; (top right) © Christie's Images/CORBIS; **487–489** Courtesy of Photofest; **492** © Archivo Iconografico, S.A./CORBIS; **495** Photo by Frances Magee; **498** (top) © The Art Archive/CORBIS; **499** (top) National Portrait Gallery, London; (bottom) Carol O'Malia; **502** Courtesy of Photofest; **504** © Dennis Marsico/CORBIS; **504–505** (background) andhedesigns/IstockPhoto; **505–509** Courtesy of Photofest; **511** (middle) Photo by Alfonso Diaz; **518–522** Courtesy of Photofest; **526** (bottom left) © The Art Archive/CORBIS; **528–553** Courtesy of Photofest; **555** Photo by Gary Tamin; **559–573, 579–581** Courtesy of Photofest; **583** Photograph by Danilo Vitoriano; **587–590** Courtesy of Photofest; **596** (left) Photo by Denise Leon; (middle) GNU Free Documentation License; **597** Courtesy of Photofest; **599** Photo by Sanja Gjenero; **606–614** Courtesy of Photofest; **615** (bottom) Photo by Marcin Pawelec; **616** (top) Photo Courtesy of Maxine Kumin; **617** (top left) © Bettmann/CORBIS; (top right) © 20th Century Fox/Shooting Star; (bottom right) © Hulton-Deutsch/CORBIS; **621** Photograph by Christopher Rayan; **624** (left) © Geoffrey Clements/CORBIS; (middle) Art Resource, NY; (right) © Christie's Images/CORBIS; **626–627** (background) © William Whitehurst/CORBIS; **628** (top) © North Carolina Museum of Art/CORBIS; (bottom) Archive Photos; **629** © Bettmann/CORBIS; **630** © Alley Cat Productions/Brand X/CORBIS; **631** © Bettmann/CORBIS; **634** © Robert Mitchell; **646** From *A Raisin in the Sun* book cover by Lorraine Hansberry, copyright © 1958, 1959, 1966, 1984, 1986, 1987. Used by permission of Random House, Inc.; Jacket Cover from *Romeo and Juliet/West Side Story* by William Shakespeare and Norris Houghton. Used by permission of Dell Publishing, a division of Random House, Inc.; Book cover from *An Enemy of the People* by Henrik Ibsen. Copyright © 1999 by Dover Publications, Inc. Reprinted by permission; Book cover for *Shaking Hands with Shakespeare: A Teenager's Guide to Reading and Performing the Bard* by Allison Wedell Schumacher (New York: Kaplan Publishing/Simon & Schuster, 2004). Used by permission of Kaplan Publishing/Simon & Schuster Adult Publishing Group; (bottom right) Cover from *The Miracle Worker* by William Gibson. Copyright © 1988 by William Gibson. Reprinted by permission; **647** © Tom Stewart/CORBIS

Unit 5

658–659 (top left) © Peter Adams/zefa/CORBIS; (bottom, left to right) Library of Congress; © Bettmann/CORBIS; Library of Congress; Library of Congress; Courtesy of Walker Brents; © Bettmann/CORBIS; **660** (left) © Peter Adams/zefa/CORBIS; **663** (top) www.stockxpert.com; (bottom) © Archivo Iconografico, S.A./CORBIS; **664** Musées Royaux des Beaux-Arts, Brussels; **670** (top) Photo by Marie Jeanne Iliescu; **673** GNU Free Documentation License; **677** Laurence Gough/www.stockxpert.com; **678** (top) Photo by Kaycee Howell; (bottom) Library of Congress; **679** *Still Life of a Salmon on a Riverbank in a Mountainous Landscape,* Russell, John (1745–1806)/Private Collection, Photo © Bonhams, London, UK/The Bridgeman Art Library; **681** © Images.com/CORBIS; **689** Simon & Schuster Publishing. From *The Three Little Wolves and the Big Bad Pig* by Eugene Trivizas and Helen Oxenbury. Text copyright © 1993 by Eugene Trivizas. Illustrations © 1993 by Helen Oxenbury. Reprinted by permission of Simon & Schuster Publishing; **690** (bottom) Library of Congress; **691** *The Keepsake* (oil on canvas), Bunce, Kate Elizabeth (1858–1927)/© Birmingham Museums and Art Gallery/The Bridgeman Art Library; **693** © Bettmann/CORBIS; **697** Stock Xchng; **699** © DLILLC/CORBIS; **701** © Krause, Johansen/Archivo Iconografico, S.A./CORBIS; **702** © Corey Hochachka/Design Pics/CORBIS; **703** (top right) GNU Free Documentation License; **707** © Douglas Kirkland/CORBIS; **709** (left) Library of Congress; **710** (bottom) Patricia R. Isaacs/Parrot Graphics; **713** © Kevin Fleming/CORBIS; **715** © The Corcoran Gallery of Art/CORBIS; **720** (left) GNU Free Documentation License; (middle) © Wolfgang Kaehler/CORBIS; **721** Photo by Jin Neoh; **726** © CORBIS; **729** © Alexander Burkatovski/CORBIS; **731** *Polyphemus attacking sailors in their boat,* 1855 (oil on canvas), Decamps, Alexandre Gabriel (1803–60)/Musee des Beaux-Arts, Rouen, France, Peter Willi/The Bridgeman Art Library; **734** (top left) GNU Free Documentation License; (top right) *Neptune's Horses,* illustration for 'The Greek Mythological Legend,' published in London, 1910 by Walter Crane © Bibliotheque des Arts Decoratifs, Paris, France/Archives Charmet/The Bridgeman Art Library; **738** (middle) Photo by Shawn Pais; **739** © Michael Maslan Historic Photographs/CORBIS; **740** Photo by Russell Hugo; **742** Photo by Irena Svidovsky; **745** Circe Pouring Poison into a Vase and Awaiting the Arrival of Ulysses (w/c), Burne-Jones, Sir Edward (1833–98)/Private Collection/The Bridgeman Art Library International; **749** © Charles & Josette Lenars/CORBIS; **755** © Underwood & Underwood/CORBIS; 757 © Smithsonian Institution/CORBIS; 760 (top) Library of Congress; **762** (top left) Photo by Pam Roth; (middle) Library of Congress; (right) Konstantin Kalishko/www.stockxpert.com; **764** (bottom) © Stapleton Collection/CORBIS; **765** ©

National Gallery Collection; By kind permission of the Trustees of the National Gallery, London/CORBIS; **767** Photo by Gaston Thauvin; **768** Philip Lange/ www.stockxpert.com; **785** (left) Library of Congress; **787** (top) Roxana Gonzalez Leyva/www.stockxpert. com; (bottom) *Penelope weaving a shroud for Laertes her father-in-law while she awaits the return of her husband Odysseus,* 1895 by Max Klinger © Private Collection/The Stapleton Collection/The Bridgeman Art Library; **788** (right) Roxana Gonzalez Leyva/www. stockxpert.com; **790** (top left) © Peter Adams/zefa/ CORBIS; **791** © Comstock/CORBIS; **792** (left) James Whitmore/Time & Life Pictures/Getty Images; (right) '*Dare you face such a monster as this?*' illustration for 'How Perseus vowed a Rash Vow,' from The Heroes of Greek Fairy Tales, by Charles Kingsley (1819–75) (colour litho), Davie, Howard (fl. 1914–44)/ © Private Collection/The Bridgeman Art Library; **795** *Study for Perseus and the Graiae,* 1880 by Sir Edward Burne-Jones © The Makins Collection/The Bridgeman Art Library; **796** © Christie's Images/CORBIS; **798** (top) © Richard T. Nowitz/CORBIS; (bottom) © Bettmann/ CORBIS; **800** © Catherine Karnow/CORBIS; **803** © Macduff Everton/CORBIS; **805** (left) The Granger Collection, New York; (right) *Young Princess,* 1930 (oil on canvas), Guirand de Scevola, Lucien (1871–1950)/Musee des Beaux-Arts, Mulhouse, France, Giraudon/The Bridgeman Art Library; **808** © Bettmann/CORBIS; **810** (left) © Abilio Lope/ CORBIS; (right) © Christine Osborne/CORBIS; **812** (top left to right) Book cover for *The Children of Odin: The Book of Northern Myths* by Padraic Colum, illustrated by Willy Pogany. Copyright © 2004. Used with permission of Aladdin Paperbacks, an imprint of Simon & Schuster Children's Publishing; Hachette Book Group. Cover from *Mythology: Timeless Tales of Gods and Heroes* by Edith Hamilton. Copyright © 1942 by Edith Hamilton. Reprinted by permission; Cover illustration from *Folklore, Myths, and Legends* by Donna Rosenberg. Illustrated by Ophelia Chamblis. © 1997 NTC Publishing Group. Reproduced by permission of The McGraw-Hill Companies. *The Odyssey* by Homer ISBN: 978-1-58049-389-5. Copyright © 2006 Prestwick House. Reprinted by permission of Prestwick House Inc.; Cover from *Oedipus Rex* by Sophocles. Copyright © 2005. Copyrighted by Prestwick House, Inc. Reprinted by permission; *The Iliad* by Homer ISBN: 978-1-58049-670–4. Copyright © 2007 Prestwick House. Reprinted by permission of Prestwick House Inc.; **816** © Bettmann/CORBIS

Unit 6

824–825 (top left) © Martyn Goddard/CORBIS; (top right) © Digital Art/CORBIS; (bottom, left to right) Courtesy of Maya Angelou; Library of Congress; Photo courtesy of Anna Quindlen; © Oscar White/CORBIS; Library of Congress; © E.O. Hoppé/CORBIS; **826** (top left) © Martyn Goddard/CORBIS; (top right) © Digital Art/CORBIS; **828** The New York Public Library/Art Resource, NY; **828–829** © Tim Wright/CORBIS; **830** (background) © Pat O'Hara/CORBIS; (middle) Archive Photos; **831** (top left) © Jon Sparks/CORBIS; (right) Photo by Samuel Rosa; **833** (top) © Lester Lefkowitz/ CORBIS; (bottom) Photo courtesy of Anna Quindlen; **834** © Anthony Redpath/CORBIS; **835** Photodisc/ Getty Images; **836** (top) © Bob Rowan; Progressive Image/CORBIS; (bottom) Chronicle/Mark Costantini; **837** © Bob Rowan; Progressive Image/CORBIS; **840** © Keith Philpott/Time & Life/Getty Images; **843** Montclair Art Museum, Museum Purchase, Acquisition Fund 1997.33.2; **846** © Sandro Vannini/CORBIS; **849** © Oscar White/CORBIS; **851** (left) © Gabe Palmer/CORBIS; (middle) © Robert Llewellyn/CORBIS; (top right) Photo by Melodi T.; (bottom right) Photo courtesy of Mary Oliver; **853** (top) © Bettmann/ CORBIS; (bottom) Courtesy of Maya Angelou; **854** © CORBIS; **856** (left) © Images.com/CORBIS; (middle) Library of Congress; (right) © George Shelley/CORBIS; **856–857** © George Shelley/CORBIS; **858** (background) © Ken Rosenthal/CORBIS; (bottom) Library of Congress; **860** (left) © Martyn Goddard/CORBIS; (right) © Digital Art/CORBIS; **862** © Christopher Felver/CORBIS; **863** © Images.com/CORBIS; **864** © Digital Art/CORBIS; **866** © Rosa & Rosa/CORBIS; **868** © Bettmann/CORBIS; **870–871** © Martyn Goddard/CORBIS; **872** © David Hockney; **874** (top left) Paulus Rusyanto/www.stockxpert.com; (bottom left) AP Photo/Evalyn Shapiro; (middle) Photo by Hannah Boettcher; (right) Natalia Bratslavsky/www .stockxpert.com; **875** (top) © 2008 Andy Warhol Foundation for the Visual Arts/ARS, New York/Photo: The Andy Warhol Foundation, Inc./Art Resource, NY; (bottom left) © Martyn Goddard/CORBIS; **876** (background) © Jim Zuckerman/CORBIS; (bottom) Library of Congress; **879–882** © Wolfgang Kaehler/ CORBIS; **886** (bottom) AP/WIDE WORLD PHOTOS; **887** Mikael Damkier/www.stockxpert.com; **889** © 2008 Artists Rights Society (ARS), New York/SIAE, Rome/© Estate of Giacomo Balla/SuperStock; **892** © Don Mason/Brand X/CORBIS; **894** (background) © Images.com/CORBIS; (bottom) AP/WIDE WORLD

PHOTOS; **897** Reed E. Brewer; **900** © AMET JEAN PIERRE/CORBIS SYGMA; **901** © James Leynse/CORBIS; **902** © Bettmann/CORBIS; **903** © CORBIS; **904** (bottom) AP/WIDE WORLD PHOTOS; **907** © Bettmann/CORBIS; **909** © Lanny Ziering/Brand X/CORBIS; **911** (top left) Photo by Cris DeRaud; (top right) © E. O. Hoppé/CORBIS; **912** Photo courtesy of William McDonough; **912–913** © Alberto Estevez/epa/CORBIS; **920** Farrar, Straus and Giroux, LLC. Jacket design from *Cradle to Cradle* by William McDonough and Michael Braungart. Copyright © 2002 by William McDonough and Michael Braungart. Reprinted by permission of North Point Press, a division of Farrar, Straus and Giroux, LLC.; **922** © Luca Da Ros/Grand Tour/CORBIS; **924** Book cover for *The Old Man and the Sea* by Ernest Hemingway (New York: Scribner/Simon & Schuster, 1996). Used by permission of Scribner, an imprint of Simon & Schuster Adult Publishing Group; Cover for *Blue Highways* by William Least Heat-Moon. Reprinted by permission of Little, Brown and Company, a division of Hatchette Book Group USA.; Cover photograph from *Leaving Home* by Hazel Rochman and Darlene Z. Campbell. Cover photograph © 1988 by Tony Stone Images/Donovan Reese. Cover design by Michele N. Tupper. Cover © 1998 by HarperCollins Publishers. Used by permission of HarperCollins Publishers. Cover photograph from *Memory Boy* by Will Weaver. Cover photography © 2003 by Sandra Nydegger. Cover © 2003 by HarperCollins Publishers. Used by permission of HarperCollins Publishers. Book cover for *Fahrenheit 451* by Ray Bradbury. (New York: Simon & Schuster, 2003). Used by permission of Simon & Schuster Adult Publishing Group. *The Ear, the Eye, and the Arm* by Nancy Farmer. Jacket painting © 1994 by Charles A. Bibbs. Reprinted by permission of Orchard Books, an imprint of Scholastic, Inc.; **927** © Keith Philpott/Time & Life/Getty Images; **928** HarperCollins Publishers. Thumbnail image of book cover from *On Writing Well* by William Zinsser. Collins; 30th Anniversary Edition (May 9, 2006). Copyright © 2006 by William K. Zinsser. Reprinted by permission of HarperCollins Publishers; **938** (top left) John Sloan: *The City from Greenwich Village,* 1992. © Artists Rights Society (ARS) New York; (top right) © Ron Chapple/CORBIS; (bottom left) © Digital Art/CORBIS; (bottom right) © Peter Adams/zefa/CORBIS

Reading Strategies & Skills/Literary Elements

Vocabulary & Spelling

Grammar & Style

Writing

Research & Documentation

Applied English

Speaking & Listening

Test-Taking Skills

Index of Titles and Authors

A

B

C

D

E

F

Y

Z

For Your Reading List